MW00817642

A Testimony of Jesus Christ - Volume 1

A Commentary on the Book of Revelation

Preface
Introduction
Revelation 1-14

...for the testimony of Jesus is the spirit of prophecy
(Rev. 19:10)

Revision 2.1

Copyright

This commentary is freely available and may be distributed with the following restrictions:

Published by SpiritAndTruth.org, Camano Island, WA U.S.A. 98282

Garland, Anthony C., 1957-

A Testimony of Jesus Christ - Volume 1 :

A Commentary on the Book of Revelation / Anthony C. Garland

Includes bibliographical references.

ISBN-13: 978-0-9788864-1-7

ISBN-10: 0-9788864-1-0

1. Bible. N.T. Revelation I-XIV—Commentaries.

Table of Contents

Volume 1

Volume 2

1 - Preface

1.1 – Copyright

1.2 - Acknowledgments

First and foremost, I thank my Lord and Savior Jesus Christ Who opened my eyes to the truth and sustained me during this project. May this work, in some small way, bring You glory. I also am grateful for my wife, Deb. For 13 years she lived with an unbelieving husband while petitioning God on my behalf. Her faithful support and encouragement made this work possible. She also spent many hours proofreading the commentary and providing detailed suggestions.

Beryl Cahoon provided invaluable assistance spending many hours proofreading the commentary and the associated slide shows. Steve Lewis reviewed an early draft of the introduction, provided numerous corrections to the associated slide shows, and provided much-appreciated encouragement when the work seemed overwhelming. Even though I have had considerable help in finding and correcting errors, whatever errors remain are my responsibility.

Dr. Mal Couch of *Tyndale Theological Seminary* (http://www.tyndale.edu) first suggested the project of producing a detailed course on the Book of Revelation. Preparation for teaching that course eventually led to the production of this commentary. I am also indebted to Dr. Couch and the instructors at Tyndale Seminary for an affordable education in Systematic Theology and Biblical languages.

Igor Stelmachenko provided website support so the commentary and associated slide shows could be published for internet use. Mike McCorkle and Hugh and Celia Johnston showed great patience living next door to a recluse for an extended period.

Brandon Staggs' excellent *SwordSearcher Bible Study Program* (http://www.swordsearcher.com) greatly facilitated access to my notes while making it possible to efficiently incorporate Scripture information into the commentary. The magnitude of my task was *greatly* reduced by his excellent program. I also relied heavily upon *Libronix Bible Software* (http://www.logos.com) for work in the original Greek and for access to an extensive set of digital study resources.

Connecticut College's Wetmore Print Collection[1] provided non-copyrighted images of Albrecht Durer's famous woodcuts.[2]

Several individuals and ministries granted permission for their copyrighted materials to appear within this commentary. See *Special Permission*[1.3].

The developers of the *Python Programming Language* (http://www.python.org) are to be thanked for an extremely productive scripting language. Without the Python language, converting the marked-up original text into an extensively cross-referenced, formatted, final version would have been much more difficult. Python was also used to automatically generate the topic and Scripture indexes.

I am especially indebted to the many men of God who journeyed through the book of Revelation ahead of me and took the time and effort to leave a path of "breadcrumbs" for those who would follow later. Their down-to-earth, literal interpretation of the book of Revelation blows as a fresh breeze in the midst of an ocean of allegory and symbolic conjecture. Many of these men have already gone on to glory: Barnhouse,[3] Bullinger,[4] Larkin,[5] McClain,[6] Morris,[7] Newell,[8] Scott,[9] Seiss,[10] Trench,[11] and Walvoord.[12] Others are still with us: Fruchtenbaum,[13] MacArthur,[14] Pentecost,[15] and Thomas.[16] How much poorer we would be without their stewardship of the torch of literal, grammatical-historical interpretation so that we might "keep the words of the prophecy of this book" (Rev. 1:3; 22:7)!

Notes

1 See *www.conncoll.edu/visual/wetmore.html*.

2 See *www.conncoll.edu/visual/Durer-prints/index.html*.

3 Donald Grey Barnhouse, *Revelation* (Grand Rapids, MI: Zondervan Publishing House, 1971).

4 E. W. Bullinger, *Commentary On Revelation* (Grand Rapids, MI: Kregel Publications, 1984, 1935).

[5] Clarence Larkin, *The Book of Revelation* (Glenside, PA: Rev. Clarence Larkin Estate, 1919).

[6] Alva J. McClain, *The Greatness Of The Kingdom* (Winona Lake, IN: BMH Books, 1959).

[7] Henry Morris, *The Revelation Record* (Wheaton, IL: Tyndale House Publishers, 1983).

[8] William R. Newell, *Revelation: Chapter by Chapter* (Grand Rapids, MI: Kregel Publications, 1994,c1935).

[9] Walter Scott, *Exposition of The Revelation* (London, England: Pickering & Inglis, n.d.).

[10] J. A. Seiss, *The Apocalypse: Lectures on the Book of Revelation* (Grand Rapids, MI: Zondervan Publishing House, 1966).

[11] Richard Chenevix Trench, *Commentary on the Epistles to the Seven Churches in Asia* (Eugene, OR: Wipf and Stock Publishers, 1861).

[12] John F. Walvoord, *The Revelation of Jesus Christ* (Chicago, IL: Moody Press, 1966).

[13] Arnold G. Fruchtenbaum, *The Footsteps of Messiah*, rev ed. (Tustin, CA: Ariel Ministries, 2003).

[14] [John MacArthur, *Revelation 1-11 : The MacArthur New Testament Commentary* (Chicago, IL: Moody Press, 1999)], [John MacArthur, *Revelation 12-22 : The MacArthur New Testament Commentary* (Chicago, IL: Moody Press, 2000)].

[15] J. Dwight Pentecost, *Things to Come: A Study in Biblical Eschatology* (Grand Rapids, MI: Zondervan Publishing House, 1958).

[16] [Robert L. Thomas, *Revelation 1-7* (Chicago, IL: Moody Press, 1992)] and [Robert L. Thomas, *Revelation 8-22* (Chicago, IL: Moody Press, 1995)].

1.3 - Special Permission

We gratefully acknowledge the following ministries and individuals who granted permission to include copyrighted materials herein.

- **Ariel Ministries** granted permission to include diagrams from [Arnold G. Fruchtenbaum, *The Footsteps of Messiah*, rev ed. (Tustin, CA: Ariel Ministries, 2003)].[2]
- **Todd Bolen** of *www.BiblePlaces.com* granted permission to include photos of places of significance to the book of Revelation.

Because these materials are copyrighted, they may not be extracted from this commentary for use in derivative works. See the *Copyright*[1.1].

Notes

1 Arnold G. Fruchtenbaum, *The Footsteps of Messiah*, rev ed. (Tustin, CA: Ariel Ministries, 2003).

2 Ariel Ministries, P.O. Box 3723, Tustin, CA 92781. *www.Ariel.org*.

1.4 - About the Author

Author Tony Garland

	Tony holds the *Masters of Theological Studies (M.T.S.)* and *Doctor of Theology* degrees from *Louisiana Baptist Theological Seminary* (http://www.lbu.edu) and the *Advanced Diploma in Systematic Theology (Th.M.)* and *Advanced Diploma in Prophetic Studies* from *Tyndale Theological Seminary* (http://www.tyndale.edu). Tony is an ordained minister of the gospel (nondenominational) and administers the Christian website *www.SpiritAndTruth.org*. He can be contacted at *contact@SpiritAndTruth.org*. Tony earned a *Bachelor's of Science* degree in Electrical Engineering from the University of Washington and has worked in the field of software engineering for several decades.

1.5 - Revision History

Revisions

Revision	Date	Description
2.1	December 18, 2006	Typographical corrections.
2.0	November 8, 2006	Converted generic quotes to right- and left-hand quotes. Typographical corrections.
1.28	September 21, 2006	Restructured the table comparing the *The Structure of the Letters*[4.15.1.4] to the *Seven Churches*[5.2.66] of Asia to work better with *Libronix* (http://www.logos.com). Typographical corrections.
1.27	August 2, 2006	Modified names of *SwordSearcher* book and commentary files to protect compatibility with future versions of SwordSearcher. Typographical corrections.
1.26	July 22, 2006	Typographical corrections.
1.25	July 10, 2006	Typographical corrections. Long-overdue update of print-format edition.
1.24	May 18, 2006	Added quote from *Irenaeus*[5.2.34] in commentary on *Revelation 7:4*[3.7.4]. Added citation from Waymeyer in *Understanding Symbols and Figures*[2.7.4]. Minor correction in *Babylon is Jerusalem?*[4.1.3.4]. Typographical corrections.
1.23	January 7, 2006	Corrected missing cross-references within *Topic Index*[5.4]. Typographical corrections.
1.22	January 3, 2006	Expanded commentary on *Revelation 17:10*[3.17.10]. Added citation from the *Jerome Biblical Commentary* to *Nebuchadnezzar's Dream and Daniel's Vision*[4.3.1]. Added chart describing *Key Interpretive Issues in Revelation 20:1-6* to commentary on *Revelation 20:1*[3.20.1]. Html versions of the commentary now available with both short and long page sizes. Typographical corrections.
1.21	November 12, 2005	Added accents to transliterations within *SwordSearcher* version. Typographical corrections.
1.20	November 3, 2005	Corrected alphabetization of *Glossary*[5.2] entries. Restored secondary index entries in *Topic Index*[5.4] which were omitted in some formats. Added new section contrasting *Babylon and the New Jerusalem*[3.17.18.1]. Moved commentary at end of *Revelation 17:4*[3.17.4] which was incorrectly placed at the introduction of *Revelation 17*[3.17]. Added a citation by Dr. John Niemelä to commentary on *Revelation 5:9*[3.5.9]. Added book by Waymeyer to *Additional Resources on the Millennial Kingdom*[4.11.10]. Typographical corrections.
1.19	October 8, 2005	Corrected problem which caused omission of entries in scripture index for books of Daniel and Zechariah in some formats. The *Scripture Index*[5.5] now lists each verse within a verse range, not just the first verse.

Revision	Date	Description
		Typographical corrections.
1.18	September 15, 2005	Corrected errors in section links for SwordSearcher version. Modified instructions on how to *use the commentary within SwordSearcher*[2.2.2.2]. Typographical corrections.
1.17	September 6, 2005	Revised the section on the *Rejection*[2.10.1] of the Book of Revelation to remove an erroneous statement and citation indicating that the Westminster Confession of Faith rejected the Apocalypse from the *Canon*[5.2.12]. Typographical corrections.
1.16	June 16, 2005	Added footnote to commentary on *Revelation 13:3*[3.13.3]. Fixed *Automatic Lookup*[2.2.2.7] example. Added a citation to *The Millennial Kingdom in the Early Church*[4.11.9]. Typographical corrections.
1.15	April 14, 2005	Added related passages to commentary on *Revelation 12:1*[3.12.1]. Revised *Revelation 19:20*[3.19.20] and *Beast Worshipers are Unique*[4.4.3.4]. Typographical corrections.
1.14	February 10, 2005	Added citation to *Additional Resources on the Rapture*[4.14.10]. Corrected missing section numbers from verse-by-verse commentary within the *Libronix PBB version* (http://www.SpiritAndTruth.org/download/libronix/index.htm). Typographical corrections.
1.13	January 1, 2005	Typographical corrections in automatic transliteration of Greek. Added *notice of registration*[1.1] with United States Copyright Office effective July 8, 2004. Moved mislocated paragraph to end of *Revelation 14:20*[3.14.20].
1.12	December 2, 2004	Added information to *Babylon is Jerusalem?*[4.1.3.4]. This is the first version available for use with the free *e-Sword* Bible study software. Corrected Greek transliteration error where initial smooth breathing mark was not being removed.
1.11	November 23, 2004	Corrected problem in SwordSearcher and Libronix PBB versions where verse ranges only included the first verse in the range.
1.10	November 10, 2004	Added topic milestone markers to the *Topic Index*[5.4] so that topic index entries operate in the active index of the Libronix PBB version.
1.9	November 8, 2004	Corrected heading levels in *Topic Index*[5.4] and *Scripture Index*[5.5] which were causing problems for the table of contents within the Libronix PBB version.
1.8	October 31, 2004	Corrected minor formatting inconsistencies concerning citations.
1.7	October 30, 2004	The HTML version and the Libronix Personal Book version now generate individual files for every section in the commentary. This greatly reduces individual page size leading to improved performance loading a new page.
1.6	October 26, 2004	First version available for use with the *Sword Searcher* (http://www.spiritandtruth.org/download/SwordSearcher/index.htm) Bible study program.
1.5	October 15, 2004	Modifications to improve operation of the *Libronix PBB version* (http://www.spiritandtruth.org/download/libronix/index.htm) of the

Revision	Date	Description
		commentary: (1) Section titles at the top of each page no longer use H1 formatting codes which confused Libronix's notion of levels in the table of contents; (2) Replaced navigation buttons which appear in each section with text links to work around what appears to be a problem with linked images within the Libronix PBB compiler. Typographical corrections, including corrections to numerous Bible addresses with incorrect chapter or verse numbers.
1.4	October 12, 2004	Moved *Acknowledgments*[1.2], *Special Permission*[1.3], *Copyright*[1.1], *About the Author*[1.4], and *Revision History* under a new *Preface*[1] section at the beginning of the table of contents. Modified the *Topic Index*[5.4] for Libronix PBB versions to limit the number of entries at each topic. (The full index is available on the web at *www.SpiritAndTruth.org/id/revc.htm?Topic_Index* (http://www.SpiritAndTruth.org/id/revc.htm?Topic_Index).)
1.3	October 8, 2004	Greek transliteration now includes macrons to differentiate *eta* from *epsilon* and *omega* from *omicron*. Hebrew transliteration now differentiates between various vowels. Collapsed abbreviated *Table of Contents* (0). Added citation by Svigel to *Revelation 3:14*[3.3.14]. Expanded *Additional Resources on the Rapture*[4.14.10]. Added a citation to the section titled *Book of Mormon*[4.17.2.4.2.1] which discusses DNA evidence against the idea that Native Americans are descendants of a lost tribe of Israel. Fixed citations in *Revelation 9:7*[3.9.7]. Expanded commentary on *Revelation 1:7*[3.1.7]. Typographical corrections. This is the first version available in Libronix PBB format for use with the *Libronix Bible Study program* (http://www.spiritandtruth.org/download/libronix/index.htm).
1.2	April 22, 2004	Removed diagram of *Daniel's Outline of the Future* which previously appeared in the section titled *Nebuchadnezzar's Dream and Daniel's Vision*[4.3.1]. We obtained initial permission to include this image in digital versions of the commentary, but were unable to procure permission for printed media. Copyright notices are now directly marked on all copyrighted images. Typographical corrections.
1.1	April 14, 2004	Related topics are now in alphabetical order. Added new section: *Tables and Figures*[5.3]. Typographical corrections.
1.0	March 27, 2004	First draft of completed commentary. Revised *Beasts, Heads, and Horns*[4.3] diagram so it can be more easily printed. Glossary and topical index items are now included in the expanded table of contents so they will be found in searches. Fixed capitalization within Scripture passages. Rearranged related topics to be in alphabetical order. The scripture index is now separated into a separate file for each Bible book. Added new section *Acknowledgments*[1.2]. Typographical corrections.
0.26	March 20, 2004	Added new section: *Revelation 22*[3.22]. Typographical corrections.
0.25	March 14, 2004	Added new section: *Revelation 21*[3.21]. Typographical corrections.
0.24	March 07, 2004	Added new section: *Revelation 20*[3.20]. Added new section: *Millennial Kingdom*[4.11]. Typographical corrections.
0.23	February	Added new section: *Revelation 19*[3.19]. Added new section: *Marriage of the*

Revision	Date	Description
	29, 2004	*Lamb*[4.10]. Revised commentary at *Revelation 1:1*[3.1.1], and *Revelation 1:2*[3.1.2] concerning the testimony of Jesus. Typographical corrections.
0.22	February 21, 2004	Added new section: *Revelation 18*[3.18]. Typographical corrections.
0.21	February 14, 2004	Added new section: *Revelation 17*[3.17]. Added new section: *Babylon and the Harlot*[4.1]. Added new section: *Audio Course*[2.1]. Added new map to *Sheep in Bozrah*[3.12.6.1]. Typographical corrections.
0.20	February 8, 2004	Added new section: *Revelation 16*[3.16]. Added new section: *Campaign of Armageddon*[4.5]. Typographical corrections.
0.19	February 3, 2004	Added new section: *Revelation 15*[3.15]. Typographical corrections.
0.18	January 30, 2004	Added new section: *Revelation 14*[3.14]. Added new section: *Finding Your Way Around*[2.2.2.2]. Added buttons to verse-by-verse commentary which provide access to the audio teaching associated with each verse. Added new diagram from *Charting the End Times* to *Nebuchadnezzar's Dream and Daniel's Vision*[4.3.1]. Typographical corrections.
0.17	January 23, 2004	Added new section: *Revelation 13*[3.13]. Revised section: *Nero*[4.12]. Typographical corrections. Added new *Glossary*[5.2] entries which point to their corresponding articles under *Related Topics*[4].
0.16	January 17, 2004	Added new section: *Revelation 12*[3.12]. Added new section: *Beasts, Heads, and Horns*[4.3]. Typographical corrections.
0.15	January 7, 2004	Added new section: *Revelation 11*[3.11]. Added new section: *Temple of God*[4.16]. Added new section: *The Plagues of Egypt and the Tribulation*[2.13.7]. Added new section: *Events of the 70th Week of Daniel*[2.13.5.4]. Added new section: *Prophetic Year*[2.13.5.2]. Revised existing section: *Supernatural Origin?*[4.2.7] Typographical corrections.
0.14	December 24, 2003	Added new section: *Revelation 10*[3.10]. Typographical corrections.
0.13	December 18, 2003	Added new section: *Revelation 9*[3.9]. Added new section: *Five: Provision, Fullness, Grace*[2.7.5.3.4]. Added new subsection concerning the *Beast*[5.2.9]: *Relation to the Pope*[4.2.8]. Typographical corrections.
0.12	December 4, 2003	Added new section: *Revelation 8*[3.8]. Added new section: *When Does the Day of the Lord Dawn?*[2.13.3.1]. Typographical corrections.
0.11	November 28, 2003	Fixed problem with links between files under Netscape (URL's contained DOS back slashes which are now converted to forward slashes). Typographical corrections.
0.10	November 24, 2003	Added new section: *Revelation 7*[3.7]. Added new section: *Ten Tribes Lost?*[4.17]. Typographical corrections.
0.9	November 18, 2003	Added new section: *Revelation 6*[3.6]. Added new section: *Zechariah's Horses*[4.19]. Added wood cut images by Albrecht Durer. Typographical

Revision	Date	Description
		corrections. Added parallel companion bible viewer. Added ability to open bible from commentary for each verse.
0.8	November 11, 2003	Added new section: *Revelation 5*[3.5]. Added new section: *Camp of Israel*[4.7.2]. Typographical corrections.
0.7	November 5, 2003	Added new section: *Revelation 4*[3.4]. Added new section: *Four Gospels*[4.7]. Typographical corrections.
0.6	October 30, 2003	Added new section: *Revelation 3*[3.3]. Added new section: *Rapture*[4.14]. Added new section: *Book of Life*[4.4]. Typographical corrections.
0.5	October 20, 2003	Added new section: *Revelation 2*[3.2]. Added new section: *Crowns*[4.6]. Added new section: *Jezebel*[4.9]. Added new section: *Worldly Churches*[4.18]. Added new section: *Who is the Overcomer?*[4.15.1.3]. Revised *Seven Churches of Asia*[4.15]. Added new picture of Domitian Gold Coins to *Failure in Fulfillment*[4.12.3]. Typographical corrections.
0.4	October 9, 2003	Added a section titled *Automatic Lookup*[2.2.2.7] which describes how to automatically open the commentary at a specified section or verse. Added first draft of verse-by-verse commentary for *Revelation 1*[3.1]. Added first draft of a section titled the *Seven Churches of Asia*[4.15]. Added first draft of a section titled *Imminency*[4.8].
0.3	September 15, 2003	Added support for automatically opening the HTML commentary by chapter and verse, section number, or fragment of the section title. Some examples: *index.htm?2.1* opens the commentary at section 2.1; *index.htm?symbols* opens the commentary at the first section which has the word 'symbols' in its title; and *index.htm?1:10* opens the commentary at chapter 1 and verse 10.
0.2	September 08, 2003	Incorporated feedback from reviewers. Added a new section on *the symbolic meaning of the number two*[2.7.5.3.1]. Added new diagrams illustrating the recapitulation and sequential views of the *Literary Structure*[2.14].
0.1	August 16, 2003	First draft of all introductory subjects. Introduction without verse-by-verse commentary.
0.0	May 2003	Began background study for introduction.

2 – Introduction

2.1 - Audio Course

A companion audio course on the book of Revelation is available over the internet from

http://www.SpiritAndTruth.org/teaching/5.htm

The course includes audio recordings of many of the background topics as well as verse-by-verse teaching through the entire book of Revelation. The course is available in a variety of formats and can be download to your computer for more convenient access or future reference.

2.2 - As We Begin

2.2.1 - An Invitation

We invite the reader to journey along with us as we explore what the last book of the Bible, the book of Revelation[1] has to say concerning a simple carpenter born 2,000 years ago in Bethlehem, Israel. Although many recognize that the death of Jesus has had a greater impact upon the world than that of any other person of history, relatively few realize how much He will intervene in history *yet to come* as He proves Himself to a skeptical world as being much more than a simple carpenter: the King of kings and Lord of lords risen from the dead.

If you do not yet know Jesus, we urge you to consider the importance of believing in Him:

> For God so loved the world that He gave His only begotten Son, that whoever believes in Him should not perish but have everlasting life. For God did not send His Son into the world to condemn the world, but that the world through Him might be saved. He who believes in Him is not condemned; but he who does not believe is condemned already, because he has not believed in the name of the only begotten Son of God. (John 3:16-18)

> Thomas said to Him, "Lord, we do not know where You are going, and how can we know the way?" Jesus said to him, "I am the way, the truth, and the life. **No one comes to the Father except through Me.**" (John 14:5-6) [emphasis added]

> God our Savior . . . desires all men to be saved and to come to the knowledge of the truth. For *there is* one God and one Mediator between God and men, *the* Man Christ Jesus, who gave Himself a ransom for all, to be testified in due time. (1Ti. 2:3-6)

We invite you to consider the free gift offered in the final chapter of the Bible:

> And the Spirit and the bride say, "Come!" And let him who hears say, "Come!" And let him who thirsts come. Whoever desires, let him take the water of life freely. (Rev. 22:17)

If you already know this carpenter personally, may your knowledge of Him be increased by our study of the book of Revelation.

2.2.2 - Housekeeping Matters

In this section, we discuss some practical matters related to the use of this commentary.

2.2.2.1 - Section Numbers

Because this commentary is being made available in a wide variety of formats (including digital formats), it is not practical to rely upon page numbers to locate information. Instead, numbers are used to designate the section within which related information appears. Sections are numbered in a hierarchical fashion where subsections include the section number of their containing section. For example, section 5 will have subsections numbered 5.1, 5.2, 5.3, etc. Section 5.1 will have subsections numbered 5.1.1, 5.1.2, 5.1.3, and so on.

2.2.2.2 - Finding Your Way Around

Digital versions of the commentary contain navigation controls which facilitate movement through the text. The following controls are located at the top and bottom of each major section.

Navigation Aids in the Electronic Version

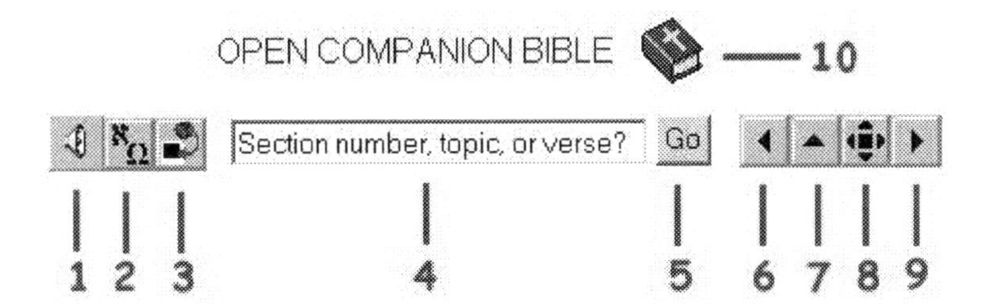

Each control in the diagram above is described below:

1. **Audio Course** - Click on this button to listen to the companion audio course on the book of Revelation.
2. **Hebrew and Greek Fonts** - Click on this button to obtain the necessary Hebrew and Greek fonts for viewing the original Bible languages in the text. See *Hebrew and Greek Fonts*[2.2.2.6].
3. **Download** - Click on this button to download the commentary from our website to your computer. This allows the commentary to be viewed when disconnected from the internet. It also provides faster access for those with a slow internet connection.
4. **Find Entry** - Type a section number, topic, or Bible address of interest. Press the *Go* button (or type [ENTER] on the keyboard) to open the related section, topic, or address. To open section *1.3*, type *1.3.* To find the topic *symbol*, type *symbol.*[2] To open this section you are reading from anywhere in the commentary, type *navigating* . To open the verse-by-verse commentary associated with Revelation 3:10, type *3:10* or *Rev. 3:10.*
5. **Go** - Press this button (or type [ENTER] on the keyboard) to find the section number, section heading, or Bible address which appears in the *Find Entry*.
6. **Previous** - Press this button to go to the preceding topic (the previous major section heading).
7. **Up** - Press this button to go to the section which contains this section.
8. **Table of Contents** - Opens the *Table of Contents*[2]. There is also an *Expanded Table of Contents*[5.1] in the *Reference Information*[5] which lists every section heading in the entire commentary.
9. **Next** - Press this button to go to the following topic (the next major section heading).
10. **Companion Bible** - Click on the Bible icon to open or close the companion Bible. When the companion Bible is open, the Bible text appears in a parallel viewing frame. Clicking on a Bible address causes the parallel Bible to move to the related address while the main text remains stationary. When the companion Bible is closed, the full viewing area is devoted to the text and clicking on a Bible address moves the entire viewing area to the Bible. Use the browser *BACK* button to return to the main text.

2.2.2.3 - Cross-References

Several types of cross-references are found within the text.

1. **Glossary Entry** - Key words and phrases are explained in the glossary. Glossary entries are followed by a section cross-reference in superscript. For example: *Amillennialism*[5.2.1].
2. **Section Title** - A cross-reference to a related section title appears in italics. The related section number appears within superscripted brackets. For example: *Why Another Commentary on Revelation?*[2.2.3].

2.2.2.4 - New King James Version

This commentary utilizes the *New King James Version* (NKJV) English text based upon the Greek *Textus Receptus* (*TR*[5.2.79]) which stands in the line of the *Majority Text* (*MT*[5.2.45]).[3] We feel this text has several advantages:[4]

1. The NKJV text provides a readable, modern text.
2. Because of its close affinity with the historic *King James Version* (KJV), the NKJV indirectly benefits from the many historic reference works based on the KJV.[5]
3. We are unconvinced by arguments that the *Critical Text* (*NU*[5.2.49])[6] necessarily represents an improvement over the traditional text.[7]
4. The NKJV text provides helpful footnotes where the *Critical Text* (NU) and the *Majority Text* (MT) differ from the *Textus Receptus* (TR).

Although there are many variations in the Greek Text of the book of Revelation, they are mainly associated with minor aspects of the text and do not present undue difficulty in understanding the message.[8]

2.2.2.5 - Use of Bible Addresses

All book names within Bible addresses appear in one of two forms: (1) the full formal name (e.g., Revelation), or (2) a standardized abbreviation. The standardized abbreviations are: **Gen., Ex., Lev., Num., Deu., Jos., Jdg., Ru., 1S., 2S., 1K., 2K., 1Chr., 2Chr., Ezra, Ne., Est., Job, Ps., Pr., Ecc., Sos., Isa., Jer., Lam., Eze., Dan., Hos., Joel, Amos, Ob., Jonah, Mic., Nah., Hab., Zep., Hag., Zec., Mal., Mtt., Mark, Luke, John, Acts, 1Cor., 2Cor., Gal., Eph., Php., Col., 1Th., 2Th., 1Ti., 2Ti., Tit., Phm., Heb., 1Pe., 2Pe., 1Jn., 2Jn., 3Jn., Jude, Rev**.[9]

Citations from other works appear *verbatim* with the following exceptions: (1) Bible addresses for which the book of Revelation is assumed, which omit an explicit book name, have been modified to include an initial book name designating the book of Revelation; (2) Bible addresses which employ abbreviated book names have been converted to use the standardized book abbreviations (above); (3) Bible addresses for single-chapter books which omit the chapter number (e.g., “Jude 5”) have been augmented with an initial chapter number of “1” (e.g., “Jude 1:5”). These changes have been made to standardize Bible addresses to facilitate the automated conversion and adaptation of this text for inclusion in computer-based study tools.

2.2.2.6 - Hebrew and Greek Fonts

The digital version of the commentary displays the original languages of the Bible using the free *Gentium*[10] and *SBL Hebrew* [11] fonts available on the internet.

If you are viewing this commentary in a digital format, you may need to download and install the fonts in order to view the original Hebrew or Greek characters. Wherever Hebrew or Greek occurs in this commentary, a transliteration into Roman characters is included for those who cannot read the original languages or who cannot access the Hebrew and Greek fonts. See the following footnote for examples of Hebrew and Greek words and their corresponding transliteration.[12]

2.2.2.7 - Automatic Lookup

The *HTML version of this commentary* (http://www.spiritandtruth.org/id/revci.htm) supports the ability to automatically open at a section or chapter and verse. To perform an automated lookup, include a search string specifying the section number, section name, or Bible address of interest. For example, to open the commentary at this section, specify: *www.spiritandtruth.org/id/revc.htm?Automatic Lookup* (http://www.spiritandtruth.org/id/revc.htm?Automatic Lookup). To open the commentary at section number 1.6, specify a search string of *?1.6*. To open the commentary at Revelation chapter 1 and verse 10, specify: *?1:10*. If you downloaded the HTML commentary for offline use, pass the search string to the *index.htm* file in the top level directory of the commentary, for example: *index.htm?Automatic*

Lookup.

2.2.2.8 - Endnote References

This commentary draws from references which exist in both digital and traditional paper media. Citations to references in traditional book or article form typically make use of the page number to locate the citation. While this means of locating a citation is viable for books in print form and for some forms of digital media, many digital references do not support traditional pagination. Therefore, a different means of locating a citation is required. Moreover, even those references which currently exist in print may eventually be more readily available in digital format. Wherever possible, we have chosen to indicate the location of citations by Bible address (e.g., *Rev. 12:10*) rather than page number. This is not possible in all cases—as when citing material from a nonbiblical source or which does not deal with the verse-by-verse treatment of the Bible text. It is our expectation that over time this approach will prove to be more digital-friendly for the use of this work in conjunction with other study aids in electronic format.

2.2.3 - Why Another Commentary on Revelation?

If one were to attempt to climb to the moon upon a stairway made of books published upon a single topic, the informed person would choose to build that staircase out of biblical commentaries. Next to the Bible itself, the most voluminous stream of publication down through history must be the writing of men and women who have attempted to understand and explain the biblical text. The number of commentaries, dictionaries, devotionals, and other study aids which focus upon the Word of God is truly staggering.

Out of this vast stream of biblical interpretation, perhaps the largest tributary consists of commentaries upon the book of Revelation, otherwise known as *The Apocalypse*. The sheer number of commentaries on the last book of the New Testament is a daunting consideration for anyone who would attempt to contribute to this flow of words which has spanned centuries and occupied some of the best minds and most devoted spirits mankind has been graced with by God. When scanning the footnotes or bibliography of one of the many modern commentaries on the book of Revelation, one is immediately overwhelmed by the breadth of material which has been written on this book.

Any writer who considers casting his small pebble into such a mighty flow must ask himself what his work could possibly contribute to the already large body of material on the subject? Why attempt to extend the work of giants who have gone before? Will it not be equivalent to painting over the face of a finished diamond? Surely, close attention must be given to the motives and goals of such a task!

It is from such a perspective that we offer this work. It is not our intention to supersede or improve upon those which have gone before, but to glean from their work while achieving the following goals:

1. **Unrestricted Use** - To provide a commentary which is not subject to the royalty and permission limitations so prevalent in our times. *A primary goal* of this work is to provide a modern commentary on the book of Revelation which may be copied and freely distributed by any means and for any purpose. This is particularly important in our current age of digital study tools and worldwide distribution via the internet. It is our desire that this commentary would be freely available for reading or inclusion with any of the many free or low-cost Bible-study programs which are now available.[13] The *copyright*[1.1] for this commentary embraces this goal.
2. **Use of Modern Technology** - To present the commentary using modern text-processing, cross-referencing, and presentation technology. This facilitates the ease with which the material can be read when using a computer, with or without an accompanying digital Bible text.
3. **Introduction to Other Works** - To guide the inquiring student toward what we believe are the most valuable and trustworthy works available on the book of Revelation. Fortunately, after dismissing those works which compromise the core values of Evangelicalism or are written by those lacking the illumination of the Holy Spirit because they have not been "born again," the number is reduced substantially.[14] Readers will find additional aids for the study

of the book of Revelation within the footnotes and *bibliography*[5.6].

4. **A Policy of Inoculation** - It is our desire to alert the unfamiliar reader concerning some of the potential *pitfalls*[2.2.10] which accompany a study of Revelation, and the Bible in general.

2.2.4 - Attacks upon the book of Revelation

As we consider this last book of the Bible, we would do well to bear in mind the strategy of the enemy which has long sought to undermine a plain acceptance and understanding of this capstone of God's revelation. The confusion which exists concerning the interpretation of the book of Revelation is one of many evidences which reflect his desire that this important part of God's Word might not have its intended effect among the saints. In fact, the two "bookends" of the Bible, Genesis and Revelation, are of foundational importance in revealing the purposes and plan of God.

If the authority of Genesis can be unseated, then the rest of God's Word which is constructed upon it, will also be seriously eroded. This, then, is a key aspect of the admittedly clever but unsupportable theory of evolution which substitutes random events for the Grand Designer. If evolution were true, then the entire gospel of Jesus Christ collapses.

As one atheist has observed:[15]

> Without Adam, without the original sin, Jesus Christ is reduced to a man with a mission on the wrong planet. Sin becomes not an ugly fate due to man's disobedience, but only the struggle of instincts. Christianity has fought, still fights, and will fight science to the desperate end over evolution, because evolution destroys utterly and finally the very reason Jesus' earthly life was supposedly made necessary. Destroy Adam and Eve and the original sin, and in the rubble you will find the sorry remains of the son of god. Take away the meaning of his death. If Jesus was not the redeemer who died for our sins, and this is what evolution means, then Christianity is nothing! Christianity, if it is to survive, must have Adam and the original sin and the fall from grace or it cannot have Jesus the redeemer who restores to those who believe what Adam's disobedience took away. [16]

Similar spiritual elements which are at work attempting to undermine the trustworthiness of the book of Genesis are also busily attempting to undermine the message of the book of Revelation. Morris observes the importance of both Genesis and Revelation as antidotes for existentialism and postmodernism which now characterize secular philosophy:

> It is small wonder that the great Enemy of God's truth has directed his most intense attacks against Genesis and Revelation, denying the historicity of the former and the perspicuity of the latter. With neither creation nor consummation—neither beginning nor ending—all that we would have is the existential present, and this unfortunately has become the almost universal emphasis of modern philosophy and religion.[17]

Not only do the books of Genesis and Revelation serve as important moorings for understanding our place in the scheme of God's universe, but the book of Revelation serves also as God's unveiling to His saints of important future events. The master deceiver is well aware of this and has specially targeted this book for attack.

> The Apocalypse not only reveals much concerning the person and work of the Man of Sin, but it describes his doom, as it also announces the complete overthrow of the Trinity of Evil. This, no doubt, accounts for much of the prejudice which obtains against the study and reading of this book. It is indeed remarkable that this is the only book in the Bible connected with which there is a distinct promise given to those who read and hear its prophecy (Rev. 1:3). And yet how very rarely it is read from the pulpits of those churches which are reputed as orthodox! Surely the great Enemy is responsible for this. It seems that Satan fears and hates above every book in the Bible this one which tells of his being ultimately cast into the Lake of Fire. But 'we are not ignorant of his devices' (2Cor. 2:11). Then let him not keep us from the prayerful and careful perusal of this prophecy which tells of those things .which must shortly come to pass.[18]

What may be surprising to the newer believer is the source of these attacks: from both outside and *within* Christianity. Of these two, the latter is more damaging.[19]

2.2.5 - Avoidance within Christianity

As has been long observed, the book of Revelation is not often taught from the pulpits of Christianity by the very men whom God has raised up for the purpose of serving as balanced, in-depth guides to the truths therein.

> There is a widespread prejudice against the study of the Apocalypse. Though it is the great prophetic book of the New Testament, the last of all the writings of *Inspiration*[5.2.33], a special message from the ascended Saviour to His Churches on earth, and pressed upon every one's attention with uncommon urgency, there are religious guides, sworn to teach "the whole counsel of God," who make a merit of not understanding it, and of not wishing to occupy themselves with it.[20]

Even the greatest commentator of the Reformation, John Calvin, avoided writing a commentary on Revelation.[21]

One side-effect of this avoidance of the book of Revelation by pastors tasked with edifying the saints is that others who are less qualified step in and attempt to do the job in their place. Due to its seemingly mysterious nature and wealth of symbols, the curiosity of believers is aroused. If they are unable to find solid teaching about the book from their local church pulpit, they naturally look elsewhere. Unfortunately, most of the alternative sources are lacking in intimacy with our Lord, biblical understanding, or are motivated to gain followers and notoriety by "tickling the ears" of the saints, as Paul warned Timothy (2Ti. 4:3-4).

2.2.6 - Hiding or Revealing?

The intent of the book of Revelation is provided by the very first word of the first verse: Ἀποκάλυψις [*Apokalypsis*][22] which Strong defines as "**1** a laying bare, making naked. **2** a disclosure of truth, instruction. 2A concerning things before unknown. 2B used of events by which things or states or persons hitherto withdrawn from view are made visible to all. **3** manifestation, appearance."[23] The emphasis shared by all these varied meanings is *making known* or *revealing* things which previously were not known and is rendered by our English word *revelation* which has a similar meaning: "**1.a.** The act of revealing or disclosing. **b.** Something revealed, especially a dramatic disclosure of something not previously known or realized."[24] That it is God's intent to *reveal* information is made plain later in the same verse where it is said that God gave the Revelation to Jesus **"to show His servants."** Clearly, the book of Revelation is not meant to obscure, but to reveal! Yet many would admit to finding the last book of the Bible difficult to understand, even puzzling—almost as if written to frustrate the very goal stated in the first verse. [25]

It is our belief that this *tension* between God's desire to reveal and the fact that many are unable to understand the book of Revelation stems from a principle which Jesus spoke about. Like many of Jesus' teachings, it is a disturbing teaching which is very important to grasp.

After Jesus had been rejected by the religious leaders of the Jews, Matthew records:

> On the same day Jesus went out of the house and sat by the sea. And great multitudes were gathered together to Him, so that He got into a boat and sat; and the whole multitude stood on the shore. Then He spoke many things to them in *parables*, saying. . . (Mtt. 13:1-3)

This is the first mention of the word "*parable*[5.2.54]" by Matthew and underscores an essential shift in the teaching ministry of Jesus.[26] Previously, Jesus had not relied heavily upon the use of parables for teaching. Matthew identifies this shift for the reader:

> All these things Jesus spoke to the multitude in parables; and **without a parable He did not speak to them** (Mtt. 13:34) [emphasis added]

At first, one might be tempted to interpret this change in teaching style to Jesus' desire to impart deep truths through simple illustrations. Such an understanding is *partly* true, but there is another more ominous aspect of the use of parables which is more germane to our topic at hand—understanding the book of Revelation. Toussaint explains:

> According to the etymology of the word "parable" παραβολή [*parabolē*] is the act of placing one thing beside another so that a comparison may be made between them. As a result the word came to

> mean a comparison, illustration, or figure. [Henry Barkclay Swete, *The Parables of the Kingdom* , p. 1.] . . . The key to the purpose of these parables is found in the Lord's own explanation (Mtt. 13:11-18). He says that He uses parables at this juncture for **two purposes**—to reveal truth and **to conceal it.** To the ones who accept the Messiah the truth and interpretation of the parables is revealed (Mtt. 11:25-26; 13:11-16). On the other hand, to those who have **hardened their hearts** the truth is veiled by the parables (Mtt. 11:25-26; 13:11-15). [emphasis added][27]

Here then is a principle which all who seek to understand God's Word must come to grips with: the Word of God is like a two-sided coin. One side *reveals* His truth to those who seek Him. The other side *hides* that same truth from those who have hardened their heart against Him. Jesus Himself explained it best:

> He answered and said to them, "Because it has been given to you to know the mysteries of the kingdom of heaven, but to them it has not been given. For whoever has, to him more will be given, and he will have abundance; but whoever does not have, even what he has will be taken away from him. Therefore I speak to them in parables, because seeing they do not see, and hearing they do not hear, nor do they understand. And in them the prophecy of Isaiah is fulfilled, which says: 'Hearing you will hear and shall not understand, and seeing you will see and not perceive.' " (Mtt. 13:11-14 cf. Isa. 6:9-10)

The surprising and rather difficult aspect of this teaching of Jesus is to some *it has not been given.* Jesus spoke of this need for spiritual regeneration to receive revelation when Nicodemus came visiting one night. Jesus told Nicodemus, "Most assuredly, I say to you, unless one is born-again, he cannot see the kingdom of God." (John 3:3). This need to be born-again reflects the fact that those who have not come to faith in Christ are unable to understand the things of God. Paul also wrote of it: "But the natural man does not receive the things of the Spirit of God, for they are foolishness to him; **nor can he know *them*,** because they are **spiritually discerned**" [emphasis added] (1Cor. 2:14).

Isaiah related the same principle. Unless men have the proper attitude and heart toward God, He will keep things hidden from them and frustrate their attempts at understanding:

> Pause and wonder! Blind yourselves and be blind! They are drunk, but not with wine; they stagger, but not with intoxicating drink. For the LORD has poured out on you the spirit of deep sleep, and has closed your eyes, namely, the prophets; and He has covered your heads, *namely*, the seers. The whole vision has become to you like the words of a book that is sealed, which *men* deliver to one who is literate, saying, "Read this, please." And he says, "I cannot, for it *is* sealed." Then the book is delivered to one who is illiterate, saying, "Read this, please." And he says, "I am not literate." Therefore the Lord said: "**Inasmuch as these people draw near with their mouths and honor Me with their lips, but have removed their hearts far from Me, and their fear toward Me is taught by the commandment of men**, therefore, behold, I will again do a marvelous work among this people, a marvelous work and a wonder; for the wisdom of their wise *men* shall perish, and the understanding of their prudent *men* shall be hidden." (Isa. 29:9-14) [emphasis added]

Here we meet with the first of several caveats which must be considered when attempting to understand the book of Revelation. Unless you, the reader, are "born-again," you will not understand God's Word—including that which is recorded in the book of Revelation. Even if you are born-again, commentaries and study aids produced by those who have not experienced regeneration are of very limited, even negative, value. This alone eliminates massive volumes of verbiage by those who lack the illumination of the Holy Spirit.[28] For how can those who lack the essential means of spiritual understanding ever hope to teach spiritual truth to others? The very symbols and allusions within God's Word are intended *by design* to conceal spiritual truth from the unregenerate. Yet many commentators throughout history have continued in this vain attempt to rely on purely natural insight to explain this spiritual book. The fruitlessness of such attempts are perhaps no more evident than in prophetic portions of Scripture which employ symbols like those found in the book of Revelation. "Prophecy therefore must be expressed in symbolic language in order that only the faithful and the spiritually discerning might know. Symbols confuse unbelieving skeptics without unnecessarily frustrating believing Christians."[29] Although there is clearly an intent by God to hide truth from those without eyes to see, Tan notes this is not the primary purpose of prophecy: "Prophecy is given more primarily to reveal the future to believers than to veil it from unbelievers."[30]

Another source of difficulty is the variety of interpretations which result from those who undertake to study the book and explain it to others. "It is doubtless true that no other book, whether in sacred or profane literature, has received in whole or in part so many different interpretations."[31] Many of these interpretations are more enigmatic than the book itself. "The literary genius G.K. Chesterson once quipped, 'Though St. John the Evangelist saw many strange monsters in his vision, he saw no creatures so wild as one of his own commentators.' "[32] This variety of interpretive results has been damaging to the cause of Christ and was certainly not His intention when He first gave it to His servant John.[33]

This diversity of interpretive results serves to *obscure* rather than *reveal* the message which God intended His saints to understand and receive a blessing from (Rev. 1:3; 22:7, 14). If God Who created language also created the human brain, surely He did so having in mind the *sufficiency* of communication between His creature and Himself and from creature to creature. If language and man's intellect is sufficient and God's revealed Word is Holy and perfect, what accounts for the wide variations in understanding attributed to the book of Revelation? In a word: *hermeneutics*[5.2.26]!

Although we treat the issues in more depth in our discussion of *Interpreting Symbols*[2.7], here we will simply note that unless a uniform approach to interpretation based on the normal rules of communication is extended to every part of God's Word, then the perspicuity of Scripture is greatly compromised. This can be seen in the huge variation of interpretive results by those who depart from these rules of grammatical historical interpretation. The large variety of meanings attributed to the book of Revelation are the result of using a faulty hermeneutic. This is one of the many tools used by the enemy of God to undermine the understanding of His Word. When one restricts the interpretive variations to those who employ a literal hermeneutic, the range of possibilities dwindles significantly resulting in much agreement and thus, the perspicuity of the Scriptures is preserved. One can only wonder why those who employ techniques which yield hugely varying interpretations fail to see the variance in their results as irrefutable evidence of the faultiness of their approach!

No, it is God's intent that we understand the message He has given. Although we may never understand all that He has revealed, it is not His purpose to frustrate or confuse (1Cor. 14:33). While it is our firm conviction that much may be known with confidence, it would be foolhardy to lay claim to a complete understanding. As Pink has observed:

> To speculate about any of the truths of Holy Writ is the height of irreverence: better far to humbly acknowledge our ignorance when God has not made known His mind to us. Only in His light do we see light. Secret things belong unto the Lord, but the things which are revealed (in Scripture) belong unto us and to our children. . . . As the time of the manifestation of the Man of Sin draws near, God may be pleased to vouchsafe a fuller and better understanding of those parts of His Word which make known "the things which must shortly come to pass."[34]

2.2.7 - The Importance of Historical Perspective

As we will see when we come to the various *systems of interpretation*[2.12], maintaining the proper historical perspective is of utmost importance. In particular, two extremes must be avoided: (1) assuming that everything written in the book applies exclusively to *our day*; (2) assuming that everything written in the book applies exclusively to *John's day*. While this may seem obvious to some, it is amazing how often interpretation runs astray of these guidelines by overemphasizing one or the other of these two extremes.

Hindson explains the tendency which is most prevalent in the time of the reader:

> There is always a great temptation to read about the future through the eyes of the present! From our current standpoint in history, we presume to speculate on how the events predicted in the Revelation will eventually be fulfilled. **The problem is that each generation tends to assume that it is the terminal generation and that the end will come in their lifetime**. [emphasis added][35]

This has been the bane of historical and futurist interpretations of Scripture and has led otherwise careful interpreters into the trap of date-setting when they should have known better.

> [Hal] Lindsey taught that within a generation (a generation equals forty years) of Israel's becoming a nation again, the Lord would return (*Late Great Planet* , p. 43). This was based upon his interpretation that the fig tree in Matthew 24:32 is a symbol for the reconstitution of Israel as a nation. Thus, the generation (Mtt. 24:34) that saw Israel become a nation would also see the Second Coming. Since Israel became a nation in 1948, many believe that Lindsey implied Christ's return would occur by 1988. . . . none of Lindsey's mentors agreed with his view.[36]

The unfortunate result of such errors has been the discrediting of the most valid interpretive system applied to the book of Revelation: (*futurism*[2.12.5]). This is throwing the baby out with the bath-water.

Another common danger is to see all of Scripture through the eyes of the salvation history of our own experience. For those who have come to Christ since the Day of Pentecost, this is the perspective of the *Church.*

> No matter what part of the Bible may we read, the one object seems to be to "find the Church.". . . This arises from our own natural selfishness. "We" belong to the Church, and therefore all "we" read "we" take to ourselves, not hesitating to rob others of what belongs to them. . . . On this system of interpretation the Bible is useless for the purposes of Divine revelation. . . . And yet it is on this same principle that the Apocalypse is usually treated. Everywhere the Church is thrust in: John . . . represents the Church; the living creatures, or Cherubim . . . are the Church; the four and twenty elders . . . are the Church; the 144,000 . . . are the Church, the great multitude . . . is the Church; the "women clothed with the sun" . . . is the Church; the man child . . . is the Church; the bride . . . is the Church; the "New Jerusalem" . . . is the Church.[37]

While we might disagree with some of the foregoing examples, the general tendency is no doubt valid: a tendency to read past distinctions in the text and to read "ourselves" into passages which are really focused on believers in another age. Here we must use caution since "all Scripture is given by *inspiration*[5.2.33] of God, and is profitable for doctrine, for reproof, for correction, for instruction in righteousness, that the man of God may be complete, thoroughly equipped for every good work" (2Ti. 3:17). But whereas all Scripture *is profitable*, not all Scripture *is written to the same specific audience*. This is especially true of the prophetic passages of Scripture which are written *primarily* to those who will live through the times described and only *secondarily* to the rest of the saints throughout history.[38] Here, we are touching on the foundational issues of *dispensationalism*[5.2.15]: a belief that a careful reading of Scripture while recognizing its self-consistent nature results in the understanding that God has dealt with different people in different ways as biblical history and progressive revelation have unfolded. When we ignore these distinctions found in God's Word, our understanding of His message suffers.

The flip-side of our tendency to find the "church" everywhere in Scripture is a failure to recognize the Jewishness of God's Word. Especially our lack of familiarity with God's promises made to national Israel throughout the Old Testament. Even when we have studied these promises of God from the older books, many incorrectly assume these are no longer to be literally understood. Instead they subject them to spiritual interpretation in a vain attempt to replace Israel with the Church. The failure to grasp the Jewishness of much of what transpires throughout Scripture, but especially in the book of Revelation, has led many interpreters astray. No more so than in their attempt to understand and explain allusions made in the Apocalypse using pagan or historic sources which are tangential or even opposed to the principles of God.[39] We discuss these and other issues related to *the interpretation of symbols*[2.7] in greater depth elsewhere.

Another error to beware of is artificially limiting the scope of the events described within the book of Revelation. The scope can be limited in numerous ways. Historically, there is a tendency to neglect vast ages of time which have a bearing on the visions John sees, but which don't conveniently fit with the polemic purpose of the interpreter. For example, many Reformers, intent on using every weapon at their disposal to separate from Rome, tended to limit their understanding of the harlot of Revelation 17 to the machinations of the Roman Catholic system. Geographically, the historical school of interpretation has tended to limit the scope of events portrayed in the book to only those of significance to Western Christianity or even Europe:

> To limit [the scope of the Apocalypse] to Popery, or to Christendom (so called) is we believe, wholly to miss the scope of the Book; and committing the mistake condemned by true logic—vis., of putting a part (and a small part too) for the whole. The awful conflict is of far wider extent than this. It exceeds all the general petty views of its scope; as affairs of State transcend those of a Parish Vestry. . . . the scope of the book, . . . is the winding up of the affairs of the whole creation, and the fixing of the eternal states of all things in heaven and on earth. . . . While many fritter away its solemn scenes in the common-place history of Europe, there are others who see beyond.[40]

The careful interpreter will understand this capstone of God's revelation as closing up all history covering a worldwide scope and will strive to avoid artificially limiting his interpretation where the text itself does not.[41] Anderson has observed, "The bible is not intended for the present dispensation only, but for the people of God in every age."[42] The correct interpretation will recognize the benefit of the entire book of Revelation for all readers of all historic ages and perspectives yet without denying specific prophetic settings peopled by different saints of God in different historic situations. These historical and prophetic scenes are described from both the vantage point of heaven and that of earth:

> We have here . . . a doctrine of the *history* of the consummation . . . an exposition of the *nature* of history. The book is a revelation of the connection between things that are seen and things that are not seen, between things *on earth* and things *in heaven*; a revelation which fuses both into one mighty drama; so that the movements of the human action, and the course of visible fact, are half shrouded, half disclosed, amid the glory and the terror of the spiritual agencies at work around us, and of the eternal interests which we see involved. . . . it becomes more plain that the earth is the battlefield of the kingdoms of light and darkness.—*Canon*[5.2.12] Bernard, *Progress of Doctrine in the New Testament*[43]

2.2.8 - Overemphasis on Extra-biblical Sources

There is an endless amount of material written about and urged as essential to understanding the book of Revelation. Most authors recognize the *OT*[5.2.51] context from which the book of Revelation springs, but some assert the need to go ever farther afield in the quest to find related material. Thus, not only must we understand the historical context and setting necessary for grammatical historical interpretation, we should seek the explanation of symbols and their intended meaning from secular and even pagan source material. We believe this to be an incorrect emphasis on extra-biblical material.

While it is certain that elements of the book of Revelation are intimately connected with the historical setting of the recipients (e.g., the letters to the churches of Asia), commentators too often *assume* this cultural/historical connection extends to the rest of the book where no such direct connection may be established. For example, Osborne states: "It is clear in Revelation that one of the primary problems of the believers in the province of Asia is some form of emperor worship (Rev. 13:4, 14-17; 14:9; 15:2; 16:2; 19:20; 20:4)."[44] It is one thing to recognize the significance of emperor worship to the immediate readers at the time the book of Revelation was written. It is quite another to assert that a proper understanding of prophetic passages which reveal events in a potentially distant future are dependent upon the events of the time of the writer. This goes too far and fails to appreciate the pattern established throughout Scripture by prophetic passages which although written and entrusted to an immediate readership serve to set forth events to come for the benefit of God's people yet unborn (Ps. 22:30; 102:18; John 17:20; 20:29; Rom. 15:4).

The unintended but real result of this over-emphasis on extra-biblical material is an implicit denial of the sufficiency of Scripture (Ps. 19:1-14; John 8:31; 1Cor. 4:6; 2Ti. 3:15-17; Heb. 4:12-13; 2Pe. 1:3, 19-21; Jude 1:3) and a subtle, but disastrous drawing of the reader ever further afield from the *inspired*[5.2.33] Word of God in search of gold which, more often than not, is *fool's gold.* This is especially problematic for the new believer who is ill-equipped to dredge through non-*canonical*[5.2.12] writings such as the *pseudepigrapha*[5.2.61] and *apocrypha*[5.2.5] while avoiding catastrophe. Commentators who encourage this route are akin to blind guides who leave blindfolded travelers at the edge of a precipice to wander at their pleasure. Such action is in direct contradiction to the mandate of God's Word for those more experienced to *proactively guide and guard* both themselves and those under their influence (Acts 20:28-29; Col. 2:8; 1Ti. 6:20; 1Pe. 5:2-3). The truths of God are not to be taught by the university model—where the widest smorgasbord of ideas is presented for the ungrounded to sample. Instead, we are to guard our minds and to cast down non-canonical writings and ideas which attempt to assert their influence above the very inspired Word of God (Rom. 1:21-22; 1Cor. 1:19; 2Cor. 10:5; Col. 2:3, 8, 18; 2Pe. 3:16-18). Not only is this emphasis on extra-biblical sources dangerous, but it results in all manner of incorrect conclusions as pagan or legendary ideas form the basis for the interpretation of inspired symbols. Nowhere is this perhaps more evident than in the far-fetched identifications proffered for the Woman of Revelation 12.

This emphasis on extra-biblical material becomes so acute that the implication for the simple child of God is that an understanding of the last book of the Bible is essentially beyond his grasp unless he immerses himself in the socio-political details of the late first-century, *including the broad study of pagan beliefs, practices, and symbols* of the secular society. Such an emphasis fails to understand the guidelines which the divine Author of the book has set forth for His children (Ps. 101:3; Isa. 33:15; Php. 4:8) and undermines the perspicuity of Scripture because most saints through the ages have lacked and continue to lack access to the extra-biblical materials these authors assert as essential to our understanding of this important book.

Another deleterious side-effect of the over-emphasis on extra-biblical material for an understanding of the Apocalypse is the blurring of the distinction between inspired writings versus uninspired writings. When the boundary between the *inerrant*[5.2.32] and the speculative and even fraudulent is minimized or overlooked, the results are predictable: questionable conclusions result and the student of Scripture begins to equate the uninspired writings of secular writers with the matchless and unique written Word of God. This is the well-traveled path to religious liberalism and even apostasy which has been a key tool of Satan throughout history and in our own day.

Within this commentary, we make occasional reference to extra-biblical writings, mainly when they provide insight into thought patterns, beliefs, and historical events of their time. For example, in the discussion of *related passages and themes*[2.13] we make mention of *Jewish rabbinical writings*[2.13.2] because these help illustrate the common understanding of Jewish rabbis regarding events related to the book of Revelation. We are not using the Rabbis to teach about the book of Revelation, but as a point of evidence that the Old Testament was understood by early rabbis to teach a future time of peril coming upon the world. It is our conviction that those similarities which do occur between extra-biblical writings and inspired Scripture reflect a *dependence of the extra-biblical material upon the Scripture.* It has been our observation that many scholars assume exactly the opposite—that extra-biblical myths and beliefs had great influence upon the writers of Scripture.

2.2.9 - Simplicity over Academics

As J. Vernon McGee was fond of observing, "Remember. . . [God] is feeding *sheep*—not *giraffes!*." Nowhere is this observation perhaps more relevant than to the topic at hand.

If our tone regarding the dangers of various streams of thought regarding the interpretation of the book of Revelation sounds overly negative, perhaps it is in reaction to the painful, laborious, and often depressing task of hours spent wading through numerous commentaries which are deeply academic and highly acclaimed by some, but which are void of faith and spiritual insight. Worse, they propose a seemingly endless series of fanciful or disjointed interpretations served up with a *large dose of unbelief and skepticism.* With rare exception, the words of former U.S. President Dwight D. Eisenhower could describe many of these works: "An intellectual is a man who takes more words than necessary to tell more than he knows."

Much of what passes for enlightened inquiry is an endless series of conjectures and discussions centered on a number of highly-questionable assertions made, for the most part, by unbelievers and their allies, liberal academics. These ever-taller ivory towers are impressive at first sight, until one learns to recognize the house-of-cards foundation upon which they are built. The sooner the believer recognizes these tangents as the distractions which they are, the less time will be spent attempting to understand and subsequently refute ideas which contradict the teachings of Jesus. We are speaking here of ideas such as the Documentary Hypothesis, Deutero-Isaiah theories, redaction criticism and others which have consumed an *enormous* amount of energy and time while yielding little if any fruit.[45] For those who are born-again, the simple words of Jesus fell these academic constructions. For those who are *not* born-again, we suggest that there is a more pressing issue than academic distractions concerning the book of Revelation—such as one's stance in regard to these infrequently quoted verses from another of John's writings: John 3:18-19, 36.

Let us say up-front that the approach we have chosen is unlikely to appeal to academics who place greater emphasis on interacting with each other's often questionable theories than on understanding the text and edifying the saints. Our approach here is not encyclopedic nor does it favor critical scholarship.[46] While recognizing alternate views, the emphasis is upon an understanding of the text itself and its priority over secondary commentary.

2.2.10 - A Policy of Inoculation

Someone has said "*every* writer has biases, but only *some* admit to it." It is not our intention here to provide an unbiased tour of a wide variety of views concerning the Apocalypse. There are many other works which the reader could refer to which fill that function. Here, we will practice a policy of 'inoculation' in regard to alternate views. That is, we intend to set forth enough information concerning the alternative view for readers to be aware of its major features. We also provide information refuting aspects of the view which we find most problematic. Neither the alternate view nor the refutation will proceed in great detail, but will include suitable references for those who wish to pursue the subject in greater depth. It is our hope that in the same way that an inoculation injects a small amount of a deadly disease into the human body so that it may build up its natural defenses, an understanding of aspects of alternate views will help the reader understand the problems accompanying them and so avoid the mistake of endorsing questionable ideas mainly because they are "new" or "different."[47]

Some of the matters we discuss are not simply differences in view within Evangelical ranks, but touch on basic issues concerning the nature of the Scriptures—which have been undermined by many who purport to lead others into a deeper understanding of Scripture. Teachers who endorse questionable views concerning the *inspiration*[5.2.33], *inerrancy*[5.2.32], and authorship of Holy Scripture are adept at dressing their skepticism within the garb of inference, making it less obvious to the inexperienced student of Scripture. We hope to make these implicit teachings more explicit where needed.

2.2.11 - Dispensational, Premillennial, Pretribulational Exposition

The reader should know that this commentary is written from the perspective of a *dispensational*[5.2.15], *premillennial*[5.2.58], and *pretribulational*[5.2.60] view of Scripture as we believe that this is what God's Word teaches when rightly interpreted.

By way of background, let us state that we came to salvation and spent the first five years of our Christian walk in a church which endorsed *preterism*[2.12.2]. The book table at the church featured books by authors such as David Chilton and embraced both *Dominion Theology*[5.2.17] and *Replacement Theology*[5.2.63]. During these five years, we learned many valuable things for which we will eternally be grateful. Yet the place of prophecy in the Word of God and the book of Revelation specifically were seldom, if ever taught. Having a better grasp of the issues and interpretive systems involved, we now understand that the book of Revelation was seen as having *already passed its point of relevance*. Having believed it was written primarily for first-century believers describing political events of their day, all fulfilled by the *hyperbolic*[5.2.27] language thought to be found in the book, the book was relegated to serving as a devotional text for Christian living. While it is undeniable that one great purpose of the book of Revelation is to inspire the saints of all ages, especially those in times of intense persecution, this is not the *only* or even *primary* purpose of the book.

Even though raised in a *preterist*[5.2.59] environment, as our understanding of the Word of God grew over time, it became clear that a plain reading of Scripture (we didn't know about *grammatical historical interpretation* or *hermeneutics*[5.2.26]) portrayed a very different picture than that what we had been taught. It has been our observation since that time that many who are trained to observe details and integrate the teachings of Scripture into a self-consistent whole wind up in the dispensational, premillennial camp.[48] Not because we hold this *a priori* understanding, but because the Scriptures, when interpreted in a consistently literal way where figures of speech and symbols are duly recognized as such and handled in their normative fashion, evidence differences in the requirements which God prescribes to different groups at different times.[49] For example, Scripture maintains a consistent distinction between the role of the nation Israel and the Church, [50] and sets forth Jesus as returning *prior* to the Millennium (Rev. 19-20).

This may disappoint those who find the "straightjacket" of literal interpretation too constraining. Some favor the broad vistas of devotional creativity and alternative understandings which result from non-literal interpretation. But it is our opinion that the very breadth of such vistas is strong indication of their unsoundness for they evidence an "unknowability" which undermines the value of the book of

Revelation itself. If the stated purpose of the Revelation is for God to "show His servants things which must shortly take place" (Rev. 1:1), what value can there be in allegorical or devotional interpretation which misplaces the locus of understanding from the actual words of the text to the mind of the reader? How are His servants to *know* when the results of non-literal interpretation abound in variety of meaning? The variety of results evidenced by non-literal interpretation serve as strong evidence against its suitability for the purpose stated by God.[51]

2.2.12 - Learning God's Way

Each of us that comes to the book of Revelation would do well to consider the words of Paul to the Corinthian church:

> And I, brethren, could not speak to you as to spiritual *people* but as to carnal, as to babes in Christ. I fed you with milk and not with solid food; for until now you were not able *to receive it*, and even now you are still not able. (1Cor. 3:1-2)

Although Paul is admonishing the Corinthian believers regarding their lack of maturity, as evidenced by relational confrontation among them (1Cor. 3:3), the inability to teach mature subjects to immature believers is also evident. The writer to the Hebrews echoes this principle:

> Therefore, leaving the discussion of the elementary *principles* of Christ, let us go on to perfection, not laying again the foundation of repentance from dead works and of faith toward God, of the doctrine of baptisms, of laying on of hands, of resurrection of the dead, and of eternal judgment. And this we will do if God permits. (Heb. 6:1-3)

The writer hopes to avoid conveying the same foundational knowledge previously related, but to go on to more advanced principles.

There is a progression found in God's Word. Many of its foundational truths are extremely simple and readily understood. Other truths are less evident and require a long-term foundation of Scriptural knowledge upon which the Holy Spirit builds our understanding. As Gregory the Great succinctly observed: "Holy Scripture is a stream of running water, where alike the elephant may swim, and the lamb walk."[52]

This explains why God's Word is fresh and powerful for both the new believer and the elderly saint—the "lamb" is refreshed in the shallows of the stream while the "elephant" plunges into the depths. But a problem may develop when the "lamb" decides to take matters into its own hands and undertake a *short-cut* straight for deeper waters. It will quickly find itself out of its depth, and in the case at hand, confused.

There is a head-on collision between the fast-food, instant-gratification mentality of our society and the way in which the Holy Spirit reveals the truths of God's Word to the *diligent* student. In our rush to plumb the depths of Scripture, we neglect the reality that the truths therein are often presented like peeling an onion—layer by layer God leads us deeper in His Word. He is not a God of our making and most certainly not a "God of the short-cut." He is the antithesis of "have it *your* way" and instead favors the spiritual tortoise over the hare.

Numerous times we have observed eager believers who are not yet truly acquainted with the basics of God's Word charge ahead attempting to master the book of Revelation. This is guaranteed to be unfruitful and even dangerous. God *owes us nothing!* Let us keep that in mind as we approach this book! If we are not ready for certain revelation and understanding, *so be it!*. Let's rest in that fact and trust God to give us what we need when we need it. To attempt to "push" into the book or to "cram" for long hours to force the understanding from the text is manifestly sin as it substitutes our selfish desire for elevated knowledge over trust in the gentle leading and guidance of the Holy Spirit as we invest *daily* in God's Word.

Ultimately, if we persist in a strong-armed insistence in "obtaining the goods" from a passage which we are not spiritually ready for, it may even become dangerous. We become open for deception as Satan or our flesh will readily provide a substitute for that which God, in His ultimate wisdom, has not yet given us. Thus, by pressing too hard or too soon to master a passage, we often wind up with an incorrect or superficial understanding of its true contents. The damage comes when we turn around and teach that which we don't understand. We also suffer as we grow satisfied and rest in an understanding which is in fact not a true understanding.

Instead, why not allow for puzzlement and wonder in our exploration of the book? When we encounter things we don't understand (not *if*, but *when*), why not simply "put them on the shelf" and pray about them? Over time, God will bring the key that helps unlock the puzzle. In the meantime, enjoy the journey and depend upon His Spirit to gradually bring your understanding to maturity.

2.2.13 - Focus is Christ

As we enter our study of the book of Revelation, it will serve us well to remember that the book is "the revelation *of Jesus Christ*" (Rev. 1:1). As the angel tells John later in the book "the **testimony of Jesus** is the spirit of prophecy" [emphasis added] (Rev. 19:10). Jesus made a similar statement when He criticized the Jewish religious leaders, "You search the Scriptures, for in them you think you have eternal life; and **these are they which testify of Me**" [emphasis added] (John 5:39). How many commentators, hoping to lead us into a deeper understanding of this book have themselves fallen into the same error as the "searchers" of Jesus' day? "But you are not willing to come to Me that you may have life" (John 5:40). May we not fall into the trap of searching the Scriptures for reasons *other than* to find our Lord![53]

> The central theme of the Apocalypse is given in the title to the book. It is "the revelation of Jesus Christ which God gave Him to show to His bond-servants the things which must shortly take place" (Rev. 1:1). Jesus Christ is the central theme of the Revelation. He is the most important key to understanding the book. He is both the author of the Revelation and the subject of it.[54]

When studying the book of Revelation, it is easy to become distracted from this central theme because there is so much going on—visions being seen, seals being opened, trumpets blown, bowls poured forth, judgments taking place, and so on. There can also develop a sense of morbid fascination with the details revealed regarding the two beasts (Rev. 13). Yet as believers, our primary motivation while awaiting the return of Jesus is to watch for *our Lord* , not the man of sin (Mtt. 24:42; 25:13; Mark 13:33, 35, 37; Luke 12:36-40; 21:36; 1Cor. 1:7; 16:13; Php. 3:20; 1Th. 1:10; 5:6; 2Ti. 4:8; Tit. 2:13; Heb. 9:28; 2Pe. 3:12; Rev. 3:2-3; 16:15). As we wait for Him, the book of Revelation provides a greater insight into His status today, no longer a man of sorrows, but the risen and glorified Lord!

> The book of Revelation is the only book in the New Testament that presents Jesus Christ as He really is today. The gospels introduce Him as the "man of sorrows, and familiar with suffering" during his incarnation. Revelation presents Him in His true glory and majesty after His resurrection and ascension into heaven, never again to be reviled, rebuked, and spat upon.[55]

The focus of the book of Revelation upon Christ and His return to institute His perfect, earthly kingdom can be seen in the numerous titles which John records:

> The book of Revelation is preeminently the 'Revelation of Jesus Christ' (Rev. 1:1). It describes Him by many titles, including 'the faithful witness' (Rev. 1:5); 'the firstborn of the dead' (Rev. 1:5); 'the ruler of the kings of the earth' (Rev. 1:5); 'the Alpha and the Omega' (Rev. 1:8; 21:6); 'the first and the last' (Rev. 1:17); 'the living One' (Rev. 1:18); 'the One who holds the seven stars in His right hand, the One who walks among the seven golden lampstands' (Rev. 2:1); 'the One who has the sharp two-edged sword' (Rev. 2:12); 'the Son of God' (Rev. 2:18); the One 'who has eyes like a flame of fire, and feet like burnished bronze' (Rev. 2:18); the One 'who has the seven Spirits of God and the seven stars' (Rev. 3:1); the One 'who is holy, who is true' (Rev. 3:7); the holder of 'the key of David, who opens and no one will shut, and who shuts and no one opens' (Rev. 3:7); 'the Amen, the faithful and true Witness' (Rev. 3:14); 'the Beginning of the creation of God' (Rev. 3:14); 'the Lion that is from the tribe of Judah' (Rev. 5:5); 'the Root of David' (Rev. 5:5); the Lamb of God (e.g., 5:6; 6:1; 7:9-10; 8:1; 12:11; 13:8; 14:1; 15:3; 17:14; 19:7; 21:9; 22:1); the 'Lord, holy and true' (Rev. 6:10); the One who 'is called Faithful and True' (Rev. 19:11); 'The Word of God' (Rev. 19:13); the 'King of kings, and Lord of lords' (Rev. 19:16); Christ (Messiah), ruling on earth with His glorified saints (Rev. 20:6); and 'Jesus - the root and the descendant of David, the bright morning star' (Rev. 22:16).[56]

The book of Revelation claims to be prophecy (Rev. 1:3; 10:7, 11; 22:7, 10, 18, 19). But, as the angel explains to John "the testimony of Jesus is the spirit of prophecy" (Rev. 19:10).[57]

It is with a devotional heart and a longing for our Lord which we should enter into our study of this book rather than an idle or morbid fascination with events to come. Without the proper focus, we risk turning this masterful message of Jesus Christ intended for personal response into a cold documentary of future events. Make no mistake: future events are here foretold, but the *purpose* of the events and their revelation to us is to glorify Jesus and to draw men to Himself. May it be so!

2.2.14 - The Primacy of Scripture

Now we come upon a subject of great importance: the primacy (ultimate importance) of Scripture. While the *inspiration*[5.2.33] and *inerrancy*[5.2.32] of Scripture is often heard on the lips, in *practice* we often demonstrate confusion on this matter. I'm speaking here of our tendency to be drawn away from the Scriptures themselves into secondary sources of lower quality. Satan is a master at using motivation, whether good or bad, and is adept at diluting our exposure to the very Words of God in favor of the fodder of man. One of his most fruitful avenues to distract believers from direct exposure to God's Word is a biblical commentary such as this. If he can draw us ever further afield through our pursuit of secondary material, he stands a better chance of separating us from the truth of God's Word. We begin to subsist on man's moldering and stale bread in place of the Bread of Life. If this is done in a gradual enough manner over time, our taste buds lose the ability to distinguish the difference. This is a dangerous diet which is both filling and utterly empty!

Yet such is the situation in many of the academies today. Forever commenting on the comments of commentators of the inspired Scriptures, the mountain of words grows ever higher and more distant from the centrality of God's Word. In our fleshly pursuit of knowledge and status, Satan is happy to provide whatever material is needed for our journey away from God. Is this not the central error of the rabbinical schools where such great priority is placed on the study of the secondary teachings of famous rabbis that precious little time is left for God's original message to dispel the darkness? What value is there in mastering Maimonides or Rashi if it precludes a basic understanding of Isaiah's Suffering Servant (Isa. 53)? Men grow in education and learning while the devil leans back and smiles!

We are not against education or human teaching. To hold such a view would be to contrary to the Scriptures themselves which indicate that God has given us *fallible human teachers* in order that we would be edified and equipped for the work of the ministry (Eph. 4:1; 2Ti. 2:24).[58] Yet as we seek to understand God's Word, it is of utmost importance that we understand the relative priority among the different sources of instruction we utilize.

Bible Study Target

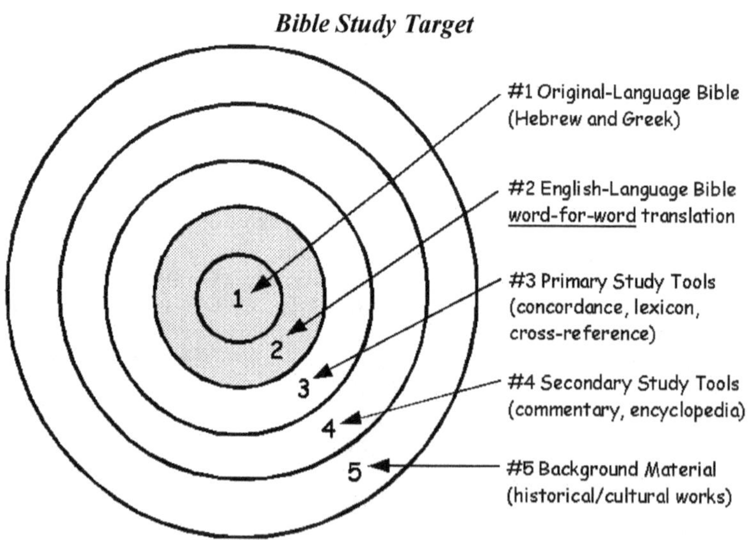

Lest someone say that *all* we need do is to remain within the inner two rings, we counter that this will not result in a mature understanding of all that God intends. For example, if we were to *completely* neglect extra-biblical history, how are we to benefit fully from Gabriel's words to Daniel: "the people of the prince who is to come shall destroy the city and the sanctuary" (Dan. 9:26)? Scripture nowhere records the nationality of the people who destroyed Jerusalem and God's House. If it were not from the historic record, we would not know that it was *Titus of Rome* who destroyed Jerusalem and the *Temple*[5.2.73] (Mtt. 24:2) and thus, be able to conclude that the "prince who is to come" is related to the Roman people.

This tension between the desire to stay immersed in God's inerrant Word versus understanding the broader context of history within which the Bible plays out and to benefit from God-given human teachers is a continual dilemma for the serious student, one that is a matter for much prayer and wisdom. Many have followed a path leading toward the edges of the target, eating stale bread and imbibing the dangerous elixir of academic liberalism only to find themselves shipwrecked in matters of faith and salvation. Fewer, but also impoverished, are those who refuse to wander beyond the center two rings. These remain ignorant of important factors which would greatly enrich their understanding of our Lord and His Word.[59] It is with an eye to recognizing the need to spend time in all rings of the diagram, yet avoiding the dangers of overdependence upon the outer rings which motivates this discussion.

The table below describes the various rings of the *Bible Study Target* and provides representative works which fall within each ring. (Consult the *Bibliography*[5.6] for additional information on the texts mentioned below.)

Rings of Biblical Study

Ring	Category	Description	Examples
1	Original-Language Bible	God's inspired Word in the original languages (Hebrew and Greek). [60]	• Hodges, *The Greek New Testament According To The Majority Text*[61] • Aland, *The Greek New Testament*[62] • Maurice A. Robinson, and William G. Pierpont, *The New Testament in The Original Greek : Byzantine Textform*[63] • *Biblia Sacra Utriusque Testamenti Editio Hebraica et Graeca*[64] • K. Elliger, and Rudolph, *Biblia Hebraica Stuttgartensia*[65] • Aron Dotan, *Biblia Hebraica Leningradensia*[66]
2	English-Language Bible[67]	*Word-for-word* translation of the Hebrew and Greek texts.[68]	KJV, KJ2000, NKJV, ASV, NASB, LITV, MKJV
3	Primary Study Tools	Concordances, Cross-references, Language Tools. These tools are denoted as *primary* because they help us to understand the raw biblical text while *minimizing* man-made interpretation.	• Strong, *The Exhaustive Concordance of the Bible*[69] • Robert L. Thomas, ed., *New American Standard Exhaustive Concordance*[70, 71] • Torrey, *The Treasury of Scripture Knowledge*[72, 73], • W. E. Vine, *Vine's Expository Dictionary of Old and New Testament Words*[74] • Frederick William Danker, and Walter Bauer, *A Greek-English Lexicon of the New Testament and Other Early Christian Literature*[75] • Spiros Zodhiates, *KJV Hebrew-Greek Key Study Bible*[76] or Spiros Zodhiates,

Ring	Category	Description	Examples
			NASB Hebrew-Greek Key Study Bible[77] • Jay P. Green, and Maurice A. Robinson, *A Concise Lexicon to the Biblical Languages*[78]
4	Secondary Study Tools	Dictionaries, encyclopedias, commentaries. These tools are denoted as *secondary* because although they can be of great value to our understanding, they also unavoidably include the biases of the authors. If we derived our primary understanding of the text from these sources, we will be 'tainted' (sometimes dramatically so) by the 'spin' which different interpreters bring to their understanding of the Bible. The dangers here are subtle, but can be far-reaching and take a long time to overcome until additional Bible study in rings 1-3 corrects misperceptions that have been learned.	• Geoffrey W. Bromiley, ed., *International Standard Bible Encyclopedia*[79] • Merrill K. Unger, R. Harrison, Frederic F Vos, and Cyril J. Barber, *The New Unger's Bible Dictionary*[80] • John F. Walvoord, and Roy B. Zuck, eds., *The Bible Knowledge Commentary*[81] • C. I. Scofield, *The Scofield Study Bible*[82] • John MacArthur, *The MacArthur Study Bible*[83] • etc. [84]
5	Background Material	Historical and cultural works which help to anchor the biblical revelation within the historic setting and culture in which it was first written.	There are a large number of works which fall into this category. A small representative sample is given here: • Nathan Ausubel, *The Book of Jewish Knowledge*[85] • Eli Barnavi, *A Historical Atlas of the Jewish People*[86] • Alfred Edersheim, *Bible History, Old Testament*[87] • Alfred Edersheim, *The Life and Times of Jesus The Messiah*[88] • Alfred Edersheim, *The Temple: Its Ministry and Services*[89] • Flavius Josephus, *The Complete Works of Josephus*[90] • *Encyclopedia Judaica - CD-ROM Edition Version 1.0*[91] • Philip Birnbaum, *Encyclopedia of Jewish Concepts*[92]

Ring	Category	Description	Examples
			• etc.

The observant reader will notice that as we move outward from the center of the target toward the outer rings, the number of study sources dramatically increases. *This is a blessing and a curse*: a blessing because of the many excellent resources which enable us to better understand the Bible, its times, and historical context; a curse because only the inner-most ring contains the *inspired and inerrant* Words of God. To the degree the secondary works draw our attention away from the center of the target, we are in danger. One need only observe the many young men of God who have gone off to seminary returning as highly "educated" liberal skeptics.[93]

Our advice is to concentrate on the inner-most three rings, especially as a new believer. **As soon as we find ourselves spending the larger share of our time outside of ring #3, let that be cause for alarm and motivate us to scurry back to the Bread of Life itself and feed upon its supernatural qualities** (Ps. 119; Heb. 4:12; 1Pe. 1:23).

The observant reader will also notice that we have just now recommended he minimize his time spent in ring #4—the very ring within which he is currently feeding by the mere fact that he is reading these words! Yet the truth remains, as much as it is our desire to see the reader blessed by this commentary, we would be doing a disservice if we failed to warn him that such fare cannot be the mainstay of his biblical diet. Although the Words of *Scripture* herein are life, the reader, aided by the Holy Spirit within him, should carefully judge whether the associated commentary remains true to God's Word.

Notes

1 Also known as the *Apocalypse of Jesus Christ*.

2 Topics are searched for within section titles, *glossary entries*[5.2], and *index entries*[5.4]. The first section title, glossary entry, or index entry containing the word or phrase is opened.

3 Scripture taken from the New King James Version. Copyright ©982 by Thomas Nelson, Inc. Used by permission. All rights reserved.

4 [Zane C. Hodges, and Arthur L. Farstad, *The Greek New Testament According To The Majority Text* (Nashville, TN: Thomas Nelson Publishing, 1985)]. We are aware that many prefer the KJV text. We have neither the mandate nor opportunity here to consider the arguments for and against the KJV text.

5 e.g., [James Strong, *The Exhaustive Concordance of the Bible* (Ontario: Woodside Bible Fellowship, 1996)], [R. Torrey, *The Treasury of Scripture Knowledge* (Oak Harbor, WA: Logos Research Systems, 1995)].

6 Kurt Aland, and Bruce M. Metzger, *The Greek New Testament* (Stuttgart, Germany: German Bible Society, 1983).

7 Neither space nor subject permit a more elaborate treatment of the relative merits and weaknesses of the *heuristics* upon which the critical Greek text depends. It is evident that many of the textual decisions underlying the *Critical Text* hinge upon unproven generalizations which are essentially unknowable on a case-by-case basis. In essence, the "algorithm" by which the textual variations are transformed into the "best" text is non-determinative and subjective. For an example which reveals these problems, see the commentary on *Revelation 5:9*[3.5.9]. Also see [Bruce M. Metzger, *A Textual Commentary on the Greek New Testament* (Stuttgart, Germany: Deutsche Bibelgesellschaft, 1994)] for additional details. The book of Revelation has fewer extant manuscripts than other books of the *NT*[5.2.48]. "The *MSS*[5.2.43] of Revelation are few compared to those of other NT literature. Thus, of the important early witnesses, only three *papyri*[5.2.53] and scarcely half a dozen *uncials*[5.2.80] of the Apocalypse are extant. While there are over a thousand *minuscule*[5.2.41] MSS for each of most of the other books, Revelation has a total of only about 250."—Alan F. Johnson, *Revelation: The Expositor's Bible Commentary* (Grand Rapids, MI: Zondervan Publishing House, 1966), 12.

8 "It should, however, be observed that the variants relate very largely to differences in the order of words, to the use or omission of the article or a connective, and to syntactical construction. Numerous as the variants are, they are not of a kind to cause uncertainty in a single paragraph taken as a whole."—Isbon T. Beckwith, *The Apocalypse of John* (Eugene, OR: Wipf and Stock Publishers, 2001), 411.

[9] Recognizing that no single set of Bible book abbreviations is optimum in terms of length, readability, and interoperation with other study aids, we are mainly interested in standardization to facilitate digital processing of this document.

[10] *http://scripts.sil.org/cms/scripts/page.php?site_id=nrsi&item_id=Gentium* (http://scripts.sil.org/cms/scripts/page.php?site_id=nrsi&item_id=Gentium)

[11] *http://www.sbl-site.org/Resources/default.aspx*

[12] Greek transliteration examples: εὐαγγέλιον [*euangelion*], μυστήριον [*mystērion*], ὑπερ [*hyper*], ῥαββι [*hrabbi*], ʼΙσραηλ [*Israēl*], ʼΙεροσόλυμα [*Ierosolyma*]. Hebrew transliteration examples: אָדָם [*`ādām*], אֶרֶץ [*`erets*], יִשְׂרָאֵל [*yisrā`ēl*], יְרוּשָׁלַיִם [*yᵉrûshālayim*], אֱלֹהִים [*`ĕlōhîm*].

[13] See *www.e-sword.net*, *www.swordsearcher.net*, *www.SpiritAndTruth.org*, and others.

[14] John 14:26; 16:13-14; 1Cor. 2:10-13; Eph. 3:5; 1Jn. 2:20, 27.

[15] How one might wish that all believers had as good a grasp of the essential relationship of Genesis to the gospel as this enemy of the cross!

[16] Bozarth, G. R., *The Meaning of Evolution*, American Atheist, 1978, 20:30.

[17] Henry Morris, *The Revelation Record* (Wheaton, IL: Tyndale House Publishers, 1983), 21.

[18] Arthur Walkington Pink, *The Antichrist* (Oak Harbor, WA: Logos Research Systems, 1999, 1923), s.v. "Antichrist in the Apocalypse."

[19] This is due to the fact that most believers automatically know to test unbiblical philosophy and teaching by God's Word. What is more damaging, are teachers who appear to fall within the pale of Christianity, but whose views concerning Revelation deny essentials of the faith or its prophetic relevance for the future.

[20] J. A. Seiss, *The Apocalypse: Lectures on the Book of Revelation* (Grand Rapids, MI: Zondervan Publishing House, 1966), v.

[21] "John Calvin, the greatest commentator of the Reformation, who wrote commentaries on the other books, did not attempt to write a commentary on Revelation."—John MacArthur, *Revelation 1-11 : The MacArthur New Testament Commentary* (Chicago, IL: Moody Press, 1999), 1.

[22] The definite article ("the") does not appear within the Greek text.

[23] Strong, *The Exhaustive Concordance of the Bible*.

[24] *American Heritage Online Dictionary*, Ver. 3.0A, 3rd ed. (Houghton Mifflin, 1993).

[25] Even Luther admitted: "Even if it were a blessed thing to believe what is contained in it, no man knows what that is."—Alva J. McClain, *The Greatness Of The Kingdom* (Winona Lake, IN: BMH Books, 1959), 6.

[26] Jesus began using parables later on the same day (Mtt. 13:1) on which the unpardonable sin was committed (Mtt. 12:24-31).

[27] Stanley D. Toussaint, *Behold The King: A Study of Matthew* (Portland, OR: Multnomah Press, 1980), 168-169.

[28] John 14:26; 16:13-14; 1Cor. 2:10-13; Eph. 3:5; 1Jn. 2:20, 27.

[29] Mal Couch, *Classical Evangelical Hermeneutics* (Grand Rapids, MI: Kregel Publications), 72.

[30] Paul Lee Tan, *The Interpretation of Prophecy* (Dallas, TX: Bible Communications, Inc., 1993), 139.

[31] Beckwith, *The Apocalypse of John*, 1.

[32] Randall Price, *The Coming Last Days Temple* (Eugene, OR: Harvest House Publishers, 1999), 308.

[33] "No other part of Scripture has proved so fascinating to expositors, and no other part has suffered so much at their hands."—Merrill C. Tenney, *Interpreting Revelation* (Peabody, MA: Hendrickson Publishers, 1957), 13.

[34] Pink, *The Antichrist*, s.v. "foreword."

[35] Edward Hindson, *Revelation: Unlocking the Future* (Chattanooga, TN: AMG Publishers, 2002), 2.

[36] Thomas Ice, *"Harold L. Lindsey,"* in Mal Couch, ed., *Dictionary of Premillennial Theology* (Grand Rapids, MI: Kregel Publications, 1996), 242.

[37] E. W. Bullinger, *Commentary On Revelation* (Grand Rapids, MI: Kregel Publications, 1984, 1935), 1-2.

[38] Matthew 24 serves as an excellent illustration. The primary audience of this passage will live during a time when there will be a *holy place* —a temple standing in Jerusalem (Mtt. 24:15), will be living in Judea (Mtt. 24:16), and living under conditions of the Mosaic Law (Mtt. 24:20).

[39] "If we count up the number of Old Testament passages quoted or alluded to in the New Testament, we find that the gospel of Matthew has a very large number, amounting in all to 92. The Epistle to the Hebrews comes higher still with 102. . . . when we turn to the Apocalypse, what do we find? . . . No less than 285 references to the Old Testament. More than three times as many as Matthew, and nearly three times as many as the Epistle to the Hebrews. We ask whether this does not give the book of Revelation a very special connection with the Old Testament, and with Israel? **It is undoubtedly written about the people of the Old Testament who are the subjects of its history**." [emphasis added]—Bullinger, *Commentary On Revelation*, 6-7.

[40] Bullinger, *Commentary On Revelation*, 111-112.

[41] The extreme of historical and geographical limitation is represented by the *preterist interpretation*[2.12.2] which sees the entire book written to 1st-Century readers and concerning events localized in either the fall of Jerusalem or the fall of Rome.

[42] Robert Anderson, *The Coming Prince* (Grand Rapids, MI: Kregel Publications, 1957), 171*.

[43] Bullinger, *Commentary On Revelation*, 123-134.

[44] Grant R. Osborne, *Revelation* (Grand Rapids, MI: Baker Academic, 2002), 6.

[45] "The roots of the present Age of Apostasy began in Europe, particularly with German rationalism, where the *inerrancy*[5.2.32] of the Scriptures was denied with the development of biblical criticism and the documentary hypothesis."—Arnold G. Fruchtenbaum, *The Footsteps of Messiah*, rev ed. (Tustin, CA: Ariel Ministries, 2003), 72.

[46] Perhaps the greatest weapon of critical scholarship is its academic *mandate* that other views engage its speculative theories else lose a hearing. This mandate denies the rule of faith of the believer and our trust in God's written revelation. Believers do not exercise a 'blind faith,' but neither should we waste precious time interacting with speculative theories which only serve to keep us from a deeper understanding of what God has revealed.

[47] Here we might pause to observe that many who have defected from solid doctrinal positions based upon the Word of God have done so because they never truly understood the position they initially endorsed. Having ridden on a "straw horse," it became all too easy for others to push them off and lead them elsewhere.

[48] Being trained as an electrical engineer, we soon found other engineers which reached similar conclusions. Men like Clarence Larkin, Henry Morris, and Robert Thomas.

[49] One need only contrast the different instructions given by God pertaining to the eating of meat to see the essence of dispensationalism: Gen. 1:29; 9:3; Deu. 12:15; Isa. 11:7; 65:25; Rom. 14:2; 1Ti. 4:3.

[50] "Of the twenty-seven uses in the Gospel of Luke and Acts, Jervell concludes: 'In Luke's writings Israel always refers to the Jewish people. At no time does it serve to characterize the church, i.e., it is never used as a *technical term*[5.2.72] for the Christian gathering of Jews and Gentiles.' "—Robert L. Saucy, *"Israel and the Church: A Case for Discontinuity,"* in John S. Feinberg, ed., *Continuity And Discontinuity* (Westchester, IL: Crossway Books, 1988), 245.

[51] Like a helium balloon in the wind, once the 'tether' of literal/normative interpretation is cut, the interpreter is 'free' to *drift* further and further afield from the intended understanding.

[52] Johnson, *Revelation: The Expositor's Bible Commentary*, vii.

[53] Ps. 40:7; Luke 18:31; 24:27, 44; John 5:39, 46; Acts 8:35; 10:43; Heb. 10:7.

[54] Hindson, *Revelation: Unlocking the Future*, 7.

[55] Tim LaHaye, *Revelation Unveiled* (Grand Rapids, MI: Zondervan Publishing House, 1999), 9-10.

[56] MacArthur, *Revelation 1-11 : The MacArthur New Testament Commentary*, 2.

[57] "He is the source of all prophecy, and all prophecy moves toward a fulfillment by Him with a view toward His own glory."—Fruchtenbaum, *The Footsteps of Messiah*, 351.

[58] Eze. 34:3, 15; John 21:17; Acts 2:42; 6:2-4; 11:25-26; 20:27; Eph. 4:11; 1Ti. 3:2; 4:6, 11, 13, 16; 5:17-18;

2Ti. 2:15, 24; Tit. 1:9; 2:1.

59 Nowhere is this perhaps more evident than in the ignorance of Jewish culture which has denuded western Christian commentary throughout history.

60 Students who do not know the original languages can derive considerable insight into the original languages by the use of some of the tools in ring #3.

61 Hodges, *The Greek New Testament According To The Majority Text.*

62 Aland, *The Greek New Testament.*

63 Maurice A. Robinson, and William G. Pierpont, *The New Testament in The Original Greek : Byzantine Textform* (Southborough, MA: Chilton Book Publishing, 2005).

64 *Biblia Sacra Utriusque Testamenti Editio Hebraica et Graeca* (Stuttgart, Germany: German Bible Society, 1994).

65 K. Elliger, and Rudolph, *Biblia Hebraica Stuttgartensia* (Stuttgart, Germany: German Bible Society, 1977).

66 Aron Dotan, *Biblia Hebraica Leningradensia* (Peabody, MA: Hendrickson Publishers, 2001).

67 Readers whose primary tongue is other than English would utilize the Scriptures in their native tongue.

68 Translations which utilize *dynamic equivalency*, such as the NIV, and those which are paraphrases (such as *The Message*) are not suited for detailed Bible study.

69 Strong, *The Exhaustive Concordance of the Bible.*

70 Robert L. Thomas, ed., *New American Standard Exhaustive Concordance* (Anaheim, CA: Foundation Publications, 1998).

71 An exhaustive concordance for the NKJV is available, but it lacks support for Strong's number and a Hebrew and Greek dictionary.

72 Torrey, *The Treasury of Scripture Knowledge.*

73 The older *Treasury of Scripture Knowledge* is more widely-available, but is not as complete or accurate as the newer version by Jerome Smith. [Torrey, *The Treasury of Scripture Knowledge*]

74 W. E. Vine, *Vine's Expository Dictionary of Old and New Testament Words* (Nashville, IL: Thomas Nelson Publishers, 1996).

75 Frederick William Danker, and Walter Bauer, *A Greek-English Lexicon of the New Testament and Other Early Christian Literature* (Chicago, IL: University of Chicago Press, 2000).

76 Spiros Zodhiates, *KJV Hebrew-Greek Key Study Bible* (Chattanooga, TN: AMG Publishers, 1991).

77 Spiros Zodhiates, *NASB Hebrew-Greek Key Study Bible* (Chattanooga, TN: AMG Publishers, 1990).

78 Jay P. Green, and Maurice A. Robinson, *A Concise Lexicon to the Biblical Languages* (Lafayette, IN: Sovereign Grace Publishers, Inc., 1987).

79 Geoffrey W. Bromiley, ed., *International Standard Bible Encyclopedia* (Grand Rapids, MI: William B. Eerdmans Publishing Co., 1979, 1915).

80 Merrill K. Unger, R. Harrison, Frederic F Vos, and Cyril J. Barber, *The New Unger's Bible Dictionary* (Chicago, IL: Moody Press, 1988).

81 John F. Walvoord, and Roy B. Zuck, eds., *The Bible Knowledge Commentary* (Wheaton, IL: SP Publications, 1983).

82 C. I. Scofield, *The Scofield Study Bible* (New York, NY: Oxford University Press, 2002, 1909).

83 John MacArthur, *The MacArthur Study Bible* (Nashville, TN: Word Publishing, 1997).

[84] Many works in this category, such as [David Noel Freeman, ed., *The Anchor Bible Dictionary* (New York, NY: Doubleday, 1996, c1992)], are so compromised by academic liberalism that we cannot recommend them except for comparative study by mature, well-grounded saints. Even then, the value-per-page of many works in this category is extremely low. The hugely-popular *NIV Study Bible* is not recommended. As mentioned elsewhere, the NIV translation is not suitable for in-depth study and the commentary attending the *NIV Study Bible* is compromised by an attempt to appeal to too many interpretive positions.

[85] Nathan Ausubel, *The Book of Jewish Knowledge* (New York, NY: Crown Publishers, 1964).

[86] Eli Barnavi, *A Historical Atlas of the Jewish People* (New York, NY: Schocken Books, 1992).

[87] Alfred Edersheim, *Bible History, Old Testament* (Peabody, MA: Hendrickson Publishers, 1995).

[88] Alfred Edersheim, *The Life and Times of Jesus The Messiah* (Peabody, MA: Hendrickson Publishers, 1993).

[89] Alfred Edersheim, *The Temple: Its Ministry and Services* (Peabody, MA: Hendrickson Publishers, 1994).

[90] Flavius Josephus, *The Complete Works of Josephus* (Grand Rapids, MI: Kregel Publications, 1981).

[91] *Encyclopedia Judaica - CD-ROM Edition Version 1.0* (Jerusalem: Judaica Multimedia, 1997).

[92] Philip Birnbaum, *Encyclopedia of Jewish Concepts* (New York, NY: Hebrew Publishing Company, 1995).

[93] "Apostasy would first begin in a denominational school and thus affect the training of ministers who were to fill the pulpits of the churches of those denominations. Eventually, more and more liberals took over the pulpits, and more and more churches became liberal themselves. So throughout the first two decades of the twentieth century, apostasy took over the schools and trained ministers for denominational churches."—Fruchtenbaum, *The Footsteps of Messiah*, 73.

2.3 - Audience and Purpose

A great variety of opinion attends the identification of the purpose and the audience for whom John wrote. Some of this can be attributed to confusion, but there can be no doubt that the varied motives of interpreters play a large role in the discussion. For if it were possible to restrict the role of the book of Revelation to a particular audience or narrow purpose, then its relevance to believers occupying other geographic or historic positions will necessarily be reduced. The reader must know that this is a driving motive behind some interpretations which aspire to relegate John's message to the dustbin of history in order to avoid the conclusion that many events described therein are yet future.

2.3.1 - Can't God Prophesy?

Perhaps the most puzzling statements encountered in the discussion of the purpose of the book of Revelation are those which assert that this most prophetic of New Testament books is not about predictive prophecy:

> The fact [is] clear, that the book is not a prediction of the great movements in the world and the Church in the later centuries of European history, or in the centuries which are yet to come. . . . these and many like inquiries all proceed from an utter misconception of the character of prophecy.[1]

> St. John did not write a textbook on prophecy. Instead, he recorded a heavenly worship service in progress.[2]

While we might agree that the book of Revelation is not a *textbook* and records a heavenly worship service, to imply the book is not about prophecy goes too far. Even Chilton himself seems inconsistent on this point. [3]

Beckwith confidently tells us that the book cannot be about "great movements in the world," whether in European history (which we would tend to agree with) "nor in . . . centuries yet to come." With a stroke of the pen he asserts that God had no intention of revealing historical events yet future. Even Chilton must admit: "John himself reminds us repeatedly, [the book] is a prophecy."[4] Not just a prophecy, but "completely in keeping with the writings of the other Biblical prophets."[5]

And how did God utilize the other biblical prophets? As all interpreters ought to be quick to recognize, prophecy was never given *primarily* for its predictive content. It was always given with an emphasis on *motivating* its hearers to repent and return to God. Perhaps the quintessential example is that of the prophet Jonah who was sent to a people he despised and delivered a prophetic message which had its intended effect of turning the Ninevites to God and avoiding judgment (Jonah 3:5-10). The minute we lose sight of the motivational motor behind God's prophetic Word is the time when we begin to distort and cheapen what God wants us to understand. And so it is with the book of Revelation. It is a book of *revealing*, especially of the true character and righteous judgment of Jesus Christ. This message is set within the context of real-world history with an emphasis on a coming time of wrath and judgment which should serve as a *huge motivator* for those who do not yet know Jesus Christ to consider their error! But for all this, it is equally an error to deny the plain predictive aspects of biblical prophecy. One need only consider how Herod was informed of the *predicted* birth place of the Messiah (Mtt. 2:5-6 cf. Mic. 5:2) or how Jesus arranged to ride into Jerusalem on a donkey (Mtt. 21:2-5 cf. Zec. 9:9) in order to fulfill Zechariah's *prediction* concerning the Messiah in order to see that prophecy includes a predictive element. Has not God Himself said:

> Remember the former things of old, for I *am* God, and *there is* no other; *I am* God, and *there is* none like Me, **Declaring the end from the beginning**, and from ancient times ***things*** **that are not *yet* done**, saying, 'My counsel shall stand, and I will do all My pleasure,' (Isa. 46:9-10) [emphasis added]

Why would these interpreters be so quick to assert that John's message is light on prophetic content or not really dealing with predictive events anchored in history? The answer lies in their motives. They desire to interpret the book from a *preterist*[5.2.59] perspective which denies the future application of its contents. Let the reader beware: much of what is written concerning the book of Revelation is flavored by the predisposition of the commentator. It is our intent in the introduction to our work to attempt to acquaint the reader with a number of these predispositions so that he will be better equipped to judge for himself the validity of the conclusions of such interpreters.

In response to those who minimize the predictive element of the book of Revelation, Couch states: "Why can't Revelation be a treasure house for the prophetical archaeologist if it is indeed a book of prophecy? Can't God write prophecy? Can't He give us the plan of the ages?"[6]

> It is important to understand what the book claims for itself. The words *prophecy*, *prophesy*, *prophesying*, *prophet*, and *prophets* are forms used twenty-one times in the writing. And the way these words are used leaves no doubt that the book is forecasting events yet to come. No other New Testament book uses this term about itself in such a clear way.[7]

This prophetic content is not intended for mere head-knowledge, but like *all of God's written revelation*, it must travel the 18 inches from our head to our heart with the express design of affecting a change in our daily living:

> The anticipation of seeing Jesus when he comes should cause us to live and act in a godly manner. As John wrote, we will be like Jesus when He appears (1 John 3:2), and so "every one who has this hope fixed on Him purifies himself, just as He is pure" (1Jn. 3:3). [Peter] also wrote of this cleansing effect of prophecy when he wrote about the new heavens and the new earth. "Beloved, since you look for these things, be diligent to be found by Him in peace, spotless and blameless" (2 Peter 3:14).[8]

2.3.2 - Overemphasis on Immediate Audience or Events

Although the principles of grammatical historical interpretation duly recognize the importance of the immediate audience of God's revelation,[9] this fact cannot be used to undercut God's ability to reveal events far future from the day of the immediate readers. When interpreters overemphasize the immediate audience, it makes it difficult to see how God could reveal future events to those same readers without running foul of the limited scope of such interpreters. Indeed, this is the case in the book before us. When the application to the immediate audience dominates the purpose of the book, then interpreters tend to search the local history of the first readers in an attempt to find events which, in their mind, "match" the events described by God. Two such examples are the Roman practice of emperor worship[10]and the myth that *Nero*[5.2.46] would revive from the dead.[11]

Such interpretations do not match the plain meaning of the text. Emperor worship was not a serious factor at the time of Nero, especially in Asia (see the discussion concerning the *date*[2.11] when the book was written). Nor did Nero fulfill the biblical requirements of the beast (Nero committed suicide in 68 AD whereas the beast is cast *alive* into the Lake of Fire *at the return of Jesus Christ* , Rev. 19:20). Nor has Nero been revived in the intervening centuries. (We discuss reasons why Nero cannot be the *Beast*[5.2.9] of Revelation *elsewhere*[4.12].)

One wonders if God doesn't ask Himself, "How can I tell these people about events future to the time of the recipients of My revelation without them attempting to find everything I say fulfilled in their own time?"

2.3.2.1 - Misunderstood Motive

Another stumbling block to an accurate interpretation of the book of Revelation is attributing the wrong motives to its authorship. To listen to some commentators, one gets the idea that the Book was written only after long and careful thought by John upon the geopolitical climate of his day and the impact the culture was having upon the affairs of the church:

> One thing that can probably be agreed upon by the majority of commentators is that a contributing reason for John's motive in writing is the perceived discrepancy in the Christian audience between, on the one hand, belief that the kingdom had been inaugurated, that God was sovereign over history, and that Christ would soon return to conclude history and, on the other hand, the reality that forces of evil continued to exist, to dominate culture and even flourish, while oppressing believers to varying degrees. How did the truth of the gospel relate practically and specifically to the difficult cultural, social, political, and economic realities.[12]

The reader should not miss the fact that John has just been "reinterpreted" from an obedient servant simply responding to the commands of His Lord (Rev. 1:19; 2:1, 12; 3:1, 7, 14; 4:1; etc.) into a savvy geopolitical analyst complete with his *own* motives!

Another frequently heard, but incorrect, motive is found in devotional and inspirational content. "St. John's primary concern in writing the book of Revelation was just this very thing: to strengthen the Christian community in the faith of Jesus Christ's Lordship, to make them aware that the persecutions they suffered were integrally involved in the great war of history."[13]

Again, the problem is not in recognizing that the book of Revelation does provide great spiritual encouragement and even immediate instructions for the *seven churches*[5.2.66] of Asia, but it is manifestly unbiblical to assert that this was John's *primary* task and to imply that John had *his own* motivations for writing the book.

2.3.2.1.1 - Anti-Supernatural Motive for Writing

Here we must discuss a common thread which runs throughout many works on the book of Revelation and which is particularly troubling. It is the hallmark of much which passes for academic learning in our times. *Anti-supernaturalism*: a prevalent bias against the supernatural and an overt reliance upon the natural. A substitution of the rational and analytical capabilities of man for the revealed truth and intervention of God. An elevation of learned opinion over the simple statements of Holy Writ.

There is no shortage of interpreters who are quick to attribute the writing of the book of Revelation to causes *other than* the direct intervention and command of God upon John: "It was **natural** that the Church of the first century should produce such a writing, for Christian hope centered in the coming of the kingdom of God and his Christ." [emphasis added][14] "The major thrust of Revelation is not sociopolitical but theological. John is more concerned with countering the heresy that was creeping into the churches toward the close of the first century than in addressing the political situation."[15]

These opinions, although from learned sources, are directly opposed to the simple statements of the book itself, which Mills correctly recognizes:

> [His motive] **is simply to fulfill his charge to faithfully record the vision he had been privileged to see** . However, this same verse provides us with a clue to the divine purpose in the book, for it was, firstly, to provide a divine assessment of the condition of the churches which it addresses (the things which are), and then, secondly, to record 'the things which shall take place after these things.' This last purpose is prophetic, as is clearly stated in Rev. 1:3; and this provides a clue as to the major purpose of the book. [emphasis added][16]

Where these anti-supernatural interpreters would have us envision John pondering for some number of months over the potential letter which he planned to write, carefully considering various purposes and ideas which he hoped to frame in *his* message, the biblical reality is miles apart. "John was writing as fast as he could to record the visions he was seeing."[17]

Peter had this to say concerning "John's motive:"

> And so we have the prophetic word confirmed, which you do well to heed as a light that shines in a dark place, until the day dawns and the morning star rises in your hearts; knowing this first, that no prophecy of Scripture is of any private interpretation, for **prophecy never came by the will of man**, but holy men of God spoke *as they were* moved by the Holy Spirit. (2Pe. 1:19-21) [emphasis added]

2.3.2.2 - Relevance to the Immediate Audience

A frequent assertion by those who are not in favor of the book of Revelation describing future events is that if the book were to describe events yet future to the time of the hearers, then it would necessarily be irrelevant:

> A predictive work which is totally unrelated to its own day could have no meaning for its readers because they would be unable to bridge the gap of thought between themselves and its prophecies. One might as well give a textbook on thermo-nuclear fission to a medieval monk and expect him to understand it as to present a work of complete prediction of the future to a man of any era and assume that he would profit by it unless some means were established by which he could connect his own times with the events which were to come.[18]

> If we go along with *dispensational*[5.2.15] interpreters in finding the *Rapture*[5.2.62] of the church at Revelation 4:1, then the book becomes largely irrelevant, not only to the original readers, but also to all Christians of any age. . . . This leaves it far from obvious why Christians should take an interest in such

> events, or why God wished to reveal them.[19]

One wonders if these same commentators ever considered Isaiah's unmatched prophecy of the Suffering Servant? What value might this have had to his *immediate* readership living between 739 and 686 BC?[20] According to their criteria it must have been "largely irrelevant" to Isaiah's contemporaries since it sets forth in great detail the crucifixion of our Lord at least six centuries before the actual events. Obviously, these interpreters are aware of the many prophetic examples such as Isaiah, but choose to treat them differently because they have no bearing on events *yet future to our own time*.

This insistence that all the events of the book of Revelation must pertain to the immediate hearers is without foundation and runs directly counter to the whole tenor of prophetic revelation throughout Scripture. Even many of those who lived as contemporaries of John failed to understand their contemporary Scriptures as being fulfilled in their day.[21]

Moreover, aspects of the prophecies themselves were not necessarily understood by the prophet himself, not to mention his contemporaries: "Interpreters of the Revelation should bear in mind two important passages: 1Pe. 1:12; 2Pe. 1:20, 21. Doubtless much which is designedly obscure to us will be clear to those for whom it was written as the time approaches."[22]

> To use the argument that the book must be understood by the first generation of Christians completely as a refutation of the futuristic position is not reasonable nor backed by the study of prophecy in Scripture in general. . . . it is strange that such an objection should be considered weighty. Much of the prophecy of the Bible deals with the distant future, including the Old Testament promises of the coming Messiah . . . the difficulty with this point of view is twofold: (1) Prophecy, as given in the Scripture, was not necessarily understandable by the writer or his generation, as illustrated in the case of Daniel (Dan. 12:4, 9). It is questionable whether the great prophets of the Old Testament always understood what they were writing (cf. 1 Peter 1:10-12). (2) It is of the nature of prophecy that often it cannot be understood until the time of the generation which achieves fulfillment.[23]

2.3.2.2.1 - The Present Value of Future Events

Tenney explains that God's prophetic word is relevant for all readers in all ages:

> Even though the Revelation may not find its fulfilment in the events of the present day nor even within the next century, it may still be relevant to the present situation. . . . One of the marvels of the written Word of God is its perennial relevance to every time and situation. Its principles are universally applicable, although its predictions may fit only one specific era. . . . There are four ways in which Revelation may be meaningful for this present age: (1) by giving to us the divine estimate of history; (2) by predicting the future to a definite degree; (3) by contributing theologically to the structure of Christian thought; and (4) by offering a spiritual stimulus to daily living.[24]

2.3.3 - Purpose

The biblical interpreter who does not suffer from anti-supernaturalism will forgo attempts to plumb the depths of John's psyche to establish the purpose of his writing. Instead, he will recognize that John himself *had no purpose!* But that *God*, by direct supernatural intervention, simply told John to write. And as a dutiful servant, John did just that!

The purpose of the book is not found in John, but in the plain statements given in the book and by an understanding of the content of the book. Mills provides an excellent summary:

> The divine purpose in this book can be seen as threefold. The first purpose is to reveal Christ in His deistic glory. Chapter 1 introduces the risen Christ as possessing all the effulgence of the glory of the Father and also presents Him in a judgmental capacity (the sword of Rev. 1:16). The purpose of revealing Christ in this glory is to depict clearly and unmistakably His deity-a fact which was already under question by some heretical sects-and also to present Him in an unmistakable judgmental role. This purpose, stated in chapter 1, pervades the whole book; . . . The second purpose is explicit in Chapters 2-3, and meets the particular needs and circumstances of particular churches at a particular time. . . . to address the needs of the *seven churches*[5.2.66], and **thereafter to leave a body of admonition, commendation, and promise which would be applicable to the Church Age** . . . . The third purpose, achieved in Chapters 4-22, is to confirm the apocalyptic and millennial prophecies of the Old Testament. With the emergence of the mystery age, the Church Age, questions would understandably arise as to whether God's program had been abandoned, modified or whatever. The purpose of these nineteen

chapters is to reaffirm these prophecies, to consolidate and supplement them into a fuller and more chronological record. . . A secondary purpose is to give the Church a focus for the hope that each believer has by giving a preview of the *Millennial Kingdom*[5.2.39] and of the eternal life which follows it. Revelation thus completes the New Testament argument by summarizing and consolidating those Old Testament prophecies of the Messianic Age of Righteousness which were unfulfilled at the end of the apostolic age, and by clarifying that these prophecies were still to be fulfilled at, or just prior to, our Lord's second advent, at which time He will set up the earthly kingdom prophesied in the Old Testament (we now know this as the Millennial Kingdom from Revelation 20). Secondly, Revelation also completes the New Testament presentation of Jesus Christ by displaying Him in His eternal glory, thereby refuting any attempt to leave Jesus as merely human or less than fully God. And thirdly, Revelation addresses the needs of the Church at the end of the apostolic age, thus leaving a picture of a Church as diverse as that which has succeeded it, and, consequently, a body of principles which provide admonition, commendation, and promise that is applicable throughout the Church Age. [emphasis added][25]

Notes

1 Isbon T. Beckwith, *The Apocalypse of John* (Eugene, OR: Wipf and Stock Publishers, 2001), 303.

2 David Chilton, *The Days of Vengeance* (Tyler, TX: Dominion Press, 1987), xii.

3 "The book of Revelation is not an apocalyptic tract; it is, instead, as St. John himself reminds us repeatedly, a *prophecy* (Rev. 1:3; 10:11; 22:7, 10, 18-19), completely in keeping with the writings of the other biblical prophets."—Chilton, *The Days of Vengeance*, 27.

4 Chilton, *The Days of Vengeance*, 27.

5 Chilton, *The Days of Vengeance*, 27.

6 Mal Couch, *"Interpreting the Book of Revelation,"* in Mal Couch, ed., *A Bible Handbook to Revelation* (Grand Rapids, MI: Kregel Publications, 2001), 51.

7 Mal Couch, *"The Literary Structure of Revelation,"* in Mal Couch, ed., *A Bible Handbook to Revelation* (Grand Rapids, MI: Kregel Publications, 2001), 81.

8 Mal Couch, *"Bibliology in the Book of Revelation,"* in Mal Couch, ed., *A Bible Handbook to Revelation* (Grand Rapids, MI: Kregel Publications, 2001), 89.

9 That's what *historico* means—the historical context is key to understanding the text.

10 "Revelation presupposes that Christians were being required to participate to some degree in the *imperial cult*[5.2.31] (e.g., Rev. 13:4-8, 15-16; 14:9-11; 15:2; 16:2; 19:20; 20:4)."—Gregory K. Beale, *The Book of Revelation: A Commentary on the Greek Text* (Grand Rapids, MI: William B. Eerdmans Publishing Co., 1999), 5.

11 "Some commentators argue that some passages in Revelation reflect a 'revival of Nero' myth, especially Rev. 13:3-4 and 17:8, 11, which speak of the demise of the beast and subsequent revival. The Nero myth held that Nero would return from the dead and lead a Parthian army against the Roman Empire. If these texts reflect the myth, then Revelation is better dated later than earlier, since presumably it took time for the myth to arise, develop, and circulate after Nero's death in 68 AD."—Beale, *The Book of Revelation: A Commentary on the Greek Text*, 17.

12 Beale, *The Book of Revelation: A Commentary on the Greek Text*, 28.

13 Chilton, *The Days of Vengeance*, 39.

14 Beckwith, *The Apocalypse of John*, 156.

15 Alan F. Johnson, *Revelation: The Expositor's Bible Commentary* (Grand Rapids, MI: Zondervan Publishing House, 1966), 4.

16 Monty S. Mills, *Revelations: An Exegetical Study of the Revelation to John* (Dallas, TX: 3E Ministries, 1987), s.v. "Introduction."

17 Edward Hindson, *Revelation: Unlocking the Future* (Chattanooga, TN: AMG Publishers, 2002), 4.

[18] Merrill C. Tenney, *Interpreting Revelation* (Peabody, MA: Hendrickson Publishers, 1957), 137.

[19] Steve Gregg, *Revelation Four Views: A Parallel Commentary* (Nashville, TN: Thomas Nelson, 1997), 42.

[20] John MacArthur, *The MacArthur Study Bible* (Nashville, TN: Word Publishing, 1997), 952.

[21] "The full text of *The Didache* was rediscovered little more than a hundred years ago, in a codex found in Constantinople in 1873. This document proves that those who actually lived through the events of A.D. 70 regarded Matthew 24:29-31—the entire Olivet Discourse—as yet-unfulfilled prophecy."—John MacArthur, *"Signs in the Sky,"* in Tim LaHaye, and Thomas Ice, eds., *The End Times Controversy* (Eugene, OR: Harvest House Publishers, 2003), 112.

[22] C. I. Scofield, *The Scofield Study Bible* (New York, NY: Oxford University Press, 2002, 1909), Rev. 1:1.

[23] John F. Walvoord, *The Revelation of Jesus Christ* (Chicago, IL: Moody Press, 1966), 21-23.

[24] Tenney, *Interpreting Revelation*, 194, 195.

[25] Mills, *Revelations: An Exegetical Study of the Revelation to John*, s.v. "Introduction."

2.4 – Theme

While it seems tempting to identify a primary theme of the book of Revelation, it appears that there are actually a number of themes which receive great emphasis within the book: *the sovereignty of God*, *worship of God*, and *the arrival of God's Kingdom*.

2.4.1 - The Sovereignty of God

One the most prevalent doctrines throughout Scripture is the sovereignty of God (Job 9:17; 33:13; Ecc. 3:14; Isa. 46:10-11; Mtt. 10:29; Eph. 1:11) and the book of Revelation is no exception. Within the book of Revelation, God's sovereignty is *demonstrated* by His powerful intervention in the events of history. From the opening of the first seal by the Lamb (Rev. 6:1) to the pouring forth of the seventh bowl, whereupon God pronounces "It is done!" (Rev. 16:17), it is manifestly clear that the physical and spiritual events which transpire are the direct result of God's initiative.

> This sovereign might is seen in the incredible use of ἐδόθη [*edothē*] (. . . "was given"), a divine passive that points to God's control of the events. This verb is used frequently in the book (Rev. 6:2, 4, 8, 11; 7:2; 8:2, 3; 9:1, 3, 5; 11:1, 2; 12:14; 13:5, 7, 14, 15; 16:8) and is especially clustered in the passages on the four horsemen (Rev. 6:1-8) and the activities of the beast (Rev. 13:5-15). In other words, even the actions of the forces of evil are controlled by God. Everything they do comes only by the permission of God.[1]

The very descriptions of God throughout the book emphasize the immutability of His purposes, which presents a threat to those who oppose Him but provides ultimate security for those who trust in Him.

> Revelation presents a sovereign God whose purposes must be victorious. He is almighty (Rev. 1:8), everlasting (Rev. 4:8), seated upon the throne of the universe (Rev. 4:2), the Creator of all things (Rev. 4:11). His authority is greater than that of evil (Rev. 12:10), and His name is the security of those who trust in Him (Rev. 14:1).[2]

The sovereignty of God is manifest in the visions of heaven and His throne, an image which occurs some forty-six times in the book. [3] God's sovereign control is illustrated by His role as Creator (Rev. 3:14; 4:11; 10:6) and the necessity of His sustenance for its continuance (Rev. 20:11; 21:1). [4]

2.4.2 - Worship of God

The first question of the *Westminster Confession* asks: "What is the chief and highest end of man?" To which the following answer is given: "Man's chief and highest end is to **glorify God**, and fully to enjoy him forever." [emphasis added] Like God's sovereignty, the theme of God's glory stretches from Genesis to Revelation. His manifest presence among His people is represented by His abiding glory (*shekinah* , Ex. 14:10; 16:10; 24:15-16; 40:34; Lev. 9:23; Num. 14:10; 16:19, 42; 20:6; 2Chr. 7:1; Isa. 4:5; 35:2; 40:5; Eze. 1:28; 3:23; 9:3; 10:18; Acts 9:3).

Here in the last book of the Bible, God's glory is seen through the visions and choruses of worship and praise offered up to God. From the first chapter, the glory of God and John's response are clearly revealed (Rev. 1:17).

> Worship is one of [the book's] strongest emphases. The first vision of the book brought the writer prostrate before the figure of the living Christ who appeared to him on Patmos. Through the long series of visions that followed there are repeated references to worship. . . . The implication of the book is that worship is a token of the genuineness of spiritual life now. The contrast between the saved and the lost in Revelation could be called a contrast in worship, since the latter worship the beast (Rev. 13:4, 8, 12, 15). Man is made to worship someone, and if he will not have the true God, he will inevitably turn to a false idol.[5]

Tenney notes the importance of worship in an ongoing celestial commentary of the events transpiring on earth below.[6]

Poetic Expressions of Praise

Title	Passage	Participants	Occasion
Tersanctus: "Holy, holy, holy"	Rev. 4:8	Living Creatures	Constant worship
"Worthy art Thou" in Creation	Rev. 4:11	Twenty-four Elders	Worship by Elders
"Worthy art Thou" in Redemption	Rev. 5:8-10	Living Creatures and Elders	Lamb's assumption of rights
"Worthy is the Lamb"	Rev. 5:11-12	Angels, Living Creatures, Elders	Lamb's assumption of rights
"Unto him that sitteth"	Rev. 5:13	Every created thing	Lamb's assumption of rights
"Salvation unto our God"	Rev. 7:9-10	Great multitude	Sealing of 144,000
"Amen. Blessing. . ."	Rev. 7:11-12	Angels	Sealing of 144,000
"The kingdom of the world"	Rev. 11:15	Great voices	Seventh angel
"We give thee thanks"	Rev. 16:18	Elders	Seventh trumpet
"Great and marvellous"	Rev. 15:2-4	Victors over *Beast*[5.2.9]	Seven last plagues
"Four Hallelujahs"	Rev. 19:1-8	Great multitude, Elders, Living Creatures, Great voices	Fall of Babylon, Marriage of Lamb

Whenever the reader is tempted to focus on the enormity of the events transpiring on the earth below, the scene shifts to the heavens above, the ultimate source of what is transpiring, and the destination of the glory derived from all that transpires in His creation. "No matter how many parentheses and digressions may be introduced, the Revelation maintains the celestial setting for terrestrial events. Behind the changing panorama of human history described under the symbolic pictures abides the unchanging reality of an eternal world in which God's purpose is unfailing and His Christ victorious."[7]

The importance of glory and its expression through worship is also evident in the degree to which Satan parodies God in a short-lived attempt to subvert God's glory for himself.

> Indeed, everything Satan does is a parody or "great imitation" of what God has already done. The mark of the beast (Rev. 13:16-17) in the right hand or forehead is a mere copy of God sealing the saints in the forehead (Rev. 7:3). The false trinity (the dragon, beast, and false prophet, Rev. 16:13) is an obvious copy of the triune Godhead. The mortal wound that is healed (Rev. 13:3, 12) imitates the death and resurrection of the Lord. The dragon giving the beast his power; throne, and "great" authority (Rev. 13:2) copies the relationship between God and Christ. The demand for the nations to worship the beast and dragon (Rev. 13:8, 14-15) follows the constant commands in Scripture to worship God.[8]

Here in the book of Revelation the attempt of the *creature* to occupy the role of the *Creator* comes to its vain conclusion (Isa. 14:13-14; Mtt. 4:9; Luke 4:7; Rev. 13:4, 8, 12, 15; 14:11; 16:2; 19:20). Near the close of the book, the angel informs John and those who would read or hear this prophecy that it is *God* Who alone is to be worshiped (Rev. 22:9).[9]

2.4.3 - The Arrival of God's Kingdom

When the New Testament opens, we find John the Baptist preaching, "Repent, for the **kingdom** of heaven is at hand" (Mtt. 3:2) [emphasis added]. Later, when John was imprisoned, Jesus too preached, "the gospel of the **kingdom** of God" (Mark 1:14). During this time of Jesus' early ministry while his disciples *had no understanding of His destiny on the cross*, they too announced, "The **kingdom** of heaven is at hand" (Mtt. 10:7) [emphasis added]. At the time of these early pronouncements, there is no additional explanation given to the hearers concerning the nature of this kingdom. It is evident that these pronouncements were in keeping with the expectations set forth by the very promises of God in the Old Testament. Promises which would have been familiar to the "lost sheep of the house of Israel" (Isa. 49:5; Mtt. 10:5-6; 15:24; Mark 7:27; John 1:11; Acts 10:36).

> Thus, read in the light of its evident Old Testament context, the phrase 'kingdom of heaven' does not refer to a kingdom located in heaven as opposed to the earth, but rather to the coming to earth of a kingdom which is heavenly as to its origin and character.[10]

After the religious leaders of the Jews committed the ultimate sin of blaspheming the Holy Spirit by attributing the works of Jesus to demon-possession (Mtt. 12:24-31; Mark 3:22, 28-30; Luke 11:15; John 7:20), Jesus began using parables to teach *new truths* concerning this kingdom (Mtt. 13, especially Mtt. 13:52). An important new truth which Jesus began to reveal was the *delay* before the kingdom of God would come fully on earth: "Now as they heard these things, He spoke another *parable*[5.2.54], because He was near Jerusalem and **because they thought the kingdom of God would appear immediately**" (Luke 19:11) [emphasis added]. [11]

When the disciples asked Jesus how to pray, His example included a petition to the Father to bring about His kingdom *on earth* (Mtt. 6:10).[12] Later, Jesus told His disciples that in the "regeneration" they would sit on thrones judging the twelve tribes of Israel (Mtt. 19:28). Immediately prior to his ascension, the disciples asked about the coming of the kingdom: "Lord, will You at this time restore the kingdom to Israel?" (Acts 1:6). Jesus never corrected this expectation of the kingdom of God on earth, but indicated that the *timing* of its arrival was yet future and that in the meantime a special period of time characterized by the permanent indwelling of the Holy Spirit to move the gospel across the world was the more immediate task (Acts 1:7-8).

> Jesus had just been speaking for forty days of the kingdom of God (Acts 1:4), and no doubt the content of his discussions prompted this question. Christ's answer must not be understood to be a denial of the hope reflected in this question, a hope firmly founded upon the provisions of the Davidic Covenant and the predictions of the prophets (Isa. 11:11; 55:3), but a confirmation of it. If the disciples were mistaken in this hope, this would have been a most opportune time to correct them, but Christ did not (John 14:2; 20:29; Rom. 15:8). Yet, misunderstanding this, many expositors have gone far astray in their understanding of the prophetic plan of God revealed in Scripture. Misunderstanding on this point is virtually fatal to understanding Biblical prophecy as a whole.[13]

This last book of the Bible includes key events related to God's kingdom coming *to earth* and its extension into the eternal state. The King extends His rightful rule over all the nations (Rev. 12:5; 19:15). Here is recorded the final defeat of the kingdoms of man (Ps. 2:1-2; Dan. 2:34-35, 44-45; Rev. 1:5; 19:15-21), the ushering in of the *Millennial Kingdom*[5.2.39] on earth (Rev. 11:15; Rev. 20:4), the demise of the kingdom of Satan (Rev. 20:2, 10), and the permanent dwelling of the King among His subjects (Rev. 21:3; 22:3).

Although relatively little is said concerning the *earthy* nature of the Millennial Kingdom in Revelation 20:4, this is but a small slice of all that God has said concerning this time of peace and great blessing upon the earth: Isa. 2:1-4; 9:7; 11:1-16; 60:1-12; 65:17-25; Jer. 23:3-8; 31:31-40; Eze. 37:15-28; Eze. 44-48; Zec. 8:1-17; 14:8-11; Mic. 4:1-8. That this period cannot refer to the eternal state (Rev. 21, 22) is clear for it includes the continuance of physical birth, (Isa. 65:23), sin (Isa. 60:12; 65:20), and physical death (Isa. 65:20).

> The belief in the Messianic Kingdom does not rest on this passage [Rev. 20:4] alone. In fact, it hardly rests on it at all. The *basis* for the belief in the Millennial Kingdom is twofold. *First*: there are the unfulfilled promises of the Jewish covenants, promises that can only be fulfilled in a Messianic Kingdom. *Second*: there are the unfulfilled prophecies of the Jewish prophets. . . . The only real contribution that the book of Revelation makes to the knowledge of the Kingdom is to disclose just how long the Messianic kingdom will last—namely one thousand years—for which the term *Millennium* is used. This is the one key truth concerning the Kingdom that was not revealed in the Old Testament.[14]

See *Millennial Kingdom*[4.11].

Tenney identifies three *NT*[5.2.48] principles which receive special emphasis within the Revelation: *judgment*, *redemption*, and the *establishment of the kingdom of God*.

> Judgment, redemption, and kingdom are interrelated parts of the public establishment of God's salvation. judgments are the fate of the unrepentant and the unredeemed, as the kingdom is the destiny of the redeemed believers. Redemption exempts one from judgment, and makes him ready for the

kingdom.[15]

This redemptive work of God goes beyond the establishment of a *mediatorial* kingdom ruled by Jesus in Jerusalem for one thousand years. It includes the redemption of all that was originally given to man and the restoration of conditions prior to the Fall (Gen. 3:6, 14-19). See the discussion concerning *Genesis and Revelation as Bookends*[2.13.8] for more information on the complete restoration brought about through the events recorded in the book of Revelation.

The arrival of God's kingdom on earth is inseparably linked with the arrival of the King Himself. "The return of Jesus to this earth is the central theme of this book. It will deal with events leading up to, accompanying, and following the Second Coming."[16] The kingdom has no temporal power prior to the Second Coming.[17] This emphasis on the *imminent*[5.2.30] coming of Jesus Christ is found in many statements throughout the book (Rev. 1:7; 2:25; 3:3, 11; 16:15; 19:11-16; 22:7, 12, 20). This last book of the Bible amplifies the teaching found throughout the NT that believers are to live in constant expectation of His return.[18]

2.4.4 - A Worldwide Revival

It should not be missed that in accordance with God's desire that all should come to repentance (2Pe. 3:9), the events of the book of Revelation are intended to serve as a final call to those who God knows will yet respond to the message of the gospel. This can be seen in the special ministries of the 144,000 Jewish servants (Rev. 7, 14), the two witnesses (Rev. 11:3), and the angel proclaiming the gospel message worldwide (Rev. 14:16). In response to their testimony, a large number of people will come to faith in Christ, although many will be martyred (Rev. 6:9-11; 7:13-14).[19]

Those who refuse to respond to the gospel message are shown to be unbending in their rejection of God and without any hint of repentance (Rev. 9:20-21; 16:9, 11, 21). Thus, the events preceding the Second Coming of Christ serve as a global "threshing" where the wheat (believers) is separated from the chaff (unbelievers) by the extreme tests which come upon the world (Luke 21:34-36; Rev. 3:10). In our sorrow over the destiny of the chaff, let us not overlook the wheat which is harvested to the glory of God (Rev. 14:14-16).

Notes

1 Grant R. Osborne, *Revelation* (Grand Rapids, MI: Baker Academic, 2002), 32.

2 Merrill C. Tenney, *Interpreting Revelation* (Peabody, MA: Hendrickson Publishers, 1957), 198.

3 "One of the predominant images is that of God on his throne . . . occurring forty-six times."—Osborne, *Revelation*, 33.

4 "The ultimate proof of his control over this world is that he both created and sustains it."—Osborne, *Revelation*, 32-33.

5 Tenney, *Interpreting Revelation*, 199-200.

6 Tenney, *Interpreting Revelation*, 36-37.

7 Tenney, *Interpreting Revelation*, 37.

8 Osborne, *Revelation*, 34.

9 One might also wonder whether the judgments which are poured out upon the *earth* are an indication that those dwelling upon the earth have placed undue emphasis upon the earth, while neglecting its Creator. Perhaps this is an indication of the fully-developed fruit of unbridled environmentalism which includes an idolatrous worship of the earth.

10 Alva J. McClain, *The Greatness Of The Kingdom* (Winona Lake, IN: BMH Books, 1959), 280.

11 The future aspect of the kingdom is found throughout Scripture: Ps. 110:1; Dan. 7:11-14, 21-22, 25-27; Mtt. 6:2; 7:21-22; 19:28; 25:31; 26:29; Mark 14:25; Luke 11:2; 19:11, 15; 21:31; 22:16-18, 29-30; 23:51; Acts 1:6-7; 14:22; 1Cor. 15:24; 2Ti. 4:1; Heb. 2:8; Rev. 3:21; 11:15, 17; 12:10; 19:20.

12 "Bauckham asserts that Revelation as a whole can be seen as the fulfillment of the first three petitions of the

Lord's Prayer: May your name be made sacred, your kingdom come, and your will be done, on earth as it is in heaven. The earthly scene, where his name is not made sacred and his will not done, is soon to be transformed by the sovereign action of the enthroned God."—Osborne, *Revelation*, 33.

13 Jerome Smith, *The New Treasury of Scripture Knowledge* (Nashville, TN: Thomas Nelson Publishers, 1992), Acts 1:6.

14 Arnold G. Fruchtenbaum, *The Footsteps of Messiah*, rev ed. (Tustin, CA: Ariel Ministries, 2003), 381.

15 Tenney, *Interpreting Revelation*, 30-31.

16 Fruchtenbaum, *The Footsteps of Messiah*, 15.

17 "The papacy has ever grasped at 'temporal power.' She wants to rule the world *now*, before Christ comes—thus *proving* herself false; . . . God's saints, with their Lord, await expectantly the Father's time."—William R. Newell, *Revelation: Chapter by Chapter* (Grand Rapids, MI: Kregel Publications, 1994,c1935), 60.

18 This is known as the doctrine of *imminency* which states that the return of Jesus for His church (the *Rapture*[5.2.62]) can occur at *any moment* without warning. There are *no preconditions* —events which must transpire—before He comes. The *pretribulation*[5.2.60] rapture position is the only position which preserves the doctrine of imminency in that every other rapture position holds that the Rapture takes place after the beginning of the Tribulation. If Jesus could truly come "tonight," but the Tribulation (Daniel's 70th week) cannot start until *Antichrist*[5.2.3] signs a covenant with Israel (Dan. 9:27), then mid- or post-tribulation Rapture is not 'imminent.' NT passages which teach the imminency of His return include: 1Cor. 1:7; 4:5; 15:51-52; 16:22; Php. 3:20; 4:5; 1Th. 1:10; 2Th. 3:10-12; Tit. 2:13; Jas. 5:7-9; 1Jn. 2:28; Rev. 3:11; 22:7, 12, 17, 20.

19 "By means of the 144,000 Jews, God will accomplish the second purpose of the Great Tribulation, that of bringing about a worldwide revival."—Fruchtenbaum, *The Footsteps of Messiah*, 179-180.

2.5 - Anti-supernatural Bias

A watchful eye must be kept whenever referring to source material outside of Scripture, especially in regard to the attitudes and assumptions of the writers of same. Even those who think of themselves as fundamentally[1] conservative in outlook and upholders of evangelical distinctives (e.g., inspiration, *inerrancy*[5.2.32]) may be found proposing ideas which are at odds with these foundational understandings of the Scriptures.

Couch identifies key elements of evangelicalism:

> A great many within the evangelical camp hold strongly to the doctrines of revelation, inspiration, and even inerrancy of the original texts of Scripture. Since the Reformation, evangelicals as a whole claim to take the Word of God literally, reading the prophets and apostles in a literal manner and accepting the historicity of the Scriptures at face value.[2]

The importance of these evangelical distinctives has been recognized by Thomas:

> Since about the middle of the twentieth century, a movement known as evangelicalism has had a considerable impact in thwarting the advance of liberalism in Christian circles. Evangelicals have been a major force in the creation of new organizations, seminaries, denominations, and local churches that honor the Bible as the inerrant Word of God.[3]

McGrath writes:

> Evangelicalism is historic Christianity. Its beliefs correspond to the central doctrines of the Christian church down the ages . . . In its vigorous defense of the biblical foundations, theological legitimacy, and spiritual relevance of these doctrines, evangelicalism has shown itself to have every right to claim to be a modern standard bearer of historic, orthodox Christianity. . . . the future of Christianity may come increasingly to depend on evangelicalism.[4]

Whenever evangelical principles are compromised, there will always be serious repercussions. As is often the case where Satan is afoot, the results are typically subtle and take time to come to full fruition —like introducing a small amount of poison into a fresh cool drink which the drinker doesn't detect until it eventually takes its deadly toll. Nowhere is this implicit denial of evangelical distinctives more evident than in historical-critical discussions of authorship, the dependency of source material, and appeal to extra-biblical literature as the key to understanding the divine message.[5] As Couch observes, the problem is not with the historical-critical approach itself, but with the bias of those who practice it. "Historical-critical interpretation in and of itself is not bad, it is an intelligent, research-oriented approach to the determination of Scripture. Many of the scholars who employed this method, however, held an **anti-supernatural bias**." [emphasis added][6]

Because of the correlation between biblical Christianity and evangelicalism, some commentators realize it is advantageous to suppress their opposition to evangelical principles. Herein lies the danger: some commentators who claim to be evangelical in outlook endorse liberal *methodologies* which in essence deny evangelicalism. They often embrace rational skepticism which is the foundation of an anti-supernatural worldview. "By adopting the methodologies of those who are less friendly to a high view of Scripture, most evangelical specialists have surrendered traditional, orthodox understandings of historicity."[7] Although Thomas deals primarily with the application of liberal principles to the synoptic gospels, many of the same principles populate popular commentaries on the book of Revelation in our day.

This accommodation of liberal principles by those who claim to be evangelical was noted by Schaeffer: "The evangelical church has accommodated to the world spirit of the age. First, there has been accommodation on Scripture, so that many who call themselves evangelicals hold a weakened view of the Bible and no longer affirm the truth of all the Bible teaches- . . . As part of this, many evangelicals are now accepting the higher critical methods in the study of the Bible."[8] Schaeffer recognizes the high view of Scripture as the dividing line between those who are truly evangelical and those who are not: "Holding to a strong view of Scripture or not holding to it is the watershed of the evangelical world. . . . evangelicalism is not consistently evangelical *unless there is a line drawn* between those who take a full view of Scripture and those who do not."[9] **Let the reader beware!** Much of what would pass itself off as evangelical commentary on the book of Revelation is not truly so—having embraced anti-supernatural presuppositions which are rejected by evangelicalism.

In accord with our stated *policy of inoculation*[2.2.10], we will spend some time helping our reader to more easily identify when anti-supernatural bias is afoot so that he may be aware of its presence and avoid its consequences.

By way of introduction, we offer the following example: "It seems likely that John has written his book carefully to signify the perfect plan of God and the completeness of his work."[10] Can you identify the hint of anti-supernatural bias in the preceding quote discussing John's motive for writing the book? Although admittedly a subtle example, the anti-supernatural bias is evident in the word *carefully*. This commentator is saying between the lines that the book of Revelation is a *carefully constructed literary work* which we are to implicitly assume is of *human origin, thought, purpose, and design*. Here we see one of the key characteristics (and dangers) of anti-supernaturalism: it communicates on two levels. On the surface level are explicit statements which may condone evangelical principles. Below the surface is an implicit denial of same. The effect is much like a friend, who upon gaining the reader's trust, sets about slowly and methodically to betray that trust.[11]

Other cases are more easily detected. For example, it is fairly commonplace to encounter discussion concerning the authorship of John suggesting it was written by a person of *another name*. But this asks the reader to endorse the notion that God has packaged His message of divine perfection within a lie (claiming to be written by John, but actually written by someone with another name)! Another commonly-encountered attitude of academic sophistication is a blatant disregard for inerrancy, such as found in redaction-critical theories whose *implicit* denial of inspiration is exceeded only by their creativity and appeal to total speculation. Aune believes "the author composed several different apocalyptic tracts for a variety of reasons over twenty to thirty years and then decided to combine them into a single document."[12] Never mind the introduction to the Apocalypse which says otherwise.[13] Those who spawn these elaborate constructions may have sincere intentions and believe they are performing a service for Christ, but such is the nature of deceivers who are more effective having been deceived themselves (2Ti. 3:13). History illustrates one of Satan's main tools against the church to be well-meaning believers who lacked an appreciation for the long-term effects of the fully-developed fruit of their 'contribution' to Christ.[14] As has been observed: "The road to hell is paved with good intentions."

2.5.1 - Implicit Denial of Evangelical Principles

To aid the reader in his appreciation of the various ways in which anti-supernatural bias enters in, we offer the following examples from well-known commentators.

We find Beckwith denying the historicity of Genesis and attributing the contents of Daniel to myth:

> In the first period of biblical history, that contained in the first eleven chapters of the book of Genesis, we have a **legendary story** of a primitive age before the separation of mankind into the tribes that formed the nations of the earth. . . . In tracing the external features of the story to an **early legend** we do not, it must be observed, change the religious character of the narrative. [emphasis added][15]
>
> The figure of the *Beast*[5.2.9] is **derived from tradition**. There ran through ancient mythologies and Hebrew folk-lore legends of a monster opposing itself to supreme powers in conflicts which symbolized the struggle of chaos against order, evil against good, death against life. **Some form of that myth suggested to the author of Daniel** (7) the figures of the beasts of his vision, and the same source furnished . . . our Apocalyptist's representation of Satan in the form of a dragon-monster. [emphasis added][16]

Couch identifies such views as reflecting a low view of Scripture known as *limited inerrancy*[5.2.32]:

> The term *limited inerrancy* means that the Bible, when speaking of matters of faith and practice (i.e., salvation, principles relating to the Christian life, etc.), is free from error. But in matters of science, history, or biography, it can be supposed that there are mistakes. While God *inspired*[5.2.33] the writers in matters of salvation and living for Christ, He left them on their own [without supernatural assistance] when it came to other matters. Characteristic beliefs associated with *limited inerrancy* are . . . the book

> of Daniel was written around 150 B.C. instead of 536 B.C.; Adam and Eve are not historical persons, but figures meant to reveal spiritual truths.[17]

Fiorenza and Beale attribute the motive for John's writing as being his own (but see Rev. 1:11, 19), that John fails to consider *OT*[5.2.51] context, and supposed that John *deliberately transforms* the material to arrive at his *own thesis*:

> Fiorenza points to the anthological style of John . . . "He does not interpret the OT but uses its words, images, phrases, and patterns as a language arsenal in order to make his own theological statement or express his own theological vision." Beale lists reasons why many believe John fails to consider the OT context: . . . [including] his prophetic spirit that causes him to center on his own authority rather than that of the OT . . . I argue . . . John is faithful on the whole to the OT context but nevertheless transforms it deliberately by applying it to his thesis.[18]

One can only wonder at the anti-supernatural nature of such statements which attribute the Revelation to the initiative and genius of John rather than what the text itself records: that John merely recorded what he was *told and shown*.[19] The visions given John were dutifully recorded on-the-fly, as is evidenced by the need to interrupt John in the midst of writing in order to suppress certain facts from the record: "Now **when** the seven thunders uttered their voices, I was **about to write**: but I heard a voice from heaven saying, 'Seal up the things which the seven thunders uttered, and do not write them' " [emphasis added] (Rev. 10:4).

Swete tells us that the book of Daniel, an essential foundation for understanding the book of Revelation, was written *after* the events it records (committing a prophetic misdemeanor of some sort), and wasn't written by Daniel, regardless of the statement of Jesus to the contrary (Mtt. 24:15; Mark 13:14):

> [The book of Daniel] seems to belong to the interval B.C. 168-165, the years during which the hand of Antiochus Epiphanes lay heavy on the Jewish people. The writer's purpose is to strengthen the religious section of the nation under this supreme test of their faith and loyalty. He is carried back in the Spirit to the days of the Exile, and identifies himself with Daniel, a Jewish captive at Babylon, who is represented as foreseeing a series of great visions . . . **From the standpoint of the writer all events later than the age of Daniel are *ex hypothesi* future.** [emphasis added][20]

Collins, in commentating on the five kings of Revelation 17:10, seems incredulous that John might actually be recording *true prophecy*—prediction in advance of the actual events:

> The five who have fallen would be the five emperors immediately preceding Domitian, namely, Galba, Otho, Vitellius, Vespasian, and Titus. The one who has not yet come must be Nerva, who indeed 'remained,' i.e., ruled, for only a short time (96-98 C.E.). This is the solution of Victorinus (comm. in apoc. 17:10). There are two problems with this solution. How did the author know that Nerva would remain a short time? **Was this genuine prophecy? Or was it eschatological dogma that happened to be historically accurate?** [emphasis added][21]

It hardly need be said that an expositor who denies supernatural prophecy is a most unlikely guide to the most prophetic book of the New Testament!

A common element among these skeptical guides to the book of Revelation is their refusal to accept the source of John's visions as being determined and provided by God. They consistently attempt to attribute the visions to John's *own motives and creative abilities* working from borrowed sources:

> In many cases it is difficult, if not impossible, to identify the source of John's imagery. Some find the raw material for this plague [Rev. 8:8] in the volcanic action of the area. . . . Others look to Jewish apocalyptic for the source of the imagery.[22]

What a contrast are the comments of those who truly represent the evangelical viewpoint. For example, Thomas undercuts the oft-heard anti-supernatural sophistry concerning John's literary borrowing of the apocalyptic *genre*[5.2.22]: "the literary genre of inspired writings was **not the choice** of the human author, but was an inevitable result of the manner in which **God chose** to reveal his message to that prophet. This, of course, distinguishes them from uninspired but similar works whose writers did, in fact, choose a particular genre." [emphasis added][23]

Seiss also recognizes the dangers of reliance upon the theories of men. We would do well to adopt his approach when reading what John recorded: "Candid readers will hardly deny [this work] the merit of .

. . straightforwardness in the treatment of Divine things, simplicity . . . direct leaning on the Sacred Word over against the stilted theories and rationalistic systems of men."[24]

Is it any wonder that it is the "common man," whom academics often look down on with scorn, whom God has trusted to carry forward the common-sense meaning of His Word? Academies will come and go, theories will incessantly rise to be debunked, but the simple meaning of the Word once entrusted to the saints (Jude 1:3) will be faithfully carried forward by those who seek God in simplicity and are guided by His Spirit into all truth (John 14:26; 16:13-14; 1Cor. 2:10-13; Eph. 3:5; 1Jn. 2:20, 27).

As we discuss the *date*[2.11] of the book of Revelation, its *authorship*[2.9], and its *audience and purpose*[2.3], the attentive reader will notice the anti-supernatural biases of many who attempt to contribute to an understanding of the book. Let us be wary of such speculation and cling to the basic elements as set forth by the very Word of God.

Notes

1 "In 1910, the General Assembly of the Presbyterian Church issued the Five Fundamentals of the Faith, which included: *first*, the *inspiration*[5.2.33] of the Scriptures; *second*, the Virgin Birth; *third*, the substitutionary atonement; *fourth*, the resurrection of Jesus; and *fifth*, the miracles of Jesus. Those who subscribed to these five points were labeled 'Fundamentalists,' and so a new word was coined. . . . The General Assembly issued these in 1910 and reaffirmed them in 1916 and 1923."—Arnold G. Fruchtenbaum, *The Footsteps of Messiah*, rev ed. (Tustin, CA: Ariel Ministries, 2003), 73.

2 Mal Couch, *Classical Evangelical Hermeneutics* (Grand Rapids, MI: Kregel Publications), 11.

3 Robert L. Thomas, *"The 'Jesus Crisis': What Is It?,"* in Robert L. Thomas, and F. David Farnell, eds., *The Jesus Crisis: The Inroads of Historical Criticism into Evangelical Scholarship* (Grand Rapids, MI: Kregel Publications, 1998), 13.

4 Thomas, "*The "Jesus Crisis": What Is It?*," 13.

5 For an excellent treatment of this topic, see [Thomas, "*The "Jesus Crisis": What Is It?*"] and [Gerhard Maier, *The End of the Historical-Critical Method* (St. Louis, MO: Concordia Publishing House, 1977)].

6 Couch, *Classical Evangelical Hermeneutics*, 20.

7 Thomas, "*The "Jesus Crisis": What Is It?*," 13.

8 Francis A. Schaeffer, *The Complete Works of Francis A. Schaeffer* (Wheaton, IL: Crossway Books, 1982), 5:320-321.

9 Schaeffer, *The Complete Works of Francis A. Schaeffer*, 333.

10 Grant R. Osborne, *Revelation* (Grand Rapids, MI: Baker Academic, 2002), 17.

11 Perhaps the most powerful weapon of Satan is the packaging of truth with deadly error. As we take in the truth, we often fail to spit out the error which rides along with it.

12 Osborne, *Revelation*, 28.

13 Compare Aune's elaborate construction with Osborne: "The unity of language and thought in the book is so extensive that many recent commentators assume unity and do not even discuss redactional theories."—Osborne, *Revelation*, 27.

14 One wonders how often these contributions are fueled by pride rather than a godly reverence for and belief in the sufficiency of what God has set forth. How many modern-day paraphrases of God's verbally inspired Word fall prey to this very error?

15 Isbon T. Beckwith, *The Apocalypse of John* (Eugene, OR: Wipf and Stock Publishers, 2001), 4.

16 Beckwith, *The Apocalypse of John*, 393.

17 Couch, *Classical Evangelical Hermeneutics*, 18.

18 Osborne, *Revelation*, 25-26.

19 How would such rational skepticism fly when faced with the need to explain the *personal motives* and *natural origin* of Isaiah in writing his 53rd chapter?

[20] Henry Barclay Swete, *The Apocalypse of St. John* (Eugene, OR: Wipf and Stock Publishers, 1998, 1906), xx.

[21] Adela Yarbro Collins, *"Book of Revelation,"* in David Noel Freeman, ed., *The Anchor Bible Dictionary* (New York, NY: Doubleday, 1996, c1992), 5:700.

[22] Robert H. Mounce, *The Book of Revelation* (Grand Rapids, MI: William B. Eerdmans Publishing Co., 1977), 186.

[23] Robert L. Thomas, *Revelation 1-7* (Chicago, IL: Moody Press, 1992), 29.

[24] J. A. Seiss, *The Apocalypse: Lectures on the Book of Revelation* (Grand Rapids, MI: Zondervan Publishing House, 1966), v.

2.6 - The Genre of the book of Revelation

Expositors of the book of Revelation seem to spend a considerable amount of time discussing the *genre*[5.2.22] of the book. The American Heritage Dictionary defines *genre* as "A category of artistic composition, as in music or literature, marked by a distinctive style, form, or content."[1] Many commentators hold that the distinctive style of the book of Revelation is *apocalyptic* or a combination of apocalyptic with other styles.[2] But as Thomas observes, this tends to confuse matters since precise definitions of *genre* and *apocalyptic* are vague:

> No consensus exists as to a precise definition of genre, so discussion attempting to classify portions of the *NT*[5.2.48], including Revelation, are at best vague. . . . A recent trend among some scholars has been to view Revelation as primarily apocalyptic. This complicates the problem of definition even further because in addition to disagreement about what constitutes genre, uncertainty also prevails regarding a definition of apocalyptic.[3]

While we would agree that the book of Revelation contains elements which are often understood as apocalyptic (e.g., visions, use of symbols, catastrophic events), we are concerned that many commentators fail to clearly distinguish between the *inspired*[5.2.33] writing of John and the *uninspired* writings of other apocalyptic works.[4]

2.6.1 - Motivation for Categorizing as Apocalyptic

When commentators emphasize the importance of the *genre*[5.2.22] of the book of Revelation, it is often with an eye to erasing distinctions between the Apocalypse of John and other uninspired apocalyptic works.[5] By classifying the book of Revelation as *apocalyptic* it then becomes fashionable to suggest that the same motives, sources, and "after-the-fact prophecy" which characterize the uninspired writings are also at work in John. Here again we see the *anti-supernatural*[2.5] biases of the interpreters at work: [6]

Having categorized John's work as representative of the *apocalyptic genre*, commentators then make assertions which are contrary to a straight-forward reading of the text:

- The book should not be interpreted literally.[7]
- The prophetic content is motivated by a desire to be optimistic.[8]
- The book likely represents the work of redactors.
- The book is a political document employing *hyperbolic*[5.2.27] literary forms.
- The book is primarily devotional rather than containing actual facts of history.[9]

We disagree with these conclusions and the artificial comparison of the book of Revelation with uninspired apocalyptic writings. From our point of view, prophecy is prophecy and the normative literal approach to interpretation is not negated simply because a book utilizes symbols and records events of great importance and magnitude. Suggesting that God gives revelation so that present difficulties can be understood as "illusory" is a gross misrepresentation of the inspirational element of His Word and smacks of cults such as Christian Science.

2.6.2 - Different from Apocalyptic Genre

Thomas rightly recognizes that the book is primarily prophetic and that overemphasizing the *genre*[5.2.22] of apocalyptic will result in a distortion of its message:

> In light of Revelation's self-claims (e.g., Rev. 1:3; 22:18-19) and how well it fulfills the qualifications of *NT*[5.2.48] prophecy, the best overall characterization of the literary style of the Apocalypse is to call it prophetic. A blending of genres such as prophetic-apocalyptic or prophetic-apocalyptic-epistolary is not the best answer because it does not allow for the preeminence of the book's prophetic content.[10]

In addition, Mounce mentions a number of dissimilarities between Revelation and apocalyptic literature: the author considers his work to be prophecy; the work is not pseudonymous—John writes in his own name; the writer is not pessimistic but maintains balance; the present age sets forth the redemptive activity of God in history rather than being a meaningless prelude to the end; the moral urgency of the book; and the lack of esoteric knowledge secretly preserved from antiquity.[11]

Johnson mentions a number of factors which indicate that the Apocalypse should not be lumped in with non-*canonical*[5.2.12] writings of apocalyptic genre.[12] He concludes: "the reader would do well to reexamine every method of interpreting Revelation that rests on this assumed similarity. . . . In no case can it be demonstrated that John depends on the assumed knowledge among his readers of the Jewish apocalyptists for clarify of meaning. On the other hand, he is everywhere dependent on the *OT*[5.2.51] canonical books."[13]

Our advice is to be wary when encountering lengthy treatments on the *apocalyptic genre* of the book as they often lay the groundwork for anti-supernatural assumptions which follow. These assumptions often deny the self-claims of the book and fail to see its place within the larger framework of biblical prophecy running throughout Scripture.[14]

Notes

1 *American Heritage Online Dictionary*, Ver. 3.0A, 3rd ed. (Houghton Mifflin, 1993).

2 "It is universally recognized that Revelation is composed of three genres: apocalyptic, prophecy, and letter."—Grant R. Osborne, *Revelation* (Grand Rapids, MI: Baker Academic, 2002), 12.

3 Robert L. Thomas, *Revelation 1-7* (Chicago, IL: Moody Press, 1992), 23-24.

4 Woods identifies attributes typical of apocalyptic writings: "Extensive use of symbolism, vision as the major means of revelation, angelic guides, activity of angels and demons, focus on the end of the current age and the inauguration of the age to come, urgent expectation of the end of earthly conditions in the immediate future, the end as a cosmic catastrophe, new salvation that is paradisal in character, manifestation of the kingdom of God, a mediator with royal functions, dualism with God and Satan as the leaders, spiritual order determining the flow of history, pessimism about man's ability to change the course of events, periodization and determinism of human history, other worldly journeys, the catchword glory, and a final showdown between good and evil."—Andy Woods, *What is the Identity of Babylon In Revelation 17-18?*.

5 Bullinger lists representative non-*canonical*[5.2.12] apocalyptic writings: *The Sibylline Oracles* (180 B.C. - 350 A.D.); *The Testaments of the Twelve Patriarchs* (130 B.C. - 10 A.D.); *The Psalms of Solomon* (70 - 40 B.C.); *The Book of Jubilees* (40 - 10 B.C.); *The Ascension of Isaiah* (1 - 100 A.D.); *The Assumption of Moses* (14 - 30 A.D.); *The Apocalypse of Baruch* (50 - 90 A.D.); *The Book of Enoch* (200 - 260 A.D.). [E. W. Bullinger, *Commentary On Revelation* (Grand Rapids, MI: Kregel Publications, 1984, 1935), 121n*] Walvoord mentions the following additional *pseudepigrapha*[5.2.61] : *Letters of Aristeas, III and IV Maccabees, Psalms of Solomon, Secrets of Enoch, Sibylline Oracles, The Syriac Apocalypse of Baruch, The Testament of the Twelve Patriarchs, The Apocalypse of Adam, The Apocalypse of Elijah, The Apocalypse of Zephaniah, Testament of Abram, Isaac, and Jacob* as well as Christian apocalyptic works subsequent to the book of Revelation: *Anabaticon and Pauli, Revelation of St. Steven and Thomas, The Decree of Gelasius, The Apocalypse of Peter, The Apocalypse of Paul, A Spurious Apocalypse of John, The Apocalypse of Sedrach*, and *The Apocalypse of the Virgin*. [John F. Walvoord, *The Revelation of Jesus Christ* (Chicago, IL: Moody Press, 1966), 24-25]

6 "The apocalyptists followed a common practice of rewriting history as prophecy so as to lend credence to their predictions about that which still lay in the future."—Robert H. Mounce, *The Book of Revelation* (Grand Rapids, MI: William B. Eerdmans Publishing Co., 1977), 18.

7 "The main objection is that it interprets Revelation without sufficient sensitivity to its literary form, giving a straightforward, literal reading of the book, rather than using a figurative approach, which would be more appropriate to the book's symbolic genre."—Gregory K. Beale, *The Book of Revelation: A Commentary on the Greek Text* (Grand Rapids, MI: William B. Eerdmans Publishing Co., 1999), 161.

8 "It is impossible to distinguish ultimately between prophecy and apocalyptic, for the latter is an extension of the former . . . certain differences do in part distinguish the two forms: prophecy tends to be oracular and apocalyptic visionary, and prophecy has a certain optimistic overtone (if the nation repents, the judgment prophecies will not occur), while apocalyptic tends to be pessimistic (the only hope lies in the future rather than the present)."—Osborne, *Revelation*, 13.

[9] Collins emphasizes the devotional aspect over the factitive: “the visions guide readers into a transcendent reality that takes precedence over the current situation and encourages readers to persevere in the midst of their trials. The visions reverse normal experience by making the heavenly mysteries the real world and depicting the present crisis as a temporary, illusory situation.”—Osborne, *Revelation*, 14.

[10] Thomas, *Revelation 1-7*, 28.

[11] Mounce, *The Book of Revelation*, 23-24.

[12] Alan F. Johnson, *Revelation: The Expositor's Bible Commentary* (Grand Rapids, MI: Zondervan Publishing House, 1966), 5.

[13] Johnson, *Revelation: The Expositor's Bible Commentary*, 6.

[14] “There is no *inherent* harm in a literary genre; there is only harm or danger in how a scholar may use such genre against a document.”—Bernard Ramm, *Protestant Biblical Interpretation*, 3rd rev. ed. (Grand Rapids, MI: Baker Book House, 1970), 144.

2.7 - Interpreting Symbols

It is readily apparent that the book of Revelation is unique among New Testament books in its heavy use of symbols. What is not so apparent is how much the approach one takes to understanding the symbols flavors the understanding of the text. Fruchtenbaum has observed the tendency toward two extremes:

> The existence of these symbols has led to two extremes. One extreme states that the existence of these symbols shows that this book cannot be understood and must simply be interpreted in terms of a general conflict between good and evil, the good winning out in the end. Beyond this, they say the book is not to be understood in any great detail. This is how the book has suffered from its enemies. In the second extreme, the symbols are used for unchecked speculation, sensationalism, and all kinds of guesswork in trying to interpret these symbols in terms of current events. Such speculation has resulted in farfetched interpretations, and changes are made as current events change. It has also led to date-setting. In this area, the book of Revelation has suffered at the hands of its friends. There is a balance between the two extremes.[1]

The schemes which interpreters have proposed in order to try and "understand" the book of Revelation run from one extreme to the other, but most often deny a straight-forward reading in favor of obscure theories involving the symbols it contains:

> E. Boring has summarized an approach to interpretation of symbols in the Apocalypse that has come to be widely held. In his view, the symbols are not to be decoded into propositional language that refers to objective realities, but are to be left as nonobjectifying pictorial language that only points to ultimate categories of language. . . . Revelation's language **does not adhere to the laws of logical propositional language** and is noninferential because John attempts to communicate the reality of God's transcendent world by words bounded by space and time. [emphasis added][2]

One wonders how the book can claim to be revealing information *to show His servants* (Rev. 1:1) if the language failed to "adhere to the laws of logical propositional language and is noninferential"?

In this section, we discuss what is perhaps the most important aspect of studying the book of Revelation: *how to read and understand the text*. While this may sound simple, it is amazing how frequently the principles of normative reading and comprehension are jettisoned when expositors come to the book of Revelation.

2.7.1 - The Importance of Meaning

Most interpreters of the book of Revelation admit that they bring with them a certain amount of "interpretive baggage"—biases and pre-understandings which flavor their assessment of the facts of history and the text. These have a huge effect upon the interpretation of the book of Revelation for two primary reasons:

1. The book is often categorized as being written in an apocalyptic literary *genre*[5.2.22] by design.
2. The book contains numerous symbols.

Once a work is defined to be apocalyptic in genre, the door is opened to a wide array of interpretive treatments as it becomes fashionable to understand the surface-level literary work on the basis of hidden, mysterious, or unstated secondary meaning below the text itself. The inclusion of symbols leads in this direction as various interpreters see license in the symbology for a further separation between the meaning of the text and the *real intent* of the author. The wider the gap which can be asserted between the text itself and the intended meaning of the author, the greater the room for conjecture and supposition by the interpreter.

When given free reign with the book of Revelation, the sad result of such license is often the very negation of the stated purpose of the book of Revelation:

> The Apocalypse ("unveiling") has become *Apocrypha*[5.2.5] ("hidden"). This should not be. The book was written to *show* those things which were coming to pass, not to obscure them in a maze of symbolism and dark sayings. Great blessing was promised to all who would read (or even hear) the

> *words* of the book of this prophecy (Revelation 1:3), but how could anyone be blessed by words he could not even understand?[3]

Even when the interpreter forgoes a tendency to look for meaning "below" the text, there are still a variety of ways in which meaning can be understood:

> Some identify the meaning with the human author's intention, while others hold that meaning is identical with God's intention. Still others claim that meaning is as broad as the *canonical*[5.2.12] interpretation of the text. And finally, there are a group of *NT*[5.2.48] scholars who would identify apostolic *hermeneutics*[5.2.26] with first-century Jewish hermeneutics.[4]

Feinberg identifies the following ways to define meaning:

1. The intention of the author.
2. The understanding of the author.
3. The understanding of the readers in the prophet's day.
4. The significance (application) of the text.
5. The use of the text elsewhere in the NT.

Thus, it becomes vital to spend some time discussing the way in which meaning comes from the text.

2.7.2 - The Art and Science of Interpretation

The practice of interpretation is known as *hermeneutics*[5.2.26].

> The word *hermeneutics* is ultimately derived from Hermes the Greek god who brought the messages of the gods to the mortals, and was the god of science, invention, eloquence, speech, writing, and art. As a theological discipline hermeneutics is the science of the correct interpretation of the Bible.[5]

Bible study consists of three primary steps: *observation*, *interpretation*, and *application*.[6]. After observing the text, interpretation should yield the understanding of God's Word which He intended resulting in its fruitful application in the life of the reader. If interpretation goes astray, then a proper understanding will not result and the application of God's message to the life of the reader will not be what God intended.

Our position is that the book of Revelation is to be interpreted normally, like any other writing, and especially like the rest of the Scriptures. We part company here from those who seek to classify the book as being representative of the *apocalyptic genre*[5.2.22] so they can apply a mystical or spiritual "spin" to the text and make it mean all manner of things.

D.L. Cooper gives a reasonable definition of normal interpretation in his *Golden Rule of Interpretation*[5.2.24]:

> When the plain sense of Scripture makes common sense, seek no other sense, therefore, take every word at its primary, ordinary, usual, literal meaning unless the facts of the immediate context, studied in the light of related passages and axiomatic and fundamental truths, indicate clearly otherwise.—*The Golden Rule of Interpretation*, D.L. Cooper[7]

The rule includes the important phrase, *studied in the light of related passages*. This is the biblical equivalent of a "safety net." In the same way that trapeze artists performing on the high-wire are protected by a net below which catches them in the event of a fall, comparing Scripture with Scripture provides a doctrinal "safety net" to keep the interpreter from "falling" into an inconsistent understanding or interpretation. This principle is also known as *the Analogy of Scripture* or *Systematic Theology*: the systematic study of the Scriptures across all the books of the Bible to arrive at a self-consistent understanding of any particular topic. This principle is founded upon the *inerrancy*[5.2.32] and *inspiration*[5.2.33] of Scripture. That the inspired books, being ultimately the work of the Holy Spirit (2Pe. 1:19-21), are without error and consistent in their teaching from Genesis 1:1 through Revelation 22:21. When we encounter what *seems* to be an inconsistency (commonly referred to as a "Bible Difficulty"), we must assume that the problem is one of our own understanding and *not* God's Word.

The experienced student of the Word will recognize how frequently what appeared to be contradictory turned out, upon further insight, study, and illumination, to be by design.[8]

Notice that the Golden Rule holds that we adhere to the plain sense of Scripture and not seek any other sense *unless* there are good reasons for doing otherwise. These reasons must be found in the immediate context of the passage under study or related passages. It is not sufficient to simply classify the book of Revelation as an apocalypse and therefore *turn the rules of interpretation upside-down* as does this commentator:

> A failure to take full account of [the apocalyptic] feature has led to some of the most outlandish teachings on this book by some whose rule of interpretation is "literal, unless absurd." Though this is a good rule when dealing with literature written in a literal genre, **it is the exact opposite in the case of apocalyptic literature, where symbolism is the rule, and literalism the exception**. [emphasis added][9]

Notice how this commentator appeals to the *apocalyptic genre* in order to dismiss normative interpretation and to assert that we should *avoid* normative interpretation in favor of pure symbolic conjecture! The easy answer to this proposal is to simply ask, "*Whose symbolic interpretation?*" No real answer can be given. This is because there in an infinite variety of interpretations possible when using symbolic conjecture. The result is that no two interpreters hold to the same meaning except in a handful of areas. This fact alone disqualifies a non-literal framework because it has *factually demonstrated* its bankruptcy at conveying a reliable message from God. In effect, it makes the book of Revelation unknowable by man.

The recommendation that normalcy be inverted reminds us of our high-school literature class where we read Melville's *Moby Dick* and then spent weeks guessing at obscure, hidden, multiple meanings which the author "might" have intended. It was great fun and students were awarded an "A" for creativity, but I often thought of how Melville would likely turn in his grave if he heard the things he was *supposed* to have communicated! But interpreting God's Holy Word is the antithesis of the high-school literature class, for here *creativity* is awarded a grade of "F!"

Why do we insist on normalcy in our interpretation of *all* of Scripture? Couch identifies a number of reasons:

> Those who are committed to a *normal* reading of Scripture offer at least three reasons: *First*, the obvious purpose of language is to enable effective communication between intelligent beings. Words have meaning and in their normal usage are intended to be understood. . . . God is the originator of language. When He spoke audibly to man, He expected man to understand Him and respond accordingly. Likewise, when God speaks to man through the inspired writings of His apostles and prophets, He expects man to understand and respond accordingly. . . . A *second* reason for a *normal* reading of Scripture concerns the historical fulfillment of prophecy. All the prophecies of the Old and New Testament that have been fulfilled to date have been fulfilled literally. . . . Thus, . . . all prophecies which are yet to be fulfilled will be fulfilled literally. A *third* reason concerns logic. If an interpreter does not use the normal, customary, literal method of interpreting Scripture, interpretation is given over to the unconstrained imagination and presuppositions of the interpreter.[10]

Neglect of this last reason is most evident in the widely-varying imaginative interpretations of the non-literal interpreters. Once the "tether of normative interpretation" is cut, the helium balloon of the interpreter's imagination floats ever further afield from the intended meaning of the text. **This single factor accounts for the majority of nonsense which is offered as commentary on the book of Revelation.**

As an example of how quickly those who forsake literal interpretation choose to ignore the pattern of previously-fulfilled literal prophecy, Couch's second reason for normalcy, consider Beale's statement which asserts that the plagues in Revelation are unlikely to be literal like those recorded elsewhere in Scripture:

> The parallel with Exodus does not supply unambiguous demonstration in support of a literal fulfillment. All that it shows is that the two descriptions are homologous, that is, that they have an essential relation in some manner. But the nature of that relation needs to be determined. Are they homologous in their physical form and effects, or in theological significance, or both? The images depicted certainly refer to actual events **on the referential level.**. . . In Revelation the fire and hail are to be understood on the symbolic level as representing particular facets of divine judgment that can be drawn out further by thorough **exegesis of the theological meaning of this particular Exodus plague.** [These] **speak of**

> **God depriving the ungodly of earthly security**. [emphasis added][11]

Beale denies literal fire and hail in the book of Revelation as found elsewhere in Scripture asserting that the reader is to seek for a *theological meaning* beyond the plain text. The fire and hail are themselves no longer important, but the theological meaning *behind* the text is now primary. But *who* determines the meaning behind the text and *how* is it determined? A perusal of the writings of expositors employing this approach readily reveals the enormous subjectivity which enters upon the process of answering these questions to arrive at an interpretation.

Another key advantage of normal interpretation is it is *minimal*, contributing the barest interpretive layer over the inspired text from God. "The *best* interpretation of a historical record is *no* interpretation but simply letting the divine Author of the record say what He says and assuming He says what He means."[12] The "thicker" the layer of interpretation required to make sense of the underlying text, the greater the danger that the commentator will wind up adding to or subtracting from the meaning intended by God (Rev. 22:18-19).[13] This minimalist interpretation is the way a reader would most likely understand the text when absent from the guidance of an allegorical interpreter.

> If one were on a desert island and read Revelation for the first time, how would he normally interpret the book? The answer would be "actual and literal," unless there was an *amillennialist*[5.2.1] and allegorist around to say, "No, no, these events are not real! They have some hidden meaning that no one is sure of, but don't let that bother you!"[14]

In opposition to the practice of literal interpretation, some interpreters grossly misrepresent what it means to interpret literally:

> Would we understand the Twenty-third Psalm properly if we were to take it "literally"? Would it not, instead, look somewhat silly? In fact, if taken literally, it would not be *true*: for I daresay that the Lord *doesn't* make every Christian to lie down in literal, green pastures.[15]

As Ramm explains, literal interpretation is not the ridiculous caricature that the previous commentator attempts to portray it as:

> To interpret Scripture literally is not to be committed to a "wooden literalism," nor to a "letterism," nor to a neglect of the nuances that defy any "mechanical" understanding of language. Rather, it is to commit oneself to a starting point and that starting point is to understand a document the best one can in the context of the normal, usual, customary, tradition range of designation which includes "tacit" understanding.[16]

Literal interpretation recognizes variations in the style of the text and maintains a consistency of interpretation driven by the text itself, not the predilections of the interpreter:

> It is not true that the *premillennialists*[5.2.58] require every single passage to be interpreted literally without exception. They do hold, on the other hand, that if the language is symbolic, it is to be governed by the laws relating to symbols; if figurative, by the laws dealing with figures; if typical, by the laws connected with types; if literal, by the laws of non-figurative speech.[17]

All interpreters utilize this normal literal approach *most of the time*. For example, in interpreting John's words:

> I, John, both your brother and companion in the tribulation and kingdom and patience of Jesus Christ, was on the island that is called Patmos for the word of God and for the testimony of Jesus Christ. (Rev. 1:9)

There is almost universal agreement that the "island that is called Patmos" is Patmos! And that John is located on that island, and that he is there due to his connection to the Word of God. Where the difference comes in, is that some interpreters *change their interpretive process* when they encounter passages employing symbols, prophecy, or especially controversial doctrine. In these passages, they jettison normal interpretation in favor of conjecture about symbols thereby reducing the text into an allegory concerning spiritual principles.

This "dual hermeneutic" is employed much like the gearshift in an automobile. On the major "freeway" of the gospel text, they generally stay in literal gear. But when a prophetic off-ramp or doctrinal mountain looms ahead, they shift into a non-literal gear. This inconsistency leads to all manner of confusion and allows for the most amazing conclusions which are often in *complete contradiction* to the plain meaning of the text! McClain recognizes this "gearshift" between two systems of interpretation:

> It should be clear, however, that regardless of the terms chosen to designate the anti-millenarian scheme of prophetical interpretation, it is a combination of two different systems, shifting back and forth between the spiritualizing and literal methods. The hermeneutical plow is pulled by 'an ox and an ass.' For this reason, the scheme may be appropriately be called eclectical.[18]

Even those who use literal interpretation when viewing *OT*[5.2.51] passages in the light of the *NT*[5.2.48] often fall into this inconsistent approach when they come to the book of Revelation:

> Two or three generations ago, students of prophecy received incalculable help from the simple discovery that when the Holy Spirit spoke of Judea and Jerusalem in the Old Testament Scriptures He meant Judea and Jerusalem, and not England and London; and that when He mentioned Zion He did not refer to the Church. But strange to say, few, if any of these brethren, have applied the same rule to the Apocalypse. Here they are guilty of doing the very thing for which they condemned their forebears in connection with the Old Testament - they have 'spiritualised.' . . . What then? If to regard 'Jerusalem' as meaning *Jerusalem* be a test of intelligence in Old Testament prophecy, shall we be counted a heretic if we understand 'Babylon' to mean *Babylon*, and not Rome or apostate Christendom?[19]

Couch describes the two main approaches to interpretation as they relate to prophecy:

> Among evangelicals there are generally two major camps regarding how prophetic passages should be read. Amillennialists will generally allegorize large portions of the prophetic Word, especially passages that speak of the Second Advent of Christ and the establishment of the one thousand year literal Davidic kingdom. In contrast, premillennialists, following the teaching of the early church, treat the Second Coming with the same literal hermeneutic as they would the First Coming of Jesus. They hold that the Bible, from Genesis to Revelation, should be understood literally from a normal reading unless typology or poetry is used. And even then, premillennialists believe that "literalness" is implied behind the figure of speech or illustration used.[20]

The most serious charge that can be leveled against non-literal interpretation is that of perverting the promises of God. God's promises, both in the OT and NT, were given to specific recipients using words which they understood in the context in which they lived and in which the promises were given. When a nonliteral view of these passages is adopted, this robs the original recipients of the promises as God gave them:

> Adopting a nonliteral view of the Old Testament kingdom prophecies raises some disturbing questions: What did those prophecies mean to those to whom they were addressed? If prophecies seemingly addressed to Israel really apply to the church (which did not exist at that time), did God give revelation that failed to reveal? And if those prophecies were meant to apply symbolically to the church, why were they addressed to Israel? What meaning could such prophecies have in their historical settings? Ironically, many who spiritualize Old Testament prophecies reject the futurist interpretation of Revelation because it allegedly robs the book of its meaning for those to whom it was written. Yet they do the very same thing with the Old Testament kingdom prophecies.[21]

God's promises involve both ends of the communication channel: the things God said and *what those who received His promises understood them to mean in the original context*. It is not permissible, after the fact, to make what God said mean something different which would have been entirely foreign to those who originally received His word. Allegorization and spiritualization do just that.

2.7.3 - The Rise of Allegorical Interpretation

Because the book of Revelation is categorized as *apocalyptic* literature and contains numerous symbols, it undergoes a great deal of abuse due to allegorical interpretation. But what exactly is allegorical (also known as *mystical*[22]) interpretation and where did it come from?

Zuck offers the following description of *allegorization*:

> Allegorizing is searching for a hidden or secret meaning underlying but remote from and unrelated in reality to the more obvious meaning of a text. In other words the literal reading is a sort of code, which needs to be deciphered to determine the more significant and hidden meaning. In this approach the literal is superficial, the allegorical is the true meaning.[23]

Completely in line with Zuck's description is the following statement by Trench regarding his understanding of the New Jerusalem (Rev. 21:2):

> The dream of an actual material city to be let down bodily from heaven to earth, . . . has been cherished in almost all ages of the Church by some, who have been unable to translate the figurative language of Scripture into those **far more glorious realities** of the heavenly πολιτεία [*politeia*], whereof those figures were the vesture and the outward array. [emphasis added][24]

Notice how the language of Trench confirms the statement of Zuck: the allegorical meaning represents *far more glorious realities*. The literal text represents figures which are the *vesture* and *outward array*. According to Trench, the true (allegorical) meaning is "clothed" by the representation of the literal text. Presumably, the interpreter must remove this outer garment of literal text to see the deeper and *more glorious* reality beyond.[25] Trench doesn't inform us that each interpreter that does so finds a *different* glorious reality![26]

Using allegorical interpretation, it is possible to "find" all manner of meanings beyond the plain sense of the text:

> To cite a few examples [of allegorical *hermeneutics*[5.2.26]]: The journey of Abraham from Ur of the Chaldees to Haran is interpreted as the imaginary trip of a Stoic philosopher who leaves sensual understanding and arrives at the senses. The two pence given by the Good Samaritan to the innkeeper has the hidden meanings of Baptism and the Lord's Supper. The river Euphrates means the outflow of manners and is not an actual literal river in Mesopotamia. Pope Gregory the Great's interpretation of the Book of Job is equally disheartening: 'The patriarch's three friends denote the heretics; his seven sons are the twelve apostles; his seven thousand sheep are God's faithful people; and his three thousand hump-backed camels are the depraved Gentiles!'[27]

While it is tempting to chuckle at these examples from early Christianity, what is alarming is how often equally obscure results attend modern interpreters of the book of Revelation.

So where did this tendency begin? Evidence is lacking within Scripture that Jesus or the Apostles understood the Old Testament in this way.

> The allegorical interpretation of Sacred Scriptures cannot be historically proved to have prevailed among the Jews from the time of exile, or to have been common with the Jews of Palestine at the time of Christ and His apostles. Although the Sanhedrim and the hearers of Jesus often appealed to the Old Testament according to the testimony of the New Testament writers, they give no indication of the allegorical interpretation. Even Josephus has nothing of it.[28]

The flowering of allegorical interpretation as applied to Scripture can be traced to Jews in Alexandria Egypt who were interested in accommodating the *OT*[5.2.51] Scriptures to Greek philosophy as a tool for removing or reinterpreting what were considered embarrassing anthropomorphisms and immoralities in the OT.

> Two names stand out in Alexandrian Jewish allegorization: Aristobulus and Philo. Aristobulus, who lived around 160 B.C., believed that Greek philosophy borrowed from the Old Testament, and that those teachings could be uncovered only by allegorizing. . . . Philo (ca. 20 B.C. - ca. A.D. 54) . . . sought to defend the Old Testament to the Greeks and, even more so, to fellow Jews. He was led to allegorize the Old Testament, . . . because of his desire to avoid [seeming] contradictions and blasphemies.[29]

Observe how often Christian aberrations have arisen from a faulty attempt to defend the Scriptures before skeptics. *Preterism*[5.2.59], and its belief that non-believers reject Scripture because Jesus' prediction to come "soon" was misunderstood, is a recent example.

Clement of Alexandria (A.D. 155-216) was influenced by Philo and proposed a system of interpretation where any passage of the Bible might have up to five meanings.[30] Thereafter, Origin, who studied Platonic philosophy and is thought to have been a pupil of Clement, went so far as to say that Scripture itself demands that the interpreter employ the allegorical method.

> Amillennialist Schaff is fair when he describes the great hermeneutical failings of *Origen*[5.2.50]: "His great defect is the neglect of the grammatical and historical sense and his constant desire to find a hidden mystic meaning. He even goes further in this direction than the Gnostics, who everywhere saw transcendental, unfathomable mysteries."[31]

> [Origen] lays down the principle that the true meaning of prophecy is to be found only by going beyond

> the literal and historical sense to the spiritual; and he says specifically of the Apocalypse that the mysteries **hidden in it** can be understood only in this way. His whole interpretation of the book is therefore spiritual rather than literal. [emphasis added][32]

Origen's interpretive approach had great influence on those who would follow in the Middle Ages, as did Augustine (354-430) who, like Philo, saw allegorization as a solution to Old Testament problems.[33] The allegorical system of interpretation prevailed throughout most of the Middle Ages:

> During the Middle Ages, the fourfold sense of Scripture was taught. Medieval scholars took Origen's threefold sense—the literal, the moral, and the spiritual—and subdivided the spiritual into the allegorical and the anagogical. As schoolman Thomas Aquinas affirmed, 'The literal sense is that which the author intends, but God being the Author, we may expect to find in Scripture a wealth of meaning.' An example of how the fourfold sense was worked out during the Middle Ages is Gen. 1:3, 'Let there be light.' Medieval churchmen interpreted that sentence to mean (1) Historically and literally—An act of creation; (2) Morally—May we be mentally illumined by Christ; (3) Allegorically—Let Christ be love; and (4) Anagogically—May we be led by Christ to glory.[34]

Although Aquinas endorsed looking beyond the primary meaning of the author, he did recognize some of the dangers of allegorization. "Aquinas put forward a threefold argument against allegory: (1) it is susceptible to deception; (2) without a clear method it leads to confusion; and (3) it lacks a sense of the proper integration of Scripture."[35] All three of these significant drawbacks are evident in much interpretation of the book of Revelation today.

> Augustine's allegorical interpretation of Bible prophecy dominated the understanding of eschatology during the medieval period. It found acceptance also with the Roman church and among the leaders of the Reformation. Even today, Augustinian eschatology is held by large segments of the Christian church.[36]

Even the Reformers, who cast off the darkness of Medieval allegorization in so many areas, failed to escape the influence of those who went before them in their understanding of the book of Revelation.[37]

As we've observed in the origination of this method of interpretation, there was a *motive* for its use. This remains the case today. At times it has simply been unbelief:

> As someone has said, "The Book of Revelation isn't hard to understand—it's hard to *believe!*" The main reason why so many have resorted to allegorical interpretations is that they have found the literal meaning of its prophecies difficult to accept, scientifically, and aesthetically, and have tried to "explain" them on some less offensive basis.[38]

At other times, the motive has been to teach unorthodox doctrines twisted from the proper understanding of the text, something which has been with us all along:

> Metaphysical cults, theosophical cults, divine science cults, pantheistic cults all base their interpretation of Holy Scripture on the theory that the meaning of Scripture is plural. The first meaning is the ordinary historical or grammatical one; and the second meaning is the one the cultist brings to Scripture from the particular metaphysical system or religious system he is pushing.[39]

Even as far back as *Tertullian*[5.2.75], the dangerous freedom offered by figurative interpretation for manipulating the meaning of the text was recognized. "On the proper method of interpreting prophecy Tertullian stated: "Now to upset all conceits of this sort, let me dispel at once the preliminary idea on which they [heretics] rest their assertion that the prophets make all their announcements in figures of speech. Now if this were the case, the figures themselves could not possibly have been distinguished, inasmuch as the verities would not have been declared, out of which the figurative language is stretched. And, indeed, if all are figures, where will be that of which they are the figures? How can you hold up a mirror for your face, if the face nowhere exists? But, in truth, all are not figures, but there are also literal statements.""[40]

As we will see as we progress, allegorical interpretation is frequently used by Christians who hope to avoid the plain implication of the teaching of Scripture. Christian Reconstructionists utilize forms of allegorical interpretation in order to work around passages in the book of Revelation which do not conveniently fit into the newspaper events surrounding the times prior to 70 A.D. Since John's writings clearly indicate a coming time of wrath and judgment upon the earth, their motive is to attempt to remove this reality in favor of a more optimistic future for Christianity:

> Reconstructionism's interest in this subject stems from its optimistic outlook regarding Christianity's ability to gain control of secular society. Because Revelation is admittedly pessimistic in this regard, the system's scheme for disposing of this unfavorable evidence is to relegate its fulfillment almost entirely to the past, to a time prior to A.D. 70.[41]

Those who stand opposed to God's promises made to the Jewish nation find the plain sense of Revelation 20 much to their disliking as it suggests the fulfillment of the *Messianic Kingdom*[5.2.39] prophecies scattered throughout the OT. Again, allegorical interpretation provides the "solution" in that the thousand years (Rev. 20:4) becomes an indefinite period and the physical rule and reign with Christ represents the current spiritual standing of the believer. Never mind that interpreting the first resurrection (Rev. 20:4-5) as being *spiritual* and the second (Rev. 20:12) as *literal* runs rough-shod over the rules of sound hermeneutics.

The net result of allegorical interpretation is to place a veil of darkness over God's divine Word. It takes that which God has graciously revealed to the saints and subjects it to the dark vagaries of human imagination and speculation. The result is predictable. Those who major in it remain as much in the dark regarding the Second Coming of Jesus as many Jews were in relation to His predicted suffering at the First Coming.[42]

Concerning the inconsistency of the allegorical method and the damage which results, Seiss notes:

> Good and able men have satisfied themselves with it; but, on the same principles of interpretation, there is not a chapter in the Bible, nor a doctrine of our holy religion, which could not be totally explained away. By a happy inconsistency do they not so treat other portions of Scripture, or they would transmute the whole Revelation of God into uncertainty and emptiness.[43]
>
> Having examined a long list of these symbolic and allegorical interpretations, and followed the processes by which their authors have tried to apply them, I have not found one which does not completely break down under the weight of its own cumbrous unfittingness. They each and all fail to explain the facts and relations of the record, and treat John as a half-demented sentimental old man, trying to make a grand poem out of a few dim anticipations touching the earthly fortunes of the Church, which could have been better told in one well-written chapter. They are, at best, the wild guesses of men who have never got hold of the real thread of the matter, whilst under the necessity of saying something.[44]

2.7.4 - Understanding Symbols and Figures

Having discussed the prevalence and dangers of allegorical interpretation, we now discuss how to understand the many symbols and figures found throughout the book of Revelation. This is the area where many commentators, in our view, take a wrong turn. They utilize the symbolic content of the book as license to depart from normative interpretation which then fuels their departure from the plain meaning of the text.

As we previously mentioned, one way in which this is done is by using the symbolic imagery within the book to cast it into the *apocalyptic genre*[5.2.22], similar to many uninspired (and fraudulent) writings which contain similar literary devices. Once this is done, interpreters such as *Gregg* (2.7.2) can attempt to turn *hermeneutics*[5.2.26] on its head. Another approach, perhaps best illustrated by Beale, is to see in the symbols a sort of encoding in which the truth of God's message is veiled in symbols for transport across the page. The use of symbols becomes an "obvious" indication that non-literal interpretation is *intended.* Beale uses one of *several* possible meanings of a single Greek word to justify hundreds of pages of non-literal exposition:

> Σημαίνω [*Sēmainō*] ["signified," Rev. 1:1] can overlap with the more general and abstract idea of "make known" in the sense of "indicate," "declare," "be manifest." But its more concrete and at least equally common sense is "show by a sign," "give (or make) signs (or signals)," or "signify" . . . σημαίνω [*sēmainō*] typically has the idea of symbolic communication when it is not used in the general sense of "make known." . . . Of its five other *NT*[5.2.48] occurrences, two have the sense of "make known" (Acts 11:28; 25:27), . . . three others are in John's Gospel where it summarizes Jesus' pictorial description of crucifixion (John 12:33; 18:32; 21:19). . . . The symbolic use of σημαίνω [*sēmainō*] in Daniel 2 defines the use in Rev. 1:1 as referring to symbolic communication and not mere general conveyance of information . . . [indicating] that a symbolic vision and its interpretation is going to be

> part of the warp and woof of the means of communication throughout Revelation. . . . Some commentators contend that since Revelation sometimes explicitly explains the meaning of an image in a vision there is a "presumption that, where expressions are not explained, they can normally be interpreted according to their natural [i.e., literal] meaning, unless the context clearly indicates otherwise". . . . But the results of the analysis of Rev. 1:1 indicated that **this rule should be turned on its head: we are told in the book's introduction that the majority of the material in it is revelatory symbolism . . . Hence, the predominant manner by which to approach the material will be according to a non-literal interpretive method.** [emphasis added][45]

Elsewhere Beale states:

> As we have seen, Rev. 1:1 programmatically introduces the pictorial visions of the book as **having a symbolic meaning without any one-to-one relation to literal historical events.** [emphasis added][46]

Having conveniently dispatched normative hermeneutics, Beale fails to offer anything substantive in its place. As with all interpretations which major on "symbolic meanings," the meaning is to be found in *the interpreter's own ideas*. Contrary to Beale's assertion that the symbols are "without any one-to-one relation to literal historical events," Osborne follows most literal interpreters in recognizing the symbols as *representing* literal events and personas.[47]

As Thomas observes, Beale has made the mistake of confusing the way in which the revelation was made (via symbols) with how it should be interpreted by those who follow:

> The verb ἐσήμανεν [*esēmanen*] ("he signified") in Rev. 1:1 furnishes an advance notice of the symbolic nature of God's communication with John. This has nothing to do with how the resultant communication should be interpreted, . . . [interpreters] fail to distinguish between the process of revelation and that of interpretation.[48]

It is also frequently the case that commentators attempt to utilize the appearance of one symbol as license to treat the entire passage in a symbolic way.[49]But each symbol must be treated individually as there are numerous cases where symbols are embedded among non-symbolic vision.

> Once a prophecy is found to contain symbols, interpreters often succumb to the temptation of treating everything else in that prophecy as symbolic. . . . The presence of symbols in a prophecy, however, does not indicate that everything else in that prophecy is symbolical. The designation of symbols must be on an individual basis. Each symbol must be carefully examined, weighed, and adequately supported by strong evidence before a symbolical designation is made. Symbols are not cheaper by the dozen.[50]

Symbols are frequently employed in the book of Revelation within similes where resemblance is emphasized.[51]

> Revelation is interpreted from a *literal* base, taking into account *comparative language* that points to a literal ultimate meaning. Two words indicate that comparative language is being used: ὥς [*hōs*] and ὅμοιος [*homoios*]. *Hos* and words related to it are used sixty-eight times in Revelation and approximately 416 elsewhere in the New Testament. *Homoios* is used twenty-two times in Revelation and about twenty-six times in the rest of the New Testament. Both words are used for comparison and should be translated "Like, as, like as, it seemed to be, something like, etc." [Often, *hos*] indicates John is comparing what he sees (something beyond his own experience or comprehension) to the closest known object with which he is familiar. . . . John uses comparative language to describe a literal event, not a symbolic or even figurative event, and certainly not an allegorical event.[52]

Symbols employed within simile have several advantages over other literary forms of communication. A simile can carry a *richness of communication* which a simple non-symbolic statement cannot (e.g., the description of the *Beast*[5.2.9] in Rev. 13:2). Simile is also used when that which is being described exceeds the experience of the writer and the symbol is the best analogy at hand for the writer to convey the *sense* of what he is seeing (e.g., the description of the demonic locusts in Rev. 9:7-10). The utilization of simile *is not license for interpreting the comparisons within the text as some form of purely symbolic communication.*

As for determining whether a literal object or figurative symbol is involved, we note several guidelines:

> *First*, the interpreter should accept as symbols that which is so designated in the context or seen under the harmony of prophecy. . . . *Second*, the interpreter should accept as symbols those elements that are

truly impossible in the realm of reality, taking care to note that eschatological times are real times. . . . [But the] prophetic Scriptures contain many descriptions of the future that are possible or plausible. In such instances, the interpreter should not assign these to the realm of symbolism.[53]

To these we may add a third from Tan:

The determination of what is figurative and what nonfigurative in prophecy is a question centuries old. From Augustine's *De Doctrina Christiana* to the present, interpreters have attempted to give different rules and guidelines. . . . the key to determining the figurative from the nonfigurative lies in ascertaining whether a given word or act is at variance with the essential nature of the subject being discussed. If a word or act, taken in the literal sense, fails to harmonize with either the flow of thought in the text or context, or with the analogy of Scripture, it is to be understood as figurative. Otherwise, it is nonfigurative.[54]

As an example, Tan's guideline can be applied productively in the case of the binding of Satan:

Then I saw an angel coming down from heaven, having the key to the bottomless pit and a great chain in his hand. He laid hold of the dragon, that serpent of old, who is *the* Devil and Satan, and bound him for a thousand years (Rev. 20:1-2)

To answer the question whether the chain is literal, one need only observe that Satan is spirit and cannot be bound by material objects. Therefore, the chain is *figurative* of the bondage under which Satan will be placed. Learning to identify which aspects of a passage are figurative and which are literal is essential for correct interpretation:

Some seem to believe that if *anything* in a given passage is symbolic, then *everything* must be symbolic . . . . In contrast, the approach recommended here can be illustrated by considering the statement, "It was raining cats and dogs outside." . . . The key to a correct interpretation is (a) to recognize that there can be both literal and figurative elements in the same text and (b) to seek to discern which aspects of the text fal into which category. In this illustration, for example, "It was raining . . . outside" should be taken *literally*, and the "cats and dogs" should be taken *figuratively*. Both the literal and the figurative function together to communicate that it was raining very hard.[55]

Perhaps the most difficult aspect of determining whether a passage conveys figurative or literal events is found in the fact that prophetic content can span periods of time far beyond the time when the vision was first given. Thus, things which seemed clearly to be figurative at the time of writing due to their impossibility (e.g., the two hundred million horsemen in Rev. 9:16; the peoples, tribes, tongues, and nations viewing the dead bodies of the two witnesses in Rev. 11:9) later become literally possible (e.g., a large world population; the advent of worldwide broadcasting).

Writing almost one-half century ago, Tenney observed:

The object like a burning mountain cast into the sea (Rev. 8:8), the opening of the bottomless pit (Rev. 9:2), and many other episodes must be interpreted symbolically if they are to be taken as applying to current or to past history. If they are yet to come, they may be a more accurate description of actual phenomena than most expositors have realized, for the physical and psychical researches of recent years have opened to the mind of man worlds that in John's time were completely unknown. The atom bomb, guided missiles, and the scientific devices of modern warfare have made the Apocalypse seem much less apocalyptic [dramatic *hyperbole*[5.2.27]] than it did fifty years ago.[56]

The fact that Revelation 19 sets forth the Second Coming of Christ which has obviously not yet occurred renders unlikely the stance of Osborne and others who hold that all the symbols found in the book were understood by the original readers:

We no longer need to guess what modern events may be prophesied, for *every* symbol was understandable to the first-century readers. . . . we seek . . . the background knowledge from the first century to unlock the tensive symbols and to see what the original readers would have understood when they read them. This is not a perfect science, of course, and **scholars debate the background behind each symbol.** [emphasis added][57]

Since some of the symbols relate events which have not yet been fulfilled, we cannot simply assert they were all understood by the original readers. For one thing, it is highly unlikely that the original readers had access to the entire corpus which came to be recognized as the *canon*[5.2.12] of Scripture, thereby lacking perhaps the most important key to understanding some of the symbols in the book of Revelation: the comparison of related passages (analogy) of Scripture. (See our discussion on the *audience and purpose*[2.3] of the book for more on this.) The insistence that all symbols were understood by the readers of John's day ignores the reality that not even John understood everything which he saw (Rev. 7:13-14). It is important to notice that John is told to write, "what you *see* " (Rev. 1:11) rather than what he *understood.* In other words, John was to record his *immediate* experiences and visions. He was not given the vision and then told to cogitate over it for a period of time to eventually produce a literary masterpiece in the apocalyptic genre perfectly understandable to first century readers!

Fortunately, many of the symbols are explained in their immediate context. And we are also blessed with the entire corpus of *inspired*[5.2.33] Scripture which we can apply to gain an understanding of what John relates.[58]

It is worth mentioning another aspect of symbols in prophetic Scripture: the tendency of literal interpreters to render symbolic descriptions by way of literal drawings. While these may be interesting or even provocative, it is generally a disservice to the prophetic text to utilize the symbols in such a way. Trench observes the priority of symbolism within the Jewish tradition as being that of conveying truth rather than rendering form:

> This description of the glorified Lord (Rev. 1:16), . . . may suggest a few reflections on the apocalyptic, and generally the Hebrew symbolism, and on the very significant relations of difference and opposition in which it stands to the Greek. Religion and Art for the Greek ran into one another with no very signal preponderance of the claims of the former over the latter. Even in his religious symbolism the sense of beauty, of form, of proportion, overrules every other, and must at all costs find its satisfaction; so that the first necessity of the symbol is that it shall not affront, that it shall satisfy rather, the aesthetic sense. . . . But with the Hebrew symbolism it is altogether different. The first necessity there is that the symbol should set forth truly and fully the religious idea of which it is intended to be the vehicle. How it would appear when it clothed itself in an outward form and shape, whether it would find favour. . . as satisfying the conditions of beauty, this was quite a secondary consideration; may be confidently affirmed not to have been a consideration at all; . . . but rather that it should remain ever and only a purely mental conception, the unembodied sign of an idea;—I may observe, by the way, that no skill of delineation can make the Cherubim themselves other than unsightly objects to the eye.[59]

The results of such renderings are often held up to ridicule as the result of the literal method of interpretation. But this misunderstands the purpose of such symbols as being primarily art form rather than representative of characteristics which are not as easily conveyed textually. All the more so when such figures are described by simile providing a definite clue that the image conveyed by the text is only an approximation of the reality being described.

2.7.5 - Understanding Numbers

We find numbers employed throughout Scripture, but perhaps no more densely packed than in the book of Revelation. Two opposite errors are often encountered when dealing with numbers in Scripture: (1) numbers are interpreted symbolically to derive fanciful teachings; (2) numbers are treated strictly literally and their symbolic significance is denied. We hope to avoid both of these extremes in our approach to the book.

2.7.5.1 - The Abuse of Numbers

Concerning the abuse of biblical numerology,[60] Trench has well observed:

> In all speculations upon numbers we may very profitably lay to heart the wise caution of Fuller, [*A Pisgah Sight of Palestine,* b. iii. c. 6.] . . . "For matter of numbers fancy is never at a loss. . . . But such as in expounding of Scripture reap more than God did sow there, never eat what they reap thence, because such grainless husks, when seriously threshed out, vanish all into chaff."[61]

This caution applies not only to numbers, but to the interpretation of symbols and typology. In the case of numerology, symbols, and typology, God undeniably conveys *more* than the surface text itself suggests, *the problem is in determining how valid* are the additional insights one may gain. As soon as the meaning attributed to a number, symbol, or type is carried beyond what God intended to convey, then we are eating Fuller's "grainless husks." So due caution must be exercised, especially by teachers.[62]

Beale provides us with illustrations of the most common abuse of numbers: a denial of any literal value and substituting a figurative meaning in its place:

> The seven kings [of Rev. 17:10] are not to be identified with any specific historical rulers but represent rather the oppressive power of world government throughout the ages, which arrogates to itself divine prerogatives and persecutes God's people.[63]

> The name "Christ" appears seven times and the name "Jesus" fourteen times. "The Lamb" is used of Christ twenty-eight times, seven bringing the Lamb and God together. The 7 x 4 appearances of this title underscore the universal scope of the Lamb's complete victory. . . . Twelve is the number of God's people, which is squared to indicate completeness and multiplied by one thousand to connote vastness. [Rev. 7:4; 14:1][64]

Notice how Beale puts his interpreter's "spin" on the numbers in order to deny their literalness with phrases like *to indicate* and *to connote*.

Some interpreters seem to despair of dealing with the numbers in the book of Revelation in any sort of literal way. This can be carried to such an extreme as to totally deny any literal meaning while *failing to provide a figurative understanding in its place*:[65] Here we meet with both confusion (we can't know what the numbers mean) and *anti-supernaturalism*[2.5] (we can't know the *writer's intention*—never mind that he was told simply to record what he was shown).

When it comes to numbers and their meaning in the book of Revelation, it is not uncommon for interpreters to ask the reader to exchange his gold (the number's literal meaning) for fool's gold (a fanciful, vague interpretation, or perhaps no interpretation at all). It may be valid in some cases to understand an additional well-recognized figurative meaning connoted by a number, but this should not be done *in lieu of its literal value*. There were, after all, twelve *actual* sons of Israel (Gen. 35:22-26) and Jesus ministered to twelve *actual* disciples (Mtt. 10:2-5).

2.7.5.2 - Literal Understanding of Numbers

In studying the book of Revelation, one is immediately struck by the prevailing bias of many commentators *against* understanding numbers in their normative, literal way. For example, the length of half of Daniel's seventieth week is described in a number of related passages (Dan. 7:25; Dan. 9:27; 12:7; Rev. 11:2-3; 12:6, 14; 13:5). This obvious strong witness to understanding this period in a literal way is simply set aside for another meaning:

> We cannot insist on a literal meaning for the three and a half years of the tribulation period or the thousand years of the millennium. They could be literal, but the numbers function symbolically in the book and probably signify a lengthy period of time that is under God's control.[66]

We are being asked to trade gold for fool's gold! Rather than understand three and a half as denoting a specific period of time specified by God,[67] we are asked to accept the alternate meaning which our interpreter says is *probably* correct!

There is a strong bias against literal understanding of numbers in the book of Revelation. Even when the text seems quite explicit as to the identification of what is being described, commentators refuse to take the text at face value:

> Let us consider the meaning of numbers in the book. . . . While some (Seiss, Walvoord, Thomas) tend to consider them literally, they are forced to some **creative interpretations** , for example, regarding the 144,000 who are sealed in Rev. 7:4-8. Walvoord . . . believes this means that 12,000 sealed in each tribe are those selected to be God's special witnesses through the tribulation period, but it seems more likely that the numbers in the book are meant symbolically **as was common in ancient apocalypses**. [emphasis added][68]

Notice how those who adhere to a literal interpretation and who arrive at a uniform understanding are said to be employing "creative interpretations." That the exact opposite is the case can be easily demonstrated by noting the wide variation in interpretation among the commentators who take the 144,000 Jews as being non-Jews. Here again we see an appeal to the literary *genre*[5.2.22] including a host of non-*canonical*[5.2.12] writings to undermine the straightforward text. We are told that we should not understand the 144,000 Jews to be 144,000 individuals nor Jews, because this book is to be read like any other "ancient apocalypse" where symbols serve as the vehicle for communicating inspirational musings and obscure political inferences. Never mind that the text goes to great lengths to make sure we know these are Jews (each of the twelve tribes is individually listed) and their appearance at this point in the events of the book of Revelation is in perfect accord with the doctrine of the believing Jewish remnant which runs throughout Scripture (1K. 19:18; 2K. 19:4, 30; 21:14; 25:22; Isa. 1:9; 6:13; 7:3; 10:20-22; 28:5; 37:4, 31-32; 46:3; 59:21; 65:8; Jer 5:10; 5:18; 23:3; 50:20; Eze. 5:3; 6:8-10; 9:8, 11; Eze. 11:13; Joel 2:32; Mic. 2:12; 7:18; Zec. 11:10; 13:8-9; Rom. 9:6, 27; Rom. 11:5, 17, 25; Gal. 6:16; 1Pe. 1:1; Rev. 12:17).[69]

We believe the correct view on the interpretation of numbers within the book of Revelation is to understand them in their primary, literal sense, but to also recognize biblical numerology where certain numbers appear with special emphasis throughout Scripture and carry additional meaning beyond the bare facts they record:

> The fact is that no number in Revelation is verifiably a symbolic number. On the other hand, the nonsymbolic usage of numbers is the rule. It requires multiplication of a literal 12,000 by a literal twelve to come up with 144,000 in Rev. 7:4-8. The churches, seals, trumpets, and bowls are all literally seven in number. The three unclean spirits of Rev. 16:13 are actually three in number. The three angels connected with the last three woes (Rev. 8:13) add up to a total of three. The seven last plagues amount to exactly seven. The equivalency of 1,260 days and three and a half years necessitate a nonsymbolic understanding of both numbers. The twelve apostles and the twelve tribes of Israel are literally twelve (Rev. 21:12-14). The *seven churches*[5.2.66] are seven literal cities. Yet confirmation of a single number in Revelation as symbolic is impossible.[70]

> Numbers may be understood literally, but even when understood in this way, they often carry with them also a symbolical meaning. Hence the number seven, . . . refers to seven literal churches . . . Yet by the very use of this number (which speaks of completion or perfection) the concept is conveyed that these were representative churches which in some sense were complete in their description of the normal needs of the church.[71]

For example, we understand that God completed His creation within a literal six-day period and rested on the seventh (Gen. 2:1; Ex. 20:11; 31:17). We also understand that He did this *by design* as a pattern to establish the working week for man (Ex. 20:9; 23:12; 31:15; etc.). The number has a two-fold significance. *First*, it has a literal meaning: the creation spanned six 24-hour days. *Second*, it has a symbolical meaning: the number seven carries the meaning of rest or completion. To deny the primary literal meaning in order to major on the secondary symbolism would be an error. So too would be an interpretation which denies the secondary symbolism.

When we interpret numbers primarily in their literal sense, we are in the company of the earliest interpreters to whom the Scriptures were entrusted: the Jews. Prior to the *rise of allegorical interpretation*[2.7.3] , the rabbis understood the Scriptures in the same way as literal interpreters today. For example, the last 'seven' of Daniel's seventy sevens (Dan. 9:24-27) are understood as a literal period of seven years.[72]

When we read the book of Revelation, we do not enter some strange *Alice in Wonderland* world where normative communication is set aside in favor of speculation. Those commentators who do so would never dream of applying similar methods of interpretation to other passages of Scripture. In the gospels they understand twelve apostles as twelve apostles, three days as three days, and so on.

The existence of symbols and categorization of writing as *apocalyptic genre* are not license for jettisoning the primary literal meaning of numbers.

2.7.5.3 - The Symbolic Meaning of Numbers

Having established the primacy of understanding numbers in their literal sense, we must also recognize biblical numerology: the study of the use of numbers throughout Scripture to convey meaning beyond the literal value. This is a large subject which we cannot treat with much depth other than to describe the symbolism conveyed by some of the most frequently found numbers in the book of Revelation. Even though many numbers clearly have an associated symbolism found in their pattern of usage throughout Scripture, not every occurrence of a given number necessarily carries the symbolic value.

2.7.5.3.1 - Two: Witness

The number two appears in the book of Revelation in association with the two witnesses (Rev. 11:3, 10) who are the "two olive trees and two lampstands standing before the God of the earth" (Rev. 11:4). These witnesses (μάτυσιν [*matysin*] from μάρτυς [*martys*] from which we derive *martyr*), furnish a testimony (μαρτυρίαν [*martyrian*]) of the power and judgment of God to a rejecting world. They serve as witnesses both before and after their death: by the miraculous powers which God grants them while living (Rev. 11:5-6) and by their subsequent resurrection which causes great fear to fall on those who see them rise (Rev. 11:11).

The basis for two as the number of witness is found in the Law of Moses which prescribes that judgments be made on the basis of at least two witnesses (Num. 35:30; Deu. 17:6; 19:5; 1K. 21:10 cf. Mtt. 18:16; 2Cor. 13:1).

God, Who can swear by no other, frequently employs the two witnesses of 'heaven and earth' to underscore His promises (Deu. 4:26; 30:19; Ps. 50:4; Isa. 1:2) as did Moses (Deu. 31:28; 32:1).[73] The two-fold use of God's created order as a witness is found within a frequently misunderstood passage in the book of Revelation where a sign consisting of "a women clothed with the **sun**, with the **moon** under her feet" [emphasis added] (Rev. 12:1) appears. Here, the ordinances of the *sun* and *moon* serve as witnesses to the promises which God makes elsewhere to this woman: that the *nation of Israel* (Jer. 31:35-36) and the *Davidic throne* (Ps. 89:35-37; Jer. 33:20-22) will never cease to exist before Him.

Throughout the New Testament, reference is made to "the law and the prophets" as the two-fold witness against those who reject God (Mtt. 5:17; 7:12; 11:13; 22:40; Luke 16:16; 24:44; John 1:45; Acts 13:15; 24:14; 28:23; Rom. 3:21). For example, Paul states: "But now the righteousness of God apart from the law is revealed, **being witnessed by the Law and the Prophets**" [emphasis added] (Rom. 3:21). The importance of this witness is emphasized in Jesus' teaching concerning the rich man and Lazarus in Luke 16. When the rich man, tormented in *hades*, appealed to Abraham to warn his five brothers to avoid his fate, Abraham responds:

> Abraham said to him, 'They have Moses and the prophets; let them hear them.' And he said, 'No, father Abraham; but if one goes to them from the dead, they will repent.' But he said to him, 'If they do not hear Moses and the prophets, neither will they be persuaded though one rise from the dead.' (Luke 16:29-31)

It is no accident that it is Moses (representing the law) and Elijah (representing the prophets) who appear with Jesus on the Mount of Transfiguration (Mtt. 17:3; Mark 9:4; Luke 9:30). Many have noted the similarity between the miraculous activities of the two witnesses of Revelation 11 and those of Moses and Elijah recorded in the Old Testament. Regardless of the actual identity of the two Revelation witnesses (see commentary on Rev. 11:3-13), the similarity of their ministry to that of Moses and Elijah seems intended to underscore their role as witnesses to *the law* and *the prophets*.

Within the "unholy trinity" of the *Beast*[5.2.9], the *False Prophet*[5.2.20], and Satan, it is significant that there are *two* human personages: the *two beasts* which rise from the sea and the earth, respectively (Rev. 13:1, 11). These two men stand as witnesses to the depravity of man, as empowered by Satan. Both are *beasts*, both *rise* from distinct human populations (the sea being a reference to *Gentile* nations and the earth a possible reference to the *Jewish* nation). The second beast has *two horns* which may emphasize his special role as a *witness to the first beast*, to whom he directs the attention and worship of those who dwell upon the earth.

2.7.5.3.2 - Three: Life, Resurrection, Completeness, the Trinity

The number three appears in the book of Revelation in association with the doxological triad (Rev. 4:8; cf. Isa. 6:3), the amount of grain sold for a set price during famine conditions (Rev. 6:6), the remaining trumpet judgments to be sounded (Rev. 8:13), the number of plagues by which a third of mankind is killed (Rev. 9:18), the amount of time during which the two witnesses lie dead before their resurrection (Rev. 11:9, 11), the number of demonic spirits associated with the "unholy trinity" (Rev. 16:13),[74] the division of Jerusalem by the great earthquake (Rev. 16:19), and the number of gates on each side of the wall of the New Jerusalem (Rev. 21:13).

In association with the number three, we observe that in the six days of creation, God pronounces the work of each day as "good" with the exception of day two (Gen. 1:6-8). It appears that the pronouncement expected for day two is held until the third day. Thus, the third day is pronounced "good" twice (Gen. 1:10, 12). Some have called the third day, the "day of double blessing." It appears that our attention is drawn to the third day and it is pronounced as "doubly" good because the third day is the day on which *life* first appears. [75] Not only does life first appear on day three of creation week, but Jesus is raised on the third day.[76] The raising of the two witnesses on the *third* day (Rev. 11:11) correlates with this association of life or resurrection with day three.

Yet in the book of Revelation, the majority of the appearances of three seem to connote completeness, much like the way leaven (sin) works its way *completely* through the *three* measures of meal (Mtt. 13:33; Luke 13:21).[77] This would seem to be the case in Revelation 8:13 where the final three woes are set apart as being of special significance. Here again, three denoting completeness or thoroughness.[78] The complete eternality of God is expressed as the One "who is and who was and who is to come" (Rev. 1:8), indicating His complete oversight of events within the domain of time.

Another significant use of three is in reference to the Trinity (Rev. 16:13). For example, the threefold repetition of "Holy" in Revelation 4:8 may refer to each of the persons of the Trinity (or as some have observed, merely be a Semitic artifact—a triplet denoting *intensity* , cf. Eze. 21:27; Jer. 22:29).[79] The thrice repetition of six as the number of the Beast (Rev. 13:18) signifies the mimic of the true Trinity by the "unholy trinity" consisting of the beast from the sea (Rev. 13:1), beast from the earth (Rev. 13:11), and Satan (the dragon, Rev. 13:4). Three unclean spirits like frogs come out of this unholy trinity and perform signs to gather the kings of the earth and all the world to do battle against God (Rev. 16:13-14). Here there seems to be a reference to completeness as well as triunity—they lead the *entire world* in opposing God.[80]

2.7.5.3.3 - Four: the Entire World, the Earth

The number four appears in the book of Revelation in association with the living creatures (Rev. 4:6, 8; 5:6, 8; 6:1, 8; 14:3; 15:7; 19:4), the four horsemen of the first seven seals (Rev. 6:1-8), the four angels (Rev. 7:1-2) standing on the four corners of the earth (Rev. 7:1) holding back the four winds of the earth (Rev. 7:1), the four horns of the altar (Rev. 9:13), the four angels bound at the great river Euphrates (Rev. 9:14) who are released to kill a third of all mankind, and the four corners of the earth to which Satan travels to gather the final battle (Rev. 20:8).

The symbolic meaning of the number four in the book of Revelation seems clear: it is the signature of the world or of global effect.[81]

> Four . . . is the signature of the world . . . . Four is stamped every where on this the organized world. Thus, not to speak of the four elements, the four seasons, neither of which are recognized in Scripture, we have the four winds (Eze. 37:9; Mtt. 24:31; Rev. 7:1); the four corners of the earth (Rev. 7:1; 20:8); the four living creatures, emblems of all creaturely life (Rev. 4:6), and each of these with four faces and four wings (Eze. 1:5-6); the four beasts coming up from the sea, and representing the four great world-empires which in the providence of God should succeed one another (Dan. 7:3); the four metals composing the image which sets forth the same phases of empire (Dan. 2:32-33); the four Gospels, or the four-sided Gospel, in sign of its designation for all the world; the sheet tied at the four corners (Acts 10:11; 11:5); the four horns, the sum total of the forces of the world as arrayed against the Church (Zec. 1:18); the enumeration, wherever this is wished to be exhaustive of the inhabitants of the world by four, kindreds, tongues, peoples, and nations (Rev. 5:9 cf. 7:9; 10:11; 11:9; 14:6; 17:15). For other significant enumerations by four, see Eze. 14:21; John 5:3; Rev. 6:8. [82]

The first four of the seven seals, the "four horsemen of the apocalypse" (Rev. 6:1-8), are each represented by a rider on a horse whose action has *worldwide* effects. The worldwide or global connotation of the number four derives from the directions of the compass (North, South, East, West, cf. Eze. 7:2) and may be why there are four living creatures which are *around* the throne (Rev. 4:6) surrounding it in all four primary directions. This same directional emphasis is seen in the camp of Israel which camped around the *tabernacle*[5.2.69] in the wilderness in these four primary directions (Num. 2:1-34; 23:10). This same arrangement is reflected in the tribal names associated with the twelve gates surrounding the New Jerusalem: 3 tribal names written on the gates in each of the four directions (Rev. 21:13). The living creatures seen by John bear a striking resemblance to Ezekiel's cherubim[83] (Eze. 1:10; 10:14) which appear to support the "chariot throne" of God as it travels in *any direction* (Eze. 1:12; 10:16-17), yet with notable differences. Each of Ezekiel's cherubim have *four* faces (a cherub or ox, a man, a lion, and an eagle) whereas John's *four* living creatures each have a different face (a calf, a man, a lion, and an eagle). See *Four Gospels*[4.7].

The global emphasis of the number four is also seen in the *four* angels which kill a third of *all mankind*.[84]

2.7.5.3.4 - Five: Provision, Fullness, Grace

The number five appears in the book of Revelation in association with the time period (five months) during which the locusts torment those men without the seal of the living God (Rev. 9:5, 10) and as the number of kings which have fallen when John is shown the mystery of Babylon (Rev. 17:10).

Although perhaps more subtle than other biblical numerology, five appears to be associated with the idea of provision, fullness, or grace. The waters of the flood were on the earth *five* months (150 days) before they subsided (Gen. 7:24). In the reunion of Joseph with his brothers, Benjamin's serving was *five* times that of the other brothers (Gen. 43:34). Benjamin was given *five* changes of garments (Gen. 45:22) whereas his brothers were only given one. When *five* of Joseph's brothers are presented before Pharaoh, it is to obtain the best land for their flocks (Gen. 47:2-6). David selected *five* stones with which to slay Goliath (1S. 17:40).[85] When David lacked provisions, he requested *five* loaves of bread (1S. 21:3). Jesus fed the multitudes using *five* loaves of bread (Mtt. 24:17; Mark 6:38; 8:19; Luke 9:13; John 6:9). See also [Bullinger, *Number in Scripture: Its Supernatural Design and Spiritual Significance*, 135-149].

From these examples we conclude that those upon whom the locusts are unleashed for *five months* (Rev. 9:5, 10) receive the full provision of torment which God has in store for them.

2.7.5.3.5 - Six: Man's Incompleteness, Human Will

The number six appears in the book of Revelation in association with the six wings of the living creatures (Rev. 4:8)[87] and the number of the *Beast*[5.2.9] (666, Rev. 13:18).

Since man was created on the sixth day (Gen. 1:26-27), six is considered to be the 'number of man.' The repetition of the number thrice in association with the number of the Beast is understood to denote the 'trinity of man' or 'satanic trinity' (Satan, the Beast, and the false prophet). "Six is the number of man, who was created on the sixth day. In Revelation 13:18 it represents the number of the ultimate man, the *Antichrist*[5.2.3]: 666."[88]

The number six seems to denote specifically the will and independence of man (i.e., sin) as evidenced by the mention of the number of fingers and toes of men who were notably powerful in their defiance of God (2S. 21:20; 1Chr. 20:6).[89]

Six also denotes incompleteness, being one less than seven, the number of completeness or perfection. The Menorah has one central stem out of which six stems branch (Ex. 25:32-33). Some see this as an indication of man's incompleteness (the six branches) made complete only with the addition of Messiah (the central branch). As Jesus said, "I am the vine, you *are* the branches. He who abides in Me, and I in him, bears much fruit; for without Me you can do nothing." (John 15:5) In the same way that six days of work are incomplete without the seventh day of rest, man's utmost effort when *independent of God* results in incompleteness and failure.

> *Six* days were appointed to him for his labour; while *one* day is associated in sovereignty with the Lord God, as His rest. *Six*, therefore, is the number of *labour* also, of man's labour as apart and distinct from God's rest. . . . the number is significant of *secular completeness*.[90]

In the book of Revelation is presented the final great effort of the *human secular system* to achieve its ends apart from God. The cataclysmic events in response to the unbridled will of man are God's ultimate reminder of man's innate inability and deficiency apart from God, which the earth-dwellers refuse to acknowledge to the bitter end.

Among the enemies of God marked by the number six: we find Goliath, whose height was *six* cubits, having *six* pieces of armor and a spear's head weighing *six* hundred shekels of iron (1S. 17:4-7); Nebuchadnezzar, whose "image" was *sixty* cubits high and *six* cubits wide (Dan. 3:1); and Antichrist, whose number is *six* hundred and *sixty-six* (Rev. 13:18). Even Solomon at the height of his earthly glory received a *mere six* hundred and *sixty-six* talents of gold (1K. 10:14) each year and sat on a throne of *only* six steps (1K. 10:19). Solomon, in his advanced human wisdom, great power and influence, but eventual drift from God, illustrates characteristics shared by the Antichrist of the end.

Throughout history, the best that man can produce by every available means and effort of rebellious will is "666" which falls short of God's triune completeness ("777").

2.7.5.3.6 - Seven: Perfection, Completeness

The number seven is the most frequently encountered number in the book of Revelation:

> Even the most careless reader of the Apocalypse must be struck by the manner in which almost every thing there is ordered by sevens. Thus, besides the *seven Churches*[5.2.66], and their seven Angels, we have already in this first chapter the seven Spirits (Rev. 1:4), the seven candlesticks (Rev. 1:12), the seven stars (Rev. 1:16); and further on, the seven lamps of fire (Rev. 4:4), seven seals (Rev. 5:1), seven horns and seven eyes of the Lamb (Rev. 5:6), seven heavenly Angels with their seven trumpets (Rev. 8:2), seven thunders (Rev. 10:3), seven heads of the dragon, and seven crowns upon these heads (Rev. 12:13), the same of the beast rising out of the sea (Rev. 13:1), seven last plagues (Rev. 15;1); seven vials (Rev. 15:7), seven mountains (Rev. 17:9), seven kings (Rev. 17:10); not to speak of other recurrences, not so obvious, of this number seven as the signature of the Book; as for instance, the distribution of the entire Book into seven visions, the sevenfold ascription of glory to the Lamb (Rev. 5:12), and to God (Rev. 7:12).[91]

Hindson lists the following 'sevens' in the book: churches (Rev. 1:4-20; 2-3); spirits (Rev. 1:4; 3:1; 4:5; 5:6); lampstands (Rev. 1:12-20; 2:1); stars (Rev. 1:16-20; 2:1; 3:1); lamps of fire (Rev. 4:5); seals (Rev. 5:1-5); horns (Rev. 5:6); eyes (Rev. 5:6); angels (Rev. 8:2-6); trumpets (Rev. 8:2-6); peals of thunder (Rev. 10:3-4); seven thousand people (Rev. 11:13); heads (Rev. 12:3; 13:1; 17:3-9); diadems (Rev. 12:3); angels (Rev. 15:1-8; 21:9); plagues (Rev. 15:1-8; 21:9); bowls (Rev. 15:7; 17:1; 21:9); mountains (17:9); kings (17:10-11); beatitudes (Rev. 1:3; 14:13; 16:15; 19:9; 20:6; 22:7, 14); "I ams" of Christ (Rev. 1:8, 17, 18; 2:23; 21:6; 22:13, 16).[92] Tenney notes seven beatitudes (Rev. 1:3; 14:13; 16:15; 19:9; 20:6; 22:7; 22:14).[93] Hindson notes: "David Hocking observes that the concept of our Lord's soon return is emphasized seven times in the Revelation by the words 'shortly' or 'quickly' [Rev. 1:1; 2:16; 3:11; 11:14; 22:7; 22:12; 22:20)."[94] Morris mentions seven "I ams" of Christ (Rev. 1:8, 11, 17, 18; 21:6; 22:13, 16) and seven doxologies in heaven (Rev. 4:9-11; 5:8-13; 7:9-12; 11:16-18; 14:2-3; 15:2-4; 19:1-6).[95]

As mentioned in our discussion of six, the number seven is understood to denote 'perfection' in the sense of completion. God created in six days and *rested* on the seventh.[96] This is the main symbolism of the number seven in the book of Revelation. The *seven* churches are representative of *all* churches. The *seven* Spirits represent the perfect omniscience of the Holy Spirit.[97]The seven seals, trumpets, and bowls denote the completeness of God's worldwide judgment.[98]

The prevalence of seven throughout the book of Revelation has also been recognized as signifying this book as the final revelation of God to complete the *canon*[5.2.12] of Scripture: [99]

> Almost certainly one of the primary reasons [for the preponderance of sevens] is to emphasize that this *is* the last book of the Bible! In fact, the book closes with a grave warning against anyone who would pretend to add anything further to God's *inspired*[5.2.33] Word (Revelation 22:18).[100]

> It seems likely that John has written his book carefully to signify the perfect plan of God and the completeness of his work.[101]

With the final acts recorded in the book of Revelation, God *completes* His mighty act of redemption and renewal thus restoring His creation to the condition it had prior to the entrance of sin.[102]

2.7.5.3.7 - Twelve: Jewish Tribes, Completeness

The number twelve appears in the book of Revelation as the twelve thousand Jews from each of the twelve tribes (Rev. 7:5-8, 14:1), the woman's garland of twelve stars (Rev. 12:1), the twelve gates of the New Jerusalem named after the twelve tribes and attended by twelve angels (Rev. 21:12), the twelve foundations of the New Jerusalem named after the twelve apostles (Rev. 21:14), the length, breadth, and height of the city being twelve thousand furlongs (Rev. 21:16), the twelve pearls at the twelve gates (Rev. 21:21), and the twelve fruits of the tree of life, yielding its fruit each month (Rev. 22:2).

The primary symbolism denoted by the number twelve is its dominant association with the sons of Jacob, the twelve tribes of Israel (Gen. 35:22; 49:28). Since Israel is God's elect [103] and Jesus chose twelve apostles,[104] it may be that God's sovereign choice is also reflected in this value. But even in Jesus' selection of twelve apostles, a direct relationship to the twelve tribes of Israel is intended (Mtt. 19:28; Luke 22:30).

In the book of Revelation, nearly all occurrences of twelve, with the exception of the fruit of the tree of life (Rev. 22:2), are related to the tribes of Israel and reflect the intense "Jewishness" of the book. [105] As we shall see in our discussion of *related passages and themes*[2.13], the fulfillment of Old Testament prophecies concerning the nation Israel is a key to understanding much of what takes place in the book of Revelation. Hence, the preponderance of twelve.

Some have seen twelve as denoting 'unity in diversity' in that individuals (the tribes, the apostles) are considered as a unified people of God.[106] Still others have found in the number the idea of completeness with the twelve tribes representing *all Israel* and twelve months representing a *complete year*.[107]

2.7.5.4 - Searching for Meaning in all the Wrong Places

Among commentators of the last book of the Bible, a stark dividing line can be seen in regard to where they go looking for an understanding of the symbols which they encounter in the text. The three main sources which are appealed to are *pagan mythology*, *Jewish apocryphal*[5.2.5] *writings*, and *the Old Testament*. Depending upon which of these three sources one emphasizes, a quite different picture of John's communication emerges. The decision of where to go looking for meaning is perhaps second only to *the art and science of interpretation*[2.7.2] in its effect upon the resulting understanding. It is our belief that those who utilize pagan mythology and uninspired Jewish apocrypha in order to understand the book of Revelation have a deficient view of the perspicuity and *sufficiency* of the *inspired*[5.2.33] Scriptures (Ps. 19:1-14; John 8:31; 1Cor. 4:6; 2Ti. 3:15-17; Heb. 4:12-13; 2Pe. 1:3, 19-21; Jude 1:3).

Some commentators assume a near equivalence among these three sources in the pursuit of meaning.

> The sources for interpreting them [symbols] come from the *OT*[5.2.51], intertestamental literature, and the Greco-Roman world—in other words, in the common world of the original readers in the province of Asia.[108]

> Though the OT, Judaism, *NT*[5.2.48], and immediate context of the Apocalypse provide the primary background for its imagery, much work remains to be done on surveying the various sources of the Greco-Roman world to broaden the multiple ideas associated with many of the images in the Apocalypse.[109]

Others go so far as to assert that the meaning of the book of Revelation *cannot* be found within the confines of inspired Scripture because certain symbols are not treated therein: "The Apocalyptist, however, does not limit himself to O.T. imagery, but has much that is **his own**, or that belongs to the common stock of the later apocalyptic. **The Woman with Child [Rev. 12:1-2] has no parallel in the O.T.**" [emphasis added][110]

Is it really true that God delivered inspired Scripture to John for our understanding, but expects us to search extra-biblical sources for the necessary keys? And what of those who only have the inspired Word of God at their disposal, but lack the historical and cultural materials which some commentators assert are necessary? It is one thing to recognize that access to historical and cultural writings may *enhance* our understanding of biblical material. It is quite another to say that it is a *requisite* for our understanding. The latter view effectively denies the sufficiency of Scripture and elevates extra-biblical material on a par with inspired Scripture in making the latter dependent upon the former.

In contrast to these views, Thomas observes: "An attempt has been made to elevate extra-biblical material referred to by John to the level of the OT among his sources. Yet no conclusive evidence proves that he used sources, written or oral, outside the OT."[111] Those who assert John's dependence upon outside sources are unable to provide clear-cut examples and often are simply reflecting the *anti-supernaturalism*[2.5] so prevalent in academic circles today. Beale wisely cautions:

> In recognizing the presence of allusions to sources other than the OT, whether Jewish or Greco-Roman . . . One must be circumspect in the search for dependence on such other literary sources and resist the temptation to find parallels where there are none.[112]

2.7.5.4.1 - Searching Pagan Mythology

Perhaps the most perplexing view is that the meaning for symbols in the book of Revelation is to be found within the pagan mythology of the reader's day. This is akin to saying we are to find the jewels of God laying in the bottom of a secular trash can!

> Fiorenza says the symbols have a special communicative function in addressing the social world of the original readers, thus opening up a new symbolic world for them. It is our task to uncover that symbolic world.[113]

> A major breakthrough in the scholarly study of Revelation was the recognition of the source and character of its images and narrative patterns. These were not composed freely by the author to comment on the current situation; in other words, they are not primarily allegories invented to comment on current affairs. Further, these images and narrative patterns were not simply borrowed from the "Old Testament" and cannot be understood fully in terms of such borrowing. They can be understood appropriately and in depth only in the context of [Ancient Near East] and Greco-Roman myth.[114]

What is all the more amazing is the tendency of some to understand the symbols of the book in light of pagan myth *despite* clear parallels to *OT*[5.2.51] passages:[115]

Not only are we urged to look to secular sources for important meaning, but secular sources for which today we only have fragmentary evidence as to their original contents at the time of John's writing. If we are dependent upon cultural writings which are mostly lost to history for a complete understanding of Scripture, than what can be said of the self-claims of Scripture as being sufficient?

As has been recognized by some, this supposed dependence upon pagan mythology is largely an *a priori* assumption and has not been clearly demonstrated. Commenting on the unlikelihood of crowns representing a victor (rather than a royal ruler) in the Apocalypse, Trench observes: "nowhere else in the Apocalypse is there found a single image drawn from the range of heathen antiquity. The Book moves exclusively in the circle of Jewish imagery."[116] In regard to the various and ingenious explanations for the "white stone" of Rev. 2:17, Trench observes:

> All these explanations, and others which it would be tedious to enumerate, even if they were more satisfactory, and they appear to me most unsatisfactory, are affected with the same fatal weakness, namely, that they are borrowed from *heathen* antiquity, while this Book moves exclusively within the circle of sacred, that is, of Jewish, imagery and symbols, nor is the explanation of its symbols in any case to be sought beyond this circle.[117]

Even some who have devoted immense effort and time in an attempt to understand the dependence of material within the book of Revelation upon the social setting of the day candidly admit the tentative nature of their case.[118]

We concur with Unger: "The importation of mythological identifications with pagan deities or astrological lore . . . is not only futile but sacrilegious."[119]

2.7.5.4.2 - Searching Jewish Apocryphal Writings

Another frequently cited source of symbolism within the book of Revelation is the various uninspired Jewish *apocryphal*[5.2.5] writings:

> Symbols and other suggestions are derived very frequently from the Old Testament, sometimes from

> common Hebrew folk-lore, and in some instances apparently from apocalyptic sources not preserved to us. There are passages in which critics are probably right in finding traces of the influence of some unknown apocalyptic writing.[120]

> [The assumption of the two witnesses] into heaven (Rev. 11:12) accords with that of Elijah (2K. 2:11), and with that of Moses as stated in *The Assumption of Moses*, mentioned by Clement of Alexandria and Origin. In this instance the Revelation seemingly assumes the familiarity of its readers with apocryphal literature.[121]

Beckwith says that John incorporates common Hebrew folk-lore (non-truths) and bases meaning upon material which is unknown and in any case is not available to us. From the similarity of the ministry of one of the two witnesses with that of Moses, Tenney infers one *must be* Moses and therefore the reader is assumed to be in need of information from *The Assumption of Moses* to understand this fact. These are claims which are quite out of proportion with the hard evidence. Most often, our inability to understand some symbol in the book is not based upon the unavailability of an unknown apocalyptic writing, but our *ignorance of the Old Testament*[2.7.5.5]. Further, familiarity with *The Assumption of Moses* is not required in order for one of the two witnesses to be Moses. Not to mention that there are reasons for supposing that neither of the two witnesses is Moses himself, but other Jews yet to be born.

Swete observes:

> There is no evidence that any one of [the noncanonical apocalypses] has served him as a 'source'; coincidences between the work of John and the extant Jewish books are nearly limited to minor points connected with the imagery and diction. Under the circumstances it is more than precarious to postulate sources of which nothing is known.[122]

What many mistake as the *dependence* of John upon noncanonical apocalyptic writings is their common allusion to events from the Old Testament:

> The general nature of the Revelation has been described as both *apocalyptic* and *prophetic*. Jewish apocalyptic literature can be seen in Isaiah 24-27, Ezekiel 38-39, Daniel 7-12, and Zechariah 9-14. Similar elements appear in the apocryphal books of Enoch, Baruch, Fourth Ezra, the Ascension of Isaiah, and the Apocalypse of Zephaniah. **But none of these are quoted in the Revelation, which draws most of its symbolic imagery from the *canonical*[5.2.12] Old Testament books.** [emphasis added][123]

2.7.5.5 - The Importance of the Old Testament

The main reason we have a tendency to look outside of Scripture for insights in our attempt at understanding the symbols within the book of Revelation is our ignorance of the Old Testament. Like *Swete's assertion* (2.7.5.4) that the woman with child (Rev. 12:1-2) has no parallel in the Old Testament, our lack of insight into *OT*[5.2.51] themes can cause us to prematurely go looking in extra-biblical material for answers.

> [Unlike apocalyptic writings] St. John's . . . symbols are not obscure ravings hatched from a fevered imagination; they are rooted firmly in the Old Testament (and the reason for their *seeming* obscurity is that very fact: We have trouble understanding them only because we don't know our Bibles).[124]

The text itself gives clear indication where we need to look for greater understanding:

> But in the days of the sounding of the seventh angel, when he is about to sound, the mystery of God would be finished, **as He declared to His servants the prophets**. (Rev. 10:7 cf. Dan. 12:9; Amos 3:7) [emphasis added]

Thus, the analogy of Scripture (Scripture interprets Scripture) is an important key to unlocking the meaning of passages which we find puzzling:[125]

Commentators disagree as to the exact number of allusions to the Old Testament, but agree to their prevalence throughout: [126]

> No book of the New Testament is so thoroughly steeped in the thought and imagery of the Hebrew Scriptures.[127]

> [The Apocalypse's] relationship with the Old Testament can scarcely be overemphasized. . . . it is

> remarkable how the Old Testament is never explicitly quoted, but continually echoed and reapplied.[128]

> The range of OT usage includes the Pentateuch, Judges, 1-2 Samuel, 1-2 Kings, Psalms, Proverbs, Song of Solomon, Job, and the major and the minor prophets. Roughly more than half the references are from the Psalms, Isaiah, Ezekiel, and Daniel, and in proportion to its length Daniel yields the most. . . . Among the allusions to Daniel, the greatest number are from Daniel 7.[129]

> According to Swete . . . there are 46 references to Isaiah, 31 to Daniel, 29 to Ezekiel, 27 to the Psalms, and then Genesis, Deuteronomy, Jeremiah, Joel, and Zechariah.[130]

> There are hundreds of places where John alludes in one way or another to the OT Scriptures. Swete mentions that of the 404 verses of the Apocalypse, 278 contain references to the Jewish Scriptures (p. cxxxv). UBS's Green *NT*[5.2.48] (2d ed.) cites over five hundred OT passages in connection with the book (pp. 897-920).[131]

> There are over five hundred references to the Old Testament in the book of Revelation. The following is a list of such references, but it makes no claim to being exhaustive or complete. . .[132]

The importance of our familiarity with the Old Testament in order to understand the book of Revelation cannot be overstated! As we attempt to demonstrate in our discussion of *Related Passages and Themes*[2.13], the vantage point of the Old Testament is required because the book of Revelation extends and concludes various themes, problems, and promises which find their basis in the Old Testament. Without a knowledge of the Old Testament, we are like math students looking at the answers in the back of the textbook, but without any knowledge of the questions they were intended to answer! We will inevitably find ourselves 'guessing' as to the true meaning intended by God.

It was this recognized dependence of the book of Revelation upon the Jewish Old Testament which led to its authority being challenged by those with an anti-Semitic bent.[133] Entering the book of Revelation with an anti-Jewish or overt allegorical slant to one's interpretation of the Old Testament is a sure recipe for disaster.

When we come to find an OT explanation for the symbols in the book of Revelation, we may safely assume we have arrived. There is no reason to go beyond the text of Scripture in search of what is often simply speculation. "If the text is sufficiently explained in . . . terms [of the Old Testament], why look further? May not the local allusions be in essence gratuitous and unnecessary speculations?"[134]

2.7.5.6 - Is It Really So Difficult?

In the end, understanding the book of Revelation is not nearly as mysterious and difficult as many would have us believe. True, it contains some of the more difficult passages of Scripture and we have yet to meet any individual who can claim to have mastered all its depths. Still, the basic framework and intended meaning of the book *must* be understandable by those who are born-again and search it with zeal, prayer, and a sincere heart. For it to be otherwise would be a denial of God's ability to communicate to His saints. Perhaps we may not understand every issue, but the parts which are important for us to grasp are imminently within our reach. Jesus Himself said as much (Mtt. 11:25; Luke 10:21; Luke 24:25; cf. 2Pe. 1:19; Rev. 1:3).

> If God is the originator of language and if the chief purpose of originating it was to convey His message to humanity, then it must follow that He, being all-wise and all-loving, originated sufficient language to convey all that was in His heart to tell mankind. Furthermore, it must also follow that He would use language and expect people to understand it in its literal, normal, and plain sense.[135]

> There is little that is really new in the Revelation. Its varied contents are largely an amplification of what is to be found in the preceding scriptures. Each of its figures and symbols are explained if not on its own pages, then somewhere within the compass of the written Word.[136]

> There are symbols, but the Bible itself will explain what these symbols mean either by direct statement or through a comparison of the usage of the symbol elsewhere in the Scriptures. The meaning of the symbols will not be determined by speculation.[137]

2.7.5.7 - The Importance of Right Relationship

As necessary as familiarity with the Old Testament is to an understanding of the book of Revelation, it is not sufficient. We must add to it a right relationship with the ultimate Author of the book lest we fall prey to the condition of Israel in Isaiah's day:

> Pause and wonder! Blind yourselves and be blind! They are drunk, but not with wine; they stagger, but not with intoxicating drink. For the LORD has poured out on you the spirit of deep sleep, and has closed your eyes, namely, the prophets; and He has covered your heads, *namely*, the seers. The whole vision has become to you like the words of a book that is sealed, which *men* deliver to one who is literate, saying, "Read this, please." And he says, "I cannot, for it *is* sealed." Then the book is delivered to one who is illiterate, saying, "Read this, please." And he says, "I am not literate." Therefore the Lord said: "Inasmuch as these people draw near with their mouths and honor Me with their lips, but have removed their hearts far from Me, and their fear toward Me is taught by the commandment of men, therefore, behold, I will again do a marvelous work among this people, a marvelous work and a wonder; for the wisdom of their wise *men* shall perish, and the understanding of their prudent *men* shall be hidden." (Isa. 29:9-14)

We must recognize that our wisdom depends upon God and He will not share intimacy of understanding with those who feign a devotion or whose motivations are impure. Ultimately, it is not *knowledge* we desire, but *God Himself.*

> And you will seek Me and find *Me*, when you search for Me with all your heart. (Jer. 29:13)

Notes

[1] Arnold G. Fruchtenbaum, *The Footsteps of Messiah*, rev ed. (Tustin, CA: Ariel Ministries, 2003), 11.

[2] Gregory K. Beale, *The Book of Revelation: A Commentary on the Greek Text* (Grand Rapids, MI: William B. Eerdmans Publishing Co., 1999), 65.

[3] Henry Morris, *The Revelation Record* (Wheaton, IL: Tyndale House Publishers, 1983), 20.

[4] Paul D. Feinberg, *"Hermeneutics of Discontinuity,"* in John S. Feinberg, ed., *Continuity And Discontinuity* (Westchester, IL: Crossway Books, 1988), 112.

[5] Bernard Ramm, *Protestant Biblical Interpretation*, 3rd rev. ed. (Grand Rapids, MI: Baker Book House, 1970), 11.

[6] Kay Arthur, *How To Study Your Bible* (Eugene, OR: Harvest House Publishers, 1994), 9-10.

[7] J. Dwight Pentecost, *Things to Come: A Study in Biblical Eschatology* (Grand Rapids, MI: Zondervan Publishing House, 1958), 44.

[8] One of the best examples is the apparent contradiction between the genealogies of Christ given by Matthew 1 and Luke 3. The solution to this dilemma reveals the masterful genius of God in His curse of Jeconiah (Jer. 22:30; 36:30). Indeed, "the *Divine* is in the details!"

[9] Steve Gregg, *Revelation Four Views: A Parallel Commentary* (Nashville, TN: Thomas Nelson, 1997), 11.

[10] Mal Couch, *Classical Evangelical Hermeneutics* (Grand Rapids, MI: Kregel Publications), 36-37.

[11] Beale, *The Book of Revelation: A Commentary on the Greek Text*, 54.

[12] Morris, *The Revelation Record*, 13.

[13] This leads to a general rule of thumb. Although there are notable exceptions, *the more weighty the commentary, the more likely it will mislead the reader in his understanding of the book of Revelation.*

[14] Mal Couch, *"Interpreting the Book of Revelation,"* in Mal Couch, ed., *A Bible Handbook to Revelation* (Grand Rapids, MI: Kregel Publications, 2001), 49.

[15] David Chilton, *The Days of Vengeance* (Tyler, TX: Dominion Press, 1987), 28.

[16] Ramm, *Protestant Biblical Interpretation*, 121.

[17] Charles Feinberg, *Premillennialism or Amillennialism* (Grand Rapids, MI: Zondervan Publishing House, 1936), 50.

[18] Alva J. McClain, *The Greatness Of The Kingdom* (Winona Lake, IN: BMH Books, 1959), 144.

19 Arthur Walkington Pink, *The Antichrist* (Oak Harbor, WA: Logos Research Systems, 1999, 1923), s.v. "Antichrist and Babylon."

20 Couch, *Classical Evangelical Hermeneutics*, 11.

21 John MacArthur, *Revelation 12-22 : The MacArthur New Testament Commentary* (Chicago, IL: Moody Press, 2000), Rev. 20:1.

22 "Literal is not opposed to spiritual but to figurative; spiritual is an antithesis on the one hand to material, and on the other to carnal (in a bad sense). The Literalist is not one who denies that figurative language, that symbols are used in prophecy, nor does he deny that great spiritual truths are set forth therein; his position is simply, that the prophecies are to be normally interpreted (i.e., according to the received laws of language) as any other utterances are interpreted-that which is manifestly literal being regarded as literal, and that which is manifestly figuratively being so regarded. The position of the Spiritualist is not that which is properly indicated by the term. He is one who holds that certain portions are to be normally interpreted, other portions are to be regarded as having a mystical sense. The terms properly expressive of the schools are normal and mystical." John Peter Lange, *A Commentary on the Holy Scripture: Revelation*, p. 98.

23 Roy B. Zuck, *Basic Bible Interpretation* (Colorado Springs, CO: Cook Communications, 1991), 29.

24 Richard Chenevix Trench, *Commentary on the Epistles to the Seven Churches in Asia* (Eugene, OR: Wipf and Stock Publishers, 1861), 185.

25 "In the history of allegorical interpretation of Scripture it is not denied that there is a literal, historical, or grammatical sense to Scripture, but it is depreciated. It is the 'fleshly' or the 'superficial' understanding of Scripture."—Ramm, *Protestant Biblical Interpretation*, 124.

26 "Among non-literal prophetic interpreters, a state of virtual interpretive chaos exists. It is rare, for instance, to see a well-ordered or definitive work by an *amillennial*[5.2.1] interpreter setting forth positively and consistently his prophetic interpretations. On the contrary, the amillennial writings usually concentrate on attacking and ridiculing the *premillennial*[5.2.58] position. This approach is probably one of necessity, for amillennialists seldom agree with each other in specific interpretations of prophecy except to be against the earthly millennium."—Paul Lee Tan, *The Interpretation of Prophecy* (Dallas, TX: Bible Communications, Inc., 1993), 73.

27 Tan, *The Interpretation of Prophecy*, 37-38.

28 George H. N. Peters, *The Theocratic Kingdom* (Grand Rapids, MI: Kregel Publications, 1978, 1884), 50.

29 Zuck, *Basic Bible Interpretation*, 30-31.

30 Zuck, *Basic Bible Interpretation*, 35.

31 Couch, "*Interpreting the Book of Revelation*," 58-59.

32 Isbon T. Beckwith, *The Apocalypse of John* (Eugene, OR: Wipf and Stock Publishers, 2001), 323.

33 "Augustine proposed seven rules of interpretation by which he sought to give a rational basis for allegorization."—Zuck, *Basic Bible Interpretation*, 39.

34 Tan, *The Interpretation of Prophecy*, 53.

35 Rodney Petersen, *"Continuity and Discontinuity: The Debate throughout Church History,"* in John S. Feinberg, ed., *Continuity And Discontinuity* (Westchester, IL: Crossway Books, 1988), 26.

36 Larry V. Crutchfield, *"Revelation in the New Testament,"* in Mal Couch, ed., *A Bible Handbook to Revelation* (Grand Rapids, MI: Kregel Publications, 2001), 32.

37 "Though the Reformers had come out of the interpretive darkness into the light of literal and historical hermeneutics, they still clung to allegorical details in their attempt to understand the book of Revelation."—Mal Couch, *"How Has Revelation Been Viewed Interpretively?,"* in Mal Couch, ed., *A Bible Handbook to Revelation* (Grand Rapids, MI: Kregel Publications, 2001), 40.

38 Morris, *The Revelation Record*, 25.

39 Ramm, *Protestant Biblical Interpretation*, 111.

40 Crutchfield, "*Revelation in the New Testament*," 25.

41 Robert L. Thomas, *Revelation 1-7* (Chicago, IL: Moody Press, 1992), 20.

42 "The question is if these allegorizing commentators are not as much in the dark in relation to the **second coming and the glory that should follow**, as the Jews were in relation to His **First Advent and His atoning suffering and death**." [emphasis added]—Arnold Fruchtenbaum, *"The Little Apocalypse of Zechariah,"* in Tim LaHaye, and Thomas Ice, eds., *The End Times Controversy* (Eugene, OR: Harvest House Publishers, 2003), 270.

43 J. A. Seiss, *The Apocalypse: Lectures on the Book of Revelation* (Grand Rapids, MI: Zondervan Publishing House, 1966), Rev. 11:3.

44 Seiss, *The Apocalypse: Lectures on the Book of Revelation*, Rev. 12:7-12.

45 Beale, *The Book of Revelation: A Commentary on the Greek Text*, 51.

46 Beale, *The Book of Revelation: A Commentary on the Greek Text*, 48.

47 "Revelation is a symbolic book, but that does not mean the symbols do not depict literal events."—Grant R. Osborne, *Revelation* (Grand Rapids, MI: Baker Academic, 2002), 16.

48 Thomas, *Revelation 1-7*, 35.

49 "It must be noted, however, that not every object seen in a vision is symbolic. Neither is it true that because some objects in a vision are symbolic, everything else in that vision must be symbolic."—Couch, *Classical Evangelical Hermeneutics*, 71.

50 Couch, *Classical Evangelical Hermeneutics*, 73-74.

51 "In which one thing explicitly (by using *like* or *as*) resembles another."—Zuck, *Basic Bible Interpretation*, 148.

52 Couch, *Classical Evangelical Hermeneutics*, 258-259.

53 Couch, *Classical Evangelical Hermeneutics*, 73-74.

54 Tan, *The Interpretation of Prophecy*, 137-138.

55 Matthew Waymeyer, *Revelation 20 and the Millennial Debate* (The Woodlands, TX: Kress Christian Publications, 2001, 2004), 99-100.

56 Merrill C. Tenney, *Interpreting Revelation* (Peabody, MA: Hendrickson Publishers, 1957), 142-143.

57 Osborne, *Revelation*, 16.

58 "The interpretation of such figures is not left up to the reader's imagination or ingenuity. They must be defined and explained, unambiguously, either in the immediate context or in the broader context of the historical and prophetic Scriptures which John could assume his readers should already have mastered."—Morris, *The Revelation Record*, 24.

59 Trench, *Commentary on the Epistles to the Seven Churches in Asia*, 42-43.

60 The study of how numbers are used within the Bible.

61 Trench, *Commentary on the Epistles to the Seven Churches in Asia*, 61-62.

62 No more so than in the case of typology wherein truths concerning God can be ascertained, but never in a way suitable for teaching as doctrine.

63 Beale, *The Book of Revelation: A Commentary on the Greek Text*, 23.

64 Beale, *The Book of Revelation: A Commentary on the Greek Text*, 61.

65 "It is not to be supposed that a specific meaning attaches invariably to a given numerical symbol, so that we could substitute this as a paraphrase in all cases; in view of the vagueness characterizing the style of visions we may presume that the writer himself did not always have a precise intention in mind."—Beckwith, *The Apocalypse of John*, 251.

66 Osborne, *Revelation*, 17-18.

67 Years based on factors related to Dan. 9:24-27.

68 Osborne, *Revelation*, 17.

69 The forward to Osborne's work, a volume within the *Baker Exegetical Commentary on the New Testament* states: "the contributors share a belief in the trustworthiness and essential unity of Scripture" yet when the

distinctions between *inspired*[5.2.33] and uninspired writings are minimized or ignored, the unity of Scripture is denied and the trustworthiness of Scripture is denigrated to the level of uninspired works. Here the author seems to place Scripture on a par with "ancient apocalypses."

70 Robert L. Thomas, *Revelation 8-22* (Chicago, IL: Moody Press, 1995), 408.

71 John F. Walvoord, *The Revelation of Jesus Christ* (Chicago, IL: Moody Press, 1966), 28.

72 "Looking at the Scriptures from a normative standpoint gives the Jews and Christians the same interpretation. Raphael Patai, quoting from the rabbinical writings, says, 'Things will come to such a head that people will despair of Redemption. This will last seven years. And then, unexpectedly, the Messiah will come. . . . At the end of the seventh [year] the son of David will come.' "—Couch, "*Interpreting the Book of Revelation*," 64.

73 Significantly, "in the beginning, God created the heavens and the earth" (Gen. 1:1) which thereafter were available to serve as "witnesses" of all that would follow.

74 Satan, the *Beast*[5.2.9], the *False Prophet*[5.2.20].

75 Inanimate life such as grass and trees was created on the third day. The animated "living creatures" (שֶׁרֶץ נֶפֶשׁ [*sherets nephesh*]) were not created until days five and six.

76 "That [the] two expressions [*after three days* and *on the third day*] were understood to mean the same thing seems clear from Mtt. 27:63-64 which says: 'We remember that impostor said, while He was yet alive, After three days I will rise again. Command therefore that the sepulchre be made sure until the third day.' "—Graham W. Scroggie, *A Guide to the Gospels* (Grand Rapids, MI: Kregel Publications, 1995, 1948), 569-570. "Jesus predicted that He would die and be raised on the third day (Mtt. 16:21; Mark 8:31; Luke 9:22). . . . Jesus"body was laid in the tomb on the evening of the day of preparation (Friday), the day before the Sabbath (Mtt. 27:62; 28:1; Mark 15:42; Luke 23:54, 56; John 19:31, 42). The women returned home and rested on the Sabbath (Saturday, Luke 23:56). Early on the first day of the week (Sunday), they went to the tomb (Mtt. 28:1; Mark 16:1-2; Luke 24:1; John 20:1) which was empty. Furthermore, on the same day He arose from the grave, Jesus walked with two disciples on the road to Emmaus (Luke 24:13), and they told Him that their Master was crucified and 'now it is the third day since this occurred" (Luke 24:21). . . . The most frequent reference to Jesus"resurrection is that it occurred on the third day (not the fourth day) (Mtt. 16:21; 17:23; 20:19; 27:64; Luke 9:22; 18:33; 24:7, 21, 46; Acts 10:40; 1Cor. 15:4). . . . There are four passages (Mtt. 27:63; Mark 8:31; 9:31; 10:34) which speak of Christ's resurrection as occurring 'after three days," but this is speaking of the same time period as on "the third day". . . The three Markan passages are paralleled by one or two of the other Synoptic Gospels, and in each case the other Synoptic does not use "after three days" as Mark does but "on the third day" (Mark 8:31 = Mtt. 16:21 / Luke 9:22; Mark 9:31 = Mtt 17:23; Mark 10:34 = Mtt. 20:19 / Luke 18:33)."—Harold Hoehner, *Chronological Aspects of the Life of Christ* (Grand Rapids, MI: Zondervan, 1977), 71-72.

77 "The threes of the Bible represent triads of completeness."—Walter L. Wilson, *A Dictionary of Bible Types* (Peabody, MA: Hendrickson Publishers, 1999), 419.

78 "*Three* denotes *divine* perfection; *Seven* denotes *spiritual* perfection; *Ten* denotes *ordinal* perfection; and *Twelve* denotes *governmental* perfection."—E. W. Bullinger, *Number in Scripture: Its Supernatural Design and Spiritual Significance* (Grand Rapids, MI: Kregel Publications, 1967), 107.

79 "In the cry of the four living creatures ("Holy, holy, holy," Rev. 4:8) Hindson sees an indication of the Trinity (59) rather than an emphatic Semitic triplet. What kind of threefold existence would he find in triplets like "a ruin, a ruin, a ruin" (Eze. 21:27) or "land, land, land" (Jer. 22:29)?"—William D. Barrick, *"Review of 'The Book of Revelation' by Hindson,"* in Richard L. Mayhue, ed., *The Master's Seminary Journal*, vol. 13 no. 2 (Sun Valley, CA: The Master's Seminary, Fall 2002), 284.

80 Not every *individual*, but individuals from every *nation, tongue, tribe, and region.*

81 "This number denotes God's government of men and affairs upon the earth."—Wilson, *A Dictionary of Bible Types*, 180.

82 [Trench, *Commentary on the Epistles to the Seven Churches in Asia*, 63-64]. An exception to Trench's comments regarding the four seasons may be found in the mention of "seedtime" (spring), "harvest" (fall), "winter and summer" in Gen. 8:22.

83 The word *cherubim* is the Hebrew equivalent to *cherubs*. The *-im* ending being the equivalent of our plural ending *-s*.

84 Contrary to the assertions of *preterists*[2.12.2] who attempt to localize the global events of the book of Revelation to the Roman Empire.

85 David probably selected one stone for Goliath and four more for each of Goliath's brothers. The four brothers of Goliath (2S. 21:22) included *Ishi-Benob* (2S. 21:16), *Saph* or *Sippai* (2S. 21:18; 1Chr. 20:4), *Lahmi* (2S. 21:19; 2Chr. 20:5) and an unnamed brother (2S. 21:20-21; 1Chr. 20:6-7). Along with Goliath, who was killed by David (1S. 17:4, 49-50), there were five brothers (1S. 17:40) of the same father, a giant from Gath (2S. 21:22; 1Chr. 20:8).

86 Bullinger, *Number in Scripture: Its Supernatural Design and Spiritual Significance*, 135-149.

87 Each of Isaiah's seraphim also had six wings (Isa. 6:2), two of which were used to cover the face, two to cover the feet, leaving two to fly.

88 Edward Hindson, *Revelation: Unlocking the Future* (Chattanooga, TN: AMG Publishers, 2002), 6.

89 "The great giant had six fingers on each hand, and six toes on each foot, for he represented the perfect example of that race of giants."—Wilson, *A Dictionary of Bible Types*, 374.

90 Bullinger, *Number in Scripture: Its Supernatural Design and Spiritual Significance*, 150.

91 Trench, *Commentary on the Epistles to the Seven Churches in Asia*, 57-58.

92 Hindson, *Revelation: Unlocking the Future*, 7.

93 Tenney, *Interpreting Revelation*, 180.

94 Hindson, *Revelation: Unlocking the Future*, 8.

95 Morris, *The Revelation Record*, 30.

96 "Seven as a number of completeness is also apparent from the seven days of creation in Genesis 1, which is the complete period of God's work of creating."—Beale, *The Book of Revelation: A Commentary on the Greek Text*, 58.

97 "The seven 'eyes' describe the perfect omniscience of the Holy Spirit (Zechariah 3:9)."—Wilson, *A Dictionary of Bible Types*, 363.

98 "Other examples of completeness are the seven seals, seven trumpets, and seven bowls, which are so numbered in order to underscore the completeness of God's worldwide judgment and salvation."—Beale, *The Book of Revelation: A Commentary on the Greek Text*, 59.

99 Although some restrict this warning to the book of Revelation only, it seems significant that no other *NT*[5.2.48] book closes with a warning even remotely similar.

100 Morris, *The Revelation Record*, 30-31.

101 Osborne, *Revelation*, 17.

102 "God completed His mighty work of creating, constructing, and energizing the entire cosmos and all its creatures in the very first seven-day period of history. Because of sin and the curse, He has since been accomplishing His might work of redeeming and saving the creation. One day this work also will be completed."—Morris, *The Revelation Record*, 31.

103 Ex. 3:7, 15, 18; 6:6; 19:5-6; Lev. 20:26; Deu. 4:34, 37; 7:6-8; 10:15; 14:2; 26:18-19; 2S. 7:23; 1K. 8:53; 1Chr. 16:13; 17:21; Ps. 105:6; 106:6-7; 135:4; Isa. 41:8; 43:1, 10; 44:1; 45:4; Jer. 10:16; Mtt. 24:22; Rom. 9:4; Rom. 11:5.

104 Mtt. 4:19; 9:9; Mark 1:17, 20; 2:14; Luke 5:27; 6:13; John 1:43; 6:70; 15:16; 17:6; Acts 1:2; Rom. 1:1, 6-7; Gal. 1:15.

105 Recognition of this very emphasis was a factor which led some to initially oppose acceptance of the book within the *canon*[5.2.12].

106 "Twelve . . . represents completeness as well as the accompanying idea of unity in diversity, as in the one nation Israel composed of twelve tribes. the twelve apostles mirror the same reality for the people of God in the *NT*[5.2.48] period."—Beale, *The Book of Revelation: A Commentary on the Greek Text*, 59.

107 "Twelve is the number of completeness. There are twelve tribes of Israel, twelve apostles of Christ, twenty-four elders (a double twelve), tree of life has twelve types of fruit (Rev. 22:2), New Jerusalem has twelve gates guarded by twelve angels (Rev. 21:12), the city has twelve foundations (Rev. 21:14). There are twelve precious stones adorning the foundation stones and twelve pearls (Rev. 21:19-21). There are also multiples of twelve: Each of the twelve tribes contains 12,000 people, making a total of 144,000 (12,000 times 12); the

wall measures 144 cubits (12 times 12)."—Hindson, *Revelation: Unlocking the Future*, 6.

108 Osborne, *Revelation*, 17.

109 Beale, *The Book of Revelation: A Commentary on the Greek Text*, 58.

110 Henry Barclay Swete, *The Apocalypse of St. John* (Eugene, OR: Wipf and Stock Publishers, 1998, 1906), cxxviii.

111 Thomas, *Revelation 1-7*, 41.

112 Beale, *The Book of Revelation: A Commentary on the Greek Text*, 79.

113 Osborne, *Revelation*, 15.

114 Adela Yarbro Collins, *"Book of Revelation,"* in David Noel Freeman, ed., *The Anchor Bible Dictionary* (New York, NY: Doubleday, 1996, c1992), 5:704.

115 "John painted verbal pictures in such a way as to ring bells in the minds of his readers, many of whom were former pagans and would have been familiar with some of these myths; he did so partly to put his readers' mythological background into biblical perspective. John can utilize even legends in order to conduct polemics against the ungodly world that formulates the myths. For example, the 'seven heads' in Rev. 12:3 appears to come not from the OT, but from cosmological traditions depicting the seven-headed sea monster Lotan."—Beale, *The Book of Revelation: A Commentary on the Greek Text*, 18.

116 Trench, *Commentary on the Epistles to the Seven Churches in Asia*, 110.

117 Trench, *Commentary on the Epistles to the Seven Churches in Asia*, 129-130.

118 "The strength of the whole case is in the whole argument. Many parts are acknowledged to be tentative, if only because the fragmentary nature of the evidence precludes a false dogmatism. . . . The fragmentary state of the evidence in fact needs to be strongly emphasized."—Colin J. Hemer, *The Letters to the Seven Churches of Asia in Their Local Setting* (Grand Rapids, MI: William B. Eerdmans Publishing Company, 1989), 7. "The objection may be raised that the whole thesis of this book proceeds from the assumptions about the local applicability which may simply not be true. It may be said that a caution in the particular is here combined with an unjustified overconfidence about the legitimacy of the whole undertaking."—Hemer, *The Letters to the Seven Churches of Asia in Their Local Setting*, 22.

119 Merrill F. Unger, *Unger's Commentary on the Old Testament* (Chattanooga, TN: AMG Publishers, 2002), Dan. 8:10.

120 Beckwith, *The Apocalypse of John*, viii.

121 Tenney, *Interpreting Revelation*, 191.

122 Swete, *The Apocalypse of St. John*, xlix.

123 Hindson, *Revelation: Unlocking the Future*, 1.

124 Chilton, *The Days of Vengeance*, 26.

125 "The Book of Revelation depends on the Old Testament much more than does any other New Testament book. This fact alone should warn us that we cannot begin to fathom its meaning apart from a solid grasp of the Bible as a whole."—Chilton, *The Days of Vengeance*, 30.

126 Also see Swete [Swete, *The Apocalypse of St. John*, cxxxv-cxlviii] for a list of references to Greek versions of the Old Testament made by the Apocalypse.

127 Swete, *The Apocalypse of St. John*, xlix.

128 Hemer, *The Letters to the Seven Churches of Asia in Their Local Setting*, 13-14.

129 Beale, *The Book of Revelation: A Commentary on the Greek Text*, 77.

130 Osborne, *Revelation*, 25.

131 Alan F. Johnson, *Revelation: The Expositor's Bible Commentary* (Grand Rapids, MI: Zondervan Publishing House, 1966), 15.

132 Fruchtenbaum, *The Footsteps of Messiah*, 801-808.

133 "The first major figure to challenge the authoritative status of the book of Revelation was Marcion, presumably because of its strong ties to the Jewish Scriptures."—Collins, "*Book of Revelation*," 5:695.

[134] Hemer, *The Letters to the Seven Churches of Asia in Their Local Setting*, 26.

[135] Charles C. Ryrie, *Dispensationalism* (Chicago, IL: Moody Press, 1995), 81.

[136] Pink, *The Antichrist*, s.v. "Antichrist in the Apocalypse."

[137] Fruchtenbaum, *The Footsteps of Messiah*, 12.

2.8 - Style of Writing

It has been observed that the style of the Greek within the book of Revelation differs significantly from that of the gospel of John. This has been frequently used to intimate that the author, although describing himself as John (Rev. 1:1, 4, 9; 21:2; 22:8), is a different John than the Apostle. (See the discussion concerning the *authorship*[2.9] of the book.) Our purpose here is to briefly discuss these differences in style and to suggest possible reasons why this is so.

The Greek of the book of Revelation has been categorized as "more primitive" or "rougher" than that of John's Gospel. This is primarily due to the violation of some of the normal rules of Greek grammar. Charles claimed it contained more grammatical irregularities than any other Greek document of the ancient world.[1]

> Most of these *solecisms*[5.2.68] are disagreements in case, number, gender, or person. Other instances sometimes included in discussion of the solecisms are not outright transgressions of ordinary grammatical rules but are better categorized as peculiar variants in style.[2]

Tenney describes a specific example: "For instance, this phrase, 'from him who is and who was and who is to come' (Rev. 1:4) should be translated literally: 'From he who is, and from he was, and from he who is coming.' The case of the noun after the preposition 'from' is wrong; the second expression is a finite verb and not a participle; and the third expression is used in the same way as the first."[3]

Some have suggested that the differences in style might reflect the aging of John between the writing of his Gospel and the book of Revelation, but this seems unlikely.[4]Others have concluded from these differences that the author of the book of Revelation cannot be the author of John's Gospel. Still others point to possible reasons for the appearance of these irregularities.

Tenney sees the *irregularity mentioned above* (2.8) as being evidence of the Hebraic material and thought of the author:

> The reason for this strange rendering is that the Greek had no past participle of the verb "to be," and so the author used a finite form. Furthermore, the case did not change because evidently the entire expression had become stereotyped as a title, and so did not alter the construction to fit the context. **The writer translated a Hebrew title directly and literally into Greek without attempting to conform to the Greek idiom.** He thought in Hebrew or Aramaic; he wrote in Greek. The relative certainty of this fact shows that the book of Revelation does not emanate chiefly from Greek and pagan sources. [emphasis added][5]

Beale too observes a correlation between the irregularities and Old Testament allusions:

> A significant number of these irregularities occur in the midst of *OT*[5.2.51] allusions. A number of expressions appear irregular because John is carrying over the exact grammatical forms of the allusions, often from the various versions of the Greek OT and sometimes from the Hebrew. He does not change the OT grammatical form to fit the immediate syntactical context in Revelation, so the OT expression sticks out like a sore thumb. . . . the solecisms of the Apocalypse function in this way.[6]

Robertson sees the textual anomalies as reflecting a heavy dependence upon the *Septuagint*[5.2.65].[7] Others suggest that John's writing style was affected by the emotionally vivid content given in rapid succession. [8]Another possibility is that John utilized an amanuensis (secretary) when writing the Gospel, but was unable to do so on Patmos.[9]

An additional factor to consider is that other of John's writings contain significant grammatical irregularities:[10]

> Without any question there are unusual grammatical features in the Apocalypse, but what about John's other writings, his first epistle, for example? Are there not extreme grammatical irregularities here, too? . . . Unusual grammatical phenomena are by no means limited to the Apocalypse in the apostle John's *canonical*[5.2.12] writings. If John deviated from the normal usage in 1 John, why could he not have done so in the Apocalypse?[11]

The grammatical departures do not appear to be due to the ignorance of the writer, but appear intentional, perhaps in order to emphasize theological subtleties.[12]

Regardless of the reasons for the stylistic oddities of the Greek of the book of Revelation, it has not adversely affected its literary impact:

> But from whatever cause or concurrence of causes, it cannot be denied that the Apocalypse of John stands alone among Greek literary writings in its disregard of the ordinary rules of syntax, and the success with which syntax is set aside without loss of perspicuity or even of literary power. The book seems openly and deliberately to defy the grammarian, and yet, even as literature, it is in its own field unsurpassed.[13]

Notes

1 "Charles claimed it contained more grammatical irregularities than any other Greek document of the ancient world. he accounted for this with his famous dictum that 'while [John] writes in Greek, he thinks in Hebrew, and the thought has naturally affected the vehicle of expression.' "—Gregory K. Beale, *The Book of Revelation: A Commentary on the Greek Text* (Grand Rapids, MI: William B. Eerdmans Publishing Co., 1999), 96.

2 Beale, *The Book of Revelation: A Commentary on the Greek Text*, 101-102.

3 Merrill C. Tenney, *Interpreting Revelation* (Peabody, MA: Hendrickson Publishers, 1957), 14.

4 "The gospel of John was probably written between A.D. 85 and 90, the epistles of John in the early nineties, and the Apocalypse about A.D. 95."—Robert L. Thomas, *Revelation 1-7* (Chicago, IL: Moody Press, 1992), 18.

5 Tenney, *Interpreting Revelation*, 14.

6 Beale, *The Book of Revelation: A Commentary on the Greek Text*, 101.

7 "It is not so much particular Hebraisms that meet us in the Apocalypse as the flavor of the *LXX*[5.2.38] whose words are interwoven in the text at every turn."—A. T. Robertson, *A Grammar of the Greek NT in the Light of HistoricalResearch* (Nashville, TN: Broadman Press, 1934), 135.

8 "Some have suggested that the message was so emotional and vivid that John struggled to keep up with the flashes of dramatic revelation coming on him."—Mal Couch, *"The Literary Structure of Revelation,"* in Mal Couch, ed., *A Bible Handbook to Revelation* (Grand Rapids, MI: Kregel Publications, 2001), 69.

9 "It is also possible that John used an amanuensis (secretary) when he wrote the gospel and the epistles (as Paul did; Rom. 16:22)—something he could not have done while writing Revelation in exile on Patmos."—John MacArthur, *Revelation 1-11 : The MacArthur New Testament Commentary* (Chicago, IL: Moody Press, 1999), 6. "There is plausibility in the suggestion that the superior smoothness of the Greek of the Gospel and various linguistic differences are due at least in part to the employment of a Greek amanuensis. . . . Paul wrote most of his epistles by the hand of another."—Isbon T. Beckwith, *The Apocalypse of John* (Eugene, OR: Wipf and Stock Publishers, 2001), 356.

10 "While the solecistic anacolutha of the Apocalypse have no parallel on any large scale in the Gospel, there is a considerable number of unusual constructions which are common to the two books."—Henry Barclay Swete, *The Apocalypse of St. John* (Eugene, OR: Wipf and Stock Publishers, 1998, 1906), cxxiii.

11 Thomas, *Revelation 1-7*, 7-8.

12 "his departures from Greek usage are pretty certainly not due to ignorance; his general correctness and his Greek vocabulary show him to have possessed an adequate command of the language."—Beckwith, *The Apocalypse of John*, 345.

13 Swete, *The Apocalypse of St. John*, cxx.

2.9 – Authorship

When one considers the contribution of the book of Revelation to the completion of the *canon*[5.2.12], its prophetic emphasis, and its teaching concerning controversial doctrines,[1] it is not surprising to find opposition to the book throughout its history. This opposition has centered in an attack upon its *canonicity*[2.10] in conjunction with a denial of its apostolic authorship.[2]

As we discussed previously, the *style of writing*[2.8] of the original Greek text raised additional questions as to the authorship of the book. The primary reason given for rejecting John the Apostle as author is the style of the Greek.

Here we should mention that the entire area of textual and New Testament criticism is fraught with difficulties in lack of objectivity. "The subject presents one of these questions in New Testament criticism in which mental bent, apart from the bias of prejudgment, is chiefly influential in determining the conclusion reached."[3] Critics often come to the subject with preconceptions which result in an underemphasis on *objective* evidence in favor of overemphasis on *subjective* evidence.

An example of objective evidence would be *external evidence* such as the testimony of early Church Fathers as to the authorship. Subjective evidence usually consists of *internal evidence* derived from an analysis of the text itself. The problem with internal textual evidence, as used in textual criticism, is that it is highly malleable and easily conformed to the biases of the critic. Johnson recognizes the contribution which presuppositions play in the conclusions reached and notes how unfruitful textual analysis has been in attempting to shed light on the authorship of the book:

> The evidence that allegedly argues against a single author revolves around a number of internal difficulties. These fall into four categories: (1) the presence of doublets—the same scene or vision described twice; (2) sequence problems—persons or things introduced seemingly for the first time when in fact they had already been mentioned; (3) seeming misplaced verses and larger sections; and (4) distinctive content within certain sections that does not fit the rest of the book. In each case, however, there are satisfying alternative explanations. In fact, **the difficulties just named stem more from the reader's presuppositions than from the text itself.** Dissection of the text has been notoriously unfruitful in yielding further light on the book itself. [emphasis added][4]

Guthrie makes the pithy observation regarding Dionysius' attack on Johannine authorship: "In this Dionysius foreshadowed, as a man born before his due time, those modern schools of criticism which have peopled early Christian history with a whole army of unknown writers, whose works attained as great a prominence as their authors obtained obscurity."[5] As Guthrie has noted, the critics would have us believe that works of great prominence, such as the book of Revelation, accepted as part of the canon, must have been written by one or more obscure authors now lost to the mists of history. The critical tendency has become so prevalent and applied so widely to biblical texts that proving that the book of Revelation somehow differs essentially from John's Gospel no longer provides the conclusion that it's author can't be John! "Dissimilarity with the Gospel neither proves nor disproves the apostolic authorship of the Apocalypse (since more often than not the Gospel is held by modern critics to be the work of **someone other** than John the apostle)" [emphasis added][6].

When approaching the issue of the authorship of the book of Revelation, we should bear these two factors in mind: *First*, greater emphasis should be placed on the testimony of the early church (objective evidence) than analysis of internal factors within the text (subjective evidence); *Second*, attacks upon the Apostolic authorship are often coupled with an attempt to discredit the book and an attendant opposition to its doctrines (e.g., its Jewish emphasis, a literal millennium).

2.9.1 - Apostolic Authorship Opposed

Opposition to the Apostolic authorship of the book of Revelation was initiated because its teachings were thought to be incompatible with the rest of the New Testament or to be too Jewish in emphasis. A Roman presbyter by the name of Caius who held the book of Revelation to be inconsistent with other parts of the New Testament first attributed the authorship to Cerinthus rather than John the Apostle. Caius' criticisms were refuted by Hippolytus, but the issue was not put to rest. [7]

Marcion, a second-century *Gnostic*[5.2.23], who rejected much of the New Testament because of his anti-Semitic stance, also rejected the book of Revelation holding that its authorship was not apostolic.[8]

By the middle of the third century, opposition to apostolic authorship had also arisen from Dionysius the Great, the bishop of Alexandria. Although he felt that the book was *inspired*[5.2.33], his opposition to millenarianism (the belief in a literal one thousand-year kingdom on earth, Rev. 20:4) was thought to have been one of the key factors which brought about his denial of apostolic authorship.[9] Dionysius also based his rejection of apostolic authorship upon an analysis of the differences between the text of the book of Revelation and that of John's Gospel. Thomas has since shown that Dionysius' analysis was flawed.[10] As bishop of Alexandria, Dionysius had great influence and his conclusions were to color the acceptance of the book of Revelation as part of the *canon*[5.2.12] within the eastern church for years to come. (We discuss this in greater depth in our treatment of the *acceptance of the book of Revelation into the canon*[2.10].)

Eusebius[5.2.19] followed Dionysius in rejecting apostolic authorship and attributed the authorship to a different John.[11] Eusebius believed that *Papias*[5.2.52]'s mention of a "John the Elder" identified a different John at Ephesus from John the apostle and that this John wrote the book of Revelation. But there are reasons for understanding this mention by Papias as being the self-same John of the fourth gospel.[12]

Rejection of apostolic authorship continued in various places, especially the eastern church, right up to the time of the Reformation. Erasmus, Luther, and Zwingli all regarded the book as non-apostolic, largely because of their opposition to its teaching of a literal thousand-year-reign of Christ on earth. Both Luther and Calvin more or less ignored the book.[13]

2.9.2 - Alternatives to the Apostle John

The author of the book of Revelation claims to be simply, "John" (Rev. 1:1, 4, 9; 21:2; 22:8). While most throughout church history have understood the author to be the Apostle John, others have suggested it to be the work of other men named John or even those not named John. Osborne has identified seven main alternatives suggested as author of the book: [14]

> There have been several suggestions: (1) John the apostle; (2) the elder John; (3) John Mark; (4) John the Baptist; (5) another John; (6) Cerinthus; and (7) someone using the name of John the apostle as a pseudonym.[15]

To this list, we could add a recent eighth suggestion that the book is a composite work of several authors. Swete observes the weaknesses of this eighth suggestion:

> It is taken for granted by some recent authorities that the Apocalypse is a composite work. But does this conviction rest on more than the reiterated assertion of writers who have found in the analysis of the book a fascinating field for intellectual exercise? When the enquirer investigates the grounds on which the hypotheses of compilation rests, . . . The phenomena which suggest diversity of authorship admit for the most part of another explanation; they may well be due to the method of the author or the necessities of his plan.[16]

As we mentioned above, such theories are based upon an overt emphasis on *subjective* internal evidence.[17] Even then, there is significant internal evidence of the unity of the book for those with eyes to see.[18]

The proposal which has received the greatest attention is that the book of Revelation is the work of a "John the Presbyter," a second John besides the Apostle who resided at Ephesus. This idea hinges entirely upon a fragment from *Papias*[5.2.52] which is only preserved for us by *Eusebius*[5.2.19]. The idea of a *different* John was called attention to by Eusebius, yet church history prior to that time is silent as to this possibility:

> Except in an obscure fragment of Papias, preserved in Eusebius *H. E.* III. 39, no mention of the Presbyter John is found before the fourth century. Eusebius is the first to point out the existence of such a person as evidenced by the fragment which he preserves from the introduction to Papias'book . . . It must be said that the sole explicit historical evidence for the existence of John the Presbyter, as

> distinguished from the Apostle, is this passage of Papias. And while we are compelled to interpret the passage as witnessing to his existence, yet there remains the extraordinary fact . . . that no other trace of such a person appears till about the beginning of the fourth century, when Eusebius called attention to the significance of Papias' language, though Papias' book had been well known through the centuries.[19]

This suggestion of Eusebius is still popular among some today, although Swete notes that we know almost nothing about this figure, which is odd if indeed he *were* the author of such an important work. "Perhaps no conjecture hazarded by an ancient writer has been so widely adopted in modern times. A conjecture it still remains, for no fresh light has been thrown on the enigmatic figure of John the Elder. But this circumstance has not prevented scholars from confidently attributing to him one or more of the Johannine group of writings."[20]

Along with "John the Elder," some, such as Calvin, have suggested John Mark (the author of the book of Mark).[21]But this seems unlikely because there is no evidence in the New Testament or the early church of John Mark being associated with the Asian church[22] nor are there any significant linguistic similarities between Mark's gospel and the book of Revelation.[23]

2.9.3 - Internal Evidence

2.9.3.1 - Subjectivity of Internal Evidence

The two main areas of evidence for determining the authorship of the book are *internal* and *external*. Internal evidence is based on the contents of the book itself as set forth by the text and includes its self-claims, attributes, and grammatical signature. As we mentioned above, internal evidence is generally less reliable than external evidence. Not because the evidence itself is inherently flawed, but because determining which internal attributes of the book are of significance in relation to authorship and what those attributes *imply* concerning the author is fraught with subjective assessment.

> There is severe danger in relying solely on internal evidence for conclusions about authorship when there is a strong consensus of ancient tradition covering the same. One's use of internal criteria can and often does become quite subjective, allowing him to prove just about anything he sets out to prove. Sometimes, when there is no such consensus among the ancients, one must rely on internal matters, as is the case with the epistle to the Hebrews. But to use internal evidence to counteract a consistent tradition coming from the earliest period of church history is very ill-advised.[24]

To help the reader more readily appreciate the subjective nature of drawing inferences solely from internal textual evidence, we need only cite the bogus conclusion of Collins in regard to the book of Revelation:

> The most significant internal evidence for the date of Revelation is to be found in its references to the destruction of a city called Babylon (14:8; 16:19; 17:5; 18:2, 10, 21). It is highly unlikely that the author of Revelation would have been interested in the conquest of the historical Babylon by the Persians in the 6th century B.C.E. or in the occasions on which it was sacked during the period of the wars among the successors of Alexander. It is even less likely that the author hoped for the destruction of a fortified town called Babylon at the head of the delta of Egypt that was the headquarters of a Roman legion during the early empire. . . . The explanation [by the angel] that follows makes clear that the woman represents the city of Rome. . . . The use of this symbolic name is thus an important indication of the date of Revelation. It implies that the work was written after the destruction of the temple by Titus, that is, after 70 C.E.[25]

To Collins, the mention of Babylon at the time of the author is an obvious indicator that he must be describing Rome, not Babylon. And John must desire the destruction of Rome because the Roman Empire had destroyed Jerusalem by the time of John's writing. Therefore, the book must have been written after 70 A.D. While this author agrees that the book of Revelation was written later than 70 A.D., this is a precarious position based on a faulty set of assertions! Collins' subjectivity in his assessment of the internal evidence is evident. He totally ignores the possibility that this prophetic book (Rev. 1:3, 19; 10:7, 11; 22:6-7, 10, 18-19) may be describing literal Babylon in the far distant future to John's time. Thus is illustrated a major weakness in the use of internal evidence: the subjective nature of its application often results in taking a wrong fork in the road of interpretation which renders all subsequent conclusions void. So with internal evidence, we must proceed with caution.

2.9.3.2 - Simplicity of Title

Many have noted the simplicity of the title given by the author as simply "John." This in itself is evidence for the apostleship of the author:

> The writer avouches himself as "John;" but, though there may have been other men named John in the Church at this time, John the Presbyter and others, still it is well-nigh impossible to conceive any other but John *the Apostle* who would have named himself by this name alone, with no further style or addition. We instinctively feel that for any one [*sic*] else there would have been an affectation of simplicity, concealing a most real arrogance, in the very plainness of this title. Who else, without this arrogance, could have assumed that thus to mention himself was sufficient to ensure his recognition, or that he had a right to appropriate this name in so absolute a manner to himself?[26]

The writer is evidently known to the readers and needs no specific introduction. "The opening words lay no emphasis upon the call and authorization of the prophet (contrast Isa. 6; Jer. 1). His identity and authority are known to readers to whom he needs no introduction."[27] Beale notes that the form of identification, lacking any specific claim to apostleship, also renders the use of "John" as a pseudonym by some other writer unlikely: "If an unknown author were attempting to identify himself with a well-known Christian figure like the apostle John, he would probably call himself not just 'John' but 'John the apostle.' "[28] Hilgenfield concurs: " 'An unknown John,' remarks Hilgenfield, 'whose name has disappeared from history, leaving hardly any trace behind it, can scarcely have given commands in the name of Christ and the Spirit to the *seven churches*[5.2.66].' "[29]

2.9.3.3 - Authority of Author

Then too, the authority which the author wields within the text can also be best explained if written by John the Apostle:

> It is worth noting that the author of the Apocalypse exercised an authority over the Asian churches that went beyond that normally associated with *NT*[5.2.48] prophets. This leads to the conclusion that although he wrote as a prophet, he functioned among his churches as an apostle.[30]
>
> He commends the Church of Ephesus for trying and convicting "them which *say they are apostles* , and are not," by which he implies his own undoubted claim to apostolic *inspiration*[5.2.33] (Rev. 2:2), as declaring in the seven epistles Christ's will revealed through him.[31]

2.9.3.4 - Textual Similarities

Others have highlighted what they see as differences in the text between the book of Revelation and John's Gospel, but there are many similarities as well. Only in these two books is Jesus called the λόγος [*logos*] in the *NT*[5.2.48]. Smalley "argues that the three main christological titles—Word, Lamb of God, and Son of Man—are so similar between the Gospel and the Apocalypse that they suggest unity of authorship."[32] Haupt comments on the prominence of μαρτυρία [*martyria*] as a signature of John's writings, also found in the Apocalypse. Haupt also notes the frequent use of triplets and septets as a signature of John's gospel. In the opening chapters of all three of John's writings, we find a reference to Jesus as the "Word" (John 1:1; 1Jn. 1:1; Rev. 1:2).[33]

The frequent use of "overcome" also appears to be a signature of John:

> The use of νικα˜ν [*nikan*] , with [the single exception of Rom. 12:21] is exclusively St. John's; and the frequent recurrence of it on the one side in his Gospel and Epistles, and on the other in the Apocalypse (thus compare John 16:32; 1Jn. 2;13-14; 5:4-5, with Rev. 2:11, 17, 26; 3:5, 12, 21; 12:11; 21:7), constitutes an interesting point of contact between the language of this Book and of those others whereof he was the author as well.[34]

Fausset observes John's unique use of the Greek diminutive for "Lamb," "The Greek diminutive for 'Lamb' (*arnion* , literally, 'lambkin') occurs twenty-nine times in the Apocalypse, and the only other place where it occurs is John 21:15. In John's writings alone is Christ called directly 'the Lamb' (John 1:29, 36)."[35] Osborne favors the view that the Apocalypse was written by John the Apostle and cites a number of similarities:

> (1) the only two books in the NT to argue for the deity of Christ on the basis of the "oneness motif" between God and Jesus are John and the Apocalypse; (2) they share a similar theme—God seeking to bring the world to repentance; (3) Mounce observes that the same Greek verb (*ekkenteo*) used in the *Septuagint*[5.2.65] version of Zec. 12:10 appears both in John 19:37 and Rev. 1:7, but appears nowhere else in the NT; (4) the identification by Ozanne of words and phrases common to John and the Apocalypse such as "conquer," "keep the word," "keep the commandments," "dwell," "sign," "witness," "true."[36]

Swete provides a list of some 27 phrases found in common in various parts of the book as evidence of a single author.[37] Thomas provides an extensive review of common vocabulary and syntactical similarities between Revelation and the other writings of the apostle John.[38]

Swete observes that the differences found between the book of Revelation and John's other writings which are thought to indicate a different author are overrated and fail to take into account the differences in the content and themes of the books:

> It is to be remembered that whereas the simple narrative of the Evangelist demands for the most part only commonest words of daily life, the Apocalyptist deals with a great variety of subjects, some of which call for a liberal use of special terms. . . . the enumeration of articles of merchandize in Rev. 18:11-13 is responsible for twelve of the words peculiar to this book, and the list of precious stones in Rev. 21:19f. for ten more.[39]

2.9.4 - External Evidence

2.9.4.1 - Testimony of the Early Church

As we have noted, the external evidence should be granted greater weight than internal evidence due to its less subjective nature. As Thomas noted above, it would be foolish of us to reject the early and objective evidence of historical witness in favor of late, subjective theories of internal grammatical and textual analysis.[40]

The earliest testimony to the Apostle John as author appears to be that of *Justin Martyr*[5.2.36]. He appeals to the book of Revelation as an acknowledged work of John the Apostle.[41] (See Beckwith for an extended treatment of the church tradition that John ministered at Ephesus after his release from Patmos and died of old age in Asia Minor. [Beckwith, *The Apocalypse of John*, 366-392].) His testimony is of special significance because he lived for some time at Ephesus amidst the *seven churches*[5.2.66] of Revelation 2 and 3 who were direct recipients of the book and because some of Revelation's original readers would still have been alive to refute or correct him on this point if need be.[43]Justin's testimony was echoed by Irenaeus, *Tertullian*[5.2.75], Clement of Alexandria, and *Origen*[5.2.50]. [44]

Another early witness is that of Papias. As bishop of Hierapolis near Laodicea, one of the seven churches(Rev. 3:14), his testimony to apostolic authorship is especially weighty.[45]He placed great emphasis on oral teaching derived from those who once knew the apostles and is less likely to have simply repeated the written tradition of others.

Victorinus (d. c. A.D. 304) also states that the book of Revelation was written by John the Apostle during the reign of Domitian. "Victorinus of Pettau states that John was banished (*damnatus*) by Domitian to a mine or quarry (*metallum*) on the island of Patmos, where he saw the revelation (in Apoc. 10:11). In another passage, he explicitly says that the work was written during the time of Domitian (in Apoc. 17:10)."[46]

Fausset observes that the weight of such historic testimony, especially in view of its contemporary locale and time to that of the book of Revelation, is convincing.[47]

> Tregelles well says [New Testament Historic Evidence], "There is no book of the New Testament for which we have such clear, ample, and numerous testimonies in the second century as we have in favor of the Apocalypse. The more closely the witnesses were connected with the apostle John (as was the case with Irenaeus), the more explicit is their testimony. That doubts should prevail in after ages must have originated either in ignorance of the earlier testimony, or else from some supposed intuition of

what an apostle *ought* to have written. The objections on the ground of internal *style* can weigh nothing against the actual evidence. It is in vain to argue, a priori, that John could not have written this book when we have the evidence of several competent witnesses that he *did* write it."[48]

2.9.4.2 - Testimony of Enemies of the Early Church

Sometimes enemies can be friends. Such is the case regarding the contribution to this topic of the testimony by those who opposed the early church. Ladd notes the opposition of the Alogi who opposed the doctrine of Jesus as "the Word." They rejected the book of Revelation as they did all literature by John the Apostle, thus attesting the early tradition of John the Apostle as author.[49]The witness of early *Gnosticism*[5.2.23] also attributes authorship to John the Apostle:

> An important witness for the apostolic authorship of Revelation has more recently come from the Gnostic materials discovered in 1945 at Chenoboskion in Upper Egypt. One of the documents is the *Apocryphon of John* , which cites Revelation 1:19 and claims to be written by "John, the brother of James, these who are sons of Zebedee." Helmbold cites authorities who date the *Apocryphon* as early as the end of the first century and notes that in any event it cannot be given a date much later than about AD 150.[50] Those who deny apostolic authorship of the book of Revelation must explain how it came to be that this important body of prophetic revelation was given through an individual who lacked the intimacy with God which characterizes other revelatory writers within Scripture? In other instances, especially significant passages in the Word of God are given through individuals who have a special intimacy with God. For example, the Torah (Pentateuch—first five books of the Bible) were given through Moses whom God spoke with "face to face" (Num. 12:7-8). Next to Jesus, no other prophet had the status and access to God as Moses (Deu. 18:18). In the case of prophetic revelation of the distant future, Daniel is also unique. Having no sin on record[51] and called "greatly beloved" of God (Dan. 9:23; 10:11, 19), it was through him that God chose to give prophecies of great significance to the subjects of the book of Revelation. Are we now to hold that this capstone of all prophetic revelation, the book of Revelation, is the work of some obscure secondary and not the Apostle John? How much more sound to expect God to entrust this important work to the "disciple whom Jesus loved" (John 19:26; 20:2; 21:7, 20).
>
> Here we find the disciple whom Jesus so dearly loved. John had been with the Savior since the beginning. He had left the family fishing business to follow the carpenter from Nazareth. He was in the "inner circle" with Peter and James. At the Last Supper, he was seated next to Jesus and leaned over on his shoulder to talk to Him. He was the *only* disciple to show up at the cross. It was there that Jesus entrusted the care of His mother, Mary, to His beloved disciple (John 19:25-27).[52]

It is against the very character of God, as revealed throughout Scripture, to entrust such a significant work to someone whose identity the critics would have us believe has been lost to history.

If external evidence of historic testimony is given primacy, especially that of those closest to the time and area of authorship, then it seems best to understand the human author as the Apostle John who had the great privilege of being the servant through whom God would close the *canon*[5.2.12].[53]

Notes

1 e.g., the existence, timing, and nature of the Millennium and the description of a future time of catastrophic events coming upon the earth.

2 "The determining factor in New Testament canonization was *inspiration*[5.2.33], and the primary test was apostolicity . . . If it could be determined that a book had apostolic authority, there would be no reason to question its authenticity or veracity."—Norman L. Geisler, and William E. Nix, *A General Introduction to the Bible* (Chicago, IL: Moody Press, 1986), 283.

3 Isbon T. Beckwith, *The Apocalypse of John* (Eugene, OR: Wipf and Stock Publishers, 2001), 354.

4 Alan F. Johnson, *Revelation: The Expositor's Bible Commentary* (Grand Rapids, MI: Zondervan Publishing House, 1966), 7.

5 John MacArthur, *Revelation 1-11 : The MacArthur New Testament Commentary* (Chicago, IL: Moody Press, 1999), 5.

6 Robert H. Mounce, *The Book of Revelation* (Grand Rapids, MI: William B. Eerdmans Publishing Co., 1977),

29.

7 "A zealous anti-*Montanist*[5.2.42] the Roman presbyter Caius in the time of Zephyrinus (pp. 199-217) wrote a Dialogue against the Montanist Proclus in which he attributed the Apocalypse to Cerinthus . . . [finding] various discrepancies between it and the other parts of the New Testament. . . . Caius criticism was . . . taken up and refuted by Hippolytus."—Beckwith, *The Apocalypse of John*, 340. "Cerinthus . . . resided in Ephesus around the turn of the first century. Included in his heretical potpourri of doctrines was the notion that at Christ's second coming a millennium characterized by sensuous pleasures would be established."—Larry V. Crutchfield, *"Revelation in the New Testament,"* in Mal Couch, ed., *A Bible Handbook to Revelation* (Grand Rapids, MI: Kregel Publications, 2001), 26.

8 "The first to reject apostolic authorship was Marcion, the second-century Gnostic who rejected all non-Pauline books (apart from an edited version of Luke) . . . because of their Jewish influence. Dionysius . . . was the first to develop a series of arguments for his position, . . . Dionysius believed that 'another (unknown) John' wrote Revelation."—Grant R. Osborne, *Revelation* (Grand Rapids, MI: Baker Academic, 2002), 3.

9 "Toward the middle of the third century Dionysius the Great, bishop of Alexandria, in his opposition to millenarianism and apparently influenced by Caius, took up anew the question of the authenticity of the Apocalypse . . . concluding that the John who wrote it was not the Apostle, he nevertheless accepted it as divinely inspired . . . The criticism of so illustrious a figure in the church as Dionysius could not fail to exert influence, especially in Egypt and the east."—Beckwith, *The Apocalypse of John*, 341.

10 "Twelve of the nineteen terms or expressions with which Dionysius says the Apocalypse has no connection or affinity . . . *are* found in the book, some of them with great frequency."—Robert L. Thomas, *Revelation 1-7* (Chicago, IL: Moody Press, 1992), 6-7.

11 "Following in his [Dionysius'] footsteps Eusebius, . . . bishop of Caesarea . . . saw a second John as the author of the book."—Beckwith, *The Apocalypse of John*, 341.

12 [Osborne, *Revelation*, 3], [MacArthur, *Revelation 1-11 : The MacArthur New Testament Commentary*, 6].

13 "The Dutch reformer Desiderius Erasmus, German reformer Martin Luther, and Swiss reformer Ulrich Zwingli . . . all regarded it as a nonapostolic work. All three did so largely because it teaches a literal thousand-year earthly reign of Christ. Essentially, John Calvin and Luther simply ignored John's Revelation."—Crutchfield, "*Revelation in the New Testament*," 33.

14 It should be noted that several of these options are directly at odds with a belief in the *inspiration*[5.2.33] of Revelation and its inclusion in the *Canon*[5.2.12]. For example, if the book was written by Cerinthus or using a pseudonym, then we have what would amount to divine *inerrancy*[5.2.32] set forth within the framework of a lie.

15 Osborne, *Revelation*, 2.

16 Henry Barclay Swete, *The Apocalypse of St. John* (Eugene, OR: Wipf and Stock Publishers, 1998, 1906), xlviii.

17 The facts of the internal textual elements themselves are not subjective, but deciding which are important and what they mean is highly subjective.

18 "Swete points to twenty-seven phrases in the early chapters that are matched up by nearly the same wording in the final chapters. 'Such coincidences leave no doubt that the same writers has been at work.' "—Mal Couch, *"The Literary Structure of Revelation,"* in Mal Couch, ed., *A Bible Handbook to Revelation* (Grand Rapids, MI: Kregel Publications, 2001), 70.

19 Beckwith, *The Apocalypse of John*, 362,366.

20 Swete, *The Apocalypse of St. John*, clxxii.

21 "As for the authorship of the Apocalypse, Calvin suggested John Mark as a good candidate."—Crutchfield, "*Revelation in the New Testament*," 34.

22 "There is nothing in the New Testament or early tradition associating [John] Mark in this way with the Asian church."—Beckwith, *The Apocalypse of John*, 347.

23 "There exist no significant linguistic similarities between Mark's gospel and the Apocalypse, nor does the Evangelist display characteristics of a visionary possessed of a strong prophetic consciousness."—Mounce, *The Book of Revelation*, 25.

24 Thomas, *Revelation 1-7*, 10.

25 Adela Yarbro Collins, *"Book of Revelation,"* in David Noel Freeman, ed., *The Anchor Bible Dictionary* (New York, NY: Doubleday, 1996, c1992), 5:700.

26 Richard Chenevix Trench, *Commentary on the Epistles to the Seven Churches in Asia* (Eugene, OR: Wipf and Stock Publishers, 1861), 2-3.

27 Colin J. Hemer, *The Letters to the Seven Churches of Asia in Their Local Setting* (Grand Rapids, MI: William B. Eerdmans Publishing Company, 1989), 30-31.

28 Gregory K. Beale, *The Book of Revelation: A Commentary on the Greek Text* (Grand Rapids, MI: William B. Eerdmans Publishing Co., 1999), 34.

29 Walter Scott, *Exposition of The Revelation* (London, England: Pickering & Inglis, n.d.), 431n.

30 Mounce, *The Book of Revelation*, 26.

31 A. R. Fausset, *"The Revelation of St. John the Divine,"* in Robert Jamieson, A. R. Fausset, and David Brown, *A Commentary, Critical and Explanatory, on the Old and New Testaments* (Oak Harbor, WA: Logos Research Systems, Inc., 1997, 1877), Rev. 1:1.

32 Osborne, *Revelation*, 5.

33 Thomas, *Revelation 1-7*, 4-5.

34 Trench, *Commentary on the Epistles to the Seven Churches in Asia*, 90-91.

35 Fausset, "*The Revelation of St. John the Divine*," Rev. 1:1.

36 Osborne, *Revelation*, 5.

37 Swete, *The Apocalypse of St. John*, xlii-xliv.

38 Thomas, *Revelation 1-7*, 11-15.

39 Swete, *The Apocalypse of St. John*, cxvi.

40 Unfortunately, the tendency of academics is to reject historical witness in favor of novel theories. It is not clear whether this is fueled simply by the need for new Ph.D. topics or simply a reflection of human pride.

41 "The earliest testimony recorded is that of *Justin*, who lived some time at Ephesus, the center of the region to which the book was sent, at a date when the generation to which it first came had not yet passed away."—Beckwith, *The Apocalypse of John*, 349.

42 Beckwith, *The Apocalypse of John*, 366-392.

43 "The testimony of Justin and *Irenaeus*[5.2.34] is especially significant, since they lived in Ephesus and Smyrna when some of Revelation's original readers would still have been alive. That the church could have been mistaken about who wrote Revelation virtually from the time it was written is inconceivable."—MacArthur, *Revelation 1-11 : The MacArthur New Testament Commentary*, 4.

44 "Justin Martyr in the mid-second century wrote that the apostle John was the author (*Dialogue with Trypho* 81.4), and this became the accepted view (so also Irenaeus, *Against Heresies* 4.20.11; Tertullian, *Against Marcion* 3.14.3; Clement of Alexandria, *Paedagogus* 2.108; Origen, *De principiis* 1.2.10)."—Osborne, *Revelation*, 2-3. "Irenaeus . . . a younger contemporary of *Papias*[5.2.52] and Justin . . . makes frequent and explicit reference to the Apocalypse as that of "John the disciple of the Lord" and he shows distinctly that by this term he means John the Apostle. From this time on the same testimony appears generally in the fathers, *e.g.* Clement of Alexandrian, Tertullian, Origen, etc."—Beckwith, *The Apocalypse of John*, 349-350.

45 "Papias . . . recognized the book, according to Andreas, as *inspired*[5.2.33], . . . from the manner in which Andreas refers to Papias' view of the book, . . . he regarded him as agreeing with his own opinion, that the author was the Apostle."—Beckwith, *The Apocalypse of John*, 349. "Papias was bishop of Hierapolis, near Laodicea, one of the seven churches."—Fausset, "*The Revelation of St. John the Divine*," Rev. 1:1.

46 Collins, "*Book of Revelation*," 5:700.

47 "These testimonies of persons contemporary with John's immediate successors, and more or less connected with the region of the seven churches to which Revelation is addressed, are most convincing."—Fausset, "*The Revelation of St. John the Divine*," Rev. 1:1.

48 Fausset, "*The Revelation of St. John the Divine*," Rev. 1:1.

[49] "The first opposition to its apostolicity came from the Alogi (*ca.* A.D. 170), who opposed the Logos doctrine of the Fourth Gospel and therefore rejected all Johannine literature. The Alogi therefore testify indirectly to the Johannine tradition and to the tradition that the Gospel and Revelation came from the same hand."—G. E. Ladd, *"Revelation, Book of,"* in Geoffrey W. Bromiley, ed., *International Standard Bible Encyclopedia* (Grand Rapids, MI: William B. Eerdmans Publishing Co., 1979, 1915), 4:172.

[50] Mounce, *The Book of Revelation*, 28.

[51] But being a sinner nonetheless (Rom. 3:19).

[52] Edward Hindson, *Revelation: Unlocking the Future* (Chattanooga, TN: AMG Publishers, 2002), 20.

[53] "Indeed, it would be a serious mistake to regard John as the originator of this book, for it would then become merely a human being's comments and prediction of the future, which would deprive the book of all its authority and impact. We therefore need to recognize, right at the outset, that this book was virtually dictated by God, and that John was merely the privileged scribe who recorded what he saw and heard (this is not to suggest that God dictated all Scripture, but this certainly holds good in large measure for Revelation)."—Monty S. Mills, *Revelations: An Exegetical Study of the Revelation to John* (Dallas, TX: 3E Ministries, 1987), s.v. "Introduction."

2.10 - Acceptance into the Canon

Three factors are difficult to separate in any consideration of the book of Revelation: the uniqueness of its *style of writing*[2.8]; the question of its *authorship*[2.9]; and its acceptance into the *canon*[5.2.12] of the New Testament. These three factors are interrelated in that each of them depends to some extent upon the others.[1] Most frequently, the unique *style of writing* has been used as evidence against apostolic *authorship*, which in turn has been used to reject the book from the *canon* of Scripture. We have already discussed the first two of these interrelated factors and here we spend some time looking at historic attitudes toward the book of Revelation from the perspective of its acceptance into the canon. We need to also be aware of a fourth factor which is the ultimate explanation of many of the attacks upon the authority of the book. "the canonical fortunes of no book hinged more on personal prejudice and theological bias than that of the Revelation of John."[2]

In other words, the pattern of events in history has often run in the opposite direction: *First*, a teaching found in the book is opposed; *Second*, a desire developed to reject the teaching by rejecting the book; *Third*, an attempt is made to undermine its apostolic authority by attributing its writing to someone other than John the Apostle; *Fourth*, differences in writing style between the book and John's other writings provided a potential means to reject apostolic authorship.

The two teachings of the book which have probably been most opposed have been the millennial reign of Christ on earth (Rev. 20:4) and the prophetic certainty of a time of great upheaval and judgment coming upon the earth prior to the establishment of the reign of Christ. The former was a key reason for the rejection of the book among some in the early church who viewed any fulfillment of Old Testament promises involving the Jews with great disdain. The latter is more frequently under attack in our own day by those who hold to *Dominion Theology*[5.2.17] or Christian Reconstructionism.[3] We touch on Dominion Theology's attempts to "reinterpret" passages which speak of a future time of tribulation in our discussion of *systems of interpretation*[2.12].

2.10.1 - Rejection

The first substantial opposition to the book of Revelation arose in the second century in response to the teachings of the cult of Montanism. *Montanus*[5.2.42] appealed to the book to support some of his teachings. Those who opposed his teachings called into question the validity of the book he employed for his doctrines.[4] Montanism taught an extravagant view of the *Millennial Kingdom*[5.2.39] which placed great emphasis upon material and sensual aspects. Although the Millennial Kingdom *will* be a time of great material blessing, many felt that Montanus misrepresented the emphasis of New Testament teaching which is focused upon a denial of the flesh in favor of greater spiritual realities.[5] This led the church to emphasize the purely spiritual aspects over the material aspects of God's blessings—an imbalance which is still with us today. This opposition to the materialism of Montanus and to a literal Millennial Kingdom in favor of a spiritual emphasis went hand-in-glove with the growing tendency to employ *allegory in interpretation*[2.7.3].

> To . . . leaders in the Eastern church, millennialism was nothing more than a Jewish concept that appealed to Christians' baser sensual appetites rather than to their higher spiritual nature. . . . Early on, Augustine held millenarian views. But he abandoned that doctrine for the superficial reason that some millenarians had envisioned a kingdom age of unparalleled fruitfulness featuring banquet tables set with excessive amounts of food and drink. He favored . . . a spiritualized interpretation of the Apocalypse. . . . Augustine articulated an *amillennial*[5.2.1] view in which no future thousand-year earthly millennium was expected.[6]

Yet a belief in a literal thousand-year-reign had been the view held by those in the very early church who had closest contact with the living apostles.[7]

As we mentioned in our discussion of the *authorship*[2.9] of the book, Dionysius, bishop of Alexandria, felt that John the Apostle was not the author of the book. Although Dionysius was careful not to reject the book out-of-hand, his views had a large effect upon the Eastern Church and led to doubts by many who followed him.

> Criticism, . . . from so distinguished a Bishop as Dionysius . . . could not fail to carry weight in Egypt and the Greek-speaking East, shaking the faith of many in the apostolical authorship of the Apocalypse, and therefore in its *canonical*[5.2.12] authority. In the fourth century *Eusebius*[5.2.19] is unable to speak positively as to its canonicity . . . Cyril of Jerusalem, a few years later, not only omits the Apocalypse from his list of canonical books, but seems definitely to exclude it from private as well as public use . . . it finds no place in the Laodicean list of 363, or in that of Gregory of Nazianzus; . . . In Eastern Syria the Apocalypse was either still unknown or it was ignored; it formed no part of the Peshitta New Testament. Junilius, . . . in the sixth century, is silent about the book; Ebedjesu, a Nestorian Bishop in the first year of the fourteenth century, still passes it over without notice in his list of New Testament books. . . . Neither Theodore, Chrysostom, or Theodoret is known to have quoted the Apocalypse. . . . As late as the beginning of the ninth century Nicephorus places it among the *antilegomena* with the Apocalypse of Peter.[8]

> *Origen*[5.2.50]'s pupil, Dionysius, bishop of Alexandria . . . opposed the chiliastic views of Nepos, a bishop in Egypt, and believed that linguistic differences with the Gospel of John as well as differences in thought and style meant that the Apostle John was not the author. His influence led to serious doubts in the East. Eusebius . . . said Revelation was written by John the Elder and refused to consider it canonical. Other Eastern Fathers who doubted it were Cyril of Jerusalem, Chrysostom, Theodore of Mopsuestia, and Theodoret of Cyrsu. As a result it was not in the canonical list at the Council of Laodicea in 360, . . . *Athanasius*[5.2.7] accepted it completely . . . and it is in the official canonical list at the Council of Carthage in 397.[9]

> Among those who either distinctly declared against it, or seem to have used it with reserve, were Cyril of Jerusalem, Gregory Nazianzen, Amphilochius of Iconium, Chrysostom, Theodoret.[10]

The opposition of the Eastern Church showed some weakening in the third Council of Carthage (A.D. 397) which finally included it in the list of canonical books,[11]but the book was not fully accepted by the Eastern Church until the Third Council of Constantinople in A.D. 680.[12]

Although the book was endorsed and enjoyed a wide circulation by the Western Church from a very early date (see below), an attitude of opposition or indifference toward the book continued even until the time of the Reformation. It may be surprising today to read of Martin Luther's attitude toward the book. He rejected its divine *inspiration*[5.2.33],[13]placed it last in his New Testament along with other books he felt had relatively little value,[14] and made a quite disappointing statement in view of the claim of the book to be the "Revelation of Jesus Christ": "In 1522 Martin Luther wrote of the Revelation, 'My mind cannot use itself to the Book, and to me the fact that **Christ is neither taught nor recognized in it**, is good and sufficient cause for my low estimation.' Though he modified his view some years later, to the end Luther remained doubtful about the book's authenticity." [emphasis added][15]

Luther was not alone in his disdain for the book of Revelation. It was rejected from the canon by Zwingli[16]and Calvin never produced a commentary on it.

2.10.2 - Acceptance

The acceptance of the book of Revelation by the Western Church was markedly different than that of the Eastern Church.[17]Perhaps this was because the Western Church had more direct knowledge of its author since the *seven churches*[5.2.66] of Asia were its direct recipients. Beckwith lists the following Church Fathers who accepted the Apocalypse: *Papias*[5.2.52], bishop of Hierapolis; *Justin Martyr*[5.2.36]; *Irenaeus*[5.2.34], presbyter and bishop of Lyons (Gaul); Theophilus, bishop of Antioch (in Syria); *Tertullian*[5.2.75] of Carthage; and Clement of Alexandria.[18] The early acceptance of the book of Revelation in the very area to which it was addressed is strong evidence of its rightful canonicity. "If the Apocalypse were not the *inspired*[5.2.33] work of John, purporting as it does to be an address from their superior to the seven churches of Proconsular Asia, it would have assuredly been rejected in that region; whereas the earliest testimonies in those churches are all in its favor."[19]

> In the literature of the second half of the second century, evidence begins to reveal wide circulation of

> the Apocalypse. Andreas quotes Papias about Revelation 12:7 ff. Irenaeus refers to old copies of the book and to people who knew John. Other early authors who mention the book are Justin, *Eusebius*[5.2.19], Apollonius, and Theophilus the Bishop of Antioch. It is referred to a number of times in the *Epistle of the Churches of Vienne*. Other references to the book abound. Tertullian . . . quotes from eighteen out of the twenty-two chapters . . . and cites it as Scripture. Some literature from the period seems to refer to the book using similar phraseology, e.g., the *Shepherd of Hermas*, which refers to the great tribulation, and the *Acts of Perpetua and Felicitas*, which according to Swete abounds in imagery similar to the book of Revelation. The circulation and wide use of the book as Scripture are evident by the beginning of the third century.[20]

> The Apocalypse seems to have been accepted almost from the beginning in the Western church . . . it appears to have been recognized by Papias . . . and may be reflected by *Ignatius*[5.2.28] . . . it was accepted by Justin Martyr, Irenaeus, Tertullian, Hippolytus, Clement of Alexandria, and Origin. It was included in the earliest list of *canonical*[5.2.12] works, the Muratorian Canon, in the latter part of the second century.[21]

The book was accepted as canonical in the West much earlier than the East. "full acceptance in the canon was recognized in the Festal Letter of *Athanasius*[5.2.7] written from Alexandria in 367. The Damasine Council (382) and the Council of Carthage (397) ratified this by officially including it in the canon of New Testament Scriptures."[22]

Today, the book of Revelation is well-established in the canon of Scripture. Its extensive connections with the Old Testament and undeniable relationship to *related passages of Scripture*[2.13], especially its many parallels with the book of Genesis, make it impractical to dismiss as uninspired or inconsistent with the rest of Scripture. Yet there are still those who oppose its teachings.

Earlier the battle over the authority of its teachings took place in relation to its canonization, but now the battle rages over how it is to be *interpreted*[2.12]. Opposition to its plain teachings in our own time has come on two fronts: a rejection of the predicted time of upheaval and judgment to come upon the earth prior to the return of Christ and a rejection of His subsequent reign for one thousand years upon the earth following His return. By *overemphasizing the symbolic nature*[2.7.4] of the text or associating the text with the *genre*[5.2.22] of obscure Jewish *apocryphal*[5.2.5] works, today's commentators attempt to persuade the student to approach the text in a way which allows the denial of these realities. Yet, as we shall see, these are plainly the teachings of this most fascinating book of the New Testament.

Notes

1 "The determining factor in New Testament canonization was *inspiration*[5.2.33], and the primary test was apostolicity . . . If it could be determined that a book had apostolic authority, there would be no reason to question its authenticity or veracity."—Norman L. Geisler, and William E. Nix, *A General Introduction to the Bible* (Chicago, IL: Moody Press, 1986), 283.

2 Larry V. Crutchfield, *"Revelation in the New Testament,"* in Mal Couch, ed., *A Bible Handbook to Revelation* (Grand Rapids, MI: Kregel Publications, 2001), 23.

3 Dominion theology does not undermine the book by explicitly attacking its authority, but by implicitly undermining its teachings through a method of interpretation which denies any application to events of the future.

4 "In the middle of the second century the heterodox teachings of Montanus precipitated the first substantial opposition to the Apocalypse of John. . . . Because Montanus appealed to the book of Revelation for support of his extreme views, Montanism cast a dark shadow of doubt over the book of Revelation."—Crutchfield, "*Revelation in the New Testament*," 26.

5 "The opposition to the heresy of Montanism, which made great use of the Apocalypse and gave extravagant form to its millennial teaching, caused it to be either rejected or differently interpreted."—Isbon T. Beckwith, *The Apocalypse of John* (Eugene, OR: Wipf and Stock Publishers, 2001), 323. "A number of church fathers rejected the book because of the *chiliast*[5.2.13] debate and its use by the Montanists."—Grant R. Osborne, *Revelation* (Grand Rapids, MI: Baker Academic, 2002), 22. "In the second century, the Alogi, a group of anti-Montanists in Asia Minor, rejected the Apocalypse on the basis of its unedifying symbolism and because they held it to contain errors of fact (*eg*., no church existed at Thyatira at that time)."—Robert H. Mounce, *The*

Book of Revelation (Grand Rapids, MI: William B. Eerdmans Publishing Co., 1977), 38.

6 Crutchfield, "*Revelation in the New Testament*," 27,31.

7 "The most explicit reference in Scripture to the thousand-year millennial reign of Christ is found in Revelation 20. It is a significant fact that the early adherents of *premillennialism*[5.2.58] (or chiliasm, as it was first called), either had direct contact with John, the longest living apostle, or with his most famous disciple *Polycarp*[5.2.55]."—Crutchfield, "*Revelation in the New Testament*," 24.

8 Henry Barclay Swete, *The Apocalypse of St. John* (Eugene, OR: Wipf and Stock Publishers, 1998, 1906), cxi-cxii.

9 Osborne, *Revelation*, 23.

10 Beckwith, *The Apocalypse of John*, 341.

11 "The first action relating to the scriptures taken by a synod is that of the counsel of Laodicea, not far from 360. . . . It adopted an ordinance forbidding the reading of uncanonical scriptures in public worship. And in the list of canonical books given, the Apocalypse is wanting. . . The third council of Carthage (397) adopted a decree regarding the scriptures to be read in service, and the Apocalypse, in keeping with the universal opinion of the Western Church from the earliest times, was included in the list of canonical books,"—Beckwith, *The Apocalypse of John*, 342.

12 "The Revelation of John finally received official acceptance in the Eastern church at the Third Council of Constantinople (A.D. 680)."—Crutchfield, "*Revelation in the New Testament*," 32.

13 "In reference to Revelation, Luther wrote in 1522 that he could find 'no trace' of evidence that the book 'was written by the Holy Spirit.' In other words, he rejected its divine inspiration."—Crutchfield, "*Revelation in the New Testament*," 33.

14 "Martin Luther . . . [rearranged] his New Testament into sections which reflected his own attitude about the various books. In the front of his New Testament he placed those books he valued most. Another section, which he placed in the back of his Bible, included the New Testament works he felt had relatively little value (Hebrews, James, Jude, and Revelation)."—Crutchfield, "*Revelation in the New Testament*," 33.

15 Harold D. Foos, *"Christology in the Book of Revelation,"* in Mal Couch, ed., *A Bible Handbook to Revelation* (Grand Rapids, MI: Kregel Publications, 2001), 105.

16 "The only book he apparently excluded from the canon was the Apocalypse."—Crutchfield, "*Revelation in the New Testament*," 34.

17 "No other writing of the New Testament can claim in comparison with the Apocalypse more abundant and more trustworthy evidence that it was widely known at an early date."—Beckwith, *The Apocalypse of John*, 337.

18 Beckwith, *The Apocalypse of John*, 338-339.

19 A. R. Fausset, *"The Revelation of St. John the Divine,"* in Robert Jamieson, A. R. Fausset, and David Brown, *A Commentary, Critical and Explanatory, on the Old and New Testaments* (Oak Harbor, WA: Logos Research Systems, Inc., 1997, 1877), Rev. 1:1.

20 John F. Walvoord, *The Revelation of Jesus Christ* (Chicago, IL: Moody Press, 1966), 14-15.

21 Osborne, *Revelation*, 23.

22 Monty S. Mills, *Revelations: An Exegetical Study of the Revelation to John* (Dallas, TX: 3E Ministries, 1987), s.v. "Introduction."

2.11 – Date

Having discussed the *authorship*[2.9] and *acceptance*[2.10] of the book of Revelation, we now turn our attention to an examination of the various dates proposed for when the book was written. Dates for the book have been proposed from as early as A.D. 41 to as late as A.D. 117, although the majority of scholars have placed it between A.D. 54 and A.D. 96.[1]

Our treatment of the date the book was written is intended mainly to acquaint the unfamiliar reader with the significance of the topic and the major arguments presented in support of the most popular dates. The works cited here provide additional background for those who are interested in delving into this matter further.

2.11.1 - Significance of the Date

The significance of the date of the book of Revelation depends to a great degree on the *interpretive system*[2.12] one holds. The *Preterist Interpretation*[2.12.2] *requires* that the book be written during the reign of *Nero*[4.12] before the destruction of Jerusalem in A.D. 70. If the book proves to have been written after A.D. 70, then the entire basis of the *preterist*[5.2.59] interpretation collapses. Other systems of interpretation are not so sensitive to the date of writing, since their interpretive frameworks do not connect the events of the book as directly to the events attending the fall of Jerusalem.

The reason the preterist position is intent on dating the book before A.D. 70 is twofold: *First* , they insist that the theme of the book centers on the near-term destruction of Jerusalem prophesied by Jesus (Luke 21:22).[2] *Second,* modern preterism is often associated with the Christian Reconstruction movement which holds to *Dominion Theology*[5.2.17] which cannot accept a worldwide rejection of Christ and a time of global judgment prior to His return. Those who accept the teaching that the book of Revelation predicts a future time of judgment coming upon the earth are seen as 'defeatists,'[3] so there is significant motivation to try to prove an early date over against the traditional late date.[4]

The reader should be aware of the major weakness of those who *depend upon* an early date for their interpretation: "The danger of dependence on a particular date for the writing of Revelation is aptly stated by Howard Winters: 'When the interpretation depends upon the date, the interpretation can never be more certain than the date itself—if the date is wrong, then, of necessity the interpretation is wrong.' "[5]

> In a review of fellow preterist David Chilton's commentary on Revelation, entitled *The Days of Vengeance*, Kenneth Gentry observes, "If it could be demonstrated that Revelation were written 25 years after the Fall of Jerusalem, Chilton's entire labor would go up in smoke." Another preterist, R. C. Sproul, observes, "If the book was written after A.D. 70, then its contents manifestly do not refer to the events surrounding the fall of Jerusalem—unless the book is a wholesale fraud, having been composed after the predicted events had already occurred."[6]

For systems of interpretation other than the preterist, the date is not critical. Either an early or a late date for the writing of the book of Revelation will not significantly affect the understanding of the book. But if the book of Revelation proves to have been written *after* the fall of Jerusalem in A.D. 70, then the preterist interpretation can be rejected.

Hitchcock has noted the narrow date range which modern preterism depends upon for its interpretation of the book. He also observes that many of those who support an early date do not necessarily support a date as early as is required by the modern preterists:

> While it is true that many scholars do hold to a pre-70 date for Revelation, it is critical to observe that the preterist position requires more than just a pre-70 date. According to Gentry, Revelation anticipates the destruction of Jerusalem (August A.D. 70), the death of *Nero*[5.2.46] (June A.D. 68), and the formal imperial engagement of the Jewish war (spring A.D. 67). Therefore, for preterists, the earliest Revelation could have been written . . . is the beginning of the Neronic persecution in November A.D. 64, and the latest possible date . . . is spring A.D. 67. The date Gentry favors is A.D. 65. . . . the problem Gentry faces is that almost all of the scholars he lists in support of his position do not actually support

his position at all. These early-date advocates hold an early date, but not an early-enough date to support the preterist position.[7]

Although there are other early-date advocates, the most vocal advocates of our time have a specific agenda: to localize the prophetic content of the book of Revelation in both time (prior to A.D. 70) and place (events surrounding Jerusalem and within the boundaries of the historic Roman Empire). This agenda provides two key results: *First*, the future judgment of the "*earth dwellers*[5.2.18]" and tribulation upon the earth is moved to the past clearing the way for Christian Reconstructionism and dominion. *Second*, the events of Revelation are poured out specifically upon the *Jews* rather than the entire disbelieving world. In concert with *Replacement Theology*[5.2.63], they believe the nation of Israel has been irrevocably *replaced* by the Church in the program of God.

It is our belief that when all the evidence is taken into account, the traditional late date is supported. But even if the early date turns out to be valid in the end, it still would not prove that the events of the book are found exclusively in the events of the past. In other words, the early date is *necessary* for the preterist interpretation, but not *sufficient* to prove that the text applies *strictly* to the immediate readers of John's day.

2.11.2 - The Nature of Internal Evidence

As we saw when discussing the *authorship*[2.9] of the book, there are two primary sources of evidence available when analyzing a biblical text: *internal* and *external*. We also noted that the interpretation of internal evidence is especially subject to subjective bias. External evidence has the advantage of being less subject to the bias of the interpreter.[8]

Those who favor an early date for the book of Revelation, and who wish to minimize the external evidence in favor of a later date, would have us place a greater emphasis on internal evidence than external evidence. "Conservative Christianity must recognize that the essential and determinative evidence ought to be drawn from the *internal* testimony of the scriptural record itself, when it is available."[9] The key point of contention in regard to the use of internal evidence is found in Gentry's last phrase: *when it is available*. Leaving aside the interpretation of internal evidence which has its own problems, the determination of what *constitutes* internal evidence is highly problematic. Most often, the selection of internal evidence is driven by the *a priori* stance of the interpreter. What one interpreter sees as being "determinative" and "conclusive," another interpreter sees as indicative of something else entirely.

For example, Hemer understands Revelation 6:6 as being significant internal evidence of a late date: "We adduce reasons for accepting the view that Rev. 6:6 alludes to an edict issued by Domitian in AD 92 to restrict the growing of vines in the provinces . . . and connect this with the contemporary setting of the Philadelphian letter."[10] Here lies the problem: who determines when a textual artifact is connected with a historical situation approximate to the time of writing? Hemer is sure that Domitian's edict restricting the growing of vines is the source for John's puzzling statement in Revelation 6:6. Yet many other interpreters see no such connection and understand the passage in an entirely different light. The crux of the matter is determining when historical *similarity* equates to textual *dependence* or *identity*? This involves a huge amount of subjectivity on the part of the interpreter.

It is also frequently the case that the internal evidence results from the view which the interpreter has brought to the text, which is then used in support for the view: "As we will see . . . the book of Revelation is primarily a prophecy of the destruction of Jerusalem by the Romans. This fact alone places St. John's authorship somewhere before September of A.D. 70."[11]

Here we see half of an "interpretive circle" which operates in the interpretation of internal evidence by early date advocates: the book is obviously a prediction of the destruction of Jerusalem and therefore *must* have been written prior to the event. The other half of this circle is as follows: the book was written before A.D. 70 and therefore must have the destruction of Jerusalem in view as its major theme. Internal evidence which contradicts this conclusion is minimized or reinterpreted.[12]

The main problem with internal evidence is that it is subject to too many conflicting interpretations. What one person believes is "significant" internal evidence for their particular view is often possible to explain in totally different ways. The identity of the seven kings and seven heads of Revelation 17:9-11 is one such commonly-used piece of internal "evidence." "[Gentry takes] the contemporary reign of the sixth king in Rev. 17:9-11 and the integrity of the temple and Jerusalem in Rev. 11:1-13 to exemplify arguments that are 'virtually certain' proof of a date some time in the sixties."[13] But, as Mounce observes, it is inadvisable to utilize something as evidence which is subject to such a diversity of interpretations. "The interpretation of the seven heads of the beast set forth in Rev. 17:10-11 is also presented as favoring the early date. Here again the divergence of opinion regarding this figure precludes the advisability of attempting to build a chronology on it."[14]

It is our position that internal evidence is highly overrated in the field of biblical studies as is evident from its fruitlessness. This is plainly evident in the conclusions drawn from academic considerations of internal evidence drawn from the four gospels.[15]

2.11.3 - Evidence for an Early Date

2.11.3.1 - Internal Evidence for an Early Date

Aspects of the text of the book of Revelation have been understood by some as being indicative of an earlier date.

Chilton holds that since Scripture teaches that all prophecy would be complete by the end of the 70th week of Daniel (Dan. 9:24-27) and since the book of Revelation contains prophetic material, therefore the book must have been written prior to the end of Daniel's 70th week:

> We have *a priori* teaching from Scripture itself that all special revelation ended by A.D. 70. The angel Gabriel told Daniel that the "seventy weeks" were to end **with the destruction of Jerusalem** (Dan. 9:24-27); and that period would also serve to "seal up the vision and prophecy" (Dan. 9:24). In other words, special revelation would stop—be "sealed up"—by the time Jerusalem was destroyed. [emphasis added][16]

We concur with Chilton's basic premise: prophecy and vision *will* be sealed up at the conclusion of the 70 weeks of Daniel. But Chilton assumes the 70th week is completed with the destruction of Jerusalem in A.D. 70—a view which is fundamentally flawed. [17] This is the interpretive equivalent of "two wrongs don't make a right." Here is revealed another Achilles heel of reliance upon internal evidence: it is too easily subject to cross-correlation which seems supportive, but is not necessarily related. Chilton misinterprets the meaning of a passage in Daniel to "prove" his interpretation of John's passage, but both interpretations are in error.

Edersheim held that the many allusions in John's Gospel and the book of Revelation to aspects of priestly service in the Temple inferred that John had close association with the priestly line (John 18:15-16) and that the Temple was still in service at the time both books were written.

> These [allusions] naturally suggest the twofold inference that the book of Revelation and the Fourth Gospel must have been written before the Temple services had actually ceased, and by one who had not merely been intimately acquainted with, but probably at one time an actor in them. . . . it seems highly improbable that a book so full of liturgical allusions as the book of Revelation—and these, many of them, not too great or important points, but to *minutia*—could have been written by any other than a priest, and one who had at one time been in actual service in the Temple itself, and thus become so intimately conversant with its details, that they came to him naturally, as part of the imagery he employed.[18]

While we might concur with Edersheim's observations concerning John's knowledge of priestly duties and the allusions found in his works, all that seems to be necessary is for John to have had such knowledge at some point during his life. Clearly, the Temple *was* in operation during the times recorded by John's Gospel (John 2:14-19). But does John's acquaintance with the Temple *necessitate* that its service was contemporaneous with the *writing* of the book of Revelation? The obvious answer is, "no." Any writer's knowledge is cumulative: it is often the case that a writer expresses knowledge gained from an earlier point in his life. This is not at all unusual. Further, there is no reason why direct revelation from God, as is the case with the book of Revelation, might not convey details not previously known to the prophet. Let the reader pause to make note of this frequent pattern involving internal evidence: what *could possibly be true* is asserted as being *requisite*. The former interpretation of the evidence is nearly always admissible, but the latter conclusion does not necessarily follow. This leap from "would seem" to "must" is commonly found in arguments based on internal evidence.

An entire category of internal evidence surrounds the assertion that the *Beast*[4.2] of Revelation (Rev. 11:7; 13:1-18; etc.) is to be understood as a veiled political reference to *Nero*[4.12]. At least three aspects of the life of *Nero*[5.2.46] are said to be found in John's description of the *Beast*[5.2.9]: *First* , Nero's persecution of Christians (Rev. 13:7); *Second* , the myth that after his death Nero would come to life again (cf. Rev. 13:3, 14; 17:8, 11); *Third* , the "number of the name" of the Beast (Rev. 13:16-18) matches that of "Caesar Nero."[19] While it is true that similarities can be found between the final Beast of world history and Nero (or many other anti-Christian leaders of history), similarity does not prove identity. The major problem with interpreting Nero as the Beast is that Nero doesn't even come close to fulfilling numerous details of the text—not the least of which is being killed, resurrected, and then cast *alive* into the Lake of Fire at the *Second Coming* of Christ (Rev. 19:20). Nero committed suicide never to rise again. We discuss these issues in greater depth in our discussion of *Nero*[4.12].

What is probably considered to be the most significant internal evidence for a pre-A.D. 70 date by early date advocates is John's mention of a Temple in Revelation 11: "We wholeheartedly concur with Adams's [*sic*] assessment that the fact that the Temple was standing when Revelation was written is 'unmistakable proof that Revelation was written before 70 A.D.' "[20] ` While we would concur with the last portion of Gentry's statement. *If* the Temple were standing when Revelation was written, then it is indeed unmistakable that Revelation was written prior to the destruction of the Temple. The problem is with the first part of the statement. Gentry equates John's *mention* of a Temple as being equivalent to the *fact* that the Temple stood at that time.[21] His statement goes beyond the demonstrable facts. Gentry continues, "How could John be commanded to symbolically measure what did not exist?"[22] Here again, the assertions of the early date advocates go far beyond what can be reliably concluded (or proven) from the text itself. As many have observed, a similar pattern has been established within the book of Ezekiel where the prophet is given a vision of another Temple at a time when no Temple stood[23] and Ezekiel's temple is also measured. Clearly, Ezekiel's mention of a Temple, including not only measurements as in John, *but myriads of details far in excess of John* stand as unassailable evidence against the claim that mere mention of a Temple by John proves as *fact* that he wrote prior to the destruction of Herod's Temple in A.D. 70. Not only is this pattern of prophetic revelation concerning a future Temple found in Ezekiel, but also in Daniel (Dan. 9:27; 12:11):

> The chief *preterist*[5.2.59] argument for the Neronic date from Revelation is the mention of the temple in Revelation 11:1-2. . . . this interpretation fails to take into account the Old Testament prophetic parallels. . . . especially Daniel and Ezekiel. In both of these Old Testament prophetic books a Temple is mentioned that is not in existence at the time the author is writing. . . . Ezekiel received news of the destruction of the temple in Jerusalem in Ezekiel 33. However, after receiving the news, in Ezekiel 40-48, Ezekiel, like John, receives a vision of a Temple that, if taken literally, has never existed up to this day. Moreover, Ezekiel, like John, is told to measure the Temple he sees in his vision.[24]

Even *if* Herod's Temple were to have been standing at the time John wrote, the Temple he mentions in Revelation 11 could still have been a future Temple. After all, Zechariah, writing *during the Second Temple era*, described a Temple future to his day.[25] Significantly, Zechariah also mentions measurement in association with the revelation he was given.

The internal evidence which early-date advocates assert as *proof* of a pre-A.D. 70 date for the book of Revelation falls short. In each case, the interpretation of the evidence is either flawed or overstated. At most, the evidence makes a case for the *possibility* of a pre-A.D. 70 date, but cannot be taken as objective evidence of this as a necessity.

2.11.3.2 - External Evidence for an Early Date

We now turn to the external evidence for an early date. This evidence tends to be less subjective and therefore more significant than the internal evidence.

Johnson cites several early documents which suggest that Paul borrowed from the pattern of the seven letters in the book of Revelation in writing his epistles: "Some external evidence for the early date exists in the Muratorian Fragment (170-190) and the Monarchian Prologues (250-350). These documents claim that Paul wrote to *seven churches*[5.2.66] following the pattern of John's example in Revelation. But this would date the book before the Pauline Epistles!"[26] This is not very strong evidence because it really is just an early form of the sort of arguments which characterize textual criticism (internal evidence). As we have mentioned, similarity does not prove identity.[27]

It has also been held that *Papias*[5.2.52] indicates, in relation to Jesus' prophecy of Mark 10:39, that John was martyred *contemporaneously* with his brother James. Since James was martyred in A.D. 63, this would make a late date for the book of Revelation impossible.[28]Papias' statement is preserved in the writings of "George the Sinner" of the 9th century:

> After Domitian, Nerva reigned one year. He re-called John from the island and allowed him to live in Ephesus. At that time he was the sole survivor of the twelve disciples, and after writing the Gospel that bears his name was honored with martyrdom. For Papias, the bishop of Hierapolis, who had seen him with his own eyes, claims in the second book of the *Sayings of the Lord* that he was killed by the Jews, thus clearly fulfilling, together with his brother, Christ's prophecy concerning them and their own confession and agreement about this.—George the Sinner (9th century), *Chronicle*[29]

Papias' statement simply says that like James, John was "killed by the Jews." It does not necessarily follow that they perished at the same time. It appears that George the Sinner understood John's martyrdom to have been after his return from Patmos at the conclusion of Domitian's reign. Thus the statement of Papias does not necessitate an early date for John's death. Moreover, church tradition relates that although John came to Ephesus in A.D. 66,[30]he survived at least until the time of Trajan (A.D. 98 - 117).[31]

The major external evidence offered by early date advocate Gentry involves a forced and unconvincing reinterpretation of a key late-date testimony. This in itself is an indication of the dearth of external evidence for an early date. The controversy surrounds the interpretation of an important statement made by Irenaeus (ca. A.D. 180):

> We will not, however, incur the risk of pronouncing positively as to the name of *Antichrist*[5.2.3]; for if it were necessary that his name should be distinctly revealed in this present time, it would have been announced by him who beheld the apocalyptic vision. For that was seen no very long time since, but almost in our day, towards the end of Domitian's reign.[32]

Schaff comments on the statement of Irenaeus: "The traditional date of composition at the end of Domitian's reign (95 or 96) rests on the clear and weighty testimony of Irenaeus, is confirmed by Eusebius and Jerome, and has still its learned defenders. . ."[33] Even though Schaff's own views concerning the date differed from the "learned defenders" he mentions, [34] it is clear that he understands the statement of Irenaeus in its straightforward sense. Irenaeus is stating that it was *the apocalyptic vision* which was seen toward the end of Domitian's reign.

Early date advocates, such as Gentry, attempt to obscure the plain statement of Irenaeus by casting a shadow over its interpretation:

> The most serious potential objection to the common translation has to do with the understanding of ἑωράθη [*eōrathē*], "was seen." What is the subject of this verb? Is it "him who saw the Apocalypse" (i.e., John) or "the Apocalypse"? What of these two antecedents "was seen" "almost" in Irenaeus's time and near "the end of the reign of Domitian"?[35]

Gentry wants to insert doubt where none exists in order to perform his *preterist*[5.2.59] 'sleight of hand.' He reverses the plain sense of the text, having us understand that it was *John* which was seen towards the end of Domitian's reign, not *the apocalyptic vision.* Gentry goes to great lengths in his attempt to undermine the obvious reading of Irenaeus. If he is not successful at this, he suggests that the Latin translation is in error. And if that doesn't persuade the reader, he spends several more pages convincing the reader that Irenaeus isn't a reliable witness anyhow: "If Irenaeus's famous statement is not to be re-interpreted along the lines of the argument as outlined above . . . it may still be removed as a hindrance to early date advocacy on [other] grounds."[36] Hitchcock counters Gentry's attempt at reinterpreting Irenaeus:

> There are four simple points that render Gentry's position highly suspect. First, the nearest antecedent to the verb "it was seen" is "the apocalypse" . . . David Aune observes, "Further the passive verb *eorathe*,

> 'he/she/it was seen,' does not appear to be the most appropriate way to describe the length of a person's life. . ." Second the verb "was seen" fits perfectly the noun *apokalupsis*. . . Third, if John were the intended subject . . . Irenaeus . . . would have surely said that John lived into the reign of Trajan, a fact that Irenaeus knew well. Fourth, the vast majority of scholars . . . have accepted the fact that this statement refers to the time the Apocalypse was seen.[37]

It should also be recognized where early-date advocate Gentry is eventually headed with his argument: an identification of Nero as the *Beast*[5.2.9] of Revelation. He conveniently omits the statements of Irenaeus immediately following those in question which clearly indicate that Irenaeus had *no such notion of Nero as the Beast*:

> But when this Antichrist shall have devastated all things in this world, he will reign for three years and six months, and sit in the temple at Jerusalem; and then the Lord will come from heaven in the clouds, in the glory of the Father, sending this man and those who follow him into the lake of fire; but bringing in for the righteous the times of the kingdom, that is, the rest, the hallowed seventh day; and restoring to Abraham the promised inheritance, in which kingdom the Lord declared, that "many coming from the east and from the west should sit down with Abraham, Isaac, and Jacob."[38]

> A few commentators have suggested that "it was seen" should be translated "he [John] was seen," so that the phrase does not mean the Apocalypse was written during Domitian's time but only that John was seen during Domitian's time. But "the Apocalypse" is the closest antecedent, and the Latin translation of Irenaeus supports this understanding of the clause. The majority of patristic writers and subsequent commentators up to the present understand Irenaeus's words as referring to the time when the Apocalypse "was seen." In the same context, Irenaeus discusses various possible identifications for the number of the "beast" (666). **But he does not entertain the possibility that the beast is to be identified with Nero, and he even rejects the possibility that the beast is to be identified with any Roman emperor at all.** [emphasis added][39]

Here is a man writing approximately 110 years *after the death of Nero* and infinitely closer than us to the culture and events of that time who understands the Beast of Revelation to be *yet future*. No wonder Gentry fails to mention this, because the *full context* of Irenaeus' statement undermines the main thesis of the preterists! Irenaeus understands the Beast to be a future world figure who will reign for a literal three and one-half years (Rev. 11:2; 13:5) and be destroyed *at the Second Coming of Christ* ushering in the *Messianic Kingdom*[5.2.39] (predicted by the *OT*[5.2.51]) upon the earth. Gentry is trying to bend the simple statement of an early church *futurist*[2.12.5] to serve the modern-day *preterist*[2.12.2] agenda.

2.11.4 - Evidence for a Late Date

Having examined the main evidence in support of an early date for the book of Revelation, we turn now to the evidence supporting a late date, near the end of the reign of Domitian (A.D. 95-96).

2.11.4.1 - Internal Evidence for a Late Date

As with the evidence for an early date, we will examine both internal and external evidence. We repeat our previous caution concerning the nature of internal evidence. Most of it is highly subjective and very tentative in nature and should be regarded with a suitably skeptical eye.

2.11.4.1.1 - Changes since the Writing of the Epistles

An entire class of internal evidence falls into the general category of differences which have been noticed between the epistles and the book of Revelation. These differences are thought to provide evidence of a significant span of time between the time the epistles were written and the writing of the book of Revelation. Some of the epistles are thought to have been written near the time of the early date suggested for the book of Revelation (e.g., A.D. 66-67 for 2 Timothy; 67-68 for 2 Peter). If the book of Revelation was written at approximately the same time as the epistles, how do we account for the differences which have been observed?

In the book of Revelation, John writes about the conditions prevailing in the *seven churches*[5.2.66] of Asia. In two of the churches (Ephesians, Laodicea), the conditions described by John seem to differ from that described by the epistles:

> If John wrote Revelation in A.D. 64-67, then the letter to the church at Ephesus in Revelation 2:1-7 overlaps with Paul's two letters to Timothy, who was the pastor of the church when Paul wrote to him. . . . Yet Paul makes no mention of the loss of first love or the presence of the *Nicolaitans*[5.2.47] at Ephesus in his correspondence with Timothy. Neither does he mention these problems in his Ephesian epistle, which was probably written in A.D. 62.[40]

> On the question, *When* the Apocalypse was given, we have a certain amount of implicit evidence here (Rev. 2:4-5), in this reproach with which the Lord reproaches the Ephesian Angel; such as has its value in confirming the ecclesiastical tradition which places it in the reign of Domitian, as against the more modern view which gives the reign of *Nero*[5.2.46] as the date of the composition of this Book. It has well been observed that in St. Paul's Epistle to the Church of Ephesus there are no signs, nor even presentiments, of this approaching spiritual declension with which the great Searcher of hearts upbraids it here. . . . Those who place the Apocalypse in the reign of Nero hardly allow ten years between that condition and this—too brief a period for so great and lamentable a change. It is inconceivable that there should have been such a letting go of first love in so brief a time. . . . Place the Apocalypse under Domitian, and thirty years will have elapsed since St. Paul wrote his Epistle to Ephesus—exactly the interval which we require, exactly the life of a generation. The outlines of the truth are still preserved; but the truth itself is not for a second generation what it was for the first.[41]

Similar changes have been noted in the Laodicean Church:

> The church at Laodicea was the only one of the seven churches (and possibly Sardis) that did not receive any commendations in Revelation 2-3. In his letter to the Colossians, probably written in A.D. 60-62, Paul indicates that the church was an active group (Colossians 4:13). He mentions the church three times in his letter (Col. 2:2; 4:13, 16). It would certainly take more than two to seven years for the church to depart so completely from its earlier acceptable status such that absolutely nothing good could be said about it in Revelation.[42]

Another significant difference between the book of Revelation and the epistles concerns the *Nicolaitans*[4.13]. At the time of the book of Revelation, the Nicolaitans appear to be a well-established and distinct heretical sect with a well-known title. For all their prominence in the letters to the seven churches (Rev. 2:6, 15), absolutely no mention is made of them in the epistles which otherwise spend considerable time warning against heretical tendencies.[43]

Perhaps even more significant is the lack of mention of Paul within the book of Revelation. Paul had a profound and lengthy ministry at Ephesus—the church addressed by one of the letters of the book of Revelation (Rev. 2:1-7). If Paul ministered in Ephesus for almost 3 years beginning in A.D. 52[44]and John wrote within just 12-16 years of Paul's ministry (as held by early date advocates), it seems very unusual that there was not the slightest inference about Paul in any of the letters to the Asian churches. But if John wrote much later, near the end of the 90s, then something more than 40 years would have passed and the generation which saw Paul's ministry would no longer be living.

> Revelation 2:1-7 makes no mention of the great missionary work of Paul in Asia Minor. On his third missionary journey Paul headquartered in Ephesus for three years and had a profound ministry there. If John wrote in A.D. 64-67, then the omission of any mention of Paul in the letters to the seven churches of Asia Minor is inexplicable. However, if John wrote 30 years later to second-generation Christians in the churches, then the omission is easily understood.[45]

2.11.4.1.2 - Emperor Worship

There has been much discussion and disagreement concerning the significance of emperor worship in relation to establishing the date of the book of Revelation. As we mentioned in our discussion of the internal evidence for the early date, there are those who consider the worship of the Roman Emperors to be one of the keys to identifying the *Beast*[5.2.9] of Revelation with *Nero*[5.2.46]. So much so that they understand the events of the book as primarily centering around the Emperor Cult associated with the Roman Caesars, thereby interpreting it to be a veiled political document of John's day.

The primary problem with understanding emperor worship at John's time as a major contributor to dating the book lies in the assumption that much of what is described within the book relates to Rome and the Caesars of that time. But this is not as obvious as some would assume. *First*, the persecutions which the *seven churches*[5.2.66] are said to be undergoing are not *necessarily* a reflection of the emperor cult. *Second*, the association of the Beast with the current emperor of Rome is uncertain. *None* of the Roman emperors are known to have fulfilled the specific predictions set forth by John, unless God be accused of the extensive use of *hyperbole*[5.2.27] throughout the prophecy. In fact, none of the specifics revealed concerning the activities of the Beast can be definitively assigned to any of the Roman emperors. Therefore, it is our feeling that any allusions to emperor worship thought to be in the text are dubious and of only secondary value in establishing a date with any reliability.

The main argument in favor of the late date in relation to emperor worship is found in the belief that at the time of Nero, emperor worship (where the emperor was regarded as god) had not fully come to the fore: "He was not tempted like his predecessors to imagine himself divine, preferring to gain credit for brilliant endowments of a human type. He shrank from the title of *Divus* and the erection of temples in his honour, because they seemed to forebode the approach of death, and Nero loved life better than a shadowy immortality."[46]

At a *later* date, under Domitian, emperor worship is said to have developed more fully,[47] "It is known that Domitian went beyond his predecessor in asserting his own divinity."[48]

> More important for the [dating] issue here is that Nero was not deified, though there is some evidence that he wished to be. However, there was no widespread demand that he be recognized as such. . . . the coins of the 90s prove Domitian's megalomania; they show even his wife was called the mother of the divine Caesar. . . . the *imperial cult*[5.2.31] was apparently much more developed and prominent in Domitian's day than it was in Nero's time.[49]

> Under Nero and his successors down to Domitian, the emperor-cult continued as one of the established religious institutions, but its progress is not signalized by edicts enforcing it, or by notorious persecutions arising from it. It is in the reign of Domitian (81-96) that we reach an insistence upon the cultus more vehement and more threatening for the future. . . . Clement of Rome, contemporary with Domitian, refers to his course in the quite general words 'the sudden and repeated calamities and adversities which have befallen us.'[50]

> We are told by ancient Roman writers that toward the end of Domitian's reign there was more chaos in the cultural and social spheres of the Empire than in any prior time. Furthermore, we are informed that Domitian insisted on greater divine titles than earlier emperors in order to increase his tyrannical hold on the reigns of government. Those refusing to acknowledge these new titles were persecuted.[51]

Whatever the case may be, it is our feeling that the state of emperor worship at the time of John is not a reliable indicator of the date of the book, whether early or late, because it cannot be clearly shown that the events within the book which *appear similar* are in fact *truly related*. Especially given the global and eschatological focus of this last book of the Bible.

2.11.4.1.3 - Other Evidence

A handful of other lines of evidence are seen as supporting the late date.

Some have seen the independent spirit of the Laodicean church in Revelation 3:17 as an allusion to the city's unaided reconstruction after a severe earthquake during the reign of *Nero*[5.2.46].[52]The completion of the reconstruction, undertaken without assistance by Rome, is seen to have required more time than a Neronian date for the book of Revelation.[53]

The mention of opposition to the churches at Smyrna and Philadelphia from "synagogues of Satan" (Rev. 2:9; 3:9) is seen to be more likely under Domitian than Nero. Under the reign of Domitian, Christianity was increasingly no longer viewed as a sect within the umbrella of Judaism, and had the advantage of being a legally-permitted well-established faith. Also, in A.D. 90, a curse was inserted into the synagogue service with the intention of flushing out any believers in Jesus as Messiah.

> An explanation is offered of the 'synagogues of Satan' at Smyrna and Philadelphia (Rev. 2:9; 3:9) which links them with conflicts operative under Domitian. It is further argued that the occasion was provided by the conjunction of that emperor's policy with the insertion of the curse of the Minim in the *Shemoneh 'Esreh* in about AD 90. The aftermath of the controversy may be traced in a problem passage in *Ignatius*[5.2.28] (ad Philad. 8.2) as it affected one of the very churches under discussion.[54]

Although we recognize the weakness of internal evidence in general, we note that Hemer, one of few who has studied the cultural allusions of the book of Revelation in great detail, concludes:

> I started with a provisional acceptance of the orthodox Domitianic dating, and have been confirmed in that view by further study. . . . We accordingly reaffirm the Domitianic date of the letters in the light of the kind of evidence here considered, while recognizing that many of these indications are uncertain. Cumulatively they align themselves with the case widely accepted on other grounds that the Revelation was written about AD 95.[55]

2.11.4.2 - External Evidence for a Late Date

2.11.4.2.1 - Early Testimony

As mentioned previously, a major early testimony to the late date of the book of Revelation is found in the statement by *Irenaeus*[5.2.34] (ca. 130-200) to the effect that John's apocalyptic vision was seen *towards the end of Domitian's reign*:

> We will not, however, incur the risk of pronouncing positively as to the name of *Antichrist*[5.2.3]; for if it were necessary that his name should be distinctly revealed in this present time, it would have been announced by him who beheld the apocalyptic vision. For that was seen no very long time since, but almost in our day, towards the end of Domitian's reign.[56]

As we mentioned above, a straightforward reading of the statement of Irenaeus indicates that it was the *vision*, not *John*, that was seen during the reign of Domitian. *Eusebius*[5.2.19] (b. ca. 260) certainly understood it in that light. "In the *Chronicle*, Eusebius lists these events in the fourteenth year of Domitian: 'Persecution of Christians and under him the apostle John is banished to Patmos and sees his Apocalypse, as Irenaeus mentions.' "[57]

Eusebius also records that "ancient Christian tradition" held that John had been banished under Domitian:

> But after Domitian had reigned fifteen years and Nerva succeeded to the empire, the Roman Senate, according to the writers that record the history of those days, voted that Domitian's honors should be cancelled, and that those who had been unjustly banished should return to their homes and have their property restored to them. It was at this time that the apostle John returned from his banishment in the island and took up his abode in Ephesus, according to an ancient Christian tradition.[58]

It appears that Eusebius drew some of his material from Hegesippus:

> Eusebius says, "After Domitian had reigned fifteen years, Nerva succeeded. The sentences of Domitian were annulled, and the Roman Senate decreed the return of those who had been unjustly banished and the restoration of their property. *Those who committed the story of those times to writing relate it.* At that time, too, the story of ancient Christians relates that the apostle John, after his banishment to the island, took up his abode at Ephesus." The key phrase here is, "Those who committed the story of those times to writing relate it." To whom is Eusebius referring? The context indicates he is referring to Hegesippus, whom he has just referred to twice as a source for his information.[59]

Although there is no doubt that subsequent testimony within the early church was influenced by Irenaeus, nonetheless it will be seen that this view has strong support, which would seem unlikely if a *bona fide* alternate view of an early date also had currency in the early church.

Tertullian[5.2.75] (ca. 160-220) and *Origen*[5.2.50] (ca. 185-254) support the late date.[60] Although they do not specifically say that John was banished by Domitian, Jerome and Eusebius interpreted Tertullian as holding this view:

> While Tertullian [c. A.D. 160-220] does not specifically say that John was banished to Patmos during the reign of Domitian, he is credited by Jerome with doing so. In addition, Eusebius quotes Tertullian's *Apology 5*, which was written in A.D. 197, and then follows with his own statements that reveal he interpreted Tertullian as following the prevailing tradition of placing John's exile under Domitian.[61]

Clement of Alexandria (c. 150-215) in his *Quis Salvus Dives* (*Who Is the Rich Man That Shall Be Saved?*) cites the story handed down of John being removed from Patmos to Ephesus upon the death of "the tyrant." The "tyrant" is likely Domitian rather than *Nero*[5.2.46] because Eusebius cites Clement with Irenaeus as a witness to the Domitian exile.[62]

The late date is attested to by the mid-second century *Acts of John*,[63]and Victorinus (d. ca. 304) who wrote the first commentary on the book of Revelation:

> Victorinus [d. c. A.D. 304], who wrote the first commentary on Revelation . . . at Revelation 10:11 notes: "He says this, because when John said these things he was in the island of Patmos, condemned to labor of the mines by Caesar Domitian. There, therefore, he saw the Apocalypse; and when grown old, he thought that he should at length receive his quittance by suffering, Domitian being killed, all his judgments were discharged. And John being dismissed form the mines, thus subsequently delivered the same Apocalypse which he had received from God." Commenting further upon Revelation 17:10, Victorinus states, "The time must be understood in which the written Apocalypse was published, since then reigned Caesar Domitian."[64]

Jerome, writing around 390, continues the witness of the late date:

> In two places, Jerome stated clearly that John was banished under Domitian. First, in his *Against Jovinianum* (A.D. 393), Jerome wrote that John was "a prophet, for he saw in the island of Patmos, to which he had been banished by the Emperor Domitian as a martyr for the Lord, an Apocalypse containing boundless mysteries of the future." Second, Jerome's most specific statement is found in his *Lives of Illustrious Men*, where he writes about John's banishment: "In the fourteenth year then after Nero, Domitian having raised a second persecution, he was banished to the island of Patmos, and wrote the Apocalypse, on which *Justin Martyr*[5.2.36] and Irenaeus afterwards wrote commentaries."[65]

Although opponents of the late date would have us understand this abundant witness as a single statement by Irenaeus uncritically echoed by those that followed, it stands to reason that if there had been a significant historic witness otherwise, there would necessarily be more indication in the historic record.

2.11.4.2.2 - Nature of Christian Persecution

We discussed previously the bearing which *emperor worship*[2.11.4.1.2] might have as internal evidence on the question at hand. There, we were dealing with a specific form of persecution related to the requirement to worship the Roman Emperor. We treated this as internal evidence because the connection between emperor worship and the description of the *Beast*[5.2.9] and persecution of believers is tentative.

Here we look at persecution *in general* during the time of *Nero*[5.2.46] and Domitian. The connection between generic persecution and the churches of Asia, especially Smyrna, is more definite than that of emperor worship. The letters to the *seven churches*[5.2.66] are clearly written to reflect actual conditions experienced by those churches at the time of writing. Although they say nothing *explicit* in relation to emperor worship, the fact of Christian martyrdom is undeniable (Rev. 2:10, 13).

Beale prefers the later date because of indications that general Christian persecution intensified near the end of the first century:

> The letters in Revelation suggest that Jewish Christians were tempted to escape persecution by seeking some form of identification with Jewish synagogues, which were exempted from emperor worship, and that Gentile Christians were tempted to compromise with trade guild cults and even the emperor cult in order to escape persecution. Such a situation is more likely to have been present toward the end of the first century rather than earlier.[66]

There is even record of Christian persecution involving both execution and exile under Domitian:

> Dio Casius records that Domitian executed the aristocrat Flavious Clemens and banished his wife Flavia Domitilla because of "atheism" (ἀθεότης [*atheotēs*]). . . . Dio's full statement views "atheism" as "a charge on which many others who drifted into Jewish ways were condemned." A similar but later statement affirms that Domitian's persecution was explicitly two-pronged, being directed against "*maiestas* [treason]" or against "adopting the Jewish mode of life." . . . With particular reference to Flavia Domitilla, inscriptions and Christian tradition affirm that she professed Christianity, which would have made her a prime candidate for a charge of "atheism" by those believing in the deity of the emperor.[67]

Beale also notes that evidence is lacking that Nero's persecution of Christians extended beyond Rome to Asia Minor as reflected by the letters to the seven churches there.[68]

The different treatment of Peter and Paul (executed) versus John (banished) is more difficult to explain if all three occurred under Nero's reign:

> Church history consistently testifies that both Peter and Paul were executed in Rome near the end of Nero's reign. *Preterists*[5.2.59] maintain that during this same time the apostle John was banished to Patmos by Nero. Why would Nero execute Peter and Paul and banish John? This seems inconsistent. The different punishments for Peter and Paul as compared with John argue for the fact that they were persecuted under different rulers. Moreover, there is no evidence of Nero's use of banishment for Christians.[69]

Overall, it seems that evidence of Christian persecution in the book of Revelation is more characteristic of the reign of Domitian than that of Nero.

2.11.4.2.3 - The Church at Smyrna

Some have observed that the church at Smyrna may not have existed until almost the time of *Nero*[5.2.46] allowing precious little time for it to have earned a reputation suitable for the commendation given by Christ (Rev. 2:8-11).[70]*Polycarp*[5.2.55], bishop of Smyrna, writing to the Philippians (ca. 110) indicates that the church at Smyrna post-dated Paul's ministry, which is more in keeping with a late date:

> In his letter to the Philippians written in about A.D. 110, Polycarp says that the Smyrnaeans did not know the Lord during the time Paul was ministering. "But I have not observed or heard of any such thing among you, in whose midst the blessed Paul labored, and who were his letters of recommendation in the beginning. For he boasts about you in all the churches—those alone, that is, which at that time had come to know the Lord, **for we had not yet come to know him**." [emphasis added][71]

2.11.4.2.4 - John in Asia

Thomas notes that if John arrived in Asia Minor in the late 60s, the early date must overcome problems of timing:

> A second reason for preferring the later date is the timing of John's arrival in Asia. According to the best information, he did not come to Asia from Palestine before the late 60s, at the time of the Jewish revolt of A.D. 66-70. This was after Paul's final visit to Asia in A.D. 65. . . . A Neronic dating would hardly allow time for him to have settled in Asia, to have replaced Paul as the respected leader of the Asian churches, and then to have been exiled to Patmos before *Nero*[5.2.46]'s death in A.D. 68.[72]

Notes

1 "The book of Revelation has been dated as early as Claudius (AD 41-54) and as late as Trajan (AD 98-117). . . . The majority of scholars place the composition of the Apocalypse either during the reign of Domitian (AD 81-96) or toward the end or immediately after the reign of *Nero*[4.12] (AD 54-68)."—Robert H. Mounce, *The Book of Revelation* (Grand Rapids, MI: William B. Eerdmans Publishing Co., 1977), 31-32.

2 "The early date is especially important to those viewing the main intention of the book as prophecy of the *imminent*[5.2.30] destruction of Jerusalem: interpreters who hold to the early date generally understand the book primarily as a polemic against apostate Jewish faith."—Gregory K. Beale, *The Book of Revelation: A Commentary on the Greek Text* (Grand Rapids, MI: William B. Eerdmans Publishing Co., 1999), 4.

3 "[Gentry] associates cultural defeatism and retreatist pietism with assigning a late date to Revelation and wants to date the book before A.D. 70 so as to have biblical support for the implementation of long-term Christian cultural progress and dominion."—Robert L. Thomas, *"Theonomy and the Dating of Revelation,"* in Richard L. Mayhue, ed., *The Master's Seminary Journal*, vol. 5 (Sun Valley, CA: The Master's Seminary, 1994), 187-188.

4 "Based on the historical evidence, the date, therefore, must be before the death of Domitian, who was assassinated in A.D. 96, as the apostle was apparently released from his exile shortly after this."—John F. Walvoord, *The Revelation of Jesus Christ* (Chicago, IL: Moody Press, 1966), s.v. "Latest Possible Date."

5 Mark Hitchcock, *"The Stake in the Heart—The A.D. 95 Date of Revelation,"* in Tim LaHaye, and Thomas Ice, eds., *The End Times Controversy* (Eugene, OR: Harvest House Publishers, 2003), 124.

6 Hitchcock, "*The Stake in the Heart—The A.D. 95 Date of Revelation*," 123.

7 Hitchcock, "*The Stake in the Heart—The A.D. 95 Date of Revelation*," 125.

8 This is not to deny the influence of bias upon the interpretation of *all* evidence. For example, evolutionists and creationists are faced with the same objective evidence, but arrive at a totally different interpretation of the evidence.

9 Kenneth L. Gentry, *Before Jerusalem Fell: Dating the Book of Revelation* (Atlanta, GA: American Vision, 1998), 113.

10 Colin J. Hemer, *The Letters to the Seven Churches of Asia in Their Local Setting* (Grand Rapids, MI: William B. Eerdmans Publishing Company, 1989), 4.

11 David Chilton, *The Days of Vengeance* (Tyler, TX: Dominion Press, 1987), 4.

12 Jerusalem is mentioned separately from Babylon and Jerusalem is not known to have been referred to as "Babylon" any time prior to A.D. 70. Yet it is *Babylon* which is the object of God's total destruction (Rev. 18), not Jerusalem.

13 Thomas, "*Theonomy and the Dating of Revelation*," 186.

14 Mounce, *The Book of Revelation*, 35.

15 Robert L. Thomas, *"The 'Jesus Crisis': What Is It?,"* in Robert L. Thomas, and F. David Farnell, eds., *The Jesus Crisis: The Inroads of Historical Criticism into Evangelical Scholarship* (Grand Rapids, MI: Kregel Publications, 1998).

16 Chilton, *The Days of Vengeance*, 5.

17 "The text that Jesus cited concerning the *Temple*[5.2.73]"s desecration, Dan. 9:27, predicts that the one who desecrates this Temple will himself be destroyed. By contrast, those who destroyed the temple in A.D. 70 (in fulfillment of Jesus" prediction)—the Roman emperor Vespasian and his son Titus—were not destroyed but returned to Rome in triumph carrying vessels from the destroyed Temple."—Thomas Ice, *"The Great Tribulation is Future,"* in Kenneth L. Gentry, and Thomas Ice, *The Great Tribulation: Past or Future?* (Grand Rapids, MI: Kregel Publications, 1999), 126. "However, if this interpretation is taken [that the abomination of desolation refers to the worship of the Roman standards in the temple precincts], Mtt. 24:16-20 is difficult if not impossible to explain. By then it would be too late for the followers of the Lord Jesus to escape; the Romans had already taken the city by this time. D.A. Carson notes, 'by the time the Romans had actually desecrated the temple in A.D. 70, it was too late for anyone in the city to flee.' "—Ice, "*The Great Tribulation is Future*," 138.

18 Alfred Edersheim, *The Temple: Its Ministry and Services* (Peabody, MA: Hendrickson Publishers, 1994), s.v. "ch. 7."

19 "The name which fits the circumstances most admirably is that of the nefarious Nero Caesar."—Gentry, *Before Jerusalem Fell: Dating the Book of Revelation*, 198.

20 Gentry, *Before Jerusalem Fell: Dating the Book of Revelation*, 168.

21 What is perhaps more significant than John's mention of a Temple is the lack of explicit mention of the destruction of Jerusalem in A.D. 70. Although this may seem unusual, neither is it conclusive evidence of an early date. The destruction of Jerusalem would have been widely known to readers of his day obviating any need to discuss it. Moreover, the major focus of the book involves events of global magnitude preceding the Second Coming of Christ—events which are at least 1900 years beyond the Roman destruction of Jerusalem.

22 Gentry, *Before Jerusalem Fell: Dating the Book of Revelation*, 173.

23 "The twenty-fifth year of the captivity, and the fourteenth year after the city was smitten, i.e., taken and reduced to ashes, are the year 575 before Christ."—Carl Friedrich Keil, and Franz Delitzsch, *Commentary on the Old Testament* (Peabody, MA: Hendrickson, 2002), Eze. 40:1.

24 Hitchcock, "*The Stake in the Heart—The A.D. 95 Date of Revelation*," 140.

25 "When [Zec. 1:16] was written, the Second Temple was still standing so the reference can only be to the rebuilding of the Temple the Romans destroyed in 70 AD." *Israel Today Magazine*, April 2001, 22.

26 Alan F. Johnson, *Revelation: The Expositor's Bible Commentary* (Grand Rapids, MI: Zondervan Publishing House, 1966), 10.

27 How much better to understand the parallel between Paul's church epistles and the seven letters of Revelation

as evidence of common authorship by the Holy Spirit.

28 "Thus it is obvious that James died in the year A.D. 63, for that is the date on the ossuary lid. Which brings us to the very date that Josephus, the great first century historian, said of James, one of the first early church leaders, who was martyred for his faith in A.D. 63. It also agrees with Dr. Luke, author of the book of Acts that describes the scene in Acts 12:2."—LaHaye, *"Newsletter,"* in Thomas Ice, ed., *Pre-Trib Perspectives* (Dallas, TX: Pre-Trib Research Center, January 2003), 2.

29 J. B. Lightfoot, and J. R. Harmer, *The Apostolic Fathers*, 2nd ed. (Grand Rapids, MI: Baker Book House, 1989), 318.

30 "Tradition claims that John had come to Ephesus in A.D. 66. That meant he had been there for nearly thirty years. . . . By A.D. 95, he was an old man—probably in his eighties."—Edward Hindson, *Revelation: Unlocking the Future* (Chattanooga, TN: AMG Publishers, 2002), 20.

31 "*Irenaeus*[5.2.34] and others record that John, the theologian and apostle, survived until the time of Trajan [A.D. 98-117].—*Eusebius*[5.2.19], *Chronicle*"—Lightfoot, *The Apostolic Fathers*, 313.

32 Alexander Roberts, James Donaldson, and A. Cleveland Coxe, *Ante-Nicene Fathers Vol. I* (Oak Harbor, WA: Logos Research Systems, 1997), s.v. "ECF 1.1.7.1.5.31."

33 Philip Schaff, and David Schley Schaff, *History of the Christian Church* (Oak Harbor, WA: Logos Research Systems, 1997, 1916), 1.XII.101.

34 Schaff goes on to state that the internal evidence favors an earlier date,"The internal evidence strongly favors an earlier date between the death of *Nero*[5.2.46] (June 9, 68) and the destruction of Jerusalem (August 10, 70)."—Schaff, *History of the Christian Church*, 1.XII.101., but as we have pointed out, external evidence should take precedence over internal evidence which is subject to greater interpretive bias.

35 Gentry, *Before Jerusalem Fell: Dating the Book of Revelation*, 48-49.

36 Gentry, *Before Jerusalem Fell: Dating the Book of Revelation*, 61.

37 Hitchcock, "*The Stake in the Heart—The A.D. 95 Date of Revelation*," 128-129.

38 Roberts, *Ante-Nicene Fathers Vol. I*, s.v. "ECF 1.1.7.1.5.31."

39 Beale, *The Book of Revelation: A Commentary on the Greek Text*, 20.

40 Hitchcock, "*The Stake in the Heart—The A.D. 95 Date of Revelation*," 146.

41 Richard Chenevix Trench, *Commentary on the Epistles to the Seven Churches in Asia* (Eugene, OR: Wipf and Stock Publishers, 1861), 77.

42 Hitchcock, "*The Stake in the Heart—The A.D. 95 Date of Revelation*," 148.

43 "The Nicolaitan party, of which there is no certain trace in the Epistles of St. Paul, is now widely distributed and firmly rooted."—Henry Barclay Swete, *The Apocalypse of St. John* (Eugene, OR: Wipf and Stock Publishers, 1998, 1906), cxvii. "The existence of a distinct heretical sect with the well-known title, the Nicolaitans, presupposes some distance in time from the apostolic epistles (in which they are not even hinted at)."—Mounce, *The Book of Revelation*, 34.

44 "Leaving Corinth in the spring of A.D. 52, Paul paid a brief visit to Palestine and then traveled overland to Ephesus, chief city of the province of Asia, which he made his base for the next phase of his activity, lasting nearly three years (Acts 20:31)."—F. F. Bruce, *"Paul the Apostle,"* in Geoffrey W. Bromiley, ed., *International Standard Bible Encyclopedia* (Grand Rapids, MI: William B. Eerdmans Publishing Co., 1979, 1915), 3:716.

45 Hitchcock, "*The Stake in the Heart—The A.D. 95 Date of Revelation*," 147.

46 Swete, *The Apocalypse of St. John*, lxxxiv.

47 Yet not all agree. David Aune, writing in the forward to Hemer states: "Hemer affirms the historicity of "the Domitianic persecution," though scholarship during the last twenty-five years has shown that an official and empire-wide persecution under the reign of Domitian has no firm historical basis but was in fact a Christian legend which reached full-blown form with *Eusebius*[5.2.19] of Caesarea in the early fourth century AD."—Hemer, *The Letters to the Seven Churches of Asia in Their Local Setting*, xviii.

48 Swete, *The Apocalypse of St. John*, lxxxii.

49 Grant R. Osborne, *Revelation* (Grand Rapids, MI: Baker Academic, 2002), 6-7.

50 Isbon T. Beckwith, *The Apocalypse of John* (Eugene, OR: Wipf and Stock Publishers, 2001), 200,204.

51 Beale, *The Book of Revelation: A Commentary on the Greek Text*, 5.

52 "The city of Laodicea was destroyed by an earthquake in A.D. 17 in the reign of Tiberius (A.D. 14-37) and again in A.D. 60 when Nero was emperor (A.D. 54-68)."—Mal Couch, *"Interpreting the Book of Revelation,"* in Mal Couch, ed., *A Bible Handbook to Revelation* (Grand Rapids, MI: Kregel Publications, 2001), 52.

53 "Rev. 3:17 has been connected with Laodicea's unaided recovery from the earthquake of Nero's reign . . . but I argue the strong probability that the reference is to a later stage of reconstruction, mentioned in the earlier *Sibylline Oracles* (4.108 of about AD 80), and occupying a full generation between the disaster and the time of Domitian."—Hemer, *The Letters to the Seven Churches of Asia in Their Local Setting*, 4.

54 Hemer, *The Letters to the Seven Churches of Asia in Their Local Setting*, 4.

55 Hemer, *The Letters to the Seven Churches of Asia in Their Local Setting*, 5,3.

56 Roberts, *Ante-Nicene Fathers Vol. I*, s.v. "ECF 1.1.7.1.5.31."

57 Hitchcock, "*The Stake in the Heart—The A.D. 95 Date of Revelation*," 134.

58 Hitchcock, "*The Stake in the Heart—The A.D. 95 Date of Revelation*," 134.

59 Hitchcock, "*The Stake in the Heart—The A.D. 95 Date of Revelation*," 127.

60 "Clement of Alexandria, Tertullian, and Origen all support the late date, but . . . they don't specifically say that John was banished by Domitian."—Hitchcock, "*The Stake in the Heart—The A.D. 95 Date of Revelation*," 138.

61 Hitchcock, "*The Stake in the Heart—The A.D. 95 Date of Revelation*," 123.

62 Hitchcock, "*The Stake in the Heart—The A.D. 95 Date of Revelation*," 123.

63 "The *apocryphal*[5.2.5] book *The Acts of John* clearly states that John wrote the book of Revelation on Patmos during Domitian's reign."—Gordon Franz, *"Was 'Babylon' Destroyed when Jerusalem Fell in A.D. 70?,"* in Tim LaHaye, and Thomas Ice, eds., *The End Times Controversy* (Eugene, OR: Harvest House Publishers, 2003), 222.

64 Hitchcock, "*The Stake in the Heart—The A.D. 95 Date of Revelation*," 133.

65 Hitchcock, "*The Stake in the Heart—The A.D. 95 Date of Revelation*," 135.

66 Beale, *The Book of Revelation: A Commentary on the Greek Text*, 13.

67 Beale, *The Book of Revelation: A Commentary on the Greek Text*, 6-7,9.

68 "There is no evidence that Nero's persecution of Christians in Rome extended also to Asia Minor, where the churches addressed in the Apocalypse are located."—Beale, *The Book of Revelation: A Commentary on the Greek Text*, 12.

69 Hitchcock, "*The Stake in the Heart—The A.D. 95 Date of Revelation*," 149.

70 "As suggested by many commentators, the very existence of the church at Smyrna suggests a later date, since it is possible that the church was not even established until 60-64 A.D."—Beale, *The Book of Revelation: A Commentary on the Greek Text*, 17.

71 Hitchcock, "*The Stake in the Heart—The A.D. 95 Date of Revelation*," 147.

72 Robert L. Thomas, *Revelation 1-7* (Chicago, IL: Moody Press, 1992), 22.

2.12 - Systems of Interpretation

We now arrive at the *major fork in the road* in understanding the book of Revelation. If you have traveled with us thus far, you are aware of various factors which influence how one understands this last book of the Bible. We've discussed how *anti-supernaturalism*[2.5] and categorizing the book as *apocryphal genre*[2.6] can contribute toward a tendency to see the book as *hyperbole*[5.2.27] or a veiled political document. We've also discussed the importance of how *symbols are interpreted*[2.7] and *the importance of meaning*[2.7.1] for a proper *interpretation*[2.7.2] to result. We also mentioned attacks upon the authority of the book by way of questioning its *apostolic authorship*[2.9] and *acceptance into the canon*[2.10]. All of these aspects are brought together in the topic at hand: the various systems of interpretation through which the text of the book is understood.

Ice identifies the major approaches to interpreting prophecy which are typically found when studying the book of Revelation:

> There are four approaches to interpreting prophecy, and all related to time: past, present, future, and timeless. These are known as *preterism*[2.12.2] (past), *historicism*[2.12.4] (present), *futurism*[2.12.5] (future), and *idealism*[2.12.3] (timeless).[1]

We would add a fifth approach known as *eclectic*[2.12.6] (mixed).

Systems of Interpretation Compared

Name	Time Period	Revelation Chapters 4-19
Preterism[2.12.2]	past	Describes the destruction of Jerusalem in A.D. 70 or the fall of Rome in A.D. 476.
Historicism[2.12.4]	present	Describes major events of Christian history spanning from John's time to the Second Coming of Christ.
Futurism[2.12.5]	future	Describes a future period prior to the Second Coming of Christ.
Idealism[2.12.3]	timeless	Describes spiritual truths. Good will eventually prevail over evil. Readers are encouraged in their current trials.
Ecclectic[2.12.6]	mixed	Typically favors idealism while borrowing some elements from other systems.

Each "system of interpretation" approaches the text with a different set of presuppositions and necessarily derives a *different* understanding of the meaning conveyed by the book. Here is the source of the primary "confusion" over the book and why so many despair of grasping its contents. Not only are there a number of major interpretive systems applied to the book, but within each system there is a certain amount of variation in understanding the secondary features of the text. The amount of interpretive variation *within* each interpretive system ranges from relatively little (futurist) to large and substantial (historicist, idealist, eclectic).[2]

In keeping with the previously stated *Golden Rule of Interpretation*[5.2.24], we believe that the *Futurist Interpretation*[2.12.5] is the correct approach to understanding the book of Revelation. It results in the most consistent understanding among practitioners of any one system and has the benefit of being applicable across the entire body of Scripture from Genesis to Revelation. It also has the advantage of being the normal way most people read throughout the day and is as equally applicable to understanding a breakfast menu as an owner's manual for an automobile.

When we use literal interpretation, we retain the eschatological worldview of the contemporaries of Jesus and the New Testament:

> The Dead Sea Scrolls offer to us a window into the eschatological worldview of Jesus and the New

> Testament. **Their eschatology followed a literal interpretation of prophetic texts** and a numerological calculation of temporal indicators in judgment and pronouncements, and understood a postponement of the final age, while not abandoning their hope of it. In many ways their eschatology was not dissimilar from modern Christian *premillennialism*[5.2.58] and reveals that as a system of interpretation, premillennialism is more closely aligned to the first-century Jewish context than competing eschatological systems. [emphasis added][3]

Our treatment of the book will make mention of alternative interpretations at important junctures, but to attempt to mention them all would only lead to hopeless confusion and a commentary spanning thousands of pages which might never be completed! "It is nearly impossible to consider all the interpretive options offered by people holding the other three views."[4]

Nevertheless, it is important to understand each of the popular systems in order to grasp how widely different results can be derived from the identical text.

2.12.1 - The Importance of Interpretation

The importance of having an objective guide to interpret the text can be seen in the following comments of Gregg who has taught the book of Revelation over a considerable period of time. "Over the next decade, I found myself favoring first one view and then another as I became aware of the merits of each."[5] "Revelation was written to be understood and to confer a blessing upon its readers, . . . Some readers may be curious about my own approach to the book of Revelation. It is not my desire to showcase my own opinions (**which have changed a number of times and may do so again in the future**) . . . " [emphasis added][6]

When those who purport to guide the inexperienced shift between the major interpretive views, is it any wonder many despair of ever understanding this book? The adverse effects of a waffling teacher upon his students is surely one of the reasons why teachers will receive greater judgment (Jas. 3:1). "Many are told that scholars themselves are woefully divided as to the meaning of this prophecy. And if godly men who study God's Word cannot figure out its meaning, how can the average Christian? With such a comprehensive and interpretive mountain to climb, Revelation unfortunately remains a closed book to many people."[7]

If experienced teachers are so unsure about how to approach the text that they admit they may be teaching quite different conclusions to the next batch of students who follow their guidance, how valuable can such guidance be in the first place? Such an approach denies the perspicuity of Scripture and the stated intention God gives for the book (Rev. 1:1, 3)!

Gregg's words above underscore the importance of being consistent in one's system of interpretation. If one is unsure about the principles underlying how to read and understand the text, then confusion and lack of conviction are sure to be the result. This can hardly result in the blessing promised by God (Rev. 1:3).

Since every interpreter makes a commitment, implicitly if not explicitly, to a particular system of interpretation, it is important to recognize errors which result when any one of the systems is taken to an unbiblical extreme:

> A return to the Biblical text is the only recourse in this strife of opposing theories. The truth in each [interpretive system] is drawn from its accord with the statements of Revelation; the error in each arises from an overextension of the truth or from an exaggeration of some one interest.[8]

In the treatment of interpretive systems which follows, considerably more space is devoted to describing the *preterist*[5.2.59] system. Although it is our view that only the futurist interpretation properly reflects the intended meaning of the text and that the other views are to be faulted in their departure from literal *hermeneutics*[5.2.26], we spend extra time on preterism because of its seeming rise in popularity at the time of our writing. It is our hope to expose the major shortcomings of the approach so that some who might have been swayed by its teachings are better able to discern the dangers.

For an excellent chart by Daniel Atkin, Robert Sloan, and Craig Blaising summarizing and comparing the views of the different interpretive systems with respect to the book of Revelation, see [Trent C.

Butler, Chad Brand, Charles Draper, and Archie England, eds., *Broadman and Holman Illustrated Bible Dictionary* (Nashville, TN: Broadman and Holman Publishers, 2003), s.v. "Revelation"].

2.12.2 - Preterist Interpretation

The term "*preterism*[5.2.59]" is based on the Latin *preter*, which means "past." Preterism understands certain eschatological passages which are yet future as having *already been fulfilled.* All biblical interpreters understand that certain prophecies have been fulfilled, but preterists differ in that they interpret a greater portion of Scripture as already having come to pass. There are different types of preterism resulting from differences in views as to which passages have been fulfilled and what events they were "fulfilled" by.

2.12.2.1 - Types of Preterism

Mild or *partial preterism*[5.2.59] holds that most of the prophecies of Revelation were fulfilled in either the fall of Jerusalem (A.D. 70) or the fall of the Roman Empire (A.D. 476), but the Second Coming of Christ is yet future. This form of preterism is orthodox and is the most frequent view encountered in our day.

> Moderate preterism has become, in our day, mainstream preterism. Today it appears to be the most widely held version of preterism. Simply put, moderates see almost all prophecy as fulfilled in the A.D. 70 destruction of Jerusalem, but they also believe that a few passages still teach a yet future second coming (Acts 1:9-11; 1Cor. 15:51-53; 1Th. 4:16-17) and the resurrection of believers at Christ's bodily return. . . . In addition to R.C. Sproul, some well-known moderate preterists include Kenneth L. Gentry, Jr., Gary DeMar, and the late David Chilton (who converted to full preterism after all his books were published).[10]

Full, *extreme*, or *consistent* preterism holds that all the prophecies of Revelation are already fulfilled, that we are currently living spiritually in the "new heavens and new earth" and denies a future bodily return of Jesus. Full or consistent preterism is heretical.

> Extreme or full preterists view themselves as "consistent" preterists. . . . Extreme preterists believe that "the second coming MUST HAVE already occurred, since it was one of the things predicted in the O.T. which had to be fulfilled by the time Jerusalem was destroyed" . . . This means there will never be a future second coming, for it already occurred in A. D. 70. Further, there will be no bodily resurrection of believers, which is said to have occurred in A.D. 70 in conjunction with the second coming. Full preterists believe that we now have been spiritually resurrected and will live forever with spiritual bodies when we die. . . . Full preterists say . . . we are now living in what we would call the eternal state or the new heavens and new earth of Revelation 21-22. Champions of this view include the originator of full preterism,. . . J. Stuart Russell . . . Max R. King and his son, Tim . . . David Chilton . . . Ed Stevens, Don K. Preston, John Noe, and John L. Bray.[11]

Although mild (partial) preterism is considered orthodox, full (extreme, consistent) preterism denies the bodily Second Coming of Christ and so is outside of orthodoxy. While one is most likely to encounter the mild preterist view in reading commentaries on the book of Revelation, one should be aware of the tendency of mild or partial preterism to develop into full or consistent preterism, thus crossing the line between orthodoxy and heresy. "Extreme preterism is sometimes known as 'consistent preterism' because it consistently applies the principles of preterism to all prophecy. If moderate preterists were consistent, they unavoidably would be extreme preterists, and would have to deny the reality of the eternal state."[12]

Since full (extreme, consistent) preterism is heretical and less frequently encountered, we will focus primarily upon mild (moderate, partial) preterism which seems to be increasingly popular in our day.

In its approach to the book of Revelation, partial preterism divides into two primary views concerning what events are foretold by the book: "Preterists hold that the major prophecies of the book were fulfilled either in the fall of Jerusalem (AD 70) or the fall of Rome (AD 476)."[13] "The second form of preterist interpretation holds that Revelation is a prophecy of the fall of the Roman Empire, 'Babylon the Great,' the persecutor of the saints, in the fifth century A.D. The purpose of the book is to encourage Christians to endure because their persecutors assuredly will be judged."[14]

2.12.2.2 - The Motivations of Preterism

Although all *preterists*[5.2.59] insist that their view of Scripture is the best way to understand and explain the text, it is useful to understand that some preterists are influenced in their tendency to interpret future passages as having been already fulfilled by a variety of motives. One motive is to respond to the criticism of skeptics who have pointed out that Jesus' promises to come *soon* have not yet materialized. Preterists believe that their view that Jesus has come in a "spiritual way" prior to A.D. 70 vindicates the Bible in the eyes of such skeptics (e.g., Bertrand Russell). But tailoring interpretation to favor non-believers is unlikely to win them to Christ.

> Do preterists think that Bertrand Russell, or anyone else who is antagonistic to the Christian faith, is going to be convinced that the Bible is God's Word by arguing that Jesus came in A.D. 70? A preterist coming [of Christ] is a pathetic coming. It does no honor. . . to the integrity of Scripture. The substitutionary atonement of Christ, the Trinitarian nature of the Godhead, and many other [doctrines], are all truths that come from Scripture, but also truths that invite the attack of agnostics, atheists, humanists, and secularists. Why is it, when we come to prophecy, that suddenly we must tailor our interpretation to suit non-believers?[15]

As we have previously mentioned, there is also the motivation to remove what appears to be a coming global judgment out of the path of Christian reconstructionism and dominion. How are Christians to be motivated to convert the governmental institutions of the world through political action if the book of Revelation, understood in a normal way, seems to describe an unparalleled time of persecution and global catastrophe in divine response by God to global apostasy on the part of the nations?

> [Gentry] associates cultural defeatism and retreatist pietism with assigning a late date to Revelation and wants to date the book before A.D. 70 so as to have biblical support for the implementation of long-term Christian cultural progress and dominion. This probably reflects his basic motivation for the early dating of Revelation: a desire for an undiluted rationale to support Christian social and political involvement.[16]

If it is not practical to undermine the authority of the book, then the next best thing is to reinterpret its teachings in a way which sweeps its predictive revelation aside. This is accomplished within preterism by moving the future back to the past.[17]

But how could what appears to be a global time of unparalleled trouble (Dan. 12:1; Jer. 30:7; Mtt. 24:21; Mark 13:19; Rev. 3:10; 7:14) be moved from the future to the past? The way preterism accomplishes this shift is to explain that the book's description of a coming time of tribulation involving *Babylon* and the *earth dwellers*[5.2.18] is actually a veiled description of God's wrath being poured out on *Jerusalem* and the *Jews* in the destruction of Jerusalem by Rome in A.D. 70.

> The Preterist will be glad to remind the futurist that the opening verses of Revelation chapter one indicate a first-century fulfillment: "The Revelation of Jesus Christ, which God gave unto him, to shew unto his servants things which must *shortly come to pass*. . . for the time *is at hand* " (Rev. 1:1, 3). For the preterist, the book of Revelation was written around A.D. 68 and it has the same focus as the Olivet Discourse: some impending disaster in the immediate future that will affect the ancient Roman world. What might that be? Preterists unanimously point to the destruction of Jerusalem in A.D. 70.[18]

The events of the book are understood as describing this time period, localized to the events of Rome and the Mediterranean, and during which *Nero*[5.2.46] (most commonly) occupies the role of the *Beast*[5.2.9] of Revelation 13. In the destruction of Jerusalem, the Jewish state finds its ultimate judgment and complete rejection while the blessings of the kingdom are transferred to the "New Israel," the Church. Never mind that John uses completely different terms to describe the primary recipients of God's wrath, the preterist manages to maneuver Israel into place as the recipient of God's judgment. " 'The preterist perspective . . . sees . . . Babylon the Great' represent[ing] apostate Israel, who aids Rome in oppressing Christians. Accordingly, part of the purpose of the book is to encourage Christians that their Jewish persecutors will be judged for their apostasy and to assure the readers that they are now the true Israel."[19] The preterist identifies the Beast of Revelation with pagan Rome which Daniel sees as the object of final judgment, but then insists that it is *apostate Israel* that is the focus of God's judgment in the book of Revelation.[20]

Although many preterists are devout, conservative, and orthodox in their views, the preterist system of interpretation has also attracted liberal and neo-orthodox interpreters who tend to view the Scriptures as a textbook for sociological progress and minimize its supernatural and judgmental elements.[21]

In summary, preterism is often fueled by several underlying motivations: *First*, a desire to move the time of tribulation described by the book of Revelation from the future into the past. This removes a major stumbling block to the view of *Dominion Theology*[5.2.17] as embraced by Christian reconstructionists that all the world's institutions will eventually come under the sway of Christianity through the worldwide dissemination and progression of the gospel. *Second*, a desire to reinterpret the many passages in both *OT*[5.2.51] and *NT*[5.2.48] which speak of a future time of restoration and blessing involving the *nation* Israel as applying to the Church. Israel's rejection of Messiah Jesus is seen as an irrecoverable error necessitating the replacement of Israel by the Church as the spiritual inheritor of previous promises to Israel.[22] *Third*, an attempt to interpret Scripture in a way which minimizes the objections of skeptics. *Fourth*, a desire on the part of more liberal preterists to avoid taking predictive prophesy as supernatural and descriptive of events to come.

2.12.2.3 - The Beginning of Preterism

As will become evident in our discussion of the *futurist system of interpretation*[2.12.5], the early church was not *preterist*[5.2.59] in its outlook.

> Dr. Henry Alford summarized the early history of preterism this way: "The Praeterist view found no favour, and was hardly so much as thought of, in the times of primitive Christianity. Those who lived near the date of the book itself had no idea that its groups of prophetic imagery were intended merely to describe things then passing, and to be in a few years completed."[23]

Justin Martyr[5.2.36] (c. 100-165), who would have been in a position to know believers who had lived through the events of *Nero*[5.2.46] and the fall of Jerusalem, knows nothing of preterism:

> Justin Martyr . . . certainly knew many believers who had lived through the events of A.D. 70. He also clearly regarded the second coming of Christ as a future event. . . . Justin, who could not have written much more than fifty years after the destruction of Jerusalem, still saw a **future fulfillment** of both the Tribulation prophecies and the return of Christ in glory. [emphasis added][24]

The *Didache* or *Teaching of the Twelve* (dated as early as A.D. 70 or soon thereafter) evidences a futurist interpretation of the Olivet Discourse, one of the favorite passages frequently used in support of the preterist view.[25]

Most cite the Spanish Jesuit Alcasar, who died in 1614, as the first real preterist.[26]Even then, his development of a preterist interpretation is seen to be in response to the Reformers having identified Babylon with the Roman church and a need to provide an alternative understanding:

> [Alcazar's] work was not free from controversial bias. The Reformers had identified Babylon with the Roman church, and had succeeded in making the Revelation a powerful controversial weapon in their favor. In order to offset this interpretation, Alcazar attempted to show that Revelation **had no application to the future**. [emphasis added][27]

Tenney puts his finger on the heart-beat of preterism. The same motivation fueled Alcasar as modern preterists: a desire to show that what God appears to have predicted concerning the future is in fact not coming upon the earth. It is our conviction that preterism is helping to lay the groundwork to undermine the predictions of the book of Revelation so that a future apostate Church lacks an understanding of the anti-Christ role it occupies prior to His return.

It seems that the further we get from the events of John's day, the more popular it becomes to understand events of his day as having "fulfilled" the predictions of the book of Revelation. But what is especially troubling about this trend is that evidence seems totally lacking that those much closer to the events and culture of John's day had any notion of the preterist perspective:[28]

> If the preterist contention that the prophecies of the Olivet Discourse and Revelation were fulfilled in the first century is true, then why is there no evidence that the early church understood these prophecies in this way? . . . There is zero indication, from known, extant writings, that anyone understood the New Testament prophecies from a preterist perspective.[29]

2.12.2.4 - Hermeneutics of Preterism

Although a full discussion of the *hermeneutics*[5.2.26] of *preterism*[5.2.59] is beyond the scope of our purpose here, it is helpful to understand some key aspects concerning how preterists approach the interpretation of Scripture in general, and the book of Revelation in particular.

The hermeneutics of preterism places great emphasis on all passages which convey the notion of "soon" or could be understood as teaching that certain events should have occurred near to the time of the New Testament.

The preterist system of interpretation involves a "slippery slope" where some so-called "time texts" are said to have already been fulfilled (Rev. 1:3; 2:16; 3:11), whereas other equivalent time texts are left as possibly future (e.g., Rev. 22:20). The "slippery slope" begins with mild preterism, and leads toward full (extreme) preterism which denies the Second Coming of Christ (heresy). The basic tension preterism has is if *some* of the passages which state that Jesus'coming is "near" *must* indicate His return within the generation that heard these statements, then why not *all* such passages? Yet if this view is applied to all such passages consistently (the view of *consistent preterism*), then passages such as Revelation 22:20, "Surely, I am coming quickly," which an overwhelming number of commentators hold to refer to His physical, bodily return, must also have been fulfilled and so all of Jesus' promises about His Second Coming must have *already occurred.* The problem here is that the preterist approach denies the doctrine of *imminency*[5.2.30]. (See our discussion of *Imminency*[4.8].)

Preterists believe in the doctrine of imminency, but deny that passages which teach the any-moment return of Christ have in view His literal Second Coming. "Our study of the New Testament is drastically off-course if we fail to take into account the apostolic expectation of an imminent Coming of Christ (not the Second Coming) which would destroy 'this generation' of Israel and fully establish the New Covenant Church."[30] But Scripture teaches that the any-moment coming of Jesus is not just a symbolic "cloud coming" of preterism which is neither discernible by the skeptical world nor by His Church,[31] rather, He may come at any moment *to gather the Church to Himself* (John 14:1-3; 1Th. 4:13-18; 1Cor. 15:51-53).

So one thing to notice concerning the hermeneutics of mild preterism is its inconsistent treatment of passages concerning the coming of Christ. It tends to place as many Second Coming passages in the past as possible, taking care not to post-date passages which are especially germane to Christ's bodily Second Coming and risk falling into the heresy of full preterism. This is what happened with the late David Chilton. His commentary on the book of Revelation, written while a mild preterist, takes Revelation 22:6-7 as having been fulfilled in the first-century.[32]Eventually he came to believe that all Second Coming passages found their fulfillment in the first century and became a full preterist, denying a future bodily return of Christ.

> It seems that more and more preterists are becoming hyperpreterists. . . . [mild preterism's view] opens the door for people to move into the heretical position of hyper-preterism. . . . we have already seen the late David Chilton take this route. Walt Hibbard, the former owner of Great Christian Books (previously known as Puritan and Reformed Book Company), once a reconstructionist, moved from partial to full preterism. . . . Once a person accepts the basic tenets of preterism, it is hard to stop and resist the appeal to preterize all Bible prophecy.[33]

> Most preterists stop short of allegorizing away the bodily return of Christ (the error of *hyper*-preterism). But it is frankly hard to see how any preterist could ever give a credible refutation of hyper-preterism from Scripture, given the fact that the hermeneutical approach underlying both views is identical. Hyper-preterists simply apply the preterist method more consistently to *all* New Testament prophecy.[34]

The preterist interpreter views all prophetic passages through a set of glasses which *require* that nearly all time indicators such as "soon," "quickly," "near," "at hand," etc. be understood as having had a first century fulfillment. As we mentioned above, for the preterist who holds to a yet future literal bodily return of Christ, there are at least *some* passages concerning His return which do not have a first-century fulfillment (e.g., Rev. 22:20). The problem for the preterist then becomes one of determining which passages teach an imminent return which he will allow to stretch out for nearly 2000 years like the futurist, and which to assert as being already fulfilled by a non-physical *cloud coming* of Christ. For wherever a "time text" is associated with the return of Jesus which the preterist believes *requires* a first-century fulfillment, an invisible, spiritual coming of Christ "must" have occurred. But this gets tricky because non-literal, invisible "comings" are a dime a dozen—being impossible to objectively validate since there are no witnesses.[35] Here is the Achilles Heel of the preterist hermeneutic: when and when not to "go spiritual" in understanding a passage.

While the initial dilemma is restricted mostly to Second Coming passages, it soon extends outward to a myriad of prophetic predictions because in order to find a first-century fulfillment to the many details which Scripture has revealed as yet future, the preterist is forced into searching historic documents in a sort of "newspaper exegesis after-the-fact" to find *some* event or persona who has a similarity to the Scriptural text.

> Preterists search first century "newspapers" to see what events fit in with their scheme of first-century fulfillment. Though futurists are often charged with practicing "newspaper exegesis," preterists are the real masters of the art. Interestingly, for the preterist, the closer we move to the time of the Lord's physical return, the *farther* we get from the events they believe are indicated in the book of Revelation.[36]

Sometimes a similar event or persona is found, although never one that fulfills the *details* of the text for a careful reader. Other times the record of history is unable to produce. This eventuates a symbolic interpretation or spiritualization of the text because some prophetic events are completely lacking a first-century analog. Thus enters another characteristic of preterist interpretation: a flipping back and forth between taking the text literally or symbolically:

> The biggest problem with the preterist position is the lack of consistent hermeneutics. They work hard to find historical evidence of [literal] prophetic fulfillment in the destruction of Jerusalem in A.D. 70. Any time an event described in a prophecy cannot be linked to an actual historical event, preterists immediately resort to a symbolic interpretation of the text. . . . What are the criteria for taking something literally? When does something become symbolic?[37]

> Preterists are inconsistent when they interpret Revelation's numbers. On the one hand, they interpret the numbers 42 (Revelation 13:5), 666 (Revelation 13:8), and 1, 5, and 7 (Revelation 17:10) in a straightforward, literal fashion. On the other hand, preterists contend that the numbers 1,000, 12,000, and 144,000 are purely symbolic.[38]

The preterist hermeneutic is like a vehicle with two gears. The route along the text proceeds in first gear (literal interpretation) until a "bump" appears in the road (lack of historic fulfillment). Then the preterist shifts to second gear (symbolic or figurative interpretation) to get over the bump before dropping back into first gear.

Since preterism sees almost all of the book of Revelation as having already been fulfilled in the past, it holds that nearly the entire book is focused solely on the readership of John's day.[39]One wonders how many first-time readers of the book of Revelation who arrive without any special bias would reach the following conclusion of preterism?

> **The Book of Revelation is not about the Second Coming of Christ.** It is about the destruction of Israel and Christ's victory over His enemies in the establishment of the New Covenant Temple. In fact, as we shall see, the word *coming* as used in the book of Revelation never refers to the Second Coming. Revelation prophesies the judgment of God on apostate Israel. [emphasis added][40]

2.12.2.5 - Damaging God's Word

There are so many problems and dangers associated with *preterism*[5.2.59], it is difficult to know how to enumerate them. Here we will touch on our main concerns regarding this system of interpretation and the damage it does to God's Word:

1. **A Denial of Predictive Prophecy** - Preterism removes the capstone of God's written revelation. The last book of the Bible no longer includes information covering the entire sway of history through the physical Second Coming of Christ, but has largely spent its significance as a historical document concerning events over 1900 years ago involving Rome and Israel. All that remains is a hazy notion that somehow the eternal state must be what we are experiencing on earth now.[41]
2. **A Denial of Global Judgment** - Preterism localizes the book of Revelation making it nearly impossible to see how God *could* have described events truly global and future if that *had*

been His intent.[42]

3. **A Denial of Reality** - If we are in the new heavens and new earth of Revelation 21-22 as preterists would have us believe, then Scripture means nothing. Either that, or we need to begin embracing a dualistic view of reality which denies our common senses, similar to that of Christian Science. The transition set forth in the creation of a new heavens and a new earth and a complete removal of the curse of Genesis is simply not evident to any objective observer. If this is the new heavens, Jesus was a charlatan.[43] Moreover, it would be news to most people in the world that the decisive victory of Satan portrayed in the book of Revelation has already been accomplished.[44]
4. **A Blurring of *Canonical*[5.2.12] Boundaries** - Preterism majors on searching first-century non-canonical writings for "fulfillments" to predictive prophecy. The results are predictable. Teaching and writing by preterists invariably draws almost as heavily from non-canonical writings (the "fulfillments") as Scripture (the predictions). We have witnessed the effects of this blurring of the boundary of the canon firsthand, especially on new untaught believers. The result is the elevation of faulty historic writings and the denigration of *inerrant*[5.2.32] Scripture. There is also the danger of pointing inexperienced believers to errant and uninspired *apocryphal*[5.2.5] and historical writings as the main diet in the place of God's Holy Word.[45]
5. **A Denial of the *Imminent*[5.2.30] Second Coming** - As more and more passages dealing with Christ's return are interpreted as first-century "cloud comings," the imminent expectation of His Second Coming, so central to the expectation of the New Testament, fades. Commenting on the writing of commentaries, preterist Chilton observes, "Indeed, if my eschatology is correct, **the Church has many more years left** to write many more words!" [emphasis added][46] So much for an expectation of the imminent return of our Lord!

2.12.3 - Idealist Interpretation

Mounce and Osborne provide a good summary of the idealist approach to interpreting the book of Revelation

> Its proponents hold that Revelation is not to be taken in reference to any specific events at all but as an expression of those basic principles on which God acts throughout history. . . . The idealist approach continues the allegorical interpretation which dominated exegesis throughout the medieval period and still finds favor with those inclined to minimize the historical character of the coming consummation. . . . Its weakness lies in the fact that it denies to the book any specific historical fulfillment.[47]

> This popular approach argues that the symbols do not relate to historical events but rather to timeless spiritual truths. . . . As such, it relates primarily to the church between the advents, that is, between Christ's first and second comings. Thus it concerns the battle between God and evil and between the church and the world at all times in church history. . . . The millennium in this approach is not a future event but the final cycle of the book . . . describing the church age.[48]

By employing allegorical interpretation, the book is reduced to a symbolic exhibition of good versus evil. "The more moderate form of allegorical interpretation, following Augustine, . . . regards the book of Revelation as presenting in a symbolic way the total conflict between Christianity and evil or, as Augustine put it, the City of God versus the City of Satan."[49]

Idealists have much in common with *preterists*[5.2.59] in that they avoid an understanding of the book of Revelation which would seem to be describing future events. Here again, there is an overemphasis on the readers of John's day, as if the book were only written to describe historic events of their time and hold devotional value for those that follow:

> Its flaw is not so much in what it affirms as in what it denies. Many idealists could be classed as preterists, since they hold that the imagery of the Apocalypse is taken from its immediate world, and that the prevailing conditions of Domitian's reign are reflected in the symbolic episodes that fill its pages. They refuse to assign to them any literal historical significance for the future, and they deny all predictive prophecy except in the most general sense of the ultimate triumph of righteousness. "The

problem with this alternative is that it holds that Revelation does not depict any final consummation to history, whether in God's final victory or in a last judgment of the realm of evil."[5150]

Idealist Calkins summarizes idealism in five propositions:

> 1) It is an irresistible summons to heroic living. 2) The book contains matchless appeals to endurance. 3) It tells us that evil is marked for overthrow *in the end.* 4) It gives us a new and wonderful picture of Christ. 5) The Apocalypse reveals to us the fact that history is in the mind of God and in the hand of Christ as the author and reviewer of the moral destinies of men.[52]

Thus, the capstone of biblical revelation, chock full of self-proclaimed prophetic relevance, is reduced to something akin to a devotional.[53]

Idealism also suffers from an inconsistency of interpretation where small sections are interpreted literally, but then the interpreter reverts back to symbolism and allegory. There is no clear or consistent means for determining when this shift should occur. A fundamental mistake is made when the fact that John is receiving revelation *through* a series of visions is seen as license to hold that John's communication is something less than logically coherent.

> They have John in a sort of "dream world" until their personally contrived formula has him revert to a literal mode of predicting the future in more precise terms. To be sure, the bulk of the Apocalypse resulted from John's prophetic trance(s) . . . (Rev. 1:10; 4:2; 17:3; 21:10). There is, however, no justification for equating such a trance with a dream where logical coherence is nonexistent. Though in some sort of ecstatic state, John's spirit was wide awake and its powers were exercised with unusual alertness and clarity.[54]

In our view, the idealist interpretation has only one aspect to commend it: an appreciation of the value of the realities recorded in the book of Revelation to all the people of God throughout history. Especially to those who face great trials, persecution, or even martyrdom. With this, we wholeheartedly agree. In almost every other way, we oppose the idealist interpretation because it violates the *Golden Rule of Interpretation*[5.2.24] and makes an accurate historical understanding of the events God has revealed almost impossible.

The bankruptcy of this approach is best illustrated by the huge variation in the interpretive results of its practitioners. If the idealist interpretation is the correct one, then the true meaning of the book of Revelation cannot be reliably determined. But then perhaps it would not matter if the book were given only to inspire the saints!

2.12.4 - Historicist Interpretation

The historicist system of interpretation understands the book of Revelation as setting forth the major events of Christian history spanning the time of John until the present.[55] "Historicist interpreters generally see Revelation as predicting the major movements of Christian history, most of which have been fulfilled up to the time of the commentator."[56] "Proponents of this method have tended to take Rev. 2-19, including the seals, trumpets, and bowls as well as the interludes, as prophetic of salvation history, that is, the development of church history within world history."[57] This view has also been called the *continuist* view.[58]

The beginning of historicism has been attributed to Joachim of Fiore (12th century) or Nicolas of Lyra (died 1340).

> This approach began with Joachim of Fiore in the twelfth century. He claimed that a vision had told him the 1,260 days of the Apocalypse prophesied the events of Western history from the time of the apostles until the present. The Franciscans followed Joachim and like him interpreted the book relating to pagan Rome and the papacy (due to corruption in the church). Later the Reformers . . . also favored this method, with the pope as the *Antichrist*[5.2.3].[59]

> Nicolas of Lyra (teacher of theology at Paris, died 1340) . . . Abandoning the theory of recapitulation, he finds in the course of the book prediction of a continuous series of events from the apostolic age to the final consummation. The seals refer to the period extending into the reign of Domitian; in the later parts are predicted the Arian and other heresies, the spread of Mohammedism, Charlemagne, the Crusades, and other historical details.[60]

The historicist view has been the interpretive approach of numerous well-known individuals: Albert Barnes, Bengel, Elliott, Martin Luther, Joseph Mede, Isaac Newton, Vitringa, William Whiston, and John Wycliffe.[61] See Ice for a summary of historicist interpretation of Revelation 6-19 (that of Albert Barnes).[62]

One of the problems the historicist view encounters is that the events of the book of Revelation appear to be clustered within a relatively short time period (Rev. 11:2-3; 12:6, 14; 13:5). In order to apply this period to history from the time of John to that of the interpreter, the 1260 days of the time period are understood as "prophetic days" and interpreted as years

> The principal difficulty in the way was to dispose of the predictions which limited the final stage of Antichrist's career to forty-two months, or twelve hundred sixty days. This was accomplished by what is known as the "year-day" theory, which regards each of the 1260 days as "prophetic days," that is, as 1260 years, and thus sufficient room was afforded to allow for the protracted history of Roman Catholicism.[63]

A variation on this approach was to use the 2,300 days of Daniel 8:14 to arrive at yet a longer period of time.[64]

One of the primary motives behind the full development of historicism was a desire to interpret the book of Revelation as an anti-Roman Catholic polemic where the *Beast*[5.2.9] was seen as denoting the pope and the papacy. This suited the needs of the enemies of the "Babylonish" papacy, especially during the Reformation. "This method of interpreting the book of Revelation achieved considerable stature in the Reformation because of its identification of the pope and the papacy with the beasts of Revelation 13. Thiessen lists Wycliffe, Luther, Joseph Mede, Sir Isaac Newton, William Whiston, Elliott, Vitringa, Bengel, and Barnes as adherents of this approach."[65] Pink sees historicism and its anti-pope focus as being a key contributor to the rise of *postmillennialism*[5.2.56]

> The dominant view which has been held by Protestants since the time of the Reformation is that the many predictions relating to the Antichrist describe, instead, the rise, progress, and doom of the papacy. This mistake has led to others, and given rise to the scheme of prophetic interpretation which has prevailed throughout Christendom. When the predictions concerning the Man of Sin were allegorized, consistency required that all associated and collateral predictions should also be allegorized, and especially those which relate to his doom, and the kingdom which is to be established on the overthrow of his power. When the period of his predicted course was made to measure the whole duration of the papal system, it naturally followed that the predictions of the associated events should be applied to the history of Europe from the time that the Bishop of Rome became recognized as the head of the Western Churches. It was, really, this mistake of Luther and his contemporaries in applying to Rome the prophecies concerning the Antichrist which is responsible, we believe, for the whole modern system of post-millennialism.[66]

Historicism suffers with idealism in the variety of interpretations which arise from its proponents

> Elliott, in his *Horae Apocalypticae* , holds that the trumpets (Rev. 8:6-9:21) cover the period from A.D. 395 to A.D. 1453, beginning with the attacks on the Western Roman empire by the Goths and concluding with the fall of the Eastern empire to the Turks. The first trumpet was the invasion of the Goths under Alaric, who sacked Rome; the second was the invasion under Genseric, who conquered North Africa; the third was the raid of the Huns under Attila, who devastated central Europe. The fourth was the collapse of the empire under the conquest of Odoacer. The locusts of the fifth trumpet were the Moslem hordes that poured into the west between the sixth and eighth centuries, and the sixth judgment of the four angels bound at the Euphrates (Rev. 9:14) was the growth and spread of the Turkish power.[67]

> This has led to endless speculation that is totally without biblical support. Identifications have included monks and friars as "locusts," Muhammad as the "fallen star," Alaric the Goth as the first trumpet, Elizabeth I as the first bowl, Martin Luther as the angel of Sardis, Adolf Hitler as the red horse.[68]

The key problem for historicism is the need to constrain the events of the book of Revelation into the historic mold brought to the text by the interpreter. Since different interpreters give priority and attention to different historical events or geographical regions, the results predictably vary. Moreover, when the chain of events of the book mismatch those of the historic period, there is the need to leave literal interpretation for the flexibility of spiritual interpretation. Thus, an inconsistent interpretive approach results.[69] John Hendrik de Vries decries the historical method of interpretation: "It turns exegesis into an artful play of ingenuity."[70]

Historicism is not very popular today. This is partly because of its consistent failure to account for the actual events of history to our own time.[71]The variation in results obtained by proponents has also been so great that it tends to invalidate the approach.[72]Osborne lists a number of weaknesses of the system, including: (1) an identification only with Western Church history; (2) the inherent speculation involved in the parallels with world history;[73] (3) the fact that it must be reworked with each new period of world history.[74]

> The historicist position, . . . suffers from the inability of interpreters of this school to establish a specific verifiable criterion of judgment whereby positive identification for the fulfillment of specific prophecies can be proved to be historically fulfilled by specific events in world history, in historical instances of fulfillment to which most of the interpreters of this school could agree. The method requires the student of Revelation to go outside the Bible and seek for the fulfillment of predictions in the past events of world history, and to one not well taught in history the method is impossible to carry out, leaving the book of Revelation largely closed to the ordinary reader.[75]

> The historical interpreters differ so much among themselves that we may well ask, Which one of them are we to believe? It is this very diversity which has caused so many earnest students to put the Apocalypse aside in despair.[76]

Modern advocates of historicism include the Seventh-Day Adventists and the followers of the late David Koresh of Waco, Texas.[77]

2.12.5 - Futurist Interpretation

The approach to interpreting the book of Revelation which has gained perhaps the widest exposure of all systems of interpretation in recent times is the futurist interpretation. This is a result of a number of seminaries in the recent past which have championed a literal interpretative approach to all of Scripture within a framework which understands related Old Testament passages and promises involving Israel, and which distinguishes between Israel and the Church. The futurist interpretation is the basic interpretive framework behind the hugely popular *Left Behind* series of novels by authors Tim LaHaye and Jerry Jenkins.[78]

Futurism derives from the consistent application of literal *hermeneutics*[5.2.26], the *Golden Rule of Interpretation*[5.2.24], across the entire body of Scripture, including the book of Revelation. Contrary to the claims of many of its critics, it is not an *a priori* view which is imposed on the text.[79] As evidenced by the testimony of the early Church, futurism is the most natural result of a plain reading of the text and the way that most unbiased readers would understand the book on their first reading.

Futurism gets its label from its refusal to see unfulfilled passages as having been fulfilled by *approximately similar* events in the past. Hence, it holds that many of the events in the book of Revelation await future fulfillment:

> The futurist generally believes that all of the visions from Revelation 4:1 to the end of the book are yet to be fulfilled in the period immediately preceding and following the second advent of Christ. The reason for the view is found in the comparison of Revelation 1:1, 19 and 4:1.[80]

> Futurists see eschatological passages being fulfilled during a future time, primarily during the seventieth week of Daniel, at the second coming of Christ, and during the millennium. While all *dispensationalists*[5.2.15] are futurists, not all futurists are dispensationalists. Futurists are also the most literal in their interpretation of prophecy passages. Dr. Tenney says: "The more literal an interpretation that one adopts, the more strongly will he be construed to be a futurist."[81]

Osborne summarizes the two primary forms taken by futurism:[82]

> There are two forms of this approach, dispensationalism and what has been called "classic *premillennialism*[5.2.58]." Dispensationalists believe that God has brought about his plan of salvation in a series of dispensations or stages centering on his election of Israel to be his covenant people. Therefore, the church age is a parenthesis in this plan, as God turned to the Gentiles until the Jewish people find national revival (Rom. 11;25-32). At the end of that period, the church will be raptured, inaugurating a

> seven-year tribulation period in the middle of which the *Antichrist*[5.2.3] will make himself known (Rev. 13) and instigate the "great tribulation" . . . At the end of that period . . . Christ returns in judgment, followed by a literal millennium (Rev. 20:1-10), great white throne judgment (Rev. 20:11-15), and the beginning of eternity . . . Classical premillennialism is similar but does not hold to dispensations. Thus there is only one return of Christ, after the tribulation period (Mtt. 24:29-31; cf. Rev. 19:11-21) and it is the whole church, not just the nation of Israel, that passes through the tribulation period.[83]

Futurism was undeniably the system of interpretation held by the majority in the early church. "Variations of this view were held by the earliest expositors, such as *Justin Martyr*[5.2.36] (d.165), *Irenaeus*[5.2.34] (d.c.195), Hippolytus (d.236), and Victorinus (d.c.303)."[84] Modern futurists wholeheartedly agree with the statement of Jerome, writing in A.D. 393: "John . . . saw . . . an Apocalypse containing boundless mysteries **of the future**"[85] As early as Irenaeus (130-200) and Hippolytus (170-236), basic futuristic concepts such as the remaining week of Daniel's seventy weeks (see our discussion of *related passages and themes*[2.13]) had already become evident:

> When Knowles deals with the next major contributors—Irenaeus (130-200) and his disciple Hippolytus (170-236)—he describes their views as "undoubtedly the forerunners of the modern dispensational interpreters of the Seventy Weeks." Knowles draws the following conclusion about Irenaeus and Hippolytus: ". . .we may say that Irenaeus presented the seed of an idea that found its full growth in the writings of Hippolytus. In the works of these fathers, we can find most of the basic concepts of the modern futuristic view of the seventieth week of Daniel ix. That they were dependent to some extent upon earlier material is no doubt true. Certainly we can see the influence of pre-Christian Jewish exegesis at times, but, by and large, we must regard them as the founders of the school of interpretation, and in this lies their significance for the history of exegesis."[86]

Because futurism is a result of literal hermeneutics (see below) and the early church was spared the damaging effects of *allegorical interpretation*[2.7.3], the early church also understood Scripture to teach a future, one-thousand-year reign of Christ on earth in fulfillment of *OT*[5.2.51] promises of the *Messianic Kingdom*[5.2.39].[87]This was a widespread view among early interpreters:

> [Justin Martyr] asserts that it teaches a literal Millennial Kingdom of the saints to be established in Jerusalem, and after the thousand years the general resurrection and judgment. . . . Irenaeus . . . finds in the book the doctrine of *chiliasm*[5.2.13], that is, of an earthly Millennial Kingdom. . . . Hippolytus is a chiliast . . . identifies . . . Antichrist, who was represented by Antiochus Epiphanes and who will come out of the tribe of Dan, will reign 3 1/2 years, persecuting the Church and putting to death the two Witnesses, the forerunners of the parousia (held to be Elijah and Enoch). . . . Victorinus . . . understands the Revelation in a literal, chiliastic, sense . . . The two witnesses are Elijah and Jeremiah; the 144,000 are Jews who in the last days will be converted by the preaching of Elijah . . . the false prophet, will cause the image of Antichrist to be set up in the temple at Jerusalem.[88]

Notice that Victorinus, writing well in advance of modern futurists, but *after the destruction of Jerusalem in A.D. 70*, sees the *Temple*[5.2.73] of Revelation as being a *future* Temple, just like modern futurists.

Unfortunately, with the *rise of allegorical interpretation*[2.7.3] and the opposition of the heresy of Montanism (which utilized an extravagant form of millennial teaching drawn from the book of Revelation),[89]the futurist view fell into disfavor, not to be seen in a favorable light again for over a thousand years.[90]

During the Reformation, literal interpretation flourished in response to the allegorical methods employed throughout the Middle Ages by the Roman Church. However, the Reformers never fully extended literalism to prophetic passages and key Reformers did not fully appreciate the book of Revelation.

The primary fork in the road between futurism and all other systems of interpretation concerning the book of Revelation comes in the refusal of the futurist to be imprecise with the details of God's revelation.[91] For example, when a passage states that a man "performs great signs, so that he even makes fire come down from heaven on the earth in the sight of men" (Rev. 13:13), the futurist expects fulfillment to involve: (1) a man; (2) performing great signs in a similar way that great signs were performed in the OT and by Christ in the gospels; (3) who calls down literal fire from literal heaven as was done in the OT; (4) viewed by other men. He then asks the simple question: Is there any reliable historic record of such an event since the time of John's writing? The obvious answer is, "No!" Hence this event awaits future fulfillment. It really is that simple!

There is a strong connection between literal interpretation and futurism: "The more literal an interpretation that one adopts, the more strongly will he be construed to be a futurist."[92] Literal interpretation allows the text to speak for itself:[93]

Critics frequently misrepresent futurism as if it places its *entire* emphasis on understanding the book of Revelation as applying to the future: "The futurist position especially encounters the difficulty that the book would have had **no significant relevance for a first-century readership**." [emphasis added][94]

This is a major misunderstanding of the futurist position which holds that the early chapters of the book are specifically addressed to the then-existing churches in Asia Minor and fully appreciates the historical setting and contents of these passages. Moreover, futurism concurs with Swete that the events of the book of Revelation are relevant in *every* age as a great source of blessing and security for persecuted believers:

> In the Epistle of the Churches of Vienne and Lyons, written in 177 to their brethren in Asia and Phrygia, which bears many signs of the use of the Apocalypse by the Christian societies of South Gaul during the troubles in the reign of Marcus Aurelius. . . . It is impossible to doubt that the roll which contained St John's great letter to the parent Churches in Asia was often in the hands of the daughter Churches in Gaul, and perhaps accompanied the confessors to the prisons where they awaited the martyr's crown.[95]

The critics of futurism require complete primary relevance of the *entire book* for the readers of John's own day. But those most closely associated with the culture and times of the readers evidence no such requirement! The witness of Justin Martyr and Irenaeus is especially important because they both had close association with the earliest Christians who would have been familiar with the times during which John wrote the book of Revelation. Even so, they fail to understand the events recorded in the book in the way in which preterists or idealists insist, but reflect the futurist view. Writing in the early 2nd century, they were much better positioned than we to understand the relevance of John's message to their times! Are they to be accused of being guilty of making the book "irrelevant?"

The mistake being made is constraining the book of Revelation as if it had only a *single* purpose. No matter which view is taken, if one fails to understand the many purposes of the book, the interpretive result will be the lacking. Preterist Chilton remarks: "No Biblical writer ever revealed the future merely for the sake of satisfying curiosity: The goal was always to direct God's people toward right action in the present. . . . The prophets told of the future **only** in order to stimulate godly living." [emphasis added][96] If Chilton were correct, then there would be little reason for prophecy to be *predictive*. The fact is, the prophets gave prophecy for more reasons than merely the stimulation of godly living. This was indeed an important reason, but not the only reason. The many fulfilled prophecies *testifying to the identity of Jesus* at His First Coming provide an abundant counter example to Chilton's claim.

It is a misrepresentation of the futurist interpretation to assert that it denies the relevance of the text to the first-century readership. This is tantamount to saying that appreciating the prophetic predictions throughout Scripture essentially denies the relevance of the same passages to those who originally received them. The pattern of prophetic passages throughout Scripture is clearly one of both immediate local application and future prediction. Even in cases where there is no immediate local application by way of historical events (e.g., Isa. 53), the passages still contain inestimable worth to the original recipients in setting forth the will of God as well as inspirational value in the sure hope of what God will do in the future (Rom. 8:24-25). In the Apocalypse, this dual application of prophetic Scripture (both immediate/local and future/remote) is made explicit in the organizational framework set forth by Christ (Rev. 1:19) and in the setting off of the seven epistles from the remaining material.

Other criticisms of futurism are manifestly silly. Gregg denies futurists the right to use the analogy of Scripture (Scripture interprets Scripture):

> A major feature of the Tribulation expected by *futurists* is its seven-year duration, divided in the middle by the Antichrist's violating a treaty he had made with Israel and setting up an image of himself in the rebuilt Jewish temple in Jerusalem. Yet none of these elements can be discovered from a literal interpretation of any passage in Revelation. . . . The *futurist* believes that Revelation 20 describes a

> period of world peace and justice with Christ reigning on earth from Jerusalem, though no part of this description can be found in the chapter itself, taken literally. This observation does not mean that this futurist scenario cannot be true. But it must be derived by reading into the passages in Revelation features that are not plainly stated.[97]

Gregg would have futurists interpret the book of Revelation as if it were delivered with no connection to existing prophetic information given by God. Never mind what the rest of Scripture has to say about Israel, Daniel's seventy weeks, Jacob's trouble, the Great Tribulation predicted by Jesus, or other matters. Those who attempt a comprehensive understanding of Scripture by bringing together *everything* God has said on related subjects are accused of "reading into" passages that which is simply not there!

Obviously, care needs to be exercised when connecting passages which seem to have related aspects, but if a good case can be made for a correlation, then the interpreter who fails in this synthesis is failing in his task before God. Chiding futurists who correlate the *little horn*[5.2.37] of Daniel (Dan. 7:8), the man of sin of Paul (2Th. 2:3), and the *Beast*[5.2.9] of Revelation (Rev. 13:1) because of obvious and intentional similarities given in Scripture, but *providing no sensible or profitable synthesis in its place* is a pattern frequently demonstrated by critics. This is the primary reason why futurists can offer a systematic and detailed outline of eschatological events while the other systems fail to provide anything even remotely similar. It almost seems that the critics of futurism dislike the certainty and coherence it offers in its interpretation of prophecy. But if God supernaturally gave the *inspired*[5.2.33] Scriptures through a single author (the Holy Spirit), why shouldn't such coherence and correlation be expected?

To the futurist, the book of Revelation has relevancy to John, to the *seven churches*[5.2.66] of Asia, to the Church throughout history, and to the saints all the way through the Second Coming of Christ and into the eternal state. Now *that's* relevancy!

> The book of Revelation is important to us because it portrays the world as a global village. Entering the twenty-first century, no better expression describes our earth and its people. Besides a mushrooming population, other factors are pushing all humanity together, such as an interlinking economy, jet age transportation, and satellite communications.[98]

We believe in the futurist interpretation of the book of Revelation. This is because we are convinced of the Golden Rule of Interpretation as the key to properly understanding God's Revelation. This is true of all written communication where the desire of the author is to convey a clear message rather than to puzzle or obscure). It is our conviction and experience that applying the Golden Rule from Genesis to Revelation will result in a futurist interpretation of Scripture and is the only reliable means of accurately knowing what God intended to the degree we may understand Him as His finite creatures.

2.12.6 - Ecclectic Interpretation

The final system of interpretation we discuss briefly is that of an eclectic interpretation. This system picks and chooses elements from each of the other interpretive systems and applies them at different places in the text. It is the ultimate "interpretive smorgasbord" whose proponents proclaim combines the best from each system. "The solution is to allow the *preterist*[5.2.59], idealist, and futurist methods to interact in such a way that the strengths are maximized and the weaknesses minimized."[99] This sounds appealing and is in keeping with the trend towards diversity so prevalent in our day. Rather than struggle within the restrictive framework of any one system, why not "have them all?"

The answer, once again, is *hermeneutics*[5.2.26], hermeneutics, hermeneutics! Thomas identifies the Achilles Heel of the eclectic approach: "It leaves to human judgment the determination of where the details of a text end and its general picture begins. Allowing this liberty for subjective opinion cannot qualify as objective interpretation."[100]

One can't simply combine the elements from disparate systems of interpretation, for they are often at odds with one another. Therefore, the *subjectivity* (a word to be avoided in interpretation) of the interpreter now rules over the choice of *when* to use *which* system. Obviously, different interpreters will make this decision differently across the text and the results will be as eclectic as the system itself. This, too, is a bad thing if you believe that God's Word has one primary meaning which He desires all

His saints to understand.

Taking one example from Beale:

> Accordingly, no specific prophesied historical events are discerned in the book, except for the final coming of Christ to deliver and judge and to establish the final form of the kingdom in a consummated new creation—though there are a few exceptions to this rule. . . . ([e].g., Rev. 2:10, 22 and 3:9-10, which are unconditional prophecies to be fulfilled imminently in the specific local churches of Smyrna, Thyatira, and Philadelphia).[101]

Here Beale arbitrarily and personally decides that "no specific prophesied historical events are discussed," but then immediately makes equally arbitrary exceptions. And if things which are said to three of the *seven churches*[5.2.66] can be held to be "unconditional prophecies," why not the many other prophecies throughout the rest of the book? We submit that no two eclectic interpreters will make the same distinctions as to which portions of the text are to be treated historically, literally, symbolically, figuratively, or devotionally. Therefore, a reliable meaning *cannot be derived* from such an approach. This is not to say that futurists unanimously agree about the precise details of related matters, but it is easily demonstrated that they arrive at a much narrower variation in understanding—a cluster of "near hits" around the center of the target while the eclectic interpreters are scattered all over the target.

A growth in popularity of the eclectic interpretation is to be expected given our postmodern age, for the eclectic system of interpretation has much in common with it: *First*, the tendency to embrace all paths as being approximately equivalent; *Second*, the desire to avoid treating other views negatively; *Third*, the willingness to allow for a variety of interpretations of what truth is (*your* truth is *your* truth, *my* truth is *my* truth). The Word of God's objective claim that there is a *single* path to truth undermines the claims of an eclectic approach much as it does the claims of postmodernism.

Those who advocate this view are often idealists who recognize some of the weaknesses of their system and desire to dabble in aspects of the other systems. The resulting interpretation is highly varied and idealistic in overall tone.

Notes

1 Thomas Ice, *"What Is Preterism?,"* in Tim LaHaye, and Thomas Ice, eds., *The End Times Controversy* (Eugene, OR: Harvest House Publishers, 2003), 18.

2 The astute reader will recognize the smaller variation in the interpretive results of the futurist system as an implicit endorsement of its validity.

3 Randall Price, *"Dead Sea Scrolls, Eschatology of the,"* in Mal Couch, ed., *Dictionary of Premillennial Theology* (Grand Rapids, MI: Kregel Publications, 1996), 91.

4 John MacArthur, *Revelation 1-11 : The MacArthur New Testament Commentary* (Chicago, IL: Moody Press, 1999), 11.

5 Steve Gregg, *Revelation Four Views: A Parallel Commentary* (Nashville, TN: Thomas Nelson, 1997), 1.

6 Gregg, *Revelation Four Views: A Parallel Commentary*, 4.

7 Mal Couch, *"Why is Revelation Important?,"* in Mal Couch, ed., *A Bible Handbook to Revelation* (Grand Rapids, MI: Kregel Publications, 2001), 16.

8 Merrill C. Tenney, *Interpreting Revelation* (Peabody, MA: Hendrickson Publishers, 1957), 144.

9 Trent C. Butler, Chad Brand, Charles Draper, and Archie England, eds., *Broadman and Holman Illustrated Bible Dictionary* (Nashville, TN: Broadman and Holman Publishers, 2003), s.v. "Revelation."

10 Ice, "*What Is Preterism?*," 22-23.

11 Ice, "*What Is Preterism?*," 23-24.

12 Larry Spargimino, *"How Preterists Misuse History to Advance their View of Prophecy,"* in Tim LaHaye, and Thomas Ice, eds., *The End Times Controversy* (Eugene, OR: Harvest House Publishers, 2003), 19.

13 Robert H. Mounce, *The Book of Revelation* (Grand Rapids, MI: William B. Eerdmans Publishing Co., 1977), 41.

[14] Gregory K. Beale, *The Book of Revelation: A Commentary on the Greek Text* (Grand Rapids, MI: William B. Eerdmans Publishing Co., 1999), 45.

[15] Spargimino, "*How Preterists Misuse History to Advance their View of Prophecy*," 26-27.

[16] Robert L. Thomas, *"Theonomy and the Dating of Revelation,"* in Richard L. Mayhue, ed., *The Master's Seminary Journal*, vol. 5 (Sun Valley, CA: The Master's Seminary, 1994), 187-188.

[17] Idealism is also guilty of reinterpreting the book to avoid the obvious implications of a horrific time yet future coming upon the world.

[18] Spargimino, "*How Preterists Misuse History to Advance their View of Prophecy*," 9.

[19] Beale, *The Book of Revelation: A Commentary on the Greek Text*, 44.

[20] "The prophecies of Daniel 2 and 7 alluded to throughout the Apocalypse foresee a last judgment of the evil nations, not primarily of unbelieving Israel. Interestingly, these preterist interpreters identify the beast of Daniel 7 in Rev. 13:1ff. with a pagan nation (Rome), which Daniel then sees as the object of final judgment. But then they identify apostate Israel elsewhere in the book as the main object of Daniel's prophesied final judgment."—Beale, *The Book of Revelation: A Commentary on the Greek Text*, 44.

[21] "Since the preterist and idealist interpretations are not committed to predictive prophecy in Revelation, they tend chiefly to be advocated today by liberal or neo-orthodox interpreters. To them, Revelation is merely a statement of faith in sociological progress and the eventual triumph of a more equable world order."—Henry Morris, *The Revelation Record* (Wheaton, IL: Tyndale House Publishers, 1983), 26. "The [preterist] view [is] held by a majority of contemporary scholars, not a few of whom are identified with the liberal interpretation of Christianity."—Alan F. Johnson, *Revelation: The Expositor's Bible Commentary* (Grand Rapids, MI: Zondervan Publishing House, 1966), 13.

[22] Regardless of statements by Paul to the contrary: Rom. 11:11-12.

[23] Thomas Ice, *"The History of Preterism,"* in Tim LaHaye, and Thomas Ice, eds., *The End Times Controversy* (Eugene, OR: Harvest House Publishers, 2003), 45.

[24] John MacArthur, *"Signs in the Sky,"* in Tim LaHaye, and Thomas Ice, eds., *The End Times Controversy* (Eugene, OR: Harvest House Publishers, 2003), 113.

[25] "The full text of *The Didache* was rediscovered little more than a hundred years ago, in a codex found in Constantinople in 1873. This document proves that those who actually lived through the events of A.D. 70 regarded Matthew 24:29-31—the entire Olivet Discourse—as yet-unfulfilled prophecy."—MacArthur, "*Signs in the Sky*," 112.

[26] "[A] Spanish Jesuit, Alcasar (died 1614), was the first to interpret the entire *premillennial*[5.2.58] part of Revelation (chaps. 4-19) as falling totally within the age of the Apocalyptist and the centuries immediately following. . . . Alcasar was a thoroughgoing 'preterist.' "—Mounce, *The Book of Revelation*, 40-41.

[27] Tenney, *Interpreting Revelation*, 136.

[28] Contrast the following statement with the claims of Gary North who writes in the publisher's preface to Chilton: "[the preterist] viewpoint is an old one, stretching back to the early church."—David Chilton, *The Days of Vengeance* (Tyler, TX: Dominion Press, 1987), xv.

[29] Ice, "*The History of Preterism*," 39.

[30] Chilton, *The Days of Vengeance*, 575.

[31] "The nature of the event has to do with a 'Cloud Coming' of Christ . . ."—Kenneth L. Gentry, *Before Jerusalem Fell: Dating the Book of Revelation* (Atlanta, GA: American Vision, 1998), 123.

[32] "In case we might miss it, he says again, at the close of the book, that 'the Lord, the God of the spirits of the prophets, sent His angel to show to His bond-servants the things which must shortly take place' (Rev. 22:6). Given the fact that one important proof of a true prophet lay in the fact that his predictions came true (Deu. 18:21-22), St. John's first-century readers had every reason to expect his book to have immediate significance."—Chilton, *The Days of Vengeance*, 42.

[33] Thomas Ice, *"Some Practical Dangers of Preterism,"* in Tim LaHaye, and Thomas Ice, eds., *The End Times Controversy* (Eugene, OR: Harvest House Publishers, 2003), 426.

[34] MacArthur, "*Signs in the Sky*," 111.

[35] Isn't this the very reason why the Scriptures indicate the return of Jesus will be visible, global, and

unmistakable?

36 Spargimino, "*How Preterists Misuse History to Advance their View of Prophecy,*" 20.

37 Gordon Franz, *"Was 'Babylon' Destroyed when Jerusalem Fell in A.D. 70?,"* in Tim LaHaye, and Thomas Ice, eds., *The End Times Controversy* (Eugene, OR: Harvest House Publishers, 2003), 236.

38 Andy Woods, *"Revelation 13 and the First Beast,"* in Tim LaHaye, and Thomas Ice, eds., *The End Times Controversy* (Eugene, OR: Harvest House Publishers, 2003), 243.

39 "[Preterists assume] that the book uses a future orientation not to describe future reality but to challenge the situation of the original readers. There are two main variations within preterist interpretation: those who see the book describing events leading to the predicted judgment of apostate Israel and the destruction of the Jewish *Temple*[5.2.73] in A.D. 70 and those who understand its focus as describing the situation of the Christian church within the Roman Empire (the conflict between church and state)."—Grant R. Osborne, *Revelation* (Grand Rapids, MI: Baker Academic, 2002), 1. Osborne mentions a third variation which has more in common with the idealist interpretation, providing "a spatial interaction between the earthly and the heavenly so as to give new meaning to the present situation."—Osborne, *Revelation*, 19.

40 Chilton, *The Days of Vengeance*, 43.

41 "The preterist has an interpretation which has a firm pedestal, but which has no finished sculpture to place on it."—Tenney, *Interpreting Revelation*, 144.

42 Concerning Revelation 10:11 wherein John is told, "And he said to me, 'You must prophesy again about many peoples, nations, tongues, and kings.'," Chilton says, "St. John's prophecy regarding the destruction of Israel and the establishing of the New Covenant will encompass the nations of the world. . . . John is to extend the proclamation of [the] Gospel to all nations."—Chilton, *The Days of Vengeance*, 270. But this is a misreading of the text. The text states that what John will yet reveal in the book is *about* these global entities not *to* them. The passage has nothing to do with proclaiming the gospel, but everything to do with proclaiming the revelation which is being given to John which *concerns* these peoples, nations, tongues, and kings. The fact is, the destruction of Jerusalem in A.D. 70 is just not that big of a deal to the modern man in Siberia and is not what is in view.

43 "The city of God, described in the last chapters of the book, is obviously unrealized. Even if it be regarded as a symbol of some perfect state of human society, it has not yet been achieved. The preterist view simply does not account adequately for the claim of Revelation to be a prediction of the future."—Tenney, *Interpreting Revelation*, 137.

44 "The major problem with the preterist position is that the decisive victory portrayed in the latter chapters of the Apocalypse was never achieved. It is difficult to believe that John envisioned anything less than the complete overthrow of Satan, the final destruction of evil, and the eternal reign of God."—Mounce, *The Book of Revelation*, 41-42. "[Mild preterist] Gentry actually believes we are in some way in the new heavens and the new earth of Revelation 21-22. If this is true, then we all must be living in the ghetto side of the New Jerusalem. But there is no ghetto in the New Jerusalem."—Ice, "*Some Practical Dangers of Preterism,*" 420.

45 "Because of their first-century template for interpreting Bible prophecy, preterists come close to investing certain historians with canonic authority. . . . Should Josephus's writings become the sixty-seventh book of the Bible?"—Spargimino, "*How Preterists Misuse History to Advance their View of Prophecy,*" 219.

46 Chilton, *The Days of Vengeance*, xiii.

47 Mounce, *The Book of Revelation*, 43.

48 Osborne, *Revelation*, 20.

49 John F. Walvoord, *The Revelation of Jesus Christ* (Chicago, IL: Moody Press, 1966), 17.

50 Tenney, *Interpreting Revelation*, 143.

51 Beale, *The Book of Revelation: A Commentary on the Greek Text*, 48.

52 Ice, "*What Is Preterism?,*" 21.

53 Robertson says, "There seems abundant evidence to believe that this apocalypse, written during the stress and storm of Domitian's persecution, was intended to cheer the persecuted Christians with a view of certain victory at last, but with **no scheme of history in view.**" [emphasis added]—Mal Couch, *Introductory Thoughts on Revelation* (Ft. Worth, TX: Tyndale Theological Seminary, n.d.). [emphasis added]

54 Tenney, *Interpreting Revelation*, 1:34.

55 One of the problems with this approach is that as Jesus delays in His coming, the "present" is constantly changing requiring a re-analysis of the "fit" between the events given by John and the span of history.

56 Beale, *The Book of Revelation: A Commentary on the Greek Text*, 46.

57 Osborne, *Revelation*, 19.

58 Mal Couch, *Classical Evangelical Hermeneutics* (Grand Rapids, MI: Kregel Publications), 258.

59 Osborne, *Revelation*, 18.

60 Isbon T. Beckwith, *The Apocalypse of John* (Eugene, OR: Wipf and Stock Publishers, 2001), 329.

61 "This [view] was held by Martin Luther, Isaac Newton, Elliott, and others."—Mal Couch, *"Interpreting the Book of Revelation,"* in Mal Couch, ed., *A Bible Handbook to Revelation* (Grand Rapids, MI: Kregel Publications, 2001), 47. "This method of interpreting the book of Revelation achieved considerable stature in the Reformation because of its identification of the pope and the papacy with the beasts of Revelation 13. Thiessen lists Wycliffe, Luther, Joseph Mede, Sir Isaac Newton, William Whiston, Elliott, Vitringa, Bengel, and Barnes as adherents of this approach."—Walvoord, *The Revelation of Jesus Christ*, 18.

62 Ice, "*What Is Preterism?*," 19.

63 Arthur Walkington Pink, *The Antichrist* (Oak Harbor, WA: Logos Research Systems, 1999, 1923), s.v. "intro."

64 "This spiritualistic approach is built upon the day/year theory, whereby 1260 days (literally 3 1/2 years) mentioned in Daniel and Revelation cover the time (1260 years) of the domination of Antichrist over the church. Another variation is to apply the day/year theory to the 2,300 days of Daniel 8:14. Thus, the historicist attempts to figure out when Antichrist came to power (i.e., the Roman Church and the papacy) by adding 1,260 or 2,300 years to arrive at the time of the second coming and the defeat of Antichrist."—Ice, "*What Is Preterism?*," 18.

65 Walvoord, *The Revelation of Jesus Christ*, 18.

66 Pink, *The Antichrist*, s.v. "intro."

67 Tenney, *Interpreting Revelation*, 138.

68 Edward Hindson, *Revelation: Unlocking the Future* (Chattanooga, TN: AMG Publishers, 2002), 14.

69 "The historicist is constantly confronted with the dilemma of a far-fetched spiritualization in order to maintain the chain of historical events, or else if he makes the events literal in accordance with the language of the text he is compelled to acknowledge that no comparable events in history have happened."—Tenney, *Interpreting Revelation*, 138.

70 Walvoord, *The Revelation of Jesus Christ*, 19-20.

71 "The deterrent to a strictly dated interpretation of Revelation is the failure of all such schemes that have hitherto been proposed. No matter how the figures and intervals in it have been pressed and twisted to yield results, no clear parallel to the current era has yet been devised."—Tenney, *Interpreting Revelation*, 135.

72 "Proponents of this view living at different periods of church history cannot agree with one another, since they limit the meaning of the symbols only to specific historical referents contemporary with their own times."—Beale, *The Book of Revelation: A Commentary on the Greek Text*, 46.

73 *Preterism*[5.2.59] suffers from this same weakness, although in a more restricted historic time-frame.

74 Osborne, *Revelation*, 19.

75 Jerome Smith, *The New Treasury of Scripture Knowledge* (Nashville, TN: Thomas Nelson Publishers, 1992), Rev. 4:1.

76 E. W. Bullinger, *Commentary On Revelation* (Grand Rapids, MI: Kregel Publications, 1984, 1935), Rev. 8:7.

77 "Those who followed events surrounding David Koresh in Waco, Texas, may be interested to know that he, along with [Seventh-Day] Adventists, are among the few historicists of contemporary times. This view was popular from the time of the Reformation to the beginning of the twentieth century, and has diminished since."—Ice, "*What Is Preterism?*," 18.

78 Dr. Tim LaHaye is a noted futurist theologian having published numerous works on prophecy, some of which we draw on in this work. See the *bibliography*[5.6].

79 We can offer our own experience in support of this claim. Having been born-again and taught for five years within a Church which embraced *preterism*[5.2.59], it was our own careful study of the details of Scripture *across the entire span of books* which caused us to reject preterism in favor of what we only later came to understand was called futurism.

80 Tenney, *Interpreting Revelation*, 139.

81 Ice, "*What Is Preterism?*," 21.

82 There is also a form of *extreme futurism* in which even the first three chapters of the book of Revelation are seen as yet future. [Bullinger, *Commentary On Revelation*]

83 Osborne, *Revelation*, 20-21.

84 Johnson, *Revelation: The Expositor's Bible Commentary*, 12.

85 "In two places, Jerome stated clearly that John was banished under Domitian. First, in his *Against Jovinianum* (A.D. 393), Jerome wrote that John was 'a prophet, for he saw in the island of Patmos, to which he had been banished by the Emperor Domitian as a martyr for the Lord, an Apocalypse containing boundless mysteries of the future.' "—Mark Hitchcock, *"The Stake in the Heart—The A.D. 95 Date of Revelation,"* in Tim LaHaye, and Thomas Ice, eds., *The End Times Controversy* (Eugene, OR: Harvest House Publishers, 2003), 135.

86 Thomas Ice, *"The 70 Weeks of Daniel,"* in Tim LaHaye, and Thomas Ice, eds., *The End Times Controversy* (Eugene, OR: Harvest House Publishers, 2003), 350.

87 "The early church fathers believed in a literal, thousand-year, earthly reign of Christ because they interpreted the teachings of Revelation in a normal rather than mystical way."—Larry V. Crutchfield, *"Revelation in the New Testament,"* in Mal Couch, ed., *A Bible Handbook to Revelation* (Grand Rapids, MI: Kregel Publications, 2001), 25.

88 Beckwith, *The Apocalypse of John*, 320.

89 "The opposition to the heresy of Montanism, which made great use of the Apocalypse and gave extravagant form to its millennial teaching, caused it to be either rejected or differently interpreted."—Beckwith, *The Apocalypse of John*, 323.

90 "This was the method employed by some of the earliest fathers (e.g., Justin, Irenaeus, Hippolytus), but with the triumph of the allegorical method . . . after *Origen*[5.2.50] and of the *amillennial*[5.2.1] view after Augustine and Ticonius, the futurist method (and chiliasm) was not seen again for over a thousand years."—Osborne, *Revelation*, 20.

91 As we noted earlier, this is one reason why many who are trained in the sciences and engineering tend toward this view of Scripture. Being trained in logic and the analysis of details, we reject the approximate "fulfillments" and interpretations of the other systems in favor of a God Who fulfills His predictions down to the gnat's eyelash.

92 Tenney, *Interpreting Revelation*, 142.

93 "Dispensationalism is actually built on the idea of letting the Bible speak for itself with a normal, literal hermeneutic. If simple rules of grammar and observation are put into place, the Scriptures will begin to make sense, from Genesis to Revelation."—Couch, "*Why is Revelation Important?*," 41.

94 Beale, *The Book of Revelation: A Commentary on the Greek Text*, 47.

95 Henry Barclay Swete, *The Apocalypse of St. John* (Eugene, OR: Wipf and Stock Publishers, 1998, 1906), xciii.

96 Chilton, *The Days of Vengeance*, 27.

97 Gregg, *Revelation Four Views: A Parallel Commentary*, 41.

98 Couch, "*Why is Revelation Important?*," 17.

99 Osborne, *Revelation*, 21.

100 Robert L. Thomas, *Revelation 1-7* (Chicago, IL: Moody Press, 1992), 35.

101 Beale, *The Book of Revelation: A Commentary on the Greek Text*, 48.

2.13 - Related Passages and Themes

When we come to the book of Revelation, it is important to understand how interwoven its contents are with *inspired*[5.2.33] writings which precede it in the *canon*[5.2.12] of Scripture. The book is not an independent document disconnected from the rest of Scripture and intended only for the angels of the *seven churches*[5.2.66].[1] Nor is it constrained to dealing only with the events of the readers of John's day. It must be seen for what it truly is: *the capstone of God's revelation to man.* Beyond this book, nothing more has been revealed by God to His Church for over 1900 years. Therefore, the wise reader will keep the following points in mind:

1. The book of Revelation is not a "head without a body." It is *intimately connected* with the previous revelation of God, especially promises and predictions which have not yet found fulfillment.
2. The book of Revelation is God's message to His people intended to guide them *during the entire period* from the departure of Christ through the day of Christ's return.

We make the mistake of "truncating" God's message when we fail to interpret its contents within the broad continuum of God's revelation to man and His historical work upon the earth.

Since the book of Revelation describes events during the "crisis" of the final rejection of God by the world prior to the coming of Jesus Christ, we should expect these events to also appear elsewhere in the Scriptures because of their great importance. And indeed they do. Our purpose in this section is to help the reader become aware of related passages and themes which bear upon an interpretation of the book of Revelation. Without a knowledge of these related passages and themes, it becomes difficult—even problematic—to understand the events conveyed by John in this final book of Scripture.

In the following discussion, we focus on the major parallels between the book of Revelation and key passages elsewhere in Scripture. But, as was mentioned in our discussion of the *interpretation of symbols*[2.7], there are literally hundreds of passages throughout the Bible and especially the Old Testament, which are connected to the book of Revelation. These will come to light as we make our way through the *Commentary*[3].

2.13.1 - Trouble Ahead

A major theme throughout Scripture is the impending arrival of God's Kingdom *on earth.* Although the Kingdom will be a time of great blessing, peace, and prosperity upon the earth, Scripture reveals that *the arrival of God's Kingdom on earth is characterized by conflict and judgment.*

> Why do the nations rage, and the people plot a vain thing? The kings of the earth set themselves, and the rulers take counsel together, against the LORD and against His Anointed, *saying*, "Let us break Their bonds in pieces and cast away Their cords from us." He who sits in the heavens shall laugh; the Lord shall hold them in derision. Then He shall speak to them in His wrath, and distress them in His deep displeasure: "Yet I have set My King On My holy hill of Zion." I will declare the decree: The LORD has said to Me, "You *are* My Son, today I have begotten You. Ask of Me, and I will give *You* The nations *for* Your inheritance, and the ends of the earth *for* Your possession. You shall break them with a rod of iron; You shall dash them to pieces like a potter's vessel." (Ps. 2:1-9)

This psalm records the general opposition of man to the rule of God, especially by the leaders of men. The divine response to this rejection includes wrath and a promise that Jesus will 'break them' and 'dash them.' These are not terms describing gradual Christian conversion and enlightenment which will one day encircle the globe as men continually turn to God. Rather, this psalm describes the *radical intervention* by God into human history to overthrow the rejection of His King.

God's climactic intervention in the affairs of a rejecting world to establish His kingdom on earth is the theme of numerous other passages. For example:

> You watched while a stone was cut out without hands, which struck the image on its feet of iron and clay, and broke them in pieces. Then the iron, the clay, the bronze, the silver, and the gold were crushed together, and became like chaff from the summer threshing floors; the wind carried them away so that no trace of them was found. And the stone that struck the image became a great mountain and filled the

> whole earth. (Dan. 2:34-35)
>
> And in the days of these kings the God of heaven will set up a kingdom which shall never be destroyed; and the kingdom shall not be left to other people; it shall break in pieces and consume all these kingdoms, and it shall stand forever. Inasmuch as you saw that the stone was cut out of the mountain without hands, and that it broke in pieces the iron, the bronze, the clay, the silver, and the gold-the great God has made known to the king what will come to pass after this. The dream is certain, and its interpretation is sure. (Dan. 2:44-45)

In Nebuchadnezzar's dream, interpreted by God through Daniel, an image made of various metals representing a series of kingdoms is described. Significantly, the dream includes the vision of a stone "cut without hands" which *strikes* the image resulting in the various metals being "crushed." The imagery here is violent, sudden and dramatic—the exact opposite of the gradual worldwide conversion which *postmillennialists*[5.2.56] expect to be the fruit of the gospel spreading across the earth.

> I was watching; and the same horn was making war against the saints, and prevailing against them, until the Ancient of Days came, and a judgment was made *in favor* of the saints of the Most High, and the time came for the saints to possess the kingdom. Thus he said: 'The fourth beast shall be a fourth kingdom on earth, which shall be different from all *other* kingdoms, and shall devour the whole earth, trample it and break it in pieces. The ten horns *are* ten kings *Who* shall arise from this kingdom. And another shall rise after them; He shall be different from the first *ones*, and shall subdue three kings. He shall speak *pompous* words against the Most High, shall persecute the saints of the Most High, and shall intend to change times and law. Then *the saints* shall be given into his hand for a time and times and half a time. 'But the court shall be seated, and they shall take away his dominion, to consume and destroy *it* forever. Then the kingdom and dominion, and the greatness of the kingdoms under the whole heaven, shall be given to the people, the saints of the Most High. His kingdom *is* an everlasting kingdom, and all dominions shall serve and obey Him.' (Dan. 7:21-27)

Daniel's dream and visions record yet another abrupt transition. Prior to the "judgment in favor of the saints," the "horn was **making war against the saints, and prevailing against them**" [emphasis added]. This passage describes events immediately prior to the coming of God's kingdom on earth. This coming of God's kingdom is something which Jesus instructed His disciples and by extension, all believers throughout the ages to pray for (Mtt. 6:10). Did the kingdom come in this sense at the crucifixion and resurrection of Jesus? No. We know this from the conditions which the Lord set forth in the prayer: "Your kingdom come. **Your will be done On earth** as *it is* in heaven." [emphasis added] Until God's will is being done "on earth as in heaven," the kingdom of God has not come in the sense Jesus would have us pray for, nor in the way the previous passages describe.

Idealists interpret these passages as symbolizing *spiritual* conflict rather than *physical* conflict whereas *preterists*[5.2.59] tend to see these passages as *hyperbolic*[5.2.27] descriptions of first-century events. But literal interpretation and the many passages indicating that the earth will reject the knowledge of God (Mtt. 24:10-12; 2Th. 2:3; 1Ti. 4:1-3; 2Ti. 3:1-9; 2Pe. 2:3-7) indicate that Christianity will not gradually subsume the social and political institutions of earth resulting in a "Golden Age." Rather, the world system is predicted to eventually *reject and intensely persecute* the people of God. It is only by the *direct intervention of God* and *by His own hand* that peace and justice will prevail. See *Campaign of Armageddon*[4.5].

As in previous *dispensational*[5.2.15] tests of mankind,[2] this age will also end in trouble. The Scriptures frequently describe the events attending this period using the term *tribulation.*

> The term *tribulation* is used in several different ways in Scripture. It is used in a non-technical, non-eschatological sense in reference to any time of suffering or testing into which one goes. It is so used in Matthew 13:21; Mark 4:17; John 16:33; Romans 5:3; 12:12; 2 Corinthians 1:4; 2 Thessalonians 1:4; Revelation 1:8-9. It is used in its technical or eschatological sense in reference to the whole period of the seven years of tribulation, as in Revelation 2:22 or Matthew 24:29. It is also used in reference to the last half of this seven year period, as in Matthew 24:21.[3]

Several well-known titles are applied by Scripture to this coming time of trouble: *the Day of the Lord*[5.2.14], *the Time of Jacob's Trouble*, and *the Great Tribulation.*

The Tribulation precedes the Messianic Kingdom on Earth [4]

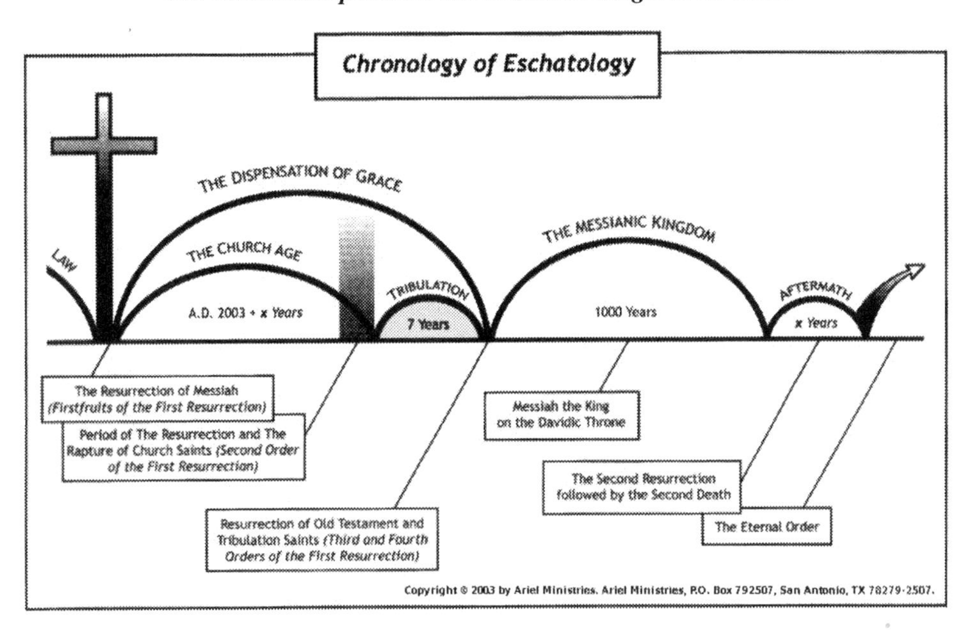

> The concept of trouble or tribulation is associated will all three [titles]: the Day of the Lord in Zep. 1:14-17, the Time of Jacob's Trouble in Jer. 30:7, and the Great Tribulation in Dan. 12:1 [Jesus' Great Tribulation statements in Mtt. 24:21, 29 were a reference to Daniel 12:1, indicating that Daniel is referring to the Great Tribulation]. All three of these Old Testament passages use the same word for trouble. The Hebrew scholars who produced the *Septuagint*[5.2.65] used the Greek word for tribulation to translate this Hebrew word for trouble in Zephaniah 1:15 and Daniel 12:1, showing they understood that both the Day of the Lord and the Great Tribulation will be characterized by tribulation.[5]

This time of trouble is unavoidably connected with "the problem of man." This problem is as old as Satan: **pride.** It is God's express purpose to turn man's pride to humility in "the Day of the Lord."

> Enter into the rock, and hide in the dust, from the terror of the LORD and the glory of His majesty. The lofty looks of man shall be humbled, the haughtiness of men shall be bowed down, and the LORD alone shall be exalted in that day. For **the day of the LORD of hosts** *Shall come* upon everything proud and lofty, upon everything lifted up-And it shall be brought low- upon all the cedars of Lebanon *that are* high and lifted up, and upon all the oaks of Bashan; upon all the high mountains, and upon all the hills *that are* lifted up; upon every high tower, and upon every fortified wall; upon all the ships of Tarshish, and upon all the beautiful sloops. The loftiness of man shall be bowed down, and the haughtiness of men shall be brought low; the LORD alone will be exalted in that day. (Isa. 2:10-17) [emphasis added]

2.13.2 - Jewish Rabbinical Thought

Because this future time of trouble is so clearly portrayed in many *OT*[5.2.51] passages, it should come as no surprise that the Jewish rabbis understood the world would be subjected to cataclysmic events before Messiah would come.[6] "According to the *Babylonian Talmud*, 'The advent of the Messiah was pictured as being preceded by years of great distress.' "[7]

> The idea became entrenched that the coming of the Messiah will be preceded by greatly increased suffering, . . . the pangs of the Messianic times are imagined as having heavenly as well as earthly sources and expressions. From Above, awesome cosmic cataclysms will be visited upon the earth: . . . These will be paralleled by evils brought by men upon themselves: . . . This will last **seven years**. And then, unexpectedly, the Messiah will come. [emphasis added][8]

> *The Babylonian Talmud* states, "Our Rabbis taught: In the seven-year cycle at the end of which the son of David will come . . . at the conclusion of the septennate, the son of David will come" (*Sanhedrin*, 97a, p. 654). [The word *septennate* refers to a period of seven years.][9]

> Another Jewish source known as the *Bereshit Rabbah* states: *If you shall see the kingdoms rising*

against each other in turn, then give heed and note the footsteps of the Messiah (XLII:4).[10]

Where did the rabbis get such ideas? From the Word of God when normally interpreted as the small sample of passages we have given above demonstrates!

2.13.3 - The Day of the Lord

A frequently found phrase throughout Scripture related to this time of trouble is *the Day of the Lord*[5.2.14] (Isa. 2:10-22; 13:6, 9; Jer. 46:2, 10; Eze. 13:5, 9, 14, 21, 23; 30:3-6, 8, 19, 25-26; Dan. 9:1-27; Joel 1:15; 2:1, 11, 31; 3:14; Amos 5:18, 20; Ob. 1:15; Zep. 1:7, 14; Zec. 14:1; Mal. 4:5; Acts 2:20; 1Th. 5:2; 2Pe. 3:10). This particular day is seen to be so unique and significant that it is also referred to as simply, *that day* (Isa. 2:11, 17; 2:20; 4:2; Joel 3:18; Mark 13:32; Luke 21:34; 2Ti. 1:12, 18; 4:8).

> The Day of the Lord refers to God's special interventions into the course of world events to judge His enemies, accomplish His purpose for history, and thereby demonstrate who He is—the sovereign God of the universe.[11]

There is some disagreement concerning whether the phrase "Day of the Lord" refers just to the time of tribulation, or whether it also includes the thousand-year reign of Christ on earth which follows.

> The most common biblical term for the seven years of Tribulation in both testaments is the *Day of Jehovah* or *Day of the Lord.* There are many who use the term, the Day of the Lord, to apply to both the Tribulation and the *Messianic Kingdom*[5.2.39]. This is generally based on the assumption that the phrases, the Day of the Lord and *that day*, are synonymous. While it is true that the expression, that day, has a wide meaning that includes both the Tribulation and the Messianic Kingdom, in those passages where the actual phrase, the Day of the Lord (Jehovah) is used, they never refer to the Millennium, but always to the Tribulation.[12]

We believe there are reasons to understand the phrase as including the millennial reign:

1. Peter's description of the Day of the Lord appears to include events following the Millennium (2Pe. 3:10-12 cf. Rev. 20:11; 21:1).[13]
2. The phrases *this day* and *that day* are not disconnected terms, but involve demonstrative pronouns which make little sense in the absence of any antecedent. The antecedent is seen to be *the Day of the Lord* (Isa. 2:12 cf. 2:20; Joel 3:14 cf. Joel 3:18).

Nevertheless, the phrase *Day of the Lord* is uniformly connected with darkness and judgment, whereas the phrases *this day* and *that day* do appear to be associated with the positive era subsequent to the initial dark elements of the day.[14]

The two-fold nature of the day is characterized by a time of intense darkness followed by incredible blessings:

> The future Day of the Lord will have at least a twofold nature. First, it will be characterized by darkness and a tremendous outpouring of divine wrath upon the world (Joel 2:1-2; Amos 5:18-20; Zep. 1:14-15; 1Th. 5:1-11). Amos 5:18-20 emphasizes that this will be the total nature of the Day of the Lord for God's enemies. It will bring no divine light or blessing to them. This will be the nature of the Day of the Lord during the 70th week of Daniel. Second, the Day of the Lord will also be characterized by light, an outpouring of divine blessing, and the administration of God's rule. The Prophet Joel, after talking about the darkening of the sun, moon, and stars and God's Day of the Lord judgment of the armies of the nations gathered in Israel (Joel 3:9-16), foretold great divine blessing "in that day" (Joel 3:17-21). In addition, the Prophet Zechariah, after discussing the future Day of the Lord, when all nations will war against Jerusalem and the Messiah will come to the earth to fight against the nations (Zec. 14:1-5), indicated that although the earlier part of "that day" will be characterized by darkness, the latter part will be characterized by light (Zec. 14:6-7), great blessing (Zec. 14:8), and God's rule over the earth (Zec. 14:9). This will be the nature of the Day of the Lord in the Millennium. . . . Just as each day of creation and the Jewish day consisted of two phases—a time of darkness ("evening") followed by a time of light ("day") [Gen. 1:4-6]—so the future Day of the Lord will consist of two phases, a period of darkness (judgment) followed by a period of light (divine rule and blessing). . . . First, during the 70th week of Daniel it will be characterized by darkness and a tremendous outpouring of divine wrath upon the world. Second, during the Millennium it will be characterized by light, an outpouring of divine blessing, and the administration of God's rule over the whole world.[15]

This dual nature results from both a *sequential* division (judgment bringing in the Kingdom of God on earth followed by the blessings of the millennial reign of Christ) and a *spiritual* division (the enemies of God will experience only the judgment whereas the people of God will experience the blessings of the millennial reign).

> Since, . . . the present day of Satan and rebellious mankind involves their rule of the world system, the future Day of the Lord would not truly be *His* day if it did not involve His rule of the world system during the Millennium. How could the Day of the Lord fully demonstrate who He is—the sovereign God of the universe—without the sovereign exercise of His rule in visible form over the entire world?[16]

Day of the Lord passages can be difficult to interpret because of the close association of near-term (historic judgments of Israel's enemies) and far-term aspects (astronomical signs). Interpretation in many of these passages is complicated somewhat by the *Law of Double Reference* (clearly evidenced in passages such as Zec. 9:9-10; Isa. 61:1-2 cf. Luke 4:18-21; Mic. 5:2-4):

> This law observes the fact that often a passage or a block of Scripture is speaking of two different persons or two different events which are separated by a long period of time. In the passage itself they are blended into one picture, and the time gap between the two persons or two events is not presented by the text itself. The fact that a gap of time exists is known because of other Scriptures. . .[17]

This has led to some difference of opinion as to whether the phrase *Day of the Lord* applies strictly to the future time of God's direct intervention to bring the rule of Messiah or whether it also includes other "days of the Lord" in past history—significant days when God intervened on behalf of Israel (e.g. Jer. 46:1-10).

> The Bible indicates that there have been several Days of the Lord in the past in which God demonstrated His sovereign rule by raising up several nations to execute His judgement on other nations. He raised up Assyria to judge the northern kingdom of Israel during the 700s B.C. (Amos 5:18, 20), Babylon to judge the southern kingdom of Judah during the 600s and 500s B.C. (Lam. 1:12; 2:1, 21-22; Eze. 7:19; 13:5; Zep. 2:2-3), Babylon to judge Egypt and its allies during the 500s B.C. (Jer. 46:10; Eze. 30:3), and Medo-Persia to judge Babylon during the 500s B.C. (Isa. 13:6, 9).[18]

But among literal interpreters, there is no question that **the** *Day of the Lord* is yet future because it entails cataclysmic events and astronomical signs which are not to be taken as mere *hyperbole*[5.2.27] (Isa. 2:19-21; Joel 2:2-10, 30-31; Zec. 14:12; Acts 2:20; 2Pe. 3:10).

> Isaiah 34:1-8 and Obadiah 15 describe a Day of the Lord when God will judge all nations or Gentiles of the world. None of the past Days of the Lord involved divine judgement of all the nations. . . . In light of this, we can conclude that the Day of the Lord of Isaiah 34 and Obadiah must be future. . . . in 1 Thessalonians 5:1-11 the Apostle Paul referred to a Day of the Lord that was future beyond the time when he wrote his epistle and that would bring sudden, inescapable destruction upon the unsaved of the world.[19]

There appear to be many different titles employed within Scripture to designate this intense time of judgment coming upon the earth.

> Following the translation found in the American Standard Version of the 1901 edition, these names include [in the Old Testament]: The Time of Jacob's Trouble (Jer. 30:7); The Seventieth Week (a seven) of Daniel (Dan. 9:27); Jehovah's Strange Work (Isa. 28:21); Jehovah's Strange Act (Isa. 28:21); The Day of Israel's Calamity (Deu. 32:35; Ob. 1:12-14); The Tribulation (Deu. 4:30); The Indignation (Isa. 26:20; Dan. 11:36); The Overflowing Scourge (Isa. 28:15, 18); The Day of Vengeance (Isa. 34:8; 35:4; 61:2); The Year of Recompense (Isa. 34:8); The Time of Trouble (Dan. 12:1; Zep. 1:15); The Day of Wrath (Zep. 1:15); The Day of Distress (Zep. 1:15); The Day of Wasteness (Zep. 1:15); The Day of Desolation (Zep. 1:15); The Day of Darkness (Zep. 1:15; Amos 5:18, 20; Joel 2:2); The Day of Gloominess (Zep. 1:15; Joel 2:2); The Day of Thick Darkness (Zep. 1:15; Joel 2:2); The Day of the Trumpet (Zep. 1:16); The Day of Alarm (Zep. 1:16). The New Testament names and designations include: The Day of the Lord (1Th. 5:2); The Wrath of God (Rev. 15:1, 7; 14:10, 19; 16:1); The Hour of Trial (Rev. 3:10); The Great Day of the Wrath of the Lamb of God (Rev. 6:16-17); The Wrath to Come (1Th. 1:10); The Wrath (1Th. 5:9; Rev. 11:18); The Great Tribulation (Mtt. 24:21; Rev. 2:22; 7:14); The Tribulation (Mtt. 24:29); The Hour of Judgment (Rev. 14:7).[20]

The *Day of the Lord* includes the judgments described within the book of Revelation which are poured out upon the earth, Israel, Babylon, and the *earth dwellers*[5.2.18]. Passages such as Isaiah 2:10-22 appear to have a direct correlation to the sixth seal (Rev. 6:12-17)[21] whereas Joel 3:1-16 and Zechariah

14:1-3 describe God's judgment of the armies of the world (Rev. 16:12-16; 19:11-21).[22]

2.13.3.1 - When Does the Day of the Lord Dawn?

A point of confusion arises when determining when the *Day of the Lord*[5.2.14] begins. Some of the passages concerning this period *appear* contradictory

1. Paul indicates that the day comes unexpectedly during a time of relative peace and safety: "The day of the Lord so comes as a thief in the night. for **when they say 'peace and safety!'** then sudden destruction comes upon them" [emphasis added] (1Th. 5:2-3). Peter also indicates the unexpected and sudden arrival of the day: "But the day of the Lord will come as a thief in the night, in which the heavens will pass away with a great noise, and the elements will melt with fervent heat; both the earth and the works that are in it will be burned up" (2Pe. 3:10).
2. The proclamation by the *earth dwellers*[5.2.18] *in response to* the cosmic signs of the sixth seal indicate they understand the Day of the Lord has already begun. "Hide us . . . for the great day of His wrath has come and who is able to stand?" (Rev. 6:16-17).
3. Jesus indicates that cosmic signs occur *immediately after the tribulation of those days,* (Mtt. 24:29).
4. Joel says dramatic cosmic signs precede the sixth seal: "And I will show wonders in the heavens and in the earth: blood and fire and pillars of smoke. **The sun shall be turned into darkness and the moon into blood before** the coming of the great and awesome day of the LORD" [emphasis added] (Joel 2:30-31).
5. Zephaniah says silence in heaven will indicate that the Day of the Lord is "at hand" (Zep. 1:7). There is one-half hour of silence prior to opening the seventh seal (Rev. 8:1).

The first two passages imply that the Day of the Lord begins early in the judgment process—prior to the opening of the seventh seal (Rev. 8:1). The last three passages imply that the Day of the Lord must begin *after* the sixth seal, possible with the opening of the seventh seal.

If Paul is correct, then the Day of the Lord cannot begin at a time when severe judgments have *already* been poured out and the earth is reeling from their effects. From Paul's passage, it would appear that the Day of the Lord could not begin after some of the seals have been opened because the first four seals result in worldwide war, bloodshed, famine, disease, and death. One could hardly describe the situation on earth after the first six seals as being one of "peace and safety." But how can we account for the statements of Joel and Zephaniah which seem to imply that the Day of the Lord would begin later—at the opening of the seventh seal or even later?

Answering this question is more important than it might seem because understanding when the Day of the Lord begins is an important aspect of understanding the timing of the *rapture*[4.14]. If God's wrath is poured forth on the Day of the Lord, then the church is taken up prior to the day. If the day begins with the opening of the first four seals by the Lamb (Rev. 6:2-8), then the church is taken up prior to that point (a *pretribulational*[5.2.60] *rapture*[5.2.62]). If the day begins with the opening of the seventh seal (Rev. 8:1), then the church could be on earth during the first six seal judgments (a pre-wrath rapture).[23] The pretribulation rapture view holds that God's wrath begins with the opening of the first seal (Rev. 6:1), whereas the pre-wrath rapture view holds that none of the first six seals involve God's wrath and that His wrath only begins with the opening of the seventh seal. Therefore, pre-wrath advocates argue that the Day of the Lord does not begin until the opening of the seventh seal. Both positions believe the church is spared from God's wrath and will be taken up prior to the Day of the Lord, but differ in their understanding of *when* the Day of the Lord begins.

Regarding the seemingly contradictory statements of Paul, Joel, Zephaniah, and John: how do we solve this "bible difficulty?" For one, we remember the *Golden Rule of Interpretation*[5.2.24]: that Scripture interprets Scripture. The Word of God is given by the Holy Spirit and so is self-consistent. Whatever "contradiction" we see must be a result of our lack of understanding.

So which is it? Does the day come as a thief, *unexpectedly* upon a relatively tranquil world? Or does it come after dramatic cosmic signs and the first six seals wreak worldwide havoc? The answer appears to be . . . *both!* In understanding the various uses of the phrase *Day of the Lord*, Showers identifies both a *broad* and a *narrow* sense:

> The biblical expression "the Day of the Lord" has a double sense (broad and narrow) in relationship to the future. The broad sense refers to an extended period of time involving divine interventions related at least to the 70th week of Daniel and the thousand-year Millennium. . . . Concerning this broad sense, A. B. Davidson wrote: "Though the "Day of the Lord," as the expression implies, was at first conceived as a definite and brief period of time, being an era of judgment and salvation, it many times broadened out to be an extended period. From being a day it became an epoch." . . .in the narrow sense it refers to one specific day—the day on which Christ will return to the earth from heaven with His angels.[24]

Thus, the phrase, *Day of the Lord*, can denote the entire period from when the initial judgments of God are first manifested (at a time of relative peace and safety) through the end of the Millennium (the broad sense) or it can denote the *specific day* upon which Christ physically returns to earth to destroy the armies gathered against Him (Rev. 19:11-21).

When Paul refers to the day coming "as a thief . . . when they say peace and safety," he is referring to the Day of the Lord in its broad sense. There will be no warning—there is no prophetic precondition that warns of the coming of the Day of the Lord in its broad sense—it is *imminent*[4.8]. When the earth dwellers react to the cosmic shaking of the sixth seal, they understand the Day of the Lord to already be in progress—the broad definition. Peace and safety are long gone—having been taken by the previous seals—and with these cosmic disturbances, it has become evident that it is *God Himself* who is behind the global disruption.

When Joel indicates that cosmic signs occur "before" the Day of the Lord, he is speaking of the narrow sense—the precise *24-hour period* in which Jesus Christ will return to earth physically in judgment (Rev. 19:11-21).[25] When Zephaniah speaks of silence in heaven indicating that the Day of the Lord is "at hand" (Zep. 1:7 cf. Rev. 8:1), he too uses the phrase in its narrow sense:

> Be silent in the presence of the Lord GOD; for the day of the LORD *is* at hand, for the LORD has prepared a sacrifice; He has invited His guests. And it shall be, in the day of the LORD'S sacrifice, that I will punish the princes and the king's children, and all such as are clothed with foreign apparel. (Zep 1:7-8)

Notice Zephaniah's emphasis on a *sacrifice* attending the Day of the Lord. A sacrifice which involves kings and princes. This speaks, in an eschatological sense, of the *very day* on which Jesus returns physically to earth and defeats the armies gathered against Him (Rev. 19:17-19). This can also be seen in the statement made by John concerning the spirits of demons which gather the kings of the earth "to gather them to the battle **of that great day of God Almighty**" [emphasis added] (Rev. 16:14). This is long after the opening of the first seal, the sixth seal, and even the seventh seal.

The Day of the Lord begins, in its broad sense, when peace and safety is taken from the earth (possibly during the opening of the first seal, certainly by the opening of the second). By the time of the sixth seal, the world is *already* in chaos, but the cosmic disturbances make plain even to the earth dwellers that God's wrath is already in progress. The cosmic signs of the sixth seal and the silence before opening the seventh seal precede the Day of the Lord in its narrow sense—they occur before the final intervention of Jesus in the final destruction of His enemies prior to establishing the *Millennial Kingdom*[5.2.39].

When these uses of the phrase are understood, we see that the day begins in the broadest sense when "peace and safety" are taken away when the day comes as a "thief in the night." It is our belief that this occurs no later than the opening of the second seal. We disagree with the pre-wrath rapture position which holds that God's wrath, and the Day of the Lord, does not begin until the opening of the seventh seal. We believe that God's wrath is associated with *all seven seals* and that the church will be taken up before this time. See *Rapture*[4.14].

2.13.4 - Jacob's Trouble and the Great Tribulation

Two other titles which are related to the coming *Day of the Lord*[5.2.14] are *the Time of Jacob's Trouble* and *the Great Tribulation*.[26] Notice that all three involve the concept of an *unparalleled* time of trouble. *Unparalleled* implies two things concerning the time periods involved:

1. Since there cannot be more than one *unparalleled* time of trouble, their time periods must overlap.[27]
2. These events have not transpired in the past.[28]

Regarding the timing of the Great Tribulation, Jesus said

> "Therefore when you see the 'abomination of desolation,' spoken of by Daniel the prophet, standing in the holy place" (whoever reads, let him understand), "then let those who are in Judea flee to the mountains. Let him who is on the housetop not go down to take anything out of his house. And let him who is in the field not go back to get his clothes. But woe to those who are pregnant and to those who are nursing babies in those days! And pray that your flight may not be in winter or on the Sabbath. For then there will be great tribulation, such as has not been since the beginning of the world until this time, no, nor ever shall be. And unless those days were shortened, no flesh would be saved; but for the elect's sake those days will be shortened." (Mtt. 24:15-22)
>
> Jesus referred to this Daniel 9:27 "overspreading of abominations" in Matthew 24:15. Then He said, "then shall be Great Tribulation, such as was not since the beginning of the world to this time, no, nor ever shall be" (Mtt. 24:21), thereby indicating that the Great Tribulation will begin when the overspreading of abominations of Daniel 9:27 occurs. Since the Great Tribulation will begin when the overspreading of abominations occurs in the middle of the 70th week, we can conclude that the Great Tribulation will begin in the middle of the 70th week of Daniel, or after the first three and one-half years of that seven-year period have transpired.[29]

Notice Jesus says, "let those who are in Judea flee to the mountains" and "pray that your flight may not be . . . on the Sabbath." There is an explicit Jewish element to this entire passage. This is because the events are related to *the Time of Jacob's Trouble* described by Jeremiah:

> 'For behold, the days are coming,' says the LORD, 'that I will bring back from captivity My people Israel and Judah,' says the LORD. 'And I will cause them to return to the land that I gave to their fathers, and they shall possess it.' Now these *are* the words that the LORD spoke concerning Israel and Judah. For thus says the LORD: 'We have heard a voice of trembling, of fear, and not of peace. Ask now, and see, whether a man is ever in labor with child? So why do I see every man *with* his hands on his loins like a woman in labor, and all faces turned pale? Alas! For that day *is* great, so that none *is* like it; and it *is* the time of Jacob's trouble, but he shall be saved out of it.' (Jer. 30:3-7)

Notice several important aspects within this passage:

1. **Jacob is Israel** - Jacob fathered the 12 tribes and was given the name Israel by God (Gen. 32:28). Thus, this is describing a time of trouble specifically for the Jews.
2. **Gathering in the Land** - This time of trouble occurs *after* Israel is gathered back in the Promised Land.
3. **Birth Pangs** - The passage refers to every man acting "like a woman in labor." How similar this is to the words of Jesus, "All these are the beginning of sorrows" (Mtt. 24:8). *Sorrows* (ωδιν [*ōdin*]) indicates "a pang or throe, **especially of childbirth**." [emphasis added][30]
4. **A Unique Day** - There is *no other day like it.*
5. **Results in Salvation** - "But he shall be saved out of it." Although the Jews undergo an extremely troubling time, salvation comes at the end.[31]

The Jewish aspect of this period can also be seen in the wider context of Micah's well-known prophecy concerning the birthplace of Messiah:

> Now gather yourself in troops, O daughter of troops; He has laid siege against us; they will strike the judge of Israel with a rod on the cheek. But you, Bethlehem Ephrathah, *Though* you are little among the thousands of Judah, *yet* out of you shall come forth to Me The One to be Ruler in Israel, Whose goings forth *are* from of old, from everlasting. **Therefore He shall give them up, until the time *that* she who is in labor has given birth; then the remnant of His brethren shall return to the children of Israel.** And He shall stand and feed *His flock* In the strength of the LORD, in the majesty of the name of the LORD His God; and they shall abide, for now He shall be great to the ends of the earth. (Mic. 5:1-4) [emphasis added]

Scripture record's *two* pregnancies in relation to Messiah. The first labor terminates in the First Coming of Messiah (Rev. 12:2-4). The second labor terminates in the ushering in of the *Millennial Kingdom*[5.2.39]. It is this second period of labor, subsequent to the going forth of Messiah from Bethlehem, which Micah sets forth. This second labor leads to the millennial age: "For now He shall be great to the ends of the earth." The time of Jacob's trouble describes the labor pains associated with the second pregnancy.

> "She who travaileth" does not refer to Israel bringing forth (giving birth to) Messiah, but to her last-day Tribulation travail (Jer. 30:5-7) in bringing forth a believing remnant, . . . Israel's greatest and most anguishing sufferings of all her long and checkered history of woe will take place during the coming Great Tribulation (Rev. 8:1-20:3). Her terrible travail pains that in God's plan precede the joy of birth (cf. Mic. 4:9; cf. John 16:21), will bring forth a regenerated nation to enter the joy of the Kingdom, which will be as unparalleled as the agony that introduces it.[32]

This period is mentioned in the book of Revelation and also Daniel which provides additional details as to its duration:[33]

> Revelation 12 states the length of time this persecution and hiding of the Jews in the wilderness will last . . . it will last 1,260 days (Rev. 12:6) . . . Revelation 12:14 states that Israel will hide in the wilderness from Satan for "a time, and times, and half a time." Daniel 7:25 uses this identical time designation for the length of time that the *Antichrist*[5.2.3] will persecute the saints of the 70th week. . . . Revelation 13:5-7, when referring to this same persecution of 70th-week saints by the Antichrist, declares that it will last for 42 months, which equal three and one-half years. . . . The Jews will be persecuted and will hide in a wilderness area for three and one-half years, exactly one-half of the seven-year 70th week. . . . the Great Tribulation will be finished when God has completely shattered the obstinate rebellion of the nation of Israel against Him [Dan. 9:24; 12:7]. In other words, the Great Tribulation will end when Israel's rebellion against God's rule ends.[34]

Scofield summarizes the character of this unique period:

> The elements of the tribulation are: (1) The cruel reign of the "beast out of the sea" (Rev. 13:1), who, at the beginning of the three and a half years, will break his covenant with the Jews (by virtue of which they will have re-established the temple worship, Dan. 9:27), and show himself in the temple, demanding that he be worshipped as God (Mtt. 24:15; 2Th. 2:4). (2) The active interposition of Satan "having great wrath" (Rev. 12:12), who gives his power to the *Beast*[5.2.9] (Rev. 13:4, 5). (3) The unprecedented activity of demons (Rev. 9:2, 11); and (4) the terrible "bowl" judgments of Rev. 16.[35]

Although the book of Revelation indicates that all those living on the earth immediately prior to the return of Jesus will be involved in troublesome times, this is especially true for the Jews. This is because God applies judgment first and more fully to those who have greater revelation and responsibility (Amos 3:2; Luke 12:48).[36]

> While it is true that all will suffer during that time, Israel will suffer more so. The basic reason for this lies in Israel's relationship to God as God's first born (Ex. 4:22) and, therefore, Israel receives double, both in blessing and cursing. The principle that Israel receives double for all her sins is stated in Isaiah 40:1-2 . . . It is also found in Jeremiah 16:16-18. The principle of Israel's receiving double for all her sins is the reason why the Tribulation is uniquely the Time of Jacob's Trouble.[37]
>
> Stanton shows the Jewish character of the period by saying: "The tribulation is primarily Jewish. This fact is borne out by Old Testament Scriptures (Deu. 4:30; Jer. 30:7; Eze. 20:37; Dan. 12:1; Zec. 13:8-9), by the Olivet Discourse of Christ (Mtt. 24:9-26), and by the book of Revelation itself (Rev. 7:4-8; 12:1-2, 17 etc.). It concerns 'Daniel's people,' the coming of 'false Messiah,' the preaching of the 'gospel of the kingdom,' flight on the 'sabbath,' the temple and the 'holy place,' the land of Judea, the city of Jerusalem, the twelve 'tribes of the children of Israel,' the 'son of Moses,' 'signs' in the heavens, the 'covenant' with the Beast, the 'sanctuary,' the 'sacrifice and the oblation' of the temple ritual—these all speak of Israel and prove that the tribulation is largely a time when God deals with His ancient people prior to their entrance into the promised kingdom."[38]

Our study of the book of Revelation will greatly benefit by keeping in mind the purposes God has for this period of time:

> The first purpose is to make an end of wickedness and wicked ones (Isa. 13:9; Isa. 24:19-20) . . . The second purpose of the Tribulation is to bring about a worldwide revival (Rev. 7:1-7) . . . The Third purpose of the Tribulation is to break the power of the stubborn will of the Jewish nation (Dan. 12:5-7;

Eze. 20:33-38).[39]

The Old Testament presents at least five purposes for the Tribulation. **1** . The Tribulation will complete the decreed period of national Israel's judicial hardening as punishment for its rejection of the messianic program, which the partial return from exile did not remove and which culminated in the national rejection of Jesus (Isa. 6:9-13; 24:1-6; cf. John 12:37-41; Rom. 11:7-10). **2** . It will produce a messianic revival among Jewish people scattered throughout the world (Deu. 4:27-30; cf. Rev. 7:1-4; Mtt. 24:14). **3** . The Tribulation will convince the Jewish nation of their need for the Messiah in order to produce a national regeneration (Dan. 12:5-7; Jer. 31:31-34; Eze. 20:34-38; 36:25-27; 37:1-14; Zec. 12:9-13:2; Isa. 59:20-21). This will result in a massive return of Jews to the land of Israel (Zec. 8:7-8; Eze. 36:24; 37:21). **4** . It will end the time of the Gentiles and effect the deliverance of the Jewish people from Gentile dominion (Isa. 24:21-23; 59:16-20; cf. Mtt. 24:29-31; Mark 13:24-27; Rom. 11:25). **5** . The Tribulation will purge the earth of wicked people in order to establish the Messianic Kingdom in righteousness (Isa. 13:9; 24:19-20; Eze. 37:23; Zec. 13:2; 14:9; Isa. 11:9). This violent reduction of the world's unbelieving population will result from the divine judgments unleashed throughout the Tribulation (Rev. 6-18), climaxing with the Battle of Armageddon under King Messiah (Rev. 19) and His purge of rebel Jews and oppressive Gentiles at the end of the Tribulation (Eze. 20:33-38; Mtt. 25:31-46).[40]

2.13.5 - The 70th Week of Daniel

Another period set forth by the *OT*[5.2.51] which involves a time of calamity with Jewish focus is the *70th week of Daniel* (Dan. 9:24-27). This prophecy was introduced to Daniel by Gabriel as follows:

> Seventy weeks are determined for your people and for your holy city, to finish the transgression, to make an end of sins, to make reconciliation for iniquity, to bring in everlasting righteousness, to seal up vision and prophecy, and to anoint the Most Holy. (Dan. 9:24)

Notice that the entire period is determined for *Daniel's people* and *Daniel's holy city*. These are none other than the *Jews* and *Jerusalem. The entire scope of this prophecy pertains to the Jews*. While it is beyond our purposes here to deal with the entire prophecy in all its detail, we pause to note that at least two aspects of the introduction infer a fulfillment yet future even to our own day:

1. **To finish the transgression**: If this refers to a specific transgression, (and some believe it does because the noun translated 'the transgression,' חַטָּאת [*chattā`t*], is singular), that transgression involves the rejection of her Messiah by the Jewish nation. Since the majority of Jews still are opposed to the notion of Jesus Christ as their Messiah, this has not yet happened.
2. **To seal up vision and prophecy**: Neither has this been completed. Sealing does not mean that all vision and prophecy would simply be delivered to the saints (e.g., the close of the *canon*[5.2.12]), but that all vision and prophecy will find *fulfillment*.[41]

2.13.5.1 - Weeks of Years

The word translated "weeks" simply means "sevens" and can be shown from the context to be seventy sevens *of years*:

> Each year of [the Babylonian] captivity represented one seven-year cycle in which the seventh or Sabbath year had not been observed. Thus it is clear that the context refers to years, not days.[42]

The usage of the Hebrew word for "sevens" elsewhere in Daniel also argues that weeks of days are not meant here:

> The Hebrew word shabua is found only in one other passage of the book (Dan. 10:2-3), where the prophet states that he mourned and fasted "three full weeks." Now here it is perfectly obvious that the context demands "weeks" of days. . . And significantly, the Hebrew here reads literally "three sevens of days." Now if in the ninth chapter, the writer intended us to understand that the "seventy sevens" are composed of days, why did he not use the same form of expression adopted in chapter ten?[43]

> There are four good reasons for believing that the "seven" intended here is a period of seven years: (1) Daniel has just been concerned about years (Dan. 9:1-2). (2) It is impossible to fit the events of verses 24–27 into 490 days or weeks. (3) In the only other place where Daniel uses the word week, he qualifies it by adding the word days (Dan. 10:2-3). (4) Finally, the fact that Dan. 9:27 speaks of a covenant being

broken at the half-way point of the seventieth seven agrees well with Dan. 7:7, 12, 25; and Rev. 12:14, which speak of three-and-one-half years as one-half of a week.[44]

2.13.5.2 - Prophetic Year

Further, these 70 x 7 = 490 *years* can be shown to consist of exactly 360 days each. They are not based on the year of our modern calendar which is either 365 days (normal year) or 366 days (leap year) long. This reflects historical differences in how the calendar year has been adjusted to account for the fact that the astronomical year is not an exact number of days.

The astronomical year consists of approximately 365 days. If we treated each year as exactly 365 days, the calendar date would slowly advance further and further ahead of the astronomical year becoming out of step with the seasons. We solve this inaccuracy by appending an extra day onto the month of February on leap year. However, in the past there have been different solutions employed for handling this problem:

> With modern astronomy one can reckon a year very precisely as being '365.24219879 days, or 365 days, 5 hours, 48 minutes, 45.975 seconds.' However, in ancient times various systems were used. When one investigates the calendars of ancient India, Persia, Babylonia and Assyria, Egypt, Central and South America, and China it is interesting to notice that they uniformly had twelve thirty-day months (a few had eighteen twenty-day months) making a total of 360 days for the year and they had various methods of intercalating days so that the year would come out correctly. Although it may be strange to present-day thinking, it was common in those days to think of a 360-day year.[45]

The more recent Jewish Calendar utilized a combination of the sun and moon:

> It is called "lunar-solar" because it allowed the sun's orbit to mark the years' beginning but based the beginning of months on observation of the phases of the moon. The first appearance of the new moon would mark the new month. According to the Talmud, the priests would watch for this and proclaim it by sending messengers and blowing trumpets. The first problem is that the moon's circuit is about 29 1/2 days, forcing a vacillation between a 30-day and a 29-day month; and second, that 12 of these moon/months equal 354 1/4 days, about 11 days short of the solar year. From the Babylonians the Hebrews learned to add an extra month every two or three years. In rabbinical times this "intercalary" month was inserted seven times in 19 years.[46]

Yet we have evidence from the time of Noah that months did not alternate in length between 30 days and 29 days. The book of Genesis indicates a 5-month period as being *exactly* 150 days in length, or five 30-day months:

> The time measurements encountered in Genesis chapters 7 and 8 are the result of a lunar calendar. Gen. 7:11 states the flood began on the seventeenth day of the second month, and it ended on the seventeenth day of the seventh month (Gen. 8:4), exactly five months. Both Gen. 7:24 and 8:3 declare the waters were upon the earth 150 days. Assuming each month is the same length, they would have 30 days apiece. Skeptics say that is a big assumption because the story does not cover an entire year, and thus doesn't take into account any days the ancients may have added on to their year.[47]

It appears that the earlier Jewish calendar may have been simpler than the "lunar-solar" system. "Ussher found that the ancient Jews and the Egyptians did not use a year based on the moon. Instead they had a year made up of 12 months, each 30 days long. At the end of the year they tacked on 5 days. Every 4 years they added 6 days."[48] We also have indication in Scripture that a simpler 360-day calendar is found within prophetic passages:

- Daniel indicates a period of seven years as the final "week" of the seventy weeks, but which is divided in half (Dan. 9:24). The period of half of this final week of years is denoted by "time, times, and half" (Dan. 7:25; 12:7), or *one, two, and one-half* = 3.5 years.
- John records the duration of the period during which Jerusalem will be trampled by the Gentiles as "forty-two months" (Rev. 11:2). If twelve 30-day months are used, this period corresponds exactly to 3.5 years of 360 days each.
- The two witnesses are said to prophesy for "one thousand two hundred and sixty days" (Rev. 11:3) which is also exactly 42 months of 30 days each or 3.5 years of 360 days each.
- The woman who flees from the dragon is fed by God for "one thousand two hundred and sixty days" (Rev. 12:6) which is also described as "time and times and half a time" (Rev.

12:14). Thus 1,260 days = 3.5 years of 360 days each.

- The beast is given authority for "forty-two months" (Rev. 13:5). This probably corresponds to the "one thousand two hundred and sixty days" during which the dragon persecutes the woman. It is also said to be "time and times and half a time" (Dan. 7:25). Thus 42 months of 30 days each = 3.5 years of 360 days each = 1,260 days.

When the various evidences are considered, it seems best to conclude:

1. Daniel's "weeks" are weeks of *years*.
2. The prophetic year consists of *360 days*.

2.13.5.3 - The Final Week

Daniel's seventy sevens of years are divided into three sequences: seven sevens, sixty-two sevens, and a final seven (Dan. 9:25-27). After the seven and sixty-two sevens (sixty-nine total), "Messiah shall be cut off" (Dan. 9:26). Thus the sixty-ninth week is seen to come to an end *before* the crucifixion of Christ. Several events are seen to transpire after the sixty-ninth week, but *before* the last week begins. These include the cutting off of Messiah and the destruction of Jerusalem by Rome.

> And **after** the sixty-two weeks Messiah shall be cut off, but not for Himself; and the people of the prince who is to come shall destroy the city and the sanctuary. The end of it *shall be* with a flood, and till the end of the war desolations are determined. (Dan. 9:26) [emphasis added]

It is only after these events that the last week begins:

> **Then** he shall confirm a covenant with many for one week; but in the middle of the week he shall bring an end to sacrifice and offering. And on the wing of abominations shall be one who makes desolate, even until the consummation, which is determined, is poured out on the desolate. (Dan. 9:27) [emphasis added]

It appears that the final week begins when the "prince who is to come" (Dan. 9:26) confirms a covenant "with the many for one week." This final seven years is known as *The 70th Week of Daniel*. Notice Gabriel mentions that it is in *the middle of the week* that he shall "bring an end to sacrifice and offering." This would be after the covenant had been in place three and one-half years.

Since the book of Revelation deals with the final stages of Jewish and Gentile history prior to the return of Messiah, it is no surprise to find the same time period set forth in relation to events it records (Rev. 11:2-3; 12:6, 14; 13:5).

> [The] period of totalitarian world rule under the beast is predicted to be just "forty-two months" before he is defeated and the millennium begins (Revelation 13:4, 5; 19:20). Before that period is still another period of "1260 days," marked by the unrestrained prophesying and miraculous works of "two witnesses" (Revelation 11:3), whose influence is finally overcome by the "beast" as he consolidates his world power (Revelation 11:7). These two periods—1260 days and forty-two months—are obviously consecutive and each corresponds to a period of three-and-a-half years, . . . a final seven-year period of earth history immediately prior to the millennium. The last half of this period apparently contains the events described in Chapters 12-19. Correspondingly, the first half of the period is outlined in Chapters 4-11.[49]

> Chapters 4-19 are believed to synchronize with Daniel's Seventieth Week (Dan. 9:24 . . .). The great tribulation begins at the middle of the "week," and continues three and a half years (Rev. 11:3-19:21). The tribulation is brought to an end by the appearing of the Lord and the battle of Armageddon (Mtt. 24:29, 30; Rev. 19:11-21).[50]

The book of Revelation provides further details corresponding to this final seven year period of Gabriel's prophecy given to Daniel. The final fulfillment of all that Gabriel prophesied to Daniel concerning the Jews and Jerusalem is part and parcel of the revelation given to John and recorded in the book of Revelation.

2.13.5.4 - Events of the 70th Week of Daniel

The parallels between Revelation and Daniel's 70th week have not gone unnoticed.[51] Although it is impossible to know with certainty the absolute sequence among all the events recorded by Scripture associated with the final week, the timing of some of the more significant events can be established.[52]

Events during the First Half of the 70th Week

Event	Scriptures
Antichrist[5.2.3] establishes covenant with many in Israel.	Dan. 9:27
144,000 Jews sealed for protection.	Rev. 7:1-8
Jews sacrifice and worship at the temple in Jerusalem.	Dan. 9:27; Rev. 11:1
Two witnesses prophesy and torment the *earth dwellers*[5.2.18].	Rev. 11:3-6
Seven seals opened, six of seven trumpets sounded.[53]	Rev. 6:1-17; Rev. 8:1-9:21

Events during the Middle of the 70th Week

Event[54]	Scriptures
Beast given authority.[55]	Dan. 7:25; Rev. 13:5
Two witnesses killed and resurrected.[56]	Rev. 11:7-12
Antichrist violates covenant.	Dan. 7:25; 9:27
Sacrifice halted at the temple in Jerusalem.	Dan. 9:27
Abomination of Desolation.	Dan. 9:27; 11:31; [57] 12:11; Mtt. 24:15; Mark 13:14; 2Th. 2:4; Rev. 13:15[58] See commentary on *Revelation 13:15*[3.13.15].
Jews flee persecution.	Mtt. 24:15-20; Mark 13:14-18 ; Rev. 12:6, 14

Events during the Last Half of the 70th Week

Event	Scriptures
Seventh trumpet sounded.[59]	Rev. 11:15
Beast and his image kill the saints.	Dan. 7:21, 25; 8:24; Rev. 7:9-16; 12:11; 13:7, 15; 20:4
Seven bowls poured out.[60]	Rev. 16:1-21
Jews recognize and call for Messiah Jesus.	Lev. 26:40-42; Hos. 5:15-6:3; Zec. 13:9; Mtt. 23:39; Luke 13:35
Campaign of Armageddon[4.5] & Second Coming	Isa. 63:1-6; Joel 3:9-16; Zec. 12:1-9; 14:1-5; Rev. 16:12-16; 19:17-21

2.13.5.5 - The 70th Week in Relation to the Book of Revelation

The following simplified outline from Fruchtenbaum illustrates how Daniel's 70th week (the Tribulation) relates to the overall chronology of the events in the book of Revelation .[61]

The Tribulation in the book of Revelation

Passage	Description
Rev. 1:1-3	Introduction.
Rev. 1:4-8	Salutation.
Rev. 1:9-20	The Things That John Saw.
Rev. 2:1-3:22	The Things Which Are.
Rev. 4:1-5:14	Events in Heaven Preceding the Great Tribulation.[62]
Rev. 6:1-9:21	**First Half of the Tribulation.**
Rev. 10:1-14:20	**Events of the Middle of the Tribulation.**
Rev. 15:1-16:21	**The Second Half of the Tribulation.**
Rev. 17:1-18	Ecclesiastical Babylon (Recurrence: First Half).[63]
Rev. 18:1-24	Political Babylon (Recurrence: Second Half).
Rev. 19:1-20:3	The Second Coming and Aftermath.
Rev. 20:4-6	The *Messianic Kingdom*[5.2.39].
Rev. 20:7-14	The Aftermath of the Messianic Kingdom.
Rev. 21:2-22:5	The Eternal Order.
Rev. 22:6-21	Conclusion.

2.13.6 - The Synoptic Gospels

Further evidence that the book of Revelation sets forth future events is found in the parallels between what the book of Revelation records and the answers Jesus gave in response to the questions of the disciples regarding the sign of His coming. "Now as He sat on the Mount of Olives, the disciples came to Him privately, saying, 'Tell us, when will these things be? And what *will be* the sign of Your coming, and of the end of the age?' " (Mtt. 24:3) Jesus' response as they sat on the Mount of Olives is known as *The Olivet Discourse* and is recorded in the synoptic gospels. Since the disciples asked about the signs of His Second Coming and the end of the age, and the book of Revelation also records events leading up to His Second Coming, we expect to find a close correlation between the two. "Thematic parallels between the birth pangs of the synoptics (Mtt. 24:4-8; Mark 13:5-8; c.f. Luke 21:8-19) and the first six seals of the Apocalypse (Rev. 6:1-11) show a definite correlation between the events described in the passages."[64] "A comparison of Christ's description of the beginning of birth pangs in Matthew 24:5-7 with the first four seals of Revelation 6:1-8 indicates that the beginning of birth pangs and the first four seals are the same thing."[65]

John McLean identifies the following parallels between the Olivet Discourse and the book of Revelation.[66]

Parallels Between the Olivet Discourse and the Seal Judgments of Revelation

Event	Revelation 6	Matthew 24	Mark 13	Luke 21
False messiahs, false prophets.	Rev. 6:2	Mtt. 24:5, 11	Mark 13:6	Luke 21:8
Wars.	Rev. 6:2-4	Mtt. 24:6-7	Mark 13:7	Luke 21:9
International discord.	Rev. 6:3-4	Mtt. 24:7	Mark 13:8	Luke 21:10
Famines.	Rev. 6:5-8	Mtt. 24:7	Mark 13:8	Luke 21:11
Pestilences.	Rev. 6:8	-	-	Luke 21:11
Persecution, martyrdom.	Rev. 6:9-11	Mtt. 24:9	Mark 13:9-13	Luke 21:12-17
Earthquakes.	Rev. 6:12	Mtt. 24:7	Mark 13:8	Luke 21:11
Cosmic phenomena.	Rev. 6:12-14	[Mtt. 24:29][67]	[Mark 13:24-25]	Luke 21:11

Here we see the characteristic "fingerprint of the Holy Spirit" in the Scriptures. Individual men writing at different times, who lack detailed information from the other writers of Scripture, achieve consistency in describing the same topics or events.

Many who have studied the Olivet Discourse understand the "abomination of desolation" mentioned by Jesus (Mtt. 24:15) as marking the dividing point of the final seven years:

> Christ introduced and discussed the *beginning* of birth pangs (Mtt. 24:4-8) *before* He introduced the abomination of desolation and the Great Tribulation (Mtt. 24:15-21), and it appears that He introduced and discussed events in chronological order in this section of Matthew 24. This implies that the beginning of birth pangs will precede the abomination of desolation (of the middle of the 70th week) and the Great Tribulation (of the second half of the 70th week) and therefore will occur during the first half of that seven-year period.[68]

2.13.7 - The Plagues of Egypt and the Tribulation

There are numerous similarities between the plagues with which God afflicted Egypt resulting in the Exodus of Israel and the plagues of the Tribulation. This correspondence is intentional and is an indication of the correspondence between the recorded facts of past history and the prophesied facts concerning the future:

1. **Literal Plagues** - In the same way that the plagues of Egypt were literal and historical events, so the plagues of the Tribulation period will be too.[69]
2. **Testing the Unrepentant** - In the same way that Pharaoh of the Exodus refused to repent (Ex. 7:13, 23; 8:15, 19, 22; 9:34), the *earth dwellers*[5.2.18] will refuse to repent during the Tribulation (Rev. 2:21; 6:16-17; 9:20; 16:9, 11, 21). The plagues test the opponents of God demonstrating the hardness of their hearts (Rev. 3:10). God gains glory in the events of their judgment (Ex. 7:3; 9:16; 11:9; Rom. 9:17-22).
3. **Establishing a Kingdom** - The plagues of Egypt resulted in the overthrow of Egypt and the birth of the theocratic kingdom of Israel. The plagues of the Tribulation result in the overthrow of the system of *Antichrist*[5.2.3] and usher in the *Millennial Kingdom*[5.2.39] establishing the reign of God on earth.

> There is a definite parallel between the supernatural preparation for the kingdom in history under Moses and the supernatural judgments which shall be poured out upon a rebellious world in preparation for the future Millennial Kingdom of our Lord Jesus Christ at His second advent. There is the same insolent challenge to the true God on the part of the Gentile powers (Ps. 2:1-3). There will be a similar gracious but infinitely greater preliminary miracle [like Ex. 7:12]—the *Rapture*[5.2.62] of the Church—warning men of the supremacy of Jehovah and the ultimate defeat of all who rebel against Him. There will be the same swift progression in the severity of the divine judgments which follow, and even a striking parallel in the nature of the judgments (cf. Rev. 6:1-17 through 18). There will be the same victorious outcome,

the destruction of the antichrist and his armies in the judgment of Armageddon, and deliverance of the people of Israel (Rev. 19:1-21). There will be another song of victory, significantly referred to as 'the song of Moses. . . and the song of the Lamb' (Rev. 15:1-3).[70]

The Plagues Compared

Plague	Egypt	Tribulation
#1 - Water becomes blood.	Ex. 7:20; Ps. 105:29	Rev. 8:8-9; 11:6; 16:3-6
#2 - Frogs	Ex. 8:6; Ps. 105:30	Rev. 16:13[71]
#3 - Lice	Ex. 8:24; Ps. 105:31	Rev. 11:6?[72]
#4 - Flies	Ex. 9:6	Rev. 11:6?[73]
#5 - Food source (livestock) destroyed	Ex. 9:6	Rev. 8:9[74]
#6 - Boils	Ex. 9:10	Rev. 16:2
#7 - Hail	Ex. 9:23; Ps. 105:32	Rev. 8:7; 16:21
#8 - Locusts	Ex. 10:13; Ps. 105:34	Rev. 9:3
#9 - Darkness	Ex. 10:22; Ps. 105:32	Rev. 8:12; 9:2; 16:10
#10 - Death of Firstborn	Ex. 12:29; Ps. 105:36	-

At the completion of the plagues of Egypt, God parted the Red Sea (Ex. 14:21; Ne. 9:11) allowing Israel to escape from Egypt and travel to Mount Sinai where Moses was given the Law and the *theocracy*[5.2.76] of Israel was established. The gathering of Israel at the end of the Tribulation will be by similar miraculous power.

> The LORD will utterly destroy the tongue of the Sea of Egypt; with His mighty wind He will shake His fist over the River, and strike it in the seven streams, and make *men* cross over dry-shod. There will be a highway for the remnant of His people who will be left from Assyria, as it was for Israel in the day that he came up from the land of Egypt. (Isa. 11:15-16)

> I will also bring them back from the land of Egypt, and gather them from Assyria. I will bring them into the land of Gilead and Lebanon, until no *more room* is found for them. He shall pass through the sea with affliction, and strike the waves of the sea: all the depths of the River shall dry up. Then the pride of Assyria shall be brought down, and the scepter of Egypt shall depart. "So I will strengthen them in the LORD, and they shall walk up and down in His name," says the LORD. (Zec. 10:10-12)

The result will be the establishment of the Millennial Kingdom on earth (Rev. 20:4-6). See *The Arrival of God's Kingdom*[2.4.3].

2.13.8 - Genesis and Revelation as Bookends

Having explored the parallels between events in the book of Revelation and passages which speak of a future time of trouble for both the world and the Jews, we now expand our scope to consider the role which Revelation plays as an opposite "bookend" to Genesis. "Ponder for a moment about the books you have in your study. What keeps most of them in a tidy, neat row? The bookends! Consider the books of Genesis and Revelation. They are the 'bookends' of the Word of God."[75]

> The Book of Revelation is the sequel to the Book of Genesis, the two books together bounding all history and bounding all of God's revelations to mankind. They constitute the alpha and omega of God's written Word, the Book of Beginnings and the Book of Unveilings.[76]

Given the extensive list of correlations which follow, it is hard to imagine how some in history could have questioned the role of the book of Revelation within the *canon*[5.2.12]. Once these relationships are seen, it becomes clear how important the book of Revelation is to the completion of God's revelation to man and how inadequate are the views which restrict the events of the book of Revelation to an exclusively first-century fulfillment.[77]

Many questions which are posed when interpreting Genesis can be easily furnished by an understanding of Revelation and vice versa. For example, consider the creation of the sun and moon on day *four* of creation week (Gen. 1:14-17) whereas light is said to have been created on the *first* day (Gen. 1:3). The oft-heard question is "how could there be light prior to the creation of the sun?" Many elaborate theories about the sun and moon actually being created earlier than day four and then "unveiled" or made to appear on that day could be instantly disposed of by the study of the light source which John records in the eternal state (Rev. 21:23).[78]

Morris offers the following instructive comparisons between the probationary (and subsequently cursed) world described in Genesis and the eternal (and redeemed) world described in Revelation.[79]

Probationary versus Eternal World

Genesis (probationary world)	Revelation (eternal world)
Division of light and darkness (Gen. 1:4).	No night there (Rev. 21:25).
Division of land and sea (Gen. 1:10).	No more sea (Rev. 21:1).
Rule of sun and moon (Gen. 1:16).	No need of sun or moon (Rev. 21:23).
First heavens and earth finished (Gen. 2:1-3).	New heaven and earth forever (Rev. 21:2).
Man in a prepared garden (Gen. 2:8-9).	Man in a prepared city (Rev. 21:2).
River flowing out of Eden (Gen. 2:10).	River flowing from God's throne (Rev. 22:1).
Tree of life in the midst of the garden (Gen. 2:9).	Tree of life throughout the city (Rev. 22:2).
Gold in the land (Gen. 2:12).	Gold in the city (Rev. 21:21).
Bdellium and the onyx stone (Gen. 2:12).	All manner of precious stones (Rev. 21:19).
God walking in the garden (Gen. 3:8).	God dwelling with His people (Rev. 21:3).
The Spirit energizing (Gen. 1:2).	The Spirit inviting (Rev. 22:17).
Bride formed for her husband (Gen. 2:21-23).	Bride adorned for her husband (Rev. 21:2).
Command to multiply (Gen. 1:28).	Nations of the saved (Rev. 21:24).
Garden accessible to the Liar (Gen. 3:1-5).	City closed to all liars (Rev. 21:27).
Man in God's image (Gen. 1:27).	Man in God's presence (Rev. 21:3).
Man the probationer (Gen. 2:17).	Man the heir (Rev. 21:7).

Cursed versus Redeemed World

Genesis (cursed world)	Revelation (redeemed world)
Cursed ground (Gen. 3:17).	No more curse (Rev. 22:3).
Daily sorrow (Gen. 3:17).	No more sorrow (Rev. 21:4).
Sweat on the face (Gen. 3:19).	No more tears (Rev. 21;4).
Thorns and thistles (Gen. 3:18).	No more pain (Rev. 21:4).
Eating herbs of the field (Gen. 3:18).	Twelve manner of fruits (Rev. 22:2).
Returning to the dust (Gen. 3:19).	No more death (Rev. 21:4).
Coats of skins (Gen. 3:21).	Fine linen, white and clean (Rev. 19:14).
Satan opposing (Gen. 3:15).	Satan banished (Rev. 20:10).
Kept from the tree of life (Gen. 3:24).	Access to the tree of life (Rev. 22:14).
Banished from the garden (Gen. 3:23).	Free entry to the city (Rev. 22:14).
Redeemer promised (Gen. 3:15).	Redemption accomplished (Rev. 5:9-10).
Evil continually (Gen. 6:5).	Nothing that defiles (Rev. 21:27).
Seed of the woman (Gen. 3:15).	Root and offspring of David (Rev. 22:16).
Cherubim guarding (Gen. 3:24).	Angels inviting (Rev. 21:9).

We may extend this list with comparisons from Bullinger.[80]

Genesis versus Revelation

Genesis	Revelation
Man in God's image (Gen. 1:26).	Man headed by one in Satan's image (Rev. 13).
Man's religion, art, and science, resorted to for enjoyment apart from God (Gen. 4).	Man's religion, luxury, art, and science, in their full glory judged and destroyed by God (Rev. 18).
Nimrod, a great rebel and King, and *hidden* anti-God, the founder of Babylon (Gen. 10:8-10).	The *Beast*[5.2.9], the great Rebel, a King, and *manifested* anti-God, the reviver of Babylon (Rev. 13, 17-18).
A flood from God to destroy an evil generation (Gen. 6-9).	A flood from Satan to destroy an elect generation (Rev. 12).
Marriage of first Adam (Gen. 2:18-23).	Marriage of last Adam (Rev. 19).
A bride sought for Abraham's son (Isaac) and found (Gen. 24).	A Bride made ready and brought to Abraham's Son (Rev. 19:9).
Man's dominion ceased and Satan's begun (Gen. 3:24).	Satan's dominion ended and man's restored (Rev. 22).

Notes

1 Rev. 2:1, 8, 12, 18; 3:1, 7, 14.

2 e.g., Adam and Eve in the Garden of Eden, mankind prior to the flood of Noah, Israel's rejection of Messiah at the First Coming of Christ

3 J. Dwight Pentecost, *Things to Come: A Study in Biblical Eschatology* (Grand Rapids, MI: Zondervan Publishing House, 1958), 170.

4 Copyright ©003 Ariel Ministries (*www.ariel.org*), P.O. Box 3723, Tustin, CA 92781. This image appears by *special permission*[1.3] and may not be duplicated for use in derivative works. [Arnold G. Fruchtenbaum, *The Footsteps of Messiah*, rev ed. (Tustin, CA: Ariel Ministries, 2003), 2].

5 Renald E. Showers, *Maranatha, Our Lord Come* (Bellmawr, NJ: The Friends of Israel Gospel Ministry, 1995), s.v. "Trouble Ahead."

6 Christians recognize that Messiah comes twice and that the cataclysm is associated with His *second* coming. Judaism "missed" Messiah at His First Coming and so interprets Second Coming passages as preceding His initial arrival.

7 *The Babylonian Talmud*, Shabbath, 118a., cited in Showers, *Maranatha, Our Lord Come*, 21.

8 Raphael Patai, *The Messiah Texts* (Detroit, MI: Wayne Statue University Press, 1979), 95-96.

9 Renald E. Showers, *The Pre-Wrath Rapture View* (Grand Rapids, MI: Kregel Publications, 2001), 14.

10 Fruchtenbaum, *The Footsteps of Messiah*, 634.

11 Showers, *Maranatha, Our Lord Come*, 38.

12 Arnold Fruchtenbaum, *"The Day of the Lord,"* in Mal Couch, ed., *Dictionary of Premillennial Theology* (Grand Rapids, MI: Kregel Publications, 1996), 87.

13 Fruchtenbaum understands Peter (2Pe. 3:10-12) as describing the result of judgments described in the book of Revelation which are poured out prior to the Second Coming. Others see Peter as describing the final destruction of the very elements comprising the heavens and earth to be replaced by the new heavens and earth. Peter's point seems to be on the *total annihilation* of all that is material. Understanding this fact is to inoculate believers from the temptation and distraction of materialism. Another possibility is that Peter is referring to the regeneration which precedes the Millennium (Isa. 65:17). This is the view of Peters: "This Kingdom is preceded by the conflagration of 2Pe. 3:10-13. This *is self-evident* , since the Kingdom is identified with the establishment of 'the new heavens and new earth' of Isa. 65:17 and 66:22. Peter *expressly* alludes to these two passages in Isaiah and *appropriates them* as descriptive of 'the new heavens and new earth' presented by himself, in the specific phraseology, 'according to promise.' The *Millennial* new heavens and new earth *thus claimed* by the Apostle, and which are associated with the Kingdom itself, are *necessarily preceded* by the fire, described. . . . some have wrongfully . . . endeavored to locate this fire *after* the thousand years."—George H. N. Peters, *The Theocratic Kingdom* (Grand Rapids, MI: Kregel Publications, 1978, 1884), 2:506.

14 "[Some] wish to extend the period of the Day of Jehovah to include the Millennium and the Aftermath, but a study of the term in every passage will show that it is never used in any context except that of the Tribulation. While other expressions, such as *that day* or *in that day*, are used for both the Tribulation and the Millennium, the term *the Day of Jehovah*, is never used for anything outside the Great Tribulation."—Fruchtenbaum, *The Footsteps of Messiah*, 183.

15 Showers, *Maranatha, Our Lord Come*, 32-33,39.

16 Showers, *Maranatha, Our Lord Come*, 33-34.

17 Fruchtenbaum, *The Footsteps of Messiah*, 4.

18 Showers, *Maranatha, Our Lord Come*, 31.

19 Showers, *Maranatha, Our Lord Come*, 31-32.

20 Fruchtenbaum, *The Footsteps of Messiah*, 176.

21 "Isaiah 2:10-22 describes a Day of the Lord that will involve the sixth seal described by the Apostle John in Revelation 6:12-17."—Showers, *Maranatha, Our Lord Come*, 31.

22 "Joel 3:1-16 and Zechariah 14:1-3, 12-15 refer to a Day of the Lord that will involve God's judgment of the armies of all the nations of the world, when those armies gather in Israel to wage war against that Nation and the city of Jerusalem [Rev. 16:12-16] and when the Messiah comes to war against them [Rev. 19:11-21]."—Showers, *Maranatha, Our Lord Come*, 32.

23 Marvin Rosenthal, *The Pre-Wrath Rapture of the Church* (Nashville, TN: Thomas Nelson Publishers, 1990).

24 Showers, *Maranatha, Our Lord Come*, 35,39.

25 The problem of cosmic signs prior to the day can also be resolved by realizing that there are numerous cosmic signs associated with the period of the end and the cosmic signs of the sixth seal, although probably the most dramatic to that point, may not be the first.

26 "The Scriptures indicate that the Day of the Lord, the Time of Jacob's Trouble, and the Great Tribulation have several things in common. First, the concept of trouble or tribulation are associated with all three . . . Second, the concept of an unparalleled time of trouble is identified with all three [Joel 2:1-2; Jer. 30:7; Dan. 12:1 cf. Mtt. 24:21] . . . Third, the term 'great' is used for all three . . . Fourth, the concept of birth pangs is associated with all three . . . Fifth, the expression 'that day' is used for all three . . . Sixth, Israel's future repentance or spiritual restoration to God is associated with all three . . . These comparisons demonstrate that several of the same concepts and terms are associated with the Day of the Lord, the Time of Jacob's Trouble, and the Great Tribulation . . . they indicate that the Day of the Lord will cover or at least include the same time period as the Time of Jacob's Trouble and the Great Tribulation."—Showers, *Maranatha, Our Lord Come*, 41-42.

27 "Both the Time of Jacob's Trouble (Jer. 30:6-7) and the Great Tribulation (Mtt. 24:21) are described as the unparalleled time of trouble. Since there can only be one such time, both will cover the same time period. The Great Tribulation will begin in the middle of the seven-year 70th week. We know this because Jesus indicated that the Great Tribulation will begin with the abomination of desolation (Mtt. 24:15-21), which will take place in the middle of the 70th week (Dan. 9:27). . . . Since the Great Tribulation will begin in the middle and terminate at the end of the 70th week and will cover the same time period as the Time of Jacob's Trouble, the Time of Jacob's Trouble will also cover the entire second half of the 70th week."—Showers, *Maranatha, Our Lord Come*, 23-24.

28 They must necessarily eclipse all the world wars and the horrors of the holocaust unless God be accused of exaggeration.

29 Showers, *Maranatha, Our Lord Come*, 43.

30 James Strong, *The Exhaustive Concordance of the Bible* (Ontario: Woodside Bible Fellowship, 1996), G5604.

31 How different this is from the interpretation which *preterists*[5.2.59] force upon Matthew 24! The destruction of Jerusalem in A.D. 70 involved no intervention by God on behalf of the Jews.

32 Merrill F. Unger, *Unger's Commentary on the Old Testament* (Chattanooga, TN: AMG Publishers, 2002), Mic. 5:3.

33 See *Prophetic Year*[2.13.5.2].

34 Showers, *Maranatha, Our Lord Come*, 44-46.

35 C. I. Scofield, *The Scofield Study Bible* (New York, NY: Oxford University Press, 2002, 1909), Rev. 7:14.

36 "It has been denied that God"s people were actually worse than the pagans about them, but reckoning must be in proportion to spiritual knowledge and privileges enjoyed. The judgments of God are always relative to light and privilege granted. . . The Latins have a pointed saying: *Corruptio optimi pessima* ('The corruption of the best issues in the worst.")"—Charles Feinberg, *The Prophecy of Ezekiel: The Glory of the Lord* (Chicago, IL: Moody Press, 1969), 37.

37 Fruchtenbaum, *The Footsteps of Messiah*, 282-283.

38 Pentecost, *Things to Come: A Study in Biblical Eschatology*, 237.

39 Fruchtenbaum, *The Footsteps of Messiah*, 177-181.

40 Randall Price, *"Old Testament References to The Great Tribulation,"* in Mal Couch, ed., *Dictionary of Premillennial Theology* (Grand Rapids, MI: Kregel Publications, 1996), 415.

41 "The implications of this phrase may include all of the following: (1) God will put His seal of authentication on all true revelations, (2) These forms of revelation will cease, (3) Prophecies will be fulfilled, and (4) Nothing else is to be added to His plans and revelations (as implied by the seal). When Christ comes back, there will be no more need for visions and prophecies."—Charles H. Ray, *"A Study of Daniel 9:24-17, Part II,"* in *The Conservative Theological Journal*, vol. 5 no. 16 (Fort Worth, TX: Tyndale Theological Seminary, December 2001), 306-307.

42 Harold Hoehner, *Chronological Aspects of the Life of Christ* (Grand Rapids, MI: Zondervan, 1977), 118.

43 Pentecost, *Things to Come: A Study in Biblical Eschatology*, 243.

44 *King James Version Study Bible* (Nashville, TN: Thomas Nelson, 1997, c1988), Dan. 9:24.

45 Hoehner, *Chronological Aspects of the Life of Christ*, 135-136.

46 Trent C. Butler, Chad Brand, Charles Draper, and Archie England, eds., *Broadman and Holman Illustrated Bible Dictionary* (Nashville, TN: Broadman and Holman Publishers, 2003), 252-253.

47 Ray, "*A Study of Daniel 9:24-17, Part II*," 321.

48 James Ussher, *The Annals of the World* (Green Forest, AR: Master Books, 1658, c2003), 114-115.

49 Henry Morris, *The Revelation Record* (Wheaton, IL: Tyndale House Publishers, 1983), 27.

50 Scofield, *The Scofield Study Bible*, Rev. 1:1.

51 "Textual correlations that develop the expansion and chronological framework of the Seventieth Week of Daniel [indicate that] Daniel 9:27 equals Rev. 6:12-17."—John A. McLean, *"Structure of the Book of Revelation,"* in Mal Couch, ed., *Dictionary of Premillennial Theology* (Grand Rapids, MI: Kregel Publications, 1996), 376.

52 We have purposefully excluded events whose relative timing we view to be less certain. A more detailed list could be prepared, but would be more likely to contain errors. For a more detailed development, see [Fruchtenbaum, *The Footsteps of Messiah*, 204,240,276].

53 The difficulty of establishing with certainty the timing of the seal, trumpet, and bowl judgments relative to other events of the Tribulation can be seen by the great amount of discussion concerning the subject. It is our belief that the judgments through the sixth trumpet could all occur within the first half of the week since the ascendancy of the beast is not seen in the judgments until the time of the first bowl under the seventh trumpet (Rev. 11:15 cf. Rev. 16:2). It seems the abomination of desolation must have occurred prior to the pouring out of the first bowl because it targets the *Beast*[5.2.9] worshipers (Rev. 16:2).

54 These events do not all transpire in one instant, but are initiated at the midpoint of the week.

55 The ascendancy and authority of the beast is strictly subject to God's control.

56 Their witness is ended by the ascendancy of the beast (Rev. 11:7) at the end of the first half of the week, whereas the last half of the week ends in the destruction of the beast (Rev. 19:20). "During the first half of the week he is in his mortal stage. In the last half he is in his *superhuman* stage; . . . This eighth verse therefore refers to the mid-career of the Beast; and the point of the vision is the moment between the mortal and superhuman stages; *i.e.*, between chapters 12 and 13."—E. W. Bullinger, *Commentary On Revelation* (Grand Rapids, MI: Kregel Publications, 1984, 1935), Rev. 17:8.

57 Although Daniel 11:31 was fulfilled by Antiochus Epiphanes, it stands as an example of the future event which Jesus spoke of (Mtt. 24:15).

58 Although the man of sin will initially sit in the temple of God and present himself as God (2Th. 2:4). Since he is not God, he lacks omnipresence. So it appears that an image is erected in the temple which then receives worship on his behalf (Rev. 13:15). This allows him to conduct other activities associated with his conquest and rule.

59 The timing of the seventh trumpet is approximate and is difficult to establish with certainty. From the description of the first bowl (under the seventh trumpet), it would seem that the last trumpet would occur near the midpoint of the week, just as the beast has established global control and the false prophet is instituting his worship. No mention is made of the beast or his worshipers until after the sixth trumpet (Rev. 9:13 cf. Rev. 11:7). The prelude to the bowl judgments—which are under the seventh trumpet—includes "those who have victory over the beast, over his image and over his mark and over the number of his name" (Rev. 15:2). These are in heaven, having overcome the *image of the beast*[5.2.29] by martyrdom. Since they overcame the image, the image must be in place prior to the seven bowls pouring forth. If the image is set up at the midpoint of the last week, then the bowl judgments must be in the last half. The seventh trumpet must occur prior to the first bowl.

60 It appears that the judgments of the seventh trumpet, which include the seven bowls, must occur after the midpoint of the week. For when the first bowl is poured forth, it targets those who have received the mark of the beast and worship his image (Rev. 16:2). This would most naturally follow his proclamation as God (2Th. 2:4) and the construction of an idol in his image which receives worship (Rev. 13:15). Moreover, prior to the pouring forth of the bowls, John sees martyrs who refused to worship the image of the beast. Thus, the bowls

must come after the setting up of the image which occurs at the midpoint of the last week.

61 Fruchtenbaum, *The Footsteps of Messiah*, 8-10.

62 [Fruchtenbaum, *The Footsteps of Messiah*, 9,175] applies the term *Great Tribulation* to the entire seven years whereas other interpreters apply it to only the last half of this period.

63 Fruchtenbaum believes the *Harlot*[5.2.25] in Revelation 17 differs from the city Babylon in Revelation 18. We believe the Harlot and the city are one and the same.

64 McLean, "*Structure of the Book of Revelation,*" 374.

65 Showers, *Maranatha, Our Lord Come*, 25.

66 [Thomas Ice, *"The Olivet Discourse,"* in Tim LaHaye, and Thomas Ice, eds., *The End Times Controversy* (Eugene, OR: Harvest House Publishers, 2003), 165] Also see [Showers, *Maranatha, Our Lord Come*, 25].

67 Items in brackets added by this author.

68 Showers, *Maranatha, Our Lord Come*, 25.

69 We disagree with allegorical interpreters who dismiss a literal correspondence between the plagues of Egypt and the Tribulation. Beale is representative of this line of thought: "The parallel with Exodus does not supply unambiguous demonstration in support of a literal fulfillment. All that it shows is that the two descriptions are homologous, that is, that they have an essential relation in some manner. But the nature of that relation needs to be determined. Are they homologous in their physical form and effects, or in theological significance, or both? The images depicted certainly refer to actual events on the referential level.. . . In Revelation the fire and hail are to be understood on the symbolic level as representing particular facets of divine judgment that can be drawn out further by thorough exegesis of the theological meaning of this particular Exodus plague. [These] speak of God depriving the ungodly of earthly security."—Gregory K. Beale, *The Book of Revelation: A Commentary on the Greek Text* (Grand Rapids, MI: William B. Eerdmans Publishing Co., 1999), 54. If one reads the Exodus account through the same interpretive lens as Beale, one would likely be led to deny the literal nature of the entire history of the Exodus, much less the plagues. Indeed, many liberal theologians do just that!

70 Alva J. McClain, *The Greatness Of The Kingdom* (Winona Lake, IN: BMH Books, 1959), 56.

71 Although not an infestation or plague of frogs, the representation of the unclean spirits as frogs is undoubtedly meant as a reminder of the frogs of the Exodus.

72 Lice are not specifically mentioned, but may be among the plagues brought by the two witnesses.

73 Flies are not specifically mentioned, but may be among the plagues brought by the two witnesses.

74 This is not a direct correlation, but a similarity. In both cases, the food source of the enemies of God is destroyed. In other judgments, crops were also destroyed: Ex. 9:22-23; Ps. 105:33-35 cf. Rev. 8:7.

75 Mal Couch, *"Why is Revelation Important?,"* in Mal Couch, ed., *A Bible Handbook to Revelation* (Grand Rapids, MI: Kregel Publications, 2001), 16.

76 Morris, *The Revelation Record*, 14.

77 The creation evangelism organization *Answers in Genesis* (www.AnswersInGenesis.org) correctly emphasizes the need to take the Scriptures literally "from the very first verse." Without an understanding of the cause of man's problem, there is no need for a savior. If Adam and Eve were not literal, what need have we of Jesus? Wouldn't it be wonderful if this "back to Genesis" emphasis on literal interpretation were taken "ahead to Revelation" and applied there too?

78 Asking this question evidences a lack of familiarity with the doctrine of God's *Shekinah* (abiding) Glory: Gen. 3:8, 24; 15:17; Ex. 3:2; 13:21-22; 14:19-20, 24; Ex. 16:10; 19:18; 24:15-16; 33:18-23; 34:5-6; 40:34; Lev. 9:6, 23; Num. 14:10, 22; 16:19, 42; 20:6; Deu. 5:25-26; 33:16; 1K. 8:10-11; 2Chr. 7:1; Isa. 4:5; 35:2; 40:5; 58:8; 60:3; Eze. 1:28; 3:23; 9:3; 10:18; 43:2-4; Hag. 2:7-9; Zec. 2:5; Mtt. 16:27; 17:2; 24:30; Mark 9:3; Luke 2:8-9; 9:29; John 1:14; Acts 2:3; 9:3; 22:6; 26:13; Heb. 1:3; 2Pe. 1:16-17; Rev. 1:14-16; 15:8; 21:3; 21:23

79 Morris, *The Revelation Record*, 22.

80 Bullinger, *Commentary On Revelation*, 58-59.

2.14 - Literary Structure

All interpreters who come to the Scriptures are faced with attempting to grasp the literary structure of the text. It doesn't take the new believer very long to discover that passages which one had always assumed were strictly sequential are found, upon further investigation, to be presented in a nonsequential fashion suitable to the purposes of the writer. This becomes most evident by studying a *parallel gospel* which presents each gospel writer's material in parallel columns.[1]

Some of the same issues arise when we come to the book of Revelation. How is the presentation of John to be understood? Are the seals, trumpets, and bowls sequential? Or do similarities between some of them imply the different passages are describing different details concerning the same event (repetition or *recapitulation*)? This process is complicated by the wide variety of conclusions interpreters reach concerning the literary structure of the book. Depending upon what elements of the book are seen as most determinative in outlining the material, different results are obtained.

> A blessing and curse of John's Apocalypse are the many commentators who have attempted to interpret the book. This is especially true of the many outlines proposed for its literary structure. The diverse proposals are a maze of interpretative confusion.[2]
>
> This rather complete lack of consensus about the structure of Revelation should caution the reader about accepting any one approach as definitive.[3]

Although there are many different views concerning the structure of the book of Revelation, two primary views have been recognized: the *sequential view* and the *simultaneous* or *recapitulation view*. Most other views are a variation on one of these. "The basic structural question is whether John intended his readers to understand the visions recorded in his work in a straightforward chronological sense or whether some form of recapitulation is involved."[4]

> The structure of the Apocalypse is determined, in part, by one's understanding of whether the three septet [sets of seven] judgments are sequential or simultaneous. The sequential view understands the seals, trumpets, and bowls as successive judgments that proceed out of each other. The simultaneous view sees a recapitulation of the septets in which the judgements are parallel to each other. Each recapitulation reviews previous events and adds further details.[5]
>
> A fundamental issue in discerning the plan of the book of Revelation is how to explain the numerous parallel passages and repetitions within it. The book itself suggests that the number seven is an ordering principle by presenting seven messages, seven seals, seven trumpets, and seven bowls. The parallels between the trumpets and bowls are especially close and seem repetitious. Some commentators have explained the repetition as the result of the use of sources. Others have seen the repetition as part of the author's literary design. The literary design has been seen as describing a linear sequence of events within history, including the past, present, and future. Another theory is that the same historical and eschatological events are described several times from different points of view.[6]

Other ways of dividing and organizing the book are also possible. For example, making a primary division based upon different visions,[7]emphasizing the contrast between scenes in heaven versus their results on earth,[8]or some other literary artifact such as spiritual transitions. Tenney calls attention to the fourfold literary structure marked by transitions where John "was transported in consciousness to a new scene of action where spiritual realities and future events were disclosed to him."[9]

In the Spirit

Section Topic	Transition Verse	Phrase	Location
Prologue: Christ Communicating	Rev. 1:1	-	-
Christ in the Church	Rev. 1:9-10	"I was in the Spirit on the Lord's Day"	"on the island that is called Patmos"
Christ in the Cosmos	Rev. 4:1-2	"Immediately I was in the Spirit"	"up here" (heaven)
Christ in Conquest	Rev. 17:3	"So he carried me away in the Spirit"	"into the wilderness"
Christ in Consummation	Rev. 21:10	"And he carried me away in the Spirit"	"to a great and high mountain"
Epilogue: Christ Challenging	Rev. 22:6	-	-

2.14.1 - Recapitulation of Events

The author of the earliest surviving commentary, Victorinus of Pettau, subscribed to the recapitulation view.[10]This view emphasizes similarities between elements of the three series of symbols (seals, trumpets, bowls) and understands the similarities as an indication of identity. Although there are many variations on this scheme, the following diagram illustrates the general idea. The passages describing the trumpet judgments are seen as depicting additional details concerning the earlier seal judgments. Similarly, the passages describing the bowl judgments are understood as elaborating on the previous trumpet judgments. See [Beale, *The Book of Revelation: A Commentary on the Greek Text*, 128] for a more elaborate example.

Recapitulation of Events

Seals	1	2	3	4	5	6	7
	↕	↕	↕	↕	↕	↕	↕
Trumpets	1	2	3	4	5	6	7
	↕	↕	↕	↕	↕	↕	↕
Bowls	1	2	3	4	5	6	7

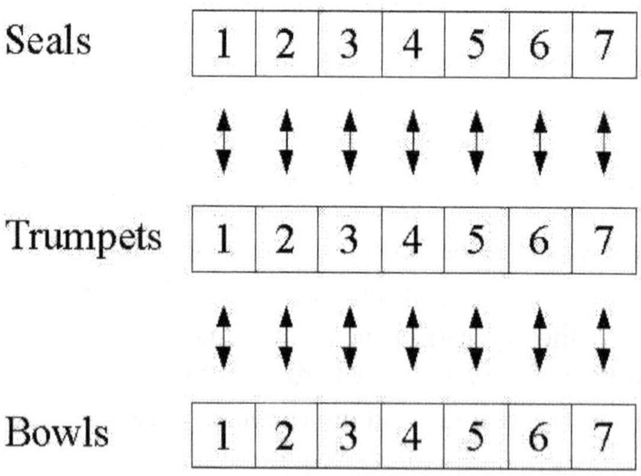

Often, a *similar event* (e.g., an earthquake) found in association with two judgments leads to their association.

> Alford, following Isaac Williams, draws attention to the parallel connection between the Apocalypse and Christ's discourse on the Mount of Olives, recorded in Mtt. 24:4-28. The seals plainly bring us down to the second coming of Christ, just as the trumpets also do (compare Rev. 6:12-17; 8:1, and Rev. 11:15), and as the vials also do (Rev. 16:17): all three run parallel, and end in the same point. Certain "catchwords" (as Wordsworth calls them) connect the three series of symbols together. They do not succeed one to the other in historical and chronological sequence, but move side by side, the subsequent

> series filling up in detail the same picture which the preceding series had drawn in outline. . . . the earthquake that ensues on the opening of the sixth seal is one of the catchwords, that is, a link connecting chronologically this sixth seal with the sixth trumpet (Rev. 9:13; 11:13): compare also the seventh vial, Rev. 16:17, 18. The concomitants of the opening of the sixth seal, it is plain, in no full and exhaustive sense apply to any event, save the terrors which shall overwhelm the ungodly just before the coming of the Judge. . . . the loosing of the four winds by the four angels standing on the four corners of the earth, under the sixth seal, answers to the loosing of the four angels at the Euphrates, under the sixth trumpet.[12]

Other times it is a *similarity in pattern* which leads interpreters in this direction:

> The strongest argument for the recapitulation view is the observation of repeated combined scenes of consummative judgment and salvation found at the conclusions of various sections throughout the book. The pattern of these scenes is always the same, consisting of a depiction of judgment followed by a portrayal of salvation; cf. respectively Rev. 6:12-17 and 7:9-17; 11:18a and 11:18b; 14:14-20 and 15:2-4; 16:17-21, including 17:1-18:24, which functions as an intensified judicial conclusion of the whole book, and 19:1-10; 20:7-15 and 21:2-8, including the following section of 21:9-22:5, which serves as an intensified salvific conclusion to the entire book.[13]

Even *similarity of phrase* has been seen as indicating recapitulation:

> A third phrase which recurs four times, and which may serve as a division point is "thunders, voices, lightnings, and an earthquake [Rev. 4:5; 8:5; 11:19; 16:18]." . . . The last three mark respectively the conclusions of the judgments of the seals, the trumpets, and the bowls, and have consequently been interpreted by some to indicate that their judgments are concurrent, or at least continuous. Does the repetition of the phrase mean that the same reaction takes place three times, or that there are three types of judgments of increasing intensity converging at the same point?[14]

The main weakness of the recapitulation view is that it emphasizes *similarity* between passages over *distinct differences* which remain. But, *similarity does not equal identity*. Those who believe that details are intentionally revealed in the text for the reader to notice are unlikely to embrace the recapitulation view because it glosses over these differences.

2.14.2 - Sequential Events

The sequential view understands the general flow of the book and especially the series of seal, trumpet, and bowl judgments as following a chronological sequence. Similarities between different chronological judgments are understood as part of God's design, but not necessitating identity because differences in the text make plain that identity is not involved. In the most widely-held sequential view, the events attending the seven bowls are subsumed within the seventh trumpet and the events of the seven trumpets are subsumed within the seventh seal.

Sequential Events

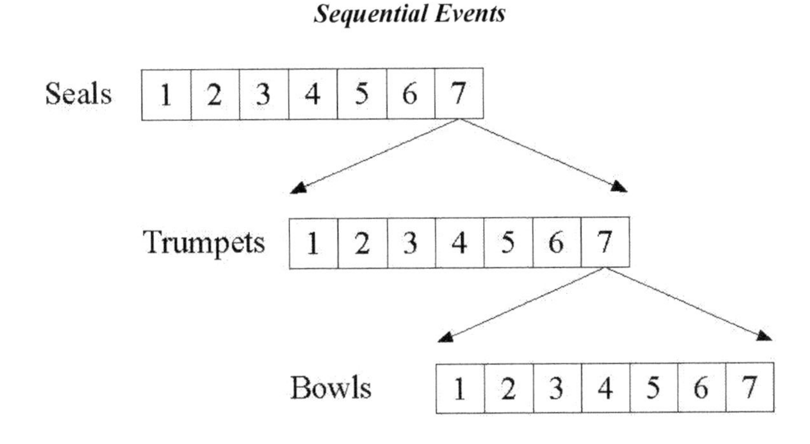

> We can understand this development by a simple illustration. We have all seen firework displays in which giant rockets are shot into the air exploding into a great ball of fire. This, as it falls toward the earth, bursts into a great number of balls of fire of various colors which, as they fall further toward the earth, burst again into smaller balls of various colors. So it is with the judgments of God. At first we see

> nothing but a sealed scroll. As the seals are removed each one appears to be a judgment and we would expect that when we come to the last seal, it would be the last judgment. But, instead, the last seal discloses seven angels, each with trumpets. These, in turn, are various judgments, and the seventh trumpet, in turn, reveals not another single judgment, but seven vials of the wrath of God. In both instances there is a series of seven with the last disclosing seven more. In addition to this structure there is a parenthesis between the sixth and the seventh in all three series.[15]

The more literal one's interpretation, the more one will tend to follow the sequential view. The more one emphasizes literary *genre*[5.2.22] and symbolism and moves further afield from the *Golden Rule of Interpretation*[5.2.24], the more likely the recapitulation structure or other literary structure will find appeal.

While the sequential view holds the basic flow of the book to be chronological, it does not preclude recapitulation in some of the related visionary scenes which are not strongly anchored within the sequence.[16]The reasons given for the sequential view include:

> There are five principal arguments for the basic futurist perspective. (1) It is argued that Rev. 1:19 divides the whole book into three temporal parts . . . (2) Rev. 4:1b ("I will show you what must happen after these things") affirms . . . that the visions of wrath in the remainder of the book are to occur after the events of the church age . . . (3) It is assumed that the order of the visions generally represents the order of future events . . . (4) If the order of the seals, trumpets, and bowls does not portray historical events in the order of their historical occurrence, and if the trumpets and the bowls are not subsumed within the seals, then . . . the trumpets and the bowls are separated from the introductory throne vision of Rev. 4:1-5:14, from which the seals and the rest of the visions in the book seem to naturally flow. (5) The increasing intensity of the judgments throughout the book is another argument.[17]

> Each set of judgments is more intense and destructive than the previous ones. The second trumpet destroys one-third of seas while the second bowl turns all of the seas into blood (Rev. 8:8-9; 16:3). . . . Although there are many similarities between the septets, the differences are more crucial and determinative. The seals generally differ in content from the trumpet and bowl plagues. There is no parallel alignment between the first, fifth, and seventh judgments of the septets. . . . The two Greek phrases καὶ εἶδον [*kai eidon*] and μετὰ ταῦτα [*meta tauta*] indicate a sequential movement . . . a chronological movement . . . The seven seals are followed by the seven trumpets, and the seven bowls follow the seven trumpets . . . The bowls evidence a sequential pattern as they are called "the last, because in them the wrath of God is finished" (Rev. 15:1). . . . The seventh trumpet is linked to the seven bowls. The 144,000 people are an example of an event under a trumpet judgment following a seal judgment. One hundred and forty-four thousand people are protectively sealed on their foreheads after the sixth seal and before the release of the plague by the four angels (Rev. 7:1-8). The fifth trumpet brings a demonic plague on humankind and torments "only the men who do not have the seal of God on their foreheads" - the sixth seal precedes the demonic plague of the fifth trumpet.[18]

> When the seventh seal is opened (Rev. 8:1-5), no immediate events as such follow on earth—except for the earthquake—as in the first six seals, unless the opening of the seventh seal includes among its events the blowing of the seven trumpets of judgment (Rev. 8:6-11:15). This appears to be precisely the case. . . . The seventh trumpet likewise is not immediately followed by any specific events on earth (Rev. 11:15ff.), except for an earthquake and a hailstorm (Rev. 11:19). However, just before the seventh trumpet is sounded, we read, "The second woe has passed; the third woe is coming soon" (Rev. 11:14). When the seven angels prepare to pour out "the seven last plagues," symbolized by the bowls, we read that with these bowls "God's wrath is completed" (Rev. 15:1, 7). Thus it seems reasonable to identify the content of the seventh trumpet with the seven bowls of judgment (Rev. 16-19).[19]

Another reason why the bowl judgments cannot represent a recapitulation of the previous trumpet or seal judgments is found in the difference in access to the heavenly *Temple*[5.2.73] during the period of the judgments. Due to the great significance of the final bowl judgments, the heavenly Temple is closed for their duration (Rev. 15:8). Yet in the midst of the seal and trumpet judgments, the Temple is not sealed (Rev. 7:15; 11:19; 14:15, 17; 15:6). This indicates that the bowl judgments (Rev. 16) cannot be merely descriptive of further detail related to the corresponding trumpet or seal judgments, but are unique in themselves and must occur at an entirely different period of time which follows upon the opening of the seals and sounding of the trumpets. See commentary on *Revelation 15:8*[3.15.8] and *Revelation 16:17*[3.16.17].

One of the frequently-heard criticisms of the sequential view is that it lacks sensitivity to the literary form or apocalyptic genre of the book.[20]

As the reader recognizes by now, the single largest factor which divides interpreters of the book is *how literal* one takes its contents. Whenever literary genre, apocalyptic similarities, and devotional qualities are elevated in importance over a literal interpretation, the result will most likely be non-futurist and embrace significant recapitulation.

By adopting a recapitulation view, it can be argued that one of the key values of the book of Revelation is forfeited, its guidance in organizing related passages:

> The value of the book of Revelation is not that it provides a lot of new information, but rather that it takes the scattered Old Testament prophecies and puts them in chronological order so that the sequence of events may be determined. . . . This is the reason for so many references to the Old Testament.[21]

Perhaps one of the simplest sequential organizations offered is that of Morris.[22]

Sequential Chronology

Chapters	Description	Duration
Rev. 1-3	Church Age	Unknown Duration
Rev. 4-19	Period of Judgment	Seven Years
Rev. 20	Kingdom Age	One Thousand Years
Rev. 21-22	Eternal Age	Endless Years

2.14.3 - Structural Outline

It is our conviction that the events of the book are mainly sequential and flow naturally from the threefold division given by John in Revelation 1:19. We will follow an outline derived from the work of McLean.[23]

I. Prologue: *Things Which You Have Seen* (Rev. 1:1-20)
II. Letters to the *Seven Churches*[5.2.66]: *Things Which Are* (Rev. 2:1-3:22)
III. Future Revealed: *Things Which Shall Take Place After These Things* (Rev. 4:1-22:5)
- A. God's Wrath/Great Tribulation (Rev. 4:1-19:21)
  - 1. Introduction to the Seven Seal Judgments (Rev. 4:1-5:14)
    - a) Throne of God in heaven (Rev. 4:1-11)
    - b) The Scroll of the Lamb (Rev. 5:1-14)
  - 2. The Six Seal Judgments (Rev. 6:1-7:17)
    - a) First Seal: White horse (Rev. 6:1-2)
    - b) Second Seal: Red horse (Rev. 6:3-4)
    - c) Third Seal: Black horse (Rev. 6:5-6)
    - d) Fourth Seal: Ashen horse (Rev. 6:7-8)
    - e) Fifth Seal: Martyrs under the altar (Rev. 6:9-11)
    - f) Sixth Seal: Great day of God's wrath (Rev. 6:12-17)
    - g) Narrative Preview: Redeemed of God (Rev. 7:1-17)
      - (1) Sealing of the 144,000 (Rev. 7:1-8)
      - (2) Martyrs from the great Tribulation (Rev. 7:9-17)
  - 3. The Seventh Seal: Seven Trumpets (Rev. 8:1-18:24)
    - a) Breaking Seventh Seal: introduction to the Seven Trumpets (Rev. 8:1-6)
    - b) First Trumpet: one-third of the earth destroyed (Rev. 8:7)
    - c) Second Trumpet: one-third of the sea destroyed (Rev. 8:8-9)
    - d) Third Trumpet: one-third of the water destroyed (Rev. 8:10-11)
    - e) Fourth Trumpet: one-third of the celestial destroyed (Rev. 8:12)
    - f) Introduction to the Three Woes (Rev. 8:13)
      - (1) Fifth Trumpet: First Woe, men tormented (Rev. 9:1-12)

(2) Sixth Trumpet: Second Woe, one-third of mankind killed (Rev. 9:13-11:14)
(3) Seventh Trumpet: Third Woe, the Seven Bowls (Rev. 11:15-18:24)
(a) Seventh Trumpet, proclamation of God's kingdom (Rev. 11:15-19)
(b) Narrative Synopsis (Rev. 12:1-14:13)
i) A Woman, Male child, Satan in conflict (Rev. 12:1-6)
ii) Angelic war in heaven (Rev. 12:7-12)
iii) War on earth (Rev. 12:13-17)
iv) *Beast*[5.2.9] out of the sea (Rev. 13:1-10)
v) Beast out of the earth (Rev. 13:11-18)
vi) Narrative Preview (Rev. 14:1-13)
(c) Introduction to the Seven Bowls (Rev. 14:14-15:8)
i) Son of Man with a sickle (Rev. 14:14-16)
ii) Wine press of God's wrath (Rev. 14:17-20)
iii) Seven angels of the Seven plagues (Rev. 15:1)
iv) Worship of God and the Lamb (Rev. 15:2-4)
v) Seven angels receive the Bowls (Rev. 15:5-8)
(d) Seven Bowl Judgments (Rev. 16:1-18:24)
i) First Bowl: malignant sores (Rev. 16:1-2)
ii) Second Bowl: sea destroyed (Rev. 16:3)
iii) Third Bowl: rivers destroyed (Rev. 16:4-7)
iv) Fourth Bowl: scorching heat (Rev. 16:8-9)
v) Fifth Bowl: darkness (Rev. 16:10-11)
vi) Sixth Bowl: preparation for war (Rev. 16:12-16)
vii) Seventh Bowl: worldwide destruction (Rev. 16:17-21)
viii) Narrative Synopsis (Rev. 17:1-18:24)
[a] Description and Destruction of the *Harlot*[5.2.25] (Rev. 17:1-18)
[b] Condemnation and Destruction of Babylon (Rev. 18:1-24)
4. The Advent of Jesus Christ (Rev. 19:2-21)
a) Introduction and praise of the advent (Rev. 19:1-10)
b) Parousia of Jesus Christ (Rev. 19:11-16)
c) Judgment of the beast, false prophet, and people (Rev. 19:17-21)
B. *Millennial Kingdom*[5.2.39] (Rev. 20:1-10)
1. Satan is bound in the abyss (Rev. 20:1-3)
2. Saints resurrected (Rev. 20:4-6)
3. Final judgment of Satan (Rev. 20:7-10)
C. Great White Throne Judgment (Rev. 20:11-15)
D. The New Jerusalem (Rev. 21:1-22:5)
IV. Epilogue (Rev. 22:6-21)

Notes

1 See [A. T. Robertson, *A Harmony of the Gospels* (New York, NY: Harper Collins Publishers, 1950)] and [Robert L. Thomas, *A Harmony of the Gospels* (San Francisco, CA: Harper Collins Publishers, 1978)].

2 Gregory K. Beale, *The Book of Revelation: A Commentary on the Greek Text* (Grand Rapids, MI: William B. Eerdmans Publishing Co., 1999), 108.

3 Robert H. Mounce, *The Book of Revelation* (Grand Rapids, MI: William B. Eerdmans Publishing Co., 1977), 46.

4 Mounce, *The Book of Revelation*, 45.

5 John A. McLean, *"Structure of the Book of Revelation,"* in Mal Couch, ed., *Dictionary of Premillennial Theology* (Grand Rapids, MI: Kregel Publications, 1996), 373.

6 Adela Yarbro Collins, *"Book of Revelation,"* in David Noel Freeman, ed., *The Anchor Bible Dictionary* (New York, NY: Doubleday, 1996, c1992), 5:696.

7 "The *seven visions* are as follows: (1) *Seven churches*[5.2.66] (Rev. 1:9-3:22); (2) Seven seals (Rev. 4:1-8:1);

(3) Seven trumpets (Rev. 8:2-11:19); (4) Seven symbolic figures (Rev. 12:1-14:20); (5) Seven bowls (Rev. 15:1-16:21); (6) Seven judgments (Rev. 17:1-19:10); (7) Seven triumphs (Rev. 19:11-22:5)."—Edward Hindson, *Revelation: Unlocking the Future* (Chattanooga, TN: AMG Publishers, 2002), 5.

8 "When God has described a scene as taking place 'in Heaven', and caused Heavenly voices to give the key to what is to follow in another scene which immediately takes place 'on earth'; and this is done *seven* consecutive times; is it not strange that writers on the Apocalypse should overlook this exceedingly simple arrangement."—E. W. Bullinger, *Commentary On Revelation* (Grand Rapids, MI: Kregel Publications, 1984, 1935), 117.

9 Merrill C. Tenney, *Interpreting Revelation* (Peabody, MA: Hendrickson Publishers, 1957), 32-33.

10 "This position was taken by Victorinus of Pettau, the author of the oldest surviving commentary (d. ca. 304)."—Collins, "*Book of Revelation,*" 5:696.

11 Beale, *The Book of Revelation: A Commentary on the Greek Text*, 128.

12 A. R. Fausset, *"The Revelation of St. John the Divine,"* in Robert Jamieson, A. R. Fausset, and David Brown, *A Commentary, Critical and Explanatory, on the Old and New Testaments* (Oak Harbor, WA: Logos Research Systems, Inc., 1997, 1877), Rev. 1:1.

13 Beale, *The Book of Revelation: A Commentary on the Greek Text*, 121.

14 Tenney, *Interpreting Revelation*, 34.

15 Donald Grey Barnhouse, *Revelation* (Grand Rapids, MI: Zondervan Publishing House, 1971), 155.

16 "This article argues for the successive view of the septet judgements, that is, the trumpets sequentially follow the seals, and the bowls sequentially follow the trumpets. The successive structure does not negate a recapitulation of other visionary scenes that preview eschatological events to come (Rev. 7:9-17; 14:8-13)."—McLean, "*Structure of the Book of Revelation,*" 373.

17 Beale, *The Book of Revelation: A Commentary on the Greek Text*, 118-120.

18 McLean, "*Structure of the Book of Revelation,*" 374.

19 Alan F. Johnson, *Revelation: The Expositor's Bible Commentary* (Grand Rapids, MI: Zondervan Publishing House, 1966), 71.

20 "The main objection is that it interprets Revelation without sufficient sensitivity to its literary form, giving a straightforward, literal reading of the book, rather than using a figurative approach, which would be more appropriate to the book's symbolic genre."—Beale, *The Book of Revelation: A Commentary on the Greek Text*, 161.

21 Arnold G. Fruchtenbaum, *The Footsteps of Messiah*, rev ed. (Tustin, CA: Ariel Ministries, 2003), 10-11.

22 Henry Morris, *The Revelation Record* (Wheaton, IL: Tyndale House Publishers, 1983), 28.

23 McLean, "*Structure of the Book of Revelation,*" 376-377.

3 – Commentary

3.1 - Revelation 1

3.1.1 - Revelation 1:1

Up to this point, we have spent considerable time discussing background information in order to better prepare the reader for the verse-by-verse exposition to follow. Having read the background material, the reader should now be equipped to understand the principles behind the method of our exposition and the liabilities we believe attend competing views.

Moving forward, we will place greater emphasis upon exposition than refuting alternate views, although we will continue to make mention of them at key places in the text.[1]

See the *Introduction*[2] for a discussion of various background topics related to the book of Revelation.

The Revelation

The first word of this book, Ἀποκάλυψις [*Apokalypsis*], should be kept in mind by the reader throughout the book. For it is God's intention to *reveal* rather than *conceal*:

> In the New Testament, *apokalypsis* always has the majestic sense of God's unveiling of himself to his creatures, an unveiling that we call by its Latin name *revelation*. . . . It depicts the progressive and immediate unveiling of the otherwise unknown and unknowable God to his church throughout the ages.[2]

The clearness and lucidity (perspicuity) of the Scriptures is their consistent theme (Deu. 29:29; Pr. 13:13; Isa. 5:24; Isa. 45:19; Mtt. 11:25; Mtt. 24:15; Luke 10:21, 26; 24:25; 2Ti. 3:16; 2Pe. 1:19). Yet if Scripture is meant to be understood, why do we have such a difficult time understanding it, and especially this book? Our problem is not so much the difficulty of understanding, but our own idolatry and rebellion. We are unwilling to *study* to know God and to *submit* in obedience to that which may be known. We are more interested in other pursuits than in seeking God through His revealed words of life (John 6:63, 68). As is often the case where Scripture is concerned, our inability to understand is more a reflection of our lack of zeal than the difficulty which attends the interpretation of God's Word. When the average person in our country spends multiple hours in front of a television set *daily*, but "just can't find the time" to read God's Word, the issue is not one of time management, but *idolatry*.

When we come to this last book of Scripture, our lack of preparation is evidenced all the more because what God intends as *revelation*, we see as *mystery*. Yet Paul holds that revelation is the antithesis of mystery (Rom. 16:25). This book is not intended to be a veiled document full of mysterious symbols, but an unveiling and clarification of things which have heretofore not been revealed by God.[3] In order to grasp the meaning of this *revelation*, we need a foundation in the rest of Scriptures, and especially the Old Testament. (See *The Importance of the Old Testament*[2.7.5.5].)

There are several reasons why we believe that this book is not intended to be enigmatic. First, we believe that a chief purpose of God was the creation of language to communicate with man. If this is so, then the intellect of man and the clarity of language must be sufficient for this task:

> If God is the originator of language and if the chief purpose of originating it was to convey His message to humanity, then it must follow that He, being all-wise and all-loving, originated sufficient language to convey all that was in His heart to tell mankind. Furthermore, it must also follow that He would use language and expect people to understand it in its literal, normal, and plain sense.[4]

Second, we have the pattern established by the rest of Scripture. "It is unthinkable to believe that God would speak with precision and clarity from Genesis to Jude, and then when it comes to the end abandon all precision and clarity."[5] It is not God's intention to train us how to read and understand 65 books of the Bible and then "throw us a curve" in the 66th book by expecting that we adopt an entirely different approach. (See the discussion regarding *The Art and Science of Interpretation*[2.7.2].)

So it is our duty here to make sense of this book, based upon what *related passages*[2.13] reveal concerning its central *themes*[2.4], while reading the text in the same way as the rest of Scripture.

of Jesus Christ

The central question surrounding this phrase is whether Jesus Christ is the *source* of the revelation (subjective genitive) or being *described* by the revelation (objective genitive).

Elsewhere, a very similar Greek phrase ἀποκαλύψεως Ἰησοῦ Χριστοῦ [*apokalypseōs Iēsou Christou*] is used by Paul: "For I neither received it from man, nor was I taught *it*, but *it came* through the revelation of Jesus Christ" (Gal. 1:12).[6] It would seem that in Galatians the genitive Ἰησοῦ Χριστοῦ [*Iēsou Christou*] is subjective rather than objective, for Paul is discussing the *source* of his revelatory knowledge. It did not come through man, nor was it taught, but it *came* through the revelation of Jesus. Jesus was the source of Paul's revelation, not man.

In favor of the objective genitive (Jesus as the object being revealed), is the oft-expressed longing of the *NT*[5.2.48] writers for His appearing (1Cor. 1:7; 2Th. 1:7; 1Pe. 1:7). In these passages, the appearing of Jesus is referred to as the "revelation of Jesus Christ." Apart from the glimpses provided within this book and elsewhere in the NT, the true character and glory of Christ is yet hidden. When He appears, His glory will no longer be veiled and all men everywhere will understand that He is God.[7]

If "context is king" in interpretation, then the next phrase would indicate we are to take this as the subjective genitive: "which God gave Him to show His servants."[8] The emphasis here is on Jesus Christ as the *source* of the revelation being given to John.

Wallace suggests the possibility that this is a *plenary genitive* indicating the revelation is both *from* Christ and *about* Christ.[9] However, as Thomas has observed, such an understanding violates the basic interpretive principle that the original author had *only one* intended meaning.[10]

The context favors the subjective genitive (the revelation is *from* Jesus Christ), but we should be aware that throughout Scripture, Jesus is involved with revelation in at least three ways:

1. He is the *source* of revelation (Gal. 1:12; 1Pe. 1:11; Rev. 1:1).
2. He is the *object* of revelation (Luke 24:44; 1Cor. 1:7; 2Th. 1:7; 1Pe. 1:7; Rev. 1:11-18; 5:6-10; 19:11-16). "Many fail to see the centrality of Jesus Christ in this volume. . . . [Some] become preoccupied with the identification of events and persons other than our Lord. Many seem to be more interested in the *Antichrist*[5.2.3] than in Jesus Christ."[11]
3. His *incarnation* is the revelation of God to man (Isa. 9:1-2; John 1:14, 18; 12:45; 14:8-9; Col. 1:15; 2:9; Heb. 1:2; 1Jn. 1:2).

Paul makes plain that the revelation he received was not the result of teaching he received from men. In other words, *biblical revelation is not by human insight or instruction.* It is the unveiling of that which was previously unknown *and would forever remain unknown* if God had not graciously granted us His self-disclosure. This is why the natural world can never be classified as the 67th book of the Bible, for the "revelation" it provides is not biblical revelation. It is subject to the finding out of man and the manner in which it is discerned is subject to the flawed interpretations and theories of fallen men. This alone tells us why Genesis takes precedence over the speculative investigation of prehistory by modern science. Scriptural revelation, the direct revelation of God, has no equal.

It is for these very reasons that biblical revelation is *always initiated by God* and never by man. It was the Lord who opened Hagar's eyes so that she saw water nearby (Gen. 21:19). It was the Lord who revealed the Angel of the Lord blocking Balaam's way (Num. 22:31). The Lord opened the eyes of Elisha's servant so that he might see the angelic host (2K. 6:17). Moses would have remained a man unknown to history if the Lord had not made His ways known to him (Ps. 103:7). Peter's declaration of Jesus as "the Christ" would not have occurred without the direct revelation of the Father (Mtt. 16:17). The disciples on the road to Emmaus would not have understood Christ in the Scriptures apart from the initiative of God (Luke 24:45). This too is the foundation of prophecy—the revealing of that which is yet future and which no man could ever plumb (Isa. 48:5-8). Hence, it is the unique signature of God alone. This revelation of God is a key ministry of the Holy Spirit Whom Jesus said would "take of what is Mine and declare *it* to you" (John 16:14).

Biblical revelation is not confined to the head, but spans the 18 inches of wilderness from the head to the heart. It results not in a cold apprehension of *facts*, but in a response of *faith* which births the soul into newness of life. It was the Lord Who opened Lydia's heart "to heed the things spoken by Paul" (Acts 16:14) resulting in the first believer in Thyatira, destined to become the site of a thriving Church addressed directly by our Lord in this book (Rev. 2:18). The mind of the unbeliever remains without revelation, blinded to the things of God. The veil over his mind is unresponsive to the efforts of man (John 1:13), but is "taken away in Christ" (2Cor. 3:14). No one can know the Father except those to whom "the Son wills to reveal *Him*" (Luke 10:22).

Here we come away with a foundational theme of Scripture: man is *wholly dependent* upon God. Without God, man has no hope. It is only by God's gracious revelation that light enters into our depraved darkness. John could write none of the Revelation if it were not for God's initiative totally apart from John. This fact alone renders many of the discussions concerning *"John's motive for writing"*[2.3.2.1] null and void.

which God gave Him

Some have taken this as an indication that Jesus did not know the content of the Revelation which was provided by the Father. When Jesus came in the incarnation, He "made Himself of no reputation, taking the form of a bondservant, *and* coming in the likeness of men" (Php. 2:7). Between His birth of the virgin Mary and His ascension to the Father, Jesus exhibited traits of His humanity. As a child, He *grew in stature and wisdom* (Luke 2:40, 52). He *learned* by the things that He suffered (Heb. 5:8), and when speaking to His disciples concerning His Second Coming, He admitted of limitations to His earthly knowledge: "But of that Day and hour no one knows, not even the angels in heaven, **nor the Son**, but only the Father." [emphasis added] (Mark 13:32).

Yet these characteristics of His humanity were recorded prior to His ascension and glorification (John 16:14; 17:5). It seems unlikely that Jesus, the very Source of "the Spirit of Christ" who "testified beforehand the sufferings of Christ, and the glories that would follow" (1Pe. 1:11) and the Agent of what is revealed to John (Rev. 1:10), would lack the information related in this book. It seems best to understand the revelation as a gift from the Father which recognizes the role distinctions within the Trinity (John 5:20; 1Cor. 15:28).

The members of the Trinity are co-equal, yet occupy *different roles* within the plan and purposes of God. Here, the Father gives revelation to the Son. To the unfamiliar reader, this might seem to imply an inferior position of Jesus in relation to the Father. Not so. Within the Trinity there is a beautiful harmony of perfect cooperation to affect God's purpose. The submission of the Son to the Father is that of a perfect *voluntary* servanthood (Isa. 49:6; 50:10; 52:13; 53:11; Mtt. 12:18; John 5:19). It is by this motivation that Jesus delivers His kingdom to God the Father (1Cor. 15:24-28). It was the love of Jesus both for mankind and to fulfill the will of the Father which caused him to make "Himself of no reputation, taking the form of a bondservant, *and* coming in the likeness of men" (Php. 2:7). This is to be the model of those who follow Him. We submit not because it is required, but out of obedience to His Word and a desire to follow His example.[12]

to show His servants

The Revelation is not just for John, nor just for the *Seven Churches of Asia*[4.15], but *for all saints of all ages*[2.3]. "Here, then, in the Prologue are five links in the chain of authorship: God, Christ, his angel, his servant John, and those servants to whom John addressed his book [the *seven churches*[5.2.66] and the saints of all ages]."[13]

The revelation is to be shown to His *servants* (literally, 'slaves'). These are they who hear His voice (John 10:3, 16, 27; Acts 22:14; Heb. 3:7, 15; 4:7) and respond in faith. Those who lack faith in the Son are unable to comprehend what is shown here:

> This is why unbelievers find the book of Revelation incomprehensible; it was not intended for them. It was given by the Father to the Son to show to those who willingly serve Him. Those who refuse to acknowledge Jesus Christ as Lord cannot expect to comprehend this book. "A natural man," explains Paul, "does not accept the things of the Spirit of God, for they are foolishness to him; and he cannot understand them, because they are spiritually appraised" (1Cor. 2:14).[14]

For more on the spiritual conditions necessary for an understanding of this book and the Scriptures in general, see *Hiding or Revealing?*[2.2.6].

must

The things which God has prophesied are *guaranteed* to transpire (Dan. 2:29, 45; Mtt. 24:6; 26:54; Mark 13:7; Luke 21:9) for "Scripture cannot be broken" (John 10:35). The things which transpire here are not without Scriptural foundation and this is the very reason they *must* take place. See *Related Passages and Themes*[2.13].

shortly take place

Shortly is ἐν τάχει [*en tachei*]. Considerable discussion attends the meaning of this phrase. Three alternatives are before us:

1. The phrase requires all of the events set forth in the book to have transpired within the lifetimes of John's initial readers (the *preterist interpretation*[2.12.2]).
2. The phrase denotes events which may be in the distant future, but which transpire in rapid sequence once they begin.
3. The phrase denotes closeness in time, but from God's perspective.

The phrase ἐν τάχει [*en tachei*] ("shortly") occurs in the following NT passages:

- "he will avenge them *speedily*" (Luke 18:8) God will avenge His elect who cry out day and night though *he bears long* with them.
- "Arise *quickly*" (Acts 12:7)
- "going there *shortly*" (Acts 25:4)
- "get out of Jerusalem *quickly*" (Acts 22:18)
- "And the God of peace will crush Satan under your feet *shortly*" (Rom. 16:20)
- "I hope to come to you *shortly*" (1Ti. 3:14)
- "things which must *shortly* take place" (Rev. 22:6) (after which Jesus says "I am coming quickly" ἔρχομαι ταχύ [*erchomai tachy*])

Of these uses, the majority favor an understanding of "closeness in time." However, three of the passages utilize this phrase to describing events which are delayed for long time periods (Luke 18:8; Rom. 16:20; Rev. 22:6). Even moderate *preterists*[5.2.59], who hold to a future bodily Second Coming of Christ, take the last passage as denoting a time period lasting at least 2,000 years:

> Gentry cites Revelation 22:7-9 as a reference to the yet future second coming. This creates a contradiction within Gentry's brand of preterism. Since Revelation 22:6 refers to the whole book of Revelation, it would be impossible to take *tachos* as a reference to A.D. 70 (as Gentry does) and at the same time hold that Revelation 22:7-9 teaches the second coming.[15]

As Mills observes, it is impossible to restrict the sense of *en tachei* to the lifetime of John's readers:[16]

> The Greek noun translated 'shortly' is used only twice in Revelation, once in Rev. 1:1 and again in 22:6, thus effectively bracketing the whole book. **The prophecies bracketed by these 'shortlys' include letters addressed to churches that existed two millennia ago (chapters 2-3), clear descriptions of Christ's physical return to this earth (Rev. 1:7; 19:19-27 [*sic*]), and a prediction of His reign on earth for one thousand years (Rev. 20:4). Both uses of this word, then, must be understood as having the same sense and yet embrace, at the absolute minimum, a period of nearly three millennia.** Therefore, only two interpretations present themselves: either, when the events start occurring they will proceed rapidly, or that the whole sweep of history is seen from a divine perspective in which one thousand years is as but a day (2Pe. 3:8). [emphasis added][17]

The use of this same verb within the *LXX*[5.2.38] also provides evidence for a long delay in fulfillment:

> It is significant to note that the *Septuagint*[5.2.65] uses *tachos* in passages which even by the most conservative estimations could not have fulfillments within hundreds or even thousands of years. For example, Isaiah 13:22 . . . was written around 700 B.C. and foretold the destruction of Babylon, which occurred at the earliest in 539 B.C. Similarly, Isaiah 5:26 speaks of the manner, not the time frame, by which the Assyrian invasion of Israel "will come with speed *swiftly*."[18]

Since *en tachei* can span long periods of time, the question then becomes one of whether it denotes the *manner* in which events will transpire (rapidly) or the *certainty and imminency*[5.2.30] attending the events?

> It may be that the stress [in Rev. 22:20] is on the certainty of the coming or on the immediacy of the coming. But one's view does not hinge on the futuristic present, but on the adverb ταχύ [*tachy*]. The force of the sentence may then mean, "Whenever I come, I will come *quickly*," in which case the stress is on the *certainty* of the coming (cf. Matt 28:8). Or, it may mean, "I am on my way and I intend to be there very *soon*."[19]

Some understand the primary meaning of *en tachei* in this passage as denoting the *manner* in which the events transpire:

> tachy does not mean soon but swiftly. It indicates rapidity of action, as is well seen in its accurate use in the medical compound tachycardia (tachy and kardia = the heart), which does not mean that the heart will beat soon, but that it is beating rapidly. Of course, the swift action may take place at the very same time, as in Mtt. 28:7-8 . . .—G. H. Lang, *The Revelation of Jesus Christ: Selected Studies* (Miami Springs, FL: Conley & Schoettle Publishing Co., 1945, 1985), 387-88.[20]

> Not only is there a preponderance of lexical support for understanding the *tachos* family as including the notion of "quickly" or "suddenly," there is also the further support that all the occurrences in Revelation are adverbs of manner. These terms are not descriptive of *when* the events will occur and our Lord will come, but rather, descriptive of the *manner* in which they will take place when they occur.[21]

> Both futurists and nonfuturists . . . agree that the idea of *tachos* here has to do with *swiftness* of execution when the prophetic events begin to take place. . . . Both certainty and rapidity of action are involved here. Whatever seeming delay there is, action is certain and it will be swift.[22]

Although this meaning is possible, it does not seem to be the best understanding of the meaning here because, "To say that the relief will come 'suddenly' offers no encouragement, but to say that it will come 'soon' does."[23] It seems more likely that *en tachei* emphasizes the certainty and *imminency*[4.8] of the events:[24]

> The presence of *en tachei* in Rev. 1:1 shows that for the first time the events predicted by Daniel and foreseen by Christ stood in readiness to be fulfilled. Therefore, John could speak of them as imminent, but earlier prophets could not.[25]

> Either '*tachus* ' means that when the events occur they will be rapid, or the whole sweep of history is seen from a divine perspective where one thousand years is as but a day (2Pe. 3:8). The latter must be preferred as the former leaves unresolved the tension that part of Revelation relates to churches that existed two millennia ago. This understanding readily accepts as completely honest and trustworthy the doctrine of the imminent return of Christ; expressed in human terms, then, '*tachus*' denotes imminence and not immediacy. The irony of this situation is that those scholars who take '*tachus*' literally end up allegorizing the text, and those scholars who take the text literally end up seeking an unusual meaning for this word! The only satisfactory position I can see is therefore to regard '*tachus*' as being used in a technical sense—a sense understood as being within the whole biblical framework of the doctrine of the imminent return of Christ.[26]

See *Imminency*[4.8].

signified it

Ἐσήμανεν [*Esēmanen*]. The same root word is used in John 12:33, σημαίνων [*sēmainōn*], where Jesus describes His death on the cross by indicating He will be lifted up from the earth in the same way as Moses lifted up the serpent on a pole. Elsewhere, Agabus *indicated* by the Spirit that there was to be a worldwide famine (Acts 11:28). The appearance of this term does not justify a departure from the *Golden Rule of Interpretation*[5.2.24] when *interpreting symbols*[2.7] as some hold. It merely indicates a way of communicating which includes symbol or analogy. Although symbols occur, they reside within a textual framework which is subject to normative interpretation with due recognition of the meaning conveyed by the symbols. "This symbolism . . . in no way gives license for a departure from the normal grammatical-historical system of hermeneutics. To clarify this point Govett proposes that *esemanen* be translated 'represent.' The revelation given to John, symbolic though it be, is to be interpreted just as one would interpret the rest of the Bible."[27] "This term evidently meant a kind of communication that is neither plain statement nor an attempt at concealment. It is figurative, symbolic, or imaginative, and is intended to convey truth by picture rather than by definition."[28]

The revelation has already been signified from the perspective of the reader: "John's use of the aorist *emartyresen*, then, is best explained by his adoption of the perspective of his readers in regard to his composition of this book. When they received it, his testimony as recorded in its pages would be a thing of the past."[29]

See *Interpreting Symbols*[2.7].

angel

An angelic host shows John the Revelation. One of the seven angels who had the seven bowls filled with the seven last plagues (Rev. 21:9). This angel was specifically sent to show John the things which must shortly take place (Rev. 22:6, 16). Here, as elsewhere in Scripture, an angel serves as the intermediary by which revelation is given to man:

> Angels were used for the revelation of the Law of Moses (Acts 7:53; Gal. 3:19; Heb. 2:2). They were active in the presenting of the prophetic truth to Daniel (Dan. 7:16-27; 8:16-26; 9:20-27; 10:1-12:13) and to Zechariah (Zec. 1:9; 2:3; 4:1, 5; 5:5; 6:4, 5). Angels were used to announce the birth of John to Zacharias (Luke 1:11-20) and the birth of Jesus to Mary (Luke 1:26-38) and to Joseph (Mtt. 1:20-21).[30]

Some suggest that the angel actively contributed to the train of visionary events which passed before John:

> The office of the angel, as I take it, was, to form the connection between John's senses or imagination and the things which he was to describe, making to pass in review before him what was only afterwards to take place in fact. How this was done, I cannot say: but as the devil could take Jesus to a high mountain and show him at one view "all the kingdoms of the world, and the glory of them," I am sure that it falls sufficiently within the sphere of angelic natures thus to picture things to man; and that when commissioned of the Lord for the purpose, no good angel is wanting in ability to be the instrument in making John *see* whatever visions he describes in this book.[31]

This seems unlikely given that John was said to be "in the Spirit" (Rev. 1:10)—the Holy Spirit is elsewhere the agent by which such visionary events are presented.

The phrase "And I saw. . ." occurs no less than forty times.[32] This indicates John's primary role as a scribe rather than an author.

3.1.2 - Revelation 1:2

bore witness

An epistolary aorist, referring to the perspective of the readers of this book once it had been completed.[33]

who bore witness to the word of God

The phrase *word of God* is a signature of the Apostle John and occurs in John 1:1; 1Jn. 1:1; 2:14; 5:7 *TR*[5.2.79]; Rev. 1:2; 19:13. This is strong evidence that John the Apostle is indeed the *author*[2.9] of this work, as tradition holds. There are many parallels between Jesus and God's revealed word:

> Among the parallels between Jesus and Scripture are 1) their eternality; 2) their production by the Holy Spirit; 3) a divine message embodied in earthly form; 4) the accommodation of man's limited intellect; 5) perfect—without sin; 6) having unique divine authority; 7) rejected by man; 8) victorious over foes; 9) revealed by faith; 10) bearing witness one to another; 11) the sole means of revelation of the Father; 12) called the Word of God.[34]

In the same way that Jesus was fully human and yet without error (divine), the written word of God was given through human vessels who were superintended by the Holy Spirit so that the result is *inerrant*[5.2.32].

testimony of Jesus Christ

There are two ways which the *testimony of Jesus Christ* may be understood:

- **Jesus is the Subject** - The testimony was *provided by* Jesus. He is its *source* (subjective genitive). Both here and in Rev. 19:10, the grammatical evidence points toward taking this as the subjective genitive (the testimony born by Jesus Christ—which God gave Him).[35]
- **Jesus is the Object** - The testimony is *about* Jesus (objective genitive). He is the One

> *revealed* by the testimony. John was banished to Patmos "for the testimony of Jesus Christ" (Rev. 1:9). This almost certainly refers to persecution resulting from his testimony *about* Jesus. When the fifth seal is opened, John sees martyrs "who had been slain for the word of God and for the testimony which they held" (Rev. 6:9). When the two witnesses finish their testimony, the beast ascends from the bottomless pit and overcomes them (Rev. 11:7). The saints who overcome Satan do so by the (spoken) word of their testimony (Rev. 12:11). The enraged dragon goes forth to make war against those who "have the testimony of Jesus Christ" (Rev. 12:17). At the start of the *Millennial Kingdom*[5.2.39], John sees "the souls of those who had been beheaded for their witness to Jesus (μαρτυρίαν Ἰησοῦ [*martyrian Iēsou*], testimony of Jesus)" (Rev. 20:4). In these situations, Scripture records persecution as the *result* of holding the testimony. This cannot refer to merely *receiving* a testimony from Jesus. It must refer to *giving* that testimony forth in the face of opposition. This objective sense would also be in accord with what John records concerning the role of John the Baptist (John 1:7). Many other passages indicate that Jesus is the primary object of prophetic revelation: the "volume of the book" is written of Him (Ps. 40:7; Luke 18:31; 24:27, 44; John 5:39, 46; Acts 8:35; 10:43; Heb. 10:7).

A survey of various passages concerning the testimony of Jesus Christ indicates that Jesus is *both* the subject and the object of testimony. Prophetic motivation is *from Jesus*: "the Spirit of Christ . . . testified" (1Pe. 1:11). It is also *about Jesus*: "indicating . . . beforehand the sufferings of Christ and the glories that would follow" (1Pe. 1:11). The relationship of the saints to the testimony of Jesus concerns both aspects: (1) we receive the testimony provided by the Holy Spirit, the Spirit of Christ; (2) we are charged with delivering the testimony concerning Jesus to others. The ministry of the saints can be found entirely within the phrase: *Knowing Him to make Him known.* If either part of this "ministry equation" is neglected, our testimony suffers.[36]

3.1.3 - Revelation 1:3

Blessed *is* he

Luther's comments underscore the need for a consistently literal interpretation of this book: "Even if it were a blessed thing to believe what is contained in it, no man knows what that is."[37] For if different *interpretive views*[2.12] render wholly different meanings, then what blessing *could* be derived and how could the prophecy be kept? How can one keep what one is not sure one has in the first place?

One reason for such blessing is undoubtedly to be found in the close ties between this book and all the rest of Scripture: "The reason is easy to understand. Since so much of this book is based on the Old Testament, a proper study of it will require a study of the Old Testament, resulting in a more comprehensive knowledge of the Bible."[38] This is one of seven unique blessings found in Revelation for:

1. He who reads and those who hear the words of this prophecy (Rev. 1:3).
2. The dead who die in the Lord during part of the Tribulation (Rev. 14:13).
3. He who watches and keeps his garments (Rev. 16:15).
4. Those who are called to the marriage supper of the Lamb (Rev. 19:9).
5. He who has part in the first resurrection (Rev. 20:6).
6. He who keeps the words of this prophecy (Rev. 22:7).
7. Those who do His commandments (Rev. 22:14).

See commentary on *Revelation 1:1*[3.1.1] regarding the perspicuity of Scripture.

he who reads and those who hear

The phrase denotes a single reader who reads the letter out loud in the midst of a congregation of listeners. At the time the book was written, writing materials were expensive and scarce. Nor was there an inexpensive means for producing copies of a written document—tedious copying by hand being the means of replication. Generally, a Christian assembly might only have access to a single copy of a document so written works were often read so that their contents might be accessible to the wider assembly.[39]

the words

The message of God is not conveyed by some existential and personal encounter. Rather, it is conveyed by *words*. God has specifically chosen normative language as the mode for communicating what He wants us to know and keep. This is the basis for the *Golden Rule of Interpretation*[5.2.24] discussed in the *introduction*[2.7.2].

Scripture makes plain that the Word of God is a detailed message conveyed by individual *words* , not mere concepts (Jos. 8:35; Jer. 26:2; Mtt. 5:18; Luke 16:17; John 5:46; John 17:8; Acts 24:14; Rom. 3:2; Rom. 16:26; 1Cor. 14:37; Rev. 22:7, 18-19). Jesus Himself said that not one jot or one tittle will "pass from the law till all be fulfilled" (Mtt. 5:18). A "jot" refers to the smallest Hebrew character: י, *yod*. A "tittle" is the fraction of a pen stroke which distinguishes similar Hebrew characters, for example the tiny overhang in the upper right which distinguishes a dalet (ד) from a resh (ר). This tiny pen stroke distinguishes words which appear almost identical, but with meanings as different as "to stand" (אָמַד [`*āmad*] ) and "to speak" ( אָמַר [`*āmar*]).

It has become fashionable to promote the idea that Scripture conveys information primarily at the level of *concepts* rather than *words*. But one must appreciate that the building blocks for expressing thoughts are individual words. And without the precision of individual words, both in their meaning and preservation, the thoughts and intent of the original author *cannot be reliably determined* . This, in part, explains the emphasis of Scripture on the very words themselves as evidenced by the reliance of Jesus on grammatical subtleties in His arguments employing the Scriptures (Mtt. 22:31, 42-45; John 10:35; Gal. 3:16).

The importance of the individual words of Scripture is also illustrated by the sober warning which attends those who would add or remove *words* from this prophecy given to John. This is the heart of the issue as to which translation is best suited for study. It is our view, and that of others knowledgeable on the subject, that the *best* translation is one which follows a policy of *formal equivalence* where the very meaning of the individual words is preserved as closely as possible. While it is an undeniable fact that all translations involve interpretation by the translators, some translations involve *more interpretation* than others. It is these translations, which employ thought-for-thought *dynamic equivalence*, which are to be avoided:

> There is an Italian proverb which says, "Translators are traitors" (*Traddutore, traditore*; "Translators, traitors"), and it's true. All translation loses meaning. All translators are traitors to the actual meaning. There is no such thing as a noninterpretive translation. . . . Are you going to translate words [formal equivalence] and be interpretive, or are you going to translate meaning [dynamic equivalence] and be **more interpretive?** [emphasis added][40]

The concept is this: as a disciple of Jesus Christ, we want the minimum distance between the *inspired*[5.2.33] *inerrant*[5.2.32] text and our own understanding. A word-for-word (formal equivalence) translation tends to minimize the interpretive layer which separates us from the original. A thought-for-thought translation (dynamic equivalence) steps in to interpret things for us. What is particularly damaging about the latter is that ambiguity in the text—involving issues that we as students of the Word need to wrestle with and recognize involves ambiguity—is masked by the interpretive decisions of the thought-for-thought translators. In effect, they are performing both translation *and interpretation*. It is the latter which we seek to minimize:

> Translators have to ask themselves, "What am I going to do with ambiguity?" If the Greek or Hebrew isn't clear, when it can mean several different things, what am I going to do? The KJV, NASB, RSV, and ESV generally answer that question, "Leave it alone. If we can reproduce in English the same ambiguity that is present in the Greek, then we will leave it ambiguous. We will not make up the reader's mind." On the other hand, the NIV will not leave any ambiguity. They make up the reader's mind whenever they feel it is necessary, and the NLT goes to even greater lengths than the NIV.[41]

One helpful rule of thumb on this matter is as follows: *the only reliable translations for detailed study are those which include italicized words.* These translations use *formal equivalence* as evidenced by the italicized words which signify phrases and conjunctions added by the translators for clarity of reading, but for which no corresponding words exist in the original language text. This also helps the careful student to know when he is standing on solid ground (words not in italics) or thin ice (italicized phrases).[42]

Now it is certainly true that every believer is a "translation" of God's Word and not necessarily a word-for-word representation. God uses our testimony, even though imperfect, to witness of Christ and the Bible to others around us. This is as it should be. We need not always carry a Bible with us and read from it with precision for people to hear and respond in faith. Yet, when it comes to studying God's Word where we have a choice of which *written text* to study and how close we adhere to the original, this is another matter entirely. We should always opt to stay as close to the Words of the Master as possible.

This is illustrated by the popular game where people sit in adjacent positions and a story is told by the person on one end of the row of chairs. Each person in line whispers the story to the next person in line. When the story reaches the opposite end of the line, it is retold to all. It is amazing to observe how the story has changed little-by-little as it goes along until significant differences have occurred between its source and its destination. The student of God's Word ought to be concerned about how many chairs separate him from the Words of the Master. Some of those chairs might be unavoidable—perhaps the student is unable to learn the original languages of the Bible so he must depend upon a translation into his own tongue. Yet why choose to sit two or three chairs *further* away from the Master by using a paraphrase which allows His Word to be distorted and misunderstood?[43]

this prophecy

This book is not merely an allegory or devotional treatise extolling the eventual victory of good over evil. The events described within this book are *bona fide* prophecy and include the prediction of actual historical events. See *Can't God Prophesy?*[2.3.1]

and keep those things which are written

Keep is the present active participle τηροῦντες [*tērountes*], "while holding fast." The saints are told to "be continually hanging on to" the things which John writes. This requires focus and energy and implies the need for watchfulness in order to avoid having them taken away.

One aspect of keeping *those things which are written* involves a proper interpretation of their meaning. For it is possible to keep the words (Rev. 22:7), but with their incorrect meaning. The result is that the things written herein are not properly kept for they are not properly understood. One example of such corruption of the things written would be *amillennialism*[5.2.1] which holds that there is no future earthly kingdom of a thousand years (Rev. 20:4-6), but that the kingdom period has already begun. Keeping the words in such a way as to denude them of their meaning is no preservation at all.

Another aspect of keeping *those things which are written* is the preservation of both the content and proper interpretation of the text and *passing it on to each successive generation.* Jesus' haunting words come to mind: "Nevertheless, when the Son of Man comes, will He really find faith on the earth?" (Luke 18:8b). This is where an understanding of church history can be a great boon to the saints of any age in that they come to appreciate their position within the stream of biblical history and doctrine which flows from Genesis to the Second Coming of Christ. Without such understanding, it is unlikely that we will *keep those things which are written* in the way God intended.

The *things which are written* include both prophetic revelation concerning events in history, but also important exhortations concerning the *application* of the message within this book. The Psalm writer admonishes the saints to keep God's precepts (Ps. 119:4). James tells us to be doer's of the Word and not just hearers only (Jas. 1:22). We are told to watch and keep our garments, lest we "walk naked and they see *our* shame" (Rev. 16:15). Christianity is not a passive intellectual exercise, but an *active application and promulgation* of the message of God (Mtt. 24:42-44; 25:13).

We would do well to remember the response of Jesus to the woman who blessed His mother Mary:

> And it happened, as He spoke these things, that a certain woman from the crowd raised her voice and said to Him, "Blessed *is* the womb that bore You, and *the* breasts which nursed You!" But He said, "More than that, blessed *are* those who hear the word of God and keep it!" (Luke 11:27-28)

the time is near

The Greek phrase is καιρὸς ἐγγύς [*kairos engys*]. *Kairos* is a key eschatological term indicating a coming time of crisis associated with the last times.[44]

> The word used in Revelation 1:3 . . . is *kairos* . It does not speak of an era or time span, but signifies "the right time," "the right moment," "the opportune time." It is used in Galatians 4:4 wherein the Bible states, "But when the fulness of the time [*kairos*] was come, God sent forth His son. . ." Christ came at just the right moment. The time was "ripe" for the coming of God's Son.[45]

> [*Engus*] can refer to any event predicted by the prophets, as when Mark indicates that "the time [*kairos*] is fulfilled, and the kingdom of God is at hand [engus]" (Mark 1:15). Something was "at hand" that has to do with *kairos* time. It was the Kingdom hope and aspiration of every Old Testament Jew who knew the writings of the Hebrew prophets.[46]

This word for "time" differs from *chronos* which generally refers to what we would call chronological time:

> Καιρός [*Kairos*] ("time") frequently has a technical sense in the NT, referring to the end times when the earthly kingdom of Israel will be instituted (cf. Acts 1:7; 3:20; 1Th. 5:1). The events of this book are thus identified with the last of the critical epoch-making periods foreordained of God. From the perspective of prophetic anticipation this period is declared to be ἐγγύς [*engys*] ("near").[47]

> Time does not translate *chronos*, which refers to time on a clock or calendar, but *kairos*, which refers to seasons, epochs, or eras. The next great era of God's redemptive history is near.[48]

James makes an almost identical statement using the same Greek verb concerning the coming of the Lord for believers (not in judgment): "Therefore be patient, brethren, until the coming of the Lord. See *how* the farmer waits for the precious fruit of the earth, waiting patiently for it until it receives the early and latter rain. You also be patient. Establish your hearts, for the coming of the Lord is at hand (ἤγγικεν [*ēngiken*])" (Jas. 5:7-8). The meaning in James is that "of approaching in time . . . [and concerns] the Lord's return."[49] Peter uses the same term: "the end of all things is at hand" (1Pe. 4:7).

As with the previous statement concerning things *which must shortly take place* (Rev. 1:1), this perspective of time is that of God and concerns the last times when prophetic predictions would come to pass. "Some interval, however, is presupposed between the vision and its fulfillment, otherwise it would be futile to write the visions down, and to arrange for their circulation throughout the churches. A certain career is anticipated for the book of Revelation."[50]

Preterist interpreters[2.12.2] generally argue that this phrase must denote fulfillment in the lifetime of John's readers. Yet they are not consistent on this point when the phrase occurs elsewhere:

> This creates a contradiction within [moderate] *preterism*[5.2.59]. Since Rev. 22:6 is a statement referring to the whole book of Revelation, it would be impossible to take tachos as a reference to A.D. 70 . . . and at the same time hold that Rev. 20:7-9 teaches the Second Coming. [Moderate preterists] must either adopt a view similar to futurism, or shift to the extreme preterist view that understands the entire book of Revelation as past history, thus eliminating any future Second Coming and resurrection.[51]

A better way to understand the text, as in *verse 1*[3.1.1], is denoting the *imminency*[5.2.30] of the events John records. See *Imminency*[4.8].

3.1.4 - Revelation 1:4

John

This simple statement identifying the writer as "John" is evidence for the traditional view of *John the Apostle as author*[2.9]. For what other John would designate himself simply as "John" when "John *the Apostle*" was the most prominent "John" amongst the Asian churches during this period? If it had been another "John," he would have clarified so. John was ideally suited to write to these churches because he had been living in Asia Minor and ministering among the churches since approximately A.D. 66.[52]

seven churches which are in Asia

See *Seven Churches of Asia*[4.15] . The names of the *seven churches*[5.2.66] are listed in Revelation 1:11.

Although the text to follow addresses each church in turn, the book of Revelation is addressed to all seven churches for all seven churches are to benefit from its contents and to learn from those things which are said concerning the other churches (Rev. 2:7, 11, 17, 29; 3:6, 13, 22).

See *Seven: Perfection, Completeness*[2.7.5.3.6].

from Him who is and who was and who is to come

This is a reference to God the Father as can be seen by the Son being mentioned in the following verse "and from Jesus Christ" (Rev. 1:5).

This unusual grammatical construction is comprised of a present participle (ὁ ω῎ν [*ho ōn*], *he who is*), an imperfect verb (ὁ ἦν [*ho ēn*], *he was*) and another present participle (ὁ ἐρχόμενος [*ho erchomenos*], *he who is coming*). A more literal rendering might be, "the *One who is* and the *He was* and the *coming One*".

Several unusual aspects of this grammatical construction have been noted:

> Another rare grammatical phenomenon of this title is the finite verb *en* doing duty for a participle (Simcox). It is modified by a definite article and is parallel with participles in the first and third members of the expression. The reason for this peculiarity lies in a limitation of the verb εἰμί [*eimi*] ("I am"), which has no participial form to express continuing action in past time. The writer wanted to describe the Father's being by including His eternal and continuing existence prior to the present moment. The imperfect indicative was the only linguistic device for doing so.[53]

Regarding "who is" (nominative) following the preposition "from," Wallace observes:

> This is the first and worst grammatical *solecism*[5.2.68] in Revelation, but many more are to follow. There are two broad options for how to deal with it: Either the author unintentionally erred or he intentionally violated standard syntax. If unintentional, it could be due to a heavily Semitized Greek, or merely represent the level of linguistic skill that a minimally educated man might achieve (as in the vulgar *papyri*[5.2.53]). Either of these is doubtful here because (1) such a flagrant misunderstanding of the rudiments of Greek would almost surely mean that the author simply could not compose in Greek, yet the Apocalypse itself argues against this; (2) nowhere else does the Seer use a nominative immediately after a preposition (in fact, he uses ἀπό [*apo*] 32 times with a genitive immediately following). If intentional, the question of what the author intends. Few scholars would disagree with Charles'assessment [R.H. Charles, *A Critical and Exegetical Commentary on the Revelation of St. John*]: "The Seer has deliberately violated the rules of grammar in order to preserve the divine name inviolate from the change which it would necessarily have undergone if declined. Hence the divine name is here in the nominative." It would be like one American saying to another, "Do you believe in 'We the People?' " If the question had been, "Do you believe in us the people?" the allusion to the Preamble to the Constitution would have been lost.[54]

The phrase is to be regarded as an indeclinable proper name[55] meant to be familiar to readers of the Greek Old Testament who read of the name which God revealed to Moses at the burning bush, 'Εγώ εἰμι ὁ ὢν [*Egō eimi ho ōn*], "I AM WHO I AM" (Ex. 3:14, *LXX*[5.2.38]).

Although the phrase denotes God's eternality, it also emphasizes one of the themes of this book: His soon coming. "Such a means of referring to the future also heightens the focus upon the *imminence*[5.2.30] of His coming: He who is already on His way may arrive at any moment."[56]

> It is difficult to understand how so many should assume without further question that ὁ ἐρχόμενος [*ho erchomenos*] [the coming one] here is=ὁ ἐσόμενος [*ho esomenos*] [the one who shall be], and that thus we have the eternity of God expressed here so far as it can be expressed, in forms of time: "He who was, and is, *and shall be.*" But how ὁ ἐρχόμενος [*ho erchomenos*] should ever have this significance is hard to perceive. . . . What is the key-note to this whole Book? Surely it is, "I come quickly. The world seems to have all things its own way, to kill my servants; but I come quickly." With this announcement the Book begins, Rev. 1:7; with this it ends, Rev. 22:7, 12, 20 and this is a constantly recurring note through it all, Rev. 2:5, 16; 3:11; 6:17; 11:18; 14:7; 16:15; 18:20.[57]

seven spirits

Isaiah provides a list of qualities of the Spirit which shall rest upon the Messiah who shall come from the stem of Jesse (David's father): "The Spirit of the LORD shall rest upon Him, the Spirit of wisdom and understanding, the Spirit of counsel and might, the Spirit of knowledge and of the fear of the LORD" (Isa. 11:2).[58] In the fourth chapter, John calls our attention to "Seven lamps of fire *were* burning before the throne, which are the **seven Spirits of God**" [emphasis added] (Rev. 4:5). These Spirits are also said to be "seven eyes, which are the Seven Spirits of God sent out unto all the earth" (Rev. 5:6). The omniscience of the Holy Spirit is in view and His worldwide ministry, also mentioned by Zechariah (Zec. 4:6-10). One of His worldwide ministries is convicting "of sin, and of righteousness, and of judgment" (John 16:8). He provides the breath of life to all the world's creatures (Gen. 2:7; Job 34:14-15). He strives with all men to restrain sin (Gen. 6:3; 20:6; 2Th. 2:6-7).

Here, the Spirits are specifically said to be Spirits *of God* making the connection to Isaiah 11:2 more plausible and denoting seven different aspects of the Holy Spirit Who was poured out on the Anointed One (the *Mashiach* or *Christos*).

That these spirits are not angels[59] is seen from their elevation on a par with the other two members of the Trinity: "The seven Spirits might conceivably refer to a group of angelic beings. But coming between references to the Father and the Son it is more probable that this is an unusual way of designating the Holy Spirit."[60]

The number of spirits matches the number of lampstands and would seem to represent the activity of Christ through the Holy Spirit in and to the seven churches (Zec. 4:6). The epistle to each church closes with the admonition, "He who has an ear, let him hear what the Spirit says to the churches" (Rev. 2:7, 11, 17, 29; 3:6, 13, 22).[61]

See *Seven: Perfection, Completeness*[2.7.5.3.6].

3.1.5 - Revelation 1:5

and from Jesus Christ

Within this simple greeting can be found a neglected doctrine of paramount importance: the Trinity. The greeting is from each member of the Trinity: from *Him who is and who was and who is to come* (the Father), from *the seven Spirits who are before His throne* (the Holy Spirit), and from *Jesus Christ* (the Son). Before we have even begun to plumb the depths of the amazing statements made concerning Christ in the verses to follow, *His divinity* is already in plain view before us.

the faithful witness

Among the unique titles of Jesus, He is "called Faithful and True" (Rev. 19:11). Here, we see His character as God, Who cannot lie (Num. 23:19; Rom. 3:4; Tit. 1:2; Heb. 6:18). Where God is involved, other witnesses are unnecessary, for God bears truthful and reliable witness of Himself (John 8:14). The *witness* of Christ was *faithful* in that He finished the work which the Father had given Him (John 17:4), manifesting the Father's name to His disciples (John 17:6) and resisting the temptation to circumvent the cross (Luke 22:42-44). In His incarnation, Jesus provided a witness of God to man (Isa. 9:1-2; John 1:14, 18; 12:45; 14:8-9; Col. 1:15; 2:9; Heb. 1:2; 1Jn. 1:2).

firstborn from the dead

He is the firstborn from the dead "that in all things He may have the preeminence" (Col. 1:18). He thus establishes the pattern for all His brethren who will also rise from the dead (Rom. 8:29).

The term "firstborn" (πρωτότοκος [*prōtotokos*]), emphasizes not His *generation*, but His *position* (Ps. 89:27) [the *LXX*[5.2.38] uses the same Greek term (Psalm 88:28 in the LXX)].[62]

> The Greek term πρωτότοκο [*prōtotoko*] could refer either to first in order of time, such as a first born child, or it could refer to one who is preeminent in rank. M. J. Harris, *Colossians and Philemon* (EGGNT), 43, expresses the meaning of the word well: "The 'firstborn' was either the eldest child in a family or a person of preeminent rank. The use of this term to describe the Davidic king in Ps. 88:28 LXX (=Ps 89:27 EVV), 'I will also appoint him my firstborn (πρωτότοκο [*prōtotoko*]), the most exalted of the kings of the earth,' indicates that it can denote supremacy in rank as well as priority in time. But whether the proto- element in the word denotes time, rank, or both, the significance of the -tokos element as indicating birth or origin (from τίκτω [*tiktō*] give birth to) has been virtually lost except in reference to literal birth." In Col. 1:15 the emphasis is on the priority of Jesus'rank as over and above creation (cf. Col. 1:16 and the 'for' clause referring to Jesus as Creator).[63]

A connection with Psalm 2 is seen in that Christ is here *firstborn from the dead* ("begotten," Ps. 2:7 cf. Acts 13:33; Heb. 1:5; Rom. 1:4) and *ruler over the kings of the earth* (Ps. 2:8). It was at His resurrection that His divine Sonship was made manifest and attested by the Father (Acts 13:33; Rom. 1:4).[64]

Although not the first to be raised from the dead, Christ is the first to be resurrected to obtain a glorified body never to die again (1Cor. 15:35-44). "There were resurrections before His in the Old Testament (1K. 17:17-23; 2K. 4:32-36; 13:20-21), and He Himself raised others during His earthly ministry (Mtt. 9:23-25; Luke 7:11-15; John 11:30-44)."[65] Yet all of these who were resurrected prior to Christ continued to age and eventually died again.[66]

> Christ is indeed "*the first begotten of the dead* ," notwithstanding that such raisings from the grave as that of the widow's son, and Jairus's daughter, and Lazarus, and his who revived at the touch of Elisha's bones (2K. 13:21), went before. There was for them no repeal of the sentence of death, but a respite only; not to say that even during their period of respite they carried about with them a body of death. Christ first so rose from the dead, that he left death forever behind Him, did not, and could not, die any more (Rom. 6:9); in this respect was "the first-fruits of them that slept" (1Cor. 15:20, 23), the Prince of life (Acts 3:15).[67]

> The resurrection of Christ is unique because He is the first instance of that transformation which the resurrection effects. It is more than a resuscitation of mortal flesh, such as took place in the cases of Jairus' daughter or of Lazarus, for they underwent no essential change of the body. . . . they were restored to their friends; but there is not a hint that they were made physically immortal, or that death did not overtake them at some later date.[68]

ruler over the kings of the earth

The rule of Jesus over the kings of the earth is by divine right, not by the willing acceptance of the kings themselves (Ps. 2; Dan. 2:34-35, 44-45; 7:11-14, 24-27). For the world will *reject the reign of God*[2.13.1]. The *arrival of God's kingdom on earth*[2.4.3] is a major theme of this prophecy given through John and culminates in the destruction of the armies of the kings of the earth at the Second Coming of Christ (Rev. 19:11-21).

While it is true that Jesus is the ruler over all men *today* , most do not realize this to be the case. A time is coming when the knowledge of the Lord will extend over the face of the entire earth and there will no longer be difference of opinion regarding Who is in control (Isa. 2:3; 11:9; Mic. 4:2; Zec. 14:8-11).

who loved us

"Loved," (Ἀγαπῶντι [*Agapōnti*]) is a present participle, He *is loving* (present tense) us. The love of God for us is demonstrated in many ways, but chiefly, in the way in which He gave His Son on our behalf: "For God so loved the world that He gave His only begotten Son, that whoever believes in Him should not perish but have everlasting life" (John 3:16). The "so" in this oft-quoted verse is not only speaking of the *degree* of God's love, but the *way in which it was manifested*—by the giving of His Son.[69] This is made clear by the context of the passage, and especially the preceding verses: "And **as** Moses lifted up the serpent in the wilderness, **even so** must the Son of Man be lifted up, that whoever believes in Him should not perish but have eternal life" [emphasis added] (John 3:14-15).

In his epistle, John also explained the giving of Jesus on the cross as a *demonstration* of God's love. "In this the love of God was manifested toward us, that God has sent His only begotten Son into the world, that we might live through Him. In this is love, not that we loved God, but that He loved us and sent His Son *to be* the propitiation for our sins" (1Jn. 4:9-10). This love of God is not restricted to the Father giving the Son, but includes *the Son giving Himself* (Eph. 5:2). Our love of God is not natural, but in reaction to His first having loved us (1Jn. 4:19).

The degree of God's love for us is fathomless. Yet God desires our finite minds to attempt to comprehend it as best we are able. The depth of His love is demonstrated by an ongoing study of what is said concerning the relationship between the Father and the Son (John 1:1; 17:5, 25) and the agonizing cost to God in order to redeem us (Mtt. 27:46; Mark 15:34). This cost is all the more amazing when our condition as enemies of God is considered (Rom. 5:6-10).

Our inability to worship God correlates with our ignorance of His Word. For it is by His Word that we come to an ever deeper understanding of the intimacy between the Father and the Son and the painful rent in that fabric necessary to secure our undeserved redemption. Emotional worship experiences in and of themselves can never substitute for a response based upon a Scriptural understanding of His love for us, as limited as it may ultimately be.

washed us

NU[5.2.49] has "freed" (λύσαντι [*lysanti*]) whereas *MT*[5.2.45] has "washed" (λούσαντι [*lousanti*]) - a difference of a single Greek letter. Scripture describes both as being true of the believer who has been set free (Mtt. 20:28; Gal. 3:13; 4:5; 1Ti. 2:6; Heb. 9:12; 1Pe 1:18; Rev. 5:9; 14:3-4) and washed, a picture of spiritual cleansing (Ps. 51:4; Isa. 1:16-18; Eze. 36:25; Acts 22:16; Eph. 5:26; Tit. 2:14; 3:5; Heb. 1:3; 9:14; 2Pe. 1:9). The imagery of the immediate passage, *in His own blood* , argues for the latter as does internal evidence elsewhere in the book (Rev. 7:14).

Whereas *loved us* is in the present tense, *washed us* is in the aorist tense. The provision for our redemption, His death on the cross which washes away all our sin both past and future, is accomplished and its full merits are applied in full the *moment* we believe. Yet He *continually* loves us.

in His own blood

A bloodless gospel is an ineffectual gospel. For it is by the spilling of blood that God has chosen to atone for sin (Lev. 17:11; Heb. 9:22).[70]

Why did God choose blood for this purpose? Ultimately, we may never know, for the "secret things belong to the LORD our God" (Deu. 29:29). Scripture reveals that the use of blood for atonement is related to its life-giving qualities (Gen. 9:4). The "life of the flesh is in the blood" (Lev. 17:11). "Life" in this verse is Hebrew נֶפֶשׁ [*nephesh*], the same term which is translated "soul" where Scripture records the once-for-all atonement made by Isaiah's Suffering Servant: "Yet it pleased the LORD to bruise Him; He has put *Him* to grief. When You make His **soul** an offering for sin" [emphasis added] (Isa. 53:10). By His blood atonement, Jesus was prophesied to "sprinkle many nations" (Isa. 52:15), thus fulfilling the many *OT*[5.2.51] types pointing to Him.

It was by blood sacrifice that the first man and woman were covered in response to their sin (Gen. 3:21). It was by blood sacrifice that the first men were to approach God (Gen. 4:4). It was by a blood sacrifice that God established His covenant with Abraham (Gen. 15:9-21). It was by blood placed on the door posts and lintel that the Jews were "covered" from the destroyer Who passed over Egypt taking the firstborn of each family (Ex. 12:23). It was by the sprinkling of blood that the Mosaic Law was ratified between God and the Israelites (Ex. 24:8). Ever since the bloodless offering of Cain (Gen. 4:3-5), man has attempted to approach God by some other means than that which God Himself has established. These would try to circumvent the single path which God requires: "Jesus said to him, 'I am the way, the truth, and the life. No one comes to the Father except through Me.' " (John 14:6)

This necessity of blood offering is offensive to man, and we believe intentionally so. For it is a messy business and continual reminder of man's lack of righteousness (Rom. 3:23) and his desperate need of the "righteousness of God," a righteousness which is *freely given* rather than *earned* (Rom. 3:21-26; 2Cor. 5:21; Php. 3:9). Yet many prefer to continue in the way of religion rather than relationship, offering up their own puny works in a vain attempt to justify themselves before a perfect and Holy God (Rom. 10:3). Religion preserves our pride, whereas relationship requires us to cast it aside.

See *Hide and Seek*[4.16.1].

3.1.6 - Revelation 1:6

made us kings and priests

In both *NU*[5.2.49] and *MT*[5.2.45], the Greek has *appointed us a kingdom* (singular), *priests to God.* A similar difference occurs in Revelation 5:10. The singular form (a kingdom) would be in keeping with the original calling of Israel to be "a kingdom of priests" (Ex. 19:6). Some have noted the Jewish audience of Peter's epistle and rightly understood 1Peter 2:9 as being a reminder to his readers of the original calling of the Jews (Ex. 19:6). Yet in this book the concept is unmistakably broadened to include all those who trust in Christ, whether Jew or Gentile, from among every "tribe and tongue and people and nation" (Rev. 5:10). Our priesthood is made possible by our "great High Priest who has passed through the heavens, Jesus the Son of God" (Heb. 4:14), therefore we have complete and full access to the Father. "Let us therefore come boldly to the throne of grace, that we may obtain mercy and find grace to help in time of need." (Heb. 4:16).

Whether we are to be "kings and priests" or "a kingdom [of] priests," it is clear that believers will co-rule with Christ during His coming earthly reign (Rev. 20:4-6). This future reign will not come to pass until after *Antichrist*[5.2.3] has his time on the world stage and a judgment is made in favor of the saints (Dan. 7:18, 25-27).[71]

Both now and in the future, our function is primarily *priestly*. That is, we are to minister *to God*. Here we run into an extremely important distinction which has not been adequately appreciated among many who lead God's people. Our primary responsibility is to minister *to God* and not *to men*. Our focus is to be *God-ward* rather than *man-ward*. We are to "offer up spiritual sacrifices to God through Jesus Christ" (1Pe. 2:5). As we take care to minister to God, He will minister to men through us.

The focus of our ministry is the New Covenant (2Cor. 3:6), not the Law of Moses, and is characterized by a series of contrasts and seeming contradictions (2Cor. 6:4-10). Our lives should evidence a consistency of living whether with the people of God or with unbelievers: "God intends the eventual abolition of all distinctions between holy and profane, sanctified and common (Zec. 14:20-21)."[72]

In one sense, there has been and will only ever be a single "kingdom of God." This is His universal dominion over His entire creation. Yet, in another sense, God has chosen to use men as mediators of His rule during periods of history.[73]

The progression of the kingdom of God is revealed in stages:

> The progression of the "kingdom of God" is gradually revealed. What is this kingdom in principle if it is not the sphere where God reigns? In the Scriptures we can trace for it seven distinct steps: 1. Paradise . . . (Gen. 1:31) 2. The *theocracy*[5.2.76] of Israel . . . 3. The kingdom announced by the prophets . . . (1S. 7:8; Isa. 11:1-16) 4. The kingdom offered and rejected in the gospels . . . (Mtt. 4:17; Luke 17:21; Luke 10:9-11) 5. The kingdom hidden in the heart . . . (John 3:3-5; Col. 1:13) 6. The thousand year reign . . . (Rev. 20:1-10) 7. The eternal kingdom in heaven . . . (2Ti. 4:18; 2Pe. 1:10-11).[74]

Our rule is not contingent upon our status in the world, but upon our position in Christ:

> Let men despise and contemn religion as they may, there is empire connecting with lowly discipleship, royalty with penitence, and prayers, and sublime priesthood with piety. Fishermen and taxgatherers, by listening to Jesus, presently find themselves in apostolic thrones, and ministering as priests and rulers of a *dispensation*[5.2.15], wide as the world, and lasting as time. Moses, by his faith, rises from Jethro's sheepfold to be the prince of Israel; and Daniel, from the den of condemnation and death, to the honour and authority of empire; and Luther, from his cell, to dictate to kings and rule the ages. There is not a believer, however obscure or humble, who may not rejoice in princely blood, who does not already wield a power which the potencies of hell cannot withstand, and who is not on the way to possess eternal priesthood and dominion.[75]

to Him be glory and dominion

The nearest antecedent is the Son to which glory and dominion are given, literally *into the ages of the ages* (εἰς τοὺς αἰῶνας τῶν αἰώνων [*eis tous aiōnas tōn aiōnōn*]). Yet elsewhere it is said that God will not share His glory with another (Isa. 48:11). Clearly, Jesus is God!

3.1.7 - Revelation 1:7

He is coming

The *OT*[5.2.51] Scriptures predicted a "coming one" (Deu. 18:15-18; Ps. 2; 22; 118:26; Isa. 9:6; 48:16; 53; 61:1; Jer. 23:5-8; Dan. 9:25; Mic. 5:2; Zec. 2:8-11; 6:12-15; etc.). This was the expectation of those among whom Jesus ministered (John 1:21; 1:45; 6:14; 7:40). John the Baptist knew of these predictions and sent his disciples to Jesus inquiring, " 'Are You the **Coming One** (ἐρχόμενος [*erchomenos*]), or do we look for another?' " [emphasis added] (Mtt. 11:3; Luke 7:19). Peter and Stephen explained it was Jesus who fulfilled these predictions (Acts 3:22; 7:37).

Yet this Coming One represented a Scriptural enigma. At times, He was said to be victorious king who would reign forever (Num. 24:17; Isa. 9:6-7). But He was also forsaken, despised, rejected, and crushed (Ps. 22; Isa. 53). How could these seeming contradictions be reconciled? Some chose to apply these passages to two different individuals, a "suffering Messiah" (Messiah ben-Joseph) and a "victorious Messiah" (Messiah ben-David).[76] Others held that the fulfillments were mutually exclusive and which would eventuate depended upon the obedience of Israel.[77]

The key which unlocks this mystery is the resurrection of Messiah (Ps. 16:10; Isa. 53:10). He would come once, die for the sins of the world, be resurrected back to life, and come a second time in judgment. His First Coming, death, and resurrection are now past. All that remains is His reappearance as described to John here and elsewhere in the *NT*[5.2.48]. "It has been estimated that one out of every twenty-five verses in the New Testament refers to the Second Coming."[78]

> Jesus came the first time in humiliation; He will return in exaltation. He came the first time to be killed; He will return to kill His enemies. He came the first time to serve; He will return to be served. He came the first time as the suffering servant; He will return as the conquering king. The challenge the book of Revelation makes to every person is to be ready for His return.[79]

He *is coming* (present tense) and every eye *will see* Him (future tense). The grammar places the event on the edge between the present and the future—the *futuristic present*. It is 'about to occur.' It is *imminent*[5.2.30]:

> The verb form ἔρχεται [*erchetai*] is an example of the futuristic use of the present tense, the future connotation being provided by the word's meaning. The idea is that Christ is already on His way, i.e., He is in the process of coming and hence *will* arrive. This use of the present tense enhances emphasis on the imminence of that coming (cf. ἔρχομαι [*erchomai*] , John 14:3).[80]
>
> This same verb is used directly or indirectly eleven more times in this book in reference to the return of Christ (cf. Rev. 1;4,8; 2:5, 16; 3:11; 4:8; 16:15; 22:7, 12, 20 [twice]), seven coming from the lips of Christ Himself (Rev. 2:5, 16; 3:11; 16:15; 22:7, 12, 20). The current verse obviously is the theme verse for the whole book.[81]

See *Imminency*[4.8].

with clouds

Clouds are often associated with the glory of the Lord. Clouds were often one aspect of the visible manifestation of the Lord's presence (Ex. 16:10; 19:9, 16; 24:15-16; 34:5; 40:34; Deu. 5:22). Clouds indicated His presence over the mercy seat where He dwelt between the cherubim (Lev. 16:2). During Solomon's prayer dedicating the *Temple*[5.2.73], he recognized God's habitation as the dark cloud (2Chr. 6:1). In response, the glory of the Lord filled the Temple (2Chr. 7:1), no doubt including a manifestation of clouds. The psalmist understood dark clouds to be God's canopy (Ps. 18:11; Ps. 97:2).

The manifestation of God by clouds indicates His localized presence on the earth, among men:

> the *Shechinah Glory*[5.2.67] is the visible manifestation of the presence of God. It is the majestic presence or manifestation of God in which He descends to dwell among men. Whenever the invisible God becomes visible, and whenever the omnipresence of God is localized, this is the Shechinah Glory. The usual title found in Scriptures for the Shechinah Glory is the glory of Jehovah, or the glory of the Lord. The Hebrew form is Kvod Adonai, which means "the glory of Jehovah" and describes what the Shechinah Glory is. The Greek title, Doxa Kurion, is translated as "the glory of the Lord." Doxa means "brightness," "brilliance," or "splendor," and it depicts how the Shechinah Glory appears. Other titles give it the sense of "dwelling," which portrays what the Shechinah Glory does. The Hebrew word Shechinah, from the root shachan, means "to dwell." The Greek word skeinei, which is similar in sound as the Hebrew Shechinah (Greek has no "sh" sound), means "to *tabernacle*[5.2.69]" . . . In the Old Testament, most of these visible manifestations took the form of light, fire, or cloud, or a combination of these. A new form appears in the New Testament: the Incarnate Word.[82]

The visible manifestation of God indicating the place where he *dwelt* has been called the "Shekinah" glory from the Hebrew verb שָׁכַן [*shākan*] meaning "dwell, live among, inhabit, abide, stay, remain, camp, i.e., to live or reside in a place, usually for a relatively long amount of time (Gen. 9:27)."[83] See *The Abiding Presence of God*[4.16.2].

> The cloud is probably not to be interpreted as a vapor cloud or as a storm cloud, but as a cloud of glory

> betokening the presence of God. . . . The "cloud," then, may be the cloud of the Shekinah, which led the children of Israel out of Egypt and through the desert, and which overshadowed the Tabernacle and the Temple (Ex. 13:21-22; 40:34; Num. 9:15-16; 2Chr. 7:2-3).[84]

When Jesus revealed His glory to Peter, James and John on the Mount of Transfiguration, the voice of the Father spoke from within a bright cloud saying, "This is My beloved Son in whom I am well pleased. Hear Him!" (Mtt. 17:5). Jesus explained His appearance with the clouds to be the sign of His coming (Mtt. 24:30) and His mention of "coming on the clouds of heaven" (Mtt. 26:64) was understood by the high priest as a blasphemous claim (Mtt. 26:64-65). He tore his garments in response, a clear indication of his understanding of what Jesus was claiming (Dan. 7:13).

John's mention here of Jesus coming *with clouds* is an allusion from the book of Daniel which records the presentation of the Son to the Father: "I was watching in the night visions, and behold, *One* like the Son of Man, coming with the clouds of heaven! He came to the Ancient of Days, and they brought Him near before Him." (Dan. 7:13). This presentation of the Son is to receive His kingdom (Dan. 7:14) and does not take place until all of His enemies are made His footstool (Ps. 110:1). This includes His future enemy, Daniel's "*little horn*[5.2.37]" (Dan. 7:8, 20-21). At present, He is seated at the right hand of the Father awaiting that day. The Son *began* the period of sitting at the right hand and waiting for His enemies to be made His footstool at His ascension (Acts 2:32-35; Heb. 10:11-13). His earthly kingdom did not come at the time of His ascension, but occurs when He rises from His seat beside the Father and descends to take up His Davidic throne on earth (Mtt. 25:31; Luke 1:32-33).[85]

At other times, the Lord is said to ride "on a swift cloud" (Isa. 19:1). It is such a passage which provides the basis for the *preterist*[5.2.59] interpretation which holds that this verse is describing a "cloud coming" in judgment upon a nation. Such a judgment in the OT was not attended by a literally visible manifestation of God. Yet here, we are explicitly told that *every eye* will see Him. Not just the "clouds of judgment," but *Him* ! This return of Jesus will be with clouds, bodily, and visible as the angels informed His disciples at the time of His ascension (Acts 1:9-11). His return is the subject of the latter portion of Revelation 19. If this were a "judgment coming" of Christ in A.D. 70 upon the Jews of Jerusalem as the preterists claim, what relevance would that have to the *seven churches*[5.2.66] of Asia who were hundreds of miles away and virtually unaffected by the event?[86]

As our discussion regarding the *Date*[2.11] the Revelation was written shows, the best evidence supports a late date near the end of Domitian's reign when John had the vision (A.D. 95-96). That being the case, the "coming" described here cannot refer to the "cloud coming in judgment" to destroy Jerusalem in A.D. 70 as the *Preterist Interpretation*[2.12.2] holds.

every eye will see Him

This phrase would seem to be almost intentionally aimed at undercutting the claims of various cults and aberrations of Christianity which have taught non-visible fulfillments of the coming of Jesus in history past. His future coming will be visible to *every eye*. This simple fact destroys the claims of preterism that this "cloud coming" occurred spiritually in 70 A.D. with the destruction of Jerusalem and the ending of the Jewish state.[87]

While mild preterism is not a cult, it shares this aberrant teaching that the coming of Jesus here is not a visible coming. "The crucifiers would see Him coming in judgment—that is, they would *understand* that His coming would mean wrath on the land."[88] Notice the preterist sleight of hand. The verse states that every eye will *see Him*, whereas DeMar states that it is an *understanding* of His *judgment* that is being described. These are not the same thing. DeMar realizes the difference and attempts to overcome this liability: "Equating 'seeing' with 'understanding' is not Scripture twisting. It is a common biblical metaphor."[89] Yet there are fundamental differences between this passage and those DeMar offers in support of the preterist view. Here, the passage states that *every eye* will see. If the preterist interpretation is correct and the "seeing" is an "understanding of judgment," then why didn't the *entire nation* of Israel "understand" and turn to Christ at the destruction of Jerusalem? Apparently, the vast majority of Jews had no idea of the correlation between the destruction of Jerusalem and the "coming of Jesus" which the preterists maintain and which John states *every eye* would see. "Seeing" is describing literal visibility by every eye, not an abstract "understanding" by a few Jews.

even they

A subgroup from among *every eye*, establishing the global nature of the manifestation of Christ.

Both Jews *and* Gentiles are responsible for the crucifixion of Jesus (Acts 4:27-28). It was *Jewish mouths* (Mark 15:13; Luke 23:21; John 19:6, 14-16) together with *Gentile hands* (John 19:23) which crucified Jesus. Ultimately, it was the sin of all mankind which sent Jesus to the cross (Rom. 4:25). Yet this passage refers to the Jews who have a particular responsibility (Acts 3:12-15) because Jesus is their promised national Messiah (Rom. 9:4-5). The Jewish generation which witnessed the crucifixion of Messiah made the fearful mistake of pronouncing a curse upon themselves and their children: "And all the people answered and said, 'His blood [be] on us and on our children.' " (Mtt. 27:25). So it is Jews who will specially mourn when they realize their grave error and the historical destruction it has wrought. As Lightner observes: "You don't put kings on crosses, you put them on thrones!"

even they who pierced Him

"Pierced" is ἐξεκέντησαν [*exekentēsan*]. John uses this identical Greek word in John 19:37 when quoting Zechariah 12:10. These are the only two places in the entire NT where this particular verb appears—another piece of evidence that the Apostle John was the writer of both books.[90]

The one who is coming is the one who they pierced—Jesus Christ. Yet Zechariah (Zec. 12:10) tells us that it is *God* who they pierced (Hebrew דָּקָרוּ [*Dāqhārû*] - "drive through, pierce, stab, run through, i.e., make physical impact with a sharp implement"[91]). "The weapon associated with [Hebrew] daqar is usually the sword, though a spear is the instrument in Num. 25:8."[92] Not only were spikes driven through Jesus' hands and feet, but He was pierced with a spear (John 19:34). Comparing Zechariah 12:10 with this verse, we see once again that Jesus is identified as God! Isaiah prophesied that He would be "wounded" ("pierced," NASB), Hebrew הָלַל [*hālal*].[93] "John is the only one of the Evangelists who records the piercing of Christ's side. This allusion identifies him as the author of the Apocalypse."[94]

Some hold that "every eye" describes all Israel whereas "even they that pierced" describes a subgroup from among the Jews who are more directly responsible for the crucifixion. But Zechariah defines those who pierced Him using terms which are synonymous with all Israel:

> And I will pour **on the house of David and on the inhabitants of Jerusalem** the Spirit of grace and supplication; then they will look on Me whom they pierced. Yes, they will mourn for Him as one mourns for *his* only *son*, and grieve for Him as one grieves for a firstborn. Zec. 12:10 [emphasis added]

Here, Zechariah identifies "they who pierced" (Revelation 1:7) as being all Israel-not a subset specifically held responsible for the crucifixion of Messiah from among a larger group of Jews.

> The recipients of the spiritual blessing [identical with those who mourn] will be (1) "the house of David," through whom the promise of the Messianic-Davidic Kingdom was made (2S. 7:8-16), and through whom it will be realized (Luke 1:31-33); and (2) "the inhabitants of Jerusalem"—the whole saved remnant of Israel, by metonymy, the capital representing the whole nation (cf. 1K. 20:34, where "Samaria," the capital, represents the nation).[95]

> The fact that only the inhabitants of Jerusalem are named, and not those of Judah also, is explained correctly by the commentators from the custom of regarding the capital as the representative of the whole nation. And it follows . . . from this, that in v. 8 also the expression "inhabitants of Jerusalem" is simply an individualizing epithet for the whole of the covenant nation. But just as in v. 8 the house of David is mentioned emphatically along with these was the princely family and representative of the ruling class, so is it also in v. 10, for the purpose of expressing the thought that the same salvation is to be enjoyed by the whole nation, in all its ranks, from the first to the last.[96]

Also, if "they who pierced" is to be understood as a subgroup from among the Jewish nation, how does one establish the precise boundary between all the Jews living at the time of Christ versus those who contributed to His crucifixion? And what does contributing to His crucifixion entail? Direct persuasion, such as manifested by the Jewish religious leaders? Does incitement by the crowd count? What about Jews who were not present at Jerusalem at the crucifixion, but opposed Jesus' ministry? And how does such a distinction between some Jews and not others square with the generational curse pronounced by and upon the Jews in general (Mtt. 27:25)?

all the tribes

In many places, *tribes* (φυλαι [*phylai*]) specifically denotes the Jewish tribes (e.g., Mtt. 19:28; Luke 2:36; 22:30; Acts 13:21; Rom. 11:1; Heb. 7:13; Php. 3:5; Jas. 1:1; Rev. 5:5; 7:4-9; 21:12). Elsewhere, especially when appearing in the phrase *all the tribes* , it has a more global meaning (e.g., Mtt. 24:30; Rev. 1:7) over against *the twelve [Jewish] tribes* (Mtt. 19:28; Luke 22:30; Acts 26:7; Jas. 1:1; Rev. 21:12). Φυλαι [*Phylai*] is differentiated from *nation* (ἔθνος [*ethnos*]), *people* (λαός [*laos*]), and *tongue* (γλῶσσα [*glōssa*]) in Rev. 7:9; 11:9; 13:7.

of the earth

The closely-related phrase "all the families of the earth" appears in several places in the OT (Gen. 12:3; 28:14; Amos 3:2; Zec. 14:17). In all of these contexts, the phrase clearly refers to the global community (not just the tribes of Israel).[97] It is through Abraham's seed that "all the families of the earth" (Gen. 12:3; 28:14) will be blessed.[98] God says to Israel, "You only have I known of all the families of the earth." (Amos 3:2) Whichever "of the families of the earth does not go up to Jerusalem to worship the King" (Zec. 14:17) during the Millennium will not receive rain. These families include "the family of Egypt" (Zec. 14:18). In each of these OT passages, the *Septuagint*[5.2.65] renders the phrase using the same Greek term (φυλαι [*phylai*]) found here.[99][100]

There is a close connection between this passage and Zechariah 12. Preterists make the same mistake in both passages of trying to limit the scope to Israel and Jerusalem. But the Zechariah passage is clearly describing a time "when all nations of the earth are gathered against [Jerusalem]" (Zec. 12:3). And the outcome of the battle is entirely different than the destruction of Jerusalem in A.D. 70: "In that Day the LORD will defend the inhabitants of Jerusalem. . . I will seek to destroy all the nations that come against Jerusalem." (Zec. 12:8-9). But nothing of the kind happened in A.D. 70. In the preterist "fulfillment" of these related passages, a *single* nation (Rome), unopposed by God, attacked Jerusalem completely destroying both the city and the Temple, resulting in the death of over 1 million Jews.[101]

> [preterists conclude] that "earth" means the land of Israel, as in Zec. 12:12 and that the "tribes" in Rev. 1:7 must be the literal Israelite tribes, who are being judged in 70 A.D. in fulfillment of the Zechariah 12 prophecy. But there are difficulties with this perspective. First, Zechariah 12 does not prophesy Israel's judgment but Israel's redemption. Furthermore, the Zechariah citation is combined with Dan. 7:13, which also refers to the eschatological deliverance, not judgment of Israel.[102]

The global context is also evident because John has just said that Jesus is "the ruler over the **kings** of the earth" [emphasis added] (Rev. 1:5). The plural *kings* indicates a wider area than just the land of Israel argued by preterists. There were not multiple kings over the Jews at the time of John's vision.

> The weightiest consideration of all appears to be the worldwide scope of the book. "Those who dwell on the earth" (Rev. 3:10; 6:10; 8:13; 11:10 [twice]; 13:8, 12, 14 [twice]; 17:2, 8) are the objects of the wrath that is pictured in its pages, and evidence points to the multi-ethnic nature of this group. The scope of the judgments of the book is also worldwide, not localized (e.g., Rev. 14:6; 15:4). Besides this, the people on whom these judgments fall do not respond by repenting.[103]

Further evidence against the preterist attempt to interpret Revelation as concerning the A.D. 70 judgment of Israel is found in a comparison of Ezekiel 3 with Revelation 10. Both prophets, Ezekiel and John, are given books to eat. Both books are sweet to the taste, but bitter once digested. Both books contain prophecy. However, one *significant difference* occurs between what Ezekiel and John ingest: Ezekiel eats a message intended for *Israel* but John eats a message for *all nations*. Ezekiel is told to prophesy to the "house of Israel, not to many people of unfamiliar speech" (Eze. 3:6) whereas John "must prophesy again about many peoples, nations, tongues, and kings" (Rev. 10:11). The message of John is **about many peoples, nations, tongues, and kings**. What more could God say to make its global extent clearer? See commentary on *Revelation 10:11*[3.10.11]. [104].

mourn

The word κόψονται [*kopsontai*] refers to the act of beating one's breast as an act of mourning.[105] Jesus refers to this event when all the tribes of the earth will mourn (κόψονται [*kopsontai*] , Mtt. 24:30). There it is said to be in response to "The sign of the Son of Man" which will "appear in heaven." This sign appears in *heaven*—visible worldwide and cannot be restricted to the region of

Israel as preterists maintain.

The Jews will mourn because of the awful realization of the truth of the crucifixion of their own Messiah and the subsequent record of history triggered by this most colossal mistake of all history:

> Israel must, indeed, be dumb if one asks them today: Tell me, pray: How can it be that the Eternal sent the fathers out of their land into captivity in Babylon for only seventy years, on account of all the abominations and idolatry by which they for centuries defiled the Holy Land:—and now Israel has been dispersed among all peoples for over eighteen hundred years, and Jerusalem, the city of the great King, is trodden down by the nations until this day? What, then, is the great and terrible blood-guiltiness which perpetually prevents you from dwelling in peace in the land of your fathers?—But Israel is not willing to know! And yet it is precisely its sin against its Messiah that is indeed the root of Israel's misery.[106]

The Gentiles too will mourn as they realize the truth of Christianity which they have steadfastly rejected, and the inescapable fact of their impending judgment. John records the astonishing hardness of heart of the "*earth dwellers*[5.2.18]" at the time of the end. Even in the face of overwhelming evidence of God's existence, sovereignty, and power, they will not repent (Rev. 16:9, 11, 21). It is our belief that this is one reason Paul says, "now *is* the day of salvation" (2Cor. 6:2). For every day, every hour, every minute that a person continues to reject the knowledge of God makes it more likely they will *never turn* to accept the free offer of salvation.[107]

> Brethren, I do not wonder that worldlings and half-Christians have no love of this doctrine, or that they hate to hear about Christ's speedy coming. It is the death knell of their gaieties and pleasures—the turning of their confidence to consternation—the conversion of their songs to shrieks of horror and despair. There is a day coming, when "the loftiness of man shall be bowed down, and the haughtiness of man shall be made low;" [Isa. 2:11, 17][108]

3.1.8 - Revelation 1:8

I am

A trademark of the book of John which records the self-identification of Jesus using this phrase. Jesus said unless you believe "I am" (John 8:24), you will die in your sins. He said that before Abraham "I am" (John 8:58), an intentional reference to the self-existent One of Exodus (Ex. 3:6, 14) for which the Jews attempted to stone Him.[109] It was before the power of this declaration of deity that those who came to arrest Jesus fell back: "Now when he said to them "I am," they drew back and fell to the ground" (John 18:6).

the Alpha and the Omega, the Beginning and the End

This complete title is applied both to the Father (Rev. 21:6) and to the Son (Rev. 22:13). The phrase is also applied to the Son in two parts (Rev. 1:11; 2:8). It is clear that the title can apply to both Father and Son and is therefore yet another clear indication of the deity of the Son.

The use of a very similar phrase by Isaiah underscores the uniqueness of God: "Besides Me *there is* no God" (Isa. 44:6). Alpha, being the first letter of the Greek alphabet (as our "A") stands for the "beginning." Omega, being the last letter of the Greek alphabet (as our "Z") stands for the "end." Because God existed from before all time and will exist beyond all time, there is no room for another God (Isa. 43:10). Throughout the Father's preexistence, the Son was with Him (John 1:1-3; 8:54; Col. 1:17).

the Lord

Designating someone as "Lord," especially in John's day, could have serious implications. It was a title which Christians did not use lightly: " 'Lord' (*kyrios*) means that the bearer was worthy of divine recognition and honor. The apostolic writers and early believers were well aware of this meaning. *Polycarp*[5.2.55], for example, died as a martyr rather than call Caesar *kyrios*."[110]

who is and who was and who is to come

See commentary on *Revelation 1:4*[3.1.4]. Some see grammatical evidence identifying the speaker here as the Father.[111] Yet the switch to the Father here after the Son has just been the subject (Rev. 1:7) and prior to similar statements by the Son (Rev. 1:11, 17) seems too abrupt.[112] Elsewhere we discuss the role of the *Antichrist*[5.2.3], empowered by Satan, as the *Master Imitator*[4.2.5]. Pink notes the correlation between this phrase describing God's self-existence and the phrase applied to Antichrist: "Christ is referred to as Him 'which was, and is, and is to come' (Rev. 4:8); the Antichrist is referred to as him that 'was, and is not; and shall ascend out of the bottomless pit' (Rev. 17:8)."[113]

the Almighty

Ὁ παντοκράτωρ [*Ho pantokratōr*] ("the Almighty") is derived from ὁ πάντων κρατῶν [*ho pantōn kratōn*] ("the one who holds all") and is rendered in the *LXX*[5.2.38] for שַׁדַּי [*shadday*] in the book of Job and צְבָאוֹת [*tsᵉbā`ōt*] ("hosts") elsewhere.[114] It is a reference to God's sovereignty and might, His command of powerful force.

3.1.9 - Revelation 1:9

I, John

John also refers to himself this way in Rev. 21:2 and 22:8, perhaps indicating an awareness of his unworthiness and inadequacy in serving as the chosen vessel for such great revelation (Rev. 22:8). The only other writer to refer to himself in such a way was Daniel (Dan. 7:28; 9:2; 10:2).

brother

Like Peter before him (1Pe. 5:1), John emphasizes his equality with other believers. The leadership hierarchy which now characterizes many church bodies of our day was unknown to John.[115] He saw himself as a fellow believer and servant of Christ (Rev. 1:1).

> At the time of the vision, he was the only remaining apostle, and perhaps the only survivor of those with whom Christ had personally conversed. He was therefore the most interesting and exalted Christian then living upon the earth—a most reverend and venerable man. But he was as humble and meek as he was high in place.[116]

tribulation. . . kingdom. . . patience

Although the earthly kingdom is yet future, those who believe in Jesus have *already* been "conveyed . . . into the kingdom of the Son" (Col. 1:13). The same triplet occurs in Acts 14:22.

Patience is better rendered "perseverance" (ὑπομονη [*hypomonē*]). It is through patience that the believer bears fruit (Luke 8:15). By patience those who are in the midst of tribulation are able to possess their souls (Luke 21:16-19; Rev. 13:10; 14:9-12). It is the *perspective* and *position* of the believer which enables him to stand through trials and situations which otherwise would be insurmountable. When cancer strikes or an unexpected automobile accident leaves a loved one paralyzed, our eternal perspective based upon the truth of the Scriptures is the remedy for utter hopelessness. When all else fails and our resources are depleted, we can and must stand upon God's Word, being convinced of our unshakable position in Christ and the perspective that this life is not all there is. It is but a "shadow" and a "vapor" by which we are prepared for eternity to come.

island called Patmos

A small Greek island off the coast of modern-day Turkey.

Patmos near Asia Minor

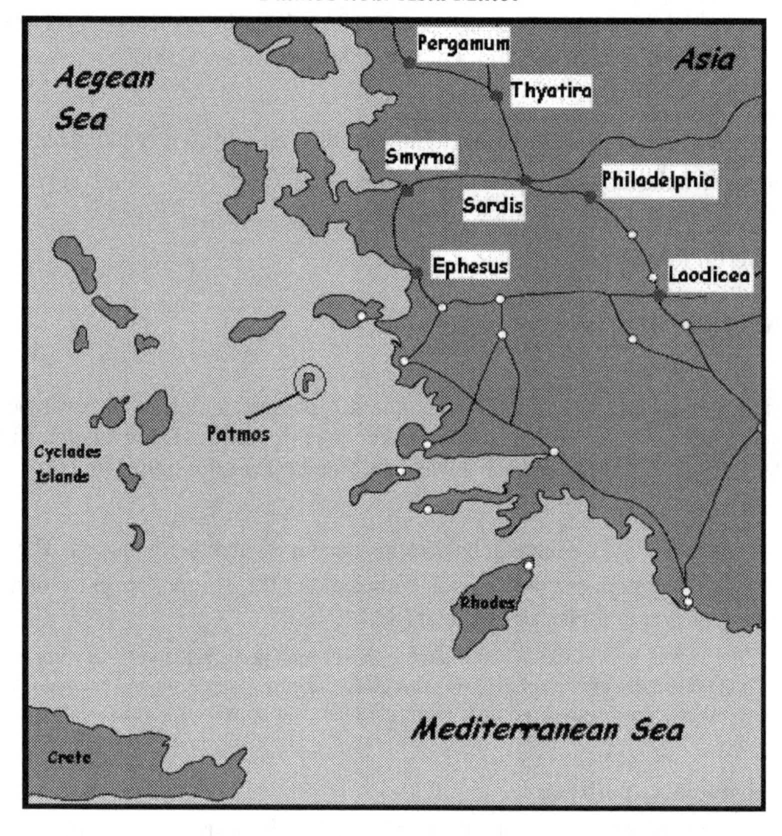

The island is one of a group of about fifty islands called the Dodecanese. Patmos is located between two other islands named Icaria and Leros. Patmos, shaped like a crescent with its horns facing eastward, was a safe place for vessels to anchor during storms and was therefore important to navigators. It was the last stopping place when traveling from Rome to Ephesus and the first stopping place on a return trip to Rome. Being a rocky and barren place, it was chosen as a penal settlement by the Romans, as were other islands in the group. Early Christian tradition says John was sent here during Domitian's reign over Rome (A.D. 81-96) and was forced to work in the mines. Another tradition adds that when Domitian died, John was permitted to return to Ephesus.[117]

The Island of Patmos [118]

Less than a year ago I passed that island. It is a mere mass of barren rocks, dark in colour and cheerless in form. It lies out in the open sea, near the coast of Western Asia Minor. It has neither trees nor rivers, nor any land for cultivation, except some little nooks between the ledges of rocks. There is still a dingy grotto remaining, in which the aged Apostle is said to have lived, and in which he is said to have had this vision. A chapel covers it, hung with lamps kept burning by the monks.[119]

The Church of the Apocalypse [120]

It is a frequent pattern within Scripture that great revelation was often given to those close to God *while in captivity outside Israel and while Jerusalem lay in ruins* . We think of Ezekiel, Daniel, and now John. Often, the greatest revelation from God occurs when least expected and in the most unusual places (e.g., Paul in Arabia, Gal. 1:15-17.)

for the word of God and for the testimony of Jesus Christ

Some have suggested the John sought out Patmos on a mission to preach the gospel to its inhabitants. But this seems highly doubtful since many more people lived in the mainland population centers in Asia and we have no record of John initiating any such trip. It is much more likely, as tradition records, that John was banished to Patmos contrary to his own desires. "According to Victorinus, John though aged, was forced to labor in the mines located at Patmos."[121] "Tacitus refers to the use of such small islands for political banishment (*Annals* 3.68; 4.30; 15.71). *Eusebius*[5.2.19] mentions that John was banished to the island by the emperor Domitian in A.D. 95 and released eighteen months later by Nerva (*Ecclesiastical History* 3.20. 8-9)."[122]

> It has been sometimes asked, *When* was that prophecy and promise fulfilled concerning John, that he should drink of his Lord's cup, and be baptized with his Lord's baptism (Mtt. 20:22)? . . . Origin, however, no doubt gave the right answer long ago. . ., Now—in this his banishment to Patmos; not thereby denying that there must have been a life-long φλῖψις [*phlipsis*] for such a one as the Apostle John, but only affirming that the words found their most emphatic and crowning fulfilment now.[123]
>
> Restricted to a small spot on earth, he is permitted to penetrate the wide realms of heaven and its secrets. Thus John drank of Christ's cup, and was baptized with His baptism (Mtt. 20:22).[124]

Under Domitian, history records the banishment of Christians who were considered "atheists" because they refused to pay homage to Caesar or to Roman gods:

> Dio Casius records that Domitian executed the aristocrat Flavious Clemens and banished his wife Flavia Domitilla because of "atheism" (ἀθεότης [*atheotēs*]). . . . Dio's full statement views "atheism" as "a charge on which many others who drifted into Jewish ways were condemned." A similar but later statement affirms that Domitian's persecution was explicitly two-pronged, being directed against "*maiestas* [treason]" or against "adopting the Jewish mode of life." . . . With particular reference to Flavia Domitilla, inscriptions and Christian tradition affirm that she professed Christianity, which would have made her a prime candidate for a charge of "atheism" by those believing in the deity of the emperor.[125]

Opposition is to be the expectation for those who truly carry the uncompromising message of the cross. The testimony *of* Jesus which John was banished for is most naturally understood to be opposition that which he testified *about* Jesus (objective genitive). "The nominal Christian and the formalist the world cannot hate, for they are of it, and it will love its own; but the Johns and Pauls must go into banishment, or give their necks to the state block."[126] When we are accepted by the world, it is time for serious self-examination. See commentary on *Revelation 1:2*[3.1.2].

3.1.10 - Revelation 1:10

in the Spirit

All prophetic revelation has its origin in the Holy Spirit (1Pe. 1:20-21) and never from man (Gal. 1:12-16; 2:2). Mysteries, things which are *unknown and unknowable by man* , are revealed only by the Spirit (Eph. 3:3). Often, spiritual revelation by the Holy Spirit involves a transporting of the prophet, physically or in a vision, to a different location where information is revealed (Eze. 8:3; 11:24; 37:1; Dan. 8:2; 2Cor. 12:2; Rev. 4:2; 17:3; 21:10).

Here, John mentions he was *in the Spirit* indicating that what he is about to describe involves supernatural revelation by means of a vision. This statement puts an end to all speculation as to the *motives and initiative*[2.3.2.1] of John himself in writing the book of Revelation. For John didn't *write* the book, he *recorded* it!

Revelation from the Spirit is found both in the *OT*[5.2.51] and *NT*[5.2.48].[127] Being 'in the Spirit' in the sense John describes is not something initiated by man. It is a sovereign action initiated by God in order to impart divine instruction. As Ezekiel describes it: "the hand of the Lord was upon him" (Eze. 1:3).

Luke describes the similar experience of Peter (Acts 10:10) and Paul (Acts 22:17) as an "ecstasy" (ἔκστασις [*ekstasis*]):

> A throwing of the mind out of its normal state, alienation of mind, whether such as makes a lunatic or that of a man who by some sudden emotion is transported as it were out of himself, so that in this rapt condition, although he is awake, his mind is drawn off from all surrounding objects and wholly fixed on things divine that he sees nothing but the forms and images lying within, and thinks that he perceives with his bodily eyes and ears realities shown him by God.[128]

Peter, Paul, and John were *passive recipients* of that which God initiated. In this sense, the experience is diametrically opposed to the ecstatic frenzies associated with cultish prophets (1K. 18:28) and some modern movements wherein the person *actively participates* in bringing about an altered state of consciousness.

the Lord's Day

There are several views concerning the meaning of this passage. One view holds that it refers to Sunday, the first day of the week. The phrase uses the same adjective ("Lord's") as does Paul when describing the Lord's Supper: "Therefore when you come together in one place, is it not to eat the Lord's Supper (κυριακὸν δεῖπνον [*kyriakon deipnon*])" (1Cor. 11:20)?

> Deissmann has proven (Bible Studies, p. 217f; Light, etc., p. 357ff) from inscriptions and *papyri*[5.2.53] that the word (Grk: kuriakos, Strongs: G2960) was in common use for the sense "imperial" as imperial finance and imperial treasury and from papyri and ostraca that (Grk: heemera, Strongs: G2250) (Grk: Sebastee, Strongs: G4575) (Augustus Day) was the first day of each month, Emperor's Day on which money payments were made (cf. 1Cor. 16:1f). It was easy, therefore, for the Christians to take this term, already in use, and apply it to the first day of the week in honor of the Lord Jesus Christ's resurrection on that day (Didache 14, *Ignatius*[5.2.28] Magn. 9).[129]

Others note that Sunday, which came to be the day of Christian worship, is nowhere else referred to using this phrase, but is described instead as "the first day of the week" (Mtt. 28:1; Mark 16:2, 9; Luke 24:1; John 20:1, 19; Acts 20:7; 1Cor. 16:2).

It also appears that John's use of the phrase predates its use among Christians to designate the day of Christ's resurrection.[130]

Another view is that the phrase does not describe the first day of the week, but denotes the eschatological "*Day of the Lord*[5.2.14]":[131]

> However, such an interpretation is open to the objection that (1) such a meaning has no relevance to the context; (2) the term is never so applied in Scripture, where the day of Christian worship is uniformly

> called the "first day of the week"; (3) such an interpretation does not agree with the Patristic understanding of the verse; (4) the interpretation is a reading back into the text of a term subsequently applied to Sunday. The term "Lord's day" is better understood as John's way of expressing the common Hebrew term "day of the Lord," in a manner in Greek which places the emphasis upon "Lord's" (by placing it in an initial position) in the same manner as the Hebrew expression places emphasis upon "Lord" (by placing it in the final position) in "day of the Lord." Supposing the expression refers to Sunday cannot account for the presence of the Greek article "the" used in the expression. When the article is lacking, there are several possible explanations to account for the fact, but when an interpretation cannot account for the presence of the Greek article, the interpretation stands self-condemned (J. B. Smith, Comm. on Revelation, Appendix 5, p. 320). The expression "on the Lord's day" would better be translated "in the Lord's day," as a reference to this specific prophetic time period. The Greek preposition *en* is more usually rendered "in," only once in Revelation is it translated "on," in the expression "on the earth," Rev. 5:13. Everywhere else where *en* is followed by the word "day" it is rendered "in" (Rev. 2:13. 9:6. 10:7. 11:6. 18:8). Understanding this term to refer to the "day of the Lord" emphasizes that the events which transpire in the third division of the book ("things which shall be hereafter") are events which take place during the "day of the Lord," a future time which begins at the Great Tribulation and concludes with the judgment of the Great White Throne at the end of the Millennium, and specifically ties in the prophecies of this book with the rest of Scripture relating to this coming day.[132]

> The key that unlocks the door to the understanding of this book is, we believe, that it relates to **The Day of the Lord** , and not to any tradition which limits the reception of this Vision to a particular day of the week; and that day Sunday. . . . Thus did Abraham also see Christ's Day. He saw it, and rejoiced, and was glad. It must have been "in Spirit," whatever meaning we may put upon the expression. There was no other way of his seeing Christ's Day; and that is the way in which it says John saw "the Lord's Day." . . . The majority of people, being accustomed from their infancy to hear the first day of the week called the Lord's Day, conclude in their own minds that day is thus called in Rev. 1:9 because that was the name of it. But the contrary is the fact: the day is so called by us because of this verse. In the New Testament this day is *always* called "the first day of the week." (See Mtt. 28:1; Mark 16:2, 9; Luke 24:1; John 20:1, 19; Acts 20:7; 1Cor. 16:2). Is it not strange that in this one place a different expression is thought to refer to the same day? And yet, so sure are the commentators that it means Sunday, . . . There is no evidence of any kind that "the first day of the week" was ever called "the Lord's Day" before the Apocalypse was written. That it should be so called afterwards is easily understood, and there can be little doubt that the practice arose from the misinterpretation of these words in Rev. 1:9.[133]

A difficulty with this view is the difference in wording when compared with the phrase "Day of the Lord" found elsewhere in the NT: "Some feel that John was transported into the future day of the Lord, the prophetic day of God's great judgment and the return of Christ . . . The major objection to this is that John does not use the common expression for the eschatological 'day of the Lord' (*hemera kyriou*)."[134] "The Greek phrase translated the Lord's day (τη κυριακη ἡμερα [*tē kyriakē hēmera*]) is different from the one translated 'the Day of the Lord' (τη ἡμερεα του κυριου [*tē hēmerea tou kyriou*], or ἡμερεα κυριου [*hēmerea kyriou*] ; cf. 1Cor. 5:5; 1Th. 5:2; 2Th. 2:2; 2Pe. 3:10) and appears only here in the New Testament."[135] Proponents of the eschatological view attempt to explain this difference as one of the Hebraism's in Revelation.[136]

A third view is that John is describing neither a day of the week nor the "Day of the Lord," but is referring to his condition in the Spirit:

> It does not refer to a specific day of the week, such as the Sabbath (Saturday) or Sunday. Rather, it was a day in which John was enraptured by prophetic and divine ecstasy and received divine revelation. It was a day in which he fell under the control of the Holy Spirit and was given prophetic *inspiration*[5.2.33]. Thus, for him, it was a "lordy day."[137]

as of a trumpet

Much of what John sees or hears is new, different, or unearthly and therefore difficult to describe precisely. John frequently employs simile in which two different, but similar things are compared. Later, this same voice will beckon John to heaven saying, "come up here" (Rev. 4:1).

Elsewhere in Scripture, trumpets attend events of great importance. A trumpet announced the manifestation of God's presence upon Mount Sinai (Ex. 19:16; 20:18). The year of jubilee when all debts were forgiven was heralded by the blast of a trumpet (Lev. 25:9). The sounding of trumpets attended the downfall of Jericho (Jos. 6:4-20). A trumpet will attend God's overthrow of the kingdoms of the earth (Ps. 45:7) and warns that the Day of the Lord is at hand (Joel 2:1). A trumpet signals the gathering of the Church at the *Rapture*[5.2.62] (1Cor. 15:42; 1Th. 4:6) and of the elect prior to the *Millennial Kingdom*[5.2.39] (Mtt. 24:31). Trumpets also attend significant events in this book (Rev. 8:2, 6, 13; 9:14). Here, we do not have a trumpet, but a voice *as of* a trumpet, signifying its power and the attention it commands.

3.1.11 - Revelation 1:11

I am the Alpha and the Omega, the First and the Last

God is said to be "everlasting" (Gen. 21:33). He "inhabits eternity" (Isa. 57:15) and is without beginning and without end: "from everlasting to everlasting" (Ps. 90:2). This appellation is especially reminiscent of that given by Isaiah: "Thus says the LORD, the King of Israel, and his Redeemer, the LORD of hosts: 'I *am* the First and I *am* the Last; besides Me *there is* no God' " (Isa. 44:6).

Whoever said Jesus never claimed to be God need look no further. For the next verse leaves absolutely no doubt that it is the *Son* Who is applying to Himself titles which are reserved exclusively for *God* (Isa. 41:4; 48:12; Rev. 21:6; 22:13)! This is consistent with the *OT*[5.2.51] where the promised Son is referred to as "Everlasting Father" (Isa. 9:6).

God is the unique "uncaused first cause," "Before Me there was no God formed, nor shall there be after Me" (Isa. 43:10). He is self-existent and outside of the limitations of time. This is why *He alone* can predict the future:

> Tell and bring forth *your case*; yes, let them take counsel together. Who has declared this from ancient time? *Who* has told it from that time? *Have* not I, the LORD? And *there is* no other God besides Me, a just God and a Savior; *there is* none besides Me. (Isa. 45:21)

God's existence outside of time is a unique identifying feature of His character which God challenges any other to try and duplicate:

> Let them bring forth and show us what will happen; let them show the former things, what they *were*, that we may consider them, and know the latter end of them; or declare to us things to come. (Isa. 41:22)

This is but one of many reasons why we choose to trust the text of Genesis over after-the-fact and error-prone interpretation of distant history by modern science.

See commentary on *Revelation 1:8*[3.1.8].

write what you see

Literally, "what you *are seeing* [you] *write!*" The verb "see" (Βλέπεις [*Blepeis*]) is in the present tense. John's contribution will be as a moment-by-moment observer, recording the events and scenes which are brought before him while in the Spirit. This, no doubt, accounts in part for the *lack of grammatical polish*[2.8] which has been observed in the Greek text. This is not a carefully crafted literary document containing sophisticated themes originating in John's own mind. John is continually reminded to "write" as he experiences the various scenes of the Revelation (Rev. 1:11, 19; 2:1, 8, 12, 18; 3:1, 7, 12, 14; 10:4; 14:13; 19:9; 21:5). This would seem to support the view that John is making a moment-by-moment record of the scenes which he is being shown. As with other writers of Scripture, the Holy Spirit is superintending the process, but it seems unlikely that John is given the time or luxury of carefully analyzing and crafting that which he records.

to the seven churches

Tradition holds that John left Jerusalem in the late sixties of the first century, prior to the destruction of Jerusalem by Rome. He went to Asia where he became the recognized leader of the Asian churches, following in the footsteps of Paul's earlier missionary work which directly or indirectly founded many of the churches mentioned here.

> The epistolary form of address immediately distinguishes this book from all other Jewish apocalyptic works . . . None of the pseudepigraphical works contains such epistolary addresses. John writes to actual, historical churches, addressing them in the same way the *NT*[5.2.48] epistles are addressed.[138]

(See *The Genre of the book of Revelation*[2.6] for more on the literary *genre*[5.2.22] of apocalyptic.)

The *seven churches*[5.2.66] are listed in the same order as their respective letters appear in Revelation 2 and 3. It has been suggested that their order indicates the natural route messengers would take to deliver copies of the letter to the seven churches.[139]

See *Seven Churches of Asia*[4.15].

which are in Asia

This is neither Asia nor even Asia Minor, but what we would today know as the region of western Turkey.

> In the New Testament, as generally in the language of men when the New Testament was written, Asia meant not what it now means for us, and had once meant for the Greeks, one namely of the three great continents of the old world. . ., nor yet even that region which geographers about the fourth century of our era began to call "Asia Minor;" but a strip of the western seaboard containing hardly a third portion of this . . . its limits being nearly identical with those of the kingdom which Attalus the Third bequeathed to the Roman people. Take "Asia" in this sense, and there will be little or no exaggeration in the words of the Ephesian silversmith, that "almost throughout all Asia" Paul had turned away much people from the service of idols (Acts 19:26; cf. ver. 10); word which must seem to exceed even the limits of an angry *hyperbole*[5.2.27] to those not acquainted with this restricted use of the term.[140]

> The "Asia" of which the Scriptures speak is not the great continent of Asia, or even of Asia Minor, but only the western part of Asia Minor, directly south of the Black Sea. The whole of it does not include a larger territory than the single state of Pennsylvania.[141]

3.1.12 - Revelation 1:12

I turned to see

John is about to enter into the experience of many other prophets who were given a revelation of the glory of the Lord, usually near the beginning of their prophetic ministry. We think of Moses (Ex. 33:22-23; 34:5-6), Ezekiel (Eze. 1), Isaiah (Isa. 6), Daniel (Dan. 10:5-6), and Paul (Acts 9:3; 22:6). John had been given a previous taste of God's glory on the Mount of Transfiguration with Peter and James (Mtt. 17:1; Mark 9:2; Luke 9:29).[142]

St. John Beholding the Seven Candelabra [143]

seven golden lampstands

The symbolism of these lampstands is explained: "the seven lampstands which you saw are the *seven churches*[5.2.66]" (Rev. 1:20). The churches *bear* light, but are not the *source* of light (Mtt. 5:14-16; John 1:4-5, 7-9; 5:32-35; Eph. 5:11-13; Php. 2:15).

> The "*seven candlesticks*" . . . are intended to send us back, to the seven-branched candlestick, or candelabrum, which bears ever the same name of λυχνία [*lychnia*] in the *Septuagint*[5.2.65] (Ex. 25:31 cf. Heb. 9:2); the six arms of which with the central shaft . . . made up the mystical seven, each with its several lamp (λύχνος [*lychnos*] , Zec. 4:2).[144]

See *Interpreting Symbols*[2.7]. See *symbolic meaning of seven*[2.7.5.3.6].

3.1.13 - Revelation 1:13

in the midst

The Levites, who performed the priestly duty of the *OT*[5.2.51], camped around the glory of the Lord which resided in the *Tabernacle*[5.2.69] (Num. 1:50; 1Chr. 9:27). The glory of the Lord was in the "midst" of the Levitical priests. The lampstands, which represent the churches (Rev. 1:20), made up of believers who are priests unto God (Rev. 1:6), also have the glory of the Lord in their midst (Mtt. 18:20).[145]

Unlike other religions of the world, the Christian is not serving a famous *mortal* man whose body is now long moldering in the grave. Christ's corpse is unavailable because He is risen and active among His Church as the body of Christ continues to minister on the earth in His absence.

Unlike the glory of God in the OT which departed from the people of God due to their sin (1S. 16:14; Ps. 51:11; Eze. 8:6; 9:3; 10:4, 18-19; 11:22-23; Hos. 5:14), each *NT*[5.2.48] believer is indwelt and *permanently sealed* with the Holy Spirit (John 6:27; 14:16; 2Cor. 1:22; Eph. 1:13; 4:30).[146] He is in the midst of His Church, and will remain there "for the day of redemption" (Eph. 4:30).

the seven lampstands

In the OT, the Menorah was made of a single central shaft to which six (or eight) branches were joined, the entire assembly being a single affair. Here, we have seven individual lamps, representing the seven typical (and historical) churches which represent the witness of Christ through the church. The central shaft joining these seven lamps and providing the oil for their continued illumination is Christ Himself (John 15:5). Some have seen in the separate lampstands a reference to the dispersion of the Jews.[147]

Son of Man

In a remarkable passage in the OT "a likeness with the appearance of a man" (Eze. 1:26) is seen high above the throne. His form is clothed in brilliant radiance which Ezekiel describes as "the likeness of the glory of the LORD" (Eze. 1:27). This is the One Who was seen by Stephen just prior to his death (Acts 7:56). Consistent with the description found in *Revelation 1:7*[3.1.7] , this is the One who is presented to the Ancient of Days in the book of Daniel (Dan. 7:13) and who is to receive "dominion and glory, and a kingdom" (Dan. 7:14). Jesus applied this term to Himself in the gospels (Dan. 7:13; Mtt. 24:30; 26:64; Mark 13:26; 14:62; Luke 21:27). Jesus is both the "Son of God" and "Son of Man." These two titles hint at the mystery of the incarnation, where all the fullness of God dwelt in human form (Col. 2:9). Jesus, as the "Son of God," is divine and without sin. As the "Son of Man," he was begotten of Mary in the line from David, Abraham, and Adam (Mtt. 1:1, 6; Luke 3:31, 34, 38; Rev. 12:1-5). His divinity and virgin birth provide the necessary perfection by which His death could atone for the sins of the world (Isa. 53:9; John 8:46; 14:30; 2Cor. 5:21; Heb. 4:15; 7:26; 9:14; 1Pe. 1:19; 2:22; 1Jn. 3:5). Although He is truly a man (Php. 2:7; Heb. 2:17), He is unique from all other men in His sinless perfection (Rom. 8:3).

As the "Son of Man," His humanity provides for His role as the judge (John 5:27) and kinsman-redeemer (*Goel* , 1Ti. 2:5)[148] of mankind (Rev. 5:4-5); to taste of death (Heb. 2:14); and to restore the dominion lost by the first man Adam.[149]

One like the *Son of Man* appears again in Rev. 14:14 where He reaps a harvest from the earth.

garment down to the feet

Apparently a reference to His priestly garments. "The *long* robe is every where in the East the garment of dignity and honour (Gen. 37:3; Mark 13:38 [*sic*]; Luke 15:22)—the association of dignity with it probably resting originally on the absence of the necessity of labor."[150]

girded about the chest

The high priest wore a priestly "sash" around his priestly garment at the height of the breast (Ex. 28:4; 28:39; 39:29; Lev. 8:7; 16:4). But this sash was not made of gold (see below). A garment reaching to the feet was impractical for those who were laborers and came to denote a position of status. The seven angels of Rev. 15:6 are similarly girded.

> The ordinary girding for one actively engaged was *at the loins* (1K. 2:5; 18:46; Jer. 13:2 cf. Luke 12:35; Eph. 6:14; 1Pe. 1:13); but Josephus expressly tells us that the Levitical priests were girt higher up, about the breast . . . favouring, as this higher cincture did, a calmer, more majestic movement.[151]

Christ has an unchangeable priesthood because He continues forever (Heb. 7:14). "Therefore He is also able to save to the uttermost those who come to God through Him, since He always lives to make intercession for them." (Heb. 7:25).

with a golden band

How similar John's vision is to that of Daniel by the Tigris (Dan. 10:5-6). Daniel saw "a man . . . whose waist *was* girded with gold of Uphaz" (Dan. 10:6). His visitor had eyes like torches of fire and feet like burnished bronze and spoke with a voice like the voice of a multitude. Yet it seems that Daniel's visitor could not have been the Son of Man which John sees here, for how could the prince of Persia (an angelic being influencing the kingdom of Persia) have ever withstood the Lord of Glory (Dan. 10:13)? And when did God ever require help (Dan. 10:13)?[152]

3.1.14 - Revelation 1:14

like wool, as white as snow

In Daniel's vision, it is the Ancient of Days (the Father) who's "hair of His head *was* like pure wool" (Dan. 7:9). Here it is that of the Son of Man. John is being shown the glory of the Son, which He had with the Father "before the World was" (John 17:5).

> It is evident that His ultimate glory was veiled in order to make possible a ministry to His disciples in scenes on earth. After His ascension into heaven, Christ never appeared again apart from His glory. In Acts 7:56, Stephen saw Christ standing at the right hand of the Father in the midst of the glory of God. In the appearance of Christ to Paul recorded in Acts 9:3-6, the glory of Christ was such that Paul was blinded. A similar experience befell the Apostle John in Revelation 1:12-20 where John fell at the feet of Christ as one dead when he beheld the glory of Christ in His resurrection.[153]

Wool and *snow* also speak of His sinless purity (Isa. 1:18). A hypothetical question which might be asked (on a par with the question whether Adam and Eve had belly buttons) is whether Jesus would have had gray hair if he had not been crucified but lived? Since death is the wages of sin and Jesus knew no sin, we can infer the answer would be "no." The hair white as wool is not a description of age or wisdom, but the incendiary brightness of His glory:

> The white hairs of old age are at once the sign and the consequence of the decay of natural strength, in other words, of death commencing; . . . Being then this, how can the white hairs, the hoary head which is the sign of weakness, decay, and the approach of death, be ascribed to Him who, as He is *from* everlasting, so also is He *to* everlasting? . . . How then shall we explain this hair *"white like wool"?* It is a part of the transfiguration in light of the glorified person of the Redeemer; a transfiguration so complete that it reaches to the extremities, to the very hairs of the head.[154]

eyes like a flame of fire

His eyes are singled out as being like *a flame of fire* . This evokes the image of a gaze which instantly pierces the deepest darkness to lay bear all sin. It is a reference to His omniscience, omnipresence, and judgment. There is no evil activity of men which Jesus does not see (Job 28:24; Ps. 90:8; 94:9; 139:23; Pr. 15:3). There is no den of iniquity so dark that Jesus is not there (Job 34:22; Ps. 139:7; Jer. 23:24; Amos 9:2). There is no work of man which will go unjudged by His piercing gaze (1Cor. 3:15; 2Cor. 5:10; Heb. 4:13). Truly, God *is* an all-consuming fire (Num. 11:1; Deu. 5:25; 9:3; 2K. 1:10; Ps. 50:3; 78:63; Isa. 33:14; Luke 9:54; Heb. 12:29; Rev. 11:5).

When speaking to the church at Thyatira, after mentioning His "eyes like a flame of fire" (Rev. 2:18), Jesus continues, "I know your works" (Rev. 2:19). He says to the same church, "all the churches shall know that I am He who searches the minds and hearts. And I will give to each one of you according to your works" (Rev. 2:23).

His piercing eyes are an identifying description in Rev. 19:12. It is impossible to escape His gaze! "And there is no creature hidden from His sight, but all things *are* naked and open to the eyes of Him to whom we *must give* account" (Heb. 4:13).

3.1.15 - Revelation 1:15

His feet

It would appear that His feet were unshod:

> They were no doubt bare; as were the feet of the Levitical priesthood ministering in the sanctuary. We are no where indeed expressly told of these that they ministered barefoot, but every thing leads us to this conclusion. Thus while all the other parts of the priestly investiture are described with the greatest

minuteness, and Moses accurately instructed how they should be made, there is no mention of any covering for the feet. Then again the analogy of such passages as Ex. 3:5; Jos. 5:15, and the fact that the *moral* idea of the shoe is that of defense against the *defilements* of the earth, of which defilements there could be none in the Holy Place, all this irresistibly points to the same conclusions.[155]

fine brass, refined in a furnace

The etymology of χαλκολίβανος [*chalkolibanos*] [*fine brass*] being uncertain, it may be intended to describe the resulting hardness of brass after the refining process, this being an allusion to the treading or trampling down of those who are unbelieving or unfaithful (Ps. 58:10; 68:23; Isa. 63:3; Rev. 2:18-29; 19:15). It is in reality an unknown metal.[156]

> Bochart sees in χαλκολίβανος [*chalkolibanos*] [*fine brass*], a hybrid formation, the combination of a Greek word and a Hebrew, χαλκός [*chalkos*], and לִבֵּן [*libbēn*] = "albare," to make white; brass which in the furnace has attained what we call *"white head."* . . . If this be correct, the χαλκολίβανο [*chalkolibano*] will not be *"fine brass"* or the "shining," but the "glowing brass." This conclusion is very much strengthened by the following phrase, *"as if they burned in a furnace;"*[157]

> It has often been suggested that our term was familiar to the important local guild of bronze-workers [in Thyatira, Rev. 2:18] . . . I suggest then that an alloy of copper with metallic zinc was made in Thyatira, the zinc being obtained by distillation. This was a finer and purer brass than the rough and variable coinage-alloy. . . . The product, I suggest, was known there as χαλκολίβανος [*chalkolibanos*], which I conjecture to be a 'copulative compound', literally rendered 'copper-zinc', λίβανος [*libanos*] being an unrecorded word, perhaps peculiar to the trade, for a metal obtained by distillation, and so derived from the verb λείβω [*leibō*].[158]

Refined is πεπυρωμένης [*pepyrōmenēs*]: "Make red hot, cause to glow, heat thoroughly . . . By such heating precious metals are tested and refined (Job 22:25; Ps. 11:7; 65:10; Pr. 10:20)."[159]

voice as the sound of many waters

The phrase *sound of many waters* is used to describe the sound of a multitude (Isa. 17:12-13; Rev. 19:6) or noise like the tumult of an army (Eze. 1:24). Here, as in other passages, it is the sound attributed to a *single* voice. Daniel heard such a voice in his vision by the Tigris (Dan. 10:6). Ezekiel also heard a similar voice in his vision of the glory of the Lord returning to the east gate of the *Millennial Temple*[4.16.5.10] (Eze. 43:2). In Ezekiel and in Revelation 1:15 and 14:2, it appears to be the voice of God Himself. For reasons mentioned in *Revelation 1:13*[3.1.13], the voice Daniel heard was most likely that of a mighty angel.[160]

3.1.16 - Revelation 1:16

in His right hand seven stars

These *stars* are the seven angels of the churches as explained in *Revelation 1:20*[3.1.20] . The picture of the stars being within His right hand (the side of favor) is of great comfort to believers for what Christ grasps in His hand cannot be snatched away (John 10:28-29). The angels and the churches they are associated with need not fear any but God Himself.

> Christ, we feel sure, could not have placed Himself in the relation which He does to them, as holding in his hand the seven stars, walking among the seven golden candlesticks, these stars being the Angels of the Churches, and the candlesticks the Churches themselves, unless they ideally represented and set forth, in some way or other, the universal Church, militant here upon earth.[161]

See the discussion of the identity of the angels at *Revelation 1:20*[3.1.20]. See *Seven: Perfection, Completeness*[2.7.5.3.6].

out of His mouth went a sharp two-edged sword

A heavy broadsword:

> It [ῥομφαια [*hromphaia*], *sword*] is properly the long and heavy broadsword . . ., which the Thracians and other barbarous nations used; and as such to be distinguished from the μάχαιρα [*machaira*] , the sacrificial knife, or short stabbing sword; . . . The word occurring six times in the Apocalypse, only

> occurs once besides in the New Testament (Luke 2:35).[162]

Some have obtained fanciful interpretations regarding the *two-edged* sword, such as representing both "the old and the new law."[163]

The sword goes *out of His mouth* in agreement with all the creative acts of God which were *spoken forth* by the Word of God (Gen. 1:3, 6, 9, 11, 14, 20, 24, 26; 2Pe. 3:5). It is for this reason that Jesus is the *Word* (λόγος [*logos*]). The speaking forth of God's will can bring creation *or destruction*. Isaiah informs us that the mouth of the Messiah is "like a sharp sword" (Isa. 49:2) and with His lips He will "slay the wicked" (Isa. 11:4). The Word spoken through the prophets is a weapon in the hand of God (Hos. 6:5). It is the *only offensive weapon* of the Christian (Eph. 6:17). Its power as a sword is seen in its ability to pierce "even to the division of soul and spirit" and discern "the thoughts and intents of the heart" (Heb. 4:12). The Word of God has *already* slain His enemies because it sets forth their impending doom in words "which cannot be broken" (John 10:35). That which is prophecy today, will be accomplished history tomorrow. It is in this sense that Jesus slays His enemies with the sword of His mouth (2Th. 2:8; Rev. 2:12, 16; 19:15). The sword signifies His judicial power which will be in accordance with His Word (Mtt. 25:31-32; John 5:22; Acts 10:42; 17:31; Rom. 2:16; 14:10; 2Cor. 5:10; 2Ti. 4:1; 1Pe. 4:5; Rev. 20:12).

like the sun

This is now the second time that John has been privileged to see the Savior's glory shining from His face like the son (Mtt. 17:2).. At the Mount of Transfiguration, Peter, James, and John were given a preview of "the Son of Man coming in His kingdom" (Mtt. 16:28). This glorious vision which John beholds is some small indication of what the entire world will behold at the Second Coming of Christ.

> I urge you in the sight of God who gives life to all things, and *before* Christ Jesus who witnessed the good confession before Pontius Pilate, that you keep *this* commandment without spot, blameless until our Lord Jesus Christ's appearing, which He will manifest in His own time, *He who is* the blessed and only Potentate, the King of kings and Lord of lords, who alone has immortality, **dwelling in unapproachable light**, whom no man has seen or can see, to whom *be* honor and everlasting power. Amen. (1Ti. 6:13-16) [emphasis added]

See *Interpreting Symbols*[2.7].

3.1.17 - Revelation 1:17

fell at His feet as dead

This is the unrehearsed response of all who have been privileged to see the glory of the Lord (Isa. 6:4; Eze. 1:28; 3:23; 43:3; 44:4; Dan. 8:17; 10:8, 16-17; Mtt. 17:6; Acts 9:4). It is as much in recognition of the power and might of God as in a realization of their utter unworthiness (Jdg. 6:22; 13:22; Isa. 6:5, 7). "The beloved disciple, who had handled the Word of life, lain in his Lord's bosom in the days of his flesh, can as little as any other endure the revelation of his majesty."[164]

laid His right hand on me

Daniel experienced a similar loss of all strength at the imposing presence of his visitor by the river Tigris (Dan. 10:8). He too was told not to be afraid and was touched in a similar act of restoration (Dan. 10:10). When Ezekiel was overcome by the glory of the Lord (Eze. 1:28), the Holy Spirit restored him to his feet (Eze. 2:1-2). Although years had passed, perhaps this brought to mind John's previous experience on the Mount of Transfiguration where John had his first glimpse of the glory of Jesus and was similarly restored (Mtt. 17:6-7).

do not be afraid

The unavoidable response of those who saw even a glimpse of His glory is that of fear. Yet how cavalier we are today in our attitude toward the Maker of a myriad of galaxies! We, who dare not even touch a 60-watt light bulb without wearing protective gloves, often treat Him as our "Genie on call."[165] We haven't the slightest notion or appreciation of His holiness, even daring to think that worship is about pleasing us—expressing our dislike if the music is not to our taste or we are unable to drink coffee during the "worship service." How much we are in need of a glimpse of His glory that we might have a Scriptural fear of the Lord![166] A lack of fear for God is the characteristic of His *enemies* (Ps.

36:1; Jer. 2:19; 5:24; Rom. 3:18) and "fear" is one of His titles (Gen. 31:42, 53).

Yet the fear that His children are to have is not the cowering response of a creature fearing retribution. It is the healthy, reverent, fear one would have toward a human father of perfect discipline and unconditional love, if one were to exist. Coupled with the recognition of power and great might is a deep comfort in the realization that God is also our Protector. As Paul observed, "If God *is* for us, who *can be* against us" (Rom. 8:31)? When we look into the face of the Judge of the Universe, it is our Savior's face we will see!

I am the First and the Last

See commentary on *Revelation 1:11*[3.1.11].

3.1.18 - Revelation 1:18

I am He who lives

John calls Him ὁ ζῶν [*ho zōn*], "the living one" (present, active participle). "Life" is an essential attribute of God Who is consistently described as "the living one" over and against other idols and gods who are lifeless.[167]

and was dead

Here is the fatal text for those, such as Jehovah's Witnesses, who maintain that Jesus Christ is not fully God. *For when did God die* except for Jesus on the cross? In this verse is a contradiction so profound that it would be the height of nonsense if it were not also the manifestation of the genius of God: that God Himself would take on the form of a man, to come in the flesh, to be oppressed by men, and nailed to a tree! The infinite and omnipotent *Creator* bound Himself in time and space and stooping to be abused by His finite and puny *creatures* (Mtt. 26:67-68; Luke 22:64). "I the source of all life stooped even to taste of death"[168] (Heb. 2:9). Yet such is the depth of God's love for us that He endured such shame!

The Maker of the universe
As man to man was made a curse;
The claims of law which He had made
Unto the uttermost He paid.

His holy fingers made the bough
That grew the thorns that pierced His brow;
The nails that pierced His hands were mined
In secret places He designed.

He made the forest whence there sprung
The tree on which His body hung;
He died upon a cross of wood,
Yet made the hill on which it stood.

The throne on which He now appears
Was His from everlasting years -
But a new crown adorns His brow,
And every knee to Him shall bow.

—F. W. Pitt, *Maker of the Universe*

How unnatural eternal life seems to us from our current perspective. Yet this was God's design prior to the entrance of sin:

> Christ sets Himself forth here as the overcomer of death natural; which it must always be remembered is rather death *unnatural;* for man was made for immortality (Gen. 2:17), and death is the denial and reversal of the true law of his creation (Rom. 5:12).[169]

The work of Jesus makes possible the wonderful promise set forth later in this book which describes the condition of those who place their trust in Him: "There shall be no death" (Rev. 21:4). Jesus reiterates this fact to encourage the persecuted church at Smyrna (Rev. 2:8).

When confronted with members of any non-Christian religion, here is the central issue at stake: *Is Jesus God or is He not?* Only orthodox Christianity will assert His full divinity. It is fruitless to engage in lengthy interaction with all such cults who deny His divinity because every other issue pales into insignificance compared to this central issue. This particular verse is of great benefit for it removes all "wiggle room" from those who would try to deny that Jesus Christ is the One here described as "the First and the Last" Who is "alive forevermore" for the same was also "dead!" Until the cult member can answer you, "When did God die?" there is little point in further discussion.

> This purpose of revealing the deity of Christ is thus seen to permeate the whole book, and **no unbiased reader of Revelation can reach any conclusion other than that Christ is God**, with the full endorsement and approval of the Father. He has received His throne from the hand of God, unlike Satan who tried to usurp the office. Jesus Christ's powers and attributes are all those of deity. **Any doubt of His deity must be laid to rest**. [emphasis added][170]

behold, I am alive forevermore

Literally, Καὶ ὁ ζῶν, καὶ ἐγενόμην νεκρὸς καὶ ἰδοὺ ζῶν εἰμι εἰς τοὺς αἰῶνας τῶν αἰώνων [*Kai ho zōn, kai egenomēn nekros kai idou zōn eimi eis tous aiōnas tōn aiōnōn*], "I am the living one and I was dead and behold living I am into the ages of the ages."[171]

The Son has eternal life and has been given authority over all flesh by the Father. For this reason, Jesus is able to give eternal life to as many as the Father has given Him (John 17:2). This is the basis for His amazing statement to Thomas. "Jesus said to him, 'I am the way, the truth, and the life. No one comes to the Father except through Me.' " (John 14:6). Jesus is "the life." *He alone* , among men, has immortality (1Ti. 6:16) and offers it to those who come to Him. The eternal life which Jesus offers is not some future promise, but is granted the instant a person believes on Him: "Jesus said to her, 'I am the resurrection and the life. He who believes in Me, though he may die, he shall live. And whoever lives and believes in Me shall never die. Do you believe this?' " (John 11:25-26).

During His earthly ministry, Jesus demonstrated that He was "the life," in numerous ways. The Law of Moses stated that lepers were unclean (Lev. 13:44-45). They were to be separated from others and to cry 'unclean! unclean!' in order to warn others of their presence. To touch a leper or any of his clothing made one unclean and also carried the very real risk of infection. It was unthinkable to touch a leper! Yet when lepers approached Jesus for healing, Jesus did the unthinkable, He *touched them!* But instead of Jesus getting leprosy, the lepers got "Jesus-sy"—they were instantly healed (Mtt. 8:3; Mark 1:41; Luke 5:13)! Because Jesus is "the life," it is impossible that He could be defiled. Instead, His life-giving power went out to others in the performance of healing miracles and the restoration of the dead to life (Mark 5:41-42; Luke 7:14-15; Luke 8:54-55; John 11:43-44).

The primary demonstration that Jesus is "the life" is found in His resurrection from the dead. "Jesus answered and said to them, 'Destroy this temple, and in three days **I will raise it up**' " [emphasis added] (John 2:19); "Therefore My Father loves Me, because I lay down My life that **I may take it again**" [emphasis added] (John 10:17). Not only would Jesus rise from the dead, but *He Himself* would be the agent of His resurrection![172]

> Then ὁ ζῶν [*ho zōn*] expresses not so much that he, the Speaker, "lived," as that He was "the Living One," the Life (John 1:4; 14:6), αὐτοζωή [*hautozōē*], having life in Himself, and the fountain and source of life to others. . . . To Him belongs *absolute being* (ὄντως εἶναι [*ontōs einai*]), as contrasted with the *relative* being of the creature, with the life which be no life, seeing that it inevitably falls under the dominion of corruption and death, so soon as it is separated from him, the source from which it was derived[173]

Christ says, "*behold*," emphasizing that His demonstration of life beyond the grave is of paramount importance, for Christ's resurrection bears witness that those who trust in Him will likewise rise from the dead (John 14:19; Rom. 6:8-9). If it were not for the fact of the resurrection—without the "Living One"—Christianity would be meaningless (1Cor. 15:12-17).

keys of Hades and of Death

With rare exception, all who enter this life face the certainty of physical death. In some passages, death and Hades are personified as enemies of the living (Hos. 13:14; Rev. 6:8), for it is by death that people enter Hades.[174]

The reference to *keys* points to many passages in which the entrance to death and Hades is described as being controlled by *gates* (Job 38:17; Ps. 9:13; 107:18; Isa. 38:10; Mtt. 16:18). Those who are held therein, are described as "prisoners" (Isa. 24:22; 1Pe. 3:19). As in real life, keys in Scripture denote the power to lock and unlock, to open and shut (Isa. 22:22; Mtt. 16:19; Rev. 3:7; Rev. 9:1; 20:1-3).[175] The keys *of Hades and of Death* unlock the gates of Hades and death so that those who would previously have been held securely by death and Hades are now set free to eternal life. Whereas death holds the bodies of men, Hades holds their souls.[176] Jesus' offer of eternal life to those who accept Him overcomes the power of Hades and death (1Cor. 15:55). In this sense, death and Hades were "raided" by Jesus Who liberated man who was destined to this fate by the curse (Gen. 3:19). Jesus is the "firstfruits of those who have fallen asleep" (1Cor. 15:20) and in His resurrection demonstrated dominion over death. It is *because* Jesus is the "living One" that He has the *keys of Hades and Death.* His resurrection "turned the key" in the gates of Hades and death liberating us to eternal life. Our liberation grants us freedom from the bondage of the fear of death (Heb. 2:15).

> What millions have gone down beneath [the power of death], and are now held by it! Every acre of the earth is full of them, and the bottom of every sea. I have seen their grim skeletons on mountain summits, eight thousand two hundred feet above the level of the sea; and I have walked upon their ashes more than a thousand feet below that level. And from far deeper depths to still more elevated heights, on all the slopes and hillsides, and in all the fields and valleys of the earth, death's victims lie in fetters of darkness, silence and dust. Even on the life-powers of the Son of God were these manacles made fast. But by him they were also opened: for he hath the keys of death.[177]

3.1.19 - Revelation 1:19

the things which you have seen

This phrase introduces the key verse for interpreting the main sections of the book. *The things which you have seen* includes those things revealed to John prior to addressing the *seven churches*[5.2.66] (Revelation 1).[178]

the things which are

The things that attend John's present time, which are set forth in the letters to the *seven churches*[4.15] found in Revelation 2 and 3.[179]

the things which will take place after this

The things yet future to John's time, constituting most of the remainder of the book, from Revelation 4 onward: "Where is the dividing line in Revelation between a symbolic view of the present and a symbolic view of the future? . . . The answer seems to be contained in Rev. 4:1, where the voice of a trumpet summoned the seer to heaven to see 'the things which must come to pass hereafter.' "[180]

The conjunction καὶ [*kai*] can be translated by "and," "even," or "both." The question arises as to whether there are three divisions or only two?

> Does Christ give John a chronological outline as a key to the visions in the book? Many think he does. If so, are there three divisions: "seen," "now," and "later"? Or are there two: "seen," i.e., "now" and "later"? In the latter case, where does the chronological break take place in the book?[181]
>
> The passage may be rendered: "Write the things which thou sawest, both the things which are and the things which shall be hereafter." Such a rendering is grammatically possible, though it is not favored by the majority of expositors. If correct, it means that Revelation relates only to the present and to the future, not to the past at all.[182]

The threefold division seems most natural and has been favored by most interpreters:

> The advantage of this outline is that it deals in a natural way with the material rather than seizing on incidentals as some expositors have done or avoiding any outline at all, as is true of other expositors. It is not too much to claim that this outline is the only one which allows the book to speak for itself without artificial manipulation and which lays guidelines of sufficient importance so that expositors who follow this approach have been able to establish a system of interpretation of the book of Revelation, namely, the futurist school.[183]

See the *Structural Outline*[2.14.3] given in our discussion of the *Literary Structure*[2.14] of the book.

after this

Literally, μετὰ ταῦτα [*meta tauta*], "after these [things]," plural.

3.1.20 - Revelation 1:20

mystery

As is frequently the case within Scripture, the answers to our questions are "in the back of the book" (in this case, the back of the *chapter*). Jesus explains the mystery of the seven stars and seven golden lampstands.[184]

> A "mystery" in the constant language of Scripture is something which man is capable of knowing, but only when it has been revealed to him by God (Mtt. 18:11; Rom. 11:25; Eph. 6:19; 1Cor. 13:2), and not through any searching of his own.[185]

Many of the fanciful interpretations offered for this book can be reigned in by the simple process of carefully observing what the book offers in the way of explaining the meaning of symbols: "This verse points up the fact that, when symbols are used in the book of Revelation, they are explained internally, not subject to imaginative suggestions by allegorizing expositors."[186]

seven stars

Due to their brightness and location in heaven, angels are often represented as stars (Job 38:7; Isa. 14:13; Rev. 9:1). See *Seven: Perfection, Completeness*[2.7.5.3.6].

There are *seven* stars, not *twelve* . The number of stars is an important aspect for differentiating this group of stars from another group of stars mentioned elsewhere (Gen. 37:9; Rev. 12:1). These are said to be the churches of Asia Minor. The twelve stars of Revelation 12:1 represent the twelve tribes of Israel, *not the church.*

angels of the churches

Here we enter upon perhaps the most difficult interpretive question in this chapter: the identity of these angels? Each of the primary views is attended with some difficulty:

The Identity of the Angels

Identity	For	Against
Heavenly guardian angels of the churches	The term "angel" describes heavenly beings elsewhere in the book of Revelation.[187]	The angels are charged, *as individuals*, with various sins. Elect angels do not sin.[188] The complexity of communication: why would the revelation be given from God to Jesus to a heavenly angel to John (a man) to another heavenly angel (the star) and then to the church?[189] Why would elect angels, known for their steadfast service and power, be said to be protected in the right hand of the Son of Man? The awards for the overcomer correspond to those promised to redeemed *humans* . Angels do not partake of the tree of life (Rev. 2:7), cannot be imprisoned by men or killed (Rev. 2:10-11), are not written in the *Book of Life*[5.2.10] (Rev. 3:5), nor will they reign over the

Identity	For	Against
		nations (Rev. 2:26-27; 3:21). If the angel is a heavenly guardian angel, then almost all that is said of him must be strictly representative of the people within the church he guards.
Human messengers from the churches[190]	The term "angels" is occasionally used of human messengers.[191] Human messengers may have been sent to Patmos for the purpose of meeting with John and carrying a copy of the letter back to each church.[192] There are fewer problems attending this view. "The view that takes the *angeloi* as men who are representatives of the churches, but are without a unique leadership function appears to be the most probable choice, largely because objections to it are easier to answer than objections to the other . . . views."[193]	Human messengers are never called "stars" (but see Gen. 37:9 cf. Rev. 12:1; Dan. 12:3).[194] Why would secondary human messengers be held personally responsible as individuals for the sins of the church?[195]
A Human leader of the church in each city (elder or bishop)[196]	The angels are individually responsible for the spiritual welfare of the churches and are protected in the right hand of the Son of Man.[197]	There is no precedent within Scripture or church history for referring to church leaders as "angels."[198] Even apostles with great authority, such as Peter and John, refer to themselves merely as "elder" (1Pe. 5:1; 2Jn. 1:1; 3Jn. 1:1).[199] NT church leadership consists of a plurality of elders.[200] The individual leader could not be personally responsible for the character of the entire church.[201] Cities such as Ephesus probably had multiple house churches.[202]
Personifications of the churches[203]	The close identification between each "angel" and the character of the church. Christ speaks to the churches both in the singular and plural.	Lack of scriptural evidence for the personification of congregations of believers. "Stars" or "angels" are not used this way anywhere else. In assigning sin to a personification, ambiguity remains as to who is truly responsible. This view would make the stars and lampstands virtually identical.[204]

In most cases, the grammar of the letters to each church implicates each *individual angel*. This is reflected by the preponderance of verb forms in the second-person *singular*. Yet the things which are said to the angel include aspects which could only be true of the wider church membership. In some cases, the grammar itself reflects a broader application. For example, in the letter to the angel of the church of Smyrna, seven of the Greek words indicate the angel is an individual (second-person *singular, you*). Yet three words indicate the larger church membership (second-person *plural, you all*).

> To the angel [singular] . . . I know your [singular] works . . . but you [singular] are rich . . . You [singular] do not fear . . . those things which you [singular] are about to suffer . . . the devil is about to throw some of you [plural] into prison . . . that you [plural] may be tested, and you [plural] will have tribulation . . . You [singular] be faithful . . . and I will give you [singular] the crown of life. (Rev. 2:8-10)

Since a number of individuals are to be thrown into prison to be tested, the promise of the crown of life cannot be strictly for the individual angel, but surely must apply to all those who remain faithful. We should take care not to make too much of the grammatical distinctions between the single angel and the plural congregation.

When all these factors are considered, it would appear that the best solution is one that takes the "angels" as human messengers or leaders of the churches while recognizing that much of what Christ says to the angel as an *individual* is also meant for the *entire church*.[205]

In our commentary on the individual letters to the seven churches, we will interpret the comments directed to each *singular* angel as being descriptive of the entire congregation.

Notes

1 As teachers, our primary calling is to make the Scriptures known. "The best defense is a strong offense."

2 Richard Chenevix Trench, *Synonyms of the New Testament* (Peabody, MA: Hendrickson Publishers, 1989), 371.

3 To be sure, many aspects of this revelation are set forth elsewhere in Scripture, but not in the completeness or sequence shown John.

4 Charles C. Ryrie, *Dispensationalism* (Chicago, IL: Moody Press, 1995), 81.

5 John MacArthur, *Revelation 1-11 : The MacArthur New Testament Commentary* (Chicago, IL: Moody Press, 1999), Rev. 1:1.

6 In Galatians, *apocalypse* appears in the genitive whereas in Revelation 1:1 it is in the nominative.

7 "Some accept the words as if they were meant to express the revealment of the Revelation. This I take to be a mistake . . . It is not the Apocalypse which is the subject of the disclosure. This book is not the Apocalypse of the Apocalypse, but THE APOCALYPSE OF JESUS CHRIST. . . . If 'The Revelation of Jesus Christ' meant nothing more than certain communications made known by Christ, I can see no significance or propriety in affixing this title to this book, rather than to any other books of holy Scripture. Are they not all alike the revelation of Jesus Christ, in this sense? Does not Peter say of the *inspired*[5.2.33] writers in general, that they were moved by the Spirit of Christ which was in them? Why then single out this particular book as 'The Revelation of Jesus Christ,' when it is no more the gift of Jesus than any other inspired book?"—J. A. Seiss, *The Apocalypse: Lectures on the Book of Revelation* (Grand Rapids, MI: Zondervan Publishing House, 1966), 16. "These opening words in the book present two major ideas about Christ. First, this book is an unveiling *by* or from Him, that is, a revelation of the future that God gave Him to give to us through His servant. Second, the book is an unveiling *concerning* Jesus Christ, an unveiling in which God makes known to us the future and Christ's role in it. The second of these seems more prominent. Though this book certainly is a revelation *by* Jesus Christ, it is foremost a revelation or unveiling *of* Him."—Harold D. Foos, *"Christology in the Book of Revelation,"* in Mal Couch, ed., *A Bible Handbook to Revelation* (Grand Rapids, MI: Kregel Publications, 2001), 104.

8 So [Henry Barclay Swete, *The Apocalypse of St. John* (Eugene, OR: Wipf and Stock Publishers, 1998, 1906)], [M. R. Vincent, *Vincent's Word Studies* (Escondido, CA: Ephesians Four Group, 2002)], and [A. T. Robertson, *Robertson's Word Pictures in Six Volumes* (Escondido, CA: Ephesians Four Group, 2003)].

9 "Is the revelation that which *comes from* Christ or is it *about* Christ? In Rev. 22:16 Jesus tells John that his angel was the one proclaiming the message of the book to John. Thus, the book is certainly a revelation *from*

Christ (hence, we may have a subjective genitive in Rev. 1:1). But the revelation is supremely and ultimately *about* Christ. Thus, the genitive in Rev. 1:1 may also be an objective genitive. The question is whether the author intended both in Rev. 1:1. Since this is the title of his book—intended to describe the whole of the work —it may well be a plenary genitive."—Daniel B. Wallace, *Greek Grammar Beyond the Basics - Exegetical Syntax of the New Testament* (Grand Rapids, MI: Zondervan Publishing House and Galaxie Software, 1999, 2002), 120.

10 "Wallace has fallen into the same pit as have so many others by his neglect of the basics of *hermeneutics*[5.2.26]. One of his glaring errors violates the principle of single meaning. In his consideration of a category he calls the 'Plenary Genitive,' he labors the point that a particular passage's construction may be at the same time both objective genitive and subjective genitive. . . . Wallace consciously rejects the wisdom of past authorities . . . His volume could have been helpful, but this feature makes it extremely dangerous."—Robert L. Thomas, *Evangelical Hermeneutics* (Grand Rapids, MI: Kregel Publications, 2002), 158.

11 Foos, "*Christology in the Book of Revelation*," 105.

12 This equality among the persons of the Trinity while fulfilling different roles well-illustrates the principle of *equality of value, but difference in role* so essential to the biblical family unit. The man and the women are absolutely equal in value before God, yet occupy different roles if the harmony and synergy God intended is to come to fruition in the family unit. The man is to be the leader (1Cor. 11:3; Eph. 5:22-24; Col. 3:18) while demonstrating sacrificial love toward his wife (Eph. 5:25; Col. 3:19). This delicate balance within the family unit requires self*less*ness. It is self*ish*ness which factors large in divorce.

13 Alan F. Johnson, *Revelation: The Expositor's Bible Commentary* (Grand Rapids, MI: Zondervan Publishing House, 1966), 21.

14 MacArthur, *Revelation 1-11 : The MacArthur New Testament Commentary*, Rev. 1:1.

15 Thomas Ice, *"Preterist 'Time Texts'," *in Tim LaHaye, and Thomas Ice, eds., *The End Times Controversy* (Eugene, OR: Harvest House Publishers, 2003), 105.

16 An exception to this statement can be made in the case of full preterism which holds that the entire book of Revelation has already been fulfilled. But this is outside of orthodox Christianity.

17 Monty S. Mills, *Revelations: An Exegetical Study of the Revelation to John* (Dallas, TX: 3E Ministries, 1987), s.v. "Introduction."

18 Ice, "*Preterist "Time Texts"*," 105.

19 Wallace, *Greek Grammar Beyond the Basics - Exegetical Syntax of the New Testament*, 536.

20 *The Conservative Theological Journal*, vol. 4 no. 13 (Fort Worth, TX: Tyndale Theological Seminary, December 2000), 304-305.

21 Ice, "*Preterist "Time Texts"*," 104.

22 Mal Couch, *"The War Over Words,"* in Tim LaHaye, and Thomas Ice, eds., *The End Times Controversy* (Eugene, OR: Harvest House Publishers, 2003), 295.

23 Robert L. Thomas, *Revelation 1-7* (Chicago, IL: Moody Press, 1992), 55.

24 " 'Soonness' means imminency in eschatological terms."—Johnson, *Revelation: The Expositor's Bible Commentary*, 21.

25 Thomas, *Revelation 1-7*, 56.

26 Mills, *Revelations: An Exegetical Study of the Revelation to John*, Rev. 1:1.

27 Thomas, *Revelation 1-7*, 56.

28 Merrill C. Tenney, *Interpreting Revelation* (Peabody, MA: Hendrickson Publishers, 1957), 186.

29 Thomas, *Revelation 1-7*, 59.

30 Arnold G. Fruchtenbaum, *The Footsteps of Messiah*, rev ed. (Tustin, CA: Ariel Ministries, 2003), 12.

31 Seiss, *The Apocalypse: Lectures on the Book of Revelation*, 20.

32 Tenney, *Interpreting Revelation*, 34.

33 Robertson, *Robertson's Word Pictures in Six Volumes*.

34 Rene Pache, *The Inspiration & Authority of Scripture* (Salem, WI: Sheffield Publishing Company, 1969), 35-40.

35 [Thomas, *Revelation 1-7*, 58-59], [Robertson, *Robertson's Word Pictures in Six Volumes*].

36 Most often, we are too eager to make Him known without truly knowing Him (Luke 10:38-42). When we do this, we misrepresent our Lord and present a caricature of God to a skeptical world.

37 Alva J. McClain, *The Greatness Of The Kingdom* (Winona Lake, IN: BMH Books, 1959), 6.

38 Fruchtenbaum, *The Footsteps of Messiah*, 13.

39 Contrast this with our own day which enjoys unprecedented ability to duplicate and distribute materials worldwide, but where Christian teaching and worship music suffers at the hands of restrictive *copyrights*[1.1] (Mtt. 10:8).

40 William D. Mounce, *Greek for the Rest of Us* (Grand Rapids, MI: Zondervan, 2003), 30.

41 Mounce, *Greek for the Rest of Us*, 30.

42 As a case in point, suppose we are studying the Scriptural teaching on Israel? We use a concordance or computer search to find all the occurrences of the word "Israel" in the *NT*[5.2.48]. Using the NIV translation, we find Ephesians 3:6 among the verses listed: "This mystery is that through the gospel the Gentiles are heirs **together with Israel**, members together of one body, and sharers together in the promise in Christ Jesus.". Yet in the Greek below this verse, the word "Israel" (Ισραηλ [*Israēl*]) never appears! This may seem like a fine point to some, especially since in this particular verse the idea captured by the NIV would seem correct. But over the long haul it is problematic to rely on a dynamic equivalency translation for study—you simply do not know when you are looking at a detail which is not there in the original. We suppose such translations may be suitable for devotional study—that is, if you don't mind having flawed devotions.

43 "The Message" is one such paraphrase which distorts God's Word to such a degree that it undermines the very *Message* after which it was titled! How close must we come to violating Revelation 22:18-19 before we realize we are doing a *disservice* to God's Word?

44 "One of the chief eschatological terms. ὁ καιρὸς [*ho kairos*] *the time of crisis, the last times*"—Frederick William Danker, and Walter Bauer, *A Greek-English Lexicon of the New Testament and Other Early Christian Literature* (Chicago, IL: University of Chicago Press, 2000), 394.

45 Larry Spargimino, *"How Preterists Misuse History to Advance their View of Prophecy,"* in Tim LaHaye, and Thomas Ice, eds., *The End Times Controversy* (Eugene, OR: Harvest House Publishers, 2003), 142-143.

46 Spargimino, "*How Preterists Misuse History to Advance their View of Prophecy*," 143.

47 Thomas, *Revelation 1-7*, 61.

48 MacArthur, *Revelation 1-11 : The MacArthur New Testament Commentary*, s.v. "Time does not translate ."

49 Danker, *A Greek-English Lexicon of the New Testament and Other Early Christian Literature*.

50 Nicoll.

51 Kenneth L. Gentry, and Thomas Ice, *The Great Tribulation: Past or Future?* (Grand Rapids, MI: Kregel Publications, 1999), 112.

52 Thomas, *Revelation 1-7*, 130.

53 Thomas, *Revelation 1-7*, 65.

54 Wallace, *Greek Grammar Beyond the Basics - Exegetical Syntax of the New Testament*, 62-63.

55 Swete, *The Apocalypse of St. John*, 5.

56 Thomas, *Revelation 1-7*, 66.

57 Richard Chenevix Trench, *Commentary on the Epistles to the Seven Churches in Asia* (Eugene, OR: Wipf and Stock Publishers, 1861), 6-7.

58 There is some uncertainty as to whether Isaiah lists seven Spirits, or only six (in this case "Spirit of the LORD" being seen as a summary of the six which follow). It seems likely, given the use of seven throughout Scripture, that Isaiah lists these attributes to indicate the *fullness* of the Holy Spirit.

59 "Some writers say these verses are speaking of the seven angels who are before the throne of God (Rev. 8:2)."—Russell L. Penney, *"Pneumatology in the Book of Revelation,"* in Mal Couch, ed., *A Bible Handbook to Revelation* (Grand Rapids, MI: Kregel Publications, 2001), 115. "Other interpreters understand the designation as a reference to the seven archangels of Jewish tradition. In 1 Enoch 20:1-8 they are listed as Uriel, Raphael, Raguel, Michael, Saraquael, Gabriel, and Remiel (cf. Tobit 12:15; Esd. 4:1; Dan. 10:13)."—Robert H. Mounce, *The Book of Revelation* (Grand Rapids, MI: William B. Eerdmans Publishing Co., 1977), 69.

60 Robert P. Lightner, *"Theology Proper in the Book of Revelation,"* in Mal Couch, ed., *A Bible Handbook to Revelation* (Grand Rapids, MI: Kregel Publications, 2001), 92.

61 Johnson, *Revelation: The Expositor's Bible Commentary*, 24.

62 "The verb [τικτωο [*tiktōo*], Strongs: G5088] which is one of the components of [πρωτότοκος [*prōtotokos*] ,Strongs: G4416) 'first-begotten or born,' is everywhere in the New Testament used in the sense of 'to bear or to bring forth,' and has nowhere the meaning 'beget,' unless James 1:15 be an exception."—Vincent, *Vincent's Word Studies*, s.v. "The verb [."

63 *New Electronic Translation : NET Bible*, electronic edition (Dallas, TX: Biblical Studies Press, 1998), Col. 1:15.

64 "I should rather put this passage in connection with Ps. 2:7, 'Thou art my son; this day have I begotten Thee.' It will doubtless be remembered that St. Paul (Acts 13:33; cf. Heb. 1:5) claims the fulfillment of these words not in the eternal generation before all time of the Son; still less in his human conception in the Blessed Virgin's womb; but rather in his resurrection from the dead; 'declared to be the Son of God with power by the resurrection from the dead' (Rom. 1:4)."—Trench, *Commentary on the Epistles to the Seven Churches in Asia*, 12.

65 MacArthur, *Revelation 1-11 : The MacArthur New Testament Commentary*, Rev. 1:5.

66 "He was not the first who rose from the dead, but the first who so rose that death was thenceforth impossible for Him (Rom. 6:9)."—Vincent, *Vincent's Word Studies*, Rev. 1:5. Those who were raptured, such as Enoch (Gen. 5:24) and Elijah (2K. 2:11), did not taste of death.

67 Trench, *Commentary on the Epistles to the Seven Churches in Asia*, 11.

68 Tenney, *Interpreting Revelation*, 118.

69 "The Greek adverb οὕτως [*houtōs*] can refer (1) to the degree to which God loved the world, that is, to such an extent or so much that he gave his own Son . . . or (2) simply to the manner in which God loved the world, i.e., by sending his own son . . . Though the term more frequently refers to the manner in which something is done, . . . the following clause . . . plus the indicative (which stresses actual, but [usually] unexpected result) emphasizes the greatness of the gift God has given. With this in mind, then, it is likely (3) that John is emphasizing both the degree to which God loved the world as well as the manner in which He chose to express that love. This is in keeping with John's style of using double entendre or double meaning. Thus, the focus of the Greek construction here is on the nature of God's love, addressing its mode, intensity, and extent."—*New Electronic Translation : NET Bible*, John 3:16.

70 The following verses may be studied for further insight into the atoning characteristics of Christ's blood: Gen. 9:4; Ex. 12:23; 24:8; Lev. 17:11; Isa. 52:15; Zec. 9:11; Mtt. 26:28; 27:4; Luke 22:20; John 19:30; Acts 20:28; Rom. 5:9; 1Cor. 10:16; Eph. 1:7; 2:13; Col. 1:14, 20; 2:14-15; Heb. 9:12, 14, 22; 10:19, 29; 11:28; 12:24; 13:12, 20; 1Pe. 1:18-19; 1Jn. 1:7; 5:8; Rev. 1:5; 5:9; 7:14; 12:11.

71 Israel will have a unique place as "priests of the Lord" (Isa. 61:5-6) during the *Millennial Kingdom*[5.2.39].

72 Trench, *Commentary on the Epistles to the Seven Churches in Asia*, Rev. 1:6.

73 For more on this topic, see [McClain, *The Greatness Of The Kingdom*] and [George H. N. Peters, *The Theocratic Kingdom* (Grand Rapids, MI: Kregel Publications, 1978, 1884)].

74 Pache, *The Inspiration & Authority of Scripture*, 106.

75 Seiss, *The Apocalypse: Lectures on the Book of Revelation*, 29.

76 "The first messiah, 'Messiah son of Joseph,' who suffered in Egypt would come to suffer and die to fulfill the servant passages [Isa. 49:1-26; 53]. The second messiah, 'Messiah son of David,' would then come and raise the first Messiah back to life. He would then establish His Kingdom to rule and to reign."—Arnold G. Fruchtenbaum, *Messianic Christology* (Tustin, CA: Ariel Ministries, 1998), 57.

77 "As described in Talmud (Sanhedrin 98a): 'Rabbi Joseph the son of Levi objects that it is written in one place "Behold one like the son of man comes with the clouds of heaven," but in another place it is written "lowly and riding upon an ass." The solution is, if they be righteous he shall come with the clouds of heaven, but if they not be righteous he shall come lowly riding upon an ass.' ' "—Fruchtenbaum, *Messianic Christology*, 66.

78 MacArthur, *Revelation 1-11 : The MacArthur New Testament Commentary*, Rev. 1:7.

79 MacArthur, *Revelation 1-11 : The MacArthur New Testament Commentary*, Rev. 1:7.

80 Robertson, *Robertson's Word Pictures in Six Volumes*, s.v. "The verb form ."

81 Thomas, *Revelation 1-7*, 76.

82 Fruchtenbaum, *The Footsteps of Messiah*, 500.

83 James Swanson, *Dictionary of Biblical Languages With Semantic Domains : Hebrew (Old Testament)*, electronic ed. (Oak Harbor, WA: Logos Research Systems, 1997), Rev. 1:7.

84 Tenney, *Interpreting Revelation*, 121.

85 See Revelation 3:11 which clarifies the distinction between the throne of the Father versus the throne of the Son.

86 Even preterists admit that some cloud coming passages relate to the Second Coming. "Preterists such as Gentry do see some passages that have 'cloud language' as referring to the Second Coming (Acts 1:9-11; 1Th. 4:13-17)"—Thomas Ice, *"Hermeneutics and Bible Prophecy,"* in Tim LaHaye, and Thomas Ice, eds., *The End Times Controversy* (Eugene, OR: Harvest House Publishers, 2003), 79. "Another hermeneutical shortcoming of preterism relates to the limiting of the promised coming of Christ in Rev. 1:7 to Judea [the destruction of Jerusalem in 70 AD]. What does a localized judgment hundreds of miles away have to do with the seven churches of Asia? John uses two long chapters in addressing those churches regarding the implications of the coming of Christ for them. For instance, the promise to shield the Philadelphian church from judgment (Rev. 3:10-11) is meaningless if that judgment occurs far beyond the borders of that city."—Thomas, *Revelation 1-7*, 225.

87 An awkward reality for preterists is the reestablishment of the Jewish state in the Promised Land. If it were to have been finally destroyed in A.D. 70 by the wrath of God as preterists maintain, evidently God did an incomplete job.

88 Gary DeMar, *Last Days Madness* (Atlanta, GA: American Vision, 1994), 162.

89 DeMar, *Last Days Madness*, 162.

90 "The choice of ἐκκεντέω [*ekkenteō*] to render the Hebrew דָּקַר [*Dāqhar*] of Zec. 12:10 in John 19:37 and Rev. 1:7 adds strength to the case that the two books had the same author. Both uses differ from the *LXX's*[5.2.38] obviously erroneous choice of κατορχέω [*katorcheō*] to render the same Hebrew word."—Thomas, *Revelation 1-7*, 82.

91 Swanson, *Dictionary of Biblical Languages With Semantic Domains : Hebrew (Old Testament)*, Rev. 1:7.

92 Robert Laird Harris, Gleason Leonard Archer, and Bruce K. Waltke, *Theological Wordbook of the Old Testament* (Chicago, IL: Moody Press, 1999, c1980), s.v. "449a."

93 "In the messianic passage Isa. 53:5, 'wounded' (KJV margin 'tormented'; jb 'pierced through') follows the divine smiting (Isa. 53:4). The Poel form used . . . is similar to that in Isa. 51:9; cf. 'pierced by the sword' (Pual, Eze. 32:26). The quotation in John 19:12 ('they shall look on him whom they have pierced') is from Zec. 12:10 but this Isa. 53:5 uses another verb (דָּקַר [*dāqhar*]) 'pierced through fatally' (usually in retribution). In Jer. 51:4 and Lam. 4:9 דָּקַר [*dāqhar*] is used as a synonym of הָלַל [*hālal*]."—Harris, *Theological Wordbook of the Old Testament*, s.v. "#660."

94 A. R. Fausset, *"The Revelation of St. John the Divine,"* in Robert Jamieson, A. R. Fausset, and David Brown, *A Commentary, Critical and Explanatory, on the Old and New Testaments* (Oak Harbor, WA: Logos Research Systems, Inc., 1997, 1877), Rev. 1:7.

95 Merrill F. Unger, *Unger's Commentary on the Old Testament* (Chattanooga, TN: AMG Publishers, 2002), 2040.

96 Carl Friedrich Keil, and Franz Delitzsch, *Commentary on the Old Testament* (Peabody, MA: Hendrickson, 2002), 10:609.

97 "The problem with interpreting Revelation 1:7 to refer to the land of Israel is that all the other uses of the exact phrase 'all the tribes of the earth' in the original language always has a universal nuance (Gen. 12:3; 28:14; Ps. 72:17; Zec. 14:17)."—Ice, "*Preterist "Time Texts"*," 99.

98 The distinction between Abraham's *seed* and *all the families of the earth* makes plain that the families are a superset beyond the physical seed. Where Gen. 12:3 is cited in Acts 3:25, the word for "families" is πατριαὶ [*patriai*].

99 " 'all the tribes of the earth' refers to all nations in every one of its Septuagint occurrences (πᾶσαι αἱ φυλαὶ τῆς γῆς [*pasai hai phylai tēs gēs*] , Gen. 12:3; 28:14; Ps. 71:17; Zec. 14:17)."—Gregory K. Beale, *The Book of Revelation: A Commentary on the Greek Text* (Grand Rapids, MI: William B. Eerdmans Publishing Co., 1999), 26.

100 Preterists respond to this evidence from the Septuagint by noting that where the Septuagint renders "tribes" as φυλαι [*phylai*], the underlying Hebrew is מִשְׁפְּחֹת [*mishppechōt*] - a different Hebrew word from the more frequently encountered word for "tribe" which describes Israel: שֵׁבֶט [*shēbet*]. They claim that by rendering both שֵׁבֶט [*shēbet*] and מִשְׁפְּחֹת [*mishppechōt*] as "tribes," the Septuagint loses the precision of the underlying Hebrew text. We agree, but what does it have to do with the evidence before us? The observation that the Septuagint renders both shebet and מִשְׁפְּחֹת [*mishppechōt*] by φυλαι [*phylai*] ("tribes") provides further evidence against the preterist contention that φυλαι [*phylai*] is a *technical term*[5.2.72] which always denotes Israelite tribes. This response of the preterists is simply a smoke screen, which when considered carefully, actually supports the opposite conclusion.

The fact is that the Septuagint, translated by Hebrew rabbinical scholars familiar with the use of Greek in times much nearer to the NT than our own, renders two different Hebrew words-denoting both Jewish tribes and non-Jewish tribes or families-as φυλαι [*phylai*] This leads us to conclude that φυλαι [*phylai*] is not a technical term denoting only Jewish tribes. It can have different meanings which are dependent upon the context. This is also obvious from the numerous qualifiers which appear in conjunction with φυλαι [*phylai*]: "tribes of the earth," "the twelve tribes," "every tribe," etc. Why would these additional qualifiers be necessary if φυλαι [*phylai*] always referred to Israelite tribes as preterists claim?

101 [Fruchtenbaum, *The Footsteps of Messiah*, 638]. If one seeks evidence for how far astray interpretation can go where the meaning of a passage is *entirely reversed* from its intended meaning, one can do no better than the *preterist interpretation*[2.12.2] of Zechariah 12 through 14.

102 Beale, *The Book of Revelation: A Commentary on the Greek Text*, 26.

103 Thomas, *Revelation 1-7*, 79.

104 See [Tony Garland, *"Revelation 1:7 - Past or Future?,"* (n.p. 2004) in *The Conservative Theological Journal*, vol. 9 no. 27 (Fort Worth, TX: Tyndale Theological Seminary, August 2005)]

105 Danker, *A Greek-English Lexicon of the New Testament and Other Early Christian Literature*.

106 Erich Sauer, *The Dawn of World Redemption* (Grand Rapids, MI: Eerdman's Publishing Company, 1951, c1964), 118-119.

107 Having personally sat with those in their dying days who continue to reject God's free and gracious offer of salvation when they have nothing to lose and everything to gain, we have gained a genuine appreciation regarding the fearful consequences of the continual rejection of the gospel offer.

108 Seiss, *The Apocalypse: Lectures on the Book of Revelation*, 81.

109 It was the Angel of the Lord who met Moses in the burning bush (Ex. 3:2) and who made claims that no ordinary angel dare make (Ex. 3:14). Indeed, it was no ordinary Angel, but the preincarnate Messiah (John 1:14, 18).

110 Foos, "*Christology in the Book of Revelation*," 107.

111 Thomas, *Revelation 1-7*, 11.

112 John F. Walvoord, *The Revelation of Jesus Christ* (Chicago, IL: Moody Press, 1966), 40.

113 Arthur Walkington Pink, *The Antichrist* (Oak Harbor, WA: Logos Research Systems, 1999, 1923), s.v. "Comparisons between Christ and the Antichrist."

114 Thomas, *Revelation 1-7*, 81.

115 See the discussion of the *Nicolaitans*[4.13] for the view that they may have contributed to the development of church hierarchy where none was intended beyond that of elders, deacons, and the flock.

116 Seiss, *The Apocalypse: Lectures on the Book of Revelation*, 35.

117 Thomas, *Revelation 1-7*, 87.

118 Copyright ©003 *www.BiblePlaces.com*. This image appears by *special permission*[1.3] and may not be duplicated for use in derivative works.

119 Seiss, *The Apocalypse: Lectures on the Book of Revelation*, 86.

120 Copyright ©003 *www.BiblePlaces.com*. This image appears by *special permission*[1.3] and may not be duplicated for use in derivative works.

121 Walvoord, *The Revelation of Jesus Christ*, 41.

122 Johnson, *Revelation: The Expositor's Bible Commentary*, 28.

123 Trench, *Commentary on the Epistles to the Seven Churches in Asia*, 19.

124 Fausset, "*The Revelation of St. John the Divine*," Rev. 1:9.

125 Beale, *The Book of Revelation: A Commentary on the Greek Text*, 6-7,9.

126 Seiss, *The Apocalypse: Lectures on the Book of Revelation*, 86.

127 Gen. 26:2, 24; 46:2; Num. 12:6; 1S. 3:15; 1K. 22:19; Job 33:15; Isa. 1:1; 6:1; Eze. 1:3; 8:3; 11:24; Dan. 2:19; 7:2; 8:1, 16; 9:21; 10:1; Joel 2:28; Acts 2:17; 9:10-12; 10:3, 11; 11:5; 16:9-10; 18:9; 22:18; 23:11; 26:19; Rev. 1:10; 4:2; 9:17.

128 James Strong, *The Exhaustive Concordance of the Bible* (Ontario: Woodside Bible Fellowship, 1996), G1611.

129 Robertson, *Robertson's Word Pictures in Six Volumes*, Rev. 1:10.

130 "Some have assumed from this passage that ἡμέρα κυριακή [*hēmera kyriakē*] was a designation of Sunday already familiar among Christians. This however, seems a mistake. The name had probably its origin here."—Trench, *Commentary on the Epistles to the Seven Churches in Asia*, 23.

131 "Sunday belongs indeed to the Lord, but the Scriptures nowhere call it 'the Lord's day.' None of the Christian writings, for 100 years after Christ, ever call it 'the Lord's day.' . . . I can see no essential difference between ἡ Κυριακη ἡμερα [*hē Kyriakē hēmera*]—*the Lord's day,*— and ἡ ἡμερα Κυριου [*hē hēmera Kyriou*]—*the day of the Lord*. They are simply the two forms for signifying the same relations of the same things. . . . And when we come to consider the actual contents of this book, we find them harmonizing exactly with this understanding of its title. It takes as its chief and unmistakable themes what other portions of the Scriptures assign to the great day of the Lord."—Seiss, *The Apocalypse: Lectures on the Book of Revelation*, 18.

132 Jerome Smith, *The New Treasury of Scripture Knowledge* (Nashville, TN: Thomas Nelson Publishers, 1992), s.v. "Not Sunday."

133 E. W. Bullinger, *Commentary On Revelation* (Grand Rapids, MI: Kregel Publications, 1984, 1935), xvi-xvii, 9.

134 Johnson, *Revelation: The Expositor's Bible Commentary*, 29.

135 MacArthur, *Revelation 1-11 : The MacArthur New Testament Commentary*, Rev. 1:10.

136 "Objection has been taken to the interpretation of 'the Lord's Day' here, because we have (in Rev. 1:9) the adjective 'Lord's' instead of the noun (*in regimen*), 'of the Lord,' as in the Hebrew. But *what else could it be called in Hebrew?* Such objectors do not seem to be aware of the fact that there is no adjective for 'Lord's' in Hebrew; and therefore the *only way of expressing* 'the Lord's Day' is by using the two nouns, 'the day of the Lord'—which means equally 'the Lord's Day' (Jehovah's day)."—Bullinger, *Commentary On Revelation*, 11-12.

137 Fruchtenbaum, *The Footsteps of Messiah*, 16.

138 Johnson, *Revelation: The Expositor's Bible Commentary*, 23.

139 Swete, *The Apocalypse of St. John*, 14.

[140] Trench, *Commentary on the Epistles to the Seven Churches in Asia*, 4.

[141] Seiss, *The Apocalypse: Lectures on the Book of Revelation*, 56.

[142] Interestingly, John is the only gospel writer who does not record his experience on the Mount of Transfiguration except if John 1:14 be taken as a reference to it.

[143] Albrecht Durer (1471 - 1528). Image courtesy of the *Connecticut College* (http://www.conncoll.edu/visual/Durer-prints/index.html) *Wetmore Print Collection* (http://www.conncoll.edu/visual/wetmore.html).

[144] Trench, *Commentary on the Epistles to the Seven Churches in Asia*, 23.

[145] The context of Mtt. 18:20 infers that Jesus will be present in any gathering of believers to grant both authority cand guidance concerning matters of church discipline.

[146] The intended permanence of sealing may be seen in the following examples: (1) the tomb (Mtt. 27:66); (2) Jesus' testimony (John 3:33); (3) Jesus sealed by the Father (John 6:27); (4) witnessed during the Tribulation (Rev. 7:3); (5) what the seven thunders uttered (Rev. 10:4); (6) Satan during the Millennium (Rev. 20:3).

[147] "Here, the scattered condition of the nation [of Israel] is just as distinctly indicated by the fact that the seven lamps are no longer united in one lamp-stand. The nation is no longer in the Land, for Jerusalem is not now the centre; but the people are 'scattered' in separate communities in various cities in Gentile lands. So that just as the *one* lamp-stand represents Israel in its unity, the *seven* lamp-stands represent Israel in its dispersion; and tells us that Jehovah is about to make Jerusalem again the centre of His dealings with the earth."—Bullinger, *Commentary On Revelation*, 72.

[148] *Goel* is a Hebrew term describing the person who is next of kin and his respective duties: to buy back what his poor brother has sold and cannot himself regain (Lev. 25:25-26); to avenge any wrong done to a next of kin, particularly murder (Num. 35:19-27); to purchase land belonging to one deceased who was next of kin and to marry his widow and to raise up children for the deceased (Ru. 2:20; 4:14). Boaz, the kinsman-redeemer of the book of Ruth (Ru. 4) is a type of Christ as our kinsman-redeemer.

[149] It is instructive to study the following parallels between Adam and Christ: **1)** Adam was created in God's image, Christ is the manifestation of God in the flesh; **2)** Adam's disobedience brought condemnation leading to death, Christ's obedience brought justification leading to life; **3)** Those who are 'in Adam' die, those who are 'in Christ' have eternal life (1Cor. 15:22); **4)** Adam is the 'son of God' (Luke 3:38) as is Christ (both were directly created by God); **5)** All men are 'born once' in Adam, believers are 'born again' in Christ; **6)** The first Adam became a living being (Gen. 2:7), the last Adam became a life-giving Spirit (1Cor. 15:45); **7)** Adam is from the earth—made of dust (Gen. 2:7), Christ is from heaven; **8)** Adam lost dominion, Christ regained it. **9)** A tree bore Adam's downfall, a tree bore Christ's victory. **10)** Adam's body was animated by the breath of God (Gen. 2:7), the body of Christ is animated by the breath of God (1Cor. 12:13).

[150] Trench, *Commentary on the Epistles to the Seven Churches in Asia*, 31.

[151] Trench, *Commentary on the Epistles to the Seven Churches in Asia*, 32.

[152] Some interpreters separate Daniel 10 into two separate passages, the first part (Daniel 10:1-9) being a vision of Christ and the second part (Daniel 10:10-21) involving an angelic being who required assistance (Dan. 10:13, 21). We believe several factors favor understanding the same heavenly being as being in view throughout the chapter.

[153] John F. Walvoord, *Jesus Christ Our Lord* (Chicago, IL: Moody Bible Institute, 1969), 204-205.

[154] Trench, *Commentary on the Epistles to the Seven Churches in Asia*, 33.

[155] Trench, *Commentary on the Epistles to the Seven Churches in Asia*, 35.

[156] Robertson, *Robertson's Word Pictures in Six Volumes*.

[157] Trench, *Commentary on the Epistles to the Seven Churches in Asia*, 37.

[158] Colin J. Hemer, *The Letters to the Seven Churches of Asia in Their Local Setting* (Grand Rapids, MI: William B. Eerdmans Publishing Company, 1989), 111-112,116.

[159] Danker, *A Greek-English Lexicon of the New Testament and Other Early Christian Literature*, 731.

[160] This return of the glory of the Lord to the *Millennial Temple*[5.2.73][5.2.40] ends the most recent departure of God from His Temple which occurred when Jesus departed to the Mount of Olives (Mtt. 23:37-39). It is for this reason that His "house" in Jerusalem has been desolate for these long ages. See The Abiding Presence of

God .

161 Trench, *Commentary on the Epistles to the Seven Churches in Asia*, 27.

162 Trench, *Commentary on the Epistles to the Seven Churches in Asia*, 40.

163 Augustine in [Trench, *Commentary on the Epistles to the Seven Churches in Asia*].

164 Trench, *Commentary on the Epistles to the Seven Churches in Asia*, 45.

165 The term *Genie* is derived from the Arabic word for demon: *Jin*.

166 The fear of God is a major theme of Scripture: Gen. 31:42, 53; Ex. 1:17; 15:11; 20:20; Jos. 4:24; 1K. 18:3; 2Chr. 19:7, 9; Job 9:34; 23:15-16; 25:1; 28:28; Ps. 5:7; 89:7; 111:10; 115:13; 119:38, 120; 128:4; 145:19; Pr. 2:5; 8:13; 9:10; 10:27; 14:26; 15:16, 33; 16:6; 19:23; 22:4; 23:17; 24:21; 31:30; Ecc. 5:7; 8:12; 12:13; Isa. 8:13; 11:3; 33:5; 50:10; 57:11; 59:19; Jer. 5:22-24; Hab. 3:16; Luke 12:5; Acts 9:31; 10:2, 35; 2Cor. 5:13; 1Pe. 3:15; Rev. 19:5.

167 Ex. 3:6; Deu. 5:26; Jos. 3:10; 1S. 17:26, 36; 2K. 19:4, 16; Ps. 42:2; 84:2; Isa. 37:4, 17; Jer. 10:10; 23:36; Dan. 6:20, 26; Hos. 1:10; Mtt. 16:16; 22:32; 26:63; John 6:69; Acts 14:15; Rom. 9:26; 2Cor. 3:3; 6:16; 1Ti. 3:15; 4:10; 6:17; Heb. 3:12; 9:14; 10:31; 12:22; Rev. 7:2.

168 Trench, *Commentary on the Epistles to the Seven Churches in Asia*, 47.

169 Trench, *Commentary on the Epistles to the Seven Churches in Asia*, 48.

170 Mills, *Revelations: An Exegetical Study of the Revelation to John*, Rev. 1:17.

171 "*And the living, and I became dead, and behold, I am living for evermore.*"—Trench, *Commentary on the Epistles to the Seven Churches in Asia*, 47.

172 The resurrection is attributed to all three members of the Trinity. To Jesus: John 2:19; 10:17. To the Father: Acts 4:10; 10:41; Rom. 4:24; 6:4; 8:11. To the Holy Spirit: 1Pe. 3:18.

173 Trench, *Commentary on the Epistles to the Seven Churches in Asia*, 42.

174 The word death probably refers to the location of the body, whereas Hades refers to the location of the immaterial part of man—his soul. *Israel My Glory*, July/August 2001, 22. The former describes the *state* of the dead whereas the latter describes the *location* of the dead. [Thomas, *Revelation 1-7*, 112] "Hades is the unseen world where all who die reside. It includes both Paradise (Luke 23:43) and Gehenna (Luke 12:5)—Abraham's bosom and the state of torment and anguish (Luke 16:22-28)."—Robert L. Thomas, *Revelation 8-22* (Chicago, IL: Moody Press, 1995), 433.

175 "The Rabbinical proverb said: 'There are four keys lodged in God's hand, which He committeth neither to angel nor to seraph: the key of the rain, the key of food, the key of the tombs, and the key of a barren woman.' "—Vincent, *Vincent's Word Studies*, Rev. 1:18.

176 Seiss, *The Apocalypse: Lectures on the Book of Revelation*, 48.

177 Seiss, *The Apocalypse: Lectures on the Book of Revelation*, 47.

178 "I favor understanding 'the things which you have seen' as linked to Rev. 1:2, and thus to be the authority to write John's Gospel . . . , though others see this as indicating chapter 1. . . . Allowing my understanding of 'the things which you have seen,' then, the first chapter becomes very much part of chapters 2-3."—Mills, *Revelations: An Exegetical Study of the Revelation to John*, Rev. 1:19.

179 Some see this phrase as being descriptive of the things John saw in the previous phrase: "Write therefore what things thou sawest *and what they are*, . . . even what things are about to happen hereafter."—Bullinger, *Commentary On Revelation*, 159.

180 Tenney, *Interpreting Revelation*, 39.

181 Johnson, *Revelation: The Expositor's Bible Commentary*, 33.

182 Tenney, *Interpreting Revelation*, 39.

183 Walvoord, *The Revelation of Jesus Christ*, 48.

184 To study the use of "mystery" in the *NT*[5.2.48], see Mark 4:11; Rom. 11:25; 16:25; 1Cor. 2:7; 13:2; 15:51; Eph. 1:9; 3:3-4, 9; 5:32; 6:19; Col. 1:26; 2:2; 4:3; 2Th. 2:7; 1Ti. 3:9, 16; Rev. 1:20; 10:7; 17:7.

185 Trench, *Commentary on the Epistles to the Seven Churches in Asia*, 51.

186 Henry Morris, *The Revelation Record* (Wheaton, IL: Tyndale House Publishers, 1983), 45.

187 Variations of the word *angel* occur 72 times in this book, and unless the references to these angels of the churches be excepted, all mentions are of divine beings. Angels are ministering spirits actively involved in other aspects of God's plan. "True churches of the Lord have individual angels assigned for their guidance and watch-care. This fact is hardly surprising in view of the innumerable company of angels (Hebrews 12:22) and their assigned function as ministering spirits of those who are heirs of salvation (Hebrews 1:14). Individual believers have angels assigned to them (Matthew 18:10; Acts 12:15). Angels are present in the assemblies during their services (1 Corinthians 11:10) and are intensely interested in their progress (1 Corinthians 4:9; Ephesians 3:10; 1 Timothy 3:16; 5:21; Hebrews 13:2; 1 Peter 1:12)."—Morris, *The Revelation Record*, 45.

188 "How could *holy* Angels be charged with such delinquencies as are laid to the charge of some of the Angels here (Rev. 2:4; 3:1, 15)?"—Trench, *Commentary on the Epistles to the Seven Churches in Asia*, 52.

189 "The complexity of the communication process is one thing that raises problems with it. It presumes that Christ is sending a message to heavenly beings through John, an earthly agent, so that it may reach earthly churches through angelic representatives. . . . An even more decisive consideration against the view of guardian angels lies in the sinful conduct of which these angels are accused. Most of the rebukes of [Revclation] chapters 2-3 are second person singular, messages that look first at the individual messengers and presumably through them to the churches they represent."—Thomas, *Revelation 1-7*, 117.

190 "This rare and difficult reference should be understood to refer to the heavenly messengers who have been entrusted by Christ with responsibility over the churches and yet who are so closely identified with them that the letters are addressed at the same time to these 'messengers' and to the congregation (cf. the plural form in Rev. 2:10, 13, 23-24)."—Johnson, *Revelation: The Expositor's Bible Commentary*, 34.

191 Αγγελος [*Angelos*] is occasionally used of human *messengers*. Examples include John the Baptist (Mtt. 11:10; Mark 1:2), the messengers sent to Jesus by John the Baptist (Luke 7:24), the spies hidden by Rahab (Jas. 2:25) and possibly the leaders of the *seven churches*[5.2.66], if these are to be understood as human leaders (Rev. 2:1, 8, 12, 18; 3:1, 7, 14). "In the *Septuagint*[5.2.65] ἄγγελος [*angelos*] is used in rare instances of a human messenger of God (Mal. 2:7; 3:1; cf. 1:1, where the *LXX*[5.2.38] so renders the name or title "Malachi" itself). In the New Testament it twice denotes simply an emissary (Luke 9:52; Jas. 2:25). Elsewhere it is always used of a supernatural being. The idea of an angel as the guardian of the nation is found in Dan. 12:1, as guardian of the individual in . . . Mtt. 18:10; Acts 12:15."—Hemer, *The Letters to the Seven Churches of Asia in Their Local Setting*, 32.

192 "Some think these men journeyed to Patmos to receive the finished book of Revelation from the hands of John, and that they returned to their respective cities and shared the message."—Mal Couch, *"Ecclesiology in the Book of Revelation,"* in Mal Couch, ed., *A Bible Handbook to Revelation* (Grand Rapids, MI: Kregel Publications, 2001), 128.

193 Thomas, *Revelation 1-7*, 118.

194 "[The idea that the angel is a human messenger] is at first sight attractive, for "messenger" is the primary meaning of ἄγγελος [*angelos*] , and the book may indeed have been distributed through messengers delegated by each church to tour its district. But . . . usage favours "angels" and the emissary could not be made representative of the community. Nor could he be readily symbolized by the "stars" of Rev. 1:20."—Hemer, *The Letters to the Seven Churches of Asia in Their Local Setting*, 33.

195 "But in answering a letter by a messenger, men write *by* him, they do not usually write *to* him; nor is it easy to see where is the correspondency [*sic*] between such messengers, subordinate officials of the Churches, and stars; or what the *'mystery'* of the relation between them then would be; or how the Lord should set forth as an eminent prerogative of his, that He held the seven stars, that is, the seven messengers, in his right hand (Rev. 2:1)."—Trench, *Commentary on the Epistles to the Seven Churches in Asia*, 56-57.

196 "The Angel in each Church is one; but surely none can suppose for an instant that there was only one presbyter, or other minister serving in holy things, for the whole flourishing Church of Ephesus, or of Smyrna; and that we are in this way to account for the single Angel of the several Churches. . . . What can he be but a bishop?"—Trench, *Commentary on the Epistles to the Seven Churches in Asia*, 53-54.

197 "The spiritual significance is that these angels are messengers who are responsible for the spiritual welfare of these seven churches and are in the right hand of the Son of Man, indicating possession, protection, and sovereign control. As the churches were to emit light as a lampstand, the leaders of the churches were to project light as stars."—Walvoord, *The Revelation of Jesus Christ*, 45.

198 "In early noncanonical Christian literature no historical person connected with the church is ever called an

angelos."—Johnson, *Revelation: The Expositor's Bible Commentary*, 34. "Who shall authorize us to understand the word 'angels' as having any connection with the Church of God? No one ever heard (until quite recent times) of such a title being given to any church officer either in Scripture, in history, or in tradition."—Bullinger, *Commentary On Revelation*, 161.

199 "If 'angel' means 'pastor' here, it is used with this meaning here and nowhere else. If the Lord Jesus meant the pastors of the churches, why did He not *say* 'pastors?' Or why did He not say 'elders,' a term which is used in the New Testament as essentially synonymous with 'pastors,' and which is later used twelve times in Revelation?"—Morris, *The Revelation Record*, 45.

200 Acts 11:30; 14:23; 15:2-4; 20:17, 28; 21:18; Php. 1:1; 1Th. 5:12; Tit. 1:5; Heb. 13:17; Jas. 5:14; 1Pe. 5:1-5.

201 "The individual could scarcely be held responsible for the character of the church, and there is no unambiguous evidence for the idea of episcopal authority in the churches of the Revelation, though it looms large in *Ignatius*[5.2.28] twenty years later."—Hemer, *The Letters to the Seven Churches of Asia in Their Local Setting*, 33.

202 "In a city the size of Ephesus, by this time, there must have been a large number of house-churches meeting separately from one another."—Thomas, *Revelation 1-7*, 128.

203 "Personifications of the prevailing spirit."—Mounce, *The Book of Revelation*, 86.

204 "This gives the required sense, but raises problems in the usage of symbolism. The "stars" and the "lampstands" of Rev. 1:20 are made virtually the same thing. Some writers justify this conception by regarding the "angel" as the heavenly counterpart of the earthly church."—Hemer, *The Letters to the Seven Churches of Asia in Their Local Setting*, 33.

205 Bullinger suggests an alternate view on the basis that these congregations may have exhibited customs carried over from the Judaism of the synagogue: "The Bible student is at once confronted with an overwhelming difficulty. He has read the Epistles which are addressed to the churches by the Holy Spirit through the Apostle Paul; and, on turning to the Epistles in Rev. 2 and 3, he is at once conscious of a striking change. He finds himself suddenly removed from the ground of *grace* to the ground of *works*. He meets with church-officers of whom he has never before heard; and with expressions with which he is wholly unfamiliar: and he is bewildered. . . . we do meet with the word Angel in connection with the *Synagogue* . . . [the] 'Angel of the Assembly,' who was the mouthpiece of the congregation. His duty it was to offer up public prayer to God for the whole congregation. Hence his title; because, as the messenger of the assembly, he spoke to God for them. When we have these facts in our hands, why arbitrarily *invent* the notion that 'angel' is equivalent to Bishop, when there is not a particle of historical evidence for it?"—Bullinger, *Commentary On Revelation*, 63, 66.

3.2 - Revelation 2

3.2.1 - Revelation 2:1

Having been commissioned by Christ to write "the things which you have seen, and the things which are, and the things which will take place after this" (Rev. 1:19), John now records "the things which are"—Jesus' assessment of the condition of the *Seven Churches of Asia*[4.15] at the time John wrote. This subject will occupy Revelation 2 and 3 until John is called up to heaven at the beginning of Revelation 4 in order to witness and record "the things which will take place after this."

The evaluation, exhortation, and promises which Jesus gives to each of the *seven churches*[5.2.66] provide important insights into the conditions of the early church. The seven letters to the churches also challenge *us today* to examine our own lives to see which attributes of the seven churches, whether good and bad, are evident in our own lives?

the angel

See the discussion concerning the identity of the angel at *Revelation 1:20*[3.1.20].

the church of Ephesus

See *Seven Churches of Asia*[4.15].

At the time of John's writing, Ephesus was an important seaport city of the Roman province of Asia. Today, the site is stranded several miles from the sea on the edge of a swampy alluvial plain and the former harbor is marked by a reed-bed.[1] Ephesus was famous for its *Temple*[5.2.73] of Artemis (Diana in Latin), 425-feet long by 220-feet wide with each of its 120 columns donated by a king, one of the seven wonders of the world (Acts 19).[2]

Temple of Artemis at Ephesus [3]

> The presence of the temple of Artemis (Diana) added to the commercial importance of Ephesus, for two reasons. First, the temple was regarded as sacrosanct throughout the Mediterranean world and thus became the primary banking institution of Asia Minor. Second, pilgrims swelled the population and contributed substantially to Ephesian business, especially during the festivals of Artemis (March/April). So prominent was the city that during the early Christian period the population of Ephesus probably exceeded a quarter million.[4]

The important place which Artemis held in the city, both religiously and commercially, can be seen by the riot which ensued in reaction to Paul's ministry (Acts 19:24-41). One of the months of the calendar was named after Artemis and a yearly celebration was held in her honor.[5] The ancient temple of the great goddess identified with Artemis stood less than a mile outside the walls of the city.[6] Ephesus also participated in the *imperial cult*[5.2.31] where temples were built to Claudius, Hadrian, and Severus.[7] Magic was a thriving art at Ephesus. Scripture records the value of books burned by those who practiced magic as "fifty thousand *pieces* of silver" (Acts 19:19).[8]

Ephesus also had a reputation as a seat of learning. Paul is recorded as having taught at one such established school, the *School of Tyrannus* (Acts 19:9). Ephesus was the scene for Justin's *Dialogue with Trypho*.[9]

Ephesus was probably listed as the first city of the seven to receive the letter from John due to its proximity to Patmos (see *Seven Churches of Asia*[4.15] map) and its key location on major overland routes:

> Ephesus lay at the intersection of two ancient major overland routes: the coastal road that ran north through Smyrna and Pergamum to Troas (near ancient Troy); and the western route to Colossae, Hierapolis, Laodicea, and regions of Phrygia and beyond. Ephesus can also be viewed as the starting-point of a type of postal route . . . running north to Pergamum and southwest through Sardis to Laodicea.[10]

Although Paul ministered extensively at Ephesus: "The first arrival of the gospel in Ephesus is unrecorded. According to Acts 2:9 Jews resident in Asia were present in Jerusalem on the day of Pentecost. And we are told of "disciples" in Ephesus before Paul's arrival, though they are represented as imperfectly instructed [Acts 19:1ff; Acts 18:24ff]."[11]

Paul first visited Ephesus on his second missionary journey (Acts 18:19-28) and on his third missionary journey taught there for a period of almost three years (Acts 20:31). Paul wrote his first letter to the Corinthian church from there.[12] It was at Ephesus that Apollos, a disciple of John the Baptist, was instructed by Aquila and Priscilla (Acts 18:24-26). When returning from his third missionary journey to Jerusalem, Paul passed by Ephesus, but stopped in Miletus. From there, he sent for and met with the elders of the church at Ephesus (Acts 20:17). The church at Ephesus had plural eldership well in advance of John's writing this letter (which adds to the difficulties attending the identification of the angel of the church—see commentary on *Revelation 1:20*[3.1.20]). Paul asked Timothy to remain in Ephesus in his absence (1Ti. 1:3) and wrote his epistle to the Ephesian church in A.D. 60-62 (after his third missionary journey, A.D. 53-57) which was delivered by Tychicus (Eph. 6:21).

Tradition holds that the John left Jerusalem prior to its destruction and in about A.D. 66 relocated to Ephesus which was his main place of ministry during the closing years of his life. If Mary were still alive, she would have undoubtedly traveled with him (John 19:27).

> About 5 km (3 mi) from Ephesus was constructed the Basilica of St. John. John is supposed to be buried there. But Meinardus asks which John, since according to Eusebius (HE iii.3) *Papias*[5.2.52], the famed second-century bishop of Hierapolis, "asserts there were also two tombs in Ephesus, and that both are called John's even to this day." This church erected to the memory of John is not to be confused with the Church of the Virgin Mary in which the Council of Ephesus was held in A.D. 431, when Nestorius was condemned in the *Theotokos* issue. . . . The stones and pillars [of the Temple of Artemis] were used in the construction of both the great Basilica of St. Sophia at Constantinople and the early Church of St. John at Ephesus. . . . Although Ephesus lies in ruins today, the railway station nearby is called Ayasoluk, a corruption of Gk *hagios Theologos*, "the holy theologian," a well-known reference in Eastern Christendom to the beloved Evangelist.[13]

holds the seven stars in His right hand

The titles which Jesus assumes in each letter are primarily derived from Revelation 1:12-18 and are tailored to the message which attends each letter. Here, The Ephesian church has lost its first love (Rev. 2:4). Jesus reminds them that it is He Who is the protector of the stars—they are held in His right hand, secure and in a position of favor (John 10:27-30). He has not left them, but they have *left Him* (Deu. 31:6, 8; Jos. 1:5; Mtt. 28:20; Heb. 13:5). See commentary on *Revelation 1:16*[3.1.16].

walks in the midst

He is the One in the midst of the churches and will always be with them (Mtt. 28:20), even if they have forsaken a close relationship with Him (Rev. 2:4). See commentary on *Revelation 1:13*[3.1.13].

3.2.2 - Revelation 2:2

I know

Perfect tense, οἶδα [*oida*], "I have known." His knowledge of their past works results in the commendations and exhortations which presently follow.[14] Christ is omniscient. See commentary on *Revelation 1:14*[3.1.14].

labor and patience

The Ephesian church had worked hard and born a consistent load of service.

The Christian life, though full of joy, is also attended by much labor and hardship (2Cor. 11:27). Continual labor requires continual patience. Believers are to persevere and not grow weary (Isa. 40:31; Gal. 6:9; 2Th. 3:13; Heb. 12:3). Those who die in the Tribulation are said to obtain rest from their labors and their works follow them (Rev. 14:13).

cannot bear

The Ephesian church did not bear those who were evil. This must refer to the Scriptural application of church discipline to protect the gathering from those who were not truly of them (Mtt. 18:17; 1Cor. 5:5; 1Ti. 6:3-5):

> The sphere in which the Angel of Ephesus had the chief opportunity of manifesting this holy intolerance of evil-doers was, no doubt, that of Church-discipline, separating off from fellowship with the faithful those who named the name of Christ, yet would not depart from iniquity (2Ti. 2:19).[15]

A letter written by *Ignatius*[5.2.28] (A.D. 98-117) mentions this commendable characteristic of the Ephesian church:

> But I have learned that certain people . . . have passed your way with evil doctrine, but you did not allow them to sow it among you. You covered up your ears in order to avoid receiving the things being sown by them—Ignatius, *The Letter of Ignatius to the Ephesians*[16]

tested those

The Ephesian church was diligent in evaluating those who ministered in their midst.

All things are to be tested by the measure of God's Word (Isa. 8:20) and the fruit which is produced (Mtt. 7:16). This is especially true of those things which are *claimed to be of the Spirit of God* , but are not (1Th. 5:2; 1Ti. 4:1; 1Jn. 4:1; Rev. 2:20). The most serious threats to the Christian assembly *come from within* (Acts 20:29-31; 1Ti. 1:3-4).

Peter warned of false teachers who would pattern themselves after the false prophets of the *OT*[5.2.51]:

> But there were also false prophets among the people, even as there will be false teachers among you, who will secretly bring in destructive heresies, even denying the Lord who bought them, *and* bring on themselves swift destruction. And many will follow their destructive ways, because of whom the way of truth will be blasphemed. By covetousness they will exploit you with deceptive words; for a long time their judgment has not been idle, and their destruction does not slumber. (2Pe. 2:1)

When the church accepts these false teachers, and fails to confront their error, then "the way of truth will be blasphemed." A key attribute of such teachers is their *deception*—appearing to be what they are not. They are all the more effective in their convincing zeal since *they themselves are deceived* (2Ti. 3:13).

It is a lamentable fact in our time that the Church seems unwilling to test its own. Application of the guidelines set forth by the *NT*[5.2.48] writers is seen as judgmental or quenching the Spirit. Yet it was the Spirit Himself who *inspired*[5.2.33] the writers who urge us through the pages of Scripture to proactively guard doctrine! The NT makes plain how essential this testing is to the health of the assemblies. Shouldn't we expect that Satan will concentrate his greatest efforts at the very 'ground zero' of God's work upon the earth—within the local Christian assembly? We cannot say that we have not been warned: "test the spirits, whether they are of God" (1Jn. 4:1)!

say they are apostles

These were not apostles in the sense of having seen the risen Christ (Acts 1:21-22; 1Cor. 9:1) since John alone survived at the time of writing.[17]

Paul had previously warned the Ephesian church about the need to *watch for* false teachers:

> For I know this, that after my departure savage wolves will come in among you, not sparing the flock. Also from among yourselves men will rise up, speaking perverse things, to draw away the disciples after themselves. Therefore watch, and remember that for three years I did not cease to warn everyone night and day with tears. (Acts 20:29-31)

Paul mentioned such false apostles when writing to the church at Corinth and was not hesitant to cut off their "ministry":

> But what I do, I will also continue to do, that I may cut off the opportunity from those who desire an opportunity to be regarded just as we are in the things of which they boast. For such *are* false apostles, deceitful workers, transforming themselves into apostles of Christ. And no wonder! For Satan himself transforms himself into an angel of light. Therefore *it is* no great thing if his ministers also transform themselves into ministers of righteousness, whose end will be according to their works. (2Cor. 11:12-15)

A key attribute of those who are not what they appear to be is their *self proclamation*. In the church of Thyatira, it was *Jezebel*[5.2.35] who *called herself* a prophetess (Rev. 2:20). Paul says that they *transform themselves* , patterning their deceit after Satan who transforms himself into an angel of light. This transformation would be entirely effective if the church did not have the Word of God and gifts of spiritual discernment to expose such imposters (1Cor. 12:10). Spiritual discernment is necessary because the natural mind is ineffective in the spiritual realm where the seduction takes place (Mtt. 24:24; Mark 13:22; 2Th. 2:9-11; 1Ti. 4:1). The power of seduction by demonic spirits may be assessed by noting how easily deceiving spirits convince the kings of the earth to participate in the height of folly: going to war *against God* (Rev. 16:13-14)!

3.2.3 - Revelation 2:3

persevered

The Ephesians had in common their *perseverance* (ὑπομονὴν [*hypomonēn*]) with John's *patience* (Rev. 1:9), the trait of faithfully waiting while "abiding under" or bearing a heavy load. Patience and perseverance are qualities which attend selflessness, for they seek things other than self (Rom. 2:7). Perseverance is produced by tribulation (Rom. 5:3). What God has revealed afore time helps us remain patient under conditions we might not otherwise tolerate because we have hope (Rom. 15:4).

have labored

The Ephesian church had dutifully labored to produce fruit (Tit. 3:8, 14). These labors were evidence of the reality of their faith (Jas. 2:17-26). The Ephesian church had a clean bill of health *from an external perspective*.

My name's sake

Jesus predicted that the Ephesians and all believers would be reviled, hated, and persecuted for His *name's sake* (Mtt. 5:11; 10:22). It is extremely important that we take care that our persecution is for *His name's* sake rather than for *our name's* sake. How often do we abuse His name to defend insensitivity or rudeness on our part? When the world hates or persecutes us, is it truly because of *His name*? Are there times when we deserve the treatment which we have justly earned, but rationalize it by incorrectly attributing it to our position in Christ?

Anything done for His *name's sake* must be done with His *character* . Since we are called by His name (Acts 15:17; Jas. 2:7), when our actions contravene the Word of God, we *profane* His name (Lev. 19:12; 20:3; 22:2, 32; Pr. 30:9; Isa. 48:11; 52:5; Jer. 34:16; Eze. 20:9, 14, 22, 30; 36:21-23; 39:7).

3.2.4 - Revelation 2:4

Nevertheless

Despite the good works and patience, there is something lacking in the Ephesian church. How sobering it is to hear the Lord say "nevertheless" after a word of commendation!

left your first love

"Left" is ἀφῆκες [*aphēkes*] meaning "to send away. . . . to bid going away or depart. . . . of a husband divorcing his wife,"[18] to "give up, abandon . . . Rev. 2:4."[19] "Note, the word is '*leave*,' not '*lose*.' To love lies in the power of the will, otherwise it would not be commanded. . . . This is the beginning of that decline which ends in Laodicea."[20]

The Ephesian church had fallen prey to the same fate as Israel before them (Jer. 2:1-9):

> Moreover the word of the LORD came to me, saying, "Go and cry in the hearing of Jerusalem, saying, 'Thus says the LORD: "I remember you, the kindness of your youth, the love of your betrothal, when you went after Me in the wilderness, in a land not sown. Israel *was* holiness to the LORD, the firstfruits of His increase. All that devour him will offend; disaster will come upon them," says the LORD.' "

God reminds Israel of "the love of *her* betrothal," when they sought after Him in the wilderness. Although the nation lacked many things in the wilderness, they had a zeal and hunger for the Lord. This is analogous to the zeal and hunger we had for God when He first calls us from the "wilderness" of the world. At that time, nothing else was as important as our *relationship* with Him!

> Hear the word of the LORD, O house of Jacob and all the families of the house of Israel. Thus says the LORD: "What injustice have your fathers found in Me, that they have gone far from Me, have followed idols, and have become idolaters? Neither did they say, 'Where *is* the LORD, Who brought us up out of the land of Egypt, Who led us through the wilderness, through a land of deserts and pits, through a land of drought and the shadow of death, through a land that no one crossed and where no one dwelt?' "

God relates the next stage in Israel's flagging relationship with Him. They have "gone far from" Him and have begun to follow *idols*. They have forgotten the wonders He did when they were rescued from a desperate situation and now other things have begun to eclipse the importance of intimacy with God. God specifically mentions Israel's having "followed idols"—the nation is turning its attention elsewhere.

> "I brought you into a bountiful country, to eat its fruit and its goodness. But when you entered, you defiled My land and made My heritage an abomination. The priests did not say, 'Where *is* the LORD?' And those who handle the law did not know Me; the rulers also transgressed against Me; the prophets prophesied by Baal, and walked after *things that* do not profit. Therefore I will yet bring charges against you," says the LORD, "And against your children's children I will bring charges."

The nation has now drifted so far apart from God that "those who handle the law did not know Me." This is a *very serious state of affairs!* The very people who should know God and accurately represent Him, no longer "know Me." How similar this sounds to the sobering words of Jesus:

> Many will say to Me in that Day, 'Lord, Lord, have we not prophesied in Your name, cast out demons in Your name, and done many wonders in Your name?' And then I will declare to them, '**I never knew you**; depart from Me, you who practice lawlessness!' (Mtt. 7:22-23) [emphasis added]

If Jesus never knew them then they could not have truly known Him. Yet they are actively ministering *in His name*—attributing their activities to His character! The disturbing reality is that it is possible to think one is actively "serving God," but without a true relationship with Him. Even in the case where we begin following after Him, time and circumstances often turn our hearts aside. When Solomon grew old, "his wives turned his heart after other gods; and his heart was not loyal to the LORD his God, as *was* the heart of his father David" (1K. 11:4).

Our priority must ever be relationship over service (works). This is the essential message of the incident involving Mary and her sister Martha related by Luke. Martha's priority was serving whereas "Mary . . . sat at Jesus' feet and heard His word" (Luke 10:39). Martha was so focused on serving that she missed a golden opportunity to listen to her Lord. Jesus summarized the actions of the two sisters: "Martha, Martha, you are worried and troubled about many things. But one thing is needed, and Mary has chosen that good part, which will not be taken away from her" (Luke 10:41-42).

Time spent sitting at the Master's feet will never be taken away from us. Although some fret that such time reduces our ability to serve, the result is actually the opposite. Our devotion, motivation, and understanding of God are deepened causing an increase in the fruit of God's ministry *through us.* Our ministry and service must be grounded in and out of our love for Him (Heb. 6:10-12). We are "priests to His God," our primary focus is God-ward, *only then* man-ward. Instead of waning, our love for Him is to be continually increasing (Php. 1:9).

The Ephesian church had lost its focus. They had taken their eyes off of *Jesus* and were now focusing on their *works* done for His name. This is the essence of idolatry.

The condition of the Ephesian church at the time of John appears considerably different to that when Paul wrote his epistle. "See the Ephesians' first love, Eph. 1:15. This epistle was written under Domitian, when thirty years had elapsed since Paul had written his Epistle to them."[21] This is evidence for a *late date*[2.11] for the writing of the book of Revelation.

3.2.5 - Revelation 2:5

Remember

Remembering is the first in a three-step process. All three steps (*remember*, *repent*, and *do* the first works) are in the imperative tense: remember! . . . repent! . . . do! The Ephesians were commanded to go back in their minds to an earlier time when their motivation and fellowship with Christ had been different.

An important function of festivals, signs, and altars is to help men remember the earlier works of God and the dedications they made (Gen. 9:15-16; Num. 15:39-40; Deu. 16:13; Jos. 22:10, 27-28).

repent

If the Ephesian church were to repent and return to their first love, they would find that God is also once again closer to them (Zec. 1:3).

> Properly speaking, *metanoein* is "to know *after*" as *pronoein* is "to know *before*"; *metanoia* is "afterknowledge" . . . The next step that *metanoia* signifies is the change of mind that results from this afterknowledge. Thus *Tertullian*[5.2.75] wrote: "In the Greek language the word for repentance is not derived from the admission of a fault but from a change of mind." . . . Last of all *metanoia* signifies a resulting change of conduct. . . . Only in Scripture and in the works of those who were dependent on Scripture does *metanoia* predominantly refer to a change of mind, to taking a *wiser* view of the past, to "the soul's perception of the wicked things it has done."[22]

Repentance includes a recognition of wrong-doing *together with* a decision to move in a different direction: "Repent therefore and be converted, that your sins may be blotted out, so that times of refreshing may come from the presence of the Lord" (Acts 3:19).

from where you have fallen

Their current estate is said to be *lower* than before. As they drifted *apart* from God in their relationship, their spiritual state also *declined. have fallen* is in the perfect tense—the fall had already taken place, but Jesus is concerned with their *present spiritual condition.*

do the first works

The Ephesian church was not lacking in works, but the *motivation* for the works had changed and was now adversely affecting the results. "Not the *quantity*, but the *quality*, of . . . works was now other and worse than once it had been."[23] How often has this been the case in Christian history when works of mercy, intended to exhibit the character of Christ and to point people to the solution of their ultimate need, suffer a gradual reduction in their zeal and focus on Christ. The result is that the Christian organization becomes just one more social institution doing "good works," but failing to engage the culture with the priority of salvation.

The solution is found in retracing our steps back to where we went astray and calling upon the Lord as we did at the first. After straying in Egypt, Abraham returned to "the place where his tent had been at the beginning, between Bethel and Ai, to the place of the altar which he had made there at first. And there Abraham called on the name of the Lord" (Gen. 13:3-4).

> But **recall the former days in which, after you were illuminated, you endured a great struggle with sufferings**: partly while you were made a spectacle both by reproaches and tribulations, and partly while you became companions of those who were so treated; for you had compassion on me in my chains, and joyfully accepted the plundering of your goods, knowing that you have a better and an enduring possession for yourselves in heaven. Therefore do not cast away your confidence, which has great reward. (Heb. 10:32-35) [emphasis added]

> Instantly, let us say, this is *not* a call to "*Christian service*" or "renewed activity." Ephesus had toil,

> patience, intolerance toward evil, patience in suffering,—*everything*. But the "first works" are the goings forth of *affection* to Christ, freely, devotedly, as in our first love.[24]

I will come

The *futuristic present*, ἔρχομαι [*erchomai*] is in the present tense: "I am coming." His impending arrival is *imminent*[5.2.30]![25]

remove

Κινήσω [*Kinēsō*] (from which we get the word kinetic) can also mean to "shake," "move," "provoke," "stir." This may be indicating not only that the lampstand will be *removed*, but that it will be *disturbed* in such a way as to disperse its membership elsewhere to form new churches (Mtt. 10:23; Acts 8:4). "The seat of the Church has been changed, but the Church itself survives."[26] Even if a church remained physically present at Ephesus, if its membership failed to return to their first love, then the essential Christian testimony of the church would be curtailed. "Without genuine Christians remaining, it is impossible for a church to produce light."[27]

Those with illumination bear greater responsibility for bearing fruit. When we fail to bear fruit, God raises up others in our stead (Mtt. 21:43; Mark 12:9; Luke 20:16). This would be the destiny of the Ephesian church if it did not repent.

> Gibbon (*Decline and Fall*, c. lxiv.), . . . writes like one who almost believed that the threatenings and promises of God did fulfill themselves in history: In the loss of Ephesus the Christians deplored the fall of the first Angel, the extinction of the first candlestick, of the Revelations; the desolation is complete; and the temple of Diana or the church of Mary will equally elude the search of the curious traveller. The circus and three stately theatres of Laodicea are now peopled with wolves and foxes; Sardis is reduced to a miserable village; the God of Mahomet, without a rival or a son, is invoked in the mosques of Thyatira and Pergamus, and the populousness of Smyrna is supported by the foreign trade of the Franks and Armenians. Philadelphia alone has been saved by prophecy, or courage. . . . Among the Greek colonies and Churches of Asia, Philadelphia is still erect—a column in a scene of ruins,—a pleasing example that the paths of honour and safety may sometimes be the same.[28]

The lampstand at Ephesus was indeed removed. "I have before me a picture of the Ephesus of today—a ruined archway, a Moslem dwelling, and a forbidding castle, 'midst desolate hills. No lampstand for Christ where once Paul labored three years, night and day with tears!"[29]

3.2.6 - Revelation 2:6

hate the deeds

The Ephesian church had left their first love, but had not left their former hatred for evil. Their hatred for evil was the diametric opposite of the tolerance of the church in Pergamum toward the teachings and deeds of the *Nicolaitans*[5.2.47] (Rev. 2:14-15).[30]

God hates the *deeds* and the *doctrine* (Rev. 2:13). God hates evil ways (Pr. 8:13), abominable activities (Jer. 44:4), a false oath (Zec. 8:17), and insincere offering (Jer. 44:4; Amos 5:21). Believers are to have no fellowship with such unfruitful works and are to expose them (Eph. 5:11; 2Jn. 1:9).

Nicolaitans

See *Nicolaitans*[4.13].

you hate . . . I also hate

Both verbs are in the present tense—both the Ephesian church and Jesus are in *ongoing* opposition to the works of the Nicolaitans.

3.2.7 - Revelation 2:7

He who has an ear

"Every man 'hath an ear' naturally, but he alone will be able to hear spiritually to whom God has given 'the hearing ear'; whose 'ear God hath wakened' and 'opened.' "[31]

let him hear

Each letter closes with this imperative command which is very similar to Jesus' invitations in the synoptic gospels (Mtt. 11:15; 13:9, 43; Mark 4:9, 23; Luke 8:8; 14:15).[32] It is Christ's desire that "those who hear the words of this prophecy" (Rev. 1:3) not only *hear* the subject matter, but *understand* its significance. This phrase recognizes the reality that those whose hearts are not open to Christ may hear (or read) the *words*, but will not *understand* the message: "The natural man does not receive the things of the Spirit of God, for they are foolishness to him; nor can he know *them*, because they are spiritually discerned" (1Cor. 2:14). See *Hiding or Revealing?*[2.2.6].

If we desire that God would reveal more to us, we must first respond in obedience to that which has already been revealed. If we fail to respond to what He has already revealed, then we stand to lose what we already understand (Mark 4:24-25; Luke 8:18). Thus is the dilemma of the lukewarm Christian who believes he sees and hears, but has become blind and deaf (Rev. 2:16-17).

> [The seven letters] are also accompanied with a seven times repeated entreaty and command to hear what is said in them. And yet there is not another portion of Scripture, of equal extent and conspicuity, to which so little attention has been paid.[33]

what the Spirit says

Christ had been speaking but now it is the Spirit who speaks - a declaration of Christ's deity and a testimony to the *inspiration*[5.2.33] of Scripture. When Jesus promised to send another helper (παρακλητον [*paraklēton*]), the Spirit of Truth, He said, "I will not leave you orphans; **I will come to you**." [emphasis added] (John 14:18). It is the Spirit of Christ, the Holy Spirit, Who initiates prophecy (1Pe. 1:11). He is the source of all spiritual revelation and illumination (John 14:17; 15:26; 16:13).

to the churches

Each letter is given for the benefit of all *seven churches*[5.2.66]. The book of Revelation is given to: (1) John; (2) each individual church; (3) all seven churches; (4) all churches of all time; (5) all believers in every age (Rev. 2:7, 11, 17, 29; 3:6, 13, 22; 13:9). See *Seven Churches of Asia*[4.15].

him who overcomes

The appearance of this phrase is an indication of John's apostolic authorship. "It is characteristic of John, occurring once in the Gospel, six times in the First Epistle, sixteen times in the book of Revelation, and elsewhere only Luke 11:22; Rom. 3:4; 12:21."[34] See *Authorship*[2.9]. See *Who is the Overcomer?*[4.15.1.3]

tree of life

The tree of life originally stood in the Garden of Eden (Gen. 2:9). By partaking of its fruit, man had eternal life. But through the Fall, man lost access to the tree (Gen. 3:22-24).

The tree of life is a common motif for righteousness and wisdom in Scripture (Ps. 1:3; Pr. 3:18; 11:30; 13:12; 15:4) for it is by righteousness and wisdom that life is lived to the full. For this reason, the Jews referred to the Word of God as the "tree of life". "[Torah scrolls are] written on parchment, sewn together, rolled onto wooden rollers called *eytz chayeem* (tree of life), and read regularly in the synagogue."[35]

During the present age, while man is barred from the tree of life, God has provided *another tree of life*: the cross of Jesus Christ. Those who place their trust in His atoning work upon the cross *have* eternal life (John 3:14-16).[36] Even though every man has been bitten by the Serpent (Gen. 3:15), by merely looking upon this tree in faith, he will be healed (Num. 21:9).

In the eternal state, believers will once again obtain full access to the tree of life (Rev. 22:2, 14). The promise made to the overcomer is an essential element of salvation. In the eternal state, man will still be *dependent* upon God for access to the tree of life (Rev. 22:2) because *independence from God* is sin.

Paradise of God

Significantly, the church which had lost its first love was given the promise of access to a tree which was in the midst of the garden wherein God and Adam used to have sweet fellowship (Gen. 3:8). This is the very essence of the *first love* which the Ephesians had left.

Paradise "Παράδεισος [*Paradeisos*] was originally a Persian word, denoting an enclosed garden, especially a royal park."[37] "Among the Persians a grand enclosure or preserve, hunting ground, park, shady and well watered, in which wild animals, were kept for the hunt; it was enclosed by walls and furnished with towers for the hunters."[38] Although Paradise was initially associated with the Garden of God (Gen. 2:8; 13:10; Isa. 51:3; Eze. 28:13; 31:5), the meaning of the term has changed with time: "We may thus trace παράδεισος [*paradeisos*] passing through a series of meanings, each one higher than the last; from any garden of delight, which is its first meaning, it comes to be predominantly applied to the Garden of Eden; then to the resting-place of separate souls in joy and felicity; and lastly, to the very heaven itself."[39] "What was originally a garden of delight has taken on the connotation of the new heavens and the new earth."[40]

Prior to the cross, paradise was a compartment within Hades (Luke 16:22-23). At His crucifixion, Jesus told the repentant thief, "today you will be with Me in Paradise" (Luke 23:43). The location of paradise after the victory of Jesus on the cross moved to heaven, for Paul was "caught **up** into Paradise" [emphasis added] where he heard inexpressible words (2Cor. 12:4). Essentially, the term describes the abode of righteous men upon death:

> It is a term describing the abode of the righteous ones, no matter where that above may be at any point in time.... from Adam until the Ascension of Jesus, Paradise was in Abraham's Bosom. From the Ascension of Jesus until the end of the Millennium, Paradise is in Heaven. Then, after the Millennium and for all eternity, Paradise will be in the New Jerusalem on the new earth.[41]

3.2.8 - Revelation 2:8

the angel

See the discussion concerning the identity of the angel at *Revelation 1:20*[3.1.20].

Trench suggests that *Polycarp*[5.2.55] may have been "the angel of the church in Smyrna":

> Knowing as we do that at a period only a little later than this, Polycarp was bishop there, a very interesting question presents itself to us, namely, whether he might not have been bishop now; whether he may not be the Angel of whom this epistle is addrest [*sic*]. There is much to make this probable. . . . It is true indeed that we have thus to assume an episcopate of his, which lasted for more than seventy years; for the "good confession" of Polycarp did not take place till the year 168, while the Apocalypse was probably written in 96. . . . As early as AD 108 *Ignatius*[5.2.28] . . . found Polycarp the bishop . . . of the Church of Smyrna . . . We have only to extend his episcopate twelve years *a parte ante*, and he will have been Angel of Smyrna when this Epistle was addrest [*sic*] to that Church. Is there any great unlikelihood in this? His reply to the Roman Governor who tempted him to save his life by denying his Lord, is well known . . . that he could not thus renounce a Lord whom for eighty and six years he had served . . . [These eighty-six years] represent no doubt the years since his conversion. Counting back eighty-six years from the year 168, being that of his martyrdom, we have AD 82 as the year when he was first in Christ. This will give us fourteen years as the period which will have elapsed from his conversion to that when this present Epistle was written, during which time he may very well have attained the post of chiefest honour and toil and peril in the Church of Smyrna. *Tertullian*[5.2.75] indeed distinctly tells us that he was consecrated bishop of Smyrna *by St. John* . . . and *Irenaeus*[5.2.34], who affirms that he had himself in his youth often talked with Polycarp, declares the same[42]

the church of Smyrna

See *Seven Churches of Asia*[4.15].

Temple of Athena in Old Smyrna [43]

Like Ephesus at the time of John, Smyrna was a coastal city which commanded the trade of the Levant.[44] It was noted as a center of learning, especially in science and medicine and claimed to be the birthplace of Homer.[45] Polycarp presided here as bishop.[46] Smyrna is represented today by Izmir, the third city of Turkey and the largest in Asia Minor until overtaken by the recent growth of Ankara.[47]

> Many writers of that time referred to it as the loveliest city of Asia. Smyrna had a magnificent natural situation and setting at the end of a long, protected inlet of the Mediterranean which gave it a natural harbor well sheltered from the elements. The harbor was compact and easily defended in time of war by simply drawing a chain across its entrance. The city itself began at the harbor and covered the undulating ground between the harbor and the Pagos, a hill covered by temples and public buildings. These noble buildings encircled this hill, and the locals proudly called these the crown of Smyrna (see Rev. 2:10).[48]

The meaning of the name Smyrna, *myrrh* or *bitter*, "Smyrna means 'bitter,' certainly an appropriate description for the lot of Christians who lived there."[49] is associated with death:

> In the New Testament the word σμύπ΄α [*smypa*] occurs only twice (Mtt. 2:11 and John 19:39) and a derivative form once (Mark 15:23). Commentators note the enormous quantity of myrrh and aloes brought by Nicodemus for the burial of Jesus. Use of these spices evidently accorded with normal Jewish practice (cf. John 11:44), except that their quantity in this case represented a costly act of devotion to Jesus, resembling that of Mary (John 12:2-11), Jesus there applied the lesson of her gift to his forthcoming burial (John 12:7; cf. Mark 14:8; Mtt. 26:12).[50]

> So much has been idly written upon names, not a little most idly on the names of these *seven Churches*[5.2.66], and the mystical meanings which they contain, that one shrinks from any seeming fellowship in such foolish and unprofitable fancies; and yet it is difficult not to remember here that σμύρνα [*smyrna*], the name of this suffering Church which should give out its sweetness in persecution and in death, is a subform of μύῤῥα [*myrhra*] . . . [which] . . . served for embalming the dead (John 19:39) . . ., went up as incense before the Lord (Ex. 30:23), was one of the perfumes of the bridegroom (Ps. 45:8), and of the bride (Sos. 3:6)[51]

Significantly, this is the church of tribulation and martyrdom. Ignatius, in his *Epistle to the Smyrnaeans* recognized the ongoing zeal of the church at Smyrna: "I observed that you are established in an unshakable faith, having been nailed, as it were, to the cross of the Lord Jesus Christ in both body and spirit and firmly established in love by the blood of Christ."[52]

This is one of only two churches (Philadelphia being the other) for which Christ gives no word of criticism.

the First and the Last

Jesus emphasizes His eternality, especially in relation to *eternal life* because this is the church which is to suffer martyrdom and to which He holds out the promise of the "crown of life" (Rev. 2:10). See commentary on *Revelation 1:11*[3.1.11] and *Revelation 1:17*[3.1.17].

who was dead, and came to life

Literally, "became dead."[53] Jesus reiterates His victory over death. It was of paramount importance that the saints at Smyrna understand their possession of eternal life for they would be asked to "be faithful until death" (Rev. 2:10). Although the devil could destroy the body, he could do no more (Mtt. 10:28; Luke 12:4). See commentary on *Revelation 1:18*[3.1.18].

3.2.9 - Revelation 2:9

I know

See commentary on *Revelation 2:2*[3.2.2].

tribulation and poverty

The connection between tribulation and poverty is found in the likelihood that their goods were plundered due to persecution for their faith (Heb. 10:34). How contrary is the condition of the church at Smyrna from that of the church in Laodicea which was lacking persecution and abounding in goods (Rev. 3:17). Yet, the Smyrnaean church received no word of *condemnation* while the Laodicean church received no word of *commendation*!

poverty

"Greek has two words for poor: *penia* means having nothing superfluous, *ptocheia* means abject poverty, destitution. [This verse] uses the latter."[54]

you are rich

The church at Smyrna could not be accurately judged by external measures. As Trench observes: "there are both poor rich-men and rich poor-men in his sight."[55] The riches of the church at Smyrna were laid up in heaven (Mtt. 6:20; 19:21; Luke 12:21; Jas. 2:5). "There is one who makes himself rich, yet has nothing; And one who makes himself poor, yet has great riches" (Pr. 13:7).

Material goods have no ultimate value, but will all be destroyed. Knowledge of this reality should bring a shift in priorities towards spiritual things which are truly lasting (2Pe. 3:10-11). The church at Laodicea had great material prosperity, but Christ said they were "wretched, miserable, poor, blind, and naked" (Rev. 3:17).

who say they are Jews but are not

This church of martyrdom faced its most intense opposition from those who at one time were closest to God. "Three sources of antagonism to Christians emerge in these seven messages, Jewish (here), pagan (Rev. 2:13), and heretical (Rev. 2:24)."[56]

That these "Jews" are the natural seed of Abraham can be seen by the description of their assembly place as a *synagogue*[57] and by the analogy of Scripture (Rom. 2:28-29; 9:6; Php. 3:2-3). These were the unbelieving Jews of Smyrna, who had physical circumcision, but lacked the circumcision of the heart:

> For he is not a Jew who *is one* outwardly, nor *is* circumcision that which *is* outward in the flesh; but *he is* a Jew who *is one* inwardly; and circumcision *is that* of the heart, in the Spirit, not in the letter; whose praise *is* not from men but from God. (Rom. 2:28-29)

Such Jews relied upon their physical decent from Abraham, but denied him as father by their actions. John the Baptist warned the Pharisees and Sadducees, "and do not think to say to yourselves, "We have Abraham as *our* father." For I say to you that God is able to raise up children to Abraham from these stones" (Mtt. 3:9).

> They answered and said to Him, "Abraham is our father." Jesus said to them, "If you were Abraham's children, you would do the works of Abraham. But now you seek to kill Me, a Man who has told you the

> truth which I heard from God. Abraham did not do this. You do the deeds of your father." Then they said to Him, "We were not born of fornication; we have one Father—God." (John 8:39-41)

Paul noted that only a subset of the Jews were "the Israel of God" (Gal. 6:16). This believing remnant within Israel were the true Jews:[58]

> But it is not that the word of God has taken no effect. For they *are* not all Israel who *are* of Israel, nor *are they* all children because they are the seed of Abraham; but, "In Isaac your seed shall be called." That is, those who *are* the children of the flesh, these *are* not the children of God; but the children of the promise are counted as the seed. (Rom. 9:6-8)

He warned the Philippian church to beware of the "mutilation" (a euphemism for the physically circumcised unbelieving Jews, Gal. 5:12):

> Beware of dogs, beware of evil workers, beware of the mutilation! For we are the circumcision, who worship God in the Spirit, rejoice in Christ Jesus, and have no confidence in the flesh, though I also might have confidence in the flesh. If anyone else thinks he may have confidence in the flesh, I more so: (Php. 3:2-4)

The unbelieving Jews were the major threat to the early church (Acts 13:50; 14:2, 5, 19; 17:5). This threat was compounded because Christians initially enjoyed protection from Rome by being considered a sect within Judaism. Since Judaism enjoyed protection as a recognized religion by Rome, so long as Christianity was seen as a sect within Judaism, persecution was minimal. But the fundamental rift between Judaism and Christianity eventually brought persecution, not only by the Jews, but also from Rome.

synagogue of Satan

The local synagogue in Smyrna opposed the Christian assembly, as did the synagogue in Philadelphia (Rev. 3:9).[59]

The gathering of Christians at Smyrna is "church" ἐκκλησίαις [*ekklēsiais*], whereas the gathering of these blasphemers is "synagogue" συναγωγὴ [*synagōgē*]. The difference in words is significant making it unlikely that Jesus is describing some other group of Christians who hold faulty doctrine concerning their Jewishness. Some interpreters take this verse as describing Christian groups who hold to *Replacement Theology*[5.2.63]. While we are opposed to Replacement Theology, such an interpretation appears to us to be a subversion of this text to serve the ends of the interpreter rather than accurate exegesis.[60] Jesus tells the Philadelphian church that members of the *synagogue of Satan* "say they are Jews and are not" (Rev. 3:9). They undoubtedly were Jews in the national sense—physical offspring of Abraham—but lacked faith in Messiah Jesus.

Persecution by the Synagogue was something that Jesus had promised (Mtt. 23:34; Mark 13:9; Luke 21:12; John 16:12) and Paul had experienced (Acts 9:20-23; 13:45-50; 14:2; 17:5-10; 18:6, 28; 19:9; 22:22). "[This] shocking statement affirmed that those Jews who hated and rejected Jesus Christ were just as much Satan's followers as pagan idol worshipers (cf. John 8:44)."[61] Persecution by the unbelieving Jews was heightened by the belief that they alone had the true understanding of God:

> The measure of their former nearness to God was the measure of their present distance from Him. In the height to which they were lifted up was involved the depth to which, if they did not continue at that height, they must inevitably fall; and this, true for them, is true also for all[62]

This persecution by Judaism was especially troubling because it meant the loss of the protection Christianity initially enjoyed while considered a sect within Judaism:

> The letters in Revelation suggest that Jewish Christians were tempted to escape persecution by seeking some form of identification with Jewish synagogues, which were exempted from emperor worship, and that Gentile Christians were tempted to compromise with trade guild cults and even the emperor cult in order to escape persecution. Such a situation is more likely to have been present toward the end of the first century rather than earlier.[63]

> According to Roman law, religions were considered illegal outside their country of origin, . . . The only exception to this law was Judaism, the practice of which was allowed throughout the Empire. Christians were probably considered a sect of Judaism until 70 A.D., though they likely would not have been completely disassociated from Judaism in the minds of pagans in the years following 70 A.D. After that date, Judaism made formal attempts to dissociate itself from Christianity.[64]

> Judaism had a special privilege that the Romans allowed only them, freedom from worshiping the Roman gods and participating in the Greco-Roman cults. Christianity was considered part of Judaism at least through the Jewish War (A.D. 66-70) and also benefited from this privilege. However, Judaism tried more and more to separate itself from Christianity and get the Roman Empire to recognize that Christianity was not exempt. . . . the Romans imposed on Jews [the Judean tax] that allowed the Jews freedom from participation in the *imperial cult*[5.2.31]. Christians refused to pay this tax; thus the Jews denounced Christians as not being true Judeans and as being troublemakers.[65]

The intensity of the hatred of the Smyrnaean Jews for Christians was illustrated in the burning of *Polycarp*[5.2.55] some years later: "[The martyrdom of Polycarp] was in the year 165, but the attitude of the Asian Jew towards Christianity had been determined at least seventy years before."[66] "The most striking instance [of persecution by Jews] actually relates to Smyrna: the Jews gathered fuel on the Sabbath for the burning of Polycarp (*Mart. Pion.* 4; Cadoux, pp. 378-79)."[67] "These things happened with such swiftness, quicker than words can tell, the crowd swiftly collecting wood and kindling from the workshops and baths, the Jews being especially eager to assist in this, as is their custom."[68]

Although it seems best to understand the text as describing unbelieving Jews (true physical offspring of Abraham, Isaac, and Jacob), some have noted the trend among cults (e.g., Jehovah's Witnesses, British Israel) of claiming to be "Jews," "One common element among cults is to claim to be the 'real' Jews by declaring themselves to be the 144,000 Jews or the ten lost Tribes of Israel."[69]

If the Jews had recognized their Messiah, what is here described as *a synagogue of Satan* could have been described as the "church of the living God."

3.2.10 - Revelation 2:10

you are about to suffer

The Smyrnaeans were about to enter a time of testing. God often warns his servants prior to a time of trial (Eze. 2:3-7; Mtt. 10:16-31; Luke 9:23-24; John 16:1-4; Acts 9:16). This gives the saints His *perspective* and great hope knowing that He recognizes what they are going through and yet it remains within His sovereign will and purpose to leave them there (Luke 22:31-32; Rom. 8:28).

the devil is about to throw

The *devil* is called διάβολος [*diabolos*], a compound of δια [*dia*] ("against") and βαλλω [*ballō*] ("to throw"). He is the accuser of the brethren (Rev. 12:10) who "throws against" them his accusations (Job 1:6; Zec. 3:1-2).

Oppression often comes by way of *people* , but Scripture identifies the motivating powers behind the scene (Eph. 6:12). The early church understood this fact:

> There is nothing more remarkable in the records which have come down to us of the early persecutions, and in this point they singularly illustrate the Scripture before us, than the sense which the confessors and martyrs, and those who afterwards narrate their sufferings and their triumphs, entertain and utter, that these great fights of affliction through which they were called to pass, were the immediate work of the devil, and no mere result of the offended passions, prejudices, or interests of men. The enemies of flesh and blood, as mere tools and instruments, are nearly lost sight of by them in a constant reference to satan as the invisible but real author of all.[70]

When members of the church at Smyrna found themselves in prison, they were to understand that it was *spiritual powers* which had placed them there. This would make it easier to bear the Tribulation and especially to pray for those who persecuted them (Mtt. 5:44).

that you may be tested

The knowledge that their tribulation was within the plan and design of God would provide immeasurable comfort.

God makes use of evil for His own purposes: He allowed a lying spirit to go forth (1K. 22:22; 2Chr. 18:21); He allows Satan to test His saints (Job 1:12; 2:6; Luke 22:31; 2Cor. 12:7; Rev. 20:8); and wayward believers to be chastened by evil (1Cor. 5:5; 1Ti. 1:20). God even uses demons in judgment (Rev. 9:15; 16:14). God allowed Satan to test Jesus in order to illustrate His sinless impeccability (Mtt. 4:1).

> God sifting and winnowing the man to separate his chaff from his wheat, the devil sifting and winnowing him in the hope that nothing else but chaff will be found in him (Luke 22:31).[71]

Scripture is full of God's testing of men. He already knows what is in a man, but does the man? Usually not. Testing makes it self-evident (Gen. 22:1; Ex. 15:25; 16:4; 20:20; Deu. 8:2, 16; 13:3; Jdg. 2:22; 3:1, 4; 2Chr. 32:31; Job 23:10; Ps. 11:4-5; 105:19; Isa. 48:10; Jer. 12:3; 20:12; Luke 4:1; 22:31; Jas. 1:12; Rev. 2:10).

ten days

The briefness of this period may be intended as a motivation for endurance (Isa. 26:20; Ps. 30:5; Mtt. 24:22; 2Cor. 4:17; 1Pe. 1:6)[72]. Hemer suggests the phrase betrays the language of the arena where the Smyrnaean saints might meet their supreme test.[73]

Some have seen the days as allusions to ten historical periods of persecution:

> [To] those who interpret here [an] allusion to the ten persecutions which the Church is often said to have passed through, during the three hundred years of its conflict with heathen Rome . . . it has been objected that this enumeration of exactly ten persecutions is altogether arbitrary; that, if we include in our list only those which had some right to be called general, as extending over the whole Roman empire, the persecutions would not be so many; if all those which reached any one city or province, they would be many more.[74]

It seems best to take this time period as representing ten literal days: "The ten days are literal and refer to an unknown persecution within a definite period of time during the generation to which this message was addressed,"[75] "In the book of Revelation, time zones, be they days, months, or years, are always quite literal, and it is best to take these ten days as being the same."[76] For a survey of different views regarding the meaning of the *ten days* see [Thomas, *Revelation 1-7*, 168-170].

until death

How sobering to receive a personal message from Jesus requesting we remain faithful to the point of death! He Who knows all things is asking these at Smyrna to prepare for the ultimate witness!

The phrase speaks of intensity rather than chronology. "It needs hardly be observed that this *'unto death'* is an intensive, not an extensive, term. Christ does not mean, 'to thy life's end,' contemplating life under the aspect of time; but 'to the sharpest and worst which the enemy can inflict upon thee, even to death itself.' "[78]

At a later date, *Polycarp*[5.2.55], bishop of Smyrna, proved faithful "until death":

> We learn from that precious document, the *Epistle of the Church of Smyrna* recording the martyrdom of Polycarp, that Jews [those of the *synagogue of Satan*] joined with heathens in crying out in the amphitheatre that the Christian bishop should be cast to the lions; and when there was a difficulty about this, that he should be burned alive; which being granted, the Jews, as was their wont . . . were forwardest in bringing logs for the pile; they, too, doing all that lay in their power to hinder the remains of the martyr from being delivered to his followers for burial.[79]

The death of His saints throughout history stands as the ultimate witness to the belief in eternal life provided to those who have believed upon His name (Rev. 12:11).

crown of life

They were to understand that death would be merely a transition for them. An exit from this world and an entry into His presence where all suffering is behind. "The thought then is that the time of interim suffering is likely to terminate in actual death, not the mere threat of it, but that death for the Christian is the prelude to life."[80]

The crown of life represents eternal life, and as here, is found in association with steadfast continuance in the faith (Jas. 1:12):

> But in accordance with your hardness and your impenitent heart you are treasuring up for yourself wrath in the day of wrath and revelation of the righteous judgment of God, who "will render to each one according to his deeds": **eternal life to those who by patient continuance in doing good seek for glory, honor, and immortality**; but to those who are self-seeking and do not obey the truth, but obey unrighteousness—indignation and wrath. (Rom 2:5-8). [emphasis added]

The church at Smyrna was told to be *faithful* to receive the crown, for temptation and weariness are ever near along the Christian path (Rev. 3:11). See *Crowns*[4.6].

3.2.11 - Revelation 2:11

let him hear what the Spirit says to the churches

See commentary on *Revelation 2:7*[3.2.7].

He who overcomes

See *Who is the Overcomer?*[4.15.1.3]

shall not

The double-negative οὐ μὴ [*ou mē*] emphasizing the impossibility of being hurt by the second death. "It is the strongest negative assertion about the future of which the Greek language is capable."[81]

second death

Although members of the church would experience martyrdom (the first death), they would be assured of avoiding the dreaded second death—the Lake of Fire. See *Births, Deaths, and Resurrections*[3.20.6.1]. It is by way of the *second birth*, being "born again," that a person moves from the category of the second resurrection to the first resurrection. Over those, "the second death has no power" (Rev. 20:6). The promise to the overcomer is given to all those who come to faith in Jesus Christ—they need not fear the second death, being cast into the *Lake of Fire* (Rev. 20:14). No believer ever finds his way to the second death. "But the cowardly, unbelieving, abominable, murderers, sexually immoral, sorcerers, idolaters, and all liars shall have their part in the lake which burns with fire and brimstone, which is the second death" (Rev. 21:8).

3.2.12 - Revelation 2:12

the angel

See the discussion concerning the identity of the angel at *Revelation 1:20*[3.1.20].

the church of Pergamos

See *Seven Churches of Asia*[4.15].

Temple of Dionysus in Pergamum [82]

> Pergamos, now Bergamo, the ancient metropolis of Mysia, and the residence of the Attalian kings, is situated on the river Ciacus, about sixty miles north of Smyrna, in long. 27 degrees East lat. 39 degrees 11 minutes North. It still retains some measure of its ancient importance; containing a population of about 15,000 souls, and having nine or ten mosques, two churches, and one synagogue.[83]

Pergamos served as the capital of Alexander's successor, Lysimachus and was bequeathed to Rome by Attalus III. At one time "it had a vast library of 200,000 volumes, which was moved by Antony to Egypt and presented to Cleopatra."[84]

> Pergamum was a university city, famous for its library of 200,000 parchment scrolls, second only in size to the library of Alexandria in Egypt. Indeed, parchment was invented in Pergamum, for when its king decided to establish a library and enticed Alexandria's librarian to head up his library, the Egyptian king banned the export of *papyrus*[5.2.53] to Pergamum. This forced Pergamum's scholars to find an alternate writing material, and they invented parchment. Parchment lasts much better than papyrus, so this invention played a big part in preserving the Bible for us.[85]

> It used to be common to credit Eumenes II, king of Pergamum shortly after 200 B.C., with the invention of parchment. Eumenes was building up his library to rival the great library of King Ptolemy in Alexandria. The king of Egypt moved to cut off the supply of papyrus to Pergamum, and in response Eumenes was forced to develop "parchment." This story is true if taken in the sense that Eumenes was the first to make use of parchment or leather; for long before the second century, animal skins for writing were unquestionably in use. In Egypt, for example, mention is made of leather documents as far back as 2500 B.C. . . . So Eumenes was by no means the first to use animal skins for writing, although he may have developed and perfected a better process for treating the skins. Whatever the case, Pergaumum and parchment are indisputably connected, the word "parchment" being derived from the Greek term *pergamene*.[86]

> The fame of Pergamum rested chiefly on its religious preeminence. A tetrad of local deities, Zeus Soter, Athena Nicephoros, Dionysius, Kathegemon, Asklepios Soter, presided over the city; the temple of Athena almost crowned the acropolis, and beneath it, on the slope of the hill and visible from the agora, stood a great *al fresco* altar of the Pergamene Zeus. Still more celebrated was the Pergamene cult of Asklepios, to whose temple there was attached a school of medicine which attracted sufferers from all quarters. . . . What Artemis was to Ephesus, such was Asklepios to Pergamum.[87]

Asklepios was the deity of medicine: "Aesculapius (whence our word 'scalpel') being worshiped, commonly under the sign of a coiled snake on a pole (note Numbers 21:8-9)."[88]

the sharp two-edged sword

The significance in Christ's title can be seen in the *doctrinal errors* of the Balaamites (Rev. 2:14) and *Nicolaitans*[5.2.47] (Rev. 2:15) which are being promoted by some in the church at Pergamum. These doctrinal errors are judged by the teachings found in the Word of God. "It is the first negative introduction of Christ because the Pergamum church faced *imminent*[5.2.30] judgment."[89] See commentary on *Revelation 1:16*[3.1.16].

3.2.13 - Revelation 2:13

I know

See commentary on *Revelation 2:2*[3.2.2].

where Satan's throne is

In Pergamum., two saviors competed with the One True Savior. Asklepios, associated with the serpent, was said to be savior because of his healing power.[90] Zeus was also considered a savior. Some believe this reference to *Satan's throne* goes beyond a general recognition of the pagan religious practices which flourished at Pergamum and denotes the throne-like altar of Zeus Soter, so dominant as to typify Satanic heathendom.[91] The obsessive serpent-motif of its sculptures and the title 'Sotre' [savior], like a blasphemous parody of its Christian use would alike give point to this identification.[92] "The most splendid monument of Pergamum was the 'altar of Zeus,' 12 m (40 ft) high, that once crowned its acropolis and was later reconstructed in East Berlin. . . . This lofty pagan shrine could have been the 'Satan's throne.' "[93]

It is also possible the phrase *Satan's throne* may principally be in recognition of the place of Pergamum in relation to emperor worship:

> Most commentators see the principal or only background in the position of Pergamum as the centre of emperor worship. This was the present threat to the church, and the reminder that Christ has the 'sharp two-edged ῥομφαία [*romphaia*]' is then set against the proconsul's *ius gladii*. It was on this ground that the Christian faced the actual threat of Roman execution. . . . It is well known that Domitian required to be addressed as *dominus et deus* ["Lord and God"].[94]

> Inscriptions proclaim the dignity of the city as the first in Asia to erect a temple to Augustus; and as it was the first, so it continued to be the chief Asian set of the emperor-cult.[95]

> The major threat to Christians in Pergamum came from its role as a center of emperor worship in Asia, a function that went with it being the capital city. Caesar worship required each citizen, once a year, to offer a pinch of incense to Caesar on his altar and profess him as Lord. The citizen was then given a certificate valid for one year which allowed him to worship whatever god or gods he preferred with impunity.[96]

Satan's throne may also denote the activities of the secret mystery religions at Pergamum:

> Alexander Hislop, in his famous book *Two Babylons*, gave much documentation to show that Pergamos had inherited the religious mantle of ancient Babylon when Babylon fell in the days of Belshazzar. The priests, who had kept the secrets of the ancient mystery religious centered at Babylon ever since the days of Nimrod, were forced to migrate at that time, transferring what amounted to the headquarters of Satan's religious system away from Babylon north and west to Pergamos.[97]

Antipas

A faithful saint, unknown to history, but not missed in the records of Christ. Precious is the death of His saints (Ps. 116:15)! His name means either *like the Father*[98] or *against all*.[99] Nothing reliable is known of him, although "according to tradition he was burned to death in a bronze bull. Little else is know of him, but his testimony must have been dramatic and the knowledge of his sacrifice widespread."[100] It is likely that Antipas died for refusing to worship the emperor. "Antipas, the city's Christian martyr, was the victim of Rome, because only the imperial cultus had the power of capital punishment."[101] He had been faithful until death and had earned the crown of life (Rev. 2:10).

3.2.14 - Revelation 2:14

Balaam

What a mix of zeal and error at this church! Antipas had stood firm in faith to the point of death, yet others within the same fellowship were promoting unscriptural teaching.

A number of commentators understand the conjunction which begins *Revelation 1:15*[3.1.15] as an indication of an emphatic comparison made between Balaam and the *Nicolaitans*[5.2.47].[102] It is thought that the doctrine of the Nicolaitans may have promoted licentiousness, in common with that of Balaam. Both are treated in our discussion of the *Nicolaitans*[4.13].

> The teaching of Balaam was encouragement of corruption by intermarriage resulting in fornication and idolatry. No doubt in the city of Pergamum intermarriage with the pagan world was a real problem. Because civil and religious life were so intertwined, for believers to accept social engagements probably meant some involvement with paganism.[103]

stumbling block

Σκάνδαλον [*Skandalon*] can be used to describe a trap, more specifically the trigger of the trap upon which the bait is laid.[104] In the case of Balaam, the bait which brought about the downfall of Israel was the desire of the men for sexual relations with the women of Moab. And so we come upon the tragic pattern of temptation, brought about both by Satan and our flesh. That which God has ordained for His purposes is twisted in unnatural ways to become the means of our downfall. Sexual relations, designed as the means of procreation within the confines of marriage (1Cor. 7:2; Heb. 13:4), becomes the lure leading to fornication and adultery.

This warping aspect of ungodly desire is in view when Paul writes to the believer's in Rome telling them to "reckon yourselves dead indeed to sin" (Rom. 6:10), for they had "died with Christ" (Rom. 6:8). The believer is to be dead to sin: *dead things do not respond to stimulus.* It is by stimulus of our ungodly desires that Satan and our flesh achieve their most damaging results. Satan is a master at providing what we desire, be it status, wealth, or a host of other *wants* so long as he is successful at getting us to compromise and participate in an ungodly activity.

Jesus did not succumb to the tempter because there was nothing within the desire of Jesus that was outside of the will of the Father (John 14:30). Therefore, Satan lacked a "handle" by which he could manipulate the Son of God (Mtt. 4:3). Jesus warns us not to be the instrument by which bait is placed (Mtt. 18:7). Even our Christian liberty can become a stumbling block for others (1Cor. 8:9).

things sacrificed to idols

Εἰδωλόθυτα [*Eidōlothyta*] "refers to sacrificial meat, part of which was burned on the altar, part was eaten at a solemn meal in the temple, and part was sold in the market for home use."[105] This message was mainly to Gentile converts at Pergamum since Judaism prohibited this practice (Num. 25:2; Ps. 106:28; Dan. 1:8). The church at Pergamum was integrated into the culture, rather than being *set apart.*

> [Christians] were expected to pay their "dues" to trade guilds by attending annual dinners held in honor of the guilds' patron deities. Homage to the emperor as divine was included along with worship of such local deities.[106]

The dietary restrictions imposed upon Gentiles by the Jerusalem Council (Acts 15:20, 15:29) were out of concern for retaining Gentile fellowship with Jewish believers. Paul allows such meat sacrificed to idols to be eaten (1Cor. 8:7; 10:18-33), but only when it does not cause offense to brothers. Here the issue was one of compromising the witness of the church within the pagan culture and partaking of pagan practices which were associated with such banquets. These dinners included the eating of meat sacrificed to idols as well as licentious behavior. See *Worldly Churches*[4.18].

to commit sexual immorality

Πορνεῦσαι [*Porneusai*]: "To give one's self to unlawful sexual intercourse."[107] This may have referred either to physical relations connected with the pagan feasts or be a description of the idolatry practiced by the church at Pergamum which participated in pagan ritual.

3.2.15 - Revelation 2:15

thus you also have

The phrase *thus . . . also have* indicates "a similarity between the teaching of Balaam and the *Nicolaitans*[5.2.47]."[108]

The problem for the church at Pergamum was not that Nicolaitans existed in the city, but that they were *within the church.* We are to separate from those who call themselves believers, but deny Christ by their actions (1Cor. 5:11).

Nicolaitans

See *Nicolaitans*[4.13].

3.2.16 - Revelation 2:16

repent

An imperative command: repent!

I will come to you quickly

A futuristic use of the present tense, ἔρχομαι [*erchomai*], *I am coming.* If the saints at Pergamum do not repent, His arrival is *imminent*[5.2.30]! He is already on His way! Here it seems best to understand *quickly* as denoting a spiritual coming in judgment upon the *Nicolaitans*[5.2.47]. No mention of such a sect extends beyond the early church. "This 'coming,' like that of Revelation 2:5, is not our Lord's second advent, but His entering *personally* and that *quickly*, upon their affairs *judicially*."[109]

sword of my mouth

If Trench is correct in correlating the *Nicolaitans* with the *doctrine of Balaam* , then this may be an allusion to Num. 31:8 (cf. Jos. 13:22; Num. 22:31).[110] The church at Pergamum had not been upholding sound biblical teaching. The teaching of the Nicolaitans did not measure up to the "Sword of the Spirit," the Word of God (Eph. 6:17) and would be defeated. See commentary on *Revelation 1:16*[3.1.16].

3.2.17 - Revelation 2:17

let him hear what the Spirit says to the churches

See commentary on *Revelation 2:7*[3.2.7].

overcomes

See *Who is the Overcomer?*[4.15.1.3]

hidden manna

The *manna* is set in direct contrast to the *things sacrificed to idols*. The church was eating *earthly pagan* food, but the overcomer is promised *heavenly* food from above.

When Israel was in the wilderness, God supernaturally provided manna for their food. Manna was something like white coriander seed and tasted like wafers made of honey (Ex. 16:31; Num. 11:7). The manna was provided for a period of forty years (Ex. 16:35) until Israel crossed the Jordan (Jos. 5:12). Manna provided life in a barren wilderness and is even called "angel's food" (Ps. 78:23-25).

In an intentional comparison between Himself and the feeding of Israel in the wilderness, Jesus fed the multitude (John 6:1-14). Afterwards, Jesus taught the significance of the event, which was not found in the miracle itself, but in what it *signified*:

> "Our fathers ate the manna in the desert; as it is written, 'He gave them bread from heaven to eat.' " Then Jesus said to them, "Most assuredly, I say to you, Moses did not give you the bread from heaven, but My Father gives you the true bread from heaven. For the bread of God is He who comes down from heaven and gives life to the world." Then they said to Him, "Lord, give us this bread always." And Jesus said to them, "I am the bread of life. He who comes to Me shall never hunger, and he who believes in Me shall never thirst." (John 6:31-35)

Jesus is the true manna which gives eternal life. The manna in the wilderness sustained the Israelites for a time, but they still died in the wilderness:

> "I am the bread of life. Your fathers ate the manna in the wilderness, and are dead. This is the bread which comes down from heaven, that one may eat of it and not die. I am the living bread which came down from heaven. If anyone eats of this bread, he will live forever; and the bread that I shall give is My flesh, which I shall give for the life of the world." (John 6:48-51)

The overcomer has faith in Christ and is a partaker of His flesh given on our behalf. Thus he has eternal life:

> "As the living Father sent Me, and I live because of the Father, so he who feeds on Me will live because of Me. This is the bread which came down from heaven—not as your fathers ate the manna, and are dead. He who eats this bread will live forever." (John 6:57-58)

This manna is said to be *hidden*. "There can, I think, be no doubt that allusion is here to the manna which at God's express command Moses caused to be laid up before the Lord in the Sanctuary (Ex. 16:32-34; cf. Heb. 9:4). This manna, as being thus laid up in the Holy Place, obtained the name of 'hidden.' "[111]

> The allusion is ultimately traceable to Ex. 16:32-34, where the Lord commanded a sample of manna to be preserved as a memorial for future generations. Tradition was quick to explain its subsequent disappearance. It was taken to have been originally kept in the ark of the covenant (cf. Heb. 9:4), and on the destruction of Solomon's temple Jeremiah, according to 2 Macc. 2:4-7, was warned to take the *tabernacle*[5.2.69], the ark and its contents to Sinai and there hide them underground. There they would remain until the coming of the Messiah, when Jeremiah would reappear and deposit them in the new Messianic temple in Jerusalem. A variant in *2 Baruch* 6:7-10, ascribing their concealment to an angel, is almost contemporary with the Revelation. neither of these passages mentions manna, but its inclusion in

this tradition is inferred from Heb. 9:4 and explicit in the Rabbinic sources (so Yoma 52b).[112]

Christ Himself may be considered *hidden manna*, being no longer visible since His ascension:

> Life eternal commences on this side of the grave, and not first on the other; and here in the wilderness Christ is the bread from heaven, the bread of God, the true manna, of which those that eat shall never die (John 6:31-33, 48-51). Nay, more than this; since his Ascension he is in some sort a *"hidden manna"* for them now.[113]

> The fact that the manna is described as "hidden," points to the mystery of eternal life, a mystery that is only perceived through faith. The hidden (or secret) manna seems to be the bread of life which is a secret from all who have not experienced the saving grace of Jesus Christ.[114]

Eating the manna may also be an allusion to participation in the marriage supper of the Lamb (Rev. 19:9).[115] Bullinger sees a literal fulfillment in the nourishment of Israel in the future wilderness (Rev. 12:14).[116]

From the perspective of the saints at Pergamum, the *hidden manna* was a reminder of God's provision in spite of deprivation. "The person leaving the state church might be deprived of his job and welfare. But in spite of what he may be deprived of, God will provide his sustenance."[117]

white stone

In understanding the *white stone*, we meet with a tendency of many interpreters to derive an understanding of scriptural imagery from pagan cultural practices.[118] See *Searching for Meaning in all the Wrong Places*[2.7.5.4].

A number of alternative interpretations have been offered for the meaning of the *white stone*.

1. **Token of Innocence** - A white pebble was placed in a ballot box by a Greek judge pronouncing a sentence of acquittal (a black pebble indicating condemnation). *Stone* is ψῆφον [*psēphon*]: "The word means (lit.) pebble, but has a secondary meaning of 'vote,' for the same word is used in Acts 26:10."[119] "There are many opinions on what the white stone represents, but when we note that Acts 26:10 uses the same Greek word for 'vote,' then we can advance a strong case that the white stone may well represent a vote of innocence. It then depicts the believer's new character and symbolically denotes the purity which flows from the cleansing from sin that takes place at conversion."[120] "This white stone is absolution from the guilt of sin, alluding to the ancient custom of giving a white stone to those acquitted on trial and a black stone to those condemned."[121]

2. **Token of Privilege** - A *tessera* (also called ψῆφος [*psēphos*]) was given at Olympic games to the victor with subsequent attendant social privileges. Allusion has been seen to yet another kind of *tessera*, one supposedly given to a gladiator at his discharge from the arena, exempting him from the obligation to risk his life again there. Many such tokens survive. They take the form of elongated rectangular tablets of bone bearing the name of a man, the letters 'SP', and the day and year, often incised in sequence on the four faces.[122]

3. **Token of Initiation** - A token of initiation into the cult of Asklepios. "Roman examples were sometimes dated on the first of January, a day said to have been a festival of Asklepios. None of the known specimens is from Pergamum, but the importance of the Asklepios cult there . . . lends a strong circumstantial appeal to the theory."[123]

4. **Good Omen** - Reflecting the practice of a person who placed a white or black pebble for each happy or unhappy day into an urn. At his death, the colors were totaled to rate the happiness of his life.

5. **High Priest's Headdress** - "One explanation links the white stone with the platelet of gold that graced the high priest's headdress (Ex. 28:36-37). The words inscribed on it were 'Holiness to the Lord.' According to this interpretation the overcomer will wear a headdress with a precious stone, on which shall be engraved the new name which belongs to the new Lord of the new kingdom, a name equivalent in value to that of Jehovah under the Old

Testament, which no one but the high priest knew how to utter."[124]

6. **High Priest's Breastplate** - "Another explanation from Jewish customs is that the imagery of the white stone originated with the twelve stones in the high priest's breastplate. The names of each of the twelve tribes in Israel were inscribed on the stones. One difficulty with this view is that the stones in the breastplate were not white (Ex. 28:17-21). Another problem is that while the priest's breastplate had twelve stones, Revelation 2:17 mentions only one stone."[125]

7. **Urim and Thummim** - Trench supposes the white stone may be a diamond, the same stone which is the Urim and Thummim.[126] "The stone is *white* or 'bright,' the Greek term λευκό [*leuko*] can refer either to the color white (traditional here) or to an object that is bright or shining, either from itself or from an outside source of illumination."[127] "The word Urim means 'light,' answering to the color white. None but the high priest knew the name written upon it, probably the incommunicable name of God, 'Jehovah.' The high priest consulted it in some divinely appointed way to get direction from God when needful. The 'new name' is Christ's (compare Rev. 3:12, 'I will write upon him My new name'): some new revelation of Himself which shall hereafter be imparted to His people, and which they alone are capable of receiving. The connection with the 'hidden manna' will thus be clear, as none save the high priest had access to the 'manna hidden' in the sanctuary."[128] "A third explanation for the white stone is based on the Urim and Thummim in the high priest's breastplate. The Urim and Thummim may have been stones, with names meaning 'lights' and 'perfections,' related to the revelation of God's will (Ex. 28:30; Num. 27:21; Deu. 33:8; 1S. 28:6). This suggestion seems possible for several reasons. (a) The promised stone in Revelation 2:17 could be white in the sense that it will have a whitish glisten. If Urim means lights, then it too could have had a whitish appearance. (b) Any engraving on the Urim was known only to the priest. This corresponds with the name written on the promised stone known only by the person who receives it. (c) Since the hidden manna Christ promised in the same verse is analogous to the Old Testament manna, the white stone could also be analogous to an Old Testament stone. It appears then that if Christ intended His audience to see an analogy between His white stone and the Urim, His reward would be experiencing God's will fully."[129] "The white stone presumably is a sparkling diamond, perhaps answering to the *Urim* ('lights') also worn in Aaron's breastplate (Leviticus 8:8). . . . [This was] were worn by the high priest when he would enter into the holy place into the presence of the Lord. He alone could then have access to the ark of the covenant wherein reposed the hidden manna."[130]

8. **Stone Tablets of the Law** - "A fourth explanation in Jewish custom for the white stone connects it with the stones on which God inscribed His moral will (i.e., the Ten Commandments). Rosscup, who suggests this view, points out that this connection 'could be directly relevant . . . to sins at Pergamum committed against God"s moral standard (Rev. 2:14-23). As the overcomer received and honored the Word disclosing God's Person and will, Christ assures [him] that he is to receive the ultimate disclosure of God's Person and will. His symbol for this is the 'white stone." ' This view is also possible for several reasons. (a) It is consistent in seeing both the manna and the stone as imageries from the same era in Israel's history. (b) It fits with other rewards in Revelation 2 which also reach back to the Old Testament (e.g., the tree of life [Rev. 2:7], from Genesis 2 and 3; the crown of life, not the second death [Rev. 2:10-11], going back also to Genesis 2 and 3; the rod of authority and the morning star [Rev. 2:26-28], from Psalm 2 and Numbers 24). (c) The idea of what 'God had written' (Rev. 2:17) is also emphasized with regard to the stones of the Law (Ex. 32:15-16). (d) The Lord made His name prominent and repeated it in writing on the stones of the Law, as in Exodus 20. (e) This view also suits the context of Revelation 2. Standing against the sin-darkening environment, the overcomer honors the value of God's moral law associated with His will (Rev. 2:14-15; cf. Rev. 2:20-23). So Christ will honor him with the ultimate enjoyment that relates to knowing and doing God's will."[131]

We believe it is inappropriate to base the interpretation of symbols within the book of Revelation upon *pagan, non-Jewish cultural practices*[2.7.5.4] . The Bible is an *inspired*[5.2.33] Jewish book (Rom. 3:2;

9:4), so we should not expect to find our answers in practices or beliefs which are considered blasphemous by God. When we apply the *Golden Rule of Interpretation*[5.2.24], *we compare Scripture with Scripture* to gain an understanding of the text. If this premise is true, and we believe it is, then it rules out all but the last four views as being contenders for understanding the *white stone*.

Of the last four views, we believe the last two views are most likely connected with this passage.

The *white stone* does not stand alone in our text for *on the stone* there will be *a new name written*. Observe several characteristics concerning this passage: (1) the gift given is a *stone*; (2) the stone is *white*; (3) the stone is *written* upon; (4) the writing conveys a *name*. We believe these factors connect the stone with the Stone Tablets of the Law given to Moses and upon which was recorded God's moral law, the *Ten Commandments* (Ex. 20:1-17; 24:12; 34:2, 29). Throughout Scripture, names convey the *character* of the one bearing the name. It is no coincidence that when God met with Moses for the second time to write the tablets of the law, He proclaimed His *character* (Ex. 34:6-7). The record of the law written on stone is a reflection of God's character.

As for the *white* aspect of the stone, we note the command given to Joshua when the law was renewed prior to crossing the Jordan:

> And it shall be, on the day when you cross over the Jordan to the land which the LORD your God is giving you, that you shall set up for yourselves large stones, and **whitewash them with lime. You shall write on them all the words of this law**, when you have crossed over, that you may enter the land which the LORD your God is giving you, 'a land flowing with milk and honey,' just as the LORD God of your fathers promised you. Therefore it shall be, when you have crossed over the Jordan, *that* on Mount Ebal you shall set up these stones, which I command you today, and you shall **whitewash them with lime**. And there you shall build an altar to the LORD your God, an altar of stones; you shall not use an iron *tool* on them. You shall build with whole stones the altar of the LORD your God, and offer burnt offerings on it to the LORD your God. You shall offer peace offerings, and shall eat there, and rejoice before the LORD your God. And you shall write very plainly on the stones all the words of this law. (Deu. 27:2-8) [emphasis added]

This command was later fulfilled by Joshua (Jos. 8:32). The written law upon the tablets of stone was a picture of how one day God would write the law upon tablets of flesh:

> You are our epistle written in our hearts, known and read by all men; clearly you are an epistle of Christ, ministered by us, written not with ink but by the Spirit of the living God, not on tablets of stone but on tablets of flesh, that is, of the heart. (2Cor. 2:2)

The *white stone* may be a memorial to the law in that it records a *new name* which expresses the character of God to which the believer is being conformed (Rom. 8:29; 1Cor. 15:49; 2Cor. 3:18; Php. 3:21; Col. 3:10).

There is a textual variant at Revelation 15:6 which mentions a white stone, but is generally thought to be a transcriptional error. See commentary on *Revelation 15:6*[3.15.6].

new name written

There are two possibilities concerning this *new name*. Either it is a new name given to the *overcomer* or it is the new name *of God* given to the overcomer in the church at Philadelphia (Rev. 3:12).

> This may indicate one or more of three main ideas. First, the name might be a new name Christ will give to each believer. It will be appropriately different for each overcomer and no one except the one who receives it will know the name. Second, the name might be the same for all believers. It will be known to all victors (all believers) just as the things of God are known (in different degree) to all believers (1Jn. 2:20, 27; 1Cor. 2:15-16). This view also fits with the Lord's promises in Isaiah that He will give to His people—all of them in common—a "new name" (Isa. 62:2; cf. 56:5; 65:15). Third, the name might be that of God the Father or of Christ Himself, a common heritage for all overcomers. In favor of this view is the parallel passage in Revelation 3:12, which says the name Christ will give is God's own name. (Further support is in Revelation 14:1 and 22:4, which refer to God's name on the foreheads of the 144,000 and all believers in the New Jerusalem.) This name could be a name of God that He deems appropriate for His own as an expression of the fact that they belong to Him (cf. Isa. 56:5; 62:2; 65:15). Also, as already noted, the white stone may allude to the stones of the Law on which God wrote His name (Ex. 20).[132]

The name is *new*: "Gr. *kainos* , new in quality, use, application, or character, as opposed to being new in time; see Mtt. 9:17 where contrasting terms occur together, kainos being second, applied to wineskins which were not brand new (as was the wine), but simply not having been used before, unused. See the use of kainos at John 13:34."[133]

Isaiah described how God would give a name to those who follow after Him—even to those who were not Jews:

> Even to them I will give in My house and within My walls a place and a name better than that of sons and daughters; I will give them an everlasting name that shall not be cut off. Also the sons of the foreigner who join themselves to the LORD, to serve Him, and to love the name of the LORD, to be His servants-everyone who keeps from defiling the Sabbath, and holds fast My covenant—even them I will bring to My holy mountain, and make them joyful in My house of prayer. Their burnt offerings and their sacrifices *Will be* accepted on My altar; for My house shall be called a house of prayer for all nations. The Lord GOD, who gathers the outcasts of Israel, says, yet I will gather to him *Others* besides those who are gathered to him. (Isa. 56:5-8)

Whether the name is that of God or a new name given the believer, it describes the new character and inheritance of the believer (2Cor. 5:17; Eph. 4:24) who has been adopted into the family of God. "The new name is the name of adoption: adopted persons took the name of the family into which they were adopted."[134]

no one knows except him

The name is secret—known only to the one who receives the stone. Full disclosure of the things of God is reserved for those who share intimacy with Him, who know Him and are known by Him. This pattern is seen in the great revelation given to those who had an especially close relationship with God such as Moses, Daniel, and John (Ps. 25:14; Mtt. 11:27). God spoke to Moses "face to face, as a man speaks to his friend" (Ex. 33:11). Daniel was "greatly beloved" of God (Dan. 9:23; 10:11, 19). John was the disciple "whom Jesus loved" (John 13:23; 20:2; 21:7, 20).

The name is unknown, as is Jesus' new name (Rev. 3:12; Rev. 19:12). This recalls the mysterious, but unrevealed name attending the Angel of the Lord and Son of God throughout Scripture. The name is hinted at, but never revealed: when Jacob wrestled with the Angel and was named Israel (Gen. 32:29); when the Angel announced the birth of Samson to his parents (Jdg. 13:6, 18); in the question concerning the Son of God (Pr. 30:4); and in God's new name to be written on the overcomer (Rev. 3:12).

Him may refer to the *category of all overcomers*—that the new name of God is only known to believers. If it refers to the *individual*, then it would seem to imply that a different name is revealed to each overcomer.[135] If the latter, then the name may be that given to the individual overcomer, or perhaps a different name revealing one of the many facets of God's character is given to each.

receives it

The one who *knows* the name is the one who receives the *stone*. "*It* refers not to the *name*, but to the *stone* (containing the *name*)."[136]

3.2.18 - Revelation 2:18

the angel

See the discussion concerning the identity of the angel at *Revelation 1:20*[3.1.20].

church in Thyatira

See *Seven Churches of Asia*[4.15].

Thyatira means "sacrifice of labor; odor of affliction."[137]

***Excavations at Thyatira*[138]**

> Thyatira is very rarely mentioned in ancient literature, and its site is covered by the modern town of Akhisar, which betrays few outward signs of its past and whose presence has prevented excavation. . . . Thyatira is first know to us as a Seleucid colony, whose foundation is ascribed to Seleucus Nicator at the time of his war with Lysimachus. . . . The increasing abundance of later inscriptions suggests that Thyatira, still of limited importance at the time of the Revelation, reached a peak of prosperity in the second and third centuries. The words of Rev. 2:19 were addressed to a growing church in a growing city.[139]

> The most outstanding feature in Thyatiran life was probably the institution of trade-guilds. . . . At Thyatira there were guilds of bakers, potters, workers in brass, tanners, leather-cutters, workers in wool and flax, clothiers, dyers; the workers in wool and the dyers were probably the most numerous, for the manufacture and dyeing of woollen goods was a Lydian speciality, in which Thyatira excelled.[140]

> Not surprisingly, religion played no major role in Thyatira's way of life, for it was not a major center of Caesar worship or Greek worship; its local god was Tyrimnus, a horse mounted god, armed with a battle-ax and a club. The only notable thing about Thyatira religiously was that it was home to the oracle Sambethe, an oracle presided over by a female fortune teller.[141]

This church may have been established from Paul's ministry to Lydia (Acts 16:14). "At the riverside at Philippa Lydia, a seller of purple of Thyatira became the first recorded Christian convert in Macedonia (Acts 16:14)."[142]

> Thyatira was famous for a purple or crimson dye manufactured from the madder root, which was a cheap rival for the expensive Phoenician murex dye made from a particular marine shellfish. Acts 16:14 attests to this specialty, for the Philippian convert, Lydia, was a seller of purple fabrics who hailed from Thyatira (she was 300 miles from her home city).[143]

Son of God

Frequent allusions to Psalm 2 in the letter to Thyatira underscore both the judgment of *Jezebel*[5.2.35] and her children (Rev. 2:22-23) and the promises made to the overcomer who is given "power over the nations" (Rev. 2:26). (See Rev. 2:18 cf. Ps. 2:9; Rev. 2:26 cf. Ps. 2:8; Rev. 2:27 cf. Ps. 2:9.[144]) This is the first instance in the letters to the *seven churches*[5.2.66] where the self-identification of Christ is in the form of a title rather than a descriptive attribute.[145]

eyes like a flame of fire

The church at Thyatira had been allowing Jezebel to promote her unscriptural teaching in their midst (Rev. 2:20), but not the slightest detail had escaped the eyes of the Master. As discussed in *Revelation*

1:14[3.1.14], the *eyes like a flame of fire* indicate His omniscience and omnipresence. He is well aware of what is happening within the church at Thyatira, especially those things he opposes (Rev. 2:20).

feet like fine brass

Fine brass is translated from a word of unknown derivation (only occurring here and in Revelation 1:15) which probably denotes bright shining metal or perhaps its purity or hardness. See commentary on *Revelation 1:15*[3.1.15].

The imagery of both eyes and feet is that of impending judgment upon Jezebel and her children (Rev. 2:22-23). The judgment will serve as a witness of His omniscience: "All the churches shall know that I am He who searches the minds and hearts" (Rev. 2:23).

3.2.19 - Revelation 2:19

I know

See commentary on *Revelation 2:2*[3.2.2].

your works, love, service, faith, ... your patience

The ministry ("service," διακονίαν [*diakonian*]) of the saints at Thyatira evidenced the fruit of the Spirit (Gal. 5:22). Their faith was real and made evident by their works (Tit. 3:8, 14; Jas. 2:22). The grammar implies that *love, service, faith*, and *patience* may be an elaboration of their *works* and that their *love* and *faith* are evidenced by their *service* and *patience*. [146]

the last *are* more than the first

"This highly commendable state of affairs was the opposite of what had happened in Ephesus (cf. Rev. 2:5; cf. Mtt; 12:45; 2Pe. 2:10)."[147]

3.2.20 - Revelation 2:20

Nevertheless

The works done at Thyatira did not stand on their own for good works are necessary, *but not sufficient* in Christian service. The world is full of organizations which focus on beneficent works to fellow man. This cannot be the measure of acceptability to God because many of these organizations embrace beliefs and practices which are directly opposed to God's Word (e.g., Shriners, Masons). Therefore, works alone say nothing about an organization's *relationship with God*. It is the sharing of the Gospel of Jesus Christ that makes service Christian.

you allow

In contrast to the church in Ephesus which could not bear false apostles and hated the *Nicolaitans*[5.2.47], the church at Thyatira tolerated a false prophetess, *Jezebel*[5.2.35].

We ourselves do not need to *actively teach or promote error* to come under Christ's corrective judgment. All we need do is *tolerate* those in our midst who do so. The failure to confront those teaching error in our midst is a fundamental error of the modern church and reflects a generation of church-goers more likely to quote Matthew 7:1 than John 3:16.

that woman Jezebel

See *Jezebel*[4.9].

The *MT*[5.2.45] indicates that *Jezebel* may have been the wife of the angel of the church.[148]

calls herself a prophetess

Scripture recognizes numerous women who fulfilled the role of *prophetess* : Miriam, sister of Aaron (Ex. 15:20); Deborah (Jdg. 4:4); Huldah (2K. 22:14); Noadiah (Ne. 6:14);[149] Isaiah's wife (Isa. 8:3);[150] Anna (Luke 2:36); the daughters of Philip the evangelist (Acts 21:9).[151] But nowhere does it record a true prophetess that is *self-proclaimed*.

Jezebel may have been a prophetess of sorts, but her prophetic powers were not from God. "Employing her intellectual faculties in the service of Satan, and not of God; but claiming *inspiration*[5.2.33], and probably possessing it, wielding spiritual powers, only they were such as reached her from beneath, not such as descended on her from above."[152] The Thyatiran church was making the serious mistake of attributing her spiritual powers to God. Unlike the Ephesian church (Rev. 2:2), they had failed to "test the spirits" (1Jn. 4:1).

Perhaps the most telltale aspect of those who are not truly hearing from God is their incessant self-proclamation.[153] This is often evidence of *pride* and an inability to produce the genuine gift of the Spirit which they claim. God's Word indicates a different pattern for those who would serve Him in humility: "Let another man praise you, and not your own mouth; A stranger, and not your own lips" (Pr. 27:2), "For not he who commends himself is approved, but whom the Lord commends" (2Cor. 10:18).

This problem was not unique to the church at Thyatira, for Ezekiel's day experienced it:

> Likewise, son of man, set your face against the daughters of your people, **who prophesy out of their own heart**; prophesy against them, and say, 'Thus says the Lord GOD: "Woe to the *women* who sew *magic* charms on their sleeves and make veils for the heads of people of every height to hunt souls! Will you hunt the souls of My people, and keep yourselves alive? And will you profane Me among My people for handfuls of barley and for pieces of bread, killing people who should not die, and keeping people alive who should not live, **by your lying to My people who listen to lies**?" 'Therefore thus says the Lord GOD: "Behold, I *am* against your *magic* charms by which you hunt souls there like birds. I will tear them from your arms, and let the souls go, the souls you hunt like birds. I will also tear off your veils and deliver My people out of your hand, and they shall no longer be as prey in your hand. Then you shall know that I *am* the LORD. Because with lies you have made the heart of the righteous sad, whom I have not made sad; and you have strengthened the hands of the wicked, so that he does not turn from his wicked way to save his life. Therefore you shall no longer envision futility nor practice divination; for I will deliver My people out of your hand, and you shall know that I *am* the LORD." ' (Eze. 13:17-23) [emphasis added]

How similar this sounds to the modern church which has no shortage of self-proclaimed "prophetesses" who frequent various conferences, peddling their ministries as being inspired by the Holy Spirit while teaching concepts which contradict God's Word.

to teach

"In her own eyes, Jezebel's alleged special revelations from God qualified her as an authoritative teacher in the church. Some others agreed and she became a recognized leader."[154] Scripture indicates that although women can have great wisdom (Pr. 31:26) and work alongside men instructing other believers (Acts 18:26), in the assembly they are not to occupy teaching roles over men (1Cor. 14:34; 1Ti. 2:12). The reason for this prohibition is not *cultural* , but reflects God's created order (1Ti. 2:13) and recognizes differences between men and women (1Ti. 2:14). The teaching role of women is *primarily* to be instructing other women (Tit. 2:3-4) and children (2Ti. 1:5, 3:15).

> The sin, apparently involving the majority of the Thyatira church's members, was twofold. First, they violated the biblical teaching that women are not to be teachers or preachers in the church (1Ti. 2:12). That led them to tolerate the woman Jezebel, who calls herself a prophetess. They compounded their error of permitting her to teach by allowing her to teach error.[155]

In our own day, this Scriptural restriction on the teaching role of women has been twisted by the feminist agenda which distorts the Scriptures using techniques not unlike that of "Christian homosexuals" who deny the plain meaning of the text. As a result, the Christian church is reaping the whirlwind with self-proclaimed prophetesses as well as female "bishops" and pastors usurping roles which God has ordained strictly for men. If a woman believes "God is calling her to be a pastor," she should think again! God does not contravene His own word.

seduce

is πλανᾳ˜ [*plana*] meaning "To cause to stray, to lead astray, lead aside from the right way."[156] Most often, it denotes *deception*, which by its very nature leads astray. Our ability to be led correlates with the strength we give to our desires. Jezebel's seduction was much like that of the Balaamites in the church at Pergamum (Rev. 2:14). See the discussion of *stumbling block* at *Revelation 2:14*[3.2.14].

eat things sacrificed to idols

Jezebel led the church at Thyatira into the same error as the Balaamites in the church at Pergamum:

> Satan seems to have used commerce to undercut the church in Thyatira, for unless one was a member of a trade guild, one had little hope of commercial prosperity; indeed, one's commercial existence was in jeopardy. Two characteristics of these guilds were incompatible with Christianity: first, they held banquets, often in a temple, and these banquets would begin and end with a formal sacrifice to the gods, so the meat eaten at these affairs was meat offered to idols (Acts 15:29). Second, these functions were, as would be expected, occasions of drunken revelry and slack morality.[157]

> Pagan worship was associated with trade guilds in that each guild had its guarding god. Guilds for wool workers, linen workers, manufacturers of outer garments, dyers, leather workers, tanners, potters, bakers, slave dealers, and bronze smiths were known. Membership in a guild was compulsory if one wanted to hold a position. . . . Guild members were expected to attend the guild festivals and to eat food, part of which had been offered to the tutelary deity and which was acknowledged as being on the table as a gift from god. At the end of the feast grossly immoral activities would commence.[158]

See *Worldly Churches*[4.18]. See commentary on *Revelation 2:14*[3.2.14].

3.2.21 - Revelation 2:21

I gave her time

Herein is the evidence of God's grace which is so often turned against Him. Those who complain that a perfect and loving God would not allow such evil in the world need to stop and consider that if He were to step into history at the very next instant to remove all evil, *they themselves* would be guaranteed a place in the Lake of Fire (Rev. 20:15)! Peter explains that the delay of God in judging evil is motivated by His longsuffering and that none should perish. "The Lord is not slack concerning *His* promise, as some count slackness, but is longsuffering toward us, not willing that any should perish but that all should come to repentance" (2Pe. 3:9).

repent

God gave *Jezebel*[5.2.35] time to recognize her error and to change her conduct accordingly, to *repent*: It is always God's desire that men and women would repent and avoid judgment (Eze. 18:30-32; 33:11-15). Concerning the word *repent*, see commentary on *Revelation 2:5*[3.2.5].

she did not repent

Jezebel had been given time to recognize her wickedness and repent, but she would not. Here is introduced the pattern of the enemies of God throughout this book. Even in the face of clear evidence of God's disapproval, those who have set their hearts against Him *refuse* to repent (Rev. 9:20-21; 16:9-11).

We often assume lack of repentance indicates a lack of understanding or the knowledge of evil. Yet Scripture indicates repentance has less to do with the *head* and more to do with the *heart* which is hardened toward God (Ex. 7:13, 23; 8:15, 19, 32; 9:34; Rom 2:5).

3.2.22 - Revelation 2:22

I will cast

A futurist use of the present tense, βαλλω [*ballō*], the judgment is *imminent*[5.2.30] as if it had already begun.

sickbed

Although κλίνην [*klinēn*] may refer to a bed occupied by a sick person (Mtt. 9:2; Mark 7:30; Luke 5:18; Acts 5:15), it may also refer to a couch used for other purposes (Mark 4:21; Luke 8:16; 17:34). Here, the reference to eating things sacrificed to idols would seem to imply a *dining couch*. The root from which it is derived, κλινω [*klinō*], has the meaning "to cause to lean, make to slope or slant"[159] from which we get our word *incline*. This *bed* may refer to a couch on which *Jezebel*[5.2.35] and those who followed her teaching would recline during the pagan feasts.[160] "Ramsay . . . strongly maintained here a reference to the dining-couch of the guild-feasts. It seems likely enough that there are allusions which escape us here through our ignorance of the inner life of the guilds, but the primary meaning is probably "sick-bed"."[161]

Her bed of whoredom will be changed into a bed of anguish.[162]

those who commit adultery

The *adultery* here referred to may have been literal—in connection with the licentious aspects of the guild feasts—or spiritual.

Τοὺς μοιχεύοντας [*Tous moicheuontas*], "those who commit adultery," "A Hebrew idiom, the word is used of those who at a woman's solicitation are drawn away to idolatry, i.e. to the eating of things sacrificed to idols"[163] (Eze. 16:37-41). The activity of Jezebel is a type representing the *Harlot*[5.2.25] of Revelation 17: "With whom the kings of the earth committed fornication, and the inhabitants of the earth were made drunk with the wine of her fornication" (Rev. 17:2).

great tribulation

This exact phrase appears both in Matthew's gospel and later in this book (Mtt. 24:21; Rev. 2:22; 7:14). Although in the context of the letter to Thyatira, it seems best to understand the phrase in its non-technical sense as denoting a personal time of great trouble for the unrepentant prophetess,[164] there are also reasons to take the phrase in its technical sense:

> Since the encouragement to the faithful in Rev. 2:25-26 refers to His second advent, the case for a technical eschatological meaning . . . is still stronger. In consideration that the main body of the Apocalypse (Revelation 4-19) includes a detailed description of this future period, it is exegetically sound to conclude that the threat to the followers of Jezebel is that of being thrust into this period of unparalleled misery.[165]

Even if the Tribulation relates specifically to the woman Jezebel in the church at Thyatira, it does not preclude understanding the passage as a type denoting the fate of the apostate church. The apostate church of the last days, which does not participate in the *Rapture*[5.2.62], remains on earth to enter the Great Tribulation.[166] See *Jacob's Trouble and the Great Tribulation*[2.13.4].

unless they repent

She was already given time and did not repent (Rev. 2:21). Now God gives *one last chance* before bringing judgment. Such is the mercy and grace of God. "The very time during which ungodly men are heaping up for themselves greater wrath against the day of wrath, was a time lent them for repentance (Rom. 2:4; 2Pe. 3:9), if only they would have understood the object and the meaning of it."[167]

their deeds

MT[5.2.45] and *NU*[5.2.49] texts have εργων αὐτῆς [*ergōn autēs*] ("deeds of her") whereas *TR*[5.2.79] has ἔργων αὐτων [*ergōn autōn*] ("deeds of them").

3.2.23 - Revelation 2:23

will kill her children with death

A futuristic use of the present tense: "I am killing". An indication of *imminency*[5.2.30] of the judgment. "Kill with death is a Hebraism for slay with most sure and awful death; so 'dying thou shalt die' (Gen. 2:17)."[168]

Jezebel[5.2.35]'s *children* are probably those who follow her spiritual teaching. "The children of Jezebel possibly included actual illegitimate children of her promiscuity, but the term more definitely refers to her converts. As Timothy was a 'son' of Paul (1 Timothy 1:2) 'in the faith,' so Jezebel had won many to her hedonistic brand of pseudo-Christianity."[169] God will cut them off as were Ahab and Jezebel's children by Jehu (2K. 10:6-7).

shall know

Middle voice, γνώσονται [*gnōsontai*]: "the churches *themselves* shall know."

The judgment of God often serves two purposes: to chasten or eliminate the one being judged; and to serve as warning to others who might otherwise follow a similar path (Deu. 17:13; 19:20; 21:21). The one who led the children of Israel to worship other gods was to be stoned so "all Israel shall hear and fear, and not again do such wickedness as this among you" (Deu. 13:11). When judgment fell upon

Ananias and Sapphira, "great fear came upon all the church and upon all who heard these things" (Acts 5:11).

minds and hearts

Νεφροὺς καὶ καρδίας [*Nephrous kai kardias*], kidneys and hearts, but translated *minds and hearts*.[170] Here is the explanation of Christ's selection of title in the letter to Thyatira: "the Son of God, who has eyes like a flame" (Rev. 2:18). Nothing escapes his gaze. See commentary on *Revelation 1:14*[3.1.14].

God alone searches the minds and hearts, for we ourselves cannot. The condition of our fallen mind and deceitful heart make it an impossible task. "The heart *is* deceitful above all *things*, and desperately wicked; who can know it? I, the LORD, search the heart, *I* test the mind, even to give every man according to his ways, according to the fruit of his doings" (Jer. 17:9-10).

Christ knows the heart of men. "Now when He was in Jerusalem at the Passover, during the feast, many believed in His name when they saw the signs which He did. But Jesus did not commit Himself to them, because He knew all *men*, and had no need that anyone should testify of man, for He knew what was in man" (John 2:23-25).

according to your works

The fellowship in Thyatira, consisting both of believers and unbelievers, would be judged according to their works. The threat of being judged according to our works should send a shiver up the spine of all who are acquainted with their own depravity as a member of Adam's race. Yet multitudes are unaware of how far short their works fall when measured against the requirements of a perfect and Holy God. Rather than recognizing their desperate need of the righteousness of Christ, they continue forward trusting in their own righteousness (Luke 10:29; 18:9; John 9:41; Rom. 10:3) unaware that before God it "is as filthy rags" (Isa. 64:6).

Eventually, God will grant them what they desire—the opportunity to stand before Him and be judged according to *their works*:

> And I saw the dead, small and great, standing before God, and books were opened. And another book was opened, which is *the Book* of Life. And the dead were judged according to their works, by the things which were written in the books. (Rev. 20:12)

At the resurrection of the unsaved dead, the dead are judged according to their works as recorded in "the books." These books will reveal their lack of perfection. Then, another book, the "*Book of Life*[5.2.10]" will be consulted to verify that they have not availed themselves of the blood of Christ to obtain the *righteousness provided by God* (Rom. 3:5, 21-26; 10:3; 2Cor. 5:21; Php. 3:9; Jas. 1:20). Lacking both perfection and a relationship with the Perfect One, they will find their destiny in the Lake of Fire (Rev. 20:15).

Believers too will be judged for their works. But the judgment they face is infinitely different than that of the nonbeliever for it is a judgment *for rewards*. Even if the believer is devoid of works, he himself escapes the wrath of Almighty God (1Cor. 3:13-15), for his righteousness is provided by God Himself (Jer. 23:6).[171]

Biblical faith is to bring forth the fruit of the Spirit and the works thereof which are an indication of true faith:

> It is indeed one of the gravest mischiefs which Rome has bequeathed to us, that in a reaction and protest, itself absolutely necessary, against the false emphasis which she puts on works, unduly thrusting them in to share with Christ's merits in our justification, we often fear to place upon them the true; being as they are, to speak with St. Bernard, the "via regni" [way of royalty], however little the "causa regnandi" [cause of royalty].[172]

3.2.24 - Revelation 2:24

to you . . . and to the rest

You is plural (ὑμῖν [*hymin*]). The question then becomes if *you* refers to the members of the Thyatiran church (and not just the angel), then who are *the rest*? The *MT*[5.2.45] and *NU*[5.2.49] do not have the conjunction "and" (καὶ [*kai*]), and read *to you, the rest*. The *TR*[5.2.79] *kai* could possibly be translated by "even," that is *to you . . . even the rest*. In either case, it appears that *you* and *the rest* denote the same group of individuals: the members of the church at Thyatira beside the angel. Christ's words which have been primarily addressed to the angel (Rev. 2:18, see commentary on *Revelation 1:20*[3.1.20]), are now explicitly broadened to the entire fellowship.

depths of Satan

> Two explanations of 'the deep things of Satan' are widely held: (1) that the phrase is an ironical retort to the claims of *Jezebel*[5.2.35]'s followers to esoteric knowledge of 'the deep things of God'; (2) that the opposition actually boasted of a knowledge of 'the deep things of Satan', saying that the spiritual man should experience all evil to demonstrate his superiority over it.[173]

> He ventures into Satan's strongholds to demonstrate the powerlessness of the enemy over him, or else to learn the real nature of sin in this firsthand way.[174]

> Some may have felt that they could attend trade guild festivities honoring patron gods or acknowledge Caesar as god if called to, since close association with idolatry would enable a Christian to "know the deep things of Satan" (Rev. 2:24) and his inner council. Such knowledge purportedly would allow Christians to know the satanic opponents' deceptive methods so well that they could all the better defeat Satan in the future.[175]

A trademark of all mystery religious and secret societies is the teaching that true knowledge lies below the surface, only attainable by the initiate. By mysterious activities, they purport to know "the deep things of God" (1Cor. 2:10). These "deep mysteries" stand in stark contrast to the simple gospel of Jesus Christ which is hidden from those who *purport to be wise* , but revealed to babes (Ps. 8:2; Mtt. 11:25; Luke 10:21; 2Cor. 11:3).

> The Magians from Babylon continually spoke of their "*deep* things," their "inner knowledge," just as the Theosophists, Christian Scientists, Spiritualists, and "Unity" devotees do today (simply ancient *Gnosticism*[5.2.23] revived!). The Lord sees through all the enemy's delusions and "mysteries"; they are not "deep" to *Him*. . . . It is no sign of spirituality to be familiar with Satanic psychic or demonic "depths."[176]

> They taught, as we know, that it was a small thing for a man to despise pleasure and to show himself superior to it, while at the same time he fled from it. The true, the glorious victory was, to remain superior to it even while tasting it to the full; to give the body to all the lusts of the flesh, and yet with all this to maintain the spirit in a region of its own, uninjured by them; and thus, as it were, to fight against pleasure with the arms of pleasure itself; to mock and defy Satan even in his own kingdom and domain.[177]

The fatal error of such cultish systems is overconfidence in the ability of man and a woeful underestimate of the appetite of the flesh and the schemes of the devil. Weaving webs of sophistry, the resulting philosophy often exchanges truth for error:

> The veneration of the serpent was but the logical development of a theory, the germ of which is common to many of the Gnostic sects. Proceeding on the assumption that the creator of the world is to be regarded as an evil power, a thing in hostility to the supreme God, it follows as a natural consequence that the fall of man through disobedience to the command of his maker must be regarded, not as a transgression against the will of the supreme God, but as an emancipation from the authority of an evil being. The serpent, therefore, who tempted mankind to sin, is no longer their destroyer but their benefactor. He is the symbol of intellect, by whose means the first human pair were raised to the knowledge of the existence of higher beings than their creator. This conception, consistently carried out, would have resulted in a direct inversion of the whole teaching of Scripture; in calling evil good and good evil; in converting Satan into God and God into Satan. [178]

Scripture makes plain we are not called to focus on the darkness, but to focus on the light (Php. 4:8). Paul warned the Colossians against such worldly philosophy which stands opposed to the simplicity which is in Christ:

> Beware lest anyone cheat you through philosophy and empty deceit, according to the tradition of men, according to the basic principles of the world, and not according to Christ. For in Him dwells all the fullness of the Godhead bodily; and **you are complete in Him**, who is the head of all principality and power. (Col. 2:8-10) [emphasis added]

The pattern of those who purport to plumb the depths of Satan is one of *bondage*, not *liberty*.

"Promising liberty to others, being themselves servants of corruption."[179]

3.2.25 - Revelation 2:25

hold fast

An aorist imperative, κρατήσατε [*kratēsate*], "you all hold fast!"[180] Similar instructions are given to the Philadelphian church (Rev. 3:11).

The church at Thyatira was to actively hold onto the good things they had until the coming of Christ (Rev. 2:19). They must be held *fast* in the face of active opposition by the flesh, the devil, and enemies of the church. This is the theme throughout Scripture for those who seek after God.

> I have chosen the way of truth; Your judgments I have laid *before me*. I **cling** to Your testimonies; O LORD, do not put me to shame! I will **run the course** of Your commandments, for You shall enlarge my heart. Teach me, O LORD, the way of Your statutes, and I shall **keep it** *to* the end. Give me understanding, and I shall **keep** Your law; indeed, I shall **observe it** with *my* whole heart. Make me walk in the path of Your commandments, for I delight in it. (Ps. 119:30-35) [emphasis added]

The Christian life is like a greased pole that we are either *actively* climbing up or *passively* sliding down. There is no opportunity to remain stationary.

until I come

The *imminent*[5.2.30] coming of Jesus is an important theme throughout this book (Rev. 1:7. 22:7, 20). That this coming is not a spiritual coming can be seen by the context. The promises of the next few verses are for "he who overcomes until the end" (Rev. 2:26) and include being given authority at the commencement of the millennial reign (Rev. 20:4). See *Imminency*[4.8]. See *Theme*[2.4].

3.2.26 - Revelation 2:26

he who overcomes

See *Who is the Overcomer?*[4.15.1.3]

keeps my works

Jesus spoke of the need for endurance, especially as lawlessness would abound and the love of many grew cold (Mtt. 24:12-13). There are many distractions which can undermine fruitful and consistent development in the Christian life. In the *parable*[5.2.54] of the four soils, Jesus explained that the devil is partly to blame, but that some lacking any root will fall away due to temptation. Still others have their potential works choked by the cares, riches, and pleasures of life. But those who have a noble and good heart hear the word and bear fruit *with patience* (Luke 8:11-15).

Keeping His works requires abiding (μενω [*menō*]) in His word (John 8:31-32). To abide is to "live, dwell, lodge . . . [and is used] of someone who does not leave the realm or sphere in which he finds himself"[181]. Thus, we are to be immersed and *live in* His Word. Otherwise we will not be His disciples and whatever we keep won't be *His works*.

until the end

For the believer, the *end* arrives when either we step through the doorway from this life into the presence of God (2Cor. 5:8) or we remain alive until the coming of the Lord (John 14:3; 1Th. 4:15).

power over the nations

This power can only be given to the overcomer by One who has such power (Gen. 49:10; Ps. 2; Eze. 21:27).[182]

power is εξουσίαν [*exousian*]: "The power exercised by rulers or others in high position by virtue of their office."[183] This authority is not innately the overcomer's, but is *granted* to him by virtue of his *identity with Christ*, for it is Christ who is destined to "rule all nations with a rod of iron" (Rev. 12:5; 19:15). The overcomer will "reign with Him a thousand years" (Rev. 20:6).

3.2.27 - Revelation 2:27

he shall rule them

This promise is closely related to that given to the Laodicean overcomer: "I will grant to sit with Me on My throne as I also overcame and sat down with My Father on His throne." See commentary on *Revelation 3:21*[3.3.21]. See commentary on *Revelation 1:6*[3.1.6]. See commentary on *Revelation 20:6*[3.20.6].

This power *will* be given, He *shall* rule. It is yet future, at the time of the millennial reign of Christ on earth (Mtt. 25:21-23; Luke 19:17-19; Rev. 20:4-6). Of particular interest concerning the timing of this power being granted to the overcomer is the *parable*[5.2.54] Jesus told "because they thought the kingdom of God would appear immediately." In this parable, the nobleman who goes to a far country to receive a kingdom is Jesus returning to the right hand of the Father. The kingdom is received just prior to His Second Coming (Luke 19:15), *after* the *little horn*[5.2.37] is defeated and "the time came for the saints to possess the kingdom" (Dan. 7:22-27). The servants who remain faithful in His absence, like the overcomers at Thyatira, are given authority over cities (Luke 19:11-19). At the end of the *Millennial Kingdom*[5.2.39] when Christ has put down the last of His foes (Rev. 20:9-10), He will then deliver the kingdom to God the Father (1Cor. 15:24-28). The reign of the overcomer extends beyond the Millennial Kingdom into the eternal state (Rev. 22:5).

rod of iron

Unlike other scepters, this scepter is of *iron* indicating His divine prerogative to rule and the impossibility of disobedience. This is a "breaking scepter" (Rev. 12:5; 19:15). "The Lord *is* at Your right hand; He shall execute kings in the day of His wrath. He shall judge among the nations, He shall fill *the places* with dead bodies, He shall execute the heads of many countries" (Ps. 110:5-6).

dashed to pieces

See *Trouble Ahead*[2.13.1].

The allusion here is to Psalm 2. The dashing will take place when Jesus' rule is extended to the ends of the earth—at His return to establish the Millennial Kingdom (Rev. 20:4-6).[184]

> Ask of Me, and I will give *You* the nations *for* Your inheritance, and the ends of the earth *for* Your possession. You shall break them with a rod of iron; You shall dash them to pieces like a potter's vessel. (Ps 2:8-9)
>
> The Hebrew word for "Thou shalt *break*," and that for "Thou shalt *rule*," only differ in their vowels; their consonants are identical; at the same time the parallelism of the latter half of the verse, "Thou shalt dash them in pieces like a potter's vessel," leaves no doubt that "Thou shalt break" was the intention of the Psalmist.[185]
>
> Christ shall rule them with a sceptre of iron to make them capable of being ruled with a scepter of gold; severity first, that grace may come after.[186]

During the millennial reign, the saints are destined to execute vengeance on the nations and judge according to the written judgment of God (Ps. 149:5-9).

like potter's vessels

"The allusion . . . is apt in view of the known existence of a guild of potters in Thyatira."[187] The clay of the potter was originally intended to be formed and fashioned according to the purpose of the potter (Isa. 29:16; 64:8; Jer. 18:1-11). Since the clay refuses to serve its intended purpose, it is the right of the potter to dash it to pieces (Isa. 41:25; 45:9; Dan. 2:35, 43-44).

received from My Father

God cares as much or more about the *means* as the *ends*. Many Christians would do well to remember this when seeking the miraculous from questionable sources. The Son would only receive the kingdom from the *Father*, not from *Satan* (Luke 4:5-8).

There is a divine chain of authority: Father to Son to believer. The Son has authority because He is under authority and likewise the believer. This authority is forfeited when the chain is broken. The centurion, in explaining *his* authority said that he, like Jesus, was also *under* authority (Luke 22:29).

All things have been given to Jesus by the Father (Mtt. 11:27). Jesus can bestow a kingdom because His Father bestowed one upon Him (Luke 22:29).

3.2.28 - Revelation 2:28

morning star

Christ Himself is said to be the morning star (Rev. 22:16).[188] What is the purpose of the morning star, but to serve as an indicator of the approaching dawn? Those who see the morning star are encouraged by the fact that the long night is almost over and soon the sun will shine in its brilliance dispelling all traces of darkness.

The current period, between the ascension of Christ and His Second Coming, is the "night."

> I wait for the LORD, my soul waits, and in His word I do hope. My soul *waits* for the Lord more than those who watch for the morning-*Yes, more than* those who watch for the morning. (Ps. 130:5-6)

> And so we have the prophetic word confirmed, which you do well to heed as a light that shines in a dark place, until the day dawns and the morning star rises in your hearts (2Pe. 1:19)

Isaiah 24 sets forth the *Day of the Lord*[5.2.14] and the awful destruction and judgment which attend it. (See *Trouble Ahead*[2.13.1].) In the middle of the passage, Isaiah mentions the "dawn." "Therefore glorify the LORD in the dawning light, the name of the LORD God of Israel in the coastlands of the sea" (Isa. 24:15).

Yet, the destruction which attends the Day of the Lord is itself an indicator that the long night is nearly over and that the sun will soon rise:

> "For behold, the day is coming, burning like an oven, and all the proud, yes, all who do wickedly will be stubble. And the day which is coming shall burn them up," says the LORD of hosts, "That will leave them neither root nor branch. But to you who fear My name the Sun of Righteousness shall arise with healing in His wings; and you shall go out and grow fat like stall-fed calves." (Mal. 4:1-2)

Psalm 46 indicates a time of great upheaval upon the earth, at which God intervenes to rescue Jerusalem "at the break of dawn" (see Zec. 12). His intervention is followed by a time of universal peace (Isa. 2:4; 9:5, 7; 14:7; Hos. 2:18; Zec. 9:10):

> God *is* our refuge and strength, a very present help in trouble. Therefore we will not fear, **Even though the earth be removed, and though the mountains be carried into the midst of the sea; *Though* its waters roar *and* be troubled, *though* the mountains shake with its swelling**. Selah *There is* a river whose streams shall make glad the city of God, the holy *place* of the *tabernacle*[5.2.69] of the Most High. God *is* in the midst of her, she shall not be moved; **God shall help her, just at the break of dawn**. The nations raged, the kingdoms were moved; He uttered His voice, the earth melted. The LORD of hosts *is* with us; the God of Jacob *is* our refuge. Selah. Come, behold the works of the LORD, Who has made desolations in the earth. **He makes wars cease to the end of the earth; He breaks the bow and cuts the spear in two**; He burns the chariot in the fire. Be still, and know that I *am* God; **I will be exalted among the nations, I will be exalted in the earth!** The LORD of hosts *is* with us; the God of Jacob *is* our refuge. Selah (Ps. 46:1-11) [emphasis added]

When the *Millennial Kingdom*[5.2.39] arrives, it will be a glorious day upon the earth during which the sun shall shine:

> Arise, shine; for your light has come! And the glory of the LORD is risen upon you. For behold, the darkness shall cover the earth, and deep darkness the people; but the LORD will arise over you, and His glory will be seen upon you. The Gentiles shall come to your light, and kings to the brightness of your rising. (Isa. 60:1-3)

You in this passage is the *earthly Jerusalem* which will be the center of Christ's reign during the thousand years (Rev. 20:4-6).[189]

The morning star rises prior to the dawn:

> The "morning star" comes before "the day" dawns; the "sun" shines during "the day"; Jesus is both. As the morning star, He is seen by few: as the sun, He is seen by all. Those who watch not merely for the sun, but for the morning star, properly heed the cautions and injunctions relating to the posture of

watching.[190]

> We have in the "Morning Star" an implied reference to the first stage of the Advent, the thief-like coming for the saints, and to obtain it indicates that we are worthy of the better resurrection, or (if living) of the translation. The mention of this in such a connection is also exceedingly significant of the exaltation of the saints to coheirship with the Christ when the morning breaks.[191]

Christ has just mentioned a *scepter* and now mentions a *star* , both elements of the prophecy of Balaam (Num. 24:17). In Balaam's prophecy, the *star* is seen first followed by the *scepter*. This accords with the view that the morning star will rise *prior to* the reign of Messiah on the earth.

> Assuredly, I say to you, this generation will by no means pass away till all things take place. Heaven and earth will pass away, but My words will by no means pass away. But take heed to yourselves, lest your hearts be weighed down with carousing, drunkenness, and cares of this life, and that Day come on you unexpectedly. For it will come as a snare on all those who dwell on the face of the whole earth. Watch therefore, and pray always that you may be counted worthy to escape all these things that will come to pass, and to stand before the Son of Man. (Luke 21:32-36)

The morning star given to the overcomer in Thyatira may be the promise of a visitation *prior to* the dawn—participation in the *Rapture*[5.2.62] of the church by all true believers and thus avoiding the last part of the night, the Great Tribulation, immediately before the dawn of the Millennial Kingdom. "Perhaps it also refers again to His second coming—this time in its very first aspect, when He comes to catch up into His presence those who believe on Him (1 Thessalonians 4:16-17)."[192] See *Rapture*[4.14].

At the very least it denotes the blessing of the continual expectancy of His coming:

> Into the heart of the faithful believer comes that wondrous *expectancy* of His coming , which John elsewhere describes as having our "hope set on him" (1 John 3:3). This is the experience of the believer who awakes out of sleep (Romans 13:11), who by the grace of God hears His voice when He says, "Awake, thou that sleepest, and arise from among the dead (ones), and Christ shall shine upon thee" (Ephesians 5:13). . . . so these spiritually awakened or aroused find Christ's coming arising as the day-star in their hearts (2 Peter 1:19).[193]

3.2.29 - Revelation 2:29

let him hear what the Spirit says to the churches

See commentary on *Revelation 2:7*[3.2.7].

Notes

1 Colin J. Hemer, *The Letters to the Seven Churches of Asia in Their Local Setting* (Grand Rapids, MI: William B. Eerdmans Publishing Company, 1989), 35.

2 Robert L. Thomas, *Revelation 1-7* (Chicago, IL: Moody Press, 1992), 129.

3 Copyright ©003 *www.BiblePlaces.com*. This image appears by *special permission*[1.3] and may not be duplicated for use in derivative works.

4 G. L. Borchert, *"Ephesus,"* in Geoffrey W. Bromiley, ed., *International Standard Bible Encyclopedia* (Grand Rapids, MI: William B. Eerdmans Publishing Co., 1979, 1915), 115.

5 "In the Ephesian calendar the month of the spring equinox was named after Artemis . . . and during that month the city celebrated a yearly festival in honour of the goddess."—Henry Barclay Swete, *The Apocalypse of St. John* (Eugene, OR: Wipf and Stock Publishers, 1998, 1906), lvii.

6 Hemer, *The Letters to the Seven Churches of Asia in Their Local Setting*, 35.

7 Robert H. Mounce, *The Book of Revelation* (Grand Rapids, MI: William B. Eerdmans Publishing Co., 1977), 86.

8 "Acts 19:19 hints that the church in Ephesus was very large indeed, for 50,000 pieces of silver represents 50,000 days' wages, which, at a daily wage of $100, was equivalent to $5,000,000. Now, if each person burned an average of $250 worth of books on magic, that value would represent 20,000 people; and even if every second person in the church was involved in magic this would require a church of, very conservatively,

40,000 members. (Do four-member Christian families on average own $1,000 worth of Christian books?) This, too, is simply an estimate of the size of the Ephesian church before three years of Paul's ministry was completed (Acts 20:31—church history claims an Ephesian church of 100,000 members in John Chrysostom's day)."—Monty S. Mills, *Revelations: An Exegetical Study of the Revelation to John* (Dallas, TX: 3E Ministries, 1987).

9 "[Ephesus had a] reputation as a seat of learning. . . . according to *Eusebius*[5.2.19] Ephesus is the scene of Justin's Dialogue with Trypho."—Swete, *The Apocalypse of St. John*, lvi.

10 Borchert, "*Ephesus*," 115.

11 Hemer, *The Letters to the Seven Churches of Asia in Their Local Setting*, 39.

12 J. A. Seiss, *The Apocalypse: Lectures on the Book of Revelation* (Grand Rapids, MI: Zondervan Publishing House, 1966), 56.

13 Borchert, "*Ephesus*," 116-117.

14 "[The perfect tense] describes an event that, completed in the past . . . has results existing in the present time (i.e., in relation to the time of the speaker). ... the perfect tense is used for 'indicating not the past action as such but the present state of affairs resulting from the past action.' "—Daniel B. Wallace, *Greek Grammar Beyond the Basics - Exegetical Syntax of the New Testament* (Grand Rapids, MI: Zondervan Publishing House and Galaxie Software, 1999, 2002), 572.

15 Richard Chenevix Trench, *Commentary on the Epistles to the Seven Churches in Asia* (Eugene, OR: Wipf and Stock Publishers, 1861), 72.

16 J. B. Lightfoot, and J. R. Harmer, *The Apostolic Fathers*, 2nd ed. (Grand Rapids, MI: Baker Book House, 1989), 89.

17 "A wider group of authoritative apostles existed [then those which had seen the Lord]. James the Just, Barnabas, Paul, Silas, Andronicus, and Junias were also apostles (Acts 14:14; Rom. 16:7; 1Cor. 15:7; Gal. 1:18; 1Th. 2:6)."—Thomas, *Revelation 1-7*, 137.

18 James Strong, *The Exhaustive Concordance of the Bible* (Ontario: Woodside Bible Fellowship, 1996), G863.

19 Frederick William Danker, and Walter Bauer, *A Greek-English Lexicon of the New Testament and Other Early Christian Literature* (Chicago, IL: University of Chicago Press, 2000).

20 William R. Newell, *Revelation: Chapter by Chapter* (Grand Rapids, MI: Kregel Publications, 1994,c1935), 38-39.

21 A. R. Fausset, *"The Revelation of St. John the Divine,"* in Robert Jamieson, A. R. Fausset, and David Brown, *A Commentary, Critical and Explanatory, on the Old and New Testaments* (Oak Harbor, WA: Logos Research Systems, Inc., 1997, 1877), Rev. 2:4.

22 Richard Chenevix Trench, *Synonyms of the New Testament* (Peabody, MA: Hendrickson Publishers, 1989), 270-272.

23 Trench, *Commentary on the Epistles to the Seven Churches in Asia*, 80.

24 Newell, *Revelation: Chapter by Chapter*, 39-40.

25 "The present tense may be used to describe a future event, . . . it typically adds the connotations of immediacy and certainty."—Wallace, *Greek Grammar Beyond the Basics - Exegetical Syntax of the New Testament*, 535.

26 Fausset, "*The Revelation of St. John the Divine*," Rev. 2:5.

27 Thomas, *Revelation 1-7*, 147.

28 Trench, *Commentary on the Epistles to the Seven Churches in Asia*, 187-188.

29 Newell, *Revelation: Chapter by Chapter*, 40.

30 Thomas, *Revelation 1-7*, 147.

31 Fausset, "*The Revelation of St. John the Divine*," Rev. 2:7.

32 A. T. Robertson, *Robertson's Word Pictures in Six Volumes* (Escondido, CA: Ephesians Four Group, 2003).

33 Seiss, *The Apocalypse: Lectures on the Book of Revelation*, 67.

34 M. R. Vincent, *Vincent's Word Studies* (Escondido, CA: Ephesians Four Group, 2002), Rev. 2:7.

35 *Israel My Glory*, May/June 2001, 23.

36 "It is suggested that the phrase "tree of life" may have carried the connotation of the cross of Christ to the original readers of Rev. 2:7."—Hemer, *The Letters to the Seven Churches of Asia in Their Local Setting*, 55.

37 Hemer, *The Letters to the Seven Churches of Asia in Their Local Setting*, 50.

38 Strong, *The Exhaustive Concordance of the Bible*, G3857.

39 Trench, *Commentary on the Epistles to the Seven Churches in Asia*, 95.

40 Thomas, *Revelation 1-7*, 153.

41 Arnold G. Fruchtenbaum, *The Footsteps of Messiah*, rev ed. (Tustin, CA: Ariel Ministries, 2003), 755-756.

42 Trench, *Commentary on the Epistles to the Seven Churches in Asia*, 97-98.

43 Copyright ©003 *www.BiblePlaces.com*. This image appears by *special permission*[1.3] and may not be duplicated for use in derivative works.

44 "The countries bordering on the eastern Mediterranean Sea from Turkey to Egypt."—*American Heritage Online Dictionary*, Ver. 3.0A, 3rd ed. (Houghton Mifflin, 1993), s.v. "Levant."

45 Thomas, *Revelation 1-7*, 159.

46 "[Polycarp] may have been a young man in the church which first received the present letter. He evidently came much under its influence."—Hemer, *The Letters to the Seven Churches of Asia in Their Local Setting*, 65.

47 Hemer, *The Letters to the Seven Churches of Asia in Their Local Setting*, 60.

48 Mills, *Revelations: An Exegetical Study of the Revelation to John*, Rev. 2:8.

49 Thomas, *Revelation 1-7*, 158.

50 Hemer, *The Letters to the Seven Churches of Asia in Their Local Setting*, 64.

51 Trench, *Commentary on the Epistles to the Seven Churches in Asia*, 111-112.

52 Lightfoot, *The Apostolic Fathers*, 110.

53 Vincent, *Vincent's Word Studies*.

54 Mills, *Revelations: An Exegetical Study of the Revelation to John*, Rev. 2:9.

55 Trench, *Commentary on the Epistles to the Seven Churches in Asia*, 100.

56 Thomas, *Revelation 1-7*, 164-165.

57 The term συναγωγὴ [*synagōgē*] is used only once for a Christian place of assembly. (Jas. 2:2).

58 For more on the believing remnant, see 1K. 19:18; 2K. 19:4, 30; 21:14; 25:22; Isa. 1:9; 6:13; 7:3; 10:20-22; 28:5; 37:4, 31-32; 46:3; 59:21; 65:8; Jer. 5:10, 18; 23:3; 50:20; Eze. 5:3; 6:8-10; 9:8; 9:11; 11:13; Joel 2:32; Zec. 11:10; Mic. 2:12; 7:18; Zec. 13:8-9; Rom. 9:6, 27; Rom. 11:5, 17, 25.

59 "Has Christ a Church, then Satan has his "synagogue" (Rev. 2:9)."—Arthur Walkington Pink, *The Antichrist* (Oak Harbor, WA: Logos Research Systems, 1999, 1923), s.v. "The Antichrist will be the Son of Satan." See *Master Imitator*[4.2.5].

60 "This method of identifying Jews is hard-pressed to produce any exegetical support either within the Apocalypse or in the rest of the *NT*[5.2.48]. Besides this, if they had called themselves Jews in this mystical sense, why would they be named as the principle source of calumny against the church? . . . It is inexplicable why a person who was not a physical descendant of Abraham would claim to be so and then turn to persecuting fellow-Christians without recanting this claim. The context demands that the offenders be of the physical descent of Abraham."—Thomas, *Revelation 1-7*, 165.

61 John MacArthur, *Revelation 1-11 : The MacArthur New Testament Commentary* (Chicago, IL: Moody Press, 1999), 71.

62 Trench, *Commentary on the Epistles to the Seven Churches in Asia*, 102.

63 Gregory K. Beale, *The Book of Revelation: A Commentary on the Greek Text* (Grand Rapids, MI: William B. Eerdmans Publishing Co., 1999), 13.

64 Beale, *The Book of Revelation: A Commentary on the Greek Text*, 30-31.

65 Grant R. Osborne, *Revelation* (Grand Rapids, MI: Baker Academic, 2002), 11.

66 Swete, *The Apocalypse of St. John*, lxxxix.

67 Hemer, *The Letters to the Seven Churches of Asia in Their Local Setting*, 67.

68 Lightfoot, *The Apostolic Fathers*, 140.

69 Fruchtenbaum, *The Footsteps of Messiah*, 64.

70 Trench, *Commentary on the Epistles to the Seven Churches in Asia*, 104.

71 Trench, *Commentary on the Epistles to the Seven Churches in Asia*, 105.

72 Trench, *Commentary on the Epistles to the Seven Churches in Asia.*

73 "We have thus at least the attestation of this form of expression at Smyrna. . . . there is reason to think that John"s words may have recalled to the Christian the language of the arena. An appearance at some great festival there might well await those who were 'faithful unto death"."—Hemer, *The Letters to the Seven Churches of Asia in Their Local Setting*, 69.

74 Trench, *Commentary on the Epistles to the Seven Churches in Asia*, 107.

75 Thomas, *Revelation 1-7*, 170.

76 Fruchtenbaum, *The Footsteps of Messiah*, 53-54.

77 Thomas, *Revelation 1-7*, 168-170.

78 Trench, *Commentary on the Epistles to the Seven Churches in Asia*, 108.

79 Trench, *Commentary on the Epistles to the Seven Churches in Asia*, s.v. "Martyrdom of Polycarp."

80 Hemer, *The Letters to the Seven Churches of Asia in Their Local Setting*, 71.

81 Thomas, *Revelation 1-7*, 174.

82 Copyright ©003 *www.BiblePlaces.com*. This image appears by *special permission*[1.3] and may not be duplicated for use in derivative works.

83 Jerome Smith, *The New Treasury of Scripture Knowledge* (Nashville, TN: Thomas Nelson Publishers, 1992), Rev. 2:12.

84 Merrill K. Unger, R. Harrison, Frederic F Vos, and Cyril J. Barber, *The New Unger's Bible Dictionary* (Chicago, IL: Moody Press, 1988), s.v. "Pergamum."

85 Mills, *Revelations: An Exegetical Study of the Revelation to John*, Rev. 2:12.

86 Neil R. Lightfoot, *How We Got the Bible*, 3nd ed. (Grand Rapids, MI: Baker Books, 2003), 18-19.

87 Swete, *The Apocalypse of St. John*, lviii-lix,lxiii.

88 Henry Morris, *The Revelation Record* (Wheaton, IL: Tyndale House Publishers, 1983), 57.

89 MacArthur, *Revelation 1-11 : The MacArthur New Testament Commentary*, 83.

90 "Asklepios . . . was also designated "Soter", and was closely identified with the serpent. Though he had celebrated shrines elsewhere he was preeminently the *Pergameus deus* [God of Pergamus]."—Hemer, *The Letters to the Seven Churches of Asia in Their Local Setting*, 85.

91 "The designation of Pergamum as the place where 'Satan's throne' is (Rev. 2:13) probably refers to Pergamum's being the official Asian center for the *imperial cult*[5.2.31]."—R. North, *"Pergamum,"* in Geoffrey W. Bromiley, ed., *International Standard Bible Encyclopedia* (Grand Rapids, MI: William B. Eerdmans Publishing Co., 1979, 1915), 3:768.

92 Hemer, *The Letters to the Seven Churches of Asia in Their Local Setting*, 85.

93 North, "*Pergamum*," 3:768.

94 Hemer, *The Letters to the Seven Churches of Asia in Their Local Setting*, 85-86.

95 Swete, *The Apocalypse of St. John*, lix.

[96] Mills, *Revelations: An Exegetical Study of the Revelation to John*, Rev. 2:13.

[97] Morris, *The Revelation Record*, 57.

[98] "Probably short for Ἀντίπατρος [*Antipatros*], 'like the Father.' "—Danker, *A Greek-English Lexicon of the New Testament and Other Early Christian Literature*.

[99] "Antipas. i.e. against all."—Smith, *The New Treasury of Scripture Knowledge*, Rev. 2:13.

[100] Mal Couch, *"Ecclesiology in the Book of Revelation,"* in Mal Couch, ed., *A Bible Handbook to Revelation* (Grand Rapids, MI: Kregel Publications, 2001), 138.

[101] Thomas, *Revelation 1-7*, 184.

[102] "What is the point of the emphatic comparison (οὕτως . . . καὶ σύ . . . ὁμοίως [*houtōs . . . kai sy . . . homoiōs*]) between Balaam and the Nicolaitans?"—Hemer, *The Letters to the Seven Churches of Asia in Their Local Setting*, 88.

[103] Fruchtenbaum, *The Footsteps of Messiah*, 56.

[104] Trench, *Commentary on the Epistles to the Seven Churches in Asia*, 118.

[105] Danker, *A Greek-English Lexicon of the New Testament and Other Early Christian Literature*.

[106] Beale, *The Book of Revelation: A Commentary on the Greek Text*, 30.

[107] Strong, *The Exhaustive Concordance of the Bible*, G4203.

[108] Mills, *Revelations: An Exegetical Study of the Revelation to John*, Rev. 2:15.

[109] Newell, *Revelation: Chapter by Chapter*, 51.

[110] Trench, *Commentary on the Epistles to the Seven Churches in Asia*.

[111] Trench, *Commentary on the Epistles to the Seven Churches in Asia*, 124.

[112] Hemer, *The Letters to the Seven Churches of Asia in Their Local Setting*, 94-95.

[113] Trench, *Commentary on the Epistles to the Seven Churches in Asia*, 125.

[114] Mills, *Revelations: An Exegetical Study of the Revelation to John*, Rev. 2:17.

[115] "Eating the 'hidden manna' is but another way of picturing what can also be represented as the joyous boon of feasting at the Messianic banquet (cf. Rev. 19:9)."—James E. Rosscup, *"The Overcomer of the Apocalypse,"* in *Grace Theological Journal*, vol. 3 no. 1 (Grace Seminary, Spring 1982), 279.

[116] E. W. Bullinger, *Commentary On Revelation* (Grand Rapids, MI: Kregel Publications, 1984, 1935), 91.

[117] Fruchtenbaum, *The Footsteps of Messiah*, 56.

[118] Interpreters frequently look to pagan sources when they mistakenly believe Scripture offers no clues: "The 'white stone' (Rev. 2:17) has no precedent in the Old Testament."—Merrill C. Tenney, *Interpreting Revelation* (Peabody, MA: Hendrickson Publishers, 1957), 190.

[119] Mills, *Revelations: An Exegetical Study of the Revelation to John*, Rev. 2:17.

[120] Mills, *Revelations: An Exegetical Study of the Revelation to John*, Rev. 2:17.

[121] Matthew Henry, *Matthew Henry's Commentary on the Whole Bible : Complete and Unabridged in One Volume* (Peabody, MA: Hendrickson, 1996, c1991), Rev. 2:17.

[122] Hemer, *The Letters to the Seven Churches of Asia in Their Local Setting*, 99.

[123] Hemer, *The Letters to the Seven Churches of Asia in Their Local Setting*, 100.

[124] Daniel Wong, *"The Hidden Manna and the White Stone,"* in *Bibliotheca Sacra*, vol. 155 no. 617 (Dallas, TX: Dallas Theological Seminary, January-March 1998), 351.

[125] Wong, "*The Hidden Manna and the White Stone*," 351.

[126] Trench, *Commentary on the Epistles to the Seven Churches in Asia*, 132.

[127] *New Electronic Translation : NET Bible*, electronic edition (Dallas, TX: Biblical Studies Press, 1998), Rev. 2:17.

128 Fausset, "*The Revelation of St. John the Divine*," Rev. 2:17.

129 Wong, "*The Hidden Manna and the White Stone*," 352.

130 Morris, *The Revelation Record*, 59.

131 Wong, "*The Hidden Manna and the White Stone*," 353.

132 Wong, "*The Hidden Manna and the White Stone*," 353.

133 Smith, *The New Treasury of Scripture Knowledge*, 2Jn. 1:5.

134 Henry, *Matthew Henry's Commentary on the Whole Bible : Complete and Unabridged in One Volume*, Rev. 2:17.

135 "Clearly the new name is the recipient's own name, a new one, reflecting his status as belonging to Christ. This is verified in its being a secret name given to the man himself."—Thomas, *Revelation 1-7*, 202.

136 Trench, *Commentary on the Epistles to the Seven Churches in Asia*, Rev. 2:17.

137 Smith, *The New Treasury of Scripture Knowledge*, Rev. 2:18.

138 Copyright ©003 *www.BiblePlaces.com*. This image appears by *special permission*[1.3] and may not be duplicated for use in derivative works.

139 Hemer, *The Letters to the Seven Churches of Asia in Their Local Setting*, 106-107.

140 Swete, *The Apocalypse of St. John*, lix-lx.

141 Mills, *Revelations: An Exegetical Study of the Revelation to John*, Rev. 2:18.

142 Hemer, *The Letters to the Seven Churches of Asia in Their Local Setting*, 109.

143 Mills, *Revelations: An Exegetical Study of the Revelation to John*, Rev. 2:18.

144 Trench, *Commentary on the Epistles to the Seven Churches in Asia*.

145 Bullinger, *Commentary On Revelation*, 186.

146 Thomas, *Revelation 1-7*, 211.

147 Thomas, *Revelation 1-7*, 213.

148 "The textual question may be summarily treated. Two *uncial*[5.2.80] manuscripts (A and 046 == Q, of the 10th century) and many cursives and versions insert σοῦ [*sou*] [your] after τὴν γυναῖκα [*tēn gynaika*] [the woman/wife]. The decisive weight of textual authority however appears against this (א, C, etc.), and the addition is readily explained by dittography."—Hemer, *The Letters to the Seven Churches of Asia in Their Local Setting*, 117.

149 Noadiah opposed Nehemiah in his work of reconstruction.

150 "Isaiah's wife was called a prophetess because the son to whom she gave birth was prophetic of the Assyrian conquest."—John MacArthur, *The MacArthur Study Bible* (Nashville, TN: Word Publishing, 1997), Isa. 8:3.

151 Although the daughters are not called *prophetesses*, they are said to *prophesy*.

152 Trench, *Commentary on the Epistles to the Seven Churches in Asia*, 140.

153 "Now to do this was to take the place of the Spirit, who indeed spake 'not from Himself,' but 'what He heard' from the Lord in glory."—Newell, *Revelation: Chapter by Chapter*, 54.

154 Thomas, *Revelation 1-7*, 215.

155 MacArthur, *Revelation 1-11 : The MacArthur New Testament Commentary*, 100.

156 Strong, *The Exhaustive Concordance of the Bible*, G4105.

157 Mills, *Revelations: An Exegetical Study of the Revelation to John*, Rev. 2:20.

158 Thomas, *Revelation 1-7*, 207-208.

159 Henry George Liddell, Robert Scott, and Henry Stuart Jones, *A Greek-English Lexicon. With a revised supplement, 1996.*, With a revised supplement, 1996 (Oxford, England: Oxford University Press, 1996).

[160] The word may refer to dining or a dining couch: "Dining Eze. 23:41; Mark 4:21; 7:30; Luke 8:16; 17:34; dining couch Mark 7:4."—Danker, *A Greek-English Lexicon of the New Testament and Other Early Christian Literature*, 436.

[161] Hemer, *The Letters to the Seven Churches of Asia in Their Local Setting*, 121.

[162] Newell, *Revelation: Chapter by Chapter*, 57.

[163] Strong, *The Exhaustive Concordance of the Bible*, G3431.

[164] A *technical phrase*[5.2.72] has the same or similar meaning regardless of context. The meaning of a non-technical phrase varies with context.

[165] Thomas, *Revelation 1-7*, 221.

[166] "This means that unlike the true Church, the Roman Catholic Church will go into the Great Tribulation and will play a role during that time."—Fruchtenbaum, *The Footsteps of Messiah*, 60.

[167] Trench, *Commentary on the Epistles to the Seven Churches in Asia*, 141.

[168] Fausset, "*The Revelation of St. John the Divine*," Rev. 2:23.

[169] Morris, *The Revelation Record*, 62.

[170] "The only things left in the body cavity by the Egyptian embalmers."—Danker, *A Greek-English Lexicon of the New Testament and Other Early Christian Literature*, s.v. "nephras."

[171] If the life of a professing believer is truly devoid of all good works, then Scripture indicates the profession is suspect (Jas. 2:14-26).

[172] Trench, *Commentary on the Epistles to the Seven Churches in Asia*, 144.

[173] Hemer, *The Letters to the Seven Churches of Asia in Their Local Setting*, 122.

[174] Thomas, *Revelation 1-7*, 228.

[175] Beale, *The Book of Revelation: A Commentary on the Greek Text*, 32.

[176] Newell, *Revelation: Chapter by Chapter*, 59.

[177] Trench, *Commentary on the Epistles to the Seven Churches in Asia*, 145.

[178] Vincent, *Vincent's Word Studies*, Rev. 2:24.

[179] Trench, *Commentary on the Epistles to the Seven Churches in Asia*, 145.

[180] Here is an example of a verb in an aorist tense which implies *continuous* action.

[181] Danker, *A Greek-English Lexicon of the New Testament and Other Early Christian Literature*, s.v. "meno."

[182] Rabbinic interpretation associated the title Shiloh with the Messiah: a midrash takes "Shiloh" to refer to "King Messiah" (Genesis R. 98.13), the Babylonian Talmud lists "Shi'loh" as one of the names of the Messiah (Sanhedrin 98b), and Medieval Jewish Biblical expositor Rashi makes the following comment: "Shiloh - i.e. King Messiah whose is the Kingdom." Note that Eze. 21:25-27 was given to Zedekiah, the last king of the Davidic dynasty. Shiloh means "to he whose it is" or "to he who it belongs" or "he whose right it is" or "to whom kingship belongs" (Midrash Rabbah 98).

[183] Danker, *A Greek-English Lexicon of the New Testament and Other Early Christian Literature*, s.v. "exousian."

[184] "It would appear that this section is eschatological in nature and looks 1) to the Millennium when all nations and peoples will acknowledge Christ as king and 2) to Jerusalem as His royal capital (cf. Eze. 28:25, 26; Joel 3:9-17; Mic. 5:4-15)."—MacArthur, *The MacArthur Study Bible*, Ps. 149:6-9.

[185] Trench, *Commentary on the Epistles to the Seven Churches in Asia*, 148.

[186] Trench, *Commentary on the Epistles to the Seven Churches in Asia*, 149.

[187] Hemer, *The Letters to the Seven Churches of Asia in Their Local Setting*, 125.

[188] Elsewhere, Satan is called הֵילֵל בֶּן־שָׁחַר [*hêlēl bēn-shāchar*] , "shining one [or Lucifer], son of the morning," (Isa. 14:12).

[189] Those who take this passage as describing the *New Jerusalem* have difficulty explaining this verse: "Whereas

you have been forsaken and hated, so that no one went through *you*, I will make you an eternal excellence, a joy of many generations" (Isa. 60:15). When was the *New Jerusalem* forsaken and hated? See also Isa. 62.

[190] George H. N. Peters, *The Theocratic Kingdom* (Grand Rapids, MI: Kregel Publications, 1978, 1884), 2:317.

[191] Peters, *The Theocratic Kingdom*, 2:418.

[192] Morris, *The Revelation Record*, 63.

[193] Newell, *Revelation: Chapter by Chapter*, 61.

3.3 - Revelation 3

3.3.1 - Revelation 3:1

Jesus dictates letters to the remaining three of the *Seven Churches of Asia*[4.15]. This chapter completes the record of "the things which are" (Rev. 1:19). The reader is encouraged to "have ears to hear what the Spirit says to the churches", even down to our own day.

the angel

See the discussion concerning the identity of the angel at *Revelation 1:20*[3.1.20].

church in Sardis

See commentary on *Seven Churches of Asia*[4.15].

Sardis

Sardis was the ancient capital of Lydia.

Temple of Artemis at Sardis [1]

Sardis was known for its great wealth and may have been the earliest kingdom (7th century B.C.) to use minted coins.[2]

> In John's time it was a trade center known for textile manufacture, dyeing, and jewelry. Sardis had been Lydia's capital and was proverbial for its riches. To this day, our idiom "as rich as Croesus" acknowledges this fact, for Croesus was the king of Sardis who had almost unlimited riches, yet who led the Lydian empire into defeat and decline. Sardis epitomized the complacency, softness and degeneration which invariably ultimately accompany wealth.[3]

It was also considered a mountain fortress[4] which was very difficult to capture, except through the negligence of the defenders:

> At the approach of Alexander, . . . the Sardians hastened out to surrender their city without resistance. . . . the place was again captured by Antiochus III in 214 BC through the negligence of the defenders. [5]

> The rock on which Sardis was built is friable, which means that while the slopes were precipitous, because of the cracks and faults, it was climbable. One of Cyrus'soldiers had noticed a Sardian soldier climbing down this slope to retrieve a helmet he had dropped, and so concluded that the slopes were negotiable in that particular spot. So that night he led a party of Persian troops up to the citadel by following the fault in the rock. When they reached the battlements they found them unguarded, for the

> Sardians considered themselves too safe to need a guard. The battle of King's Mountain in American history is similar to the Sardian collapse, for in that battle the rebels scaled a redoubt while the English relaxed in false confidence of their security. Astonishingly, Sardis did not learn from experience, for two centuries later one of Antiochus' soldiers repeated this feat and again led the capture of an unguarded city which had resisted siege for a year. Twice, the Sardians lost their city because they were too complacent to watch! This historical background underlies Christ's injunction to watchfulness (Rev. 3:2-3), and Rev. 3:3 alludes to the means by which the city was lost twice before—a thief in the night.[6]

A large temple dedicated to the Asiatic goddess Cybele stood at Sardis:

> Excavations . . . unearthed . . . an exceptionally large (160 by 300 feet) temple dedicated to Artemis. Its seventy-eight Ionic columns (of which two are still standing) are each fifty-eight feet in height. . . . It was dedicated to a local Asiatic goddess usually referred to as Cybele, who was identified with the Greek Artemis. This patron deity was believed to possess the special power of restoring the dead to life [cf. Rev. 3:1].[7]

Being situated in a mountainous region, the city was earthquake-prone:

> Sardis, like neighboring Philadelphia, suffered a catastrophic earthquake in AD 17. . . . this was nothing less than the sudden collapse of a great part of the mountain and the consequent disappearance of much of the very site of the original fortress-city.[8]

> Because of the earthquake, which drove them from the city proper, and because of the fertility of the soil, many of the people had turned to farming as a means of livelihood, specifically to the cultivation of vineyards. Apparently, because of famine, in A.D. 92 Domitian issued an edict that at least half the vineyards in the provinces be cut down and no new ones planted. This action was designed to increase production of corn which the Empire needed badly. This crisis affected Philadelphia more critically than any other, because no city of Asia depended on the fruit of the vine more than it. Dionysius, god of wine, was the principal deity.[9]

(Some correlate Domitian's edict with Revelation 6:6, although we believe it to be unlikely.) In the second century, Melito was bishop of this city. [10] but Christianity was completely exterminated in the Hermus Valley in the Middle Ages.[11]

In more recent times, Sardis has none of its previous opulence:

> Sardis, the once proud capital of Lydia, and the residence of its opulent monarchs, is now reduced to a wretched Turkish village called Sart, the habitation of herdsmen, buffaloes, and oxen, situated at the foot of mount Tmolus, on the banks of the Pactolus, between 30 and 40 miles east from Smyrna. The ruins of Sardis are peculiarly grand, and lift up their heads, as if to assert their ancient glory; but it now contains not a single Christian family.[12]

The derivation of the name Sardis is uncertain as is the meaning, having been given as *remnant*, "[Some] have derived it from the Hebrew, and have assigned it the signification of *remnant*, or *an escaped few*."[13] *those escaping*, [J. Dwight Pentecost, *Things to Come: A Study in Biblical Eschatology* (Grand Rapids, MI: Zondervan Publishing House, 1958), 152] *renovation*, [Pentecost, *Things to Come: A Study in Biblical Eschatology*, 152] *the sun*, [Smith, *The New Treasury of Scripture Knowledge*, Rev. 3:1] *red ones*, [Smith, *The New Treasury of Scripture Knowledge*, Rev. 3:1] and *prince of joy*.[18]

seven Spirits of God

See commentary on *Revelation 1:4*[3.1.4]. Christ emphasizes to this church that He is the source of the *seven Spirits of God* (John 15:26; 16:7) because of His assessment that they *are dead* . It is the specialty of the third Person of the Trinity, the Holy Spirit, to bring forth life from that which is a lifeless wilderness (Gen. 1:2):

> Jesus answered, "Most assuredly, I say to you, unless one is born of water and the Spirit, he cannot enter the kingdom of God. That which is born of the flesh is flesh, and that which is born of the Spirit is spirit. Do not marvel that I said to you, 'You must be born again.' The wind blows where it wishes, and you hear the sound of it, but cannot tell where it comes from and where it goes. So is everyone who is born of the Spirit." (John 3:5-8)

Prior to the Day of Pentecost, Jesus explained that it was the Holy Spirit that would be the source of "rivers of living water" which would flow out of the heart of those believing in Him (John 7:37-39).

This life-giving Spirit was poured forth on the Day of Pentecost (Acts 2:33). It was on this day that the *body of Christ* was first animated by the *Spirit of Christ* (Rom. 8:9). As God had first breathed the "breath of life" to animate dust from which he formed man (Gen. 2:7), so each believer is animated by the Holy Spirit when he comes to spiritual life and is joined to the body of Christ (1Cor. 12:12-13). Christ is here emphasizing the Spirit as the means by which they might *strengthen the things which remain, that are ready to die* (Rev. 3:2).

> It need hardly be observed how important a witness this verse, when the right interpretation of *"the seven Spirits"* has been seized, bears to the faith of the Western Church on that great point upon which it is at issue with the Eastern, in respect, namely, of the procession of the Holy Ghost. he is indeed the Spirit of the Father *and the Son.*[19]

seven stars

The stars are the angels of the churches. If elders, they are to be men "full of the spirit" (Acts 6:3-5; 11:24). See commentary on *Revelation 1:16*[3.1.16] and *Revelation 1:20*[3.1.20].

I know

See commentary on *Revelation 2:2*[3.2.2].

have a name that you are alive

Alive is ζῇς [*zēs*]: "Which needs to be distinguished from the word-group of βίος [*bios*] ('life'). The former refers to inner life, the latter to external."[20] Christ emphasizes the wide divergence between how the church of Sardis *appears to men* and how it *appears to God.* This underscores a theme which runs throughout Scripture: that those without the Spirit of God are unable to see the world through the eyes of God. The church of Sardis had made *for themselves* a *name. Name* is here used to represent fame, reputation, or character. Thus the Sardians were following in the sin of Babel. "And they said, 'Come, let us build ourselves a city, and a tower whose top *is* in the heavens; let us make a name for ourselves, lest we be scattered abroad over the face of the whole earth' " (Gen. 11:4).

but you are dead

Jesus says they are *dead*—in the sense of being disconnected from the Father, just as the prodigal (Luke 15:24, 32).

> One commentator has said, "Their state is described in a single word—soulless profession-they had a name to live but were dead. It is not scandalous wickedness, but decent death; the form retained, the heart gone; Christ owned in word, ignored in deed; creeds correct, conduct respectable, life departed . . . sound doctrine and outward propriety . . . affections not only waning, but gone. His name held, His Word read, His truth owned, Himself forgotten." . . . When the human spirit does not control some part of the body, there is said to be a partial paralysis. Some pressure upon a nerve center or some other abnormality may cause one foot to be dragged or one hand to be withered instead of maintaining the normal participation in the life of the body. The Holy Spirit should govern and direct the Church which is the Body of Christ.[21]

The *activity* of a fellowship can often be mistaken as an indication of life. But Scripture makes plain that works and activity in and of themselves are no reliable indicator of spiritual life for it is possible for an active fellowship to be comprised of the "living dead" (Mtt. 8:22; Luke 9:60; 1Ti. 5:6). "Go throughout Christendom . . . and you will often find the Gospel in a coffin."[22] "The letter does not speak of persecution (why would Satan bother to persecute a dead church?)."[23]

> It is vain to boast of a correct creed, of right theories, of sound doctrine, if there be no practical godliness, no good works, no positive virtues and active charities and labours. Orthodoxy is important, but orthodoxy alone will not do. The most orthodox in this list is depicted as the deadest. . . . There are, indeed, such things as "dead works;" works that have no life-connection with piety; works put on from without, and not brought forth from within; fruits tied upon the tree, and not the product of its life; which are not at all characteristics of true religion. There may be prayers, vigils, fasts, temples, altars, priests, rites, ceremonies, worship, and still be no true piety. Heathenism has all these.[24]

True spiritual life comes to the "living dead" by way of spiritual regeneration (Eph. 5:14) and is characterized by the presence and leading of the Holy Spirit (Eze. 1:12, 20; Mtt. 4:1; Luke 2:27; Acts 8:29; 10:19; 13:2; 16:9-10; 18:5).

3.3.2 - Revelation 3:2

be watchful

A present tense imperative participle (γίνου γρηγρῶν [*ginou grēgrōn*]) : "you be continually watching!" The command to the church at Sardis is the same found throughout Scripture to all believers. They are to be *continuously watching*. "It is not merely the call to be awake; it is to remain awake, to keep a vigil as a watchman in the midst of a sleeping encampment."[25]

The Sardian church was to *be watchful* because of the weakness of the flesh. " 'Watch and pray, lest you enter into temptation. The spirit indeed *is* willing, but the flesh *is* weak' " (Mtt. 26:41). They were to *watch themselves*:

> But take heed to yourselves, **lest your hearts be weighed down with carousing, drunkenness, and cares of this life, and that Day come on you unexpectedly**. For it will come as a snare on all those who dwell on the face of the whole earth. Watch therefore, and pray always that you may be counted worthy to escape all these things that will come to pass, and to stand before the Son of Man. (Luke 21:34-36) [emphasis added]

They were also to *watch others* in order to guard the fellowship:

> Therefore take heed to yourselves and to all the flock, among which the Holy Spirit has made you overseers, to shepherd the church of God which He purchased with His own blood. For I know this, that after my departure savage wolves will come in among you, not sparing the flock. Also from among yourselves men will rise up, speaking perverse things, to draw away the disciples after themselves. Therefore watch, and remember that for three years I did not cease to warn everyone night and day with tears. (Acts 20:28-31)

If they would not watch, then He would come upon them as a thief (Rev. 3:3). Unlike the "secure sinner," those who watch will not be taken by surprise.

strengthen the things which remain

The church of Sardis had need of endurance and was to press forward and strengthen those things which had not already died. Evidently, their fellowship had been drawing back from God's calling:

> For you have need of endurance, so that after you have done the will of God, you may receive the promise: "For yet a little while, *and* He who is coming will come and will not tarry. Now the just shall live by faith; but if *anyone* draws back, My soul has no pleasure in him." (Heb. 10:36-38)

But the Sardian church would be unable to strengthen the things which remain except for a renewed dependence upon the Holy Spirit. For in their own efforts, they were totally incapable of what Jesus here commands.[26] Again we see the purpose for Christ's title as "He who has the seven Spirits of God" when writing to this dying church.

that are ready to die

The branches were almost completely disconnected from the life-giving vine (John 15:5).

works perfect

Perfect is πεπληρωμένα [*peplērōmena*] rather than τέλεια [*teleia*] indicating works previously prepared and appointed but having been unfulfilled (Eph. 2:10). The works that they had (Rev. 3:1) were done to please or impress men and thus their *motivation* was fatally flawed. In this, the Sardian church was following in the footsteps of the religious leaders of Jesus' day: "But all their works they do to be seen by men. They make their phylacteries broad and enlarge the borders of their garments" (Mtt. 23:5). "Even so you also outwardly appear righteous to men, but inside you are full of hypocrisy and lawlessness" (Mtt. 23:28).

before God

Before *men*, the works were impressive and gave the church a name, but before *God* they were wood, hay, and stubble leaving their appointed true works of God unfulfilled. See *Worldly Churches*[4.18].

The *NU*[5.2.49] and *MT*[5.2.45] differ from the *TR*[5.2.79] here having *My God* . See Revelation 3:12.

3.3.3 - Revelation 3:3

remember . . . how you have received

The church at Sardis is given a command similar to that of the Ephesian church: to remember what they had earlier received and practiced. Inattention had played a significant part in their drift away from life toward death (Heb. 2:1).

hold fast

τήρει [*tērei*], a present tense imperative: "continually hold fast!" Like those who would be blessed by "the words of this prophecy" (Rev. 1:3), the church at Sardis would need to actively *keep* the things they had heard.

repent

See commentary on μετανοια [*metanoia*] at *Revelation 2:5*[3.2.5].

if you will not watch

Christians are to watch: (1) for Christ; (2) themselves lest they drift; (3) others lest false brethren or teachers pervert what they have received. Here the emphasis is upon watching for Christ (Mtt. 24:42; 25:13; Mark 13:33, 35; Mark 13:37; Luke 12:36-40; 21:36; 1Cor. 1:7; 16:13; Php. 3:20; 1Th. 1:10; 5:6; 2Ti. 4:8; Tit. 2:13; Heb. 9:28; 2Pe. 3:12; Rev. 3:2-3; Rev. 16:15).

as a thief, and you will not know what hour

Coming *as a thief* always denotes an unexpected coming in judgment because a *thief* comes to rob and destroy. Christ is never said to come for His church *as a thief*. "The first phase of the Lord's coming is as a bridegroom and the second phase is as a thief. He does not come upon His bride as a thief and He does not come upon the apostates and unregenerate world as a bridegroom."[27] Here, the phrase would remind the Sardian church of the historical fall of the city (see commentary on *Revelation 3:1*[3.3.1]):

> The city had been captured twice in its history, once in 549 B.C. by Cyrus of Persia and again in 195 B.C. by Antiochus the Great, while its inhabitants were indifferently resting in its supposed impregnability. Would Christians there allow the same to happen to them at the hands of one whom they had made their spiritual opponent?[28]

Some believe the immediate context of the letter argues for understanding this threat as pertaining to a localized spiritual coming in judgment:

> The context of Rev. 3:3b requires that the term "like a thief in the night" does not here refer to the *rapture*[5.2.62], but rather to Christ coming in judgment like that threatened to the church at Ephesus (Rev. 2:5), for this coming can be averted by repentance, but that cannot apply to the rapture. Here the "thief" aspect is a reminder drawn from the embarrassing history of the city.[29]

At a time when the Sardian church least expected Him, judgment would fall on the local assembly. Yet even here when a local application appears in view, we find Scripture teaching a general principle which will apply at the time of the end. "The threat here is not related to His second coming, but is that the Lord would come and destroy the Sardis church if there is no revival. It can also be extrapolated into a warning of the judgment that faces all dead churches at Christ's return."[30]

There are indicators that the coming could be eschatological: "In other alleged cases of Christ's coming for special judgment (cf. Rev. 2:5, 16, 22-23), consequences are explicitly stated, but here no such penal result is given. Apparently it is understood to be Christ's punishment of disloyalty at His second advent."[31]

Elsewhere, Scripture relates that the *Day of the Lord*[5.2.14] will come in a similar manner:

> For you yourselves know perfectly that the day of the Lord so comes as a **thief** in the night. For when they say, "Peace and safety!" then sudden destruction comes upon them, as labor pains upon a pregnant woman. And they shall not escape. But you, brethren, are not in darkness, so that this Day should overtake you as a **thief**. You are all sons of light and sons of the day. We are not of the night nor of darkness. Therefore let us not sleep, as others *do*, but let us watch and be sober. For those who sleep, sleep at night, and those who get drunk are drunk at night. But let us who are of the day be sober, putting on the breastplate of faith and love, and *as* a helmet the hope of salvation. For God did not appoint us to wrath, but to obtain salvation through our Lord Jesus Christ, who died for us, that whether we wake or

sleep, we should live together with Him. (1Th. 5:2-10) [emphasis added]

But the day of the Lord will come as a **thief** in the night, in which the heavens will pass away with a great noise, and the elements will melt with fervent heat; both the earth and the works that are in it will be burned up. (2Pe. 3:10) [emphasis added]

On the Day of the Lord, Jesus comes *as a thief* in judgment upon an unsuspecting world:

But as the days of Noah *were*, so also will the coming of the Son of Man be. For as in the days before the flood, they were eating and drinking, marrying and giving in marriage, until the day that Noah entered the ark, and did not know until the flood came and took them all away, so also will the coming of the Son of Man be. Then two *men* will be in the field: one will be taken and the other left. Two *women will be* grinding at the mill: one will be taken and the other left. Watch therefore, for you do not know what **hour** your Lord is coming. But know this, that if the master of the house had known what **hour** the **thief** would come, he would have watched and not allowed his house to be broken into. Therefore you also be ready, for the Son of Man is coming at an **hour** you do not expect. (Mtt. 24:37-44)[32] [emphasis added]

Take heed, watch and pray; for you do not know when the time is. *It is* like a man going to a far country, who left his house and gave authority to his servants, and to each his work, and commanded the doorkeeper to watch. Watch therefore, for you do not know when the master of the house is coming—in the evening, at midnight, at the crowing of the rooster, or in the morning— lest, coming suddenly, he find you sleeping. And what I say to you, I say to all: 'Watch!' (Mark 13:33-37)

Let your waist be girded and *your* lamps burning; and you yourselves be like men who wait for their master, when he will return from the wedding, that when he comes and knocks they may open to him immediately. Blessed *are* those servants whom the master, when he comes, will find watching. Assuredly, I say to you that he will gird himself and have them sit down *to eat*, and will come and serve them. And if he should come in the second watch, or come in the third watch, and find *them* so, blessed are those servants. But know this, that if the master of the house had known what **hour** the **thief** would come, he would have watched and not allowed his house to be broken into. Therefore you also be ready, for the Son of Man is coming at an **hour** you do not expect. (Luke 12:35-40)[33] [emphasis added]

"Behold, I am coming as a **thief**. Blessed *is* he who watches, and keeps his garments, lest he walk naked and they see his shame." (Rev. 16:15) [emphasis added]

Christ's coming as a thief has no reference to His coming for the church at the rapture. His thief-like coming occurs at the day of the Lord. Since Paul tells the Thessalonians they were well acquainted with the prophetic truth concerning the day of the Lord, this day is not to be identified with the Rapture, about which Paul did need to write to clarify their understanding. The day of the Lord begins with the Great Tribulation, and ends with the close of the Millennium. Those who shall "not escape" (1Th. 5:3) are those who are not brethren, who fail to watch and pray (Luke 21:36), are not counted worthy to escape, and therefore go on into the tribulation period.[34]

Paul said much the same thing to the Thessalonian church as Jesus says here to the church at Sardis—to the faithful who remain watching, Christ will *not come as a thief*:

For you yourselves know perfectly that the day of the Lord so comes as a thief in the night. For when they say, "Peace and safety!" then sudden destruction comes upon them, as labor pains upon a pregnant woman. And they shall not escape. **But you, brethren, are not in darkness, so that this Day should overtake you as a thief.** You are all sons of light and sons of the day. We are not of the night nor of darkness. Therefore let us not sleep, as others *do* , but let us watch and be sober. (1Th. 5:2-6) [emphasis added]

See *Trouble Ahead*[2.13.1].

will not

The negation here is with οὐ μέ [*ou me*], the strongest possible form of negation in Koine Greek.[35] No matter the resolve, awareness, or intelligence of those who fail to continuously watch, they will be spiritually deceived and will not know the time.

3.3.4 - Revelation 3:4

a few even in Sardis

God never lumps the faithful in with the errant in his assessment. Even in the midst of a wicked culture, there are those who trust in Him which He will never forsake (Gen. 6:9; 18:25; 19:22; Jos.

6:17).

not defiled their garments

Before coming to faith, these few were wearing "filthy rags" in comparison to the righteousness required by God (Isa. 64:6). Having trusted in Christ, His righteousness has been imputed to them and they are positionally holy. Even then, in their walk, they could become defiled by fleshly activities of the world (Jas. 1:27; Jude 23). By confessing their sins, these few had steadfastly remained in close fellowship with God (1Jn. 1:9).

shall walk with me

The picture of *walking* is two-fold: (1) the faithful are presently guided by the Spirit to walk in His ways (Gen. 5:22; 1S. 2:9; Job 23:14; Ps. 37:5, 23; 40:2; 66:9; 119:133; Pr. 3:6; 16:9; 19:21; 20:24; Isa. 2:3; 30:21; 48:17; Jer. 6:16; 10:23; Rom. 8:1, 4-6; Gal. 5:16); (2) in the future, the redeemed will have full fellowship with God as did Adam in the Garden of Eden (Gen. 3:8; Rev. 21:3; 22:3-4).

in white

They will wear *white* garments in contrast to the "filthy garments" they wore prior to coming to faith:

> Now Joshua was clothed with filthy garments, and was standing before the Angel. Then He answered and spoke to those who stood before Him, saying, "Take away the filthy garments from him." And to him He said, "See, I have removed your iniquity from you, and I will clothe you with rich robes." And I said, "Let them put a clean turban on his head." So they put a clean turban on his head, and they put the clothes on him. And the Angel of the Lord stood by. (Zec. 3:3-5)

These are those whose sin has been atoned by the blood of Jesus, who "wash their garments in the blood of the Lamb." Those at Sardis in John's day are to be followed by a constant stream of faithful throughout history culminating in those who stand firm to obtain the crown of life during the Great Tribulation (Rev. 7:9-17). Those slain for the word of God and for the testimony they held are given white robes to wear (Rev. 6:9-11). The *white* color speaks of the righteousness of Christ, but also of the marriage garments worn by His bride and those who attend the wedding feast who are found to be "spotless and without blemish" and "white and clean":

> But when the king came in to see the guests, he saw a man there who did not have on a wedding garment. (Mtt. 22:11)

> "Let us be glad and rejoice and give Him glory, for the marriage of the Lamb has come, and His wife has made herself ready." And to her it was granted to be arrayed in fine linen, clean and bright, for the fine linen is the righteous acts of the saints. . . . And the armies in heaven, clothed in fine linen, white and clean, followed Him on white horses. (Rev. 19:7-14)

> Husbands, love your wives, just as Christ also loved the church and gave Himself for her, that He might sanctify and cleanse her with the washing of water by the word, that He might present her to Himself a glorious church, not having spot or wrinkle or any such thing, but that she should be holy and without blemish. (Eph 5:25-27)

they are worthy

Their worthiness is found in the worthiness of Him on Whom they have believed. Those who were at one time invited to the wedding, but rejected the Bridegroom were not worthy to attend. "Then he said to his servants, 'The wedding is ready, but those who were invited were not worthy" (Mtt. 22:8). Those with faith in Christ are adopted into God's family and are found worthy to attain the resurrection of life (Luke 20:34-36, the *first resurrection*, see commentary at *Revelation 2:11*[3.2.11]).

> God's Word does not refuse to ascribe a *worthiness* to men (Mtt. 10:10-11; 22:8; Luke 20:35; 21:36; 2Th. 1:5, 11); although this worthiness must ever be contemplated as *relative* and not *absolute*; as resting on God's free acceptance of an obedience which would fain be perfect, even while it actually *is* most imperfect, and on this his acceptance and allowance of it alone.[36]

3.3.5 - Revelation 3:5

overcomes

See *Who is the Overcomer?*[4.15.1.3]

clothed in white garments

See commentary on *Revelation 3:4*[3.3.4]. *Clothed* is περιβαλεῖται [*peribaleitai*], the overcomer will *cause himself* to be clothed in white.[37] The overcomer will be *clothed in white garments* like those in Laodicea who are counseled "to buy ... white garments, that you may be clothed, that the shame of your nakedness may not be revealed" (Rev. 3:18). This clothing *covers* nakedness, reminding us of the Hebrew word for *atonement*, כָּפַר [*kūppar*]: "*pual* - to be covered over."[38] The *white garments* are a symbol of redemption (Rev. 4:4; 5:8-9; 7:9-17). The sin of the overcomer will be removed from God's sight by being covered by the "righteousness of God" (Rom. 3:5, 21-26; 10:3; 2Cor. 5:21; Php. 3:9; Jas. 1:20).

Some have also seen the *white garments* as a possible allusion to the glorified state of the redeemed (Dan. 12:3; Mtt. 13:43; Rom. 8:19, 23; Php. 3:21).

> The armies of heaven who appear with the warrior Messiah are "arrayed in fine linen, white and pure" (Rev. 19:14). It would seem, therefore, that the white garments promised to the overcomer in Rev. 3:5 represent an attire appropriate to the heavenly state. Since they are made white by washing in the blood of the Lamb (Rev. 7:13), the figure is highly appropriate to portray justification.[39]

I will not

This is emphatic: a double negative (Luke 21:33; John 6:37; 8:51; 13:8; Rev. 2:11).

blot out his name from the Book of Life

The church at Sardis had a name and likely had an official roll containing the names of those who attended. Yet it was dead. Jesus directs the church members to be concerned whether they are in the *Book of Life*[5.2.10] rather than the church role. See *Book of Life*[4.4].

confess his name

Christ taught the same in the gospels—that whoever would confess Him before men, in turn, He would confess before His Father and the angels (Mtt. 10:32; Luke 12:8). What powerful incentive this is for our witness of Him in the face of skeptics and mockers! When standing before such men, let us consider ourselves to be standing before the very throne of the Father in our confession of the Son. "Coming immediately after the promise of not erasing the overcomer's name from the book of life, this promise implies that on that future day of reckoning the judge will acknowledge the names written in the book as those who belong to Him."[40]

3.3.6 - Revelation 3:6

let him hear what the Spirit says to the churches

See commentary on *Revelation 2:7*[3.2.7].

3.3.7 - Revelation 3:7

the angel

See the discussion concerning the identity of the angel at *Revelation 1:20*[3.1.20].

church in Philadelphia

See commentary on *Seven Churches of Asia*[4.15]. Philadelphia was built by Attalus Philadelphus, king of Pergamum (died 138 BC) from which it derives its name.

Architrave Fragment at Philadelphia [41]

Philadelphia is twenty-seven miles E.S.E. from Sardis[42] and suffered frequent earthquakes, one of which nearly destroyed it during the reign of Tiberius Philadelphia.

> Philadelphia, so called from its founder, Attalus Philadelphus, still exists in the town called Allah-shear, "the city of God." . . . The number of houses is said to be about 3000, of which 250 are Greek, the rest Turkish; and the Christians have twenty-five places of worship, five of them large and regular churches, a resident bishop, and twenty inferior clergy.[43]

He who is holy,

Here again we see the deity of Christ (and the Trinity) in the application of a title by the Son which is uniquely the Father's. This title is applied to יהוה [*yhwh*] in the *OT*[5.2.51] (Isa. 6:3; 40:25; 43:15). The holiness of Jesus is a reflection of his identification with the Father in the Godhood. "I and *My* Father are one" (John 10:30). "*Hagios* characterizes Jesus, not so much as the sinless one, but as one especially set apart, belonging exclusively to God."[44]

There is only *one* who is holy, an attribute required as the perfect sacrifice (Isa. 53:4-11; Heb. 10:14). No other man could bear the sins of other men since they could not even bear their own sin (Heb. 7:27). He is holy not only in the sense of being *perfect and without sin* (Isa. 53:9; John 8:46; 14:30; 2Cor. 5:21; Heb. 4:15; 7:26; 9:14; 1Pe. 1:19; 2:22; 1Jn. 3:5), but because of his *uniqueness and separateness*—there is none other like Him. "And you shall be holy to Me, for I the Lord am holy, and have separated you from the peoples, that you should be Mine" (Lev. 20:26). His name is "Holy" (Isa. 57:15) and he is righteous in all His ways (Ps. 145:17). He is the "Holy One" Who the Father had promised would not be allowed to see corruption (Ps. 16:10) and thus would be raised from the dead.

The holiness of God is the subject of great angelic praise throughout Scripture (Isa. 6:3; Rev. 4:8). All those in the spiritual realm, even the demons, recognize this attribute of Christ (Mark 1:24). Yet, this truth was sadly lacking on earth where the "Holy One" was denied by unholy men who asked for a murderer in His place (Acts 3:14; 4:27).

He who is true

Another attribute of the Trinity: God cannot lie (Num. 23:19; Rom. 3:4; Heb. 6:18; Tit. 1:2). Jesus tells the Laodiceans that His witness is faithful and *true* (Rev. 3:14)—what He says is *undeniable* in its accuracy. This is why it is He who will judge and avenge the blood of the martyrs (Rev. 6:10; 19:11). Because He Himself is *true*, His "words will by no means pass away" (Mtt. 24:35).

key of David

The *key* indicates the governmental authority of *David*.[45] He is the promised king Who will rule from the throne of David (2S. 7:13-17; Ps. 89:4, 28; Isa. 9:7; 16:5; Jer. 23:5; 33:15; Amos 9:11; Zec. 6:13; Mtt. 19:28; 25:31; Luke 1:32; Acts 2:30).

Jacob prophesied that a ruler would arise from the tribe of Judah (Gen. 49:10). Isaiah prophesied of a coming child with an eternal kingdom that would rule from David's throne (Isa. 9:6-7). Gabriel repeated this promise to Mary at the annunciation: "He will be great, and will be called the Son of the Highest; and the Lord God will give Him the throne of His father David" (Luke 1:32).

The *key of David* was laid on the *shoulder* of Eliakim who acted as prime minister and who determined who would be allowed to see King Hezekiah. He also would make decisions only the king could overthrow. His was a position of great authority and trust:

> Then it shall be in that Day, that I will call My servant Eliakim the son of Hilkiah; I will clothe him with your robe and strengthen him with your belt; I will commit your responsibility into his hand. He shall be a father to the inhabitants of Jerusalem and to the house of Judah. The key of the house of David I will lay on his shoulder; so he shall open, and no one shall shut; and he shall shut, and no one shall open. I will fasten him *as* a peg in a secure place, and he will become a glorious throne to his father's house. (Isa. 22:20-23)

> This key was properly handled by the king (Rev. 3:7), and therefore by the "house-mayor" only in his stead. The power of the keys consisted not only in the supervision of the royal chambers, but also in the decision who was and who was not to be received into the king's service. There is a resemblance, therefore, to the giving of the keys of the kingdom of heaven to Peter under the New Testament. But there the "binding" and "loosing" introduce another figure, though one similar in sense; whereas here, in the "opening" and "shutting," the figure of the key is retained.[46]

The key being *laid on his shoulder* speaks of *committing responsibility into his hand* and alludes to Isaiah's prophecy of the ultimate Davidic ruler:

> For unto us a Child is born, unto us a Son is given; **And the government will be upon His shoulder**. And His name will be called Wonderful, Counselor, Mighty God, Everlasting Father, Prince of Peace. Of the increase of *His* government and peace *There will be* no end, upon the throne of David and over His kingdom, to order it and establish it with judgment and justice from that time forward, even forever. The zeal of the LORD of hosts will perform this. (Isa. 9:6-7) [emphasis added]

Being both God and man, in the line of David (Mtt. 1:1, 6; Luke 3:31), Christ alone has the authority to open the scroll initiating the judgments which usher in the Davidic kingdom upon the earth. "But one of the elders said to me, 'Do not weep. Behold, the Lion of the tribe of Judah, the Root of David, has prevailed to open the scroll and to loose its seven seals.' " (Rev. 5:5).

Some interpreters see these keys as being identical with the keys of the kingdom of heaven (Mtt. 16:19; Heb. 3:6).[47] Peter was given the keys to the kingdom and was personally present when each of the 3 person groups (Jews, Samaritans, and Gentiles: Acts 1:8) first received the Holy Spirit.[48] Jesus chastised the scribes and Pharisees, "But woe to you, scribes and Pharisees, hypocrites! For you shut up the kingdom of heaven against men; for you neither go in yourselves, nor do you allow those who are entering to go in" (Mtt. 23:13). Instead, authority to enter the kingdom of heaven was entrusted to a simple fisherman (Mtt. 16:19). The authority of heaven stands behind the Spirit-led decisions of the church (Mtt. 18:18; John 20:23).

Concerning the keys of Hades and Death, see commentary on *Revelation 1:18*[3.1.18].

He who opens and no one shuts

ὁ ἀνοιγων καὶ οὐδὲς κλείσει [*ho anoigōn kai oudes kleisei*]: "the one presently opening and no one shall shut". He is *actively* holding open the door such that no one else can shut it.

shuts and no one opens

κλείων καὶ οὐδεὶς ἀνοίγει [*kleiōn kai oudeis anoigei*]: "while presently shutting and no one is presently opening". He is *actively* shutting things which are to remain shut. Men must respond while the door is held open by God for once it is shut, there is no recourse for entry:

> And while they went to buy, the bridegroom came, and those who were ready went in with him to the wedding; and the door was shut. (Mtt. 25:10)

> When once the Master of the house has risen up and shut the door, and you begin to stand outside and knock at the door, saying, 'Lord, Lord, open for us,' and He will answer and say to you, 'I do not know

you, where you are from.' (Luke 13:25)

3.3.8 - Revelation 3:8

I know

See commentary on *Revelation 2:2*[3.2.2].

open door

Θύραν ἐνεῳγμένην [*Thyran eneōgmenēn*]: "a door while having been opened" (perfect tense) - the door now stands open after *having been opened* by Jesus. Although Jesus is knocking at a *shut* door in Laodicea (Rev. 3:20), at Philadelphia He Himself holds the door *open* such that *no one can shut it*. This door in Philadelphia could represent the door of evangelism and illumination without which human promulgation of the gospel falls on unreceptive ears (Luke 24:45; Acts 14:27; 16:14; 1Cor. 16:9; 2Cor. 2:12; Col. 4:3). See commentary on *Revelation 3:20*[3.3.20].

In view of the mention of the *key of David* (Rev. 3:7) and *synagogue of Satan* (Rev. 3:9), it seems more likely the door provides entrance into the *Messianic Kingdom*[5.2.39] where Christ will rule from the throne of David (see commentary on *Revelation 3:21*[3.3.21]).[49]

> It speaks of a sure entrance into the Messianic Kingdom, promised to this church as a reward for their faithfulness. No one, not even those of "the synagogue of Satan," can shut them out. Jewish opponents would seek to deny Gentiles, such as Christians in this city, entrance into the Messianic Kingdom.[50]

In view of Jesus' subsequent promise to the overcomer, "I also will keep you from the hour of trial which shall come upon the whole world" (Rev. 3:10), perhaps this door that is held open and which no man can shut is a sure pathway to heaven for the faithful at the time of the *Rapture*[5.2.62]: "After these things I looked, and behold, a **door** standing **open** in heaven. And the first voice which I heard was like a trumpet speaking with me, saying, 'Come up here, and I will show you things which must take place after this.' " [emphasis added] (Rev. 4:1). See *Rapture*[4.14].

a little strength

Even though they have but little strength, they will be able to avail themselves of the door since Christ ensures it remains open. Some believe this should be translated without the indefinite article, "little strength" as an indication of weakness rather than power.[51] The ministry of the church at Philadelphia would be all the more effective because in their strength their accomplishments would be undeniably of God (2Cor. 12:9; Php. 4:13). Others believe that the commendations given to this church are an indication of their spiritual vitality so that this phrase "must refer to the church's limited influence because of its numerical smallness."[52]

kept My word

The church at Philadelphia had faithfully kept His word. They had preserved its meaning and applied it to their own lives. They were blessed with those who keep the words of this prophecy (Rev. 1:3; 22:7). It is by keeping his word—and the commandments therein—that the Philadelphian church *demonstrated* the depth of their love for Him (John 14:21-24).

In our own day, there are many pressures attempting to dissuade believers from keeping His word. "We are asked by some to abandon Genesis to 'science,' salvation by redemption to anthropology, the life of the Spirit to psychology, the very Word itself to higher criticism."[53]

not denied My name

They had not denied Him by their words (Mtt. 10:32-33; 26:70-72; Luke 12:8-9; 1Jn. 2:22-23) or through their actions (Pr. 30:9; Acts 3:13-15; 1Ti. 5:8). In the midst of the ultimate test, the church at Pergamos held fast to His name and did not deny His faith. (See commentary on *Revelation 2:13*[3.2.13].) In the days of the Tribulation, many will deny His name by taking the name of another (John 5:43; Rev. 13:17; 14:11).

3.3.9 - Revelation 3:9

synagogue of Satan, who say they are Jews and are not

See commentary on *Revelation 2:9*[3.2.9].

but lie

ψεύδονται [*pseudontai*], present tense, middle voice: *they themselves are presently lying.* They are making this ongoing claim themselves.

worship before your feet, and to know that I have loved you

In the local context, Christ would converts who were formerly of the "synagogue of Satan" to the Philadelphian church.[54] The worship would not be *to* the Philadelphian believers, but *before* them in recognition that God has *loved* them and favored them (Dan. 2:46-47).[55] "That the persecuting Jews would one day be forced to come and worship before your feet does not mean that the latter will be worshiped as deities, but they will be sitting enthroned with Christ (Rev. 3:21), before whom, someday, every knee will bow (Php. 2:10)."[56]

This is an allusion to numerous passages in the *OT*[5.2.51] which indicate that in the Millennium, Gentiles will come and bow down to Israel in recognition that God is with them (Isa. 45:15; 49:22-23; 60:14-16). Zechariah described a time when Gentiles would honor faithful Jews because, "we have heard *that* God *is* with you":

> Thus says the LORD of hosts: "Peoples shall yet come, inhabitants of many cities; the inhabitants of one *city* shall go to another, saying, 'Let us continue to go and pray before the LORD, and seek the LORD of hosts. I myself will go also.' Yes, many peoples and strong nations shall come to seek the LORD of hosts in Jerusalem, and to pray before the LORD." Thus says the LORD of hosts: "In those days ten men from every language of the nations shall grasp the sleeve of a Jewish man, saying, 'Let us go with you, for we have heard *that* God *is* with you.' " (Zec. 8:20-23)

In the *church age*, just the opposite is true—God elevates the faithful, both Gentile and Jew, over the national Jew who rejects Messiah Jesus.[57] The unique role of favor enjoyed by the Church is intended to provoke the unbelieving Jewish nation to jealousy (Deu. 32:21; Isa. 65:1-2; Rom. 10:19-21; 11:11, 14; Rev. 3:9). "What the Jews expected from the pagans, they themselves will be forced to render to the followers of Jesus."[58]

> In light of the general nature of the application of all seven of these messages, the prophecy must look forward to the time when the whole church enters the *Messianic Kingdom*[5.2.39]. The people of Israel will have an entirely different attitude toward the church as Christ's bride because they will by then have turned to Christ themselves.[59]

This verse does not distinguish *Gentiles* from *Jews*, but *faithful* from *faithless*. The Philadelphian church included *Jewish* believers (Rom. 9:27).

> In connexion with this promise, there is an interesting passage in the Epistle of *Ignatius*[5.2.28] to this same Philadelphian Church (c. 6), implying the actual presence in the midst of it, of converts from Judaism, who now preached the faith which once they persecuted.[60]

The formerly non-believing Jews from the *synagogue of Satan* would *worship before* their believing *Jewish* countrymen as well as the believing Gentiles. (Lest we forget, the writer of the Revelation is himself a son of Abraham by birth!)

God *loved* them as was *demonstrated* by the cross (John 3:14-17; Rev. 1:5). "In this is love, not that we loved God, but that He loved us and sent His Son *to be* the propitiation for our sins" (1Jn. 4:10).

3.3.10 - Revelation 3:10

to persevere

Perseverance is especially needed in the midst of adversity. Jesus said that it would be by patience that believers "possess your souls" (Luke 21:16-19). *Persevere* is ὑπομονῆς [*hypomonēs*], which may include the idea of expectation related to the promise to be kept from the hour:

> Arndt and Gingrich hold that the word *hupomone* sometimes meant '(patient) expectation.' They

> indicated that is its meaning in the expression 'patience of Jesus Christ' in Revelation 1:9 and that perhaps that is its meaning in Revelation 3:10. . . . One thing in favor of this view is Christ's exclamation in Rev. 3:11, 'Behold I come quickly, hold that fast which thou hast.'[61]

keep you from the hour of trial

A large body of discussion attends this phrase. The debate centers on whether *from* (εκ [*ek*]) here denotes *out of* or *through*. Is the promise to keep the church *out of* the trial or to preserve it *through* the trial?

Proponents of the *kept through* view observe other passages where εκ [*ek*] can have this meaning.[62] They also observe examples in Scripture where God's people are protected in the midst of God's judgment:

> On the very same day Noah and Noah's sons, Shem, Ham, and Japheth, and Noah's wife and the three wives of his sons with them, entered the ark. (Gen. 7:13)

> Now the blood shall be a sign for you on the houses where you *are*. And when I see the blood, I will pass over you; and the plague shall not be on you to destroy *you* when I strike the land of Egypt. (Ex. 12:13)

> Come, my people, enter your chambers, and shut your doors behind you; hide yourself, as it were, for a little moment, until the indignation is past. For behold, the LORD comes out of His place to punish the inhabitants of the earth for their iniquity; the earth will also disclose her blood, and will no more cover her slain. (Isa. 26:20-21)

> "Do not harm the earth, the sea, or the trees till we have sealed the servants of our God on their foreheads." . . . They were commanded not to harm the grass of the earth, or any green thing, or any tree, but only those men who do not have the seal of God on their foreheads. (Rev. 7:3; 9:4)

Proponents of the *kept from* view point to the fact that the most natural use of εκ [*ek*] indicates *out of* and that if the alternate meaning were in view, another more suitable preposition would have been used.[63] They too can point to passages which support their view—where the faithful are *removed* prior to God's judgment:

> And Enoch walked with God; and he *was* not, for God took him. (Gen. 5:24)

> And Abraham came near and said, "Would You also destroy the righteous with the wicked? Suppose there were fifty righteous within the city; would You also destroy the place and not spare *it* for the fifty righteous that were in it?" . . . Then he said, "Let not the Lord be angry, and I will speak but once more: suppose ten should be found there?" And He said, "I will not destroy *it* for the sake of ten." (Gen. 18:23-32)

> And he said to him, "See, I have favored you concerning this thing also, in that I will not overthrow this city for which you have spoken. Hurry, escape there. For I cannot do anything until you arrive there." Therefore the name of the city was called Zoar. (Gen. 19:21-22)

The problem cannot be solved simply by appeal to similar passages since *both models* of protection are found in Scripture. This is because saints occupying different roles in history find themselves in different situations with regard to what God is doing in their midst. There is not a "one size fits all" approach to how God chooses to protect the faithful: at the time of Noah's flood, Enoch "walked with God and he *was* not, for God took him" (Gen. 5:24), yet Noah and his family were preserved *through* the flood within the Ark (Gen. 7:13). We believe that by these typological examples, God is teaching us that some saints will be raptured whereas others—who come to faith later—will be protected in the midst of His wrath.

But, the simple answer to the question at hand is found by reading the promise more carefully, for the promise is not to be kept from *the trial*, but from *the hour of trial*. The church will not even experience the trial for it will be *kept from the hour* when the trial is visited upon the earth.

> Christ promised to keep these church saints form the *time period* characterized by the testing Christ had in mind. If the Lord had meant that He would keep them from just the testing itself, He could have made that very clear by omitting the words 'the hour' and simply saying, 'I will keep you from the testing.'[64]

When the all-important word *hour* is factored into the discussion, it becomes clear that the promise relates to the *time* of trial and not its effects. "When Jesus in his human nature prayed 'remove this cup from me [Mark 14:36; Luke 22:42],' and the parallel or equivalent request, 'save me from this hour

[John 12:27],' he was not praying to be spared during the hour, but to be kept from it, which settles the meaning of the expression here."[65] Too often, commentators fail to grasp this important distinction. For example:

> It is far from clear that the removal of Christians from the earth would be the only possible way in which Jesus could *keep* His people *from* **the wars and plagues** anticipated to occur at that time. [emphasis added][66]

But this line of reasoning is flawed because the verse says nothing about being kept from *wars and plagues*—the promise is to be kept from the *hour* or *time*.

A serious problem with the *kept through* view is that God's promise is of little merit in view of the fact that Scripture records multitudes of the faithful will suffer violent death during this period (Dan. 7:21, 25; 8:24; Rev. 7:9-16; 12:11; 13:7; 20:4):[67]

> Even if the church saints were to be shielded from the testing of God's wrath will bring on the earth in the period of testing Christ had in mind, the Scriptures (Rev. 6:9-11; 13:7, 15; 20:4) make it clear that many of the saints alive on the earth during that period will be martyred by unbelievers. Thus, even though they will not be put to death by God's wrath, they will still experience violent death as if they had not been shielded from God's wrath. This militates against the answer that Christ will shield or protect the saints in or through that period of testing.[68]

> This verse does not say that the Church will be merely kept safe *during* the trial, but it will be kept *from the very hour* of trial, that is, from the very *time* of it. This requires a removal before the Tribulation ever occurs. If Revelation 3:10 means that the Church will be kept safe during the Tribulation, then something goes terribly wrong. Throughout the Tribulation, saints are being killed on a massive scale (Rev. 6:9-11; 11:7; 12:11; 13:7, 15; 14:13; 17:6; 18:24). If these saints are Church saints, they are *not* being kept safe and Revelation 3:10 is meaningless. Only if Church saints and Tribulation saints are kept distinct does the promise of Revelation 3:10 make any sense.[69]

This *hour of trial* is said to *come upon the whole world* (see below) and cannot relate to the destruction of Jerusalem in A.D. 70 as some hold for there was no need to protect the Philadelphian church from events hundreds of miles distant which had offered no direct physical threat to Asia Minor. This promise relates to a unique time of trial yet future that all believers shall escape due to their participation in the *Rapture*[5.2.62]. In this, the passage has in common a typological and future application like that of Revelation 2:20-22 where *Jezebel*[4.9] is cast into *great tribulation*. See commentary on *Revelation 2:22*[3.2.22]. See *Rapture*[4.14].

which shall come

τῆς μελλούσης ἔρχεσθαι [*tēs mellousēs erchesthai*], *the one about to come*. "The participle τῆς μελλούσης [*tēs mellousēs*] ('which is about to') modifies ὥρας [*hōras*], 'hour,' rather than πειρασμοῦ [*peirasmou*], 'trial,' showing that it is the hour, not the trial, that is prominent in the statement."[70]

the whole world

Some *interpreters*[2.12.2] take *world* (οἰκουμένης [*oikoumenēs*]) as denoting the land in Israel or the Mediterranean in order to find fulfillment in the events attending Rome and the destruction of Jerusalem in A.D. 70.

> In A.D. 68, the death of *Nero*[5.2.46], and the civil wars that followed, greatly threatened the stability of the Roman Empire, until Vespasian was made emperor in A.D. 70. During this same period (A.D. 66-70), the Jews were embroiled in a fight for the survival of their nation against the Romans . . . which they lost.[71]

It is true that this term is used in contexts where its scope is not global (Luke 2:1; Acts 11:28; 17:6; 19:27). However the term is also used in a global sense elsewhere (Mtt. 24:14; Luke 4:5; Luke 21:26; Acts 17:31; Rom. 10:18; Heb. 1:6; 2:5; Rev. 12:9; 16:14).

> This same expression is used in Revelation 16:14 to refer to the kings of the whole inhabited earth gathering together to battle at Armageddon in conjunction with the sixth bowl judgment . . . it was used in Jesus' statement concerning the preaching of the gospel of the kingdom in all the inhabited earth to all nations during the future tribulation period (Mtt. 24:14 [cf. Rev. 14:6]). In both of these passages, it

> must refer to the entire inhabited earth, not just the Roman Empire.[72]

Thus, it is not a *technical term*[5.2.72] and it's meaning is determined by the context. Even if we permit the *preterist interpretation*[2.12.2] that *world* here means all the *known* world, the events of Nero in Rome and the fall of Jerusalem in A.D. 70 had little impact at Philadelphia in Asia Minor:

> The Neronian persecution was limited to Rome as far as the data tell us, and there is no evidence for it extending to the province of Asia at that time.[73]

> What does a localized judgment hundreds of miles away have to do with the *seven churches*[5.2.66] of Asia? John uses two long chapters in addressing those churches regarding the implications of the coming of Christ for them. For instance, the promise to shield the Philadelphian church from judgment (Rev. 3:10-11) is meaningless if that judgment occurs far beyond the borders of that city.[74]

The context of the book of Revelation and the events which it describes—the wrath of God being poured forth on an unbelieving world prior to the return of Christ—argue for the global sense here. This time was described by Jesus in terms which are clearly global:

> For then there will be great tribulation, such as has not been since the beginning of the world until this time, no, nor ever shall be. And unless those days were shortened, no flesh would be saved; but for the elect's sake those days will be shortened. (Mtt. 24:21-22)

> For it will come as a snare on all those who dwell on the face of the whole earth. Watch therefore, and pray always that you may be counted worthy to escape all these things that will come to pass, and to stand before the Son of Man. (Luke 21:35-36)

Of special interest is Jesus' statement recorded by Mark. In describing the uniqueness of this time, He mentioned *since the beginning of creation*, another indication of global scope. This is in contrast with the words told Daniel by the angel that it would be the most unique time *since there was a nation* when describing its effects upon the Jewish nation (Dan. 12:1).

> For *in* those days there will be tribulation, such as has not been **since the beginning of the creation** which God created until this time, nor ever shall be. And unless the Lord had shortened those days, no flesh would be saved; but for the elect's sake, whom He chose, He shortened the days. (Mark 13:19-20) [emphasis added]

An early teaching from the Didache alludes to this passage and takes it in a global sense:

> For as lawlessness increases, they will hate and persecute and betray one another. And then the deceiver of the world will appear as a son of God and "will perform signs and wonders," and the earth will be delivered into his hands, and he will commit abominations the likes of which have never happened before. (5) Then **all humankind will come to the fiery test**, and "many will fall away" and perish [emphasis added][75]

3.3.10.1 - Earth Dwellers

to test those who dwell upon the earth

Both Isaiah and Zephaniah described this day:

> For behold, the LORD comes out of His place to punish the inhabitants of the earth for their iniquity; the earth will also disclose her blood, and will no more cover her slain. (Isa. 26:21)

> The great day of the LORD *is* near; *It is* near and hastens quickly. The noise of the day of the LORD is bitter; there the mighty men shall cry out. That day *is* a day of wrath, a day of trouble and distress, a day of devastation and desolation, a day of darkness and gloominess, a day of clouds and thick darkness, a day of trumpet and alarm against the fortified cities and against the high towers. "I will bring distress upon men, and they shall walk like blind men, because they have sinned against the LORD; their blood shall be poured out like dust, and their flesh like refuse." Neither their silver nor their gold shall be able to deliver them in the day of the LORD'S wrath; but the whole land shall be devoured by the fire of His jealousy, for He will make speedy riddance of all those who dwell in the land. (Zep 1:14-18)

The tribulation and wrath associated with this coming hour is intended *to test* those whose home, citizenship, and focus is earthward rather than heavenly.[76]

The phrase *those who dwell upon the earth* takes on a soteriological/eschatological meaning in the book of Revelation for it denotes the *unsaved at the time of the end who steadfastly continue in their rejection of God.* In contrast to the faithful who are *aliens* and *sojourners* upon the earth (Lev. 25:23; Num. 18:20, 23; 1Chr. 29:15; Ps. 39:12; 119:19; John. 15:19; 17:14, 16; Php. 3:20; Heb. 11:13; 1Pe. 2:11) and whose hope is heavenward (Heb. 11:13-16; Rev. 13:6), these that *dwell* upon the earth are trusting in man and his environment.[77] These are the spiritual offspring of the humanists of our day. Believers are not among these earth dwellers, for the earth dwellers ultimately hate believers:[78] "If you were of the world, the world would love its own. Yet because you are not of the world, but I chose you out of the world, therefore the world hates you" (John 15:19). When the earth dwellers give us praise and are in love with us, then it is time for us to reassess the validity of our heavenly witness.

The time of testing will come unexpectedly upon "those who dwell on the face of the whole earth" (Luke 21:35). They will suffer through a time of testing like none before and they will endure both the wrath of God (Rev. 6:16-17) and Satan (Rev. 12:12)! They will be subjected to incredible deception (2Th. 2:11; Rev. 13:12-14; 17:8),[79] will worship both Satan and the *Antichrist*[5.2.3] (Rev. 13:4, 8) and willingly participate in the slaughter of those who remain faithful to God (Rev. 6:10; 11:10). Even though every nation, tribe, tongue, and people will hear the gospel during this time of testing, the majority will stand confirmed in their rejection of God (Rev. 14:6):

> All the classes [of men named here] literally reside on the earth, but the phrase referred to is one of moral signification and import. They are apostates from Christianity, having deliberately and determinately rejected the heavenly calling, and chosen the earth. *God* may have heaven; *they* are determined to have the earth as their place and portion.[80]

> All of these Revelation references to "them that dwell upon the earth" clearly indicate that they will be unsaved people of the future period of testing who will never get saved. . . . In spite of the devastating horrors of the sixth trumpet, which will kill one-third of mankind, the earth-dwellers will not repent of their wicked deeds (Rev. 9:20-21). The fourth bowl will cause people to be scorched with great heat; the fifth bowl will cause excruciating pain; and the sixth bowl will cause hailstones weighing approximately 94 pounds each to bombard people. Although they will recognize that these are God's wrath judgments, the earth-dwellers will blaspheme Him rather than repent (Rev. 16:1, 7, 8-11, 21).[81]

See *Beast Worshipers are Unique*[4.4.3.4]. Like the believers of Philadelphia, those who trust in Christ prior to this time will be *kept from the hour* . Yet Scripture also records numerous saints who will come to faith during this horrific period and will walk through the events of their day—often ending in the ultimate witness—death (Rev. 7:9-16; 12:11; 13:7; 20:4).

Some suggest that the *trial* or test of this time period will have at least three purposes: (1) to serve as a witness to God (Dan. 11:35; 12:10); (2) to purge the rebels from Israel and turn the elect to God (Zec. 13:7-9; Mark 13:13); (3) to demonstrate the unrepentant state of the *earth dwellers*[5.2.18].[82] Even as the *earth dwellers* remain steadfast in their rejection of God, the believing Jewish remnant will swell:

> "Awake, O sword, against My Shepherd, against the Man who is My Companion," says the LORD of hosts. "Strike the Shepherd, and the sheep will be scattered; then I will turn My hand against the little ones. And it shall come to pass in all the land," says the LORD, "*That* two-thirds in it shall be cut off *and* die, but *one*-third shall be left in it: I will bring the *one-third* through the fire, will refine them as silver is refined, and test them as gold is tested. They will call on My name, and I will answer them. I will say, 'This *is* My people'; and each one will say, 'The LORD *is* my God.' " (Zec. 13:7-9)

Only the faithful will dare risk supporting the Jewish faithful during this massive outpouring of anti-Semitic and anti-Christian sentiment (Mtt. 25:31; Rev. 12:13). See *Trouble Ahead*[2.13.1].

3.3.11 - Revelation 3:11

I am coming quickly

"The placement of this fifth promise at this point is clear implication that the deliverance of the faithful will occur in conjunction with His coming. It holds open the possibility that His coming will happen before this generation passes, but does not guarantee it. This heightens the expectancy of Christ's coming soon, a possibility which is stressed further by the presence of *tachy* ('soon')."[83] See commentary on *Revelation 1:1*[3.1.1]. See *Imminency*[4.8].

hold fast

κράτει [*kratei*], a present tense imperative: "be continually holding fast!" The same thought as those who are blessed in Revelation 1:3.

that no one may take your crown

The crown *of life* was promised to the overcomer in Smyrna (Rev. 2:10). Since a specific crown is not identified, "Perhaps here the more general meaning of victory attached to *stephanon* should remain undefined."[84] See *Crowns*[4.6].

3.3.12 - Revelation 3:12

overcomes

See. *Who is the Overcomer?*[4.15.1.3]

I will make him a pillar in the temple

Some have seen this as an allusion to the pillars in Solomon's *Temple*[5.2.73]. "The reference here to Solomon is unmistakable. He it was who built the temple, and put in its porch those mysterious pillars 'Jachin [*i.e., He shall establish*] and Boaz [*i.e., In it is strength*]' (1K. 7:13-22; 2Chr. 3:17)."[85] Others find the analogy flawed in this instance:

> To find any allusion here . . . to the two monumental pillars, Jachin and Boaz, which Solomon set up, not in the temple, but in the open vestibule before the temple (1K. 7:21; 2Chr. 3:15, 17), I must say, appears to me quite beside the mark; and if there were any question on this point, the words which follow, *"and he shall go no more out,"* appear entirely decisive upon this point. These famous pillars were *always without* the temple; they would therefore have served very ill to set forth the blessedness of the redeemed, who should be *always within* it.[86]

The language has much in common with *Temple* language elsewhere in the *NT*[5.2.48] which is applied to the body of the believer and the presence of the indwelling of the Holy Spirit. See *Temple of the Believer*[4.16.5.5].

Since there is no *Temple* in the New Jerusalem (Rev. 21:22), this promise may be similar to the promise concerning the Millennium made to the Thyatiran overcomer (Rev. 2:27) and denote participation in the *Millennial Temple*[5.2.40] during the Messianic Age.[87] Some view the entire New Jerusalem as a "temple." See *New Jerusalem*[4.16.5.11].

The image of the *pillar* also evokes passages where the righteous are compared to fruitful trees "planted in the house of the Lord" (Ps. 92:12-14), God's *house* being the Temple (John 2:16).

go no more out

This is perhaps the most precious promise among all the promises given the overcomer. For this phrase relates to *fellowship with God!* The entire message of Scripture, from Genesis 1 to Revelation 22, can be found within this pregnant phrase. See *Hide and Seek*[4.16.1]. To the overcomer in Philadelphia is the promise of the fulfillment of that *first love* so lacking in Ephesus, to walk once again in full fellowship with God (Gen. 3:8; 5:24; Rev. 21:3, 22).

write on him the name of My God

The written name indicates character and ownership (Num. 6:27; John 1:12). These will be owned by God and molded according to His character. They are "sons of God" (Mtt. 5:9; Luke 20:36; John 1:12; Rom. 8:14, 19; Gal. 3:26). In the Tribulation, the 144,000 Jews have the Father's name written on their foreheads (Rev. 14:1) which identifies whose they are and provides for their protection (Rev. 7:3; 9:4). Here, the name is recorded on all the redeemed in the eternal state (Rev. 22:4).

In the last days, Satan will provide his own imitation of this identification (Rev. 13:16-17; 17:5; 20:4). See *Master Imitator*[4.2.5].

Previously, a new name was written on a stone given to the overcomer at Pergamos. See commentary on *Revelation 2:17*[3.2.17].

name of the city of My God

Jerusalem will have a new name during the Millennium:

> The Gentiles shall see your righteousness, and all kings your glory. You shall be called by a new name,

> which the mouth of the LORD will name. (Isa. 62:2)

> At that time Jerusalem shall be called The Throne of the LORD, and all the nations shall be gathered to it, to the name of the LORD, to Jerusalem. No more shall they follow the dictates of their evil hearts. (Jer. 3:17)

> "All the way around *shall be* eighteen thousand cubits; and the name of the city from *that* day *shall be*: THE LORD *IS* THERE." (Eze. 48:35)

The Lord will name the millennial Jerusalem "The Throne of the LORD" and "THE LORD *IS* THERE" indicating the presence of Messiah Jesus who will rule from the throne of David in the midst of the city.[88]

However this name is that of the *New Jerusalem* and is not said to be *new*.[89] The name is applied to the overcomer as a declaration of his right to citizenship in the eternal city (Rev. 21:2). Citizenship *declared* now (Php. 3:20) will be *realized* there.

This verse may also contain an allusion to an event of Philadelphian history whereby the city took a new name:

> The gratitude of the victims to the emperor is . . . variously attested . . . A huge pedestal found at Puteoli bears a dedicatory inscription to Tiberius surrounded by the names of Asian cities, . . . The name 'Philadelphea' [*sic*] is fully preserved. Later coins and inscriptions of some of these cities show that they assumed an imperial name or cognomen about this time. . . [Philadelphia] takes the name 'Neocaesarea' . . . The concept of Philadelphia as a new city with a new name to honour the divine emperor whose patronage had restored its fortunes has again been related to Rev. 3:12.[90]

city of My God

Earthly Jerusalem has been chosen by God. He has put His name there (1K. 8:48; 11:13, 36; 14:21; 2Chr. 6:6, 38; 12:13; Ps. 132:13; Isa. 49:14-16). Yet for all its glory, even in the Millennium when it is restored (Isa. 60; (62), the earthly Jerusalem is not the final destiny of the saints or the abode of God's presence. For at the end of the Millennium there will be a "new heavens and new earth" (Rev. 21:2) and a *New Jerusalem* which will be the ultimate destiny of the saints.

Elsewhere, Jesus also refers to the Father as *My God* (Mtt. 27:46; John 20:17; cf. Eph. 1:17; Heb. 1:8-9). We are Christ's and Christ is the Father's (1Cor. 3:23).

New Jerusalem

New is καινῆς [*kainēs*], new in quality. The *New Jerusalem* bears little similarity to the Jerusalem of our time or of the Millennium (Rev. 20:4-6). This is not the millennial city, which many Scriptures declare will be restored to prominence among the nations. It is the eternal abode of the saints:

> In Holy Scripture there are two Jerusalems: the one is on earth in the land of Palestine; the other is 'above' in heaven (Gal. 4:25-26; Heb. 12:22). Now the Old Testament prophets speak of a city which, in the coming Kingdom, shall be reclaimed from Gentile power, rebuilt, restored to the historic nation of Israel, and made the religious center of the world. This Jerusalem cannot be the 'heavenly Jerusalem,' for that city is impeccably holy, the eternal dwelling of the true God, and has never been defiled or marred by human sin and rebellion. Any such notion is to the highest degree impossible and absurd. All predictions of a restored and rebuilt Jerusalem must therefore refer to the historical city of David on earth.[91]

which comes down out of heaven

This is the "Jerusalem above" (Gal. 4:24), the "heavenly Jerusalem," the ultimate goal and destination of all the saints (John 14:2-3; Heb. 13:14).

> But you have come to Mount Zion and to the city of the living God, the heavenly Jerusalem, to an innumerable company of angels, to the general assembly and church of the firstborn *who are* registered in heaven, to God the Judge of all, to the spirits of just men made perfect. (Heb. 12:22-23)

She comes down *out of heaven* as a "bride, the Lamb's wife":

> Then one of the seven angels who had the seven bowls filled with the seven last plagues came to me and talked with me, saying, "Come, I will show you the bride, the Lamb's wife." And he carried me away in the Spirit to a great and high mountain, and showed me the great city, the holy Jerusalem, descending out of heaven from God. (Rev. 21:9-10)

She is referred to as a *bride* and *wife* for this is the final residence of the wife of the Lamb (Rev. 19:7).

My new name

New is καινο˜ν [*kainon*], new in quality. This new name, which denotes a yet unrevealed aspect of the character of Jesus (Rev. 3:12; 19:12) will be written on the overcomer. This recalls the mysterious, but unrevealed name attending the Angel of the Lord and Son of God throughout Scripture. The name is hinted at, but never revealed: when Jacob wrestled with the Angel and was named Israel (Gen. 32:29); when the Angel announced the birth of Samson to his parents (Jdg. 13:6, 18); in the question concerning the Son of God (Pr. 30:4); and in God's new name to be written on the overcomer (Rev. 3:12).

The overcomer is intimately identified with He who overcame (John 16:33). That the overcomer bears the names of both the Father and the Son is yet another clear statement of the deity of Christ—for God the Father would never share ownership or identity with any non-God.

3.3.13 - Revelation 3:13

let him hear what the Spirit says to the churches

See commentary on *Revelation 2:7*[3.2.7].

3.3.14 - Revelation 3:14

the angel

Some have suggested this particular angel to be Archippus (Col. 4:17) who was named as the first bishop of Laodicea in the *Apostolical Constitutions* (viii. 46)[92].

> Lightfoot has suggested however from Col. 4:17 that Archippus, presumably the son of Philemon (Philemon 2), held responsibility in the church in Laodicea. The two cities were only ten miles apart, and Col. 4 suggests habitual communication between them.[93]

See the discussion concerning the identity of the angel at *Revelation 1:20*[3.1.20].

church of the Laodiceans

See commentary on *Seven Churches of Asia*[4.15]. Laodicea was in southern Phrygia, midway between Philadelphia and Colosse.

Bathhouse Arches at Laodicea [94]

It was known as *Laodicea on the Lycus* to distinguish it from at least five other cities bearing the same name. Previously Diospolis, then Rhoas, then rebuilt by Antiochus the Second, king of Syria, and named after his wife Laodice (whom he divorced and who later poisoned him).[95]

Laodicea was known as an independent and wealthy city where wool was a major source of commerce. "It has often been observed that Laodicea was a banking centre. Cicero cashed his bills of exchange there on his arrival in his province of Cilicia in 51 BC."[96]

> The city suffered grievously in the Mithridatic war, but presently recovered again; once more in the wide-wasting earthquake in the reign of Tiberius, but was repaired and restored by the efforts of its own citizens, without any help asked by them from the Roman senate (Tacitus, *Annal.* xiv. 27).[97]
>
> The prosperity of the city was illustrated following a great earthquake of A.D. 60, which destroyed the city and other cities around it. As was its habit, the Roman government offered substantial aid in rebuilding the devastation. Yet Laodicea was not among those cities who received help. Whether the government refused to offer it because of their great wealth, or Laodicea refused it because they did not need it, is debated. Whatever the case, the reason was wealth.[98]
>
> In 62 BC the proconsul Flaccus confiscated large amounts of Jewish gold bound for Jerusalem, among them the sum of over twenty pounds weight at Laodicea. . . . the sums collected may represent the totals of temple-tax from their respective districts. It has been calculated that the amount from Laodicea would imply a population of 7,500 adult Jewish freemen in the district.[99]

Aspects of the letter from Christ appear to allude to commercial activities in Laodicea:

> Laodicea was a great garment manufacturing center and pioneered mass-produced, and therefore cheap, outer garments. These garments used the wool of the vast flocks of sheep that grazed the high plateaus in the vicinity. Laodicea was proud of its garment industry and its well-clothed citizens—this adds pertinence to the nakedness of Rev. 3:17. This verse draws on another aspect of Laodicean pride, too, for the city was a noted medical center with a famous school at the temple of the Carian god, Men. This medical school was world famous for two products in particular, an ointment for the ears and one for the eyes. To aid in exporting these medications, the doctors of Laodicea developed a process of converting the ointment to powder which was compressed into tablets. The comment of Rev. 3:18 is thus ironic; in their pride, the church members of Laodicea did not recognize that they were spiritually blind.[100]

The name Λαοδίκεια [*Laodikeia*] is a compound from Λαός [*Laos*] ("people") and δίκη [*dikē*] ("judgment," "rule"). Thus the city was aptly named for the letter which Christ here writes:

> Its name designates it as the Church of mob rule, *the democratic Church*, in which everything is swayed and decided by popular opinion, clamour and voting; and hence a self-righteousness and self-sufficient Church.[101]
>
> Laodicea . . . means "people ruling." This is set in contrast to God's ruling in the church. It is a church entirely ruled by men, for the Holy Spirit is not present and doing His ministry of guiding.[102]

Although Paul mentions this church in his epistle to the Colossians (Col. 2:1; 4:13-16) and it remained a significant church for a number of centuries as witnessed by an important council concerning the *canon*[5.2.12] of Scripture which was held there in AD 361—the *Council of Laodicea*, at the time of John's writing, the leadership of the church appears to have been inverted from Scriptural guidelines. Paul had previously warned Timothy concerning the consequences of the sheep ruling in place of spirit-led Shepherds:

> For the time will come when they will not endure sound doctrine, but according to their own desires, *because* they have itching ears, they will heap up for themselves teachers; and they will turn *their* ears away from the truth, and be turned aside to fables. (2Ti 4:3-4)

the Amen

Derived from the Hebrew term אָמֵן [*`āmēn*] which denotes certainty, a reliable support:

> The basic root idea is firmness or certainty. In the Qal it expresses the basic concept of support and is used in the sense of the strong arms of the parent supporting the helpless infant. The constancy involved in the verbal idea is further seen in that it occurs in the Qal only as a participle (expressing continuance). The idea of support is also seen in II Kings 18:16, where it refers to pillars of support.[103]

the Faithful and True Witness

"Christ's attributes of sincerity and truth come to the forefront as He deals with those whose alleged devotion to Him is only superficial and not substantial."[104] He will shortly deliver an assessment of the Laodicean church which is unique in its total lack of commendation. No other of the *seven churches*[5.2.66] fairs as poorly in His assessment. Therefore, He emphasizes the accuracy and trustworthiness of what He is about to say. In scenes of judgment, we find an emphasis on the reliability of His witness because it is a requirement for Holy judgment (Rev. 19:11). His words are worthy to have faith exercised upon them (Rev. 21:5; 22:6):

> The word [πιστός [*pistos*]] is employed in two very different senses in the New Testament as elsewhere, in an active and a passive,—now as trusting or believing (John 20:27; Acts 14:1), now as trustworthy or to be believed (2Ti. 2:22; 1Th. 5:27; 1Jn. 1:9). Men may be πιστοί [*pistoi*] in both senses, the active and the passive, as exercising faith, and as being worthy to have faith exercised upon them; God can be πιστός [*pistos*] only in the latter.[105]

Again, we find Jesus applying to Himself titles which are descriptive of the Father (Jer. 42:5). Being God, Jesus can do nothing but witness of the truth. What other man could make the claim of Jesus, "If I bear witness of Myself, My witness is true" (John 8:14-18)?

> Pilate therefore said to Him, "Are You a king then?" Jesus answered, "You say *rightly* that I am a king. For this cause I was born, and for this cause I have come into the world, that I should bear witness to the truth. Everyone who is of the truth hears My voice." Pilate said to Him, "What is truth?" And when he had said this, he went out again to the Jews, and said to them, "I find no fault in Him at all." (John 18:37-38)

These characteristics will allow for His just rule during the Millennium:

> His delight is in the fear of the Lord, and He shall not judge by the sight of His eyes, nor decide by the hearing of His ears; but with righteousness He shall judge the poor, and decide with equity for the meek of the earth; He shall strike the earth with the rod of His mouth, and with the breath of His lips He shall slay the wicked. Righteousness shall be the belt of His loins, and faithfulness the belt of His waist. (Isa. 11:3-5)

See commentary on *Revelation 1:5*[3.1.5].

the Beginning of the creation of God

This meaning of *beginning* here may be *author* or *efficient cause*[106] and does not indicate that He was a product of creation:

> This is a favorite Arian prooftext, cited to prove that Jesus is not eternal, but had a beginning, Jesus being understood by them to be the first-created creature of God, through whom God created all else in the universe. The underlying Greek word, *arche*, may be understood in a passive sense, and rendered "the beginning," as the A.V., or more correctly understood in the active sense, and rendered "the beginner," source, origin, or principle of creation. Since God is eternal, and Jesus is God, the passive sense is not suited to the context, as being out of harmony with the many representations of Christ John has already given, whereby he in citing or alluding to Old Testament passages has applied to Jesus Christ in the book of Revelation what is in the Old Testament spoken of Jehovah.[107]
>
> Not he whom God created first, but as in Col. 1:15-18, the Beginner of all creation, its originating instrument. All creation would not be represented adoring Him, if He were but one of themselves.[108]

Having analyzed the use of ἀρχή [*archē*] (*beginning*) in the *Septuagint*[5.2.65] and throughout the *NT*[5.2.48], Svigel concludes the meaning here is primarily that of governmental rule and the phrase here should be rendered, "the supreme Authority over the creation of God."[109]

Jesus is the Beginning and End (Rev. 21:6; 22:13), both the *author* of and ruler over creation (Gen. 1:1; John 1:1-3; 1Cor. 8:6; Eph. 3:9; Col. 1:15-17; Heb. 1:2).[110] See commentary on *Revelation 5:12*[3.5.12] and *Revelation 5:13*[3.5.13].

3.3.15 - Revelation 3:15

I know

See commentary on *Revelation 2:2*[3.2.2].

cold

ψυχρὸς [*psychros*]: "in mind: of one destitute of warm Christian faith and the desire for holiness."[111]

hot

ζεστός [*zestos*], used of " 'boiling' water."[112]

I could wish

It is always and constantly God's desire that men would fear Him and keep His commandments, but men still choose to walk in their own counsels (Deu. 5:29; Ps. 81:10-13).

you were cold or hot

Here we have what would seem to be an allusion to the marginal water supply of Laodicea:

> Rudwick and Green emphasize that the site of Laodicea was chosen for its position at an important road-junction. 'It lacked a natural water-supply, for there are no springs on the site, and the Lycus River dries up in summer' (p. 177). The remains of a remarkable aqueduct of stone pipes indicate that the people derived water from a source south of the city, perhaps from the hot mineral springs near Denizli, the modern town five miles distance. This would have cooled only slowly in the pipes, and on arrival the supply would have been tepid and its effect emetic.[113]
>
> The people of Laodicea had built an aqueduct to supply their city, but the water was lukewarm and impure. The remains can still be seen, and thick deposits of calcium carbonate inside the pipes witness plainly to the worth of the water which once flowed through them. The words of Rev. 3:14-15 must have hit home powerfully in Laodicea: the writer said that the church was as useless and distasteful as that bad water.[114]

Aqueduct at Laodicea [115]

Some have pondered why Jesus would rather have *cold.* This is explained by realizing that the only thing God hates more than lack of faith is *hypocritical* faith. Inconsistency of conviction is more damaging and irretrievable than the wrong conviction. Scripture is replete with the theme of the need for the people to make a clear choice between God or the alternative (Jos. 24:15; 1K. 18:21; Eze. 20:39; Zep. 1:5; Mtt. 6:24). "There is no one farther from the truth in Christ than the one who makes an idle profession without real faith."[116] It is the double-minded man, like "the wave of the sea driven and tossed by the wind," who should not "suppose he will receive anything from the Lord" (Jas. 1:5-8).

Here, the *cold* and *hot* relate to their spiritual condition:

> The *hot* are the truly saved believers. The *cold* are those who are not believers and do not claim to be believers. The *lukewarm* are those who do claim to believe in Jesus, but are not truly regenerate believers.[117]

> How shall we then understand this exclamation of the Saviour, . . . namely, by regarding the *"cold"* here as one hitherto untouched by the powers of grace. There is always hope of such an one, that, when he does come under those powers, he may become a zealous and earnest Christian. He is not one on whom the grand experiment of the Gospel has been tried and has failed. But the *"lukewarm"* is one who has tasted of the good gift and of the powers of the world to come, who has been a subject of Divine grace, but in whom that grace has failed to kindle more than the feeblest spark. The publicans and harlots were *"cold,"* the Apostles *"hot."* The Scribes and Pharisees, . . . were *"lukewarm."*[118]

3.3.16 - Revelation 3:16

you are lukewarm

The church was no longer a light shining in the darkness. It appears to have been at peace with its enemies: the *synagogue of Satan*:

> Antiochus settled a community of two thousand Jews in Laodicea after expelling them from Babylon. By 62 BC the governor of the city became alarmed at the amount of currency the Jews were exporting to pay the temple tax and so placed an embargo on currency (exchange control is nothing new!), and consequently seized one hundred and twenty pounds weight [Hemer gives the figure of *twenty* pounds, p. 182.] of gold as contraband in Laodicea and Apameia. This gold was worth about 15,000 days'wages in those days, and as the temple tax was the equivalent of two days' wages, this means there were at least 7,500 Jewish men (besides women and children) in these cities. When John wrote this letter more than a century later, given the prosperity of the city, the Jewish population was probably considerably higher. The significance of this probability is that, while Christians elsewhere in Asia were persecuted by the Jews (e.g., Rev. 2:9; 3:9), there is no mention of persecution in this city with so large a Jewish population. This silence speaks volumes, for the Christian church in Laodicea was so complacent and self-sufficient in its wealth that it had ceased to be effective for Christ; so much so that its traditional persecutor, the Jews, considered it benign.[119]

See *Worldly Churches*[4.18].

vomit you out

An equivalent threat to that given to the Ephesian angel of removing his lampstand (Rev. 2:5). "Recent travellers with difficulty discovered one or two Christians in the poor village of Iski-hissar, which stands on the site which Laodicea occupied of old."[120] When conditions become so bad that repentance and return are not forthcoming, God turns men loose to their own destruction and loss (Jer. 15:1-4; Zec. 11:9; Rom. 1:20-28).

3.3.17 - Revelation 3:17

you say

λέγεις [*legeis*], *you are presently saying.*

I am rich

The attitude of the city of Laodicea had infected the church. "It is evident that the Christians of Laodicea shared the self-sufficiency of their fellow-townsmen, and carried it into the sphere of their relations with God and Christ."[121] Self-sufficiency is the death-knell of relationship with God for *independence of God is sin* ! The town had independently recovered from a devastating earthquake in the reign of Tiberius (A.D. 14-37, Luke 3:1) without asking for or receiving help from the Roman senate.[122] Its riches and success had influenced the thinking of its residents. Pride and self-sufficiency had crept into the culture and the culture had crept into the church.

I am rich, πεπλύτηκα [*peplytēka*], is *I have become rich*, (perfect tense). The emphasis is on the *result*—now being rich—so it is translated as a present tense.[123] Here we see the curse of blessing for Scripture records that where men receive God's blessing they soon drift away from the very source of their blessing. Everywhere, the pattern of history is that of a revolving wheel:[124]

1. Men suffer lack and affliction and turn to God.
2. God responds to repentance with provision and blesses.
3. Men glory in their condition of prosperity and grow cold toward God.
4. Judgment falls and the wheel goes around again.

Man seems unable to experience provision from God without misplacing its source as his own achievements (Jer. 9:23-24; Hos. 12:8-9; Luke 12:16-21) which then becomes the focus leading to evil:

> Now godliness with contentment is great gain. For we brought nothing into *this* world, *and it is* certain we can carry nothing out. And having food and clothing, with these we shall be content. But those who desire to be rich fall into temptation and a snare, and *into* many foolish and harmful lusts which drown men in destruction and perdition. For the love of money is a root of all *kinds of* evil, for which some have strayed from the faith in their greediness, and pierced themselves through with many sorrows. (1Ti. 6:6-10)

How different was the condition of the Laodicean church from those in Smyrna (Rev. 2:9)!

have need of nothing

It appears the Laodiceans highly valued their independence and that they refused the offer of Rome to help rebuild following the earthquake. Many of the rebuilt structures included the inscription ἐκ τῶν ἰδίων [*ek tōn idiōn*] ("out of our own resources").[125]

God had warned the children of Israel of how their sin could pervert His blessing:

> Beware that you do not forget the LORD your God by not keeping His commandments, His judgments, and His statutes which I command you today, lest-*when* you have eaten and are full, and have built beautiful houses and dwell *in them*; and *when* your herds and your flocks multiply, and your silver and your gold are multiplied, and all that you have is multiplied; when your heart is lifted up, and you forget the LORD your God who brought you out of the land of Egypt, from the house of bondage; who led you through that great and terrible wilderness, *in which were* fiery serpents and scorpions and thirsty land where there was no water; who brought water for you out of the flinty rock. (Deu. 8:11-15)

Agur, the son of Jakeh, understood the danger of the lack of need leading to independence from God:

> Remove falsehood and lies far from me; give me neither poverty nor riches-Feed me with the food allotted to me; lest I be full and deny *You*, and say, "Who *is* the LORD?" Or lest I be poor and steal, and profane the name of my God. (Pr. 30:8-9)

do not know

The Laodicean's had no idea of their condition for they were spiritually blind (Hos. 7:8-9; Luke 6:42).

you are

σὺ εἶ [*sy ei*], emphatic: *you . . . you are.*

wretched and miserable

They were *wretched,* ταλαίπωρος [*talaipōros*]—*afflicted*[126], and *miserable,* ἐλεεινὸς [*eleeinos*]—*pitiable.*[127] They themselves were afflicted but did not know their condition, hence they were pitiable.

poor

They were poor in the wrong way: *spiritually* rather than *physically*. See commentary on *Revelation 2:9*[3.2.9].

blind

They *do not know* because they are *blind.* Scripture makes plain that those who are sure of their sight are most often sightless (Isa. 42:18-20; John 9:39-41). So it was with the Laodicean church. Of all the churches which Jesus wrote to, this church was the *least likely* to respond to His exhortation because it was sure of its health and vision.

> But sin makes blind and man cannot perceive his corruption (Eph. 4:18; Rev. 3:17). He believes in the good within himself and deifies his own nature (2Th. 2:3-4): 'Mankind is deity seen from below.' So long as he believes that, he will never lay hold of the redemption (Mtt. 9:12).[128]

So it is with many churches in our day who are convinced that their social activities and programs are an indicator of their spiritual health. Having lost all capability of introspection by the measure of God's Word, they are unable to assess their condition by anything other than pragmatic measures and ministry statistics. As they grow in influence and numbers, their willingness to admit of the need for correction continually wanes until they reach a condition much like that of the Laodicean church.

naked

They had not watched nor kept their garments so now they were naked (Rev. 16:15). Their shame was evident to all but themselves, for they were blind to their own nakedness.

3.3.18 - Revelation 3:18

I counsel you to buy from Me

The language is meant to speak to the merchants of the city, some of whom would have been members of the church:

> He who might have commanded, prefers rather to counsel; He who might have spoken as from heaven, conforms Himself, so far as the outward form of his words reaches, to the language of earth. To the merchants and factors of this wealthy mercantile city He addresses himself in their own dialect. . . . Would it not be wise to transact their chief business with Him?[129]

Salvation is *free* for no man has the necessary riches to contribute even one penny toward the cost of his own salvation. And to do so would be the height of blasphemy since it would deny the sufficiency of the sacrifice of God's own Son (Col. 2:14; Heb. 7:27; 9:12, 28). On the other hand, Scripture also records that true salvation and service for the Lord costs *everything* (Luke 14:33).

> The price which they should pay was this, the renunciation of all vain reliance on their own righteousness and wisdom; the price which in another Epistle St. Paul declared he had so gladly paid, that so he might himself win Christ (Php. 3:7-8); the [forsaking all], ἀποτάσσεσται πα˜σα [*apotassestai pasa*] , which the Lord long before had declared to be the necessary condition of his discipleship (Luke 14:33).[130]

gold. . . white garments. . . eye salve

The remedies for the previously-stated ills, for they were *poor*, *naked*, and *blind* (Rev. 2:17).

refined in the fire

Not just gold, but *refined* gold which has been purified by fire:

> In this you greatly rejoice, though now for a little while, if need be, you have been grieved by various trials, that the genuineness of your faith, *being* much more precious than gold that perishes, though it is tested by fire, may be found to praise, honor, and glory at the revelation of Jesus Christ. (1Pe. 1:6-7)

The Laodiceans church needed true spiritual gold which would stand the test of the bema seat of Christ:

> Now if anyone builds on this foundation *with* gold, silver, precious stones, wood, hay, straw, each one's work will become clear; for the Day will declare it, because it will be revealed by fire; and the fire will test each one's work, of what sort it is. (1Cor. 3:12-13)

white garments

The mention of *white garments* would be especially noteworthy since Laodicea was known for its production of high quality glossy black wool:

> Commentators . . . have seen allusion to the clothing industry of Laodicea and in particular a contrast with the glossy black wool of its sheep. Knowledge of the breed rests primarily upon Strabo: 'The country around Laodicea produces sheep remarkable not only for the softness of their wool, in which they surpass even that of Miletus, but also for its raven-black color.[131]

"Laodicea's wools were famous. Christ offers infinitely whiter raiment."[132] The same white garments which are promised to the overcomer in Sardis (Rev. 3:4-5). See commentary on *Revelation 3:4*[3.3.4].

be clothed, that the shame of your nakedness may not be revealed

The Laodicean church had walked in the steps of Adam and Eve before them—they had attempted to *clothe themselves* to cover their nakedness (Gen. 3:7-11). Yet the fig leaves sewn by Adam and his wife were not sufficient in God's sight—animal sacrifice was needed to atone for sin when *God provided* their clothing (Gen. 3:21). The Laodicean church had *religion*, but was lacking *relationship* . They had attempted to substitute their own righteousness (Pr. 20:6; 21:2; Mtt. 5:20; Luke 10:29; 18:9) for the righteousness that can only come from God (Rom. 10:3). They were clothed in see-through garments of their own works—naked but unable to see their condition. They needed to purchase from God the robes of righteousness:

eye salve that you may see

The *eye salve* may allude to the early practice of ophthalmology associated with the city:

> We have explicit evidence for the connection of Laodicea with a leading figure of first-century ophthalmology. . . . local people today find medicinal value in bathing their eyes in the Hierapolis waters, the alum content apparently being the beneficial [*sic*] agent. . . . the city probably marketed extensively and profitably an ointment developed locally from available materials, whose exact composition may have been kept secret from commercial rivals.[133]

The Laodicean's needed the illuminating work of the Holy Spirit so that they may more clearly see their own nakedness and realize their need of clothing. "The Spirit convinces of sin, and by this ['eye salve'] we must understand the illuminating grace of the Holy Ghost, which at once shows to us God, and in God and his light ourselves."[134] They needed the illumination of the Holy Spirit so they could see their condition accurately, just as the "seven eyes" saw them (Rev. 4:6). See *Hiding or Revealing?*[2.2.6]

3.3.19 - Revelation 3:19

As many as I love, I rebuke and chasten

The Laodicean church could take comfort in the fact that Christ had written a letter of rebuke to them for it was an indication of his ongoing love for them. They were not so far gone that He would leave them silently to their own devices. Like a loving Father, God chastens those who would be His sons (Deu. 8:5; 2S. 7:14; Heb. 12:5-8).

be zealous

ζήλευε [*zēleue*], *be continually full of zeal* (present-tense). The same root word as "hot" in Revelation 3:15. Although God said "I could wish you were cold or hot" (either state being preferable to lukewarm hypocrisy), He still prefers that they be *hot*. The Laodicean church-goer was to *earnestly desire*, *pursue*, and *strive after* God.[135] He could no longer remain a *church-goer*, but would need to become a *God-chaser*.

repent

See commentary on μετανοια [*metanoia*] at *Revelation 2:5*[3.2.5].

3.3.20 - Revelation 3:20

I stand at the door and knock

I stand is ἕστηκα [*hestēka*], perfect tense: *I have stood. Knock* is κρούω [*krouō*], present tense: *I am knocking*. He has been standing for a period of time and is *still* awaiting their response to his continual knocking. The knocking is accompanied by the voice of the bridegroom. When the bride lacks sufficient zeal and is slow to respond, the bridegroom has already withdrawn (Sos. 5:1-6). If the Laodicean church was truly *zealous* , they would have already opened the door (Luke 12:35-36).

The irony here in that Christ is outside *His own church*, desiring to be invited back in![136] The love of God and His desire to rectify the condition in Laodicea is reflected in the manner in which the God of the universe steadfastly waits outside the Laodicean door.

> He at whose door we ought to stand, for He *is* the Door (John 10:7), who, as such, has bidden *us* to knock (Mtt. 7:7; Luke 11:9), is content that the whole relation between Him and us should be reversed, and instead of our standing at his door condescends Himself to stand at ours.[137]

Some have seen in this *door* an allusion to a monumental gate in the city.[138] Elsewhere, Jesus is Himself the door (John 10:9) providing full access to heaven and God (Heb. 10:19-20).

hears My voice

The voice is intentionally contrasted with the knock:

> So far as we may venture to distinguish between the two, . . . to see in the voice the more inward appeal, the closer dealing of Christ with the soul, speaking directly by his Spirit to the spirit of the man; in the knocking those more outward gracious dealings, of sorrow and joy, of sickness and health, and the like, which He sends, and sending uses for the bringing of his elect, in one way or another, by smooth paths or by rough, to Himself.[139]

All men have ears, but not all hear His voice. See commentary on *Revelation 2:7*[3.2.7].

come in to him

Wallace argues from the grammar that this verse cannot denote an offer of salvation. He observes that Christ is promising to come *in to the presence of* (πρὸς αὐτόν [*pros auton*]) the one who opens the door, not *into* the sphere of his person.[140] But this is not essential for the verse to denote the fellowship associated with salvation. Elsewhere, salvation is described as the Father and Son coming *to* (not *into*) the believer:

> "He who has My commandments and keeps them, it is he who loves Me. And he who loves Me will be loved by My Father, and I will love him and manifest Myself to him." Judas (not Iscariot) said to Him, "Lord, how is it that You will manifest Yourself to us, and not to the world?" Jesus answered and said to him, "If anyone loves Me, he will keep My word; and My Father will love him, and We will come **to him [πρὸς αὐτόν [*pros auton*]]** and make Our home with him." (John 14:21-23) [emphasis added]

Yet the context offers little to support an evangelistic emphasis:

> The verse contains nothing of the gospel message as such—no mention of substitutionary atonement, of Christ's resurrection, of repentance, of faith in the person and work of Christ. Neither is there anything in the adjacent context about these vital matters. Yet evangelists and personal workers everywhere commonly employ this verse as a gospel invitation. God, in His grace, does occasionally use it to help bring an unsaved person to Christ, since it does enjoin a proper attitude of openness to God's call, but that is not its intent. It is addressed only to compromising, lukewarm Christians in compromising, lukewarm churches, and it is they whom Christ is seeking to draw back to Himself.[141]

and dine with him

After coming under the Mosaic Covenant, Moses, Aaron, Aaron's sons, and seventy of the elders of Israel "saw God" and "ate and drank" in His presence (Ex. 24:8-11). Dining conveys the idea of intimate fellowship (Luke 19:5-7; John 13). Jesus says he will *dine with him* in ongoing fellowship and intimacy as soon as the door is opened. There is also the promise of dining with Him at the marriage supper of the Lamb (Mtt. 22:1-14; 25:1-13; 26:29; Luke 22:16; Rev. 19:9). "The consummation of this blessed intercommunion shall be at the Marriage Supper of the Lamb, of which the Lord's Supper is the earnest and foretaste."[142] Jesus has promised not to partake of the Passover meal until he dines with believers in the *Millennial Kingdom*[5.2.39] (Mtt. 8:11; Mtt. 26:29; Mark 14:25; Luke 22:18).

3.3.21 - Revelation 3:21

overcomes

See *Who is the Overcomer?*[4.15.1.3]

sit with Me

They will sit with Him and share His rule in the same way He sits at the right hand of the Father and shares His rule. See commentary on *Revelation 2:26*[3.2.26] and *Revelation 2:27*[3.2.27].

on My throne

An amazing manifestation of grace. Those who were about to be spewed from his mouth are invited to sit with Him on His throne.[143]

> The promise . . . is an extension of the promise Christ made to the Twelve while on earth that they would not only eat and drink with Him in His kingdom, but also sit upon twelve thrones judging the twelve tribes of Israel (cf. Mtt. 19:28; Luke 22:29-30). Paul expanded the promise to include all Christians as rulers and the broadened domain of the world, not just Israel (cf. 1Cor. 6:2).[144]

Jesus clarifies a point which is often confused today: He is not now sitting on *His throne*, but is seated at the right hand of the Father on the *Father's throne*.

> There is a most important *dispensational*[5.2.15] teaching in this verse. There are those who think that the Church is the kingdom and that there is to be no literal kingdom on earth. Here the Lord says that at the present time He is not upon His own throne.[145]

Jesus taught that there would be a delay in the coming of His kingdom (Mtt. 6:10; Luke 11:2; 19:11-15; Acts 1:6-7). Its arrival is yet future and will be indicated by signs (Luke 21:31). It occurs after the *Antichrist*[5.2.3] has his day (Dan. 7:11-14, 21-22, 25-27; Rev. 19:20), after the seventh angel sounds his trumpet (Rev. 11:15-17), after Satan is cast down (Rev. 12:10), when Christ returns to judge the sheep and the goats (Mtt. 25:31; 2Ti. 4:1), in the regeneration when the apostles will rule over the tribes of Israel (Mtt. 19:28; Luke 22:29-30) and believers co-rule (Rev. 20:4-6), when He drinks wine and eats the Passover again with His followers (Mtt. 26:29; Mark 14:25; Luke 22:16-18).

> This passage, in harmony with Luke 1:32, 33; Mtt. 19:28; Acts 2:30, 34, 35; 15:14-16, is conclusive that Christ is not now seated upon His own throne. The Davidic Covenant, and the promises of God through the prophets and the Angel Gabriel concerning the *Messianic kingdom*[5.2.39] await fulfilment.[146]

> Several factors indicate that David's throne is separate and distinct from God's throne in heaven. *First* , several descendants of David have sat on his throne, but only one of his descendants ever sits on the right hand of God's throne in heaven. That descendant is Jesus Christ (Ps. 110:1; Heb. 8:1; 12:2). *Second* , David's throne was not established before his lifetime (2S. 7:16-17). By contrast, since God has always ruled over His creation, His throne in heaven was established long before David's throne (Ps. 93:1-2). *Third* , since God's throne in heaven was established long before David's throne and since God's throne was established forever (Lam. 5:19), then it was not necessary for God to promise to establish David's throne forever (2S. 7:16) if they are the same throne. *Fourth*, David's throne was on the earth, not in heaven. David and his descendants who sat on his throne exercised an earthly, ruling authority. They never exercised ruling authority in or from heaven. By contrast, as noted earlier, the Bible indicates that God's throne is in heaven. *Fifth* , the Bible's consistent description of David's throne indicates that it belongs to David. When God talked to David about his throne, God referred to it as "thy throne" (2S. 7:16; Ps. 89:4; 132:12). When God mentioned David's throne to others, He referred to it as "his throne" (Ps. 89:29; Jer. 33:21), "David's throne" (Jer. 13:13), and "the throne of David" (Jer. 17:25; 22:2, 4; 22:30). By contrast, the Scriptures' consistent description of the throne in heaven indicates that it belongs to God the Father. [147]

According to Trench, this is a greater position than the role given to the apostles over the tribes of Israel (Mtt. 19:28).[148]

He is currently seated to the right hand of the Father on *the Father's* throne. In the Millennium, He will take up *his* throne (Mtt. 25:31). In the eternal state, it appears the two thrones become synonymous (1Cor. 15:24-25; Rev. 22:1, 3).

as I also overcame

It is by Jesus' identity as the overcomer and their identification with Him that believers are overcomers. See *Who is the Overcomer?*[4.15.1.3].

sat down with my Father on His throne

After His ascension, Jesus sat down at the right hand of the Father. This is his present position (Mark 16:19; Rom. 8:34; Eph. 1:20; Col. 3:1 Heb. 1:3; 8:1; 10:12; 12:2; 1Pe. 3:22). Jesus told the high priest that he would see the Son of Man "sitting at the right hand of the Power" (Mtt. 26:64). He stood up at the death of His witness Stephen (Acts 7:55-56), but this was not yet the time to receive the kingdom and return to rule for He must remain seated until His enemies are made His footstool (Ps. 110:1; Mtt. 22:44). Eventually, He will be presented before the Ancient of Days to receive the kingdom (Dan. 7:13-14) initiating His return and subsequent rule from the throne of David (Luke 1:33; Mtt. 5:31-32; Rev. 19:11-21; 20:4-6).

> This, the grandest and crowning promise, is placed at the end of all the seven addresses, to gather all in one. It also forms the link to the next part of the book, where the Lamb is introduced seated on His Father's throne (Rev. 4:2, 3).[149]

3.3.22 - Revelation 3:22

let him hear what the Spirit says to the churches

See commentary on *Revelation 2:7*[3.2.7].

> After reading the seven letters to the *seven churches*[5.2.66], we cannot escape the fact that compromise of God's word is anathema to Christ and is the root of all Christian weakness. Let us each individually resolve to uphold the full teaching of our Lord and Savior—in the strength He provides.[150]

This is the *last mention* of "church" (εκκλησία [*ekklēsia*]) in the book of Revelation until the closing remarks: "I, Jesus, have sent My angel to testify to you these things for the churches. I am the root and the descendant of David, the bright morning star." (Rev. 22:16). As we note elsewhere, the Jewishness of the book of Revelation was recognized early on and contributed to a reluctance to recognize its *canonicity*[2.10] . This is a reflection of what we have just observed: the absence of the church from the events following chapters 2 and 3. We believe this is intentional and indicates that the saints who experience the Tribulation period come to faith after the *Rapture*[5.2.62] of the church. This includes a significant Jewish witness (Rev. 7:4-8; 11:3-13; 14:1-5).

> The fact that parts of Revelation contain no reference to the church but make many references to Israel has been recognized by scholars who do not advocate a *Pretribulation*[5.2.60] Rapture of the church. For example, the Roman Catholic scholar, C. Van Den Biesen, state, "The Apocalypse abounds in passages which bear no specific Christian character but, on the contrary, show a decidedly Jewish complexion."[151]

It is important to understand that the pretribulational rapture view is not *derived from* this observation, but that it is founded upon other passages. The emphasis on the church in chapters 2 and 3 followed by a complete omission of any mention of the church in the events of judgment spanning chapters 6 through 19 is but one of numerous evidences in Scripture which indicate that the church will not endure the Tribulation. See *Rapture*[4.14].

Notes

1 Copyright ©003 *www.BiblePlaces.com*. This image appears by *special permission*[1.3] and may not be duplicated for use in derivative works.

2 *American Heritage Online Dictionary*, Ver. 3.0A, 3rd ed. (Houghton Mifflin, 1993), s.v. "Lydia."

3 Monty S. Mills, *Revelations: An Exegetical Study of the Revelation to John* (Dallas, TX: 3E Ministries, 1987), Rev. 3:1.

4 "Even at dates later than the Revelation "to capture the acropolis of Sardis" was proverbially "to do the impossible"."—Colin J. Hemer, *The Letters to the Seven Churches of Asia in Their Local Setting* (Grand Rapids, MI: William B. Eerdmans Publishing Company, 1989), 133.

5 Hemer, *The Letters to the Seven Churches of Asia in Their Local Setting*, 133.

6 Mills, *Revelations: An Exegetical Study of the Revelation to John*, Rev. 3:1.

7 Robert H. Mounce, *The Book of Revelation* (Grand Rapids, MI: William B. Eerdmans Publishing Co., 1977), 109.

8 Hemer, *The Letters to the Seven Churches of Asia in Their Local Setting*, 134.

9 Robert L. Thomas, *Revelation 1-7* (Chicago, IL: Moody Press, 1992), 272.

10 "Melito, a name we hear seldom now, but the titles of whose works inspire us with a deep regret for their almost entire loss, was bishop of Sardis, being the only illustrious name connected with this Church, in the latter half of the second century (Neander, *Kirch. Gesch.* i. 3, p. 1140)."—Richard Chenevix Trench, *Commentary on the Epistles to the Seven Churches in Asia* (Eugene, OR: Wipf and Stock Publishers, 1861), 152.

11 Thomas, *Revelation 1-7*, 242.

12 Jerome Smith, *The New Treasury of Scripture Knowledge* (Nashville, TN: Thomas Nelson Publishers, 1992),

Rev. 3:1.

13 J. A. Seiss, *The Apocalypse: Lectures on the Book of Revelation* (Grand Rapids, MI: Zondervan Publishing House, 1966), 71.

14 J. Dwight Pentecost, *Things to Come: A Study in Biblical Eschatology* (Grand Rapids, MI: Zondervan Publishing House, 1958), 152.

15 Pentecost, *Things to Come: A Study in Biblical Eschatology*, 152.

16 Smith, *The New Treasury of Scripture Knowledge*, Rev. 3:1.

17 Smith, *The New Treasury of Scripture Knowledge*, Rev. 3:1.

18 Smith, *The New Treasury of Scripture Knowledge*, Rev. 3:1.

19 Trench, *Commentary on the Epistles to the Seven Churches in Asia*, 153.

20 Thomas, *Revelation 1-7*, Rev. 3:1.

21 Donald Grey Barnhouse, *Revelation* (Grand Rapids, MI: Zondervan Publishing House, 1971), 66-67.

22 Barnhouse, *Revelation*, 68.

23 John MacArthur, *Revelation 1-11 : The MacArthur New Testament Commentary* (Chicago, IL: Moody Press, 1999), Rev. 3:4.

24 Seiss, *The Apocalypse: Lectures on the Book of Revelation*, 73.

25 Barnhouse, *Revelation*, 68.

26 "This doctrine of Total Inability, which declares that men are dead in sin, does not mean that all men are equally bad, nor that any man is as bad as he could be, nor that any one is entirely destitute of virtue, nor that human nature is evil in itself, nor that man"s spirit is inactive, and much less does it mean that the body is dead. What it does mean is that since the fall man rests under the curse of sin, that he is actuated by wrong principles, and that he is wholly unable to love God or to do anything meriting salvation. . . . Man is a free agent but he cannot originate the love of God in his heart. . . . As the bird with a broken wing is 'free" to fly but not able, so the natural man is free to come to God but not able."—Loraine Boettner, *The Reformed Doctrine of Predestination* (Phillipsburg, NJ: Presbyterian and Reformed Publishing Company, 1932), 61-62.

27 Barnhouse, *Revelation*, 70.

28 Thomas, *Revelation 1-7*, 255.

29 Mills, *Revelations: An Exegetical Study of the Revelation to John*, Rev. 3:3.

30 MacArthur, *Revelation 1-11 : The MacArthur New Testament Commentary*, 114.

31 Thomas, *Revelation 1-7*, 253.

32 This passage does not describe the Rapture of the church as Luke's account makes especially clear: " 'I tell you, in that night there will be two *men* in one bed: the one will be taken and the other will be left. Two *women* will be grinding together: the one will be taken and the other left. Two *men* will be in the field: the one will be taken and the other left.' And they answered and said to Him, 'Where, Lord?' So He said to them, 'Wherever the body is, there the eagles will be gathered together' " (Luke 17:34-37). Those who are *taken* are like those who *perished* in the flood of Noah. Jesus indicates they are taken in *judgment* as many parallel passages which describe birds feeding on carrion make plain: Deu. 28:26; Job 39:30; Eze. 39:4, 17-20; Jer. 7:33; 12:9; 15:3; 16:4; 19:7; Mtt. 24:28; Luke 17:37; Rev. 19:17-18.

33 Once again, the context of this passage is *judgment* as can be seen by the verses which follow: "But if that servant says in his heart, "My master is delaying his coming," and begins to beat the male and female servants, and to eat and drink and be drunk, the master of that servant will come on a day when he is not looking for *him*, and at an hour when he is not aware, and will cut him in two and appoint *him* his portion with the unbelievers. And that servant who knew his master's will, and did not prepare *himself* or do according to his will, shall be beaten with many *stripes*. . . . I came to send fire on the earth, and how I wish it were already kindled!" (Luke 12:45-49).

34 Smith, *The New Treasury of Scripture Knowledge*, Rev. 3:3.

35 *New Electronic Translation : NET Bible*, electronic edition (Dallas, TX: Biblical Studies Press, 1998), Rev. 3:3.

36 Trench, *Commentary on the Epistles to the Seven Churches in Asia*, 164.

37 "the one who conquers *will cause himself to be clothed* in white clothing. Like Gal. 5:12, this is an example of a causative direct middle. Direct middles are not uncommon with verbs meaning 'to put on clothes.' "—Daniel B. Wallace, *Greek Grammar Beyond the Basics - Exegetical Syntax of the New Testament* (Grand Rapids, MI: Zondervan Publishing House and Galaxie Software, 1999, 2002), 424.

38 James Strong, *The Exhaustive Concordance of the Bible* (Ontario: Woodside Bible Fellowship, 1996), H3722.

39 Mounce, *The Book of Revelation*, Rev. 3:5.

40 Thomas, *Revelation 1-7*, 264.

41 Copyright ©003 *www.BiblePlaces.com*. This image appears by *special permission*[1.3] and may not be duplicated for use in derivative works. *Architrave*: The lowermost part of an entablature in classical architecture that rests directly on top of a column. Also called epistyle.

42 Smith, *The New Treasury of Scripture Knowledge*, Rev. 3:7.

43 Smith, *The New Treasury of Scripture Knowledge*, Rev. 3:7.

44 Thomas, *Revelation 1-7*, 273.

45 "By Metonymy of the Adjunct, whereby the sign is put for the thing signified, 'key' is put for governmental authority, of which it is the sign."—Smith, *The New Treasury of Scripture Knowledge*, Rev. 3:7.

46 Carl Friedrich Keil, and Franz Delitzsch, *Commentary on the Old Testament* (Peabody, MA: Hendrickson, 2002), 7:262.

47 Trench, *Commentary on the Epistles to the Seven Churches in Asia.*

48 Although Paul is commissioned as the apostle to the Gentiles in Acts 9:1-43, it is Peter who first takes the gospel to the Gentiles in Acts 10:1-48. Why? Because it is Peter who has the keys to the kingdom.

49 Mounce, *The Book of Revelation*, Rev. 3:8.

50 Thomas, *Revelation 1-7*, 278.

51 Trench, *Commentary on the Epistles to the Seven Churches in Asia.*

52 Thomas, *Revelation 1-7*, 279.

53 Barnhouse, *Revelation*, 75.

54 Thomas, *Revelation 1-7*, 280.

55 "The passage does not mean that believers are to be worshiped. It is merely at their feet that the unbelievers shall kneel as they are forced to acknowledge that Christ is God, and that every detail of the Scripture is eternal and true."—Barnhouse, *Revelation*, 76.

56 Steve Gregg, *Revelation Four Views: A Parallel Commentary* (Nashville, TN: Thomas Nelson, 1997), 76.

57 "Rev. 3:9, . . . refers to Isaianic prophecies that the Gentiles will come and bow down before Israel and recognize Israel as God's chosen people (Isa. 45:14; 49:23; 60:14). This Jewish hope has been turned upside down. Note it is the Jewish persecutors of Christians whom God will make to submit to the church. This reversal of Isaiah's language is probably a conscious attempt to express the irony that the submission that unbelieving ethnic Jews hoped to receive from Gentiles, they themselves will be forced to render to the church."—Gregory K. Beale, *The Book of Revelation: A Commentary on the Greek Text* (Grand Rapids, MI: William B. Eerdmans Publishing Co., 1999), 94.

58 Alan F. Johnson, *Revelation: The Expositor's Bible Commentary* (Grand Rapids, MI: Zondervan Publishing House, 1966), Rev. 3:9.

59 Thomas, *Revelation 1-7*, 282.

60 Trench, *Commentary on the Epistles to the Seven Churches in Asia*, 177.

61 Renald E. Showers, *Maranatha, Our Lord Come* (Bellmawr, NJ: The Friends of Israel Gospel Ministry, 1995), 209-210.

62 "To be kept *in* temptation, not to be exempted *from* temptation (τηρεῖν εκ [*tērein ek*] not being here==τηρεῖν ἀπό [*tērein apo*] , Jas. 1:27; Pr. 7:5 cf. 2Th. 3:3); a bush burning, and yet not consumed (cf.

Isa. 43:2)."—Trench, *Commentary on the Epistles to the Seven Churches in Asia*, 178. "The words τηρήσω ἐκ [*tērēsō ek*] are to be understood from John 17:15: God's people shall receive special protection in the trial rather than exemption from it (ἀπό [*apo*] ; cf. also 2Pe. 2:9)."—Hemer, *The Letters to the Seven Churches of Asia in Their Local Setting*, 164.

63 "The idea of the saints being shielded from the testing while living within and through its time period also would have been expressed more clearly through the use of another preposition, either *en* (meaning 'in') or *dia* (meaning 'through') [thus, 'I will keep you *in* or *through* the time period of testing'] rather than *ek*."—Showers, *Maranatha, Our Lord Come*, 212.

64 Showers, *Maranatha, Our Lord Come*, 211.

65 Smith, *The New Treasury of Scripture Knowledge*, Rev. 3:10.

66 Gregg, *Revelation Four Views: A Parallel Commentary*, 76.

67 "If Gundry's view of Rev. 3:10 is correct [that the church will be guarded and preserved during God's testing of earth-dwellers during the Tribulation], then one is left with the colossal problem of reconciling the fact that multitudes of believers will die under the fierce persecution of *Antichrist*[5.2.3] during the Tribulation and yet God supposedly will preserve His people physically through the Tribulation."—Keith H. Essex, *"The Rapture and the Book of Revelation,"* in Richard L. Mayhue, ed., *The Master's Seminary Journal*, vol. 13 no. 1 (Sun Valley, CA: The Master's Seminary, Spring 2002), 29-30.

68 Showers, *Maranatha, Our Lord Come*, 212.

69 Arnold G. Fruchtenbaum, *The Footsteps of Messiah*, rev ed. (Tustin, CA: Ariel Ministries, 2003), 155.

70 Thomas, *Revelation 1-7*, 288.

71 Gregg, *Revelation Four Views: A Parallel Commentary*, 77.

72 Showers, *Maranatha, Our Lord Come*, 214.

73 Grant R. Osborne, *Revelation* (Grand Rapids, MI: Baker Academic, 2002), 8.

74 Thomas, *Revelation 1-7*, 225.

75 J. B. Lightfoot, and J. R. Harmer, *The Apostolic Fathers*, 2nd ed. (Grand Rapids, MI: Baker Book House, 1989), 158.

76 "The temptation brings out the fidelity of those kept by Christ and hardens the unbelieving reprobates (Rev. 9:20, 21)."—A. R. Fausset, *"The Revelation of St. John the Divine,"* in Robert Jamieson, A. R. Fausset, and David Brown, *A Commentary, Critical and Explanatory, on the Old and New Testaments* (Oak Harbor, WA: Logos Research Systems, Inc., 1997, 1877), Rev. 3:10. Note, however, that this verse indicates that it is those who dwell on the earth who are the object of the testing, *not the faithful*.

77 This fact explains why the events of Revelation include great judgments poured out upon the natural systems of the earth for the earth has become an idol of worship for the *earth dwellers*[5.2.18].

78 Some may say that earth dwellers do not *hate* believers, but simply tolerate them. This is only true to the extent the local culture has been influenced by the salt and light of believers. When darkness increases, hatred of the earth dwellers towards believers escalates dramatically, for believers remind them of God's righteous judgment which they desire to throw off.

79 This spiritual deception will be so powerful that only those who have come to faith will have the needed supernatural protection to overcome it.

80 Walter Scott, *Exposition of The Revelation* (London, England: Pickering & Inglis, n.d.), Rev. 11:9.

81 Showers, *Maranatha, Our Lord Come*, 216-217.

82 The idea that the trial is also to *refine believers* is contradicted by this verse which states that the ones to be tested are the ones who "dwell upon the earth"—a technical term in the book of Revelation for those who remain unrepentant during the events of the end. "This same expression occurs in Revelation 6:10; 11:10; 13:8, 12, 14; 14:6 and 17:8. In its usage it is not giving us a geographical description but rather a moral classification."—Pentecost, *Things to Come: A Study in Biblical Eschatology*, 197.

83 Thomas, *Revelation 1-7*, Rev. 3:11.

84 Thomas, *Revelation 1-7*, 291.

[85] E. W. Bullinger, *Commentary On Revelation* (Grand Rapids, MI: Kregel Publications, 1984, 1935), 96.

[86] Trench, *Commentary on the Epistles to the Seven Churches in Asia*, 182.

[87] Fruchtenbaum, *The Footsteps of Messiah*, 65.

[88] "Heb. *Jehovah shammah.* i.e. *The Lord is there*. Signifying the personal presence of Messiah who will reign visibly in Israel."—Smith, *The New Treasury of Scripture Knowledge*, Eze. 48:35.

[89] Trench believes it will be "The Lord is there" (Eze. 48:35). [Trench, *Commentary on the Epistles to the Seven Churches in Asia*]

[90] Hemer, *The Letters to the Seven Churches of Asia in Their Local Setting*, 157.

[91] Alva J. McClain, *The Greatness Of The Kingdom* (Winona Lake, IN: BMH Books, 1959), 244.

[92] Trench, *Commentary on the Epistles to the Seven Churches in Asia*, 190.

[93] Hemer, *The Letters to the Seven Churches of Asia in Their Local Setting*, 181.

[94] Copyright ©003 *www.BiblePlaces.com*. This image appears by *special permission*[1.3] and may not be duplicated for use in derivative works.

[95] "The new city was established by Antiochus II (261-246 BC) and named after his first wife Laodice, whom he divorced in 253."—Hemer, *The Letters to the Seven Churches of Asia in Their Local Setting*, 180.

[96] Hemer, *The Letters to the Seven Churches of Asia in Their Local Setting*, 191.

[97] Trench, *Commentary on the Epistles to the Seven Churches in Asia*, 189.

[98] Thomas, *Revelation 1-7*, Rev. 3:14.

[99] Hemer, *The Letters to the Seven Churches of Asia in Their Local Setting*, 182.

[100] Mills, *Revelations: An Exegetical Study of the Revelation to John*, Rev. 3:14.

[101] Seiss, *The Apocalypse: Lectures on the Book of Revelation*, 72.

[102] Fruchtenbaum, *The Footsteps of Messiah*, 66.

[103] Robert Laird Harris, Gleason Leonard Archer, and Bruce K. Waltke, *Theological Wordbook of the Old Testament* (Chicago, IL: Moody Press, 1999, c1980), 1.41.

[104] Thomas, *Revelation 1-7*, 300.

[105] Trench, *Commentary on the Epistles to the Seven Churches in Asia*, 191.

[106] "Waterland defines *Arke* (beginning), 'that is, author or efficient cause' (Works, vol. 2, p. 53)."—Smith, *The New Treasury of Scripture Knowledge*, Rev. 3:14.

[107] Smith, *The New Treasury of Scripture Knowledge*, Rev. 3:14.

[108] Fausset, "*The Revelation of St. John the Divine*," Rev. 3:14.

[109] Michael J. Svigel, *"Christ as Arche in Revelation 3:14,"* in *Bibliotheca Sacra*, vol. 161 no. 642 (Dallas, TX: Dallas Theological Seminary, April-June 2004), 225.

[110] See also Pr. 8:22-30 where wisdom is personified with attributes much like those of Jesus: having intimate fellowship with the Father, eternal generation, beside the Father as a master craftsman, the delight of the Father.

[111] Strong, *The Exhaustive Concordance of the Bible*, G5593.

[112] Frederick William Danker, and Walter Bauer, *A Greek-English Lexicon of the New Testament and Other Early Christian Literature* (Chicago, IL: University of Chicago Press, 2000), 337.

[113] Hemer, *The Letters to the Seven Churches of Asia in Their Local Setting*, 188.

[114] Tim Dowley, ed., *The History of Christianity* (Minneapolis, MN: Fortress Press, 1995), 72.

[115] Copyright ©003 *www.BiblePlaces.com*. This image appears by *special permission*[1.3] and may not be duplicated for use in derivative works.

[116] John F. Walvoord, *The Revelation of Jesus Christ* (Chicago, IL: Moody Press, 1966), Rev. 3:15.

[117] Fruchtenbaum, *The Footsteps of Messiah*, 66.

[118] Trench, *Commentary on the Epistles to the Seven Churches in Asia*, 195-196.

[119] Mills, *Revelations: An Exegetical Study of the Revelation to John*, Rev. 3:14.

[120] Trench, *Commentary on the Epistles to the Seven Churches in Asia*, 191.

[121] Henry Barclay Swete, *The Apocalypse of St. John* (Eugene, OR: Wipf and Stock Publishers, 1998, 1906), lxi.

[122] Trench, *Commentary on the Epistles to the Seven Churches in Asia*, 189.

[123] "Intensive Perfect (a.k.a. Resultative Perfect). . . . The perfect may be used to emphasize the results or present state produced by a past action. The English present often is the best translation for such a perfect. This is a common use of the perfect tense."—Wallace, *Greek Grammar Beyond the Basics - Exegetical Syntax of the New Testament*, 574.

[124] In our own day and culture, we are experiencing stage 3 and nearing stage 4.

[125] Hemer, *The Letters to the Seven Churches of Asia in Their Local Setting*, 193.

[126] Strong, *The Exhaustive Concordance of the Bible*, G5005.

[127] Danker, *A Greek-English Lexicon of the New Testament and Other Early Christian Literature*, 249.

[128] Erich Sauer, *The Dawn of World Redemption* (Grand Rapids, MI: Eerdman's Publishing Company, 1951, c1964), 50.

[129] Trench, *Commentary on the Epistles to the Seven Churches in Asia*, 201-202.

[130] Trench, *Commentary on the Epistles to the Seven Churches in Asia*, 203.

[131] Hemer, *The Letters to the Seven Churches of Asia in Their Local Setting*, 199.

[132] Fausset, "*The Revelation of St. John the Divine*," Rev. 3:18.

[133] Hemer, *The Letters to the Seven Churches of Asia in Their Local Setting*, 198.

[134] Trench, *Commentary on the Epistles to the Seven Churches in Asia*, 206.

[135] Strong, *The Exhaustive Concordance of the Bible*, G2206.

[136] Gregg, *Revelation Four Views: A Parallel Commentary*, 80.

[137] Trench, *Commentary on the Epistles to the Seven Churches in Asia*, 211.

[138] "This ostentatious self-sufficiency reached a climax when the reconstruction was completed by the erection of great public buildings at the expense of individual citizens in the years immediately preceding the Domitianic date of the Revelation [in response to the earthquake of *Nero*[5.2.46]'s reign]. The monumental triple gate thus donated may have been in mind in the writing of Rev. 3:20."—Hemer, *The Letters to the Seven Churches of Asia in Their Local Setting*, 208.

[139] Trench, *Commentary on the Epistles to the Seven Churches in Asia*, 212.

[140] "The crucial phrase for our purposes is 'I shall come in to him.' This text has often been taken as a text offering salvation to a lost sinner. Such a view is based on two assumptions: (1) that the Laodiceans, or at least some of them, were indeed lost, and (2) that εἰσελεύσομαι πρὸς [*eiseleusomai pros*] means 'come into.' Both of these assumptions, however, are based on little evidence. With reference to the first assumption, that those in the Laodicean church were not believers, it is important to note that in the preceding verse, the resurrected Lord declares, 'Those whom I love, I reprove and discipline.' Here φιλεω [*phileō*] is used for 'love' a term that is never used of God/Jesus loving unbelievers in the *NT*[5.2.48]. (Indeed, it would be impossible for God to have this kind of love for an unbeliever, for it routinely speaks of enjoyment and fellowship. ἀγαπα [*agapa*] , rather, is the verb used of God's love for unbelievers [cf. John 3:16], for it frequently, if not normally, speaks of commitment and, when used with God/Jesus as the subject, the idea is often of an unconditional love.) This φιλεω [*phileō*] must be applied to the Laodiceans here, for the verse concludes, 'Be zealous, therefore, and repent.' The inferential οὖ [*ou*] connects the two parts of the verse, indicating that the Laodiceans are to repent because Christ loves (φιλεω [*phileō*]) them! The second assumption is that εἰσελεύσομαι πρὸς [*eiseleusomai pros*] means 'come into.' Such an assumption is based on a less than careful reading of the English text! The ASV, NASB, RSV, NRSV, for example, all

correctly render it 'come in to.' (Note the space between the prepositions.) The idea of 'come into' would be expressed with eij as the independent preposition and would suggest a penetration into the person (thus, spawning the idea of entering into one's heart). However, spatially πρό [*pro*] means toward, not into. In all eight instances of εἰσέρχομαι πρὸς [*eiserchomai pros*] in the NT, the meaning is 'come in toward/before a person' (i.e., enter a building, house, etc., so as to be in the presence of someone), never penetration into the person himself/herself. In some instances, such a view would not only be absurd, but inappropriate (cf. Mark 6:25; 15:43; Luke 1:28; Acts 10:3; 11:3; 16:40; 17:2; 28:8). What, then, can we say that this verse is affirming? First, we should answer in the negative: it is not an offering of salvation. The implications of this are manifold. Among other things, to use this text as a salvation verse is a perversion of the simplicity of the gospel. Many people have allegedly 'received Christ into their hearts' without understanding what that means or what the gospel means. Although this verse is picturesque, it actually muddies the waters of the truth of salvation. Reception of Christ is a consequence, not a condition, of salvation. As far as the positive meaning of this verse, it may refer to Christ having supremacy in the assembly or even to an invitation (and, consequently, a reminder) to believers to share with him in the coming kingdom. But to determine which of these is correct is beyond the scope of grammar. All grammar can tell us here is which view is almost certainly not correct—namely, that which sees this as an offering of salvation."—Wallace, *Greek Grammar Beyond the Basics - Exegetical Syntax of the New Testament*, 381.

[141] Henry Morris, *The Revelation Record* (Wheaton, IL: Tyndale House Publishers, 1983), Rev. 3:20.

[142] Fausset, "*The Revelation of St. John the Divine*."

[143] Morris, *The Revelation Record*, Rev. 3:21.

[144] Thomas, *Revelation 1-7*, 325.

[145] Barnhouse, *Revelation*, 84.

[146] C. I. Scofield, *The Scofield Study Bible* (New York, NY: Oxford University Press, 2002, 1909), Rev. 3:21.

[147] Renald Showers, *Israel My Glory*, January/February 2001, 30.

[148] Trench, *Commentary on the Epistles to the Seven Churches in Asia.*

[149] Fausset, "*The Revelation of St. John the Divine*," Rev. 3:21.

[150] Mills, *Revelations: An Exegetical Study of the Revelation to John*, Rev. 3:22.

[151] Showers, *Maranatha, Our Lord Come*, 246.

3.4 - Revelation 4

3.4.1 - Revelation 4:1

Having completed the letters to the *Seven Churches of Asia*[4.15], John is called up to the throne room in heaven where he is given a vision of God the Father on His throne.

After these things

The phrase is μετὰ ταῦτα [*meta tauta*] and indicates a transition from "the things which are" (Rev. 1:19), the letters written to the *Seven Churches of Asia*[4.15] in chapters 2 and 3. John enters upon the second of the two major time periods into which this revelation is divided: "the things which will take place after this". See *Structural Outline*[2.14.3].

a door *standing* open

Standing open is ἠνεῳγμενη [*ēneōgmenē*], perfect tense: "a door already having been opened." The door was opened prior to John seeing it and now stood ajar. In Revelation 3:8 Jesus set an open door before the Philadelphian church. This door is not for evangelism, but provides passage for John to heaven to be shown the events recorded hereafter.

There are numerous parallels between this passage and the vision recorded by Ezekiel. Ezekiel did not mention a *door*, but said "the heavens were opened and I saw visions of God" (Eze. 1:1). The "heavens were opened" at Jesus' baptism (Mtt. 3:16; Luke 3:21), the stoning of Steven (Acts 7:56), Peter's vision of the unclean animals (Acts 10:11), and at the Second Coming of Christ (Rev. 19:11).

the first voice which I heard *was* like a trumpet speaking with me saying

This is probably better translated as: "The first voice I had heard speaking to me like a trumpet said."[1] This is the voice John heard at the first, on the Lord's day, which sounded like a trumpet (Rev. 1:10).[2] See commentary on *Revelation 1:10*[3.1.10].

Come up here

Having written the letters to the churches, John is called "to Heaven that he might look down upon all that should follow from the point of view of Heaven itself. . . . Any true understanding of the course of world events must be based on Heaven's perspective of those events. Further it may be said that here is a typical teaching in the very act of John's translation to Heaven for the vision that is to follow. . . . all believers will be caught up to Heaven before the judgment is actually poured out upon the earth."[3] Yet many commentators are averse to seeing any possible connection between the experience of John recorded here and the *Rapture*[5.2.62] of the church:

> There is no convincing reason why the seer's being "in the Spirit" and being called into heaven typifies the rapture of the church any more than his being taken into the wilderness to view Babylon indicates that the church is there in exile. The phrase relates to the experience of the seer, and not necessarily to that of the church.[4]

> This phrase is taken by many to prove the *pretribulation*[5.2.60] Rapture of the church. This text, however, cannot prove anything about the Rapture, for to apply this to the Rapture one must take John to be a type of the church, the call to "come up hither" a type of the shout-command at the Rapture, and the third heaven as the destination of believers at the Rapture, all of which are tenuous connections at best. One cannot base a doctrine on a type, and proof of the timing of the Rapture must rest upon the direct statements of Scripture elsewhere. There is no need to search the Apocalypse for a direct mention of the pretribulation Rapture of the church, when the doctrine is clearly stated elsewhere.[5]

> Many *Premillennialists*[5.2.58] see the Rapture of the Church in this verse, but this requires somewhat of an allegorical interpretation. Following *The Golden Rule of Interpretation*[5.2.24] , this verse merely contains an invitation for John to come to Heaven in vision (Rev. 4:2) in order that God can show him *the things which must come to pass hereafter*.[6]

We concur with Smith that this text cannot *prove* anything about the Rapture and that the pretribulational timing of the Rapture rests upon other passages and Biblical teaching, but we cannot agree with Tenney that this passage has not even a *typological* relationship to the Rapture. Nor do we agree with Fruchtenbaum that recognizing typology here is akin to allegory. Are we "allegorizing" when we understand the serpent on the pole in Numbers 21 as a type pointing to the cross? By this measure, Jesus would have to be said to be an allegorical interpreter (John 3:14-16).

As Smith even recognizes, there are significant parallels between this verse *in its setting* and the Rapture:

1. Like John, the saints will hear a verbal command at the Rapture (1Th. 4:16).
2. Like John, the destination of those raptured is heaven (John 14:1-3; 1Th. 4:17).
3. Like John, those raptured are *in Christ* —members of the Church which was created on the Day of Pentecost (1Cor. 12:13).
4. John hears a voice *as* a trumpet. The raptured saints hear a voice *and* a trumpet (1Cor. 15:52; 1Th. 4:16).
5. The command John hears, "Come up here!", also attends the *resurrection* of the two witnesses (Rev. 11:12).

The context also emphasizes the transition between "the things which are" and the "things which will take place after these [things]" (Rev. 1:19). John has just finished writing the seven letters to *seven churches*[5.2.66] dictated by Jesus. These letters are *full* of the church. Yet the word church (εκκλησία [*ekklēsia*]) in the last verse of chapter three is the *final* appearance of the word until Revelation 22:16 —long after "the things which must take place" introduced here. Surely the similarities between this passage and aspects of the Rapture coupled with the dramatic transition which attends the introduction of this chapter are more than pure coincidence!

We find it puzzling why believers are content to recognize subtle typology concerning Christ found in Abraham's offering of Isaac (Gen. 22) or the serpent on the pole in the wilderness (Num. 21), yet are unwilling to allow for seeing typological hints concerning the Rapture in other passages such as this? If Boaz, Ruth, and Naomi are understood to represent Jesus, the Church, and Israel in the book of Ruth, why is it considered out-of-bounds to notice similar parallels between this verse and what is taught elsewhere concerning the Rapture of the Church, *especially given its context*? We believe this bias against understanding typology of the Rapture in this verse wrong-headed and believe that the Holy Spirit *intended* to *support* here what is explicitly taught elsewhere. See *Rapture*[4.14].

I will show you

This is the primary purpose of the Revelation being given John (Rev. 1:1, 19; 22:6). The scenes in the book of Revelation often follow a pattern where a heavenly setting is described followed by an earthly setting:

> Each Vision "in heaven" is preparatory to the Vision afterwards seen "on earth"; and what is seen "on earth" is the carrying out of the Vision previously seen "in heaven." The one is mutually explanatory of the other. The heavenly Vision explains what is going to take place upon the earth; and the utterances in each heavenly Vision set forth the special object of the earthly events which are to follow. The former Vision of each pair, is therefore, the key to the latter.[7]

As with all of history, it is critical that the interpreter of events transpiring upon the earth has access to the perspective of God. For without His perspective, all is chaos and disarray. All the more so at the end of history when events upon the earth become extremely chaotic and destructive—seemingly without purpose or plan. Yet as is shown John and conveyed to us, the events are carefully orchestrated and *initiated* by God Himself as He finally moves His hand to take back that which was lost in the Garden and legally regained at the cross. It is from this heavenly perspective that the great events of judgment in the pages to come must be understood. To those saints living during the time of the end, John's revelation—wherever a copy might be procured—will be of inestimable value!

things which must take place after this

The things to come are *sure* for they *must* take place. God's prophetic word cannot be broken (John 10:35). This is why the sword extends from the *mouth* of Jesus—the will of God, once having been spoken forth, is unstoppable (Rev. 1:16; 19:15). *After this* is perhaps better translated *after these [things]*. It is the same phrase which begins the verse: μετὰ ταῦτα [*meta tauta*]. This verse follows "the things which are" and Jesus is now introducing the next major topic—the things which are yet future to John's time.

3.4.2 - Revelation 4:2

I was in the Spirit

Once again, John was "in the Spirit," as he was at the beginning of his vision (Rev. 1:10). Ezekiel described his similar experience as the hand of the Lord being upon him (Eze. 1:3; 3:14). Later, he records: "the Spirit lifted me up between earth and heaven, and brought me in visions of God to Jerusalem" (Eze. 8:3). In subsequent visions, the Spirit took Ezekiel to Chaldea (Eze. 11:24) and to the valley of dry bones (Eze. 37:1). Paul was caught up to the third heaven in a similar experience, although he does not mention the Spirit's involvement (2Cor. 12:1-2). Being "in the Spirit" refers not only to spiritual or physical transport to a new location or vantage point, but to a unique empowerment by the Spirit to receive special revelatory communication from God (Eze. 2:2; 3:12-14; Gal. 1:16; 2:2; Eph. 3:3). Although the text does not explicitly say so, John was probably *transported* to heaven. The command was for him to "come up here." The Spirit transports John to the wilderness (Rev. 17:2) and a great and high mountain (Rev. 21:10) later in the book.

***One* sat on the throne**

Prior to being given great revelation, prophets are often exposed to the glory of God. Earlier, John saw the glorified Jesus. Now he will be shown the throne room in heaven. Isaiah had a similar vision of God on His throne (Isa. 6:1). This is where Jesus is presented to the "Ancient of Days" to receive His kingdom (Dan. 7:9-14). In Ezekiel's vision, "on the likeness of a throne *was* a likeness with the appearance of a man" (Eze. 1:26). Isaiah also saw Him: "I saw the Lord sitting on a throne, high and lifted up, and the train of His robe filled the temple" (Isa. 6:1b).

See commentary on *Revelation 1:12*[3.1.12].

The One sitting is God the Father, not Christ, for Christ comes to the One on the throne to receive the scroll with the seven seals (Rev. 5:1-7). This is the One whose wrath, along with that of the Lamb, is poured out upon the *earth dwellers*[5.2.18] (Rev. 6:16-17) and to Whom, along with the Lamb, salvation belongs (Rev. 7:10).

He is sitting *on the throne* which emphasizes His ultimate rule and control of all that transpires in the book (Rev. 4:5, 9, 10; 5:1, 6, 7, 13; 6:16. 7:10, 15; 16:17; 19:4; 20:11-15; 21:5). Even the final manifestation of evil is dependent upon permission being granted from the Father (Rev. 3:21; 6:4; 7:2; 13:7, 14, 15). God is completely sovereign over the affairs of history, yet those who participate in sin are fully responsible moral agents (Acts 2:22-23). God's *throne* is prominent throughout the book and indicates His ultimate role as *judge* (Rev. 20:11).[8]

Hundreds of years before John, Ezekiel saw the same One seated on His *chariot throne*:

> And above the firmament over their heads *was* the likeness of a throne, in appearance like a sapphire stone; on the likeness of the throne *was* a likeness with the appearance of a man high above it. Also from the appearance of His waist and upward I saw, as it were, the color of amber with the appearance of fire all around within it; and from the appearance of His waist and downward I saw, as it were, the appearance of fire with brightness all around. Like the appearance of a rainbow in a cloud on a rainy day, so *was* the appearance of the brightness all around it. This *was* the appearance of the likeness of the glory of the LORD. So when I saw *it*, I fell on my face, and I heard a voice of One speaking. (Eze. 1:26-28)

Ezekiel was overcome by what he saw. Here, no mention is made of John collapsing under the vision of God's glory as occurs so frequently elsewhere (Isa. 6:5; Eze. 1:28; 3:23; Dan. 10:8; Mtt. 17:6; Mark 9:6; Acts 9:4; Rev. 1:17). Perhaps this is because John had already been strengthened by Christ following his collapse at the earlier revelation of the risen Christ (Rev. 1:17).

What John sees is not some immaterial spiritual revelation, but a *real material place*:

> Heaven is a material place. John saw a throne. If the objection is that he was in the Spirit and that it might be a spiritual throne, we would answer that the body of Jesus Christ was raised from the dead and that our Lord said, "Handle me, and see; for a spirit hath not flesh and bones, as ye see me have" (Luke

> 24:39); and it was that body which ascended into Heaven. There must be a material Heaven or there was no ascension, and if there was no ascension, there was no resurrection, and if there was no resurrection, there is no salvation.[9]

3.4.3 - Revelation 4:3

like a jasper

Jasper describes the light of, foundation, and walls of the holy Jerusalem (Rev. 21:11, 18-20). It was the last of the twelve stones representing the twelve tribes of Israel which were mounted in the breastplate of the high priest (Ex. 28:20; 39:13). When Satan was in the Garden of God, his covering included precious stones like jasper (Eze. 28:13-14). "Modern ignorance of ancient terminology makes precise identification of the stones quite tentative (Morris). Probably the equation of *iaspidi* ('jasper stone') to the modern jasper which is dull and opaque (Alford) is wrong because the modern stone is hardly considered costly as the text implies."[10] "From Rev. 21:11, where it is called most precious, which the jasper was not, Ebrard infers it was a diamond."[11]

like a sardius stone

"The sardius, better known in our day as the carnelian, is red. Hengstenberg quotes ancient authorities who call it 'blood-colored' and takes it to describe the righteous wrath of God, the color of the fire of divine anger."[12] This stone is also mentioned as part of Satan's covering in the Garden of God (Eze. 28:13). It is the sixth foundation stone of the holy Jerusalem (Rev. 21:19) and the first of the twelve stones representing the twelve tribes of Israel in the breastplate of the high priest (Ex. 28:17; 39:10). The inclusion of both the first stone, *sardius*, and last stone, *jasper* from the breastplate denote the idea of *all Israel, first and last, beginning and end*, or *alpha and omega* (Rev. 1:8, 17; 2:8).

> The jasper and the sardine stone are the first and last of these twelve stones [representing the tribes of Israel]. The jasper represented Reuben, the first of the tribes, since Reuben was the firstborn of Jacob. The sardine stone represented Benjamin, the youngest of the twelve sons of Jacob. In other words, the two stones represented the first and the last and therefore may be regarded as including all the other stones in between, that is, the whole of the covenanted people.[13]

Most see the references to precious stones here (and in Eze. 28) as a description of brilliant colored lights which radiate from God and His throne (Eze. 1:26-28): "We need not find symbolism in each element of the vision; it is enough to allow the archetypical imagery to create the impression of transcendent glory."[14]

a rainbow around the throne

The brilliant light emanating from the throne resembled a rainbow of *emerald* hues. The *rainbow* was given as a sign following Noah's flood to *remind God* of His covenant never again to destroy all flesh with a flood (Gen. 9:13-16; Isa. 54:9-10). Ezekiel saw this same rainbow as the brightness around the throne (Eze. 1:28). The world that was previously perished in the flood. In the chapters to follow, the judgment will be by *fire* (2Pe. 3:5-7).

> As the rainbow was first reflected on the waters of the world's ruin, and continues to be seen only when a cloud is brought over the earth, so another deluge, namely, of fire, shall precede the new heavens and earth: the Lord, as here, on His throne, whence (Rev. 4:5) proceed "lightnings and thunderings," shall issue the commission to rid the earth of its oppressors.[15]

The rainbow is *around* the throne implying a full circle like a halo.[16] A rainbow adorns the head of the mighty angel whose cry precedes the seven thunders (Rev. 10:1-3).

like an emerald

The color of the third stone of the high priest's breastplate (Ex. 28:17; 39:10) and also associated with Satan's covering in the Garden of God (Eze. 28:13). The stone of the fourth foundation of the holy Jerusalem (Rev. 21:19).[17]

3.4.4 - Revelation 4:4

around about

Multitudes surround God's throne (1K. 22:19; Rev. 5:11; 7:11), but in concentric positions. Those closest to God appear to occupy positions of special service, blessing, and favor. The elders occupy a position of prominence near the throne along with the four living creatures (Rev. 4:6-9). The Lamb is also in their midst (Rev. 5:6).

on the thrones

These elders appear to co-reign with the Father in some lesser capacity. This brings to mind the promises made to the apostles wherein they will rule over the twelve tribes in the regeneration (Mtt. 19:28) and the promises made in the previous chapters to the overcomer (Rev. 2:26-27; 3:21 cf. Rev. 20:4, 6). Nowhere in Scripture do we see mention of elect *angels* occupying thrones.[18] Later, during the *Millennial Kingdom*[4.11], we find *humans* which sit upon thrones (Rev. 20:4).

Daniel's vision of the Ancient of Days mentions "thrones" which "were put in place" prior to a court being seated (Dan. 7:9-19). The court's judgment results in the destruction of the beast and the removal of the dominion of the other beasts (Dan. 7:12). This is the "judgment . . . made *in favor* of the saints of the Most High" when "the time came for the saints to possess the kingdom" (Dan. 7:22). The saints will be given into the hands of the beast for "a time and times and half a time" (Dan. 7:25; 9:27; 12:7; 11:2; 11:3, 13:5)[19] but the court shall be seated and "take away his dominion, to consume and destroy *it* forever" (Dan. 7:26). The only other mention of *thrones* (plural) in this book are those occupied by saints who take part in the first resurrection and rule and reign during the Millennium (Rev. 20:4). These elders comprise the court which will be seated and rule against the beast bringing about his eventual overthrow and ushering in the *Millennial Kingdom*[5.2.39] (Rev. 19, 20). Paul revealed that saints would be entrusted with the judgment of such weighty matters. "Do you not know that the saints will judge the world? . . . Do you not know that we shall judge angels?" (1Cor. 6:2-3).

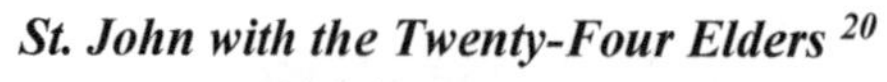

St. John with the Twenty-Four Elders [20]

twenty-four elders

The twenty-four elders repeatedly worship the Father (see commentary on *Revelation 4:10*[3.4.10]). One of the elders comforts John explaining that Jesus has prevailed to loose the seven-sealed scroll (Rev. 5:5). Later, an elder explains to John the identity of those coming out of the Great Tribulation (Rev. 7:13-14). The 144,000 with the Father's name on their foreheads sing a new song before these elders and the living creatures (Rev. 14:3). A wide range of opinions attends the identification of these elders. "There are at least thirteen different views of their identity, ranging from the twenty-four ruling stars (or judges) in the heavens to the simple figure of wholeness and fullness."[21]

> Attempts to identify the elders have fallen into two broad categories, one saying that they are men and the other that they are angels. Each category has three variations, the former one saying that the men are either representatives of Israel, representatives of the church, or representatives of both. The latter category sees the angels as representatives either of the *OT*[5.2.51] priestly order or of the faithful of all ages, or as a special class or college of angels.[22]

Whether to understand the elders as *human* or *angelic* beings turns on several factors:

1. Can the term "elder" describe an angel?[23]
2. Do angels wear crowns, symbols of reward not found in association with angels elsewhere?

3. Do elect angels sit on thrones, although never mentioned elsewhere?
4. Is the textual variant at Revelation 5:9, which explicitly includes the elders among the redeemed, the preferred reading?

The *elders* are πρεσβυτέρους [*presbyterous*], presbyters. Frequently translated 'elders' (67 times in the KJV). The term is never used of angelic beings:

> Nowhere else in Scripture is the term [elder] used to describe celestial or angelic beings. This term is used of humans in positions of authority either in the synagogue or church.[24]

> *Presbuteroi* (elders) is never used in Scripture to refer to angels, but always to men. It is used to speak of older men in general, and the rulers of both Israel and the church. There is no indisputable use of *presbuteroi* outside of Revelation to refer to angels. (Some believe that "elders" in Isaiah 24:23 refers to angels, but it could as well refer to humans.) Further, "elder" would be an inappropriate term to describe angels, who do not age.[25]

The number of the elders, *twenty four* is seen by some as symbolizing the twelve tribes of Israel (written on the gates of the New Jerusalem, Rev. 21:12) and the twelve apostles of the Lamb (written on the twelve foundations of the city, Rev. 21:14). Thus, they suggest twelve of the elders represent OT saints and the other twelve *NT*[5.2.48] saints.

> That these twenty-four represent the heads of the twelve tribes of Israel and the twelve apostles is abundantly confirmed in Scripture. When we come to the description of the new Jerusalem, we find twelve messengers at the gates and on the gates the names of the twelve tribes of the children of Israel, while the names of the twelve apostles are on the foundations of the city (Rev. 21:12-14). Our Lord promised the disciples that they should sit upon twelve thrones judging the twelve tribes of Israel (Mtt. 19:28; Luke 22:30). So it is that believers of all ages are seen here.[26]

Yet the Lord said the apostles would judge the twelve tribes "in the regeneration, when the Son of Man sits on the throne of His glory" (Mtt. 19:28). This does not take place until His Second Coming when the Millennial Kingdom is established (Mtt. 25:31; Rev. 20:4). This scene in heaven precedes that time by at least seven years for the Lamb has not yet taken the scroll from the Father to loose the first of its seven seals (Rev. 5). So it is not clear that OT saints are pictured here. The time at which this vision occurs within the sequence of events shown John implies that the elders are *already* in heaven prior to the events of *The 70th Week of Daniel*[2.13.5]. We believe that passages such as Daniel 12:1-2 imply that OT saints are not resurrected until *after* this *time of Jacob's Trouble*[2.13.4] —prior to the Millennial Kingdom (Rev. 20:4). To be sure, the souls of OT saints are in paradise (heaven at this time), but it seems unlikely that they would have received rewards (i.e., crowns) or rule on thrones prior to the resurrection attending the Millennial Kingdom.[27]

Others note the parallel with the twenty four divisions which David and Zadok made of the sons of Aaron for their priestly service (1Chr. 24:1-5). Rather than twelve OT saints and twelve NT saints, the number *twenty four* could merely represent the *priestly* role of the NT saints:

> The figure 24 is probably taken from 1 Chronicles 24, where David divided the Tribe of Levi into 24 courses to represent the whole. Since the Church is a kingdom of priests, these 24 elders represent the Church as a whole. This actually provides [another] clue to the fact that the 24 elders represent the Church and not angels.[28]

The events of the Tribulation period which follows argue against their identification with Israel:

> Some believe the elders represent Israel. But while individual Jews have been and will continue to be redeemed throughout history, at the time of this vision the nation as a whole had not yet been redeemed. Their national judgment and salvation (Rom. 11:26) comes during the Tribulation (chaps. 6-19), largely as a result of the evangelistic efforts of the 144,000 (introduced in chap. 7). When the twenty-four elders are first introduced, those events are yet to take place.[29]

Various lines of evidence suggest they represent the redeemed of the present church age.[30]

> The biblical description seems to point to believers of this present church age. They are already in heaven (Rev. 4-5) before the opening of the seal judgments (Rev. 6). They are sitting on thrones before God (Rev. 4:4). Angels never sit in the presence of God. However, Christ promised church-age believers that they would sit with Him on His throne (Rev. 3:21). God positionally has made all believers today sit

> together in the heavenly places in Christ (Eph. 2:6). The elders are clothed in white robes (Rev. 4:4). Church-age believers are promised such pure clothing (Rev. 3:5, 18; 19:7-8). The elders have crowns of gold on their heads (Rev. 4:4). . . . Believers in the churches are promised such crowns (Rev. 2:10; 3:11). In the Epistles, believers are also promised crowns for spiritual accomplishments (1Cor. 9:25; 1Th. 2:19; 2Ti. 4:8; Jas. 1:12; 1Pe. 5:4). Holy angels do not wear crowns, but believers can and will wear them. . . . The elders are set in contrast to angels (Rev. 5:11). The term *presbuteros* (elder) is never used of angels in the Bible. The word denotes maturity and growth. Holy angels could not be designated with this term because they were all created at the same time. . . . The more plausible explanation of the twenty-four elders is that they represent the redeemed of this present church age.[31]

> Among the well-known commentators who regard these elders as representative of the Church are Alford, Barnes, Benson, Binney, Carpenter, Clarke, Clemance, Book, Crafer, Crosby, Dusterdieck, Fausset, Girdlestone, Godet, Gray, Henry, [Hengstenberg], Holden, Kiyper, Milligan, Plummer, Roberson, Scott, Sheppard, Simcox, Slight, Smith, Swete, Weidner.[32]

If these represent saints of the church age,[33] then we have another piece of evidence in favor of a *pretribulational*[5.2.60] *rapture*[4.14]: "Here then is yet another proof that the Church shall not pass through the Tribulation, for we find these singers in Heaven before the beginning of the judgments."[34]

> As John beholds certain subjects of redemption, robed, and crowned, and enthroned, as priests and kings in heaven, we here have (let it be noted) positive demonstration, that, at the time to which this vision relates, a resurrection and a translation *have already taken place* . . . .They occupy these thrones, while yet the closed book, which brings forth the seals and trumpets, lies untouched in the hand of Him that sits upon the throne. They see it there, and they vote the Lamb worthy to open it. They behold Him taking it up, and fall down and worship as He holds it. They are in their places when heaven receives the accession of the multitude which come "out of the great tribulation" (Rev. 7:11-14). They have their own distinct positions when the still later company of the hundred and forty-four thousand gather round the Lamb on Mount Sion. And they are spectators of the judgment of great Babylon, and sing Alleluia in glory as they see her fall (Rev. 19:4).[35]

Elders will also rule with Christ from Jerusalem in the Millennial Kingdom (Isa. 24:23).

clothed in white robes

The elders are *clothed* in *white* which speaks of a covering for sin provided by Christ's atonement on behalf of the saints. See commentary on *Revelation 3:4*[3.3.4] and *Revelation 3:5*[3.3.5].

There is some question as to whether the elders include themselves among the redeemed mentioned in Revelation 5:9 as textual variants attend the text. The *TR*[5.2.79] and *MT*[5.2.45] texts indicate the elders are redeemed whereas the *NU*[5.2.49] text does not. See commentary on *Revelation 5:9*[3.5.9].

crowns of gold

Crowns is στεφάνους [*stephanous*]. The crowns may indicate that the elders are among those who have been made "kings and priests" (or "a kingdom *of* priests" , NU text) as is promised the overcomers (Rev. 2:10; 3:11). See commentary on *Revelation 1:6*[3.1.6] . They were awarded these crowns, yet they repeatedly cast them before the Father's throne in recognition of the superiority and source of their blessing (Rev. 4:10).[36] "When all earthly crowns and thrones have perished, the redeemed ones of Christ will be at the beginning of their reign. How small then will appear the great majesties of earth, and how insignificant the power they have to bestow!"[37]

In Scripture, angelic beings are never promised nor found wearing crowns. Yet some suggest the elders to be angels. Crowns (other than those worn by God) are typically associated with rewards attending judgment. The judgment of angels would likely take place after this scene in heaven because: (1) the saints participate in their judgment—presumably after having been glorified (1Cor. 6:3); and 2) significant events attending the angelic realm have yet to transpire before they can be judged. "If this passage is regarded as chronologically before the time of the tribulation which succeeding chapters unfold, it would seem to eliminate the angels, as at this point they have not been judged and rewarded since their judgment seems to come later."[38] This assumes the angelic judgment by the saints is for both *reward* and *punishment*. If these crowns are not associated with reward, or the angelic judgment is only for punishment from which the elect angels are exempt, then the plausibility of the elders being angels encounters fewer difficulties.

See *Crowns*[4.6].

3.4.5 - Revelation 4:5

lightnings, thunderings, and voices

These portend the magnificence and glory of the Father and bring reverent fear to those who experience them, as when God revealed Himself to the children of Israel at Mount Sinai (Ex. 19:16-18; Heb. 12:18-21) and to Ezekiel (Eze. 1:13). In this book, thunder attends moments of great significance and impending *judgment* (Rev. 8:5; 10:3; 11:19; 16:17-18; 19:6 cf. Ex. 9:23-34; 1S. 2:10; 7:10; 1S. 12:17-18; 2S. 22:14; Ps. 18:13; 104:7). "This is the faint rumbling of the judgment that shall come forth against mankind out of Christ, against the empire of Satan, and the farthest worlds of the universe. Now there is a premonition of judgment, but soon worlds shall perish."[39] "These demonstrate that the throne is one of judgment, and that wrath is about to proceed from it."[40]

The *voices* may be those of the "seven thunders" whose utterance John is told not to record (Rev. 10:3-4). " 'The thunderings express God's threats against the ungodly: there are voices in the thunders (Rev. 10:3), that is, not only does He threaten generally, but also predicts special judgments' [Grotius]."[41]

seven lamps

These *lamps* are said to be the *seven Spirits of God* which are *burning before the throne*. See commentary on *Revelation 1:4*[3.1.4]. These are not the "seven lampstands" which are the churches (Rev. 1:12, 20), but represent the Holy Spirit Who is the source of light (illumination) and Who empowers the seven lampstands. Their continual *burning* is an indication of judgment (Mtt. 3:11) and zeal (Acts 2:3), for nothing escapes the penetrating witness of the Holy Spirit (Gen. 15:17; Rev. 3:1; 5:6). The lamps are associated with *lightnings* and *thunderings* and are *burning* as an indication of the time of judgment which follows.

> "For behold, the day is coming, burning like an oven, and all the proud, yes, all who do wickedly will be stubble. And the day which is coming shall burn them up," says the LORD of hosts, "That will leave them neither root nor branch." (Mal. 4:1)

See *Trouble Ahead*[2.13.1].

3.4.6 - Revelation 4:6

sea of glass, like crystal

Those who achieve victory over the beast (by not loving their lives to the death, Rev. 12:11) are seen standing on this *sea of glass* before the throne. There, it is said to be "mingled with fire" possibly indicating the brilliance of light radiating from the *crystal* -like structure (Rev. 15:2).

Moses, the sons of Aaron, and the elders of Israel saw something similar when they met with God on Mount Sinai:

> Then Moses went up, also Aaron, Nadab, and Abihu, and seventy of the elders of Israel, and they saw the God of Israel. And *there was* under His feet as it were a paved work of sapphire stone, and it was like the very heavens in *its* clarity. (Ex. 24:9-10)

This sea may also symbolize the "river of life" which flows from the temple during the Millennium (Eze. 47:1-9) and proceeds from the throne in the eternal state (Rev. 22:1), where there is no more sea (Rev. 21:1). Both are said to be like *crystal*.[42] Corresponding to the bronze laver in the *tabernacle*[5.2.69] and Solomon's *Temple*[5.2.73] (Ex. 38:8; 1K. 7:23), the sea pictures the washing away of uncleanness by Christ's atonement. This *sea of glass* is under the throne, but was seen above from Ezekiel's perspective below the chariot throne (Eze. 1:22-26).[43]

> Thank God the laver [in heaven] will be turned to crystal. The day will come when one of the saints will ever need confession. . . . I shall never have to go to the Heavenly Father again to tell Him I have sinned. . . The laver is of crystal only because I and all the saints of all the ages will have been made like into the Lord Jesus Christ. There will be no more sin. This is one of the reasons why it will be Heaven.[44]

See commentary on *Revelation 15:2*[3.15.2].

around the throne

These creatures are around the throne, whereas in Ezekiel's vision the similar creatures are *in the midst* of the cloud of fire (Eze. 1:5).

four living creatures

There are *four* creatures indicating the universal character of their representation (see the *symbolic meaning of four*[2.7.5.3.3]). They are *Living creatures*, ζῷα [*zōa*]: "to denote beings that are not human and yet not really animals of the usual kind . . . Of the four peculiar beings at God's throne, whose description Rev. 4:6-9 reminds us of the ζῷα [*zōa*] in Eze. 1:5ff, the cherubim. See also Rev. 5:6, 8, 11, 14; 6:1, 3, 5-7; 7:11; 14:3; 15:7; 19:4."[45] Ezekiel also sees *four living creatures*, τεσσάρων ζῳιων [*tessarōn zōiōn*] (Eze. 1:5-22; 3:13; 10:1-20). Ezekiel's creatures have close similarity to these:

1. They attend the throne.
2. They are winged.
3. Aspects of their character represent a lion, an ox (or calf), a man, and an eagle.

But there are also significant differences:

1. Ezekiel's creatures had four wings whereas these have six.
2. Ezekiel's creatures *each* had all four faces of a man, a lion, an ox, and an eagle whereas these each have *one* of the characteristics.[46]
3. No mention is made of Ezekiel's creatures themselves having eyes—although the wheels they attend are full of eyes. These creatures *themselves* are full of eyes.

Similarity does not make identity and we must conclude that these living creatures, while probably cherubim, are different in identity to Ezekiel's cherubim (Eze. 10:20). Since Isaiah's seraphs had six wings, perhaps these creatures are of that order (Isa. 6:2, 6).

It appears that these creatures attend God's stationary throne whereas Ezekiel's cherubim attend God's *chariot throne* which transports the manifestation of His glory (Ps. 18:10; Eze. 10:19-20; 11:22). We first meet with cherubim in their service of God guarding the way to the tree of life after the expulsion of Adam and Eve from the Garden (Gen. 3:24).[47]

Satan was created as one of these cherubim serving at God's throne until he fell (Eze. 28:14). "Here are the living ones, in every way his equals, yes, infinitely his superiors, since they have access to all of the power of God. These are not with him in his rebellion. They are ready to carry into effect the orders of divine judgment."[48]

These living creatures call John's attention to the effects of the Lamb's loosening of the first four seals whereupon the four horsemen of the Apocalypse ride forth (Rev. 6:1-7). One of the four living creatures gives the final seven bowls of God's wrath to the seven angels who will pour forth the seven plagues.

> After the Flood, the *Teraphim* (probably a corruption of the Cherubim) were made in imitation of them and became objects of worship [Gen. 31:19, 34-35; Jdg. 17:5; 18:14, 17-18, 20; 1S. 15:23; 19:13, 16; 2K. 23:24; Eze. 21:21; Hos. 3:4; Zec. 10:2]. The remembrance of them was carried away by the scattered nations (Gen. 10), and probably the Assyrian sculptures are traditional corruptions of the Cherubim, for they consisted of a *man* with an *eagle's* head; a *lion* or a *winged bull* with a *human* head.[49]

The cherubim attend God's throne. The writer of Hebrews informs us that the things in the earthly sanctuary were a model of the ultimate reality in heaven above (Heb. 9:24). In the earthly Tabernacle and Temple, we find these *living creatures* portrayed at each end of the Ark of the Covenant and on the veil separating the holy place (Ex. 26:31; 36:35). Their images attended God's glory which was said to "dwell between the cherubim" above the mercy seat (Ex. 25:22; Num. 7:89; 1S. 4:4; 2S. 6:2; 1K. 7:29; 2K. 19:15; 1Chr. 13:6; 2Chr. 5:7; 6:41; Ps. 80:1; 99:1; Isa. 37:16; Eze. 41:18). See *The Abiding Presence of God*[4.16.2], *A Heavenly Pattern*[4.16.4].

lion . . . calf . . . man . . . eagle

The symbolism conveyed by these faces is the subject of much discussion.

> The interpretations of the symbols of the four living creatures are, of course, numerous and varied. Some of them are: the four Evangelists or Gospels; the four elements; the four cardinal virtues; the four faculties or powers of the human soul; the Lord in the fourfold great events of redemption; the four patriarchal churches; the four great apostles, the doctors of the Church; the four principal angels, etc. [50]

As we discuss elsewhere, the *interpretation of symbols*[2.7] can often lead in unbiblical directions, especially to the degree that non-biblical sources provide the source for their interpretation. When other passages within Scripture are taken into consideration, it seems the likeness of these four creatures reflect the four primary roles of Messiah Jesus revealed in the four gospels:

1. King (Matthew)
2. Servant (Mark)
3. Man (Luke)
4. God (John)

Evidence in support of this view is presented in our discussion of the *Four Gospels*[4.7].

3.4.7 - Revelation 4:7

The simile of the first two and the last are like animals (lion, calf, flying eagle). The description of the third centers on its *face* being like that of a man. Nothing is said concerning the likeness of the remainder of its body.

3.4.8 - Revelation 4:8

having six wings

The cherubim Ezekiel saw had four wings (Eze. 1:11-12) whereas these creatures have six wings like the seraphim which Isaiah saw attending the throne (Isa. 6:2, 6). "In Isa. 6:2 we read, 'Each had six wings: with twain he covered his face (in reverence, as not presuming to lift up his face to God), with twain he covered his feet (in humility, as not worthy to stand in God's holy presence), and with twain he did fly [in obedient readiness to do instantly God's command].' "[51]

full of eyes

Eyes indicate great intelligence (Eze. 1:18; 10:12; Dan. 7:8, 20; Rev. 1:14; 2:18; 5:6; 19:12). These creatures are near the apex of God's created order (Eze. 28:12-15).[52]

around and within

"John's object is to show that the six wings in each did not interfere with that which he had before declared, namely, that they were 'full of eyes before and behind.' The eyes were *round* the outside of each wing, and up the *inside* of each when half expanded, and of the part of body in that inward recess."[53] "Being so full of eyes positioned in this manner, they are able to move their wings without ever disrupting their vision."[54]

Holy, holy, holy

Isaiah's seraphim made a similar pronouncement concerning God's uniqueness (Isa. 6:3). Praises of God's holiness are said to "enthrone" Him (Ps. 22:3). "Who *is* like You, O LORD, among the gods? Who *is* like You, glorious in holiness, fearful in praises, doing wonders?" (Ex. 15:11). Worship of God is a major theme of this book as He brings about the redemption of creation in the culmination of history. See *Worship of God*[2.4.2]. Three denotes completeness or may reflect the Trinity. See *Three: Life, Resurrection, Completeness, the Trinity*[2.7.5.3.2].

Almighty

παντοκράτωρ [*pantokratōr*], see commentary on *Revelation 1:8*[3.1.8].

Who was and is and is to come

ὁ ἦν καὶ ὁ ω"ν καὶ ὁ ἐρχόμενος [*ho ēn kai ho ōn kai ho erchomenos*] , the same phrase as is found in Revelation 1:4, 8, but with the 1st and 2nd titles reversed. Comprised of a verb and two participles: "The *he was* and the *who is* and the *coming one*". This unusual grammatical construction is discussed in the commentary on *Revelation 1:4*[3.1.4].

3.4.9 - Revelation 4:9

Whenever the living creatures give glory

This is a repetitive event as evidenced by the future tense: δώσουσιν [*dōsousin*], *they shall give.*

who lives forever and ever

See commentary on *Revelation 1:4*[3.1.4].

3.4.10 - Revelation 4:10

the twenty-four elders fall down

Their action is tied to the doxology given by the living creatures. Whenever the creatures *shall* give glory, the elders *shall themselves* fall down: πεσοῦνται [*pesountai*] , future tense middle voice. This is repetitive and voluntary worship (Rev. 4:10; 5:8-10, 14; 11:16; 19:4). They "worship at His footstool" for "He *is* holy" (Ps. 99:5).

Him who lives forever

The one living into the ages of the ages. This is God the Father seated on His throne. How similar His identity is with that of Jesus: *the Living One, and dead I became and behold living I am into the ages of the ages* (Rev. 1:18). See commentary on *Revelation 1:18*[3.1.18]. His eternal existence is coupled with His role as Creator (see *next verse*[3.4.11]) because He alone is without previous cause. He is the unique "uncaused cause" which has always existed and from which all else was brought forth. If God were not eternal, then all eternity would have been nothingness because no agent would have preexisted creation to bring it forth. "This is the strongest possible expression for an unending eternity. We make special mention of it because later we shall see that the same phrase is used of the duration of the punishment of Satan, his captains and those of earth who have followed him."[55]

cast their crowns

They recognized the supreme worthiness of the One on the throne. Their own crowns are entirely dependent upon His grace and bestowal. "What are these crowns? . . . they are the symbols of reward. They are the prizes, which have come from God's heart of grace, given unto those who, at the best, were unprofitable servants. When we shall see the worship of the mighty cherubim, we shall realize therefore, that no crown belongs to us rightfully and we shall cast them down before the presence of Him who lives forever."[56]

See *Crowns*[4.6].

3.4.11 - Revelation 4:11

worthy to receive glory and honor and power

λαβεῖν [*labein*], present tense: *to be continually receiving.* Both the Father and the Son are *worthy to receive glory and honor and power* (Rev. 5:12). See *Worship of God*[2.4.2].

You created all things

If there could have been any doubt about Who is seated on the throne, here it is removed. He alone is *creator*, all else is *creature*. He alone is *independent*, all else is *dependent* upon Him. Recognition of this distinction is the foundation of all right worship, for worship of any other is directing to that which is *dependent* what is only for the *Originator* (Rev. 22:8-9). All worship directed elsewhere is idolatry.

Scripture reveals that all three persons of the Trinity participated in creation:

1. The Father (Gen. 1:1-31; Isa. 40:21-28; Isa. 43:1, 7; Isa. 45:12, 18; 48:13; 51:13; Acts 14:15;

17:24).

2. The Spirit (Gen. 1:2; Job 26:13; 33:4; Ps. 104:30; Isa. 42:5).

3. The Son (John 1:3; Eph. 3:9; Col. 1:16; Heb. 1:3; Rev. 3:14).

by Your will they exist and were created

His role as Creator underwrites all worship of Him, for He *alone* is Creator and all else is creature and therefore, *entirely dependent* upon His will for continued existence (Heb. 1:3). "In Him all things consist" (Col. 1:17) "For of Him and through Him and to Him are all things, to whom be glory forever. Amen" (Rom. 11:36).

TR[5.2.79] and *MT*[5.2.45] have εισι [*eisi*], *exist*. *NU*[5.2.49] has ἦσαν [*ēsan*], *existed*. The past tense emphasizes the creative act. The present tense emphasizes their ongoing existence by His will.

Were created, ἔκτισας [*ektisas*], the aorist tense typically denotes past time. God *finished* creation and then rested (Gen. 2:2-3; Ex. 20:11; 31:17). "When the *NT*[5.2.48] refers to creation... it always refers to a past, completed event—an immediate work of God, not a still-occurring process of evolution."[57] Even *if* it were somehow possible for complex life forms to arise by chance,[58] the notion is precluded by Scripture. Creation is not an ongoing process.[59]

Here we need to alert the reader of the danger of allowing the chapter break between chapters 4 and 5 to destroy the flow of the text. There is an intimate connection between the words of the cherubim and elders concerning *creation* and the events of the next chapter where the Lamb takes the seven-sealed scroll. For here the subject is *creation* and there it will be *redemption*. Not redemption *positionally* which was accomplished at the cross, but *experientially*. Not just redemption of saved men, but of the *entire created order* (Rom. 8:18-22) which has been subject to Satan since the fall (Mtt. 4:8; Luke 4:6; John 12:31; 14:30; 16:11; 2Cor. 4:4; 1Jn. 5:19; Rev. 13:1; 13:7).

> Thus, *creation* is the subject of the first great utterance of the *Zoa* and the Elders. Their words announce the blessed fact that the judgments which are about to take place, have for their great object the removal of the curse [Gen. 3:14-19], and of all unholiness from the earth; and the ending of creation's groaning and travail.[60]

Notes

1 *New Electronic Translation : NET Bible*, electronic edition (Dallas, TX: Biblical Studies Press, 1998), Rev. 4:1.

2 Many red-letter Bibles seem unwilling to identify the voice as being that of Jesus for they render the words of this voice in black but the words of the voice speaking in Revelation 1:10-11 in red. An exception is the KJ2000 Bible, *http://life-equals-jesus.org/Couric/KJ2Khome.html*, available from *http://www.spiritandtruth.org/download/tools/index.htm*.

3 Donald Grey Barnhouse, *Revelation* (Grand Rapids, MI: Zondervan Publishing House, 1971), 88.

4 Merrill C. Tenney, *Interpreting Revelation* (Peabody, MA: Hendrickson Publishers, 1957), 141.

5 Jerome Smith, *The New Treasury of Scripture Knowledge* (Nashville, TN: Thomas Nelson Publishers, 1992), Rev. 4:1.

6 Arnold G. Fruchtenbaum, *The Footsteps of Messiah*, rev ed. (Tustin, CA: Ariel Ministries, 2003), 165.

7 E. W. Bullinger, *Commentary On Revelation* (Grand Rapids, MI: Kregel Publications, 1984, 1935), 211.

8 God's throne appears in Rev. 1:4; 3:21; 4:2-6, 9-10; 5:1, 6-7, 11, 13; 6:16; 7:9-11, 15, 17; 8:3; 12:5; 13:2; 14:3, 5; 16:10, 17; 19:4-5; 20:11; 21:5; 22:1, 3.

9 Barnhouse, *Revelation*, 89.

10 Robert L. Thomas, *Revelation 1-7* (Chicago, IL: Moody Press, 1992), 342.

11 A. R. Fausset, *"The Revelation of St. John the Divine,"* in Robert Jamieson, A. R. Fausset, and David Brown, *A Commentary, Critical and Explanatory, on the Old and New Testaments* (Oak Harbor, WA: Logos Research Systems, Inc., 1997, 1877), Rev. 4:2.

12 Barnhouse, *Revelation*, 90.

13 John F. Walvoord, *The Revelation of Jesus Christ* (Chicago, IL: Moody Press, 1966), 104.

14 Alan F. Johnson, *Revelation: The Expositor's Bible Commentary* (Grand Rapids, MI: Zondervan Publishing House, 1966), Rev. 4:3.

15 Fausset, "*The Revelation of St. John the Divine*," Rev. 4:3.

16 Thomas, *Revelation 1-7*, 343.

17 Mounce observes: "Ex. 28:17-21 lists the twelve stones, each inscribed and representing a tribe in Israel. Note that the jasper and the carnelian (sardius) are the last and the first (Benjamin and Reuben; cf. Gen. 49:3-27). On this basis the emerald (no. 4) would stand for the tribe of Judah."—Robert H. Mounce, *The Book of Revelation* (Grand Rapids, MI: William B. Eerdmans Publishing Co., 1977), 134. But in the list of stones given by Exodus 28:17, the emerald is listed as the *third* stone—the last in the first row of three—and would represent the tribe of *Levi*, not Judah.

18 "Nowhere in Scripture do angels sit on thrones, nor are they pictured ruling or reigning. Their role is to serve as 'ministering spirits, sent out to render service for the sake of those who will inherit salvation' (Heb. 1:14; cf. Mtt. 18:10)."—John MacArthur, *Revelation 1-11 : The MacArthur New Testament Commentary* (Chicago, IL: Moody Press, 1999), Rev. 4:4.

19 Daniel 11:3 probably denotes the first half of the 7-year period. The remaining 3.5 years are the time of the beast's dominion.

20 Albrecht Durer (1471 - 1528). Image courtesy of the *Connecticut College* (http://www.conncoll.edu/visual/Durer-prints/index.html) *Wetmore Print Collection* (http://www.conncoll.edu/visual/wetmore.html).

21 Johnson, *Revelation: The Expositor's Bible Commentary*, Rev. 4:4.

22 Thomas, *Revelation 1-7*, 344.

23 In support of identifying the elders with angels, [Thomas, *Revelation 1-7*, 345] notes the *Septuagint*[5.2.65] rendering of 'elders' in Isa. 24:23 refers to a heavenly assembly. But the context of the passage is the Messianic Kingdom in which resurrected *humans* are known to function in leadership roles.

24 Fruchtenbaum, *The Footsteps of Messiah*, 167.

25 MacArthur, *Revelation 1-11 : The MacArthur New Testament Commentary*, Rev. 4:5.

26 Barnhouse, *Revelation*, 91.

27 "The entire scriptural doctrine concerning the state of the dead, forbids the idea that disembodied souls are already crowned and enthroned, although at rest in the bosom of God. . . . The coronation time, is the resurrection time; and no one can be crowned until he is either resurrected if dead, or translated if living."—J. A. Seiss, *The Apocalypse: Lectures on the Book of Revelation* (Grand Rapids, MI: Zondervan Publishing House, 1966), 104. The OT saints are not *in Christ* in the sense of having been baptized into His body (1Cor. 12:13) and are not part of the Church which was formed on the Day of Pentecost. "Even though Israel is redeemed by the blood of Christ, Israel never experienced the baptism of the Holy Spirit which placed them 'in Christ,' so this phrase can only describe those saints of the present age who are thus related to Christ."—J. Dwight Pentecost, *Things to Come: A Study in Biblical Eschatology* (Grand Rapids, MI: Zondervan Publishing House, 1958), 407. Therefore the OT saints are not raised at the *Rapture*[5.2.62] of the church when the *dead in Christ* arise (1Th. 4:16), but at a later time—prior to the Millennial Kingdom in which Israel will play a key role (Mtt. 19:28). "Resurrection is viewed as a terminating event and Israel's resurrection could not come until her program were terminated."—Pentecost, *Things to Come: A Study in Biblical Eschatology*, 410.

28 Fruchtenbaum, *The Footsteps of Messiah*, 167.

29 MacArthur, *Revelation 1-11 : The MacArthur New Testament Commentary*, Rev. 4:5.

30 For the view that they are heavenly beings, see [Bullinger, *Commentary On Revelation*, 217-220] and [Thomas, *Revelation 1-7*, 344-348]. For an extended discussion of the identity of the elders, see [Pentecost, *Things to Come: A Study in Biblical Eschatology*, 207-208, 253-258].

31 Robert G. Gromacki, *"Twenty Four Elders of Revelation,"* in Mal Couch, ed., *Dictionary of Premillennial Theology* (Grand Rapids, MI: Kregel Publications, 1996), 377-378.

32 Alva J. McClain, *The Greatness Of The Kingdom* (Winona Lake, IN: BMH Books, 1959), 469.

[33] "Identification of the twenty-four elders should not be dogmatically held, but such evidence as there is seems to point to the conclusion that they may represent the church as the Body of Christ."—Walvoord, *The Revelation of Jesus Christ*, 107.

[34] Barnhouse, *Revelation*, 91.

[35] Seiss, *The Apocalypse: Lectures on the Book of Revelation*, 104.

[36] Fruchtenbaum sees their wearing crowns as an indication that the events of these two chapters follow the bema seat judgment of believers' works. "The fact that these 24 elders are wearing these *stephanos* crowns also shows that the events described in chapters four and five occur *after* the Judgment Seat of Messiah but *before* the Marriage of the Lamb."—Fruchtenbaum, *The Footsteps of Messiah*, 167.

[37] Barnhouse, *Revelation*, 92.

[38] Walvoord, *The Revelation of Jesus Christ*, 106.

[39] Barnhouse, *Revelation*, 92.

[40] Seiss, *The Apocalypse: Lectures on the Book of Revelation*, 102.

[41] Fausset, "*The Revelation of St. John the Divine*," Rev. 4:5.

[42] Passages related to the *river of life* : Ex. 17:6; Ps. 36:8-9; 46:4; Sos. 4:15; Isa. 12:2; 44:3; 55:1; Jer. 2:13; 17:13; Eze. 47:1, 8-9; Joel 3:18; Zec. 13:1; 14:8; John 4:10; 7:37-38; 19:28; 1Cor. 10:4; Rev. 7:17; 21:6; 22:1-2, 6; 17.

[43] "Contrast the turbid 'many waters' on which the harlot 'sitteth' (Rev. 17:1, 15)."—Fausset, "*The Revelation of St. John the Divine*," Rev. 4:6.

[44] Barnhouse, *Revelation*, 94.

[45] Frederick William Danker, and Walter Bauer, *A Greek-English Lexicon of the New Testament and Other Early Christian Literature* (Chicago, IL: University of Chicago Press, 2000), 341.

[46] Only one of the creatures is said to have a *face* like a man. The other creatures are simply said to have a likeness to a lion, ox, and eagle, respectively. We should not be dogmatic about whether it was their *faces* which bore the likenesses in all four creatures.

[47] Cherubim are mentioned in Gen. 3:24; Ex. 25:18-20, 22; 26:1, 31; 36:8, 35; 37:7-9; Num. 7:89; 1S. 4:4; 2S. 6:2; 22:11; 1K. 6:23-29, 32, 35; 7:29, 36; 8:6-7; 2K. 19:15; 1Chr. 13:6; 28:18; 2Chr. 3:7, 10-14; 5:7-8; Ezra 2:59; Ne. 7:61; Ps. 18:10; 80:1; 99:1; Isa. 37:16; Eze. 9:3; 10:1-9, 14-20; 11:22; 28:14, 16; 41:18, 20, 25; Heb. 9:5.

[48] Barnhouse, *Revelation*, 97.

[49] Bullinger, *Commentary On Revelation*, 225.

[50] M. R. Vincent, *Vincent's Word Studies* (Escondido, CA: Ephesians Four Group, 2002), Rev. 4:8.

[51] Fausset, "*The Revelation of St. John the Divine*," Rev. 4:8.

[52] Johnson, *Revelation: The Expositor's Bible Commentary*, Rev. 4:8.

[53] Fausset, "*The Revelation of St. John the Divine*," Rev. 4:8.

[54] Thomas, *Revelation 1-7*, 361.

[55] Barnhouse, *Revelation*, 98.

[56] Barnhouse, *Revelation*, 98.

[57] John MacArthur, *"Creation: Believe it or Not,"* in Richard L. Mayhue, ed., *The Master's Seminary Journal*, vol. 13 no. 1 (Sun Valley, CA: The Master's Seminary, Spring 2002), 15.

[58] All objective science shows that the generation of complexity requires *intelligence*. Design requires a *designer*.

[59] "*were created*—by Thy definite act of creation at a definite time."—Fausset, "*The Revelation of St. John the Divine*," Rev. 4:11.

[60] Bullinger, *Commentary On Revelation*, 231.

3.5 - Revelation 5

3.5.1 - Revelation 5:1

Having seen the Father and His glorious throne, John's attention is now drawn to a scroll held in the Father's hand. The redeeming Lamb takes the scroll and prepares to open its seals, initiating God's judgments in the *Day of the Lord*[5.2.14] and beginning the reclamation of the earth in preparation for God's direct rule.

And I saw

John's focus now shifts from the details of the throne and the living creatures and elders to that which lays upon the right hand of "Him who sat on the throne." The scene which presents itself to John is among the most sublime in all of Scripture. If Isaiah 53 can be said to be the "holy of holies" of the *OT*[5.2.51], then perhaps Revelation 5 holds that honor in the *NT*[5.2.48].

> Where, in all the revelations of eternity, is there another such a scene? Where, in all the disclosures of God, and His awful administrations, is there another such a picture, or another such a crisis? Search the book of *inspiration*[5.2.33] from end to end, and you will find no parallel to it. [1]

right *hand*

The side of favor and strength (Ps. 20:6; 74:11; 80:17; 89:13; 98:1). This is the side at which the Son is seated awaiting His kingdom (Ps. 110:1; Dan. 7:13-14; Mark 16:19; Acts 5:31; 7:55; Eph. 1:20; Col. 3:1; Heb. 1:3; 10:12) and making intercession for His Church (Rom. 8:34). Jesus is seated "with My Father on His throne" (Rev. 3:21) and shares the power and reign of the Father (Rev. 5:13; 6:16; 7:10 cf. 1K. 2:19). The long period of waiting while He remains seated is about to come to an end.

on the throne

The position from which the Father rules the affairs of His universe (Ps. 47:8; Isa. 6:1; Dan. 7:9-10). The throne pictures both *sovereignty* and *judgment* (Rev. 20:11).

a scroll

βιβλίον [*biblion*], also rendered *book* (Rev. 1:11; 3:5; 13:8; 17:8; 20:12; 20:15; 21:27; 22:7, 9-10, 18-19). Later, a mighty angel appears with a little book βιβλαρίδιον [*biblaridion*] and cries out at which seven thunders utter their voices. John is told to seal up the things which the seven thunders utter and not write them (Rev. 10:4). The angel then declares (even swears) that "in the days of the sounding of the seventh angel, when he is about to sound, the mystery of God would be finished, as He declared to His servants the prophets." (Rev. 10:6). John is then commanded to eat the little book which will be sweet to the taste but bitter in the stomach. The book given to John, like that eaten by Ezekiel (Eze. 2:9-3:5), apparently contains prophetic pronouncements of God, of woe and judgment, which must come to pass (Rev. 10:9-11). There are similarities between this scroll and these other books. This scroll is also sealed. Great prophetic streams find their fulfillment in the opening of the scroll. These similarities have led some to suggest that the sealed scroll primarily contains prophetic information previously unrevealed which is now made known through the things shown John.

> What ought we to look for as the first thing, in the Apocalypse, which , as we have seen, has the end of the "many days" and "the time of the end" for its great subject, but the *unsealing* of this book, the sealing of which is so prominently spoken of in the book of Daniel? . . . We take it therefore that the opening of the seals of this book is the enlargement, development, and continuation of the Book of Daniel, describing, from God's side, the judgments necessary to secure the fulfilment of all that He has foretold.[2]

As attractive as this explanation may be, it falls short of explaining the emphasis placed in this chapter between the right to open the book and *redemption*. The identification of this scroll is not found only in the fact that, like other prophetic writings, it is *sealed*, but also in its close association with *redemption* (Rev. 5:9) and the events which follow upon the loosing of its seals. The scroll is inherently related to the fulfillment of a *purchase*.

Ladd suggests the scroll is a form of ancient will. "The little book is in the form of an ancient will, which was usually sealed with the seals of seven witnesses. It contains God's inheritance for His people, which is founded upon the death of His son (see Heb. 9)."[3] This view has the advantage of explaining the emphasis found here upon the death of the Lamb (Rev. 5:6, 9). The events which transpire following the loosing of the seals are directly related to Christ's *inheritance*:

> [Psalm 2:1-3] describe[s] the rebellious world forces gathered together to try to prevent God's Messiah from taking tenant possession or administration of the earth. [Psalm 2:7] records that when the Messiah confronts this challenge, He will declare what God has already decreed concerning Him: "Thou art my Son." . . . the biblical term "son" involves the concept of "heir" (Gal. 4:7). Thus, as God's Son, the Messiah is the heir of an inheritance given to Him by God. Psalm 2:8 presents God's description of that inheritance: "I shall give thee the nations for thine inheritance, and the uttermost parts of the earth for thy possession."[4]

Although the loosing of the seals results in the realization of the promised inheritance (Ps. 2:8), it seems that more than just a will is in view. A *purchase* was made at the cross, and now the deed of that purchase is being claimed by its rightful owner.

While Babylon had besieged Jerusalem, God told Jeremiah to purchase a plot of ground in Israel. Even though the land had fallen to Babylon, Jeremiah's purchase demonstrated the reality of God's promise to restore Israel back to the land (Jer. 32:14-15, 43-44). There are significant parallels between Jeremiah's deed of purchase and Messiah's redemption described in this chapter. In both cases, a purchase was made in advance and a period intervened before the possession was fully awarded at a future date.

> Although [Jeremiah] had paid the price of redemption for this cousin's land and thereby had gained the right of tenant possession, he could not take immediate, actual possession of the land for at least two reasons. First, Jeremiah was confined in prison when he paid the price of redemption (Jer. 32:2-3, 8-9). Second, his cousin's land was "already under Babylonian control" when Jeremiah paid for it. Because Israel had rebelled against God so persistently, its land inheritance had been turned over to foreigners (Lam. 5:2; Jer. 32:21-24, 28-36). The Jews (including Jeremiah) would be exiled to other countries, and their land would continue under enemy control for several decades; but then the Jews would be regathered to their homeland, and their land would be restored to their control (Jer. 32:15, 37, 41-44). Because he knew that actual possession of the land could not take place for many years, Jeremiah commanded that both deeds of purchase be placed in a secure place for a long time (Jer. 32:13-15).[5]

The purchase price has been paid, but that which has been purchased remains in the hands of usurpers. Thus, a chain of judgments are brought forth by which the purchaser takes back what He rightfully owns. In the end, the usurpers are evicted and that which has been purchased is finally in the hands of the purchaser.

> The contents of the Βιβλιον [*Biblion*] must be brought into relation to the whole chain of judicial acts which unfold from Rev. 6 on and from which there develop organically the visions of the trumpets and bowls. Hence we are not concerned merely with the 6 or 7 seals themselves, but with all the last events up to the consummation.[6]

The meaning of the scroll is best understood by recognizing the truth in each of these ideas:

- **A Catalog of Judgments** - Judgments of lament and mourning and woe attend the opening of each seal (and the subsequent trumpets and bowls). In this, the scroll is similar to Ezekiel's book (Eze. 2:9-10). "When the Lamb breaks the seals, it is not merely a disclosure of the scroll's contents, but an activation of those contents."[7]
- **Prophetic Revelation** - As the seals are removed from the scroll, events unfold which are the fulfillment of prophetic themes found elsewhere in Scripture. When the scroll has been completely unsealed and the seventh trumpet has sounded, it is said that "the mystery of God would be finished, as He declared to His servants the prophets" (Rev. 10:7). See *Related Passages and Themes*[2.13].
- **A Testament** - The testamentary nature of the scroll is seen in the fact that only the *slain* Lamb can open it (Heb. 9:15-17; Rev. 5:9). Opening the scroll ultimately brings about the outworking of unfulfilled promises of the New Covenant (Jer. 31:31-37; Rom. 11:26-27; etc.).
- **A Deed of Purchase** - By opening of the scroll, the Lamb takes as His inheritance that which He had already *purchased* (Rev. 5:9). His inheritance includes an enduring kingdom and the title deed to the earth (Ps. 2:6-8). "But what is this remarkable scroll? It is nothing less than

> the title deed to the earth itself. . . . it is clearly the antitype of all the rich typological teaching associated with the divinely specified procedures for land redemption in the Old Testament."[8] "The sealed scroll is the deed of purchase for mankind's tenant possession inheritance or administration of the earth that was forfeited when mankind fell away from God. . . . a scroll deed of purchase was made when Christ paid the redemption price to redeem mankind's tenant possession of the earth by shedding His blood on the cross."[9]

As the Lamb opens the scroll, these varied aspects of its contents work in harmony to reveal the consummation of history:

> Frequent references to the events of the seals, trumpets, and bowls appear throughout the remaining visions in Revelation . . . indicating that the content of the seven-sealed scroll ultimately includes the unfolding of the consummation of the mystery of all things, the goal or end of all history, for both the conquerors and the worshipers of the beast. In Rev. 10:7 we are told that in the days of the sounding of the seventh trumpet "the mystery of God will be accomplished, just as he announced to his servants the prophets." From this it may be concluded that the scroll contains the unveiling of "the mystery of God" that OT prophets foretold . . . Thus the "seals" conceal the mystery, which only Christ can disclose (Dan. 12:9; Rev. 10:4), of how God's judgment and his kingdom will come. . . . The scroll, then, is not only about judgment or about the inheritance of the kingdom, Rather it contains the announcement of the consummation of all history.[10]

written inside and on the back

The tablets of the Testimony containing the Ten Commandments which Moses brought from Mount Sinai were also "written on both sides; on the one *side* and on the other they were written." The writing was the work of God engraved on the tablets (Ex. 32:15-16). In the previous chapter, we saw extensive parallels between the experience and vision of John and that of Ezekiel (Eze. 1). Here is another parallel, for Ezekiel was given a book which contained "writing on the inside and the outside, and written on it *were* lamentations and mourning and woe." Legal documents are also written on both sides:

> Jeremiah signed and sealed shut one copy of the scroll deed of purchase and had witnesses sign it, apparently on the outside (Jer. 32:10, 12). Concerning this practice, Weemse wrote, "For the manner of writing the contract, he who was to buy the ground wrote two instruments; the one to be sealed with his own signet, the other he showed unclosed to the witnesses, that they might subscribe and bear witness of that which was written. *This, the witnesses did subscribe UPON THE BACK of the inclosed [sic] instrument*" . . . Gaston Maspero gave an example of an enclosed document being used as evidence. "Contracts stamped upon clay tablets have been found in Babylonia, enclosed in an envelope of clay, on the outside of which an exact duplicate of the contract is impressed: if in the course of time any disagreement arose and it was suspected that the outside text had been tampered with, the envelope was broken in the presence of witnesses to see if the inside text agreed with it or not." The fact that the sealed scroll of Revelation 5 had writing on both the inside and the outside (Rev. 5:1), in the same manner as Jeremiah's and other deeds of purchase in Israel's land redemption system, indicates that it is a deed of purchase.[11]

sealed

κατεσφραγισμένον [*katesphragismenon*], perfect tense passive: *having been sealed.* It was previously sealed and remains so. Various types of documents can be sealed. A document may contain prophetic pronouncements from the Lord concerning the future and be sealed until the time in which its contents are to be fulfilled (Dan. 8:26; 12:4-9). Other documents, such as title deeds are sealed to protect their contents from tampering until the time in which the title is claimed. Jeremiah's deed sealed this way (Jer. 32:10-14). Until the seals are broken, the contents of the book are inaccessible—they remain an unrevealed *mystery* (Isa. 29:11; Dan. 8:26; 12:4-9; Rev. 10:7). Even in our own day, when so much within Scripture has been *revealed* (Rev. 22:10), God's words remain a sealed book for many. This was the case in Isaiah's day (Isa. 29:11-14).

seven seals

In the number *seven* is found the symbolism of completion. See *Seven: Perfection, Completeness*[2.7.5.3.6]. Within these seven seals are found all the judgments to be poured out upon the earth and the *earth dwellers*[5.2.18] as part of the redemption of creation and the Lamb taking dominion over the earth. See commentary on *Revelation 5:5*[3.5.5].

All seven seals enclose the scroll as a unit. Some commentators attempt to divide the effects which flow from the opening of the seals into separate categories: the wrath of Satan versus the wrath of God. This will not do, for it is the Lamb Who is the only one found worthy to loose the seals. *He alone opens all seven seals. His initiative is as fully engaged in opening of the first seal as the last.*

> All seven are part of the same sealed scroll; all seven have the same purpose or function with regard to that scroll; all seven will be part of the irrefutable evidence that Christ is the true Kinsman-Redeemer; all seven will be broken by Christ; and all seven will be part of the same program of Christ's evicting Satan and his forces and taking permanent possession of the earth.[12]

The *sequence of events*[2.14.2] which follow from the opening of these seals indicates that *all* the judgments which following are included within the seals:

> A study of Revelation 8 through 18 indicates that the seventh seal will contain the seven trumpet and seven bowl judgments. Thus, when Christ breaks all seven seals of the Revelation 5 scroll, He will thereby instigate the total bombardment of divine wrath or judgment against the domain of Satan and his forces, which will cover the 70th week of Daniel 9 up to Christ's coming immediately after the 70th week and the Great Tribulation.[13]

3.5.2 - Revelation 5:2

Who is worthy to open

"A mighty angel shouts out a challenge for anyone to come forth who is 'worthy' to open the great scroll and its seals. All creation in heaven and earth and under the earth stood motionless and speechless. . . . no one had the authority and virtue for such a task."[14] "As the echoes of his cry recede there is only silence. The powerful archangels Michael and Gabriel do not answer. Uncounted thousands of other angels remain silent. All the righteous dead of all the ages, including Abraham, Isaac, Jacob, Joseph, Job, Moses, David, Solomon, Elijah, Elisha, Isaiah, Jeremiah, Ezekiel, Daniel, Peter and the rest of the apostles, Paul, and all the others from the church age, say nothing."[15]

The question of worthiness hinges on several factors. Only Christ has the necessary qualifications:

1. **Perfect Judgment** - A combination of perfect justice and perfect compassion. One who extends perfect mercy while not flinching from exacting perfect justice (Deu. 7:16; 13:8; 19:13, 21; 25:12; Isa. 11:4; John 7:24). "Because He is faithful [Rev. 19:11] He must discharge His office as judge, not shrinking from the administration of discipline or punishment where it is needed. Because He is true [Rev. 19:11] He cannot alter the standards of God which condemn sin. Favoritism and laxity cannot be found in Him, for He is the perfect administrator of justice in a world where injustice has long since reigned."[16]
2. **Relationship to Mankind** - Dominion of the earth was originally given to Adam (Gen. 1:26-28) from whence it was lost to Satan due to sin. "As a result of getting the first man, Adam, to join his revolt against God, Satan usurped tenant possession of the earth away from its original tenant and has been exercising administration control of the world system against God ever since. Several things indicate that this is so. For example, Satan had the authority to offer Jesus all the power and glory of the kingdoms of the world (Luke 4:5-6); Satan declared that it had been delivered (perfect passive verb) to him by someone else (Adam, Luke 4:6); Jesus called Satan 'the prince of this world' (John 12:31; 14:30; 16:11); and Paul called him 'the god of this age' (2Cor. 4:4)."[17] Dominion is to be restored by a *man*. Not just any man, but the *perfect man* (2Cor. 5:21; Heb. 4:14; 1Pe. 2:22; 1Jn. 3:5). "Just as the Israelite redeemer had to be a kinsman (a relative from the same clan and tribe) of the person who lost the tenant possession, so the Redeemer of mankind and their forfeited tenant possession of the earth had to be a kinsman (a relative of the same kind) of mankind. He had to be a human. No angel or any other kind of being would qualify."[18]
3. **Right of Possession** - Possession of that which was lost required the payment of a redemption price. The price to redeem a world lost to the ravages of sin was the shedding of truly innocent blood (Rev. 5:6, 9).
4. **Ability to Possess** - The *right* to possess is meaningless without the *might* to possess. "Martin

> Kiddle wrote: "The strong angel's challenge to find some one worthy to open the scroll and to break its seal was much more than to ask for some one capable of *revealing* the world's fate. The demand was for one able not only to disclose God's plan, but to set it in motion, accomplish it, bring it to pass.""[19]

> The possession of this book and the execution of the purpose can be entrusted only to one who is completely worthy. No ordinary man can accept the responsibility of opening its sealed pages. Paradoxically, the person who undertakes this tremendous task must be absolutely courageous and absolutely compassionate.[20]

3.5.3 - Revelation 5:3

no one . . . was able

All men, except one, are "born of Adam" and are lost in sin, and are therefore unqualified to bring about redemption (1K. 8:46; 2Chr. 6:36; Job 15:14; Pr. 20:9; Ecc. 7:20; Isa. 64:6; Rom. 3:9, 19-23; Gal. 3:22; 1Jn. 1:8-10).

> And what, indeed, have been all the endeavours of unsanctified men, in politics, in science, and in all the arts of civilization, improvement, philosophy, and even religion, but to work out this problem of successful repossession of what was lost in Adam, to attain to that forfeited perfection and supreme good which has ever danced before their imaginations.[21]

When Adam forfeited dominion in the Fall, all men born of the line of Adam fell with him (Rom. 5:12; Acts 17:26). Having inherited the sin of Adam, none is able to prevail. Herein lies the need for the virgin birth of Christ. For Christ is the only man for which the truism "Absolute power corrupts absolutely," does *not* hold.

> Throughout history there have been many pretenders to earth's throne who have sought to conquer and rule the world. The first and most powerful and notorious usurper was Satan. After his rebellion against God was crushed, he and his angelic followers were thrown out of heaven (Luke 10:18; Rev. 12:3-4), and he became the "god of this world" (2Cor. 4:4). He *inspired*[5.2.33] a host of humans to try their hand at conquest, men such as Nebuchadnezzar, Darius, Alexander the Great, the emperors of Rome, Attila the Hun, Genghis Khan, Napoleon, Lenin, Stalin, and Hitler. In the future will come the most powerful Satan-possessed human conqueror of all, the final *Antichrist*[5.2.3]. All of those men, and a host of lesser lights, have one thing in common: they failed. Only one individual has the right, the power, and the authority to rule the earth: the Lord Jesus Christ.[22]

3.5.4 - Revelation 5:4

I wept much

ἔκλαιον [*eklaion*], imperfect tense: *I was weeping*. John evidently understood the significance of the scroll and the great need to open it and to read its contents. From this we understand overwhelming sadness attends any future which continues apart from redemption. For the horrors of sin, sickness, murder, death and the warping of all things God intended for good would continue unabated for unending millennia if it were not for the cross of Christ. If God had not sent His Son—at His own initiative—mankind would have *forever* and completely remained lost. Locked within an eternity of generations darkened by depravity and pain, there would have been forever *no hope*. Aside from the cross, the history of man is one long testimony of inability to overcome the ravages of sin.

> John knew by that Spirit in which he was, what that sealed book meant. He knew that if no one was found worthy and able to take it from the hand of God, and to break its seals, that all the promises of the prophets, and all the hopes of the saints, and all the preintimations of a redeemed world, must fail.[23]

> W. A. Criswell explains why John wept: "[John's tears] represent the tears of all God's people through all the centuries. Those tears of the Apostle John are the tears of Adam and Eve, driven out of the Garden of Eden, as they bowed over the first grave, as they watered the dust of the ground with their tears over the silent, still form of their son, Abel. Those are the tears of the children of Israel in bondage as they cried unto God in their affliction and slavery. They are the tears of God's elect through the centuries as they cried unto heaven. They are the sobs and tears that have been wrung from the heart and soul of God's people as they looked on their silent dead, as they stand beside their open graves, as they

experience in the trials and sufferings of life, heartaches and disappointments indescribable. Such is the curse that sin has laid upon God's beautiful creation; and this is the damnation of the hand of him who holds it, that usurper, that interloper, that intruder, that alien, that stranger, that dragon, that serpent, that Satan-devil. 'And I wept audibly,' for the failure to find a Redeemer meant that this earth in its curse is consigned forever to death. It meant that death, sin, damnation and hell should reign forever and ever and the sovereignty of God's earth should remain forever in the hands of Satan" *[Expository Sermons on Revelation* (Grand Rapids: Zondervan, 1969), 3:69-70][24]

Thankfully, man was not left abandoned to a history of self-perpetuated depravity. For history is *HIS story*—"History, then, has its center in Jesus Christ and its goal is his triumphant reign over all the powers of the world."[25]

3.5.5 - Revelation 5:5

do not weep

μὴ κλαῖε [*mē klaie*], a present tense imperative indicating that John continued to weep.[26]

the Lion of the tribe of Judah

God had revealed that the ruler would be like a *lion*, an offspring of *Judah* (Gen. 49:9-10; Ps. 60:7). Jesus was born in the line of Judah (Mtt. 1:2-3; Luke 3:33; Heb. 7:14). Although Reuben was the firstborn, due to his sin and the sins of his brothers, the right of kingly rule fell to *Judah*:

> Actually Reuben had the right of the firstborn. Nevertheless the Messiah is not "Lion out of the tribe of Reuben." For, on account of sin (as recorded in Gen. 35:22), Reuben was deprived of his firstborn rights and the right concerning the Messiah (1Chr. 5:1; Gen. 49:3-4). The next following brothers, Simeon and Levi, were also excluded (Gen. 49:5-7) on account of their bloody deed at Shechem (Gen. 34:25). Thereupon Reuben's rights as the firstborn were divided as follows: The double share of the material inheritance (Deu. 21:15-17) went to Joseph (in Ephraim and Manasseh; 1Chr. 5:1-2); The priestly dignity (see Ex. 13:2, 13:15), having regard to Ex. 32:26-28, went to Levi (Num. 3:12, 45; 8:17-18); and The ruler's dignity (Gen. 43:1-34; 33:1-20; 48:14, 18-19) went to Judah, Jacob's fourth son (1Chr. 5:2). Therefore is the Messiah the "Lion out of the tribe of Judah" (Rev. 5:5; Gen. 49:9-10).[27]

The genealogical records of the tribes of Israel were lost in the destruction of the temple in 70 AD. This poses a problem for Judaism which, having rejected Jesus, still awaits Messiah. If Messiah comes now, how will it be determined that He is the Lion from the tribe of *Judah*?

> Messiah will have to come before the tribe of Judah loses its identity. This establishes a clear time period for the prophecy. The records by which tribal identities were maintained were kept in the Jewish *Temple*[5.2.73]. All of these records were lost with the destruction of the temple in 70 A.D. Within a few generations all the tribes of Israel, with the exception of Levi, had lost their identity. Immediately after 70 A.D. the rabbis passed laws which would preserve the identity of the priestly tribe of Levi, but Jews from the other tribes quickly lost their identity. In order for this prophecy to have significance to humans (God still knows the tribal identities), Messiah had to come before 70 A.D.[28]

Root of David

Jesus was born in the line of David (Mtt. 1:1, 6, 17, 20; Luke 1:27, 32; 3:31; Rom. 1:3; 2Ti. 2:8; Rev. 22:16), He is the "son of David" (Mtt. 9:27; 12:23; 15:22; 20:30-31; 21:9, 15; 22:42; etc.). Jesus is the "Rod from the stem of Jesse" (Isa. 11:1), the "Root of Jesse" (Isa. 11:10), David's father (Ru. 4:22).

Jesus is the fulfillment of the Davidic Covenant.[29] God made an unconditional covenant with David where He swore that his throne would be established like the sun and moon (Ps. 89:33-37). At present, there is no "throne of David" upon the earth, but there will be when the Lion has completed His work (Rev. 20:4-6) for the zeal of God will ensure it!

> For unto us a Child is born, unto us a Son is given; and the government will be upon His shoulder. And His name will be called Wonderful, Counselor, Mighty God, Everlasting Father, Prince of Peace. Of the increase of *His* government and peace *There will be* no end, **Upon the throne of David and over His kingdom**, to order it and establish it with judgment and justice from that time forward, even forever. The zeal of the LORD of hosts will perform this. (Isa. 9:6-7) [emphasis added]

As a *root* springs anew from the stump of a tree which has been cut down and *appears* to be dead, so the line leading to Messiah was preserved throughout history. "For there is hope for a tree, if it is cut down, that it will sprout again, and that its tender shoots will not cease. Though its root may grow old in the earth, and its stump may die in the ground, *Yet* at the scent of water it will bud and bring forth branches like a plant" (Job 14:7-9). This *root* was repeatedly chopped back, but never completely terminated as Satan attempted throughout history to thwart the Messianic line of promise. See commentary on *Revelation 12:4*[3.12.4].

Messianic Line from Abraham to Jesus [30]

Jesus is the promised "Branch" that would come (King, Jer. 23:5-6; Servant, Zec. 3:8; Man, Zec. 6:12; Lord, Isa. 4:2). See *Four Gospels*[4.7].

> "Behold, *the* days are coming," says the LORD, "That I will raise to **David** a Branch of righteousness; a King shall reign and prosper, and execute judgment and righteousness in the earth. In His days Judah will be saved, and Israel will dwell safely; now this *is* His name by which He will be called: THE LORD OUR RIGHTEOUSNESS." (Jer. 23:5-6) [emphasis added]

Some see the *root* as including the idea of Jesus' preexistence (cf. Mic. 5:2).[31] Although this is true (Mtt. 22:42-25), the present context deals with the origin of Jesus, not of David. *Root* here "is a metaphorical term for 'offspring.' "[32]

has prevailed

ἐνίκησεν [*enikēsen*], from the same root (νικα῀ω [*nikaō*]) which describes "he who overcomes," ὁ νικ῀ων [*ho nikōn*]. Jesus has "overcome the world" (John 16:33). Whoever is born of God shares in His inheritance as overcomer (1Jn. 5:4; Rev. 2:7, 11, 17, 26; 3:5, 12, 21; 17:14; 21:7). "At the cross He defeated sin (Rom. 8:3), death (Heb. 2:14-15), and all the forces of hell (Col. 2:15; 1Pe. 3:19). Believers are overcomers through His overcoming (Col. 2:13-14; 1Jn. 5:5)."[33]

> Christ defeated Satan and his forces when He paid the redemption price of His shed blood. Through the payment of that price, Christ defeated Satan and his forces in the sense that He gained the right to take tenant possession of the earth away from them and rule the earth as the last Adam. This truth sheds light on the meaning of Christ's statement just before He went to the cross, "the prince of this world is judged" (John 16:11). Christ's death sealed Satan's doom. At the proper time, determined sovereignly by God, Christ will exercise the right he gained at the cross to throw out the usurper.[34]

"Since [the] captivity, the royal family of Judah has not exercised rule but has remained dormant, just as a stump gives no evidence of having life. The stump of this royal family will spring to life again suddenly when its King (the Messiah or Christ) springs forth from it to rule."[35] Having *prevailed*, the

Lamb qualifies as the promised *Shiloh* (Gen. 49:10; Eze. 21:25-27). *Midrash Rabbah 98* states that Shiloh denotes "to he whose it is," "to he who it belongs," "he whose right it is," or "to whom kingship belongs."[36]

to open the scroll

Jesus has the authority to *open the scroll* because He has the key of David. See commentary on *Revelation 3:7*[3.3.7]. "God [the Father] Himself will not break a single seal of it, for the Father has ceded the prerogative of judgment"[37] (John 5:22-27).

to loose its seven seals

Having paid the ultimate price of redemption, being made sin on our behalf (Isa. 53:6; 2Cor. 5:21), the Lamb has earned the right to loose the seals bringing judgments on those who continue to reject His gracious offer of redemption (John 3:35-36). As each of these seals is loosed, additional judgment is brought upon the earth. The first six seals result in preliminary judgments (Rev. 6:1, 3, 5, 7, 9, 12). At the loosening of the seventh seal, the judgments become more pronounced as all seven trumpet judgments are within the seventh seal (Rev. 8:1-6). At the opening of the seventh seal, the first four trumpets are sounded (Rev. 8:7, 8, 10, 12). Because the last three trumpet judgments are especially severe, there is a pause in the judgments as angelic warning is given concerning the severity of the last three trumpets (Rev. 8:13). Then the first two of the final three trumpets sound (Rev. 9:1, 13). At the sounding of the final trumpet, the declaration is made: "The kingdoms of this world have become *the kingdoms* of our Lord and of His Christ" (Rev. 11:15). By this we understand the last seven bowl judgments to be subsumed within the seventh trumpet. Prior to the pouring forth of the seven bowls of wrath (Rev. 16:1-17), three more additional angelic warnings are given (Rev. 14:6-9). The judgments of God's wrath are completed in the pouring forth of the seventh bowl (Rev. 16:17). See *Sequential Events*[2.14.2].

In the loosing of all seven seals, and the subsequent trumpet and bowl judgments, Christ retakes that which He purchased at Calvary (John 19:30; Rev. 11:15; 16:16; 21:6). To bring the kingdom of God to earth, the kingdom of Satan must first be overthrown. Much of what follows in this book must be understood in the context of the overthrow of Satan's kingdom prior to the setting up of God's kingdom on earth.

> By the end of the 70th week, Satan and his forces will have drawn all the rulers and armies of the world into the land of Israel for the battle of Armageddon (Rev. 16:12-16), which will take place at Christ's Second Coming and will pit Satan and his ungodly allies against Christ and His forces (Rev. 19:11-20:3). This will be Satan's ultimate challenge to Christ's right to take tenant possession of the earth and rule it. The combined military might of rebellious mankind will be gathered to the precise location to which Christ will return to take possession of the earth, because Satan will want all the help he can get to try to prevent Christ from exercising His right (Ps. 2:1-3).[38]

> No portion of the roll is said to be *unfolded* and *read*; but simply the *seals* are successively *opened* , giving final access to its contents being read as a perfect whole, which shall not be until the events symbolized by the seals shall have been past, when Eph 3:10 shall receive its *complete* accomplishment, and the Lamb shall reveal God's providential plans in redemption in all their manifold beauties. Thus the opening of the seals will mean the successive steps by which God in Christ clears the way for the final opening and reading of the book at the visible setting up of the kingdom of Christ.[39]

See *The Arrival of God's Kingdom*[2.4.3].

3.5.6 - Revelation 5:6

four living creatures

See commentary on *Revelation 4:6*[3.4.6].

the elders

See commentary on *Revelation 4:4*[3.4.4].

a Lamb

"When John turned, he saw, not a Lion, according to the Elder's announcement, but a Lamb, according to the prior historical fact."[40] For the *Lion of Judah* must first be the *Lamb of God* in order to purchase redemption and earn the right to go forth as a Lion in judgment. Here we see the character of God—grace and mercy preceding judgment. "In one brilliant stroke John portrays the central theme of *NT*[5.2.48] revelation—victory through sacrifice."[41]

Ἀρνίον [*Arnion*], originally meant *little lamb*[42] or *young sheep*.[43] "The imagery derives from the Passover, when Jewish families were required to keep the sacrificial lamb as a household pet for four days before sacrificing it (Ex. 12:3-6)."[44] The only other occurrence of *arnion* in the entire NT is John's gospel, where it is used of the Christian community (John 21:15).[45] This is another indication that the same author wrote the book of John and the book of Revelation. See *Authorship*[2.9]. [46] "In Revelation the name 'Lamb' (*arnion*, literally, 'little lamb') is used more often than any other name or title of Christ. John called Him the Lamb twenty-eight times."[47]

Twice in John's gospel, John the Baptist refers to Jesus as "the Lamb of God," referring to His impending sacrifice which will atone for the sins of the world (John 1:29, 36). Isaiah also described the Messiah as a sacrificial lamb, a passage which Philip explained to the Ethiopian eunuch (Isa. 53:7; Acts 8:32-35). Peter describes the precious, sinless blood of Christ "as of a lamb without blemish and spot," an allusion to the Passover lamb whose blood "covered" the Israelites from the destroying angel in the plague which took the firstborn of Egypt (1Pe. 1:19 cf. Ex. 11:5-6; 12:3-13). In fulfillment of the requirement that no bones of the lamb may be broken (Ex. 12:46; Ps. 34:20), the Roman soldiers found Jesus already dead and did not break his legs as they did those of the thieves crucified beside him (John 19:33-36). Paul clearly understood Jesus to be the Passover lamb. "For indeed Christ, our Passover, was sacrificed for us" (1Cor. 5:7). It is by "the blood of the Lamb" that believers overcome the *diabolos* who "throws-against" them accusations (Rev. 12:11), for it is the blood which cleanses them of sin and provides their white robes. It is the blood of Christ which provides for their eternal life as those who are written in the "*Book of Life*[5.2.10] of the Lamb slain from the foundation of the world" (Rev. 13:8).

The *Lamb* is to be contrasted with the *beast* throughout this book.[48] The second beast who "had two horns like a lamb" may be mistaken as this lamb by those who are deceived, but he speaks "like a dragon" (Rev. 13:11). See *Master Imitator*[4.2.5]. See *A Lamb and a Beast*[3.13.8.2].

stood

ἑστηκὸς [*hestēkos*], perfect participle: having stood. The lamb had been there for some time. Having been seated to the right hand of the Father for millennia, Jesus now rises. The time of sharing the Father's throne is rapidly drawing to a close. Once He takes the scroll, as the *Root of David*, He will initiate a series of irreversible events which will result in the establishment of the Davidic kingdom upon the *earth*. See commentary on *Revelation 5:10*[3.5.10].

as though it had been slain

ἐσφαγμένον [*esphagmenon*], perfect passive participle: "of animals, especially when killed as a sacrifice slaughter, slay; metaphorically, of Jesus' atoning death as the Lamb of God."[49] By His one-time sacrifice, sin was rendered powerless to prevent those who trust in Him from right-standing before God (Heb. 9:26). It has been said, "the only man-made thing in heaven will be the scars of the Savior." Isaiah informs us, "His visage was marred more than any man, and His form more than the sons of men" (Isa. 52:14). Heaven and earth will pass away and the former things will pass (Rev. 21:1, 4), but *will the scars of Messiah ever be erased?* For they serve as a testimony of His love, His resurrection from death (John 20:20, 27), and His identity as Redeemer (Luke 24:30-31).

The slaying of God's own Son was not an afterthought in response to an unexpected rebellion. He was "slain from the foundation of the world" (Rev. 13:8).[50] Peter informs us that He was "foreordained before the foundation of the world, but was manifest in these last times" (1Pe. 1:20). It was known from all eternity that Christ would come to die for the sin of the world: there is nothing which God has not seen and provided for in advance (Isa. 45:21). Even as early as Abraham, God provided a detailed picture of the atonement of the cross when Abraham was told to offer Isaac as a picture of another Father's offering of another Son on the same mountain years yet future. As Abraham observed, "God will provide for Himself the lamb" (Gen. 22:8) and so He has! This is the pierced Lamb which "every eye will see," "even they who pierced him" (Rev. 1:7 cf. Zec. 12:10). Are *you* trusting in the slain

Lamb, Who was foreordained for *your* redemption?

seven horns

"Here is the intimation that something more than sacrifice and intercession is now to be His business."[51] The *horn* is a biblical symbol denoting power or government (1S. 2:10; 2S. 22:3; Ps. 132:13-17). The *seven* horns indicate the complete power of Christ and the finality (completeness) of His kingdom. "As a horn is the emblem of power, and seven the number of perfection, the seven horns may denote the almighty power of Jesus Christ."[52] His is the only "everlasting dominion" and kingdom "which shall not be destroyed" (Dan. 7:14). Other "horns" have risen and fallen on the world stage (Dan. 7:7-8, 11, 20, 21, 24; 8:3-12, 20-22; Rev. 12:3; 13:1, 11; 17:3, 7, 12, 16), but the "stone cut without hands" will strike all previous horns and smash them to pieces (Dan. 2:34, 45-46; 7:14). Christ is the *horn* of salvation from the lineage of the house of David (Luke 1:67-73):

> And in the days of these kings the God of heaven will set up a kingdom which shall never be destroyed; and the kingdom shall not be left to other people; it shall break in pieces and consume all these kingdoms, and it shall stand forever. Inasmuch as you saw that the stone was cut out of the mountain without hands, and that it broke in pieces the iron, the bronze, the clay, the silver, and the gold-the great God has made known to the king what will come to pass after this. The dream is certain, and its interpretation is sure. (Dan. 2:44-45)

> Then to Him was given dominion and glory and a kingdom, that all peoples, nations, and languages should serve Him. His dominion *is* an everlasting dominion, which shall not pass away, and His kingdom *the one* Which shall not be destroyed. (Dan. 7:14)

> Therefore God also has highly exalted Him and given Him the name which is above every name, that at the name of Jesus every knee should bow, of those in heaven, and of those on earth, and of those under the earth, and *that* every tongue should confess that Jesus Christ *is* Lord, to the glory of God the Father. (Php 2:9-11)

The *seven horns* may also allude to the conquest of Jericho by Joshua (his Hebrew name is *Yehoshua* meaning "YHWH saves," corresponding to *Jesus* in Greek):

> When the children of Israel first entered the land of Canaan to claim it for their own as God had promised, they encountered a wicked city barring their way. When in accord with God's command, the priests took "seven trumpets of ram's horns," the walls of Jericho tumbled down and the city and its alien inhabitants were destroyed. Thus, these "seven horns" on the Lamb may well have recalled to John the seven ram's horns of Joshua, and their effectiveness in enabling the people of God to enter on their inheritance in God's land of promise.[53]

Another similarity with the Book of Joshua is found in the pouring forth of the seventh bowl—subsumed within the sounding of the *seventh trumpet* —when the mighty city of Babylon is destroyed (Rev. 16:17-19).

seven eyes

As the text says, these are the *seven Spirits of God.* Commenting on the related passage in Zec. 3:9, Baron explains:

> The *manifold intelligence* or *omniscience* of this "Living Stone"—the seven reminding us of the sevenfold plenitude of the One Spirit of Jehovah, "the spirit of wisdom and understanding, the spirit of counsel and might, the spirit of knowledge and of the fear of the Jehovah," which should rest upon Him, and which was so wonderfully fulfilled in Him whom the New Testament seer beheld as the Lamb which had been slain [Rev. 5:6]. [54]

> Three grand qualities of the Goel [kinsman-redeemer] are thus brought to view;—*first*, sacrificial virtue, to take away sin; *second*, aggressive strength to conquer and to overcome all foes; and *third*, perfect and universal intelligence, direct from the indwelling Spirit of God in all its fulness.[55]

See commentary on *Revelation 1:4*[3.1.4].

sent out

ἀπεσταλμένοι [*apestalmenoi*], perfect passive participle: *having been sent out.* They were sent in the past and by now have *already* seen all (Zec. 4:2-10). The eyes indicate omniscience and the complete knowledge of all that is hidden for perfect judgment. There is no secret which these eyes have not viewed (Ecc. 12:14; Isa. 29:15; 40:27; Mtt. 10:26; Mark 4:22; Luke 8:17; 12:2; Rom. 2:16; 1Cor. 4:5).

See commentary on *Revelation 1:14*[3.1.14].

3.5.7 - Revelation 5:7

took the scroll

εἴληφεν [*eilēphen*], perfect tense. An aorist use of the perfect tense encountered in narratives.[56] The emphasis is on the past action rather than the continuing results. "The Greek conveys a dramatic action in the tense of the verb 'took' (perhaps a dramatic perfect?): 'He went up and took it, and now he has it.' "[57] Having stood, Christ now takes the scroll out of the hand of the Father. As Christ initiates these actions, the world slumbers below, oblivious to the thief approaching in their night.[58] "He who moved at first to create, now moves to restore. . . . The Lamb Becomes a Lion . . . in the scene before us Christ is not on the Father's throne; the age of His intercession has come to a close. We shall see Him acting in an entirely new character. . . . The age of the Church is over. This is now prophecy of the future."[59]

Here is a pivotal moment in history, *second only to the crucifixion in its import*. "This is the sublimest individual act recorded in the Apocalypse. It is the act which includes all that suffering creation, and the disinherited saints of God have been sighing, and crying, and waiting for, for all these long ages—for six thousand years of grief and sorrow."[60] "His taking of the scroll marks the initiation of proceedings to convert its contents into reality and eventually usher in the promised kingdom."[61]

After age-upon-age of death, murder, disease, and sin—while countless bones piled upon the earth below—God has waited in patience so that all that would come to Him would respond (2Pe. 3:9). Even since the cross, where the cost of sin was paid in full, justice has slept due to grace. With the Lamb's taking of the scroll, the events of history take a turn toward the impending redemption of all that is God's from the dominion of Satan and sin. Once the Lamb rises from the right hand of the Father to take the scroll, the die is cast and the program leading to the redemption of the created order moves now in rapid succession. The Son of God has begun to take the nations for His inheritance (Ps. 2:8; 82:8). He is now about to take possession of that which has been His since the cross, an everlasting dominion which shall not pass away—the one kingdom which shall not be destroyed (Dan. 7:14, 27). When the last of the seals has been loosed, triggering the trumpet and bowl judgments, it will be said, "The kingdoms of this world have become *the kingdoms* of our Lord and of His Christ, and He shall reign forever and ever!" (Rev. 11:15). "This marks the beginning of the end of the groaning of Rom. 8:22."[62]

This is no gradual conversion of the world to Christ, but the initiation of a dramatic, cataclysmic intervention into His history to reject Satan and unrepentant *earth dwellers*[5.2.18]. See *Trouble Ahead*[2.13.1].

3.5.8 - Revelation 5:8

living creatures

See commentary on *Revelation 4:6*[3.4.6].

twenty-four elders

See commentary on *Revelation 4:4*[3.4.4].

fell down

The *living creatures* and *elders* repeatedly fall before the throne in adoration and worship (Rev. 4:10; 5:14; 19:4).

harp

Harps are played by the 144,000 from the twelve tribes of Israel (Rev. 14:1-3) and all those who have victory over the beast by refusing to take the mark and worship him (Rev. 15:2). The Levites used harps as part of their priestly service ministering to God (2Chr. 5:12; 29:25), as did the psalmist (Ps. 33:2; 43:4; 71:22; 92:3; 149:3; 150:3).

golden bowls full of incense which are the prayers of the saints

It was at the hour of incense that the people were praying when the angel of the Lord appeared to

Zacharias announcing the birth of John the Baptist (Luke 1:10). The prayers of the saints—many of which have remained without answer for thousands of years— will find their fulfillment in the events to come (Rev. 19:1-2). Later, similar bowls will contain the wrath of God (Rev. 15:7). It seems we are to see a correlation between the *prayers of the saints* offered up to God as *incense* and the resulting vengeance poured forth as God's wrath. Prior to the sounding of the seven trumpets, an angel offers the *prayers of the saints* with *incense* on an altar before God. He then exchanges the contents of the censer for fire from the altar and throws it to the earth resulting in "thunderings, lightnings, and an earthquake" —all sounds of impending judgment (Rev. 8:3-5).

The continual cries of God's elect throughout history are like the fragrance of incense which rises to God (Ps. 141:1-2). "And shall God not avenge His own elect who cry out day and night to Him, though He bears long with them?" (Luke 18:7). Malachi spoke of a time when incense would be offered to God, not just in the *Temple*[5.2.73], but across the entire world. Not just by the priests of Israel, but by all the Gentiles. This offering pictures the global prayer which even now ascends from the saints as a memorial to His throne (Mal. 1:11; Acts 10:4). When on our knees we are contributing to the contents of these bowls. "And who can reckon up the volumes and oceans of such entreaties, which remain to this day unanswered? But, not one of them is lost. They are carefully treasured in golden bowls."[63]

> Why are harps and bowls full of incense, which are the prayers of the saints (Rev. 5:8), connected with the Lamb's taking the book of the inheritance? Did the prayers of the saints bring about this scene? Would our Lord have commanded His disciples to pray "Thy kingdom come, Thy will be done, as in heaven, so on earth," if (a) God had not meant to bring this to pass, and (b) if the prayers of the saints were not a vital factor in bringing about this glorious result?[64]

Some view only the elders as possessing the harps and bowls. "The fact is that the details of the following description are not appropriate to the living beings. To see them as possessing harps and bowls is unnatural, and to attribute to them priestly functions ignores the priestly function that is distinctive to the elders (Swete; Charles; Lenski)."[65] Although one of the living creatures handles a golden bowl later in the Apocalypse (Rev. 15:7), this bowl is full of wrath and is not seen to reflect a priestly function whereas the golden bowls of *incense* are priestly in function (Lev. 4:7; Num. 4:16; 1S. 2:28).

3.5.9 - Revelation 5:9

they sang

ᾄδουσιν [*adousin*], present tense: *they are singing.* A *historical present* which describes an event which has already transpired using the present tense for heightened vividness which transports the reader to the time of the action. In the *OT*[5.2.51], the tribe of Judah (meaning "praise," Gen. 29:35) led the way into battle and so it is here (Jdg. 20:18). These scenes of ecstatic heavenly worship are as lofty as the judgments which follow are severe.

Both the living creatures and the elders sing this song. This has caused some to favor the variant reading of this verse which omits the "we" from the redeemed because the living creatures, being of an angelic order, are not among the redeemed.[66] See below.

The Adoration of the Lamb [67]

a new song

New is καινὴν [*kainēn*], new in quality. The new aspect of the song may be worship motivated by the impending opening of the scroll which for so many years has remained untouched. The words of this song record the unique initiation by the Lamb of the events which rapidly lead to the climax of history and the establishment of His kingdom.

open its seals

See commentary on *Revelation 5:5*[3.5.5] . See Revelation 6:1.

You were slain

See commentary on *Revelation 5:6*[3.5.6].

your redeemed us

ἠγόρασας [*ēgorasas*]: "Literally *buy, purchase, do business in the marketplace* (Mtt. 13.44); figuratively, as being no longer controlled by sin *set free*; from the analogy of buying a slave's freedom for a price paid by a benefactor *redeem* (1Cor. 6:20)."[68] Redemption involves a *purchase* and those who are purchased are no longer their own (1Cor. 6:20; 7:23; 2Pe. 2:1). The purchased price for those *redeemed* was not made with corruptible things like silver and gold (1Pe. 1:18), but by the life of the Son of Man Who gave "His life a ransom for many" (Mtt. 20:28). The redemption in view is both soteriological (individual souls are reconciled to God) and eschatological (the original creation will be restored at last).

> Redemption has its roots and foundations in the past, but its true realization lies in the future, and connects directly with the period and transactions to which our text relates. The Scriptures everywhere point forward to Christ's Apocalypse, as the time when first the mystery shall be finished, and the long process reach its proper consummation.[69]

This is similar to Boaz's redemption of land for Naomi (Ru. 4:1-11). Like Boaz, Jesus is the *Goel*. The term *Goel* describes the person who is next of kin and his respective duties as *kinsman-redeemer* : to buy back what his poor brother has sold and cannot himself regain (Lev. 25:25-26); to avenge any wrong done to a next of kin, particularly murder (Num. 35:12-27); to purchase land belonging to one deceased who was next of kin and to marry his widow and to raise up children for the deceased (Ru. 2:20; 4:14).

There are small variations in the manuscript evidence for verses 9 and 10 which impinge on a significant theological issue: the identity of the twenty-four elders. Are the elders included among the redeemed or not? The *TR*[5.2.79] text for these two verses (reflected in the KJV and NKJV) is shown below. We have marked the places where other manuscripts differ.

> . . . For you were slain and have redeemed **us**[A] to God by Your blood out of every tribe and tongue and people and nation, and have made **us**[B] kings and priests to our God; and **we**[C] shall reign on the earth. (Rev. 5:9-10, NKJV)

- **A** - All manuscripts read "us" (ἡμα῀ς [*hēmas*]) with a *single* exception: *Codex Alexandrinus* from the fifth century omits the word.[70]
- **B** - All manuscripts read "made them" (αὐτοὺς [*autous*]) with a *single* exception: *Textus Receptus* which reads "us" (ἡμα῀ς [*hēmas*]).[71]
- **C** - All manuscripts read "they shall reign" (βασιλευσουσιν [*basileusousin*] or βασιλευουσιν [*basileuousin*]) with a *single* exception: *Textus Receptus* which reads "we shall reign" (βασιλευσομεν [*basileusomen*]).[72]

The manuscript evidence for "us" in verse 9 is overwhelming:

> Tregelles retains "us," remarking "in verse 9, *eemas*, 'us,' should certainly be read. There was an opinion, many years ago, that it rested on but slight authority. This arose through an error in a reprint of Griesbach's text; so that he was supposed to have excluded it. On this misprint interpretations were based. Now of all collated manuscripts, the Codex Alexandrinus alone omits *eemas* (and this is thought to have some support from the Ethiopic version); and one manuscript has *eemon* instead. The consent of the ancient versions has much weight in a case of this kind. It is surprising that some later editors have omitted it only on the authority mentioned." [S. P. Tregelles, *The Hope of Christ's Second Coming*, p. 69, 70 note].[73]

> Some critics and expositors have rejected this ἡμα῀ς [*hēmas*] (us), for the reason that it is omitted in the Codex Alexandrinus, and in the Ethiopic version; though the latter is not much more than a loose paraphrase. The Codex Sinaiticus, however, which was discovered in 1860, and which is of equal antiquity and authority with the Codex Alexandrinus, contains it. The Codex Basilianus, in the Vatican, contains it. The Latin, Coptic or Memphitic, and Armenian, which are of great value, contain it. And so do *all other manuscripts and versions*. And to discredit it simply and only because it does not appear in that one single Codex of Alexandria, is most unreasonable and unjust to the weight of authority for its retention.[74]

Here we encounter an excellent example of the arbitrary and subjective nature of textual criticism underwriting the *NU*[5.2.49] text which omits "us." The motives are no doubt well-intentioned as is the logic—once applied. But the guidelines employed in the selection of the preferred text from among the variant readings are flawed. Proponents of the *Critical Text* attempt to pass off as scientific analysis that which is largely arbitrary. For it is impossible to accurately restore an original text when subjective guesswork, hundreds of years after-the-fact, guides the selection process. The approach relies heavily on heuristics: general guidelines which *seem to make sense*, but *which cannot be known to actually reflect the facts*. And therein lies the vulnerability of the method. In the case at hand, we have "us" in *every significant manuscript known with the exception of one*. But that doesn't deter the "logic" of textual criticism which arrives at a conclusion rejecting the overwhelming evidence in favor of the *one exceptional reading*:[75]

> Although the evidence for τῶι θεῶι [*tō theō*] is slight, . . . this reading best accounts for the origin of the others. Wishing to provide ἠγόρασας [*ēgorasas*] with a more exactly determined object than is found in the words ἐκ πάσης φυλῆς κ.τ.λ. [*ek pasēs phylēs ktl*], some scribes introduced ἡμα῀ς [*hēmas*] either before τῶι θεῶι [*tō theō*] (94 2344 *al*) or after τῶι θεῶι [*tō theō*] (1611 1006 046 ℵ 2053 *al*), while others replaced τῶι θεῶι [*tō theō*] with ἡμα῀ς [*hēmas*] (1 2065* Cyprian *al*). Those who made the emendations, however, overlooked the unsuitability of ἡμα῀ς [*hēmas*] with αὐτούς [*autous*] in the following verse (where, indeed, the Textus Receptus reads ἡμα῀ς [*hēmas*], but with quite inadequate authority).[76]

> A number of internal factors militate against the inclusion of ἡμα῀ς [*hēmas*] as part of the text of the autograph. A most obvious one is the impossibility of reconciling the first person plural with the third person plurals what are clearly the correct readings in the next verse. . . . Such an abrupt switch from first person to third person renders the language of the song meaningless, so the reading must be judged as impossible.[77]

Here we see a bias of scholars of our age who frequently assume that those before us lacked the necessary care or intelligence to handle the text: they "overlooked the unsuitability . . . in the following verse." They would have us believe that for hundreds of years, scribes preserved an "obvious" error which "renders . . . the song meaningless." Centuries later, appealing to arbitrary and subjective guesswork, these critics reject the majority witness and elevate the single minority variant while claiming to "restore" the proper text. Such is the science of textual criticism.

While we recognize the need for textual criticism, we regret that often arbitrary and unverifiable suppositions are given precedence over manuscript evidence leading to questionable conclusions as here.

Part of the motivation for expunging "us" from this verse comes from a desire, *possibly misplaced*, to bring verse 9 into conformity with the majority of manuscripts which have "them" rather than "us" in verse 10: "Indeed, *all* the critical authorities are unanimous in substituting the 3rd person for the 1st in the next verse [verse 10]. But if so, then we *must* have the 3rd person here and not the 1st person."[78] There are two liabilities which attend such reasoning:

1. There are other possible explanations for why both 1st person ("us") and 3rd person ("them") may appear within the same song. For one, both the living creatures and the elders sing the song. Perhaps the living creatures exclude themselves ("them") while the elders include themselves ("us") within the company of the redeemed. "Revelation 5:9 has content that is appropriate to humans (the elders), while verse 10 is appropriate for angelic singers (the cherubs). John did not explain the arrangement of singers, but his words allow for an antiphonal arrangement."[79] Also, singing a song in both the 1st person and 3rd person is not without precedent (see below). "The *Hebrew* construction of the third person for the first, has a graphic relation to *the redeemed*, and also has a more modest sound than *us, priests* [Bengel]."[80] More likely, "The use of them instead of 'us' indicates the vastness and comprehensiveness of redemption. The twenty-four elders move beyond themselves to sweep up all the saints of all the ages into their paean of praise and adoration."[81]
2. One of the tenets of textual criticism is to favor the more difficult rendering. We suggest that the very existence of a majority witness which contains "us" in verse 9 and "them" in verse 10 provides ample evidence of the more difficult rendering. For scribes lacking in reverence for every *word* of the text would have likely "rectified" this tension (as do the modern critics), yet *they did not.*[82]

Pentecost provides an explanation for the variations which does not require jettisoning the majority witness of "us" in verse 9:

> Some have sought to dissociate the elders from the redemption of which they sing (Rev. 5:9) by deleting the word "us" from the text, affirming on that basis that these could not be the representatives of the church. On this point several things are to be observed. First, there is good manuscript evidence to

> include the word in the text. The word need not be deleted on textual grounds. In the second place, even if it were to be deleted it does not mean that the elders were not singing of their own redemption. In Exodus 15:13, 17, where Moses and the people of Israel are praising God for His judgment, which they manifestly experienced themselves, they sing in the third person. Scripture gives precedent, therefore, for dealing with that which is subjective as an objective fact. And in the third place, if the word were omitted and it could be proved that they were singing about a redemption which they did not experience themselves, it need not prove that the elders are not the church, for as the elders are brought into a knowledge of the judgments of God being poured out on the earth they anticipate the victory of the saints who are on the earth through these experiences and they can praise God for the redemption of these from "every kindred, and tongue, and people, and nation" (Rev. 5:9) who have experienced the tribulation, been saved in it, and who will be made "kings and priests, and shall reign on the earth," (Rev. 5:10; 20:6).[83]

by your blood

A bloodless gospel is no gospel. Without the shedding of *blood* there is no remission of sin. The redeemed of this age are "the church of God which He purchased with His own **blood**" [emphasis added] (Acts 20:28). Redemption provides for the forgiveness of sin—that which separates man from God—and was made possible "through His **blood**" [emphasis added] (Col. 1:14). This is the reason why Christ's **blood** is said to be "precious" (1Pe. 1:19).[84] See commentary on *Revelation 1:5*[3.1.5].

every tribe and tongue and people and nation

The global emphasis of this book is seen in this phrase and similar. The redeemed come out of "all nations, tribes, peoples, and tongues" (Rev. 7:9). John is told to prophesy about many "peoples, nations, tongues, and kings" (Rev. 10:11). The *earth dwellers*[5.2.18], who rejoice over the death of the two witnesses, represent the "peoples, tribes, tongues, and nations" (Rev. 11:9). The worldwide scope of the *Antichrist*[5.2.3]'s power is seen in that he is granted authority over "every tribe, tongue, and nation" (Rev. 13:7). The gospel is preached by an angel to "every nation, tribe, tongue, and people" (Rev. 14:6). The waters upon which the harlot sits "are peoples, multitudes, nations, and tongues" (Rev. 17:1, 15). The work of the Church is to reach these global peoples with the message of the gospel (Mark 16:15) and results in a global harvest of incredible diversity. The four categories denote global extent. See *Four: the Entire World, the Earth*[2.7.5.3.3].

> Behind *phyles* ("tribe") is the idea of the same descent. It is a group belonging to the same clan and united by family lineage (Lenski; Haily). People speaking the same language are intended in *glosses* ("tongue") (cf. Acts 2:4, 6, 8, 11) (Lenski; Hailey). *Laou* ("people") unites a people of the same race or stock (Hailey) or possibly of the same interests (Lenski). The group indicated by *ethnous* ("nation") is one bound together by political unity (Lenski) or perhaps, more broadly, by habits, customs, and peculiarities [Cremer].[85]

These facts all stand against the *preterist interpretation*[2.12.2] which would localize these passages to Jerusalem and the Mediterranean attending the fall of Jerusalem in A.D. 70 or the subsequent fall of Rome.

3.5.10 - Revelation 5:10

have made us

The *TR*[5.2.79] text reads as shown. The *MT*[5.2.45] and *NU*[5.2.49] texts read "have made *them*." See discussion concerning textual variants in the *preceding verse*[3.5.9].

kings and priests

The TR and MT texts read as shown. The NU text reads "a kingdom of priests." A similar variation attends Revelation 1:6 where the TR text reads as shown, but the MT text agrees with the NU text as shown here. See commentary on *preceding verse*[3.5.9]. See commentary on *Revelation 1:6*[3.1.6].

As priests, believers are ministers of the new covenant—not of the letter, but of the Spirit (2Cor. 3:6). They offer up spiritual sacrifices acceptable to God (1Pe. 2:5) while proclaiming His praises (1Pe. 2:9). They minister to God as *priests* and share His reign as *kings* (Dan. 7:27; Rev. 2:26-27; 3:21; Rev. 20:6). "Though believers are currently viewed as a royal priesthood (1Pe. 2:5, 9; cf. Ex. 19:6), this is only preliminary to the fullness of the way they will function alongside Christ in the *Millennial*

Kingdom[5.2.39]."[86] See commentary on *Revelation 2:26*[3.2.26], *Revelation 3:21*[3.3.21], and *Revelation 20:6*[3.20.6].

we shall reign on the earth

The TR text reads as shown. The MT and NU texts read "*they* shall rule." See discussion concerning textual variants in the *preceding verse*[3.5.9].

This is the same promise made earlier to the overcomer in Thyatira and Laodicea. The saints will be given power over the nations and will co-rule with Christ (Rev. 2:26-27). They will sit with Him on His throne (Rev. 3:21). They *shall* reign (future tense) *on the earth* in fulfillment of the familiar petition within the "Lord's Prayer": *Your kingdom come, Your will be done* ***on earth*** *as it is in heaven* (Mtt. 6:10). The rule will be upon *His* throne, not upon the throne of the *Father* where He currently is seated. This occurs at the Millennial Kingdom following His appearing (2Ti. 4:1; Rev. 20:4-6). The psalm writer said, "those who wait on the LORD, they shall inherit the **earth**" [emphasis added] (Ps. 37:9b). Jesus said, "Blessed are the meek, for they shall inherit the **earth**" [emphasis added] (Mtt. 5:5). There is *real, physical land* involved in the redemption which pours forth from this book. The taking back of man's dominion over the earth which was lost by Adam (Gen. 1:26, 28), and the restoration of Israel to the Promised Land (Amos 9:13-15).[87] See commentary on *Revelation 3:21*[3.3.21].

Some argue that a future earthly kingdom is out-of-step with the spiritual glories of the gospel. Yet it is completely in keeping with the promises found throughout the *OT*[5.2.51].

> But strangely enough, some of the very men who are so scornful of the alleged "materialism" of a Millennial Kingdom, are the most insistent that the Church today must make effective in society what they call the social and moral ideals of the present kingdom of God. Thus, it is our duty to vote the right ticket politically, give to the Red Cross, help the Boy Scouts, support the United Nations, endow hospitals, etc. But if a "spiritual" kingdom can and should produce such effects at the present time through the very imperfect agency of sinful men, why cannot the same thing be true in larger measure in the coming age when the rule of God will be mediated more perfectly and powerfully through the Eternal Son personally present among men as the Mediatorial King? ... The reasoning of such men at times seems very curious. If physicians conquer disease, if scientists eliminate certain physical hazards, if by legislation governments improve the quality of human existence, if wise statesmen succeed in preventing a war, etc.,—these things are often cited as evidence of the progress of a present Kingdom of God. But if the Lord Jesus Christ Himself returns to earth in person to accomplish these same things, more perfectly and universally, then we are told that such a kingdom would be "carnal."[88]

> Some people tell us that it is quite too low and coarse a thing to think of the earth in connection with the final bliss of the saints. They preach that we do but degrade and pervert the exalted things of holy Scripture, when we hint the declaration of the wise man, that "the earth endureth forever," and that over it the glorious and everlasting kingdom of Christ and His saints, is to be established in literal reality. But if the ransomed in heaven, with golden crowns upon their brows, kneeling at the feet of the Lamb, before the very throne of God, and with the prayers of all the saints, and the predictions of all the prophets in their hands, could sing of it as one of the elements of their loftiest hopes and joys, I beg to turn a deaf ear to the surly cry of "*carnal*"—"*sensual*"—"*unspiritual*"—which some would turn me from "the blessed hope." Shall the saints in glory shout "*We shall reign on the earth,*" and we be accounted heretics for believing that they knew what they were saying?[89]

3.5.11 - Revelation 5:11

living creatures

See commentary on *Revelation 4:6*[3.4.6].

elders

In favor of the view that the elders are the redeemed, they are distinguished from angels both here and in Revelation 7:11. See commentary on *Revelation 4:4*[3.4.4].

ten thousand times ten thousand

μυριάδες μυριάδων [*myriades myriadōn*], *myriads of myriads*, a countless multitude. A similar phrase describes the demonic horsemen, δισμυριάδες μυριάδων [*dismyriades myriadōn*], *two myriads of myriads*. Assuming demons are fallen angels, and only one-third of the angels fell (Rev.

12:4), then the total number of the elect angels is truly staggering, essentially *innumerable* (Job 25:3; Ps. 68:17; Dan. 7:10; Mtt. 26:53; Luke 2:13-14; Heb. 12:22).

3.5.12 - Revelation 5:12

the Lamb who was slain

See commentary on *Revelation 5:6*[3.5.6].

power . . . honor . . . glory

The same three which were earlier given to the Father in worship (Rev. 4:10-11) are now given to the *Lamb* . Yet, Scripture records that God will not give His glory to another (Isa. 42:8; 48:11). Jesus taught, "that **all should honor the Son just as they honor the Father**. He who does not honor the Son does not honor the Father who sent Him" [emphasis added] (John 5:23). Thus He prayed, "And now, O Father, glorify Me together with Yourself, with the glory which I had with You before the world was" (John 17:5). What greater statement of divinity could Jesus have made than this? "Therefore, it is proper to worship the Son, even as it is proper to worship the Father, for here it has been shown that Father and Son receive the same worship."[90] Indeed, Jesus frequently received worship at His First Coming (Mtt. 2:2; 14:33; 15:25; 28:9; 28:17; Mark 5:6; Luke 24:52; John 9:38; 20:28). Once again, we see that Jesus is God. See commentary on *Revelation 1:17*[3.1.17].

> This scene contrasts markedly with the crucifixion, an event in which all humanity rebelled against its Creator and thought to kill Him so that it could go its own irresponsible, independent way. Here, at last, Jesus Christ receives His due: full acclaim and acknowledgment by every created thing.[91]

3.5.13 - Revelation 5:13

every creature

All that is *creaturely* worships the *Creator*. This alone establishes that Jesus is not a created being—for worship of any *creature* , no matter how high, is blasphemous idolatry (Rev. 22:8-9).

> Therefore God also has highly exalted Him and given Him the name which is above every name, that at the name of Jesus every knee should bow, of those in heaven, and of those on earth, and of those under the earth, and *that* every tongue should confess that Jesus Christ *is* Lord, to the glory of God the Father. (Php 2:9-11)

in heaven and on the earth and under the earth and such as are in the sea

All of the created order—no matter their location—pay homage to the Father and the Son (Ps. 148:7-10; Php. 2:10). The fourfold division of the phrase denotes the universal creation, similar to how *the heavens and the earth* are used (Gen. 1:1), or *under the earth* may refer to those in Hades: both demons in the bottomless pit (Luke 8:31; Rev. 9:1-2; 9:11; 11:7; 17:8) and the unsaved dead who await final judgment (Rev. 20:13). See *Four: the Entire World, the Earth*[2.7.5.3.3]. Whether visible (the material realm) or invisible (the spiritual realm), all is dependent for existence every moment upon the favor and will of God. It is in this sense that Jesus is the "Beginning" and "Firstborn" over creation (Col. 1:15; 3:14).

> He is the image of the invisible God, the firstborn over all creation. For by Him all things were created that are in heaven and that are on earth, visible and invisible, whether thrones or dominions or principalities or powers. All things were created through Him and for Him. And He is before all things, and in Him all things consist. (Col. 1:15-17)

to Him who sits on the throne and to the Lamb

Both the Father and the Lamb receive equal worship. An astounding indication of the Deity of Christ and the Trinity! Only in the eternal state will we be able to fully apprehend the glory of the Father *and the Son* (John 17:24).

> I urge you in the sight of God who gives life to all things, and *before* Christ Jesus who witnessed the good confession before Pontius Pilate, that you keep *this* commandment without spot, blameless until our Lord Jesus Christ's appearing, which He will manifest in His own time, *He who is* the blessed and only Potentate, the King of kings and Lord of lords, who alone has immortality, **dwelling in unapproachable light, whom no man has seen or can see, to whom *be* honor and everlasting power** . Amen. (1Ti 6:13-16) [emphasis added]

See commentary on *Revelation 5:12*[3.5.12]. See *Worship of God*[2.4.2].

3.5.14 - Revelation 5:14

living creatures

See commentary on *Revelation 4:6*[3.4.6].

twenty-four elders

See commentary on *Revelation 4:4*[3.4.4]. The *NU*[5.2.49] and *MT*[5.2.45] texts omit *twenty-four*.

Him who lives forever and ever

Omitted from the NU and MT texts. See commentary on *Revelation 1:8*[3.1.8], *Revelation 1:11*[3.1.11], and *Revelation 1:18*[3.1.18].

Notes

1 J. A. Seiss, *The Apocalypse: Lectures on the Book of Revelation* (Grand Rapids, MI: Zondervan Publishing House, 1966), 118.

2 E. W. Bullinger, *Commentary On Revelation* (Grand Rapids, MI: Kregel Publications, 1984, 1935), 233.

3 G. E. Ladd, *"Revelation, Book of,"* in Geoffrey W. Bromiley, ed., *International Standard Bible Encyclopedia* (Grand Rapids, MI: William B. Eerdmans Publishing Co., 1979, 1915), 4:174.

4 Renald E. Showers, *Maranatha, Our Lord Come* (Bellmawr, NJ: The Friends of Israel Gospel Ministry, 1995), 97.

5 Showers, *Maranatha, Our Lord Come*, 82.

6 Gottlob Schrenk, *"Biblion,"* in Gerhard Kittel, Geoffrey William Bromily, and Gerhard Friedrich, eds., *Theological Dictionary of the New Testament* (Grand Rapids, MI: Eerdmans, 1964-c1976), s.v. "Biblion."

7 Robert L. Thomas, *Revelation 1-7* (Chicago, IL: Moody Press, 1992), 379.

8 Henry Morris, *The Revelation Record* (Wheaton, IL: Tyndale House Publishers, 1983), 96.

9 Renald E. Showers, *The Pre-Wrath Rapture View* (Grand Rapids, MI: Kregel Publications, 2001), 43.

10 Alan F. Johnson, *Revelation: The Expositor's Bible Commentary* (Grand Rapids, MI: Zondervan Publishing House, 1966), 71.

11 Showers, *Maranatha, Our Lord Come*, 81, 88.

12 Showers, *Maranatha, Our Lord Come*, 111.

13 Showers, *Maranatha, Our Lord Come*, 96.

14 Johnson, *Revelation: The Expositor's Bible Commentary*, 71.

15 John MacArthur, *Revelation 1-11 : The MacArthur New Testament Commentary* (Chicago, IL: Moody Press, 1999), Rev. 5:2.

16 Merrill C. Tenney, *Interpreting Revelation* (Peabody, MA: Hendrickson Publishers, 1957), 130.

17 Showers, *Maranatha, Our Lord Come*, 84.

18 Showers, *Maranatha, Our Lord Come*, 85.

19 Showers, *The Pre-Wrath Rapture View*, 53.

20 Tenney, *Interpreting Revelation*, 126.

21 Seiss, *The Apocalypse: Lectures on the Book of Revelation*, 118.

22 MacArthur, *Revelation 1-11 : The MacArthur New Testament Commentary*, 162.

23 Seiss, *The Apocalypse: Lectures on the Book of Revelation*, 114.

24 MacArthur, *Revelation 1-11 : The MacArthur New Testament Commentary*, 165.

25 Johnson, *Revelation: The Expositor's Bible Commentary*, 71.

26 "The prohibition is of the cessation of some act that is already in progress. It has the idea, *Stop continuing*."—Daniel B. Wallace, *Greek Grammar Beyond the Basics - Exegetical Syntax of the New Testament* (Grand Rapids, MI: Zondervan Publishing House and Galaxie Software, 1999, 2002), 720.

27 Erich Sauer, *The Dawn of World Redemption* (Grand Rapids, MI: Eerdman's Publishing Company, 1951, c1964), 157.

28 Arnold G. Fruchtenbaum, *Messianic Christology* (Tustin, CA: Ariel Ministries, 1998), 22.

29 For more on the Davidic Covenant, see 2S. 7:8-17, 19; 23:5; 1K. 11:36; 15:4; 2K. 8:19; 1Chr. 17:9-16, 27; 22:10; 2Chr. 6:15-17; 7:18; 13:5; 21:7; Ps. 2:6-8; 89:3-4; Ps 89:19-51; 132:10-12; Isa. 9:7; 11:1; 37:35; 55:3; Jer. 22:30; 23:5-6; 30:9; 33:14-17, 19-26; 36:30; Eze. 37:24-25; Hos. 3:4-5; Amos 9:11-12; Luke 1:32-33, 69-70; Acts 2:29-32; 13:22-23, 32-37; 15:16-17; Rom. 9:4.

30 Line of Messiah: Gen. 3:15; 9:1, 26; 12:2; 17:19; 21:12; 22:18; 25:23; 26:5, 2; 27:27; 28:3, 13-15; 32:9; 35:11; 48:4; 49:10; 2S. 7:12-16; 1Chr. 17:11; Jer. 22:30; 36:30; Luke 1:33.

31 "As the 'root' of David, He existed before David, that is, He is eternal. And as the 'offspring' or descendant of David, He is the rightful Heir to the throne of David, and the One who will fulfill the covenanted blessings promised to David."—Mal Couch, ed., *A Bible Handbook to Revelation* (Grand Rapids, MI: Kregel Publications, 2001), 93. "Not merely 'a sucker come up from David's ancient root' (as Alford limits it), but also including the idea of His being Himself the root and origin of David: compare these two truths brought together, Mtt. 22:42-45. Hence He is called not merely Son of David, but also David. He is at once 'the branch' of David, and 'the root' of David."—A. R. Fausset, *"The Revelation of St. John the Divine,"* in Robert Jamieson, A. R. Fausset, and David Brown, *A Commentary, Critical and Explanatory, on the Old and New Testaments* (Oak Harbor, WA: Logos Research Systems, Inc., 1997, 1877), Rev. 5:5.

32 Thomas, *Revelation 1-7*, Rev. 5:5.

33 MacArthur, *Revelation 1-11 : The MacArthur New Testament Commentary*, 167.

34 Showers, *Maranatha, Our Lord Come*, 92.

35 Showers, *Maranatha, Our Lord Come*, 90.

36 " 'The Messiah shall be called Shiloh to indicate that he was born of a woman and would therefore not be a divine being.' The amniotic sac in which the fetus is formed in the womb is called the shilyah in Hebrew. This is similar to sheloh, the Hebrew word for Shiloh. This is one of the rabbinic arguments against the divinity of Messiah."—Fruchtenbaum, *Messianic Christology*, 23. Rabbinic interpretation associated the title Shiloh with the Messiah: a midrash takes "Shiloh" to refer to "King Messiah" (Genesis R. 98.13), the *Babylonian Talmud* lists "Shi'loh" as one of the names of the Messiah (Sanhedrin 98b), and Medieval Jewish Biblical expositor Rashi makes the following comment: "Shiloh - i.e. King Messiah whose is the Kingdom." Note that Eze. 21:25-27 was given to Zedekiah, the last king of the Davidic dynasty.

37 Robert Anderson, *The Coming Prince* (Grand Rapids, MI: Kregel Publications, 1957), 173.

38 Showers, *Maranatha, Our Lord Come*, 94.

39 Fausset, "*The Revelation of St. John the Divine*," Rev. 5:1.

40 Bullinger, *Commentary On Revelation*, 237.

41 Robert H. Mounce, *The Book of Revelation* (Grand Rapids, MI: William B. Eerdmans Publishing Co., 1977), 144.

42 Although the diminutive sense may have no longer been the sense by NT times. [Frederick William Danker, and Walter Bauer, *A Greek-English Lexicon of the New Testament and Other Early Christian Literature* (Chicago, IL: University of Chicago Press, 2000), 108]

43 Johnson, *Revelation: The Expositor's Bible Commentary*, 72.

44 MacArthur, *Revelation 1-11 : The MacArthur New Testament Commentary*, 167.

45 *Arnion* occurs in the *Septuagint*[5.2.65] at Ps. 114:4, 6; Jer. 11:19; 50:45.

46 Jesus as the "Lamb" in Revelation: Rev. 5:6, 8, 12-13; 6:1, 16; 7:9-10, 14, 17; 12:11; 13:8, 11; 14:1, 4, 10; 15:3; 17:14; 19:7, 9; 21:9, 14, 22-23, 27; 22:1, 3.

47 Harold D. Foos, *"Christology in the Book of Revelation,"* in Mal Couch, ed., *A Bible Handbook to Revelation*

(Grand Rapids, MI: Kregel Publications, 2001), 106.

48 "Another object of the form Greek, *arnion*, the Lamb, is to put Him in the more marked contrast to Greek, *therion*, the *Beast*[5.2.9]."—Fausset, "*The Revelation of St. John the Divine*," Rev. 5:6. The beast in Revelation: Rev. 11:7; 13:1-4, 11-12, 14-15, 17-18; 14:9, 11; 15:2; 16:2, 10, 13; 17:3, 7-8, 11-13, 16-17; 19:19-20; 20:4, 10.

49 Timothy Friberg, Barbara Friberg, and Neva F. Miller, *Analytical Lexicon of the Greek New Testament* (Grand Rapids, MI: Baker Books, 2000), 371.

50 Passages related to the *foundation of the world* : Gen. 1:1; Pr. 8:29; Mtt. 13:35; 25:34; Luke 11:50; John 1:1; 17:24; Eph. 1:4; Heb. 4:3; 9:26; 1Pe. 1:20; Rev. 13:8; 17:8.

51 Seiss, *The Apocalypse: Lectures on the Book of Revelation*, 116.

52 Jerome Smith, *The New Treasury of Scripture Knowledge* (Nashville, TN: Thomas Nelson Publishers, 1992), Rev. 5:6.

53 Morris, *The Revelation Record*, 101.

54 David Baron, *Zechariah: A Commentary On His Visions And Prophecies* (Grand Rapids, MI: Kregel Publications, 1918), 116.

55 Seiss, *The Apocalypse: Lectures on the Book of Revelation*, 117.

56 Wallace, *Greek Grammar Beyond the Basics - Exegetical Syntax of the New Testament*, 578.

57 Johnson, *Revelation: The Expositor's Bible Commentary*, 72.

58 Mtt. 24:43; Luke 12:39; John 12:6; 1Th. 5:2, 4; 2Pe. 3:10; Rev. 3:3; 16:15.

59 Donald Grey Barnhouse, *Revelation* (Grand Rapids, MI: Zondervan Publishing House, 1971), 98, 100.

60 Seiss, *The Apocalypse: Lectures on the Book of Revelation*, 117.

61 Thomas, *Revelation 1-7*, Rev. 5:8.

62 Monty S. Mills, *Revelations: An Exegetical Study of the Revelation to John* (Dallas, TX: 3E Ministries, 1987), Rev. 5:5.

63 Seiss, *The Apocalypse: Lectures on the Book of Revelation*, 118.

64 William R. Newell, *Revelation: Chapter by Chapter* (Grand Rapids, MI: Kregel Publications, 1994,c1935), 97.

65 Thomas, *Revelation 1-7*, Rev. 5:8.

66 [Barnhouse, *Revelation*, 110] raises the question as to whether the living creatures may participate in the song having a personal experience of redemption. We feel this view has little merit. For one, Scripture is entirely silent as to this possibility. For another, upon what basis would angelic redemption be based? For Christ came as the God-*man*, born of a *woman* to regain that which was lost by the first *man* Adam. How could fallen angels profit from *human* redemption? Our ignorance concerning the angelic realm is only surpassed by our tendency toward unprofitable speculation concerning that which we cannot know.

67 Albrecht Durer (1471 - 1528). Image courtesy of the *Connecticut College* (http://www.conncoll.edu/visual/Durer-prints/index.html) *Wetmore Print Collection* (http://www.conncoll.edu/visual/wetmore.html).

68 Friberg, *Analytical Lexicon of the Greek New Testament*, 33.

69 Seiss, *The Apocalypse: Lectures on the Book of Revelation*, 111.

70 Zane C. Hodges, and Arthur L. Farstad, *The Greek New Testament According To The Majority Text* (Nashville, TN: Thomas Nelson Publishing, 1985), Rev. 5:9.

71 Hodges, *The Greek New Testament According To The Majority Text*, Rev. 5:10.

72 Hodges, *The Greek New Testament According To The Majority Text*, Rev. 5:10.

73 Smith, *The New Treasury of Scripture Knowledge*, Rev. 5:9.

74 Seiss, *The Apocalypse: Lectures on the Book of Revelation*, 108*.

75 Regarding the identification of the twenty-four elders as angels, Thomas who holds such a view, observes: "If any one of the three readings including ἡμᾶς [*hēmas*] is correct, it would mean that those singing this song are among the redeemed. This would necessitate a reconsideration of the conclusions reached above regarding the identities of the four living beings and twenty-four elders [as angels]. Unquestionable manuscript support for inclusion of the pronoun is impressive."—Thomas, *Revelation 1-7*, 410.

76 Bruce M. Metzger, *A Textual Commentary on the Greek New Testament* (Stuttgart, Germany: Deutsche Bibelgesellschaft, 1994), 666.

77 Thomas, *Revelation 1-7*, 410.

78 Bullinger, *Commentary On Revelation*, 242.

79 John Niemelä, *The Twenty-Four Elders and the Rapture* (Orange, CA: Chafer Theological Seminary, 2005), 5.

80 Fausset, "*The Revelation of St. John the Divine*," Rev. 5:9.

81 MacArthur, *Revelation 1-11 : The MacArthur New Testament Commentary*, 172.

82 This passage illustrates the elasticity of the tenets of textual criticism and how easily its practitioners abandon their own grammatical heuristics when it seems useful.

83 J. Dwight Pentecost, *Things to Come: A Study in Biblical Eschatology* (Grand Rapids, MI: Zondervan Publishing House, 1958), 257.

84 Characteristics of Christ's blood: Gen. 9:4; Ex. 12:23; 24:8; Lev. 17:11; Isa. 52:15; Zec. 9:11; Mtt. 26:28; 27:4; Luke 22:20; John 19:30; Acts 20:28; Rom. 5:9; 1Cor. 10:16; Eph. 1:7; 2:13; Col 1:14, 20; 2:14-15; Heb. 9:12, 14, 22; 10:19, 29; 11:28; 12:24; 13:12, 20; 1Pe. 1:18-19; 1Jn. 1:7; 5:8; Rev. 1:5; 5:9; 7:14; 12:11.

85 Thomas, *Revelation 1-7*, Revelation 5:9.

86 Thomas, *Revelation 1-7*, Rev. 5:10.

87 Concerning the land promises made to Israel, see: Gen. 15:7, 18; 26:4; 35:12; Ex. 3:8, 17; 6:4; 12:25; 13:5, 11; 32:13; 33:1; Deu. 1:8; 29:1, 9, 12; 30:1; 32:52; Jos. 21:43; 23:5; 1Chr. 16:18; 17:9; Ps. 105:11; Isa. 60:21; Jer. 11:5; 16:15; Eze. 37:14, 25; Amos 9:15; Acts 7:5.

88 Alva J. McClain, *The Greatness Of The Kingdom* (Winona Lake, IN: BMH Books, 1959), 520-521.

89 Seiss, *The Apocalypse: Lectures on the Book of Revelation*, 119.

90 Smith, *The New Treasury of Scripture Knowledge*, Rev. 5:12.

91 Mills, *Revelations: An Exegetical Study of the Revelation to John*, Rev. 5:8.

3.6 - Revelation 6

3.6.1 - Revelation 6:1

Having taken the scroll from the Father, the Lamb now begins to open the seals. As each seal is opened, a new judgment comes upon the earth. John is shown the judgments associated with the first six seals.

Now I saw

The chapter break is unfortunate here. Recall that the previous chapter ended with the exaltation of the Lamb and the recognition of His unique worthiness to open the scroll sealed with seven seals (see commentary on *Revelation 5:5*[3.5.5]). The scene of worship and praise which John beheld is an important *precursor* to the scenes of judgment to follow. "After five chapters of rather elaborate preparation, 'the things which must happen soon' (Rev. 1:1; 4:1) begin to unfold."[1]

when the Lamb opened

The *Lamb* had been slain to redeem men and the world *Revelation 5:9*[3.5.9]. Having paid the ultimate price, He is now worthy to *open* the first seal and initiate the steps which will lead to His global rule on earth. "Each time, with the opening of a seal, nothing is read from the scroll (Lenski), but actions occur that unquestionably match the corresponding part of the scroll exposed through each consecutive seal."[2]

None of the horrendous judgments about to take place transpire *until* the *Lamb* opens a seal. Human history records a litany of wars, natural disasters, famines, and the like, but what is about to come forth upon the earth is *completely unique*. What has transpired up to now is the routine manifestation of human selfishness, sin, and the fallen world in which man lives. As Jesus explained, "all *these things* must come to pass, but the end is not yet" (Mtt. 24:6). But with the opening of the seals by the *Lamb*, a divinely-initiated series of judgments begin which are historically unique in a number of aspects:

1. **Severity** - The judgments are more severe than any previously experienced in history. This coming day is *unique* so there is "none like it" (Jer. 30:7; Dan. 12:1; Mtt. 24:21; Mark 13:19; Rev. 3:10). (See *Jacob's Trouble and the Great Tribulation*[2.13.4].)
2. **Wrath of the Lamb** - Unlike previous times when God the Father has manifested His wrath upon nations, this is the time of the "wrath of the Lamb" (Rev. 6:16). It is the *Son*, the *Lamb of God*, Who's wrath is being manifested.
3. **The Final Flowering of Sin** - Humanism and Satanism will be at their apex on a global scale. The *ascent of man*, as humanists view human history, will have reached its apex—which is in reality its lowest point since the *ascent* is really a *descent*. At this time, there will be a full flowering of sin unique in all history for its depravity and extent.
4. **Ushering in God's Kingdom on Earth** - The wrath of the Lamb which comes forth is not merely a disconnected judgment of sin. It is part and parcel of the sweeping away of the systems of man to make way for the promised *Messianic Kingdom*[5.2.39] on earth—the only kingdom which will never pass away.

This last point, the ushering in of God's earthly kingdom, can be seen in the similarities between the events found in this book when compared with the events leading to the establishment of the first Theocratic Kingdom on earth—when Israel was delivered from Egypt.

> There is a definite parallel between the supernatural preparation for the kingdom in history under Moses and the supernatural judgments which shall be poured out upon a rebellious world in preparation for the future Millennial Kingdom of our Lord Jesus Christ at His second advent. There is the same insolent challenge to the true God on the part of the Gentile powers (Ps. 2:1-3). There will be a similar gracious but infinitely greater preliminary miracle [like Ex. 7:12]—the *Rapture*[5.2.62] of the Church—warning men of the supremacy of Jehovah and the ultimate defeat of all who rebel against Him. There will be the same swift progression in the severity of the divine judgments which follow, and even a striking parallel in the nature of the judgments (cf. Rev. 6:1-17 through 18). There will be the same victorious outcome, the destruction of the antichrist and his armies in the judgment of Armageddon, and deliverance of the

> people of Israel (Rev. 19:1-21). There will be another song of victory, significantly referred to as 'the song of Moses... and the song of the Lamb' (Rev. 15:1-3).[3]

Everything which transpires from this point forward is completely within the control of God. For it is the *Lamb* Who initiates these events and there is no judgment, famine, or plague of demons which does not ultimately serve God's purpose in what unfolds. This is seen by the frequently found phrase, *it was given* which attends both good and bad events recorded here (see commentary on Revelation 6:2).

Since it is the *Lamb* Who unleashes the events about to transpire, we are not surprised by the close correlation between the sequence of events here and those which Jesus, the Lamb of God, taught would come (see *The Synoptic Gospels*[2.13.6]).

They include:[4]

1. False Messiahs: Mtt. 24:5, 11; Mark 13:6; Luke 21:8; Rev. 6:2.
2. Wars: Mtt. 24:6-7; Mark 13:7; Luke 21:9; Rev. 6:4.
3. Famines: Mtt. 24:7; Mark 13:8; Luke 21:10; Rev. 6:5-6, 8.
4. Pestilences: Luke 21:11; Rev. 6:8.
5. Persecution: Mtt. 24:9; Mark 13:9-13; Luke 21:12-17; Rev. 6:9-11.
6. Earthquakes: Mtt. 24:7; Mark 13:8; Luke 21:11; Rev. 6:12.
7. Cosmic Phenomena: Mtt. 24:29; Mark 13:24-25; Luke 21:11; Rev. 6:12-14.

one of the seals

Concerning the significance of the seals, see commentary on *Revelation 5:1*[3.5.1].

> Each of the scroll's seven seals (cf. Rev. 5:1) represents a specific divine judgment that will be poured out sequentially on the earth. The seals encompass the entire period of the Tribulation (Rev. 3:10), culminating with the return of Christ. It seems best to understand the first four seals as taking place during the first half of the Tribulation, the fifth stretching from the first into the second half, (called the "great tribulation" in Rev. 7:14 and lasting three and one-half years; Rev. 11:2; 12:6; 13:5) and the sixth and seventh taking place during that "great tribulation." Apparently the seventh seal contains the seven trumpet judgments (Rev. 8:1-11:19) and the seventh trumpet (Rev. 11:15) contains the seven bowl judgments (Rev. 16:1-21). The seven seals thus contain all the judgments to the end when Jesus Christ returns.[5]

As the Lamb opens the seals, a sequence of events are initiated which are closely parallel to Matthew 24 (also Mark 13 and Luke 21). The first four seals are set apart from the final three in their common representation *by riders on horses*.

The Four Horsemen of the Apocalypse [6]

Showers equates the birth pangs "beginning of sorrows" of Mtt. 24:4-8 with the first four seals of Revelation 6:1-8 and places them during the first half of the 70th week of Daniel.[7] He also observes that the *Day of the Lord*[5.2.14] includes the notion of birth pangs (Isa. 13:6-10; 1Th. 5:3), so the first four seals are probably included within the first half of the 70th week (see *The 70th Week of Daniel*[2.13.5]).

> Since the beginning of birth pangs of Matthew 24 and the first four seals of Revelation 6 are the same thing, and since the broad Day of the Lord will include the beginning of birth pangs, we can conclude that the broad Day of the Lord will also include the first four seals of Revelation 6. . . . Since the beginning of birth pangs of the first half of the 70th week and the first four seals of Revelation 6 are the same thing, the divine wrath, anger, and destruction of the Day of the Lord will also be associated with the first four seals.[8]

living creatures

See commentary on *Revelation 4:6*[3.4.6].

voice like thunder

Some speculate that the *voice like thunder* of the living creature may be the source of the seven thunders which John is prevented from recording (Rev. 10:3). However, the description of this voice is probably meant to be an indication of its imposing volume to connect its command with the judgment to follow. See commentary on *Revelation 4:5*[3.4.5].

Come and see.

Ἔρχου καὶ ἴδε [*Erchou kai ide*] (*MT*[5.2.45]) or Ἔρχου καὶ ἴδου [*Erchou kai idou*] (*TR*[5.2.79]). This phrase occurs in the TR and MT texts in conjunction with the loosing of each of the first four seals (Rev. 6:1, 3, 5, 7). These translations understand the living creature to be *speaking to John.* The *NU*[5.2.49] text omits καὶ ἴδε [*kai ide*], *and see*, understanding *come* as a command issued by the living creature *to the rider of the horse* bringing him forth in judgment. This would accord well with the emphasis found on the judgments being subject to divine control.

> The cry itself is very brief—Ἔρχου [*Erchou*]! It may be equally rendered *Go*, or *Come!* Our translators give it about as often one way as the other. It does not alter the sense here whichever way we take it. It is not an address to John, as many have regarded it, and as the questionable addition to the text—*"and see"*—would seem to require. John was already on the spot, beholding all that was transpiring, and did not need to be called any nearer, or to remove any further off. And if his nearer approach or further departure had been needed in the case of the first horseman, it could not have been needed for the succeeding ones. But we find the same command repeated in each successive instance. Neither can we explain why it should be such a voice of thundering power, if it was simply to call to the seer.[9]

3.6.2 - Revelation 6:2

white horse

This *white horse* is the first of *four* horses of different colors, similar to the horses seen by Zechariah (Zec. 1:8; 6:2-6).[10] See *Zechariah's Horses*[4.19] for a discussion of the relationship between Zechariah's visions and the horsemen shown John. Within the context of the book of Revelation, white represents righteousness. "The white horse . . . emerges as an emblem of righteousness, though there is no guarantee that the righteousness is more than apparent."[11]

he who sat on it

The similarities between this rider and Christ are striking:

1. **Riding a White Horse** - Both ride upon a white horse indicating victory (Rev. 6:2; 19:11).
2. **Wearing a Crown** - Both wear a crown (Rev. 6:2; 19:12). (But Christ wears *multiple* crowns.)
3. **Overcome** - Both are "overcomers"—victorious in their pursuits (Rev. 6:2; John 16:33; 1Jn. 4:4; Rev. 3:21; 17:14).

Even so, this is not the *white horse* which carries He who is Faithful and True in Revelation 19:11. For it is *the Lamb* who has just loosed the first seal sending this horseman out. It violates all logic for the same person to be opening the seal and sending himself forth.[12] "Moreover, it would be inappropriate to have an angelic being call forth Christ or his servants."[13] If Christ rides forth here, who is it that remains in heaven to open the remaining seals?[14] This rider carries a *bow* whereas Christ's weapon is a *sword* (Rev. 2:12; 19:15). This rider is *alone* whereas Christ is followed by the armies in heaven also riding on white horses (Rev. 19:14). Finally, this rider sets forth at the beginning of the Tribulation whereas Christ rides forth at its end.

In light of related passages, it seems best to understand this rider as representing a movement which ultimately culminates in the one whom Jesus described:[15] "I have come in My Father's name, and you do not receive Me; if another comes in his own name, him you will receive" (John 5:43). To an unsuspecting world he *looks* like Messiah, the political savior of mankind, yet he is a deceiver, the *anti-* or *pseudo*-Christ. Here is documented the initial appearance of the figure of the *Antichrist*[5.2.3] upon the stage of world history. Although there will be numerous false messiahs down through history, none as convincing and successful as this final figure.[16] The Restrainer has been taken out of the way so that the Antichrist, the son of perdition, might be revealed in his own time (2Th. 2:6-7). He is the one who will be destroyed with the breath of the mouth of the Lamb (2Th. 2:8; Rev. 19:20). The church has already been taken up for she watches for Christ, not Antichrist. See *Rapture*[4.14], *Imminency*[4.8].

> The beginning of birth pangs of Matthew 24 and the first four seals of Revelation 6 are the same thing and will occur during the first half of the seven years of the 70th week. In light of the fact that the beginning of birth pangs will involve false messiahs, it would appear that the rider of the first seal will be a false messiah. . . . Since, . . . God's Holy Spirit has the function of restraining humanity's lawlessness, and since the Antichrist will be the ultimate expression of human lawlessness, it would appear that Paul was indicating in 2 Thessalonians 2:6-8 that the restraining work of the Holy Spirit is the restraint that prevents the Antichrist from being revealed until the right time. The Holy Spirit will continue that restraining work until He, as the restrainer, is removed, at which time the Antichrist will be revealed. Since, as noted earlier, only God has the authority to remove the Holy Spirit's restraint, and since the Antichrist will be revealed once that restraint is removed, we can conclude that it will be through divine activity that the Antichrist will be turned loose to conquer the world. . . . It is important to note that God declared He will raise up the foolish, idol shepherd (Zec. 11:16).[17]

> The rider on the white horse is more probably to be identified as the Antichrist. If this is not Antichrist, then Revelation does not place Antichrist on the scene of events before the middle of Daniel's Seventieth Week (in Rev. 13), and the rider is virtually unidentifiable.[18]

Pre-wrath *rapture*[5.2.62] advocate Marvin Rosenthal finds the idea of God's release of the Antichrist to be "preposterous:"

> If the seals are God's wrath, then God alone must take direct responsibility for a counterfeit religious system and the emergence of the Antichrist, for that is precisely what the first seal depicts. To attribute the emergence of the Antichrist to God is obviously preposterous. . . . To suggest that the first four seals are God's wrath is totally unfounded. It strains reason to think that once God begins His *Day of the Lord*[5.2.14] wrath, the Antichrist is able to assume control of the world.[19]

But to take any other view—that the manifestation of Antichrist is under the control of Satan or man—is opposed to biblical teaching. Even if the *restrainer* is taken to be something or someone other than God Himself (a view we do not hold), who is it that takes the Restrainer "out of the way" so that the "lawless one" is revealed (2Th. 2:6-7)? If the revealing of Antichrist is *not* subject to the precise timing and permission of God, then what are we to make of a tremendous number of biblical passages which assert the absolute sovereignty of God over all things?

Rosenthal lacks an adequate view of the sovereignty of God and how He redirects sin and the depravity of man toward His own ends. There are many examples where sin accomplishes God's purpose, yet those who sin remain fully responsible for their actions. God is not the *author* of sin, but all things *serve His purpose* in the end (Mtt. 24:26; Mark 14:21; Luke 22:22; Acts 2:22-23). See *Who is the Restrainer?*[4.14.4.2].

> The first six seals. . . are thus set here, in order to show us that these judgments do not arise from chance, but are all under Divine control. The great False Messiah of the first Seal cannot be revealed until the appointed moment shall have come and the voice from the throne gives the permissive command "Go!" The judgments cannot fall until the same command is given.[20]

a bow

The *bow* is a symbol representing strength (Job 29:20; 30:11; Eze. 39:3).

Some understand the mention of a *bow*, but no arrows as an indication of his initial deception by peace and agreement (Dan. 9:27). "The Antichrist is seen riding a white war-horse, and with bow in hand, but with no arrow fitted to it. The symbol suggests bloodless victories."[21] Like Antiochus Epiphanes before him, he would "come in peaceably, and seize the kingdom by intrigue . . . and after the league *is made* with him he shall act deceitfully" (Dan. 11:21-23).

> And in the latter time of their kingdom, when the transgressors have reached their fullness, a king shall arise, having fierce features, who understands sinister schemes. His power shall be mighty, but not by his own power; he shall destroy fearfully, and shall prosper and thrive; he shall destroy the mighty, and *also* the holy people. Through his cunning He shall cause deceit to prosper under his rule; and he shall exalt *himself* in his heart. He shall destroy many in *their* prosperity. He shall even rise against the Prince of princes; but he shall be broken without *human* means. And the vision of the evenings and mornings which was told is true; therefore seal up the vision, for *it refers* to many days *in the future*. (Dan. 8:23-

> 26)
>
> There is no question among expositors that Antiochus is in view in this prophecy. What was prophesied was fulfilled literally through him. However, the prophecy looks beyond Antiochus to a future person (the Antichrist) of whom Antiochus is only a foreshadowing. This coming one is said to "stand against the Prince of princes" (Dan. 8:25). This can be none other than the Lord Jesus Christ. Thus the prophecy must go beyond Antiochus and look forward to the coming of one whose ministry will parallel that of Antiochus. From Antiochus certain facts can be learned about the forthcoming desecrator: (1) He will achieve great power by subduing others (Dan. 8:24). (2) He will rise to power by promising false security (Dan. 8:25). (3) He will be intelligent and persuasive (Dan. 8:23). (4) He will be controlled by another (Dan. 8:24), that is, Satan. (5) He will be an adversary of Israel and subjugate Israel to his authority (Dan. 8:24-25). (6) He will rise up in opposition to the Prince of princes, the Lord Jesus Christ (Dan. 8:25). (7) His rule will be terminated by divine judgment (Dan. 8:25). So it may be concluded that there is a dual reference in this striking prophecy. It reveals Israel's history under the Seleucids and particularly under Antiochus during the time of Greek domination, but it also looks forward to Israel's experiences under Antichrist, whom Antiochus foreshadows.[22]
>
> So before the terrors of the Tribulation break loose and lead to the battle of Armageddon there will come a period of world peace. But it will be a deceptive peace, as the world is lulled into a false sense of security followed by war, famine, and death. The world's desperate desire for international peace will serve as the bait for the satanic trap. That longing for security and safety will play into the hands of Antichrist, Satan's ruler, who will convince the world that he can provide them. He will particularly deceive Israel, whose people have for so long desired peace, and he "will make a firm covenant with the many [Israel] for one week" (Dan. 9:27). Antichrist's peace pact and protection of Israel will not last, however: "in the middle of the week [the Seventieth Week of Daniel's prophecy; the Tribulation] he will put a stop to sacrifice and grain offering; and on the wing of abominations will come one who makes desolate, even until a complete destruction, one that is decreed, is poured out on the one who makes desolate" (Dan. 9:27). The false peace that Antichrist brings will come to an abrupt halt at the midpoint of the Tribulation when he desecrates the temple in Jerusalem, betrays the Jewish people, and launches deadly attacks on them (cf. Mtt. 24:4-10). There can and will be no peace until the Prince of Peace sets up His earthly kingdom (Rev. 20:1-6).[23]

Like Antiochus before him, the Antichrist plays a special role in relation to Israel during the events to come:

> God will have specific purposes for bringing Antichrist on the world scene. One purpose will be the punishment of Israel. . . . [the] desolation of Israel by the Antichrist will be part of God's judgment of the nation because it rejected its Messiah in His first coming [John 5:43]. . . . A second purpose will be the repentance of Israel. . . . God will bring the Antichrist on the world scene to play a major role in shattering [Israel's] rebellion [Dan. 12:7]. . . . A third purpose will be the judgment of the world. . . . God will judge the world by giving it the kind of ruler it deserves. . . . A fourth purpose will be the exposure of the world's unbelief. God will bring the Antichrist on the world scene and permit him to make his claim to be God to demonstrate mankind's unbelief, . . . A fifth purpose will be the instigation of the final showdown between Christ and Satan's forces and the defeat of those forces.[24]

a crown

στέφανος [*stephanos*], generally used of a victor's crown or wreath, *but not always*. A widespread, but erroneous teaching is that this crown, being a *stephanos* and not a *diadema*, indicates that the rider cannot be Christ.[25] Not so, for Christ is also found wearing such a crown (Mtt. 27:29; Mark 15:17; John 19:2, 5; Heb. 2:9). Evidence that this rider is other than Christ must be derived from other factors (see above). See *Crowns*[4.6].

was given to him

ἐδόθη [*edothē*] , passive voice. Although the rider likely believes he has gained his own crown for himself (cf. Isa. 45:1-4; Pr. 21:1; Dan 2:21; 2:37; 4:25, 31-32; 5:21), it is only his by *permission.* Everything which proceeds from the opening of the seals is subject to the permission of the one seated on the throne and the Lamb. The sovereignty of God is heavily emphasized throughout the book of Revelation—there is *nothing* which transpires that God Himself does not grant authority for it. This is seen in the frequently-found phrase *was given* which denotes the granting of permission to an agent from another, namely God (Rev. 6:2, 4, 8, 11; 7:2; 8:3; 9:1, 3, 5; 11:1; 13:5, 7, 14-15; 16:8; 19:8; 20:4). The first horseman is *granted* his crown (Rev. 6:2), the second horseman is *given* to take peace with a great sword (Rev. 6:4); Death and Hades, who ride with the third horsemen are *given* authority to kill a fourth part of the earth (Rev. 6:8), the four angels are *given* the power to hurt the earth and sea (Rev. 8:3), the star from heaven is *given* the key to loosen the demonic locusts from the abyss (Rev. 9:1) who were themselves *given* power to torment men (Rev. 9:5), the beast is *given* authority to continue for forty two months (Rev. 13:5) and to make war against the saints and overcome them (Dan. 7:25; Rev. 13:7), the fourth bowl is *given* the ability to scorch men (Rev. 16:8). All of these horrific and terrible realities—the very manifestation and flowering of sin of which God is no author—are harnessed for His purposes. The troubling and yet comforting reality is that there is *no creature* which ultimately does not *serve God's purpose* , either willingly or unwillingly. Troubling, because in the inscrutable purpose of God such evil is allowed to continue. Comforting, because everything we suffer is subject to God's approval and purpose (Job 2:6; Rom. 8:28). "How irresistible the grasp of Omnipotence on the powers and forces of evil. They are effectually bridled till the plans of God are ripe and ready for action."[26] Once the reality of God's sovereignty is understood, the bondage of Satan is seen for what it is. For Satan has *less* freedom in *rebellion* against God than he once had in obedient service of the Master.

he went out conquering and to conquer

νικων και ἵνα νικήσῃ [*nikōn kai hina nikēsē*], both *conquering* and *conquer* are from νικάω [*nikaō*], the same root as *overcomer*. Thus, he is *another overcomer* (Rev. 11:7) to be contrasted with the True Overcomer Who is Christ (Rev. 5:5; 17:14).

> He will be endowed with the most extraordinary powers, so that "he shall destroy wonderfully, and shall prosper, and practice, and shall destroy the mighty and the holy people" (Dan. 8:24). Before his exploits the fame of Alexander and Napoleon will be forgotten. None will be able to stand before him. He will go "forth conquering and to conquer" (Rev. 6:2). He will sweep everything before him so that the world will exclaim, "Who is like unto the *Beast*[5.2.9]? who is able to make war with him?" (Rev. 13:4). His military exploits will not be confined to a corner, but carried out on a vast scale. He is spoken of as the man who will "shake kingdoms" and "make the earth to tremble" (Isa. 14:16).[27]

> Ezekiel 34:23-30 says that when God establishes His covenant of peace with Israel, the covenant will result in safety, peace with nations, and the elimination of harmful beasts by famine. By contrast, when the Antichrist establishes his covenant of peace with Israel [Dan. 9:27], God will inflict the world with conditions opposite of those His covenant of peace will bring. He will unleash war (the sword) [the second seal, Rev. 6:3-4], famine (the third seal, Rev. 6:5-6), and harmful beasts (the fourth seal, Rev. 6:7-8) upon the earth to demonstrate that the Antichrist's covenant of peace is not the covenant of peace that will bring true safety, as foretold in the Old Testament.[28]

3.6.3 - Revelation 6:3

come and see

"The 'living one' who introduces this second horse does not use a voice of thunder as did the 'living one' who dispatched the first horse. This is significant, for it indicates that the first horse brings the other three horses in its train as a sequential consequence."[29] See commentary on *Revelation 6:1*[3.6.1].

3.6.4 - Revelation 6:4

fiery red

πυρρός [*pyrros*]: "As a color fiery red, red (as fire)."[30] The same color as the dragon in Revelation 12:3.

was granted

Ultimate power rests with God who allows the judgment for His purposes. See commentary on *Revelation 6:2*[3.6.2].

take peace from the earth

Although the rider on the white horse appears to conquer by means of negotiation and avoids bloodshed, this does not last. Eventually he shows his true colors as the second rider joins the ride—bringing war and death. This may correspond to the point in Daniel's vision where another "*horn* which came up, before which three fell, namely, that horn which had eyes and a mouth which spoke pompous words, whose appearance *was* greater than his fellows" (Dan. 7:20). It appears that the *little horn*[5.2.37] may only progress so far by means of peace before he is forced to go to war and assert his position with violence. Shortly after this point: "I was watching; and the same horn was making war against the saints, and prevailing against them" (Dan. 7:21 cf. Rev. 6:9-10). This is the time of the "beginning of sorrows" which Jesus spoke of (Mtt. 24:6-8). See *The Synoptic Gospels*[2.13.6].

should kill one another

σφάξουσιν [*sphaxousin*]: "To slaughter . . . Of the killing of a person by violence . . . *butcher* or *murder someone*"[31]. The same root described the Lamb "as though it had been *slain*" (Rev. 5:6). This will be a time of unprecedented bloodshed which will forever puncture the naive view of humanism that man is inherently good.

a great sword

This sword is wielded by the second horseman, but it is *sent by God*:

> For thus says the LORD God of Israel to me: "Take this wine cup of fury from My hand, and cause all the nations, to whom I send you, to drink it. And they will drink and stagger and go mad because of the sword that I will send among them." Then I took the cup from the LORD'S hand, and made all the nations drink, to whom the LORD had sent me. (Jer. 25:15-17)

This is the pattern of God's judgment to nations who reject Him—He makes them *mad* and turn upon one another (Eze. 38:21). "While Scripture does not give the details, the advances in modern weaponry suggest a terrible, unimaginable holocaust."[32]

3.6.5 - Revelation 6:5

a black horse

Black is μέλας [*melas*] which is used "Of clothing used in mourning . . . as the color of evil."[33]

a pair of scales

Here the black speaks of judgment and famine, for the rider carries a pair of scales (balances) used to weigh food and indicating its scarcity.

3.6.6 - Revelation 6:6

a quart

"The measure spoken of here is the Greek measure of capacity of very ancient usage, the choenix. As early as the time of Homer it was indicated as the amount of wage given to a workman for a full day's work (Odyssey XIX:XXVIII). Herodotus also gives this as the measure of wheat consumed by each soldier in the army of Xerxes (VIII:CLXXXVII)."[34]

wheat

σίτου [*sitou*], used of wheat in the context of hardship "as an indication of severe famine and rising prices . . . *Ignatius*[5.2.28], in his fervent longing for martyrdom, uses this symbolic language . . . *I am God's wheat* and will be ground by the teeth of the wild beasts."[35]

a denarius

That famine is intended here is evident for this amount "was a workman's average daily wage."[36] Men will work an entire day and barely procure enough to stay alive. "Ordinarily, from sixteen to twenty measures were given for a denarius."[37]

do not harm the oil and the wine

ἀδικήσῃς [*adikēsēs*], second person *singular*, imperative mood. The voice from the midst of the four living creatures is *commanding* the *one* on the black horse not to harm the oil and wine. Again, we see the judgments which pour forth are precisely under the control of God. See commentary on *Revelation 6:1*[3.6.1].

Some attempt to understand this verse in relation to an edict of Domitian restricting vine production in favor of corn:

> It is argued that Rev. 6:6 refers to Domitian's edict against vines in AD 92, a measure which may have been intended as a drastic means of increasing corn production, but which hit Philadelphia with exceptional severity because of its dependence on viticulture.[38]

> Because of the earthquake, which drove them from the city proper, and because of the fertility of the soil, many of the people had turned to farming as a means of livelihood, specifically to the cultivation of vineyards. Apparently, because of famine, in A.D. 92 Domitian issued an edict that at least half the vineyards in the provinces be cut down and no new ones planted. This action was designed to increase production of corn which the Empire needed badly. This crisis affected Philadelphia more critically than any other, because no city of Asia depended on the fruit of the vine more than it. Dionysius, god of wine, was the principal deity.[39]

This seems unlikely for the four horsemen ride out after the Lamb begins opening seals—something which remains future even to our own day. Moreover, it appears Domitian's edict was not motivated in response to famine.[40]

Others have understood the reference to *oil* as pertaining to the marking upon the foreheads of the servants of God who are anointed for protection during this time (Rev. 7:3; 9:4; 22:4), but this seems unlikely since the context concerns food supply and famine.

Another suggestion is that the common commodities are hard to come by, but luxury items will remain available for the upper classes.

> This intimates that the famine is by no means universal: yea, it suggests that side by side with abject suffering there is abundance and luxury.[41]

> Some interpreters have suggested that the brunt of the suffering falls upon the poorer classes, but the rich are left largely untouched, but this is a less likely interpretation, for while fine wine and oil could be understood of the luxuries belonging to the rich, the poorer quality product may be in view here as descriptive of the ordinary provisions used by the common people.[42]

> One of the great criticisms of the present time is that there is scarcity in the midst of plenty. This is the situation which will be accentuated a thousandfold when the *Antichrist*[5.2.3] begins his reign. It is a social maladjustment.[43]

Still another idea is that the oil and wine denote medicinal supplies. That although food will be lacking, there will be an abundance of medicine.[44] This seems unlikely in view of the catastrophic conditions (medicinal supplies require careful storage and efficient distribution) and the number of deaths inferred.

Others suggest another possibility. They point to a similar passage in 1 Samuel which records famine conditions caused by rainy conditions which destroyed the grain crop, but under which vineyards and olive trees would flourish:

> The proper understanding of the phrase "do not damage the oil and the wine" is found in an event recorded in 1 Samuel 12. . . . Samuel was threatening to call upon the Lord to bring thunder and rain as punishment. Why? . . . Heavy rains at the time of harvest would destroy the wheat, thereby bringing famine. . . As Nogah Hareuveni of Neot Kedumim, the Biblical Gardens of Israel, has pointed out: "The ripe, heavy-eared wheat can suffer from a downpour not only through physical damage from the force of the wind-driven rain, but also by rotting from the sudden moisture combined with the high temperatures that prevail in Israel by *Shavuot* (in late May-early June). This interpretation explains why the Israelites cried out to Samuel 'pray. . .to save us from death' (1S. 12:19)—from death by starvation that would follow the destruction of the grain crop.". . . "the oil and the wine," will not be affected by this rainstorm because they will have already been pollinated. In fact, the water might even help them, thus giving oil and wine for all, rich and poor alike.[45]

The reverse scenario might also be possible: that of drought. "Since the roots of the olive and vine go deeper, they would not be affected by a limited drought which would all but destroy the grain."[46] However, the nature of the famine which attends these "beginning of sorrows" (Mtt. 24:8) is probably uniquely severe in history and argues against understanding the distinction between food items as denoting a limited famine. This situation contrasts with a locust-induced famine, such as that of Joel, in which *all* crops were ruined: "The field is wasted, the land mourns; for the grain is ruined, the new wine is dried up, the oil fails" (Joel 1:10).

> The problem with taking this as a reference to limited famine is that it underrates the severity of the seals. This famine will be serious enough to make it unique in history up to that time. The world has already seen many limited famines, but never one like this. . . . So it is wrong to take a major feature such as this prohibition against hurting the oil and the wine and interpret it as a limitation on human hardship. It indicates rather the inequity that will prevail. The poor will have it extremely hard while the wealthy will experience no interruption to their luxurious lifestyle.[47]

Both oil and wine are listed among the commercial wealth of Babylon at the time of her destruction (Rev. 18:13). See commentary on *Revelation 18:13*[3.18.13].

3.6.7 - Revelation 6:7

fourth seal

This is the last seal which will loose a horse and rider. The first four seals are to be understood as a group, four being indicative of their global effects. See *Four: the Entire World, the Earth*[2.7.5.3.3].

come and see

See commentary on *Revelation 6:1*[3.6.1].

3.6.8 - Revelation 6:8

pale horse

Pale is χλωρός [*chlōros*] from which we derive *chlorophyll*, which denotes the green pigments found in plants. It may denote a mottled appearance, like the sorrel or dappled horses in Zechariah's vision. See *Zechariah's Horses*[4.19]. Here it denotes "the color of a person in sickness as contrasted with the appearance of health,"[48] for the name of the rider of the pale horse is *death* (θάνατος [*thanatos*]).

> Properly, "greenish-yellow," like young grass or unripe wheat. Homer applies it to honey, and Sophocles to the sand. Generally, "pale, pallid." Used of a mist, of sea-water, of a pale or bilious complexion. Thucydides uses it of the appearance of persons stricken with the plague (ii., 49). In Homer, it is used of the paleness of the face from fear, and so as directly descriptive of fear ("Iliad," x., 376; xv., 4). Of olive wood ("Odyssey," ix., 320, 379) of which the bark is gray.[49]

> The word to describe the fourth horse's color, *chloros* ("pale green"), is the color of grass and other vegetation in Mark 6:39 and Rev. 8:7; 9:4, but in the present connection, designates the yellowish green of decay, the pallor of death. It is a pale ashen color that images a face bleached because of terror. It recalls a corpse in the advanced state of corruption (Ford).[50]

Death, and Hades followed

Death and Hades are here personified (cf. Isa. 28:18 where Death and Sheol sign a covenant). These two are often found together in Scripture for *Hades* is the destination of the unsaved upon passing through the gateway of *death*. This seems to be their relationship here because Hades *followed* behind Death—taking in the soul and spirit of those who had first died. Elsewhere, the appearance of *Death* with *Hades* may denote the destination of the *material* and *immaterial* parts of man, respectively. For the body molders in the grave (*death*) while the spirit and soul enter the underworld (*Hades*). Thus, "Death and Hades delivered up the dead who were in them" may refer to the release of the spirit and soul of the unsaved from imprisonment in Hades to be joined with a bodily resurrection from the grave in order to stand before God in judgment (Rev. 20:13).

The eventual casting of *death* and *Hades* into the Lake of Fire (Rev. 20:14) may describe the total victory over these unsavory realities brought about by the cross of Jesus (Hos. 13:14; 1Cor. 15:21-26, 54-55; 2Ti. 1:10) or denote those destined for the lake—the unsaved dead whose bodies remained in the grave and souls remained in Hades until the Great White Throne Judgment. Jesus has the keys of *Death* and *Hades*. See commentary on *Revelation 1:18*[3.1.18]. Death and Hades either both ride the same horse, or Death is the horseman and Hades follows on foot. In either case, the two are inseparable as Hades takes in all that Death supplies.

power was given to them

Ultimate power rests with God who allows the judgment for His purposes. See commentary on *Revelation 6:2*[3.6.2].

over a fourth of the earth

A staggering judgment when seen in relation to today's population:

> If today's [1992] world population figure of five billion is used, . . . "one fourth of the earth" means that Death and Hades have authority, which they apparently will exercise, to take the lives of one and a quarter billion people. The magnitude of this catastrophe can hardly be grasped because nothing comparable has happened throughout history (Swete). If limited to two continents, which it will probably not be (Beckwith; Lenski; Mounce), it will amount to the elimination of people from two of the world's most populous ones (Walvoord).[51]

Since Thomas wrote, the world population has risen to over 6 billion [December 2003] which would result in the death of over 1.5 billion people.[52] This number would be reduced by the believers in Christ who are taken in the *Rapture*[4.14] prior to this period.

sword. . . hunger. . . death. . . beasts

The fourfold source of judgment hints at its global scope. See *Four: the Entire World, the Earth*[2.7.5.3.3]. *Sword* is ῥομφαίᾳ [*hromphaia*]: "A large and broad sword, used by barbaric peoples, especially the Thracians."[53] As has frequently been the case in the past, hunger follows war: the second horseman took peace from the earth and the effects of his ride contribute to the effectiveness of the fourth horseman. Although the third horseman brought great famine— the greatest experienced to that time—the famine now becomes even more severe. The listing of alternative forms of death pictures inescapable judgment. Those who escape death by the *sword* may die of *hunger*. Those who survive the *hunger* are likely to perish from disease (*death*).[54]

> Throughout human history, disease has killed people on a far more massive scale than war. More Union and Confederate soldiers died from disease during the Civil War than were killed in battle. An estimated 30 million people died during the great influenza epidemic of 1918-19 —more than three times as many as the estimated 8.5 million soldiers who died in battle during World War I. [55]

Those who survive the first three will be so weak as to be unable to defend themselves from wild *beasts* which will become emboldened and attack them.

> So it shall be a reproach and a taunt, an instruction and an astonishment, unto the nations that are round about thee, when I shall execute judgments on thee in anger and in wrath, and in wrathful rebukes; (I, Jehovah, have spoken it;) when I shall send upon them the evil arrows of **famine**, that are for destruction, which I will send to destroy you: and I will increase the **famine** upon you, and will break your staff of bread; and I will send upon you **famine** and **evil beasts**, and they shall bereave thee; and **pestilence and blood** shall pass through thee; and I will bring the **sword** upon thee: I, Jehovah, have spoken it. (Eze. 5:15-17) [emphasis added]

> Thus says the Lord GOD: "Pound your fists and stamp your feet, and say, 'Alas, for all the evil abominations of the house of Israel! For they shall fall by the **sword**, by **famine**, and by **pestilence**. He who is far off shall die by the **pestilence**, he who is near shall fall by the **sword**, and he who remains and is besieged shall die by the **famine**." Thus will I spend My fury upon them. (Eze. 6:11-12) [emphasis added]

From these passages we understand that what seem like intensified *natural* disturbances (war, hunger, death, attack by beasts) are in fact expressions of God's judgment. Thus God's wrath is *already* seen in the fourth seal—well in advance of the sixth and seventh seals.[56]

The picture being drawn is one of no escape. No matter which group or location a man finds himself in, there is a God-ordained judgment which will result in death:

> For thus saith the Lord Jehovah: "How much more when I send **my four sore judgments** upon Jerusalem, the **sword**, and the **famine**, and the evil **beasts**, and the **pestilence**, to cut off from it man and beast!" (Eze. 14:21) [emphasis added]

> Thus shalt thou say unto them, "Thus saith the Lord Jehovah: 'As I live, surely they that are in the waste places shall fall by the **sword**; and him that is in the open field will I give to the **beasts** to be devoured; and they that are in the strongholds and in the caves shall die of the **pestilence**.' " (Eze. 33:27)

[emphasis added]

Amos predicted this character of the day of Jehovah: "Woe unto you that desire the day of Jehovah! Wherefore would ye have the day of Jehovah? It is darkness, and not light. As if a man did flee from a lion, and a bear met him; or went into the house and leaned his hand on the wall, and a serpent bit him. Shall not the day of Jehovah be darkness, and not light? even very dark, and no brightness in it?" (Amos 5:18-20).

There is intentional irony in God's reversal of roles as men become the source of food for beasts (Gen. 9:2-3 cf. Eze. 29:5; 39:17-20; Rev. 19:17-18). When man is disobedient to God, He reverses the original divine order where man was given dominion over the beasts (Gen. 1:26-28; 9:2-3) and gives man into the hand of beasts (Lev. 26:22; Deu. 32:24). The beasts will be emboldened both because of the emaciated and sickly condition of men and the scarceness of their own food supply. "Once food becomes scarce, wild animals which generally leave man alone will begin to attack man for food."[57]

3.6.9 - Revelation 6:9

Opening the Fifth and Sixth Seals[58]

fifth seal

With the opening of the fifth seal, we break from the judgments associated with the four horsemen.

"There are no voices of command from heaven under this seal, and no messengers dispatched from the throne; for the reason that bloody persecutions of God's servants come from beneath—not from above."[59] We now leave the "beginning sorrows" spoken of by Jesus behind and enter the time of tribulation characterized by martyrdom:

> All these *are* the beginning of sorrows. **Then** they will deliver you up to tribulation and kill you, and you will be hated by all nations for My name's sake. And then many will be offended, will betray one another, and will hate one another. (Mtt. 24:8-10) [emphasis added]

The beginning of sorrows have passed and the Great Tribulation is now upon the world, a time of unprecedented martyrdom and *anti-Semitism*[5.2.64][5.2.4] (Mtt. 24:15-22; Rev. 12:6, 13-15). "The futurist interpretation takes these as the first martyrs of the tribulation of Daniel's 70th Week. The fifth seal corresponds to Mtt. 24:8-28, martyrdoms."[60]

under the altar

θυσιαστηρίου [*thysiastēriou*], used "of the altar of burnt offering in the inner forecourt of the temple at Jerusalem . . .the heavenly altar of Revelation also seems to be thought of as an altar of incense: Rev. 6:9; 8:3, 5; 9:13; 14:18; 16:7."[61] When Aaron and his sons were consecrated to the priesthood, after the blood of the bull was put on the horns of the altar of sacrifice (or burnt offering), the remaining blood was poured "beside the base of the altar" (Ex. 29:12; Lev. 8:15). This pattern was also followed for the sin offering (Lev. 4:7). The blood of the martyred saints is considered as an "offering" before God as it accumulates at the base of the altar during this time of intense persecution of all who name the name of Christ (Mtt. 24:9). "Like sacrifices, they had been slain for their testimony. Not sacrifices of atonement, but of *devotion*."[62]

> The picture of souls immediately in God's presence after death is in harmony with 2Cor. 5:8, and the fact that the martyrs are beneath the altar is consistent with the symbolism of Lev. 4:7, for the priest poured the blood of the sacrifice at the bottom of the altar, and the blood represented the life of the sacrifice (Lev. 17:11-14). So these martyrs will sacrifice their lives for God, and Heaven acknowledges this.[63]

Some see this altar to be the altar of incense rather than the altar of sacrifice.[64] Yet the location of the martyrs *under the altar* has more in common with the altar of sacrifice and there is no compelling reason to connect this altar with the altar of incense upon which the prayers of the saints are offered.

the souls

ψυχὰς [*psychas*] , these have yet to attain a resurrection body which they will receive prior to the *Millennial Kingdom*[5.2.39] (Rev. 20:4). The word can also denote *physical life*. "And they overcame him because of the blood of the Lamb, and because of the word of their testimony; and they loved not their life (ψυχὴν [*psychēn*]) even unto death" (Rev. 12:11).[65] Given the location of the martyrs *under the altar*, *souls* may be intended to convey *life*. In the same way that the "life (נֶפֶשׁ [*nph*ᵉ*sh*]) of the flesh is in the blood" (Lev. 17:11) and the blood was poured beneath the altar (Ex. 29:12), the *souls* of the martyrs reside under the heavenly altar. Though their physical life was terminated, they themselves are still very much alive:

> Their slaying, then, is not the end of them. It is not the total interruption of their being in all respects. It makes them invisible to men in the flesh, in the natural state; but it does not hinder their living on as souls, or their being visible to heavenly eyes, or to the eyes of John in his supernatural and prophetic exaltation. The holy Apocalyptist tells us that he *"saw"* them, although they "had been slain;" and heard them speaking with loud voices, though their material tongues had been burnt to ashes, and their corporeal organs of speech had been stiffened in death. It is altogether a wrong interpretation of the Scriptures which represents the dead in a state of non-existence, unconsciousness, or oblivion.[66]

who had been slain for the word of God

It is difficult to establish exactly when these saints were martyred. Some argue that they were martyred *prior* to the opening of the fifth seal, during the preceding four seals.

> A. T. Robertson, who has been acclaimed as America's premier Greek authority of the 20th century, indicates that the verb form translated "were slain" in Revelation 6:9 represents action that was completed before the action of the main verb "saw" . . . The fact that John did not see believers being

> slain, but instead saw the disembodied souls of saints who had been slain before he saw them, forces the conclusion that when Christ breaks the fifth seal, it will not cause the martyrdom of those saints . . . The martyred saints of the fifth seal will be living and dying during the first four seals.[67]

But it is difficult to avoid the emphasis a plain reading of the verse puts upon the timing of the fifth seal and the revelation of the martyrs. It seems clear that with the opening of the fifth seal God intends us to realize that we have gone past the beginning of sorrows into the actual Tribulation period. See *Trouble Ahead*[2.13.1].

By now, a heightened religious persecution attends the events upon the earth for these saints did not perish due to beasts, famine, pestilence, or war—but were *slain for the word of God* . Their testimony was seen as a dangerous and undesirable witness against the false religious system riding the beast (Rev. 17:6). At this point in the sequence of events, the *Antichrist*[5.2.3] has not yet become the center of all worship:

> [Some assume] that the fifth seal saints are martyred because they would not bow to the Antichrist. But, again, there is nothing in the context of the fifth seal to indicate this. To be sure, they are martyred for their faith. But it does not say that it was specifically for refusing to bow down to the Antichrist. The self-proclamation of deity by the Antichrist takes place at the time of the Abomination of Desolation (Mtt. 24:15; 2Th. 2:4) which, . . . happens at the midpoint of the seven years. In Revelation, that midpoint begins with chapter eleven, when the *Temple*[5.2.73] is taken over by Gentiles for 42 months (the second three and one-half years). Then Antichrist proceeds to remove all opposition by killing the two witnesses (Rev. 11) and persecuting the Jews (Rev. 12). He then proclaims himself to be God and sets up his image (Rev. 13). Only those saints in and subsequent to chapter thirteen are being killed for refusing to accept the Antichrist.[68]

> The revelation of the fifth seal makes clear that in the future time of tribulation it will be most difficult to declare one's faith in the Lord Jesus. It may very well be that the majority of those who trust Christ as Saviour in that day will be put to death. This is confirmed in Revelation 7 where another picture of the martyred dead of the tribulation is given, and in Revelation 13 where death is inflicted on all who will not worship the beast. Martyrdom in those days will be as common as it is uncommon today.[69]

the testimony which they held

Like the first martyr of the Church (Stephen, Acts 7:59) and Antipas of the church at Pergamos (Rev. 2:13) they will *hold* a consistent testimony up to and *beyond* the point of death (Rev. 12:11). They are faithful sheep whose blood is spilled for God's sake. "Yet for Your sake we are killed all day long; we are accounted as sheep for the slaughter" (Ps 44:22 cf. Rom. 8:36). Their death is as much a part of their testimony as their life. Those who "die in the Lord" have works which follow them (Rev. 14:13).

3.6.10 - Revelation 6:10

How long, O Lord

Lord is δεσπότης [*despotēs*] which emphasizes His ownership of the saints, as a master has slaves,[70] or a ruler over a household (Tit. 2:9).[71] Let us always keep in mind that He can do *whatever* He desires with His sheep. In this case, He allows their slaughter as a testimony to their faith and the evil unfolding below which will finally be judged.

judge and avenge

When God finally tramples the winepress of His wrath it is described as "the day of vengeance," for "the year of My redeemed has come" (Isa. 63:3-4). This then, is the *judgment* associated with the fifth seal—that petition of God by the martyred saints seals the fate of those who put them to death. One of the duties of the *Goel* , the nearest of kin, was to avenge the blood of the family member who had been murdered (Num. 35:19-21; Deu. 19:6; Jos. 20:3). See commentary on *Revelation 5:9*[3.5.9].

dwell on the earth

Their persecutors appear to be currently living on the earth which argues for understanding these as recent martyrs from the times described by the seals. This phrase denotes the *earth dwellers*[5.2.18] and has significance far beyond merely designating people who happen to be living upon the earth. In this book, it takes on a soteriological and eschatological sense as a *technical phrase*[5.2.72] describing those in the end times who refuse salvation, persecute the saints, and continue to blaspheme God in the midst of judgment (Rev. 3:10; 6:10; 11:10; 12:12; 13:8, 12, 14; 14:6; 17:8).[72] These are the ones being tested by this time of trial from God (Rev. 3:10) and rejoice when God's two witnesses are killed (Rev. 11:10). It is they who are subject to the wrath of both God and the devil (Rev. 12:12) and who will be deceived into worshiping the beast (Rev. 13:12, 14). Even though an angel preaches the everlasting gospel to each one (Rev. 14:6), they continue in their rejection of God to the end. Therefore, their names are not written in the *Book of Life*[5.2.10] (Rev. 17:8). See *Book of Life*[4.4].

3.6.11 - Revelation 6:11

white robe

These are the white robes promised to the overcomers, for their nakedness is clothed (Rev. 12:11 cf. Rev. 3:5, 18). This is the righteousness of God which is obtained, not by works, but by *faith* (Rom. 3:5, 21-26; 10:3; 2Cor. 5:21; Php. 3:9; Jas. 1:20). See commentary on *Revelation 3:5*[3.3.5].

a little while longer

Some see the announcement of the angel that "there should be delay no longer" as the terminus of this period (Rev. 10:6). But the context of the angel's proclamation here concerns the completion of "the mystery of God . . . as He declared to His servants the prophets" (Rev. 10:7). Perhaps the two time periods coincide in that martyrdom continues until the time of the final victory (Rev. 19).

until . . . fellow servants and their brethren . . . would be killed

Their *fellow servants and their brethren* denotes a single category. "Figure of speech Hendiadys of Nouns. 'Fellow servants and brethren' denote by this figure not two separate classes of persons, but one class, their fellow servants who were their brethren."[73]

Here again a most difficult reality presents itself. God Who has the power to step in and end this holocaust at any moment instead *chooses* to allow it to play out in all its gruesome detail. Although we will never fully apprehend His divine patience, we know that it is explained, in part, by His great mercy toward those who have not yet turned, the glorious testimony being accrued by the martyred saints, and the filling up of the cup of injustice of the perpetrators. If He were to move immediately in vengeance at the time of their request, then some would be eternally lost that are yet to become their *brethren.*

> This section of Scripture is the first intimation that the reign of *Antichrist*[5.2.3] is to witness the greatest revival that the world has ever seen. More millions will be saved under the preaching of God's witnesses in these seven years than in many times that period in this present age.[74]

Their request has much in common with the prayers of the saints in the bowls in Revelation 5:8 and is recorded by the Psalmist, "O Lord God, to whom vengeance belongs - O God, to whom vengeance belongs, shine forth! Rise up, O Judge of the earth; render punishment to the proud. Lord, how long will the wicked, How long will the wicked triumph?" (Ps. 94:1-3).

The "golden age" to be ushered in by the preaching of the gospel as all the world turns to Christ is an unscriptural myth. A golden age will come, but not by worldwide response to the gospel:

> Surely this ought to be sufficient to convince all Christians today that the gospel is not intended to cover the world, or to bring in universal peace and blessing. This *dispensation*[5.2.15] of grace (rejected) is to be followed by a dispensation of judgment. Not until after that shall Jerusalem be the centre of God's presence and government.[75]

> The Gospel, as now preached, is not, and in the present order of things never will be, triumphant. This is demonstrated in the seven Epistles, and is the common teaching of the Scriptures on the subject. A leading feature in its entire history is, that it is mostly rejected. It is universally preached "as a witness to all nations," but nations, as such, with all their patronage, have never received it, and have ever been the slayers of its witnesses.[76]

killed as they were

They are probably being slain initially at the hand of the harlot who is "drunk with the blood of the saints and with the blood of the martyrs of Jesus" (Rev. 17:6).[77] She rides the beast who probably does the actual execution at her behest. Once she is destroyed (Rev. 17:16-17), then the beast himself will carry out their martyrdom. Many will be beheaded (Rev. 20:4).

3.6.12 - Revelation 6:12

sixth seal

"It would be difficult to paint any scene more moving or more terrible than that described at the opening of the sixth seal."[78] Up to now, the effects of the first five seals, although unprecedented in their global impact, could still be explained away as an intensification of what history already records: conflict, war, death, famine, disease, and martyrdom. With the opening of the sixth seal, all such explanations vanish for the signs which attend this seal are unmistakable in their uniqueness and scope.

> The magnitude of the earthquake and cosmic disturbances that will occur when Christ breaks the sixth seal (Rev. 6:12-14) forces the conclusion that this will be an awesome expression of the wrath of God, not the work of unregenerate mankind.[79]

When the *sixth seal* is opened, there are unmistakable global signs of astronomical proportions, but the Lamb has yet to ride forth on His horse (Rev. 19:11)—He is still in heaven loosing seals. How can His riding forth to destroy the armies of the earth be *tonight* if none of these unmistakable signs have transpired? Yet Scripture teaches His coming is *imminent*[4.8]. The answer to this dilemma, as we've seen, is in recognizing that signs precede His final arrival in judgment, but not His coming as a bridegroom for His bride—a separate coming which precedes these events. See *Rapture*[4.14].

By the time of the sixth seal, the *Day of the Lord*[5.2.14] must be already underway. Having already come without warning, *like a thief in the night*, it is now made unmistakable to the *earth dwellers*[5.2.18] in the cosmic signs which attend this seal:

> Paul declared that the broad Day of the Lord will come like a thief in the night—suddenly, unexpectedly, when the victims are unprepared [1Th. 5:2]. A thief depends upon the element of surprise for success. He does not give his intended victims a forewarning of his coming. Paul's point—the unsaved will be given no forewarning of the coming of the broad Day of the Lord—rules out any of the seals of Revelation as being forewarnings of the beginning of the broad Day. For example, it rules out the sixth seal (Rev. 6:12-14) which will cause great cosmic disturbances and a major earthquake causing the people of the world to flee to the mountains in terror (Rev. 6:15-17). . . . if the disturbances of the sixth seal were a precursor to the Day of the Lord, the unsaved thereby would be given a graphic forewarning of its coming and will not be caught by surprise when it comes. Thus, the Day of the Lord would not come unexpectedly like a thief in the night.[80]

a great earthquake

The uniquely intense earthquakes which attend the judgments of the Tribulation period provide tangible evidence of God's hand in the events which transpire (Rev. 6:12; 8:5; 11:13; 16:18 cf. Mtt. 27:54). During the Tribulation, even though men understand the source of the earthquakes, most fail to repent (Rev. 6:16). A rare exception is the case of the great earthquake in Jerusalem, where those who avoid death "gave glory to the God of heaven" (Rev. 11:13).

Jesus said great earthquakes would be one of the signs of "the beginning of sorrows" (Mtt. 24:7-8). The *OT*[5.2.51] prophets also predicted a time where God would intensely shake the earth.[81] Haggai revealed that global earthquakes and the overthrow of the Gentile kingdoms would precede the return of God's glory to His (millennial) *Temple*[5.2.73]:[82]

> For thus says the Lord of hosts: 'Once more (it is a little while) I will shake heaven and earth, the sea and dry land; and I will shake all nations, and they shall come to the Desire of All Nations, and I will fill this temple with glory,' says the Lord of hosts. . . . I will overthrow the throne of kingdoms; I will destroy the strength of the Gentile kingdoms. I will overthrow the chariots And those who ride in them; the horses and their riders shall come down, every one by the sword of his brother. 'In that day,' says the Lord of hosts, 'I will take you, Zerubbabel My servant, the son of Shealtiel,' says the Lord, 'and will make you like a signet *ring*; for I have chosen you,' says the Lord of hosts. (Hag 2:6-7, 22-23)

Joel saw earthquakes associated with the mighty judgments of God poured out in the Day of the Lord, judgments which were intended to cause people to turn to God.

> The earth quakes before them, the heavens tremble; the sun and moon grow dark, and the stars diminish their brightness. The LORD gives voice before His army, for His camp is very great; for strong *is the One* who executes His word. For the day of the LORD *is* great and very terrible; who can endure it? "Now, therefore," says the LORD, "Turn to Me with all your heart, with fasting, with weeping, and with mourning." (Joel 2:10-12)

The *earthquake* affects more than just the face of the earth. Σεισμὸς [*Seismos*] means "shaking; of a storm on the sea, with waves caused by high winds [Mtt. 8:24]."[83] In the *Septuagint*[5.2.65], it is used in Joel 2:10 to describe the heavens trembling.[84] This catastrophic event extends beyond the geography of the earth to effect the cosmic realm.

the sun became black as sackcloth of hair

Jesus said that cosmic signs would be associated with the time of the end (Mtt. 24:29; Mark 13:24-25; Luke 21:11). From other considerations, we understand that the signs associated with this sixth seal are not the only cosmic signs of this time period.[85]

> The Isaiah 13:9-10 and Joel 3:14-15 passages [concerning cosmic disturbances] clearly take place *within* the Day of the Lord, . . . Joel 2:30-31 describes cosmic disturbances *before* the Day of the Lord. In the prophetic scheme of things, there are several cosmic disturbances.[86]

> There are reasons for concluding that the cosmic disturbances related to the beginning of the Joel 3 Day of the Lord and the Second Coming of Christ immediately after the Great Tribulation are not the same as those of the sixth seal. First, the cosmic disturbances of Joel 3 will occur when the armies of the nations have gathered for war in Israel. Those armies will not begin to gather for war until the sixth bowl has been poured out (Rev. 16:12-16), long after the sixth seal—one seal, seven trumpets, and five bowls after the cosmic disturbances of the sixth seal. . . . other cosmic disturbances will occur after those of the sixth seal. A third of the sun, moon, and stars will be darkened by the fourth trumpet (Rev. 8:12); the sun will be darkened by smoke from the abyss at the fifth trumpet (Rev. 9:1-2); the sun will scorch people on the earth with fire and fierce heat when the fourth bowl is poured out (Rev. 16:8-9). . . . when the cosmic disturbances of the sixth seal take place, kings, military men, and all other classes of people will run to the caves and rocks of the mountains to hide. . . . By contrast, when the cosmic disturbances immediately before the Joel 3 Day of the Lord occur after the sixth bowl, the kings and military men will not run and hide. Rather, they will remain assembled together in battle array to boldly attempt war against God, His Messiah, and the holy angels (Ps. 2:1-3; Joel 3:9-16; Zec. 12:2-9; 14:1-6, 12-14).[87]

The *sun* and *moon* were created for "signs" (Gen. 1:14).[88] They now provide indication that the events associated with this seal cannot be explained by natural phenomena—but result from the One Who controls the universe!

The darkening of the sun may be from the perspective of viewers on the earth—due to material ejected into the upper atmosphere by the earthquake or the impact of asteroids in the next verse. Although the sun is darkened, the moon continues to reflect light (as if the path light follows between the sun and moon is only minimally affected). In the fifth trumpet judgment, it is smoke which darkens the sun (Rev. 9:2).

Eventually, like the earth, the sun and moon are judged to show those who dwell on the earth Who the true source of light is—the Lord Himself. If the trend in our own day is any indication, worship of the heavenly bodies will still be prevalent at that time and so God interferes with that which man has idolized (Zep. 1:5).[89] As always, the message is to turn from *dead* idols to serve the *living* God:

> The sun shall no longer be your light by day, nor for brightness shall the moon give light to you; but the Lord will be to you an everlasting light, and your God your glory. Your sun shall no longer go down, nor shall your moon withdraw itself; for the Lord will be your everlasting light, and the days of your mourning shall be ended. (Isa. 60:19-20)

the moon became like blood

ἡ σελήνη ὅλη [*hē selēnē holē*], the *entire moon* in all its fullness. John uses simile to describe the effects upon the moon. The entire moon takes on a reddish appearance, as when atmospheric dust darkens or moisture refracts its light. The red appearance conveys the idea of judgment.

3.6.13 - Revelation 6:13

stars of heaven fell to the earth

Stars is ἀστέρες [*asteres*] from which we get the word *asteroid.* The word is also used of the supernatural manifestation which led the magi to the babe (Mtt. 2:2), Christ who is the "morning star" (Rev. 2:27; 22:16), angels (Rev. 1:16; 2:1; 3:1; 9:1), and astronomical objects (Mtt. 24:29; Mark 13:25; 1Cor. 15:41; Rev. 6:3; Rev. 8:10). Here and in Revelation 8:10 *stars* are said to fall to the earth. It seems best to understand these as asteroids or meteors for even the smallest sun would consume the entire planet should it ever fall to earth.[90]

> The stars proper are certainly still found in their places after the fulfilment of this vision. (See Rev. 8:12.) And remembering that the Scriptures often speak in the common language of men, without reference to the distinctions of science, and that even science itself still popularly speaks of "falling stars," when it means simply meteoric phenomena, it appears but reasonable that we should understand the apostle to be speaking of something of the same sort.[91]

> The most likely identification of these particular falling stars is that of a great swarm of asteroids that pummel the earth. Such an event has never occurred in historic times, but scientists have long speculated about the probability of either past or future earth catastrophes caused by encountering a swarm of asteroids.[92]

"The sixth seal presents a disturbance of nature so vast that we naturally seek to explain it as *hyperbole*[5.2.27]," [93] but this is not merely hyperbolic language.[94] (See *Interpreting Symbols*[2.7].) These are the very signs that Jesus predicted would attend the period preceding His return:

> Immediately after the tribulation of those days the sun will be darkened, and the moon will not give its light; the stars will fall from heaven, and the powers of the heavens will be shaken. **Then the sign of the Son of Man will appear** in heaven, and then all the tribes of the earth will mourn, and they will see the Son of Man coming on the clouds of heaven with power and great glory. (Mtt. 24:29-30 cf. Mark 13:24-25; Luke 23:44-45; Rev. 1:7) [emphasis added]

Isaiah had been shown this fearsome time:

> Behold, the day of the LORD comes, cruel, with both wrath and fierce anger, to lay the land desolate; and He will destroy its sinners from it. For the stars of heaven and their constellations Will not give their light; the sun will be darkened in its going forth, and the moon will not cause its light to shine. I will punish the world for *its* evil, and the wicked for their iniquity; I will halt the arrogance of the proud, and will lay low the haughtiness of the terrible. I will make a mortal more rare than fine gold, a man more than the golden wedge of Ophir. Therefore **I will shake the heavens**, and the earth will move out of her place, in the wrath of the LORD of hosts and in the day of His fierce anger. (Isa. 13:9-13) [emphasis added]

In these judgments, God is shattering the puny pillars of support which men trust in when they turn away from Him.

> See that you do not refuse Him who speaks. For if they did not escape who refused Him who spoke on earth, much more *shall we not escape* if we turn away from Him who *speaks* from heaven, whose voice then shook the earth; but now He has promised, saying, "Yet once more I shake not only the earth, but also heaven." Now this, "Yet once more," indicates the **removal of those things that are being shaken, as of things that are made, that the things which cannot be shaken may remain**. Therefore, since we are receiving a kingdom which cannot be shaken, let us have grace, by which we may serve God acceptably with reverence and godly fear. (Heb. 12:25-28) [emphasis added]

The increasingly severe judgments which fall during this period are specifically designed to remove hope in all else but God so that all creatures recognize their *utter dependence* upon the Creator. Hope placed anywhere else is idolatry. God now begins a systematic destruction of the natural order (sun, moon, stars, earth) which men have often deferred to in place of the Creator.[95] In its failure to recognize the Creator, environmentalism eventually fails in its effort to preserve the creation.

3.6.14 - Revelation 6:14

the sky receded

receded is ἀπεχωρίσθη [*apechōristhē*]. The term is used to describe the *parting* of Paul and Silas from Barnabas and Mark (Acts 15:39). The sky *receded* causing it to be "split apart" (NASB). At the appearance of the Judge at the Great White Throne Judgment, "the earth and heaven fled away and there was found no place for them" (Rev. 20:11). The psalmist predicted a time when the heavens would "grow old like a garment; like a cloak You will change them" (Ps. 102:25).

> Come near, you nations, to hear; and heed, you people! Let the earth hear, and all that is in it, the world and all things that come forth from it. For the indignation of the LORD *is* against all nations, and *His* fury against all their armies; He has utterly destroyed them, He has given them over to the slaughter. Also their slain shall be thrown out; their stench shall rise from their corpses, and the mountains shall be melted with their blood. All the host of heaven shall be dissolved, and **the heavens shall be rolled up like a scroll**; all their host shall fall down as the leaf falls from the vine, and as *fruit* falling from a fig tree. (Isa. 34:1-4) [emphasis added]

Passages such as this tempt the interpreter to jettison the literal approach and "go symbolic."[96] Yet events which are so far removed from our daily experience as to be completely foreign need not be incredible when initiated by the hand of the Almighty. It is as if we were to try to explain the design of a nuclear plant to the ant! The construction of the starry realm is far beyond our grasp and the description which meets us here is at best an approximation which only hints at the full dimensions of what transpires. Clearly, it is an enormous and terrifying sight which could not even begin to be explained by modern physics. "This is the human perception of the magnitude of the disturbance, but is not the ultimate passage of the heavens, which does not come until Rev. 20:11; . . . The impression of all these heavenly phenomena is that the universe is coming apart."[97]

In response to these events, men recognize the *wrath of the Lamb* (Rev. 6:16). Mills offers an unusual suggestion concerning the purpose for the splitting of the sky:

> In order to ensure that there is no misunderstanding on the source of these disasters, God will open the heavens for an instant, and the people on earth will be given a glimpse of God and the Lamb on their thrones (Rev. 6:16). Revelation 6:14 pictures an extended scroll suddenly being split; the two ends recoil, spring-like, around the end rod to which the scroll is attached. Suddenly, earth can peer into Heaven as Stephen did in Acts 7:56. Man sees Him who sits on the throne and the Lamb. Men will know they are experiencing the wrath of God, and this knowledge will be even more fearsome to them than the great natural catastrophes they will have endured.[98]

every mountain and island was moved out of its place

The seismic disturbances will be of such magnitude that the entire geography of the earth is permanently altered.[99] The extensive mapping of the earth, both by GPS and sonar, will eventually be for naught as in a moment every geophysical mapping database is rendered obsolete.[100] As great as this earthquake is, it is but a precursor to an even greater one associated with the seventh bowl at which "every island fled away and the mountains were not found" (Rev. 16:19). It would appear that the islands sink from sight and the mountains are leveled by God's final outpouring of wrath.

3.6.15 - Revelation 6:15

kings of the earth

These are the kings which fail to "kiss the Son, lest He be angry, and you perish in the way, when His wrath is kindled but a little" (Ps. 2:12). They are the "kings of earth who committed fornication and lived luxuriously" with Babylon, who were ruled by her, but will mourn her fall (Rev. 17:2, 18; 18:3, 9). They are the kings who "gather . . . to the battle of that great day of God Almighty" (Rev. 16:14; 19:19). Here, they are "gathered together *as* prisoners are gathered in the pit, and will be shut up in the prison" (Isa. 24:20).

the great men . . . the mighty men

μεγιστανες [*megistanes*], *the great ones* and ἰσχυροὶ [*ischyroi*], *strong ones*. These are men who do not occupy official positions of rulership or military command, but who nevertheless influence and control the affairs of men from behind the scenes: from board rooms, golf courses, and luxury yachts. They are the "captains of industry." As the globalization of our world continues, power will reside more and more in the hands of these leaders of multinational corporations.

commanders

χιλίαρχοι [*chiliarchoi*] from χιλιάς [*chilias*] *one thousand.* The leaders over a thousand troops.

Roughly equivalent to a major or colonel.[101]

every slave and every free man

Several verses indicate that even at the supposed "height" of humanism's achievements at the time of the end, slavery will not yet have been abolished worldwide (Rev. 13:16; 19:18). The emphasis is upon the comprehensive nature of the judgments. The magnitude of the disturbances coming upon the earth is such that *every man* is affected.

hide themselves in caves

Here is the classic record of man's response to his own sin—a vain attempt to hide from the omnipresent, omniscient, almighty God (Gen. 3:8; Rev. 6:16). In the irony of God, those who persecuted God's servants, who were "destitute, afflicted, tormented—of whom the world was not worthy," who "wandered in deserts and mountains, *in* dens and caves of the earth" (Heb. 11:38) now experience firsthand a similar affliction from the very hand of God.

3.6.16 - Revelation 6:16

fall on us

So intense is their fear of God's judgments that they temporarily seek even death—anything to flee from His manifest presence (Hos. 10:8; Luke 23:30; Rev. 9:6).

hide us from the face of Him

Attempting to hide from God illustrates how sin and fear warp the intellect, for it is impossible to hide from the Omnipresent One (Job 34:22). How different the motivation of the godly from the ungodly. Those with faith in Christ *desire* His presence and *seek* His face. (Ps. 17:15; Pr. 8:7; Isa. 45:19; Isa. 58:2; 65:1; Jer. 29:13; Amos 5:4). Those who reject God *fear* His presence and *flee* His face. This dichotomy is seen today in the reaction of people to the preaching of the gospel:

> For we are to God the fragrance of Christ among those who are being saved and among those who are perishing. To the one *we are* the aroma of death *leading* to death, and to the other the aroma of life *leading* to life. And who *is* sufficient for these things? (2Cor. 2:15-16)

At the scene of God's final judgment of the ungodly, there will be nowhere available to hide from His face, for heaven and earth will have fled away (Rev. 20:11). All things are naked in His sight![102]

who sits on the throne

See commentary on *Revelation 4:2*[3.4.2].

the wrath of the Lamb

Here we encounter a phrase of seeming contradiction. The *Lamb* who was silently led to the slaughter (Isa. 53:7) now metes out *wrath.* It is the *Lamb* which opens each of the seals bringing forth these judgments which are indicative of the *wrath* of God. See commentary on *Revelation 5:5*[3.5.5].

The wrath of God began earlier, when the Lamb arose from His seat to open the first seal. Now it is recognized for what it is. "It should be noted that the passage does not say that the wrath of God begins only with the sixth seal, but that only with the sixth seal do unbelievers recognize that it is the wrath of God."[103] Those on the earth are ignorant of the Scriptures. Yet even they recognize that the time of God's *wrath* has now come upon the earth (Rev. 11:18; 14:9-10, 19; 15:1, 7; 16:1, 19). See commentary on *Revelation 5:6*[3.5.6].

3.6.17 - Revelation 6:17

the great day of His wrath

The *great day* is *The Day of the Lord*[2.13.3], a unique time yet future when God will radically intervene in history to demonstrate in an irrefutable way Who He is.

> The primary Old Testament passages from which the images in the sixth seal are drawn prove that the great day must be the *Day of the Lord*[5.2.14] (Isa. 2:10-11, 19-21; 13:9-13; 34:4, 8; Eze. 32:7-8; Hos. 10:8; Joel 2:11, 30; Zep. 1:14; Mal. 4:5).[104]

> First, the expression the Day of the Lord refers to God's special intervention into world events to judge His enemies, accomplish His purpose for history, and thereby demonstrate who He is—the sovereign God of the universe (Isa. 2:10-22; Eze. 13:5, 9, 14, 21, 23; Eze. 30:3, 8, 19, 25-26). Second, several Days of the Lord already have occurred in which God demonstrated His sovereign rule by raising up nations to execute His judgement on other nations. For example, He raised up Babylon to judge Egypt and its allies during the 500s B.C. (Jer. 46:2, 10; Eze. 30:3-6). However, the Bible also foretells a future Day of the Lord.[105]
>
> At the outset of the day of the Lord, human trials will be prolonged and comparable to a woman's labor before giving birth to a child (Isa. 13:8; 26:17-19; 66:7-9; Jer. 30:6-8; Mic. 4:9, 10; cf. Mtt. 24:8; 1Th. 5:3). This phase of growing human agony will be climaxed by the Messiah's personal return to earth to terminate the period of turmoil through direct judgment.[106]

The great day which has been on the horizon for thousands of years has finally arrived. Men will experience unparalleled fear and conditions that have never before prevailed upon the earth:

> Wail, for the day of the LORD *is* at hand! It will come as destruction from the Almighty. Therefore all hands will be limp, every man's heart will melt, and they will be afraid. Pangs and sorrows will take hold of *them*; they will be in pain as a woman in childbirth; they will be amazed at one another; their faces *will be like* flames. Behold, the day of the LORD comes, cruel, with both wrath and fierce anger, to lay the land desolate; and He will destroy its sinners from it. (Isa. 13:6-9)

The proud technologies of man, and infrastructure upon which it depends, will quickly collapse in the midst of this time of divine retribution. Death will be so common that burial will be uncommon as the flesh of men is treated as so much garbage:

> The **great day** of the LORD *is* near; *It is* near and hastens quickly. The noise of the day of the LORD is bitter; there the mighty men shall cry out. That day *is* a day of wrath, a day of trouble and distress, a day of devastation and desolation, a day of darkness and gloominess, a day of clouds and thick darkness, a day of trumpet and alarm against the fortified cities and against the high towers. "I will bring distress upon men, and they shall walk like blind men, because they have sinned against the LORD; their blood shall be poured out like dust, and their flesh like refuse." (Zep 1:14-17) [emphasis added]
>
> "For behold, the day is coming, burning like an oven, and all the proud, yes, all who do wickedly will be stubble. And the day which is coming shall burn them up," says the LORD of hosts, "That will leave them neither root nor branch." (Mal 4:1-2)

Not only will God pour forth his wrath upon the Gentile nations, but the Jewish nation will also undergo a time of unparalleled trouble designed to purge out the unbelieving rebels and turn the remainder back to God. In the midst of this intense judgment, God has promised that a believing remnant will survive (see *Jacob's Trouble and the Great Tribulation*[2.13.4]):

> Now these *are* the words that the LORD spoke concerning Israel and Judah. "For thus says the LORD: 'We have heard a voice of trembling, of fear, and not of peace. Ask now, and see, whether a man is ever in labor with child? So why do I see every man *with* his hands on his loins like a woman in labor, and all faces turned pale? Alas! **For that day *is* great**, so that none *is* like it; and it *is* the time of Jacob's trouble, but he shall be saved out of it." (Jer. 30:4-7) [emphasis added]

Jesus also spoke of this fearful time:

> And there will be signs in the sun, in the moon, and in the stars; and on the earth distress of nations, with perplexity, the sea and the waves roaring; men's hearts failing them from fear and the expectation of those things which are coming on the earth, for the powers of heaven will be shaken. (Luke 21:25-26)

This is that *great day* for which the angels who did not keep their proper domain are reserved for judgment—they will be *used in judgment* against men (Rev. 9). See *The Day of the Lord*[2.13.3], *Jacob's Trouble and the Great Tribulation*[2.13.4].

The *wrath* is said to be *of the Lamb* (Rev. 6:16). This is extremely significant because those who are covered by the blood of the Lamb prior to this day (1Pe. 1:17-19) are exempted from experiencing His wrath—they are His bride (Luke 21:36; Rom. 5:9; 1Th. 5:9; Rev. 3:10). See commentary on *Revelation 3:10*[3.3.10]. See *Rapture*[4.14].

has come

ἦλθεν [*ēlthen*], aorist tense which normally denotes past time. The day *has already come* in the opening of the sixth seal. God's wrath is being poured out *prior* to the seventh seal (which initiates the seven trumpet judgments). This contradicts the pre-wrath *rapture*[5.2.62] view which holds that the seals represent "**Man's wrath** through *Antichrist*[5.2.3]" [emphasis added][107]. While it is true that the aorist tense *can* be used to describe a future event (*proleptic*),[108] it is more often used of actions which have already transpired.[109] Advocates of the pre-wrath rapture view argue that the pronouncement associated with the sixth seal is *anticipatory* of the wrath of God, and not in *reaction* to it.[110] Since the aorist can represent events either in the past or future, the form of the verb itself (aorist) cannot settle the matter. Instead, the *context* must indicate which meaning is in view. The use of this same word within the larger context of the book of Revelation argues for understanding *has come* as denoting a past or present event which has just arrived.

Mention of this specific aorist form rendered *has come* (ἦλθεν [*ēlthen*]) in the book of Revelation, include the following:

1. "Then *He came* and took the scroll" (Rev. 5:7).
2. "For the great day of His wrath *has come*" (Rev. 6:17).
3. "Another angel, having a golden censer, *came* and stood at the altar." (Rev. 8:3).
4. "The nations were angry, and Your wrath *has come*" (Rev. 11:18).
5. "Fear God and give glory to Him, for the hour of His judgment *has come*" (Rev. 14:7).
6. "Thrust in Your sickle and reap, for the time *has come* for You to reap" (Rev. 14:15).
7. "Then one of the seven angels who had the seven bowls *came*" (Rev. 17:1).
8. "Five have fallen, one is, and the other has not yet *come*" (Rev. 17:10). (It is important in this instance to observe that ἦλθεν [*ēlthen*] merely denotes *come*. The future aspect of the statement, *not yet*, comes from another word (οὔπω [*oupō*].)
9. "That great city Babylon, that mighty city! For in one hour your judgment *has come*" (Rev. 18:10).
10. "Rejoice and give Him glory, for the marriage of the Lamb *has come*" (Rev. 19:7).
11. "One of the seven angels who had the seven bowls filled with the seven last plagues *came* to me" (Rev. 21:9).

In each of these cases, the verb describes something in the past, in the present, or in the *immediate future*—having "just now" come. "The aorist may be used for stating a present reality with the certitude of a past event. This idiom is a device for emphasis. It is commonly used of a state which has just been realized, or a result which has just been accomplished, or is on the point of being accomplished. (John 13:31; Mtt. 3:17; 1Cor. 4:18)."[111] In none of its appearances in Revelation is it rendered by the translators as a true future tense (e.g., *shall come, will come, is coming*).

The pre-wrath rapture view requires its use here to be anticipatory over a period—spanning the events of the next chapter where the 144,000 are sealed and a multitude of martyrs are revealed—reaching until the seventh seal is loosed (Rev. 8:1). Within the larger context of the book of Revelation this verb form does not denote what pre-wrath rapture proponents require. The most that can be said is that in some cases it describes an event which is "just now" happening, on the boundary between the present and the future (e.g., the impending destruction of Babylon in Rev. 18:10, the arrival of the marriage of the Lamb in Rev. 19:7).

> The only time an aorist indicative speaks of something future or something about to happen, however, is if it is a dramatic aorist (H. E. Dana and Julius R. Mantey, *A Manual Grammar of the Greek New Testament* [New York: Macmillan, 1927], p. 198), a futuristic aorist (BDF, par. 333 [2]), or a proleptic aorist (Nigel Turner, *Syntax*, vol. 3 of *A Grammar of New Testament Greek* [Edinburgh: T. & T. Clark, 1963], p. 74). Some contextual feature must be present to indicate clearly these exceptional usages. No such feature exists in the context of the sixth seal, so these special uses are not options here. . . . The verb in Rev. 6:17 must be a constantative aorist looking back in time to the point in the past when the great day of wrath arrived.[112]

When we examine the immediate context of this passage—the seismic and astronomical disturbances —we find that Isaiah elsewhere attributes these phenomena as being *part of* the Day of the Lord:

> **Enter into the rock, and hide in the dust**, from the terror of the LORD and the glory of His majesty. The lofty looks of man shall be humbled, the haughtiness of men shall be bowed down, and the LORD alone shall be exalted in that day. For the **day of the LORD of hosts** *Shall come* upon everything proud and lofty, upon everything lifted up-And it shall be brought low—upon all the cedars of Lebanon *that are* high and lifted up, and upon all the oaks of Bashan; upon all the high mountains, and upon all the hills *that are* lifted up; upon every high tower, and upon every fortified wall; upon all the ships of Tarshish, and upon all the beautiful sloops. The loftiness of man shall be bowed down, and the haughtiness of men shall be brought low; the LORD alone will be exalted **in that day**, but the idols He shall utterly abolish. **They shall go into the holes of the rocks, and into the caves of the earth, from the terror of the LORD and the glory of His majesty, when He arises to shake the earth mightily. In that day** a man will cast away his idols of silver and his idols of gold, which they made, *each* for himself to worship, to the moles and bats, **To go into the clefts of the rocks, and into the crags of the rugged rocks, from the terror of the LORD and the glory of His majesty, when He arises to shake the earth mightily.** (Isa. 2:10-21) [emphasis added]

Isaiah tells us that *in that day*, not before the day, men will hide in holes of the rocks and caves.[113] They are hiding *from the terror of the LORD when He arises to shake the earth mightily.* Their hiding is not *anticipatory*, but *reactionary*. In other words, the events of the sixth seal are part of the Day of the Lord.

> The reaction of the unbelieving world to the terrors unleashed by the sixth seal will not be one of repentance (cf. Rev. 9:21; 16:11), but of mindless panic. They will finally acknowledge what believers have been saying all along, that **the disasters they have experienced are God's judgment**. [emphasis added][114]

In what way could the events of the sixth seal be said to be "**Man's** wrath" [emphasis added][115] as pre-wrath rapture advocates hold? These events occur "when **He** opened the sixth seal" [emphasis added] (Rev. 6:12). Who is *He*? The *Lamb* of Revelation 6:1! It is *Jesus Christ* who directly initiates these judgments. And how could astronomical and seismic manifestations such as these reflect the wrath of puny *men*? For *what man could cause* asteroids to fall to the earth and the sky to recede as a scroll (Rev. 6:13-14)?

> Isaiah 2:10-22 foretold the future time when people, including the proud and lofty, will flee in terror to hide in the holes of the rocks and caves of the earth "for the fear of the LORD, and for the glory of his majesty, when he ariseth to shake terribly the earth" (Isa. 2:11). . . . note that Isaiah indicated he was writing about the Day of the Lord, from which we can conclude that the Day of the Lord . . . will include the sixth seal, and that seal will involve Day of the Lord wrath.[116]

See *When Does the Day of the Lord Dawn?*[2.13.3.1]

who is able to stand

τίς δύναται σταθῆναι [*tis dynatai stathēnai*]. *Able* is present tense. The phrase could be rendered: *who is presently able to stand.* Their exclamation does not concern a *potential* future situation, as if the wrath were to begin *after* the seventh seal. They are *presently* experiencing the wrath and recognize it by the events which have just transpired which have driven them to hide in caves and in the rocks. *When the sky splits and rolls up like a scroll, mountains and islands move out of their place, and asteroids fall to earth, there is little doubt concerning the power involved—it is the judgment of God!* These events are not a precursor to God's wrath, they are the *result* of His wrath.

As Joel said, "For the day of the Lord is great and very terrible; Who can endure it?" (Joel 2:11b). It will be a time of unprecedented bloodshed and death, However, in the midst of these things, there *are some* who are able to stand because they are afforded special protection from God. The 144,000 from the twelve tribes of Israel, Jewish believers in Messiah Jesus, are protected so that their gospel mission (Rev. 7:9) can be accomplished during this time of unprecedented upheaval (Rev. 7:3-8).

As for the *earth dwellers*[5.2.18], they will remain in denial:

> But then, amazingly, even this would pass. After these few terrifying days, the stars stopped falling and the terrible shakings ceased. The survivors emerged from their shelters and began again to rationalize their resistance to God. After all, these calamities could be explained scientifically, so perhaps they had been too quick to attribute them to God's wrath. They quickly set about rebuilding their damaged

> structures and became more resolute in their opposition to the gospel of Christ.[117]
>
> The book of Revelation discredits those who hold that God is so loving and kind that He will never judge people who have not received His Son. Though the modern mind is reluctant to accept the fact that God will judge the wicked, the Bible clearly teaches that He will. The Scriptures reveal a God of love as clearly as they reveal a God of wrath who will deal with those who spurn the grace proffered in the Lord Jesus Christ. The passage before us is a solemn word that there is inevitable judgment ahead for those who will not receive Christ by faith.[118]

Dear reader, is *your* citizenship in heaven? Or do you remain an earth dweller yet?

> Friends and brethren, what a mercy that day is not yet upon us! There is a Rock to which we still may fly and pray, with hope of security in its wide-open clefts. It is the Rock of Ages. There are mountains to which we may yet betake ourselves, and be forever safe from all the dread convulsions which await the world. They are the mountains of salvation in Christ Jesus. I believe I am addressing some who have betaken themselves to them. Brethren, "hold fast the profession of your faith without wavering; for He is faithful that promised." (Heb. 10:23.) But others are still lingering in the plains of Sodom, who need to take this warning to heart as they never yet have done. O ye travellers of the judgment, seek ye the Lord while He may be found, and call upon Him while He is near! And may God in His mercy hide us all from the condemnation that awaits an unbelieving world![119]

Amen!

Notes

1 Robert L. Thomas, *Revelation 1-7* (Chicago, IL: Moody Press, 1992), Rev. 6:1.

2 Thomas, *Revelation 1-7*, Rev. 6:1.

3 Alva J. McClain, *The Greatness Of The Kingdom* (Winona Lake, IN: BMH Books, 1959), 56.

4 Keith H. Essex, *"The Rapture and the Book of Revelation,"* in Richard L. Mayhue, ed., *The Master's Seminary Journal*, vol. 13 no. 1 (Sun Valley, CA: The Master's Seminary, Spring 2002), 230.

5 John MacArthur, *Revelation 1-11 : The MacArthur New Testament Commentary* (Chicago, IL: Moody Press, 1999), Rev. 6:1.

6 Albrecht Durer (1471 - 1528). Image courtesy of the *Connecticut College* (http://www.conncoll.edu/visual/Durer-prints/index.html) *Wetmore Print Collection* (http://www.conncoll.edu/visual/wetmore.html).

7 "Both passages involve similar descriptions to the approaching end."—Renald E. Showers, *The Pre-Wrath Rapture View* (Grand Rapids, MI: Kregel Publications, 2001), 11. "The beginning of birth pangs and the first four seals are the same and . . . take place during the first half of the 70th week."—Renald E. Showers, *Maranatha, Our Lord Come* (Bellmawr, NJ: The Friends of Israel Gospel Ministry, 1995), 16. "A comparison of Christ's description of the beginning of birth pangs in Matthew 24:5-7 with the first four seals of Revelation 6:1-8 indicates that the beginning of birth pangs and the first four seals are the same thing."—Showers, *Maranatha, Our Lord Come*, 25.

8 Showers, *Maranatha, Our Lord Come*, 63.

9 J. A. Seiss, *The Apocalypse: Lectures on the Book of Revelation* (Grand Rapids, MI: Zondervan Publishing House, 1966), 125.

10 As another example of *Anti-supernatural Bias*[2.5], consider Mounce's observation: "As usual, John modifies his sources [Zechariah] with great freedom. Apparently for Mounce, it is *John* who is determining the content of his vision!"—Robert H. Mounce, *The Book of Revelation* (Grand Rapids, MI: William B. Eerdmans Publishing Co., 1977), Rev. 6:2.

11 Thomas, *Revelation 1-7*, Rev. 6:2.

12 Fausset sees this rider as "Evidently Christ, whether in person, or by His angel, preparatory to His coming again, as appears from Rev. 19:11, 12."—A. R. Fausset, *"The Revelation of St. John the Divine,"* in Robert Jamieson, A. R. Fausset, and David Brown, *A Commentary, Critical and Explanatory, on the Old and New Testaments* (Oak Harbor, WA: Logos Research Systems, Inc., 1997, 1877), Rev. 6:2.

13 Alan F. Johnson, *Revelation: The Expositor's Bible Commentary* (Grand Rapids, MI: Zondervan Publishing House, 1966), Rev. 6:2.

[14] "How the Lamb who opens the seal can be the effect of the opening, and at the same time be the rider on a white horse, we cannot understand."—E. W. Bullinger, *Commentary On Revelation* (Grand Rapids, MI: Kregel Publications, 1984, 1935), Rev. 6:2.

[15] All four riders are representative personifications of forces. With this rider, there is also a correlation to an individual which the "spirit of antichrist" brings forth (1Jn. 4:3). "This rider, like the other three, is not an individual, but a personification of a growing movement or force that will be at work during this future period."—Thomas, *Revelation 1-7*, Rev. 6:2.

[16] "Rabbi Akiba proclaimed Bar Kokhba as Messiah in A.D. 132; the whole Jewish community of Crete followed a messiah named Moses in the fifth century; Abu Issa of Isfahan raised an army of 10,000 men; and European Jewry crowned Shabbetai Zvi messiah in the seventeenth century, although he later converted to Islam!"—Randall Price, *Jerusalem In Prophecy* (Eugene, OR: Harvest House Publishers, 1998), 192.

[17] Showers, *Maranatha, Our Lord Come*, 105-108.

[18] Jerome Smith, *The New Treasury of Scripture Knowledge* (Nashville, TN: Thomas Nelson Publishers, 1992), Rev. 6:2.

[19] Marvin Rosenthal, *The Pre-Wrath Rapture of the Church* (Nashville, TN: Thomas Nelson Publishers, 1990), 142.

[20] Bullinger, *Commentary On Revelation*, Rev. 6:17.

[21] Arthur Walkington Pink, *The Antichrist* (Oak Harbor, WA: Logos Research Systems, 1999, 1923), s.v. "The Career of the Antichrist."

[22] J. Dwight Pentecost, *"Daniel,"* in John F. Walvoord, and Roy B. Zuck, eds., *The Bible Knowledge Commentary* (Wheaton, IL: SP Publications, 1983), Dan. 8:23.

[23] MacArthur, *Revelation 1-11 : The MacArthur New Testament Commentary*, Rev. 6:2.

[24] Showers, *Maranatha, Our Lord Come*, 108-109.

[25] "The Greek language has two words meaning 'crown,' One is the word *diadem*, which is a king's crown. It is the crown of a sovereign and of a person who is royal by his nature and by his position—a king. This is the kind of crown that Jesus wears."—Arnold G. Fruchtenbaum, *The Footsteps of Messiah*, rev ed. (Tustin, CA: Ariel Ministries, 2003), 160. "That the figure is not Messiah is indicated by the fact that the crown here is a *stephanos* crown, the crown of an overcomer or victor. It is not the diadem crown, the crown of sovereignty and royalty, the type of crown Messiah will wear in chapter 19."—Fruchtenbaum, *The Footsteps of Messiah*, 206. "This rider wears the conqueror's crown (*stephanos*); Christ will have a different kind of crown—the crown of kings (*diadema*)."—Showers, *Maranatha, Our Lord Come*, 105. "This rider wears a *stephanos* , a crown won as a prize; in Rev. 19:12 Christ wears many *diademas*, royal crowns."—MacArthur, *Revelation 1-11 : The MacArthur New Testament Commentary*, Rev. 6:2.

[26] Walter Scott, *Exposition of The Revelation* (London, England: Pickering & Inglis, n.d.), 155.

[27] Pink, *The Antichrist*, s.v. "The Genius and Character of the Antichrist."

[28] Showers, *Maranatha, Our Lord Come*, 62.

[29] Monty S. Mills, *Revelations: An Exegetical Study of the Revelation to John* (Dallas, TX: 3E Ministries, 1987), Rev. 6:3.

[30] Timothy Friberg, Barbara Friberg, and Neva F. Miller, *Analytical Lexicon of the Greek New Testament* (Grand Rapids, MI: Baker Books, 2000), 340.

[31] Frederick William Danker, and Walter Bauer, *A Greek-English Lexicon of the New Testament and Other Early Christian Literature* (Chicago, IL: University of Chicago Press, 2000), 796.

[32] MacArthur, *Revelation 1-11 : The MacArthur New Testament Commentary*, Rev. 6:4.

[33] Danker, *A Greek-English Lexicon of the New Testament and Other Early Christian Literature*, 499.

[34] Donald Grey Barnhouse, *Revelation* (Grand Rapids, MI: Zondervan Publishing House, 1971), 127.

[35] Danker, *A Greek-English Lexicon of the New Testament and Other Early Christian Literature*, 752.

[36] Danker, *A Greek-English Lexicon of the New Testament and Other Early Christian Literature*, 179.

[37] Fausset, "*The Revelation of St. John the Divine*," Rev. 6:6.

38 Colin J. Hemer, *The Letters to the Seven Churches of Asia in Their Local Setting* (Grand Rapids, MI: William B. Eerdmans Publishing Company, 1989), 175.

39 Thomas, *Revelation 1-7*, 272.

40 Thomas, *Revelation 1-7*, Rev. 6:6.

41 Pink, *The Antichrist*, s.v. "Antichrist in the Apocalypse."

42 Smith, *The New Treasury of Scripture Knowledge*, Rev. 6:6.

43 Barnhouse, *Revelation*, 128.

44 "For while there is a famine of food, there will be an abundance of medicine, for the *oil and wine* are not hurt. These items were used for medicinal purposes."—Fruchtenbaum, *The Footsteps of Messiah*, 219.

45 Gordon Franz, *"Was 'Babylon' Destroyed when Jerusalem Fell in A.D. 70?,"* in Tim LaHaye, and Thomas Ice, eds., *The End Times Controversy* (Eugene, OR: Harvest House Publishers, 2003), 226-227.

46 Mounce, *The Book of Revelation*, 155.

47 Thomas, *Revelation 1-7*, Rev. 6:6.

48 Danker, *A Greek-English Lexicon of the New Testament and Other Early Christian Literature*, 882.

49 M. R. Vincent, *Vincent's Word Studies* (Escondido, CA: Ephesians Four Group, 2002), Rev. 6:8.

50 Thomas, *Revelation 1-7*, Rev. 6:8.

51 Thomas, *Revelation 1-7*, Rev. 6:8.

52 See the world population clock: [*http://www.census.gov/cgi-bin/ipc/popclockw*].

53 Danker, *A Greek-English Lexicon of the New Testament and Other Early Christian Literature*, 737.

54 "Metonymy of the Effect, the effect (death) put for the cause producing it (pestilence)."—Smith, *The New Treasury of Scripture Knowledge*, Rev. 6:8.

55 MacArthur, *Revelation 1-11 : The MacArthur New Testament Commentary*, Rev. 6:8.

56 "The context of Ezekiel 5:17 (Eze. 5:12-16) indicates that the famine, beasts, pestilence, and sword of that passage are expressions of God's wrath."—Showers, *Maranatha, Our Lord Come*, 115.

57 Fruchtenbaum, *The Footsteps of Messiah*, 219.

58 Albrecht Durer (1471 - 1528). Image courtesy of the *Connecticut College* (http://www.conncoll.edu/visual/Durer-prints/index.html) *Wetmore Print Collection* (http://www.conncoll.edu/visual/wetmore.html).

59 Seiss, *The Apocalypse: Lectures on the Book of Revelation*, 140.

60 Smith, *The New Treasury of Scripture Knowledge*, Rev. 6:11.

61 Danker, *A Greek-English Lexicon of the New Testament and Other Early Christian Literature*, 366.

62 Bullinger, *Commentary On Revelation*, Rev. 6:9.

63 Mills, *Revelations: An Exegetical Study of the Revelation to John*, Rev. 6:9.

64 "The description given in Revelation seems to fit the altar of incense better than the great altar of sacrifice which stood near the door of the *tabernacle*[5.2.69]. The altar in Revelation is connected with the prayers of the martyrs (Rev. 6:9), its fire is used to light the incense of the golden censer (Rev. 8:3, 5), and its location is 'before God,' which would accord much more closely with the place of the altar of incense that stood on the border between the Holy Place and the Holy of Holies, the inner shrine of the tabernacle."—Merrill C. Tenney, *Interpreting Revelation* (Peabody, MA: Hendrickson Publishers, 1957), 171.

65 "This Greek word occurs 105 times in the New Testament, and its uses and occurrences may be classified as follows: (1) Metonymy of the Cause, 'soul' put for 'life,' which is the effect of it. The natural life of the body, Mtt. 2:20; 6:25, 25; 10:39, 39; 16:25, 25; 20:28. Mark 3:4; 8:35; 10:45. Luke 6:9; 9:56; 12:22, 23; 14:26; 17:33a; John 10:11, 15, 17; 12:25a, 25b; 13:37, 38; 15:13; Acts 15:26; 20:10, 24; 27:10, 22; Rom. 11:3; 16:4; Php. 2:30; 1Jn. 3:16, 16; Rev. 8:9; 12:11. Rendered 'soul,' Mtt. 16:26, 26; Mark 8:36, 37; Luke 12:20; 1Th. 2:8. (2) The immaterial, invisible part of man: Mtt. 10:28; Acts 2:27, 31; 1Th. 5:23; Heb. 4:12. (3) The disembodied man (2Cor. 5:3, 4; 12:2): Rev. 6:9; 20:4. (4) The seat of personality: Luke 9:24, 24; Heb. 6:19;

10:39. (5) Metonymy of Cause. The seat of perception, feeling, desire: Mtt. 11:29; Luke 1:46; 2:35; Acts 14:2 (mind), 22; 15:24. (6) Metonymy of Cause. The seat of will and purpose: Mtt. 22:37; Mark 12:30, 33; Luke 10:27; Acts 4:32; Eph. 6:6; Php. 1:27; Col. 3:23; Heb. 12:3. (7) The seat of appetite: Rev. 18:14. (8) Metonymy of Cause, soul put for person. Synecdoche of the Part, an integral part of man (individually) is put for the whole person. Used of persons or individuals: Acts 2:41, 43; 3:23; 7:14; 27:37; Rom. 2:9; 13:1; Jas. 5:20; 1Pe. 3:20; 2Pe. 2:14; Rev. 18:13. (9) Synecdoche of the Part. The expression 'my soul,' 'his soul,' etc., becomes by Synecdoche the idiom for me, myself, himself, etc. Used to emphasize the personal pronoun (a) in the first person: Mtt. 12:18; 26:38; Mark 14:34; Luke 12:19, 19; John 10:24 (us); 12:27; 2Cor. 1:23; Heb. 10:38 (soul); (b) in the second person: 2Cor. 12:15; Heb. 13:17; Jas. 1:21; 1Pe. 1:9, 22; 2:25; (c) in the third person: 1Pe. 4:19; 2Pe. 2:8. (10) Synecdoche of the Part. 'Soul' (Gr. *psyche*) is also used of animals. An animate creature, human or other: 1Cor. 15:45; Rev. 16:3. (11) The 'inward man,' seat of the new life: Luke 21:19; 1Pe. 2:11; 3Jn. 2. Compare the classification of the corresponding Old Testament term *nephesh* at Gen. 2:7 (note)."—Smith, *The New Treasury of Scripture Knowledge*, Mtt. 2:20.

66 Seiss, *The Apocalypse: Lectures on the Book of Revelation*, 142.

67 Showers, *Maranatha, Our Lord Come*, 110, 119.

68 Arnold G. Fruchtenbaum, *A Review of the Pre-Wrath Rapture of the Church* (Tustin, CA: Ariel Ministries, n.d.), 43.

69 John F. Walvoord, *The Revelation of Jesus Christ* (Chicago, IL: Moody Press, 1966), Rev. 6:9.

70 Danker, *A Greek-English Lexicon of the New Testament and Other Early Christian Literature*, 176.

71 Friberg, *Analytical Lexicon of the Greek New Testament*, 107.

72 " 'Them that dwell on the earth' is a semi-technical designation for mankind in its hostility to God."—Mounce, *The Book of Revelation*, 159.

73 Smith, *The New Treasury of Scripture Knowledge*, Rev. 6:11.

74 Barnhouse, *Revelation*, 132.

75 Bullinger, *Commentary On Revelation*, Rev. 6:11.

76 Seiss, *The Apocalypse: Lectures on the Book of Revelation*, 126.

77 "As to who is persecuting these believers, this will be answered by Revelation 17: namely, Ecclesiastical Babylon."—Fruchtenbaum, *The Footsteps of Messiah*, 220.

78 Walvoord, *The Revelation of Jesus Christ*, Rev. 6:12.

79 Showers, *Maranatha, Our Lord Come*, 119.

80 Showers, *Maranatha, Our Lord Come*, 60.

81 McLean believes this earthquake to be correlated with the timing of the Abomination of Desolation: "If the time sequence of A (the Abomination of Desolation at the midpoint of the Seventieth Week of Daniel and the tribulation of the synoptics), equals B (at this time the people flee to the mountains and women are warned about impending dangers); and the time frame of B equals C (the people cry out for the mountains to fall on them); and the reference C equals D (the sixth seal of Revelation when the wrath of God and the Lamb initiate the great day of their wrath, and people cry for the mountains to fall on them), then A (the Abomination of Desolation at the midpoint of Daniel's Seventieth Week), equals or occurs at the [same] time as D (the time of the sixth seal of the Apocalypse)."—John A. McLean, *"Structure of the Book of Revelation,"* in Mal Couch, ed., *Dictionary of Premillennial Theology* (Grand Rapids, MI: Kregel Publications, 1996), 375-376.

82 In this passage Zerubbabel typifies the Messiah.

83 Danker, *A Greek-English Lexicon of the New Testament and Other Early Christian Literature*, 746.

84 MacArthur, *Revelation 1-11 : The MacArthur New Testament Commentary*, Rev. 6:12.

85 Fruchtenbaum recognizes "five cosmic disturbances: one before the seven years, three during, and one after."—Fruchtenbaum, *A Review of the Pre-Wrath Rapture of the Church*, 25.

86 Fruchtenbaum, *A Review of the Pre-Wrath Rapture of the Church*, 25.

87 Showers, *Maranatha, Our Lord Come*, 66-69.

88 Passages describing astronomical signs: Isa. 5:30; 13:10; 24:23; 30:26; 50:3; Jer. 4:23-28; Eze. 32:7; Joel 2:10; 2:31; 3:15; Amos 8:9; Mtt. 24:29; Mark 13:24; Luke 21:25; 23:45; Acts 2:20; Rev. 6:12; 8:12; 9:2.

89 Concerning the worship of heavenly bodies: Gen. 11:4; Deu. 4:19; 17:3; 2K. 17:16; 23:5, 11; 2Chr. 33:3; Job 31:26-28; Isa. 47:13; Jer. 8:2; 10:2; 19:13; Acts 7:42; Rom. 1:25; Rev. 8:12.

90 Some believe these *stars* could refer to fallen angels. "The sixth seal marks the end of the first half of the tribulation, so these stars could be the expulsion of Satan's host from Heaven (Rev. 12:7-12 with 12:3-4)."—Mills, *Revelations: An Exegetical Study of the Revelation to John*, Rev. 6:13.

91 Seiss, *The Apocalypse: Lectures on the Book of Revelation*, 154.

92 Henry Morris, *The Revelation Record* (Wheaton, IL: Tyndale House Publishers, 1983), Rev. 6:13.

93 Mills, *Revelations: An Exegetical Study of the Revelation to John*, Rev. 6:13.

94 As we forewarned the reader in our discussion concerning *The Genre of the book of Revelation*[2.6], many interpreters part ways here from the *Golden Rule of Interpretation*[5.2.24] in favor of subjective "apocalypticism." "The details of this dramatic description of a universe in turmoil are drawn from the common stock of current apocalypticism. They are not to be taken with complete literalness. Those who first read John's description would not have bothered to debate whether or not the details were to be taken literally. They were part of a well-established tradition that went back through contemporary apocalyptic literature to the early prophetic portrayals of the day of the Lord."—Mounce, *The Book of Revelation*, 161. We might ask who decides what "complete literalness" means? Which parts are literal and which parts are not? Are the men literal? But not the stars? "The suggestion of combining symbolic and literal (Mounce) is fraught with hermeneutical difficulty."—Thomas, *Revelation 1-7*, Rev. 6:12. Also: how *would* God convey these events if they *were* literal? The *Anti-supernatural Bias*[2.5] of these interpreters makes it nearly impossible for God to tell us of catastrophic events because they always get recast as "apocalyptic" and therefore not literal.

95 Concerning worship of heavenly bodies: Gen. 11:4; Deu. 4:19; 17:3; 2K. 17:16; 23:5, 11; 2Chr. 33:3; Job 31:26-28; Isa. 47:13; Jer. 8:2; 10:2; 19:13; Acts 7:42; Rom 1:25.

96 However: "The difficulties of the symbolic interpretation are insuperable, while no difficulties whatever attend the literal interpretation."—Bullinger, *Commentary On Revelation*, 274.

97 Thomas, *Revelation 1-7*, Rev. 6:14.

98 Mills, *Revelations: An Exegetical Study of the Revelation to John*, Rev. 6:14.

99 That is, until the regeneration of the *Millennial Kingdom*[5.2.39] (Mtt. 19:28) and later, the eternal state (Rev. 21:1).

100 Even today, charts of Alaskan waters made prior to the 1964 earthquake carry a disclaimer indicating that actual depths may vary by dozens of feet from that shown on the chart.

101 Danker, *A Greek-English Lexicon of the New Testament and Other Early Christian Literature*, 881.

102 Concerning the omniscience of God: 2S. 7:19; Job 24:1; 28:24; 31:4; Ps. 69:5; 139:2-4; 147:5; Isa. 40:28; 41:21-26; 42:9; 43:9; 44:7; 45:21; 46:10; 48:3-5; Jer. 12:3; Dan. 2:10, 27; Mtt. 6:8; Luke 7:39; 12:6; Acts 15:28; Rom. 11:33; Rev. 2:23.

103 Fruchtenbaum, *The Footsteps of Messiah*, 221.

104 MacArthur, *Revelation 1-11 : The MacArthur New Testament Commentary*, Rev. 6:17.

105 Renald E. Showers, *"The Day of the Lord,"* in Elwood McQuaid, ed., *Israel My Glory* (Westville, NJ: Friends of Israel Gospel Ministry, March/April 2003), 18-19.

106 Thomas, *Revelation 1-7*, Rev. 6:17.

107 Rosenthal, *The Pre-Wrath Rapture of the Church*, 147.

108 We will use the term "prophetic" for "proleptic" since most readers are more familiar with that term.

109 "The aorist tense describes an *undefined* action that normally occurs in the past."—William D. Mounce, *Greek for the Rest of Us* (Grand Rapids, MI: Zondervan, 2003), 157, 160.

110 Rosenthal, *The Pre-Wrath Rapture of the Church*, 164-167.

111 Tommie P. Dana, and Julius R. Mantey, *A Manual Grammar of the Greek New Testament* (Toronto, Ontario: The Macmillan Company, 1955), 198.

112 Thomas, *Revelation 1-7*, 460.

[113] Rosenthal misrepresents Isaiah: "The prophet Isaiah said men would flee to the caves of the mountains immediately before the Day of the Lord."—Rosenthal, *The Pre-Wrath Rapture of the Church*, 175. This makes little sense. Why would they flee *before* that day when it is the events which *attend* the day which they recognize as being God's wrath which *cause* their flight?

[114] MacArthur, *Revelation 1-11 : The MacArthur New Testament Commentary*, Rev. 6:17.

[115] Rosenthal, *The Pre-Wrath Rapture of the Church*, 147.

[116] Showers, *Maranatha, Our Lord Come*, 120.

[117] Morris, *The Revelation Record*, Rev. 6:17.

[118] Walvoord, *The Revelation of Jesus Christ*, Rev. 6:17.

[119] Seiss, *The Apocalypse: Lectures on the Book of Revelation*, 159.

3.7 - Revelation 7

3.7.1 - Revelation 7:1

After the Lamb has opened six of the seven seals, there is a pause in the action while the servants of God are sealed for protection from the judgments to follow.

After these things

Μετὰ ταῦτα [*Meta tauta*].[1] This phrase indicates significant transitions in the development of John's vision. The judgments of the first six seals have been communicated and now a transition occurs in preparation for the seventh seal, which will contain the seven trumpets and seven bowls.

If the NU and *MT*[5.2.45] texts are correct in rendering Revelation 7:1 as *After this* rather than *After these [things]* (according to the text of the *TR*[5.2.79]), then perhaps chapter seven describes the next vision John sees which is not necessarily chronologically related to chapter six. If so, then the sealing of Israel (Rev. 7:4-9) and the killing of numerous faithful from all nations (Rev. 7:9-17) may have begun during the previous seals.[2] On the other hand, the distinction of the multitude in this chapter from those under the fifth seal (Rev. 6:9-11) argues for understanding them as chronologically distinct groups. (See Revelation 7:9 where John's vision of the multitude coming out of the Great Tribulation is said to follow the sealing of the twelve tribes.)

> Because the visions constitute a pause in the chronological progression represented by the opening of the seals, they have been called a parenthesis between the sixth and seventh seals, but there is some objection to this because the visions are an integral part of the book's movement. . . . The natural meaning of the text places the sealing and the vision as a whole just after the sixth seal. Revelation 7 is an interlude between the sixth and seventh seals. . . . The description is provided to answer the questions of Rev. 6:17 by way of showing that some will survive and even prosper spiritually under the blessing of God during earth's terrors. . . . The evidence is sufficient for placing this sealing just before the midpoint of the seven-year Tribulation, at the end of the period called "the beginning of birth pains." Though the *meta touto* indicates a change of vision, this does not mean there is no relationship to the sixth seal.[3]

In any case, what transpires in this chapter is an interlude of sorts which is not tied explicitly to any seal, but inferred as being between the sixth and seventh seals. The scene now shifts from the judgments themselves to the people of God, both Jewish and otherwise, who attend this time of wrath upon the earth:

> The great day of God's wrath has come, but the action is interrupted . . . the author introduces an intermezzo between the sixth and seventh members of the series. A change comes over the spirit of his dream. . . . it is a consoling rhapsody or *rapture*[5.2.62] designed to relieve the tension by lifting the eyes of the faithful over the foam and rocks of the rapids on which they were tossing to the calm sunlit pool of bliss which awaited them beyond. They get this glimpse before the seventh seal is opened with its fresh cycle of horrors.[4]

> Chapter 7 comes as a parenthesis between the sixth and seventh seals—a stylistic feature repeated in the trumpet sequence (Rev. 10:1-11:13) but not with the bowls (cf. Rev. 16:12-21). It is not intended to take the reader back to a time before the Four Horsemen are released in order to parallel the trumpets with the seals. It contrasts the security and blessedness which await the faithful with the panic of a pagan world fleeing from judgment. . . . Chapter 7 also serves as a dramatic interlude. It delays for a brief moment the disclosure of that which is to take place with the seventh and final seal is removed from the scroll of destiny.[5]

four angels

Four is the number of worldwide effect. See *Four: the Entire World, the Earth*[2.7.5.3.3]. This is the first of several global judgments which involve four angels. There are four angels bound at the river Euphrates which will later be released to kill a third of mankind (Rev. 9:14).

four corners of the earth

This is figurative language indicating the four main compass directions (Eze. 7:2). The angels have a ministry extending over the *entire* earth.

standing . . . holding

Standing is ἑστῶτας [*estōtas*], perfect tense, *having stood. Holding* is κρατοῦντας [*kratountas*], present tense. The angels had taken their positions earlier and were already actively restraining the winds when John saw them. This is the proverbial *calm before the storm.* "Only the detail of the sealing of the 144,000 remained before the unleashing of these destructive winds."[6]

four winds

The four major directions from which winds blow: from the East, South, West, and North. This is equivalent to saying "from every direction" (Jer. 48:36; Dan. 8:8).[7] *Wind* is also used to describe God's breath or Spirit (Eze. 37:9; Zec. 6:5) which is often used in judgment. In Pharaoh's dream, the seven years of Egyptian famine were brought about by an east wind (Gen. 41:6, 27). The plague of locusts brought upon Egypt came on the east wind (Ex. 10:13). The same east wind allowed the children of Israel to cross the Red Sea (Ex. 14:21). The east wind is often associated with God's judgment and deliverance (Ps. 48:7; 78:26; Isa. 27:8; Jer. 18:17; Eze. 19:12; Hos. 13:15; Jonah 4:8). Since there is no mention of wind in association with any forthcoming judgment here, it seems best to understand the wind as denoting the *judgment and influence of God* which is about to "blow" across the land as it had in the past. In Daniel's vision, it was the "four winds of heaven" which stirred up the "Great Sea" which brought forth the four rapacious beasts (Dan. 7:2). The sea represented the Gentile nations from which the four successive empires would arise. These same four winds control the upcoming rise of *Antichrist*[5.2.3] in judgment (Rev. 13:1). The winds speak of the impending global judgments and their initiation and sovereign control by God.[8]

Angels Restraining the Four Winds [9]

not blow on the earth, on the sea, or on any tree

These three parts of the created order will undergo God's judgment in events to come.

1. With the sounding of the first trumpet, a third of the *trees* are burned up (Rev. 8:7).
2. At the second trumpet, a third of the *sea* becomes blood (Rev. 8:8). At the pouring forth of the second bowl, the entire *sea* becomes blood as of a dead man (Rev. 16:3).
3. At the sounding of the first trumpet, a third of the *earth* is burned up (Rev. 8:7, NU and MT texts). At the pouring forth of the sixth bowl, the *earth* is utterly shaken (Rev. 16:18-20).

The *earth*, the *trees*, and especially the *sea* are all important parts of the system of nature which supports life on the planet. Because man will continue to idolize the creation rather than the Creator (Rom. 1:25), God will set about to destroy this idol. But none of this can begin until the servants of God are sealed for protection (Rev. 7:3-4). Even after the judgments have begun, the locusts from the bottomless pit are told not to harm the earth, sea or vegetation, but only men (Rev. 9:4).

Having at one time been an avid environmentalist and valuing animal life above human life, we are familiar with the pagan religious undercurrents which fuel this movement. Many environmentalists thrill to the sight of a dolphin or whale, yet despise the God of the Bible Who brought them all forth. If environmentalists thrill to a dolphin or hummingbird, how much more marvelous is the One Who spoke and they leapt into existence! He is far more worthy of wonder than the mere work of His hands! To be sure, man has not been a faithful steward of all God has given him, but to deny the Creator while attempting to save the creation is folly as events in this book make plain.

Some commentators take these as symbolic representations:

> "That no wind might blow upon the *earth* "—the scene of settled government (Rev. 10:2; Ps. 46:2); "nor upon the *sea* "—nations and peoples in anarchy and confusion (Dan. 7:2-3; Isa. 57:20); "nor upon any *tree* "—the might and pride of the earth (Dan. 4:10, 22; Eze. 31:3-9, 14-18).[10]

> These symbols are easy to interpret. The earth is Israel; the sea, the Gentiles; the trees, as we know from the famous *parable*[5.2.54] in the ninth chapter of the book of Judges, refer to those in authority.[11]

While it is true that each of these entities carries a symbolic meaning in other passages (cf. especially Rev. 13:1; 17:15), it is best to understand their use here as literal because of the related passages which follow. The locusts are commanded "not to harm the grass of the earth, or any green thing, or any tree, but only those men who do not have the seal of God on their foreheads" (Rev. 9:4). The passage concerning the locusts differentiates *men* from real *vegetation* ("any green thing"). When *trees* are destroyed, so too is the *green grass* (Rev. 8:7). When the *sea* becomes blood, *living creatures* and *ships* are affected (Rev. 8:9; 16:3). If the sea represents the nations here (as it does in Rev. 13:1 and 17:15), then what is meant by the *living creatures* and the *ships* which ply its waters? Also, when men, cities, or authorities are the recipients of judgments which follow, they are specifically denoted as such (Rev. 9:4-5, 18, 20; 11:13; 16:2, 9; 18:14-19; 19:19).

3.7.2 - Revelation 7:2

from the east

Literally, *from the rising of the sun*. Within Scripture, *east* is often the direction of the deliverance or judgment of God (Gen. 41:6, 23, 27; Ex. 10:13; 14:21; Ps. 48:7; 78:26; Isa. 27:8; Jer. 18:17; Eze. 19:12; Hos. 13:15; Jonah 4:8; Rev. 16:12). It is the direction to which the glory of the Lord departed from both Solomon's and Herod's *Temple*[5.2.73] (Eze. 10:18; 11:22-23 cf. Mtt. 23:38; 24:1-3) and the direction by which it will eventually return (Eze. 43:2-4; 44:1-2). Here, it is "the direction of God," the direction from which God's protective sealing comes prior to the unleashing of the judgments to come.

the seal

Seal is σφραγῖδα [*sphragida*]. This is not a seal itself, but "the instrument with which one seals or stamps."[12] This angel carries the means by which the one hundred and forty-four thousand will be sealed (Rev. 7:4-8, which *see*[3.7.4]). "This text does not explicitly say what this seal is, but Rev. 14:1 suggests that it is the name of the Lamb and that of His Father (cf. Isa. 44:5)."[13] Those who are to be sealed are one of three groups who survive this horrific time of judgment. Two of the groups are described in this chapter:

> Chapter 7 forms a parenthetical section between the sixth (Rev. 6:12-17) and seventh (Rev. 8:1) seals to answer that question, introducing two groups who will survive the fury of divine judgment. The first, those described in Rev. 7:1-8, are the Jewish evangelists who will be preserved on earth. They will survive the holocaust of divine wrath unleashed by the seal, trumpet, and bowl judgments. God will also protect them from the murderous efforts of *Antichrist*[5.2.3] and his henchmen to wipe out believers in the true God. Having survived the wars, famine, unprecedented natural disasters, disease, rampant, unchecked sinfulness, and savage persecution of the Tribulation, they will enter the *Millennial Kingdom*[5.2.39] alive. The second group to escape divine fury (Rev. 7:9-17) are those who will be martyred and thereby ushered into the blissful rest of heaven, where they will be preserved.[14]

The third group which survives, although not mentioned in this chapter, are those who come to faith during the Tribulation and manage to stay alive until the Second Coming. These will enter the Millennial Kingdom and form its initial populace (Mtt. 25:31-40).

of the living God

Throughout Scripture, the One True God is contrasted with dead idols who are dumb and cannot respond.[15] Nevertheless, the pattern of history is that man has more often sought help from dumb idols than from the *living God* (Deu. 5:26; 1S. 17:26; Mtt. 16:16; 1Th. 1:9-10; Heb. 12:22). In Satan's most successful ploy to keep men captive to idolatry, he mimics the *living God* by empowering the false prophet "to give breath to the *image of the beast*[5.2.29]" (Rev. 13:15). *Life-giving* power is an intrinsic characteristic of God (Luke 24:5).[16] See commentary on *Revelation 1:18*[3.1.18].

to whom it was granted to harm the earth and the sea

Every judgment is subject to God's conditional permission. See commentary on *Revelation 6:2*[3.6.2]. The *earth*, trees, and *sea* will be harmed in God's upcoming judgments. See commentary on *Revelation 7:1*[3.7.1].

3.7.3 - Revelation 7:3

harm the earth, the sea, or the trees

See commentary on *Revelation 7:1*[3.7.1].

on their foreheads

Foreheads is μετώπων [*metōpōn*], which is used to describe the location of the mark "of a branded slave."[17] The seal identifies them as belonging to God (Rev. 14:1) and may be similar to the promise given to the overcomer in Philadelphia that Jesus would "write on him My new name" (Rev. 3:12, Rev. 14:1[18]). The picture of sealing for protection by marking the servants on their *foreheads* recalls a vision shown Ezekiel in which most in Jerusalem were practicing idolatry which God was about to judge. Prior to His judgment going forth, an angel was told to "Go through the midst of the city, through the midst of Jerusalem, and put a mark on the foreheads of the men who sigh and cry over all the abominations that are done within it" (Eze. 9:4). In the judgment which followed, those without the mark (seal) of God were killed (Eze. 9:5-6).

> As blood was put upon the door of the houses of Israel in Egypt so that the angel of death would pass over these houses and strike only those which were not marked, so the seal of God is put upon the forehead of His own so that the angels of judgment, passing through the world, will know those who are God's.[19]

As *Master Imitator*[4.2.5], Satan, through the beast, will mark those who are his, who are thereafter unredeemable (Rev. 14:9-10). "Are we told that God, by His angel, will 'seal' His servants in their foreheads (Rev. 7:3), so also we read that Satan, by his angels, will set a mark in the foreheads of his devotees (Rev. 13:16)."[20]

During the time of the Tribulation, it appears there will be three categories of people:

1. Those who are sealed and protected by God for special ministry (Rev. 7:4-8; 14:1).
2. Those who accept the mark of the beast (Rev. 13:16-18) and are doomed (Rev. 14:9-10). They are not written in the *Book of Life*[4.4].
3. Those who refuse the mark of the beast, many of whom are martyred (Rev. 20:4).

In the eternal state, God's name will be on the foreheads of all the faithful (Rev. 22:4 cf. Rev. 3:12). See commentary on *Revelation 13:16*[3.13.16] and *Revelation 14:1*[3.14.1].

3.7.4 - Revelation 7:4

who were sealed

ἐσφραγισμένων [*esphragismenōn*], perfect passive participle, *ones having been sealed*. The angel recounts the total number of individuals who, by this time, have been sealed. The seal identifies those who are set apart for special protection in the midst of the judgments from God. "The mark which denotes ownership also carries with it the protection of the owner,"[21] in this case, God. The seal may not be visible to men, but is evident to God and the angels and demons who carry forth his judgment (Rev. 9:4). It is analogous to the sealing of believers today, who are baptized into the body of Christ and sealed with the Holy Spirit (2Cor. 1:22; Eph. 1:13; 4:30).

> The best analysis of the seal is that it protects against the disasters that the four winds will bring to the earth (Beckwith; Caird). The context of Rev. 7:1-3 is in preparation for the judgments of the seventh

> seal that includes the seven trumpets. Thus the sealing must refer to these judgments. The command "do not hurt" implies that after the sealing is finished, the judgments that are next in the divine program (i.e., Revelation 8) will come (Smith).[22]

Seiss suggests that in order to stand in the midst of this time of unparalleled judgment and tribulation, those who are sealed will require a special measure of spiritual enablement:

> We may, therefore, conceive of this sealing of the 144,000 as a special and extraordinary impartation of the Holy Ghost; which again connects this vision with particular Old Testament promises. By the mouth of Joel, the Lord said to Israel: "I will pour out my Spirit upon all flesh." This was indeed a general promise, but with it was coupled another, which is not so general, but particular to Israel: "And *your* sons and *your* daughters [O Jews] shall prophesy, *your* old men shall dream dreams, *your* young men shall see visions, and also upon the servants and upon the handmaidens in those days will I pour out my Spirit." Peter tells us that this began to be fulfilled in the miracle of Pentecost; but the fulfilment did not end there. There are also particulars in this passage which were not fulfilled upon the primitive Church —particulars which refer to the judgment times, and connect directly to the scenes to which this sealing of the 144,000 is related. "Wonders in heaven and earth, blood, and fire, and pillars of smoke," are spoken of; and the turning of the sun into darkness, and the moon into blood; . . . In this we distinctly recognize the occurrences under the red horseman of the second seal, the physical prodigies of the sixth seal, and the exact manifestations under the first and fifth trumpets.[23]

One hundred *and* forty-four thousand

In our discussion of *Interpreting Symbols*[2.7] , we noted the tendency of many interpreters to ignore the literal meaning of numbers whenever a cherished theological viewpoint makes the literal value given in the text unpopular. Perhaps the two most abused numbers in the entire book of Revelation are the 144,000 sealed individuals here and the 1,000 years of the millennial reign (Rev. 20). Although this passage goes to great lengths to make plain the literal nature of what is being conveyed, this hasn't stopped many from flights of interpretive fancy which substitute subjective conjecture for the plain facts:

> The name "Christ" appears seven times and the name "Jesus" fourteen times. "The Lamb" is used of Christ twenty-eight times, seven bringing the Lamb and God together. The 7 x 4 appearances of this title underscore the universal scope of the Lamb's complete victory. . . . Twelve is the number of God's people, which is squared to indicate completeness and multiplied by one thousand to connote vastness.[24]

> Twelve is the number of the tribes, and **appropriate to the Church**: three by four: three, the divine number, multiplied by four, the number for world-wide extension. Twelve by twelve implies fixity and completeness, which is taken a thousandfold in 144,000. A thousand implies the world perfectly pervaded by the divine; for it is ten, the world number, raised to the power of three, the number of God. [emphasis added][25]

No matter how specific God's Word may be concerning the identification of this group of persons, the interpreters refuse to follow the text where it leads. This is because they have theological biases which go against recognizing the obvious Jewish nature of this passage. (As we saw earlier, the Jewish nature of this book was recognized by many and led to opposition to its *acceptance into the canon*[2.10].)

> Many are so morbidly prejudiced against everything Jewish, that it is concluded in advance, that anything merciful, referring to the Israelitish race, must needs be understood some other way than as the words are written. Though all the prophets were Jews, and Jesus was a Jew, and the writer of this Apocalypse was a Jew, and all the Apostles were Jews, and salvation itself is of the Jews, and the Jews as a distinct people are everywhere spoken of as destined to continue to the world's end, it is regarded as the next thing to apostasy from the faith, to apply anything hopeful, that God has said, to this particular race. . . . No wonder, therefore, that they cannot find a consistent interpretation of a vision of grace which is predicated of Jacob's literal seed, in contradistinction from all others.[26]

Bullinger, an authority on figures of speech, holds that this number is not symbolic of some other group than the Jews, but intentionally definite:

> Alford says of this number, "No one I am aware of has taken it literally!" Very likely: but we are thankful to be an exception to the rule, and to believe what God says. There is such a thing as *Figures of Speech*, but, we ask, what Figure is used here? What is its name? The truth is that there is here no Figure whatever; but it is the simple statement of fact: a *definite* number in contrast with the *indefinite* number in this very chapter (Rev. 7:9). If the total number is not exact, then all the items which go to make it up are indefinite also. If the number is symbolical, then what number in the Book may we take as literal? . .

> . We prefer to believe God. And, believing Him, we conclude that He had reserved 7,000 in the days of Ahab (1K. 19:18; Rom. 11:4), so He will reserve 144,000 in the Great Tribulation.[27]

As is often the case within Scripture, when the plain sense of Scripture is rejected, a foothold is provided for aberrant teachings frequented by cults, in this case the Jehovah's Witnesses:

> The Jehovah's Witnesses teach that the 144,000 is the body of spirit-begotten believers who have a "heavenly hope" (Rom. 8:24. Eph. 4:4. Col. 1:5. Heb. 7:19. 1Pe. 1:3. 1Jn. 3:3). All other believers can have only an "earthly hope" (Job 14:7. Jer. 31:17. Acts 26:6). Once the Watchtower organization had more than 144,000 adherents, the teaching was developed that the "great multitude" mentioned later in the chapter (Rev. 7:9) referred to those Christians who had only an earthly hope. Jehovah's Witnesses teach that members of the "great multitude" who have only an earthly hope do not need to be born again. . . . If the claim of Jehovah's Witnesses that the heavenly hope is limited to 144,000 has any validity, the significance of that hope for anyone today is purely historical, for since this number was reached within five years of Pentecost, no person alive today could possibly lay claim to be one of that fixed number, not even the leaders of the Watchtower in Brooklyn, New York. [28]

However, the verses which follow make it clear that the sealed are *Jews*. This is in accordance with what is said later concerning the 144,000—that they are *firstfruits*,

> These sealed Jews are those who come to faith in Jesus as Messiah during the Tribulation period. They are further described as "first fruits unto God and to the Lamb" (Rev. 14:4), indicating that they compose the first stage of a final harvest of Jewish souls to be gathered later at the Lord's coming in glory. . . . These comprise the "remnant" of Jews "who keep the commandments of God, and have the testimony of Jesus Christ" (Rev. 12:17b).[29]

See commentary on *Revelation 14:1*[3.14.1].

of all the tribes of the children of Israel

Children of Israel, υἱῶν Ἰσραήλ [*huiōn Israēl*], literally: *sons of Israel*. These are the same twelve *tribes of the children of Israel* whose names are written on the gates of the New Jerusalem (Rev. 21:12). These are a specific group of people who are physical offspring of Israel and differentiated from the rest of men (Zec. 9:1). In the regeneration, Jesus said the apostles will rule over these tribes (Mtt. 19:28; Luke 22:30). "Immediately after the Translation of the heavenly saints (1Th. 4:15-17), God will work in grace amongst His ancient people, and among the Gentiles at large outside the apostate part of the world."[30]

At this point in the Revelation, we encounter one of those "Jewish elements" in the book of Revelation which seem to cause much discomfort for many commentators. Bullinger elaborates:

> Few Scriptures have suffered more at the hands of Gentile Christians than this. Notwithstanding the fact that it concerns "all the tribes of the children of Israel," and that the twelve tribes are named separately, popular interpretation insists on taking them as meaning the Church of God. Any system of interpretation which has this for its foundation may be judged and condemned at the outset as not only useless, but mischievous. Such a system has been described by Hooker as one "which changeth the meaning of words as alchemy doth, or would do, the substance of metals, making anything what it listeth; and bringeth, in the end, all truth to nothing."[31]

The unwillingness to accept the Jewishness of what is described here is evident from many commentators who refuse to take the passage at face value:

> The number scarcely refers only to Jewish Christians; rather it stands for all the members of the Church, the true Israel.[32]

> If [the number is] literal, it is necessary to suppose that this refers to the twelve tribes of the children of Israel. But on every supposition this is absurd. **Ten of their tribes had been long before carried away**, and the distinction of the tribes was lost, no more to be recovered, and the Hebrew people never have been, since the time of John, in circumstances to which the description here could be applicable. These considerations make it clear that the description here is symbolical. [emphasis added][33]

> Walvoord accepts this passage as proving that the twelve tribes are still in existence. This interpretation seriously complicates the book of Revelation by bringing in racial distinctions which no longer exist in the *NT*[5.2.48] purview. It disregards the **historical fact** that ten of the twelve tribes disappeared in Assyria and the remaining two list their separate identity when Jerusalem fell in A.D. 70. . . . The

> number is **obviously symbolic**. [emphasis added][34]

Mounce asserts that taking the passage literally "seriously complicates" the book of Revelation and asserts that *racial distinctions . . . no longer exist in the NT purview* . This would have come as a surprise to the apostle Paul who continued to describe himself as a Jew long after his conversion (Acts 21:39-22:3), said the same of Peter (Gal. 2:14-16), and spent almost three full chapters of Romans explaining to believers that God is not through with the *Jewish nation* (Rom. 9, 10, 11). At the close of this most important section of Scripture, Paul makes a statement which directly contradicts Mounce:

> For I do not desire, brethren, that you should be ignorant of this mystery, lest you should be wise in your own opinion, that **blindness in part has happened to Israel** until **the fullness of the Gentiles has come in**. And so **all Israel will be saved**, as it is written: "The Deliverer will come out of Zion, and **He will turn away ungodliness from Jacob**; for this *is* My covenant with them, when I take away their sins." Concerning the gospel *they are* enemies for your sake, but concerning the election *they are* beloved for the sake of the fathers. For the gifts and the calling of God *are* irrevocable. (Rom. 11:25-29) [emphasis added]

Elements of this short, but very important passage, reveal:

1. Paul was concerned that certain Gentile believers would *be wise in your own opinion*, namely that they would assume, like Mounce, that racial distinctions no longer exist. Not so!
2. Paul differentiates between two different groups of *believers*. Paul is doing the unthinkable, according to those with Mounce's view. He is making a distinction *among* the redeemed! And what distinction is it? He is contrasting the *fullness of the Gentiles* with *all Israel*. He is saying that God has a different emphasis and timetable for the Gentile elect and the Jewish elect! God Himself recognizes a *racial distinction* which Mounce cannot recognize.
3. The Deliverer *will come* (future tense) and turn away ungodliness from *Jacob*. The *fullness of the Gentiles* and ungodly *Jacob* can not be made one and the same without ignoring the most basic rules of interpretation. One describes Gentiles and the other Jews. Both will eventually come to faith.
4. When a Jew comes to faith in Messiah Jesus, he does not cease to be a Jew. In fact, the *exact opposite* was the concern in NT times—whether a Gentile, upon coming to faith had to become a Jew (Acts 10:45; 11:17; 15:6-29)![35]
5. When the Deliverer turns away ungodliness from Jacob (who is Israel, the father of the Jews), it is said that this is *because* of God's covenant. What covenant is that? It is the New Covenant which was originally given to Israel (Jer. 31:31). Again, what is surprising in the NT is not that Jews cease to be Jews (they don't), but that Gentiles participate in this *Jewish covenant*.

Another frequently-encountered error concerning the interpretation of this passage is the assertion that ten of the twelve tribes have been forever lost. We discuss this unbiblical myth in our section entitled *Ten Tribes Lost?*[4.17]

> This passage also teaches that the so-called "ten lost tribes" were, in fact, never lost (cf. Rev. 21:12; Matt. 19:28; Luke 22:30; Jas. 1:1). Instead, representatives from the ten northern tribes filtered south and intermingled with the two southern tribes (cf. 2Chr. 30:1-11; 34:1-9) and thus were preserved.[36]

Ladd, in his desire to avoid the plain teaching of the text, believes this list of the twelve tribes is unlike any other in the *OT*[5.2.51]:

> These twelve tribes cannot be literal Israel, because they are not the twelve tribes of OT Israel. The list here appears nowhere else in the Bible. It has three irregularities: it names Judah first, thus ignoring the OT order of the tribes; it omits Dan with no explanation (see Eze. 48:1); it mentions Joseph instead of Ephraim. Perhaps John meant by this irregular listing of the twelve tribes to designate the Israel that is not the literal Israel. . . . The twelve tribes were irregularly listed to show that true Israel is not literal Israel, but the Church.[37]

Here we meet again with *Replacement Theology*[5.2.63]—the unbiblical idea that the Church is "Israel," something *nowhere stated in Scripture*. To be sure, believers are called the spiritual seed of Abraham (Rom. 4:12-18; Gal. 3:7-8, 29), but if Scripture is any indication, there is an important distinction between the *spiritual* seed of *Abraham* and the *physical* seed of *Jacob*. For nowhere in all of Holy Writ —not *once*—is the Church denoted by the word "Israel."[38] Those who confuse the Church with Israel are just one step behind many of the cults, such as The Church of God or *British Israelism*[5.2.11], who want to oust Israel from her promises and substitute themselves instead. (For more on these movements, see *Ten Tribes Lost?*[4.17]) The Church already has her own promises so why should we try to steal Israel's too? Besides, the spiritual restoration of the Jews is attended with great blessings: "For if their being cast away *is* the reconciling of the world, what will their acceptance *be* but life from the dead?" (Rom. 11:15).

The irregularities which Ladd sees as so significant are found in other listings of the tribes. Concerning the omission of tribes, we could cite the omission of Dan from the extensive tribal genealogies of 1 Chronicles 2:10. "In the enumerations of the tribes throughout Scripture, of which there are about eighteen, the full representative number twelve is always given, but as Jacob had thirteen sons [counting the two sons of Joseph instead of the father as Jacob's] one or other is always omitted."[39]

This rotation and omission of tribal names is not unusual, as Ladd would have us believe, but is typical. "It should be noted that there is no standard way of listing the twelve tribes. There are at least nineteen different ways of listing them in the Old Testament, none of which agree with the list given here."[40]

> A careful examination of the dozen places in the Bible where all the twelve tribes are mentioned will reveal some very beautiful truths. Jacob had twelve sons who were the fathers of the twelve tribes. Joseph and two sons, Ephraim and Manasseh, whose names later were added to the list of the tribes. This gives us fourteen names out of which twelve are selected, but not always the same twelve, in presenting the truths concerning Israel. Levi, the priestly tribe, had no military duties to perform and was not given a portion of the land when the tribes entered Palestine. The portion of Levi was to be the Lord Himself (Deu. 18:1-2; Jos. 13:14). In order to fill His place both in military affairs and in the land, a new tribe had to be found so Joseph was replaced by his two sons. Leaving out the name of Levi and that of Joseph, twelve names remained.[41]

Concerning Judah being listed first, the camp of Judah led the procession of the tribes on the march (Num. 10:14). Rather than seeking to *understand* why this list omits Dan and Ephraim, Ladd merely asserts that their omission means that the phrase "children of Israel" must denote the Church. But this runs roughshod over hermeneutical principles because these 144,000 from the tribes of Israel are *contrasted* with "a great multitude . . . of all . . . tribes" (Rev. 7:9). These are different groups: one is denoted by *twelve* specific tribal names and is only *144,000* in size. The other comes from *all* tribes (and nations, peoples, and tongues) and is *innumerable*.[42]

As to why Dan and Ephraim are omitted from the list, there seems to be a ready explanation. God promises that any person *or tribe* which practices idolatry will be set apart for adversity:

> So that there may not be among you man or woman or family **or tribe**, whose heart turns away today from the LORD our God, **to go *and* serve the gods of these nations** [e.g., idolatry], and that there may not be among you a root bearing bitterness or wormwood; and so it may not happen, when he hears the words of this curse, that he blesses himself in his heart, saying, 'I shall have peace, even though I follow the dictates of my heart' -as though the drunkard could be included with the sober. The LORD would not spare him; for then the anger of the LORD and His jealousy would burn against that man, and every curse that is written in this book would settle on him, and the LORD would blot out his name from under heaven. And **the LORD would separate him from all the tribes of Israel for adversity**, according to all the curses of the covenant that are written in this Book of the Law. (Deu. 29:18-21) [emphasis added]

When the tribe of Dan migrated north from their original location, they persuaded a renegade Levite in Ephraim to join them, along with his graven image. After overthrowing Laish and renaming the town Dan, they set up the carved image and a priesthood attended it (Jdg. 18:19-30). Thereafter, the town of Dan became a center for worship of one of the golden calves which Jeroboam promoted as an alternative to worship at Jerusalem during the divided kingdom (1K. 12:28-30; 2K. 10:29).

> The Lord's estimation of Dan and his idolatry can be seen in the decreasing role of the tribe in scriptural history. In the twenty different listings of the tribes, Dan is generally far down and often is the last in the list. Consider, for example, the order of march in the wilderness: "And the standard of the camp of the children of Dan set forward, which was over the rear guard of all the camps throughout their hosts; and

> over its host was Ahiezer, the son of Ammishaddai" (Num. 10:25). [See *Camp of Israel*[4.7.2] .] Dan was the last tribe to receive its inheritance in the Promised Land (Jos. 19:47-49). Most striking is the total omission of Dan from the extensive tribal genealogies of 1 Chronicles 2:10! These scriptural facts should be remembered when facing the often-asked question of why Dan is omitted in the 144,000 Jews sealed in the Tribulation period (Rev. 7:4-8). Evidently this is due to the problem of idolatry which plagued this tribe throughout its history.[43]

Also, when Deborah and Barak led Israel to war in the time of the judges, the tribes sent men to fight, but not Dan. Dan's failure to participate is remarked upon in Scripture: "Why did Dan remain on ships?" (Jdg. 5:17).

Ephraim also was involved with idolatry:

> Interestingly, Jeroboam's idols were placed in the tribes of Dan and Ephraim (i.e., Bethel, 1K. 12:29). Thus, in the Revelation 7 listing, Dan was replaced by Levi (Rev. 7:7) and Ephraim was replaced by his father Joseph (Rev. 7:8), while his brother Manasseh was included to complete the twelve (Rev. 7:6).[44]

> The tribes of Dan and Ephraim are omitted from the list which follows, being replaced by Levi and Joseph. The reason for Ephraim's omission is suggested by Hos. 4:17. For possible reasons for Dan's omission see the related texts . . . (Lev. 24:10-16. Deu. 29:18-21. Jdg. 18:2-31. 1K. 12:26-33). Dan and Ephraim are included in Ezekiel's prophecy of their inheritance in the eternal earthly kingdom of Christ (Eze. 48:1-6, 32), demonstrating God's faithfulness to his covenant and promise (Lev. 26:44. Mal. 3:6. Rom. 11:29. 15:8).[45]

Although Dan is omitted here, this should not be taken as an indication that the tribe of Dan will perish due to lack of protection during the Tribulation. "In the end grace triumphs and Dan is named first in the future distribution of land amongst the tribes (Eze. 48:2), but while being first mentioned, it is the furthest removed from the temple, being situated in the extreme north."[46]

Some understand the omission of Dan as an indication that the *Antichrist*[5.2.3] will arise from Dan:[47]

> He who shall come claiming the kingdom for himself, and shall terrify those men of whom we have been speaking, having a name containing the aforesaid number [666], is truly the abomination of desolation. This, too, the apostle affirms: "When they shall say, Peace and safety, then sudden destruction shall come upon them." And Jeremiah does not merely point out his sudden coming, but he even indicates the tribe from which he shall come, where he says, "We shall hear the voice of his swift horses from Dan; the whole earth shall be moved by the voice of the neighing of his galloping horses: he shall also come and devour the earth, and the fulness thereof, the city also, and they that dwell therein." [Jer. 8:16] This, too, is the reason that this tribe is not reckoned in the Apocalypse along with those which are saved.—*Irenaeus*[5.2.34], *Against Heresies*, v.xxx.ii[48]

Yet, in our discussion of *The Beast*[4.2] we identify reasons which indicate a Gentile origin for the Antichrist. See the discussion of whether the *Beast*[5.2.9] will be *Jewish or Gentile?*[4.2.3]

There is also the possibility that the omission of Dan and Ephraim are not as significant as many think, perhaps mainly motivated to maintain symmetry.[49]

The sealed are said to be "servants of God" (Rev. 7:3) and "follow the Lamb wherever He goes" perhaps indicating a unique dedication and obedience to God in the midst of the Tribulation on earth (Rev. 7:3; 14:4-5). Their ministry is probably evangelistic in nature. Isaiah described a worldwide Jewish mission to the Gentiles. The context is immediately before the gathering of the Jews for the millennial age:[50]

> I will set a sign among them; and those among them who escape I will send to the nations: *to* Tarshish and Pul and Lud, who draw the bow, and Tubal and Javan, *to* the coastlands afar off who have not heard My fame nor seen My glory. And **they shall declare My glory among the Gentiles** . Then they shall bring all your brethren for an offering to the LORD out of all nations, on horses and in chariots and in litters, on mules and on camels, to My holy mountain Jerusalem, says the LORD, as the children of Israel bring an offering in a clean vessel into the house of the LORD. (Isa. 66:19-20) [emphasis added]

It seems conclusive that these are to be used in evangelism. *First*, what else could be the purpose of a divinely-protected group in the midst of this time period but to share the truth of the gospel and save even more from doom? *Second* , their appearance is grammatically linked with the innumerable believers which John subsequently sees (Rev. 7:9-17).

> In the future, God will graciously grant Israel a second opportunity to be His witness nation, and at that time they will not fail. Led by the 144,000 evangelists (Rev. 7:1-8), Israel will be a light to the nations during the darkest hour of earth's history.[51]

> There is a decided advantage in using Jews to conduct a worldwide revival in the short timer period of 3 1/2 years. . . The modern missionary, . . . must spend approximately six years [4 years of Bible, 2 of target language] before he is fully equipped to present the gospel in a language that is not his own. . . . All of this world's major languages, and a great number of the world's minor languages, are spoken by Jews somewhere. . . . with a large segment of American Jewry being the exception, most Jews receive a good and basic understanding of the Old Testament text. . . . These Jews will already speak the languages needed. They will already have a basic knowledge of the Old Testament text. . . they could begin to preach the gospel in a very short period of time.[52]

> Our Lord says that the gospel of the kingdom is to be preached in all the world for a witness before the end shall come (Mtt. 24:14). In view of all the teaching of the Word of God on this subject, it is undoubtedly the gospel of the kingdom which is the added special message of the 144,000. Of course, they present Jesus as the Saviour. Many look to Him and are saved. But they also preach the gospel of the kingdom presenting Jesus as Messiah. They are the sealed witnesses, the 144,000 like Paul who go out with all the gifts of the Holy Spirit, having the prophecies of Joel fulfilled in themselves, as the first faint occurrences at Pentecost cannot possibly be the complete fulfillment which comes to full fruition in the last days.[53]

Along with many Gentiles who will come to faith during this troublesome time, these 144,000 Jewish believers are the initial means by which the Deliverer will begin to turn ungodliness from the Jewish nation (Rom. 11:25-26). The setting apart of a specific group from among the Jews also provides evidence that the Church Age has come to a close:

> As long as the church is on the earth there are none saved to a special Jewish relationship. All who are saved are saved to a position in the body of Christ as indicated in Colossians 1:26-29; 3:11; Ephesians 2:14-22; 3:1-7. During the seventieth week the church must be absent, for out of the saved remnant in Israel God seals 144,000 Jews, 12,000 from each tribe, according to Revelation 7:4. The fact that God is again dealing with Israel on this national relationship, setting them apart to national identities, and sending them as special representatives to the nations in place of the witness of the church, indicates that the church must no longer be on earth.[54]

The Twelve Tribes of Israel

Hagar
Sarah
Abraham
Gen 17:19; 21:12; 22:18; 26:3-5
Ishmael
Isaac + Rebekah
Ishmaelites
Arabs
(Muhammed?)
Gen 27:28; 28:3,13-14; 35:11; 48:3
Esau
Jacob/Israel
Leah
Bilhah (Rachel's)
Zilpah (Leah's)
Rachel
Edomites
Idumaeans
(Herod)
Gen 49:10
Reuben 1
Simeon 2
Levi 3
Judah 4
Dan 5
Naphtali 6
Gad 7
Asher 8
Issachar 9
Zebulun 10
Joseph 11
Benjamin 12
2S 7:12; 1Chr 17:11
David
Manasseh 1
Ephraim 2
Luke 1:33
Jesus

Scott sees significance in the grouping of the tribes which follows:

> In our English version there are three tribes named in each verse, but in reality the arrangement of the tribes as of the apostles (Mtt. 10:2-4) is in pairs: *first* , Judah and Reuben—the fourth and first sons of Leah—the former the royal tribe, the latter the representative of the nation (Gen. 49:3); *second* , Gad and Asher—the two sons of Zilpah—associated in the prophetic blessings in the last days (Gen. 49:19-20); *third* , Naphtali and Manasseh linked in the enumeration of Eze. 48:4; *fourth* , Simeon and Levi—the second and third sons of Leah—associated in the prophetic enumeration (Gen. 49:5-7), also in the Lord's revelation of Himself to saved Israel (Zec. 12:13); *fifth,* Issachar and Zabulon [*sic*]—the fifth and sixth sons of Leah, both are associated in the prophetic (Gen. 49), and in the territorial (Eze. 48) enumerations of the tribes; *sixth,* Joseph and Benjamin—the two sons of Rachel, the beloved wife of the patriarch.[55]

3.7.5 - Revelation 7:5

the tribe of Judah

The fourth son of Jacob by Leah (Gen. 29:35). Judah means *praise* (Gen. 29:35) and was in the line leading to the Messiah and led the procession of the tribes (Num. 10:14), even into battle (Jdg. 20:18 cf. 2Chr. 20:21; Ps. 149:6). See *Camp of Israel*[4.7.2]. See commentary on *Revelation 5:5*[3.5.5].

twelve thousand *were* sealed

"The number twelve in the Scripture has a special association with the idea of completion and it is also attached inseparably to the destiny of God's chosen earthly people, Israel. Immediately, of course, we think of the twelve tribes and the twelve apostles."[56] See *Twelve: Jewish Tribes, Completeness*[2.7.5.3.7].

the tribe of Reuben

The first son of Jacob by Leah (Gen. 29:32). Reuben means *see ye a son.*

the tribe of Gad

The seventh son of Jacob by Leah's handmaid, Zilpah (Gen. 30:11). Gad means *a troop.*

3.7.6 - Revelation 7:6

the tribe of Asher

The eighth son of Jacob by Leah's handmaid, Zilpah (Gen. 30:13). Asher means *happy am I.*

the tribe of Naphtali

The sixth son of Jacob by Rachel's handmaid, Bilhah (Gen. 30:8). Naphtali means *my wrestling.*

the tribe of Manasseh

One of Joseph's two sons (Gen. 41:51). Joseph was the eleventh son of Jacob by Rachel (Gen. 30:24). Manasseh means *causing to forget.* Manasseh's brother, Ephraim, is omitted from the list of those sealed. See commentary on *Revelation 7:4*[3.7.4].

3.7.7 - Revelation 7:7

tribe of Simeon

The second son of Jacob by Leah (Gen. 29:33). Simeon means *hearing.*

tribe of Levi

The third son of Jacob by Leah (Gen. 29:34). Levi means *attached,* or *joined.*

tribe of Issachar

The ninth son of Jacob by Leah (Gen. 30:18). *Issachar* means *he will bring a reward.*

3.7.8 - Revelation 7:8

tribe of Zebulun

The tenth son of Jacob by Leah (Gen. 30:20). *Zebulun* means *dwelling* or *habitation.*

tribe of Joseph

The eleventh son of Jacob by Rachel (Gen. 30:24). *Joseph* means *adding*. One of Joseph's sons,

Ephraim, is not mentioned in the list of those sealed although Manasseh is. This may not be significant since the tribe of Joseph would normally denote both Manasseh and Ephraim. See commentary on *Revelation 7:4*[3.7.4].

tribe of Benjamin

The twelfth and last son of Jacob by Rachel (Gen. 35:18). *Joseph* means *son of my right hand.*

3.7.9 - Revelation 7:9

After these things

"The connecting link, *after these things*, is chronological and also shows a cause and effect relationship between the first and second parts of Revelation seven. Thus, by means of the 144,000 Jews, God will accomplish the second purpose of the Great Tribulation, that of bringing about a worldwide revival."[57] See *A Worldwide Revival*[2.4.4].

behold

The sight which John saw was remarkable—both in its global scope and quantity. After having written the seven letters to the *Seven Churches of Asia*[4.15] , which evidence lack of zeal and the penetration of worldliness into the churches, perhaps John was surprised by the large number who eventually respond to the gospel despite the inadequacies which attend those entrusted with the Great Commission (Mtt. 28:18-20; Mark 16:15-16; Luke 24:47; John 17:18; Acts 1:8; 10:42).

a great multitude which no one could number

Here is a second group who will survive the time of God's wrath—the faithful who come out of the Great Tribulation (Rev. 7:14). Like the saints under the fifth seal (Rev. 6:9-11), the majority of these probably die for their faith. But their death—at the hands of the harlot and later, the beast—will be their ultimate victory as overcomers (Rev. 2:10, 13; 12:11). They have successfully applied the teaching of Jesus: "Do not fear those who kill the body but cannot kill the soul. But rather fear Him who is able to destroy both soul and body in hell" (Mtt. 10:28). This innumerable company of believers (cf. Rev. 7:14) indicates an innumerable company of people who come to faith in Christ during the time of the end. See *How are People Saved in the Tribulation?*[4.14.4.4]

of all nations, tribes, peoples, and tongues

A fourfold designation emphasizing the global origin of this group. See *Four: the Entire World, the Earth*[2.7.5.3.3]. That the 144,000 of Revelation 7:4 cannot be symbolic of believers in general is seen by this verse. The 144,000 were from "all the tribes **of the children of Israel**" [emphasis added] whereas these are from *all . . . tribes*. Both *OT*[5.2.51] and *NT*[5.2.48] indicate that multitudes of non-Jews will join with the believing Jewish remnant in seeking the Lamb (Isa. 11:10; Luke 2:32; Rom. 3:29-30; 9:24). Like the multitude in Revelation 5:9, these too are redeemed, but at a later date. These come out of the Great Tribulation. These have come from *all* nations, tribes, peoples, and tongues. Evidently, by this time, the gospel message has indeed been preached "in all the world as a witness to all nations" so that shortly "the end will come" (Mtt. 24:14).[58] If the scene shown John includes future saints which have yet to die in the judgments or persecution about to come, then they will have heard the preaching of the divinely commissioned angel "having the everlasting gospel to preach to those who dwell on the earth —to every nation, tribe, tongue, and people" (Rev. 14:6). See commentary on *Revelation 7:14*[3.7.14]. See *Jacob's Trouble and the Great Tribulation*[2.13.4].

stood before the throne

The same throne introduced in chapter 4 (Rev. 4:2). This multitude is in heaven, not on earth.

and before the Lamb

The Lamb is still in heaven in the midst of opening the seven seals. The rider on the white horse (Rev. 6:2) cannot be the Lamb. See commentary on *Revelation 5:6*[3.5.6] and *Revelation 6:2*[3.6.2].

clothed in white robes

Like the martyrs of the fifth seal (Rev. 6:9-11), they will be clothed in white (Rev. 6:11). Like those martyrs, they have not yet been resurrected.

> Does the fact that they were clothed in white robes and held palms in their hands require the conclusion that they are resurrected with literal, physical resurrection bodies (cf. Luke 24:36-43)? . . . when Christ broke the fifth seal, John saw under the altar in heaven the souls of saints who had been slain for the Word of God during the 70th week (Rev. 6:9-11). Since they had been slain, they were without physical bodies, and yet they were given white robes to wear (Rev. 6:11). Thus, in Revelation the wearing of a white robe did not require a resurrection body. Even bodiless souls could wear such a robe. . . . when the rich man of Luke 16 died, his body was buried (Luke 16:22), and his soul went to hell (Luke 16:23). Even though his soul was without its body, Jesus ascribed eyes (Luke 16:23) and a tongue (Luke 16:24) to his bodiless soul. . . . In spite of the fact that angels do not have physical bodies by nature, the Bible ascribes wings, faces, feet, and hands to them (Isa. 6:2, 6; Rev. 10:1-2, 5, 8, 10) and portrays them wearing clothing (Mtt. 28:2-3; Mark 16:5; Acts 1:10; Rev. 15:6). . . . Although the Bible ascribes such things as hands, feet, faces, tongues, and the wearing of clothing to human, angelic, and divine beings, it does not mean that those beings have literal, physical bodies such as resurrected people have. . . . the fact that the great multitude of Revelation 7 were clothed in white robes and held palms in their hands does not require the conclusion that they are resurrected with literal, physical resurrection bodies.[59]

See commentary on *Revelation 1:5*[3.1.5], *Revelation 3:4*[3.3.4], and *Revelation 3:18*[3.3.18].

palm branches

During the Feast of Tabernacles (*Sukkoth*), the children of Israel were to "take for yourselves on the first day the fruit of beautiful trees, **branches** of **palm** trees, the boughs of leafy trees, and willows of the brook; and you shall rejoice before the LORD your God for seven days" (Lev. 23:40). The boughs were used in the construction of makeshift dwellings (*booths*, *tabernacles*) reminiscent of the time of wilderness wandering (Lev. 23:43). In the *Millennial Kingdom*[5.2.39], all the nations will go up to Jerusalem each year to keep this feast (Zec. 14:16) which will commemorate not only the wilderness wandering under Moses, but the wilderness of Israel's dispersion among the nations after having rejected her Messiah.

> Compare Zec. 14:16, whence it appears that the earthly feast of tabernacles will be renewed, in commemoration of Israel's preservation in her long wilderness-like sojourn among the nations from which she shall now be delivered, just as the original typical feast was to commemorate her dwelling for forty years in booths or tabernacles in the literal wilderness.[60]

The waving of palm branches became a symbol of national liberation and blessing and attended the First Coming of the King to Jerusalem (John 12:13).[61] Here, they wave palm branches in anticipation of his return to Jerusalem in the events ahead.[62]

3.7.10 - Revelation 7:10

Salvation belongs to

When Jesus rode into Jerusalem on the day He presented Himself as king in fulfillment of the prophecy of Zechariah (Zec. 9:9 cf. Mtt. 21:1-11), the crowd laid palm branches under His path while crying out "Hosanna **to** the Son of David!" (Mtt. 21:9). *Hosanna*, an Aramaic word made up of the words "save" and "I pray," originally meant "save, I pray." Although it originally expressed a request —the desire for salvation—it eventually developed a "liturgical usage, a shout of praise and worship *hosanna, we praise you.*"[63] These praise the Lamb much as the people praised the King at His first presentation to Jerusalem—"*salvation belongs to* the Son of David!"[64]

Σωτηρία [*Sōtēria*] includes both *deliverance* and *preservation*.[65] These had been delivered from the persecution of the Great Tribulation and preserved through death. Salvation was completed at the cross, but its full manifestation awaits the future (Rev. 12:10; 19:1). Because salvation *belongs* to the Father and the Son it cannot be obtained anywhere else, especially not by our own works. Salvation is by grace through faith.[66]

to our God . . . and to the Lamb

God is *uniquely* the Savior. The Father spoke through Isaiah, "I, *even* I, *am* the LORD, and besides Me *there is* no savior. I have declared and saved" (Isa. 43:11). Zacharias prophesied concerning the salvation of the Lamb at His impending incarnation saying, "Blessed *is* the Lord God of Israel, for He has visited and redeemed His people, and has raised up a horn of salvation for us in the house of His servant David, as He spoke by the mouth of His holy prophets who *have been* since the world began" (Luke 1:69-70). Salvation belongs to the Father *and the Son* because the Son provided salvation through redemption (Rev. 5:9). "Nor is there salvation in any other, for there is no other name under heaven given among men by which we must be saved" (Acts 4:12).

The Son is worshiped on an equal basis with the Father (John 5:23).[67] See commentary on *Revelation 5:13*[3.5.13].

3.7.11 - Revelation 7:11

the angels . . . and the elders

The elders are differentiated from the angels (cf. Rev. 5:11). They are either a separate class of angelic beings (much like the living creatures), or they are redeemed men. See commentary on *Revelation 4:4*[3.4.4].

the four living creatures

See commentary on *Revelation 4:6*[3.4.6].

worshiped

προσεκύνησαν [*prosekynēsan*]: "Used to designate the custom of prostrating oneself before a person and kissing his feet, the hem of his garment, the ground, etc.; the Persians did this in the presence of their deified king, and the Greeks before a divinity."[68] The frequent response of the elders and living creatures (Rev. 4:10; 5:14; 11:16; 19:4). An innumerable host worships before the throne (Rev. 5:11).

3.7.12 - Revelation 7:12

blessing, glory, wisdom, thanksgiving, honor, power, might

The blessing is sevenfold indicating completeness. See *Seven: Perfection, Completeness*[2.7.5.3.6]. *Blessing* is εὐλογία [*eulogia*], from whence derives *eulogy*. Literally, *a good word. Thanksgiving* is εὐχαριστία [*eucharistia*], from whence derives *eucharist*.

See commentary on *Revelation 5:13*[3.5.13]. See *Worship of God*[2.4.2].

3.7.13 - Revelation 7:13

white robes

See commentary on *Revelation 1:5*[3.1.5], *Revelation 3:4*[3.3.4], and *Revelation 3:18*[3.3.18].

where did they come from

They are new arrivals in heaven, they were not among the multitude of the redeemed worshiping the Lamb when He first took the scroll from the Father (Rev. 5:9).

3.7.14 - Revelation 7:14

Sir

Sir is κύριε [*kyrie*] which is frequently translated *Lord.* Elsewhere, the word is translated *master* (Mtt. 6:24); *Sir* (Mtt. 13:27; John 5:7), and *lord* (Mtt. 10:24; Luke 12:36; 14:21; 16:3; John 15:15). It is the respectful address of an inferior to his superior in age or station.[69]

you know

σὺ οἶδας [*sy oidas*], emphatic: *you, you know.*

the ones who come out

ἐρχόμενοι [*erchomenoi*], present participle. They are *continually coming out*— probably the result of ongoing persecution resulting in martyrdom, although the text does not explicitly indicate martyrdom. "Present middle participle with the idea of continued repetition. 'The martyrs are still arriving from the scene of the great tribulation.' "[70] "Therefore the *Rapture*[5.2.62] of the church is not in view in this verse, since it is a single, instantaneous, and sudden event (cf. 1Cor. 15:51-52)."[71]

the great tribulation

Literally, *the tribulation, the great.* " '*The* tribulation,' points to a definite prophetic period, and not simply to tribulation in general in which *all* saints shared. '*The* great tribulation' cannot be the general troubles that affect God's people in all ages. The insertion of the definite article marks its speciality."[72] This is the unique time of intense tribulation which Jesus predicted (Mtt. 24:21). During this time, multitudes will die; both unbelievers in judgment and believers through martyrdom and harsh conditions (as these, Rev. 14:13). "And unless those days were shorted, no flesh would be saved; but for the elect's sake those days will be shortened" (Mtt. 24:22). This is the "hour of trial which shall come upon the whole world, to test those who dwell on the earth" (Rev. 3:10). This time of trouble will be especially difficult for the Jewish nation (Jer. 30:7; Dan. 12:1, 7; Mtt. 24:16-20). Yet even this Great Tribulation cannot separate the faithful from the love of Christ, for they are *overcomers* (Rom. 8:35-39). See *Who is the Overcomer?*[4.15.1.3]

As we have discussed elsewhere, the Church is not appointed to God's wrath and is exempted from this "hour or trial which God brings upon the whole world to test those who dwell on the earth" (Rev. 3:10). These believers are those who come to faith after the *rapture of the Church*[4.14].

It is interesting to note the accuracy which attends predictions made by those who take Scripture at face value. Walter Scott (1796-1861), writing well in advance of the establishment of Israel in 1948, says of this verse: " 'The great tribulation' is yet future. **It pre-supposes the Jewish nation restored to Palestine in unbelief** , to serve Gentile political ends, and brought there by the active intervention of a great maritime power (Isa. 18)." [emphasis added][73] Since 1948, Scott's words, which reflect God's Word, have come to pass. See *Trouble Ahead*[2.13.1].

washed their robes

See commentary on *Revelation 1:5*[3.1.5].

made them white

ἐλεύκαναν [*eleukanan*], used to describe making blood-red stains due to sin become white (Isa. 1:18).[74] It may picture not only their salvation (washing away their sins), but also the exchange of garments bloodied by their persecution on earth for clean garments from God.

in the blood of the Lamb

The garments of many were no doubt stained with their own blood. Still, it is the blood of the Lamb which is required for salvation. Their blood, while precious to God (Ps. 116:15) and spilled as a testimony to God, lacks any redemptive power. See commentary on *Revelation 1:5*[3.1.5] and *Revelation 5:9*[3.5.9].

3.7.15 - Revelation 7:15

Therefore

"Because they are so washed white; for without it they could never have entered God's holy heaven."[75]

before the throne of God

The entire thrust of Scripture, from Genesis to Revelation is the restoration of man to full intimacy with God. These occupy a position of great blessing in their proximity to the throne. By the sovereignty of God, these elect did not come to faith prior to the *rapture*[4.14] , but endured the most difficult time for people of faith of all history. Even so, they remained steadfast in their testimony and overcome the adversary (Rev. 12:11).

serve Him day and night in His temple

Their ministry is reminiscent of the four living creatures: "they do not rest **day or night**, saying: 'Holy, holy, holy, Lord God Almighty, Who was and is and is to come!' " [emphasis added] (Rev. 4:8). These who come out of the Great Tribulation may have a different ministry than that of the Church which is caught away prior to this time.

> As their calling and service differ from ours, so does their destiny. We, as the bride with the Bridegroom, sit upon the throne to rule and reign with the Lord of Glory. Our destiny is said to be that of rulers and judges. We are to be kings and priests (1Cor. 6:2-3; 1Pe. 2:9; Rev. 1:6). The 144,000 are to be the glorious bodyguard, the retinue of the Lamb, following Him whithersoever He goeth (Rev. 14:4). The destiny of the Gentile multitude, however, is that of temple servants.[76]

dwell among them

Dwell is σκηνώσει [*skēnōsei*]: "Literally live or camp in a tent."[77] Used by John of Jesus' incarnation when "the Word became flesh and dwelt among us" (John 1:14). This word only appears in the *NT*[5.2.48] in John's gospel and this book (John 1:14; Rev. 7:15; 12:12; 13:6; 21:3), providing evidence that the books share the same *authorship*[2.9].

Their enduring faith in the midst of the Great Tribulation provides a great testimony to the power of God and results in His dwelling among them. They realize the ultimate goal of the eternal state: "And I heard a loud voice from heaven saying, 'Behold, the *tabernacle*[5.2.69] of God *is* with men, and He will dwell with them, and they shall be His people. God Himself will be with them *and be* their God' " (Rev. 21:3). As the psalmist said, "In Your presence *is* fullness of joy; at Your right hand *are* pleasures forevermore" (Ps. 16:11).

> "He that sits upon the throne shall spread his tabernacle over them." The A.V. reads, "shall dwell among them"; a poor and utterly inadequate rendering of the divine thought herein expressed. God spread His tabernacle over the tent of meeting of old, which thus became the centre and rest of the thousands of Israel. It covered them in the desert. Two millions and a half people—the typically redeemed host of Jehovah—were sheltered from scorching suns and winters' blasts, by the huge canopy which God spread over them; it was the nation's glory and defense.[78]

His dwelling presence is directly tied to the promises which follow that the "sun shall not strike them, nor any heat." "His dwelling among them is to be understood as a secondary truth, besides what is expressed, namely, His being their covert."[79]

> When the Lord has washed away the filth of the daughters of Zion, and purged the blood of Jerusalem from her midst, by the spirit of judgment and by the spirit of burning, then the LORD will create above every dwelling place of Mount Zion, and above her assemblies, a cloud and smoke by day and the shining of a flaming fire by night. For over all the glory there *will be* a covering. And **there will be a tabernacle for shade in the daytime from the heat**, for a place of refuge, and for a shelter from storm and rain. (Isa. 4:4-6) [emphasis added]

3.7.16 - Revelation 7:16

They shall neither hunger anymore nor thirst anymore

Many of these tribulation saints no doubt suffered physical deprivation during their time of persecution (Mtt. 25:31-46; Rev. 13:17), not to mention the harsh conditions upon the earth during this time: "Their hunger talks of the famine of the third seal (Rev. 6:5-6), their deprivation of water of the third trumpet (Rev. 8:10-11), and the heat of the sun of the fourth bowl (Rev. 16:8-9). In other words, these martyrs will come from all phases of the tribulation judgments depicted in Revelation."[80]

God also satisfies the *spiritual* hunger of the longing soul (Ps. 107:9; John 4:14; John 6:35). These are among the blessed ones "who hunger and thirst for righteousness" and "shall be filled" (Mtt. 5:6).

nor any heat

In their wilderness wanderings, Israel was sheltered from the heat by the cloud which covered the camp during the day (Num. 10:34 cf. Isa. 4:4-6). Isaiah was also given revelation concerning this truth: in the day of salvation, the Father gave the Son as a covenant to the people. He would go forth to the sheep who were in darkness so that they would be fed. They would no longer hunger or thirst, nor would they suffer from the heat or sun. And He would lead them by the springs of water (Isa. 49:8-10).

Those who *reject* God will feel intense heat before His judgments are complete (Rev. 16:8).

3.7.17 - Revelation 7:17

the Lamb who is in the midst of the throne

Not only the Father dwells among them (Rev. 7:15), they will also be in intimate association with the Son who Himself is in the midst of the throne. Because of their faithful witness amidst chaos and intense persecution, they now enjoy the benefits which many others will not experience until the eternal state (Rev. 21:3; 22:3).

will shepherd them

In place of the worthless shepherd who feeds himself on the sheep (Zec. 11:15-17), they will be led by the True Shepherd out of Judah who was stricken on their behalf (Mtt. 2:6; 26:31; Mark 6:34; 14:27; John 10:2-16). God, who scattered the sheep of Israel, will one day gather them again (Isa. 40:11; Jer. 31:10; Eze. 34:11-31; Mic. 5:4; Mtt. 2:6).

living fountains of waters

He leads them to the still waters which restore the soul (Ps. 23:1-2). This is the living water which the same Shepherd promised the Samaritan woman (John 4:10-11) and which believers in the church age experience through the indwelling Holy Spirit (John 7:38-39).[81] This water is available freely to all who thirst (Rev. 21:6). It is the river of life which will ultimately be found flowing from the throne of God and the Lamb, watering the tree of life (Rev. 22:1-2). In the *Millennial Kingdom*[5.2.39], a fountain of living water will flow from Jerusalem and revive all that it touches (Eze. 47:12; Zec. 14:8).

wipe away every tear

Many of the tears they had shed were due to their experience of death—both of loved ones and themselves. But God has swallowed up death forever and promised to wipe away every tear (Isa. 25:8). In their joy, their sorrow and sighing will flee away (Isa. 35:10; 51:11). Even in the Millennial Kingdom, great joy will be experienced (Isa. 65:19). Ultimately, in the eternal state, there will be no more pain and the former things (e.g., sin and the curse) shall pass away and all cause for tears will be gone (Rev. 21:4).

> Converts during the tribulation will have to face fierce and bestial persecution at the hands of their fellow-men, and also have to endure the natural tribulations which God will unleash on all mankind as a consequence of the sins of the human race. Yes, it will be possible to be saved during the tribulation, but **it is infinitely better and imminently sensible to accept Jesus Christ as one's Savior now, before the tribulation**. [emphasis added][82]

Notes

1 The *NU*[5.2.49] text has Μετὰ τοῦτο [*Meta touto*], *After this* (singular).

2 "This ministry of the 144,000 is something that occurs throughout the entire first half and not merely after the sixth seal judgment. In fact, it is going on during the Seal judgments, and it is the means by which the fifth seal saints come to Messiah. The passage begins with *After this*, which is not chronological, but merely the next vision John sees."—Arnold G. Fruchtenbaum, *The Footsteps of Messiah*, rev ed. (Tustin, CA: Ariel Ministries, 2003), 222.

3 Robert L. Thomas, *Revelation 1-7* (Chicago, IL: Moody Press, 1992), Rev. 7:1.

4 James Moffatt, *"Revelation of St. John the Divine,"* in W. Robertson Nicoll, ed., *The Expositor's Greek Testament*, vol. V (New York, NY: George H. Doran Company, n.d.), Rev. 7:1.

5 Robert H. Mounce, *The Book of Revelation* (Grand Rapids, MI: William B. Eerdmans Publishing Co., 1977), Rev. 7:1.

6 Thomas, *Revelation 1-7*, Rev. 7:1.

7 "We use the same expression today without in any way denying that the earth is a sphere, so must allow Revelation the same latitude and not see its thought as 'primitive'!"—Monty S. Mills, *Revelations: An Exegetical Study of the Revelation to John* (Dallas, TX: 3E Ministries, 1987), Rev. 7:1.

8 "Since nowhere in Revelation do we read of the four winds actually blowing, they may be taken as representing the earthly catastrophes that occur under the trumpets and bowls."—Alan F. Johnson, *Revelation: The Expositor's Bible Commentary* (Grand Rapids, MI: Zondervan Publishing House, 1966), Rev. 7:1-3.

9 Albrecht Durer (1471 - 1528). Image courtesy of the *Connecticut College* (http://www.conncoll.edu/visual/Durer-prints/index.html) *Wetmore Print Collection* (http://www.conncoll.edu/visual/wetmore.html).

10 Walter Scott, *Exposition of The Revelation* (London, England: Pickering & Inglis, n.d.), 155.

11 Donald Grey Barnhouse, *Revelation* (Grand Rapids, MI: Zondervan Publishing House, 1971), 143.

12 Frederick William Danker, and Walter Bauer, *A Greek-English Lexicon of the New Testament and Other Early Christian Literature* (Chicago, IL: University of Chicago Press, 2000), 796.

13 Thomas, *Revelation 1-7*, Rev. 7:2.

14 John MacArthur, *Revelation 1-11 : The MacArthur New Testament Commentary* (Chicago, IL: Moody Press, 1999), Rev. 7:1.

15 Concerning lifeless idols: Deu. 4:28; 2K. 19:18; Ps. 115:4; 135:15; Isa. 37:19; 41:25; 44:9; 45:20; 46:7; Jer. 2:28; 10:5, 8, 15; 16:20; Dan. 5:23; Acts 19:26; Rev. 9:20.

16 Concerning the Living God: Ex. 3:6; Deu. 5:26; Jos. 3:10; 1S. 17:26, 36; 2K. 19:4, 16; Ps. 42:2; 84:2; Isa. 37:4, 17; Jer. 10:10; 23:36; Dan. 6:20, 6:26; Hos. 1:10; Mtt. 16:16; 22:32; 26:63; John 6:69; Acts 14:15; Rom. 9:26; 2Cor. 3:3; 6:16; 1Ti. 3:15; 4:10; 6:17; Heb. 3:12; 9:14; 10:31; 12:22; Rev. 7:2.

17 Danker, *A Greek-English Lexicon of the New Testament and Other Early Christian Literature*, 515.

18 At Rev. 14:1, in contrast to the *TR*[5.2.79] text, *MT*[5.2.45] and *NU*[5.2.49] texts indicate that the names of *both* the Father *and* the Son are written.

19 Barnhouse, *Revelation*, 144.

20 Arthur Walkington Pink, *The Antichrist* (Oak Harbor, WA: Logos Research Systems, 1999, 1923), s.v. "The Antichrist will be the Son of Satan."

21 Danker, *A Greek-English Lexicon of the New Testament and Other Early Christian Literature*, 796.

22 Thomas, *Revelation 1-7*, Rev. 7:3.

23 J. A. Seiss, *The Apocalypse: Lectures on the Book of Revelation* (Grand Rapids, MI: Zondervan Publishing House, 1966), 166.

24 Gregory K. Beale, *The Book of Revelation: A Commentary on the Greek Text* (Grand Rapids, MI: William B. Eerdmans Publishing Co., 1999), 61.

25 A. R. Fausset, *"The Revelation of St. John the Divine,"* in Robert Jamieson, A. R. Fausset, and David Brown, *A Commentary, Critical and Explanatory, on the Old and New Testaments* (Oak Harbor, WA: Logos Research Systems, Inc., 1997, 1877), Rev. 7:4.

26 Seiss, *The Apocalypse: Lectures on the Book of Revelation*, 161.

27 E. W. Bullinger, *Commentary On Revelation* (Grand Rapids, MI: Kregel Publications, 1984, 1935), 282.

28 Jerome Smith, *The New Treasury of Scripture Knowledge* (Nashville, TN: Thomas Nelson Publishers, 1992), Rev. 7:4.

29 William Varner, *Jacob's Dozen: A Prophetic Look at the Tribes of Israel* (Bellmawr, NJ: Friends of Israel Gospel Ministry, 1987), 103.

30 Scott, *Exposition of The Revelation*, 153.

31 Bullinger, *Commentary On Revelation*, 278.

32 Raymond Edward Brown, Joseph A. Fitzmyer, and Roland Edmund Murphy, eds., *The Jerome Biblical Commentary* (Englewood Cliffs, NJ: Prentice-Hall, 1996, c1968), Rev. 7:4.

33 Albert Barns, *Notes on the Bible* (Grand Rapids, MI: Baker Book House, 1884-85), Rev. 7:4.

34 Mounce, *The Book of Revelation*, 168.

35 "Scripture speaks of three categories of persons its contents concern: the Jews, the Gentiles, and the church of God (1Cor. 10:32). What is stated in Rev. 7:4 pertains to Israel—it cannot pertain to any other group. The names of the tribes of Israel are nowhere in Scripture ever applied to the Gentiles or the church of God. Even among those who (mistakenly) believe the term 'Israel' can denote the Church, some recognize the overwhelming evidence in this passage against taking 'Israel' as the Church: "It is clear that, though "Israel"

may elsewhere designate the spiritual Israel, "the elect (Church) on earth" [Alford], here, where the names of the tribes one by one are specified, these names cannot have any but the literal meaning."[83]"—Smith, *The New Treasury of Scripture Knowledge*, Rev. 7:4.

36 MacArthur, *Revelation 1-11 : The MacArthur New Testament Commentary*, Rev. 7:4.

37 G. E. Ladd, *"Revelation, Book of,"* in Geoffrey W. Bromiley, ed., *International Standard Bible Encyclopedia* (Grand Rapids, MI: William B. Eerdmans Publishing Co., 1979, 1915), 4:175.

38 The "Israel of God" of Gal. 6:16 being no exception. "As Peter Richardson observes: 'Strong confirmation of this position [i.e., that "Israel" refers to the Jews in the NT] comes from the total absence of an identification of the church with Israel until A.D. 160; and also from the total absence, even then, of the term "Israel of God" to characterize the church.' "—Johnson, *Revelation: The Expositor's Bible Commentary*, Rev. 7:1-3. In *every* instance, the word "Israel" refers to those who are of the physical seed of Jacob. See [Arnold G. Fruchtenbaum, *Israelology: The Missing Link in Systematic Theology* (Tustin, CA: Ariel Ministries, 1989), 684-690].

39 Scott, *Exposition of The Revelation*, 157.

40 MacArthur, *Revelation 1-11 : The MacArthur New Testament Commentary*, Rev. 7:4.

41 Barnhouse, *Revelation*, 148.

42 "The Gentile company (verse 9) is not numbered. The Israelitish company, on the contrary, is carefully reckoned and the result stated, not in round numbers, but in precise terms."—Scott, *Exposition of The Revelation*, 157.

43 Varner, *Jacob's Dozen: A Prophetic Look at the Tribes of Israel*, 60.

44 Varner, *Jacob's Dozen: A Prophetic Look at the Tribes of Israel*, 103.

45 Smith, *The New Treasury of Scripture Knowledge*, Rev. 7:4.

46 Scott, *Exposition of The Revelation*, 158.

47 Mills suggests that Dan will be key in leading Israel toward the Antichrist in the time of the end: "Dan has a traditional history of idolatry (Lev. 24:11; Jdg. 18:30-31; 1K. 12:28-29), and in the end times it will be no different: Dan will not recognize her Messiah, but will lead Israel in its firm covenant with the Pseudo-christ."—Mills, *Revelations: An Exegetical Study of the Revelation to John*, Revelation 7:4. As interesting as this theory might be, it requires the tribe of Dan to act in concert *as a tribe* which seems unlikely given the lack of human ability to determine the boundaries of the tribe within the Jewish population. Of course, the possibility exists that some form of genetic tracking, along with genetic material recovered from a known Danite, could provide the key to unlock *human* knowledge of the boundaries of the tribe. As we discuss elsewhere, God knows which are the offspring of each son of Jacob. See *Ten Tribes Lost?*[4.17].

48 Alexander Roberts, James Donaldson, and A. Cleveland Coxe, *Ante-Nicene Fathers Vol. I* (Oak Harbor, WA: Logos Research Systems, 1997), s.v. "ECF 1.1.7.1.5.31."

49 "A great deal of speculation and guesswork has developed as a result [of the omission of the tribe of Dan], mainly the idea that the Antichrist will come out of this tribe. . . . Others claim that the *False Prophet*[5.2.20] will arise out of the Tribe of Dan and that is why that tribe is left out. But this too, is pure speculation. There is nothing in the context to suggest either of these suppositions. The text itself does not state the reason why the Tribe of Dan is left out. The actual reason is simply to maintain the symmetry of twelve."—Fruchtenbaum, *The Footsteps of Messiah*, 222-223.

50 Unger takes this evangelistic work as occurring during the millennial age rather than in preparation for it: "The LORD will dispatch those of the Jews who escape the judgments of the Tribulation to the nations to evangelize the Gentiles of the Kingdom."—Merrill F. Unger, *Unger's Commentary on the Old Testament* (Chattanooga, TN: AMG Publishers, 2002), Isa. 66:19b. It would seem that "those among them who "escape" could refer to the sealed Jews of the Diaspora during the Tribulation period itself."

51 MacArthur, *Revelation 1-11 : The MacArthur New Testament Commentary*, Rev. 7:9.

52 Fruchtenbaum, *The Footsteps of Messiah*, 178-179.

53 Barnhouse, *Revelation*, 151.

54 J. Dwight Pentecost, *Things to Come: A Study in Biblical Eschatology* (Grand Rapids, MI: Zondervan Publishing House, 1958), 214.

55 Scott, *Exposition of The Revelation*, 158.

56 Barnhouse, *Revelation*, 145.

57 Fruchtenbaum, *The Footsteps of Messiah*, 179-180.

58 Henry Morris, *The Revelation Record* (Wheaton, IL: Tyndale House Publishers, 1983), Rev. 7:9.

59 Renald E. Showers, *Maranatha, Our Lord Come* (Bellmawr, NJ: The Friends of Israel Gospel Ministry, 1995), 248.

60 Fausset, "*The Revelation of St. John the Divine*," Rev. 7:9.

61 Regarding John 12:13: "From about two centuries earlier, the waving of palm branches had become a national, if not nationalistic, symbol, which signaled the fervent hope that a messianic liberator was arriving on the scene."—MacArthur, *Revelation 1-11 : The MacArthur New Testament Commentary*, John 12:13.

62 Fausset, "*The Revelation of St. John the Divine*," Rev. 7:9.

63 Timothy Friberg, Barbara Friberg, and Neva F. Miller, *Analytical Lexicon of the Greek New Testament* (Grand Rapids, MI: Baker Books, 2000), 416.

64 "The word [salvation] frequently carries the meaning of 'victory' in classical Greek and in the *LXX*[5.2.38] (Caird)."—Thomas, *Revelation 1-7*, Rev. 7:10.

65 Danker, *A Greek-English Lexicon of the New Testament and Other Early Christian Literature*, 801.

66 Concerning salvation by faith: Hab. 2:4; Luke 7:42, 50; Acts 13:39; Rom. 1:17; 3:20, 28; 4:2-6; 5:1, 16-18; Gal. 2:16, 21; 3:11, 24; 5:4; 6:15; Eph. 2:8-10; 2Ti. 1:9; Tit. 3:5; Heb. 10:38; Rev. 7:10.

67 Concerning worship of Jesus: Mtt. 2:2; 8:2; 9:18; 14:33; 15:25; 28:9, 17; Mtt. 20:20; Mark 5:6; Luke 24:52; John 5:18, 23; John 9:38; 20:28; Acts 7:59 cf. Ps. 31:5; Php. 2:9; Heb. 1:6; Rev. 5:13; Rev. 7:10.

68 Danker, *A Greek-English Lexicon of the New Testament and Other Early Christian Literature*, 716.

69 Moffatt, "*Revelation of St. John the Divine*," 399.

70 A. T. Robertson, *Robertson's Word Pictures in Six Volumes* (Escondido, CA: Ephesians Four Group, 2003), Rev. 7:14.

71 MacArthur, *Revelation 1-11 : The MacArthur New Testament Commentary*, Rev. 7:14.

72 Scott, *Exposition of The Revelation*, 163.

73 Scott, *Exposition of The Revelation*, 163.

74 Danker, *A Greek-English Lexicon of the New Testament and Other Early Christian Literature*, 472.

75 Fausset, "*The Revelation of St. John the Divine*," Rev. 7:15.

76 Barnhouse, *Revelation*, 153.

77 Friberg, *Analytical Lexicon of the Greek New Testament*, 350.

78 Scott, *Exposition of The Revelation*, 165.

79 Fausset, "*The Revelation of St. John the Divine*," Rev. 7:15.

80 Mills, *Revelations: An Exegetical Study of the Revelation to John*, Rev. 7:16.

81 He Who is the Living Water thirsted in dying (John 19:28): "He who began His ministry by hungering (Mtt. 4:3), ended it by thirsting (John 19:28). He who was the Rock whence Israel in the desert was refreshed (1Cor. 10:4), and He who turned the water into wine (John 2:1-25), now thirsts."—Graham W. Scroggie, *A Guide to the Gospels* (Grand Rapids, MI: Kregel Publications, 1995, 1948), 587.

82 Mills, *Revelations: An Exegetical Study of the Revelation to John*, Rev. 7:17.

83 Fausset, "*The Revelation of St. John the Divine*," Rev. 7:1.

3.8 - Revelation 8

3.8.1 - Revelation 8:1

Now that God's servants have been sealed for protection, the seventh seal can be opened. Seven angels are given seven trumpets. The first four angels sound their trumpets resulting in great devastation to the life-supporting systems of the earth. As harsh as these judgments are, they are less severe than the remaining three trumpets to come.

He opened

We must ever bear in mind that it is the Lamb who opens each of the seals initiating the judgments which befall the earth and its citizens. See commentary on *Revelation 5:5*[3.5.5] and *Revelation 6:1*[3.6.1].

seventh seal

The seventh seal *contains* the seven trumpet judgments and the seventh trumpet *contains* the seven bowl judgments.[1] The full effects of opening all seven seals include all seven trumpet judgments and the seven bowl judgments: 6 seal judgments + 6 trumpet judgments + 7 bowl judgments = 19 specific judgments in all. At the opening of the seventh seal, 6 judgments (the six seals) have passed and 13 remain (six trumpets and seven bowls within the seventh trumpet). See *Literary Structure*[2.14].

silence in heaven

"In the Jewish temple, musical instruments and singing resounded during the whole time of the offering of the sacrifices, which formed the first part of the service. But at the offering of incense, solemn silence was kept."[2] Zephaniah revealed that silence would attend the *Day of the Lord*[5.2.14] in response to the solemn occasion where He will prepare a sacrifice and invite His guests (Zep. 1:7).[3] The sacrifice will consist of the men who oppose God and the guests are the birds of heaven who will feast upon them (Rev. 19:17-18). This silence precedes the Day of the Lord in its narrow sense—the actual day when Christ returns and physically defeats the armies gathered against him. The Day of the Lord, in its broadest sense, is already in progress. See *When Does the Day of the Lord Dawn?*[2.13.3.1]

> The implication is that when the judgment about to happen becomes visible as the seventh seal is broken and the scroll unrolled, both the redeemed and the angels are reduced to silence in anticipation of the grim reality of the destruction they see written on the scroll. The half an hour of silence is the calm before the storm. It is the silence of foreboding, of intense expectation, of awe at what God is about to do.[4]

Scripture reveals a pattern of silence associated with the recognition of God's holiness and righteous judgment (Ps. 76:8-9; Hab. 2:20; Zep. 1:7; Zec. 2:13).[5]

> When Heaven falls silent for half an hour, when all the singing, glorifying, and praising ceases, there will be a deep sense of foreboding. The judgments, every righteous soul knows, must be formidable in the extreme, yet they will shudder in awe at the prospect of having to witness their administration.[6]

3.8.2 - Revelation 8:2

seven angels

These are seven specific angels who are said to stand before God. Some have identified these with angels which are named in the books of *Enoch* and *Tobit*.[7]

But God has only chosen within the pages of *inspired*[5.2.33] Scripture to reveal the names of three powerful angels: Lucifer (Isa. 14:12), Gabriel (Dan. 8:16; 9:21; Luke 1:19), and Michael (Dan. 10:13; 12:1; Jude 1:9; Rev. 12:7). It is pure speculation to attempt to identify these specific angels other than recognizing that Scripture reveals that Gabriel "stands in the presence of God" (Luke 1:19).

The Seven Angels with Trumpets [8]

> They are of particular rank and distinction, for not all angels are of the same dignity and office. Paul enumerates "dominions, principalities, and powers" [Col. 1:16] among the celestial orders. Daniel speaks of some chief princes [Dan. 10:13], Paul and Jude refer to archangels [1Th. 4:16; Jude 1:9]. Angelic beings are not, therefore, of one and the same grade. The sons of God, in general, come before him only at appointed times (Job 1:6) but the Saviour speaks of some angels who "do always behold the face of the Father which is in heaven" (Mtt. 18:10).[9]

Some believe these angels are the seven spirits before God's throne (Rev. 1:4; 3:1; 4:5; 5:6).[10] But there is strong evidence for understanding the Seven Spirits as the various manifestations of the Holy Spirit rather than angels. See commentary on *Revelation 1:4*[3.1.4].

who stand before God

When Gabriel visited Zecharias to announce the birth of John the Baptist, he said "I am Gabriel, who stands in the presence of God" (Luke 1:19). Apparently there is a group of especially powerful angels, of which Gabriel is a member, who have close access to God and stand before Him. Here we meet with another piece of evidence which argues that the twenty-four elders are not angels for they *sit* before God. See commentary on *Revelation 4:4*[3.4.4].

> These seven angelic trumpeters are elect and loyal servants of God with a position commensurate with their trust. They stand, permanently, in the presence of God Almighty; these are special angels, they are

> of Heaven's elite (Rev. 8:2)! In eastern courts the most favored courtiers had the right to enter the king's presence at all times; these angels are angels of the presence; their high rank is thus confirmed.[11]

to them were given seven trumpets

The trumpets were given to the angels by divine permission. The judgments which come forth once they are blown are initiated by God. See commentary on *Revelation 6:2*[3.6.2].

These are the next set of seven judgments in the series of seals, *trumpets*, and bowls. As the judgments progress, they escalate in intensity. The trumpet judgments are more severe than the preceding seal judgments, but less severe than the bowl judgments to follow. For example, at the second trumpet, a third of the seas become blood (Rev. 8:8). At the second bowl judgment, the remaining two-thirds of the seas become blood as of a dead man (Rev. 16:3). At the sounding of the seventh trumpet, whose effects include the bowl judgments which follow, the announcement is made: "The kingdom of the world has become the kingdom of our Lord and of his Christ, and he will reign for ever and ever." (Rev. 11:15). See *Literary Structure*[2.14].

Zephaniah associated trumpets sounding an alarm with the *Day of the Lord*[5.2.14] (Zep. 1:14-18). The seven trumpets, which ultimately lead to the fall of the great city Babylon (Rev. 18), are typified by the seven ram's horns used to overthrow Jericho in the days of Joshua (Jos. 6:4-5). "It should be carefully noted, that the order of these first four trumpet-judgments is the same as that of the bowls of wrath in chapter 16. (1) Earth; (2) Sea; (3) Rivers and fountains of waters; (4) The Sun."[12] The trumpet judgments are divided into two groups: the first four which affect the natural systems (Rev. 8:7-12) and the last three which affect men (Rev. 9:1, 13; 11:15).

> In contradistinction to the last three trumpets, the first four afflict natural objects, i.e., earth, trees, grass, rivers, and the like. The fifth and sixth have men as their special objects, and unlike the first four which are connected and interdependent, are separate and independent. In contrast to these two, the first four have only an indirect effect on mankind. Besides these differences, the voice of the eagle in Rev. 8:13 separates the trumpets into two groups (Alford, Swete, Beckwith, Sweet).[13]

3.8.3 - Revelation 8:3

another angel

Because of the intercessory service of the angel, some see him as Christ (Isa. 53:12; Rom. 8:34; John 17:15-24; Heb. 7:25; 1Ti. 2:5; Rev. 8:3).[14] But it seems unlikely that the second person of the Godhead would be denoted simply as *another angel*—as if more-or-less on a par with the other seven which are to sound trumpets. There is also a contradiction if *He* Who opens the seal in verse 1 is the Lamb Himself. The explanation that this is Christ supposes that the Lamb opens the seventh seal and then puts down the scroll to take upon Himself an entirely different role—that of offering the prayers of the saints with incense.

> Because of his priestly work, some identify him as the Lord Jesus Christ. That identification is unlikely, however, for several reasons. First, Christ is already identified in the heavenly scene as the Lamb (Rev. 5:6; 6:1; 7:17), distinguishing Him from this angel. Second, while the pre-incarnate Christ appeared as the Angel of the Lord in the Old Testament, Jesus is nowhere identified as an angel in the New Testament. Third, the reference in verse 2 [Rev. 8:2] to the seven actual angels defines the meaning of the term in this context. The angel in verse 3 [Rev. 8:3] is described as another (*allos* ; another of the same kind; cf. Rev. 7:2) angel like those in verse 2 [Rev. 8:2]. Finally, everywhere He appears in Revelation, Jesus is clearly identified.[15]

> Here the angel acts merely as a ministering spirit (Heb. 1:4), just as the twenty-four elders have vials full of odors, or incense, which are the prayers of saints (Rev. 5:8), and which they present before the Lamb.[16]

incense . . . offer it with the prayers of the saints

On the day of atonement, Aaron was instructed to take a censer full of burning coals of fire from the altar and put the incense on the fire which would form a cloud which would cover the mercy seat—where the Lord's presence was. This cloud served as a protective separation from God's presence "lest he die" (Lev. 16:12-13). The cloud shielded Aaron from the presence of God. Elsewhere, when a plague had broken out among the people, Aaron was instructed to take a censer with fire and incense among the congregation to make atonement for them. Just like *the prayers of the saints*, this act of Aaron's was described as *intercession* (Num. 16:46-48). In the *Millennial Kingdom*[5.2.39], incense will be offered to God worldwide (Mal. 1:11). Previously, the twenty-four elders (and possibly the living creatures) were said to hold "golden bowls of incense, which are the prayers of the saints" (Rev. 5:8). See commentary on *Revelation 5:8*[3.5.8]. The prayers of the saints are intercessory and also include petitions for justice, such as those of the martyrs under the altar at the fifth seal (Rev. 6:10).

> These are undoubtedly the cries of believers in the Great Tribulation against their persecutors and all who blaspheme God and Christ in that time. Their prayers, affirmed by the heavenly incense which God has provided, show that He is in agreement with the cries of the saints as they come into His presence, from which the seven trumpet judgments will be released. There is a sense of anticipation as these prayers rise before God. They will shortly be answered; God's wrath and His people's prayers are connected.[17]

upon the golden altar

The writer of Hebrews informs us that the earthly *tabernacle*[5.2.69] was but a model of a greater reality in heaven (Heb. 9:11, 24). There were two altars in the plan of the tabernacle, a larger altar of burnt offering (sacrifice) outside the holy place and a smaller altar of incense within the holy place (Lev. 4:7). It is upon the altar of incense in the heavenly temple that the prayers are offered (Ex. 30:1; Luke 1:11).

3.8.4 - Revelation 8:4

smoke of the incense, with the prayers of the saints ascended

The psalm writer recognized that the prayers of the saints served a similar purpose as incense burnt before the Lord (Ps. 141:2)—an aroma pleasing to God. The picture of prayer ascending to God is also seen when Hezekiah reinstated the Passover. Even though they were unable to observe the Passover in strict accordance with God's instructions, God was pleased with their prayers because of the pure motivation of their hearts. "Then the priests, the Levites, arose and blessed the people, and their voice was heard, and their prayer came *up* to His holy dwelling place to heaven" (2Chr. 30:27). When Cornelius prayed to God and an angel was sent to instruct him to fetch Peter to hear the gospel, it was said, "Your prayers and your alms have come up for a memorial before God" (Acts 10:4).

3.8.5 - Revelation 8:5

filled it with fire from the altar

The *fire* speaks of judgment (Mtt. 3:11-12; Luke 12:49), just as when the man in Ezekiel's vision scattered coals of fire over Jerusalem (Eze. 10:2).

threw *it* to the earth

The act of the angel with the censer prefigures the angels with the seven bowls of God's wrath (Rev. 16:1, 3, 4, 8, 10, 12, 17). Here, there is an explicit connection between the petitions of the saints and the resulting judgment, whereas the bowls contain God's own wrath.[18]

> "All this occurs in answer to the prayers of the saints. There are those who think meanly of prayer, and are always asking: 'What profit should we have if we pray unto the Almighty?' (Job 21:15.) The true answer is, 'much every way.'

There is an eye that never sleeps
Beneath the wing of night;
There is an ear that never shuts
When sink the beams of light.

There is an arm that never tires
When human strength gives way;
There is a love that never fails
When earthly loves decay.

That eye is fixed on seraph throngs;
That arm upholds the sky;
That ear is filled with angel songs;
That love is throned on high.

But there's a power which man can wield,
When mortal aid is vain,
That eye, that ear, that love to reach,
That listening ear to gain.

That power is PRAYER, which soars on high,
Through Jesus, to the throne;
And moves the hand which moves the world,
To bring salvation down!"[19]

there were noises, thunderings, lightnings, and an earthquake

Noises is φωναὶ [*phōnai*] which can also be translated as "voices" (ASV, KJV, YLT). It is translated as "noises" in Revelation 8:5 and by "sound" in Revelation 9:9. The *noises* (or "voices"), *thunderings, lightnings* and *earthquake* are all indicators of judgment. There is a direct cause-and-effect relationship between the prayers of the saints which were mingled in the censer before its contents were thrown to the earth and these indicators of impending judgment. See commentary on *Revelation 4:5*[3.4.5]. "These terms compose a FORMULA OF CATASTROPHE; and the fourfold character here denotes universality of the catastrophe in respect to the thing affected."[20] See *Four: the Entire World, the Earth*[2.7.5.3.3].

3.8.6 - Revelation 8:6

prepared themselves to sound

The sounding of the angels will be in response to the prayers of the saints which were offered with incense before the throne. Since the judgments are now to be of a greater severity than the previous six seals, great solemnity attends the moment.

> The Old and New Testaments use the trumpet as the symbol of God's intervention in history (e.g., Ex. 19:16, 19; Isa. 27:13; Joel 2:1; Zep. 1:16; Zec. 9:14; Mtt. 24:31; 1Cor. 15:52-53; 1Th. 4:16). A trumpet blast can mean one of three things in Scripture: first, an alarm; second, a fanfare to announce royalty; third, a summons to battle—the latter is appropriate in this context.[21]

> No doubt, these angels had been waiting for this particular ministry for a long time. As "ministering spirits, sent forth to minister for them who shall be heirs of salvation" (Hebrews 1:14), all of Christ's mighty angels (2 Thessalonians 1:7) are intensely occupied with the progress of His work of salvation on earth, "which things the angels desire to look into" (1 Peter 1:12). The seven "presence angels" were surely the most concerned of all, and they were fully prepared.[22]

3.8.7 - Revelation 8:7

hail

At this juncture, we once again encounter a major fork in the road of interpretation where many interpreters insist on understanding the effects of the judgments of the trumpets as being symbolic rather than literal. As we discussed in our treatment of *Interpreting Symbols*[2.7], this leads in the direction of conjecture and supposition out of which it is nearly impossible to obtain an unambiguous understanding of what God intends to *reveal*. For the reasons before stated, and because of the *Golden Rule of Interpretation*[5.2.24], we choose to allow the *context* to determine whether symbolism is in view. When we do, we find that a literal understanding of physical phenomena is most likely in view.

> We are aware that a majority of interpreters maintain that the results of this first Trumpet are not literal. They seem as anxious to get rid of the miraculous and the supernatural from Interpretation, as the Rationalists are to eliminate it from *Inspiration*[5.2.33]. But why, unless the plagues of Egypt also were not literal plagues, we cannot understand, Again we ask, Why should not these be literal judgments which are to come upon the earth? What is the difficulty? . . . To explain this away is to manifest a want of faith in the power of God, and in the Word of God. Such things have taken place on earth. Why should they not take place again?[23]

We note the similarity between the judgments found here and the *physical, literal* judgments which God poured out upon Egypt. Indeed, Isaiah indicates that literal events future to his day would rival those of the Egyptian Exodus:

> The LORD will utterly destroy the tongue of the Sea of Egypt; with His mighty wind He will shake His fist over the River, and strike it in the seven streams, and make *men* cross over dry-shod. There will be a highway for the remnant of His people who will be left from Assyria, as it was for Israel in the day that he came up from the land of Egypt. (Isa. 11:15-16)

In the seventh plague which God sent upon the Egyptians on behalf of Israel, God sent "hail, and fire mingled with the hail, so very heavy that there was none like it in all the land of Egypt since it became a nation." This judgment was sent "on man, on beast, and on **every herb of the field**" [emphasis added] (Ex. 9:22-23). Significantly, in the sounding of this angel, the same mix of fire and hail destroys a third of the trees and all the green grass. This includes grain being grown for food (see below).

Hail which is sent by God in judgment is often of a great size inflicting severe damage (Jos. 10:11; Eze. 13:11; Hag. 2:17; Rev. 16:21). In the seventh bowl judgment, the hail weighs one talent (Rev. 16:21)—ranging between 75 to 88 pounds.[24] The hail is drawn from God's "treasury of hail . . . reserved for the day of battle and war" (Job 38:22). Under the Law of Moses, the penalty for blasphemy and idolatry was stoning (Lev. 24:14-16; Deu. 13:6-10; 17:2-5). During the Tribulation period, the *earth dwellers*[5.2.18] continue in blasphemy and idolatry. Perhaps this explains why God stones them with large hailstones (Rev. 16:21).

> The language is evidently drawn from the plagues of Egypt, five or six out of the ten exactly corresponding: the hail, the fire (Ex. 9:24), the water turned to blood (Ex. 7:19), the darkness (Ex. 10:21), the locusts (Ex. 10:12), and perhaps the death (Rev. 9:18). Judicial retribution in kind characterizes the inflictions of the first four, those elements which had been abused punishing their abusers.[25]

> Hailstorms are normally isolated, yet this will be a hailstorm that will blanket and devastate an area larger than the entire North and South American continents (together they represent 28% of earth's land surface). What a fearful storm that will be. This will be the first stroke of God's scourge, a thunderstorm, or series of thunderstorms, which has no precedent, or anything even mildly approaching it in violence in man's history since the flood.[26]

See *The Plagues of Egypt and the Tribulation*[2.13.7].

fire

Fire generally speaks of judgment. When John the Baptist spoke to the Pharisees and Sadducees who came to his baptism, he called them a "Brood of vipers!" and warned them of impending judgment. He spoke of a Coming One who was greater than he who would baptize with the Holy Spirit and *fire* . Those who repented and turned to God, after the Day of Pentecost, were baptized by Jesus with the Holy Spirit and joined to the Body of Christ (1Cor. 12:13). Those who rejected God would eventually be baptized with *fire* (Mtt. 13:41-42). In the context of this baptism, John presented two alternative categories which encompass all men: wheat and chaff: "His winnowing fan *is* in His hand, and He will thoroughly clean out His threshing floor, and gather His wheat into the barn; but He will **burn up the chaff with unquenchable fire**" [emphasis added] (Mtt. 3:12). Here, the earth dwellers get their first taste of God's judging fire which ultimately culminates in the Lake of Fire (Rev. 19:20; 20:14-15).

mingled with blood

Mingled is μεμιγμένα [*memigmena*], perfect tense: *having been mingled.* "The perfect tense indicates an inseparable mix."[27] As in the Egyptian judgments, blood is included in the concoction thrown to the earth. Joel predicted this day: "And I will show wonders in the heavens and in the earth: blood and fire and pillars of smoke" (Joel 2:30). All three of these elements are present in this event as the blood is mingled with the hail and the fire causes the green grass and trees to burn generating huge plumes (pillars) of smoke.[28]

thrown to the earth

This is the first judgment specifically targeted at the destruction of life-supporting natural systems on the planet. Even now, those who reject God worship the *creature* rather than the *Creator* (Rom. 1:25). At the time of the end, God will set about destroying this idol of the earth dwellers.

> People today are very concerned about saving the environment. Fears about the depletion of the ozone layer, pollution, the destruction of the rain forests, and global warming are constantly in the news. There is a passionate concern to save endangered species, everything from whales to spotted owls to California condors, and a host of lesser-known species. For many, protecting the environment has become far more than a concern for health and safety; it has become an issue of idolatry, as they worship "Mother Nature" by trying to protect and perpetuate the earth. . . . Fallen mankind has failed to recognize and honor God as Creator, choosing instead to make a god out of the earth. But the environmental, evolutionary pantheism that devalues man, elevates animals and plants, and ignores the Creator will be severely judged. "Earth Day" that year will be a gloomy and dismal affair; in a scorched and ravaged world there will be little of the environment left to celebrate.[29]

These are the judgments which the 144,000 Israelites were sealed for protection from. See commentary on *Revelation 7:1*[3.7.1].

a third

In each of the trumpet judgments which result in death, *a third* of the population receiving the judgment perishes. A third of the trees is burned up here, *a third* of the earth is burned up (Rev. 8:7, *MT*[5.2.45] and *NU*[5.2.49] text), *a third* of the sea becomes blood (Rev. 8:8), *a third* of the sea creatures and ships are destroyed (Rev. 8:9), *a third* of the rivers is polluted (Rev. 8:10-11), *a third* of the sunlight, moonlight, and starlight is affected (Rev. 8:12), and *a third* of mankind is killed (Rev. 9:15, 18).

trees were burned up

This judgment is *literal*, just as was the similar judgment of Egypt, as recounted by the psalmist: "He turned their rain into hail, with lightning throughout their land; he struck down their vines and fig trees and shattered the trees of their country" (Ps. 105:32-33). This would include fruit-bearing trees contributing to conditions of famine. See *The Plagues of Egypt and the Tribulation*[2.13.7]. "The third seal (Rev. 6:5-6) prophesied a severe famine during which food will be horrendously expensive. Compounding this already severe food shortage will be the destruction of one-third of the earth's foliage, a destruction wreaked by hail and fire mixed with blood (Rev. 8:7)."[30]

The natural disasters which attend these judgments are a problem for those whose *interpretive system*[2.12] requires a previous "fulfillment" in history. *Preterist interpreters*[2.12.2] attempt to identify this judgment with Roman military tactics during the fall of Jerusalem:

> Chilton tries to find a literal fulfillment of Revelation 8:7 during the siege of Jerusalem in A.D. 70. He says, "Literally, the vegetation of Judea, and especially of Jerusalem, would be destroyed in the Roman scorched-earth methods of warfare." He then quotes a passage from *Wars* 6:6-8 describing the desolation of Jerusalem and the surrounding countryside caused by war. What Chilton does not say is why the Romans cut down the trees. . . . The Romans cut down the wood in order to build earthworks for the siege of Jerusalem. They didn't burn as part of a "scorched earth" policy. The actual cutting of the trees stands in marked contrast with the description of the first trumpet judgment.[31]

all green grass

Green is χλωρὸς [*chlōros*], the same word which describes the color (*pale*) of the horse attending the fourth seal (Rev. 6:8). *Grass* is χόρτος [*chortos*] which can describe "stalks of grain in their early, grass-like stages Mtt. 13:26; Mark 4:28."[32] Thus, this judgment may bring not just environmental destruction, but destroy grain production and contribute to the conditions of famine already initiated by the fourth seal.

Joel, in speaking of the locust-induced famine of his day, also speaks of the eschatological *Day of the Lord*[2.13.3]:

> Alas for the day! For the day of the LORD *is* at hand; it shall come as destruction from the Almighty. Is not the food cut off before our eyes, joy and gladness from the house of our God? The seed shrivels under the clods, storehouses are in shambles; barns are broken down, for the grain has withered. How the animals groan! The herds of cattle are restless, because they have no pasture; even the flocks of sheep suffer punishment. O LORD, to You I cry out; **For fire has devoured the open pastures, and a flame has burned all the trees of the field**. The beasts of the field also cry out to You, for the water brooks are dried up, and **fire has devoured the open pastures** . (Joel 1:15-20) [emphasis added]

Those who take *trees* and *grass* here in a symbolic way encounter a logical inconsistency. If trees represent authorities or governmental powers and grass is generally understood as representing the human race (1Pe. 1:24), then we have the situation where *all green grass* (humanity) is destroyed, but only *one-third* of the trees (authorities). "Symbolic interpretation leads to a hopeless quagmire of contradictions. For instance, the earth, grass, and trees are symbols of nations and men in the first trumpet (Rev. 8:7), but in trumpets 3, 5, and 6 these objects of nature appears side-by-side with men (Rev. 8:11; 9:4, 15)."[33] Purely symbolic interpretations render a wide variety of results here which are typically subjected to great elasticity in order to avoid such contradiction. For example, the *green grass* is taken as *Israel* rather than *mankind*.[34] It is much simpler to see these as literal, physical catastrophes which are completely in keeping with the predictions of the character of the *Day of the Lord*[5.2.14] in the *OT*[5.2.51].

The variation in interpretation among those who take these items symbolically is strong evidence against such an understanding:

> Elliott says that this first Trumpet denotes the wars of Alaric the Goth and Rhadagaisus the Vandal against the Western Roman Empire. We should never have guessed this ourselves. There is nothing about this or even like it in this Scripture. . . . One says "trees" mean princes and great men; and "grass" means men's power and glory (Wordsworth). J. N. Darby says "that which is elevated, eminent, lofty is intended by the trees; the young, feeble and aged are meant by the green grass." Wetstein says "Trees mean fortified cities; grass unwalled villages." Others say "by trees are signified apostles and great doctors; by grass, common Christians" (Paralus). Alford holds that "it appears rather to indicate a general character of the judgments, than to require any special interpretation in each particular case." To all this we have one simple remark to make—We prefer to believe God's own special interpretation of His own judgments, in the plain literal sense of the words.[35]
>
> To some, the sea is pure doctrine; the mountain, aspiring prelates; the fire, their ambition; the discoloration of the waters, the introduction of false doctrine; the fishes, the lower orders of ecclesiastics and monks; the ships, the bearers of the Gospel. To others, the mountain is Rome; its burning, the conflagration of that city by Alaric; the destruction of the ships, the plunder of its wealth. Still others see in the record, a symbol of the ravages by Attila. And I only wonder that no one has discovered that it denotes the settlement of the Mormons in Salt Lake Territory! The simple truth is, that if it does not mean what it says, as men ordinarily use language, no man can tell what it does mean; and the opinion of one is just as good, and just as *bad*, as that of another.[36]

A short sample of the varied meanings derived by various symbolic interpreters underscores the subjective nature of the entire approach:[37]

Variation in Symbolic Interpretations

Symbol	Assigned Meaning
Fiery Mountain	Satan; a great heresy; Vespasian; prelacy;[38] Rome; a system of power; the *Messianic Kingdom*[5.2.39] (Dan. 2); the Jewish state; Babylon; Zion; a heathen nation.
Sea	The nations; the church's baptismal waters; sea of Galilee; pure doctrine; confusion and anarchy; the non-Roman world.
Blood	Corruption of deadly error; introduction of false doctrine; spiritual death and apostasy.
Living Creatures	Destruction of souls; Jews; Ecclesiastics (monks); people.
Ships	Congregations; churches; cities of Palestine; bearers of the gospel; sack of Rome; commerce and means of communication; little states at the time of the Roman empire.
Trees	Men in the haughtiness of pride and position; the elect remnant.
Grass	The people of Israel; the elect remnant.
Great Star	Mohammed; Simon Magus; *Montanus*[5.2.42]; Arius; Cerinthus; Pelagius; Eleazar; Josephus; Genseric; Attila; Menander; Manes; Novatus; *Origen*[5.2.50].
Sun, Moon, Stars	Cities of Galilee and the people of the Jews; the Jewish temple, Jerusalem, and its population; the Bible, its doctrine, and the ministers of the Church; the decay of imperial government from Valens to the fall of Augustus, false doctrines and corrupt manners of the patriarchs and bishops; the great prevalence of errors, defections, apostasies, and confusions in Christendom; the subversion of the Western imperial government and its dependencies.

> The first four trumpets all deal directly with the earth. They do not symbolize political, social, or economic judgment; those types of judgment come later in Revelation. Nor do they describe any judgment that has ever happened in history in some locale or region. The trumpet judgments are actual, literal, physical events that will affect the whole earth.[39]

Some understand the destruction of all the green grass here, but subsequent reference to grass (Rev. 9:4) as license to jettison normative interpretation in recognition of the *apocalyptic literary genre*[2.6]:

> To worry about the prohibition in Rev. 9:4 against harming the grass, when in Rev. 8:7 the green grass was already burned up, or about the question of how a great star could fall from heaven in Rev. 8:10 when the stars had already fallen in Rev. 6:12, is to misunderstand the literary *genre*[5.2.22] in which the Apocalypse is written. . . . We are dealing here with a montage of divine judgments upon a recalcitrant world.[40]

These supposed logical inconsistencies are easily explained. During the opening of the sixth seal, stars fall to the earth. As we discuss in our commentary on *Revelation 6:13*[3.6.13], this does not mean that every stellar "sun" in the universe made its way to the surface of our planet! More likely, it describes a meteor shower or asteroids since human life still remains after the impact (Rev. 6:15-17) along with the sun and the moon (Rev. 8:12). Thus, there remains plenty of cosmic material to supply the needs of the star which falls here (Rev. 8:10). Concerning the grass, one wonders if such authors have ever read anything concerning the beneficial effects of fire upon rangelands? The complete burning of the grass (Rev. 8:7) and its reappearance later (Rev. 9:4) is easily explained by recognizing that the initial destruction burned the stalks of grass, but left the root system intact underground. Some time later, the grass sprouts up once again. "In most parts of the earth grass is not green the year round, but is seasonal. Burning of all the grass that is green during a particular season would leave the remainder untouched until its season of dormancy is over (Simcox)."[41]

3.8.8 - Revelation 8:8

***something* like a great mountain burning with fire was thrown into the sea**

The text is careful to differentiate between a *great mountain* and *something like* a great mountain (ὡς ὄρος μέγα [*hōs oros mega*]). The object itself is evidently not a mountain, nor is it said to *erupt* or spew into the ocean—as we might expect from a great volcanic disturbance. Instead, it is *thrown into the sea* by some agent, possibly an angel, although the text does not say. This could describe the impact of a large meteor burning upon entry to the earth's atmosphere from outer space,[42] or it could be something entirely supernatural.

Jeremiah referred to Babylon as a "destroying mountain" which God would make as a "burnt mountain" (Jer. 51:25). Here it seems that God uses a destroying mountain in judgments which will ultimately overthrow Babylon (Rev. 17, 18).

a third of the sea became blood

In the first plague which God brought upon Egypt where Aaron stretched forth his rod, all the waters of Egypt became blood (Ex. 7:19; Ps. 78:44). Here, as in Egypt, a *literal judgment* is in view because the result affects living creatures and ships ((Ps. 105:29 cf. Rev. 8:9). Later, in the pouring of the second bowl, all of the sea will become "blood as of a dead *man*" (Rev. 16:3). Like Moses, God's two witnesses will also have the power to turn water into blood (Rev. 11:6).

In the third bowl judgment, the remainder of the rivers and springs of water which were not poisoned in the judgments of the third trumpet also become blood (Rev. 16:4). Later, it will be said of the *Harlot*[5.2.25] that she is "drunk with the blood of the saints and with the blood of the martyrs of Jesus" (Rev. 17:6). During the Tribulation, God gives her literal blood to drink.

The destruction of the sea will cause tremendous upheaval to the food chain which supports all life on the planet. The divine hand is systematically removing every means by which man can continue to imagine himself as independent of the one true God.

> The price of sin will include the pangs of hunger, for not only will God ensure that the world's food supply is depleted, but He will also ensure that its meager reserves will not be bolstered, and then ensure that man's alternate food source, the sea, will be drastically depleted.[43]

> God created the sea to be a blessing to mankind, to provide food, oxygen (much of Earth's oxygen comes from the phytoplankton and algae in the world's oceans), and water from the rainstorms on the land that is originally gathered up by evaporation from the oceans. But people have repaid God's gracious provision with ingratitude and idolatry, revering the sea as the supposed source of their remotest evolutionary ancestors. As He had devastated the land environment, the true God judges the sea.[44]

In the plague of Egypt, the water turned into literal blood so it would seem a similar miraculous judgment occurs here, although it is also possible that "blood" may simply denote "death" which results from the polluted waters:

> The word translated "blood" can mean "death" and this provides a ready explanation for this passage. The prophecy may mean that the chemical composition of the waters will be so altered by the meteorite, or whatever it is that God will plunge into the ocean, that the marine life in the effected area will be killed and even metal vessels will be destroyed or ruined. As the text does not say the sea became "like"

> blood but that it "became" blood, and, as the same word is used in Rev. 16:6, this should not be taken as only describing the color of the oceans, but must be understood either literally, or with its secondary meaning of "death."[45]

See *The Plagues of Egypt and the Tribulation*[2.13.7].

3.8.9 - Revelation 8:9

living creatures in the sea died . . . ships were destroyed

Literally, *the creatures in the sea, the ones having life. Life* is ψυχὰς [*psychas*], which has many different shades of meaning, but here describes "life on earth in its external, physical aspects. (breath of) life, life-principle, soul, of animals."[46] The sea is to be taken literally because both *living creatures* and *ships* are destroyed—neither of which have biblical precedence if the sea is taken as a symbol representing the Gentile nations. See commentary on *Revelation 7:1*[3.7.1] . When Isaiah prophesied of this time, he mentioned that ships would be among those things which God destroyed as He brought down man's pride (Isa. 2:16).

> The impact will also generate unimaginably huge tsunamis (tidal waves). Those giant waves will destroy a third of the ships on the world's oceans, capsizing huge ocean-going vessels and completely swamping ports. The resulting disruption of commerce and transportation will cause economic chaos.[47]

3.8.10 - Revelation 8:10

a great star fell from heaven

Star is ἀστὴρ [*astēr*], the same root word as the "stars of heaven" which fell to earth at the opening of the sixth seal (Rev. 6:13). In both cases, the astronomical body is most likely a meteor or asteroid. See commentary on *Revelation 6:13*[3.6.13].

Some have suggested that this star is an angel, possibly even Satan.[48]

> This "great star" evidently symbolizes a distinguished ruler responsible as set in the moral firmament to give light in the dark night of the world's history, but he is an apostate personage—one under the immediate judgment of God, "burning as a torch"; in this respect like the "great mountain burning with fire." The epithet "great" is attached to the mountain, and also to the star; only in the former a corporate power or system is referred to, whereas in the latter an exalted individual is meant.[49]

This view finds support by those who understand the star, *already fallen* , in Revelation 9:1 to be this very star. Since the star there is clearly a spiritual being who unlocks the bottomless pit, then perhaps his fall is recorded here. Although there are many parallels between this verse and the fall of Satan (Isa. 14:12; Luke 10:18; Rev. 9:1; 12:4), the context appears to be describing a cosmological event involving a large physical object. This star is said to be *burning* and appears to rain down upon a wide area of the globe causing the waters to become polluted. These characteristics speak more readily of natural phenomena than a malevolent spiritual being.

As we discussed concerning *the interpretation of symbols*[2.7], once the choice is made to take physical descriptions as being symbolic, there is no end to the conjecture which attends the interpretation of what God is attempting to convey. Again, we ask the question: *If God had wanted to describe a time of extreme physical catastrophe, how would He have done so differently than what we have before us?* A second question presents itself: *How could God tell us about future physical convulsions if we forever insist on taking the text as some form of veiled apocalyptic political intrigue?* See *The Genre of the book of Revelation*[2.6].

burning like a torch

Torch is λαμπὰς [*lampas*], which was used in ancient times to describe meteors and comets.[50]

springs of water

Springs is πηγὰς [*pēgas*] which is elsewhere translated as *fountain* (Mark 5:29; Jas. 3:11; Rev. 7:17; Rev. 21:6) and *well* (John 4:6; 2Pe. 2:17). The emphasis is on water as a life-giving *source*. When men must exist without food or drink, it is lack of water which first leads to death. There is an intentional contrast between the experience of the *earth dwellers*[5.2.18] who are dependent upon these water supplies and those in the previous chapter coming out of the Great Tribulation who are led by the Lamb to living *fountains* (πηγὰς [*pēgas*]) of waters. Though it is God who made these *springs of water* to maintain physical life (Rev. 14:7), He now destroys them to demonstrate the dependence of all life upon Him. God is systematically setting about to remove all the props which allow the earth dwellers to imagine there is no God.

3.8.11 - Revelation 8:11

Wormwood

Ἄψινθος [*Apsinthos*]: "*Artemisia Absinthium*"[51]. Derived from "*absinthe*, a bitter, dark green oil made from certain strong-smelling plants with white or yellow flowers, alcoholic in effect; called wormwood from its use as a medicine to kill intestinal worms."[52] The equivalent word (also translated as *wormwood*) in the *OT*[5.2.51] is לַעֲנָה [*laănāh*], "a very unpleasant substance to consume, which may make one sick, either a root herb, leafy plant oil, or liver-bile; wormwood, i.e., a dark green bitter oil used in absinthe *Artemisia absinthium*."[53]

> [In the Old Testament] it is suggested that it is a poison derived from a root of some kind (Deuteronomy 29:18), that it is very bitter (Proverbs 5:4), and that it produces drunkenness (Lamentations 3:15) and eventual death. It is associated with another poison known as "gall" (Deuteronomy 29:18; Lamentations 3:19). This substance was used to produce a stupefying drink for Christ on the cross (Psalm 69:21; Matthew 27:34) which, however, He refused to drink.[54]

Significantly, God describes idolatry as "a root bearing bitterness of wormwood" (Deu. 29:17). Idolatry is a prevalent sin of the *earth dwellers*[5.2.18] during this time of judgment (Rev. 9:20; Rev. 13:15-16). So God judges their bitterness of *wormwood* by giving them *wormwood* to drink. This is the same judgment which God gave Israel when she rejected Him and pursued false Gods (Jer. 8:14; 9:14-16; 23:15). *Wormwood* also describes the fruit of unrighteousness, which will be a prevalent characteristic of the Tribulation period (Amos 5:7; 6:12 cf. 2Ti. 3:2-4).

At the bitter waters of Marah, Moses cast a *tree* into the waters and made them sweet (Ex. 15:25). This pictured Messiah's work on the cross which provided living water (John 7:38-39). Here, we have worm*wood* which turns the earth dwellers' water bitter. Since they would not avail themselves of the cross of Christ—today's "tree of life"—to obtain the living waters of Jesus (John 4:10), God gives them *wormwood* instead and poisonous waters which bring death rather than life. Like Moses, one of Elisha's miracles healed bitter waters and made them sweet (2K. 2:19-22).

many men died

The explicit identification of men—separately from the trees, grass, sea, ships, and living creatures in the sea—is another evidence of the need to interpret these judgments literally. If the latter represent various organizations and systems of man, why are men specifically singled out here? Many men die from drinking the poisoned waters, but many more will also die due to lack of water from the loss of one-third of the earth's aquifer.

it was made bitter

It was made bitter is ἐπικράνθησαν [*epikranthēsan*] . The same word describes the effect upon John's stomach of the book of prophecy which he is given to eat (Rev. 10:7). Here, the bitterness is so severe as to cause death. The wormwood is essentially poisonous.

3.8.12 - Revelation 8:12

the sun, . . . the moon, . . . the stars

Isaiah prophesied the darkening of all three of these sources of light during the Day of the LORD:

> Behold, the day of the Lord comes, cruel, with both wrath and fierce anger, to lay the land desolate; and He will destroy its sinners from it. For the **stars** of heaven and their constellations will not give their light; the **sun** will be darkened in its going forth, and the **moon** will not cause its light to shine. (Isa. 13:9-10) [emphasis added]

In Joel's vision of the *Day of the Lord*[5.2.14], the darkening of these same heavenly bodies attends the advance of His army (Joel 2:10-11), which are probably the demonic forces unleashed in the next chapter. The darkening of the sun, moon, and stars will be relatively frequent during the various judgments of this terrible period (Joel 3:15).

darkened

The sun became "black as sackcloth" as a result of the sixth seal judgment (Rev. 6:12). During the plagues of Egypt God brought complete darkness during the day (Ex. 10:21-23), but only a partial darkening is described here. The darkening of the sun, moon, and stars at this juncture is most likely due to cloud cover—either by smoke or other physical disturbances (Isa. 5:30; Eze. 32:6; Zep. 1:14-15; Rev. 9:2). As in Genesis, the language may reflect the perspective of the *earth dweller*[5.2.18] so that cloud or dust could obscure these cosmic bodies. Others assume the sun, moon, and stars *themselves* are directly affected: "Somehow, the visible luminaries in the heavens for a time, maybe a day, maybe several days, slow down their internal reactions in such a way as to reduce their power by a factor of one-third. The day and night, as a result are only two-thirds as bright as normal, even though the skies are completely clear of haze or anything else to obscure the light."[55] Although the text does not say that the skies are *completely clear* , it is certainly within God's power to tinker with the internal mechanism of solar power since at a later date the sun's burning will be intensified (Rev. 16:8-9). See also Jeremiah 4:23-28; Matthew 24:29; Mark 13:24; Luke 21:25; Acts 2:20. See commentary on *Revelation 6:12*[3.6.12]. See *The Plagues of Egypt and the Tribulation*[2.13.7].

a third of the day did not shine

The previous description implied the possibility of a continuous reduction in light, possibly due to intervening clouds or dust. Here, the implication is an eclipse or other supernatural phenomena where *all* light from the sun, moon, and stars is blocked for one-third of the time. It is almost impossible to estimate the means by which God could bring about this phenomena. However it occurs, it will be dramatic and unmistakable in its unnatural origin. "How the fractional darkening of the heavenly bodies can produce a reduced duration of daylight, moonlight, and starlight is a puzzle (Swete). Yet man's ability to grasp the 'how' or the cause and effect is no basis for attributing inconsistency to the author."[56]

3.8.13 - Revelation 8:13

an angel flying through the midst of heaven

The *MT*[5.2.45] and *NU*[5.2.49] texts have *eagle* (αετου [*aetou*]) instead of *angel* (αγγελου [*angelou*]). If an eagle rather than an angel, it is interesting to note that one of the living creatures was said to be "like a flying eagle" (Rev. 4:7). A few manuscripts have ἀγγέλου ὡς αἐτοῦ [*angelou hōs aetou*], *an angel like an eagle*.[57] "Since Rev. 4:7 relates to the description of one of the four living beings, it may be that John intends the eagle mentioned here to have the same significance."[58] The *midst of heaven* can describe the atmospheric heavens where birds fly (Rev. 19:17). Later, it is an *angel* (*TR*[5.2.79], MT, and NU texts) which flies through *the midst of heaven* (μεσουρανήματι [*mesouranēmati*]) having the everlasting gospel to preach (Rev. 14:6).

Woe, woe, woe

The angel announces that the judgments associated with the sounding of the final three trumpets are especially severe. "The ability of the eagle to speak . . . is insufficient ground on which to conclude it is symbolic. Animate creation other than mankind receive that ability occasionally in Scripture (cf. Gen. 3:1-5; Num. 22:28-30)."[59] The first two of the remaining three trumpets unleash demonic forces upon the world: the fifth trumpet results in the release of a demonic hoard of locusts (Rev. 9:1-12); the sixth trumpet releases four fallen angels who lead what appear to be a demonic army against mankind (Rev. 9:13-21, 11:14). In the sounding of the seventh trumpet (the third woe), after the subsequent bowl judgments have reached their climax, the kingdoms of the world will be Christ's (Rev. 11:15). The two demonic judgments and seven bowl judgments will be especially terrible for those dwelling upon the earth. Woe is also said to the inhabitants of the earth when the devil is cast down to earth (Rev. 12:12).

If it is an *eagle* (rather than an angel) which cries, perhaps it cries in anticipation of the feast of carrion which awaits it (Job 39:27-30; Luke 17:37; Rev. 19:17-18).[60]

> "Vulture" may be more appropriate than "eagle," for, in a sense, this bird will be calling its fellows to devour the carrion that will result from God's judgments (Mtt. 24:28). This vulture is a seemingly insignificant augury of the gathering of its ilk to the final judgment of Armageddon (Rev. 19:17-18), an insignificant omen which will rapidly become a voracious flood of scavengers. [61]

The threefold repetition of *woe* corresponds to the three remaining trumpets and emphasizes the completeness of the sorrow to follow. See *Three: Life, Resurrection, Completeness, the Trinity*[2.7.5.3.2]. "One reason for using [the word woe] which usually refers to great calamity is that these [judgments] will have people, not objects of nature, as their direct objects."[62]

inhabitants of the earth

Inhabitants is κατοικοῦντας [*katoikountas*], *the ones presently dwelling* upon the earth. These are the *earth dwellers*[5.2.18] who will experience the remaining severe judgments to come. These are the ones who steadfastly refuse God's mercy throughout the period of severe judgments, but continue to harden their hearts and blaspheme God (Rev. 16:21). See *Earth Dwellers*[3.3.10.1].

Dear reader, *today* is the day of salvation. If you have not yet left the ranks of the earth dwellers to join those whose citizenship is in heaven, beware! For each day of delay provides further opportunity for your heart to harden:

> "Do not harden your hearts as in the rebellion, in the day of trial in the wilderness, where your fathers tested Me, tried Me, and saw My works forty years. Therefore I was angry with that generation, and said, 'They always go astray in *their* heart, and they have not known My ways.' So I swore in My wrath, 'They shall not enter My rest.' " Beware, brethren, lest there be in any of you an evil heart of unbelief in departing from the living God; but exhort one another daily, while it is called "Today," lest any of you be hardened through the deceitfulness of sin. (Heb. 3:8-13)

Notes

1 "A study of Revelation 8 through 18 indicates that the seventh seal will contain the seven trumpets and the seven bowl judgments."—Renald E. Showers, *The Pre-Wrath Rapture View* (Grand Rapids, MI: Kregel Publications, 2001), 54.

2 A. R. Fausset, *"The Revelation of St. John the Divine,"* in Robert Jamieson, A. R. Fausset, and David Brown, *A Commentary, Critical and Explanatory, on the Old and New Testaments* (Oak Harbor, WA: Logos Research Systems, Inc., 1997, 1877), Rev. 8:1.

3 Some understand Zephaniah to be describing silence on the *earth*, whereas here it is silent in *heaven*. [Walter Scott, *Exposition of The Revelation* (London, England: Pickering & Inglis, n.d.), 169n] But Zephaniah says, "Be silent in the presence of the Lord GOD," which could certainly describe heaven.

4 John MacArthur, *Revelation 1-11 : The MacArthur New Testament Commentary* (Chicago, IL: Moody Press, 1999), Rev. 8:1.

5 "This silence, nevertheless, has made a good deal of noise in the world, especially among commentators. It would be difficult to find another point upon which there have been so many different and discordant voices."—J. A. Seiss, *The Apocalypse: Lectures on the Book of Revelation* (Grand Rapids, MI: Zondervan Publishing House, 1966), Rev. 8:1.

6 Monty S. Mills, *Revelations: An Exegetical Study of the Revelation to John* (Dallas, TX: 3E Ministries, 1987), Rev. 8:1.

7 "In 1 Enoch 20:2-8, reference is made to seven angels who stand before God and are named Uriel, Raphael, Raguel, Michael, Saraqael, Gabriel (cf. Luke 1:19) and Remiel."—Alan F. Johnson, *Revelation: The Expositor's Bible Commentary* (Grand Rapids, MI: Zondervan Publishing House, 1966), Rev. 8:2. Not all translations of 1 Enoch 20 list seven angels, some list six: "These are the names of the holy angels who watch: Suruel, . . . Raphael, . . . Raguel, . . . Michael, . . . Saraqael, . . . Gabriel."—James H. Charlesworth, *The Old Testament Pseudepigrapha - Vol. 1* (New York, NY: Doubleday, 1983), 1 Enoch 20:1-7. Raphael is also mentioned in *Tobit*: "I am Raphael, one of the seven holy angels, which present the prayers of the saints, and which go in and out before the glory of the Holy One."—*The Apocrypha: King James Version* (Oak Harbor, WA: Logos Research Systems, 1995), Tobit 12:15.

[8] Albrecht Durer (1471 - 1528). Image courtesy of the *Connecticut College* (http://www.conncoll.edu/visual/Durer-prints/index.html) Image courtesy of the *Connecticut College* (http://www.conncoll.edu/visual/Durer-prints/index.html) *Wetmore Print Collection* (http://www.conncoll.edu/visual/wetmore.html).

[9] Seiss, *The Apocalypse: Lectures on the Book of Revelation*, Rev. 8:2.

[10] E. W. Bullinger, *Commentary On Revelation* (Grand Rapids, MI: Kregel Publications, 1984, 1935), Rev. 8:2.

[11] Mills, *Revelations: An Exegetical Study of the Revelation to John*, Rev. 8:2.

[12] William R. Newell, *Revelation: Chapter by Chapter* (Grand Rapids, MI: Kregel Publications, 1994,c1935), 125.

[13] Robert L. Thomas, *Revelation 8-22* (Chicago, IL: Moody Press, 1995), Rev. 8:4.

[14] "We are satisfied that the angel-priest is Christ—our great High Priest. The service at the altars proves it—for both the brazen altar and the golden altar are referred to. No mere creature could add efficacy to the prayers of saints. . . . Further, the action recorded at the altars is of mediatorial character—one between suffering and praying saints on earth and God—and as Christianity knows of but 'one mediator between God and men, the man Christ Jesus' (1Ti. 2:5), the proof is undeniable that the angel-priest is Christ."—Scott, *Exposition of The Revelation*, 171. "This angel casts fire into the earth; and Jesus says of Himself: 'I came to cast fire into the earth; and what could I wish if it were already kindled?' . . . This angel offers the prayers of all the saints, and renders them savoury before God. Such an office is nowhere in the Scriptures assigned to angels proper, but is everywhere assigned to the Lord Jesus Christ. There would seem to be strong reason, therefore, for supposing that this Angel is really the Jehovah-Angel, and none other than the Lord Jesus Christ."—Seiss, *The Apocalypse: Lectures on the Book of Revelation*, 184-185.

[15] MacArthur, *Revelation 1-11 : The MacArthur New Testament Commentary*, Rev. 8:3.

[16] Fausset, "*The Revelation of St. John the Divine*," Rev. 8:3.

[17] MacArthur, *Revelation 1-11 : The MacArthur New Testament Commentary*, Rev. 8:4.

[18] "Symbolically, this represents the answer to the prayers of the saints through the visitation on earth of God's righteous judgments."—Johnson, *Revelation: The Expositor's Bible Commentary*, Rev. 8:5.

[19] Seiss, *The Apocalypse: Lectures on the Book of Revelation*, 187.

[20] Scott, *Exposition of The Revelation*, 173.

[21] Mills, *Revelations: An Exegetical Study of the Revelation to John*, Rev. 8:6.

[22] Henry Morris, *The Revelation Record* (Wheaton, IL: Tyndale House Publishers, 1983), Rev. 8:6.

[23] Bullinger, *Commentary On Revelation*, Rev. 8:7.

[24] Trent C. Butler, Chad Brand, Charles Draper, and Archie England, eds., *Broadman and Holman Illustrated Bible Dictionary* (Nashville, TN: Broadman and Holman Publishers, 2003), 1666.

[25] Fausset, "*The Revelation of St. John the Divine*," Rev. 8:7.

[26] Mills, *Revelations: An Exegetical Study of the Revelation to John*, Rev. 8:7.

[27] Mills, *Revelations: An Exegetical Study of the Revelation to John*, Rev. 8:7.

[28] "The specific cause of the hail and fire . . . thrown to the earth is not revealed, but from a scientific standpoint an earthquake of the magnitude and extent of the one in Revelation 8:5 would likely trigger worldwide volcanic eruptions. Besides spewing vast quantities of flaming lava (which could be blood red in appearance) into the atmosphere, the atmospheric disturbances caused by those eruptions could trigger violent thunderstorms that would produce large hail."—MacArthur, *Revelation 1-11 : The MacArthur New Testament Commentary*, Rev. 8:7.

[29] MacArthur, *Revelation 1-11 : The MacArthur New Testament Commentary*, Rev. 8:7.

[30] Mills, *Revelations: An Exegetical Study of the Revelation to John*, Rev. 8:7.

[31] Gordon Franz, *"Was 'Babylon' Destroyed when Jerusalem Fell in A.D. 70?,"* in Tim LaHaye, and Thomas Ice, eds., *The End Times Controversy* (Eugene, OR: Harvest House Publishers, 2003), 228-229.

[32] Frederick William Danker, and Walter Bauer, *A Greek-English Lexicon of the New Testament and Other Early Christian Literature* (Chicago, IL: University of Chicago Press, 2000), 884.

[33] Thomas, *Revelation 8-22*, Rev. 8:7.

[34] Scott, *Exposition of The Revelation*, 178.

[35] Bullinger, *Commentary On Revelation*, Rev. 8:8.

[36] Seiss, *The Apocalypse: Lectures on the Book of Revelation*, 195.

[37] [Bullinger, *Commentary On Revelation*, Rev. 8:7-11], [Scott, *Exposition of The Revelation*, Rev. 8:7-11], [Steve Gregg, *Revelation Four Views: A Parallel Commentary* (Nashville, TN: Thomas Nelson, 1997), Rev. 8:7-11], [Thomas, *Revelation 8-22*, Rev. 8:7-11], [Seiss, *The Apocalypse: Lectures on the Book of Revelation*, 194-199].

[38] Church government administered by prelates.

[39] MacArthur, *Revelation 1-11 : The MacArthur New Testament Commentary*, Rev. 8:7.

[40] Robert H. Mounce, *The Book of Revelation* (Grand Rapids, MI: William B. Eerdmans Publishing Co., 1977), 184.

[41] Thomas, *Revelation 8-22*, Rev. 8:7.

[42] "This is evidently a giant meteorite or asteroid, surrounded by flaming gases set ablaze by the friction of the earth's atmosphere, on a collision course with the earth. The current doomsday scenarios about an asteroid hitting the earth will come true with a vengeance."—MacArthur, *Revelation 1-11 : The MacArthur New Testament Commentary*, Rev. 8:8.

[43] Mills, *Revelations: An Exegetical Study of the Revelation to John*, Rev. 8:8.

[44] MacArthur, *Revelation 1-11 : The MacArthur New Testament Commentary*, Rev. 8:8.

[45] Mills, *Revelations: An Exegetical Study of the Revelation to John*, Rev. 8:8.

[46] Danker, *A Greek-English Lexicon of the New Testament and Other Early Christian Literature*, 893.

[47] MacArthur, *Revelation 1-11 : The MacArthur New Testament Commentary*, Rev. 8:9.

[48] "Whenever the word *star* is used symbolically, it is a common symbol of an angel, and this is the case here. The angel's name is *Wormwood*, showing the angel to be a fallen one."—Arnold G. Fruchtenbaum, *The Footsteps of Messiah*, rev ed. (Tustin, CA: Ariel Ministries, 2003), 226.

[49] Scott, *Exposition of The Revelation*, 181.

[50] MacArthur, *Revelation 1-11 : The MacArthur New Testament Commentary*, Rev. 8:10.

[51] Henry George Liddell, Robert Scott, and Henry Stuart Jones, *A Greek-English Lexicon. With a revised supplement, 1996.*, With a revised supplement, 1996 (Oxford, England: Oxford University Press, 1996), 299.

[52] Timothy Friberg, Barbara Friberg, and Neva F. Miller, *Analytical Lexicon of the Greek New Testament* (Grand Rapids, MI: Baker Books, 2000), 85.

[53] James Swanson, *Dictionary of Biblical Languages With Semantic Domains : Hebrew (Old Testament)*, electronic ed. (Oak Harbor, WA: Logos Research Systems, 1997), s.v. "a very unpleasant substance to consume, which may make one sick, either a root herb, leafy plant oil, or liver-bile; wormwood, i.e., a dark green bitter oil used in absinthe ."

[54] Morris, *The Revelation Record*, Rev. 8:11.

[55] Morris, *The Revelation Record*, Rev. 8:12.

[56] Thomas, *Revelation 8-22*, Rev. 8:12.

[57] Bruce M. Metzger, *A Textual Commentary on the Greek New Testament* (Stuttgart, Germany: Deutsche Bibelgesellschaft, 1994), 669.

[58] Johnson, *Revelation: The Expositor's Bible Commentary*, Rev. 8:13.

[59] Thomas, *Revelation 8-22*, Rev. 8:13.

[60] Concerning birds feeding upon carrion as a result of God's judgment: Deu. 28:26; Job 39:30; Eze. 39:4, 17-20; Jer. 7:33, 12:9, 15:3, 16:4, 19:7; Mtt. 24:28; Luke 17:37; Rev. 19:17-18.

[61] Mills, *Revelations: An Exegetical Study of the Revelation to John*, Rev. 8:13.

[62] Thomas, *Revelation 8-22*, Rev. 8:13.

3.9 - Revelation 9

3.9.1 - Revelation 9:1

The first two of the final three trumpets are sounded, releasing demonic judgments upon the earth. Unlike the previous four trumpet judgments, these target men rather than natural systems. Even in the face of "hell on earth," the *earth dwellers*[5.2.18] continue in their ways and refuse to repent.

Then the fifth angel sounded

This is the fifth angel of the seven which were given trumpets (Rev. 8:2). When he sounds, it brings forth the first of the remaining three woes. See commentary on *Revelation 8:13*[3.8.13].

As we've seen, once one departs from a literal interpretation of the text, there is almost no end to the speculation concerning the meaning of the text which results. And the more unusual the description of the plague, as here, the more fanciful this speculation becomes. Although we describe the problems associated with the *Historicist Interpretation*[2.12.4] elsewhere, we offer a small example of its fruits in interpreting this fifth trumpet—a demonstration of its inadequacies:

> By this [the fifth trumpet] is predicted an event, from which the world still trembles,—the French Revolution. . . . A sketch [of the French Revolution], divested of the prejudices of both sides, shall now be given. . . . This sketch unquestionably contains the substance of the French Revolution. Yet it is the work of no living pen. It is seventeen hundred years old,—The Ninth Chapter of the Apocalypse.[1]

Rather than attempting to "shoe-horn" what is related in this chapter into past historic events such as the French Revelation, how much more productive to recognize a description of something the likes of which has never yet occurred. The key to understanding the nature of the judgment associated with the fifth trumpet is found in a study of the *source* from whence the locust army, loosed by the fifth trumpet, comes and how they got there. Suffice it to say, it is not Frenchmen being held locked away in the bottomless pit!

This entire passage describes something yet future to the experience of the earth:

> I agree with Alford and De Burgh, that these *locusts from the abyss* refer to judgments about to fall on the ungodly immediately before Christ's second advent. None of the interpretations which regard them as past, are satisfactory. Joel 1:2-7; 2:1-11, is strictly parallel and expressly refers (Joel 2:11) to THE DAY OF THE LORD GREAT AND VERY TERRIBLE: Joel 2:10 gives the portents accompanying the day of the Lord's coming, *the earth quaking, the heavens trembling, the sun, moon, and stars, withdrawing their shining* : Joel 2:18, 31, 32, also point to the immediately succeeding deliverance of Jerusalem: compare also, the previous last conflict in the valley of Jehoshaphat, and the dwelling of God thenceforth in Zion, blessing Judah.[2]

a star fallen from heaven to the earth

As we previously observed, angelic beings are, at times, referred to as *stars* (Job 38:7; Isa. 14:13). That this star is not an astronomical body, but a person, can be seen by the reference to *him, he* (Rev. 9:1-2), and by his personal action of opening the bottomless pit. *Fallen* is πεπτωκότα [*peptōkota*], a perfect tense participle, *having previously fallen and now being in a fallen state*. John did not see the actual fall. At the time John saw the star, it had already fallen.

Since the star had *previously* fallen, some suggest from the immediate context that it refers to the star of the third trumpet which fell from heaven and is called Wormwood (Rev. 8:10-11):

> In the last chapter we saw it in the course of its falling. The result was the bitterness of wormwood. We now see it fallen to the earth. . . . May it not be merely that the great star has lost much of his power and is now a fallen star? It is none other than Satan himself and we shall see the details of this coming to earth in the twelfth chapter [Rev. 12:9-10].[3]

Whether this star fell in the events of the previous chapter (Rev. 8:10-11) or in the events recorded in a subsequent chapter (Rev. 12:9-10), the possibility exists that it could be Satan. If so, then the demonic locusts which he unleashes from the pit may be what is referred to, in part, when John records: "Woe to the inhabitants of the earth and the sea! For the devil has come down to you, having great wrath, because he knows that he has a short time" (Rev. 12:12). It is interesting that John uses the term *woe* to describe the results of Satan's fall while the star which falls here looses the first of three *woes*. Satan's "tail" drew a third of the stars of heaven and threw them to earth (Rev. 12:4), and he himself is cast out of heaven (Rev. 12:9). When Jesus' disciples reported their success at exorcising demons to Jesus, He said "I saw Satan fall like lightning from heaven" (Luke 10:18)—referring to the authority which they demonstrated over the powers of Satan's domain. The coming of God in the flesh to disable the accuser at the cross spelled the doom of Satan and the eventual overthrow of his rule in this world by God's coming kingdom on earth. "Now is the judgment of this world; now the ruler of this world will be cast out" (John 12:31). Jesus said that when the Holy Spirit had come, He would convict the world of judgment "because the ruler of this world is judged" (John 16:5-11). "Jesus was not speaking of Satan being cast out at that precise moment, but that his power had been broken and that he was subject to Jesus' authority."[4] If the star that had previously fallen is Satan, then there is considerable irony in the fact that he now releases his demonic horde from the very region where he himself will be confined during the *Millennial Kingdom*[5.2.39] (Rev. 20:1-3).[5]

> This we believe refers to Lucifer, or 'Day-star' (see Isa. 14:12 margin). The reference, we think, is not to his original fall, but to what is described in Rev. 12:9. The fact that the key of the abyss is given to him is in keeping with the fact that during the tribulation period God allows him free rein and suffers him to do his worst.[6]

> Satan's expulsion from Heaven and his consequent casting down (confinement) to earth will happen in the second half of the tribulation, for Rev. 12:6, 14 require this as these verses indicate that Satan's fall to earth will happen at the midpoint of the seven year tribulation.[7]

If the angel is Satan, then some see a further description of him as "the angel of the bottomless pit whose name in Hebrew *is* Abaddon, but in Greek he has the name Apollyon" (Rev. 9:11). See commentary on *Revelation 9:11*[3.9.11]. It is impossible to be dogmatic on this point, for it is also possible that the star which opens the pit is some lesser principality than Satan himself and "the angel of the bottomless pit" may be simply the highest ranking among the fallen angels *in the pit* prior to their having been loosed.

It is no accident that at the conclusion of these, the fifth and sixth trumpet judgments, we read, "But the rest of mankind, who were not killed by these plagues, did not repent of the works of their hands, **that they should not worship demons**" [emphasis added] (Rev. 9:20a). As we see in this book, God has a wry wit about His judgments, for example: "stoning" those who are guilty of blasphemy (Rev. 16:21). Here he unleashes upon the world the very beings they worship in order that they may get a fill of their ways. Incredibly, they will still refuse to repent!

to him was given

He did not have the authority to open the pit himself, it was *given by God.* The horror which this fallen star is about to unleash is entirely subject to the sovereign permission of God. See commentary on *Revelation 6:2*[3.6.2].

the key of the bottomless pit

The shaft of the abyss had been locked so that whatever or whoever was there could not escape. Now the star which had previously fallen is given the key to unlock whomever or whatever is held there! Later, an angel will be given the same key with which to lock Satan within the same compartment for the duration of the Millennial Kingdom (Rev. 20:1-2).

Elsewhere, Jesus is said to "have the keys [plural] of Hades and of Death." Since different regions of Hades are separated by a "great gulf" (χάσμα μέγα [*chasma mega*]) (Luke 16:26), perhaps the bottomless pit is also within Hades—even being the great chasm itself, although its shaft is normally sealed. Paul associated the bottomless pit (abyss) with the location of the dead (Rom. 10:7). If so, then there may be a relationship between the "keys of Hades" and this key. See commentary on *Revelation 1:18*[3.1.18].

bottomless pit

τὸ φρέατος τῆς ἀβύσσου [*to phreatos tēs abyssou*], *the shaft of the abyss. Shaft* is φρέατος [*phreatos*], a deep opening in the ground to a sealed-in well.[8] It is "the pit of the abyss (because the nether world is thought to increase in size the further it extends from the surface of the earth and so resemble a cistern, the orifice of which is narrow)."[9] In contrast with an underground spring, it is a *sealed* compartment, a “tank, cistern, reservoir.”[10] Here, it stores a *reserve* of malevolent beings. The word is also translated *pit* (Luke 14:5) and *well* (John 4:11).

The shaft leads to the *abyss* (ἀβύσσου [*abyssou*]): “from *a*, intensive, and *bussos*, a depth; akin to bathus, deep.”[11] The term is used to describe the invisible underworld which is contrasted with the sky and earth that are visible to the human eye. The abyss is discernible only by God.[12] It is said to describe “a very deep gulf or chasm in the lowest parts of the earth used as the common receptacle of the dead and especially as the abode of demons.”[13]

> The word “abyss” comes from roots meaning “without depth” and so is properly translated “bottomless.” It is apparently at the very center of the earth and so, in truth, has no bottom. Its boundaries in all directions are all ceilings; one cannot do “down” in any direction.[14]

If the shaft to the abyss was previously locked, then how did this compartment come to have occupants? How did they get in? The abyss appears to be a prison of sorts for demons, as evidenced by the request of the demons which Jesus cast out of Legion. They “begged Him that He would not command them to go out into the abyss” (Luke 8:30-31). “These demons preferred to be incarnate in swine, so deep was their horror and dread of the abyss to which some of their fellows were already confined.”[15] It appears that the demonic forces which are about to be released from the abyss were supernaturally transported there by God—reserved for the day of judgment when they will *serve God’s purposes*. “Not only that they should be then judged, but that they should be the executors of God’s judgments also in that great day which we are now studying and learning about in the Apocalypse.”[16] The locking away of these demons is described by Jude:

> And the angels who did not keep their proper domain, but left their own abode, He has reserved in everlasting chains under darkness for the judgment of the great day; as Sodom and Gomorrah, and the cities around them in a similar manner to these, having given themselves over to sexual immorality and gone after strange flesh, are set forth as an example, suffering the vengeance of eternal fire. (Jude 1:6-7)

The demons are fallen angels, some of which left their own abode and are reserved for the judgment of the *great day*. This is *The Day of the Lord*[2.13.3]. The angels themselves will not be judged at this time, but are “reserved for the judgment”—they will be used by God to torment the earth dwellers.[17] Unlike other demons which were free to roam the earth, these particular fallen angels were guilty of an especially wicked act. Similarly to the inhabitants of Sodom and Gomorrah, they had given themselves over to sexual immorality, ἐκπορνεύσασαι [*ekporneusasai*], and “gone after strange flesh.” *Strange flesh* is σαρκὸς ἑτέρας [*sarkos heteras*], *another [different] kind of flesh*. The flesh was not *allos* (similar), but *heteros* (different). This seems to point to the event prior to the flood when certain angels went after flesh of a different kind: “There were giants on the earth in those days, and also afterward, when the sons of God came in to the daughters of men and they bore *children* to them. Those *were* the mighty men who *were* of old, men of renown” (Gen. 6:4).

Some suggest that the *these* in Jude’s passage refers to *Sodom and Gomorrah*—that the cities *in a similar manner to Sodom and Gomorrah* went after strange flesh. But the grammar indicates that *these* (masculine plural) refers back to the angels (masculine plural). Sodom and Gomorrah and the cities around them gave themselves over to sexual immorality and went after strange flesh *in a similar manner to the angels*. The actions of the inhabitants of the cities is compared to that of the angels which preceded.[18]

Jude tells us that they did not keep their “proper domain,” ἀρχη [*archē*], meaning: “rule, office, domain, sphere of influence.”[19] “The idea is that certain angels acted improperly, going outside the bounds prescribed by God.”[20] The bounds which they exceeded involved their interaction with strange flesh—mingling with the daughters of men.[21] Because of this grievous sin, they are “reserved in everlasting chains under darkness.” *Darkness* is ζόφον [*zophon*], which denotes “especially the darkness of the nether regions and these regions themselves.”[22] Elsewhere, Peter uses a similar phrase to describe the situation of these same angels:

> For if God did not spare the angels who sinned, but cast *them* down to hell (ταρταρώσας [*tartarōsas*]) and delivered *them* into **chains of darkness (σειραῖς ζόφου [*seirais zophou*])**, to be reserved for judgment, and did not spare the ancient world, but saved Noah, *one of* eight *people*, a preacher of

> righteousness, bringing in the flood on the world of the ungodly; and turning the cities of Sodom and Gomorrah into ashes, condemned *them* to destruction, making *them* an example to those who afterward would live ungodly. (2Pe. 2:4-6) [emphasis added]

That these are a specific subset of sinning angels can be seen from the fact that many fallen angels remain free to roam the earth. These angels are guilty of the specific sin involving flesh of a different kind (Gen. 6:4). Those who were involved with exceedingly serious sins such as these are "bound" for subsequent release in God's judgment (Rev. 9:14).

> The "spirits now in prison" in the abyss are those "who once were disobedient—in the days of Noah." They are the demons who cohabited with human women in Satan's failed attempt to corrupt the human race and make it irredeemable (Gen. 6:1-4). . . . The demons released by Satan at the fifth trumpet may not include those who sinned in Noah's day (cf. Jude 1:6), since they are said to be in "eternal bonds" (Jude 1:6) until the final day when they are sent to the eternal Lake of Fire (Rev. 20:10; Jude 1:7). Other demons imprisoned in the abyss may be the ones released. So the pit is the preliminary place of incarceration for demons from which some are to be released under this judgment.[23]

The beast who overcomes God's two witnesses "ascends out of the bottomless pit [abyss]" (Rev. 11:7). The world is said to marvel at the beast "that was, and is not, and yet is" (Rev. 17:8). Perhaps the abyss is his abode while he "is not"—after "one of his heads" was "mortally wounded," but before "the deadly wound was healed" (Rev. 13:3). Perhaps the angels, some of which are in the abyss for having gone after strange flesh, will be involved in the origination of the beast. Or perhaps his ascent from the abyss merely indicates his empowerment by Satan (2Th. 2:9). See commentary on *Revelation 11:7*[3.11.7].

The demons which inhabit the abyss have a king, Abaddon or Apollyon: see commentary on *Revelation 9:11*[3.9.11].

3.9.2 - Revelation 9:2

he opened the bottomless pit

The *shaft* leading to the abyss was now opened allowing whatever was therein to escape.

> Jehovah once said to Job: "Have the gates of Sheol been opened unto thee? or hast thou seen the doors of the shadow of death?" (Job 37:17). There are worlds of being and of darkness upon which man has never looked. There is a tenanted abyss of which the demons know, and concerning which they besought the Saviour that He would not send them into it [Luke 8:27-31]. It is a dark and horrible prison, in which many, many strange and evil things are shut up. Satan knows of that world, and would fain bring forth its malignant inhabitants into the earth if he only dared. At last, however, he receives permission to bring them, and the fifth trumpet gives the result.[24]

smoke arose . . . like the smoke of a great furnace

The plume of smoke that arose is probably one of the "pillars of smoke" which Joel described in the "awesome day of the Lord" (Joel 2:30). A similar plume of smoke attended the destruction of Sodom and Gomorrah by fire (Gen. 19:28). Here we see further evidence that the abyss is deep within the earth and probably of a great temperature due to subterranean activity below the earth's crust. That portions of Hades are of an elevated temperature is clear from Jesus' account of the rich man and Lazarus, where the rich man cried out, "Father Abraham, have mercy on me, and send Lazarus that he may dip the tip of his finger in water and cool my tongue; for I am tormented in this flame" (Luke 16:24).

the sun and air were darkened because of the smoke of the pit

Here is another cosmic sign—the darkening of the sun. There will be numerous situations which result in the reduction of light from the sun during the Tribulation period. See commentary on *Revelation 6:12*[3.6.12] and *Revelation 8:12*[3.8.12].

3.9.3 - Revelation 9:3

out of the smoke locusts came upon the earth

As the smoke arose, other creatures arose with it. They are said to be *locusts*. We encounter another similarity between the judgments sent upon the *earth dwellers*[5.2.18] in the Tribulation and the plagues of Egypt (Ex. 10:12-15). Unlike the locusts which descended upon Egypt, these locusts are not allowed to "harm the grass of the earth, or any green thing, or any tree" (Rev. 9:4). Since the bottomless pit was previously locked and is evidently of a great temperature, natural locusts would neither find entry nor be able to survive in the pit. But these are not normal locusts, as other factors in this passage make plain.

Isaiah describes a noise of tumult at which the people shall flee—in response to the Lord rousing Himself. His plunder is said to be "As the running to and fro of locusts, **He** shall run upon them" [emphasis added] (Isa. 33:4). Notice that the judgment of the people, compared to the ravaging of locusts, is said to be the work of God. In the same way in which a natural locust plague is under the control of God's sovereign will (Joel 2:25), so too is this demonic horde of locusts. Joel also saw this end-time locust-like army of the Lord.[25]

> The earth quakes before them, the heavens tremble; the sun and moon grow dark, and the stars diminish their brightness. The LORD gives voice before **His army**, for **His camp** is very great; for strong *is the One* who executes His word. For the day of the LORD *is* great and very terrible; who can endure it? (Joel 2:10-11) [emphasis added]

> Now in this second chapter, Joel is going to give a blending of the plague of locusts together with the threat of the Assyrian army and then look down the avenue of time into the future and the *Day of the Lord*[5.2.14]. Of course the liberal theologian would say this refers simply to the locust plague and the local situation. He would like to dismiss a great deal of meaning from the Word of God. The other extreme view is to say this refers only to the Great Tribulation Period. I think we need to see that in Joel there is a marvelous blending. He moves right out of the locust plague to the Day of the Lord which is way out yonder in the future.[26]

> The prophet adopts the vantage point of the ultimate day of the Lord, and from that position he looks back to the present locust plague.[27]

> [Joel describes the] appearance . . . of horses—(Rev. 9:7). Not literal, but figurative locusts. The fifth trumpet, or first woe, in the parallel passage [to Joel] (Rev. 9:1-11).[28]

In the context of Joel, the army of God arrives in concert with *The Day of the Lord*[2.13.3] (Joel 1:15-2:11) and eventually gives way to the judgment of the nations (Joel 3:1-17). Then the blessings of the *Messianic Kingdom*[5.2.39] (Joel 3:18-21). This matches the order of events in the book of Revelation. The demonic plagues of this chapter are the first of these three stages.

> It is therefore with diffidence that we suggest, without being dogmatic, that they are, most likely, fallen angels now imprisoned in Tartarus. . . . these infernal locusts issue from 'the well of the Pit,' an expression occurring nowhere else in Scripture, and only the locusts are said to come from there. So also the term Tartarus is found nowhere but in 2Pe. 2:4. It seems likely, then, that the well of the Pit may be only another name for Tartarus (with which only fallen angels are connected), just as the Lake of Fire is only another name for Gehenna. . . . 2Pe. 2:4 simply says [fallen angels] are 'reserved unto judgment,' and we believe this means that God is holding them in Tartarus until His time comes for Him to use them as one of His instruments of judgment upon an ungodly world. The time when God will thus use them is stated in Jude 1:6 - it will be in 'the judgment of the great day' (compare Rev. 6:17 for 'the great day'. Confirmatory of this, observe that in Joel 2:11 the Lord calls the supernatural locusts 'His army,' then employed to inflict sore punishments on apostate Israel.[29]

to them was given power

The ultimate source of their power is not Satan, but God. See commentary on *Revelation 6:2*[3.6.2].

as the scorpions of the earth have power

Here is another hint that these are not normal locusts because they are given power *as the scorpions of the earth*. This phrase implies not only that these are not scorpions (being locusts), but that neither are they *of the earth*. Their origin is not of the earth. Originally, they were angels *of heaven*, but chose to follow Satan in his rebellion, and eventually committed the serious offense which led to their confinement. Now, they are *of the abyss* (Rev. 9:11). Their similarity with earthly scorpions is found in their ability to inflict a painful sting (Rev. 9:5-6). Jesus mentioned "serpents and scorpions" as representative of "the power of the enemy" (Luke 10:19).

3.9.4 - Revelation 9:4

they were commanded

Like the horseman of the third seal (Rev. 6:6), the destructive abilities of the locusts is specifically limited by the permission of God. See commentary on *Revelation 6:2*[3.6.2].

not to harm the grass of the earth, or any green thing, or any tree

Here we see the reason why the last three woes—the last three trumpets—are separated from the previous four trumpets. The first four trumpets involve judgments on *natural systems*, including vegetation, whereas the judgments of the final three trumpets target *people*. In contrast to the previous trumpet judgments (Rev. 7:3; 8:7-11), the locusts are told *not* to harm the natural system, but to attack certain men. These are not natural locusts: "This is an unusual locust that will not attack anything green—that is all the normal locust would attack. They did not attack human beings."[30]

The natural locusts of the plagues of Egypt, although supernaturally provided, illustrate the normal activities of locusts:

> For they covered the face of the whole earth, so that the land was darkened; and they ate every herb of the land and all the fruit of the trees which the hail had left. So there remained nothing green on the trees or on the plants of the field throughout all the land of Egypt. (Ex. 10:15)
>
> The flight of locusts is thus described by M. Olivier (*Voyage dans l'Empire Othoman*, ii.424): "With the burning south winds (of Syria) there come from the interior of Arabia and from the most southern parts of Persia clouds of locusts (*Acridium peregrinum*), whose ravages to these countries are as grievous and nearly as sudden as those of the heaviest hail in Europe. We witnessed them twice. It is difficult to express the effect produced on us by the sight of the whole atmosphere filled on all sides and to a great height by an innumerable quantity of these insects, whose flight was slow and uniform, and whose noise resembled that of rain: the sky was darkened, and the light of the sun considerably weakened. In a moment the terraces of the houses, the streets, and all the fields were covered by these insects, and in two days they had nearly devoured all the leaves of the plants. Happily they lived but a short time, and seemed to have migrated only to reproduce themselves and die; in fact, nearly all those we saw the next day had paired, and the day following the fields were covered with their dead bodies."[31]

How different are these locusts from natural locusts, for they avoid the very things which natural locusts devastate. Some have difficulty reconciling the instructions not to harm the green grass when in the first trumpet it was said that "all green grass was burned up" (Rev. 8:7). This is readily explained:

> The reference to the grass of the earth suggests that some time has passed since the first trumpet judgment scorched all the grass that was then in season (Rev. 8:7). The damaged grass has grown again and is to remain untouched in this plague, indicating that enough time has elapsed for a partial recovery of the earth's environment.[32]

See commentary on *Revelation 8:7*[3.8.7].

but only those men who do not have the seal of God on their foreheads

Here we see the chronological relationship in the visions related by John, for in order to be protected from these locusts, the men must have *already* been sealed. Indeed they were, in Revelation 7:4. Thus, Revelation 9 must follow chronologically after Revelation 7.

These are the 144,000 of Israel who were sealed in Revelation 7:3 which *see*[3.7.3] . Their seal protected them in the midst of the judgments of the systems of nature (Rev. 7:3; 8:7) and now it provides protection from the judgment of the demonic locusts. Here is another indicator that these are not ordinary insects: they are able to differentiate between those who have God's seal and those who do not. The seal may not be a visible mark (see commentary on *Revelation 7:4*[3.7.4]), yet these locusts are able to detect those who are sealed. The answer lies in the fact that demons have great spiritual awareness. During Jesus' ministry, demons frequently identified him as the "Son of God" or "Holy One of God," a fact which was missed by His disciples and most of those whom He taught (Mtt. 8:29; Mark 1:24; 3:11; Luke 4:33-34; 8:28). Mark informs us that Jesus "did not allow the demons to speak, because they knew Him" (Mark 1:34). Luke says "And demons also came out of many, crying out and saying, 'You are the Christ, the Son of God!' And He, rebuking *them*, did not allow them to speak, for they knew He was the Christ" (Luke 4:41). Not only did the demons recognize Jesus, but they also recognized Paul—and that he had *spiritual authority* which the seven sons of Sceva lacked since they were presumably not born again (Acts 19:14-16). Thus, these demonic locusts will be able to readily identify those which have been marked for special protection by God, whether the mark is physical or spiritual in nature.

If we are to understand the 144,000 sealed Jews in Revelation 7 to be the initial sealing of an evangelistic force and a signal of God's redemptive focus returning upon Israel (Rom. 11:25-32), then from their initial witness, many more, both Jew and Gentile, will come to know God during the Tribulation. These are those who John saw which "came out" of the Great Tribulation (Rev. 7:14). It would seem that these too will be protected from the demonic horde:[33]

> Those who have the seal of God include not only the 144,000 Jewish evangelists (Rev. 7:3-4; 14:1), but also the rest of the redeemed (cf. Rev. 22:4; 2Ti. 2:19). This seal marks them as personally belonging to God and as such protected from the forces of hell. Jesus promised the faithful members of the Philadelphia church that "He who overcomes, I will make him a pillar in the temple of My God, and he will not go out from it anymore; and I will write on him the name of My God, and the name of the city of My God, the new Jerusalem, which comes down out of heaven from My God, and My new name" (Rev. 3:12).[34]

3.9.5 - Revelation 9:5

they were not given *authority* to kill

Given is ἐδόθη [*edothē*], passive, it is divine permission which prevents them from killing their victims. It is God's intention that their victims will be unable to escape the torment of the locusts through death. This is similar to the limitation which God put on Satan in Job's testing (Job 2:6).[35] God ultimately desires to keep these people alive so that they have the opportunity to repent and turn to Him:

> After millennia of captivity, the vile demons would no doubt want to give full vent to all of their pent-up evil by slaughtering people. Certainly Satan would want to kill all the unregenerate to keep them from repenting. But God, in His mercy, will give people torment for five months (the normal life span of locusts, usually from May to September), during which they cannot die but will be given the opportunity to repent and embrace the gospel.[36]

This verse frustrates those who attempt to interpret the judgment as involving an army of human origin, for what army on earth has ever resisted killing the enemy?

to torment them for five months

In Revelation 9:10 we are told "Their power *was* to hurt men five months." It is not clear whether the ministry of the locusts is limited to that period of time or whether the effects of their sting lasts for five months. Probably the former. The time period may be intended to convey the idea of God's complete provision for their torment. Significantly, in the judgment of the flood, the waters prevailed upon the earth for the same period of time, five months (150 days, Gen. 7:24).[37] See *Five: Provision, Fullness, Grace*[2.7.5.3.4].

> The duration of the plague is fixed. It is to last "five months." A similar fixed date is given in Numbers 11:19-20: "a whole month." In 2 Samuel 24:13, also we have "seven years," "three months," and "three days," as the fixed limit of certain judgments. These periods are always taken literally. Why not this? The time limit of these infernal locusts corresponds with that of ordinary locusts, which is five months (from May to September).[38]

like the torment of a scorpion when it strikes a man

This would include both the pain of an initial sting and the subsequent pain due to an injected poison. "At least two general types of scorpion poison exist. One is a hemotoxin that causes mild to severe local effects such as edema, discoloration, and pain; the other is a dangerous neurotoxin (nerve poison) that may cause severe local and systemic effects such as convulsions, paralysis, cardiac irregularities, and death."[39]

3.9.6 - Revelation 9:6

men will seek death

They will be gripped with incredible fear (Luke 23:30; Rev. 6:16), experience intense pain (Joel 2:6), and wish to die (Jonah 4:8). Job described the anguish of those who suffer and long for death:

> Why is light given to him who is in misery, and life to the bitter of soul, who long for death, but it does not *come*, and search for it more than hidden treasures; who rejoice exceedingly, *and* are glad when they can find the grave? (Job 3:20-22)

> So that my soul chooses strangling *And* death rather than my body. I loathe *my life*; I would not live forever. Let me alone, for my days *are but* a breath. (Job 7:15-16)

will not find it

Not is οὐ μὴ [*ou mē*], a double negative emphasizing the impossibility of death. This is perhaps the most puzzling verse in the chapter. "It would seem from the sixth verse that there is an intimation of suicide attempts which are frustrated by God."[40]

they will desire to die and death will flee

They will desire is ἐπιθυμήσουοσιν [*epithymēsouosin*], *an intense desire*, elsewhere translated by *lust*. *To die* is ἀποθανεῖν [*apothanein*], present tense infinitive. The pain of the locusts is so intense that their *continual desire* will be to find release through death. But they will not find relief because death will *flee* (φεύγει [*pheugei*], present tense—continually flee). Joel was given a glimpse of this intense fear and pain: "Before them the people writhe in pain; All faces are drained of color" (Joel 2:6).

We have record in the gospels of the degree to which demons *control* their victims:

> Then they brought him to Him. And when he saw Him, immediately the spirit convulsed him, and he fell on the ground and wallowed, foaming at the mouth. So He asked his father, "How long has this been happening to him?" And he said, "From childhood. And often he has thrown him both into the fire and into the water to destroy him. But if You can do anything, have compassion on us and help us." (Mark 9:20-22)

> And when He stepped out on the land, there met Him a certain man from the city who had demons for a long time. And he wore no clothes, nor did he live in a house but in the tombs. When he saw Jesus, he cried out, fell down before Him, and with a loud voice said, "What have I to do with You, Jesus, Son of the Most High God? I beg You, do not torment me!" For He had commanded the unclean spirit to come out of the man. For it had often seized him, and he was kept under guard, bound with chains and shackles; and he broke the bonds and was driven by the demon into the wilderness. (Luke 8:27-29)

Perhaps part of the tormenting assigment of the demons is not only to sting their victims, but to ensure they remain unable to take their own lives.

> We are not told what will make man unable to commit suicide (Rev. 9:6), but can speculate that these demonic creatures, anticipating a man's actions, by simply stinging him at the crucial moment, will prevent him from suicide. What excruciating torture; driven to the point of suicide, but prevented from taking the final step by the very same torment that drives a man to the resolve to take his own life. Man will seek death by any means, even the tormenting locusts, yet they will not be permitted to kill (Rev. 9:5). [41]

3.9.7 - Revelation 9:7

The shape of the locusts was like

Up to this point, the creatures which come up out of the bottomless pit have been identified as "locusts" (Rev. 9:3). Now, John begins a series of descriptions which are similitudes—representations which approximate what he sees concerning the locusts. Comparative terms such as ὁμιόωμα [*homioōma*] (likeness, image, form, appearance), [42] ὅμοιος [*homoios*] (like, similar), [43] and ὡς [*hōs*] (as, like)[44] will occur frequently in the descriptions which follow. As elsewhere in this book, much of what John is shown exceeds anything he has seen before and so he struggles to relate the vision using similes which provide an approximation of what he is being shown. These comparative terms do not provide license for fanciful symbolism or allegorical interpretation—they represent the closest similarity which John knew for describing what he saw. If anything, they provide support for understanding John's description as closely accurate of the reality before him.

Before continuing with our study of this passage, we feel it is important to discuss how we are to understand the seemingly fantastic[45] description of the locusts (and the horses and horsemen of the sixth trumpet) which follow in this chapter. Many find their description so unbelievable that they are driven to spiritualize the passage:

> Many commentators interpret the plague as a condition of sinful life rather than an eschatological event. Hendricksen sees the description as "the operation of the powers of darkness in the soul of the wicked during this present age" (p. 147). For Hengstenberg it is the hellish spirit that penetrates the earth (I, pp. 429 ff), and for Dana, the forces of decay and corruption which God will use to undermine the Roman Empire (pp. 126 ff).[46]

As we have observed in our discussion of *Interpreting Symbols*[2.7] , the decision to depart from a literal interpretation, which recognizes figures of speech, is a serious one for it places the interpreter upon a sea of subjectivity. Moreover, if all this chapter is meant to teach is general moral principles or even the depravity of men (Jer. 17:9), then how does one explain the excessive details of the vision? What possible purpose could they serve? Why not say the same thing with far fewer words? No, what is being described here is real, literal, and important to understand in detail else God would not have "wasted" words on it.

We would ask the reader to keep in mind several considerations:

1. **Demonic Capabilities** - We know next to *nothing* concerning the demonic realm and especially the transformative capabilities of angels—be they elect or fallen. Scripture records that angels are "ministering spirits" (Ps. 104:4; Heb. 1:7, 14), yet they appear in numerous passages as anatomically accurate *human men* . When Isaiah, Ezekiel, and John are shown the seraphim and cherubim, there is considerable difficulty describing their appearance in a manner that we could possibly grasp (Isa. 6:2; Eze. 1:10; 10:14; Rev. 4:7). The description of Satan, the "anointed cherub," is equally fantastic (Eze. 28:12-14). Thus, we should not be surprised to find malevolent beings of immense spiritual and transformative powers with such fantastic descriptions. "They seem, from their description, to be a kind of *Infernal Cherubim* . The horse, the man, the lion, and the scorpion are combined in them [Rev. 4:7]."[47]
2. **Size of the Locusts** - We know nothing concerning the *size* of the demonic locusts. Depending upon their similarity to earthly locusts, they are likely between 0.5 to 7 inches (13 to 175 mm.).[48] In other words, these demon locusts *may be on the scale of insects*. The fact that they have a painful, and possibly poisonous sting, which does not kill their victims also points in this direction. For if the locusts were much larger than their largest earthly counterparts, then the sting alone could easily be a mortal wound.[49]
3. **Fantastic Appearance of Natural Insects** - When asked to describe a simple spider or dragonfly when viewed under a magnifying glass or a flea under a microscope, how many of us would resort to similes like those of John (Rev. 9:7-10, 17-19)? Most, if not all of us! The simple fact is that known insects of the natural world are almost equally bizarre—but lacking in demonic power—to those described here. Consider the following description. *The creature had four wings, each of which was covered with something like 250 thousand scales, and a tripartite body with a head as it were with six thousand eyes. Two long hair-like whips extended from its head with which it guided itself over immense distances. Its tongue was like a fire hose and one fourth the length of its body and it pranced upon six legs, the forelegs of which terminated in six needle-like spears.* A bizarre fantasy? Not at all! A female monarch butterfly.[50] A rather benign insect at that!

Once we trade in the *Golden Rule of Interpretation*[5.2.24] for the fools gold of symbolism and allegory, we embark upon a sea of conjecture concerning the identification of this judgment. Bullinger and Seiss, in defense of a literal understanding, identify the mischief which results from jettisoning a literal interpretation:

> The most common interpretation sees the fulfilment of this judgment in the Invasion of Europe by the Turks. In that case the "*star*" is seen to be Mahomet. His "fall from heaven" means that his family was

> once high and wealthy; he being an orphan and poor. "To him was given the key of the bottomless pit;" *i.e.*, "he *professed* to receive a key from God." So that in his case profession was evidently possession! How he opened the pit the interpreters do not tell us, but the "smoke" was his false teaching. Out of the pit came the *locusts*. *Arbah* in Hebrew means a locust. That is quite near enough with them for *Arabians*, though there could hardly be Mahommedans before Mahomet. . . . The "*crowns* like gold" were the turbans of linen. "*Faces* as men" means *courage*. "They had *hair* as women:" this refers to the *horse tail* decorations worn by the Pashas on their heads.[51]

> Many indeed, consider it mere fancy-work, fiction, and symbol, referring to events in the past history of the race and intended to describe quite other things than are thus literally depicted. But the account is given as an account of realities. There is no difficulty involved in the language employed. The grammatical sense is plain and obvious. Neither is there any intimation whatever of any other sense. And if any other sense was intended, there lives not a man who can tell, with any degree of certainty, what that other sense is. Many and great minds have laboured to make out an allegorical and historical interpretation of these locusts from the pit, but thus far, as Alford has justly remarked, only "an endless Babel" has been the result. Alford gives it up. Stuart gives it up. Hengstenberg gives it up. Vaughan gives it up. Others have given it up. And every candid man just give it up, on any scheme that will consistently interpret the Apocalypse as a whole, or preserve to the sacred records the credit and value which this book claims for its contents.[52]

The text compares these creatures to *locusts*. Since most of us have probably never studied the appearance and capabilities of even the *household spider* in detail, let us be wary to take John's description seriously knowing that God's severe judgment at the time of the end will certainly call forth such a devilish reality. "What God says is plain enough. He does not ask us to understand it. He asks us to *believe* it; and this, by God's help, we mean to do."[53]

horses

Joel used similar terminology to describe the locust plague of his day—and the demonic plague of this day.

> **Their appearance is like the appearance of horses**; and like swift steeds, so they run. With a noise like chariots over mountaintops they leap, like the noise of a flaming fire that devours the stubble, like a strong people set in battle array. (Joel 2:4-5) [emphasis added]

We are not alone in understanding Joel's vision of God's locust army as depicting something far beyond his immediate event—this ultimate eschatological invading army released from the pit.

> At the sight of this terrible army of God the nations tremble, so that their faces grow pale. *'Ammim* means neither people (see at 1 Kings 22:28) nor the tribes of Israel, but nations generally. Joel is no doubt depicting something more here than the devastation caused by the locusts in his own day. [54]

As will be seen by examining the many similarities between this passage and that of Joel, Joel saw both the local locust plague of his own day, but also understood it as a type (or model) of this demonic locust plague in the final *Day of the Lord*[2.13.3]. Both the natural locusts of Joel's day and the demonic locusts here represent sovereign judgments of God.[55] Like John, he resorted to similitude in comparing the locusts with horses:[56]

> Such an association is facilitated by three facts: (1) The heads of locusts and horses are similar in appearance. The German and Italian words for "locust" literally mean "hay-horse" [*Heupferd*] and "little horse" [*cavalletta*], respectively (Wolff, Joel and Amos, p. 45, n. 46; cf. also Driver, *The Books of Joel and Amos*, p. 52). (2) Both locusts and human armies advance swiftly. (3) The locusts' buzzing wings resemble the sound of chariot wheels (for accounts of the sounds made by locusts, see Driver, *The Books of Joel and Amos*, p. 52).[57]

on their heads were crowns of something like gold

John does not use simile to describe the crowns, but only the material out of which they were made. The crowns they wear also differentiates them from natural locusts. These are from among the hierarchy and rank of fallen angels (Rom. 8:38; Eph. 1:21; 3:10; 6:12; Col. 1:16; 2:10). "Alford understands it of the head of the locusts actually ending in a crown-shaped fillet which resembled gold in its material."[58] "Not actual crowns, but AS crowns. Milligan remarks that any yellow brilliancy about the head of the insect is a sufficient foundation for the figure."[59] More likely, the crowns are an indicator of the victory the locusts will enjoy over their prey. See *Crowns*[4.6].

their faces *were* like the faces of men

This indicates they are intelligent rational beings and not normal locusts.

3.9.8 - Revelation 9:8

they had hair like women's hair

Jeremiah described horses that would "come up like the **bristling** locusts" [emphasis added] (Jer. 51:27). The word for *bristling* is סָמָר [*sāmār*]: "Pertaining to a short, stiff, coarse hair or filament not soft to the touch, and possibly painful to very soft tissues as the feature of an insect whisker."[60] The participial form is used of a *nail* (Ecc. 12:11; Isa. 41:7). "Johnson suggests, 'The comparison of their hair with that of women may refer (as in other ancient texts) to the locusts' long antennae.' "[61] "An Arabic proverb compares the antlers of locusts to the hair of girls."[62] However, these are not natural locusts, so the hair that John sees appears to be long, like that of a woman.

their teeth were like lion's *teeth*

Joel describes the natural plague of locusts of his day as a "nation" with teeth of a lion:

> For a nation has come up against My land, strong, and without number; **His teeth *are* the teeth of a lion**, and he has the fangs of a fierce lion. He has laid waste My vine, and ruined My fig tree; He has stripped it bare and thrown *it* away; its branches are made white. (Joel 1:6-7) [emphasis added]

In Joel's description, the teeth are said to be lion-like because of their ability to consume and strip all vegetation bare. Here, the mention of teeth parallels Joel's locust vision and is an indication of their rapaciousness. There is no indication that the demon locusts will utilize their teeth directly against their victims—it is their tails with which they strike.[63]

3.9.9 - Revelation 9:9

breastplates

θώρακας [*thōrakas*]. This word may denote an actual breastplate or "the part of the body covered by the breastplate, *the chest*."[64] It is the word from which we get *thorax*. Interestingly, we use this word to describe insects. "Thorax: The second or middle region of the body of an arthropod, between the head and the abdomen, in insects bearing the true legs and wings."[65] See commentary on *Revelation 9:7*[3.9.7].

like the sound of chariots with many horses running into battle

The sound of their flight is compared to chariots in battle, so great is their number. Once again, Joel and John agree: "With **a noise like chariots** Over mountaintops they leap, Like the noise of a flaming fire that devours the stubble, Like a strong people set in battle array." [emphasis added] (Joel 2:5).

3.9.10 - Revelation 9:10

tails like scorpions, and there were stings in their tails

Stings is κέντρα [*kentra*] , used also of a pointed stick (Acts 9:5; 26:14) and figuratively to describe the power of death to hurt (1Cor. 15:55). The sting denotes not only the ability to pierce, but possibly also the pain of a poisonous tip, or stinger.[66] See commentary on *Revelation 9:5*[3.9.5]. The sting of some natural scorpions is extremely painful:

> Of a boy stung in the foot by a scorpion, Laborde relates that, although of a race which bears everything with remarkable patience, he rolled on the ground, grinding his teeth, and foaming at the mouth. It was a long time before his complainings moderated, and even then he could make no use of his foot, which was greatly inflamed. And such is the nature of the torment which these locusts from the pit inflict.[67]

3.9.11 - Revelation 9:11

they had a king over them

These locusts are to be contrasted with natural locusts which have no king: "The locusts have no king, yet they all advance in ranks" (Pr. 30:27). These demonic locusts *have* a king and advance like their natural counterparts:

> They run like mighty men, they climb the wall like men of war; every one marches in formation, and they do not break ranks. They do not push one another; every one marches in his own column. Though they lunge between the weapons, they are not cut down. (Joel 2:7-8)

In one of the translations of the *LXX*[5.2.38], Amos is shown a king over a swarm of locusts: "Thus has the Lord [God] shewed me; and behold, a swarm of locusts coming from the east; and, behold, one caterpillar, king Gog" (Amos 7:1).[68] Perhaps because the plague of locusts was seen by Amos as a sign of God's judgment (Deu. 28:38, 42; Amos 4:9; Joel 1:1-7), Gog—the archenemy of Israel—is pictured as their king (Eze. 38:2-3, 14, 16, 18, 21; 39:1, 11; Rev. 20:8).

angel of the bottomless pit

Regarding the phrase *of the bottomless pit* (τῆς ἀβύσσου [*tēs abyssou*]), Wallace suggests it emphasizes the *source* from whence the angel came.[69]

Abaddon

Ἀβαδδών [*Abaddōn*], a transliteration of the related Hebrew term. The Hebrew term אֲבַדּוֹן [*`ăbaddōn*] is derived from אבד [*`bd*] meaning "to perish, become lost, be ruined." It is translated by "destruction" and associated with שְׁאוֹל [*sh^e`ōl*] in Job 26:6 and Pr. 15:11, where it denotes a *place* which is seen by the omnipresence and omniscience of God. Abbadon is personified along with death (מָוֶת [*māwet*]) as having heard of the fame of elusive wisdom (Job 28:22). It is said to be the destination of a consuming fire (Job 31:12) and is associated with the grave (קֶבֶר [*qheber*]), but differentiated from it (Ps. 88:11). It is said that hell (שְׁאוֹל [*sh^e`ōl*]) and Abbadon ("destruction") are never full (Pr. 27:20). In all of these uses, it denotes a *location* which is associated with *Sheol* and the grave, but differs from them. "The rabbins have made Abaddon the nethermost of the two regions into which they divide the lower world."[70]

Some suppose him to be Satan:

> The king of these locusts is named in both Hebrew and Greek. The name that God gives to him is Abaddon or Apollyon. . . . In it, of course, is one of the titles of Satan of which there are so many in the Bible. We are reminded of the two passages in Matthew's Gospel where the Lord Himself speaks of the prince of the demons or rather where He comments on the Pharisee's use of the name, Beelzebub, whom they call the prince of the demons. . . . The Lord said, commenting on the Pharisees' thought, "If Satan cast out Satan, he is divided against himself" (Mtt. 12:26), thus linking the name of the one they called prince of demons to Satan himself.[71]

However, if Satan is taken as the fallen star to which the key is given to open the pit (presumably from the *outside*), and this angel is *from* the pit, it argues against his identification as Satan. Perhaps this angel is the highest ranking angel which has been confined within the pit for the duration of their demonic captivity? He is probably not related to the elect angel who eventually locks Satan in the pit (Rev. 20:2).

> John gives his title as the angel of the abyss. Some identify this angel as Satan, but his domain is the heavenlies (Eph. 6:12), where he is the "prince of the power of the air" (Eph. 2:2). He is not associated with the abyss until he is cast into it (Rev. 20:1-3). This angel is better viewed as a high-ranking demon in Satan's hierarchy.[72]

Others suppose this angel to be *Antichrist*[5.2.3]:

> It is the Destroyer of the Gentiles of Jer. 4:7, translated 'Spoiler' in Isa. 16:4 and Jer. 6:24. Suitable name is this for the one who is the great opponent of the Saviour. 'Destroyer' is close akin to 'Death' in Rev. 6:8. The reason why his name is given here in both Hebrew and Greek is because he will be connected with and be the destroyer of both Jews and Gentiles! But why give the Hebrew name first? Because the order in judgment, as in grace, is 'the Jew first' - see Rom. 2:9 and 1:16 for each, respectively.[73]

The beast that makes war against the two witnesses is said to ascend out of the bottomless pit (Rev. 11:7; 17:8). His coming is "according to the working of Satan, with all power, signs and lying wonders" (2Th. 2:9). His ascent from the pit may speak of his physical origin, the source of his spiritual empowerment, or both. It appears his ascent from the pit takes place when his deadly wound is healed (Rev. 13:3, 12) for John implies the order of events: "The beast that you saw [1] was, and [2] is not, and [3] will ascend out of the bottomless pit and [4] go to perdition" (Rev. 17:8a). It is unlikely that the Antichrist would be found in the pit at its initial opening, already having been emprisoned with demons for an extended period of time[74] or that he would be said to be a king *over demons*.[75] This king is an *angel*, but nowhere does Scripture refer to Antichrist as an angel. Instead, he is said to be a *man* (Dan. 7:8; 8:23; 11:37; 2Th. 2:3). Admittedly, there is considerable mystery associated with the Antichrist, especially regarding his origin, how he "is not, and will ascend" and the *means* by which his "deadly wound was healed" (Rev. 13:3). Yet, it seems unlikely that this king who is an angel refers to Antichrist. See commentary on *Revelation 13*[3.13] and *The Beast*[4.2].

This *angel* is probably neither Satan nor Antichrist, but a high-ranking fallen angel who has been king over the emprisoned demons for the duration of their time in the pit.

Apollyon

Ἀπολλύων [*Apollyōn*], the Greek translation of the Hebrew אֲבַדּוֹן [*`ăbaddōn*]. The LXX usually translates Hebrew *Abaddon* as *apoleia*, "destruction." Apollyon appears in the nominative case like a proper name would appear in quotes.[76]

Providing the name in both Greek and Hebrew is characteristic of John. "This stylistic trait of giving information in bilingual terms is peculiar to Revelation and the fourth Gospel (John 6:1; 19:13, 17, 20; 20:16)."[77] It is another piece of evidence in favor of authorship by the Apostle John. See *Authorship*[2.9]. "John uses both names to emphasize his impact on both ungodly Jews and Gentiles."[78]

3.9.12 - Revelation 9:12

One woe is past

This speaks of the first of the three woes (Rev. 8:13), the judgment of the fifth trumpet (Rev. 9:1-11). See commentary on *Revelation 8:13*[3.8.13].

Behold, still two more woes are coming

John writes *behold* because, as terrible as this first woe has been, the two remaining woes are still worse. This woe brought torment, but the second woe—the judgment of the sixth trumpet—brings the release of a demonic army the likes of which the earth has never seen (Rev. 9:13-19, 11:14) and the third woe—the judgments of the seventh trumpet—brings the seven bowls of God's wrath (Rev. 11:15; 15:7; 16:2-4, 8, 10, 12, 17).

after these things

μετὰ ταῦτα [*meta tauta*], the familiar chronological indicator which partitions John's vision.

3.9.13 - Revelation 9:13

the sixth angel sounded

This is the sixth angel of the seven which were given trumpets (Rev. 8:2). When he sounds, the second of the three final woes is brought forth. See commentary on *Revelation 8:13*[3.8.13].

> Each time the trumpet sounds, the judgment which follows is more severe than the previous one. Long ago Isaiah had prophesied that "when thy judgments are in the earth, the inhabitants of the world will learn righteousness" (Isa. 26:9). No doubt, therefore, each succeeding judgment will uncover a few reluctant "learners," but those that remain unconverted are still more stubborn and thus each visitation must increase in severity.[79]

a voice from the four horns of the golden altar

The voice comes from the golden altar upon which the prayers of the saints were offered and from which they ascended before God (Rev. 8:3-4). Mention is made of the altar to associate the judgment of the sixth trumpet with the petitions of the saints previously offered upon the altar. The voice could be that of the angel who offered the prayers of the saints upon the altar, but more likely, is the voice of the Father because that which is commanded requires the utmost in authority—the release of the bound angels.[80] The horns of the altar are intended to signify mercy, for by running to the temple and clinging to them a man could seek sanctuary (1K. 1:50-51; 2:20). But now, a voice of judgment comes from the horns of mercy.

> Shockingly, from the altar associated with mercy came words of judgment. God is a merciful, gracious, compassionate God, yet His "Spirit shall not strive with man forever" (Gen. 6:3). When this trumpet judgment occurs, the time for mercy will have passed; the altar of mercy will become an altar of judgment.[81]

3.9.14 - Revelation 9:14

saying to the sixth angel who had the trumpet

The sixth angel is tasked with the release of the four bound angels. We are not told how they are bound nor how they are released. We can assume that both their binding and release involves the direct supernatural power of God and the sixth angel is merely the instrument by which this power is administered. Their binding is most likely similar to that which will be experienced by Satan during the *Millennial Kingdom*[5.2.39] (Rev. 20:1-3) and their loosing like that of Satan at the end of the Millennium (Rev. 20:7).

release the four angels

These four angels have evidently been reserved in bondage for this special purpose of God. Since there are only four, it is likely that they are a specific group of especially malevolent or powerful angels. Even one angel, in a single night, killed one hundred and eighty-five thousand Assyrians (2K. 19:35). It appears that these four angels will be assisted in their assignment by an additional demonic army. They probably serve as commanders. The number four speaks of the worldwide effect of their destruction. See *Four: the Entire World, the Earth*[2.7.5.3.3].

The Four Angels Bound at the Euphrates [82]

who are bound

τοὺς δεδεμένους [*tous dedemenous*], perfect tense passive participle, *the ones having been bound*. They were bound in the past and remain bound up to this point in preparation for their use in judgment by God. See commentary on *Revelation 9:2*[3.9.2]. Their binding at the Euphrates is similar to the locking away of other fallen angels in the abyss. "These four angels, we are distinctly told are 'reserved unto judgment.' The word is εἰς [*eis*] *unto, with a view to* judgment (not merely to being judged)."[83] See commentary on *Revelation 9:1*[3.9.1].

Barnhouse takes these to be supernatural powers who, while bound, have actively prevented "the passing of evil forces from the east to the west."[84] When they are removed, then forces from beyond the Euphrates are allowed to come into the holy land. This seems unlikely on two counts:

1. Why would angels who are serving God on an ongoing basis by actively opposing evil be said to be *bound*? "That the four angels are bound indicates that they are demons (cf. Rev. 20:1ff.; 2Pe. 2:4; Jude 1:6), since holy angels are nowhere in Scripture said to be bound. Because holy angels always perfectly carry out God's will, there is no need for Him to restrain them from opposing His will."[85]

2. The description of the resulting invasion is so fantastic as to defy explanation as a natural army of men.[86]

at the great river Euphrates

Later, in the sixth bowl judgment, the *Euphrates* is dried up to prepare the way for the kings of the east to gather to battle against God (Rev. 16:12-14). The mention of the *Euphrates* both here and in Revelation 16:12 provides further evidence that Babylon (Rev. 14:8; 16:19; 17:5; 18:2, 10, 21) is the literal, historical city on the banks of the Euphrates.[87]

> Exactly *how* they are bound there is a mystery, of course. How anything—particularly disembodied spirits—could be chained for four thousand years in a flowing river is unknown, to say the least. . . . No doubt God is equal to the needs of the occasion, however, and can bind them in some quite appropriate and effective manner. . . . [88]

> "The Euphrates is linked with the most important events in ancient history. On its banks stood the city of Babylon; the army of Necho was defeated on its banks by Nebuchadnezzar; Cyrus the Younger and Crassus perished after crossing it; Alexander crossed it, and Trajan and Severus descended it."—*Appleton's Cyclopedia*[89]

> It was near the Euphrates that sin began, the first lie was told, the first murder was committed, and the tower of Babel (the origin of an entire complex of false religions that spread across the world) was built. The Euphrates was the eastern boundary of the Promised Land (Gen. 15:18; Ex. 23:31; Deu. 11:24), and Israel's influence extended to the Euphrates during the reigns of David (1Chr. 18:3) and Solomon (2Chr. 9:26). The region near the Euphrates was the central location of three world powers that oppressed Israel: Assyria, Babylon, and Medo-Persia. It was on the banks of the Euphrates that Israel endured seventy long, bitter, wearisome years of captivity (cf. Ps. 137:1-4). It is the river over which the enemies of God will cross to engage in the battle of Armageddon (Rev. 16:12-16).[90]

> Attention has been abundantly called by commentators to the region of the Euphrates as that place where human sin began and also Satan's empire over man; where the first murder was committed; where the first war confederacy was made (Genesis 14); and back of this it is where Nimrod began to be "a mighty one in the earth," and where the vast system of Babylonian idolatry, with its trinity of evil—"father, mother and son" originated, to deceive the whole world by the Satanic fable of "the queen of heaven." Here, moreover, as we saw in Zechariah 5, iniquity is to have its last stage on earth (see Revelation 18 also).[91]

3.9.15 - Revelation 9:15

who had been prepared

οἱ ἡτοιμασμένοι [*hoi hētoimasmenoi*], perfect tense passive participle, *the ones having been prepared.* The preparation was not their own, but that of God. God had actively held them in reserve for this specific time. They are reserved for use *in* judgment (Isa. 24:21-22; 2Pe. 2:4; Jude 1:6). Indeed, God "works all things according to the counsel of His will" (Eph. 1:11).

for the hour and day and month and year

"The one article and one preposition before the four times, unites them: . . . it denotes the appointed hour of the appointed day of the appointed month of the appointed year."[92] They were to be released at the "hour of His judgment" (Rev. 14:7), a time known only to God (Mark 13:32; Acts 1:7).[93] *This very moment*, as we contemplate the text, these powerful angels and their related demonic horde are pent up awaiting their eventual release whereupon they will rush out upon an unsuspecting world to unleash "hell on earth." The intensity of their malevolent thoughts and intentions likely escalates as they endure the ongoing frustration of their present captivity. What a horrific and fearsome judgment that will pour forth upon the *earth dwellers*[5.2.18] at the time of the end!

to kill a third of mankind

A third of the population of the earth would be killed by these four angels *and the army which they lead* (Rev. 9:16-18). Death will come by three means: fire, smoke, and brimstone. See commentary on *Revelation 9:18*[3.9.18].

The trumpet judgments share a pattern of affecting one-third of what they target. In the first trumpet judgment, a *third* of the trees were burned up (Rev. 8:7). In the second trumpet judgment, a *third* of the sea became blood, a *third* of the creatures in the sea perish, and a *third* of the ships were destroyed (Rev. 8:8-9). In the third trumpet judgment, a *third* of the rivers and springs are poisoned (Rev. 8:10-11). In the fourth trumpet judgment, a *third* of the sun, moon, and stars were struck so as to be darkened (Rev. 8:12). In the fifth and sixth trumpet judgments, all men without the seal of God are tormented, and then a *third* of them are killed.

When the second seal is opened, peace is taken from the earth and people kill one another (Rev. 6:4). When the third seal is opened, there is great famine and presumably additional deaths occur (Rev. 6:5-6). When the fourth seal is opened, Death and Hades kill "a fourth of the earth" (Rev. 6:8). If the *fourth of the earth* describes a *region*, then we can't be sure what proportion of the total population die —it would depend upon the region and the distribution of the population. If we assume that roughly one fourth of the *population* remaining alive at the time of the third horseman's ride perish in the judgments of the third seal, then less that 75 percent of the original population prior to opening the first seal remains alive. (Some died during the judgments of the second and third seals.) Additional people die in the preceding trumpet judgments (ships are destroyed, men die from drinking poisoned waters, Rev. 8:9, 11). Here an additional third *of the remaining population* perish, or one-third of the less than 75 percent which remains. *After the first six seal and six trumpet judgments, the population of the earth has been reduced by more than half.*

If the first seal were loosed today [December 2003], using the current world population of over 6 billion, and neglecting those who will be removed from the earth in the *Rapture*[4.14] prior to this time,[94] more than 3 billion would have died by the end of the sixth trumpet in the judgments from God.[95] No wonder Jesus said, "For then there shall be great tribulation, such as has not been since the beginning of the world until this time, no, nor ever shall be. And unless those days were shortened, no flesh would be saved; but for the elect's sake those days will be shortened" (Mtt. 24:21-22).

3.9.16 - Revelation 9:16

two hundred million

δισμυριάδες μυριάδων [*dismyriades myriadōn*], *two myriads of myriads*, an essentially countless number. This is a similar phrase to that found in Revelation 5:11 to describe the countless angelic host. Only here, the phrase is doubled for heightened effect.[96] The number should not be thought of as specifically denoting *two hundred million*, but a vast, essentially numberless host.[97]

Joel saw this army in his vision: "A people *come*, great and strong, the like of whom has never been, nor will there ever be any *such* after them, even for many generations" (Joel 2:2). *Strong* is עָצוּם [*ātsûm*], which can denote a "throng, multitude, i.e., pertaining to that which is a large number of countable persons (Ps 35:18)."[98] "As the morning light spreads itself over the mountains, so a people *numerous* [Maurer] and strong shall spread themselves."[99]

Some take the horses and horsemen as denoting a human army from east of the Euphrates:

> Armies of this size and sophistication have only been a feasibility in recent times (indeed, the world's population around 1600 A.D. is estimated to have been 500 million; so at the time Revelation was written the world population may well have only been 200 million—surely, only God could envisage armies of 200 million men in that day and age!). We have a prophecy of human destruction which makes World War II look insignificant.[100]

But it would seem this multitude is neither from the east (Rev. 16:12) nor human:

> To summarize why these two hundred million are demons and not Chinese, four things should be noted: *first*, they are led by four fallen angels; *second*, the location of the army is stated to be the Euphrates, where Babylon is located (which in the future will be the headquarters of the counterfeit trinity); *third*, the description given in the text rules out this army's being human; and *fourth* , the kings of the east [Rev. 16:12] are not connected with this at all.[101]

Moreover, the practical aspects of mobilizing a *human* army of such size seem insurmountable. It is not simply an issue of manpower alone:[102]

> According to General William K. Harrison (an expert in military logistics), an army of 200 million could

> not be conscripted, supported, and moved to the Middle East without totally disrupting all societal needs and capabilities ("The War of Armageddon," xerographic copy of unpublished, undated article). As General Harrison brings out on this aspect of Revelation, God has made men with certain limitations; and the actual raising and transporting of an army of the size spoken of in v. 16 completely transcends human capability. All the Allied and Axis forces at their peak in World War II were only about 70 million (*The World Almanac, 1971*, ed. L. H. Long [New York: Newspaper Enterprise Association, 1970], p. 355). Thus it seems better to understand the vast numbers and description of the horses as indicating demonic hordes.[103]
>
> Some have suggested that this is the human army referred to in Rev. 16:12 and led by "the kings from the east," noting that the Red Chinese army reportedly numbered 200 million during the 1970s. But no reference is made to the size of the army led by the kings of the East. Further, **that army arrives on the scene during the sixth bowl judgment, which takes place during the seventh trumpet, not the sixth**. [emphasis added][104]

I heard the number

John would have been unable to count their number, but was told there were *two myriads of myriads* so as to relate to his readers their essential numberless value. The vast number of the army is further evidence of the (fallen) angelic origin—for there are countless numbers of angels of which one-third fell (Rev. 7:4; 12:4).

3.9.17 - Revelation 9:17

thus I saw the horses

The previous judgment involved demonic locusts whose appearance was "like horses"—they were not horses, but a similitude. Here, John says he saw *horses*, but doesn't mention *like* or *as*, as in a similitude. These horses are not like normal horses for they breath fire out of their mouths and harm with "heads" on their tails. Yet, like horses, they are *ridden upon* by horsemen. "Perhaps they are like the fabled Centaurs—horses with human-like heads and upper bodies, in appearance like men riding horses except that the horses ridden by them are also their own bodies."[105] Again, Joel describes what is before us:

> Their appearance is like the appearance of horses; and like swift steeds, so they run. With a noise like chariots over mountaintops they leap, like the noise of a flaming fire that devours the stubble, like a strong people set in battle array. (Joel 2:4-5)

Note that when John uses simile, what he describes is *approximately* true to the vision that he is being shown. It is the *closest* thing he is familiar with to compare that which he sees. This precludes the notions of some that John was describing futuristic military weaponry with which he had no familiarity:

> John was writing to addressees with no knowledge of mechanized warfare; to them cavalry was the most formidable military force, so naturally he described his vision in terms to which his readers could relate. The mounts John saw may well be advanced military equipment (which even we may not know how to describe), but which he described using the vocabulary and references of his readers.[106]

Mills suggests that John saw something like tanks, helicopter gunships, and other modern mechanized equipment, realized that these represented some sort of unknown futuristic weaponry, and then *translated this down* in terms of cavalry images for his readers. We find this notion difficult to accept. When John uses simile, he uses the closest *object known to him* which approximates what he sees. If John had been shown modern military tanks, he would have undoubtedly mentioned something "like chariots with multiple wheels." If helicopter gunships, then he would have mentioned flight, perhaps "like an eagle," etc. He clearly saw some sort of *animals* which were mounted by *riders*. Understanding this army to be demonic in origin solves many of the conjectural problems posed by attempts to find natural fulfillments in modern warfare, recognizes their huge number, and explains how they are led by four malevolent angels.

hyacinth blue

ὑακίνθινος [*huakinthinos*]: "Either dark sapphire blue or dark red, depending on which mineral or stone is used for comparison."[107]

> The three words . . . translated fire, hyacinth and brimstone are found in no other place in the New

> Testament. The first of the words is used by Aristotle and Polybius in the sense of flaming or firing. Hyacinth is a translation of a word that is rendered by various authorities as "red color bordering on black" (Thayer), "violet or dark blue" (Bailly), while ancient writers described it as "purple and iron colored" (cit. in Liddell and Scott). In the last half of this same verse and in the following verse three plagues are further described as fire, smoke and brimstone. Each of these words is different from the three used in the description of the breastplate.[108]

the heads of the horses *were* like the heads of lions

It is unclear whether John means that the head of each horse resembled the actual appearance of the head of a lion, or merely that they shared the ferocious characteristics of a lion (1Chr. 12:8). Probably the latter since he calls them "horses."

out of their mouths came fire, smoke, and brimstone

They devour their enemies in much the same way as the two witnesses (Rev. 11:5). Fire and brimstone are the result of God's overwhelming judgment (Gen. 19:24; Deu. 29:23; Job 18:15; Ps. 11:6; Isa. 30:33; 34:9; Eze. 38:22; Luke 17:29; Rev. 14:10; 19:20; 20:10; 21:8). "A fire devours before them, and behind them a flame burns; the land *is* like the Garden of Eden before them, and behind them a desolate wilderness" (Joel 2:3a).

> No doubt this all sounds fantastic and impossible, so commentators have invented all sorts of figurative meanings to apply to these deadly horses. But these are not the first fire-breathing animals the earth has seen. Ancient nations everywhere describe fire-breathing dragons which formerly existed on earth, and the Bible describes at least one such creature, called leviathan (Job 41:19-21). There are many indications that these dragons were actually dinosaurs, and the fossil evidence does show structures on at least some dinosaurs that could well have served as mixing chambers for flammable chemicals [not to mention methane from digestive processes] that could be expelled in the form of fire and smoke.[109]

3.9.18 - Revelation 9:18

a third of mankind was killed

"The terrible slaughter will completely disrupt human society. The problem of disposing of the dead bodies alone will be inconceivable. The sickly stench of decaying corpses will permeate the world, and it will take an enormous effort on the part of the survivors to bury them in mass graves or burn them."[110] See commentary on *Revelation 9:15*[3.9.15].

3.9.19 - Revelation 9:19

their power is in their mouth and in their tails

The nearest antecedent is the *horses* (Rev. 9:17b) to which the *MT*[5.2.45] and *NU*[5.2.49] texts attest by including the phrase "of the horses" (τῶν ἵππων [*tōn hippōn*]).

their tails *are* like serpents, having heads; and with them they do harm

The demonic locusts had tails with which they stung (Rev. 9:10), but these demonic horses differ in that their tails are like *serpents* rather than scorpions—*having heads* and a mouth. The fierceness of this army can be seen in the lethal power which attends both ends of the horses. Approaching the horsemen from the rear is of little avail since their tails also harm. Some have suggested John is describing modern military weaponry, but the description and the *source* of the army (demonic, from the pit) is evidence to the contrary.

3.9.20 - Revelation 9:20

But the rest of mankind, who were not killed by these plagues

The two-thirds left from the population prior to the sounding of the sixth trumpet (Rev. 9:13), representing less than half of the original population of the earth. See commentary on *Revelation 9:15*[3.9.15].

did not repent

The very reason that *only one-third* were killed was to provide a witness and opportunity for the remaining two-thirds to repent and turn to God. Like *Jezebel*[5.2.35] of the church at Thyatira (Rev.

2:21)—who is a type for the *earth dwellers*[5.2.18] of the end—they fail to see God's gracious mercy in giving them additional time to repent.

> "Now, therefore," says the LORD, "Turn to Me with all your heart, with fasting, with weeping, and with mourning." So rend your heart, and not your garments; return to the LORD your God, for He *is* gracious and merciful, slow to anger, and of great kindness; and He relents from doing harm. (Joel 2:12-13)

But, as we shall see, the earth dwellers continue to harden their hearts with the result that stays of judgment which indicate God's mercy and forbearance are met with a continuance or even elevation of their sinful deeds (Rev. 16:8-11).

This is the purpose of what Jesus described to the church at Philadelphia: "Because you have kept My command to persevere, I also will keep you from the hour of trial which shall come upon the whole world **to test those who dwell on the earth**." [emphasis added] Much like the testing of Jesus in the wilderness following His baptism by John (Mtt. 4:1-11), this period is meant not so much to see how those being tested respond, but to demonstrate their unchanging character. The analogy of the Tribulation with its plagues to the deliverance of Israel from Egypt is found in the similarity of the character of the earth dwellers to Pharaoh: both refused to repent. In Pharaoh's case, as the plagues continued to intensify, he continued to harden his heart (Ex. 7:13, 23; 8:15, 19, 32; 9:34). So will the hearts of the earth dwellers. And yet, through the mystery of God's sovereignty, the continued opposition of the unrepentant will be used to bring Him great glory (Ex. 11:9; Rev. 19:1). The proverb writer captured the spirit of the unrepentant: "Though you grind a fool in a mortar with a pestle along with crushed grain, *Yet* his foolishness will not depart from him" (Pr. 27:22). It is God's specific purpose in the midst of judgment to bring repentance. Yet often, as here, men fail to respond to His correction:

> O LORD, *are* not Your eyes on the truth? You have stricken them, but they have not grieved; You have consumed them, but they have refused to receive correction. They have made their faces harder than rock; they have refused to return. Therefore I said, "Surely these *are* poor. They are foolish; for they do not know the way of the LORD, the judgment of their God." (Jer. 5:3-4)

> "Also I gave you cleanness of teeth in all your cities. And lack of bread in all your places; yet you have not returned to Me," says the LORD. "I also withheld rain from you, when *there were* still three months to the harvest. I made it rain on one city, I withheld rain from another city. One part was rained upon, and where it did not rain the part withered. So two *or* three cities wandered to another city to drink water, but they were not satisfied; yet you have not returned to Me," says the LORD. "I blasted you with blight and mildew. When your gardens increased, your vineyards, your fig trees, and your olive trees, the locust devoured *them*; yet you have not returned to Me," says the LORD. "I sent among you a plague after the manner of Egypt; your young men I killed with a sword, along with your captive horses; I made the stench of your camps come up into your nostrils; yet you have not returned to Me," says the LORD. "I overthrew *some* of you, as God overthrew Sodom and Gomorrah, and you were like a firebrand plucked from the burning; yet you have not returned to Me," says the LORD. "Therefore thus will I do to you, O Israel; because I will do this to you, prepare to meet your God, O Israel!" For behold, He who forms mountains, and creates the wind, Who declares to man what his thought *is*, and makes the morning darkness, Who treads the high places of the earth-The LORD God of hosts *is* His name. (Amos 4:6-13)

Most frequently, men complain that if only they had more definite information, *then* they would repent and believe. Our experience has been that the needed information is more often a smokescreen for a rebellious and unrepentant heart which has no intention of submitting to God. For we have spent many an hour in discussions with such as these—providing information and answering objections—only to find that, having answered one objection, a new one quickly arises in its place! These stand in the place of the rich man who asked that someone from the dead be sent back with *more evidence* to his brothers so that they would accept the horrible truth of the judgment ahead:

> Then he said, 'I beg you therefore, father, that you would send him to my father's house, for I have five brothers, that he may testify to them, lest they also come to this place of torment.' Abraham said to him, 'They have Moses and the prophets; let them hear them.' and he said, 'No, father Abraham; but if one goes to them from the dead, they will repent.' But he said to him, 'If they do not hear Moses and the prophets, neither will they be persuaded though one rise from the dead.' (Luke 16:27-31)

Abraham recognizes that the problem is not one of *evidence*, but a *hard heart*. They already have enough evidence to believe, but choose not to. "The fool has said in his *heart*, '*There is* no God.' " (Ps. 14:1; 53:1). Paul catalogs the damning condition of the unregenerate man (Rom. 3:10-18). Even after this catastrophic intervention, men will continue to reject God because they desire independence from God:

> The death of one-third of the earth's remaining population will be the most catastrophic disaster to strike the earth since the Flood. Yet in an amazing display of hardness of heart, the rest of mankind, who were not killed by these plagues, did not repent. It is unimaginable that after years of suffering and death under the terrifying judgments from God, coupled with the powerful preaching of the gospel by the 144,000 Jewish evangelists (Rev. 7:1-8), the two witnesses (Rev. 11:1-14), an angel in the sky (Rev. 14:6-7), and other believers (Mtt. 24:14), the survivors will still refuse to repent.[111]
>
> Man's basic sin is independence; it is not that he blatantly prefers Satan to God; it is just that he wishes not to be under God's authority. But deep down man chooses Satan because he promises independence. However, this section reveals that Satan will never deliver on his promise, but instead delivers the most vicious form of bondage.[112]

the works of their hands

The problem is not men's *hands*, but rather the *will* of men which motivates their hands. Their will is opposed to God and therefore what they produce by their *hands* does not glorify God, but rather reflects their own selfishness and sin. In the end, without God's Holy Spirit, men become creative perverts, dangerous geniuses (Gen. 11:6), bent on creating their own hell in pursuit of what they incorrectly perceive to be wisdom and intelligence. "Professing to be wise, they became fools" (Rom. 1:22).[113]

The *works* of men's hands include the very gods they bow down to (Deu. 4:28; 2K. 19:18; Ps. 115:4; 135:15; Isa. 2:8; 17:8; 37:19; 44:10-20; Jer. 1:16; 10:3-5; 25:6; Acts 7:41; 19:26). This is the thrust of the meaning here—that men continue in idolatry—giving honor and attention to everything *except* their Creator. Worshiping the *creature* (Rom. 1:25) and that which men have produced in the place of the one true God.

In the context of the Tribulation, the *image of the Beast*[4.3.2.19] is the ultimate *work of their hands* since the *False Prophet*[4.3.2.18] "deceives those who dwell on the earth . . . to make an image to the beast" (Rev. 13:14). Thus, they themselves make the ultimate *idol* (icon) of their own worship! In the delusion which God sends upon the earth (2Th. 2:11), men worship that which they themselves made rather than the God who made them.

worship demons

During the Tribulation, the ultimate devil and idol worship will take place. Men will worship the dragon (Satan) who gives authority to the beast, they will worship the beast, and even the *image* (idol) of the beast (Rev. 13:4, 8, 15). [114] Scripture indicates that although idols themselves are lifeless, the *inspiration*[5.2.33] to make and worship them is demonic in origin. To worship or sacrifice to an idol is to worship or sacrifice to demons (Lev. 17:7; Deu. 32:17). Lest the reader assume sacrifice to demons is a thing of darkened cultures of the past, we only ask how many lives are being offered up in abortion clinics in worship of the "god of convenience" in our supposedly "modern" cultures today? Not only that, but the continuance and even increase of pagan practices around the world clearly show the tendency of men apart from God. In the time of the end, it will only be worse. History records the *descent* of man, not his *ascent*.

idols of gold, silver, brass, stone, and wood

As one commentator entitled this section: "Stone Hearts and Stone Idols."[115] At the time of the end, men will worship idols made from the same basic materials as those praised by the men at Belshazzar's feast (ca. 550 BC, Dan. 5:4, 23). Some readers will no doubt scoff at the notion of idol worship in the same sense as is recorded for ancient cultures. In reply we observe:

1. Scripture makes plain that when men turn from God, there is virtually no limit to the depravity and ignorance to which they descend (Rom. 1:21-23).
2. The vantage point of western "civilized" society, benefits from a strong Judeo-Christian foundation. Although that foundation is quickly eroding, we still enjoy benefits which lag behind the erosion. Our assessment of what is possible in false worship is limited by this perspective. God's assessment is not.

3. The very idolatry described here—where inanimate items are worshiped—is taking place *today* in many pagan cultures across the globe.
4. Pagan belief is rapidly on the rise within our own culture, in the media, and on the internet. With pagan belief will come pagan worship, a return to the darkness of the past.
5. It can take many generations for godliness to permeate a culture and to reap its benefits. This can all be lost in only one or two generations. Consider that at two times in history *every person alive* knew God directly: (1) at the time of Adam and Eve and, (2) after the flood. Now stop and consider the many "lost peoples" and cultures which have no notion of God. They are "lost" in the truest sense of the word. At one time their forebears had *direct knowledge* of the God of the Bible, but intervening generations walked away from Him and darkness now prevails.
6. Worship of the *work of men's hands* extends beyond basic idols of wood, stone, and precious metals. It includes everything that man produces which is not in the service of God. Items as diverse as weapons of war, computer technology, bioengineering and genetic tampering with the basic elements of life. It is not the items themselves that are so much the issue, but the way in which they are employed. In this regard, technology is a large mirror amplifying the fallen character of men. It can be used for good or for evil, but inevitably the evil use winds up dominating. Meanwhile, man persists in his refusal to recognize his depraved nature.
7. With the *rapture of the church*[4.14], the descent into spiritual darkness will be hastened. "During the last century there has been a tremendous advance in what is called 'spiritual' but which is really spiritism or demonism. All this is to increase (until) after the believers have been removed at the *rapture*[5.2.62] of the Church. It will be the predominating state of affairs after all the believers have been taken from the earth."[116]

Commentators speak with one voice concerning the real possibility of demon-based worship becoming a reality for "modern man."

> Take Chicago: Arriving in this city at the close of 1893, (the former World's Fair) I found nearly two pages of the Saturday issue of the newspaper were taken up with the announcement of services at the various churches, and the sermons were generally on solemn subjects by godly men. In 1935, four or five announcements, at most a half a dozen, invited to places where one's soul would be safe to attend; while the announcements of Spiritualists, Theosophists, Christian Scientists, Unity followers, etc.—those cults that have direct traffic in Satan—ran into the scores. (Six orthodox, against 75 Satanic, in the *Chicago Daily News* of November 14, 1931.)[117]

> Those sophisticates of western culture who had long deluded themselves in the unscientific sophistries of modern evolutionary humanism will quickly revert to more satisfying practices of ancient evolutionary polytheistic pantheism, acknowledging the demonic powers which operate in the earth and its atmosphere under "the prince of the power of the air, the spirit that now worketh in the children of disobedience" (Ephesians 2:2). This acknowledgment will be even easier for those multitudes who had been devotees of Asian and African cultures, for these already were either pantheistic or animistic or both. For many years prior to Christ's return for His saints, there will have been a revival of occultism, astrology, spiritism, and kindred "doctrines of devils" (1 Timothy 4:1; 2 Timothy 3:13), even in western cultures, preparing the minds of men everywhere for a worldwide return to pagan idolatry in the final days of the cosmic rebellion. Great worship centers will then be erected, with grotesque images of modern art depicting the various cosmic and terrestrial forces and processes presumably controlled by the principalities and powers of the wicked one (Ephesians 6:12; 1 John 5:19), and these will become objects of worship, with men and women in effect worshiping those evil spirits which they portray and represent.[118]

> It may appear too disparaging to understand of this enlightened age, to entertain the possibility of a return to the ancient worship of images. People may feel insulted at the thought. But the way for it is opening, and the process to effect it is already going on. The minds of anti-Christian religionists everywhere are fast relapsing into the old heathenish philosophies, and I know not what is to hinder their acceptance of the religions with which those philosophies are conjoined. Modifications of them may be made, to conform them somewhat to the requirements of an altered condition of the public mind and taste; but idol-worship will again become, as it is even now becoming, the religion of some who claim to be among the most enlightened and the very illuminators of mankind. Socrates had his demon-guide.[119]

which can neither see nor hear nor walk

An intentional contrast is made between the lifeless idols which men worship (Ps. 115:7; Isa. 46:5-7) and the true living God.[120]

During the Tribulation, Satan will empower the false prophet to produce an idol which comes as close to emulating life as is possible apart from God: "He was granted *power* to give breath to the *image of the beast*[5.2.29], that the image of the beast should both speak and cause as many as would not worship the image of the beast to be killed" (Rev. 13:15).[121] Since history demonstrates the willingness of men to worship inanimate objects, this lifelike image will be irresistible to the earth dwellers—they will worship both the beast *and his image*. They will be all-the-more willing because *God will send them strong delusion, that they should believe the lie*, for "they did not receive the love of the truth, that they might be saved" (2Th. 2:10-11).

If you do not yet know God and believe it preposterous that you would worship an idol, animate or otherwise, beware! For Scripture records that aside from the protection of the Holy Spirit, those who do not know God will not be able to resist the delusion which is sent from God Himself! See commentary on *Revelation 13:15*[3.13.15].

3.9.21 - Revelation 9:21

they did not repent

See commentary on *Revelation 9:20*[3.9.20].

murders

Murder has always been prevalent upon the earth. In "civilized" societies such as ours, it is often hidden out of direct view and under the control of policies related to population control: abortion, euthanasia, and genetic engineering. During the Tribulation, there will be increased murders as those who refuse to worship the beast are "purged" from society (Dan. 9:21, 25; Rev. 13:7, 15; 16:6; 17:6; 18:24). Unrepentant murderers will have their place in the second death (Rev. 21:8). See commentary on *Revelation 2:11*[3.2.11] and *Revelation 20:14*[3.20.14].

sorceries

φαρμάκων [*pharmakōn*]: "Magic potion, charm,"[122] related to φαρμακεία [*pharmakeia*], "employment of drugs for any purpose: sorcery, magic, enchantment."[123] The term occurs in the list of the works of the flesh (Gal. 5:20) and is translated *sorcery* (*witchcraft*, KJV). It also describes the *sorcery* by which Babylon deceived all the nations (Isa. 47:9, 12; Rev. 18:23). "Used in the *Septuagint*[5.2.65] of the Egyptian sorceries (Ex. 7:22. Of Babylon, Isa. 47:9, 12)."[124]

Sorcery was forbidden by the Law of Moses (Ex. 22:18; Deu. 18:10-11) as were all practices which involved communication with the dead such as conjuring spells (Deu. 18:11), consulting mediums (1S. 28:3-9), spiritism, or calling up the dead (really the demonic realm). This included all forms of magic (Ex. 22:18; Lev. 19:31; Lev. 20:6, 27; 2Chr. 33:6; Mal. 3:5). God condemned all of these practices and was indignant that men would "*seek* the dead on behalf of the living" (Isa. 8:19). Instead, they were to seek the *living* God.

One need only view modern cartoons on television or observe the recent Harry Potter phenomenon to observe how the foundation continues to be laid for subsequent generations who will have little reservation to participate in these forbidden practices.[125]

> That people are today [1983] being prepared for an irruption of demons, however, seems very probable. The plethora of movies, television programs, and books with demonic themes, along with the latter-day mushroom growth of occult religions and practices, are all surely conditioning men to a widespread belief in Satan and his demons. Furthermore, none of this is driving men to refuge in Christ, as one might at first suppose it would.[126]

Drugs are used in association with sorcery because they place the practitioner into an altered state of consciousness whereby he or she becomes more open to contact with the demonic realm. The following account of a shaman from the Yanomamo tribe illustrates the connection between drug use and the demonic realm—a connection well-known even among "primitive" peoples:

> I recently interviewed a man who had spent most of his life communing with spirit entities. There is no doubt as to his "authenticity." He was a shaman, a medicine man and chief of his Yanomamo tribe, which resides deep in the Amazonian rain forest of Venezuela. At odds with the lie promoted in anthropological circles that the lives of primitive tribes-people are pure, natural and Eden-like and therefore best kept from outside influence —Chief Shoefoot and his peoples violent, fear-filled existence is documented in a book titled *The Spirit of the Rain Forest*, written by Mark Ritchie . . .
>
> As a young boy, Shoefoot was singled out as one sensitive to the spirit realm and subsequently initiated into the sorcerers world. Again, a shaman is one who, through knowledge and power obtained from the spirits, heals and guides his people. Although the initial process of enabling him to contact the spirits was brutal, involving days of food and water deprivation and having someone force **hallucinogenic drugs** into his system by blowing them up his nose, the spirits he met were at first benign and curiously captivating. . . . Shoefoot increased his drug intake in order to go deeper into the spirit world to find more trustworthy and benevolent spirits. That led to even more wicked spirits (Luke 11:26), greater frustration, and intense despair.[127] [emphasis added]

Some, who deny the reality of the spiritual realm, believe experiences such as those of this shaman are brought on by natural causes, such as drug use:

> I asked Shoefoot through interpreter Mike Dawson, Joe's son, who grew up among the Yanomamo, how he would answer a skeptic who thought his experiences with the spirits were nothing more than hallucinations brought on by the drugs he took. Shoefoot's 70-something-year-old eyes sparkled at the question; he enjoys responding to challenges by skeptics, especially when he speaks to university anthropology students. Its ironic that this "primitive" man considers the highly educated anthropologists who study his people naive at best, deceived at worst. He told me of knowing shamans who had many of the same spirits he had had, yet, unlike him, they did not come to know them as a result of taking drugs. Whether the contacts were made with a clear mind or in a drug-induced state, descriptions and details were nearly always identical they all communed with the same spirits.[128]
>
> During the awful days of the tribulation, the breakdown of law and order will mean that there will be no more restraints on drug use. Furthermore, the fearful judgments on the earth will drive many to drugs as a form of escapism. The merchants of the earth will gladly cooperate because of the great profits involved [Rev. 18:13].[129]

Interestingly, *Jezebel*[5.2.35] of the church of Thyatira apparently taught believers to experience "the depths of Satan" (Rev. 2:24), much like her namesake in the *OT*[5.2.51] practiced witchcraft (2K. 9:23). As we discussed previously, Jezebel at Thyatira can be seen as a type for the church which enters the Great Tribulation (Rev. 2:22) whereas those who overcome and reject her teaching will receive "the morning star" (Rev. 2:28, which *see*[3.2.28]). Those who practice sorcery will also have their part in the second death (Rev. 21:8) and will never enter through the gates of the eternal city (Rev. 22:15).

sexual immorality

πορνείας [*porneias*], from which we derive *pornography*. The word is used of "*prostitution, unchastity, fornication*, of every kind of unlawful sexual intercourse."[130]

Writing many years ago, Seiss uncannily identified the trend. One only wonders what he might say if he could see our day:

> And interlinked with these sorceries, and reacting the one on the other, will also be the general subversion of marriage and its laws, and the deluging of society with the sins of fornication and adultery. The Apostle uses the word "fornication" alone, as embracing all forms of lewdness, but as if to intimate **that marriage will then be hardly recognized any more.** And already we hear the institution of legal wedlock denounced and condemned as tyrannical, and all rules, but those of affinity and desire, repudiated as unjust. Already, in some circles, we find the doctrines of *free love* put forth and defended in the name of right, a better religion, and a higher law. And it would be strange indeed, if the revival of the old heathen philosophies and religions, which justified, sanctioned, and sanctified promiscuous concubinage, did not also bring with it a revival of all these old heathen abominations. [emphasis added][131]

The term for "sexual immorality" is also used to denote spiritual apostasy, that is, idolatry. "This usage was more easily understandable because some Semitic and Graeco-Roman cults were at times connected with sexual debauchery (cf. Hos 6:10; Jer 3:2, 9; 2K. 9:22)."[132] This is the sense in which

Babylon is condemned (Rev. 17:2, 5; 18:3; 19:2). Perhaps at the time of the end, there will also be a resurgence of idolatrous religious practices involving temple prostitution. In our own day, there is blatant disregard for the laws of marriage, even among those who take the name of Christ.

or their thefts

Theft is a broad sin which underwrites many other sins.

> The last crime in this category is that of theft. This is "the statement or general and abounding dishonesty, the obliteration of moral distinctions, the disregard of others' rights, and the practice of fraud, theft, and deceit wherever it is possible." In our day corruption in high places gives the example to all classes. The only wrong consists in getting caught.[133]

The conditions and judgments which John describes in this chapter are difficult for us to imagine. Yet if we understand the *inspired*[5.2.33] pages of Biblical history, we recognize the reality of the events attending the Genesis Flood and the tower of Babel. What man has had the capability of doing in the past can easily be repeated in the future. To those who suggest that "modern man" has thrown off such shackles, we answer with just a few words: *Chairman Mao, Stallin, Hitler, holocaust*. These were not isolated individuals, but entire *historical movements* supported by countless others. The capability of the same and worse lies before us in the pages of the book of Revelation.

> I suppose many of us tend to regard this description as fanciful, as *hyperbole*[5.2.27], and to doubt that destruction on this unimaginable scale can come to pass. However, we should recognize that such a view uses our experience as its guide, and that Hiroshima's population would doubtless have felt exactly the same if someone had prophesied the devastation one atomic bomb was about to wreak on them. But their opinion did not alter the fact one iota.[134]

> People are prone to persuade themselves that this world of sense and time is all that we need be concerned about, and hence have no fears of an unseen world of evil, and no decided or active desire for the blessings of an unseen world of good. They live only for earth, not dreaming that this brief life is only the vestibule to worlds of mightier and eternal moment. Their houses are built by the very margin of hell, and yet they rest and feast in them without a feeling of insecurity or of danger. The flames of perdition clamour after them beneath the pavements on which they walk, but they have no sense of fear or serious apprehension. God and angels are ever busy to win their attention to the ways of safety, but they turn a deaf ear and drift along as they list, crying, Peace! Peace! And so will the wicked and the unbelieving go on, until ignored and offended Omnipotence gives over the power to Satan to let loose upon them these horrid beings from the abyss, under whose torment they will wish they never had lived at all, and vainly attempt to make their escape from what they once considered their chief and only good.[135]

For those who have not yet trusted in Jesus Christ for a way back to God, now is the time to be reconciled of your sin. For each day which passes brings us closer to the fearsome realities described in this chapter: the incredible scenes of hellish torture as demonic hordes are released upon an unsuspecting world. But more frightening than all is the *lack of any willingness to repent* on the part of those left alive who dwell on the earth! **How often must one harden his heart before he reaches the point of no return?** Will you still be able to consider God's offer with an open heart tomorrow after having turned away one more time today?

Notes

[1] George Croly, *The Apocalypse of St. John* (London, England: C. & J. Rivington, 1827), 123-126.

[2] A. R. Fausset, *"The Revelation of St. John the Divine,"* in Robert Jamieson, A. R. Fausset, and David Brown, *A Commentary, Critical and Explanatory, on the Old and New Testaments* (Oak Harbor, WA: Logos Research Systems, Inc., 1997, 1877), Rev. 9:12.

[3] Donald Grey Barnhouse, *Revelation* (Grand Rapids, MI: Zondervan Publishing House, 1971), 168.

[4] John A. Martin, *"Luke,"* in John F. Walvoord, and Roy B. Zuck, eds., *The Bible Knowledge Commentary* (Wheaton, IL: SP Publications, 1983), Luke 10:18.

[5] [Robert H. Mounce, *The Book of Revelation* (Grand Rapids, MI: William B. Eerdmans Publishing Co., 1977), Rev. 9:1] suggests that the "fall" of the star merely describes the descent of an elect angel, as in "having come down" to do God's will by opening the pit. But here, the angel is said to "fall" (root πιπτω [*piptō*]) whereas

the elect angel which descends to bind Satan is said to "come down" (root, καταβαίνω [*katabainō*]). Moreover, the former is perfect tense whereas the later is present tense.

6 Arthur Walkington Pink, *The Antichrist* (Oak Harbor, WA: Logos Research Systems, 1999, 1923), s.v. "Antichrist in the Apocalypse."

7 Monty S. Mills, *Revelations: An Exegetical Study of the Revelation to John* (Dallas, TX: 3E Ministries, 1987), Rev. 9:1.

8 Timothy Friberg, Barbara Friberg, and Neva F. Miller, *Analytical Lexicon of the Greek New Testament* (Grand Rapids, MI: Baker Books, 2000), 402.

9 James Strong, *The Exhaustive Concordance of the Bible* (Ontario: Woodside Bible Fellowship, 1996), G5421.

10 Henry George Liddell, Robert Scott, and Henry Stuart Jones, *A Greek-English Lexicon. With a revised supplement, 1996.*, With a revised supplement, 1996 (Oxford, England: Oxford University Press, 1996).

11 W. E. Vine, *Vine's Expository Dictionary of Old and New Testament Words* (Nashville, IL: Thomas Nelson Publishers, 1996), s.v. "#12."

12 Frederick William Danker, and Walter Bauer, *A Greek-English Lexicon of the New Testament and Other Early Christian Literature* (Chicago, IL: University of Chicago Press, 2000).

13 Strong, *The Exhaustive Concordance of the Bible*, G12.

14 Henry Morris, *The Revelation Record* (Wheaton, IL: Tyndale House Publishers, 1983), Rev. 9:2.

15 Barnhouse, *Revelation*, 169.

16 E. W. Bullinger, *Commentary On Revelation* (Grand Rapids, MI: Kregel Publications, 1984, 1935), Rev. 9:15.

17 Later, the demons will undergo their own judgment and suffer torment: Mtt. 8:29.

18 "And the [angels (masculine plural)] who did not keep their proper domain, but left their own abode, He has reserved in everlasting chains under darkness for the judgment of the great day; as [Sodom (neuter plural)] and [Gomorrah (feminine singular)], and the [cities (feminine plural)] around them in a similar manner to [these (masculine plural)], [having given themselves over to sexual immorality (feminine plural)] and [gone after (feminine plural)] strange flesh, are set forth as an example, suffering the vengeance of eternal fire" (Jude 1:6-7).

19 Danker, *A Greek-English Lexicon of the New Testament and Other Early Christian Literature*, 112.

20 *New Electronic Translation : NET Bible*, electronic edition (Dallas, TX: Biblical Studies Press, 1998).

21 We are unable to discuss the many arguments for and against this interpretation as it is beyond the scope of our current study. When all the various considerations and related passages are taken into account, it is our view that it is difficult to escape the plain teaching of Scripture concerning this unnatural event for which specific angels have been locked away.

22 Danker, *A Greek-English Lexicon of the New Testament and Other Early Christian Literature*, 339.

23 John MacArthur, *Revelation 1-11 : The MacArthur New Testament Commentary* (Chicago, IL: Moody Press, 1999), Rev. 9:3.

24 J. A. Seiss, *The Apocalypse: Lectures on the Book of Revelation* (Grand Rapids, MI: Zondervan Publishing House, 1966), 205.

25 How different is the identification of Joel's "army" when related passages of Scripture are allowed to speak than that which is often promoted by those who hold to *dominion theology*[5.2.17] who frequently identify Joel's army as the Church!

26 J. Vernon McGee, *Thru The Bible Commentary* (Nashville, TN: Thomas Nelson, 1997, c1981), Joel 2:1.

27 Jerry Falwell, Edward D. Hindson, and Michael Woodrow Kroll, eds., *KJV Bible Commentary* (Nashville, TN: Thomas Nelson, 1997, c1994), Joel 2:1-2.

28 Fausset, "*The Revelation of St. John the Divine*," Joel 2:4.

29 Pink, *The Antichrist*, s.v. "Antichrist in the Apocalypse."

30 McGee, *Thru The Bible Commentary*, Joel 2:7.

[31] William Smith, *Smith's Bible Dictionary* (Nashville, TN: Thomas Nelson, 1997), s.v. "Locust."

[32] MacArthur, *Revelation 1-11 : The MacArthur New Testament Commentary*, Rev. 9:4.

[33] Undoubtedly some will escape this demonic horde by having previously been martyred (Rev. 7:14).

[34] MacArthur, *Revelation 1-11 : The MacArthur New Testament Commentary*, Rev. 9:4.

[35] Concerning God's use of evil for His own purposes: Jdg. 9:23; 1S. 18:10; 1K. 22:22; 2K. 19:7; 2Chr. 18:21; Job 1:12; 2:6; Isa. 37:7; Mtt. 4:1; Luke 22:31; John 19:11; 1Cor. 5:5; 1Ti. 1:20; 2Cor. 12:7; Rev. 2:10; 9:5; 9:15; 16:14; 17:17; 20:3; 20:8.

[36] MacArthur, *Revelation 1-11 : The MacArthur New Testament Commentary*, Rev. 9:5.

[37] Morris, *The Revelation Record*, Rev. 9:5.

[38] Bullinger, *Commentary On Revelation*, Rev. 9:5.

[39] *Britannica CD 99 Multimedia Edition*, s.v. "scorpion."

[40] Barnhouse, *Revelation*, 171.

[41] Mills, *Revelations: An Exegetical Study of the Revelation to John*, Rev. 9:6.

[42] Danker, *A Greek-English Lexicon of the New Testament and Other Early Christian Literature*, 567.

[43] Danker, *A Greek-English Lexicon of the New Testament and Other Early Christian Literature*, 566.

[44] Danker, *A Greek-English Lexicon of the New Testament and Other Early Christian Literature*, 897.

[45] *American Heritage Online Dictionary*, Ver. 3.0A, 3rd ed. (Houghton Mifflin, 1993), s.v. "Bizarre, as in form or appearance; strange.."

[46] Mounce, *The Book of Revelation*, Rev. 9:10.

[47] Bullinger, *Commentary On Revelation*, Rev. 9:3.

[48] "Scorpions range in size from 13 to 175 mm (0.5 to 7 inches) and have six pairs of appendages. The chelicerae, the small first pair, are used to tear apart prey. The pedipalps, the second pair, are large and have strong, claw-like pincers, which are held horizontally in front and are used as feelers and for grasping prey. The last four pairs, each equipped with a pincer, are walking legs."—*Britannica CD 99 Multimedia Edition*, s.v. "scorpion."

[49] Against this view, Mounce observes: "John apparently would have us understand the locusts to be of considerable size. Otherwise the description of hair, face, teeth, etc. would tend toward the comic."—Mounce, *The Book of Revelation*, Rev. 9:7.

[50] My description constructed from [Jules H. Poirier, *From Darkness to Light to Flight: Monarch—the Miracle Butterfly* (El Cajon, CA: Institute for Creation Research, 1995)].

[51] Bullinger, *Commentary On Revelation*, Rev. 9:12.

[52] Seiss, *The Apocalypse: Lectures on the Book of Revelation*, 207.

[53] Bullinger, *Commentary On Revelation*, Rev. 9:12.

[54] Carl Friedrich Keil, and Franz Delitzsch, *Commentary on the Old Testament* (Peabody, MA: Hendrickson, 2002), Joel 2:4-6.

[55] "So among Mohammedans, 'Lord of the locusts' is a title of God."—Fausset, "*The Revelation of St. John the Divine*," Joel 2:11.

[56] Job also compared the horse with the locust (Job 39:19-20).

[57] Robert B. Chisholm, *"Joel,"* in John F. Walvoord, and Roy B. Zuck, eds., *The Bible Knowledge Commentary* (Wheaton, IL: SP Publications, 1983), Joel 2:3.

[58] Fausset, "*The Revelation of St. John the Divine*," Rev. 9:7.

[59] M. R. Vincent, *Vincent's Word Studies* (Escondido, CA: Ephesians Four Group, 2002), Rev. 9:7.

[60] James Swanson, *Dictionary of Biblical Languages With Semantic Domains : Hebrew (Old Testament)*, electronic ed. (Oak Harbor, WA: Logos Research Systems, 1997).

61 Mal Couch, *"Angelology in the Book of Revelation,"* in Mal Couch, ed., *A Bible Handbook to Revelation* (Grand Rapids, MI: Kregel Publications, 2001), 159.

62 Fausset, "*The Revelation of St. John the Divine*," Rev. 9:8.

63 Those who suggest they will rip and tear their victims by way of their teeth are without scriptural support. That the victims are to be refused death argues against such an understanding. It is better to see the teeth as a parallelism to the destructive abilities of lions as Joel utilizes in relation to rapacious natural locusts which devour every living thing.

64 Danker, *A Greek-English Lexicon of the New Testament and Other Early Christian Literature*, 367.

65 *American Heritage Online Dictionary*, s.v. "thorax."

66 Friberg, *Analytical Lexicon of the Greek New Testament*, 228.

67 Seiss, *The Apocalypse: Lectures on the Book of Revelation*, 206.

68 "Οὕτως ἔδειξέν μοι κύριος καὶ ἰδοὺ ἐπιγονὴ ἀκρίδων ἐρχομένη ἑωθινή καὶ ἰδοὺ βροῦχος εἷς Γωγ ὁ βασιλεύσ. [*Houtōs edeixen moi kyrios kai idou epigonē akridōn erchomenē heōthinē kai idou brouchos eis Gōg ho basileuts*]"—*Septuaginta : With Morphology* (Stuttgart, Germany: German Bible Society, 1996, c1979), Amos 7:1.

69 "It is possible that this is an attributive or descriptive genitive, but genitive of source indicates origin more than character and hence seems more appropriate in this context."—Daniel B. Wallace, *Greek Grammar Beyond the Basics - Exegetical Syntax of the New Testament* (Grand Rapids, MI: Zondervan Publishing House and Galaxie Software, 1999, 2002), 110. "Metonymy of the Adjunct. The name of the pit is given to the angel of the pit, by this figure, by which the abstract is put for the concrete."—Jerome Smith, *The New Treasury of Scripture Knowledge* (Nashville, TN: Thomas Nelson Publishers, 1992), Rev. 9:11.

70 Smith, *Smith's Bible Dictionary*, s.v. "Apollyon."

71 Barnhouse, *Revelation*, 172-173.

72 MacArthur, *Revelation 1-11 : The MacArthur New Testament Commentary*, Rev. 9:11.

73 Pink, *The Antichrist*, s.v. "Antichrist in the Apocalypse."

74 Unless we adopt the theory of some that Antichrist already walked the stage of history, was slain, and will be revived yet future. Some consider a revival of Judas as possible fulfillment, but the Antichrist's deadly wound is by the sword (Rev. 13:14), whereas Judas committed suicide by hanging (Mtt. 27:5).

75 The only *man* said to rule over demons is Jesus Christ (Col. 2:10).

76 "Although ancient Greek did not have the convention of quotation marks, it could express essentially the same idea with a nominative of appellation."—Wallace, *Greek Grammar Beyond the Basics - Exegetical Syntax of the New Testament*, 60.

77 Alan F. Johnson, *Revelation: The Expositor's Bible Commentary* (Grand Rapids, MI: Zondervan Publishing House, 1966), Rev. 9:11.

78 MacArthur, *Revelation 1-11 : The MacArthur New Testament Commentary*, Rev. 9:11.

79 Morris, *The Revelation Record*, Rev. 9:13.

80 Barnhouse takes the voice to be a personification of the altar itself. [Barnhouse, *Revelation*, 174].

81 MacArthur, *Revelation 1-11 : The MacArthur New Testament Commentary*, Rev. 9:13.

82 Albrecht Durer (1471 - 1528). Image courtesy of the *Connecticut College* (http://www.conncoll.edu/visual/Durer-prints/index.html) *Wetmore Print Collection* (http://www.conncoll.edu/visual/wetmore.html).

83 Bullinger, *Commentary On Revelation*, Rev. 9:15.

84 Barnhouse, *Revelation*, 175.

85 MacArthur, *Revelation 1-11 : The MacArthur New Testament Commentary*, Rev. 9:14.

86 Unless we allow ourselves the luxury of departing from the text and imagining it to describe helicopter gunships and other modern weapons—thus falling into a trap similar to that of the *Historicist Interpretation*[2.12.4].

[87] "There is another intriguing possibility, of course. Maybe the Euphrates mentioned here is the antediluvian Euphrates rather than the Babylonian Euphrates. It is barely possible that, deep in the earth, remains the underground storage chamber which controlled the primeval flow into the garden of Eden. Though most of these caverns broke up with their fountains (controlled exit conduits) erupted to help produce the Flood, or at least in the earth's isostatic readjustments after the Flood, it must may be that the primeval source of Eden's rivers is still intact."—Morris, *The Revelation Record*, Rev. 9:14.

[88] Morris, *The Revelation Record*, Rev. 9:14.

[89] Smith, *Smith's Bible Dictionary*, s.v. "Euphrates."

[90] MacArthur, *Revelation 1-11 : The MacArthur New Testament Commentary*, Rev. 9:14.

[91] William R. Newell, *Revelation: Chapter by Chapter* (Grand Rapids, MI: Kregel Publications, 1994,c1935), Rev. 9:14.

[92] Bullinger, *Commentary On Revelation*, Rev. 9:15.

[93] Morris takes the time designation collectively as denoting a *duration* of their ministry lasting 13 months.

[94] All true believers will be taken at the *Rapture*[4.14], but it is a difficult number to accurately estimate.

[95] See the world population clock: [*http://www.census.gov/cgi-bin/ipc/popclockw*].

[96] A few manuscripts have the lesser μυριάδες μυριάδων [*myriades myriadōn*], *myriads of myriads*.

[97] "Attempts to reduce this expression to arithmetic miss the point. A 'double myriad of myriads' is an indefinite number of incalculable immensity."—Mounce, *The Book of Revelation*, Rev. 9:16.

[98] Swanson, *Dictionary of Biblical Languages With Semantic Domains : Hebrew (Old Testament)*, s.v. "#H6099."

[99] Fausset, "*The Revelation of St. John the Divine*," Joel 2:2.

[100] Mills, *Revelations: An Exegetical Study of the Revelation to John*, Rev. 9:16.

[101] Arnold G. Fruchtenbaum, *The Footsteps of Messiah*, rev ed. (Tustin, CA: Ariel Ministries, 2003), 231.

[102] Bear in mind that the passage says "two myriads of myriads" which indicates a numberless multitude rather than precisely "200 million." But for the sake of argument, a 200 million man army is assumed.

[103] Johnson, *Revelation: The Expositor's Bible Commentary*, Rev. 9:13-19.

[104] MacArthur, *Revelation 1-11 : The MacArthur New Testament Commentary*, Rev. 9:16.

[105] Morris, *The Revelation Record*, Rev. 9:17.

[106] Mills, *Revelations: An Exegetical Study of the Revelation to John*, Rev. 9:17.

[107] Friberg, *Analytical Lexicon of the Greek New Testament*, 387.

[108] Barnhouse, *Revelation*, 176.

[109] Morris, *The Revelation Record*, Rev. 9:18.

[110] MacArthur, *Revelation 1-11 : The MacArthur New Testament Commentary*, Rev. 9:15.

[111] MacArthur, *Revelation 1-11 : The MacArthur New Testament Commentary*, Rev. 9:20.

[112] Mills, *Revelations: An Exegetical Study of the Revelation to John*, Rev. 9:6.

[113] This passage explains why some members of the "North American Man-Boy Love Association," which advocates sex between adult men and young boys, are among the academic elite.

[114] *Demons* is in the accusative, which Wallace believes may be an indication of an inability to have a true personal relationship with as a false deity. "It may be significant that usually in the *NT*[5.2.48], the dative direct object is used with προσκυνέω [*proskyneō*] when true Deity is the object of worship (cf. Mtt. 14:33; 28:9; John 4:21; 1Cor. 14:25; Heb. 1:6; Rev. 4:10; 7:11; 11:16; 19:10; 22:9). The implication, in part, may be that God is a true God—one with whom human beings can have a personal relation. And usually, when false deity is worshiped, the accusative direct object is used (cf. Rev. 9:20; 13:8, 12; 14:9, 11; 20:4)."—Wallace, *Greek Grammar Beyond the Basics - Exegetical Syntax of the New Testament*, 172.

[115] Morris, *The Revelation Record*, Rev. 9:20.

[116] Barnhouse, *Revelation*, 177.

[117] Newell, *Revelation: Chapter by Chapter*, Rev. 9:20.

[118] Morris, *The Revelation Record*, Rev. 9:20.

[119] Seiss, *The Apocalypse: Lectures on the Book of Revelation*, 214.

[120] Concerning God as living: Ex. 3:6; Deu. 5:26; Jos. 3:10; 1S. 17:26, 36; 2K. 19:4, 16; Ps. 42:2; 84:2; Isa. 37:4, 17; Jer. 10:10; 23:36; Dan. 6:20, 26; Hos. 1:10; Mtt. 16:16; 22:32; 26:63; John 6:69; Acts 14:15; Rom. 9:26; 2Cor. 3:3; 6:16; 1Ti. 3:15; 4:10; 6:17; Heb. 3:12; 9:14; 10:31; 12:22; Rev. 7:2.

[121] It would appear that the ability to give life to that which is inanimate is essentially that of God alone: Gen. 2:7. Therefore, the breath given to the image of the beast must in some sense be a proximate duplication of that which God alone can do. A "lying wonder" (2Th. 2:9).

[122] Danker, *A Greek-English Lexicon of the New Testament and Other Early Christian Literature*, 854.

[123] Wesley J. Perschbacher, *The New Analytical Greek Lexicon of the New Testament* (Peabody, MA: Hendrickson Publishers, 1999), 426.

[124] Vincent, *Vincent's Word Studies*, Rev. 9:21.

[125] In response to those who believe that participating in activities such as reading the Harry Potter books is "harmless creativity" we respond with the simple question: Does it not grieve God that we will not train our children in the things of God, but readily expose them to the influence of magic? To believe otherwise is to demonstrate a lack of appreciation for our own tendencies as well as an ignorance of God's word. Moreover, God knows that even if today's train ride may seem "harmless" and not end in disaster, the eventual destination—given our dark hearts—is a *guaranteed train wreck!* His prohibitions against these practices are numerous and serious because He *alone* understands the nature of man. If we call ourselves *Christians*, then why would we participate in activities which are unbiblical and undoubtedly grieve our Lord?

[126] Morris, *The Revelation Record*, Rev. 9:6.

[127] T. A. McMahon, "The Spirits of the Lie," *The Berean Call*, November 2003. [*www.TheBereanCall.org*].

[128] McMahon continues: "Mike added that we of the sophisticated West have trouble relating to a culture in which spirits, i.e., demons, are a real, everyday part of life. However, that doesn't mean they're necessarily exclusive to the dense jungles of the Yanomamo. He said that on one autumn trip to the U.S. with Shoefoot, he was shocked as his friend, the former shaman, continually pointed out representations of spirits he had known being featured across America as it celebrated its most financially successful holiday: Halloween. Some time later, Shoefoot was given a sampling of TVs Saturday-morning cartoon characters and power figures. It was more of the same. He was not aware of the worldwide popularity of the Harry Potter books, which introduce children to sorcery and encourage them in the practice of witchcraft. As Mike explained this series of books to him, he was grieved that so many young people were being set up for the suffering and bondage that had tormented his own people."—T. A. McMahon, "The Spirits of the Lie," *The Berean Call*, November 2003. [*www.TheBereanCall.org*].

[129] Morris, *The Revelation Record*, Rev. 19:21.

[130] Danker, *A Greek-English Lexicon of the New Testament and Other Early Christian Literature*, 693.

[131] Seiss, *The Apocalypse: Lectures on the Book of Revelation*, 216.

[132] Danker, *A Greek-English Lexicon of the New Testament and Other Early Christian Literature*, 693.

[133] Barnhouse, *Revelation*, 178.

[134] Mills, *Revelations: An Exegetical Study of the Revelation to John*, Rev. 9:21.

[135] Seiss, *The Apocalypse: Lectures on the Book of Revelation*, 210.

3.10 - Revelation 10

3.10.1 - Revelation 10:1

The judgments of the first six seals and first six trumpets are now behind us. The seventh trumpet yet remains—containing the seven bowls—which is itself within the seventh seal (Rev. 8:1). In a similar way to which *chapter 7*[3.7] stood between the sixth and seventh seal judgments, this chapter is placed between the sixth and seventh trumpets and sets the stage for that final trumpet.

> These interludes encourage God's people in the midst of the fury and horror of divine judgment, and remind them that God is still in sovereign control of all events. During the interludes God comforts His people with the knowledge that He has not forgotten them, and that they will ultimately be victorious.[1]

It should be noted that the effects of the sixth trumpet may not yet be entirely complete: for the second woe is only said to be past after the ministry of the two witnesses in Revelation 11:3-13:[2]

> This part of the Apocalypse is sometimes treated as an episode, thrown between the second and third woe-trumpets, and having little or no relation to either. This is an error. We have still to deal with the blast of the sixth Trumpet. It is only in the fourteenth verse of the eleventh chapter, that we find the note of indication that the woe of the sixth Trumpet is accomplished.[3]

The theme of this chapter appears to be the declaration of God's intention and right to take possession of the earth—both land and sea—and to bring to fulfillment the many prophetic themes found in Scripture which point to the establishment of God's kingdom *on earth.* See *The Arrival of God's Kingdom*[2.4.3]. The judgments which come forth in the seventh trumpet (which include the seven bowls of God's wrath) are in many ways parallel to the judgment of the flood in the days of Noah. Jesus compared the suddenness of the judgments of the end with the suddenness with which Noah's flood arrived upon an unsuspecting populace (Mtt. 24:37-38; Luke 17:26). We see an allusion to the judgment of Noah in the rainbow which is on the head of the mighty angel who occupies the central role in this chapter (Rev. 10:1).

another mighty angel

The description of this mighty angel has significant similarities to that of deity.

3.10.1.1 - Divine Similarities

Caution is needed when attempting to establish the identity of this angel, even though the ultimate identity of the angel has little effect upon the purpose of the chapter.[4] For the discussion concerning the angel's identity often includes imprecise logic—most frequently found in the form of sweeping statements which either affirm or deny his identification as Christ based on similarities between this passage and other portions of Scripture.

For example:

> What absolutely forbids this angel being Christ is the oath sworn by the angel in Rev. 10:5-6, one that could never come from the lips of the second person of the Trinity (Beckwith, Mounce).[5]

This is faulty logic, for elsewhere Scripture readily affirms that God swears by Himself:

> For when God made a promise to Abraham, because He could swear by no one greater, **He swore by Himself**, saying, "Surely blessing I will bless you, and multiplying I will multiply you." (Heb. 6:13-14) [emphasis added]

Similar *non-sequiturs*[6] characterize much of the discussion on this subject. It seems that many interpreters arrive at chapter ten with an *a priori* view regarding the identity of the angel and simply amass snippets from supporting Scriptures in an attempt to bolster their position. Another example: some assert that this angel is Christ because of the many similarities in his description with the angel of Daniel 10.[7] But this conclusion assumes the deity of the angel in Daniel 10, an assumption which is difficult to maintain when one considers that Daniel's angel required assistance from Michael (Dan. 10:13, 21). Yet this crucial detail is not addressed.[8] Care should be exercised when evaluating the evidence both for and against the divine identification. Certainly, the appearance and activities of the angel are *remarkably similar* to that of deity.

Divine Similarities

Characteristic	Mighty Angel	Divinity
Traveling with clouds.	Rev. 10:1	Ex. 16:10; Ps. 97:2; Dan. 7:13; Mtt. 24:30; Rev. 1:7
Associated with rainbow.	Rev. 10:1	Rev. 4:3
Radiant face.	Rev. 10:1	Rev. 1:16
Feet like fire.	Rev. 10:1	Rev. 1:15
Holding a book.	Rev. 10:2	Rev. 5:8
Like a lion.	Rev. 10:3	Rev. 5:5
Swears by God.	Rev. 10:6[9]	Deu. 32:40; Heb. 6:13
Authority over land and sea.	Rev. 10:2, 5, 8	Gen. 1:9-10; Zec. 9:10; Mtt. 28:18; Eph. 1:22; Rev. 5:13

Adding to these similarities is the *OT*[5.2.51] representation of the second person of the Trinity by an angel, the *Angel of the Lord.*[10]

Yet, *Similarity does not make identity*. These similarities do not *necessitate* identifying this mighty angel as the second person of the Trinity. *Mighty angel* is ἄγγελον ἰσχυρὸν [*angelon ischyron*], the same phrase which is translated "strong angel" in Revelation 5:2. There, a strong angel asks "Who is worthy to open the scroll and to loose its seals," to which the answer will eventually come forth: "the Lion of the tribe of Judah, the Root of David has prevailed to open the scroll" (Rev. 5:5). Since the strong angel in chapter 5 is not Christ, then this mighty angel need not be understood as Christ. Later, a mighty angel (ἄγγελος ἰσχυρὸς [*angelos ischyros*]) takes up a great stone and throws it into the sea to indicate how Babylon will be destroyed (Rev. 18:21). As we have previously noted (Rev. 6:2), it seems unlikely that any of these mighty angels are to be understood as Christ because the Lamb is still in heaven in the process of loosing the seals and does not ride forth until all seven seal, trumpet, and bowl judgments have been initiated (Rev. 19:11). He is the *instigator* of all that flows forth in the judgments, but does not participate in them until His literal, bodily coming to take up His kingdom. Although the description of angels may at times be very similar to the description of God's glory (e.g., Dan. 10:4 cf. Rev. 1:14-15), this is not a reliable indicator of deity, as in the vision given to Daniel where a most glorious angel nevertheless requires the assistance of Michael to withstand other fallen angels (Dan. 10:12, 20). Moreover, on the mount of transfiguration, not only was Jesus transfigured, but Moses and Elijah also appeared in great glory (Mtt. 17:3; Mark 9:4; Luke 9:30). Thus, glorious manifestations, as here, need not necessitate a divine identification. In the phrase *another mighty angel*, *another* is αλλος [*allos*] (another similar angel) rather than ἕτερος [*heteros*] (another different angel). This angel is like other angels, whereas Christ is essentially different from angels.[11] When Christ appears in the Revelation, He receives an unambiguous title:

> Whenever Jesus Christ appears in Revelation John gives Him an unmistakable title. He is called "the faithful witness, the firstborn of the dead, and the ruler of the kings of the earth" (Rev. 1:5), the son of man (Rev. 1:13), the first and the last (Rev. 1:17), the living One (Rev. 1:18), the Son of God (Rev. 2:18), "He who is holy, who is true" (Rev. 3:7), "the Amen, the faithful and true Witness, the Beginning of the creation of God" (Rev. 3:14), "the Lion that is from the tribe of Judah, the Root of David" (Rev. 5:5), the Lamb (Rev. 6:1, 16; 7:17; 8:1), Faithful and True (Rev. 19:11), the Word of God (Rev. 19:13), and "King of Kings, and Lord of Lords" (Rev. 19:16). It is reasonable to assume that if Christ were the angel in view here He would be distinctly identified.[12]

It is our view that this angel is not Christ, but a *divine emissary* whose great glory and declarative actions indicate he is acting in the authority of God and asserting the right and intention of God to reclaim the globe in the judgments which will follow. This angel represents Christ in a similar way to which the Angel of Jehovah represented Jehovah in the OT, but with an important difference: this angel is not divine.

coming down from heaven

This phrase probably denotes angels which normally reside in heaven, perhaps even in His immediate presence. Perhaps this angel is one of the seven "presence angels" which stand before God (Rev. 8:2) and which were given the seven trumpets (Rev. 8:2). Later, another angel, not called mighty, but having *great authority*, comes *down from heaven* to announce the impending fall of Babylon (Rev. 18:1-2). The angel who binds Satan, an assignment necessitating great authority and power, also is said to come *down from heaven* (Rev. 20:1).

clothed with a cloud

Clouds generally attend the divine presence. See commentary on *Revelation 1:7*[3.1.7]. Clouds are associated with the resurrection of the two *human* witnesses (Rev. 11:12). See *Divine Similarities*[3.10.1.1].

a rainbow was on his head

The only angel said to have a rainbow on his head. This passage undoubtedly contributed to artist depictions of halos which often characterized religious artwork.[13] Here, the rainbow is a reminder of God's covenant with Noah (Gen. 9:11-17; Isa. 54:9). Fausset takes the rainbow as "the emblem of covenant mercy to God's people, amidst judgments on God's foes."[14] But this ignores the setting of the Noahic covenant which came *after* the destruction of the flood in which Noah and his family were preserved in the ark. The rainbow does not indicate a covenant with certain people over against other people for the covenant following the flood was "between God and every living creature of all flesh that *is* on the earth" (Gen. 9:16). In the more severe judgments to come within the seventh trumpet, God has promised never again to flood the entire earth as He did in the days of Noah (Isa. 54:9). Judgment must now come by a different means (2Pe. 3:5-7). The rainbow is also an indicator of God's general faithfulness to covenant. The mystery declared to the prophets (Rev. 10:7) which He has promised, is sure to come to pass. The angel's stance on both earth and sea indicate, as during Noah's flood, the global nature of the judgments which will attend his roar (Rev. 10:3).

Up to now, even though the wicked prosper, in the midst of God's direct judgment we can expect that those who know Him will be specially protected:

> You have said, 'It is useless to serve God; what profit *is it* that we have kept His ordinance, and that we have walked as mourners before the LORD of hosts? So now we call the proud blessed, for those who do wickedness are raised up; they even tempt God and go free.' Then those who feared the LORD spoke to one another, and the LORD listened and heard *them*; so a book of remembrance was written before Him for those who fear the LORD and who meditate on His name. "They shall be Mine," says the LORD of hosts, "On the day that I make them My jewels. And I will spare them as a man spares his own son who serves him." Then you shall again discern between the righteous and the wicked, between one who serves God and one who does not serve Him. "For behold, the day is coming, burning like an oven, and all the proud, yes, all who do wickedly will be stubble. And the day which is coming shall burn them up," says the LORD of hosts, "That will leave them neither root nor branch. But to you who fear My name The Sun of Righteousness shall arise with healing in His wings; and you shall go out and grow fat like stall-fed calves." (Mal. 3:14-4:2)

his face *was* like the sun

This angel has a radiant countenance like the glorious angel which Daniel saw (Dan. 10:6). See *Divine Similarities*[3.10.1.1].

his feet like pillars of fire

His burning feet speak of judgment. That which he stands upon—the earth and the nations—will be judged (Isa. 63:3-6; Rev. 14:19-20). See commentary on *Revelation 1:15*[3.1.15]. The description of this angel closely parallels that of Daniel's vision (Dan. 10:6). See *Divine Similarities*[3.10.1.1].

> Since the theme of the Exodus is always in the background of this central section of Revelation, it is quite possible that the angel's legs would recall the pillar of fire and cloud that gave both protection (Ex. 14:19, 24) and guidance (Ex. 13:21-22) to the children of Israel in their wilderness journey. Farrer notes

that the description of the angel fits his message—affirming God's fidelity to his covenants (Rev. 10:7): the bow reminding of God's promise through Noah, the pillar of fire God's presence in the wilderness, and the scroll the tablets of stone.[15]

3.10.2 - Revelation 10:2

He had a little book

The book is a βιβλαρίδιον [*biblaridion*], *little book*, rather than a βιβλίον [*biblion*], *book*.[16] This book is differentiated from the scroll held by the Lamb (Rev. 5:8). See *Divine Similarities*[3.10.1.1].

The book is similar to the scroll (or book) which Ezekiel was instructed to eat (Eze. 3:1-2). Both Ezekiel and John are told to eat the book, both books were sweet to the taste but bitter in the stomach, and both books contained prophecy which the prophet was to ingest and deliver to other men (Rev. 10:9-11 cf. Eze. 2:9-3:4). This book is "little" because it contains a relatively lesser portion of the overall prophetic content within the seven-sealed scroll loosed by the Lamb (Rev. 5:1-2). The contents of this *little book* are consumable and digestible by John whereas it is almost certain that he could never have ingested the full contents of the seven-sealed scroll. See commentary on *Revelation 5:1*[3.5.1] and *Revelation 10:11*[3.10.11].

open in his hand

Like the Lamb before the throne (Rev. 5:7-8), this angel has a book in his hand. The Lamb's book is said to be in His *right* hand but this angel appears to hold his book in his *left* hand because while holding the book he raises his right hand (Rev. 10:1, *MT*[5.2.45] and *NU*[5.2.49] texts) in an oath. Whereas the Lamb's book was originally *sealed*, this book is *open*. *Open* is ἠνεῳγμένον [*ēneōgmenon*], perfect tense passive participle, *having previously been opened* . By now the Lamb's book has had all seven seals removed (Rev. 8:1) and probably lies completely open too. As intriguing as these similarities may be, this book is undoubtedly not the seven-sealed scroll for it is said to be smaller. Moreover, unless this angel is Christ, he is among those who are unworthy to even "look at it" (Rev. 5:3), much less take hold of it (Rev. 10:8).

his right foot on the sea and *his* left *foot* on the land

That which he places his feet upon he demonstrates his authority over (Deu. 11:24). "The setting or planting of his feet on sea and land is the formal taking possession of both; or the formal expression of the purpose to do so."[17] *And* is δὲ [*de*] which often indicates an adversative relationship: *but*. *Left* is εὐώνυμον [*euōnymon*]: "Used by the Greeks as a euphemism for *left, the left hand, the left side*, as a replacement for ἀριστερός [*aristeros*] (*left*) in opposition to the right, since omens on the left were regarded as unfortunate (Mtt. 20:21)."[18] His right foot (the side of favor) is placed upon the sea *but* his left foot (the side of disfavor) is placed on the land. This is a literal depiction with a possibly additional secondary symbolism: (1) the sea and land depict the *entire physical* globe; and 2) the sea represents the Gentile nations (Rev. 13:1; 17:15) while the land may represent the Jewish nation as stewards of the Promised Land (Gen. 13:15; Lev. 25:10-28; 27:24; 2Chr. 10:7; Ps. 83:12; Joel 1:6; 3:2).[19] The authority the angel represents is complete: both geopolitically and nationally (Ps. 2:8; 89:25; Zec. 9:10; Mtt. 28:18; Eph. 1:22). The placement of the disfavored foot upon the land, if the *land* is representative of Israel, may indicate that judgment will begin with the Jewish nation—those who have the greater revelation and responsibility (Rom. 2:9 cf. Mtt. 10:15; Luke 12:47-48). See commentary on *Revelation 13:1*[3.13.1] and *Revelation 13:11*[3.13.11].

See *Divine Similarities*[3.10.1.1].

3.10.3 - Revelation 10:3

a loud voice

Like Christ, the angel spoke with a loud or great voice (Rev. 1:10). The voice of this mighty angel is also similar to that of the strong angel who asked *Who is worthy to open the scroll and to loose its seals?* (Rev. 5:2). So too, the angel ascending from the east, having the seal of the living God also cried out with a loud voice (Rev. 7:2)

as *when* a lion roars

Unlike Christ's voice, this angel's voice is not "as of a trumpet" (Rev. 1:10) or "as the sound of many waters" (Rev. 1:15), but as when a lion roars. *Roar* is μυκάται [*mykatai*] from μυκάομαι [*mykaomai*], "The verb here is originally applied to the lowing of cattle, expressing the sound, 'moo-ka-omai.' Both Aristophanes and Theocritus use it of the roar of the lion, and the former of thunder. Homer, of the ring of the shield and the hissing of meat on the spit."[20]

The great volume of the voice itself does not necessitate identifying the angel with divinity for the impressive voice of mighty angels is well attested (1Th. 4:16; Rev. 5:2; 7:2; 8:13; 12:10; 14:7, 15; 16:1; 18:2). Some who interpret this angel as Christ understand the roar as indicating His identity as the "Lion of the tribe of Judah" (Rev. 5:5)[21] (see *Divine Similarities*[3.10.1.1]), but this is unnecessary. The context indicates *lion* is used as a simile to indicate the ferocity and volume of his cry. Moreover, there are other references to lion-like attributes in Revelation besides those of Christ (Rev. 4:7; 9:8, 17; 13:2). The roaring of a lion is an allusion to passages which set forth God's ferociousness in judgment.

When Jeremiah prophesies the seventy years of captivity of Israel in Babylon to be followed by the eventual return to the land (Jer. 25:11-12), he continues to speak forth a judgment of God among "all the nations . . . to whom the LORD has sent me" (Jer. 25:17). The list of Gentile nations destined for judgment is extensive (Jer. 25:18-26) and neither will Israel be spared: " 'For behold, I begin to bring calamity **on the city which is called by My name**, and should you be utterly unpunished? You shall not be unpunished, for I will call for a sword on "all the inhabitants of the earth",' says the LORD of hosts" [emphasis added] (Jer. 25:29). In this global judgment, the LORD is said to *roar* as a *lion*. The judgment prophesied by Jeremiah involves both "His fold" (Israel) and "all flesh" (Gentile nations).

> Therefore prophesy against them all these words, and say to them: "**The LORD will roar from on high**, and utter His voice from His holy habitation; He will roar mightily **against His fold**. He will give a shout, **as those who tread** the grapes, **Against all the inhabitants of the earth**. A noise will come to the ends of the earth-For the LORD has a controversy with the nations; He will plead His case with all flesh. He will give those *who are* wicked to the sword," says the LORD. Thus says the LORD of hosts: "Behold, disaster shall go forth from nation to nation, and a great whirlwind shall be raised up from the farthest parts of the earth. And at that day the slain of the LORD shall be from *one* end of the earth even to the *other* end of the earth. They shall not be lamented, or gathered, or buried; they shall become refuse on the ground. Wail, shepherds, and cry! Roll about *in the ashes*, you leaders of the flock! For the days of your slaughter and your dispersions are fulfilled; you shall fall like a precious vessel. And the shepherds will have no way to flee, nor the leaders of the flock to escape. A voice of the cry of the shepherds, and a wailing of the leaders to the flock *will be heard*. For the LORD has plundered their pasture, and the peaceful dwellings are cut down because of the fierce anger of the LORD. He has left His lair **like the lion**; for their land is desolate because of the fierceness of the Oppressor, and because of His fierce anger." (Jer. 25:30-38) [emphasis added]

When we recall the extensive parallels between the previous chapter and Joel, it is little surprise that Joel expresses the same theme. This angel gives a *roar* as a *lion* to awaken the people of the earth in preparation for the judgment of God against *all nations*:

> Let the nations be wakened, and come up to the Valley of Jehoshaphat; for there I will sit to judge all the surrounding nations. Put in the sickle, for the harvest is ripe. Come, go down; for the winepress is full, the vats overflow-For their wickedness *is* great. Multitudes, multitudes in the valley of decision! For the day of the LORD *is* near in the valley of decision. The sun and moon will grow dark, and the stars will diminish their brightness. The LORD also will roar from Zion, and utter His voice from Jerusalem; the heavens and earth will shake; but the LORD will be a shelter for His people, and the strength of the children of Israel. (Joel 3:12-16)

The nations will soon be gathered to the Valley of Jehoshaphat (a compound from Hebrew *Yahweh* and *shaphat*, meaning "Jehovah has judged"[22]), and there God "will sit to judge all the surrounding nations" (Rev. 16:12-16, which *see*[3.16.12]). Notice too, the winepress motif, symbolized in this chapter by the mighty angel's stance: standing *upon* both sea and land. Although both the Jewish nation and the Gentile nations will be judged according to Jeremiah, Joel reminds us of an extremely important distinction between Israel and all other nations: Israel *alone* is God's chosen nation and has *unconditional everlasting promises* of divine protection (Isa. 44:21; Jer. 31:35-37; 33:20-22; Rom. 11:1, 25-29). Therefore, in the midst of the judgment of God, "the LORD will be a shelter for His people, and the strength of the children of Israel" (Joel 3:16).[23] Isaiah also records God's promise to defend Jerusalem and Mount Zion. He stirs himself "As a lion roars, and a young lion over his prey" (Isa. 31:4). See commentary on *Revelation 12*[3.12].

seven thunders uttered their voices

The voices are said to be *their* own, ἑαυτῶν [*eautōn*], indicating "intensive possession: 'their own' voices. The voices were and remained 'their own,' not shared with anyone else and therefore perpetuated (Alford)."[24] In the vision of the throne room in heaven, John heard "thunderings and voices" (Rev. 4:5). One of the living creatures whose announcement attends the opening of the first seal is said to have "a voice like thunder" (Rev. 6:1), but there are only four living creatures, not seven. Two aspects of these thunderous voices are left as a mystery for us: (1) their identity, and 2) what they said. It may be that the lion-like cry of this mighty angel was replied to by the "seven angels having the last seven plagues, for **in them the wrath of God is complete**" [emphasis added] (Rev. 15:1). The correlation between the seven thunders and the seven angels with the seven last plagues is strengthened by what the mighty angel announces, "in the days of the sounding of the seventh angel, when he is about to sound, **the mystery of God would be finished**, as He declared to His servants the prophets" [emphasis added] (Rev. 10:7). "These may have been angel-voices, the effect (thunder) being put, by *Metonymy*, for the cause."[25] On the other hand, what the seven thunders utter is apparently of great importance and divine privacy, for John is not allowed to record what is said. This argues for identifying the thunders with the very voice of God Himself in that they evidently declare *the mystery of God* which must *remain* a mystery throughout the centuries from the day of John to the time of the end.[26] The following verse indicates that the seven thunders uttered more than one message. We are probably right to assume that each of the seven thunders uttered a unique message, although we cannot be dogmatic on this point. The seven thunders and their seven utterances are an indication of the completeness of judgment which attend their declaration. See *Seven: Perfection, Completeness*[2.7.5.3.6].

One might ask whether the seven thunders are the Seven Spirits before the throne (Rev. 1:4; 4:6)? But, as we have seen, the Seven Spirits refer to the Holy Spirit and there is no record in Scripture of the Spirit speaking in a direct auditory manner.

> John had earlier noted there were thunderings proceeding from God's throne (Revelation 5:5) along with voices. It is probably that these seven thunderous voices which followed the great cry . . . were nothing less than seven pronouncements from the very throne of God.[27]

3.10.4 - Revelation 10:4

I was about to write

Since John was instructed, "What you see, write in a book" (Rev. 1:11) and "Write the things which you have seen, and the things which are, and the things which will take place after this" (Rev. 1:19), he was dutifully recording the things which he was being shown.

a voice from heaven

The source of the voice is unidentified, but ultimately of divine authority for it forbids John from recording what he had previously been instructed *by God* to record (Rev. 1:11, 19). Later, this same voice tells John to take the little book from the mighty angel (Rev. 10:8).

Seal up the things . . . do not write them

Although John's primary purpose in writing Revelation is to *reveal* (Rev. 1:1; 22:10), here he is commanded to omit the utterance of the seven thunders from the biblical record. Daniel was also told to seal up what he had been shown in a vision (Dan. 8:26; 12:4, 9). In Daniel's case, the sealing appears to denote the inability to *understand* the contents until a later time when knowledge and understanding of the Scriptures would increase. Here, the sealing pertains to the actual revelation which is completely omitted from the record. Amos records, "Surely the Lord GOD does nothing unless he reveals His secret to His servants the prophets" (Amos 3:7). This principle is not violated here because *the prophet, John, is allowed to hear* what the thunders utter, even though told not to write it down for his readers.

It is ultimately fruitless for us to speculate as to what was omitted because the reason John may not record their utterance appears to be related to the outworking of the *mystery* of God. Therefore, *it may not be known* what they said until it comes to pass—for God has not chosen to reveal their message to us.

> Here is a definite commandment from God that no indication shall be given as to the correct interpretation of the seven thunders. In spite of this, however, some commentators have attempted to do that which God forbade John to do. It seems that the reverent student of the Word of God can do nothing but pass on to that which follows.[28]

Here, we would do well to remember the words of Moses and the Psalm writer: "The secret *things belong* to the LORD our God" (Deu. 29:29) and "*It is* the glory of God to conceal a matter" (Pr. 25:2).[29]

> As the visible portion of an iceberg is only a small part of the iceberg, most of which is hidden from man's sight, so God's disclosures reveal only part of his total being and purposes.[30]

A related passage in the Psalms attributes a sevenfold aspect to the voice of the LORD. Interestingly, it is found in conjunction with a reference to God's reign as judge during the Noahic flood which we have seen is related to the global judgment set forth in this chapter:

> The voice **of the LORD** *is* over the waters; the God of glory thunders; the LORD *is* over many waters. The voice **of the LORD** *is* powerful; the voice **of the LORD** *is* full of majesty. The voice **of the LORD** breaks the cedars, yes, the LORD splinters the cedars of Lebanon. He makes them also skip like a calf, Lebanon and Sirion like a young wild ox. The voice **of the LORD** divides the flames of fire. The voice **of the LORD** shakes the wilderness; the LORD shakes the Wilderness of Kadesh. The voice **of the LORD** makes the deer give birth, and strips the forests bare; and in His temple everyone says, "Glory!" The LORD sat *enthroned* **at the Flood**, and the LORD sits as King forever. (Ps 29:3-10) [emphasis added]

Although we may not know what the seven thunders said, we can infer from the context and related passages that it concerns aspects of the remaining seven judgments (the seven bowls subsumed within the seventh trumpet) which result in the kingdoms of this world becoming the kingdoms of the Father and His Christ (Rev. 11:15). Perhaps the contents of the utterances demonstrate similar themes as that which the Psalm writer recorded.

As to their contents, perhaps they uttered "inexpressible words, which it is not lawful for a man to utter" (2Cor. 12:4). Perhaps their contents would be unbearable down through the centuries:

> So terrible are they that God in mercy withholds them, since "sufficient unto the day is the evil thereof." The godly are thus kept from morbid ponderings over the evil to come; and the ungodly are not driven by despair into utter recklessness of life. [31]

3.10.5 - Revelation 10:5

standing

ἑστῶτα [*estōta*], perfect tense participle, *while having stood.* The angel is still standing on the sea and land when he raises his hand to swear.

raised up his hand to heaven

Raising the hand was a common practice when taking an oath (Gen. 14:22; Deu. 32:40; Eze. 20:5, 15; 36:7; 47:14). The *MT*[5.2.45] and *NU*[5.2.49] texts indicate the angel raised his *right* hand, in which case the book would be held in his left hand. Another powerful angel lifted both hands before Daniel to swear "by Him who lives forever" (Dan. 12:7).

3.10.6 - Revelation 10:6

swore by Him who lives forever and ever

Here and in Daniel 12, the angels swear to underscore the unchangeable nature of the message they give. In both cases, the aspect of the message being emphasized is the *timing* with which prophesied events will take place. Daniel's angel indicated that the final period when the power of Israel would be shattered would be "times, time and half *a time*" (Dan. 12:7). Here, the angel tells John that the long history of delay where God's grace prevented Him from moving in final judgment has come to an end. See *Divine Similarities*[3.10.1.1].

There is no higher person by which one can swear than the eternal God (Rev. 1:18; 4:9).

who created heaven and . . . the earth and . . . the sea

Emphasis is placed upon the identity of God as Creator, for the declaration of the angel in this chapter is intimately connected with God repossessing the title to the earth (both land and sea, indeed the entire creation), which has been marred by the interposition of sin and Satan. Mention of God's creative acts over both the *earth* and *sea* parallels his stance (Rev. 10:2). God owns that which He has created (Gen. 2:1; 1Cor. 10:26)! See commentary on *Revelation 4:11*[3.4.11].

there should be delay no longer

χρόνος οὐκέτι ἔσται [*chronos ouketi estai*], *time no longer it will be*. "Signifying not the abolition of time, which is impossible, but that there would be no further delay or waiting (Rev. 6:10) for the accomplishment of God's covenanted and promised purposes."[32] The truth of this statement is found in the response of the devil after having been cast to earth (Rev. 12:12). Although prophetic events such as the coming of Christ for His church and the *Day of the Lord*[5.2.14] are *Imminent*[4.8]—they could begin at any time—history has evidenced a delay in the consummation of things:

> The true attitude of the Church, and that to which all the representations and admonitions of the Scriptures are framed, is to be looking and ready any day and every day for the coming of Christ to seize away his waiting and watching saints. But in faithfully assuming this attitude, and thus hoping and expecting the speedy fulfilment of what has been promised, the Church has been made to see one notable and quickening period after another pass away without bringing the consummation which was anticipated. Eve thought the promise on the point of fulfilment when Cain was born; but He whom she was expecting was yet 4,000 years away. When Simeon took the infant Savior to his bosom . . . he supposed that the time for the consummation had arrived; but it was only the preliminary advent that he had lived to witness. . . . The early Christians were lively in their expectations that yet in their day the standard of the coming One would be seen unfurled in the sky, and all their hopes be consummated; but the days of the Apostles and of the apostolic fathers passed, and still "the Bridegroom tarried." . . . Although the Saviour may come any day, and our duty is to be looking for Him every day, it is still possible that all present prognostications on the subject may fail, as they have always failed; that years and years of earnest and confident expectation may go by without bringing the Lord from heaven; and that delay after delay, and ever repeating prolongations of the time of waiting may intervene, till it becomes necessary for the preservation of the faith of God's people to hear the fresh edict from the lips of their Lord, that "*there shall be no more delay*." Though the coming of the consummation be slow, *it will come*. There is not another truth in God's word that is so peculiarly authenticated. . . . Shall we then have any doubt upon the subject? Shall we allow the failure of men's figures and prognostications to shake our confidence or obscure our hope? Shall we suffer the many and long delays that have occurred, or that ever may occur, to drive us into the scoffer's ranks?[33]

Habakkuk set forth the principle of the patience that is needed in regard to prophetic pronouncements of God: "For the vision *is* yet for an appointed time; but at the end it will speak, and it will not lie. Though it tarries, wait for it; because it will surely come, it will not tarry" (Hab. 2:3).

God's prophetic timetable is not ours. How often we forget! The result is the discrediting of His Holy Word as we misrepresent that which it teaches by making it conform to our own expectations concerning the age within which we find ourselves in the plan of history. But we must be patient! God's predictions are *sure*, but they are for an *appointed time* which He alone knows. Let us remember that! That which God has predicted "He will manifest in **His own time**" [emphasis added] (1Ti. 6:15).

3.10.7 - Revelation 10:7

in the days of the sounding of the seventh angel

This refers to the time period during which the seventh angel sounds and the final seven bowl judgments pour forth (Rev. 11:15; (16). See *Literary Structure*[2.14].

the mystery of God

A mystery is something which is unknowable by man unless revealed by God:

> The New Testament mystery doctrines (see T. Ernest Wilson, *Mystery Doctrines of the New Testament* , pp. 10-12) make an interesting study, and may be listed as follows (1) the faith, 1Ti. 3:9. (2) the church, Rom. 16:25. (3) the gospel, Eph. 6:19. (4) Jew and Gentile in one body, Eph. 3. (5) the bride, Eph. 5:32.

Rev. 19, 20. (6) seven stars and *seven churches*[5.2.66], Rev. 1:20. (7) of godliness, 1Ti. 3:16. (8) kingdom of heaven, Mtt. 13:11. (9) Israel's blindness, Rom. 11:25. (10) *rapture*[5.2.62] of the church, 1Cor. 15:51. (11) His will, Eph. 1:9. (12) of God, Rev. 10:7. (13) the indwelling Christ, Col. 1:24-29. (14) the Godhead of Christ, Col. 2:2, 9. (15) of iniquity, 2Th. 2:7. (16) Babylon, Rev. 17:5. Isa. 2:1-4.[34]

NT[5.2.48] mysteries reveal information which was not previously made known: "The mystery [of Rev. 10:7] is that there will be a series of seven climactic judgments that will destroy the satanic mystery of the man of sin. This was not revealed in the Old Testament."[35]

> The expression, "the *mystery* of God," in this connection seems to indicate all those counsels and dealings of God made known by Him to and through the Old Testament prophets, concerning His governmental proceedings with men on earth looking always toward the establishment of the kingdom in the hands of Christ. When Christ comes to take the kingdom, there will be no mystery, but, on the contrary, manifestation. "The earth shall be full of the knowledge of Jehovah, as the waters cover the sea"—that is, universally and compulsorily (Isaiah 11:9).[36]

See commentary on *Revelation 1:20*[3.1.20].

would be finished

ἐτελέσθη [*etelesthē*], prophetic aorist, which emphasizes the certainty of the future event as if it had already occurred.[37] The completion comes in the sounding of the seventh trumpet, which initiates the seven bowls of God's wrath. When the final (seventh) bowl is poured forth, "a loud voice came out of the temple in heaven, from the throne, saying, 'It is done!' " (Rev. 16:17).

> All the pain, sorrow, suffering, and evil in the world cause the godly to long for God to intervene. A day is coming when He will break His silence, a day when all the purposes of God concerning men and the world will be consummated. . . . All the atheists, agnostics, and scoffers who mocked the thought that Christ would return (2Pe. 3:3-4) will be silenced. The millennia of sin, lies, murders, thefts, wars, and the persecution and martyrdom of God's people will be over. Satan and his demon hosts will be bound and cast into the abyss for a thousand years (Rev. 20:1-3), unable any longer to tempt, torment, or accuse believers. The desert will become a blossoming garden (cf. Isa. 35:1; 51:3; Eze. 36:34-35), people will live long lives (Isa. 65:20), and there will be peace between former enemies at all levels of society—and even in the animal kingdom (Isa. 11:6-8).[38]

He declared to His servants the prophets

Declared is εὐηγγέλισεν [*euēngelisen*], *he announced good news*. The message declared to the prophets was ultimately one of good news: the gospel! Not only of Christ's provision for man's sin, but of God's ultimate reclamation of fallen creation. The complete gospel includes much more than individual redemption, but extends to the entire redemptive revelation of God:

> We, therefore, plant ourselves upon the divinest of records, and upon the most authentic, direct, and solemn of all sacred utterances, and say, that he whose gospel drops and repudiates from its central themes the grand doctrine of the consummation of all things, as portrayed in this Apocalypse, is not the true Gospel of God.[39]

As we have attempted to emphasize throughout our study, the book of Revelation is not a "head without a body." It is intimately connected with a large amount of prophetic material set forth elsewhere in Scripture. This fact alone undermines the attempt by *preterist interpreters*[2.12.2] to limit the scope of the book. For to limit the scope of Revelation to the events surrounding the judgment of Jerusalem by Rome in A.D. 70 necessitates the cutting short of all the grand prophetic themes of Scripture. Indeed, some *preterists*[5.2.59] implicitly recognize this fact when they assert that we are *already in the new heavens and new earth.* See *Preterist Interpretation*[2.12.2].

No, we must leave the preterists to follow their own dead-end path which lops off huge parts of God's prophetic program and understand the book of Revelation within the grand scheme of God's entire redemptive plan for all nations, nay, for the entire globe, nay, for all of creation! See *Related Passages and Themes*[2.13].

The phrase *the prophets* is best understood as denoting the *Old Testament* prophets because "the relative silence of NT prophecy in regard to the fulfillment of Israel's hope and kingdom is notable. The occurrences of προφήτης [*prophētēs*] in the Gospels, Acts, and the Epistles are predominantly references to *OT*[5.2.51] prophets."[40] Although what is to come is a mystery, the non-mysterious aspects of the mystery were *declared* to the OT prophets.:

> The mystery previously hidden refers to all the unknown details that are revealed from this point to the end of Revelation, when the new heavens and new earth are created. God had preached that mystery (without all the details revealed in the New Testament) to His servants the prophets in the Old Testament, and men like Daniel, Ezekiel, Isaiah, Jeremiah, Joel, Amos, and Zechariah wrote of end-time events. Much of the detail, however, was hidden and not revealed until the New Testament (for example in Mtt. 24, 25, and 2Th. 1:5-2:12), and more particularly in the previous chapters of Revelation.[41]

The mystery was declared by *God* to *His servants* (Dan. 9:6; Amos 3:7; Zec. 1:6). The prophets were not free to speculate concerning God's plan for history using their own uninspired words. They were *His servants* and *He saw to it that they obeyed* to record precisely that which He desired to have recorded in Holy Scripture! For how could He call them *servant* (even "slaves," δούλους [*doulous*]) if they did not serve His will? And what could be said of a God who was unable to control His servants —those set aside for His specific use? Those commentators who would deny the *inspiration*[5.2.33] and *inerrancy*[5.2.32] of Scripture, of which there is no shortage, must stumble on this point. Here, John tells us that what will be fulfilled is what *God declared to His servants*: that which they recorded and was preserved for our learning.

If the Lord spoke through His servants the prophets, only to have what He said be hopelessly twisted and distorted so that it was no longer inerrant *in all matters which it records*, then how could He hold men to it? Would it be fair to condemn men for eternity in flames if the very message which sets forth their doom and the offer of eternal life is itself hopelessly flawed? For even if the main message were somehow preserved (the view of partial inspiration), what man could be condemned for failing to trust in it if it could be shown that numerous passages were in error? And who is responsible for deciding what portions are the true message of God reliably preserved and which portions are not His, but flawed distortions of His original message? Clearly, views which fail to acknowledge the reliability of God's Word make Scripture akin to Swiss cheese—full of holes.[42] See *Anti-supernatural Bias*[2.5].

Since the mystery which will be finished was *declared to His servants the prophets*, we might expect that the mystery involves the consummation of a wide range of prophetic themes which run like threads throughout both testaments. Jerome Smith provides a cogent summary of what may be involved in this "ultimate mystery."

> This "mystery" which is to be finished involves (1) the resolution of the problem of evil, which was first manifest in the Garden of Eden, as the first sin seemingly interrupted the purpose for Adam and Eve in the Garden of Eden. The fall brought the attendant curse upon man and all creation, the curse now announced to be removed. The prophets speak unitedly of the coming *Messianic Kingdom*[5.2.39] as a time of regeneration, restitution, and restoration, when earth will be restored to its paradisiacal state, a time when the curse is removed (Rev. *22:3; Gen. *3:15; Isa. 11:6-9; 60:21; Zec. 14:11; Acts 3:19-21). (2) the resolution of the apparent paradox of election and free will, and a clarification to us of the orderings of providence (1Cor. 13:12; Eph. 1:11). (3) the consummation of the mystery of godliness, involving the human and divine cooperating in establishing the Davidic theocratic kingdom (Isa. 54:1; Mtt. 22:41-46; John 1:51; 1Cor. 15:50; Eph. 1:10; 1Ti. 3:16). (4) the completion of our redemption and the establishment of our inheritance (Mtt. 19:27-30; Rom. 8:23; Eph. 1:11; 4:30; Heb. 9:28; 1Jn. 3:2). (5) the pre-tribulational, *premillennial*[5.2.58] personal appearance of Christ for believers to prepare the organization of, and to set up, his kingdom before its open, public manifestation (Deu. 33:2; Isa. 11:11; 1Cor. 15:51-52; 1Th. 4:16-18; Tit. 2:13; Rev. 11:17-18). (6) the accomplishment of divine vengeance and retribution in the *Day of the Lord*[5.2.14] (Is. 61:2; 63:4; Rev. 1:10). (7) the open revelation of Christ, the overthrow of *Antichrist*[5.2.3], the investiture of the kingdom, the exaltation of the saints, the overthrow of Satan (Dan. 7:13-14; Luke 10:18; Col. 3:4; 2Th. 1:10; 2:8; Rev. 20:10). Because this finishing occurs at the beginning of the seventh trumpet (which itself is clearly premillennial), the finishing is necessarily premillennial, not *postmillennial*[5.2.56]. The theme of all the prophets is the fulfillment of the covenants and promises in the "sure mercies of David" in establishing the Messianic Kingdom, which is the kingdom of God upon earth, as our eternal inheritance (Isa. 55:3; Mtt; 5:5; Acts 1:3, 6; 13:34; 15:14-18; 28:31; Rom. 4:13; 8:17).[43]

Peter emphasized this same truth in his first sermon after the Day of Pentecost, that heaven would receive Jesus "until the times of restoration of all things, which God has spoken by the mouth of all His holy prophets since the world began" (Acts 3:21). This is an act of redemption, but on a far grander scale then human salvation alone. Our kinsman-redeemer will restore the entire created order. See commentary on *Revelation 5:2*[3.5.2].

3.10.8 - Revelation 10:8

the voice which I heard from heaven

The same voice which instructed John not to write what the seven thunders uttered (Rev. 10:4). The divine authority of this voice is seen in its command which countermanded God's earlier instructions that John was to record what he saw. Here, the divine authority is seen again in that John boldly approaches a mighty angel and tells him to turn over the book.

open in the hand

See commentary on *Revelation 10:2*[3.10.2].

who stands on the sea and on the earth

See commentary on *Revelation 10:2*[3.10.2].

3.10.9 - Revelation 10:9

Give me

One would typically expect an *imperative* mood verb here—as when commanding: *you give*. Here it is an infinitive, δοῦναι μοι [*dounai moi*], *to give to me*, probably reflecting John's tentativeness to tell such a mighty angel what to do. Even though John's authority and instruction is from heaven, it is no small thing to approach this mighty angel and *tell* him anything! John could only approach the mighty angel knowing he had received divine command to do so:

> The soul who is obedient—who yields unquestioning submission to the expressed will of God—is for the time omnipotent. He walks and acts in the strength of the Creator—the maker of heaven and earth. Fear? he knows it not. The invisible God, seen by faith, makes him invincible in the path of obedience —"immortal till his work is done."[44]

Take and eat

λάβε καὶ κατάφαγε [*labe kai kataphage*], two verbs in the imperative mood: *You take and you eat!* The response of the mighty angel to John indicates his superior power and is intended to overcome John's reluctance to touch, much less take, this important book held in the hands of such a mighty being.

Eat is from κατεσθίω [*katesthiō*] meaning: "Consume, devour, swallow."[45] The emphasis is upon John completely consuming what he is given to eat. Eating God's Word is a frequent theme of Scripture and indicates the acceptance, digesting of, meditating upon, and sustenance derived from that which is eaten (Jer. 15:16). Job declared, "I have not departed from the commandment of His lips; I have treasured the words of His mouth more than my necessary *food*" (Job 23:12). Jesus, the Word of God, referred to Himself as *the Bread of Life* (Job 23:12; John 6:27-35, 48). In the same way that God made Israel dependent upon manna, so too are His servants to be dependent upon his Word.[46]

John was told to eat prophetic revelation much like that of Ezekiel. See commentary on *Revelation 10:11*[3.10.11].

it will make your stomach bitter

Bitter is πικρανεῖ [*pikranei*], used "Of honey when wormwood is mixed."[47] How well this describes God's prophetic Word! It is honey for the obedient, but mixed with wormwood (Rev. 8:11) in the face of disobedience. This is the very essence of the Word of God. For those who follow it, it is the Word of Life. For those who reject it, it is the Word of Death. This dual nature of God's Word was understood by Paul:

> Now thanks *be* to God who always leads us in triumph in Christ, and through us diffuses the fragrance of His knowledge in every place. For we are to God the fragrance of Christ among those who are being saved and among those who are perishing. To the one *we are* the aroma of death *leading* to death, and to the other the aroma of life *leading* to life. And who *is* sufficient for these things? (2Cor. 2:14-16)

The bitterness would develop *after* John had tasted its sweetness, when its contents were fully digested. “There was *sweetness* in the assurance that the prayers of God’s Israel, who had ‘cried day and night unto Him,’ were about to be answered.”[48] But the mature student of God’s prophetic Word will come to appreciate its bitterness. The new believer, excited by the prospect of God’s intervention into history, readily exults in God’s prophetic program, but often fails to appreciate the alternate aspect of the fulfillment of God’s promises—the eternal damnation of those who have not yet trusted in Christ. The bitterness which John will experience is an appreciation of God’s grace and mercy and the realization that in the completion of the mystery of God, judgment will have overcome the current age of mercy resulting in the eternal loss of countless persons who continue in their rejection of God. For undoubtedly the book contains “lamentations and mourning and woe” (Eze. 2:10).

it will be as sweet as honey in your mouth

See commentary on *Revelation 10:10*[3.10.10].

3.10.10 - Revelation 10:10

ate it

κατέφαγον [*katephagon*], John *totally consumed or devoured* it (cf. Mtt. 13:4; 23:14; John 2:17).

St. John Swallows the Little Book [49]

sweet as honey in my mouth. But . . . my stomach became bitter

Although the initial taste was sweet, the result was bitterness. " 'Turn your stomach,' or 'be hard on your stomach' is a better translation than 'bitter' in Rev. 10:9, for we have no sense of taste in our stomachs."[50]

All of God's Holy Word is sweet (Ps. 19:10; 119:103), but especially the initial exposure to prophetic passages. Often, those who "eat" prophetic Scripture "sit on the edge of their seat" and focus on its quick fulfillment. Like a perpetual "sugar high," it provides an initial surge of energy and motivation, but will never sustain like a balanced meal of God's Word. The continual chasing after the latest prophetic conference, while superficially treating prophetic passages and never grasping important aspects of God's character—His heart for the lost and His ultimate interest in restoration over judgment—is sure to lead to disillusionment and will shipwreck the faith of some. Critics of the *Rapture*[4.14] rightfully point to those who continually overemphasize prophetic passages within a shallow framework of Scriptural understanding and are forever watching for *Antichrist*[5.2.3] rather than Christ.

> To almost all people, prophecy is sweet. Prophetic conferences draw larger audiences than virtually any other kind of conference. The voluminous sale of the more sensational prophecy books is another evidence of how "sweet" BIble prophecy has become to so many people. But if "sweetness" is all there

> is, then it is worth little. Every student of prophecy should have the second experience that John had: bitterness in the stomach. A knowledge of things to come should give every believer a burden for people. For the way of escape from these things is the *Rapture*[5.2.62], and the requirement to qualify for the Rapture is the acceptance of Messiah now. A true student of prophecy will not simply stop with the knowledge of things to come. Rather this knowledge will create the strong burden to preach the gospel to others and thereby give them a way of escape.[51]

The healthy saint is not sustained by hype, be it prophetic or charismatic, but seeks to know Christ through His Word and to make Him known with compassion and sensitivity—as Jesus walked in the gospels. The balanced study of God's Word brings a burden for the lost and a growing realization of the destiny of those who fail to respond to God's gracious offer. The desire to see God quickly judge is mitigated by a desire to see His grace prevail. Amos responded to those who desired the *Day of the Lord*[5.2.14]:

> Woe to you who desire the day of the LORD! For what good *is* the day of the LORD to you? It *will be* darkness, and not light. It *will be* as though a man fled from a lion, and a bear met him! Or *as though* he went into the house, leaned his hand on the wall, and a serpent bit him! *Is* not the day of the LORD darkness, and not light? *Is it not* very dark, with no brightness in it? (Amos 5:18-20)

3.10.11 - Revelation 10:11

he said

The *TR*[5.2.79] text has the singular form, *he said* whereas the *MT*[5.2.45] and *NU*[5.2.49] texts have the plural form, *they said.* If the former, then the mighty angel was speaking. If the latter, then perhaps both the voice from heaven and the mighty angel or several angels spoke in unison.[52]

You must prophesy again

You must is δεῖ σε [*dei se*] which indicates necessity, often to attain a certain intended result.[53] John is told to prophesy *again.* That which he has been relating up to now is *prophetic*, not some veiled political document in an *apocalyptic genre*[5.2.22]. See *The Genre of the book of Revelation*[2.6]. See *Audience and Purpose*[2.3].

Victorinus, who wrote the first commentary on Revelation, understood this phrase to indicate John's subsequent release from Patmos for how could John deliver what he must prophesy if he were to remain on Patmos?

> Victorinus [d. c. A.D. 304], who wrote the first commentary on Revelation . . . at Revelation 10:11 notes: "He says this, because when John said these things he was in the island of Patmos, condemned to labor of the mines by Caesar Domitian. There, therefore, he saw the Apocalypse; and when grown old, he thought that he should at length receive his quittance by suffering, Domitian being killed, all his judgments were discharged. And John being dismissed from the mines, thus subsequently delivered the same Apocalypse which he had received from God."[54]

about many peoples, nations, tongues, and kings

The fourfold designation: peoples, nations, tongues, kings, indicates the global scope of the message John is prophesying. See *Four: the Entire World, the Earth*[2.7.5.3.3].

Both Ezekiel's scroll and John's book are closely related. (See commentary on *Revelation 10:2*[3.10.2].) Both contain prophecy. However, a *significant difference* occurs between what Ezekiel and John ingest: Ezekiel eats a message intended for *Israel*, but John eats a message for *all nations*. Ezekiel is told to prophesy to the "house of Israel, not to many people of unfamiliar speech" (Eze. 3:6), whereas John "must prophesy again about many peoples, nations, tongues, and kings" (Rev. 10:11). The message of Revelation is **about** a multinational, multiethnic population. It is global in nature and cannot be restricted to the events of the A.D. 70 destruction of Jerusalem by Rome as *preterists contend*[2.12.2]. "It is no one Empire or Emperor that is concerned in the prophecies of the second half of the Apocalypse; not merely Rome or *Nero*[5.2.46] or Domitian, but a multitude of races, kingdoms, and crowned heads."[55] See commentary on *Revelation 1:7*[3.1.7].

The group John is to prophecy *about* includes those who "dwell on the earth," who view the bodies of slain witnesses (Rev. 11:9). This is the same group which an angel preaches the everlasting gospel to

(Rev. 14:6). These are the ones upon which the harlot, Babylon, sits (Rev. 17:15). About is ἐπι [*epi*] which can also be translated *against* (Luke 12:52-53). For much of what John relates is both *about* and *against* the *earth dwellers*[5.2.18] around the globe.

Notes

1 John MacArthur, *Revelation 1-11 : The MacArthur New Testament Commentary* (Chicago, IL: Moody Press, 1999), Rev. 10:1.

2 Thomas suggests that the sixth trumpet is closed at the end of chapter 9. "Some prefer to include Rev. 10:1-11:13 as part of the sixth trumpet judgment because of the declaration of 11:14 that at that point the second woe has passed. This conclusion is uncalled for, however, in light of the clear indication of 9:20-21 that the sixth trumpet has ended there."—Robert L. Thomas, *Revelation 8-22* (Chicago, IL: Moody Press, 1995), Rev. 10:1. But Rev. 9:20-21 says nothing specifically about the sixth trumpet being ended. All that can be said is that it indicates a definite lull in the action which immediately followed the sounding of the sixth trumpet.

3 J. A. Seiss, *The Apocalypse: Lectures on the Book of Revelation* (Grand Rapids, MI: Zondervan Publishing House, 1966), 223.

4 This can be established from the lack of any detailed, proof-positive identification found in the text. Yet there is much discussion concerning whether this angel is Christ or simply a powerful angel.

5 Thomas, *Revelation 8-22*, Rev. 10:1.

6 "*non sequitur* 1. An inference or conclusion that does not follow from the premises or evidence."—*American Heritage Online Dictionary*, Ver. 3.0A, 3rd ed. (Houghton Mifflin, 1993).

7 Henry Morris, *The Revelation Record* (Wheaton, IL: Tyndale House Publishers, 1983), 181.

8 Those commentators who understand the vision of Daniel 10:5-9 as being a theophany—a vision of God—usually see the messenger of the subsequent verses (10-21) as a *different* individual, possibly Gabriel. This allows the first vision to be that of Christ while allowing the second individual to be an angel who seeks assistance from Michael (Dan. 10:13, 21). A problem with this view is the unity of the text which argues that the same individual is in view in both sections of the passage. The arguments for and against seeing one versus two heavenly individuals in Daniel 10 are beyond the scope of our treatment here other than to recognize that the similarities between Revelation 10 and Daniel 10 are insufficient to unambiguously establish the divinity of the angel of Revelation 10.

9 Another mighty angel, who requires Michael's assistance and is therefore not divine (Dan. 10:20), swears by God (Dan. 12:7 cf. Dan. 10:5).

10 It should be noted that these were *preincarnate* appearances of Jesus. John's vision is seen after the incarnation. Concerning the Angel of the Lord: Gen. 16:7-11; 22:11, 15; Ex. 3:2; 14:19; 23:20-23; 32:34; Num. 22:22-35; Jdg. 2:1, 4; 5:23; 6:11-22; 13:3-21; 2S. 24:16; 1K. 19:7; 2K. 1:3, 15; 19:35; 1Chr. 21:12-30; Ps. 34:7; 35:5-6; Isa. 37:36; 63:9; Hos. 12:4; Zec. 1:11-12; 3:1-6; 12:8; cf. Acts 7:30-31, 35, 37-38.

11 Although, as we have observed, Christ is referred to as an angel or *messenger* in His OT appearances as the Angel of Jehovah, we are now speaking of the incarnate glorified Christ. "While the preincarnate Christ appeared in the Old Testament as the Angel of the Lord, the New Testament nowhere refers to Him as an angel."—MacArthur, *Revelation 1-11 : The MacArthur New Testament Commentary*, Rev. 10:1.

12 MacArthur, *Revelation 1-11 : The MacArthur New Testament Commentary*, Rev. 10:1.

13 "Some interpret the rainbow as the natural result of light from the angel's face refracted by the cloud in which he was arrayed."—Robert H. Mounce, *The Book of Revelation* (Grand Rapids, MI: William B. Eerdmans Publishing Co., 1977), Rev. 10:1.

14 A. R. Fausset, *"The Revelation of St. John the Divine,"* in Robert Jamieson, A. R. Fausset, and David Brown, *A Commentary, Critical and Explanatory, on the Old and New Testaments* (Oak Harbor, WA: Logos Research Systems, Inc., 1997, 1877), Rev. 10:1.

15 Mounce, *The Book of Revelation*, Rev. 10:1.

16 Although the same book is later designated as a βιβλίον [*biblion*] (Rev. 10:8).

17 E. W. Bullinger, *Commentary On Revelation* (Grand Rapids, MI: Kregel Publications, 1984, 1935), Rev. 10:2.

18 Timothy Friberg, Barbara Friberg, and Neva F. Miller, *Analytical Lexicon of the Greek New Testament* (Grand

Rapids, MI: Baker Books, 2000), 4:182.

19 "Since God was the ultimate owner of the land of Israel, since He had given tenant possession of the land to the people of Israel forever (Gen. 13:15; 2Chr. 10:7), and since the Israelites were only the tenant administrators of God's land, they were forbidden to sell the land forever [Lev. 25:23]. . . If . . . an Israelite became so poverty-stricken that he was forced to sell the portion of land that was his tenant possession, he did not sell the ownership of the land. Instead, he sold the tenant possession or administration of the portion of the land for a temporary period of time (Lev. 25:16, 25-27). . . . God required that a sold tenant possession be returned to the original tenant or his heir in the year of jubilee (Lev. 25:10, 13, 28; 27:24)."—Renald E. Showers, *Maranatha, Our Lord Come* (Bellmawr, NJ: The Friends of Israel Gospel Ministry, 1995), 78-79.

20 M. R. Vincent, *Vincent's Word Studies* (Escondido, CA: Ephesians Four Group, 2002), Rev. 10:3.

21 "We have already seen who it is that is called 'the Lion from the tribe of Judah.' "—Seiss, *The Apocalypse: Lectures on the Book of Revelation*, Rev. 10:3.

22 James Strong, *The Exhaustive Concordance of the Bible* (Ontario: Woodside Bible Fellowship, 1996), H3092.

23 This does not refer to the believers in general for nowhere are believers called *the children of Israel*. This uniquely designates the *physical seed of Jacob*. Believers are the *spiritual seed of Abraham* (Rom. 4:11-18; Gal. 3:7-8, 29). "'Abraham's seed,' therefore, is not necessarily equivalent of a Jew or a member of the people of Israel. God"s promise to Abraham encompassed both 'a great nation" and "all peoples on earth" (Gen. 12:2-3). Both of these groups, therefore, share the fulfillment of that promise in the salvation of God without being merged into each other. It is significant that when the fulfillment of the Abrahamic promise is related to the Gentiles, it is specifically this statement about "all nations," not any reference to the "great nation" or Israel, that the apostle uses as *OT*[5.2.51] support (Gal. 3:8). Again, there is sharing, but not identity."—Robert L. Saucy, *"Israel and the Church: A Case for Discontinuity,"* in John S. Feinberg, ed., *Continuity And Discontinuity* (Westchester, IL: Crossway Books, 1988), 254.

24 Thomas, *Revelation 8-22*, 76.

25 Bullinger, *Commentary On Revelation*, Rev. 10:4.

26 "As usual, interpretation has run wild as to the seven thunders. As a few illustrations may be cited: Vitringa, the seven crusades; Daubuz, the seven kingdoms which received the Reformation; Elliott, the bull fulminated against Luther from the seven-hilled city, etc."—Vincent, *Vincent's Word Studies*, Rev. 10:3. "Some would have use believe that these seven thunders are the Papal Bulls issued against Luther and the Reformation [Elliott, vol. ii., p. 100, etc.]. If this be so, then God sealed the book in vain for all know what those thunders uttered."—Bullinger, *Commentary On Revelation*, Rev. 10:4.

27 Morris, *The Revelation Record*, Rev. 10:3.

28 Donald Grey Barnhouse, *Revelation* (Grand Rapids, MI: Zondervan Publishing House, 1971), 183.

29 This is not the only portion of the divine record which is not recorded: John 20:30; 21:25.

30 Alan F. Johnson, *Revelation: The Expositor's Bible Commentary* (Grand Rapids, MI: Zondervan Publishing House, 1966), Rev. 5:4.

31 Fausset, "*The Revelation of St. John the Divine*," Rev. 10:4.

32 Jerome Smith, *The New Treasury of Scripture Knowledge* (Nashville, TN: Thomas Nelson Publishers, 1992), Rev. 10:6.

33 Seiss, *The Apocalypse: Lectures on the Book of Revelation*, Rev. 10:6.

34 Smith, *The New Treasury of Scripture Knowledge*, Rom. 16:25.

35 Arnold G. Fruchtenbaum, *The Footsteps of Messiah*, rev ed. (Tustin, CA: Ariel Ministries, 2003), 702.

36 William R. Newell, *Revelation: Chapter by Chapter* (Grand Rapids, MI: Kregel Publications, 1994,c1935), Rev. 10:7.

37 "An author sometimes uses the aorist for the future to stress the certainty of the event. It involves a 'rhetorical transfer' of a future event as though it were past."—Daniel B. Wallace, *Greek Grammar Beyond the Basics - Exegetical Syntax of the New Testament* (Grand Rapids, MI: Zondervan Publishing House and Galaxie Software, 1999, 2002), 564.

38 MacArthur, *Revelation 1-11 : The MacArthur New Testament Commentary*, Rev. 10:1.

39 Seiss, *The Apocalypse: Lectures on the Book of Revelation*, Rev. 10:7.

[40] Thomas, *Revelation 8-22*, Rev. 10:7.

[41] MacArthur, *Revelation 1-11 : The MacArthur New Testament Commentary*, 10:7.

[42] It is not our purpose here to treat the reliability of the Scriptures in great detail. For those who call Jesus "Lord," the most revealing study which can be done is to survey the NT for passages where Jesus refers to the *Scriptures* (sometimes referred to as *the Law and the Prophets*). The unbiased reader will readily appreciate that Jesus held the generation of his day responsible for their understanding and response to God *solely upon the contents of the written Scriptures* . He constantly and unfailingly points to the "Scriptures." He never recognizes a personal existential encounter with God, but identifies the ultimate truth about God as being the objective written record. What Scripture records are the very words of God: Ex. 24:4; 34:27; Num. 33:2; Deu. 31:9, 24; 31:26; 1Chr. 28:19; Isa. 8:1; Isa. 30:8; Jer. 1:9; 30:2; 36:2, 28, 32; Dan. 12:4; 1Cor. 2:13; 14:37; 1Th. 4:2, 15; Rev. 1:19; 10:4.

[43] Smith, *The New Treasury of Scripture Knowledge*, Rev. 10:7.

[44] Walter Scott, *Exposition of The Revelation* (London, England: Pickering & Inglis, n.d.), Rev. 10:9.

[45] Frederick William Danker, and Walter Bauer, *A Greek-English Lexicon of the New Testament and Other Early Christian Literature* (Chicago, IL: University of Chicago Press, 2000), 442.

[46] Interestingly, each man was to daily collect the manna for his own household. How different would our country be if each father approached bible study this way—rather than ignoring the Word or relying upon a professional clergy to gather manna for him once a week?

[47] Danker, *A Greek-English Lexicon of the New Testament and Other Early Christian Literature*, 657.

[48] Bullinger, *Commentary On Revelation*, Rev. 10:11.

[49] Albrecht Durer (1471 - 1528). Image courtesy of the *Connecticut College* (http://www.conncoll.edu/visual/Durer-prints/index.html) *Wetmore Print Collection* (http://www.conncoll.edu/visual/wetmore.html).

[50] Monty S. Mills, *Revelations: An Exegetical Study of the Revelation to John* (Dallas, TX: 3E Ministries, 1987), Rev. 10:9.

[51] Fruchtenbaum, *The Footsteps of Messiah*, 243.

[52] "'*They,*' who told John he must prophesy, we may surmise were heavenly 'watchers' *(as in Daniel 4:13, 17):* for the mind of God as to earthly judgments and prophetic programs is well known by those dwelling in the light of heaven *(compare Revelation 7:13, 14; 11:15, 21:1; 22:9)*."—Newell, *Revelation: Chapter by Chapter*, Rev. 10:11.

[53] Danker, *A Greek-English Lexicon of the New Testament and Other Early Christian Literature*, 172.

[54] Mark Hitchcock, *"The Stake in the Heart—The A.D. 95 Date of Revelation,"* in Tim LaHaye, and Thomas Ice, eds., *The End Times Controversy* (Eugene, OR: Harvest House Publishers, 2003), 133.

[55] Henry Barclay Swete, *The Apocalypse of St. John* (Eugene, OR: Wipf and Stock Publishers, 1998, 1906), Rev. 10:11.

3.11 - Revelation 11

3.11.1 - Revelation 11:1

a reed like a measuring rod

Reed is κάλαμος [*kalamos*] , the same word which described the mock scepter given to Jesus along with His crown of thorns (Mtt. 27:29). The soldiers used this "scepter" to beat Him on the head (Mtt. 27:30; Mark 15:19).

> *Kalamos* (measuring rod) refers to a reedlike plant that grew in the Jordan Valley to a height of fifteen to twenty feet. It had a stalk that was hollow and lightweight, yet rigid enough to be used as a walking staff (cf. Eze. 29:6) or to be shaved down into a pen (3Jn. 1:13). The stalks, because they were long and lightweight, were ideal for use as measuring rods.[1]

Later, one of the seven angels (having one of the seven bowls of the seven last plagues) talks with John and uses a golden reed to measure the heavenly Jerusalem (Rev. 21:15). *Measuring rod* is ῥάβδῳ [*hrabdō*] which is translated elsewhere by "rod," "staff," or "scepter."[2] This is the word used for the *rod* of iron by which the rule of Jesus is asserted (Rev. 2:27; 12:5; 19:15).

And the angel stood, saying

This phrase, *the angel stood*, is omitted by the *MT*[5.2.45] and *NU*[5.2.49] texts which render the voice speaking with John anonymously: "someone said."[3] If we follow the reading of the *TR*[5.2.79] text, then the angel speaking with John would seem to be the angel of Revelation 10 which told him he must "prophesy again about many peoples, nations, tongues, and kings" (Rev. 10:11). A few verses later, the voice speaking with John asserts ownership of the two witnesses as if speaking for God in the first person: "And I will give *power* to **my** two witnesses" [emphasis added] (Rev. 11:3a). Whether the voice is that of an angel or from the throne, the speaker has full divine authority.

measure

In Ezekiel's vision of the mountain of the Lord's house, an angelic messenger measures the *Millennial Temple*[4.16.5.10] using a measuring rod (Eze. 40:2ff). Ezekiel is told to "look with your eyes and hear with your ears, and fix your mind on everything I show you, for you *were* brought here so that I might show *them to you*. Declare to the house of Israel everything you see." (Eze. 40:4-5). Measurements were made of both the inner temple and common area (Eze. 42:15-20). Similarly, Zechariah sees a "man with a measuring line in his hand" (Zec. 2:1) who measures the dimensions of Jerusalem. The measurement appears to testify of its immense perimeter in a future time of blessing (Zec. 2:4-5).

John is told to "measure" three things: (1) the temple of God; (2) the altar; and 3) those who worship there. The temple and altar are to be literally measured whereas the presence of the worshipers is merely to be noticed and recorded.[4] The act of measuring indicates a separation between a portion which God recognizes (the *Temple*[5.2.73], altar, and worshipers) versus a portion he rejects (the outer court, see below).

> Verses 1 and 2 indicate there will be a distinction between Jew and Gentile in this period. The two earlier Jewish temples were divided into four areas: first, the sanctuary itself, which only priests (not even Levites) could enter (this is called the temple of God); second, the area the men of Israel could enter (this included the altar); third, the court of the women in which Israelite women worshiped God; and finally, the court of the Gentiles. John's instruction was to measure the first three, thus symbolizing God's interest in, and protection of, the Jewish nation. Chapter 12 confirms this interpretation, for it describes the divine protection symbolized here.[5]

temple of God

Τὸν ναὸν τοῦ θεοῦ [*Ton naon tou theou*]. The word for *temple*, ναὸν [*naon*] has two general meanings in relation to the house of God in Jerusalem. "(1) In a narrower sense, the inner sanctuary within a sacred precinct (τὸ ἱερόν [*to hieron*]) where the divine being resides *shrine, (inner) temple* (Mtt. 27.51); (2) in a broader yet specific sense, the sanctuary in Jerusalem consisting of the (outer) Holy Place and the (inner) Holy of Holies *temple* (Mtt. 26.61)."[6] The term probably refers to the Holy of Holies and the Holy Place, where only the priests were allowed access. The inner sanctuary, where the divine being resided, is where Jesus predicted the "abomination of desolation" would one day stand in the holy place (τόπῳ ἁγίῳ [*topō hagiō*] , Mtt. 24:15). The man of sin, the son of perdition, will also sit in "the temple of God τὸν ναὸν τοῦ θεοῦ [*ton naon tou theou*]" (2Th. 2:4). This refers to a rebuilt Temple yet future to our time, often called the *Tribulation Temple*[4.16.5.9].

> Five distinct temples are alluded to by the Scriptures. Solomon's temple was destroyed by Nebuchadnezzar in 587 B.C. Antiochus Epiphanes pillaged and consecrated to Jupiter the temple of Zerubbabel in 168 B.C. Herod's magnificent temple was reduced to ashes by Titus in A.D. 70. The fourth temple, the edifice described in this chapter, is to be the focus of attention during the Great Tribulation. Finally, the fifth temple will be the *Millennial Temple*[4.16.5.10] described in Eze. 40-47. [7]

Much confusion has been needlessly brought to bear upon this passage by interpreters who insist on ignoring the literal details of the description and spiritualizing nearly everything as pertaining to "the church." Barnhouse summarizes:

> One commentator has brought together on one page the interpretations of his fellows in a way that will explain much of the confusion that has arisen out of this passage. He points out that almost universally the commentators have tried to force the church into the picture that is painted here when, of course, the church is not in view at all. "The temple is here figuratively used of the faithful portion of the church of Christ." The command is given to John "to measure the temple of God" in order to call his attention to "the size of the church of God." The "altar" is again, in the mind of one commentator, "the church." The "outer court" signifies "a part of the church of Christ." The "Holy City," according to these expositors is "always in the Apocalypse the title of the church." The "two witnesses" represent "the elect church of God," says one (embracing both Jew and Christian), "and the witness which she bears concerning God, especially in the Old and New Testaments." "The twelve hundred and sixty days" constitutes the period "during which the church although trodden under foot, will not cease to prophesy." Concerning the war of the beast against them we are told, "The whole vision is symbolical, and the intention is to convey the idea that the church, in her witness for God, will experience opposition from the power of Satan" and so on and on and on. . . . "What wonder, when such diverse expressions are forced to mean the same thing, if there be endless confusion. Literalism may not solve every perplexity, but it does not lead into any such inexplicable obscurity as this."[8]

We can avoid much of this mischief by following the *Golden Rule of Interpretation*[5.2.24].

See *Temple of God*[4.16] and *Tribulation Temple*[4.16.5.9]. This Temple is to be contrasted with the "temple of God . . . in heaven" (Rev. 11:19).

the altar

The altar was the location where sacrifices were offered. We know that the *Tribulation Temple*[4.16.5.9] will have an altar because during *The 70th Week of Daniel*[2.13.5] the *Antichrist*[5.2.3] is said to make a covenant which appears to provide, in part, for sacrifices to be offered on such an altar. In opposition to his covenant "in the middle of the week he will put a stop to sacrifice and grain offering" (Dan. 9:27b). "By being mentioned separately from the *Naos* (in which was the golden altar of incense) it looks as though the brazen altar of sacrifice was intended. The word will suit either."[9]

those who worship there

τοὺς προσκυνοῦντας [*tous proskynountas*], present tense participle, *the ones presently worshiping*. At the time of the measurement, worship is in progress. There is an intentional contrast between John's instructions to measure the ones worshiping in the temple versus to leave out the outer court which is given to the nations. Worship within the temple is recognized by God, whereas the activity of the outer court is dismissed.

3.11.2 - Revelation 11:2

leave out the court which is outside the temple

Τὴν αὐλὴν τὴν ἔζωθεν τοῦ ναοῦ ἔκβαλε ἔζωθεν [*Tēn aulēn tēn ezōthen tou naou ekbale ezōthen*], a play on words: *the courtyard outside the temple you throw outside*. The phrase *throw outside* (ἔκβαλε ἔζωθεν [*ekbale ezōthen*], *expel outside*, *cast out*[10]) emphasizes the rejection of the outer court, probably due to God's disfavor.

Court is αὐλὴν [*aulēn*]: "An enclosed space, open to the sky, near a house, or surrounded by buildings."[11] The *LXX*[5.2.38] uses the identical term to describe God's courts (αὐλὴν [*aulēn*]) which are trampled (πατεῖν [*patein*]) by those who are godless in behavior, yet come offering sacrifice at the temple (Isa. 1:12, also Ex. 27:9).

> In the *Temple*[5.2.73] which had been built by Herod, in which Jesus walked when He was here upon earth, the outer court was marked off from the inner one where Israel was permitted to go and it was separated by "the middle wall of partition" (Eph. 2:14). Beyond this no Gentile could go. Paul, accused of breaking this rule, and bringing Gentiles into the holy place, was almost destroyed by angry Jews (Acts 21:28).[12]

> In the time of the Second Temple [the Jews] had erected a boundary fence, the *Soreg* , between the Court of the Gentiles and the Court of the Israelites, with a warning inscription promising death to any non-Israelite who passed beyond it into the Court of the Israelites. The New Testament (Acts 21:27-28) records a Jewish crowd's violent reaction to Paul when they mistakenly believed that he had taken a Gentile proselyte (Titus) into the Temple to offer sacrifice.[13]

it has been given

The portion of the temple which is not under the control of the Jews *has been given* to the nations to tread. Once again, we see the sovereign purpose of God in the events surrounding the temple during the Tribulation. It is *He* who has ultimately given control of the outer court to the Gentiles. See commentary on *Revelation 6:2*[3.6.2].

When Asaph contemplated the apparent success of the wicked, he lamented how God's "enemies roar in the midst of Your meeting place; they set up their banners *for* signs . . . They have defiled the dwelling place of Your name to the ground" (Ps. 74:1-7). Elsewhere, he decries, "the nations have come into Your inheritance; Your holy temple they have defiled" (Ps. 79:1). In the setting of Asaph, the temple had been completely destroyed (cf. Isa. 63:18). Here, only a portion of the temple is in the hands of the nations.

the Gentiles

Gentiles is ἔθνεσιν [*ethnesin*], often translated as *nations* in Revelation (Rev. 2:26; 5:9; 7:9; 10:11; 12:5; 13:7; 14:6; 15:4; 16:19; 17:15; 18:3; 19:15; 20:3; 21:24; 22:2). These are the *nations* which John was just told to prophesy about (Rev. 10:11). Hence, he is already beginning to fulfill that command. The emphasis on a portion of the temple precincts being given to the Gentiles (or nations) supposes that the main part of the temple proper is under the jurisdiction of non-Gentiles, that is, the Jews.

> This casting out of the court of the Gentiles because it is the court of the Gentiles, proves the present *dispensation*[5.2.15] at an end. Now Gentiles and Jews stand on the same level. The one has no prerogatives or rights above the other. In the Church there is neither Greek nor Jew, Barbarian, Scythian, bond nor free; but all nationalities and conditions in life yield to one common brotherhood and heirship. The text, therefore, tells of a new order of things. . . . the Jew is again in the foreground for the fathers' sakes, and the Gentiles are thrust back.[14]

they will tread the holy city underfoot

There is only one *holy city* within Scripture: Jerusalem (Ne. 11:1, 18; Isa. 48:2; 52:1-2; Dan. 9:24; Mtt. 4:5; 27:53). In some cases, the phrase refers to the New Jerusalem which comes down from heaven (Rev. 21:2; 22:19), but here it is clearly the earthly Jerusalem because a portion of it has been given to the nations to *tread . . . underfoot*. The treading of the holy city is typified by the similar occupation and desecration of the sanctuary by Antiochus Epiphanes in the days of the Maccabees:[15]

> Then I heard a holy one speaking; and *another* holy one said to that certain *one* who was speaking, "How long *will* the vision *be, concerning* the daily *sacrifices* and the transgression of desolation, the giving of both the sanctuary and the host to be **trampled under foot?**" And he said to me, "For two thousand three hundred days; then the sanctuary shall be cleansed." (Dan. 8:13-14) [emphasis added]

As in Daniel 11, treading underfoot speaks of having authority over the city, just as when the mighty angel *stands* on the sea and land indicating his authority over the globe (Rev. 10:2, 5). Here, the Gentiles, or nations, exert authority over the holy city while the Jews have authority over the temple of God and the altar. The trampling of the holy city also speaks of *occupation without appreciation* —the occupiers treat that which is holy as a common thing, failing to understand its significance in the eyes of God (Heb. 10:29). God has promised to make the *earthly* Jerusalem "a praise in all the earth" (Isa.

62:7), but the nations steadfastly refuse to acknowledge God's plan for Jerusalem which includes her ownership by Israel. In some settings, treading or trampling may also denote destruction (Isa. 63:18).

When Jesus responded to his disciples' question concerning when Herod's temple would be destroyed (Luke 21:7), he indicated that following the destruction of Jerusalem, the Jews would "be led away captive into all nations. And Jerusalem will be trampled by Gentiles until the times of the Gentiles are fulfilled" (Luke 21:24). Thus, this trampling is an indication that during the time period which John sees in his vision the "times of the Gentiles" have still not come to a close. "John indicates that Jerusalem is still in Gentile power and that from the beginning of the series of judgments, which this parenthesis interrupts, until the end of the Gentile dominion is three and one-half years."[16]

Jesus indicated that the trampling would take place *after* the destruction of A.D. 70—which supports the *futurist interpretation*[2.12.5] that takes this temple to be a *tribulation temple*[5.2.78] yet to be built. The *preterist interpretation*[2.12.2] holds that the trampling described here occurs *before* the temple is destroyed—for if this is Herod's temple, as they maintain, then the nations are trampling *while it still stands*. Yet the sequence indicated by Jesus (Luke 21:24) is just the opposite: *first* Jerusalem is destroyed and the Jews dispersed among the nations, *then* the trampling begins. The trampling only ends when the "times of the Gentiles" are fulfilled and jurisdiction of Jerusalem returns fully and permanently to the Jews.[17]

> The Times of the Gentiles can best be defined as that long period of time from the Babylonian Empire to the Second Coming of the Messiah during which time the Gentiles have dominion over the City of Jerusalem. This does not rule out temporary Jewish control of the city, but all such Jewish control will be temporary until the Second Coming. Such temporary control was exercised during the Maccabbean Period (164-63 B.C.), the First Jewish Revolt against Rome (A.D. 66-70), the Second Jewish Revolt (the Bar Cochba Revolt) against Rome (A.D. 132-135), and since 1967 as a result of the Six Day War. This too, is temporary, as Gentiles will yet trod Jerusalem down for at least another 3 1/2 years (Rev. 11:1-2). Any Jewish takeover of the City of Jerusalem before the Second Coming must therefore be viewed as a temporary one and does not mean that the Times of the Gentiles have ended. The Times of the Gentiles can only end when the Gentiles can no longer tread down the City of Jerusalem.[18]

It is our belief that at the liberation of Jerusalem in the Six-Day War, the bizarre circumstance where the Jews gave control of the Temple Mount back into the hands of Muslims rather than retaining control of the Mount and removing the *Dome of the Rock*[4.16.5.8] is a modern-example of the hand of God which has determined that the time has not yet been fulfilled for Israel to obtain exclusive and lasting control over all of Jerusalem. How significant it is today that most nations of the world refuse to recognize Jerusalem as the capital of Israel while pressuring the Jews to continue to subject this historic site of Judaism to support an Islamic religious site while at the same time restricting the religious access of their own people. One would think this situation sufficiently strange to obtain the attention of the atheist who denies the divine hand in history!

It is interesting that the same root word (πατεω [*pateō*]) which denotes the *trampling* of the courts in Isaiah (LXX) appears in this chapter to describe the *treading underfoot* of the holy city by the nations. Even though the nations occupy the holy city, it would seem that God's response to their activities may be akin to how he responded to the Jews when they offered sacrifices which appeared righteous externally, but when in fact their hearts were far from him:

> When you come to appear before Me, who has required this from your hand, to trample My courts? Bring no more futile sacrifices; incense is an abomination to Me. The New Moons, the Sabbaths, and the calling of assemblies-I cannot endure iniquity and the sacred meeting. Your New Moons and your appointed feasts My soul hates; they are a trouble to Me, I am weary of bearing *them*. When you spread out your hands, I will hide My eyes from you; even though you make many prayers, I will not hear. Your hands are full of blood. (Isa. 1:12-15)

***for* forty-two months**

The "holy city" which is to be tread underfoot is none other than the "holy city" upon which *the seventy weeks of Daniel*[2.13.5] are determined (Dan. 9:24), of which one-half of the final week is mentioned here as "forty-two months" and as "one thousand two hundred and sixty days" (Rev. 11:3).

The treading of the holy city is said to last forty-two months. This corresponds to half of the final week of *the 70 weeks of Daniel*[2.13.5] (Dan. 9:24-27). But which half? John is told not to measure the outer court because it "has been given" (aorist tense, typically an event occurring prior to the time of the writer) to the Gentiles. Then John is told "They will tread" (future tense) the holy city for *forty-two months*. If the treading of the holy city by the Gentiles is taken to be simultaneous with their authority over the outer court, then it occurs while the Jews are allowed to worship in the temple and sacrifice on the altar. This would be the *first half* of the final week—before sacrifices are brought to an end (Dan. 9:27) and the two witnesses are overcome by the beast (Rev. 11:3). If the treading is taken to follow the possession of the outer court by the Gentiles, then the *forty-two months* could denote the *last half* of the week: after the *Antichrist*[5.2.3] has violated his covenant (Dan. 9:27), the Abomination of Desolation occurs (Mtt. 24:15 cf. Dan. 11:31; Dan. 12:11),[19] the Antichrist exerts his global authority (Dan. 7:25; 12:7, 11-12; Rev. 13:5-8), and the Jews flee to the wilderness where they are protected by God (Mtt. 24:16-20; Rev. 12:6, 14). See *Events of the 70th Week of Daniel*[2.13.5.4]. The last half of the week is probably in view so that the termination of the *forty-two months* corresponds to the end of the "times of the Gentiles" (Luke 21:24) with the arrival of Christ and the introduction of the *Millennial Kingdom*[5.2.39]. Jeremiah prophesied the restoration which would follow *Jacob's Trouble and the Great Tribulation*[2.13.4]:

> 'Ask now, and see, whether a man is ever in labor with child? So why do I see every man *with* his hands on his loins like a woman in labor, and all faces turned pale? Alas! For that day *is* great, so that none *is* like it; and it *is* **the time of Jacob's trouble, but he shall be saved out of it**. For it shall come to pass **in that day**,' Says the LORD of hosts, '*That* **I will break his yoke from your neck, and will burst your bonds; foreigners shall no more enslave them**. But they shall serve the LORD their God, and David their king, whom I will raise up for them.' (Jer. 30:6-9) [emphasis added]

Jeremiah explains the reason the times of the Gentiles will come to an end is so that the nation of Israel will be free to serve God under the Messianic economy of the Millennial Kingdom. It is God's jealousy over His chosen nation which will bring this about. Woe to the nations who will fail to appreciate God's zeal for Israel!

> 'Therefore do not fear, O My servant Jacob,' says the LORD, 'Nor be dismayed, O Israel; for behold, I will save you from afar, and your seed from the land of their captivity. Jacob shall return, have rest and be quiet, and no one shall make *him* afraid. For I *am* with you,' says the LORD, 'to save you; **Though I make a full end of all nations where I have scattered you, yet I will not make a complete end of you**. But I will correct you in justice, and will not let you go altogether unpunished.' (Jer. 30:10-11) [emphasis added]

The forty-two months correspond to 3 1/2 years of 360-days each. See *Prophetic Year*[2.13.5.2].

3.11.3 - Revelation 11:3

my two witnesses

The *TR*[5.2.79] text indicates that it is an angel which is speaking with John (Rev. 11:1). Yet here, the speaker speaks of the two witnesses as being his own. Either (1) the angel is speaking in the first person for God; (2) the angel speaking to John is the second person of the Trinity (see *Divine Similarities*[3.10.1.1]); or (3) the voice is that of God directly from the throne.

These witnesses are said to be *my* witnesses because, like the prophets who preceded them, they are dedicated to speaking forth His word and judgments as His servants (Rev. 10:7). There are *two witnesses* because two is the number of witness prescribed by the Law of Moses (Num. 35:30; Deu. 17:6; 19:5 cf. Mtt. 18:16. 2Cor. 13:1.). See *Two: Witness*[2.7.5.3.1].

witnesses is μάρτυσιν [*martysin*] from which we get the word *martyr* . Like many of God's witnesses during the Tribulation, these two individuals will be steadfast in their faith unto death (Rev. 11:7 cf. Rev. 2:10; 12:11; 20:4). They cannot be killed until "they finish their testimony (μαρτυρίαν [*martyrian*])" (Rev. 11:7). The saints and even the angels are witnesses in the sense that they share in the "testimony (μαρτυρίαν [*martyrian*] of Jesus" (Rev. 19:10). The coming of the Holy Spirit on the Day of Pentecost was to empower the church to be a witness to Jesus (Acts 1:8; Acts 2:32; 3:15; 13:31).

Since their ministry is reminiscent of Moses (plagues, turning water to blood) and Elijah (consuming with fire, shutting off rain from heaven), their message will undoubtedly be that of both *the law* and *the prophets* —the writings which are frequently mentioned as a dual witness elsewhere (Mtt. 5:17; 7:12; 11:13; 22:40; Luke 16:16, 29; 24:44; John 1:45; Acts 13:15; 24:14; 26:22; 28:23; Rom. 3:21).

The Jewishness of this chapter, and especially the ministry of these two witnesses, must be seen within the larger context of God's promises to restore Israel. In an important parallel passage, the apostle Paul anguishes over Israel's need of the gospel:

> Brethren, my heart's desire and prayer to God for Israel is that they may be saved. . . . How then shall they call on Him in whom they have not believed? And how shall they believe in Him of whom they have not heard? And how shall they hear without a preacher? And how shall they preach unless they are sent? . . . But I say, did Israel not know? . . . I say then, have they stumbled that they should fall? Certainly not! . . . For if their being cast away is the reconciling of the world, what *will* their acceptance *be* but life from the dead? [Eze. 37] . . . God is able to graft them in again . . . For I do not desire, brethren, that you should be ignorant of this mystery, lest you should be wise in your own opinion, that blindness in part has happened to Israel until the fullness of the Gentiles has come in. And so all Israel will be saved, as it is written: "The Deliverer will come out of Zion, and He will turn away ungodliness from Jacob." (Rom. 10:1, 14-15, 19; 11:11, 15, 23, 25-26a)

These two witnesses are among the "beautiful feet" which preach the gospel of peace (Rom. 10:15) to Israel. Their ministry involves the entire earth, but takes place in Jerusalem and has all the markings of *OT*[5.2.51] Jewish prophets. They are a key element in the plan of the Deliverer to "turn ungodliness from Jacob" (Rom. 11:26) in preparation for the *Millennial Kingdom*[5.2.39] to come. "The purpose of God to make Israel and her land the centre round which He shall gather the nations, is not frustrated, but postponed. Our chapter presents the initial stages in the development of this glorious earthly purpose."[20]

The breadth of interpretations expositors have assigned to these two witnesses is legend: from literal individuals such as the apostles James and Peter[21] to symbolic ideas such as the church preaching Christ in the two testaments.[22]

There are two forks in the road of interpretation on the way to determining who these individuals might be. The first fork which separates interpreters is whether the text describes symbols, institutions, or individuals?

Symbols, Institutions, or Individuals?

Symbolic	Corporate	Literal
"Expositors within [the symbolic] category agree on one point: The witnesses are not human beings. These scholars vary, however, in their opinion of what the witnesses represent. The main interpretations in this group are these: (1) The two witnesses represent the testimony of the church from the Law and the prophets, (2) the Old and New Testaments, (3) the Word of God and the Spirit of God."[23]	"Ten views on the witnesses' identity have been suggested in this category: (1) the church in its function of witness-bearing, (2) the church represented in the east by the Paulikians and the west by the Waldenses, (3) believers who suffer martyrdom, (4) a literal group of people (i.e., the number two may be symbolic of a large multitude), (5) the Christian church and the Christian state, (6) the line of witnesses in the Eastern and Western church against the papacy, for 1,260 years (taking each day for a year, Rev. 11:3) until the sixteenth century, when it was exterminated, (7) Israel and the church, (8) the house of Israel and the house of Aaron, (9) the believing Jewish remnant	"Expositors in this category agree that the witnesses are two individuals, but they disagree on who these people are, as exemplified by the following ten interpretations: (1) Elijah and Moses, (2) Elijah and Enoch, (3) Elijah and John the Baptist, (4) Elijah and John the Apostle, (5) Elijah and an unidentified person, (6) Peter and James, (7) Peter and John, (8) Peter and Paul, (9) the two high priests, Ananus and Jesus, who nobly withstood the zealots in Jerusalem, and were massacred by them, and (10) two unknown persons who will minister in the spirit and power of Moses and Elijah in the future."[25] "These witnesses are *individuals*. No reader of the account, having no

Symbolic	Corporate	Literal
	during the tribulation, (10) the two nations descended from Abraham (i.e., the Arabs and the Israelites)."[24]	preconceived theory to defend, would ever think of taking them for bodies, or successions of people. All the early fathers, from whom we have any testimony on the subject, regarded them as two individual men."[26]

We concur with many other interpreters who see abundant evidence indicating the witnesses are to be understood as two individuals:[27]

> The classical use of μάρτυς [*martys*] is "in the sense of human attestation or testimonial." The word thus implies that the "witnesses" (μάρτυσιν [*martysin*]) are human beings. This consideration is further suggested by John's use of the article τοῖς [*tois*], which indicates specific persons. Elsewhere in the New Testament μάρτυς [*martys*] is always personal (Mtt. 18:16; Luke 24:48; Acts 1:8; 1Ti. 5:19; Heb. 10:28; Rev. 1:5). Therefore symbolic interpretations must be rejected. Second, Revelation 11:3 states that the two witnesses "shall prophesy" . . . The activity of prophesying, then, is personal and involves personal beings. This too suggests that symbolic interpretations are inadequate. Third, the overall context in which the activity of the two witnesses is described (Rev. 11:3-12) supports the preferred view. In these verses witnesses, depicted as individuals, speak (Rev. 11:3, 6); are given power to kill their enemies (Rev. 11:5); are heard, handled, and hated (Rev. 11:3, 7, 10); have mouths, ears, and feet (Rev. 11:5, 11-12); wear "sackcloth," and after their martyrdom John saw their "dead bodies" (τό πτώματα αὐτῶν [*to ptōmata autōn*] , Rev. 11:8-9). By no stretch of the imagination, then, can an interpreter regard these witnesses as other than real persons.[28]

3.11.3.1 - Who are the Witnesses?

Now we reach the second fork in the interpretive road: having established that the two witnesses are best understood as historic individuals, which individuals might they be? The most popular suggestions include: (1) the return of Moses and Elijah; (2) the return of Enoch and Elijah; (3) two future prophets who minister in the power and character of Moses and Elijah.

Identifying the Witnesses

Identity	Reasons For	Reasons Against
Moses and Elijah[29]	"Based on the miracles they are to perform, some have said they are Elijah (commanding fire to devour enemies and shutting up the sky so that it does not rain, Rev. 11:5-6; cf. 1K. 17:1; 2K. 1:10-14), and Moses (water turned to blood, the earth smitten with every plague, Rev. 11:6; cf. Ex. 7:20; 9:14 ; etc.)."[30] "Some writers argue that Moses and Elijah must be the two witnesses because their return is prophesied in Deuteronomy 18:15-18 and Malachi 4:5-6."[31] "Both [Moses and Elijah] left the earth in unusual ways. Elijah never died,	"There is nothing in Scripture that limits miracles such as these to Moses and Elijah. Elijah raised a person from the dead (1K. 17:17-24); but so did Jesus (Mark 5:35-42; Luke 8:49-56; John 11:14-44), Peter (Acts 9:36-41), and Paul (Acts 20:9-12). To argue that Moses and Elijah must be the witnesses because of the miracles mentioned, then, is weak."[35] "The expression 'like me' in Deuteronomy 18:15 seems to preclude using that verse as a means of identifying the witnesses in Revelation 11:3 [as Moses and Elijah], for the

Identity	Reasons For	Reasons Against
	but was transported to heaven in a fiery chariot (2K. 2:11-12), and God supernaturally buried Moses' body in a secret location (Deu. 34:5-6; Jude 1:9)."[32] "Moses appeared with Elijah at the transfiguration (Mtt. 17:13) . . . the law (Moses) and the prophets (Elijah) would be joining in witness unto Christ during the announcement of the coming of the King."[33] The transfiguration is connected with the second coming (Mtt. 16:28; Mark 9:1; Luke 9:27) which these prophets help usher in. Some claim that John the Baptist already fulfilled the coming of Elijah but, "The Lord's statement that John was Elijah was a statement based on contingency. John was Elijah 'if ye will receive *it* ' (Mtt. 11:14). The Lord indicated that if they received the offered kingdom John would be the one to do the work of Elijah. But they rejected this offer (Mtt. 17:12) and therefore John is precluded from being the one to fulfill the prophecy."[34] John himself indicated he was not Elijah (John 1:21).	promised prophet was not Moses, but one 'like' Moses. Also, Jesus said, 'For all the prophets and the Law prophesied until John. And if you care to accept it, he himself is Elijah, who was to come' (Mtt. 11:13-14). Christ later said, 'Elijah is coming and will restore all things; but I say to you, that Elijah already came, and they did not recognize him, but did to him whatever they wished?' (Mtt. 17:11-12). These statements of Jesus show that John the Baptist was, in a real sense, the anticipated Elijah of Malachi, though there may yet be a future fulfillment of that prophecy. The point is that while the prophecy does speak of a literal witness, the person need not be Elijah himself but one who is like Elijah (cf. Luke 1:17). This apparently is the Lord's interpretation of Malachi's prophecy (Mtt. 17:11-12). In view of this, it is not necessary to insist that Elijah the Tishbite must be one of the two witnesses."[36] "The likelihood that Elijah and Moses appeared in glorified bodies (Luke 9:30-31) on the Mount of Transfiguration is a problem for the return of Elijah as well, for since Elijah has already received a glorified body, he cannot die. An exponent of the Elijah view might respond that Elijah's appearance on the Mount of Transfiguration was not in a glorified body, for which death could never be a possibility, but 'in glory' (i.e., some other state such as the glorious characteristics manifested in Christ's own natural body at that time). It might also be argued that Moses had died and that Scripture never records a special resurrection and glorification for him, so that he may have appeared at the

Identity	Reasons For	Reasons Against
		Transfiguration only by some act of God's power to visualize his old body in a 'vision' intelligible to the disciples (Mtt. 17:9), or as Samuel was made to appear, though still actually in the state of death (1S. 28). By this logic, Elijah, like Moses, was on the Mount of Transfiguration in a vision and not a body at all. However, since Elijah was caught up into heaven in his natural body, it seems more likely that he appeared in that body (presumably glorified) on the mount. If Elijah was glorified, it would then be most appropriate to interpret Moses' body as also glorified (though some may say that this requires the assumption of a resurrection for Moses, which Scripture nowhere records, and that this is too large an assumption). If Elijah was still in his mortal body preserved for centuries by powers known only to God and enabled to appear on the mount, then, in the interest of consistency, Moses also was there in person in his mortal body. However, the fact that Moses died, and his body was buried (Deu. 34:5-8; Jude 9), makes it less likely that he reappeared in that mortal body. It seems then that both Elijah and Moses probably have already received glorified bodies of some kind and so could not die. This rules them out as candidates for a future return."[37] "An objection to this interpretation is that those blessed departed servants of God would have to submit to death (Rev. 11:7, 8), and this in Moses' case a second time, which Heb. 9:27 denies."[38] "No second coming of Moses is anywhere promised in the Word."[39] "While the transfiguration is identified with

Identity	Reasons For	Reasons Against
		the millennial age (2Pe. 1:16-19) it is nowhere identified with the tribulation period or the ministry of the witnesses."[40]
Elijah and Enoch[41]	"Some, on the basis of Jewish tradition and the wider context of Scripture, interpret the two witnesses as Elijah and Enoch. One reason is that according to an early rabbinic opinion it is believed that Enoch will rejoin Elijah for a ministry like that of the two witnesses (1 Enoch 90:31; cf. 4 Ezra 6:26). But this is simply an ancient Jewish opinion, not necessarily correct. Also there are many statements in 1 Enoch that are bizarre and questionable. Another reason for saying these witnesses will be Elijah and Enoch is that neither of these two men saw death but were translated to heaven (Gen. 5:24; 2K. 2:11). Since Hebrews 9:27 says that 'it is appointed for men to die once and after this comes judgment,' God, it is argued, must have reserved Enoch and Elijah as His witnesses for this future time. The merit of this argument is that it helps rule out Moses and others as possible candidates, for they have already died."[42] "Neither [Enoch] nor Elijah were given immortal bodies when they were translated, however, because it was necessary for Christ first to die for their sins and rise again. . . (1Cor. 15:22-23). Thus Enoch and Elijah have been waiting in heaven in their natural bodies through all the intervening ages since their respective translations."[43] "In Revelation 11:4 the word 'standing' suggests that they were already there in John's day, and must be two people who have already been translated. Thus, it is held, only Elijah and Enoch could meet this requirement."[44] "Even	"It should be pointed out, however, that since there will be a whole generation of believers who are raptured and thus will not die physically (1Cor. 15:51-57; 1Th. 4:16-17), the idea that Enoch and Elijah must return in order to die once to make Hebrews 9:27 absolutely all-inclusive, is without basis. It should also be noted that Hebrews 11:5 says that Enoch was translated 'so that he should not see death.' To allow a future return and death, then, would nullify God's promise."[46] "Those who claim them to be Enoch and Elijah base it on the fact that these two men never died, and so they will return to die in the Tribulation. Often, Hebrews 9:27 is used as evidence for 'it is appointed unto men once to die.' But it is a general principle and not an absolute rule. For example, take the word *once* : some people have died twice, namely, all those who had been resurrected in the Old and New Testaments apart from Messiah. Furthermore, what about the living Church saints? If indeed Hebrews 9:27 is an absolute rule, it would mean that all living Church saints at the *Rapture*[5.2.62] will also have to die at some time. Both I Corinthians 15:51 and I Thessalonians 4:15-17 show that Hebrews 9:27 is only a general principle. Also in the light of Hebrews 11:5 ['By faith Enoch was translated that he should not see death. . .'], it cannot be that Enoch will die in the future."[47] "Enoch is clearly said to have been *translated* , and this involves corruption

Identity	Reasons For	Reasons Against
	after His incarnation, on the mount with Peter, James, and John, [Jesus] was much arrayed in heavenly glory as Elijah who there appeared in converse with him; yet, from that holy mount, and glory, and sublime transfiguration, he came down, and suffered, and *died.* Paul was once in heaven, caught up, he knew not how, and saw and heard things he dared not tell; and yet, he came back, and preached, and suffered, and *died.* John was called up to heaven, to behold the wonders that are described in this Book; yet he also returned, and suffered, and *died.*"[45]	putting on incorruption and mortality putting on immortality (1Cor. 15:50-58). Since Elijah has already been taken into Heaven, the same is true of him, for no man in his physical state can enter Heaven (1Cor. 15:50). This means that neither Elijah nor Enoch can die, for they are now immortal."[48] Enoch seems an unlikely candidate on the grounds that he is a type for the Church which is *removed*[4.14] prior to the Tribulation as Enoch was taken before the flood.[49] "It is the stated purpose that Enoch was translated 'in order that he might not see death' (Heb. 11:5). In view of this it could hardly be stated that he will be returned to die. . . . It would seem that an antediluvian prophet would not be sent into a time when God is dealing with Israel."[50] If the nature of their ministry serves to identify the individuals, and it may not, then we have no indication for Enoch: "A further difficulty for this view is Enoch's failure to match the criteria assigned to the two witnesses."[51]
Two Future Prophets[52]	The two witnesses are taken as two unknown Jewish prophets who will minister at the time of the Tribulation. This view avoids the various problems which attend the other views. The passage does not positively identify the individuals so there is no need to find fulfillment in previous individuals having already died or been translated. "If God wished us to know He could have told us. The fact that He has not done so ought to stop our mouths."[53] "There are great difficulties in all points of view identifying the two witnesses with historical characters."[54]	Although Jesus indicated that John the Baptist served in a capacity like that of Elijah who would come prior to the day of the LORD (Mtt. 11:14), John himself indicated he was not Elijah (John 1:21). If Malachi is to be taken literally, then it is necessary for *Elijah* to come, not his *likeness* (Mal. 4:5). Both Moses and Elijah are connected with the coming of Christ in His kingdom (Mtt. 16:28; Mark 9:1; Luke 9:27) by their appearance on the Mount of Transfiguration (Mtt. 17:3; Mark 9:4; Luke 9:30). The character of the ministry of the witnesses seems to intentionally recall that of Moses and Elijah.

they will prophesy

Their ministry will be like that of John (Rev. 10:11) in that their prophesy will be global in extent, for they shall not only prophesy (which includes correction and exhortation), but they shall also torment those who dwell on the earth (Rev. 11:5-7, 10).

one thousand two hundred and sixty days

This is the first half of the final week of *the seventy weeks of Daniel*[2.13.5], before the beast reaches ascendancy and is able to overcome them (Rev. 11:7).[55] It cannot be the latter half of the week as some suggest:[56]

1. It is the *beast* who is destroyed at the close of the week (Rev. 19:20), not the witnesses. See *Events of the 70th Week of Daniel*[2.13.5.4].
2. It is more natural to understand the overthrow of the Jewish prophets as leading to the defilement of the *Temple*[5.2.73] in the Abomination of Desolation to follow. Prior to their overthrow, they are invincible and almost certainly would not allow the beast to sit in the Holy Place to declare himself as god (2Th. 2:4).[57]
3. Why would the two *Jewish* witnesses, who are key in the revival of the Jews during the Tribulation, be found in Jerusalem *after* the Jews have fled elsewhere due to the intense persecution of the dragon which begins at the midpoint of the final week (Mtt. 24:15; Rev. 12:6, 13-14)?
4. How could the beast overcome the witnesses at the *end* of the 70th week and the world throw a big celebration at the very time *Antichrist*[5.2.3] is heavily involved with the *Campaign of Armageddon*[4.5] and Christ arrives?[58]
5. The overthrow of the prophets would more naturally contribute to the rise and fame of the beast.[59]
6. If Christ returns with the resurrected saints to the earth at the end of the 70th week, why do these two resurrected witnesses ascend to heaven?

These problems disappear if the 1,260 days mentioned here are understood as denoting the first half of the week, including a powerful witness to Jerusalem culminating in the ascent of the beast to overthrow the witnesses and exert full control over the Temple, as Paul relates of the man of sin (2Th. 2:4).

in sackcloth

Sackcloth was a rough, course cloth, or a bag-like garment made of such cloth which was worn as a symbol of mourning, grief, or repentance (e.g., Jer. 4:8; 6:26; 48:37; 49:3; Amos 8:10). Its association with mourning and sorrow may have been not only due to its coarseness on the wearer, but also because it was made from black goat hair. When prophets wore sackcloth, it indicated their own brokenness over the message of doom and judgment which they themselves were delivering. Prophets were never cavalier in their dire predictions, but grieved over the judgment they proclaimed (Isa. 20:2). In this sense, the sackcloth of the two witnesses is akin to the bitterness which attended John's consumption of the little book of prophecy (Rev. 10:9-10). The sackcloth indicates the message of the two witnesses is one of impending judgment to which their listeners should respond in repentance. Although this chapter records a rare case of repentance in the judgments of God at the time of the end, it is not directly due to the testimony of the witnesses (Rev. 11:13). The pattern elsewhere is one of failure to repent (Rev. 9:21; 16:11).

These two witnesses are 1) clothed in sackcloth, 2) have a ministry matching that of previous OT Jewish prophets, and 3) minister in Jerusalem. These factors, along with the absence of the Church (see *Rapture*[4.14]) and the sealing of the 144,000 Jews (Rev. 7:4-8), argue for the Jewishness of the two witnesses.

3.11.4 - Revelation 11:4

These are

αὗτοι εἰσιν [*autoi eisin*]: *These, they are*, emphasizing the individuals.

the two olive trees

Israel is referred to by God as a "Green Olive Tree, Lovely *and* of Good Fruit" (Jer. 11:16a). The psalm writer referred to himself, one who trusted in God's mercy, as "a green olive tree in the house of God" (Ps. 52:8). The definite article (*the*) is intended to denote a specific pair of olive trees (see below).

and the two lamp stands

Lamp stands is λυχνίαι [*lychniai*], the same word which described the seven lampstands which were the *Seven Churches of Asia*[4.15] (Rev. 1:12, 20; 2:1, 5). Evidently, these two lamp stands will serve a similar purpose to the seven lampstands (the churches). As in the previous phrase, the definite article (*the*) points to a pair of olive trees and lamp stands which would be known to John. The allusion is to Zechariah's fifth vision (Zec. 4:1-14) wherein Zechariah is shown a lampstand of solid gold with seven pipes feeding seven lamps. The lamps are fed by a shared bowl of oil which stands between two olive trees into which the oil from the trees drips (Zec. 4:3, 12). When Zechariah asks an angel concerning the identity of the two olive trees and the fruitful oil-dripping branches which extend from them, the angel responds: "These *are* the two anointed ones [lit. 'sons of oil'] who stand beside the Lord of the whole earth" (Zec. 4:14). They are two who are anointed by oil (a common figure for the Holy Spirit).

> The candlestick itself—the central object of this vision—is doubtless a figurative representation of the seven-branched candlestick in the *Temple*[5.2.73]. There it stood in the Holy Place . . . not only as the emblem and representation of what the whole redeemed family shall finally be "when in union with their risen, glorified Lord they shall for ever shine in the sanctuary of God," but also as *typifying Israel's high calling in relation to the other nations*. In his midst a great light had shone—the light of the self-revelation of the glory of Jehovah—not only for his own illumination, but that he might be the candlestick, the light-bearer, and light-diffuser all around. . . . We know how terribly and sadly Israel failed to respond to God's purpose concerning Him.[60]

> It is most in harmony with the scope of these visions (one of the great objects of [the vision] was to encourage the two heads, or leaders, of the restored remnant of the nation in their task of rebuilding the Temple) to regard the olive trees as representing Joshua the high priest, and Zerubbabel the prince.[61]

The fourth (Zec. 3) and fifth (Zec. 4) visions of Zechariah are related. In the fourth vision, upon the stone which is laid before Joshua are *seven eyes* (Zec. 3:9). Similarly, the plumb line in the hand of Zerubbabel is seen by seven "eyes of the LORD which scan to and fro throughout the whole earth" (Zec. 4:10). As we have seen, these eyes represent the Holy Spirit, the "seven eyes, which are the seven Spirits of God sent out into all the earth" (Rev. 5:6b). The fifth vision concerns seven lamps which also allude to the Holy Spirit: "Seven lamps of fire *were* burning before the throne, which are the seven Spirits of God" (Rev. 4:5). Zechariah's two visions concern the work of the Holy Spirit through *two individuals* during *two restorations*:

- **Two Individuals** - The fifth vision ends with the statement that the two "sons of oil" *stand* beside the Lord of the whole earth. In the fourth vision, Joshua is said to be *standing* before the Angel of the LORD. Throughout the fourth vision, it is the high priest Joshua who is being encouraged. In the fifth vision, Zerubbabel is told that the construction of the temple will be completed " 'Not by might nor by power, but by My Spirit,' Says the LORD of hosts" (Zec. 4:6). Thus, it is by the hand of Joshua and Zerubbabel that the Holy Spirit will accomplish the restoration of the second Temple. "While in relation to the remnant of Israel at that time, and to the Temple then in building, we are to understand by these two 'sons of oil' the actual persons of Joshua and Zerubbabel, it is certain that these two, considered *merely as individuals*, do not exhaust the symbol, for the simple reason that the supply of oil for the candlestick is a vision designed to describe the *abiding*, and especially the *future* position and mission of the congregation of Israel, could not be represented as dependent on the lives of two mortal men. They must therefore be viewed standing here as types or representatives of the kingly and priestly offices to which they respectively belonged."[62]

- **Two Restorations** - In the immediate context of the fourth vision, Joshua is admonished to walk in God's ways. There is also a distant context of the vision which indicates that God will bring forth his Servant "the BRANCH" (Zec. 3:8). This is a common title of Messiah (see *Four Gospels*[4.7]) and results in the eventual cleansing *of the land* (Zec. 3:9). " 'In that day,' says the LORD of hosts, 'Everyone will invite his neighbor under his vine and under his fig tree.' " (Zec. 3:10). This speaks of a time of prosperity and peace—as in the *Millennial Kingdom*[5.2.39].[63] The fifth vision concerns the foundation of the temple (*house*) and communicates to Zerubbabel that "his hands shall also finish *it*" (Zec. 4:9). This speaks of the second temple which was underway at the time of the vision. Later, Zechariah indicates that a future individual, called "the BRANCH," will build the temple and wear *two* crowns: ruling as both priest and king.[64] Concerning this individual, Zechariah relates, "So He shall be a priest on His throne" (Zec. 6:13b), yet no high priest ever ruled on a throne nor did any king of Israel function in the office of priest. When taken together, these passages indicate both a near-term restoration (the rebuilding of Jerusalem and the temple in the days of Zerubabbel and Joshua) and a distant restoration (the restoration of Jerusalem and the temple for the Millennial Kingdom under Messiah). The meager temple of the time of Zerubbabel, which caused those who remembered Solomon's temple to weep in disappointment (Ezra 3:12-13), which was enhanced by Herod and saw the first advent of Messiah only to be destroyed by Rome in A.D. 70 due to the apostasy of the nation, would one day stand anew in the days of the *Millennial Temple*[4.16.5.10] (Eze. 40-47). "But Zechariah's prophecy also looks forward to the restoration of Israel in the Millennium (cf. Zec. 3:8-10). The olive trees and lampstands symbolize the light of revival, since olive oil was commonly used in lamps. . . . God will not bring salvation blessing from human power, but by the power of the Holy Spirit (cf. Zec. 4:6). Like Joshua and Zerubbabel, the two witnesses will lead a spiritual revival of Israel culminating in the building of a temple."[65] "[The witnesses] are the corresponding Zerubbabel and Jeshua of the final restitution."[66]

The allusion back to Zechariah's visions is further proof of the Jewishness of these individuals, but also underscores their function in bringing Israel toward the final restoration seen by Zechariah.[67] The Church Age having come to a close, the focus has shifted back to Israel in preparation of a faithful nation suitable for the Millennial Kingdom to come.

> The history of corporate Gentile Christianity is not as the shining light that "shineth more and more unto the perfect day," as some who boast in the supposed progress and speak of the conversion of the world before the glorious appearing of Christ ignorantly suppose, but rather that of a bright dawn, developing into an increasingly dark and cloudy day, and ending in blackness of darkness. And there is no hope for Christendom which continued not in the goodness of God when once it is "cut off"; nor is there any promise of the restoration and relighting of *its* candlestick when once its light has been quenched in anti-Christian apostasy. But it is different with Israel. There is always hope in his end. Not only shall the sceptre of governmental rule and the kingdom come back to the daughter of Jerusalem, after the long centuries of subjugation and oppression, but her candlestick, too, shall be restored after the long period of Israel's spiritual darkness and blindness, to shine in more resplendent glory than even in the past. This is the meaning of Zechariah's fifth vision, and it sets forth in symbol the great truth proclaimed by the former prophets in relation to Israel's future glory as the centre of light and blessing to all the nations of the earth.[68]

It is the role of the people of God, be they Israel or the Church, to shine forth so that those who do not God may "see your good works and glorify your Father in heaven" (Mtt. 5:14). This mission was fulfilled in the life of John the Baptist (John 1:7-8; 5:35) and also in Jesus (John 1:9; 3:19). In the absence of Jesus, the Church had presented the light (Rev. 1:13, 20; 2:5). Why the need for these two lampstands if the previous seven are still present on the earth? It is our view that this is additional evidence in favor of a *pretribulational*[5.2.60] *Rapture*[4.14] for the seven lampstands are not present on the earth during this period of time when the two lampstands minister.

standing before the God of the earth

Standing is ἑστῶτες [*estōtes*], a perfect tense participle, *while having stood.* They took their place before God prior to John having seen them. Here the phrase is an intentional allusion to the nearly identical phrase in the related passage in Zechariah. "These *are* the two anointed ones **who stand**

beside the Lord of the whole earth" [emphasis added] (Zec. 4:14).

Standing before the Lord describes a position of *ministry to the Lord* (Deu. 10:8; 1K. 17:1; Rev. 8:2). These two stand before God and *minister to Him* by faithfully prophesying and witnessing His word. Although their ministry appears directed toward the *earth dwellers*[5.2.18], they are in fact focused upon being pure and faithful conduits for God to speak to the nations at the time of the end.

the God of the earth

The term for *earth* is γῆς [*gēs*], which *preterist interpreters*[2.12.2] generally prefer to interpret as designating the *land of Israel* or the surrounding geographical area in order to restrict the scope of the book of Revelation to Israel in the events of A.D. 70. The global scope of Revelation is seen again here in that these witnesses stand before the God of the entire *earth* and those which they torment include "peoples, tribes, tongues, and nations" —a global population (Rev. 11:9-10).

3.11.5 - Revelation 11:5

if anyone wants to harm them

Although set forth as a conditional statement, the remainder of the passage implies that the vast majority of people strongly oppose their ministry and *do* desire to harm them, for they rejoice at their eventual death (Rev. 11:10).[69] In the eyes of the *earth dwellers*[5.2.18] who will hate these witnesses, the ability of the beast to kill them is a testimony to his invincibility. He is seen as a "savior" from these detestable prophets and their defeat no doubt elevates his status before the earth dwellers (Rev. 13:4).

fire proceeds from their mouth

Those who seek to harm the two witnesses face a similar fate to the opponents of the army of the sixth trumpet (Rev. 9:18-19). *Fire* speaks of judgment and in some cases is used figuratively to describe destruction (Jdg. 9:14, 20; Ps. 18:8). Frequently, judgment by God, in conformance to His Word, is described as being a weapon of His *mouth* (Isa. 11:4; 49:2; Hos. 6:5; 2Th. 2:8; Rev. 1:16; 19:15). In the passages just cited, there are normally clues in the context which indicate where figurative language is being employed. For example, in Judges 9 various men in the dispute are said to be "trees," "brambles," and "cedars" (Jdg. 9:14-15). In the Second Coming of Jesus, His eyes are *like* a flame of fire and He is said to be riding a horse through the sky. These textual clues prevent us from interpreting the sword that goes forth from His mouth as a literal sword extending from His face. Rather, we recognize the figurative language employed and understand the sword in His mouth as an allusion to the Word of God (Heb. 4:12) by which His enemies are judged and so justly killed. This is part of normative interpretation using the *Golden Rule of Interpretation*[5.2.24].

The passage before us is very similar to statements made by other prophets:

> Therefore I have hewn *them* by the prophets, I have slain them by the words of My mouth; and your judgments *are like* light *that* goes forth. (Hos. 6:5)
>
> Therefore thus says the LORD God of hosts: "Because you speak this word, behold I will make My words in your mouth fire, and this people wood, and it shall devour them." (Jer. 5:14)
>
> "*Is* not My word like a fire?" says the LORD, "And like a hammer *that* breaks the rock in pieces?" (Jer. 23:29)

Hosea likens the words spoken by God through the prophets to a weapon. The prophets spoke forth God's judgments which eventually resulted in the literal death of those judged. The words of the prophets are likened to a sword ("I have hewn"), but there is no literal sword in the prophets' mouths. Similarly, Jeremiah's words are likened to fire and the people wood. It would be easy to conclude from these figurative uses of fire and the mouth as a weapon that such must be the case here too. But there are important differences between the previously cited passages and what is said here. Passages wherein figurative language occurs typically contain an indication of such. For example, Hosea says, "I have hewn *them* by the prophets." Obviously, people were not literally cut in two by the prophets. This is an indication that figurative language is employed. Similarly, Jeremiah is told that the people will be made "wood"—another indicator that figurative language is in use. It is not good enough simply to establish that similar themes in related passages are figurative and therefore conclude that this passage must be too. The immediate context of the passage in question must itself provide indication that figurative language is in use.

It would seem there are three alternatives for interpreting the passage before us:

1. **Purely Figurative** - The fire which proceeds from their mouths speaks of general judgments which are spoken forth by the two witnesses. The judgments result in death, but not necessarily by literal fire.
2. **Partly Figurative** - Literal fire devours their enemies. The fire "proceeds from their mouth" in the sense that, like Elijah, they *call forth* fire from heaven upon their opponents (1K. 10:10-12).
3. **Purely Nonfigurative** - Literal fire actually proceeds directly from their mouths (like the demon horses of Rev. 9:17).

Notice that all of these alternatives are possible within the boundaries of "literal interpretation," because literal interpretation includes the recognition of figures of speech *where the context so indicates*. The question becomes, "Does the context indicate figurative language is employed?" Although figurative language describes the similarity of their identity to the "two olive trees" of Zechariah, the pattern of their ministry—and especially the judgments they bring forth—match that of non-figurative judgments found in the *OT*[5.2.51]. It would seem that we must conclude that if figurative language is afoot, it is minimal. That is, literal fire comes forth directly out of their mouths or they employ their mouths to call literal fire down from heaven.[70] A question remains: if this passage is intended to describe the ability to *call down fire from heaven* upon their enemies, how do we explain the difference in description here from other passages where fire is explicitly said to be called down from heaven (2K. 1:10-12; Rev. 13:13)?

Thus, several factors favor a purely nonfigurative interpretation regarding this judgment by fire of their enemies:

1. Clear indicators of figurative language concerning the nature of the fire or plagues are lacking.[71]
2. Literal judgments such as those described here are recorded as historical facts in the OT.
3. The fire is not said to originate in heaven as it is in other passages concerning Elijah (2K. 1:10-12) and the *False Prophet*[4.3.2.18] (Rev. 13:13).

Whether the fire comes directly from their mouths, or whether their words call it forth, it would seem that the unique miraculous authority which attends such a defensive ability is intended to manifest the divine source of their ministry (Num. 10:2; 16:35; Ps. 106:18; Heb. 12:29). The unusual nature of their response to their enemies brings to mind the incident in Numbers where Korah's household is judged:

> And Moses said: "By this you shall know that the LORD has sent me to do all these works, for *I have* not *done them* of my own will. If these men die naturally like all men, or if they are visited by the common fate of all men, *then* the LORD has not sent me. But **if the LORD creates a new thing**, and the earth opens its mouth and swallows them up with all that belongs to them, and they go down alive into the pit, **then you will understand that these men have rejected the LORD**." Now it came to pass, as he finished speaking all these words, that the ground split apart under them, and the earth opened its mouth and swallowed them up, with their households and all the men with Korah, with all *their* goods. So they and all those with them went down alive into the pit; the earth closed over them, and they perished from among the assembly. (Num. 16:28-33) [emphasis added]

Moses explains that the unusual nature of the judgment serves a specific purpose. It provides unique testimony to the *source* of the judgment (God) and the *authority* of Moses as His spokesman. So will this fire-consuming ability testify that God is the one judging the opponents of His two witnesses and that they have His full authority in their ministry.

We should also remember the unique period in which these two individuals minister. This is a time in history during which demonic powers are at a peak (Rev. 9:1-2, 13-19; 12:12) and the time of the lawless one, the *Antichrist*[5.2.3], whose coming "is according to the working of Satan, with all power, signs, and lying wonders, and with all unrighteous **deception** among those who perish" [emphasis added] (2Th. 2:9-10a). These are the days of the false prophet who "performs great signs, so that he even makes fire come down from heaven on the earth in the sight of men" (Rev. 13:13).

These unique historic factors also argue for a completely nonfigurative interpretation because these two witnesses must exhibit miraculous powers which are on a par with, or even superior to, that of the man of sin and his false prophet in an age frequented by demonic manifestations.

3.11.6 - Revelation 11:6

shut heaven

Shut is κλεῖσαι [*kleisai*]: "*shut, lock, bar*."[72] The same root is used where Jesus informs us "many widows were in Israel in the days of Elijah, when the heaven was **shut up** three years and six months, and there was great famine throughout all the land" [emphasis added] (Luke 4:25b). Jesus described the ministry of Elijah the Tishbite who said to King Ahab, "*As* the LORD God of Israel lives, before whom I stand, there shall not be dew nor rain these years, except at my word" (1K. 17:1). Elijah, by the power of God, shut the atmospheric heaven from providing rain and dew.

so that no rain falls in the days of their prophecy

James refers to the similar event in Elijah's life to underscore the power of prayer in the life of believers. "Elijah was a man with a nature like ours, and he prayed earnestly that it would not rain; and it did not rain on the land for three years and six months" (Jas. 5:17). Both Jesus and James inform us that the heaven was shut against rain for a period of *three years and six months*—a period of time matching *the days of their* (the two witnesses) *prophecy* : 1,260 days (Rev. 11:3).

> The third trumpet judgment resulted in the poisoning of one-third of the earth's fresh water supply (Rev. 8:10-11). Added to that, the three-and-one-half-year drought lasting throughout the 1,260 days of their preaching (Rev. 11:3; cf. Luke 4:25; Jas. 5:17) brought by the two witnesses will cause widespread devastation of crops and loss of human and animal life through thirst and starvation.[73]

The *lack of water* and the *sackcloth* worn by the prophets allude to a time of *fasting and mourning* on the earth which is intended to produce repentance.

See *Who are the Witnesses?*[3.11.3.1] See *Events of the 70th Week of Daniel*[2.13.5.4].

power over waters to turn them into blood

The witnesses have power like that of Moses in Egypt (Ex. 4:9; 7:17-21; Ps. 78:44; 105:29). See *Who are the Witnesses?*[3.11.3.1] See *The Plagues of Egypt and the Tribulation*[2.13.7]. The results of this plague will emulate the effects of the second trumpet judgment and the second and third bowl judgments where the seas and springs of water "become blood" (Rev. 8:8; 16:3-4).

to strike the earth with all plagues

The two witnesses will be able to initiate numerous plague judgments upon the earth as they will. The full range of plagues is not described, but we can safely assume they are similar to the plagues with which Moses and Aaron tormented Egypt. See *Who are the Witnesses?*[3.11.3.1] See *The Plagues of Egypt and the Tribulation*[2.13.7].

3.11.7 - Revelation 11:7

When they finish their testimony

As we have seen throughout the book of Revelation, the ability of the evil forces which manifest during the time of the end is entirely within God's sovereignty. These two witnesses may not be killed until they have finished their God-given task (John 17:4). So it is with all believers (John 21:18-23; Acts 20:24; 2Ti. 4:7).

the beast

Beast[5.2.9] is θηρίον [*thērion*] , which was used of wild animals (Rev. 6:8), including those which fought in the Roman arena.[74] The term is also used to describe animals as revealed in visions, such as that of Daniel (*LXX*[5.2.38]: Dan. 7:3, 5-7, 11-12, 17, 19, 23). It is the diminutive form of θήρ [*thēr*] but equivalent in meaning.[75] It is to be contrasted against the diminutive for *Lamb*, ἀρνίον [*arnion*].[76] See *Master Imitator*[4.2.5].

> This name "the Beast" contrasts the Antichrist from the true Christ as "the Lamb;" and it is a significant

> fact that by far the great majority of passages where the Lord Jesus is so designated are also found here in the Apocalypse. The "Lamb" is the Saviour of sinners; the "Beast" is the persecutor and slayer of the saints. The "Lamb" calls attention to the gentleness of Christ; the "Beast" tells of the ferocity of the Antichrist. . . Under the Law lambs were ceremonially clean and used in sacrifice, but beasts were unclean and unfit for sacrifices.[77]

Revelation mentions two different beasts: Antichrist (Rev. 13:1) and the *False Prophet*[5.2.20] (Rev. 13:11). Which beast is in view here? Evidence indicates it is Antichrist who slays the witnesses.

> The "beast" most probably refers to the future Antichrist. Five facts support this view.
>
> First, the persecutor of the witnesses is not "a beast" but "the beast" (τό θηρίον [*to thērion*]). This use of a definite article indicates that he is a figure well known to the writer. Since teaching on the Antichrist was so familiar to Jews and Christians through Old and New Testament prophecy (Dan. 7:2-25; 9:27 ; 11:35-45 ; Mtt. 24:15; Mark 13:14; 2Th. 2:3-12; 1Jn. 4:1-6), it is not impossible that John was thinking of him here.
>
> Second, since the word "beast" (θηρίον [*thērion*]) in the Apocalypse is always used with reference to the future Antichrist or his system (Rev. 13:1 ; 14:9, 11 ; 15:2 ; 16:2 ; 17:3 ; 19:20 ; 20:10) [we note one exception: Rev. 13:11], the beast in 11:7 should be seen in the same light.
>
> Third, the beast will come up out of (ἐκ [*ek*]) the abyss, that is, it will have a satanic, demonic source and character (cf. Rev. 9:1). This feature corresponds with that of the coming Antichrist in 2 Thessalonians 2:9-10.
>
> Fourth, the description of the beast as "coming up out of the abyss" (ἀναβαῖνον ἐκ τῆς ἀβύσσου [*anabainon ek tēs abyssou*] , Rev. 11:7) corresponds with the beast "about to come from the abyss" (ἀναβαίνειν ἐκ τῆς ἀβύσσου [*anabainein ek tēs abyssou*]) in Rev. 17:8 (cf. Rev. 13:1). This correspondence is illuminating, for since the beast in Rev. 17:8 probably refers to the future Antichrist with his kingdom, the same is probably the case in Rev. 11:7.
>
> Fifth, νικάω [*nikaō*] ("to overcome") is used three times in the Apocalypse with reference to the enemy of God's people (Rev. 6:2 ; 11:7 ; 13:7). Since other occurrences of the term are related directly to the coming Antichrist (Rev. 6:2 ; 13:7), the same may be true in Rev. 11:7.[78]

The definite article, *the*, implies at his first introduction here by John that he is a recognized figure:

> This beast was not mentioned before, yet he is introduced as "the beast," because he had already been described by Daniel (Dan. 7:3, 11), and he is fully so in the subsequent part of the Apocalypse, namely, Rev. 13:1; 17:8. Thus, John at once appropriates the Old Testament prophecies; and also, viewing his whole subject at a glance, mentions as familiar things (though not yet so to the reader) objects to be described hereafter by himself. It is a proof of the unity that pervades all Scripture.[79]

The individual before us is found in many passages of Scripture and given many different titles. "Across the varied scenes depicted by prophecy there falls the shadow of a figure at once commanding and ominous. Under many different names like the aliases of a criminal, his character and movements are set before us."[80]

> It is unfortunate that the great variety of names bestowed upon him has led some brethren to the conclusion that they must belong to separate persons, and has caused them to apportion these out to different individuals; only confusion can result from this. There is almost as much ground to make the Devil and Satan different persons, as there is to regard (as some do) the Beast and the Antichrist as separate entities. That the Devil and Satan are names belonging to the same person, and that the Beast and the Antichrist is the selfsame individual, is proven by the fact that identically the same characteristics under each is found belonging to the one as to the other.[81]

Pink cites the *Teaching of the Apostles* (said to be dated to the beginning of the 2nd century), the writings of Cyril (Bishop of Jerusalem in the fourth century), and Gregory of Tours (who wrote at the end of the 6th century) as evidence of the early view that the Beast is an *individual* rather than a *system*. He attributes the idea that the Antichrist was the Roman system to the Waldenses: "It is not until we reach the fourteenth century (so far as the writer is aware) that we find the first marked deviation from the uniform belief of the early Christians. It was the Waldenses,—so remarkably sound in the faith on almost all point of doctrine—who, thoroughly worn out by centuries of the most relentless and merciless persecutions, published about the year 1350 a treatise designed to prove that the system of Popery was the Antichrist."[82]

"This shows that these Witnesses are upon the earth during the thirteenth chapter; and that the Beast is on the Earth during the eleventh chapter."[83] See *The Beast*[4.2].

ascends out of the bottomless pit

Bottomless pit is ἀβύσσου [*abyssou*], the deep well within the earth where fallen angels are held. See commentary on *Revelation 9:1*[3.9.1]. See *Supernatural Origin?*[4.2.7] The beast is from the bottomless pit (Rev. 11:7; 17:8) whereas the Lamb is from heaven (John 3:13, 31; 6:33, 38, 41-42, 51). "We have not here his historical rise 'out of the *sea* ' (Rev. 13:1), but his satanic revival 'out of the bottomless *pit* ' or abyss (Rev. 11:7)."[84]

make war

A trademark of the beast, and the dragon who empowers him, is his incessant opposition to the people of God. In addition to these two witnesses, he makes war against the saints in general (Dan. 7:21, 25; Rev. 7:9-16; 12:11; 13:7; 20:4), and against the Jews in particular (Jer. 30:7; Dan. 8:24; 12:1; Rev. 12:13, 17). See *Jacob's Trouble and the Great Tribulation*[2.13.4].

overcome them, and kill them

Overcome is νικήσει [*nikēsei*] from νικάω [*nikaō*]. Here is the one who rides forth "conquering and to conquer" (Rev. 6:2). See commentary on *Revelation 6:2*[3.6.2]. This is another *external similarity* between the beast and the Lamb. See *Master Imitator*[4.2.5]. He appears to overcome in the eyes of the world, but those he kills are the true overcomers (Rev. 2:11; 12:11). See *Who is the Overcomer?*[4.15.1.3] He overcomes the witnesses after he is restored from his deadly wound:

> That this incident will happen after his resurrection from the dead is clear from the statement, *the beast that comes up from the abyss*, and he will come back from the Abyss by means of his resurrection by Satan. Along with his resurrection, the act of killing the Two Witnesses will provide another reason why mankind will worship him. All previous attempts to kill the Two Witnesses fail.[85]
>
> Immediately upon his resurrection, he kills . . . the Two Witnesses. Consequently, *their* 1,260 days must just overlap into *his* 42 months. They must have witnessed, therefore, for nearly 1,260 days during his mortal stage, before his assassination.[86]

See *Events of the 70th Week of Daniel*[2.13.5.4].

3.11.8 - Revelation 11:8

their dead bodies *will lie* in the street

Lack of burial is particularly repugnant to the Jews. "For a corpse to remain unburied or to be exhumed subsequent to burial, and thus become food for beasts of prey, was the climax of indignity or judgment (1K. 14:11; 16:4; 2K. 9:37; Ps. 79:3; Jer. 7:33; 8:1; 16:4, 6; 22:19; Eze. 29:5; Rev. 11:9)."[87] The beast and *earth dwellers*[5.2.18] purposefully leave the bodies of the witnesses unburied as an intentional dishonor and insult (Isa. 14:20; Jer. 8:2; 14:16). This is another indication of the Jewishness of the context.[88]

the great city

The same phrase is used elsewhere to describe Babylon (Rev. 14:8; 17:18; 18:10, 16, 18, 19), earthly Jerusalem (Rev. 16:19), and the heavenly Jerusalem (Rev. 21:10).[89] Both Babylon and earthly Jerusalem have great significance in the scenario of the Tribulation. One is the center of the anti-God system of Babylon (Rev. 17-18) whereas the other is the earthly city where God has placed His name (1K. 11:36; 2Chr. 33:4, 7; Dan. 9:19). It is within this latter great city, Jerusalem, that the *Tribulation Temple*[4.16.5.9] will stand which *Antichrist*[5.2.3] desecrates (Rev. 11:1-2). The identity of the city among the three possible locations (Babylon, earthly Jerusalem, heavenly Jerusalem) is established by its identification as the place "where also our Lord was crucified."

spiritually

πνευματικῶς [*pneumatikōs*] meaning "*in a manner consistent with the* (divine) *Spirit*."[90] " 'Spiritually' . . . shows this to be the language of allegory or metaphor. Neither Sodom nor Egypt is the city's real name."[91] One of the ministries of the Holy Spirit is to assess the true spiritual conditions of His subject. He is represented by "seven eyes which are the seven Spirits of God sent out into all the earth" (Rev. 5:8). His omniscient gaze burns away the dross of external representation to reveal the true character below (Rev. 4:5). It is in this sense, as seen by the Spirit, that Jerusalem is called "Sodom and Egypt."

called Sodom and Egypt

Both Sodom and Egypt typify cities which were opposed and judged by God. Sodom was an exceedingly wicked city which was overthrown for her sins by God's judgment (Gen. 13:13; 19:24). Egypt was the nation which held Israel in bondage and was judged by plagues prior to the Exodus (Ex. 1:13-14; 3:7; 20:2). Jerusalem, in her godless state, is likened to both the wicked city and the wicked nation. Even though the two witnesses exhibit a Jewish ministry located in Jerusalem, they are rejected by the majority of the inhabitants—their fellow Jews.

When Moses sang a song predicting the apostasy of Israel upon entering the Promised Land after his death, he referred to the Jewish nation as "a nation void of counsel," whose "vine *is* of the vine of *Sodom* and of the fields of Gomorrah" (Deu. 32:28-32). Isaiah used a similar analogy when describing God's rejection of Israel's insincere sacrifices: "Hear the word of the LORD you rulers of *Sodom*; give ear to the law of our God, you people of Gomorrah: 'To what purpose *is* the multitude of your sacrifices to Me?' " (Isa. 1:10). The sin of Jerusalem is said to be as the sin of Sodom in that it was flaunted openly (Isa. 3:8).[92] Even the apostate prophets are likened to the inhabitants of Sodom and Gomorrah (Jer. 23:14). When rejected by the cities of the lost sheep of the house of Israel, Jesus indicated that the cities which did not receive the apostles or their words would be considered worse off than Sodom and Gomorrah in the day of judgment (Mtt. 10:14-15; Luke 10:12). Although Jerusalem is here referred to as Sodom, Isaiah also indicated that Babylon's eventual overthrow would be like that of Sodom and Gomorrah (Isa. 13:19). Elsewhere, Ezekiel describes the Northern Kingdom (Samaria) and the Southern Kingdom (Jerusalem) as idolatrous sisters, both of which committed harlotry in their youth while in *Egypt* (Eze. 23:2-4, 19, 27). Comparison with *Egypt* recalls the idolatrous golden calf which Israel made upon departure from Egypt (Ex. 32:4, 24).

where also our Lord was crucified

The *MT*[5.2.45] and *NU*[5.2.49] texts have *their Lord* instead of *our Lord.* Although the city has the spiritual attributes of Sodom and Egypt, its identity is clearly established as Jerusalem, the place of the crucifixion (Luke 13:33; John 19:20; Heb. 13:12). Concerning those who suggest some other location than Jerusalem, Bullinger observes: "A Sunday-school child could tell us where the Lord was crucified; but these learned men cannot."[93]

3.11.9 - Revelation 11:9

***those* from the peoples, tribes, tongues, and nations**

A fourfold designation indicating global scope—all the peoples of the earth. See *Four: the Entire World, the Earth*[2.7.5.3.3]. This is the global community which John was told he "must prophesy again about" (Rev. 10:11), over which the beast is granted authority (Rev. 13:7), and upon which the harlot sits (Rev. 17:2, 15).

will see their dead bodies

The phrase "from the peoples, tribes, tongues, and nations" generally speaks of a global community which is worldwide in scope and not necessarily restricted within a single city. It is unlikely that we are to understand this as describing a group of people *from* the global community who are resident in Jerusalem at the time,[94] but that the populace of the entire globe is aware of the events which are transpiring. Television or a similar technology would be a natural explanation in our own day. Bullinger, writing before 1913 and the advent of television said: "The older commentators might have felt a difficulty in understanding how the whole earth could rejoice at an event happening in Jerusalem. But in these days of electric inventions, telephones, and wireless telegraphy, we all know how the next day the whole world sympathises or rejoices together."[95]

three-and-a-half days

The global audience will not just see the dead bodies at the time they are slain, but will continue to observe the bodies over the three-and-a-half day period. That these are not to be taken as lengthy periods, but literal days, is seen from their lack of advanced decomposition at the time of their resurrection. Their bodies would have probably remained exposed and allowed to slowly decompose over an extended period, but God intervenes and resurrects them on the third day. See commentary on *Revelation 11:11*[3.11.11]. *Three* days speaks of life and resurrection. See *Three: Life, Resurrection, Completeness, the Trinity*[2.7.5.3.2].

not allow their dead bodies to be put into graves

There are at least two reasons burial is withheld from the witnesses:

1. **Jewish Sensibilities** - One reason their bodies will remain unburied is as an intentional insult to Jewish sensibilities which consider lack of burial an indication of being judged or cursed. See commentary on *Revelation 11:8*[3.11.8].
2. **Trophies to the *Beast*[5.2.9]** - Not only will their bodies be withheld from burial, but it seems likely they will be proactively protected from disturbance by scavengers, such as birds and dogs which would normally descend upon unguarded carcasses (2K. 9:10; Ps. 79:2; Jer. 7:33; Rev. 19:17-18). They are prevented from burial and protected from scavengers because they serve as trophies which testify to the power of the beast and the victory of the world over the torment which they delivered at the hand of God. So long as they lie inert on the pavement they provide visual confirmation of the superiority of the beast (Rev. 13:4).

Graves is μνῆμα [*mnēma*] which emphasizes the purpose of a tomb as a *sign of remembrance.*[96] Instead of having their own private memorial, they serve as a public memorial to the victory of the beast.

3.11.10 - Revelation 11:10

those who dwell on the earth

This *technical phrase*[5.2.72] denotes the global populace of the time of the end who consistently oppose God (Rev. 9:20), worship the beast (Rev. 13:8), and reject the things of heaven in favor of the things of earth. They are the ones for whom the time of testing is purposefully designed (Rev. 3:10).

make merry

εὐφραίνονται [*euphrainontai*], the same root word describes "eat, drink, and **be merry**" [emphasis added] (Luke 12:19). It is used "of religious and spiritual jubilation *rejoice, celebrate, be jubilant* (Acts 2:26)."[97]

Although they make merry for a few days, their triumph will be short-lived:

> That the triumphing of the wicked is short, and the joy of the hypocrite is *but* for a moment? Though his haughtiness mounts up to the heavens, and his head reaches to the clouds, *yet* he will perish forever like his own refuse; those who have seen him will say, 'Where is he?' He will fly away like a dream, and not be found; yes, he will be chased away like a vision of the night. The eye *that* saw him will *see him* no more, nor will his place behold him anymore. (Job 20:5-9)

Although the time of the end is characterized by war and disruption, worldly enemies will unite in their hatred for these two witnesses and join hands rejoicing in their demise (Luke 23:12).[98]

send gifts to one another

So great will be their elation over the death of these two prophets that they will declare a holiday and exchange gifts with one another in celebration (Ne. 8:10-12; Est. 9:19-22). The elation of the *earth dwellers*[5.2.18] over the death of the two witnesses provides evidence of the seriousness of the plagues which they meted out during their ministry. These two witnesses were not hated solely because they represented God, but all the more so because of their effectiveness at tormenting those who were affected by their plagues.

because these two prophets tormented those who dwell on the earth

Tormented is ἐβασάνισαν [*ebasanisan*] , which can describe torture in judicial examination, general harassment, or any kind of severe distress, especially physical distress. It is used to describe the results of paralysis (Mtt. 8:6), the torment inflicted by the demonic scorpions (Rev. 9:5), the eventual torment feared by demons (Mtt. 8:29), the pain of childbirth (Rev. 12:2), and the final torment of the unsaved dead (Rev. 14:10; 20:10). As prophets, they joined a long list of God's servants who were hated by those to whom they were sent (1K. 18:17; 21:20; 22:8; Jer. 38:4; Mtt. 23:37; Luke 13:33-34; John 7:7, 25; Acts 5:33; Acts 7:54-57; Acts 17:5-7).

3.11.11 - Revelation 11:11

breath of life from God entered them

Breath is πνεῦμα [*pneuma*], also rendered *spirit*. Here it speaks of the life-giving force which animates men's bodies of clay (Gen. 2:7; Job 33:4). The return of the spirit by the power of God attended the raising of the daughter of Jairus (Luke 8:54).

Although there are significant parallels between the breath of life which animates the dead witnesses and that which will animate the nation of Israel (Eze. 37:5, 10), the spiritual restoration of the nation is not in view here. This is a literal resurrection of two individuals. The Jewish nation has not yet been spiritually revived as evidenced by the opposition to the witnesses by many residing in Jerusalem (Rev. 11:13). At this point in the events of the end, the spiritual revival of the Jews is in progress, but not yet complete (Rom. 11:25-26). See commentary on *Revelation 11:13*[3.11.13].

great fear fell on those who saw them

Those who saw is θεωροῦντας [*theōrountas*], a present tense participle, *the ones presently observing them*. The "peoples, tribes, tongues, and nations" were watching the bodies of the dead prophets for the entire period they lay in the street and now saw them stand *as they watched*! Their rejoicing is cut short as they witness the unthinkable—the two dead, partially decomposing corpses rise to their feet. What they see is manifestly impossible, yet impossible to deny. Unlike the resurrection of Jesus which was witnessed by relatively few, this resurrection is seen by an international audience of probably many more. The testimony to the superiority and victory of the beast unravels in a moment and exultation turns to *great fear* as the power of God is seen to overcome even the death inflicted by the beast. The demonstration of God's power universally results in fear, especially for those who do not know Him (Jos. 2:9; Mtt. 27:54; Acts 5:5, 11).

The phrase *those who saw them* seems to speak directly to the global community rather than denoting a subset of peoples who happen to be present in Jerusalem at the time of their resurrection. The implication is that their resurrection is seen as part of a global broadcast.

3.11.12 - Revelation 11:12

they heard

The *MT*[5.2.45] text has ἤκουσα [*ēkousa*] instead of ἤκουσαν [*ēkousan*] indicating *I heard*—emphasizing what John heard said to the two witnesses rather than what they heard.[99]

Come up here.

ἀνάβατε [*anabate*], *you all come up here* . The same command was heard by John when he arose to heaven (Rev. 4:1). See commentary on *Revelation 4:1*[3.4.1]. See *Rapture*[4.14].

they ascended to heaven in a cloud

Their ascent to heaven is much like that of Jesus following His resurrection (Acts 1:9; Rev. 12:5) and that of the Church at the *Rapture*[4.14] (1Th. 4:17). Their ascent, having been resurrected from the dead, is part of the *first resurrection*:

> Although the resurrection of the righteous is called "first" in Rev. 20:4, it is not one event but embraces a series of resurrection events, "Every man in his own order: Christ the first fruits; afterward they that are Christ's at his coming" (1Cor. 15:23). Under the single profile of the first resurrection, therefore, is

> to be comprehended the resurrection of Christ, the *rapture*[5.2.62]-resurrection of church saints, and the resurrection of tribulation saints (such as the two witnesses of Rev. 11:1-19). It also comprehends the resurrection of Old Testament saints at the end of the tribulation.[100]

See commentary on *Revelation 2:11*[3.2.11].

their enemies saw them

We are specifically told that their resurrection is seen by their enemies. Their resurrection is perhaps the greatest moment of their ministry since they manifest the power and promise of God: the power to overcome death and the promise to raise believers from the grave. This, their greatest and last testimony, is not ineffectual for it contributes to the fear of those who survive the coming earthquake and results in their apparent salvation.

3.11.13 - Revelation 11:13

a great earthquake

There are numerous earthquakes during the Tribulation. A previous great earthquake attended the opening of the sixth seal (Rev. 6:12). As great as this earthquake is, a still greater earthquake—the greatest of all recorded history—is yet to follow at the pouring forth of the seventh bowl judgment (Rev. 16:17).

a tenth of the city fell

In the subsequent earthquake associated with the seventh bowl, Jerusalem is said to be "divided into three parts, and the cities of the nations fell" (Rev. 16:19). In this lesser precursor to the final great earthquake, only one tenth of the city falls. Only a portion falls resulting in a relatively lesser death toll in order to provide opportunity for those remaining to respond in repentance and turn to God.

people

ὀνόματα ἀνθρώπων [*onomata anthrōpōn*], *names of men*, as in *the number of individuals*. Some understand this as an allusion to the removal of their names from the *Book of Life*[4.4].[101]

the rest were afraid and gave glory to the God of heaven

Since the ministry of the two witnesses occurs during the first half of the final week of Daniel, they are overcome by the beast near the midpoint of the Tribulation (see *The 70th Week in Relation to the Book of Revelation*[2.13.5.5]). During this period, it appears that the covenant of the *Antichrist*[5.2.3] is in effect (Dan. 9:27) and the Jews have control of the *Temple*[5.2.73], except for the outer court, and are able to worship and offer sacrifices there (Rev. 11:1-2). Thus, the covenant has not yet been broken, the *Abomination of Desolation* has not yet transpired, and the most intense Jewish persecution has not yet occurred (Mtt. 24:15-21; Rev. 12:6, 14, 17). Thus, it is likely that the majority of the population of Jerusalem is still Jewish up to the point that the two witnesses are killed and resurrected. This would make sense since, as we have noted, the ministry of the two witnesses is very similar to Jewish prophets of old, both in their God-given powers and their wearing of sackcloth. Although the ministry of the two witnesses obviously affects the entire world, it is uniquely Jewish and seemingly designed to have the greatest impact upon those who are Jews and who have not yet accepted Jesus as Messiah. When a tenth of the city falls, the remaining population is said to give glory to the God of heaven. Their response to the final ministry of the two witnesses—their resurrection—and the subsequent earthquake is markedly different than that of the *earth dwellers*[5.2.18] in general as recorded elsewhere in the book of Revelation for these apparently repent. The text says they fear and give glory to God! In concert with the 144,000 sealed of Israel (Rev. 7:4-8), this would appear to be further evidence of the ongoing spiritual regeneration of the Jews which Paul so plainly predicted:

> For I do not desire, brethren, that you should be ignorant of this mystery, lest you should be wise in your own opinion, that blindness in part has happened to Israel until the fullness of the Gentiles has come in. And so all Israel will be saved, as it is written: "The Deliverer will come out of Zion, and He will turn away ungodliness from Jacob; for this *is* my covenant with them, when I take away their sins." (Rom. 11:25-27)

The two witnesses are special servants of the Deliverer and through their ministry ungodliness was turned away from a portion of Jacob. In the midst of the time of Jacob's trouble, remaining aspects of the New Covenant as it relates to the Jewish nation (Jer. 31:33-34) are being fulfilled in preparation for the *Millennial Kingdom*[5.2.39] to follow.

Although some commentators connect the *resurrection of the two witnesses* with Ezekiel's promise of the spiritual regeneration of Israel (Eze. 37), it is more correct to connect the *repentance of this Jewish remnant* in Jerusalem with Ezekiel's passage, although complete fulfillment will not be realized until the Second Coming of Christ.

3.11.14 - Revelation 11:14

the second woe is past

The *woes* referred to here are the three woes which correlate with the last three trumpet judgments (Rev. 8:13). These are more severe than the previous four trumpet judgments and target *men* rather than *natural systems*. The *second* woe refers to the judgments attending the sounding of the *sixth* trumpet. This verse provides a helpful indicator which correlates the events of Revelation 10 and 11 with the trumpet judgments which were underway in Revelation 8 and 9. Although the immediate effects of the second woe (the sixth trumpet judgment) come to a close with the ending of chapter 9, we are here told that the events recorded in Revelation 10 and 11 transpire *before* the end of the second woe—that is during the times of the opening of the seven seals and the sounding of the first six trumpets. This confirms our observation that the "one thousand two hundred and sixty days" during which the two witnesses prophesy (Rev. 11:3) coincides with the *first half* of *The 70th Week of Daniel*[2.13.5]. See *The 70th Week in Relation to the Book of Revelation*[2.13.5.5].

the third woe is coming quickly

The *third* woe refers to the judgments attending the sounding of the *seventh* trumpet. This would seem to indicate that the sounding of the seventh trumpet *follows* the ministry of the two witnesses and their overthrow by the beast. The seventh trumpet must sound near the midpoint of the Tribulation or early in the second half. This would position all seven of the final bowl judgments in the last half of *The 70th Week of Daniel*[2.13.5]. See *The 70th Week in Relation to the Book of Revelation*[2.13.5.5].

Each of the final seal and trumpet judgments is set off from the previous six by an interlude during which additional information and perspective is provided and the greater severity of that which is to come is emphasized. Between the opening of the sixth and seventh seal, we are informed of the 144,000 sealed of Israel and the multitude coming out of the Great Tribulation (Rev. 7:1-17). Between the sounding of the sixth and seventh trumpet, we are told of the mighty angel standing upon the earth, the book of prophesy eaten by John, the *Tribulation Temple*[4.16.5.9] , and the ministry of the two witnesses (Rev. 10:1-11:13).[102]

3.11.15 - Revelation 11:15

seventh angel sounded

The seventh angel sounds the seventh trumpet (Rev. 8:2). This last of the seven trumpets is not to be confused with the "last trump" which attends the *Rapture*[4.14].[103]

> This cannot be what is meant by *the last trump* [1Cor. 15:52]; at the time that I Corinthians was written, John had not written Revelation. The Corinthians would not have had any knowledge of the seven trumpets. The only knowledge they would have of trumpets are those spoken of in the Old Testament, especially those of the Feast of Trumpets. *The last trump* refers to the Feast of Trumpets and the Jewish practice of blowing trumpets at this feast each year. During the ceremony there are a series of short trumpet sounds concluding with one long trumpet blast which is called the *tekiah gedolah*, the great trumpet blast. This is what Paul means by *the last trump*.[104]

> This seventh trumpet is the last of this series of seven, but not the last absolutely, and is not to be confused with the "last trump" of 1Cor. 15:52. Chronologically, the trumpet of Mtt. 24:31 must follow this seventh trumpet of Revelation, for it occurs after the Tribulation, at the open manifestation of Christ's Second Advent (Mtt. 24:30), which in the book of Revelation is recorded in Rev. 19:11-16, which is after the time expressed here. In the book of Revelation the seventh trumpet is never called "last" (Rev. 1:11, 17; 2:8, 19; 15:1. 21:9; 22:13).[105]

> The seventh trumpet covers an extended period of time, thus distinguishing it from the instantaneous

("in a moment, in the twinkling of an eye" event of the "last trumpet." Instead of calling for the moment of the *Rapture*[5.2.62] of the church, as the "last trumpet" does, the seventh trumpet calls for prolonged waves of judgment on the ungodly. It does not parallel the trumpet of 1 Corinthians 15:52, but does parallel the trumpet of Joel 2:1-2: "Blow a trumpet in Zion, and sound an alarm on My holy mountain! Let all the inhabitants of the land tremble, for the day of the Lord is coming; surely it is near, a day of darkness and gloom, a day of clouds and thick darkness."[106]

The seventh trumpet is typified by the seven trumpets of the conquest of Jericho by Joshua. See commentary on *Revelation 8:2*[3.8.2].

kingdoms of this world

MT[5.2.45] and *NU*[5.2.49] texts have *kingdom* (singular).[107]

> The use of the singular term kingdom of the world instead of the plural "kingdoms" introduces an important truth. All of the world's diverse national, political, social, cultural, linguistic, and religious groups are in reality one kingdom under one king. That king is known in Scripture by many names and titles, including the accuser (Rev. 12:10), the adversary (1 Pet. 5:8), Beelzebul (Mtt. 12:24), Belial (2Cor. 6:15), the dragon (Rev. 12:3, 7, 9), the "evil one" (John 17:15), the god of this world (2Cor. 4:4), the prince of the power of the air (Eph. 2:2), the roaring lion (1Pe. 5:8), the ruler of the demons (Mark 3:22), the ruler of this world (John 12:31), the serpent of old (Rev. 12:9; 20:2), the tempter (1Th. 3:5), and, most commonly, the devil (Mtt. 4:1) and Satan (1Ti. 5:15).[108]

The sounding of the seventh trumpet "proclaims the coming coronation of earth's rightful king, the answer to the prayer of the ages, 'thy kingdom come' [Mtt. 6:10]."[109] The seventh trumpet is typified by Zadok's blowing of the horn when Solomon was anointed as King (1K. 1:39). The coming of the kingdom of God is connected with the overthrow of Satan (Rev. 12:10) and involves the reclamation of the earth as the Lord's, but now, Satan is "god of this age" (Mtt. 4:8-9; 2Cor. 4:4). See commentary on *Revelation 20:2*[3.20.2].

> The sounding of the seventh trumpet signals God's answer to the prayer, "Your kingdom come. Your will be done, on earth as it is in heaven" (Mtt. 6:10). That answer sweeps through chapters 12-22 as God finishes His mighty work of reclaiming creation from the usurper, Satan.[110]

See commentary on *Revelation 5:1*[3.5.1].

have become

ἐγένετο [*egeneto*] , singular, prophetic aorist. The event is so certain in the sounding of the seventh angel that it is treated as if already past. However, the kingdom will not have arrived in totality until all seven bowl judgments are poured forth (Rev. 16:17) and the King Himself returns to earth to defeat the armies of the nations (Isa. 63:1-6; Zec. 12:1-9; 14:1-8; Rev. 19:11-21). That day is described by many passages of which a small sample appears below:

> All the ends of the world shall remember and turn to the Lord, and all the families of the nations shall worship before You. For the kingdom is the Lord's, and He rules over the nations. (Ps. 22:27-28).
>
> He shall have dominion also from sea to sea, and from the River to the ends of the earth. Those who dwell in the wilderness will bow before Him, and His enemies will lick the dust. The kings of Tarshish and of the isles will bring presents; the kings of Sheba and Seba will offer gifts. Yes, all kings shall fall down before Him; all nations shall serve Him. (Ps. 72:8-11)
>
> Of the increase of *His* government and peace *There will be* no end, upon the throne of David and over His kingdom, to order it and establish it with judgment and justice from that time forward, even forever. The zeal of the LORD of hosts will perform this. (Isa. 9:7)
>
> And in the days of these kings the God of heaven will set up a kingdom which shall never be destroyed; and the kingdom shall not be left to other people; it shall break in pieces and consume all these kingdoms, and it shall stand forever. (Dan. 2:44)
>
> Then to Him was given dominion and glory and a kingdom, that all peoples, nations, and languages should serve Him. His dominion *is* an everlasting dominion, which shall not pass away, and His kingdom *the one* Which shall not be destroyed. (Dan. 7:14)
>
> And the LORD shall be King over all the earth. In that day it shall be-"The LORD *is* one," and His name one. All the land shall be turned into a plain from Geba to Rimmon south of Jerusalem. Jerusalem shall be raised up and inhabited in her place from Benjamin's Gate to the place of the First Gate and the

> Corner Gate, and *from* the Tower of Hananeel to the king's winepresses. *The people* shall dwell in it; and no longer shall there be utter destruction, but Jerusalem shall be safely inhabited. (Zec. 14:9-11)

> He will be great, and will be called the Son of the Highest; and the Lord God will give Him the throne of His father David. And He will reign over the house of Jacob forever, and of His kingdom there will be no end. (Luke 1:32-33)

Not one of the above passages finds literal fulfillment in the present day Church as the adherents of *Replacement Theology*[5.2.63], *Dominion Theology*[5.2.17], and Covenant Theology claim because the sounding of the seventh trumpet remains future to our time. These passages do not speak of an *invisible spiritual* kingdom, but a *visible earthly* kingdom—the *Millennial Kingdom*[5.2.39] of Revelation 20:4-6. See *The Arrival of God's Kingdom*[2.4.3].[111]

> All attempts to equate this glorious reign of Christ over the whole earth with any past event or with the church is utterly foreign and contradictory to the clear eschatological teaching of Scripture, including especially this passage. There is no way this text can be fulfilled except by the universal reign of Jesus Christ over the whole earth—as the prophets had for so long predicted.[112]

His Christ

Christ is Χριστοῦ [*Christou*], an appellative *the Anointed One, the Messiah.*[113] This speaks of His *office* as the promised Anointed One and is a direct allusion to the Father's pronouncement concerning the Son: "Why do the nations rage and the people plot a vain thing? The kings of the earth set themselves and the rulers take counsel together against the LORD and **His Anointed**, *saying*, 'Let us break Their bonds in pieces and cast away Their cords from us.' " [emphasis added] (Ps. 2:1-2). *His Anointed* is מְשִׁיחוֹ [*meshîchō*], *the anointed of His* and is a direct parallel to τοῦ Χριστοῦ αὐτοῦ [*tou Christou autou*], *the Christ of His* . The seventh trumpet proclaims the impending fulfillment of Psalm 2, especially verses 7-9 which will be realized in the pouring forth of the final seven bowls:

> "I will declare the decree: the LORD has said to Me, 'You *are* My Son, today I have begotten You. Ask of Me, and I will give *You* The nations *for* Your inheritance, and the ends of the earth *for* Your possession. You shall break them with a rod of iron; You shall dash them to pieces like a potter's vessel.' " (Ps. 2:7-9)

See commentary on *Revelation 2:27*[3.2.27].

forever and ever

εἰς τούς αἰῶνας τῶν αἰώνων [*eis tous aiōnas tōn aiōnōn*], *into the ages of the ages*. His kingdom is without end (Ex. 15:18; Ps. 10:16; 145:13; Isa. 9:7; Dan. 2:44; 4:3; 6:26; 7:14, 18, 27; Mic. 4:7; Luke 1:33; 1Ti. 1:17; 2Pe. 1:11; Rev. 11:15).

3.11.16 - Revelation 11:16

the twenty-four elders

See commentary on *Revelation 4:4*[3.4.4].

their thrones

The thrones belong to the elders. This argues for their identification as the redeemed. See commentary on *Revelation 4:4*[3.4.4].

fell on their faces

The elders are repeatedly found prostrate before the throne in worship (Rev. 4:10; 5:8, 14; 7:11; 19:4).

3.11.17 - Revelation 11:17

the Almighty

ὁ παντοκρατωρ [*ho pantokratōr*], see commentary on *Revelation 1:8*[3.1.8].

who is and who was and who is to come

See commentary on *Revelation 1:4*[3.1.4]. *MT*[5.2.45] and *NU*[5.2.49] texts omit *and who is to come.*[114] Some see the omission of this phrase as support for the *premillennial*[5.2.58] interpretation of the Second

Coming, as an indication that He has *already come* at the time His reign is taken up.[115] The expectation for the "Coming One" is clearly set forth at the first advent when Israel expected her coming King and His kingdom (Mtt. 11:3; 21:9; Luke 7:19). They will not see the king until they ask for Him (Mtt. 23:39; Luke 13:35).

reigned

ἐβασίλευσας [*ebasileusas*], an ingressive aorist, *did begin to reign.*

3.11.18 - Revelation 11:18

the nations were angry and Your wrath has come

This refers to the rage of the nations (Ps. 2:1) exhibited throughout the Tribulation by an unrelenting opposition to God. The response of God to the anger of the nations was predicted long ago: "He shall speak to them in His wrath, and distress them in His deep displeasure" (Ps. 2:5). The nations of the Tribulation are ruled by unwise kings (Rev. 17:12; 19:19) who fail to "Kiss the Son, lest He be angry and you perish *in* the way when His wrath is kindled but a little" (Ps. 2:12).

The wrath of God speaks of the entire period of the judgments which are being loosed upon the earth, beginning with the first seal loosed by the Lamb (Rev. 6:1). Even the *earth dwellers*[5.2.18] understood that God's wrath was being poured forth at the time of the opening of the sixth seal (Rev. 6:16-17). Yet, this statement is made in response to the sounding of the seventh trumpet which proclaims a period of intensified judgment specifically characterized as seven "bowls of the wrath of God" (Rev. 15:7; 16:1). In these impending "seven last plagues . . . the wrath of God is complete" (Rev. 15:1).

See *Delivered from the Wrath to Come*[4.14.6].

the time of the dead that they should be judged

Time is καιρὸς [*kairos*]. Here it denotes a "specific character of time"[116]—the time during which God will judge the dead.

Every man, once dead, will face judgment (Heb. 9:27). To Daniel it was revealed that the time of Jacob's trouble would precede the time of the judgment of the dead and that there would be two categories of resurrection: to everlasting life and to shame and everlasting contempt (Dan. 12:1-3). Later in the book of Revelation, we will find that the timing of these two categories of the resurrected dead differs by at least one thousand years. All the righteous dead are resurrected by the advent of the *Millennial Kingdom*[5.2.39] in order to participate therein, whereas the unrighteous dead are not resurrected until after the final rebellion at the close of the Millennial Kingdom. The resurrection of the unsaved dead and their final judgment is referred to as "the second death." For the saved dead who participate in the first resurrection preceding the Millennial Kingdom "the second death has no power, but they shall be priests of God and of Christ, and shall reign with Him a thousand years" (Rev. 20:6). Although the righteous dead will stand before the judgment seat of Christ, it is for reward rather than punishment and those who trust in Christ cannot themselves be lost (1Cor. 3:13-15; 2Cor. 5:10). It is in this sense that Jesus said, "Most assuredly, I say to you, he who hears My word and believes in Him who sent Me has everlasting life, and shall not come into judgment, but has passed from death into life" (John 5:24). Believers will not undergo judgment for their sins because Christ has taken their sins upon Himself in their stead.

The judgment of all those throughout history who reject Christ occurs at the Great White Throne (Rev. 20:11). This judgment cannot transpire until every last rejecter of Christ has met physical death. This is one of the purposes found in the loosing of Satan for the final rebellion at the end of the Millennium (Rev. 20:7-9)—to manifest the last generation of Christ-rejecters prior to the judgment. The result of the Great White Throne Judgment is the assigning of varying degrees of punishment, based on works, and the casting of the unsaved dead into the Lake of Fire. "This is the second death" (Rev. 20:14). See commentary on *Revelation 20:11*[3.20.11]. Jesus promised that the overcomer would not participate in the second death. See commentary on *Revelation 2:11*[3.2.11].

Since the judgment of the dead does not occur until the close of the Millennial Kingdom, it can be seen that this passage is very forward-looking, taking in a long period of history within its purview. Thus, it is describing the *results* which flow from the outworking of the seventh trumpet. This includes the outpouring of the seven bowls of wrath (Rev. 16), the return of Christ (Rev. 19), the Millennial Kingdom (Rev. 20:4-6), and the Great White Throne Judgment (Rev. 20:11-15).[117]

that you should reward your servants the prophets and the saints

The reward of the prophets and saints is associated with Christ's return (Rev. 3:11; 22:12) and is to be contrasted with the judgment of the dead just mentioned. *The prophets* refers to both *OT*[5.2.51] and *NT*[5.2.48] prophets.[118]

> (1) "Thy servants the prophets" evidently points to those who have in all ages witnessed for God. . . . "Servants" is here qualified by the additional noun, "prophets." "Thy servants the prophets." To witness for God in a dark and evil day is a service which God never forgets. All such are peculiarly His servants. (2) "The saints." This term is the common one in the New Testament to designate the general body of believers, and is nowhere used in the New Testament Scriptures to express a select company. It is the common appellation of the redeemed in both Testaments.[119]

The rewards include the many promises found throughout Scripture (Dan. 7:18; Mtt. 5:12; 10:41; 16:27; 25:34; Luke 14:14; Rom. 2:7; 1Cor. 2:9; 2Ti. 4:8; Heb. 4:9; 11:10; 2Jn. 1:8) including those related to the inheritance of the believer (Acts 20:32; 26:18; Rom. 8:17; Eph. 1:11-14; 5:5; Col. 1:12; 3:24; Heb. 9:15; 1Pe. 1:4). This includes all the promises made to the overcomer (Rev. 2:7, 11, 17, 26; 3:5, 12, 21; 21:7) and the blessings which attend the Millennial Kingdom (see *The Arrival of God's Kingdom*[2.4.3]) and the eternal state (Rev. 21, 22).[120] See *Believer's Crowns*[4.6.3].

those who fear Your name both small and great

A healthy, reverent fear undergirds the attitude of those who trust in the Lord (Jos. 24:14; 1S. 12:24; Ps. 34:9; 85:9; 102:15; 103:11; 115:13, 14; 147:11; Ecc. 8:12; 12:13; Mic. 6:9; Luke 1:50; Rev. 19:5). *Both small and great* describes every category of mankind—all variations in physical stature, wealth, or position—are found in His kingdom (Ps. 115:13; Rev. 19:5).[121]

destroy those who destroy the earth

Destroy is from διαφθείρω [*diaphtheirō*] which can denote either physical or moral destruction.[122] Here is God's assessment of modern environmentalism—which purports to radically care for the earth while denying the Creator behind the creation and creatures which it panders to. At the Second Coming, the condition of the earth has reached the equivalent of the time of the flood where "the earth is filled with violence" (Gen. 6:13). This corruption was due to the great wickedness of man in that "every intent of the thoughts of his heart *was* only evil continually" (Gen. 6:5). This is the predictable end of unregenerate men once the Restrainer is removed and the mystery of lawlessness reaches full flower (2Th. 2:7). "The word 'destroy' is the same, actually, as 'corrupt.' Man had destroyed the earth by corrupting the earth, using it not for God's glory, but instead to satisfy his own greed and lust."[123]

Some take *those who destroy the earth* as a separate category from *the nations*, as if denoting fallen angels which are under the rule of the *Destroyer*, that is "Abaddon" and "Apollyon" (Rev. 9:11).[124] But the object of their destruction would seem to be *men* rather than the earth as stated here.

3.11.19 - Revelation 11:19

the temple of God was opened in heaven

This is the heavenly temple (Isa. 6:1-4; Rev. 7:15; 14:15, 17; 15:5-6, 8; 16:1, 17), not the earthly temple in Jerusalem (Rev. 11:1-2). The chapter begins and ends with Temples: the *earthly Temple*[5.2.73] in Jerusalem and now this Temple in *heaven* is *opened* to reveal its contents to John (and subsequently to the reader). See *Temple of God*[4.16].

the ark of His covenant

The *MT*[5.2.45] text has "the ark of the covenant *of the Lord*". *Ark* is κιβωτὸς [*kibōtos*], meaning "box, chest,"[125] and is used to describe both the Ark of the Covenant (Heb. 9:4; Rev. 11:19) and Noah's Ark (Mtt. 24:38 cf. Gen. 6:14, *LXX*[5.2.38]). The *ark of His covenant* refers to the box which stood in the Holy Place containing items which testified of God's relationship with Israel.[126] This testimony had both positive and negative aspects:

> The broken tablets of the Ten Commandments (Ex. 32:19) were a witness to the great spiritual defection and breaking of the covenant by the people—a defection which almost cost them their existence as Abraham's seed (Ex. 32:10; Deu. 9:14). The pot of manna recalled the violations committed against its gathering (Ex. 16:20) and the complaints against its provision (Num. 11:16). The rod of Aaron was a visible reminder of the treasonous spirit that sought to replace God's appointed leadership (Num. 16:1-50). . . . The pot of manna revealed God's loyal love in that He continued His constant care of the nation by giving her 'daily bread' until everyone finally reached the Promised Land (Ex. 16:35; Jos. 5:12). Aaron's budded rod was graciously given to validate God's proper priesthood (Num. 17:5; 18:6-9, 23) and to preserve the lives of those who would otherwise have perished for their complaints (Num. 17:10). Finally, the book of the Law was present with the Ark to testify to every successive generation (Deu. 4:9) that God had chosen the nation not because of anything she had done but because of His own sovereign love and gracious choice (Deu. 7:6-9).[127]

There has been much speculation concerning the location of the earthly Ark of the Covenant.

> The ark of the covenant disappeared when Nebuchadnezzar destroyed the temple and carried Judah captive into Babylon 600 years before Christ. At that time "all the vessels of the house of God, great and small, and the treasures of the house of the Lord" were also taken to Babylon (2 Chronicles 36:18), as were the brass and other metals that adorned the temple (2 Kings 25:13-20). No mention, however, was made of the ark, the most important and perhaps most costly (the ark was overlaid with gold and the mercy seat and cherubim were of pure gold) item in the temple, as well as certainly the most significant item to the writers of the accounts in 2 Kings, 2 Chronicles, and Jeremiah (chapter 52, as well as the book of Lamentations). Neither was there any mention of the ark when Cyrus commissioned the rebuilding of the temple and sent back all its vessels as well (Ezra 1:1-11).[128]

Numerous locations have been suggested for the *earthly* Ark of the Covenant:

1. Shishak took the ark to Egypt (1K. 14:25-26; 2Chr. 12:2-4, 9).
2. Nebuchadnezzar took the ark to Babylon (2K. 25:13-15; 2Chr. 36:17-19; Jer. 52:17-22; cf. *Fourth Book of Ezra* 10:19-22).
3. Jeremiah hid the ark in a cave (2 Maccabees 2:4-6; Ezra 1:9-11).[129]
4. Antiochus IV (Epiphanes) took the ark to Syria (1 Maccabees 1:21-24, 57).
5. Titus took the ark to Rome.[130]
6. The ark is hidden below the Temple Mount.[131]
7. The son of the Queen of Sheba took the ark to Ethiopia.[132]
8. The ark no longer exists and will never appear again (Jer. 3:16).[133]
9. The ark was taken to heaven by God (see below).[134]

Some suggest that this passage proves that the ark has been relocated to heaven, but Scripture informs us that the earthly Temple was patterned after a greater heavenly reality (Heb. 8:4-5; Heb. 9:1-11). Thus, within the heavenly Temple we find many of the same implements as is the earthly Temple (Rev. 4:5; 6:9; 8:3, 5; 9:13; 14:18; 16:7). The revelation of an ark in the heavenly Temple no more precludes the continued existence of the earthly ark then the existence of the heavenly altar of sacrifice means the earthly one has been relocated to heaven.

Leaving aside the question of the location of the earthly ark, as interesting as it might be, what is the significance of the ark revealed in heaven? As we noted in our commentary on *Revelation 11:5*[3.11.5], there is a unique relationship between the word of God and judgment. It is God's word which establishes the righteous requirements for obedience and underwrites the definition of righteous judgment. The appearance of the Ark of *His covenant* emphasizes that which will be used as the standard for judgment. It is because of man's willful disobedience and rebellion in the light of the standard of the law that God's righteous judgment is required. His wrath is measured by the distance between the contents of the written requirements in the ark versus the actions of sinful men.

In a similar passage, "the temple of the tabernacle of the testimony in heaven was opened." There, the tabernacle of the testimony is seen to be connected to the "seven angels having the seven plagues" (Rev. 15:5-6). The mention of *covenant* and *testimony* indicate the righteous requirement of the law which judges those who are guilty and under judgment of God's wrath (Rom. 2:12; 3:19-20). For "the law brings about wrath" (Rom. 4:15). Believers will not be subject to the written requirements which were taken away in Christ (Rom. 7:6; Col. 2:14). See commentary on *Revelation 15:5*[3.15.5].

Some believe the break between chapters 11 and 12 to be placed incorrectly and take this last verse of chapter 11 as being more closely associated with the opening verse of chapter 12.[135] Both verses begin with the same conjunction (καὶ [*kai*]) offering numerous interpretive possibilities regarding their association. The suggestion is made that the Ark of the Covenant suggests God's remembrance of Israel which explains the shift in focus to the woman with child of the next chapter. But God's promises to Israel flow primarily from other covenants (Abrahamic, Davidic, New, Land) than the Law of Moses, which the ark recalls. The Law of Moses is said to have been broken which necessitated the establishment of the New Covenant (Jer. 31:31-34). Rather than a sign of God's covenant faithfulness to Israel associated with the next chapter, it seems more natural to understand the appearance of the ark as denoting the standard of the law by which all the unredeemed stand guilty of impending righteous judgment. The mention of the manifestations of impending judgment would seem more naturally to be associated with the proclamation attending the sounding of the seventh trumpet bringing wrath than the scene of chapter 12 which sets forth Israel's struggle to bring forth Messiah.

lightnings, noises, thunderings, an earthquake, and great hail

All of these manifestations speak of impending judgments of the seven bowls (Rev. 16) which are in accord with the wrath of God based upon the righteous law as recorded in the Ark of the Covenant. See commentary on *Revelation 4:5*[3.4.5]. The ark is revealed after the sounding of the seventh trumpet (Rev. 11:15), but before the seven bowls of God's wrath are poured out on the earth (Rev. 16:1-17). When the final bowl is poured forth, the manifestations of judgment seen in this heavenly scene are *delivered to earth* : lightnings, noises, thunderings, an earthquake (Rev. 16:18) and a plague of great hail (Rev. 16:21). These manifestations underscore the connection between the heavenly Ark of the Covenant (containing the "testimony," the Ten Commandments) and the final judgment of the God-rejecting world below. See commentary on *Revelation 16:21*[3.16.21].

Notes

1 John MacArthur, *Revelation 1-11 : The MacArthur New Testament Commentary* (Chicago, IL: Moody Press, 1999), Rev. 11:1.

2 James Strong, *The Exhaustive Concordance of the Bible* (Ontario: Woodside Bible Fellowship, 1996), G4464.

3 NASB.

4 A figure of speech: "*Zeugma*. The verb measure is by this figure 'yoked' to a second object which does not fit it as equally as the first, for worshippers would not be measured but taken account of."—Jerome Smith, *The New Treasury of Scripture Knowledge* (Nashville, TN: Thomas Nelson Publishers, 1992), Rev. 11:1.

5 Monty S. Mills, *Revelations: An Exegetical Study of the Revelation to John* (Dallas, TX: 3E Ministries, 1987), Rev. 11:1.

6 Timothy Friberg, Barbara Friberg, and Neva F. Miller, *Analytical Lexicon of the Greek New Testament* (Grand Rapids, MI: Baker Books, 2000), 269.

7 W. A. Criswell, and Paige Patterson, eds., *The Holy Bible: Baptist Study Edition* (Nashville, TN: Thomas Nelson Publishers, 1991), Rev. 11:1.

8 Donald Grey Barnhouse, *Revelation* (Grand Rapids, MI: Zondervan Publishing House, 1971), Rev. 11:1.

9 E. W. Bullinger, *Commentary On Revelation* (Grand Rapids, MI: Kregel Publications, 1984, 1935), Rev. 11:1.

10 Smith, *The New Treasury of Scripture Knowledge*, Rev. 11:2.

11 Frederick William Danker, and Walter Bauer, *A Greek-English Lexicon of the New Testament and Other Early Christian Literature* (Chicago, IL: University of Chicago Press, 2000), 121.

12 Barnhouse, *Revelation*, Rev. 1:2.

13 Randall Price, *The Coming Last Days Temple* (Eugene, OR: Harvest House Publishers, 1999), 484.

[14] J. A. Seiss, *The Apocalypse: Lectures on the Book of Revelation* (Grand Rapids, MI: Zondervan Publishing House, 1966), Rev. 11:2.

[15] "The best conclusion is that the twenty-three hundred days of Daniel are fulfilled in the period from 171 B.C. and culminated in the death of Antiochus Epiphanes in 164 B.C. The period when the sacrifices ceased was the latter part of this longer period. Although the evidence available today does not offer fulfillment to the precise day, the twenty-three hundred days, obviously a round number, is relatively accurate in defining the period when the Jewish religion began to erode under the persecution of Antiochus, and the period as a whole concluded with his death. The alternate theories produce more problems than they solve."—John F. Walvoord, *Daniel: The Key to Prophetic Revelation* (Chicago, IL: Moody Bible Institute, 1971), Dan. 8:14.

[16] J. Dwight Pentecost, *Things to Come: A Study in Biblical Eschatology* (Grand Rapids, MI: Zondervan Publishing House, 1958), 213.

[17] "The period termed by our Lord the 'Times of the Gentiles', commences with the capture of Jerusalem by Nebuchadnezzar. It is a period coincident from its beginning to its close, with the treading down of Jerusalem."—Arthur Walkington Pink, *The Antichrist* (Oak Harbor, WA: Logos Research Systems, 1999, 1923), s.v. "Israel and the Antichrist."

[18] Arnold G. Fruchtenbaum, *The Footsteps of Messiah*, rev ed. (Tustin, CA: Ariel Ministries, 2003), 21.

[19] Although Daniel 11:31 was fulfilled by Antiochus Epiphanes, it stands as an example of a future desecration which Jesus spoke of (Mtt. 24:15).

[20] Walter Scott, *Exposition of The Revelation* (London, England: Pickering & Inglis, n.d.), 218.

[21] "We have no hesitation in naming St. James and St. Peter as the persons indicated."—J. Stuart Russell, *The Parousia: The New Testament Doctrine of Our Lord's Second Coming* (Grand Rapids, MI: Baker Book House, 1999, 1887), 434.

[22] Isbon T. Beckwith, *The Apocalypse of John* (Eugene, OR: Wipf and Stock Publishers, 2001), 324.

[23] Daniel Wong, *"The Two Witnesses in Revelation 11,"* in *Bibliotheca Sacra*, vol. 154 no. 615 (Dallas, TX: Dallas Theological Seminary, July-Sep 1997), 345.

[24] Wong, "*The Two Witnesses in Revelation 11*," 345-346.

[25] Wong, "*The Two Witnesses in Revelation 11*," 346-347.

[26] Seiss, *The Apocalypse: Lectures on the Book of Revelation*, Rev. 11:3.

[27] Pentecost, *Things to Come: A Study in Biblical Eschatology*, 304-313.

[28] Wong, "*The Two Witnesses in Revelation 11*," 348.

[29] So [Barnhouse, *Revelation*], [MacArthur, *Revelation 1-11 : The MacArthur New Testament Commentary*], [Robert L. Thomas, *Revelation 8-22* (Chicago, IL: Moody Press, 1995)]. See [Seiss, *The Apocalypse: Lectures on the Book of Revelation*, 248-249] for a summary of the writings of various church fathers in support of the coming of Elijah prior to the end.

[30] Wong, "*The Two Witnesses in Revelation 11*," 349.

[31] Wong, "*The Two Witnesses in Revelation 11*," 349-350.

[32] MacArthur, *Revelation 1-11 : The MacArthur New Testament Commentary*, Rev. 11:3.

[33] Pentecost, *Things to Come: A Study in Biblical Eschatology*, 306.

[34] Pentecost, *Things to Come: A Study in Biblical Eschatology*, 311.

[35] Wong, "*The Two Witnesses in Revelation 11*," 349.

[36] Wong, "*The Two Witnesses in Revelation 11*," 349-350.

[37] Wong, "*The Two Witnesses in Revelation 11*," 351-352.

[38] A. R. Fausset, *"The Revelation of St. John the Divine,"* in Robert Jamieson, A. R. Fausset, and David Brown, *A Commentary, Critical and Explanatory, on the Old and New Testaments* (Oak Harbor, WA: Logos Research Systems, Inc., 1997, 1877), Rev. 11:3.

[39] Arno C. Gaebelein, *The Revelation* (Neptune, NJ: Loizeaux Brothers, 1961), Rev. 11:3-6.

[40] Pentecost, *Things to Come: A Study in Biblical Eschatology*, 306-307.

41 So [Henry Morris, *The Revelation Record* (Wheaton, IL: Tyndale House Publishers, 1983)], [Seiss, *The Apocalypse: Lectures on the Book of Revelation*], "The ancient church, including such as *Tertullian*[5.2.75], *Irenaeus*[5.2.34], and Hippolytus, were consistent in identifying the two witnesses as Enoch and Elijah."—Thomas, *Revelation 8-22*, Rev. 11:3. See [Seiss, *The Apocalypse: Lectures on the Book of Revelation*, 248-249] for a summary of the writings of various church fathers in support of the coming of the Elijah prior to the end.

42 Wong, "*The Two Witnesses in Revelation 11*," 350-351.

43 Morris, *The Revelation Record*, Rev. 11:3.

44 Pentecost, *Things to Come: A Study in Biblical Eschatology*, 307.

45 Seiss, *The Apocalypse: Lectures on the Book of Revelation*, Rev. 11:3.

46 Wong, "*The Two Witnesses in Revelation 11*," 350-351.

47 Fruchtenbaum, *The Footsteps of Messiah*, 234-235.

48 Fruchtenbaum, *The Footsteps of Messiah*, 235.

49 Barnhouse, *Revelation*, Rev. 11:3.

50 Pentecost, *Things to Come: A Study in Biblical Eschatology*, 307.

51 Robert L. Thomas, *Revelation 1-7* (Chicago, IL: Moody Press, 1992), Rev. 11:3.

52 So [Wong, "*The Two Witnesses in Revelation 11*"], [John F. Walvoord, *The Revelation of Jesus Christ* (Chicago, IL: Moody Press, 1966)], [Pentecost, *Things to Come: A Study in Biblical Eschatology*, 308].

53 Bullinger, *Commentary On Revelation*, Rev. 11:3.

54 Walvoord, *The Revelation of Jesus Christ*, Rev. 11:3.

55 "The duration of man is often reckoned in days (Gen. 47:9, 28; Ps. 90:10, 12; 119:84), whereas judgments are sometimes reckoned in months (Gen. 8:5; Rev. 9:5, 10; 13:5)."—Smith, *The New Treasury of Scripture Knowledge*, Rev. 11:3.

56 [MacArthur, *Revelation 1-11 : The MacArthur New Testament Commentary*], [Mills, *Revelations: An Exegetical Study of the Revelation to John*]

57 "The three-and-a-half year period of the prophecy of the two witnesses corresponds to the first half of the tribulation. . . . [The] absolute rule by the beast (Revelation 13:5) apparently becomes possible only by the execution of the two witnesses by the beast (Revelation 11:7) As long as the witnesses exercise such power over both men and nature, it is impossible for the beast to acquire world power."—Morris, *The Revelation Record*, Rev. 11:6.

58 "But here in revelation 11 instead of the awful advent of the Lord from heaven 'immediately' after the killing of these witnesses, we read of a hideous celebration of their death by the nations and tribes of the earth. . . . it is at the *beginning* of the *Beast*[5.2.9]'s successful blasphemous career, *that he kills these two witnesses*."—William R. Newell, *Revelation: Chapter by Chapter* (Grand Rapids, MI: Kregel Publications, 1994,c1935), Rev. 11:14.

59 Pentecost cites English: "There is thought-provoking logic in the argument that their testimony will be given during the first half of Daniel's prophetic week, and that their martyrdom will be the first persecuting act of the Beast, after he breaks his covenant with the Jews (Dan. 9:27)."—Pentecost, *Things to Come: A Study in Biblical Eschatology*, 309.

60 David Baron, *Zechariah: A Commentary On His Visions And Prophecies* (Grand Rapids, MI: Kregel Publications, 1918), 131.

61 Baron, *Zechariah: A Commentary On His Visions And Prophecies*, 135.

62 Baron, *Zechariah: A Commentary On His Visions And Prophecies*, 136.

63 "A picture is given of a day of similar gladness and joy of heart when, on account of sin pardoned, free access to God's throne granted, and the Deliverer having come anointed with the plenitude of the Spirit and sealed by God the Father, each true Israelite would invite his friends as joyful guests to partake of festal cheer under his own vine and fig-tree. The days of peace once more are seen. The glorious era of the earthly Solomon has indeed returned in greater splendour under the reign of the Prince of Peace. 'Paradise lost' has become

'Paradise regained.' "—Baron, *Zechariah: A Commentary On His Visions And Prophecies*, 122.

64 The offices of both Joshua (priestly) and Zerubbabel (civil, or kingly) will be combined in one in Messiah and the counsel of peace shall be between both offices (Zec. 6:11-13).

65 MacArthur, *Revelation 1-11 : The MacArthur New Testament Commentary*, Rev. 11:4.

66 Seiss, *The Apocalypse: Lectures on the Book of Revelation*, Rev. 11:4.

67 We do not believe it to be coincidental that the subsequent vision of Zechariah is that of a flying-scroll wherein wickedness in the form of economic measures is transported "to build a house for it in the land of Shinar; when it is ready, *the basket* will be set there on its base" (Zec. 5:11). We see the corresponding fulfillment of Zechariah's vision in subsequent events concerning Babylon in Revelation 17 and 18.

68 Baron, *Zechariah: A Commentary On His Visions And Prophecies*, 134.

69 "The verb θέλει [*thelei*] ('desires') is present indicative and makes the assumption that some will want to harm the two."—Thomas, *Revelation 8-22*, Rev. 11:5.

70 "These men are accorded miraculous power to bring fire down from heaven—they are filled with the Holy Spirit."—J. Vernon McGee, *Thru The Bible Commentary* (Nashville, TN: Thomas Nelson, 1997, c1981), Rev. 11:5.

71 The only possible exception would be the *source* of the fire being their mouths. This could be construed as a possible indicator of figurative language. Then again, how else could God indicate literal fire directly originating in their mouths? It seems there will always be room for some uncertainty when interpreting potentially figurative passages which prophesy miraculous events because the boundary between normalcy and miraculous is highly elastic and subject to the purpose of God in any given setting.

72 Danker, *A Greek-English Lexicon of the New Testament and Other Early Christian Literature*, 434.

73 MacArthur, *Revelation 1-11 : The MacArthur New Testament Commentary*, Rev. 11:6.

74 Danker, *A Greek-English Lexicon of the New Testament and Other Early Christian Literature*, 361.

75 Friberg, *Analytical Lexicon of the Greek New Testament*, 198.

76 *Therion* describes the *Antichrist*[5.2.3] in Rev. 11:7; 13:1-4, 12, 14-15, 17-18; 14:9, 11; 15:2; 16:2, 10, 13; 17:3, 7-8, 11-13, 16-17; 19:19-20; 20:4, 10. *Arnion* describes the Lamb in Rev. 5:6, 8, 12-13; 6:1, 16; 7:9-10, 14, 17; 12:11; 13:8, 11; 14:1, 4, 10; 15:3; 17:14; 19:7, 9; 21:9, 14, 22-23, 27; 22:1, 3.

77 Pink, *The Antichrist*, s.v. "The Beast."

78 Wong, "*The Two Witnesses in Revelation 11*," 353-354.

79 Fausset, "*The Revelation of St. John the Divine*," Rev. 11:7.

80 Pink, *The Antichrist*, s.v. "intro."

81 Pink, *The Antichrist*, s.v. "Names and Titles of the Antichrist."

82 Pink, *The Antichrist*, s.v. "The Papacy Not the Antichrist."

83 Bullinger, *Commentary On Revelation*, Rev. 11:7.

84 Scott, *Exposition of The Revelation*, Rev. 19:18.

85 Fruchtenbaum, *The Footsteps of Messiah*, 250.

86 Bullinger, *Commentary On Revelation*, Rev. 17:12.

87 J. B. Payne, *"Burial,"* in Geoffrey W. Bromiley, ed., *International Standard Bible Encyclopedia* (Grand Rapids, MI: William B. Eerdmans Publishing Co., 1979, 1915), 1:556.

88 The Jewishness of Revelation contributed to its lack of acceptance in the Eastern Church. See *Acceptance into the Canon*[2.10].

89 The phrase "great city" in Revelation 16:19 probably denotes Jerusalem: "The likelihood of Babylon's being named twice (or even three times if 'the cities of the nations' refers to Babylon) in the same verse is quite remote. Revelation 11:8 has a clear identification of Jerusalem as 'the great city' (Moffat, Ford). Furthermore, its separation from 'the cities of the Gentiles (or nations)' in the next phrase indicates that Jerusalem is in view. This interpretation that does justice to this context also concurs with predicted topographical changes

that will take place around Jerusalem in conjunction with the second advent (Zec. 14:4) (Seiss). Jerusalem experienced a fairly severe earthquake earlier (Rev. 11:3), but that was only partial. This earthquake will divine the city into three parts."—Thomas, *Revelation 8-22*, Rev. 16:19.

90 Danker, *A Greek-English Lexicon of the New Testament and Other Early Christian Literature*, 679.

91 Thomas, *Revelation 8-22*, Rev. 11:8.

92 "The reference to Sodom may relate to Dan. 11:37; the *Beast*[5.2.9] may well encourage homosexual orgies, thus God's blast of 'Sodom.' "—Mills, *Revelations: An Exegetical Study of the Revelation to John*, Rev. 11:8.

93 Bullinger, *Commentary On Revelation*, Rev. 11:8.

94 Thomas, *Revelation 8-22*, Rev. 11:8.

95 Bullinger, *Commentary On Revelation*, Rev. 11:9.

96 Danker, *A Greek-English Lexicon of the New Testament and Other Early Christian Literature*, 524.

97 Friberg, *Analytical Lexicon of the Greek New Testament*, 181.

98 Demonstrating the political *parable*[5.2.54]: "My enemy's enemy is my friend."

99 "Not only does the weight of external evidence favor ἤκουσαν [*ēkousan*], but since the Seer constantly uses ἤκουσα [*ēkousa*] throughout the book (24 times), copyists were more likely to substitute ἤκουσα [*ēkousa*] for ἤκουσαν [*ēkousan*] than vice versa."—Bruce M. Metzger, *A Textual Commentary on the Greek New Testament* (Stuttgart, Germany: Deutsche Bibelgesellschaft, 1994), 672.

100 Paul Lee Tan, *The Interpretation of Prophecy* (Dallas, TX: Bible Communications, Inc., 1993), 94-95.

101 "In the letter to the church in Sardis, the Lord stated that He would not blot out of the scroll of life the names of the overcomers (Rev. 3:5). Is this not further proof that there is a book containing the record of every individual who is ever born into this lost world?"—Barnhouse, *Revelation*, Rev. 11:13.

102 This pattern does not extend to the sixth and seventh bowl judgments which are consecutive and lack any discernible gap (Rev. 16:12-21).

103 See [Pentecost, *Things to Come: A Study in Biblical Eschatology*, 188-192].

104 Fruchtenbaum, *The Footsteps of Messiah*, 149.

105 Smith, *The New Treasury of Scripture Knowledge*, Rev. 11:15.

106 MacArthur, *Revelation 1-11 : The MacArthur New Testament Commentary*, Rev. 11:15.

107 "It should be noted that the word *kingdom* is singular, and so Messiah will gain the one-world kingdom of the *Antichrist*[5.2.3]."—Fruchtenbaum, *The Footsteps of Messiah*, 273.

108 MacArthur, *Revelation 1-11 : The MacArthur New Testament Commentary*, Rev. 11:15.

109 Smith, *The New Treasury of Scripture Knowledge*, Rev. 11:15.

110 MacArthur, *Revelation 1-11 : The MacArthur New Testament Commentary*, Rev. 11:15.

111 Concerning the future aspect of the kingdom: Ps. 110:1; Dan. 7:11-14, 21-22, 25-27 (cf. Rev. 19:20); Mtt. 6:2; 7:21-22; 19:28; 25:31; 26:29; Mark 14:25; Luke 11:2; 19:11, 15; 21:31; 22:16-18, 29; 22:30; 23:51; Acts 1:6-7; 1Cor. 15:24; Heb. 2:8; 2Ti. 4:1; Rev. 3:21; 12:10; 11:15, 17; 19:20 (cf. Dan. 7:11-14).

112 MacArthur, *Revelation 1-11 : The MacArthur New Testament Commentary*, Rev. 11:15.

113 Danker, *A Greek-English Lexicon of the New Testament and Other Early Christian Literature*, 886.

114 The arbitrariness of the heuristics behind textual criticism and the prevailing bias of *Critical Text* advocates against the Byzantine texts are demonstrated in the reason given for rejecting *and who is to come* from the *Critical Text*: "The addition of ὁ ἐρχόμενος ὅτι [*ho erchomenos hoti*] . . . is a typical Byzantine accretion, in imitation of the tripartite expression in 1.4, 8; cf. 4.8."—Metzger, *A Textual Commentary on the Greek New Testament*, 672. It seems when a longer reading is favored by advocates of the *Critical Text* they reason that omissions are a common copyist error. When a shorter reading is favored then the longer reading is dismissed as a "typical Byzantine accretion." The fact that the former are errors of *omission*, whereas the latter are errors of *commission*, doesn't seem to be considered. A copyist with any reverence for the text is much more likely to commit the former (resulting in the shorter reading) than the latter (resulting in the longer reading).

Therefore, in lieu of other considerations, the longer reading should normally be favored.

115 "Millenarian writers have always insisted that a personal [Premillennial] Advent is to be witnessed under the seventh or last trumpet. Now, Bengel in his *Gnomon* has shown, that by the authority of the earliest *MSS*[5.2.43]. the phrases '*and art to come* ' in Rev. 11:17, and '*and shalt be* ' in Rev. 16:5, are to be rejected. This criticism is fully sustained by the authoritative Sinaitic MSS. discovered by Prof. Tischendorf. . . . Thy should the title of 'Who is to come,' or 'the Coming One' given in Rev. 1:4, 8 and 4:8 be omitted in 11:17 and 16:5? The reason, so corroborative of our faith, was given long ago by Ansbert (as quoted by Bengel): 'They do not here subjoin, as they are accustomed, "and Who art to come;" they speak of Him *as already present*.' This omission, as the weightiest MSS. (admitted by Anti-Millenarians, as Prof. Stuart, *Com.*) prove, is not *accidental* but *intentional*, showing that the Coming One is no longer expected to come, but *has already come*. It is a beautiful, incidental, and most powerful proof confirmatory of our position, indicative of a [Premillennial] arrival and presence."—George H. N. Peters, *The Theocratic Kingdom* (Grand Rapids, MI: Kregel Publications, 1978, 1884), 2:185.

116 Danker, *A Greek-English Lexicon of the New Testament and Other Early Christian Literature*, 395.

117 "The sounding of the seventh messenger is a prolonged blast which covers the announcement of events to take place in the distant future, even after the millennial reign of Christ has been completed."—Barnhouse, *Revelation*, Rev. 11:2.

118 "The linking of prophets with apostles in Rev. 18:20 and the angel's reference to them as 'your [John's] brethren' in Rev. 22:9 shows the impossibility of excluding NT prophets from the term."—Thomas, *Revelation 8-22*, Rev. 11:18.

119 Scott, *Exposition of The Revelation*, Rev. 11:18.

120 The reward of the believer is a vast topic spanning innumerable Scriptures from which only a small sample is listed here.

121 So too are they found in *Antichrist*[5.2.3]'s: Rev. 13:16; 19:18; 20:12.

122 Danker, *A Greek-English Lexicon of the New Testament and Other Early Christian Literature*, 190.

123 Morris, *The Revelation Record*, Rev. 11:18.

124 "The event is a fulfillment of the double prophecy, "And it shall come to pass in that day, that the Lord shall punish the host of the high ones that are on high, and the kings of the earth upon the earth" (Isa. 24:21). There can be no doubt that here is a division that recognizes Satan and his followers on the one side and the earthlings on the other."—Barnhouse, *Revelation*, Rev. 11:18.

125 Friberg, *Analytical Lexicon of the Greek New Testament*, 230.

126 Concerning the contents of the ark: Ex. 16:34; 25:16, 21; 40:20; Num. 17:10; Deu. 10:2-5; 31:26; 1K. 8:9, 21; 2Chr. 5:10; 6:11; Heb. 9:4.

127 Randall Price, *In Search of Temple Treasure* (Eugene, OR: Harvest House Publishers, 1994), 53,54.

128 Morris, *The Revelation Record*, Rev. 11:19.

129 The inventory in Ezra 1:9-11 lists gold and silver dishes, silver pans, gold and silver bowls, and other articles for a total of 5,400 items. The Ark of the Covenant is not specifically listed.

130 "Vespasian resolved to build a temple to Peace, which he finished in so short a time, and in so glorious a manner, as was beyond all human expectations and opinion: for he having now by Providence a vast quantity of wealth, besides what he had formerly gained in his other exploits, he had this temple adorned with pictures and statues; for in this temple were collected and deposited all such rarities as men aforetime used to wander all over the habitable world to see, when they had a desire to see them one after another: he also laid up therein, as ensigns of his glory, those golden vessels and instruments that were taken out of the Jewish temple."—Flavius Josephus, *The Complete Works of Josephus* (Grand Rapids, MI: Kregel Publications, 1981), s.v. "Wars VII, v7." Elsewhere, Josephus records the Holy of Holies was *empty*: "The inmost part of the temple of all was of twenty cubits. This was also separated from the outer part by a veil. **In this there was nothing at all**. It was inaccessible and inviolable, and not to be seen by any; and was called the Holy of Holies." [emphasis added]—Josephus, *The Complete Works of Josephus*, s.v. "Wars V, v 5." [emphasis added]

131 "Certain Rabbis claim to have seen the Ark in a tunnel under the Temple ground in Jerusalem. The Israeli government sealed the entrance with cement because of protests from the Arabs, because it was near the Dome of the Rock. There is no proof that the Ark is there." [*www.bibleandscience.com*]

[132] "Supposedly, King Solomon had a son by the Queen of Sheba named Menelik. When he grew up Menelik returned to Jerusalem for a copy of the Ark of the Covenant which Solomon gave to him. But Menelik secretly switched the real Ark with the replica. Menelik took the real Ark back to Ethiopia. Traditionally, Sheba is located in Saudi Arabia not Ethiopia.—[*www.bibleandscience.com*]"

[133] "Certain it is, that the ark in the future is not to be brought to light, spite of speculation and guess-work to the contrary. On this Jeremiah speaks with no uncertain voice (Jer. 3:16). The ark, the sign of Jehovah's presence and faithfulness, will no longer be needed in the palmy days of the kingdom, for *that* which it signified will then be an accomplished reality. Jehovah will have made good His unchanging grace to His people, and His throne and presence in their midst will gloriously supersede the ark in the *tabernacle*[5.2.69] and temple of old."—Scott, *Exposition of The Revelation*, Rev. 11:19.

[134] Morris, *The Revelation Record*, Rev. 11:19.

[135] [Scott, *Exposition of The Revelation*, Rev. 11:19], [Gaebelein, *The Revelation*, Rev. 11:19].

3.12 - Revelation 12

3.12.1 - Revelation 12:1

The scene which John is shown next is an extension of what has preceded. In the previous chapter, *Revelation 11*[3.11] , John was shown two witnesses who prophesied and tormented the whole world and were eventually killed in Jerusalem. The character of their ministry is that of Jewish *OT*[5.2.51] prophets and their connection with Jerusalem emphasizes their probable Jewishness. It is our view that one of their ministries is to act as witnesses in a way which is especially effective at reaching unbelieving Jews and so contribute toward the spiritual restoration of Israel prophesied elsewhere in Scripture (Jer. 31:34-37; Eze. 37; Rom. 11:25-27).

Now, the scene shifts to a series of signs which depict a woman struggling against her adversary, the dragon. This too is a *Jewish scene*, but with aspects which range all the way back to man's Fall in the Garden of Eden and the subsequent promise of a redeemer. The signs which John sees in heaven portray events which have happened and will happen on the earth.

a great sign

Sign is σημεῖον [*sēmeion*], from the same root word translated *signified* in *Revelation 1:1*[3.1.1]. It indicates that what John sees is symbolic or figurative of the reality being conveyed. This is not a real woman in the heavens standing literally on the moon! Rather, the elements which John sees *signify* truths which are not directly stated in the text, but which are conveyed by the symbolism. "A picture is worth a thousand words." In this case, the symbolism is drawn *entirely from the OT*—as one might expect since all revelation is given by the same Holy Spirit.

> And the fact that we are here told that this is a *sign*, goes far to prove that the Apocalypse in general is to be taken literally, except where indication to the contrary is given. It would be quite superfluous to tell us that this thing is a sign, and that certain things mean certain other things, except upon the assumption that whatever is not so labelled is to be taken just as it reads, . . . But, whatever else is literal in this book, the case of this woman is not.[1]

See *Interpreting Symbols*[2.7]. See commentary on *Revelation 1:1*[3.1.1].

a woman

John is introduced to a woman. She is one of a number of women found in Scripture. Within this book alone, we find four important women:

1. *Jezebel*[5.2.35] of Thyatira typifies the apostate church, which is not taken in the *Rapture*[4.14], but contributes to *The Great Harlot*[4.1.4]. See commentary on *Revelation 2:20*[3.2.20], *Jezebel*[4.9].
2. The woman before us in Revelation 12 who struggles to give birth and then flees from the dragon to the wilderness.
3. The woman of Revelation 17 who is said to be a "great *Harlot*[5.2.25]" (Rev. 17:1). See commentary on *Revelation 17:1*[3.17.1], see *The Great Harlot*[4.1.4].
4. The bride (Rev. 19:7; 21:2, 9; 22:17).

Each of these women symbolizes a spiritual system or development of importance from the perspective of God. Although the symbolism must not be missed, neither should it be overemphasized because the symbols also speak of *real people* who participate or contribute to each system of development in *real history* . So although the symbols which these women represent may span more than an individual lifetime, at any given time in history, the women consist of a portion of the human population. And so it will be with the woman before us here. She denotes a spiritual development spanning back to Eve, but also a specific group of individuals who make up that development at the time of the end, when she flees for 1260 days (Rev. 12:6).

There are two main errors which consistently arise in interpretations of this chapter. We hope to avoid both:

- **Pagan Symbolism** - Many commentators attribute the symbolism in this chapter to pagan sources. The significance of the woman, and the attendant sun and moon, is thought to be found by searching out vague similarities from pagan mythologies. But such an approach has several shortcomings. *First*, it assumes that God subjected the correct understanding of His *inspired*[5.2.33] revelation to a dependence upon uninspired and blasphemous writings of those who do not know Him. *Second* , it ignores the many evidences that suggest just the opposite: that pagan mythology is dependant upon God's inspired revelation—serving up a vague distorted echo of the truth (e.g., the heel of Achilles, Gen. 3:15). See *Searching Pagan Mythology*[2.7.5.4.1].
- **The Church is Everywhere** - Among those commentators which manage to steer clear of interpreting this woman from a background of pagan sources, another error beckons: that of pouring the Church into every passage of Scripture from the beginning of Genesis through the end of Revelation and everywhere in between. Clear clues in the text which preclude an interpretation of the woman as the Church are ignored in favor of a preunderstanding that since this woman appears to be glorious, she *must* denote the "Church Triumphant!" But this view runs roughshod over the many interpretive clues in the text before us: "By far the majority interpretation is that the woman is 'the church' which is entirely unsatisfactory and ignores all sorts of basic interpretive cues: (1) Christ birthed the church (Mtt. 16:18), not the other way around. (2) The sun/moon/stars have a direct corollary in Joseph's dream (Gen. 37:9). Sun = Joseph's Father (Jacob), moon = Jacob's mother, 11 stars = brothers (12 stars meaning all twelve tribes). Hence a strong reference to Israel. (3) The reference to 'clothed with the sun' and 'the moon under her feet' refer to many passages which declare that the promises made to Israel (especially for a Davidic ruler and the continuation of the nation) can be thwarted only if the sun and moon can be made to cease from before God (Ps. 89:35-37; Jer. 31:36). Hence the reference is to the permanence of Israel and its promises in the mind of God as evidenced by His oaths involving the sun and moon. (4) The woman travails to give birth to the man-child (singular, male) who is caught-up. This would seem a clear allusion to the promise of the seed of the woman (Gen. 3:15) and the man-child is obviously Christ and not [the *Rapture*[5.2.62] of] the church."[2]

As we shall see as we proceed through the chapter, the woman is best understood as representing *Israel*, but with elements which reflect the role of *Mary* and which stretch back all the way to *Eve* and the promise of a redeemer (Gen. 3:15). This harmonizes with the gospels which present both aspects of Messiah: his Jewish (Abrahamic) genealogy (Mtt. 1:1) and his human (Adamic) genealogy (Luke 3:23). See *Four Gospels*[4.7]. To capture all that is related concerning the woman, she must be seen as representing an historic development within God's overall plan which:

1. Originated with the promise of a redeemer to *Eve* (Gen. 3:15).
2. Led to the creation of the nation of *Israel* through whom the redeemer would come (Isa. 7:14; 9:6-7; Mic. 5:2; Rom. 9:5).
3. Found partial fulfillment in His First Coming by virgin birth from *Mary* (Isa. 7:14; Mtt. 1:25; Luke 1:34).
4. Finds ultimate fulfillment in His Second Coming to establish the *Millennial Kingdom*[5.2.39] and to rule in the line of King David of Israel (Isa. 9:7; Jer. 23:5; 30:9; Amos 9:11; Zec. 6:12-13; Luke 1:32-33; Acts 1:6; Rev. 20:4). It is this aspect, often overlooked, which explains the continued persecution of the woman *after* having birthed the Man Child.

> That Israel will play a key role in the end-time drama is not surprising. The seventieth week of Daniel's prophecy (the Tribulation) will primarily concern Israel, just as the first sixty-nine did (cf. Dan. 9:24-27). Israel's presence in the end times is consistent with God's emphatic promises of her continued existence as a nation . . . (Jer. 31:35-37; cf. 33:20-26; 46:28; Amos 9:8).[3]

3.12.1.1 - A Virgin and a Harlot

In contrast to *The Great Harlot*[4.1.4] of Revelation 17 who embodies the very origins of harlotry and blasphemy (also stretching back in history), as the deliverer of the redeemer she represents the development of God's ultimate *solution* to the problem of the *Harlot*[5.2.25]. A comparison of this woman with *The Great Harlot*[4.1.4] is instructive:

Two Women Compared

Woman with Sun and Moon	Woman who Rides the *Beast*[5.2.9]
Clothed with the sun (Rev. 12:1).	Clothed with purple and scarlet (Rev. 17:4).
A virgin (Isa. 7:14; Mtt. 1:25; Luke 1:34-35).	A fornicator (Rev. 17:4).
In pain (Rev. 12:2).	At ease, drunk (Rev. 17:4, 6; 18:7).
Stands (Rev. 12:1).	Sits (Rev. 17:3, 9, 15).
Supported by moon (Rev. 12:1).	Supported by beast (Rev. 17:3).
Head crowned (Rev. 12:1).	Head marked as harlot (Rev. 17:5).
Persecuted by dragon (Rev. 12:4, 13).	Rides beast empowered by dragon (Rev. 13:1-4; 17:3).
Flees to wilderness (Rev. 12:6, 14).	Seen from the wilderness (Rev. 17:3).
Associated with Jerusalem (Rev. 12:5 cf. Rev. 11:8).	Associated with Babylon (Rev. 17:5, 18).

clothed with the sun

Clothed is περιβεβλημένη [*peribeblēmenē*], a perfect tense participle: *having been clothed*, "cast around, wrapped in."[4] When John saw her, she had already been clothed by God and enjoyed the protection afforded by her clothing (Isa. 61:10).

Her being clothed with the sun is often the departure point for grand speculative expositions which interpret the woman as the church or specifically as Mary, the mother of Christ.[5] It is also a frequent point of departure to search pagan writings for an understanding of her interpretation. One of the problems with such an approach is that the sun is employed as a symbol in many different ways in many different writings. The key to understanding the contribution of the sun to the identity of the woman is found by examining the way the sun is used *within Scripture*.

First, it should be noted that a primary function of clothing is to provide shelter and protection from external elements.

> Thus says the Lord GOD to Jerusalem: "Your birth and your nativity *are* from the land of Canaan; your father *was* an Amorite and your mother a Hittite. *As for* your nativity, on the day you were born your navel cord was not cut, nor were you washed in water to cleanse *you* you were not rubbed with salt nor wrapped in swaddling cloths. No eye pitied you, to do any of these things for you, to have compassion on you; but you were thrown out into the open field, when you yourself were loathed on the day you were born. And when I passed by you and saw you struggling in your own blood, I said to you in your blood, 'Live!' Yes, I said to you in your blood, 'Live!' I made you thrive like a plant in the field; and you grew, matured, and became very beautiful. *Your* breasts were formed, your hair grew, **but you *were* naked and bare**. When I passed by you again and looked upon you, indeed your time *was* the time of love; **so I spread My wing over you and covered your nakedness**. Yes, I swore an oath to you and entered into a covenant with you, and you became Mine," says the Lord GOD. "Then I washed you in water; yes, I thoroughly washed off your blood, and I anointed you with oil. **I clothed you** in embroidered cloth and gave you sandals of badger skin; I clothed you with fine linen and covered you with silk." Eze. 16:3-10 [emphasis added]

Whatever the sun represents, it protects the woman in some way. "For the LORD God is a sun and shield" (Ps. 84:11a). When we examine the Scriptural use of the sun, we find both the sun and the moon often appear together as a *dual witness*. When God created the sun and moon, He said they would be "for signs and seasons, and for days and years" (Gen. 1:14). Most of us can readily understand how the sun is for "seasons, and for days and years," but in what way is the sun "for signs?"

The word for *sign* here is אוֹת [*`ōt*] which indicates a token or mark, something designed as a memorial, *to bring to remembrance*.[6] It is the same word which describes Cain's mark (Gen. 4:15), the *sign* of the rainbow (a memorial of God's covenant with Noah, Gen. 9:12), the *sign* of circumcision (a memorial of the Abrahamic covenant), the *sign* of the Passover (a memorial of the Exodus, Ex. 13:9), and the *sign* of the Sabbath (a memorial of the Mosaic covenant, Ex. 31:13). Thus, one function of the sun was to be used as a reminder in various ways. We've already seen one such use of the sun in our study of Revelation because God promised there would be *signs* in the sun and the moon at the time of the end (see commentary on *Revelation 6:12*[3.6.12]). We also know that there was a great sign via the sun when Jesus was crucified (Luke 23:45). Perhaps some of the signs of the sun in the time of the end are intended to bring the crucifixion to mind?

There is another way in which the sun serves as a sign, along with the moon. God uses the sun and the moon as dual witnesses to important promises He has made, much in the same way that He swears by heaven and earth.[7] Of particular interest to our passage, God has said that both sun and moon will be witnesses (signs) of His unconditional promise to *preserve the nation Israel*:

> Thus says the LORD, Who gives the **sun** for a light by day, the ordinances of the **moon** and the stars for a light by night, Who disturbs the sea, and its waves roar (The LORD of hosts *is* His name): **"If those ordinances depart from before Me, says the LORD, *then* the seed of Israel shall also cease from being a nation before Me forever."** Thus says the LORD: "If heaven above can be measured, and the foundations of the earth searched out beneath, I will also cast off all the seed of Israel for all that they have done," says the LORD. (Jer. 31:35-37) [emphasis added]

In relation to the events which transpire in Revelation 11 concerning the two witnesses, we note that the promise to preserve the nation Israel is found in the context of His promise to regenerate the nation —the only explicit mention of the New Covenant in the OT. This promise given through Jeremiah is essentially restated in the words of Paul: "I say then, has God cast away His people? Certainly not! For I also am an Israelite, of the seed of Abraham, *of* the tribe of Benjamin" (Rom. 11:1).

Let the reader and the nations of the world take note! **The Jews will continue as a people so long as the sun and moon remain visible in the sky!** If the enemies of Israel understood the full impact of this verse, they would immediately reprogram their missiles for a new target: they must first take out the sun and moon before they will be able to wipe out the *physical seed* of Abraham, Isaac, and Jacob!

The sun and moon not only witness of His promise to preserve the nation, but also His promise that the throne of David shall continue before Him and that there will be Levites to minister to Him:

> Once I have sworn by My holiness; I will not lie to David: his seed shall endure forever, and his throne as the sun before Me; it shall be established forever like the moon, even *like* the faithful witness in the sky. Selah (Ps. 89:35-37)

> Thus says the LORD: 'If you can break My covenant with the day and My covenant with the night, so that there will not be day and night in their season, then My covenant may also be broken with David My servant, so that he shall not have a son to reign on his throne, and with the Levites, the priests, My ministers. As the host of heaven cannot be numbered, nor the sand of the sea measured, so will I multiply the descendants of David My servant and the Levites who minister to Me.' (Jer. 33:20-23a)

As we have seen, Jesus is not now seated on the throne of David, an *earthly throne centered in Jerusalem*. These promises are important to grasp because they are key to understanding why the dragon continues to persecute the woman, even after she successfully brings forth the Man Child Who then accomplishes the crucifixion and resurrected. For what purpose could the dragon have in pursuing the woman beyond the victory of Messiah at the cross? The answer is found in understanding that God's purposes include elements which go beyond the crucifixion, but include promises and themes which are intimately connected with the Second Coming when Christ returns to earth to establish His millennial reign. See commentary on *Revelation 3:21*[3.3.21]. See *The Arrival of God's Kingdom*[2.4.3].

The promise that Israel will always exist is a key motivator behind the doctrine of the faithful remnant of Jewish believers which stretches throughout Scripture. It is part and parcel of the sealing of the

144,000 in Revelation 7:4. See commentary on *Revelation 7:4*[3.7.4].

with the moon under her feet

The emphasis in relation to the *moon under her feet* is not so much *standing upon*, as in trampling or having authority over, but *being supported*. She is clothed (sheltered) by the sun and standing (supported by) the moon. Her position is sure. (See commentary above concerning the promises of God to Israel witnessed by the sun and the moon.)

a garland of twelve stars

Garland is στέφανος [*stephanos*]. See *Crowns*[4.6]. Here we are given another evidence concerning the identification of this woman. What do these stars represent? Earlier we saw that stars represented angels of the churches (Rev. 1:20). But they were only *seven* in number, not twelve. At times, stars also represent angels (Job 38:7; Rev. 9:1; (4). Yet here the stars are not in isolation, but found with the *sun and moon*. This clearly is an allusion to Joseph's dream which mentions the sun, moon, and stars:

> Then he dreamed still another dream and told it to his brothers, and said, "Look, I have dreamed another dream. And this time, the **sun**, the **moon**, and the **eleven stars** bowed down to **me**." So he told *it* to his father and his brothers; and his father rebuked him and said to him, "What *is* this dream that you have dreamed? Shall your mother and I and your brothers indeed come to bow down to the earth before you?" (Gen. 37:9-10) [emphasis added]

The sun represents his father Jacob, the moon represents *Leah*,[8] and the eleven stars represent his eleven brothers. When we include Joseph as an additional star, we have our sun, moon, and twelve stars. This is perhaps the most important aspect of the identification of the woman: the *twelve* stars are to be understood in the sense of the *gates* (tribes) rather than the *foundations* (apostles—representing the church) of the New Jerusalem (Rev. 21:12). See *Twelve: Jewish Tribes, Completeness*[2.7.5.3.7].

3.12.2 - Revelation 12:2

being with child

ἐν γαστρὶ ἔχουσα [*en gastri echousa*], *in the womb having*. Something we should immediately notice about this entire vision is the lack of any mention of a father. This is most uncharacteristic of a Jewish writing dealing with genealogy (cf. Mtt. 1:1; Luke 3:23). The lack of a father is significant and, when combined with the rest of Scripture (Isa. 7:14; Luke 1:34), points strongly toward the virgin birth. Another point which is critical that we understand: the woman *produces* the child and not the other way around! How often commentators stumble over this simple point! If we keep in mind that the woman is the source of the child, then we avoid all sorts of confusion as to the identity of the woman in relation to the child. She is the *mother* of the child and not his offspring!

cried out in labor

κράζει [*krazei*], present tense, the woman was in the midst of birth pangs at the time John saw her. Although Scripture is replete with instances of women experiencing birth pangs, this is one instance where the pain is both symbolic and *literal* for it finds its fulfillment in the virgin birth of Christ by Mary. Yet there is more.

Remember that the book we have before us is one of *two bookends*[2.13.8] of Scripture, and that many of the themes from the beginning of creation (Gen. 1) are to be brought to consummation in the eternal state (Rev. 22). When we consider the woman *in labor* from the perspective of the grand scheme of Scripture, we think immediately of the curse. For it is at the curse, God's response to The Fall of mankind, where we see the first mention of both childbirth and labor pain:

> And the LORD God said to the woman, "What *is* this you have done?" The woman said, "The serpent deceived me, and I ate." So the LORD God said to the serpent: "Because you have done this, you *are* cursed more than all cattle, and more than every beast of the field; on your belly you shall go, and you shall eat dust All the days of your life. And I will put enmity Between you and the woman, and between your seed and her Seed; He shall bruise your head, and you shall bruise His heel." To the woman He said: "I will greatly multiply your sorrow and your conception; in pain you shall bring forth children; your desire *shall be* for your husband, and he shall rule over you." (Gen. 3:13-16)

Notice several elements of this most important passage and their correlation with the chapter before us:

1. A woman and the serpent.
2. Enmity between the woman and the serpent.
3. Conflict between her offspring and the serpent.
4. Childbirth (first mention in Genesis).
5. The woman will experience labor pains.

The ties between the curse brought about by The Fall and the events of the chapter before us are undeniable![9]

Here we see the Eve/Mary aspect of the symbolism of the woman. For Eve received the initial promise that a redeemer would come by the seed of a woman.[10] Thus is the genius of God: *through the same vessel by which mankind fell would the redeemer of mankind come forth!* The woman was first to eat of the forbidden fruit, but she would have the ultimate honor of producing the Fruit which would crush the head of the serpent![11] This promise of a redeemer must be seen as a backdrop for all Biblical history which flows forward from this point. It must never be forgotten or overlooked. In all the subsequent births, deaths, covenants, kingdoms, and promises, *this central promise of the redeeming seed through woman* is paramount in God's plan. This, and nothing less, is what is set before us in this chapter of John's vision.

We find another woman in Scripture who is in labor. Unlike this woman, she gives birth *before* her labor pain came. "Before she was in labor, she gave birth; before her pain came, she delivered a male child" (Isa. 66:7). This speaks of the suddenness of the establishment of the Jewish nation prior to the Millennium (cf. Mic. 5:3-5; Mtt. 24:8):

> The people and their land will be reborn in a day (Rom. 11:26), suddenly at the Messiah's coming (Zec. 12:10-13:1), unaccompanied by travail pains (Isa. 54:1, 4-5). . . . The figure of the male child comprehends the spiritually regenerated nation, the many sons being viewed as one under the returning Messiah, who will then be manifested as their one representative Head. . . . Will the LORD begin and not finish His work of restoring Israel?[12]

> While it has been customary for commentators to view this as the church (spiritual Israel) quickly springing up and spreading across the world, it should rather be viewed as converted Israel who will come to faith during the Tribulation Period and quickly spread the message of the gospel around the world.[13]

Thus, the labor of our woman precedes and differs from the woman of Isaiah 66. Our woman has been in labor for long ages. She labored from the first promise to Eve until its culmination in the virgin Mary:

> But when the fullness of the time had come, God sent forth His Son, born of a woman, born under the law, to redeem those who were under the law, that we might receive the adoption as sons. (Gal. 4:4-5)

No matter how definite the text before us, there will always be some who avoid the obvious in favor of another interpretation. Thus it is with those who attempt to make the woman the Church, totally reversing the symbolism of the text which indicates that she gives birth to Christ and not the other way around:

> Israel, not the Church, gave birth to Christ (Rom. 9; Mic. 5; Isa. 9:6; Heb. 7:14). In no possible sense did the Church do so. Seiss, generally very helpful, most strenuously asserts the Woman to be "the Church Universal"—whom he calls "the Mother of us all," etc. But this is a Romish relict, nothing else. The "church of all ages" is a pleasant theological dream, wholly unscriptural. No wonder Mr Seiss proceeds to call the Child "the whole regenerated purchase of the Savior's blood," though how the Mother and the Child can be thus *the same company*, even the author's utmost vehemence fails to convince you! [Seiss: Lectures 26 and 28][14]

3.12.3 - Revelation 12:3

another sign appeared in heaven

Like the woman clothed with the sun and the moon under her feet, a second sign is introduced. These two signs are meant to find juxtaposition and highlight the contest between God's promise to the woman and the intention of the dragon to undermine God's work.

fiery red dragon

Red is πυρρὸς [*pyrros*] meaning *fiery red* , like the horse which rode forth at the loosing of the second seal (Rev. 6:4). The color speaks of blood and destruction.

> With what carnage and misery has he overflooded the earth! There has never been a murder, but he caused it. There has never been a sanguinary war, but he instituted it. There has never been a death scene, but it is traceable to him. Every blight of human happiness, every failure of human peace, every sorrow of human life, has come from him. All the fiery passions that rankle in men, and break forth in deeds of violence and blood, are his inspirations.[15]

The dragon is a key player in the events of the end time. He is explained to be "that serpent of old, called the Devil and Satan" (Rev. 12:9b). It is the dragon who gives the beast his power, throne, and great authority (Rev. 13:2) and receives worship along with the beast (Rev. 13:4). His words are those spoken by the *False Prophet*[5.2.20] (Rev. 13:11). Later, a demonic spirit comes forth from the mouth of the dragon to lead the kings of the earth to the *Campaign of Armageddon*[4.5] (Rev. 16:13). Although he works intensely during the period of the end (Rev. 12:12), he is unable to prevail and is eventually cast into the bottomless pit (Rev. 20:2). The dragon is known by several names:

> Five names are given to Satan, all describing his person and his work. In the *great dragon*, his fierceness and ferociousness is seen. The *old serpent* points back to the Garden of Eden . . . In the word *devil* [*diabolos*], Satan is viewed as the accuser of all of God's children. *Satan* means adversary and in this he is seen as the opponent to God's program. As the *deceiver*, he is pointed out as the great master counterfeiter who attempts to deceive the elect and non-elect alike.[16]

> Professor Milligan says: "In these words ['devour,' Rev. 12:5] we have the dragon doing what Pharaoh did to Israel (Ex. 1:15-22), and again and again, in the Psalms and the Prophets, Pharaoh is spoken of as `the dragon'(Ps. 74:13; Isa. 27:1; 51:9; Eze. 29:3). Nor is it without interest to remember that Pharaoh's crown was wreathed with a dragon (the asp or serpent of Egypt), and that just as the eagle was the ensign of Rome, so the dragon was that of Egypt. Hence, the significance of Moses' rod being turned into a serpent."[17]

See *#15 - Dragon*[4.3.2.15].

seven heads and ten horns

Some see the seven heads and ten horns as representing the original *ten* kings of the time of the end, three of which are overcome by the *little horn*[4.3.2.25] leaving *seven* (Dan. 7:8).[18] We believe it is better to understand the heads and horns as representing *different entities* rather than different numbers (phases) of the same group of kings. We believe the seven heads represent seven sequential kingdoms of history while the ten horns represent the ten contemporaneous kings which emerge from the final kingdom (Dan. 7:7). See *Beasts, Heads, and Horns*[4.3].

The Dragon with Seven Heads [19]

Albrecht Durer's woodcut above, as beautiful and devotional as it is, fails to convey an important detail of the image seen by John: the placement of the ten horns in relation to the seven heads. Although Scripture gives no explicit indication of their arrangement, a study of related passages indicates that all ten horns are found on one head—the seventh, or last, head. "If the seven heads stand for seven successive world empires, the ten horns must be on the seventh head to agree with Daniel's placement of the ten horns at the time of the end (Dan. 7:24)."[20] See *#4 - Seven Heads/Kings*[4.3.2.4]. See *#22 - Ten Horns/Kings*[4.3.2.22].

seven diadems on his heads

Some believe *diadem* speaks of royalty whereas *stephanos* a victor. But this may be an oversimplification as these terms are not technical terms, but have an emphasis defined by the context. See *Crowns*[4.6]. Here, the seven diadems denote seven kings and seven historic kingdoms. See *#4 - Seven Heads/Kings*[4.3.2.4]. The ten horns upon the seventh head also wear ten crowns (Rev. 13:1). See *#22 - Ten Horns/Kings*[4.3.2.22]. These are the kingdoms which were delivered to Satan and through which he has dominated earthly history:

> Then the devil, taking Him up on a high mountain, showed Him all the kingdoms of the world in a moment of time. And the devil said to Him, "All this authority I will give You, and their glory; for *this* has been delivered to me, and I give it to whomever I wish. Therefore, if You will worship before me, all will be Yours." (Luke 4:5-7)

At the time of the end, he shares this authority with the *Beast*[4.3.2.16] who also has these seven heads (Rev. 13:1).

3.12.4 - Revelation 12:4

his tail drew

Drew is σύρει [*syrei*]: "To drag, pull, draw . . . in catching fish,"[21] "as moving someone or something along by force."[22] He exhibited considerable influence over the stars with his tail. He was key in their rebellion. This is not his final casting out, but his original fall in sin and corruption of a portion of the heavenly host (Isa. 14:12; Eze. 28:14). This occurred early in God's created order, prior to the temptation of Eve in the Garden of Eden (Gen. 3:1-5).

a third of the stars of heaven

Stars refer to the angels (messengers or leaders) of the churches (Rev. 1:20). They also refer to angels (Job 38:7; Rev. 9:1; (4). Here, they refer to angels which followed the dragon in his rejection of God and fall into sin (Isa. 14:12; Eze. 28:15). They are "his angels" (Rev. 12:7, 9). Since there is an innumerable host of angels (see commentary on *Revelation 5:11*[3.5.11]), one-third of such a vast number is countless. Those angels which remained in heaven are God's elect (1Ti. 5:21).

threw them to the earth

Fallen angels (demons) were on the earth well in advance of Christ's advent (Gen. 6:2-4; 1K. 22:22-23; 2Chr. 18:21-22). See commentary on *Revelation 9:1*[3.9.1].

woman who was ready to give birth

The promised birth witnessed by the law and the prophets (Gen. 3:15; Isa. 7:14; 9:6-7) was about to find fulfillment (Mtt. 1:20; Luke 1:34). See commentary on *Revelation 12:2*[3.12.2].

to devour her child

As God had prophesied, there was established ongoing enmity between the seed of the woman and the seed of the serpent (Gen. 3:15). This is born out in the lengthy pattern throughout history of attempts to destroy the line leading from Adam—through Abraham—to bring forth the promised Lion from the tribe of Judah (Gen. 49:10). See diagram and commentary at *Revelation 5:5*[3.5.5].

Historic evidence of Satan's attempt to thwart the Messianic promise is abundant: Cain's murder of Abel (Gen. 4:8); the pollution of the offspring of men by the "sons of God" with the "daughters of men" (Gen. 6:2-4);[23] Pharaoh's attempt to kill all male Hebrews (Ex. 1:16, 22; Acts 7:19); Haman's attempt to wipe out the Jews (Est. 3:6); Athaliah, Ahaziah's mother, attempts to wipe out all the royal heirs of Judah (2Chr. 22:10); Herod's slaughter of the babes in his attempt to murder Jesus (Mtt. 2:16). "The most direct attempt was, of course, in the crucifixion of Christ."[24] The importance of the line leading to the Messiah is also seen in God's supernatural intervention to allow Sarah to conceive in her old age (Heb. 11:11).

Ultimately, the seed of the serpent did in fact bruise the heel of the redeemer—at His crucifixion (John 8:44). Yet this "victory" of the serpent resulted ultimately in the bruising of his own head (Gen. 3:15). For the child overcame death and was ultimately caught up to God (see commentary on *Revelation 12:5*[3.12.5]).

as soon as it was born

Although the serpent stood before the woman over an extended period of time, he made one last attempt when the child was first born. Through Herod, the serpent ordered the slaughter of all male children in Bethlehem and its districts who were two years old and under (Mtt. 2:16).

3.12.5 - Revelation 12:5

a male child who was to rule with a rod of iron

To rule is Ποιμαίνειν [*Poimainein*]: "Herd, tend, (lead to) pasture."[25] Elsewhere, it is translated as *feed* (Luke 17:7; John 21:16; Acts 20:28; 1Cor. 9:7; 1Pe. 5:2; Jude 1:12), but also *rule* (Mtt. 2:6; Rev. 2:27; 7:17; 12:5; 19:15). Ruling, but in the sense of leading, guiding, protecting, as a shepherd.[26] A related noun, ποιμεν [*poimen*] is translated by *pastor* (Eph. 4:1) and *shepherd* (Mtt. 9:36; 25:32; 26:31; Mark 6:34; 14:27; Luke 2:8, 15-20; John 10:2, 11-16; Heb. 13:20; 1Pe. 2:25).

A rod of iron alludes to Psalm 2 which makes clear that the initial form of His rule will be violent. "They shall be dashed to pieces like the potter's vessels" (Ps. 2:8 cf. Rev. 2:27; 19:15). His rule with the rod extends through those who will co-rule with him. "Scripture clearly shows that Christ (Ps. 2:8), the man child (Rev. 12:5), the church saints (Rev. 2:26-27), the tribulation saints (Rev. 20:4-6), and indeed all the saints (Ps. 149:6-9) are to so rule."[27] The certainty of the rule of Christ and His kingdom was set forth in the sounding of the seventh trumpet (Rev. 11:15-18). See *The Arrival of God's Kingdom*[2.4.3]. See commentary on *Revelation 2:27*[3.2.27] and *Revelation 11:15*[3.11.15].

caught up

Ἡρπασθη [*Hērpasthē*]: "Take suddenly and vehemently, or take away in the sense of . . . steal, carry off drag away."[28] The same root describes how the violent *take* the kingdom *by force* (Mtt. 11:12). It describes how the "wicked one comes and *snatches away* what was sown" (Mtt. 13:19). The term is used to describe physical transportation by the power of the Holy Spirit: Philip is *caught away* from the sight of the Ethiopian eunuch and is later found in Azotus (Acts 8:39); Paul was *caught up* to the third heaven (2Cor. 12:2); and the church will be *caught up* with the dead in Christ to meet the Lord at the *Rapture*[4.14] (1Th. 4:17).

Here it is passive—an external agent (the Father) catches the child away. The same passive aspect is seen in Luke's detailed record of the event which employs a passive verb and participle to describe the ascension:

> Now when He had spoken these things, while they watched, **He was taken up (ἐπήρθη [*epērthē*])**, and a cloud received Him out of their sight. And while they looked steadfastly toward heaven as He went up, behold, two men stood by them in white apparel, who also said, "Men of Galilee, why do you stand gazing up into heaven? This *same* Jesus, who **was taken up (ἀναλημφθεὶς [*analēmphtheis*])** from you into heaven, will so come in like manner as you saw Him go into heaven." (Acts 1:9-11) [emphasis added]

The child ascends and remains until the time of restoration predicted by the prophets.

> Repent therefore and be converted, that your sins may be blotted out, so that times of refreshing may come from the presence of the Lord, and that He may send Jesus Christ, who was preached to you before, whom heaven must receive until the times of restoration of all things, which God has spoken by the mouth of all His holy prophets since the world began. (Acts 3:19-21)

The times of the restoration of all things includes the regeneration (Mtt. 19:28) which precedes the promised *Millennial Kingdom*[5.2.39] (Rev. 20:4-6). See *The Arrival of God's Kingdom*[2.4.3].

to God and His throne

Notice that the child is caught up to *God's throne* , not His own throne. He remains seated to the right hand of the Father until the time comes for Him to rule from the throne of David on earth (Dan. 7:13-14, 21-22, 26-27; Mtt. 25:31; Rev. 3:21). See commentary on *Revelation 3:21*[3.3.21].

3.12.6 - Revelation 12:6

Then the woman fled

The connective, "Then," indicates a sequence between the catching up of the child and the fleeing of the woman. But are these two events *necessarily* closely correlated in time? How soon must the flight be to the catching up of the child? Some interpreters relate this flight to that of the Jews from

Jerusalem in the destruction by Rome in 70 A.D.[29] Yet even that flight was approximately 4 decades after the ascension of Christ. Nor was there any indication of supernatural assistance as this passage describes (Rev. 12:14). Certainly nothing like the Exodus occurred in relation to the destruction of Jerusalem in 70 A.D. which would allow for the use of similar phraseology involving "wings of a great eagle."

Here we are faced with one of the characteristics of prophetic passages: events which appear side-by-side in the text can often be separated by long ages. This occurs because the prophetic vision has two characteristics which we need to be aware of. *First*, the prophets were only shown important highlights of the final development (1Pe. 1:10-11). *Second*, the full range of history was often collapsed in their view, much as when looking through a telescope. "Somewhat as a picture lacks the dimension of depth, the prophecy often lacks the dimension of time: events appear together on the screen of prophecy which in their fulfillment may be widely separated in time."[30]

There are numerous examples of this phenomenon. The First and Second Coming of Christ are juxtaposed in numerous passages (Isa. 61:1-2; Zec. 9:9-10; Mal. 3:1-2; 4:5-6; Luke 4:17-19). Yet history has shown these events to be separated by at least 1900 years. The first and second resurrections are juxtaposed (Dan. 12:2; John 5:28-29), yet they are separated by no less than 1,000 years (Rev. 20:4-6).

We have a similar sequence before us: The child is caught up and the woman flees. The child was caught up over 1900 years ago and the woman has yet to flee in the sense of this passage.

> [When] the woman flees into the wilderness . . . we meet with another, and yet more lengthened parenthesis. Between the ascension of the Man Child and the woman's flight—*yet future*—the history of Christianity comes in. The great point to lay hold of is the connection between Christ and *Israel*, not Christ and the Church, hence the two omitted parenthetic periods: (1) between the birth and ascension; (2) between the ascension and the flight.[31]

> This vision next recognizes Jesus' ascension (Rev. 12:5), and then takes up Israel's story as though the Church Age does not intervene, just as Dan 9:26 ignores the same period. The Church Age is the "mystery" of the Old Testament (Rom 11:25; 16:25), and is distinct from Israel's history.[32]

Zechariah saw the same sequence, contiguous in the text, but separated by the age of grace during which the body of Christ preaches the gospel before the focus shifts back again to Israel:

> "Awake, O sword, against My Shepherd, against the Man who is My Companion," says the LORD of hosts. "Strike the Shepherd, and the sheep will be scattered; then I will turn My hand against the little ones. And it shall come to pass in all the land," says the LORD, "*That* two-thirds in it shall be cut off *and* die, but *one*-third shall be left in it: I will bring the *one-third* through the fire, will refine them as silver is refined, and test them as gold is tested. They will call on My name, and I will answer them. I will say, 'This *is* My people'; and each one will say, 'The LORD *is* my God.' " (Zec. 13:7-9)

In Zechariah's passage, the shepherd is struck (the Great Shepherd crucified) and then the sheep are scattered. In the time of testing, only one-third survives. The remainder turn to God in faith. Can this be said of the destruction of Jerusalem in A.D. 70?

> The prophecy that *two parts . . . shall be cut off and die, but the third shall be left* in the land cannot refer contextually to the destruction wrought in Judea during the Jewish War of A.D. 67 to 70. . . . Nor can its sequel regarding *the third part* that survives the terrible time of judgment by being brought *through the fire* (Jer. 30:5-7; Mtt. 24:13) be reconciled with the facts of history under such an interpretation. The remnant of the Jews who survived the horrors of the Jewish War from A.D. 67 to 70 did not come forth refined *as silver is refined* and tested *as gold is tested*, a regenerated and spiritual people. On the contrary, the preponderating majority remained in their unbelief, were scattered worldwide, and to this day have remained in spiritual darkness, with only a *very few* believing and forming "a remnant according to the election of grace" (Rom. 11:5).[33]

Both Zechariah's passage and this passage refer to the *same events* of the time of the end. In both contexts, they are related as being immediately after the First Coming (shepherd struck, child caught up) yet an intervening age occurs. The flight of the woman takes place after the final casting out of the dragon (Rev. 12:7-12). The woman fled because of intense persecution by the dragon (Rev. 12:13-14).

Although the woman has not yet fled in the sense of this passage (where only 3.5 years exist before the return of Christ, Rev. 12:6, 14), the dragon has great enmity toward her on an ongoing basis. For, as we have mentioned, the return of Christ involves the Jews coming to repentance and calling for His return (Mtt. 23:39). And the character of His millennial reign upon earth is intensely Jewish, as indicated by a temple standing in Jerusalem. This all reflects the important fact that *God is not through with the Jews: they remain an important part of His plan* (Rom. 9-11). Therefore, we should *expect* to see great opposition by the god of this age to the chosen nation. And indeed we do! Is there any one nation which has survived persecution and pogroms as have the Jews? Can one point to any other nation which has a Holocaust like that of the Jews? A Holocaust, which destroyed some *six million* people, and is even now denied as a ruse by some—a mere six decades after the event, when the piles of shoes, teeth, and hair of the victims may still to be seen?

Even portions of the Church serve as a hireling of the dragon. Large numbers among Christianity deny Israel's right to the Promised Land and oppose her attempts to defend herself against unreasonable hostility. The same wayward Church denies God's *OT*[5.2.51] promises which are manifestly for Israel—attempting to rob them for her own purpose and producing a distorted understanding of Scripture in the process.

Although all race-related persecution is of the dragon, he has a special penchant for opposing Israel because she is a key in what remains for God's program of the end times and beyond. Unless we realize this spiritual reality, we will be forever puzzled by *anti-Semitism*[5.2.64][5.2.4]. How else does one explain the possession of *The Temple Mount*[4.16.3] by Israel, but her inability to ascend there to worship? Or her possession of Jerusalem while the nations of the world, including our own United States, refuse to recognize Jerusalem as her capital? Or what about the countless resolutions of the United Nations condemning Israel and the veritable silence from the same body in regard to hostilities by her enemies? None of this makes *logical sense* because it has nothing to do with logic! There is a *dark spiritual dimension* behind anti-Semitism and its cousin, anti-Zionism:

> You declare, my friend, that you do not hate the Jews, you are merely "anti-Zionist." And I say, let the truth ring forth from the high mountain-tops, let it echo through the valleys of God's green earth: when people criticize Zionism, they mean Jews—this is God's own truth. . . And what is anti-Zionist? It is the denial to the Jewish people of a fundamental right that we justly claim for the people of Africa and freely accord all other nations of the Globe. It is discrimination against Jews, my friend, because they are Jews. In short, it is anti-Semitism. . . Let my words echo in the depths of your soul: when people criticize Zionism, they mean Jews—make no mistake about it.—Dr. Martin Luther King, Jr., cited in *Levitt Letter*, December 2002, p. 28. [*www.levitt.com*]

> One of the darkest stains on the history of mankind has been the persistent specter of anti-Semitism. Over the centuries the Jews have faced more hatred and persecution than any other people. Much of that suffering was chastisement from God to turn the nation away from their sin and unbelief and back to Him. God repeatedly warned Israel of the consequences of disobedience (cf. Deu. 28:15-68) and punished them when they failed to obey (cf. 2K. 17:7-23). Within the paradigm of God's sovereign purpose for His people, Israel also has suffered constantly and severely at the hands of Satan, acting as God's instrument. Unlike God, however, Satan's purpose in causing the Jewish people to suffer is not remedial, but destructive. He seeks to bring them not to repentance and salvation, but to death and destruction.[34]

Among the most notable times of Jewish persecution are found the Crusades, the Inquisition, the pogroms of Russia, and the Holocaust. Sadly, the persecution of God's chosen nation has not yet reached its climax, for Scripture reveals the darkest hour is yet to come.

into the wilderness

The woman flees from the dragon. But where? She flees to the *wilderness*. Note that her flight is to a place of refuge for a period of 1,260 days (see below). This indirectly tells us *when* she flees—the precise event which triggers her flight. She flees at the middle of *The 70th Week of Daniel*[2.13.5] when sacrifice and offering is halted and the *Temple of God*[4.16] is made desolate:

> "Therefore when you see the 'abomination of desolation,' spoken of by Daniel the prophet, standing in the holy place" (whoever reads, let him understand), "then let those who are in Judea flee to the mountains. Let him who is on the housetop not go down to take anything out of his house. And let him who is in the field not go back to get his clothes. But woe to those who are pregnant and to those who are nursing babies in those days! And pray that your flight may not be in winter or on the Sabbath. For then there will be great tribulation, such as has not been since the beginning of the world until this time, no, nor ever shall be." (Mtt. 24:15-21)

We believe this event occurs just after the *Beast*[4.3.2.16] overcomes the two witnesses (Rev. 11:7). See *The Final Week*[2.13.5.3]. See commentary on *Revelation 11:3*[3.11.3]. When reading Jesus' words recorded by Matthew, one is immediately struck with the *Jewishness* of His comments which speak of a "holy place," "Judea," and the "Sabbath." This is no accident! For the words of Jesus in Matthew 24, while of value for all saints of all ages, are of *ultimate value* to the Jewish saints at the time of the end who reside in Judea and understand the signs of their times. For them, Matthew 24 will not just have a spiritual application, but a *real physical application* for it is they who will see the abomination set up at the mid-point of the Tribulation and will know to flee.

> The urgency of Christ's command to flee as soon as the abomination of desolation stands in the holy place . . . indicates that they must flee immediately—no opportunity for plane reservations, packing belongings, or anything else. The nearest desert area they can reach will be their only opportunity for survival.[35]

Her Master gives her with necessary instructions: "let those who are in Judea flee to the mountains."

Judean Wilderness West of Jericho[36]

Those who are in Judea will flee eastward to the nearest mountains. Initially, they will probably attain the Judean wilderness westward of Jericho (shown above). "Fleeing first to the 'mountains' and then on to the 'wilderness.' "[37]

In the day of Jacob's trouble (Jer. 30:7-8), the latter days (Jer. 30:24), prior to Israel's restoration for the *Millennial Kingdom*[5.2.39] (Jer. 30:9-10) God promises to give a surviving remnant grace in the *wilderness*. "Thus says the Lord: 'The people who survived the sword Found grace in the wilderness Israel, when I went to give him rest.' " (Jer. 31:2) Those who are in Jerusalem flee to the wilderness. Jews will also undergo purging among *the wilderness of the peoples*—among the nations where they have been scattered. In the same way that the rebellious of Israel fell in the wilderness and were prevented from entering the Promised Land, so too will the rebellious of Israel in the time of the end perish rather than participate in the promised Millennial Kingdom. [38]

> "*As* I live," says the Lord GOD, "surely with a mighty hand, with an outstretched arm, and with fury poured out, I will rule over you. I will bring you out from the peoples and gather you out of the countries where you are scattered, with a mighty hand, with an outstretched arm, and with fury poured out. And I will bring you into the wilderness of the peoples, and there I will plead My case with you face to face. Just as I pleaded My case with your fathers in the wilderness of the land of Egypt, so I will plead My case with you," says the Lord GOD. "I will make you pass under the rod, and I will bring you into the bond of the covenant; I will purge the rebels from among you, and those who transgress against Me; I will bring them out of the country where they dwell, but they shall not enter the land of Israel. Then you

> will know that I *am* the LORD." (Eze. 20:33-38)

3.12.6.1 - Sheep in Bozrah

where she has a place

Ὅπυ ἔχει ἐκεῖ τόπον [*Hopu echei ekei topon*], *where she is having there (a) place*. This appears to speak of a specific location within the wilderness, rather than merely fleeing to the wilderness in general. This is "her place" which the eagle takes her to (Rev. 12:14). It is a specific place which was prepared beforehand by God (Rev. 12:6).

Does Scripture give any indication where her place might be? Some think not:

> Petra, the ruins of an ancient city of Edom carved out of rock and protected by high mountain walls and with a narrow access, has been a suggested location of the "place," but this is pure speculation. The only stipulation possible is that it is a place of refuge for converted Israel during the last half of the seventieth week.[39]

While we agree that the precise identification of Petra as the place of refuge is difficult to assert dogmatically, we disagree that it is "pure speculation." There are numerous passages which pertain to the flight of the remnant and her divine protection in the wilderness. Given the importance of the preservation of a Jewish remnant, we should not be surprised by this. However, many of the passages are obscure and occur within settings which have both a local and a far-future reference and distinguishing between the two can be quite difficult. We offer some of these passages below in the hopes that they will prompt further study of this matter.

In the midst of a passage by Isaiah describing a time of destruction coming upon the people of Moab during which they would court Zion's favor for refuge, there is a stunning reversal in the scene:

> Take counsel, execute judgment; make your shadow like the night in the middle of the day; hide the outcasts, do not betray him who escapes. **Let My outcasts dwell with you, O Moab**; be a shelter to them from the **face [presence cf. Rev. 12:14]** of the spoiler. For the extortioner is at an end, devastation ceases, oppressors are consumed out of the land. In mercy the throne will be established; and One will sit on it in truth, in the *tabernacle*[5.2.69] of David, judging and seeking justice and hastening righteousness. (Isa. 16:3-5) [emphasis added]

Isaiah reverses the context and appeals to Moab for the protection of "My outcasts" (Israel). The context is a time of intense persecution and destruction which is followed by the just reign of Messiah upon the throne of David—the *Millennial Kingdom*[5.2.39].

> *Let mine outcasts dwell* (sojourn) *with thee, Moab* (the KJV correctly follows the [Masoretic Text], as over against the *LXX*[5.2.38], Syriac, and Targum, who render it: "the outcasts of Moab"). . . . The LORD was saying to Moab, through the Spirit of prophecy in Isaiah, "When My people Israel will be outcasts, be a haven to them, hiding them from their persecutors." Envisioned is that preeminent time of Israel's trouble, the Great Tribulation . . . under *Antichrist*[5.2.3], Israel's supreme "destroyer" (Rev. 12:6-13:18). . . . At the height of that persecution of the Jewish remnant, Christ will return in glory to sit upon His throne and judge the nations (Mtt. 25:46).[40]

The passage describes the path by which Moab should have sent its tribute of lambs to the king of Israel. "From Sela to the wilderness to the mount of the daughter of Zion *Jerusalem*" (Isa. 16:1 cf. 2K. 3:4-5). Sela means "Rock" and is understood to be a reference to Petra.[41] Could it be that the path by which the Moabites should have sent lambs from Petra via the wilderness to Jerusalem is to be retraced by the sheep of Israel who are scattered in the time of the end (Zec. 13:7-9)?

This occurs during the time when the Lord is testing those who dwell upon the earth (Rev. 3:10). During this time, the faithful remnant will be hidden in their chambers—reminiscent to the time of the Passover in Egypt:

> Come, my people, enter your chambers, and shut your doors behind you; hide yourself, as it were, for a little moment, until the indignation is past. For behold, the Lord comes out of His place to punish the inhabitants of the earth for their iniquity; the earth will also disclose her blood, and will no more cover her slain. (Isa. 26:20-21)

Daniel informs us that the domain of the Antichrist will have the following exceptions: "He shall also enter the Glorious Land, and many *countries* shall be overthrown; but these shall escape from his hand:

Edom, Moab, and the prominent people of Ammon" (Dan. 11:41). For some reason the Antichrist is unable to overthrow these regions which include both Bozrah and Petra.[42]

Bozrah in Southern Jordan [43]

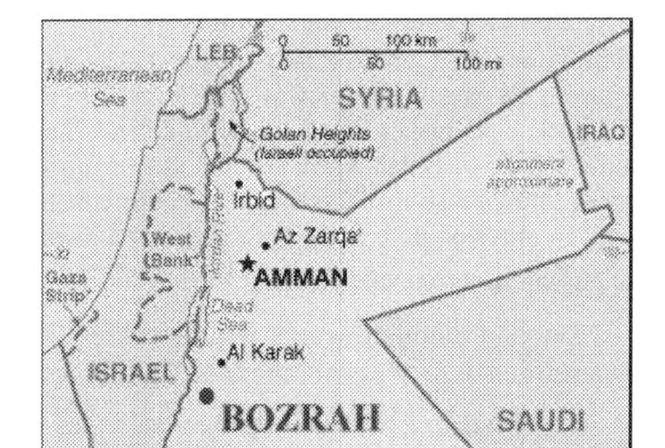

> Bozrah, the ancient capital of Edom, is without a doubt to be identified with the modern village of Buseirah, which is located in N Edom (M.R. 208018). It guards both the Kings' Highway (the major N-S route through Transjordan) and a major route W to the Wadi Arabah and thence to the Negeb and S Judah. It is also within striking distance of the Edomite copper mines in the Wadi Dana and Wadi Feinan some 10-15 km SSW. No water source has been found within the site, the main supply probably being the spring at `Ain Jenin, about one km E, which until recently was also the source for the modern village.[44]

Interestingly, several Second Coming passages also indicate that God is seen *coming from* these regions:

> Who *is* this who comes from **Edom**, with dyed garments from **Bozrah**, this *One who is* glorious in His apparel, traveling in the greatness of His strength? -"I who speak in righteousness, mighty to save." Why *is* Your apparel red, and Your garments like one who treads in the winepress? "I have trodden the winepress alone, and from the peoples no one *was* with Me. For I have trodden them in My anger, and trampled them in My fury; their blood is sprinkled upon My garments, and I have stained all My robes. For the day of vengeance *is* in My heart, and the year of My redeemed has come." (Isa. 63:1-4) [emphasis added]

> God came from Teman, the Holy One from Mount Paran. Selah His glory covered the heavens, and the earth was full of His praise. (Hab. 3:3)

> The prophet, under the form of a theophany, was given a vision of the second advent of the Messiah . . . seen coming *from Teman*, a district of **Edom**, poetically the part standing for the whole, . . . advancing *from Mount Paran* , the hilly country between Edom and Sinai (Deu. 33:2). Isaiah, in a vision of the second advent, similarly beheld the Messiah advancing in judgment upon His foes "from Edom, with dyed garments from Bozrah" (Isa. 63:1-6). [emphasis added][45]

In the Psalms, mention is made of the nation being led to Edom during a time when God has cast Israel off and is seeking help from trouble. God is appealed to as the one who will *tread down* (cf. Isa. 63:1-6) Israel's enemies:

> Who will bring me *to* the strong city? Who will lead me to **Edom?** *Is it* not You, O God, *who* cast us off? And You, O God, *who* did not go out with our armies? Give us help from trouble, for the help of man *is* useless. Through God we will do valiantly, for *it is* He *who* shall tread down our enemies. (Ps. 60:9-12 cf. Ps. 108:10-13) [emphasis added]

The reference to "strong city" is thought to refer to Petra, "*the strong city.* (Petra or Sela) the rock-built city of *Edom* (Ps. 31:21; 2K. 14:7)"[46], also known as *Sela*:

> Let the wilderness and its cities lift up *their voice*, the villages *that* Kedar inhabits. Let the inhabitants of **Sela** sing, let them shout from the top of the mountains. Let them give glory to the LORD, and declare His praise in the coastlands. The LORD shall go forth like a mighty man; He shall stir up *His* zeal like a man of war. He shall cry out, yes, shout aloud; He shall prevail against His enemies. (Isa. 42:11-13) [emphasis added]

> Petra is located in a basin within Mount Seir, and is totally surrounded by mountains and cliffs. The only way in and out of the city is through a narrow passageway that extends for about a mile and can only be negotiated by foot or by horseback. This makes the city easy to defend, and its surrounding high cliffs give added meaning and confirmation to Isaiah 33:16 . . . The name *Bozrah* means "sheepfold." An ancient sheepfold had a narrow entrance so that the shepherd could count his sheep. Once inside the fold, the sheep had more room to move around. Petra is shaped like a giant sheepfold, with its narrow passage opening up to a spacious circle surrounded by cliffs.[47]

Micah describes an assembly of Jacob, a remnant, which will be gathered into a fold (*bozrah*). The one who breaks them out is clearly a reference to Messiah, the Good Shepherd:

> I will surely assemble all of you, O Jacob, I will surely gather the remnant of Israel; I will put them together like sheep of the **fold [בָּצְרָה [Bātsrāh]]**, like a flock in the midst of their pasture; they shall make a loud noise because of *so many* people. The one who breaks open will come up before them; they will break out, pass through the gate, and go out by it; their king will pass before them, with the LORD at their head. (Mic. 2:12-13) [emphasis added]

> The LORD will "gather" from their worldwide, age-long Diaspora the elect "remnant," which will survive "the time of Jacob's trouble" (Jer. 30:5-7), the Great Tribulation (Rev. 8:1-20:3), preceding the establishment of the Kingdom over Israel (Rev. 20:4-6; Acts 1:7). . . . The saved remnant will be the nucleus of the millennial Kingdom. The LORD declared, *I will put them together like the sheep of Bozrah* (a region in Edom well known as a sheep-raising center). . . . They (the returning remnant of Israel) will follow "the breaker," the Messiah, who will break through and open the way, going up before them. They, following Him, will break through the gate and go out from their captivity to glorious freedom.[48]

An appreciation of the ultimate setting of the previous passage sheds new light on the familiar teaching of Jesus:

> Most assuredly, I say to you, he who does not enter the sheepfold by the door, but climbs up some other way, the same is a thief and a robber. But he who enters by the door is the shepherd of the sheep. To him the doorkeeper opens, and the sheep hear his voice; and he calls his own sheep by name and leads them out. And when he brings out his own sheep, he goes before them; and the sheep follow him, for they know his voice. Yet they will by no means follow a stranger, but will flee from him, for they do not know the voice of strangers. (John 10:1-5)

Will the Jewish remnant of the time of the end be in such a physical "sheepfold" of sorts? Will they be reading these very words of Jesus penned by John thousands of years before their situation—waiting for the "shepherd of the sheep" to bring out his own sheep? Only time will tell.

These references to Edom and Bozrah are indicators that at the Second Coming, God has business to take care of in Edom. That business involves the defense of his sheep, the Jewish remnant represented by the woman who flees the dragon. See *Campaign of Armageddon*[4.5].

prepared by God

ἡτοιμασμένον [*hētoimasmenon*], perfect tense passive participle, *having been prepared by God.* The preparation is made prior to her flight so that the place is ready for her upon her arrival. In the same way that the Church has a dwelling place (μοναὶ [*monai*]) prepared by Jesus in the Father's house (John 14:2 cf. Rev. 21:2), so the Jewish remnant has a place prepared in the Father's world (Isa. 26:20-21).

they should feed her

The physical needs of the woman are met in her wilderness hiding place. *They* , an indefinite plural, seems to indicate the participation of others in providing for her nourishment. In the same way that the ravens (1K. 17:2-3) and the widow of Zarephath in Sidon (1K. 17:8-15) were used as intermediaries to feed Elijah during his time of drought, so too will others be used to provide for the Jewish remnant.

During the Tribulation, there will be numerous situations involving drought and lack of provision. See commentary on *Revelation 11:6*[3.11.6] . The need for provision will be exacerbated in her case because no one will be able to buy or sell without the mark of the beast during this three and one-half years (Rev. 13:17).

We note that Elijah was fed by a *raven* (an unclean bird) and a *Gentile* widow (Luke 4:26-29). Perhaps this is a typological indication that the Jewish remnant will be provided for by Gentile means. Provision for the Jews by Gentiles during this time helps explain the context of the Sheep and Goat judgment when the nations (ἔθνη [*ethnē*], *Gentiles*) are gathered before Christ at His return and rewarded based on their provision for *His brethren* (Mtt. 25:32).[49]

God used Moses as an intermediary when He supernaturally fed Israel in her previous time in the wilderness after the Exodus where he provided water from a rock and manna from heaven:

> And they tested God in their heart by asking for the food of their fancy. Yes, they spoke against God: They said, "Can God prepare a table in the wilderness? Behold, He struck the rock, so that the waters gushed out, and the streams overflowed. Can He give bread also? Can He provide meat for His people?" Therefore the LORD heard *this* and was furious; so a fire was kindled against Jacob, and anger also came up against Israel, because they did not believe in God, and did not trust in His salvation. Yet He had commanded the clouds above, and opened the doors of heaven, had rained down manna on them to eat, and given them of the bread of heaven. Men ate angels' food; He sent them food to the full. (Ps. 78:18-25)

During her time in the wilderness, Israel will remember the days of her youth when she came up from the land of Egypt. God will speak comfort to her and she will be purged of idolatry:

> Therefore, behold, I will allure her, will bring her into the wilderness, and speak comfort to her. I will give her vineyards from there, and the Valley of Achor as a door of hope; she shall sing there, as in the days of her youth, as in the day when she came up from the land of Egypt. "And it shall be, in that day," says the LORD, "*That* you will call Me 'My Husband,' And no longer call Me 'My Master,' For I will take from her mouth the names of the Baals, and they shall be remembered by their name no more." (Hos. 2:14-17)

The context indicates this precedes the Millennial Kingdom:

> In that day I will make a covenant for them with the beasts of the field, with the birds of the air, and *with* the creeping things of the ground. **Bow and sword of battle I will shatter from the earth**, to make them lie down safely. I will betroth you to Me forever; yes, I will betroth you to Me In righteousness and justice, in lovingkindness and mercy; I will betroth you to Me in faithfulness, and you shall know the LORD. (Hos. 2:18-20) [emphasis added]

Isaiah spoke of the pure who would dwell with God and would be provided with water and bread:

> The sinners in Zion are afraid; fearfulness has seized the hypocrites: "Who among us shall dwell with the devouring fire? Who among us shall dwell with everlasting burnings?" He who walks righteously and speaks uprightly, he who despises the gain of oppressions, who gestures with his hands, refusing bribes, who stops his ears from hearing of bloodshed, and shuts his eyes from seeing evil: he will dwell on high; his place of defense *will be* the fortress of rocks; bread will be given him, his water *will be* sure. (Isa. 33:14-16)

This time of testing in the wilderness, fed by God, will result in the full conversion of those who remain alive.[50] Whereas Israel had been "not My people," then it will be said, "You *are* My people!" (Hos. 2:23).

one thousand two hundred and sixty days

This period is also described as "time and times and half a time" (Rev. 12:14). This corresponds to half of *The 70th Week of Daniel*[2.13.5] . This is the last half of the week during which the nations trample the holy city (Rev. 11:2) and the beast has authority (Dan. 7:25; Rev. 13:5). A period Jesus referred to as consisting of "great tribulation" (Mtt. 24:21). See *Prophetic Year*[2.13.5.2].

This is the period during which Daniel was told events of the end would come to fulfillment: "Then I heard the man clothed in linen, who *was* above the waters of the river, when he held up his right hand and his left hand to heaven, and swore by Him who lives forever, that *it shall be* for a time, times, and half *a time*; and when the power of the holy people has been completely shattered, all these *things* shall be finished" (Dan. 12:7). One of the purposes of this period is to shatter "the power of the holy people" to turn them back to *total dependence* upon God. In the time of *Jacob's Trouble*[2.13.4], God will both *tear* and *heal* in order to bring the Jews to recognize Jesus as Messiah and urgently seek His return on their behalf:[51]

> "For I *will be* like a lion to Ephraim, and like a young lion to the house of Judah. I, *even* I, will tear *them* and go away; I will take *them* away, and no one shall rescue. I will return again to My place till they acknowledge their offense. Then they will seek My face; in their affliction they will earnestly seek Me." Come, and let us return to the LORD; for He has torn, but He will heal us; He has stricken, but He will bind us up. After two days He will revive us; on the third day He will raise us up, that we may live in His sight. (Hos. 5:14-6:2)

> He would withdraw His favor, and His sinning people would be scattered worldwide and be *temporarily* set aside in their national election. He will remain in His place (the prophecy spanning the centuries until the second advent of Christ) until the remnant of Israel (Zec. 12:10-13:1; Rom. 11:26; Rev. 7:1-8) will *acknowledge their offense* . . . accepting the full punishment of their guilt and not considering themselves to be *not* guilty (Zec. 11:5). *And seek My face* , through faith in their future incarnate Messiah-Savior (Isa. 53:1-10). . . . This prophetically presupposes Christ's incarnation and redemptive work at the first advent and the application of His salvation to Israel at His second advent (Rom. 11:26).[52]

They will then repeat the praise which they first gave at His first advent (Mtt. 21:9), but now with genuine commitment:

> O Jerusalem, Jerusalem, the one who kills the prophets and stones those who are sent to her! How often I wanted to gather your children together, as a hen gathers her chicks under *her* wings, but you were not willing! See! Your house is left to you desolate; for I say to you, **you shall see Me no more till you say, "Blessed *is* He who comes in the name of the LORD!"** (Mtt. 23:37-39) [emphasis added]

3.12.7 - Revelation 12:7

war

Πόλεμος [*Polemos*]: "Opposite . . . peace; as a single engagement battle, fight."[53]

Michael and his angels

Michael is one of the "chief princes" who aided the heavenly messenger of Daniel against the prince of Persia and Greece (Dan. 10:13, 21). Daniel is told that Michael is "your prince" (Dan. 10:21), and "The great prince who stands *watch* over the sons of your people" (Dan. 12:1). Thus, he is uniquely associated with the protection of the Jewish people.[54] It is during the time of *Jacob's trouble*[2.13.4], when "there shall be a time of trouble, such as never was since there was a [Jewish] nation" that "shall stand up" to protect Israel (Dan. 12:1-2). Jude informs us that Michael is an "archangel" and his connection with Israel is also reflected in the fact that he "disputed about the body of Moses" with the devil (Jude 1:9).

fought with the dragon

"With what weapons and tactics this heavenly warfare will be waged is beyond our understanding. Angels cannot be injured or slain with earthly weapons, and such physical forces as we know about are not able to move spiritual beings. But these beings do operate in a physical universe, so there must exist powerful physico-spiritual energies of which we yet can have only vague intimations, . . . It is with such energies and powers that this heavenly battle will be waged."[55]

Michael and His Angels Fight the Dragon[56]

dragon and his angels

This refers to "a third of the stars of heaven" which were thrown to the earth by the tail of the dragon (Rev. 12:4). See Commentary on *Revelation 12:4*[3.12.4]. Their eventual destiny is the Lake of Fire, which was specially prepared for them (Mtt. 25:41; Rev. 20:10). Some are confined, reserved for judgment (see commentary on *Revelation 9:1*[3.9.1]).

The dragon's angels are organized by rank.

> Put on the whole armor of God, that you may be able to stand against the wiles of the devil. For we do not wrestle against flesh and blood, but against **principalities, against powers, against the rulers of the darkness of this age, against spiritual *hosts* of wickedness** in the heavenly *places*. (Eph 6:11-12) [emphasis added]

Perhaps one of the more powerful ones is the angel of the bottomless pit (Rev. 9:11). An angel which spoke with Daniel fought against high-ranking angels on his way to Daniel (Dan. 10:13, 20-21).

The existence and influence of these malevolent spiritual beings is a well-established theme of Scripture. This is why it is so important for believers to have a grasp of what Scripture reveals concerning the world which we live in. For there are forces and objectives at work that underlie the physical realm which the instrumentation of science is entirely unable to reveal. They are at work in the non-physical realm where science is blind. Yet we see their results in the workings of sin, reigns of terror, and the machinations of powerful nations and corporations through history.

> The movements of nations, their wars, their politics, and social policy, are shaped and directed by higher powers. There are angels, good and bad, who are constantly influencing men and governments, and of this [Daniel 10] is a conspicuous example. Wars and strife on earth are the reflex of opposing spiritual powers in the lower heavens.[57]

No more so than in the plight of the Jews and the illogical conditions which attend the disfavor they suffer by the majority of the world's nations. And this is exactly one of the goals of this chapter—God is revealing to us the true nature of *anti-Semitism*[5.2.64][5.2.4]. Although the world is full of destructive biases and half-truths, none is as malignant nor hell-bent as Satan's desire to destroy the woman of Revelation 12.

As significant as *his angels* are in terms of powers which influence and manipulate the world, these ranks of fallen angels are not of primary concern for the believer "because He who is in you is greater than he who is in the world" (1Jn. 4:4). "For I am persuaded that neither death nor life, nor angels nor principalities nor powers, nor things present nor things to come, nor height nor depth, nor any other created thing, shall be able to separate us from the love of God which is in Christ Jesus our Lord." (Rom. 8:38-39).

3.12.8 - Revelation 12:8

they did not prevail

Prevail is ἴσχυσεν [*ischysen*], indicating that the dragon and his angels had *insufficient power* to withstand Michael and his angels. The elect angels of God are able to defeat the most mighty of the fallen angels, including Satan (Rev. 20:2). Christ does not even condescend to participate in the conflict, for like all the angels, Satan is a *creature*, albeit a powerful one. Many people have the completely cockeyed view that the Bible concerns a battle between Satan and Christ. Nothing could be further from the truth, because Satan himself is a creature of Christ's creating (Col. 1:16). The gap between Creator and creature is inestimable. Christ could merely *blink* and Satan and all evil would instantly and permanently be vanquished. Yet he withholds their doom for His purposes, only a tiny corner of which He reveals to us—much of it in this book. For Christ, as God, to stoop to battle directly with the devil would be providing Satan with a great compliment. Hence, he is dealt with by Michael or other angelic powers, who are themselves creatures.

nor was a place found

The woman had a place prepared for her to which she fled, but the dragon no longer has a place in heaven.

any longer

Prior to this battle with Michael, the dragon had access to heaven as he does in our day. See commentary on *Revelation 12:10*[3.12.10]. See commentary on *Revelation 20:2*[3.20.2].

3.12.9 - Revelation 12:9

cast out

This is the first stage in the *de facto* fulfillment of what was previously accomplished *de jure* at Christ's First Coming (Luke 10:18; John 12:31; 16:11; Col. 2:15; Heb. 2:14; 1Jn. 3:8). The next stage occurs with his binding in the abyss (Rev. 20:1-3) after which he is released, but then cast into the Lake of Fire (Rev. 20:10).

that serpent of old

ὁ ὄφις ὁ ἀρχαῖος [*ho ophis ho archaios*], *the serpent, the ancient* . This is a direct allusion to his role as the serpent in the Garden of Eden (Gen. 3:1-4), and especially God's prophecy which set forth a number of truths concerning the serpent and the line leading to Messiah (Gen. 3:14-16):

1. God would put enmity between the serpent and the woman and between the serpent's seed and her Seed.

2. The woman's seed would bruise (crush) the serpent's head.
3. God would bring Messiah via the rebellious woman, but only through pain (of childbirth).

The reference to *serpent of old* indicates that the stand-off between the woman in labor and the serpent is an age-old situation which spans the time from Eve to the virgin Mary and beyond. Thus, the woman signifies not just *Mary*, nor just *Israel*, but the promise of a redeemer through the line of Israel stretching all the way back to the first woman, *Eve*. See commentary on *Revelation 12:1*[3.12.1].

the devil

Διάβολος [*Diabolos*], a compound word made up of δια [*dia*] (*against*) and βαλλω [*ballō*] (*to throw*). This title emphasizes his role as slanderer, *throwing* accusations *against* the saints. "*Diabolos* is the usual rendering of שָׂטָן [*sātān*], "satan," in the *LXX*[5.2.38] (e.g., Job 1:6) suggesting the two words are almost synonymous."[58]

who deceives the whole world

World is οἰκουμένην [*oikoumenēn*]: "The whole inhabited earth,"[59] with reference to those portions which are populated by humans, the region to which the gospel of the kingdom will be preached to all nations prior to the end (Mtt. 24:14). "The whole world lies *under the sway of* the wicked one" (1Jn. 5:19). By the sorcery of Babylon, the nations were deceived (Rev. 18:23).

His first target of deception was Eve (Gen. 3:4-5; 2Cor. 11:3; 2Ti. 2:14), but he has been at work deceiving nations all through history. He is the father of lies, there is no truth in him (John 8:44). Those through whom he deceives are most effective because they themselves are deceived (2Ti. 3:13).

> Educated and ignorant, king and pauper, male and female, Jew and Gentile, strong and weak, young and old, black and white—all are deceived by him. All the world's high-sounding philosophies, conceived ever so brilliantly by profound thinkers—whether pragmatism, idealism, *gnosticism*[5.2.23], determinism, hedonism, materialism, transcendentalism, existentialism, deism, or any of countless others, and regardless of the eminence of the geniuses with whose names they are associated—Aristotelianism, Platonism, Hegelianism, Marxism, Maoism, Confucianism, Buddhism, Kantianism, Freudianism—*all* are man-originated, man-centered, and man-honoring, rather than God-originated, God-centered, and God-honoring [Col. 2:8-9].[60]

His ultimate deceiving tool at the time of the end is the *False Prophet*[5.2.20] who performs great signs to deceive those who dwell on the earth (Rev. 13:13-14), those who receive the mark of the beast and worship his image (Rev. 19:20). See commentary on *Revelation 13:11*[3.13.11]. Satan empowers both the *Beast*[4.3.2.16] and the *False Prophet*[4.3.2.18] as two mighty deceivers. In a similar way that God gives power to the two witnesses who testify of God (Rev. 11:3), these two are empowered by Satan as master deceivers during a time when deception will be the rule rather than the exception. The deception will be so strong that only by the power of the Holy Spirit will the regenerate avoid succumbing to the signs and lying wonders:

> The coming of the *lawless one* is according to the working of Satan, with all power, signs, and lying wonders, and with all unrighteous deception among those who perish, because they did not receive the love of the truth, that they might be saved. And for this reason God will send them strong delusion, that they should believe the lie, that they all may be condemned who did not believe the truth but had pleasure in unrighteousness. (2Th. 2:9-12)

The False Prophet is the ultimate from among those Jesus warned of: "false prophets will rise and show great signs and wonders to deceive" (Mtt. 24:24a.).

At the Second Coming of Christ, Satan is bound in the abyss so as to halt his deceiving ministry for the duration of the Millennium (Rev. 20:3), but at the end he will be released to deceive the nations one final time (Rev. 20:8-10).

3.12.10 - Revelation 12:10

Now salvation, and strength, and the kingdom of our God and the power of His Christ have come

An equivalent statement to that which accompanied the sounding of the seventh trumpet (Rev. 11:15), but which recognizes the removal of Satan from God's heaven as a key signal of the beginning of the end. See commentary on *Revelation 11:15*[3.11.15]. The seventh trumpet is yet future to our day and so the kingdom awaits and we continue to pray, "Your kingdom come, Your will be done on earth as *it is* in heaven" (Mtt. 6:10).

> How utterly idle is the discoursing of modernists and religious educationalists and social reformers about "the kingdom." Their talk is full of "the *kingdom* this" and "the *kingdom* that"; whereas our Lord Jesus has not yet taken His kingdom. It has not yet been given Him of the Father. We are not living in kingdom days, but in days when Satan is the prince of this world and the god of this age, also, when he is accusing the saints before God. Only those born again ever *see* the kingdom of God; and "righteousness, peace, and joy in the Holy Ghost"—wholly a separate thing from human arrangements and reforms! is the only form of the kingdom of God now.[61]

See *The Arrival of God's Kingdom*[2.4.3].

strength . . . and power

Δύναμις [*Dynamis*] . . . καὶ ἡ ἐξουσία [*kai hē exousia*], better rendered *power . . . and authority.*[62] Ἐξουσία [*Exousia*] in this context carries the idea of "Authority, absolute power, warrant . . . authority and commission."[63]

His Christ

An intentional allusion to the equivalent phrase from the *OT*[5.2.51]: "The kings of the earth set themselves, and the rulers take counsel together, against the LORD and against **His Anointed**" [emphasis added] (Ps. 2:2). See commentary on *Revelation 11:15*[3.11.15].

have come

ἐγένετο [*egeneto*] , prophetic aorist. The kingdom does not arrive until the events of Revelation 19. See *The Arrival of God's Kingdom*[2.4.3]. In the cutting off of Satan's access to heaven, the kingdom is now so near (Rev. 12:12) as to be considered an accomplished fact.

the accuser of the brethren

Ὁ κατήγωρ [*Ho katēgōr*], present tense participle, *the one presently accusing*. Prior to his casting out, Satan was continuously active bringing charges against the elect. The term is used of bringing a legal charge before a judge, as in court.[64] He goes to and fro between this world and heaven as the "accuser of our brethren" (Rev. 12:10). Yet even in his missions of slander and accusation, he is strictly limited (Job 1:6-12; Zec. 3:1-5; Luke 22:31).

> Satan (along with the evil angels) has actively opposed both the holy angels and God's people since his fall. In the Old Testament, demons sought to hinder the ministry of the holy angels to Israel (cf. Dan. 10:12-13). In the present age, Satan "prowls around like a roaring lion, seeking someone to devour" (1Pe. 5:8), opposes the spread of the gospel (Mtt. 13:19, 37-39; Acts 13:10), oppresses individuals (Luke 13:10-16; Acts 10:38), and uses sin to disrupt and pollute the church (Acts 5:1-11). Believers are to be wary of his schemes (2Cor. 2:11), give him no opportunity (Eph. 4:27), and resist him (Jas. 4:7).[65]

day and night

This phrase emphasizes the ongoing nature of his activity (Rev. 4:8; 7:15; 14:11; 20:10; 21:25).

3.12.11 - Revelation 12:11

they overcame

Αὐτοὶ ἐνίκησαν [*Autoi enikēsan*], *they, they overcame* . Emphasis is placed upon the redeemed who overcame Satan by God's work. They are among the true overcomers (Rev. 2:7, 11, 17, 26; 3:5, 12, 21; 17:14; 21:7). See *Who is the Overcomer?*[4.15.1.3]

by the blood of the Lamb

Satan is able to accuse the brethren continually because the brethren continually sin (1Jn. 1:8). Thankfully, the one-time sacrifice of the Lamb of God justifies them eternally. Satan's accusations toward the believer are essentially made against the perfect righteousness of Christ. This is how "they overcame him by the blood of the Lamb." In our initial appeal to Christ for salvation, His work on the cross takes into account all our sin, both past, present, *and future* . Our sin only affects our fellowship with Him, not our standing as a justified one (1Jn. 1:9). Once we come to faith, Satan now appeals to the Judge Who is also the Justifier (Rom. 8:33).

Concerning *the blood*, see the commentary on *Revelation 1:5*[3.1.5]. Concerning *the Lamb*, see the commentary on *Revelation 5:6*[3.5.6].

testimony

The rest of her offspring have the testimony of Jesus Christ (Rev. 12:17).

they did not love their lives

They did not love is οὐκ ἠγάπησαν [*ouk ēgapēsan*], which speaks of "*love*, especially of love as based on evaluation and choice, a matter of will and action."[66] Ἀγαπάω [*Agapaō*] speaks not so much about altruism, but intensity. Jesus said the Pharisees *love* (ἀγαπάω [*agapaō*]) the best seats in the synagogue (Luke 11:43). John wrote that men *loved* (ἀγαπάω [*agapaō*] darkness (John 3:19).[67] *Lives* is ψυχήν [*psychēn*], also translated *souls* (see below).

Among these are the ones "who had been beheaded for their witness to Jesus and for the word of God, who had not worshiped the beast or his image, and had not received *his* mark on their foreheads or on their hands" (Rev. 20:4). These are they "of whom the world was not worthy" (Heb. 11:38), which include the martyrs of the fifth seal (Rev. 6:9) and many coming out of the Great Tribulation who were martyred for their faith (Rev. 7:14; 15:2).

to the death

Ἄχρι θανάτου [*Achri thanatou*], *until death* , the same phrase Jesus used when writing to the persecuted church at Smyrna (Rev. 2:10). These overcomers followed His instructions and maintained their testimony *to the point of* death and obtained the "crown of life" (Rev. 2:10). Their death was merely a gateway to the continuance of their eternal life—their souls were safe. They did not fear those who could only kill the body: "And do not fear those who kill the body but cannot kill the soul (ψυχην [*psychēn*]). But rather fear Him who is able to destroy both soul (ψυχην [*psychēn*]) and body in hell" (Mtt. 10:28).

3.12.12 - Revelation 12:12

rejoice, O heavens and those who dwell in them

The inhabitants of the heavens rejoice because the accuser has been cast down and the faithful overcomers have prevailed even through death. Heaven and her peoples also rejoice over the fall of Babylon when God avenges them (Rev. 18:20; 19:1-3). Even the fields and woods are said to rejoice over the eventual redemption of Israel (Isa. 44:23) and the arrival of Messiah to judge the earth in righteousness (Ps. 96:11-13).

Dwell is σκηνοῦντες [*skēnountes*], The same root word is used to describe how Jesus *dwelt* (tabernacled) among men in the flesh (John 1:14). The ones in heaven are no longer within reach of the *Beast*[5.2.9] who blasphemes God's *tabernacle*[5.2.69] and those which *dwell* (tabernacle) in heaven (Rev. 13:6).

Those that *dwell* in the heavens include:

1. The elect angels.
2. The church which was "kept from the hour of testing" (Rev. 3:10), having been taken in the *Rapture*[4.14].
3. Those coming out of the Great Tribulation through death, over whom God spread his *tabernacle* (Rev. 6:9-10; 7:14-15).

Ultimately, God will *dwell* (tabernacle) among men (Rev. 21:3). See *The Abiding Presence of God*[4.16.2].

Woe to the inhabitants of the earth and the sea

These are the *earth dwellers*[5.2.18]. They live in the same domain over which the mighty angel stood to declare the impending restoration of God's dominion (Rev. 10:2). Currently, it is the domain of Satan (Mtt. 4:8-10; John 12:31; 14:30; 16:11; 2Cor. 4:4).

having great wrath

Wrath is "Θυμὸς [*Thymos*], 'Anger' . . . a more turbulent word than ὀργή [*orgē*], 'wrath.' "[68] These will live through a time of *double woe* . They will experience the woe of the final trumpet judgments of God (Rev. 8:13; 9:12; 11:14) *combined with* this woe due to the great wrath of the devil. This is part of the testing which is to come upon those who dwell upon the earth. See commentary on *Revelation 3:20*[3.3.20].

he knows that he has a short time

He knows is εἰδὼς [*eidōs*], a perfect tense participle, *having known.* The emphasis is on the devil's wrath at the time of being cast down which is based on his previous knowledge of limited time. *A short time* is ὀλίγον καιρὸν [*oligon kairon*], denoting *a limited opportunity* . The intensity of his wrath reflects his desire to make the most of the short period which remains before he is bound and cast into the abyss (Rev. 20:1-3). This corresponds to the pronouncement by the mighty angel that "there should be delay no longer, but in the days of the sounding of the seventh angel . . . the mystery of God would be finished" (Rev. 10:6-7).

3.12.13 - Revelation 12:13

cast to the earth

See commentary on *Revelation 9:9*[3.9.9].

he persecuted

'Εδίωξεν [*Ediōxen*], which can also be rendered: "Drive away, drive out, run after, pursue."[69]

the woman who gave birth to the male child

See commentary on *Revelation 12:2*[3.12.2] and *Revelation 12:5*[3.12.5].

3.12.14 - Revelation 12:14

was given

Again, we see the sovereignty of God Who provides for her. See commentary concerning God's sovereignty at *Revelation 6:2*[3.6.2].

two wings of a great eagle

This phrase speaks of supernatural assistance given by God in a time of human incapability. It describes God's deliverance of Israel from Egypt by the parting of the Red Sea: "You have seen what I did to the Egyptians, and *how* I bore you on eagles' wings and brought you to Myself" (Ex. 19:4). It also connotes supernatural protection and provision, patterned after the way in which an eagle, when training a youngster to fly, pushes it out of the nest but also flies with it and catches it to bear it upwards again when needed.

> He found him in a desert land and in the wasteland, a howling wilderness; He encircled him, He instructed him, He kept him as the apple of His eye. As an eagle stirs up its nest, hovers over its young, spreading out its wings, taking them up, carrying them on its wings, *so* the LORD alone led him, and *there was* no foreign god with him. He made him ride in the heights of the earth, that he might eat the produce of the fields; He made him draw honey from the rock, and oil from the flinty rock. (Deu. 32:10-13)

The woman will be given supernatural assistance in her flight as well as supernatural protection and provision en route and upon arrival at her destination. Her strength shall be renewed so that she will not succumb to natural weariness (Isa. 40:31). Supernatural intervention had protected the *Church*[4.14] *from* the entire "hour of trial which shall come upon the whole world" (Rev. 3:10). Here, supernatural intervention protects the woman *in the midst of* the last half of the hour when "the LORD comes out of

His place to punish the inhabitants of the earth for their iniquity" (Isa. 26:20-21 cf. Zep. 2:1-3).

> Fearfulness and trembling have come upon me, and horror has overwhelmed me. So I said, "Oh, that I had wings like a dove! I would fly away and be at rest. Indeed, I would wander far off, *and* remain in the wilderness. Selah I would hasten my escape from the windy storm *and* tempest." (Ps. 55:5-8)

fly into the wilderness to her place

It is *her place*: indicating a specific location set aside for her protection. It had been previously prepared by God. She will reside there during the last half of *The 70th Week of Daniel*[2.13.5].

Judean Wilderness and Lisan Peninsula [70]

The Lisan Peninsula separates the two basins of the Dead Sea at its narrowest point. This peninsula is a likely route from the Judean wilderness to Jordan, the area of Bozrah and Petra which some passages point to in relation to the preservation of a believing remnant and the Second Coming. See *Sheep in Bozrah*[3.12.6.1].

where she is nourished

She is nourished is τρέφεται [*trephetai*], she is being "provided with food."[71] The same term describes how "your heavenly Father *feeds*" the wild birds (Mtt. 6:26; Luke 12:24). At the Sheep and Goat Judgment, it is the sheep who *fed* Jesus' "brothers" during their time of need. The term can also describe a place of nurturing (Luke 4:16). See commentary on *Revelation 12:6*[3.12.6].

for a time and times and half a time

This period is also described as "one thousand two hundred and sixty days" (Rev. 12:6). It describes the final half of *The 70th Week of Daniel*[2.13.5]. See commentary on *Revelation 12:6*[3.12.6]. See *Prophetic Year*[2.13.5.2].

from the presence of the serpent

Presence is προσώπου [*prosōpou*], she is protected from the "face, countenance"[72] of the serpent. This denotes his inability to access her. It is used "in all kinds of more or less symbolic expressions which, in large part, represent *OT*[5.2.51] usage, and in which the face is often to be taken as the seat of the faculty of seeing."[73] She is *hidden* from his access, and possibly even from his knowledge.

3.12.15 - Revelation 12:15

like a flood after the woman

Flood is ποταμόν [*potamon*] , used to describe a large quantity of water, as during a natural disaster (Mtt. 7:25; Luke 6:48; 2Cor. 11:26; Rev. 8:10; 16:4) or in great abundance (John 7:38; Rev. 22:1). Since the origin of this flood is a *sign* (the mouth of the great dragon) and the text says *like a flood* , it is best to take this as a figure of speech denoting the overwhelming military force of an adversary (Ps.

65:7; 69:2-4; 124:1-5; Isa. 8:7; 59:19; Jer. 46:7-8; Dan. 9:26; 11:21-22).

The dragon's pursuit of the woman may be a continuation of the *Beast's*[4.3.2.16] invasion of the glorious land. [74] If so, the flight of the woman does not take place until after the abomination is set up (Mtt. 24:15). Then, the invasion of the Antichrist continues in his pursuit of the woman.

> Many commentators interpret Daniel 11:41 with reference to the occupation of the land of Palestine by the *Beast*[5.2.9]. The event that causes the Beast to move in is the invasion of Palestine from the north by the King of the North (Dan. 11:40). The covenant made by the Beast (Dan. 9:27) has evidently guaranteed Israel an inviolate right to the land. Some event must be necessary to cause the Beast to abrogate his covenant. Since the covenant is said to be broken in the middle of the week (Dan. 9:27) and the invasion from the north is seen to be the cause of the breaking of the covenant (Dan. 11:41) it may be concluded that this invasion takes place in the middle of the week.[75]

carried away by the flood

Carried away is Ποταμοφόρητον [*Potamophorēton*], which denotes drowning.[76] Satan desires to drown her with his flood, but God has plans to regenerate her with His living water (Eze. 36:25-27; John 7:38-39).

3.12.16 - Revelation 12:16

the earth helped the woman

The earth itself is inanimate. This speaks of *God's help manifested through nature* , a common aspect of God's miraculous dealings with his people (Ex. 9:23-25; Jos. 10:11; Job 38:22-23; Isa. 11:15; Eze. 38:22). Perhaps the most dramatic example of the past is the parting of the Red Sea by an "unnatural" natural phenomenon: the east wind (Ex. 14:21).

the earth opened its mouth and swallowed up the flood

Swallowed is κατέπιεν [*katepien*], a compound word meaning "drink down."[77] Previously, God used *the earth* to literally swallow Korah and his household. "So they and all those with them went down alive into the pit; the earth closed over them, and they perished from among the assembly" (Num. 16:33 cf. Num. 26:10; Ex. 15:12). It seems likely that something similar will occur to those who pursue the woman.

3.12.17 - Revelation 12:17

he went to make war with the rest of her offspring who keep the commandments of God

This phrase is pregnant with *anti-Semitism*[5.2.64][5.2.4]. Although the woman now hides, representing the hidden Jewish remnant, the dragon turns to pursue *the rest of her offspring*. This should not be taken as *spiritual offspring* for the context of this chapter and the identification of the woman argue that her offspring are *physical descendants* of Abraham, Isaac, and Jacob. This is the distinction which Paul maintains when he describes the time of Israel's spiritual restoration in preparation for the *Millennial Kingdom*[5.2.39] (Rom. 11:25-26 cf. Eze. 37). It is inconsistent interpretation to make her offspring in the first portion of the chapter denote physical descendants (Jews) only and then take her offspring as spiritual descendants here.

In reference to the woman's representation of Israel, some take her to be the faithful remnant within national Israel, the "Israel of God" (Gal. 6:16).[78] In this view, she represents the spiritually regenerate among the physical descendants of Abraham, Isaac, and Jacob. This view encounters some difficulties:

- **Promised Redeemer** - The promise of a redeemer, so central to her identification in this chapter, was given to the physical seed of Abraham, Isaac, and Jacob. It did not depend upon a continuous line of God-believing Jews for its fulfillment, it was a *physical* development. Paul says that "the adoption, the glory, the covenants, the giving of the law, the service *of God*, and the promises" were given to "my countrymen **according to the flesh**" [emphasis added] (Rom. 9:3-4). One of these promises was that national Israel would produce the Messiah, regardless of the spiritual condition of the Jews (Rom. 9:5).
- **Purpose of Persecution** - It would seem that one purpose of the time of *Jacob's*

Trouble[2.13.4] is found in the purging of unbelief from national Israel. If the woman represents only the faithful remnant, who among her is purged (Eze. 20:33-38; Hos. 2:14-17)?

- **Anti-Semitism** - Once we make the woman to be the faithful remnant within national Israel, it becomes difficult to explain the nature of anti-Semitism by what is revealed here. If the woman represents only faithful Jews and she is persecuted, then shouldn't faithful Jews be the main focus of anti-Semitism? Wouldn't Christian Jews be purged by the dragon while Orthodox Jews remain relatively unscathed? Yet History reveals an even-handed persecution of the Jews, even where faith in Messiah Jesus is lacking. In some instances, such as the Crusades and the Inquisition, *lack of faith* in Messiah Jesus even brought *greater* persecution. This chapter explains the history of anti-Semitism—the persecution of Jews based on *physical descent* —better if the woman is national Israel. Even unbelieving Jews represent a dangerous potential for the dragon, for they carry forward God's promises to continue the physical nation and offer continued hope of the spiritual regeneration which Scripture promises (Jer. 31:34; Rom. 11:25-26).

This is not to say that taking the woman as national Israel is without its difficulties. For when she flees to the wilderness, not all Jews are in her midst. Here we encounter a problem similar to that of the parables: they are meant to be illustrative, but if taken to a minute level of detail, they break down. Here, the woman represents the original promise to Eve of a redeemer, realized and carried forward through the nation of Israel up to the birth of Jesus by Mary. Beyond the birth and catching away, she represents national Israel in general up until the time of her flight. During the time of the end, a subset of the Jews in Judea flee to the wilderness, whereas others do not (the 144,000 of Revelation 7:4 and Jews of the diaspora). At the point of her flight, she no longer represents all of national Israel for there will be numerous groups of Jews at the time of the end:

1. Jews protected in the wilderness, where God continues the work of purging idolatry from their midst (Hos. 2:14-17; Eze. 20:33-38).
2. The 144,000 Jews protected by God's seal, probably engaged in the work of worldwide evangelism (Rev. 7, 14).
3. Jews in the diaspora who come to faith during this time who are unable to reach the wilderness with the woman.
4. Jews in the diaspora who receive the *Antichrist*[5.2.3] and his mark (John 5:43).

The *rest of her offspring* speaks of all Jews who did not flee to the wilderness—both believing and unbelieving. The phrase is further restricted to the offspring *who keep the commandments of God.* This indicates that *during the final half week* unbelieving Jews are not the *primary* object of the dragon's warfare—for they, like unbelieving Gentiles, will take his mark and give him due worship (Rev. 13:15-18 cf. John 5:43).[79] It is *believing Jews* elsewhere around the world that are now his target. This will include the 144,000 of Israel who were sealed for protection (Rev. 7:4-8). They are described as "ones who follow the Lamb wherever He goes," which indicates they keep the commandments of God (Rev. 14:4). Besides the specially sealed 144,000, there will be many other Jews who come to faith by their ministry and that of the two witnesses during the time of Jacob's Trouble. "These are scattered followers of the Lamb who did not reach the appointed place in the wilderness prepared for the main body of people symbolized by the woman."[80] These are those Jesus referred to as "My brethren," (Mtt. 25:40) which were provided for by the "sheep" (righteous Gentiles) who are afforded entry into the Millennial Kingdom to follow.[81] These Jews will be involved in evangelism, because they *have the testimony of Jesus Christ.*[82]

We are not saying that Gentile believers will not undergo persecution. Far from it! The many passages concerning the activities of the *Beast*[4.3.2.16] and *his image*[4.3.2.19], the *False Prophet*[4.3.2.18], and the *Harlot*[4.3.2.21] make it painfully clear that *all believers—be they Jewish or Gentile* will undergo extreme danger and persecution during this time (Rev. 6:9; 7:14; 20:4). See *#20 - Saints*[4.3.2.20].

The wrath of the dragon has been building as he is frustrated at each of his attempts:

> The dragon had to redirect his anger from the Son to the woman in Rev. 12:5 when the Son escaped his

> clutches. That increased his rage. He lost his place in heaven in Rev. 12:8, 9, 12, angering him even more. At this point the woman has escaped to a place of refuge leaving him only the woman's remaining seed to vent his fury on. The repeated frustration of his efforts explains the furious persecution the dragon proceeds to inflict on the faithful.[83]

But it will be doubly difficult for the Jewish believers because God has revealed the uniquely Jewish terror of this time:

> At that time Michael shall stand up, the great prince who stands *watch* over the sons of your people; and there shall be a time of trouble, such as never was since there was a nation, *even* to that time. And at that time your people shall be delivered, every one who is found written in the book. (Dan. 12:1)
>
> Alas! For that day *is* great, so that none *is* like it; and it *is* the time of Jacob's trouble, but he shall be saved out of it. (Jer. 30:7)
>
> In the Holocaust under Hitler, one-third of the world's Jewish population died. Under the fierce persecution of the Antichrist, controlled and energized by Satan, two-thirds of the Jewish population will die [Zec. 13:7-9]. This will be the largest and most intense persecution of the Jews ever known in history.[84]
>
> Zechariah 13:8-9 indicates that only one-third of Israel will survive the tribulation and enter the millennium. This will result in an "all saved" Israel as prophesied by Romans 11:26. At the beginning of the last decade of the twentieth century there are approximately fifteen million Jews worldwide, so, if this is a guide, it suggests that about five million Jews will enter the millennium and ten million Jews will perish in the Great Tribulation.[85]

However, the dragon will not succeed in his "ultimate solution." As in the days of the Assyrian, God will protect a believing remnant:

> And it shall come to pass in that day *That* the remnant of Israel, and such as have escaped of the house of Jacob, will never again depend on him who defeated them, but will depend on the LORD, the Holy One of Israel, in truth. The remnant will return, the remnant of Jacob, to the Mighty God. For though your people, O Israel, be as the sand of the sea, **A remnant of them will return**; the destruction decreed shall overflow with righteousness. For the Lord GOD of hosts will make a determined end in the midst of all the land. (Isa. 10:20-23) [emphasis added]

The dragon fights a battle he can never win, for God has sworn that Israel will continue before Him (Jer. 31:35-37). Her continued existence is also required in order to fulfill aspects of the Abrahamic, Land, Davidic, and New Covenants which have yet to find fulfillment.[86] By the end of *Jacob's time of trouble*[2.13.4], the terms *Israel* and *Israel of God* (Gal. 6:16) will be synonymous for "all Israel will be saved" (Rom. 11:26). At that time, the *only Israel* will be a *believing Israel*:

> No more shall every man teach his neighbor, and every man his brother, saying, 'Know the LORD,' for they all shall know Me, from the least of them to the greatest of them, says the LORD. For I will forgive their iniquity, and their sin I will remember no more. (Jer. 31:34)

have the testimony of Jesus Christ

They have the testimony *provided by* Jesus Christ which they witness to others *concerning* Him. See commentary on *Revelation 1:1*[3.1.1] and *Revelation 1:2*[3.1.2].

Notes

1 J. A. Seiss, *The Apocalypse: Lectures on the Book of Revelation* (Grand Rapids, MI: Zondervan Publishing House, 1966), Rev. 12:1.

2 Elwood McQuaid, ed., *Israel My Glory* (Westville, NJ: Friends of Israel Gospel Ministry, September/October 2001), 34.

3 John MacArthur, *Revelation 12-22 : The MacArthur New Testament Commentary* (Chicago, IL: Moody Press, 2000), Rev. 12:1.

4 Monty S. Mills, *Revelations: An Exegetical Study of the Revelation to John* (Dallas, TX: 3E Ministries, 1987), Rev. 12:1.

5 "Medieval scholastic theologians . . . looked for excuses to find Mary, the mother of Jesus, in unsuspecting places. They saw her in Revelation 12, where they envisioned her incorruptibility and bodily transfiguration.

Clothed with the sun, that woman, they said, is 'the transfigured mother of Christ.' "—Mal Couch, *"How Has Revelation Been Viewed Interpretively?,"* in Mal Couch, ed., *A Bible Handbook to Revelation* (Grand Rapids, MI: Kregel Publications, 2001), 38. "The woman cannot mean, literally, the virgin mother of Jesus, for she did not flee into the wilderness and stay there for 1260 days, while the dragon persecuted the remnant of her seed."—A. R. Fausset, *"The Revelation of St. John the Divine,"* in Robert Jamieson, A. R. Fausset, and David Brown, *A Commentary, Critical and Explanatory, on the Old and New Testaments* (Oak Harbor, WA: Logos Research Systems, Inc., 1997, 1877), Rev. 12:1.

6 James Strong, *The Exhaustive Concordance of the Bible* (Ontario: Woodside Bible Fellowship, 1996), H224.

7 Concerning heaven and earth serving as witnesses: Gen. 1:1; Deu. 4:26; 30:19; 31:28; 32:1; Ps. 50:4; Isa. 1:2; Jer. 6:19; Jas. 5:12; Heb. 6:17.

8 Note that Jacob interprets the moon as representing *Leah* rather than Rachel. Rachel was already dead. The dream was not fulfilled until much later in Egypt while Leah was presumably still alive (Gen. 44:14). Her death is not mentioned until later (Gen. 49:31). "Rachel died . . . giving birth to Benjamin . . . Leah, no doubt, raised Joseph and Benjamin. . . Clearly, [in Gen. 37:10] Jacob was referring to Leah."—McQuaid, *Israel My Glory*, 34.

9 Yet how fashionable it is in our day for seemingly highly educated Christian theologians to dismiss all possibility that Genesis 3:15 speaks of the promised redeemer. They denounce the *protevangelium* (first gospel), almost as if in concert with Judaism they seek to deny the unity of both *NT*[5.2.48] and *OT*[5.2.51]. They would do well to reconsider the words of Jesus (Luke 24:27, 44; John 5:39, 46).

10 An odd phrase for an offspring in a Jewish genealogy, which hints at His virgin origin.

11 Arnold Fruchtenbaum discusses evidence that Eve expected the promised redeemer in Cain: "Literal translation: 'I have gotten a man: Jehovah'. The common English translation is not based on the Hebrew text but on the Greek *Septuagint*[5.2.65] which reads 'through God.' This was followed by the *Latin Vulgate*[5.2.81] which also reads 'through God.' The *Jerusalem Targum*, an Aramaic translation, reads 'I have gotten a man: the angel of Jehovah.' The rabbis also gave a reading here which is much closer to the original Hebrew text. The *Targum Pseudo-Jonathan* reads, 'I have gotten for a man the angel of the Lord.' Another Aramaic translation is the *Targum Onqelos* which says 'from before the Lord.' The *Midrash Rabbah* (on Gen. 22:2), the rabbinic commentary, says of Gen. 4:1 'with the help of the Lord.' Rabbi Ishmael asked Rabbi Akiba, 'Since you have served Nahum of Gimzo for 22 years and he taught that every *ach* and *rach* is a limitation but every *et* and *gam* is an extension, tell me what is the purpose of the *et* here.' He replied, 'if it is said "I have gotten a man: the Lord" it would have been difficult to interpret, hence et "with the help of the Lord" is required.' The footnote on page 181 of this Midrash says 'it might imply that she had begotten the Lord.' The rabbis clearly understood the implications of the construction and so had to make the necessary adjustments in their translation."—Arnold G. Fruchtenbaum, *Messianic Christology* (Tustin, CA: Ariel Ministries, 1998), 16.

12 Merrill F. Unger, *Unger's Commentary on the Old Testament* (Chattanooga, TN: AMG Publishers, 2002), Isa. 66:7-9.

13 Jerry Falwell, Edward D. Hindson, and Michael Woodrow Kroll, eds., *KJV Bible Commentary* (Nashville, TN: Thomas Nelson, 1997, c1994), Isa. 66:5-9.

14 William R. Newell, *Revelation: Chapter by Chapter* (Grand Rapids, MI: Kregel Publications, 1994,c1935), Rev. 12:1.

15 Seiss, *The Apocalypse: Lectures on the Book of Revelation*, Rev. 12:3.

16 Arnold G. Fruchtenbaum, *The Footsteps of Messiah*, rev ed. (Tustin, CA: Ariel Ministries, 2003), 246-247.

17 M. R. Vincent, *Vincent's Word Studies* (Escondido, CA: Ephesians Four Group, 2002), Rev. 12:4.

18 John F. Walvoord, *The Revelation of Jesus Christ* (Chicago, IL: Moody Press, 1966), Rev. 12:3.

19 Albrecht Durer (1471 - 1528). Image courtesy of the *Connecticut College* (http://www.conncoll.edu/visual/Durer-prints/index.html) *Wetmore Print Collection* (http://www.conncoll.edu/visual/wetmore.html). This woodcut does not accurately portray all that is taught concerning the dragon and its horns. The ten horns should all appear on only one of its head—the head representing the final kingdom. See *Beasts, Heads, and Horns*[4.3].

20 Robert L. Thomas, *Revelation 8-22* (Chicago, IL: Moody Press, 1995), Rev. 12:3.

21 Frederick William Danker, and Walter Bauer, *A Greek-English Lexicon of the New Testament and Other Early Christian Literature* (Chicago, IL: University of Chicago Press, 2000), 794.

22 Timothy Friberg, Barbara Friberg, and Neva F. Miller, *Analytical Lexicon of the Greek New Testament* (Grand Rapids, MI: Baker Books, 2000), 379.

23 "Seeking to produce a mongrel, half-human half-demon and thus unredeemable race of men, Satan sent demons ('sons of God'; the same Hebrew phrase refers to angels in Job 1:6; 2:1; 38:7; Ps. 29:1; 89:6) to cohabit with human women (Gen. 6:1-4)."—MacArthur, *Revelation 12-22 : The MacArthur New Testament Commentary*, Rev. 12:4.

24 Thomas, *Revelation 8-22*, Rev. 12:4.

25 Danker, *A Greek-English Lexicon of the New Testament and Other Early Christian Literature*, 683.

26 Danker, *A Greek-English Lexicon of the New Testament and Other Early Christian Literature*, 683.

27 Jerome Smith, *The New Treasury of Scripture Knowledge* (Nashville, TN: Thomas Nelson Publishers, 1992), Rev. 12:5.

28 Danker, *A Greek-English Lexicon of the New Testament and Other Early Christian Literature*, 109.

29 "The flight of the woman may in part reflect the escape of the Palestinian church to Pella at the outbreak of the Jewish war in A.D. 66 (*Eusebius*[5.2.19], *hist. Eccl* . iii.5; cf. Mark 13:14)."—Robert H. Mounce, *The Book of Revelation* (Grand Rapids, MI: William B. Eerdmans Publishing Co., 1977), Rev. 12:6.

30 Alva J. McClain, *The Greatness Of The Kingdom* (Winona Lake, IN: BMH Books, 1959), 136-137.

31 Walter Scott, *Exposition of The Revelation* (London, England: Pickering & Inglis, n.d.), 258.

32 Mills, *Revelations: An Exegetical Study of the Revelation to John*, Rev. 12:6.

33 Unger, *Unger's Commentary on the Old Testament*, Zec. 13:8.

34 MacArthur, *Revelation 12-22 : The MacArthur New Testament Commentary*, Rev. 12:13.

35 Henry Morris, *The Revelation Record* (Wheaton, IL: Tyndale House Publishers, 1983), Rev. 12:6.

36 Copyright ©003 *www.BiblePlaces.com*. This image appears by *special permission*[1.3] and may not be duplicated for use in derivative works.

37 E. W. Bullinger, *Commentary On Revelation* (Grand Rapids, MI: Kregel Publications, 1984, 1935), Rev. 12:16.

38 They perish to join the ranks of the second resurrection who remain in Hades for the duration of the Millennial Kingdom only to be resurrected for judgment at the Great White Throne and subsequent condemnation in the Lake of Fire (Rev. 20:11-15).

39 Thomas, *Revelation 8-22*, Rev. 12:14.

40 Unger, *Unger's Commentary on the Old Testament*, Isa. 15:4.

41 [Unger, *Unger's Commentary on the Old Testament*, Isa. 16:1.] "Selah is generally supposed to be the same as Petra, which in Greek signifies a rock, the celebrated capital of Arabia Petraea."—Smith, *The New Treasury of Scripture Knowledge*, 2K. 14:7.

42 "The passage [Dan. 11:41] states that while Antichrist will conquer the whole world, there nations will escape his domination: Edom, Moab, and Ammon. All three of these ancient nations currently comprise the single modern kingdom of Jordan."—Fruchtenbaum, *The Footsteps of Messiah*, 297.

43 Image courtesy of the *Perry-Castañeda Library Map Collection*, University of Texas at Austin. [*www.lib.utexas.edu/maps*]

44 Ulrich Hart, and Hübner, *"Bozrah in Edom,"* in David Noel Freeman, ed., *The Anchor Bible Dictionary* (New York, NY: Doubleday, 1996, c1992), 1:774.

45 Unger, *Unger's Commentary on the Old Testament*, Hab. 3:3-7.

46 Unger, *Unger's Commentary on the Old Testament*, Ps. 60:9.

47 Fruchtenbaum, *The Footsteps of Messiah*, 296-297.

48 Unger, *Unger's Commentary on the Old Testament*, Mic. 2:12-13.

49 The difficulty and risk of their actions at the time of the end are a demonstration of their faith.

50 It is provocative to consider some of the parallels between the temptation of Jesus and the testing of the Jewish remnant at the time of the end: Jesus is the Son of God (Mtt. 4:3), the Jewish remnant is the son of God (Hos. 11:1; Mtt. 2:15). Jesus is led to the wilderness by the Holy Spirit (Mtt. 4:1), the Jewish remnant is led to the wilderness by God (Hos. 2:14). Jesus is tempted to worship Satan (Mtt. 4:9), the Jewish remnant is tempted to worship Satan (Rev. 13:4 cf. John 5:43). Jesus refuses Satan's kingdom in favor of the kingdom of God (Mtt. 4:10), the Jewish remnant refuses Satan's kingdom in favor of the Millennial Kingdom (Hos. 2:18; Isa. 16:1-5). Jesus is fed by God (Mtt. 4:11), the Jewish is remnant fed by God (Rev. 12:6). Jesus is tempted to command that stones become bread (Mtt. 4:3), in the midst of the rock city (Sela, Isa. 16:1; 42:11) the Jewish Remnant finds bread (Rev. 12:6), much in the same way their fathers were fed upon fleeing Egypt (Deu. 8:16 cf. Rev. 2:17). During the time of Jesus' testing, Satan brings Jesus to the pinnacle (wing) of the *Temple*[5.2.73]. During the time of testing of the Jewish remnant, Satan empowers *Antichrist*[5.2.3]'s abomination on the wing of the Temple (Dan. 9:27). (Commentators differ as to whether "wing" (Dan. 9:27, NKJV, NASB) refers to a physical location within the Temple. Nevertheless, Jesus and Paul make plain the abomination will involve a desecrating authority over the Temple (Mtt. 24:15; Mark 13:14; 2Th. 2:4).)

51 "Satan knows that once Messiah returns, his freedom ends. Satan also knows that Jesus will not come back until the Jewish leaders ask Him to come back. So if Satan can succeed in destroying the Jews once and for all before they come to national repentance, then Jesus will not come back and Satan's career is eternally safe."—Fruchtenbaum, *The Footsteps of Messiah*, 311-312.

52 Unger, *Unger's Commentary on the Old Testament*, Hos. 5:15-6:2.

53 Friberg, *Analytical Lexicon of the Greek New Testament*, 321.

54 Although Scripture does not say, perhaps it was Michael who protected Daniel while in the lion's den (Dan. 6:22)?

55 Morris, *The Revelation Record*, Rev. 12:8.

56 Albrecht Durer (1471 - 1528). Image courtesy of the *Connecticut College* (http://www.conncoll.edu/visual/Durer-prints/index.html) *Wetmore Print Collection* (http://www.conncoll.edu/visual/wetmore.html).

57 Scott, *Exposition of The Revelation*, Rev. 12:7.

58 Thomas, *Revelation 8-22*, 12:9.

59 Danker, *A Greek-English Lexicon of the New Testament and Other Early Christian Literature*, 561.

60 Morris, *The Revelation Record*, Rev. 12:9.

61 Newell, *Revelation: Chapter by Chapter*, Rev. 12:10.

62 NASB.

63 Danker, *A Greek-English Lexicon of the New Testament and Other Early Christian Literature*, 278.

64 Danker, *A Greek-English Lexicon of the New Testament and Other Early Christian Literature*, 423.

65 MacArthur, *Revelation 12-22 : The MacArthur New Testament Commentary*, Rev. 12:7.

66 Friberg, *Analytical Lexicon of the Greek New Testament*, 30.

67 For other negative uses of ἀγαπάω [*agapaō*] , see John 12:43 and 2Pe. 2:15.

68 Vincent, *Vincent's Word Studies*, Rev. 12:12.

69 Danker, *A Greek-English Lexicon of the New Testament and Other Early Christian Literature*, 201.

70 Copyright ©003 *www.BiblePlaces.com*. This image appears by *special permission*[1.3] and may not be duplicated for use in derivative works.

71 Danker, *A Greek-English Lexicon of the New Testament and Other Early Christian Literature*, 825.

72 Danker, *A Greek-English Lexicon of the New Testament and Other Early Christian Literature*, 720.

73 Danker, *A Greek-English Lexicon of the New Testament and Other Early Christian Literature*, 720.

74 "This invasion of Israel sent by Satan was described in Daniel 11:41 as: *He shall enter also into the glorious land* . This is the same invasion spoken of in Revelation 11:1-2 by which the *Antichrist*[5.2.3] will succeed in

taking control of both Jerusalem and the *Temple*[5.2.73] and will commit the Abomination of Desolation."—Fruchtenbaum, *The Footsteps of Messiah*, 267.

75 J. Dwight Pentecost, *Things to Come: A Study in Biblical Eschatology* (Grand Rapids, MI: Zondervan Publishing House, 1958), 352.

76 Danker, *A Greek-English Lexicon of the New Testament and Other Early Christian Literature*, 694.

77 Danker, *A Greek-English Lexicon of the New Testament and Other Early Christian Literature*, 416.

78 Morris, *The Revelation Record*, Rev. 12:1.

79 It is unclear whether the acceptance of the mark by some *Jews* will guarantee their survival under the *Beast*[5.2.9]. Isaiah describes a "covenant with death" which God annuls: "When the overflowing scourge passes through, then you will be trampled down by it" (Isa. 28:15-18). Perhaps the rage of the dragon will be so great against the Jews that the Beast will make an exception and exterminate even those Jews who take his mark.

80 Thomas, *Revelation 8-22*, Rev. 12:17.

81 Those who take "My brethren" as denoting the family of faith face the difficulty of explaining who the sheep are? If His brothers are both Jews and Gentiles in the faith, then how can the sheep be separate from them and yet also inherit the kingdom? The actions of the sheep and their reward of entry to the kingdom demonstrate them to be among the saved. The differentiation between Jesus' brothers and the sheep cannot be based upon spiritual regeneration, but must reflect a national Jew/Gentile distinction concerning persecution at the time of the end.

82 Pentecost, *Things to Come: A Study in Biblical Eschatology*, 297.

83 Thomas, *Revelation 8-22*, Rev. 12:17.

84 Fruchtenbaum, *The Footsteps of Messiah*, 289.

85 Mills, *Revelations: An Exegetical Study of the Revelation to John*, Rev. 12:15.

86 Pentecost, *Things to Come: A Study in Biblical Eschatology*, 291-292.

3.13 - Revelation 13

3.13.1 - Revelation 13:1

In the previous chapter, we saw a dragon with seven heads and ten horns who attempted to intercept the promised child and subsequently persecuted the woman who gave birth to the child. We saw numerous indicators which pointed to the Jewish context of that chapter and its events, with the woman finally receiving supernatural assistance to reach a place of protection prepared by God (Rev. 12:6, 14). Since the dragon could not destroy the woman, he became enraged and "went off to make war with the rest of her offspring" (see commentary on *Revelation 12:17*[3.12.17]).[1]

Now, the scene shifts to describe a beast who also has seven heads and ten horns, who is closely identified with the dragon. He and another beast institute a series of satanically-empowered deceptions which bring the whole world under the sway of the beast with seven heads and ten horns, and ultimately Satan. This is the rise of the *Antichrist*[4.2],[2] whose activities are key to *The 70th Week of Daniel*[2.13.5].

By now, the *Restrainer*[4.14.4.2] has been taken out of the way resulting in the departure of the Church in the *Rapture*[4.14]. Thus, believers today will not see the rise of the *Beast*[5.2.9] and the events of this chapter, for they are to watch for the *imminent*[4.8] return of Christ, not the rise of *Antichrist*[4.2]. Even so, multitudes will come to faith during this period of intense persecution as the message of the various witnesses which God has specially equipped for the time of the end goes forth (Rev. 7:4-8; 11:3-12; 14:6).[3]

Prior to studying this chapter, we recommend the study of related topics: *The Beast*[4.2]; *Nero*[4.12]; and *Beasts, Heads, and Horns*[4.3].

I stood on the sand of the sea

The *NU*[5.2.49] text has *he stood*, that is, the dragon of the previous chapter.

> Some manuscripts read, "he stood," the change being effected by the dropping of one letter *nu* from the end of the verb *estathe*. If the letter is properly dropped, it indicates that the dragon himself stood upon the sand of the sea. If the letter is added, it means that John stood upon the sand of the sea. . . inasmuch as it is more likely that a letter be dropped than a letter added to the text, some scholars continue to feel that the Authorized Version is correct that John stood upon the sand of the sea.[4]

> Hengstenberg remarks, "One cannot decide on *external* grounds between the two [textual] readings." Authorities are divided. But a careful study of the context shews [*sic*] conclusively that it is the Seer, and not the dragon that "stood upon the sand of the sea." The apocalyptic prophet always takes his place or stand as a point of observation in keeping with the subject at hand. Thus heaven (Rev. 4:1); the sand of the sea (Rev. 13:1); the wilderness (Rev. 17:1); and a high mountain (Rev. 21:10), are respective points of view from which he can contemplate the various panoramic visions as they pass before his gaze.[5]

If it is the dragon which stands on the sand, rather than John, then it would intimate his summons of the Beast portrayed next. "The dragon, cast out of Heaven after his final defeat at the hands of Michael and his forces, comes to the earth looking for an instrument through whom he can carry on his warfare against his hated Creator and God."[6] Whether it is John or the dragon, the dragon is clearly the malevolent power behind the rise of the Beast: "The coming of the *lawless one* is according to the working of Satan, with all power, signs, and lying wonders" (2Th. 2:4).

Although elsewhere sand denotes an innumerable company, "The sand of the sea does not mean the seashore in Scriptural language. The sand, always represents an innumerable company, as will be easily seen by a comparison of the passages from the time when God promised Abraham seed as the sand of the sea in multitude. The sea is clearly shown as a symbol of the restless nations of the earth. Further in this prophecy we will see that the 'many waters' are 'peoples, multitudes, nations, and tongues' (Rev. 17:15)."[7] Here, it merely describes the position of John on the shore from where he observed the beast's rise from the water.

I saw a beast

John sees two beasts in this chapter. The first beast is closely identified with the dragon—having seven heads and ten horns. He is also the beast whose deadly wound was healed. Moreover, he is the object of worship and aided in this role by the second beast (Rev. 13:11). These characteristics identify the first beast as Antichrist, also called the *Beast*. The second beast which appears later is known as the *False Prophet*[5.2.20] (Rev. 16:13; 19:20; 20:10). As we mention in our discussion of why *Nero*[5.2.46] cannot be the Antichrist, the early church which lived much nearer to the time of Nero and the Apostle John, did not see Nero as the Beast. *Irenaeus*[5.2.34] identifies the first of St John's Wild Beasts with St Paul's Man of Sin. See commentary on *Revelation 13:4*[3.13.4].

As we discuss in *Beasts, Heads, and Horns*[4.3], the symbolism of the revelation given to both Daniel and John concerning this time of the end often blurs the distinction between an *individual* and the *government* which he leads:

> There can be no kingdom without a king, and no empire without an emperor; neither can there be a king in fact without a kingdom. We cannot consistently speak of imperial power and dominion apart from a personal head which represents and embodies that power.[8]
>
> But it is very clear from what follows in Rev. 13 that there is something more than the Empire here in view. In Rev. 13:3-8 it is a person that is before us. We are satisfied that this same person is also described, symbolically, in the opening verses. As is frequently the case in the prophetic scriptures, the king and his kingdom are here inseparably united. Rev. 13:1, 2 portrays both the Empire and its last Emperor.[9]
>
> Is the beast out of the sea a man or an empire? The answer is both. (a) The beast is a man because his number is that of a man (Rev. 13:18). Also the use of the masculine pronoun αὐτόν [*auton*] (Rev. 13:8) to refer to the neuter θηρίον [*thērion*] (Rev. 13:1-2, 4) indicates that he is a human being. In addition, parallels between the beast and the Lamb indicate that he is a person: both have followers on whose foreheads are inscribed their names (Rev. 13:16-17; 14:1), both are conquerors (Rev. 5:5; 13:7), and both receive worship (Rev. 5:8; 13:4). (b) At the same time the beast is an empire over which the man reigns. This fact is demonstrated by the symbolism of the beasts of Daniel 7.[10]

See *The Beast*[4.2]. See *#16 - Beast*[4.3.2.16].

rising up

Ἀναβαῖνον [*Anabainon*], present tense participle, *presently arising*. John saw the beast as he was rising.

out of the sea

Daniel's *four beasts*[4.3.2.8] also were seen rising from the sea (Dan. 7:2-3). The Beast's ascension from the sea speaks of the origin of his kingdom from the Gentile nations. "Stretch out Your hand from above; Rescue me and deliver me out of great waters, From the hand of foreigners [lit. *strange children*]" (Ps. 144:7). This beast shares characteristics of the first three of Daniel's beasts (all Gentile kingdoms). See commentary on *Revelation 13:2*[3.13.2]. Leviathan, the twisted serpent, representative of both Satan and the Beast, is in the sea (Isa. 27:1; Ps. 74:13).

The Beast is also said to ascend out of the bottomless pit (Rev. 11:7, 17:8). His ascent out of the bottomless pit speaks of his revival from the dead following his fatal wound. See *Supernatural Origin?*[4.2.7]

This beast arises from the sea, but the second beast arises from the *earth* or *land* (Rev. 13:11). This has caused some to expect the second beast, the False Prophet, to be Jewish in origin. See commentary on *Revelation 12:11*[3.12.11].

> These contrasting terms are indicative of the origin of the two beasts. The sea may symbolize the Gentiles (Rev. 17:15; cf. Dan. 7:2-3) and if this is the case here, the opposite term, the earth, symbolizes the Jews. There is precedence for the Gentile origin of Antichrist in the Old Testament allusions, and the Jewish identification may be strengthened if here "the earth" has technical sense of "the land" [of Israel] as it sometimes may in Revelation (Rev. 11:18; cf. Dan. 8:9).[11]

The land/sea distinction between Gentiles and Jews is seen in the parables of the hidden treasure and the pearl of great price:

> Christ's inheritance is not only the Church which is the pearl of great price for which He sold all that He had, but it also includes Israel which is the treasure hidden in the field and which He purchased with His own blood and which He hid again.[12]
>
> The treasure [Mtt. 13:45-46] represents the Jews, so it is natural that the pearl [Mtt. 13:45-46] would represent the Gentiles. Furthermore, the pearl comes from the sea, and the sea symbolizes the Gentile world (Dan. 7:2-3; Rev. 17:1, 17:15). Finally, the pearl comes from the oyster, which itself was unclean in the Law of Moses but made clean by the Law of Messiah.[13]

Some suggest that the sea indicates his rise from the abyss (Rev. 11:7; 17:8).[14]

seven heads

Like the dragon (Rev. 12:3), the Beast has seven heads. The heads represent *seven world kingdoms*[4.3.2.4] which culminate in the Beast as the seventh which had "not yet come" in John's day (Rev. 17:10). This is not a matter of conjecture for this same Beast with seven heads is ridden upon by the *Harlot*[5.2.25], the "mother of harlots and abominations of the earth" (Rev. 17:3). We are told that the seven heads are "seven mountains on which the woman sits. They are seven kings" (Rev. 17:9-10).[15] One of the heads of the Beast receives a deadly wound which is healed (Rev. 13:3). This revived head is considered as "the eighth, and is of the seven, and is going to perdition" (Rev. 17:11). The terminology describing the Beast indicates he is both a kingdom *and* its representative leader—the king.

In Daniel's night vision, he sees *four beasts*[4.3.2.8] which, when taken together, have seven heads:

> That we have here in Rev. 13:1, 2 a composite kingdom is clear from the 'seven heads.' Now note that in Dan. 7 the first, second and fourth kingdoms are not said to have more than one head, but the third has 'four heads' (Dan. 7:6). Thus the beasts of Dan. 7 have, three of them one head each, and the third four heads, or seven in all; which tallies perfectly with Rev. 13:1. . . . the four kingdoms of Dan. 7 are to be restored, and play their final parts immediately before the Millennium. If the reader will turn to Dan. 2, which is parallel with Dan. 7 - the 'image in its four parts' (the head, the breast and arms, the belly and thighs, the legs and feet) corresponding with the four beasts - it will be found that when we come to Dan. 2:45, which speaks of Christ (under the figure of 'the Stone cut out of the mount without hands' returning to earth to destroy the forces of evil, and then set up His kingdom, we discover that the Stone 'brake in pieces the iron (Rome), the brass (Greece), the clay (apostate Israel), the silver (Medo-Persia), and the gold (Babylon).' What we desire the reader to note particularly is that the Stone strikes not only the iron, but the brass, clay, silver, and gold; in fact, Dan. 2:35 tells us, expressly, they shall be 'broken to pieces together!' If, then, they are destroyed together, they must all be on the scene at the time of Christ's return to earth to inaugurate His millennial reign, and if so, each of them must have been revived and restored!![16]

Although it is true that the four beasts Daniel sees are represented in this beast with seven heads, it is unlikely that the seven heads on the beast correspond exactly with the seven heads of Daniel's four beasts. For a discussion of the problems involved, see *Daniel saw Seven Heads*[4.3.2.4.1]. See *#4 - Seven Heads/Kings*[4.3.2.4].

ten horns

Like the dragon (Rev. 12:3), the beast has ten horns. The ten horns are identified for us: "The ten horns which you saw are ten kings who have received no kingdom as yet, but they will receive authority for one hour as kings with the beast. These are of one mind, and they will give their power and authority to the beast." (Rev. 17:12-13). These are the ten horns which Daniel saw upon the fourth *terrible beast*[4.3.2.12] in his night vision (Dan. 7:7, 20) which are also said to be ten kings (Dan. 7:24). The Beast ridden by the Harlot also has ten horns (Rev. 17:3). "And the ten horns which you saw on the beast, these will hate the harlot, make her desolate and naked, eat her flesh and burn her with fire. For God has put it into their hearts to fulfill His purpose" (Rev. 17:16-17:17a) Initially, the beast supports the Harlot and she rides upon, or controls, him. Eventually the ten kings who are allied with the Beast will turn on the Harlot, throw her off and destroy her. See *#22 - Ten Horns/Kings*[4.3.2.22]. See *The Great Harlot*[4.1.4]. See commentary on *Revelation 17:16*[3.17.16].

on his horns, ten crowns

Unlike the dragon which wears crowns on its heads (Rev. 12:3), the beast's crowns are on its horns. The dragon's crowns are associated with historical *kingdoms* of which this beast is one. The beast has crowns on each of his ten horns, indicating the rule of the ten contemporaneous kings associated with the last head or kingdom. These ten horns are the same as those of the last (terrible beast) of Daniel's four beasts (Dan. 7:7). See *#22 - Ten Horns/Kings*[4.3.2.22]. See *Crowns*[4.6].

a blasphemous name

Ὄνομα βλασφημίας [*Onoma blasphēmias*], *a name blasphemous*. The *MT*[5.2.45] and NU texts have, ὀνόματα βλασφημίας [*onomata blasphēmias*], *names blasphemous*. The blasphemous name or names are an indication of his character. Daniel described this individual who "shall exalt and magnify himself above every god, shall speak blasphemies against the God of gods, and shall prosper till the wrath has been accomplished; for what has been determined shall be done" (Dan. 11:36).[17] He is also noted for his mouth speaking great things against God. See commentary on *Revelation 13:5*[3.13.5].

3.13.2 - Revelation 13:2

like a leopard . . . bear . . . lion

The characteristics of the first three beasts in Daniel's night vision contribute to this beast of the end (Dan. 7:4-6).[18] The fourth *terrible beast*[4.3.2.12] seen by Daniel is not mentioned because this *Beast*[5.2.9] *is* the embodiment of that terrible beast at the time of the end.

> It is a composite of the four beasts of Daniel's vision (Dan. 7) and must be related to them. Daniel wrote from the standpoint of the Jewish people, whose fate under the Gentile empires to come would effect the First Coming of Messiah. Revelation, written under the fourth and last of these empires, presumably after the Jewish commonwealth had been crushed, takes this picture of Gentile world power from Daniel and combines these four empires onto the picture of the future world-state. The magnificence of Babylon, the vastness of Medo-Persia, the dominating culture of Greek Macedonia, and the organizing might of Rome are united in one state that will aspire to world domination and that will achieve it.[19]

The order in which the attributes are listed, leopard then bear then lion, are reversed from what Daniel saw. This reflects John's different vantage point. Daniel, living in the days of the lion beast (Babylon), looked forward in time to see the rise of the bear (Medo-Persia), and then the leopard (Greece). John, writing in the time of the first phase of the terrible beast (Rome), looked backward in time to see them in reverse order. See *#8 - Four Beasts/Kings*[4.3.2.8].

The mention of the leopard, bear, and lion in connection with the Beast arising from the sea is in concert with what Daniel was shown concerning the *continuation* of Babylon, Medo-Persia, and Greece and their contribution to the final form of world government. "As for the rest of the beasts, they had their dominion taken away, yet their lives were prolonged for a season and a time" (Dan. 7:12). When the stone representing the *Messianic kingdom*[5.2.39] strikes the image of Nebuchadnezzar's dream, all the metals of the image are demolished together: "the iron, the clay, the bronze, the silver, and the gold were crushed together" (Dan. 2:35); "it broke in pieces the iron, the bronze, the clay, the silver, and the gold" (Dan. 2:45). Thus, attributes of all the kingdoms are found in this last beast.

Many understand this final kingdom to be a "revived Rome." This view is based on continuity expressed in Nebuchadnezzar's dream. The ten toes of the image are on its *feet* which are partly of *iron* which symbolizes Rome:

> Whereas you saw the feet and toes, partly of potter's clay and partly of iron, the kingdom shall be divided; yet the strength of the iron shall be in it, just as you saw the iron mixed with ceramic clay. And *as* the toes of the feet *were* partly of iron and partly of clay, *so* the kingdom shall be partly strong and partly fragile. As you saw iron mixed with ceramic clay, they will mingle with the seed of men; but they will not adhere to one another, just as iron does not mix with clay. And in the days of these kings the God of heaven will set up a kingdom which shall never be destroyed; and the kingdom shall not be left to other people; it shall break in pieces and consume all these kingdoms, and it shall stand forever. (Dan. 2:41-44)

Adding to this identification is the fact that Daniel is only shown *four beasts*[4.3.2.8] prior to the kingdom being given to the Son of Man (Dan. 7:11-14). In some sense, this last kingdom of the end must be a continuation of Rome.

> The final world empire will be in some sense a revival of the Roman Empire (the iron legs and ten toes of the statue in Daniel 2), but will far exceed it both in power and extent. It will be much more than a European confederacy; it will cover the entire world.[20]

It is also clear that all the previous kingdoms contribute to its characteristics. Bullinger notes that when John is told "one [kingdom] is" (Rev. 17:10), it is Rome which is in view—the next kingdom "has not yet come." He wonders how Rome can be both.[21] Yet the continuity between Rome of John's day and the form of kingdom represented by the rise of the Beast is strongly inferred by the continuance of Daniel's fourth beast until the time of the end, when it is predicted "to devour the whole earth" (Dan. 7:23). Moreover, in the famous prophecy of *Daniel's seventy weeks*[2.13.5], Daniel was told that the "people of the prince who is to come shall destroy the city and the sanctuary" (Dan. 9:26). This prophecy was fulfilled in the destruction of Jerusalem and the temple in A.D. 70 by *Rome*. Thus, the prince to come has a Roman origin. These passages argue for some form of continuity between Rome and the initial beast kingdom of the end. This should not be overemphasized since attributes of the other three beasts are also found in it.

As we progress in this chapter, we will see God sovereignly grant permission for this beastly empire to attain authority by way of empowerment from the dragon. Hosea was shown these beasts and how they would be used to tear Israel to cause her to turn back to God:

> When they had pasture, they were filled; they were filled and their heart was exalted; therefore they forgot Me. So I will be to them like a **lion**; like a **leopard** by the road I will lurk; I will meet them like a **bear** deprived *of her cubs*; I will tear open their rib cage, and there I will devour them like a lion. **The wild beast shall tear them**. O Israel, you are destroyed, but your help *is* from Me. I will be your King; where *is any other*, that he may save you in all your cities? And your judges to whom you said, 'Give me a king and princes'? I gave you a king in My anger, and took *him* away in My wrath. (Hos. 13:6-11) [emphasis added]

> The lion, bear, leopard, and wild beast . . . correspond to the world empires among which Israel is to be scattered and persecuted (Dan. 7) during the time that she is in Dispersion until she will be regathered by her covenant-keeping LORD (Eze. 37:1-28; Mtt. 24:31; Rom. 11:26).[22]

the dragon gave him his power

Paul told the church at Thessalonica that the coming of the Beast would be according to the working (ἐνέργειαν [*energeian*]) of Satan (2Th. 2:9). The Beast will be *energized* by Satan, which speaks of empowerment by a supernatural being.[23] "In him shall dwell all the fulness of the Devil bodily."[24]

> He will be Satan's parody of the God-Man. He will be an incarnation of the Devil. The world today is talking of and looking for the Super-man. This is exactly what the *Antichrist*[5.2.3] will be. He will be the Serpent's masterpiece. . . . he will be the culmination and consummation of satanic craft and power. All the evil, malignity, cunning, and power of the Serpent will be embodied in this terrible monster.[25]

We must not underestimate the connection between the dragon and the Beast. The relationship between the Beast and the dragon must be intimate, for the Beast is allowed to be the recipient of *all worship* (2Th. 2:4). This may indicate that worship toward the Beast finds its ultimate destination in the dragon by way of possession. See commentary on *Revelation 13:4*[3.13.4].

his throne and great authority

The Beast obtains his throne and authority from the dragon. During the temptation, the dragon showed Jesus "all the kingdoms of the world in a moment of time" and explained, "All this authority I will give You . . . for *this* has been delivered to me and I give it to whomever I wish" (Luke 4:6). Evidently, the Beast accepts an offer similar to that which Jesus refused. "Will not Antichrist"s kingdom be the very one which Satan offered in vain to Christ? namely, 'all the kingdoms of the world, and the glory of them" (Mtt. 4:8)."[26] Although Scripture does not say, we can infer that the Beast, probably in some private fashion, ultimately gives *his* worship to the dragon. The only alternative would be that Satan so completely indwells the Beast that the result is their near unity.

The close association of the Beast with the dragon and Babylon is seen in a passage from Isaiah which begins as a proverb against the king of *Babylon*, but contains elements which go far beyond any mortal man to identify the power behind the king—Satan:

> Take up this proverb against the king of Babylon . . . How you are fallen from heaven, O Lucifer, son of the morning! *How* you are cut down to the ground, you who weakened the nations! For you have said in your heart: 'I will ascend into heaven, I will exalt my throne above the stars of God; I will also sit on the mount of the congregation on the farthest sides of the north; I will ascend above the heights of the clouds, I will be like the Most High.' Yet you shall be brought down to Sheol, to the lowest depths of the Pit. Those who see you will gaze at you, *and* consider you, *saying: 'Is* this the man who made the earth tremble, who shook kingdoms?' (Isa. 14:4, 12-16)

The shaking of the earth and kingdoms refers to the activities of the ultimate *king of Babylon*, the Beast and his close unity and empowerment with Satan, the dragon. The fifth bowl of God's wrath is poured out "on the throne of the beast, and his kingdom" (Rev. 16:10).

3.13.3 - Revelation 13:3

one of his heads

The head which is wounded is the seventh head:

> Here *is* the mind which has wisdom: The seven heads are seven mountains on which the woman sits. They are seven kings. Five have fallen, one is, *and* the other has not yet come. And when he comes, he must continue a short time. "And the beast that was, and is not, is himself also the eighth, and is of the seven, and is going to perdition." (Rev. 17:10-11)[27]

The person of the *Beast*[5.2.9] is the king of the seventh empire (the restored Roman empire equated with Daniel's fourth beast). When he is personally killed, as head of the seventh empire, the empire also meets its demise. Some have taken the wounding of his head and his subsequent revival as describing the original Rome which disintegrated later to be revived.[28] This view does not fit the scenario because this individual did not rule at the time of John (the initial phase of Rome). Taking the wound and revival as pertaining to the disintegration of Rome after John's day and its subsequent revival at the time of the end—separated by at least 1900 years—would hardly cause the wonderment of the world which is described here which is fundamental to the ultimate worship of this individual (Rev. 13:4). It would seem that the same populace which sees the demise of his head must also witness his revival.

> It is best to identify the restoration to life with an end-time satanically controlled king who will come to the world as a false Christ. This allows for the interchangeability of the head with the whole beast—i.e., the king with his kingdom—as Rev. 13:12, 14 required. It coincides with further details to come in Rev. 17:8. It agrees with the final climactic appearance of the beast in history as a person, in concert with the vision's focus on the future. This means a future sequence that will be a close counterfeiting of Christ's death and resurrection.[29]

as if it had been mortally wounded

ὡς ἐσφαγμένην [*hōs esphagmenēn*], the identical phrase describes the "Lamb as though it had been slain" (Rev. 5:6).[30] *As if* denotes the appearance after having been slain and brought back to life. There is no reason to take this as merely a "wound" here when it describes the "slain" Lamb there.[31]

There are some who struggle with the idea that the beast could *truly die* because this would require a *literal resurrection* from the dead. Isn't this something that only God is capable of? Our very reluctance to consider this possibility provides evidence of the tremendous influence such an event would have upon those who witness such a miracle! Surely, if the *False Prophet*[5.2.20] is able to give breath to the inanimate *image of the beast*[5.2.29] (Rev. 13:15), then couldn't God also allow Satan to exercise the necessary power to raise the dead? Scripture records that saints have raised the dead (1K. 17:21; 2K. 4:34; Acts 9:40; 20:10). If God empowered the saints to do so for His purposes, why couldn't He do the same in allowing Satan to deceive those who had pleasure in unrighteousness at the end (2Th. 2:11-12)? The terms used for the death and revival of the Beast seem to point unavoidably to a *bona fide* miracle, although that which it attests to (the deity of the Beast) is false (2Th. 2:9):

> [The] view [that the beast is literally resurrected from the dead] has many more advocates down through history than some might realize. . . . It is interesting to realize that even Augustine believed like [Tim] LaHaye on this matter (The City of God, Book XX, Chapter 19). Another ancient one who held views

> similar . . . is Lactantius (early 300s) (Divine Institutes, Book VII, Chapter 17; Commentary on the Apocalypses, Chapter 13). More recent individuals include: Lewis Sperry Chafer, J. A. Seiss, Charles C. Ryrie, Leon Morris, Walter K. Price, Robert Govett and Robert Thomas.[32]

his deadly wound was healed

ἡ πληγὴ τοῦ θανάτου αὐτοῦ ἐθεραπεύθη [*hē plēgē tou thanatou autou etherapeuthē*], *the wound of the death of him was healed. Wound* is πληγὴ [*plēgē*], which often denotes a wound "as the result of a blow,"[33] although it can also denote a figurative blow of misfortune. The same word describes the plagues with which the two witnesses strike the earth (Rev. 11:6). Great emphasis is placed upon his death and revival, indicating its importance in the events which transpire at the end. It is the primary motivator for his worship (Rev. 13:12, 14; 17:11). "Man ignores the force of Jesus' resurrection, but will choose to be fooled by the Beast's recovery. Why? Jesus demands righteousness; the Beast will indulge sin."[34] See *Supernatural Origin?*[4.2.7]

Zechariah relates the payment of thirty pieces of silver for the value of Messiah at His First Coming when he was betrayed by Judas (Mtt. 26:15; 27:3). The passage then describes a "foolish . . . worthless shepherd" who will specialize in consuming the sheep. He is said to exhibit wounds affecting his arm and right eye:

> I said to them, "If it is good in your sight, give me my wages; but if not, never mind!" So they weighed out thirty shekels of silver as my wages. Then the LORD said to me, "Throw it to the potter, that magnificent price at which I was valued by them." So I took the thirty shekels of silver and threw them to the potter in the house of the LORD. Then I cut in pieces my second staff Union, to break the brotherhood between Judah and Israel. The LORD said to me, "Take again for yourself the equipment of a foolish shepherd. For behold, I am going to raise up a shepherd in the land who will not care for the perishing, seek the scattered, heal the broken, or sustain the one standing, but will devour the flesh of the fat sheep and tear off their hoofs. Woe to the worthless shepherd who leaves the flock! **A sword will be on his arm and on his right eye! His arm will be totally withered and his right eye will be blind.**" (Zec. 11:12-17) [emphasis added]

If this speaks of Antichrist, perhaps, like the resurrected Christ who retained the identifying marks of His death, so too the revived Beast will retain the marks of wounds which caused his death. They will serve to authenticate his identity as the leader who was previously slain.[35]

Preterist interpreters[2.12.2] believe the death and revival mentioned by John is a veiled reference to the *Nero*[5.2.46] revival myth, but this seems unlikely for it is a pagan notion without factual basis.[36] The revival which John records here is *real, fantastic, and miraculous* because it *results in* global worship of the Beast. Here again, we encounter deficiencies with the *Preterist Interpretation*[2.12.2]. If *Nero*[4.12] is the Beast, then any worship he may have received was *prior* to his demise by suicide. He *never rose from the dead* as described here. The worship which is attributed to the Beast results from his prior miraculous restoration. See *Revival Myth*[4.12.1]. See *Nero*[4.12].

3.13.4 - Revelation 13:4

So they worshiped the dragon who gave authority to the beast

So is the conjunction καὶ [*kai*], often translated by *and.* It links that which follows with that which preceded. In this case, it indicates that *worship of the dragon is in response to* the miraculous healing of the *Beast*[5.2.9]. This must not be missed!

- It rules out all consideration of *Nero*[4.12] as the Beast for people would hardly worship a failed legend. Whatever worship *Nero*[5.2.46] might have received, it came prior to his death by suicide.
- It explains the prominence which Scripture gives to the wounding and revival of the Beast. This is the catalyst which brings an outpouring of worship to both the dragon and the Beast. It is the *coup de grâce* of the miraculous signs empowered by the dragon.
- It recognizes the typological counterfeit of the Beast as pseudo-Christ. Christ died and rose from the dead only to be rejected by His own. The Beast dies and rises from the dead to acclaim.

It is not clear whether they worship the dragon explicitly and directly. This is most certainly possible, as some people today openly worship Satan. But it is also said that they worship the Beast. The text emphasizes the dragon as the source of authority for the Beast. This may indicate in the same way in which idol worship is understood as being worship of the demons *behind* the idols (Deu. 32:17; Ps. 106:37; Rev. 9:20), so too the worship of the Beast includes that power which is behind him. This seems even more likely because Scripture indicates that the Beast will exalt himself above *every god* and show *himself as God* (Dan. 11:36; 2Th. 2:4). Thus, worship directed to the Beast is equivalent with worship of the dragon who empowers him. At the time of the end, Satan will *almost* achieve one of his most treasured goals: universal worship (Isa. 14:14; Mtt. 4:9; Luke 4:7).

they worshiped the beast

This refers to the worship of an *individual*, not an empire.[37]

> Some wish to interpret this as a reference to the revival of the Roman Empire, . . . But a revived Roman Empire would not cause man to worship it as God any more than the revival of Poland or Israel did. . . . It is the resurrection of the man *Antichrist*[5.2.3] which creates this worship.[38]

This is the first phase of the *abomination of desolation* (Mtt. 24:15) when the man of sin himself sits in the temple of God proclaiming himself as God. His initial declaration as God will take place in the *Tribulation Temple*[4.16.5.9].

> Then the king shall do according to his own will: he shall exalt and magnify himself above every god, shall speak blasphemies against the God of gods, and shall prosper till the wrath has been accomplished; for what has been determined shall be done. He shall regard neither the God of his fathers nor the desire of women,[39] nor regard any god; for he shall exalt himself above *them* all. (Dan. 11:36-37)

> Let no one deceive you by any means; for *that Day will not come* unless the falling away comes first, and the man of sin is revealed, the son of perdition, who opposes and exalts himself above all that is called God or that is worshiped, so that he sits as God in the temple of God, showing himself that he is God. (2Th. 2:3-4)

The early church, having no knowledge of *preterism*[5.2.59], understood Paul's epistle to the Thessalonians as describing an Antichrist yet future:

> And again, speaking of Antichrist, [Paul] says, "who opposeth and exalteth himself above all that is called God, or that is worshipped [2Th. 2:4]." He points out here those who are called gods, by such as know not God, that is, idols. For the Father of all is called God, and is so; and Antichrist shall be lifted up, not above Him, but above those which are indeed called gods, but are not.—*Irenaeus*[5.2.34], *Against Heresies*, iii.vi.2[40]

The Beast, being empowered and possibly indwelt by Satan, shares the same aspirations as his master. He says in his heart:

> I will ascend into heaven, I will exalt my throne above the stars of God; I will also sit on the mount of the congregation on the farthest sides of the north; I will ascend above the heights of the clouds, I will be like the Most High (Isa. 13:13-14)

Yet, ultimately he is only a *man*:

> Yet you shall be brought down to Sheol, to the lowest depths of the Pit. Those who see you will gaze at you, and consider you, saying, 'Is this the man who made the earth tremble, who shook kingdoms, who made the world as a wilderness and destroyed its cities?' (Isa. 14:15-17)

Worship of the Beast will include worship of his image. See commentary on *Revelation 13:15*[3.13.15].

Who *is* like the beast?

The adulation of the world for the Beast is a perversion of acclaim which should go to God:

> This cry of the world, 'Who is like unto the Beast' is a travesty of the song of Moses. When celebrating Jehovah's overthrow of their enemies at the Red Sea, Israel sang, 'Who is like unto Thee, O Lord, among the Gods! Who is like Thee, glorious in holiness, fearful in praises, doing wonders!' (Ex. 15:11 cf. Ps. 89:8).[41]

Who is able to make war with him?

Not only is the power of the Beast evident in his revival, but upon his ascension from the abyss he will *make war* with the two powerful witnesses of God which have plagued the *earth dwellers*[5.2.18] (Rev. 11:7). Their overthrow further propels his ascent to fame and position. He is Satan's overcomer (see commentary on *Revelation 6:2*[3.6.2]). Yet in the end, he will make one war too many for he will take on the King of kings to his own demise. "These will make war with the Lamb, and the Lamb will overcome them, for He is Lord of lords and King of kings" (Rev. 17:14a).

His revival from the abyss, the holding pen of demons (Rev. 9:1-2), and his ability to sway the world and overcome God's prophets all point toward his demonic possession, possibly even by Satan himself (Luke 22:3):

> The Antichrist will be a man (2Th. 2:4), but at some point in his life, he will be indwelt by a powerful demon from the abyss. This demon-possessed man will be a gifted orator, an intellectual genius, possess great charm and charisma, and have immense leadership power. Added to those natural qualities will be the hellish power of Satan. The result will be a person of superhuman power, vast intelligence, and consummate wickedness.[42]

3.13.5 - Revelation 13:5

he was given a mouth speaking great things and blasphemies

As we have seen throughout this book, the actions and duration of the agents of evil are subject to God's sovereign permission (Rev. 13:7, 14-15 cf. Luke 22:31). The *great things* which he speaks are the "pompous words" which Daniel saw the *little horn*[5.2.37] speak (Dan. 7:8, 11, 20, 25). In his exaltation of himself, Daniel saw him "speak blasphemies against the God of gods" (Dan. 11:36). The *great things and blasphemies* likely speak of the same thing. "The figure [of speech] is *Hendiadys*; for the great things are his blasphemies."[43] See *#25 - Little Horn*[4.3.2.25].

he was given authority to continue

Continue is ποῖσαι [*poisai*]: "To be active."[44] The *MT*[5.2.45] text has πολεμον ποισαι [*polemon poisai*], *to make war*. See commentary on *Revelation 6:2*[3.6.2].

forty-two months

This period is equivalent to the "time and times and half a time," a three and one-half year period during which Daniel saw that the saints would be given into the hand of the little horn (Dan. 7:25). [45] See *Prophetic Year*[2.13.5.2].

This period begins at the midpoint of the week, when he violates his covenant with many in Israel (Dan. 9:27) and overcomes the two witnesses (Rev. 11:7) who had prophesied for 1,260 days (the first half of *The 70th Week of Daniel*[2.13.5]). See *Events of the 70th Week of Daniel*[2.13.5.4]. This is the time of *Jacob's trouble*[2.13.4] which shall be "for a time, times, and half *a time*; and when the power of the holy people has been completely shattered, all these *things* shall be finished" (Dan. 12:7). During this time, the holy city is being tread underfoot by the Gentiles (Rev. 11:2) and the woman, the Jewish remnant at the time of the end, is hidden in her place (Rev. 12:6, 14). See commentary on *Revelation 11:2*[3.11.2] and *Revelation 12:6*[3.12.6].

Irenaeus[5.2.34], a disciple of *Polycarp*[5.2.55] who himself knew the Apostle John, explains the passage in concert with *futurist interpreters*[2.12.5]:

> But **when this Antichrist shall have devastated all things in this world, he will reign for three years and six months, and sit in the temple at Jerusalem; and then the Lord will come from heaven in the clouds, in the glory of the Father, sending this man and those who follow him into the lake of fire**; but bringing in for the righteous the times of the kingdom, that is, the rest, the hallowed seventh day; and restoring to Abraham the promised inheritance, in which kingdom the Lord declared, that "many coming from the east and from the west should sit down with Abraham, Isaac, and Jacob."—Irenaeus, *Against Heresies*, v.xxx [emphasis added][46]

3.13.6 - Revelation 13:6

he opened his mouth in blasphemy against God, to blaspheme His name, His tabernacle, and those who dwell in heaven.

The *TR*[5.2.79] text designates as many as four targets for the blasphemy of the beast: (1) God; (2) His name; (3) His *tabernacle*[5.2.69]; and 4) those who dwell in heaven. The last three could also be taken as an elaboration of the first, *blasphemy against God consisting of...* Unlike the TR text, in the *MT*[5.2.45] and *NU*[5.2.49] texts the phrase, *those who dwell in heaven*, is not separated from the rest of the sentence by καὶ [*kai*] ("and"). Thus, *those who dwell in heaven* is taken in apposition to His tabernacle. "And he opened his mouth in blasphemies against God, to blaspheme His name and His tabernacle, *that is*, those who dwell in heaven."

those who dwell in heaven.

Τοὺς ἐν τῷ οὐρανῷ σκηνοῦντας [*Tous en tō ouranō skēnountas*], present tense participle: *those presently dwelling in heaven*. These are the ones who rejoiced over the casting out of Satan from heaven and the overcoming of Satan by the saints (Rev. 12:11-12). This includes an innumerable company of angels (Heb. 12:22; Rev. 5:11), the church having been taken in the *Rapture*[4.14] (Rev. 5:9), "The catching away of so many people of God must needs leave a deep impression behind it. The slain and abused bodies of the Two Witnesses are visibly revived, and taken up into the sky before the eyes of *Antichrist*[5.2.3]'s minions. This was a grand and most convincing evidence against him and all his infamous pretensions, a manifest token of his devilish falsity and approaching doom. And he needs above all to break it down, to cast discredit and dishonour upon it, and to root out the very idea if he can. Hence his particular railing and impatience with reference to this divine tent of the glorified ones, and his virulent blaspheming of those who tabernacle in it. . . How blessed are they who through faith and watchfulness have been accounted worthy to escape his power by being caught up to God ere he is revealed!"[47] the martyrs under the fifth seal (Rev. 6:9-11), those out of the Great Tribulation (Rev. 7:9), the two witnesses (Rev. 11:12), and others who have died prior to this point (Rev. 12:11; 20:4), many of which resisted the *Beast*[5.2.9] to attain "victory" (Rev. 15:2). The steadfast faith of believers to the point of death enrages the Beast for the threat of persecution and death is the only device available to him to coerce their worship—a worship which is motivated by the burning jealousy of the dragon who empowers him. The horrible experience of those who come out of the Great Tribulation is ultimately tempered by their intimate dwelling with God (Rev. 7:15-17). See *The Abiding Presence of God*[4.16.2].

3.13.7 - Revelation 13:7

It was granted to him

Now the *Beast*[5.2.9] is given permission to overcome the saints. This disturbing reality has been on the prophetic agenda for thousands of years:

> I was watching; and the same horn was making war against the saints, and prevailing against them, . . . He shall speak *pompous* words against the Most High, shall persecute the saints of the Most High, and shall intend to change times and law. Then *the saints* shall be given into his hand for a time and times and half a time. (Dan. 7:21, 25)

How could it be that God would grant permission for the Beast to overcome the saints? Here is where our grasp of God's sovereignty and His glory must be our sure support. As he used Pharaoh in the days of the Exodus, so too he uses the Beast in the time of the end. He has raised up the Beast for His ultimate glory.

> But indeed for this *purpose* I have raised you up, that I may show My power *in* you, and that My name may be declared in all the earth. As yet you exalt yourself against My people in that you will not let them go. (Ex. 9:16-17)

to make war with the saints

The saints at the time of the end are under tremendous persecution. They are killed by the *little horn*[5.2.37] (Dan. 7:21, 25), the *Harlot*[5.2.25] (Rev. 17:6), the Beast (Rev. 13:7), and even the *image of the Beast*[5.2.29] (Rev. 13:15). See *#20 - Saints*[4.3.2.20] . The saints are martyred during this period because they are unwilling to worship the Beast and his image (Rev. 13:15). True believers of our age will not see this war:[48]

> 2 Thessalonians 2:1-8 predicts that the rapture of the church must occur before the appearance of the *Antichrist*[5.2.3], and in Revelation 13:1-10 (cf. Rev. 6:2; 11:7) he will have appeared. This negates the possibility that the church is in view in Revelation 13:7, for it will have already been raptured.[49]

and to overcome them

See comments concerning the overcomer of *Revelation 6:2*[3.6.2].

authority was given him over every tribe, tongue, and nation

This speaks of his global control—something which was never achieved by Rome in the days of *Nero*[4.12]:

> Daniel 7:23 clearly states that at some point the Fourth Empire *devours the whole earth*. This is something Rome never did. Some attempt to make the expression mean the "then-known world," but it cannot be said that Rome even conquered the then-known world. . . . Rome did not even extend as far east as the empire of Alexander the Great. The Greeks went as far as the Indus River in India . . . Rome did not even extend that far. Furthermore, Rome never fully conquered the Parthian Empire, and that, too, was part of the known world. The area of Scotland was also part of the known world that Rome did not conquer. Rome had to build the Hadrian Wall in order to keep the nomads of northing Scotland from overrunning that part of Britain controlled by Rome.[50]

This speaks of the ultimate manifestation of Gentile power of the end as seen in *Nebuchadnezzar's dream*[4.3.1]. Remember that it is Satan who has authority over the kingdoms of the world prior to *The Arrival of God's Kingdom*[2.4.3] (see commentary on *Revelation 13:2*[3.13.2]). Since *Nero*[5.2.46]'s Rome has long passed and Christ has not yet come, it is evident that this final kingdom of Satan is yet to appear upon the stage of world history.

> A totalitarian system of unbelievable scope and power is also predicted. Every new invention of man gives him one more tool by which he can control others and enforce his will upon them. These inventions under the power of an able leader could make him the undisputed tyrant of the earth. Such a rule is foreshadowed by the beast. . . The concentration of evil in one vast system ruled by an antichrist who will be the most powerful potentate the human race has ever produced.[51]

3.13.8 - Revelation 13:8

All who dwell on the earth

The ones who not only *physically* dwell on the earth, but whose affections and complete allegiance are entirely upon the earth (Isa. 26:21; Luke 21:35; Rev. 3:10; 6:10; 11:10; 12:12; 13:8, 12, 14; 14:6; 17:8). They are to be contrasted with those whose citizenship is in heaven (John 15:19; 17:14-16; Php. 3:20; Heb. 11:13; 1Pe. 2:11). These are they whom the martyrs of the fifth seal cried out for God to avenge their deaths upon (Rev. 6:10). See *Earth Dwellers*[3.3.10.1].

will worship him

This is a defining moment for the *earth dwellers*[5.2.18], much like the unpardonable sin of Jesus' day:

> Then a third angel followed them, saying with a loud voice, "If anyone worships the beast and his image, and receives *his* mark on his forehead or on his hand, he himself shall also drink of the wine of the wrath of God, which is poured out full strength into the cup of His indignation. He shall be tormented with fire and brimstone in the presence of the holy angels and in the presence of the Lamb. And the smoke of their torment ascends forever and ever, and they have no rest day or night, who worship the beast and his image, and whoever receives the mark of his name." (Rev. 14:9-11)

Those who choose to worship the beast and take his mark are *forever lost*. Even though they have not yet died, they are *irredeemable*. See commentary on *Revelation 13:15*[3.13.15].

whose names have not been written in the Book of Life of the Lamb

Whose names have not been written is οὐ γέγραπται τὸ ὄνομα οὐτοῦ [*ou gegraptai to onoma outou*], perfect tense: *it has not been written, the name of him*. Unlike those who lacked faith in Sardis and would be blotted out of the *Book of Life*[5.2.10] (Rev. 3:5), these were never written in the book to begin with. Therefore, their destiny in the Lake of Fire is guaranteed (Rev. 20:15) since their names are not written in the Book of Life:

> The beast that you saw was, and is not, and will ascend out of the bottomless pit and go to perdition. And those who dwell on the earth will marvel, **whose names are not written in the Book of Life from the foundation of the world**, when they see the beast that was, and is not, and yet is. (Rev. 17:8) [emphasis added]

Some understand the phrase *of the Lamb* to denote a *different* book than the *Book of Life* mentioned elsewhere (Php. 4:3; Rev. 3:5; 20:12), but such a view is exegetically precarious. In their view, the *Book of Life* initially contains the names of all the living. Names are then blotted out as people die having never come to faith. The *Book of Life of the Lamb* is seen as a separate book which only contains the names of the elect and whose contents are never altered. We believe the two-book view is problematic:

- Too much emphasis is placed upon minor differences in phrasing when referring to the same book.
- The two books serve the same purpose—differentiating between the redeemed and the unredeemed. So why have two books?
- The book which the names of the *Beast*[5.2.9] worshipers have not been written in is referred to as both *the Book of Life of the lamb* (Rev. 13:8) and *the Book of Life* (Rev. 17:8). It is one and the same book.

We believe it is better to understand all references to the Book of Life as denoting a *single book* which records three categories of people:

1. **The Unsaved** - Each person to be born is written in the book. Those who die before coming to faith are blotted out.[52]
2. **The Saved** - Each person to be born is written in the book. Those who come to faith prior to death have their names retained in the book.
3. **Beast Worshipers** - The beast worshipers are a unique category of people of the time of the end. They are so hardened against God and destined to reject Him in the face of overwhelming evidence to the contrary that they are *never written* in the book (Rev. 13:8; 17:8). See *Earth Dwellers*[3.3.10.1]. See *Beast Worshipers are Unique*[4.4.3.4].

For a more complete discussion of these issues, see *Book of Life*[4.4].

lamb slain from the foundation of the world

Foundation is καταβολῆς [*katabolēs*], a compound word meaning "a throwing or laying down."[53] Christ's sacrifice was not an afterthought in the mind of God.

> And if you call on the Father, who without partiality judges according to each one's work, conduct yourselves throughout the time of your stay *here* in fear; knowing that you were not redeemed with corruptible things, *like* silver or gold, from your aimless conduct *received* by tradition from your fathers, but with the precious blood of Christ, as of a lamb without blemish and without spot. **He indeed was foreordained before the foundation of the world**, but was manifest in these last times for you. (1Pe. 1:17-20) [emphasis added]

Even before the perfect creation of Adam and Eve, God knew the end of history. This is evidenced in His provision for their first sin, spilling the innocent blood of animals to cover their nakedness (Gen. 3:21). An enormous number of types throughout the *OT*[5.2.51] predicted the coming of Christ and His sacrifice for the sins of men (see *Abraham Offers Isaac*[4.16.3.1] and *Typology and the Rapture*[4.14.9]).

The secrets of God, established from the foundation of the world, were gradually revealed through God's prophets (Ps. 78:2 cf. Mtt. 13:35; Tit. 1:1-3). In what is perhaps the "holy of holies" of the OT—Isaiah 53—God revealed that His lamb would be slain: "He was oppressed and He was afflicted, yet He opened not His mouth; He was led as a lamb to the slaughter, and as a sheep before its shearers is silent, so He opened not His mouth" (Isa. 53:7).[54]

John the Baptist understood the implications of Isaiah's passage, for when he saw Jesus he remarked: "Behold! The Lamb of God who takes away the sin of the world!" (John 1:29). See commentary on *Revelation 5:6*[3.5.6].

3.13.8.1 - From the Foundation of the World

In the sovereignty and omniscience of God, many things were determined and accomplished before or from the foundation of the world:

- God existed before the foundation (Gen. 1:1; Ps. 90:2; Isa. 40:21).
- Christ existed before the foundation (Isa. 48:16; Mic. 5:2; John 1:1; 17:5, 24).
- Christ was loved by the Father before the foundation (John 17:24).
- Wisdom was established before the foundation (Pr. 8:23).
- Believers were predestined for salvation before the foundation (Eph. 1:4; 2Ti. 1:9).
- God promised eternal life before time began (Tit. 1:2).
- Christ was foreordained before the foundation (1Pe. 1:20; Rev. 13:8).
- Unrevealed secrets of God existed from the foundation (Mtt. 13:35).
- The kingdom was prepared for the faithful from the foundation (Mtt. 25:34).
- The blood of all the prophets was shed from the foundation (Luke 11:50).
- The *Beast*[5.2.9] worshipers were not written in the *Book of Life*[5.2.10] from the foundation (Rev. 17:8).

3.13.8.2 - A Lamb and a Beast

An intentional contrast is seen between the Lamb and the *Beast*[5.2.9].

The Lamb versus The Beast

Similarity	Lamb	Beast
Slain	Before history (1Pe. 1:17-20)	At the end of history (Rev. 13:3)
Arose from the dead	Rom. 1:4	Rev. 13:3, 14; 17:8, 11
Worshiped	Mtt. 2:2; 8:2; 14:33; John 5:23; 20:28[55]	2Th. 2:4; Rev. 13:4, 8, 12, 14:9; 16:2; 19:20; 20:4

These similarities are developed further in our discussion of *Master Imitator*[4.2.5].

3.13.9 - Revelation 13:9

If anyone has an ear, let him hear.

As when Jesus taught, prior to the formation of the church, all people are enjoined to hear (Mtt. 11:15). Unlike Revelation 2 and 3, there is no mention made of the *seven churches*[5.2.66] which are *no longer present*[4.14] upon the earth.

> A textual clue found in Revelation 13:9 has led many Bible interpreters to the conclusion that those addressed in Revelation 13:10 are not the seven churches of Asia Minor but rather, consist of a different group all together. When Christ addressed the seven churches of Asia Minor in Revelation 2-3, He always used the phrase, "He who has an ear, let him hear what **the Spirit says to the churches** " (Revelation 2:7, 11, 17, 29; 3:6, 13, 22). . . . Conspicuously missing from this phrase [in Rev. 13:9] are the words "what the Spirit says to the churches." [emphasis added][56]

Those who have an ear, but choose not to hear do so because of pride. This is the major sin of the end and of our own day:

> Hear and give ear: Do not be proud, for the LORD has spoken. Give glory to the LORD your God before He causes darkness, and before your feet stumble on the dark mountains, and while you are looking for light, He turns it into the shadow of death *And* makes *it* dense darkness. (Jer. 13:15-16)

3.13.10 - Revelation 13:10

He who leads into captivity shall go into captivity; he who kills with the sword must be killed with the sword

In a passage whose context is the time of *Jacob's trouble*[2.13.4], God indicates that He will correct Israel. "Though I make a full end of all nations where I have scattered you, yet I will not make a complete end of you. But I will correct you in justice, and will not let you go altogether unpunished." (Jer. 30:11). He promises Israel's preservation and retribution in kind to those who oppress her: "Therefore all those who devour you shall be devoured; and all your adversaries, every one of them, shall go into captivity; those who plunder you shall become plunder, and all who prey upon you I will make a prey" (Jer. 30:16). Upon His arrest at the garden of Gethsemane, Jesus stated this principle, "Put your sword in its place, for all who take the sword will perish by the sword" (Mtt. 26:52b). The basis for such retribution is God's law of capital punishment established after the flood: "Whoever sheds man's blood, by man his blood shall be shed; for in the image of God He made man" (Gen. 9:5). The *Beast*[5.2.9], the *False Prophet*[5.2.20], and the *Harlot*[5.2.25] all *persecute the saints*[4.3.2.20] and so the Harlot will be ravaged according to God's will (Rev. 17:16-17) and the Beast and the False Prophet will be killed to become the first occupants of the Lake of Fire (Rev. 19:20; 20:10).

However, variations in the Greek manuscripts at this phrase indicate that retribution by justice may not be the meaning. The *MT*[5.2.45] text has: εἴ τις ἔχει αἰχμαλωσίαν, ὑπάγεὶ εἴ τις ἐν μαχαίρᾳ, δεῖ αὐτὸν ἀποκτανθῆναι [*ei tis echei aichmalōsian, hypagei ei tis en machaira, dei auton apoktanthēnai*], *if anyone [is] for captivity, [then] he is going; if anyone [is] for [the] sword, he must be killed.* In the MT text, the subject in each case is the believer—not his enemy. This appears to be a simple statement setting forth the trust which the saints must maintain in God's sovereign appointment of their role in history. If it is a saint's God-appointed role to serve as a martyr, so be it! A similar theme is found in a passage concerning God's judgment of Israel:

> And it shall be, if they say to you, 'Where should we go?' then you shall tell them, 'Thus says the LORD: "Such as *are* for death, to death; and such as *are* for the sword, to the sword; and such as *are* for the famine, to the famine; and such as *are* for the captivity, to the captivity." ' (Jer. 15:2)

Depending upon which text we follow, this passage may describe retribution by God's sure justice (Rev. 14:9-12) or the need to cling to His sovereignty in the midst of affliction (Rom. 8:28). Both are taught by Scripture.

Here is the patience and the faith of the saints

Patience is ὑπομονὴ [*hypomonē*], meaning *to abide under*. It indicates stead-fastness and perseverance while enduring toil and suffering.[57] It is through faith and patience that the promises of the believer are attained (Heb. 6:12). John was himself a "brother and companion in the tribulation and kingdom and patience of Jesus Christ . . . on the island that is called Patmos" (Rev. 1:9). Jesus recognizes the patience exhibited by the churches of Asia (Ephesus, Rev. 2:2; Thyatira, Rev. 2:19). Patience is a *command* which the Lord gives believers. Because the faithful church of Philadelphia kept this command, Jesus promised to keep them "from the hour of trial which shall come upon the whole world" (Rev. 3:10). The patience in this verse is directed to those who find themselves in the midst of the Great Tribulation—perhaps the most dangerous time of all history for believers upon the earth.

The *patience and the faith* is found *here*: in the realization of God's sovereignty. Whatever befalls these Tribulation saints, they must rest in the knowledge that it is according to God's will and that they can never perish.[58]

> Who shall separate us from the love of Christ? *Shall* tribulation, or distress, or persecution, or famine, or nakedness, or peril, or sword? As it is written: **"For Your sake we are killed all day long; we are accounted as sheep for the slaughter."** Yet in all these things we are more than conquerors through Him who loved us. (Rom. 8:35-37 cf. Ps. 44:22) [emphasis added]

God *will* avenge His elect once "*the* number of their fellow servants and their brethren, who would be killed as they *were* was completed" (Rev. 6:10-11). In the meantime, they were not to love their lives. Instead, they must hold their testimony to the point of martyrdom, knowing their death was but a gateway to a place of intimacy and rest with the Lamb in heaven (Rev. 7:14-17). Although many would die, Jesus assured them, "not a hair of your head shall be lost. By your **patience** possess your souls" [emphasis added] (Luke 21:18). These would be required to lose their lives in order to possess their souls, for to keep their lives meant taking the mark and being doomed for eternity. At all costs, they must not "draw back to perdition" (Heb. 10:36)!

Although a remnant of Jews is hidden and protected in a special place in the wilderness (Rev. 12:6, 14), the vast majority of the people of faith will be within the domain of the Beast, the persecuting *little horn*[5.2.37] (Dan. 7:21, 25). Jesus understood the intensity of this time and the resulting rarity of finding people of faith at the end:

> Then the Lord said, "Hear what the unjust judge said. And shall God not avenge His own elect who cry out day and night to Him, though He bears long with them? I tell you that He will avenge them speedily. Nevertheless, when the Son of Man comes, will He really find faith on the earth?" (Luke 18:3)

Their patience accomplishes several things: it witnesses of the reality of their faith and the glory of God; it makes them "perfect and complete" (Jas. 1:4); and it allows the cup of God's wrath toward their persecutors to fill to the brim (Rev. 14:10; 16:19).

3.13.11 - Revelation 13:11

another beast

Another is ἄλλο [*allo*]: "Generally *another* person or thing of the same kind (Acts 4:12), as contrasted with ἕτερος [*heteros*] (*another* of a different kind or form) (Gal. 1:6-7)."[59]

The Seven-Headed Beast and the Beast with Lamb's Horns [60]

Elsewhere, he is differentiated from the first beast, the *Antichrist*[5.2.3]. He is known as the *False Prophet*[5.2.20] (Rev. 19:20; 20:10). See *#18 - False Prophet*[4.3.2.18]. Some have taken this beast to describe a system or movement:

> The second beast which is described, Rev. 13:11-17, as coming out of the earth, and having two horns like unto a lamb, and speaking as a dragon, and exercising all the authority of the first beast in his sight, is referred to the papacy. The false prophet receives a similar application. So Luther, Vitringa, Bengel, Auberlen, Hengstenberg, Ebrard, and many English divines.[61]

> The commentators are in the most dire confusion on the identification . . . the Roman church, the Greek church, the French Republic, the Jesuits, the Roman theologians, the earthy carnal wisdom, including the heathen philosophies, false doctrines and the like. . . Still others identify the second beast with the heathen priesthood, the principle of inductive philosophy, witchcraft and soothsaying, divination and magic.[62]

But his attributes are personal, for salvation and damnation are individual, not institutional:[63]

> The second beast is a **specific individual** rather than a religious institution. . . . it is more likely that the singular phrase "beast" (*therion*) or "false prophet" (*pseudoprophetes*) refers to an individual rather than a religious institution. Moreover, because he spends eternity in the lake of fire (Revelation 19:20; 20:10), the false prophet is characterized as possessing an eternal soul. Such an attribute and eternal fate

> is descriptive of individuals rather than institutions. [emphasis added][64]

Together with the first *Beast*[5.2.9] and the dragon, he forms an evil trinity:

> There is a Trinity of Evil. Now it surely needs no argument to prove that these three evil persons are opposed to and are the antithesis of the three Persons in the Godhead. The Devil stands opposed to God the Father - 'Ye are of your father, the Devil,' John 8:40, etc. The Antichrist stands opposed to God the Son - his very name shows this. The remaining evil person stands opposed to God the Spirit. If this be the case, then our present task is greatly simplified: it is merely a matter of noting what is separately predicted of the two Beasts in Rev. 13 so as to ascertain which of them stands opposed to Christ and which to the Holy Spirit. . . Now there are only two arguments of any plausibility which have been advanced to support the view that it is the second Beast of Rev. 13 which is the Antichrist, but so far as we are aware no one has endeavored to show that the first Beast represents the third Person in the Trinity of Evil! Yet he must be so if the second is the Antichrist![65]

We shall see that a primary function of this second beast is much like that of the Holy Spirit in relation to Christ. For he wields equivalent power to the first beast (Rev. 13:12), yet retains no glory for himself, but constantly witnesses of the first beast, the Antichrist. And so it is with the Holy Spirit and the Son of God:

> However, when He, the Spirit of truth, has come, He will guide you into all truth; for He will not speak on His own *authority*, but whatever He hears He will speak; and He will tell you things to come. He will glorify Me, for He will take of what is Mine and declare *it* to you. (John 16:13-14)

> He is the third person of the Trinity of Evil. As there is to be an Antichrist who will both counterfeit and oppose the Christ of God, so there will be an Anti-spirit who will simulate and oppose the Spirit of God. Just as the great work of the Holy Spirit is to glorify Christ, so the one aim of the Anti-spirit will be to magnify the false christ (see Rev. 13:12). Just as the coming of the Holy Spirit at Pentecost was visibly attended by 'cloven tongues like as of fire' (Acts 2:3), so we read of the Anti-spirit that 'he doeth great wonders, so that he maketh fire come down from heaven on the earth in the sight of men' (Rev. 13:13). And just as it is the Holy Spirit who now quickens dead sinners into newness of life, so of the Anti-spirit we are told, 'He had power to give life unto the *image of the Beast*[5.2.29]' (Rev. 13:15).[66]

Some point to the religious aspect of the work of the second beast in favor of his identification as the Antichrist, or *pseudo-Christ*. But this cannot be, for it is the first beast which attains all worship, not the second. The refusal of the second beast to participate as the object of worship is fatal to any view that the second beast is the Antichrist. Moreover, the role of the Antichrist is much broader than that of a mere religious figure:[67]

> To regard the Antichrist as limited to the religious realm and divorced from the political, seems to us, to leave out entirely an essential and fundamental element of his character and career. The Antichrist will claim to be the true Christ, the Christ of God. Hence, it would seem that he will present himself to the Jews as their long-expected Messiah - the One foretold by the Old Testament prophets - and that before apostate Christendom, given over by God to believe the Lie, he will pose as the returned Christ. Therefore, must we not predict, as an inevitable corollary, that the pseudo christ, will usher in a false millennium, and rule over a mock *Messianic Kingdom*[5.2.39]? Why was it (from the human side) that, when our Lord tabernacled among men, the Jews rejected Him as their Messiah? Was it not because He failed to fulfill their expectations that he would take the government upon His shoulder and wield the royal sceptre as soon as He presented Himself to them? Was it not because they looked for Him to restore the Kingdom to Israel there and then? Is it not therefore reasonable to suppose that when the Antichrist presents himself to them, that he will wield great temporal power, and rule over a vast earthly empire? It would certainly seem so.[68]

coming up

ἀναβαῖνον [*anabainon*], present tense participle, *presently coming up* . Like the first beast (Rev. 13:1), John saw this beast as he was rising from the earth.

up out of the earth

The first beast arose out of the sea, indicating his Gentile origin (see commentary on *Revelation 13:1*[3.13.1]). This beast arises from the earth, which may indicate his Jewish origin. Although there is ample evidence of the *Gentile origin*[4.2.3] of the first beast, some suggest that the second beast is Jewish.[69] They note the lack of mention of the tribe of Dan in the 144,000 sealed of Israel (see commentary on *Revelation 7:4*[3.7.4]) and the negative prophecy of Jacob concerning Dan: "Dan shall be a serpent by the way, a viper by the path, that bites the horse's heels so that its rider shall fall backward" (Gen. 49:17). It is difficult to be dogmatic on the earth-sea distinction because the *Gentile* kingdoms which Daniel saw arise from the *sea* (Dan. 7:3) are also said to be four kings which arise from the *earth* (Dan. 7:17). Fruchtenbaum suggests the mention of earth merely denotes his humanity.[70] It almost certainly indicates his *earthiness* as opposed to that which is from heaven (John 8:23).

Although the bottomless pit is within the *earth*, the origin of this beast does not speak of the abyss.[71] The beast which arises from the bottomless pit is the one which "was, and is not" (Rev. 17:8), the first beast out of the sea with the deadly wound that was healed (Rev. 13:3). This second beast causes the *earth dwellers*[5.2.18] to worship the first beast whose deadly wound was healed (Rev. 13:12-14).

two horns

The mention of horns in conjunction with a Lamb points to the vision of the throne room prior to the opening of the first seal where John saw "a Lamb as though it had been slain, having seven horns and seven yes, which are the seven Spirits of God sent out into all the earth" (Rev. 5:6b). Horns frequently symbolize power. The Lamb has seven, the number of *completeness*[2.7.5.3.6]. This beast has two, the number of *witness*[2.7.5.3.1], for he shall serve as the ultimate witness to the first beast.

> The two horns have a pertinent significance, for two is the number of witness and just as Christ declared the Spirit of God should 'testify (lit., bear witness) of Me' (John 15:26), so the third person in the Trinity of Evil bears witness to the first Beast.[72]

like a lamb

Paul warned of Satan's "ministers," false apostles and deceitful workers which follow Satan's pattern and transform themselves into apostles of Christ (2Cor. 11:13-15). There have been many false apostles and deceitful workers since then and especially toward the time of the end, but none more convincing and containing such contrast as this False Prophet of the end. His appearance as a lamb masks his true inward nature. Who he is will not be evident from his outward appearance but, like other false prophets, determined by observing the fruit of his labors:

> Beware of **false prophets**, who come to you in **sheep's clothing**, but inwardly they are ravenous wolves. You will know them by their fruits (Mtt. 7:15-16a). [emphasis added]

> Then many false prophets will rise up and deceive many. And because lawlessness will abound, the love of many will grow cold. But he who endures to the end shall be saved. And this gospel of the kingdom will be preached in all the world as a witness to all the nations, and then the end will come. (Mtt. 24:11-14)

spoke like a dragon

Although he looks like a lamb, his verbal instructions are energized by the will of the dragon (Rev. 12:2-4, 17; 13:4). It is he who causes worship of the Beast. He *tells* those who dwell on the earth to make the image of the Beast. He is also the enforcer of the mark required in order to buy or sell. His speech like a dragon is an allusion to the introduction of deception into the human race in the Garden: "Now the serpent was more cunning than any beast of the field which the LORD God had made. And **he said** to the woman, 'Has God indeed said . . . ?' " [emphasis added] (Gen. 3:1). Like the serpent, his mouth will be employed in opposition to God's Word.

3.13.12 - Revelation 13:12

all the authority of the first beast

As the Holy Spirit in relation to Christ, so the *False Prophet*[5.2.20] has the full authority given by the dragon to the *Beast*[5.2.9] (Rev. 13:2). Perhaps the most remarkable aspect of the False Prophet is his refusal to obtain worship for himself even though he has the full authority of the Beast. Outside of the altruistic example of the Holy Spirit in relation to Christ, this is unheard of. The answer lies in the pregnant phrase which follows.

in his presence

The authority of the False Prophet is very closely controlled. He is only granted his power "in the sight of the beast" (Rev. 13:14 cf. Rev. 19:20). He is on a leash, as it were. During the end, it is the dragon's intention that ultimate authority and attention be directed to the Beast. If the dragon enters the Beast, as he did Judas (Luke 22:3), then worship of the Beast becomes the worship of Satan. If the False Prophet's authority were in any way independent of the Beast, then he could potentially direct attention to himself. The dragon is very aware of this possibility since he was the subject of the same corrupting influence of power (Isa. 14:13-14; Eze. 28:17). "It is particularly noteworthy that the second beast will have to exercise the Beast's authority in his presence—there just can be no trust between the forces of evil!"[73]

> The alliance of religion and state has a long and sad record of despotism and suppression, but the ecclesio-political union of these to human beasts will culminate in the worst period of persecution in the history of the world. . . . Each leader assists and supports the other, the king enforcing the religious authority of the prophet and the prophet persuading the world's superstitious masses that the king should be worshiped and obeyed as a god.[74]

causes the earth and those who dwell in it to worship the first beast

Note that it is the *first* beast which is worshiped (Rev. 13:4) in accordance with the predictions of Daniel (Dan. 11:36) and Paul (2Th. 2:4). The *second* beast directs worship *toward* the first and is dependent upon him for his power (Rev. 13:12). Hence the first beast is the "man of sin . . . the son of perdition," not the second. [75]

Pink notes the relative ease with which a supreme military leader such as the *Antichrist*[5.2.3] is able to step into the position of assumed deity:

> At first sight it appears strange, if not incongruous, that a military despot should be found filling the character of a religious impostor. But history shows that there is a point at which one character readily merges into the other. Political ambition, intoxicated by success, finds it an easy step from self-glorification to self-deification, and the popular infatuation as easily passes from the abject adulation of the tyrant to the adoration of the god.[76]

The False Prophet's main focus is to direct worship to the Beast. This is his key role among the world's religions at the time of the end, made all the easier by a large reduction in Christians beginning with the disappearance of the true Church in the *Rapture*[4.14] prior to the time of God's wrath (Rev. 3:10):

> True children of God are to be found in many varying shades of Christianity, sprinkled throughout Christendom. There are undoubtedly born-again individuals in the midst of all churches. They are saved in spite of the organizations and not because of the organizations. What is going to happen to all of these organizations when the true believers are *removed*[4.14] from the world? Already, in our own day, we see indications that much of the guiding force of these great organizations is in the hands of those who would deny essential truths of Scripture. This tendency will increase, and at the coming of Christ for the believers, the tares in the midst of the wheat will go on functioning as usual, all moving rapidly into one great church union, with one head of all. This religious leader will work together with the political dictator.[77]

Eventually, even a universal ecumenical religion proves to be a threat to the worship of the Beast. The Beast (empowered by the dragon) desires *all* worship personally. This may be a contributing factor in the demise of the *Harlot*[5.2.25] (Rev. 17:16), for she is the mother of worldwide spiritual idolatry and abomination (Rev. 17:5) and could otherwise compete with the Beast in the area of religion. See *The Great Harlot*[4.1.4]. The prominence of the False Prophet prior to her demise is not revealed, but we do know he is the ultimate religious figure directing worship to the Beast at the end. His role as religious leader may also fulfill Israel's expectation of a prophet (Deu. 18:15-18; John 1:21; Luke 7:19). "The false prophet arises to play the part expected of the prophet who had been announced for so long, and his role will be to tell Israel that their Messiah has come."[78] Those who worship the Beast are the *Earth Dwellers*[3.3.10.1].

whose deadly wound was healed

Deadly wound is Ἡ πληγὴ τοῦ θανάτου αὐτοῦ [*Hē plēgē tou thanatou autou*], *the wound of his death.* This recovery was not from a serious wound, but from actual death. The connection between the miraculous recovery of the Beast and his worship is emphasized again (Rev. 13:3-4). This rules out

Nero[5.2.46] and all previous people of history as candidates for the Antichrist because only *after* his revival and ascent from the abyss does the Beast receive worship as god. The only man prior to Antichrist who arose from the dead to receive worship is Christ, not Antichrist. See commentary on *Revelation 13:3*[3.13.3]. See *Supernatural Origin?*[4.2.7].

3.13.13 - Revelation 13:13

He performs great signs

We have just been told that the *False Prophet*[5.2.20] "exercises all the authority of the first beast" (Rev. 13:12). Thus, it is no surprise that he performs wondrous miracles, for he has the authority of the *Beast*[5.2.9] who himself is empowered directly by Satan:

> The coming of the *lawless one* is according to the working of Satan, with all power, signs, and lying wonders, and with all unrighteous deception among those who perish, because they did not receive the love of the truth, that they might be saved. And for this reason God will send them strong delusion, that they should believe the lie, that they all may be condemned who did not believe the truth but had pleasure in unrighteousness. (2Th. 2:9-12)

Not only will the False Prophet perform signs and lying wonders, the subjects of his deception, the *earth dwellers*[5.2.18], will be sent strong delusion *by God* to believe that which is false. It would appear that the signs themselves are *bona fide*, but what they attest to is false. Even the spirits of demons who collect the kings of the earth to Armageddon—one of whom comes out of the mouth of the False Prophet—convince by the *signs* they perform (Rev. 16:14). Thus can be seen the demonic source of the signs which the False Prophet is able to use in his deception. We are offered a small hint of that which the demonic realm can achieve when Pharaoh's sorcerers and magicians used enchantments to turn rods into serpents (Ex. 7:11), water into blood (Ex. 7:22), and brought frogs up on the land (Ex. 8:7).[79]

Let the reader attend to the importance of the matter before us: *signs are unreliable indicators of a work of God!* "Many will say to Me in that day, 'Lord, Lord, have we not prophesied in Your name, cast out demons in Your name, and done many wonders in Your name?' And then I will declare to them, 'I never knew you; depart from Me, you who practice lawlessness!' " (Mtt. 7:22-23)

> Christ's miracles, as miracles, were no evidence of His Divine mission. The real evidence was that the miracles which He wrought were the very miracles which the Prophetic Word had declared He should work, and which were *on that account* the sign and seal of His ministry, and formed His credentials from on high. This is clear from Mtt. 11:1-6. It was not that they were mere miraculous acts, but that they were what God had foretold, and the essence of their testimony was *to the truth of God's word*, rather than the power of Christ. Hence it is that they are so generally called "signs," and not merely "wonders."[80]

The earth dwellers of the end, even those who call themselves *Christians*, have fallen prey to that which is already at work in our own day: *an unbiblical reliance upon signs as evidence of God.* They have built their faith upon the wrong foundation!

Two Foundations of Faith

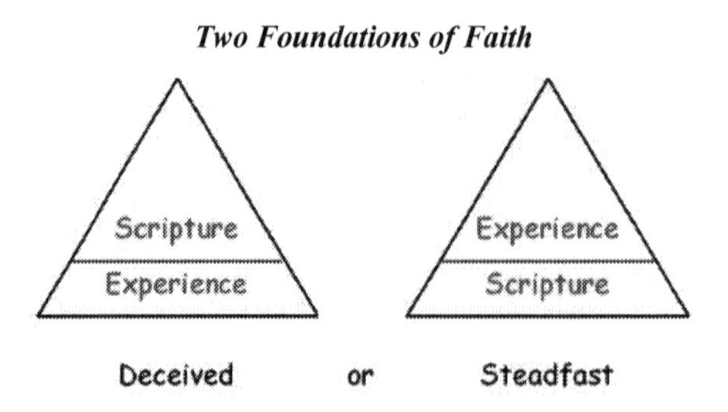

They are completely open to deception because their faith is based upon *experience* rather than *Scripture*. They validate their religious beliefs based on their own personal experience. They are the ultimate in postmodern thinking[81]—they have *their truth* which is real to them. Thus, when they see the truly miraculous signs provided by the False Prophet, they easily succumb to the desired conclusion: the Beast is god. When and if such "people of faith" are confronted with the Scriptures—assuming God's word is available at the time of the end—they will bend the Scripture and reinterpret it to validate their experience. If God's written word denies their experience, they will reject it over their personal experience. Thus, their experience will sit in judgment of God's Word.[82]

Biblical believers are to be just the opposite. Their faith is based upon God's *inerrant*[5.2.32] Scriptures. Each and every experience is *tested* against its adherence to that which God has already revealed in Scripture. When and if an experience fails the test of Scripture, it is *rejected* for we know that the Spirit of God speaks consistently. That which is *of* the Holy Spirit is in agreement with that which is *authored through* the Holy Spirit: "Beloved, do not believe every spirit, but test the spirits, whether they are of God; because many false prophets have gone out into the world" (1Jn. 4:1). Thus, the biblical believer evaluates the fruit of his experience against the measure of Scripture and avoids deception:

It is *by the signs* that the False Prophet deceives the earth dwellers to receive the mark of the Beast and worship his image (Rev. 19:20). Yet the signs are false—not in their miraculous ability, but in *what they attest to*.[83] Signs alone are not trustworthy:

> But there was a certain man called Simon, who previously practiced sorcery in the city and astonished the people of Samaria, claiming that he was someone great, to whom they all gave heed, from the least to the greatest, saying, "This man is the great power of God." And they heeded him because he had astonished them with his sorceries for a long time. (Acts 8:9-11)

> If there arises among you a prophet or a dreamer of dreams, and he gives you a sign or a wonder, and the sign or the wonder comes to pass, of which he spoke to you, saying, 'Let us go after other gods'—which you have not known—'and let us serve them,' you shall not listen to the words of that prophet or that dreamer of dreams, for the Lord your God is testing you to know whether you love the Lord your God with all your heart and with all your soul. You shall walk after the Lord your God and fear Him, and keep His commandments and obey His voice; you shall serve Him and hold fast to Him. (Deu. 13:1-4)

makes fire come down from heaven

He has an ability similar to that of God's two witnesses (Rev. 11:5). See commentary on *Revelation 11:5*[3.11.5]. Perhaps his power is even more impressive because its source *appears* to be *from heaven* . In the past, fire from heaven was associated with God's power, consuming both His adversaries (2K. 1:9-12) and His sacrifice (Num. 16:35; 1K. 18:38). The False Prophet shows the Pharisees of the end the very signs they sought as validation of Messiah when Jesus walked the earth (Mtt. 16:1). Yet all is not as it appears, for he is a great deceiver. As in the days of Job, fire will fall "from heaven" which will actually be in the service of Satan (Job 1:19). It need hardly be said that *Nero*[4.12] never had an accomplice like this!

3.13.14 - Revelation 13:14

And he deceives

Empowered by the great deceiver (Rev. 12:9), he produces the fruit of deception. The power of this deception will be unique in history. Jesus suggested that only those protected by the Holy Spirit would be able to resist his ability to convince. "For false christs and false prophets will rise and show great signs and wonders to deceive, if possible, even the elect. See, I have told you beforehand" (Mtt. 24:24-25 cf. Mark 13:22).

those who dwell

Some manuscripts in the *MT*[5.2.45] text line have τοὺς ἐμοὺς τοὺς κατοικοῦντας [*tous emous tous kataoikountas*], *those [people] of mine who dwell*. This variation in the text may hint at the explicit inclusion of John's people, the Jews, in this deception. We know from elsewhere in Scripture that the Jews will be among those who are deceived (John 5:43).

make an image to the beast

The *Beast*[5.2.9] has a problem. He claims to be god, but lacks God's omnipresence. Therefore, an icon (εἰκόνα [*eikona*]) of the Beast is to be made. While Scripture does not say, it would appear that one purpose of the icon is to occupy the place of worship in the "holy place" (Mtt. 24:15) on an ongoing basis as the focal point of worship.[84] The image serves as the center of worship allowing the Beast to go about his other affairs of state. This probably occurs after the initial declaration of deity made in the person of the Beast himself (2Th. 2:4).

> The term *abomination* refers to an image or an idol. This even is also mentioned in Matthew 24:15-16: . . . The only clue given is that it will be something *standing* (like an image or idol) in the Holy Place. . . . the Abomination of Desolation must include something more than merely the *Antichrist*[5.2.3]'s self-proclamation of deity. Furthermore, the Daniel and Matthew passages implied an image or idol that would be erected in the *Temple*[5.2.73]. . . . Thus, the two stages of the Abomination of Desolation, lasting a total of 1,290 days will be the declaration of deity by the Antichrist in the Holy of Holies followed by the setting up of his image in the same place.[85]

The fact that nothing like what is recorded in our text happened in the first century represents no problem for *preterists*[5.2.59] who find fulfillment in the time of *Nero*[5.2.46]. The details are simply *swept aside*. Typical of preterism's refusal to interpret the text at face value is the example found in Gregg:

> The making of *an image to the beast* (v. 14), or an *image of the beast*[5.2.29] (v. 15), the giving breath to the image, and the requirement that all men worship it **are difficult features to correlate with any action known to have occurred in Israel in the first century. This need not be taken literally**, however, and can simply refer to the Jew's general homage to Rome's authority. [emphasis added][86]

Here we see a first-rate example of the exegetical *gearshift* we mentioned related to the *Preterist Interpretation*[2.12.2] of this book. Their technique is to search first century documents for an approximate "fulfillment" of the literal text. When the documents cannot produce even an approximate connection, then the gear shifts to non-literal interpretation in order to move over the "speed bump." With such a fluid means of interpretation, the authority of Scripture to specify what constitutes fulfillment is subverted.

Worship of the image made to the Beast is a flagrant violation of the second of the Ten Commandments: "You shall not make for yourself a carved image—any likeness *of anything* that *is* in heaven above, or that *is* in the earth beneath, or that *is* in the water under the earth; you shall not bow down to them or serve them" (Ex. 20:4a).

See *#19 - Image of Beast*[4.3.2.19].

3.13.15 - Revelation 13:15

He was granted power to give breath to the image of the beast

The power given to the *False Prophet*[5.2.20] here is perhaps the apex of what God has ever allowed in the hands of the enemy: the power to give life. This power is intrinsic to the Creator, and He is intimately involved with the creation of each creature.[87] The False Prophet gives breath (*pneuma*) to that which is initially inanimate, as "God formed man *of* the dust of the ground, and breathed into his nostrils the breath of life; and man became a living being" (Gen. 2:7). Unlike all previous lifeless idols which have been the work of men's hands, the *image of the beast*[5.2.29] is given life. This is probably the capstone of the lying wonders which the False Prophet performs—the grand finale of his deception.

Scripture records that men have readily given worship to lifeless creations in the past:

> What profit is the image, that its maker should carve it, the molded image, a teacher of lies, that the maker of its mold should trust in it, to make mute idols? Woe to him who says to wood, 'Awake!' To silent stone, 'Arise! It shall teach!' Behold, it is overlaid with gold and silver, yet in it there is no breath at all. (Hab. 2:18-19 cf. Ps. 135:17-18; Jer. 10:14; 51:17-19)

They worship all the more so now when they see the fantastic miracle of the beast's image having come to life at the hands of the False Prophet. The image itself must be ultimately compelling because the enormity of the miracle performed by the False Prophet does not draw attention to the prophet, but all attention remains focused on the worship of the image itself and the *Beast*[5.2.9] to which it attests.[88] Some oppose the notion that the image could truly be given life. They prefer to understand "breath" as denoting *animation*. Thus, they see the image with breath as a futuristic technological mimic of life. Although this is possible, it doesn't seem to do justice to the text and the way in which *pneuma* (*breath*) denotes life-giving power elsewhere in Scripture (Gen. 2:7; Rev. 11:11). "The *pneuma* is therefore the equivalent of πνεῦμα ζωῆς [*pneuma zōēs*] ('the breath of life') so recently encountered in connection with the two witnesses."[89]

Morris suggests another possibility, that the spirit given may be an unclean spirit, or demon:

> The word in the Greek is *pneuma*, meaning "spirit" or "wind." The false prophet is enabled (by his own master, Satan) to impart a spirit to the image, but that spirit is one of Satan's unclean spirits, probably a highly placed demon in the satanic hierarchy. This is a striking case of demon possession, with the demon possessing the body of the image rather than that of a man or woman.[90]

Although it is impossible to know precisely what is inferred from the "breath" being given to the image, the results are nothing short of life—for the image exhibits apparent intelligence and speaking abilities. We must remember that the False Prophet "exercises all the authority of the first beast" (Rev. 13:12) and that the first beast is given "great authority" by the dragon. If the dragon revives the Beast and brings him back from the abyss, as evidenced by the worship of the masses, then why couldn't the False Prophet with the same measure and source of power give life to the image? Certainly this is not beyond the ability that God *could grant* if it were within His purpose to do so. Moreover, we have no examples in Scripture of the animation of inanimate objects by demonic possession. Spirits seek embodiment in living hosts (Mark 5:12). Either way, the image appears convincingly lifelike.

The image probably plays a role in the sequence of events associated with the "abomination of desolation" spoken of by both Daniel (Dan. 11:31; 12:11 cf. Dan. 9:27) and Jesus (Mtt. 24:15):

> The abomination of desolation, which the reader is to understand, includes the following elements: 1. It occurs in the Jewish *Temple*[5.2.73] in Jerusalem (Dan. 11:31; 2Th. 2:4). 2. It involves a person setting up a statue in place of the regular sacrifice in the holy of holies (Dan. 11:31; 12:11; Rev. 13:14-15). 3. This results in the cessation of the regular sacrifice (Dan. 9:27; 11:31; 12:11). 4. There will be a time of about three-and-a-half years between this event . . . and the end of the time period (Dan. 9:27; 12:11). 5. It involves an individual setting up a statue or image of himself so that he may be worshipped in place of God (Dan. 11:31; 2Th. 2:4; Rev. 13:14-15). 6. The image is made to come to life (Rev. 13:14). 7. A worship system to this false god is thus inaugurated (2Th. 2:4; Rev. 13:14-15). 8. At the end of this time period the individual who commits the act will himself be cut off (Dan. 9:27).[91]

This event concludes at the middle of the final week, after the Beast overcomes the two witnesses (Rev. 11:7). It is the signal for the flight of the Jewish remnant to the mountains and thereafter to the wilderness. See commentary on *Revelation 12:6*[3.12.6]. See *Events of the 70th Week of Daniel*[2.13.5.4]. See *#19 - Image of Beast*[4.3.2.19].

that the image of the beast should . . . speak

This idol is unlike all previous idols which were mute (Ps. 115:5; 135:16; Jer. 10:5). The False Prophet spoke as a dragon (Rev. 13:11) and that which he empowers continues in that same vain, ordering the death of those who refuse to worship.

cause as many as would not worship the image of the beast to be killed

This is the point of no return. The entire population of the earth is now divided into those who retain physical life, but forever lose spiritual life versus those who retain spiritual life, but are likely to lose physical life. The former are those who worship the Beast and his image. The latter refuse to worship at the cost of their physical lives. The only exceptions are the believing Jewish remnant which is hidden by God (Rev. 12:6, 14) and those who manage to stay alive underground within the Beast's system (Rev. 18:4).

Many of those which refuse the mark and reside within the Beast's system will be Gentiles who come to faith during this time of the end. Their survival will be precarious on two counts: (1) the Beast, his image, and the *Harlot*[5.2.25] all seek their death; and (2) they will be unable to purchase the basic necessities of life. Many of them will achieve victory over the Beast, not by survival, but by persevering in martyrdom (Rev. 7:14-17; 20:4).

Those who worship the Beast and his image and take his mark are warned by an angel concerning the seriousness of what they are about to do (Rev. 14:9). This unique global warning indicates the irreversible nature of taking the mark. Taking the mark is akin to the unpardonable sin of Jesus' day—there is no possibility of redemption once the mark is taken (Rev. 14:9-11). In stark contrast to the people of faith, they are eternally *insecure*. This is a unique situation to the time of the end. For what sin is there today from which the blood of Christ cannot redeem? Could not even the likes of a Hitler be saved if he had *truly and sincerely* repented prior to death? We answer a resounding "yes!" because we understand the priceless value of the blood of the Lamb which provides redemption for *all* sin (Rev. 5:9). For if Christ's blood cannot atone for some specific sin, then there are *two* requirements for salvation, not one: receiving Christ by faith *and* avoiding this specific sin. May it never be!

Here, as at Christ's First Coming, we have a unique situation where there is a specific act, which once participated in, moves the individual *beyond all possibility of redemption* . The act is the equivalent of eternal, permanent rejection of the Lamb. So blasphemous and foreordained are these that they are never afforded entry into the *Book of Life*[5.2.10], not even to be written and subsequently blotted out (Rev. 13:8; 17:8). Like those who commit the unpardonable sin, taking the mark is the equivalent of permanently rejecting Christ. See *Beast Worshipers are Unique*[4.4.3.4].

Those who have victory over the Beast, his image, the mark, and the number of his name are seen in heaven prior to the pouring forth of the bowl judgments (Rev. 15:2 cf. Rev. 16:2). Therefore, this command to take the mark must occur prior to the bowl judgments. Those who refuse to worship the Beast or his image and refuse his mark are "beheaded for their witness to Jesus and for the word of God" (Rev. 20:4). These live and reign with Christ in the *Millennial Kingdom*[5.2.39]. When the third bowl judgment is poured forth, the remainder of the rivers and springs become blood. An angel explains this righteous judgment of God: "For they have shed the blood of saints and prophets, and you have given them blood to drink. For it is their just due" (Rev. 16:6).

The image which requires worship is typified by Nebuchadnezzar's statue. Those who refused to bow down before it were cast into a furnace (Dan. 3:5). As the three young Hebrew men were preserved *through* the fire, so too will be those saints who live at the time of the end (Rev. 7:14; 15:2; 20:4).

3.13.16 - Revelation 13:16

he causes all, both small and great, rich and poor, free and slave

These are similar categories of persons who fled to the mountains and hid themselves in caves from the wrath of God and of the Lamb (Rev. 6:15). No matter what station or position a person has, they will all be treated absolutely equitably. Even the rich, who might normally expect to bribe their way around the requirement, have no exemption. So manic is the desire of the dragon—and his empowered *Beast*[5.2.9]—for all worship that he will treat the most powerful men on a par with the least in their requirement to render worship. In this regard, the dragon emulates the true God: "Yet He is not partial to princes, nor does he regard the rich more than the poor" (Job 34:19). The birds will exhibit similar uniform treatment of the *earth dwellers*[5.2.18] at their banquet at the second advent (Rev. 19:17).

Here again is evidence against taking *Nero*[4.12] as the Beast, for the requirement of worship is global: "The Neronian persecution was limited to Rome as far as the data tell us, and there is no evidence for it extending to the province of Asia at that time."[92]

to receive a mark

The *TR*[5.2.79] text has δῶσῃ αὐτοῖς [*dōsē autois*], *he should give* them a mark. The *NU*[5.2.49] text has δῶσιν αὐτοῖς [*dōsin autois*], *they should give them* a mark.

Mark is χάραγμα [*charagma*]: "From *charasso*, to engrave . . . denotes a mark or stamp."[93] It differs from στίγμα [*stigma*] , such as Paul carried in his body (Gal. 6:17) which indicates a mark or scar "without special design, but carrying significance."[94] The mark here probably is of a specific design so as to be recognizable. It differs in emphasis from the seal (σφραγῖδα [*sphragida*]) placed on the 144,000 of Israel (Rev. 7:2). The mark emphasizes *loyalty* to the Beast but the seal emphasizes *ownership* by God.[95] The only other occurrence of this word outside the book of Revelation is by Luke. "Therefore, since we are the offspring of God, we ought not to think that the Divine Nature is like gold or silver or stone, something **shaped** [*graven*, KJV; *formed*, NASB] by art and man's devising" [emphasis added] (Acts 17:29). It is almost certainly visible: "Made by engraving, etching, imprinting, branding,"[96] whereas the seal of God is probably invisible (Rev. 7:2). The former is discernible by supernatural powers (Rev. 7:2; Rev. 9:4), the latter by the government of the Beast.

> [DeMar] equates the mark of Revelation 13 (Rev. 13:16) with the mark that is given to the 144,000 by the Lamb. "Will Jesus implant a microchip in the foreheads of the 144,000?" he asks. Here DeMar confuses things that must not be confused. As the eternal Son of God, Jesus Christ does not need some kind of a visible mark to help Him watch over the 144,000. The *Antichrist*[5.2.3] and his minions, however, are not divine. . . . Mention of an invisible mark in one place of Scripture need not imply that the mark in all other places is invisible.[97]

> A strictly literal translation of "the mark of the beast" might imply "a picture of the beast" or "a mark made by the beast." A more satisfactory indication of the relationship between "mark" and "beast" would be "a mark showing one's relationship to the beast" or "a mark of loyalty to the beast" or "a mark of the party of the beast."[98]

> In summary, the mark of the beast would signify to the reader of the time that the recipient: worshipped the beast as divine, acknowledged the beast's authority, is devoted to the beast, and considers himself to be the beast's property or slave to command.[99]

> In the *Papyri*[5.2.53], χάραγμα [*charagma*] is always connected with the Emperor, and sometimes contains his name and effigy, with the year of his reign. It was necessary for buying and selling. It is found on all sorts of documents, making them valid; and there are many on "bills of sale." *Charagma* is therefore the *official seal.*[100]

The mark which is taken is the *same* for all:

> This mark has nothing to do with credit, as is often taught today. In a credit system, everyone must have a different number. In this case, everyone has the *same* number. The purpose of the mark will be to serve as a sign of identification of those who will own the Antichrist as their god. Only those who have this number will be permitted to work, to buy, to sell, or simply to make a living. The verse does not speak of credit cards, banking systems, a cashless society, a one-world money system, or computers, etc.[101]

It is certainly within the realm of possibility for the mark to serve both as a single identifier of allegiance to the Beast *and* a globally unique identifier. All that is required is to combine an outward visible mark (indicating shared allegiance) with an invisible digital code (indicating unique identification). The external mark would function to readily cull the obedient from the disobedient while the invisible code would provide the necessary means for digital monetary exchange in the controlled economy of the end. As is typical of Satan's schemes, the unique identifier would provide numerous *benefits* which would also serve as motivation to take the mark. The cost of refusing the mark is not just the risk of one's life, but also the inability to participate in the global market. The details of the mark are not revealed by Scripture.

on their right hand

This implies a mark on the surface of the hand. Such a mark has several advantages from the perspective of the Beast.

- It requires the worshiper to permanently deface his body as an act of homage.
- It provides a ready means to identify those without the mark.
- It is immune to the fragility of technical systems—especially given the disruptive nature of the time of the end.

On the other hand, a low-technology implementation has the disadvantage of being subject to ready falsification. Perhaps the answer is found in a combination of both externally visible and internal (implanted) technology:

> While I admit that the preposition *epi* is used, this does not consign the futurist interpretation [of an implanted mark] to sudden death. If this mark were purely on the surface of the skin, the resultant loss of skin, as happens regularly with people, would mean the mark would disappear. For this mark to have any degree of permanence it must, in some sense, be "in" the tissue. The use of επι [*epi*] doesn't really deny that. it is simply saying that the mark is visible to someone, or to some device such as a scanner. In fact the word "mark" (*charagma*) comes from the verb *charasso* which means "to cut to a point, then to inscribe." it is really not farfetched to see the phrase as describing some kind of minor surgery—a

"cutting to a point"—for the insertion of a chip that will be "inscribed" with data.[102]

This is a time in which Jesus' injunction to cut off one's hand (Mtt. 18:8) can be taken literally, for Rev. 14:9-10 and 20:4 make it plain that no one bearing the mark of the Beast will enter eternal life. Indeed, it will be better to enter eternal life maimed than to be cast into hell-fire whole.[103]

or on their foreheads

The high priest wore a plate of pure gold upon his forehead with the engraving, "HOLINESS TO THE LORD" (Ex. 28:36-38). It declared him to be one who was set aside for the purpose and ministry of God (a saint). Ezekiel was shown a vision where those to be spared God's judgment receive a mark on their foreheads (Eze. 9:4). Harlots wore a mark on their forehead identifying their harlotry (Jer. 3:3; Rev. 17:5). The 144,000 sealed of Israel have the name of the Father and of the Lamb written on their foreheads (Rev. 14:1 cf. Rev. 7:3). See commentary on *Revelation 7:3*[3.7.3].

In all of these examples, the mark identifies the category to which the person belongs and serves as an indication of character, as does the mark of the Beast. Those who take it are completely opposed to God and unwilling to repent in the face of overwhelming evidence of His judgment. See *Beast Worshipers are Unique*[4.4.3.4].

The placement of the mark on the *hand* or *forehead* brings to mind the command God gave through Moses that the children of Israel would faithfully teach His commands to their children.

And these words which I command you today shall be in your heart. You shall teach them diligently to your children, and shall talk of them when you sit in your house, when you walk by the way, when you lie down, and when you rise up. **You shall bind them as a sign on your hand, and they shall be as frontlets between your eyes** . You shall write them on the doorposts of your house and on your gates. (De 6:6-9 cf. Ex. 13:9, 16) [emphasis added]

In response to these instructions, the Jews developed phylacteries, small scrolls which contained God's law and which were bound to the hand or head. The phylacteries differ from the mark of the Beast in that they were attached to the *left* hand. "*Tefillin* (phylacteries) are small tightly rolled scrolls that contain passages from Exodus and Deuteronomy. They were placed in boxes that were tied to the head or left arm. The *mezuzot* were placed in ornamental cases that were attached to the doorpost of a house."[104] Although the mark of the Beast is on the right hand rather than the left, the similarity to the instructions given by God to Israel in remembrance of the law is striking.

3.13.17 - Revelation 13:17

no one may buy or sell

In order to enforce worship of the *Beast*[5.2.9] and his image, the mark is tied to his global economic system. Those who refuse the mark are automatically cut off from the global economy. They are driven underground to rely either upon supernatural provision (as the woman in the wilderness of Revelation 12:6) or the black market. Some manage to survive outside the global economy, including the "sheep" in the Sheep and Goat Judgment at the return of Christ to take up His kingdom(Mtt. 25:31-32). The sheep have provided for the dire needs of Jesus' "brethren" during this time, but they themselves have been without the mark. For it is not possible to take the mark and remain among the redeemed who enter the kingdom (Rev. 14:9-11).

There are several aspects of modern technology which will likely contribute to the control of the global economy under the Beast. *First*, the mark itself may be tied into a cashless system of exchange. While Scripture *does not say this*, how effective it would be to do away with all means of value exchange except for that which requires the mark. *Second*, the use of modern identifying marks, such as bar codes, on *items of commerce* facilitates tracking their whereabouts and distribution. With sophisticated inventory systems it becomes much more difficult to supply the black market "off the record."

The degree to which technology plays in the system of the end is pure speculation. It may utilize systems of identification, tracking, and exchange yet unknown to us. Or it may use the oldest of technologies—tattoos or similar. The desire of the Beast to catch every possible violator argues for a high-technology solution which is more difficult to forge. The disruptive conditions on the earth during the time of the end argue for a low-technology solution.

who has the mark or the name of the beast or the number of his name

The *TR*[5.2.79] text indicates three alternatives: (1) the mark, or (2) the name of the beast, or (3) the number of his name. The *MT*[5.2.45] and *NU*[5.2.49] texts indicate just two alternatives: the mark *which is*: (1) the name of the beast, or (2) the number of his name. In any event, the mark embodies information pertaining to the name of the Beast.

the number of his name

Most commentators take *the number of his name* to indicate the practice of *gematria*[5.2.21], where the individual letters comprising the name are given values which then contribute to a total value which is *the number*:

> The *mystic use of numbers* (the rabbinical Ghematria, γεωμετρία [*geōmetria*]) was familiar to the Jews in Babylon, and passed from them to the Greeks in Asia. It occurs in the Cabbala, in the Sibylline Books (I. 324-331), in the Epistle of Barnabas, and was very common also among the *Gnostic*[5.2.23] sects . . . It arose from the employment of the letters of the Hebrew and Greek alphabets for the designation of numbers. The Hebrew *Aleph* counts 1, *Beth* 2, etc., *Yodh* 10; but *Kaph* (the eleventh letter) counts 20, *Resh* (the twentieth letter) 200, etc. The Greek letters, with the addition of an acute accent (as ά, β΄), have the same numerical value in their order down to Sigma, which counts 200; except that σ˜ (*st*, [stigma]) is used for 6, and φ΄ (an antiquated letter *Koppa* between π and ρ) for 90. The Hebrew alphabet ends with *Tav* = 400, the Greek with *Omega* = 800. To express thousands an accent is put beneath the letter, as α, [*a,*] = 1,000; β, [*b,*] = 2,000; ι, [*i,*] = 10,000.[105]

Again, there is evidence that the number is the same for all who receive it:

> Doubtless, the invention of computers and the introduction of a "cashless society" would aid in the enforcement of an economic boycott against Christians. However, the mark is the "name of the beast or the number of his name" (Rev. 13:17) not the name or number that identifies each individual citizen.[106]

3.13.18 - Revelation 13:18

Here is wisdom

This phrase indicates that what follows constitutes a riddle of sorts requiring great wisdom to comprehend. A similar statement introduces the riddle of the *seven heads*[4.3.2.4] of the beast (Rev. 17:9). "*It is* the glory of God to conceal a matter, but the glory of kings *is* to search out a matter" (Pr. 25:2). When Daniel was puzzled about the revelation given to him, he was told that "the words *are* closed up and sealed till the time of the end. . . none of the wicked shall understand, but the wise shall understand" (Dan. 12:9-10). Although the book of Revelation is not a sealed book (Rev. 22:10), undoubtedly a similar principle attends this passage: those living at the time of the fulfillment will be best positioned to understand the full meaning of what is related. Until that time, history is full of names conjectured to fulfill the riddle of this verse. See *A Lock almost any Key will Turn*[4.12.2.3].

the number of a man

Ἀριθμὸς ἀνθρώπου [*Arithmos anthrōpou*], simply *number of man*. The definite article ("the") is not found in the Greek text. Wallace sees the missing article as an indication that the number is not of *a man*, but *the number of humankind*.[107] While this may account for the grammar, it fails to account for the previous verse wherein the article appears before both *number* and *man*: τὸν ἀριθμὸν τοῦ ὀνόματος αὐτοῦ [*ton arithmon tou onomatos autou*], *the number of the name of him* (cf. Rev. 14:11). Thus, the number seems inextricably tied to the individual. Some explain *of a man* as designating a number *as men count*.[108]

His number *is* six hundred and sixty six

Discussion on the meaning of this value and its association with individuals and movements of history is legend. "The interpretations of this number form a jungle from which escape is apparently hopeless."[109]

The numeric designator for the value 666 found in the *MT*[5.2.45] and *TR*[5.2.79] texts employs the Greek character *stigma* which is not generally used today. It occurs between *epsilon* (ε) and *zeta* (ζ). Thus it displaces *zeta* as the sixth character, giving *zeta* through *theta* the values 7 through 9, *iota* through *kappa* the values 10 through 90, and *rho* through *omega* the values 100 through 800. An additional character, *sampsi* stands at the end as 900.[110] Since our Greek font does not contain *stigma* we will represent it by a *sigma* with an accent: ς′[111]

In the TR and MT text, the value is given by the three Greek letters χξς′ [*chxs*].[112] Given the Greek alphabet of the time, the values of the three letters are: χ = 600; ξ = 60; ς′ = 6. Their sum is the infamous 666.[113] The *NU*[5.2.49] text spells out the values using words: ἑξακοσιοι ἑξηκοντα ἑξ [*hexakosioi hexēkonta hex*], *six hundred sixty six*. Among all the extant manuscript evidence, only a very few have δεκα [*deka*] (10) as the middle value resulting in 616.[114]

The *Nero*[4.12] advocates make much of the alternative value 616 because two different spellings of *Nero*[5.2.46] can account for both the value 666 and 616. This may be true. But it is but one small piece of the overall puzzle which contributes to the identity of the *Beast*[5.2.9]. Nero succeeds on this count, *but fails miserably on all others*. Nero is far from the only individual in history who meets the conditions for 666. See *A Lock almost any Key will Turn*[4.12.2.3]. Metzger suggests that the textual variation indicating 616 is best explained as an intentional modification of the original text by a scribe who saw Nero in the text.[115] See our discussion of the attempts to find fulfillment in *Nero*[4.12].

Irenaeus, who lived much nearer to the time of Nero than modern *preterists*[5.2.59] and who was a disciple of *Polycarp*[5.2.55] who knew our author, supports the reading 666:

> Such, then, being the state of the case, and this number [666] being found in all the most approved and ancient copies [of the Apocalypse], and those men who saw John face to face bearing their testimony [to it]; while reason also leads us to conclude that the number of the name of the beast, [if reckoned] according to the Greek mode of calculation by the [value of] the letters contained in it, will amount to six hundred and sixty and six; that is, the number of tens shall be equal to that of the hundreds, and the number of hundreds equal to that of the units (for that number which [expresses] the digit six being adhered to throughout . . . I do not know how it is that some have erred following the ordinary mode of speech, and have vitiated the middle number in the name, deducting the amount of fifty from it, so that instead of six decades they will have it that there is but one. (I am inclined to think that this occurred through the fault of the copyists, as is wont to happen, since numbers also are expressed by letters; so that the Greek letter which expresses the number sixty [chi, ξ] was easily expanded into the letter Iota [ι] of the Greeks.) Others then received this reading without examination; some in their simplicity, and upon their own responsibility, making use of this number expressing one decade; while some, in their inexperience, have ventured to seek out a name which should contain the erroneous and spurious number.—Irenaeus, *Against Heresies*, v.xxx[116]

He saw the number connected with the antitype of *Antichrist*[5.2.3]'s image—Nebuchadnezzar's statue. He also saw the Beast as a person yet future, not Nero:

> For that image which was set up by Nebuchadnezzar had indeed a height of sixty cubits, while the breadth was six cubits; on account of which Ananias, Azarias, and Misael, when they did not worship it, were cast into a furnace of fire, pointing out prophetically, by what happened to them, the wrath against the righteous which shall arise towards the [time of the] end. For that image, taken as a whole, was a prefiguring of this man's coming, decreeing that he should undoubtedly himself alone be worshipped by all men.—Irenaeus, *Against Heresies*, v.xxx[117]

Adding to the complexity of identifying an individual with the number are various ways in which *gematria*[5.2.21] can be performed. Harless argues for the simplest, *ragil* method:

> There are seven ways of calculating gematria in Jewish tradition. 1) *Ragil:* This method is the basis for all the other methods. Each letter of the alphabet has its own numerical value. The numerical value of a word or phrase is the sum total of the values of its letters. 2) *Katan:* All the tens and hundreds are converted to the single numbers 1 to 9. 3) *K'lali:* In this method, the value of a word is the square of the sum of the *ragil* values of each letter in that word. 4) *Millui:* This method gives a letter the numerical value of the sum of the *ragil* values of the letters that make up the name of the letter. 5) *Kolel:* This method sums the *ragil* values of the letters in a word plus the number of letters. 5) *Hakadmi:* The value of the first letter is *ragil*. The accumulated value of the second letter is its *ragil* value plus the *ragil* value of the first letter. The accumulated value of the third letter is its *ragil* value plus the accumulated value

of the second letter, *etc.* 7) *Haperati:* The value of each letter is the square of its *ragil* value. The value of the word is the sum of all the squares of its letters. It is apparent that the *k'lali, millui, kolel, hakadmi,* and *haperati* methods are unlikely to be intended in this passage, since they would tend to produce numerical values much in excess of 666. These methods also seem to be late additions not in use during the New Testament period. Only the *ragil* and *katan* methods are candidates for this calculation. *Katan* suffers from four shortcomings: 1) It would require a long name to evaluate to 666 (at least 74 letters). 2) The Talmud only uses *ragil.* 3) Therefore, *katan* is a later development and not contemporary with the Revelation. 4) Only *ragil* has an analogue in Greek and Roman culture, *katan* does not.[118]

The threefold representation of "6," the number of man, may be connected with the three key players in the kingdom of the Beast of the end: "Possibly the threefold occurrence of the number six is a vague imitation of the trinity formed by [the Beast's] association with the devil and the false prophet."[119] As we discussed in *Six: Man's Incompleteness, Human Will*[2.7.5.3.5], the number almost certainly emphasizes how the Beast, the epitome of human achievement and government at the end, falls short.[120] Others note how the value compares to the sum of the Greek letters making up the name "Christ": "According to the Greek numbering scheme Christ's name, Ἰησοῦς [*Iēsous*], is represented by I=10, η=8, σ=200, ο=70, υ=400, ς=200, which add up to 888."[121]

Various passages of Scripture hint at the character of the Beast using values which employ six, including the number of fingers and toes on the godless giants of old (2S. 21:20; 1Chr. 20:6); Goliath who had a height of *six* cubits, *six* pieces of armor, and a spear's head weighing *six* hundred shekels of iron (1S. 17:4-7); Nebuchadnezzar, whose "image" was sixty cubits high and six cubits wide (Dan. 3:1); and even Solomon's wages of *six* hundred and *sixty-six* talents of gold (1K. 10:14). See *Six: Man's Incompleteness, Human Will*[2.7.5.3.5].

Ultimately, it is fruitless for us to employ this number in speculation as to the identity of the Beast.

1. The value of the number in and of itself is too broad—too many historic names can be made to generate "666." (See *A Lock almost any Key will Turn*[4.12.2.3].)
2. The church will not be present when the Beast becomes known to the world, for she will have been taken in the *Rapture*[4.14] (2Th. 2:1-8).
3. The number of his name is perhaps the *least important clue* among many attributes which Scripture set forth concerning the identity and ministry of this individual. Certainly it is the most elastic.
4. While the Restrainer remains (2Th. 2:7), he will not be revealed. No amount of conjecture or analysis will bring him forth prior to God's timing. While there are no preconditions for the removal of the Restrainer, he could continue to restrain for decades or even centuries beyond our present time.[122]

What we *can* be sure of is that the value given in this passage will enable believers of the end, when combined with the many other Scriptural clues, to positively identify the individual. It may be that gematria is not even involved in the final understanding of the number:

> A similar use of *nous* and *sophia* occurs in Rev. 17:9, where John calls attention to the identity of the beast ridden by the harlot. What John seems to be asking for in both cases is divine discernment and not mathematical ingenuity! Believers need to penetrate the deception of the beast. John's reference to his number will help them to recognize his true character and identity.[123]

> The better part of wisdom is to be content that the identification is not yet available, but will be when the future false Christ ascends to his throne. The person to whom 666 applies must have been future to John's time, because John clearly meant the number to be recognizable to someone. If it was not discernible to his generation and those immediately following him—and it was not—the generation to whom it will be discernible must have lain (and still lies) in the future. Past generations have provided many illustrations of this future personage, but all past candidates have proven inadequate as fulfillments. Christians from generation to generation may manifest the same curiosity as the prophets of old regarding their own prophecies (cf. 1Pe. 1:10-11), but their curiosity will remain unsatisfied until the time of fulfillment arrives.[124]

For those who are in the Church Age, the number of the Beast, as fascinating a puzzle as it may be, is of relatively little importance. For the Church will not be present when he is revealed (see *Who is the Restrainer?*[4.14.4.2]). This is by *design* for we are to maintain a watch for *Christ* , not Antichrist! We are commanded to look for our bridegroom, not a coming global despot (Php. 3:20).

Notes

1 Some infer from the placement of the material of chapter 13 following upon the plight of the woman in chapter 12 that "the rest of her offspring" (Rev. 12:17) must be those who are subsequently persecuted within chapter 13. If so, then her offspring would include all who refuse to take the mark, both Jew and Gentile. [Alan F. Johnson, *Revelation: The Expositor's Bible Commentary* (Grand Rapids, MI: Zondervan Publishing House, 1966), Rev. 13:1] Yet there are valid reasons to understand her offspring as physical Jews. See commentary on *Revelation 12:1*[3.12.1].

2 We note that the term *Antichrist*[5.2.3] is not used by John in the book of Revelation. But neither is the *little horn*[5.2.37] or many of the other names which apply throughout Scripture to this individual, here designated as the first beast. See *Man of Many Names*[4.2.1].

3 "Though the Holy Spirit '[will be] taken out of the way' (2Th. 2:7) in the Tribulation, this has to do with His work of restraining sin and not with His indwelling and empowering believers."—Russell L. Penney, *"Pneumatology in the Book of Revelation,"* in Mal Couch, ed., *A Bible Handbook to Revelation* (Grand Rapids, MI: Kregel Publications, 2001), 119.

4 John F. Walvoord, *The Revelation of Jesus Christ* (Chicago, IL: Moody Press, 1966), s.v. "Some manuscripts read, "he stood," the change being effected by the dropping of one letter ."

5 Walter Scott, *Exposition of The Revelation* (London, England: Pickering & Inglis, n.d.), Rev. 13:1.

6 Donald Grey Barnhouse, *Revelation* (Grand Rapids, MI: Zondervan Publishing House, 1971), Rev. 13:1.

7 Barnhouse, *Revelation*, Rev. 13:1.

8 J. A. Seiss, *The Apocalypse: Lectures on the Book of Revelation* (Grand Rapids, MI: Zondervan Publishing House, 1966), 322.

9 Arthur Walkington Pink, *The Antichrist* (Oak Harbor, WA: Logos Research Systems, 1999, 1923), s.v. "Antichrist in the Apocalypse."

10 Daniel K. Wong, *"The Beast From The Sea in Revelation 13,"* in *Bibliotheca Sacra*, vol. 160 no. 639 (Dallas, TX: Dallas Theological Seminary, July-September 2003), 337.

11 Randall Price, *"Antichrist,"* in Mal Couch, ed., *Dictionary of Premillennial Theology* (Grand Rapids, MI: Kregel Publications, 1996), 46.

12 Barnhouse, *Revelation*, 103.

13 Arnold G. Fruchtenbaum, *The Footsteps of Messiah*, rev ed. (Tustin, CA: Ariel Ministries, 2003), 676.

14 "To say that the sea stands for the abyss carries on the *OT*[5.2.51] concept of the sea, that is the source of the satanic sea monster (cf. Job 26:12-13; Ps. 74:13-14; 87:4; 89:9-10; Isa. 27:1; 51:9-10) (Johnson). Also, Paul equates the sea with the abyss in his Rom. 10:7 citation of Deu. 30:13."—Robert L. Thomas, *Revelation 8-22* (Chicago, IL: Moody Press, 1995), Rev. 13:1.

15 Concerning inaccuracies in the KJV and NKJV, see commentary on *Revelation 17:10*[3.17.10].

16 Pink, *The Antichrist*, s.v. "Babylon and the Antichrist."

17 "Beginning with verse 36, a sharp break in the prophecy may be observed, introduced by the expression *the time of the end* in verse 35. Up to this point, the prophecy dealing with the Persian and Grecian Empires has been fulfilled minutely and with amazing precision. Beginning with verse 36, however, an entirely different situation obtains. No commentator claims to find precise fulfillment in the remainder of this chapter. Although Zöckler and others attempt to relate Daniel 11:36-45 to Antiochus, many students of Scripture have recognized from antiquity that another king must be in view. Ibn-Ezra, for example, identified this king with Constantine the Great; Rashi and Calvin referred him to the Roman Empire as a whole; and Jerome, Theodoret, and Luther, among others, identified him with the New Testament Antichrist."—John F. Walvoord, *Daniel: The Key to Prophetic Revelation* (Chicago, IL: Moody Bible Institute, 1971), Dan. 11:36.

18 "Because the leopard, lion, and bear in Revelation 13:2 are also used in Daniel 7 to depict nations, the

interpreter is alerted to the fact that John is employing symbolic language. Thus, the leopard, lion, and bear also represent nations in Revelation 13 just as they did in Daniel 7."—Andy Woods, *What is the Identity of Babylon In Revelation 17-18?*.

19 Merrill C. Tenney, *Interpreting Revelation* (Peabody, MA: Hendrickson Publishers, 1957), 188.

20 John MacArthur, *Revelation 12-22 : The MacArthur New Testament Commentary* (Chicago, IL: Moody Press, 2000), Rev. 13:1.

21 "We are at a loss to understand how this can be the Roman Empire revived! For the Beast itself is like a *leopard* (Greece) (Dan. 7:6). Its feet are those of the *bear* (Medo-Persia); and its mouth is like a *lion's* mouth (Babylon). Where is the Roman Empire here in any form? If the Beast be the Roman Empire, does he have himself, intact, for one of his own heads? The notion is only a venerable, but vain, imagination. Rome cannot be at the same time one of the heads, and yet the whole Beast himself. 'One is' (Rev. 17:10). That is said to be the Roman Empire. But it is added, 'the other is not.' Is this the Roman Empire too? Clearly not! What we have here is the embodiment and personification of the sovereignty of the world under Satanic power."—E. W. Bullinger, *Commentary On Revelation* (Grand Rapids, MI: Kregel Publications, 1984, 1935), Rev. 13:2.

22 Merrill F. Unger, *Unger's Commentary on the Old Testament* (Chattanooga, TN: AMG Publishers, 2002), Hos. 13:8.

23 Frederick William Danker, and Walter Bauer, *A Greek-English Lexicon of the New Testament and Other Early Christian Literature* (Chicago, IL: University of Chicago Press, 2000), 265.

24 Pink, *The Antichrist*, s.v. "The Genius and Character of the Antichrist."

25 Pink, *The Antichrist*, s.v. "The Man of Sin, the Son of Perdition."

26 Pink, *The Antichrist*, s.v. "The Antichrist in Revelation 13."

27 Concerning inaccuracies in the KJV and NKJV, see commentary on *Revelation 17:10*[3.17.10].

28 "The 'healing,' then, of the head of the beast, speaks of the Roman Empire, which fell in A.D. 476; the empire has a latter-day emergence, form, or development."—Wong, "*The Beast From The Sea in Revelation 13*," 346.

29 Thomas, *Revelation 8-22*, Rev. 13:3.

30 The Greek is identical with the exception of the gender of the participle: the *Lamb* is masculine, the *head* is feminine. A similar phrase appears in Revelation 13:8.

31 "Many take the phrase, *as though he had been smitten unto death* , to mean that the *Antichrist*[5.2.3] appeared to be dead but was not really. However, the same idiom is used of Messiah in Revelation 5:6, and there was no question that Messiah died."—Fruchtenbaum, *The Footsteps of Messiah*, 247.

32 Ice, *"The Death and Resurrection of the Beast, Part 2,"* in Thomas Ice, ed., *Pre-Trib Perspectives*, vol. 8 no. 23 (Dallas, TX: Pre-Trib Research Center, May 2005), 5.

33 Danker, *A Greek-English Lexicon of the New Testament and Other Early Christian Literature*, 668.

34 Monty S. Mills, *Revelations: An Exegetical Study of the Revelation to John* (Dallas, TX: 3E Ministries, 1987), Rev. 13:3.

35 "The popular Islamic picture of the Antichrist, or *Dajjal*, graphically portrays him as blind in one eye, with the word *kafir*—unbeliever—written on his forehead; his primary function is to mislead the unbelieving masses by claiming divinehood and the power to perform miracles."—Norman L. Geisler, and Abdul Saleeb, *Answering Islam* (Grand Rapids, MI: Baker Books, 1993), 113.

36 "Some have seen in the healing of the wound a reference to the Nero redivivus belief of the first century . . . It is doubtful . . . that John would have used a false rumor as a basis for this."—Wong, "*The Beast From The Sea in Revelation 13*," 346n27.

37 The preference for an individual to worship is evident from the time of Rome: "The worship of emperors . . . provided a living tangible, audible deity for men who had been accustomed to the formal routine of ritual observance. The gods of Graeco-Roman legend had no reality; and their very existence had been challenged by the philosophers. The [Roman] emperor was the living head of the state and the guardian of its welfare. . . . His abilities and deeds seemed almost superhuman to the ordinary man of the street. Here at last was a real person whose position and powers made him worthy of worship."—Tenney, *Interpreting Revelation*, 24.

38 Fruchtenbaum, *The Footsteps of Messiah*, 248.

39 Regarding the phrase, "the desire of women": "The most plausible explanation, in the light of Daniel's Jewish

background and Antichrist's prime persecuting energies that will be spent against the Jews, is that the reference is to the natural desire of Hebrew women to become the mother of the promised Messiah (Gen. 3:15), making the expression a symbol of the Messianic hope in general. The 'desire of women' would be a subjective genitive: 'that desired by women.' Favoring that interpretation is the contextual position of the phrase sandwiched between references to 'the gods of his fathers' and 'any god.' "—Unger, *Unger's Commentary on the Old Testament*, Dan. 11:37.

40 Alexander Roberts, James Donaldson, and A. Cleveland Coxe, *Ante-Nicene Fathers Vol. I* (Oak Harbor, WA: Logos Research Systems, 1997), s.v. "ECF 1.1.7.1.3.7."

41 Pink, *The Antichrist*, s.v. "Antichrist in the Apocalypse."

42 MacArthur, *Revelation 12-22 : The MacArthur New Testament Commentary*, Rev. 13:1.

43 Bullinger, *Commentary On Revelation*, Rev. 13:5.

44 Danker, *A Greek-English Lexicon of the New Testament and Other Early Christian Literature*, 682.

45 "Christ's public ministry was limited to three years and a half; so also will the *Antichrist*[5.2.3]'s final ministry be (Rev. 13:5)."—Pink, *The Antichrist*, s.v. "Comparisons between Christ and the Antichrist."

46 Roberts, *Ante-Nicene Fathers Vol. I*, s.v. "ECF 1.1.7.1.5.31."

47 Seiss, *The Apocalypse: Lectures on the Book of Revelation*, 328.

48 Wong also notes that the removal of the Restrainer (2Th. 2:6-8), the Holy Spirit, suggests a *pretribulational*[5.2.60] *rapture*[5.2.62].

49 Wong, "*The Beast From The Sea in Revelation 13*," 347.

50 Fruchtenbaum, *The Footsteps of Messiah*, 35.

51 Tenney, *Interpreting Revelation*, 196-197.

52 We uphold the unlimited atonement of Christ's blood for all of mankind. He was given for the *world* : John 3:16; 6:51; Rom. 5:18; 2Cor. 5:14-19; 1Ti. 2:4-6; Heb. 2:9; 1Jn. 2:2; 4:14.

53 James Strong, *The Exhaustive Concordance of the Bible* (Ontario: Woodside Bible Fellowship, 1996), G2602.

54 A complete scroll of Isaiah was found as part of the Dead Sea Scrolls. Dated prior to Christ, it contains this amazing chapter predicting the atoning sacrifice of Jesus Christ hundreds of years in advance. It stands as irrefutable evidence of both the *inspiration*[5.2.33] of the OT and the identity of Jesus Christ as the predicted Messiah of Israel.

55 Concerning the worship of Jesus: Mtt. 2:2; 8:2; 9:18; 14:33; 15:25; 28:9, 17; 20:20; Mark 5:6; Luke 24:52; John 5:18, 23; 9:38; 20:28; Acts 7:59; Ps. 31:5; Php. 2:9; Heb. 1:6; Rev. 5:13; 7:10.

56 Andy Woods, *"Revelation 13 and the First Beast,"* in Tim LaHaye, and Thomas Ice, eds., *The End Times Controversy* (Eugene, OR: Harvest House Publishers, 2003), 239.

57 Danker, *A Greek-English Lexicon of the New Testament and Other Early Christian Literature*, 846.

58 The importance of God's sovereignty is a teaching which is sadly lacking among many Christians today. This is a side-effect of the drift of Christianity away from a God-centered toward a man-centered frame of reference. God is seen more as a "big buddy in the sky" Whose primary role is to "make my life better." Could it be, having come to faith in Christ, in numerous cases our suffering might actually *increase?*

59 Timothy Friberg, Barbara Friberg, and Neva F. Miller, *Analytical Lexicon of the Greek New Testament* (Grand Rapids, MI: Baker Books, 2000), 44.

60 Albrecht Durer (1471 - 1528). Image courtesy of the *Connecticut College* (http://www.conncoll.edu/visual/Durer-prints/index.html) *Wetmore Print Collection* (http://www.conncoll.edu/visual/wetmore.html).

61 Philip Schaff, and David Schley Schaff, *History of the Christian Church* (Oak Harbor, WA: Logos Research Systems, 1997, 1916), 1.12.101.

62 Barnhouse, *Revelation*, 240.

63 "Most interpreters view the two Beasts as two aspects of the same thing. All seem to be agreed that they are not individuals; which is the very thing that the ordinary reader would at once take them to be. Little help,

therefore, can be expected from such guides."—Bullinger, *Commentary On Revelation*, Rom. 13:11.

64 Woods, "*Revelation 13 and the First Beast*," 248.

65 Pink, *The Antichrist*, s.v. "The Antichrist in Revelation 13."

66 Pink, *The Antichrist*, s.v. "Antichrist in the Apocalypse."

67 Those who emphasize an exclusively religious role for the Antichrist fail to appreciate the political promises found in Messiah who reigns from the throne of David upon His return. See *The Arrival of God's Kingdom*[2.4.3].

68 Pink, *The Antichrist*, s.v. "Antichrist in Revelation 13."

69 "It might well be . . . though we would not press the point, that this anti-Spirit would be a Jew, and that he would be used of Satan to deceive Israel if possible."—Barnhouse, *Revelation*, 242. "This individual is evidently a Jew, since he arises out of the earth, or land, that is Palestine (Rev. 13:11)."—J. Dwight Pentecost, *Things to Come: A Study in Biblical Eschatology* (Grand Rapids, MI: Zondervan Publishing House, 1958), 336.

70 "Whereas earlier the four beasts arose out of the sea, here they arise out of the earth. Coming out of the *sea* emphasizes their Gentile identity. Arising out of the *earth* emphasizes their humanity."—Fruchtenbaum, *The Footsteps of Messiah*, 29.

71 Not all agree: "In contrast to the first beast, who will come up out of the sea (Rev. 13:1), the second beast will come up out of the earth. Like Antichrist, the false prophet will be indwelt by a demon out of the abyss."—MacArthur, *Revelation 12-22 : The MacArthur New Testament Commentary*, Rev. 13:11. It can also be said that the Witch of Endor "saw a spirit ascending out of the earth" (1S. 28:13). Yet there is no mention elsewhere in Scripture of a source for the False Prophet from the abyss. Moreover, there is great emphasis placed upon such a source for the Beast. The silence of other passages on such a suggestion is weighty.

72 Pink, *The Antichrist*, s.v. "Antichrist in Revelation 13."

73 Mills, *Revelations: An Exegetical Study of the Revelation to John*, Rev. 13:12.

74 Henry Morris, *The Revelation Record* (Wheaton, IL: Tyndale House Publishers, 1983), Rev. 13:12.

75 "Just as the Holy Spirit calls all men to worship the resurrected Son, the False Prophet will call men to worship the resurrected counterfeit son."—Fruchtenbaum, *The Footsteps of Messiah*, 254.

76 Pink, *The Antichrist*, s.v. "The Career of the Antichrist."

77 Barnhouse, *Revelation*, 243.

78 Barnhouse, *Revelation*, 244.

79 This also indicates the level to which occult magic had developed within early Egypt. However, they were unable to bring forth lice (Ex. 8:18). See 2 Timothy 3:8.

80 Bullinger, *Commentary On Revelation*, Rev. 13:13.

81 We do postmodernism a favor here by calling it *thought!*

82 They are no better off than the Roman Catholics who are subject to the authority of the Magisterium of Rome over the Scriptures.

83 "These miracles are not counterfeit, but are used to establish false claims."—Jerome Smith, *The New Treasury of Scripture Knowledge* (Nashville, TN: Thomas Nelson Publishers, 1992), Rev. 13:14.

84 We have no information as to the *size* of the image. Since Paul informs us that the Beast will "sit as God in the temple of God" (2Th. 2:4), and Jesus tells us that the abomination stands in the "holy place" (Mtt. 24:15), it would seem unlikely for the image to be a colossal statue for it would require the removal or modification of the temple in order to stand in the holy place.

85 Fruchtenbaum, *The Footsteps of Messiah*, 257,259,260.

86 Steve Gregg, *Revelation Four Views: A Parallel Commentary* (Nashville, TN: Thomas Nelson, 1997), 300.

87 Concerning God's involvement with the inception and development of life: Ex. 21:22-23; Jdg. 13:5; Job 10:11; 31:15; Ps. 22:9-10; 119:73; 139:13; Ecc. 11:5; Isa. 44:2, 24; 49:5; Jer. 1:5. This is one of numerous reasons why abortion is morally equivalent to murder (Ex. 21:22-23). It is the interrupting by sinful man of that which God has established.

88 Here again we see the parallel between the False Prophet and the Holy Spirit: both refusing to draw attention to themselves, but dedicated to pointing to whom they serve.

89 Thomas, *Revelation 8-22*, Rev. 13:15.

90 Morris, *The Revelation Record*, Rev. 13:15.

91 Ice, *"An Interpretation of Matthew 24-25—Part XIII,"* in Thomas Ice, ed., *Pre-Trib Perspectives*, vol. 8 no. 1 (Dallas, TX: Pre-Trib Research Center, May 2003), 6.

92 Grant R. Osborne, *Revelation* (Grand Rapids, MI: Baker Academic, 2002), 8.

93 W. E. Vine, *Vine's Expository Dictionary of Old and New Testament Words* (Nashville, IL: Thomas Nelson Publishers, 1996), G5480.

94 Johannes P. Louw, and Eugene Albert Nida, *Greek-English Lexicon of the New Testament : Based on Semantic Domains* (New York, NY: United Bible Societies, 1996, c1989), 1:443.

95 Yet χάραγμα [*charagma*] *is* used of brands on animals which denotes ownership. [Danker, *A Greek-English Lexicon of the New Testament and Other Early Christian Literature*, 876]

96 Friberg, *Analytical Lexicon of the Greek New Testament*, 406.

97 Larry Spargimino, *"How Preterists Misuse History to Advance their View of Prophecy,"* in Tim LaHaye, and Thomas Ice, eds., *The End Times Controversy* (Eugene, OR: Harvest House Publishers, 2003), 25.

98 Louw, *Greek-English Lexicon of the New Testament : Based on Semantic Domains*, 1:443.

99 Hal Harless, *"666: The Beast and His Mark in Revelation 13,"* in *The Conservative Theological Journal*, vol. 7 no. 22 (Fort Worth, TX: Tyndale Theological Seminary, December 2003), 341.

100 Bullinger, *Commentary On Revelation*, Rev. 13:16.

101 Fruchtenbaum, *The Footsteps of Messiah*, 255.

102 Spargimino, "*How Preterists Misuse History to Advance their View of Prophecy*," 24-25.

103 Mills, *Revelations: An Exegetical Study of the Revelation to John*, Rev. 13:11.

104 Randall Price, *The Stones Cry Out: What Archaeology Reveals About the Truth of the Bible* (Eugene, OR: Harvest House Publishers, 1997), 279.

105 Schaff, *History of the Christian Church*, 1.12.101.

106 Harless, "*666: The Beast and His Mark in Revelation 13*," 360-361.

107 "If ἀνθρώπου [*anthrōpou*] is generic, then the sense is, 'It is [the] number of *humankind*.' It is significant that this construction fits Apollonius' *Canon*[5.2.12] (i.e., both the head noun and the genitive are anarthrous), suggesting that if one of these nouns is definite, then the other is, too. Grammatically, those who contend that the sense is 'it is [the] number *of a man*' have the burden of proof on them (for they treat the head noun, ἀριθμὸς [*arithmos*], as definite and the genitive, ἀνθρώπου [*anthrōpou*] , as indefinite—the rarest of all possibilities). In light of Johannine usage, we might also add Rev. 16:18, where the Seer *clearly* uses the anarthrous ἄνθρωπος [*anthrōpos*] in a generic sense, meaning 'humankind.' The implications of this grammatical possibility, exegetically speaking, are simply that the number '666' is the number that represents humankind. Of course, an individual is in view, but his number may be the number representing all of humankind. Thus the Seer might be suggesting here that the antichrist, who is the best representative of humanity without Christ (and the best counterfeit of a perfect man that his master, that old serpent, could muster), is still less than perfection (which would have been represented by the number seven)."—Daniel B. Wallace, *Greek Grammar Beyond the Basics - Exegetical Syntax of the New Testament* (Grand Rapids, MI: Zondervan Publishing House and Galaxie Software, 1999, 2002), 253.

108 "It is counted as men usually count. Compare Rev. 21:17, and 'a man's pen,' Isa. 8:1."—M. R. Vincent, *Vincent's Word Studies* (Escondido, CA: Ephesians Four Group, 2002), Rev. 13:18.

109 Vincent, *Vincent's Word Studies*, Rev. 13:18.

110 E. W. Bullinger, *Number in Scripture: Its Supernatural Design and Spiritual Significance* (Grand Rapids, MI: Kregel Publications, 1967), 48-49.

111 Bullinger explores the relationship between the name of the character *stigma* and the mark of this passage:

"The number 6 was stamped on the old mysteries. The great secret symbol consisted of the three letters SSS, because the letter S in the Greek alphabet was the symbol of the figure 6 . . . α = 1, β = 2, γ = 3, δ = 4, ε = 5, but when it came to 6, another letter was introduced! Not the next—the sixth letter (ζ, *zeta*)—but a different letter, a peculiar form of S, called "stigma." Now the word στίγμα [*stigma*], means *a mark*, but especially a mark made by *a brand* as burnt upon slaves, cattle, or soldiers, by their owners or masters; or on devotees who thus branded themselves as belonging to their gods. It is from στίζω [*stizō*], *to prick*, or *brand with a hot iron*. Hence it came to be used of *scars* or *wound-prints* , and it is thus used by Paul of his scars, which he regarded as the tokens of his sufferings, the marks which he bore on his body for the sake of his Lord and Master, and marking him as belonging to the one who had bought him (Gal. 6:17)."—Bullinger, *Number in Scripture: Its Supernatural Design and Spiritual Significance*, 283.

112 "The expression of this number, χξς′ [*Chxs*] consists of the *initial* and *final* letters of the word χριστός [*christos*], christ, viz., χ and ς′ with the symbol of the serpent between them, χ-ξ-ς′."—Bullinger, *Number in Scripture: Its Supernatural Design and Spiritual Significance*, 49.

113 Bullinger mentions several interesting properties associated with this value: "It is remarkable that the Romans did not use all the letters of their alphabet, as did the Hebrews and Greeks. They used only *six* letters, D, C, L, X, V, and I. And it is still more remarkable, and perhaps significant, that the sum of these amounts to 666: 1. D = 500; 2. C = 100; 3. L = 50; 4. X = 10; 5. V = 5; 6. I = 1."—Bullinger, *Number in Scripture: Its Supernatural Design and Spiritual Significance*, 284. "The number 666 has another remarkable property. It is further marked as the *concentration* and essence of 6 by being the *sum* of all the numbers which make up the *square of six!* The square of six is 36 (6^2, or 6 x 6), and the sum of the numbers 1 to 36 [36 factorial] = 666, *i.e.*, 1 + 2 + 3 + 4 + 5 + 6 + 7 + 8 + 9 + 10 + 11 + 12 + 13 + 14 + 15 + 16 + 17 + 18 + 19 + 20 + 21 + 22 + 23 + 24 + 25 + 26 + 27 + 28 + 29 + 30 + 31 + 32 + 33 + 34 + 35 + 36 = 666."—Bullinger, *Number in Scripture: Its Supernatural Design and Spiritual Significance*, 286.

114 "The only textual issue that we are concerned with is the correct reading of Revelation 13:18, και ὁ ἀριθμὸ αὐτοὺ ἑξακοσιοι ἑξήκοντα ἕξ [*kai ho arithmo autou hexakosioi hexēkonta hex*], 'and his number is six hundred and sixty-six.' This is the reading of Sinaiticus (ℵ), Alexandrinus (A), Chester Beatty *papyrus*[5.2.53] (p^{47}), many Italic manuscripts (it), the *Vulgate*[5.2.81] (Vg), and most other manuscripts including the Syrian (syr) and Coptic (cop). The Italic manuscript (it) has τεσσερακοντα [*tesserakonta*], 'forty' instead of ἑξήκοντα [*hexēkonta*] , 'sixty.' This is probably due to a scribal error confusing Revelation 14:1 with 13:18. This reading does not appear until the ninth century. Of more concern is the δεκα [*deka*] 'ten' of Ephraemi Rescriptus (ca. fifth century) and the Italic manuscript Harleianus Londiniensis (it^z, eighth century). *Irenaeus*[5.2.34] was aware of this textual variant but roundly condemned it as misleading. This strong testimony from Irenaeus and the late nature of the variant reading lend confidence that 666, not 646 or 616, is the correct reading."—Harless, "*666: The Beast and His Mark in Revelation 13*," 337.

115 "Instead of ἑξήκοντα [*hexēkonta*], which is strongly supported by P^{47} ℵ A P 046 051 all extant *minuscules*[5.2.41] it^{gig} gv $syr^{ph, h}$ $cop^{sa, bo}$ arm *al*, δέκα [*deka*] is read by C some manuscripts known to Irenaeus . . . and $Tyconius^{pt}$. According to Tishendorf's 8th ed., the numeral 616 was also read by two minuscule manuscripts that unfortunately are no longer extant . . . When Greek letters are used as numerals the difference between 666 and 616 is merely a change from ξ to ι (666 = χξς′ [*chxs*] and 616 = χις′ [*chis*]. Perhaps this change was intentional, seeing that the Greek form Nero Caesar written in Hebrew characters (נרון קסר [*nrwn qhsr*]) is equivalent to 666, whereas the Latin form of Nero Caesar [in Hebrew] (נרו קסר [*nrw qhsr*] is equivalent to 616."—Bruce M. Metzger, *A Textual Commentary on the Greek New Testament* (Stuttgart, Germany: Deutsche Bibelgesellschaft, 1994), Rev. 13:18.

116 Roberts, *Ante-Nicene Fathers Vol. I*, s.v. "ECF 1.1.7.1.5.31."

117 Roberts, *Ante-Nicene Fathers Vol. I*, s.v. "ECF 1.1.7.1.5.30."

118 Harless, "*666: The Beast and His Mark in Revelation 13*," 343-344.

119 Walvoord, *The Revelation of Jesus Christ*, s.v. "666 False Trinity."

120 "Many . . . take the view that the number 666 represents man's falling short of perfection. . . . No Greek article appears before the word 'man,' so one could render the statement, 'it is the number of man.' "—Wong, "*The Beast From The Sea in Revelation 13*," 338n2.

121 Wong, "*The Beast From The Sea in Revelation 13*," 337n2.

[122] We are not suggesting it is *likely* that he will remain for such great periods beyond our day, merely recognizing the Scriptural possibility.

[123] Johnson, *Revelation: The Expositor's Bible Commentary*, 138.

[124] Thomas, *Revelation 8-22*, Rev. 13:18.

3.14 - Revelation 14

3.14.1 - Revelation 14:1

In the previous chapter, the future looked very bleak for the saints. The *Beast*[5.2.9] arose from the sea, empowered by the dragon, and was given authority over the saints (Rev. 13:5). The *False Prophet*[5.2.20] aided the Beast in his ascendancy and worldwide worship (Rev. 13:11-13). An *image of the Beast*[5.2.29] was made which required worship of the image and of the Beast at the cost of one's life (Rev. 13:15).

Here, the focus moves back from the earth, under the control of the Beast, to the heavenly realm where the justice and sovereignty of God are once again emphasized. All is not as it appears on the earth below. For the ultimate judge is on His throne, redeeming men from the midst of the Tribulation.

> The blackest storms often give place to the loveliest sunsets. The winds and thunders exhaust themselves. The clouds empty and break. And from the calm heavens behind them comes a golden light, girthing the remaining fragments of gloom with chains of brightness, and overarching with the bow of promise the path along which the terrible tempest has just passed. Like this evening glory after the summer's gust, is the chapter on which we now enter.[1]

John is shown the firstfruits of the redeemed of Israel, an indication of many more Jews yet to come. He is also shown a threefold angelic witness:

1. The final global presentation of the gospel to all men representing their *last* opportunity to accept salvation before taking the mark of the Beast.
2. The declaration of the certain and *imminent*[5.2.30] destruction of Babylon.
3. The divine warning concerning the gravity of worshiping the Beast and taking his mark.

John is also shown the incredibly difficult conditions under which the saints of the end must prevail and the final harvest at the end of the age, the subject of so much of Jesus' teaching (e.g., Mtt. 13).

a Lamb

The *MT*[5.2.45] and *NU*[5.2.49] texts have *the Lamb*. Even though the *TR*[5.2.79] text lacks the article, there is no question *which* Lamb this is. It cannot be the second beast of the previous chapter which was "like a lamb" (Rev. 13:11). Those who follow *him* will never see Mount Zion as these do. The 144,000 have the name of the Father of this Lamb on their foreheads—a clear reference to God the Father. Hence, this is the "Lamb as though it had been slain" (Rev. 5:6).

Mount Zion

Mount Zion, also known as "the City of David" (2S. 5:7). Within Scripture, the term "Zion" is used in a variety of ways[2] and can refer to as many as three different locations:

> *David's City* . In the *OT*[5.2.51] Zion refers to Jerusalem, the city that David conquered and made a capital of the united kingdom of Israel (1Chr. 11:5; Ps. 2:6; Isa. 2:3). *The Millennial City* . In a prophetic sense, Zion has reference to Jerusalem as the future capital city of the nation Israel in the Kingdom age (Isa. 1:27; 2:3; 4:1-6; Joel 3:16; Zec. 1:16-17; 8:3-8; Rom. 11:26). *Amillennial*[5.2.1] theologians spiritualize, rather "mysticalize," the term to mean the Christian church of this age. *The Heavenly City* . The *NT*[5.2.48] also refers to Zion as the New Jerusalem (Heb. 12:22-24), the eternal city into which the church will be received (cf. Rev. 21-22).[3]

We have seen that Psalm 2 is alluded to many different times in the book of Revelation (e.g., Rev. 2:27; 11:15). And so it is here. "He who sits in the heavens shall laugh; the Lord shall hold them in derision. Then He shall speak to them in His wrath, and distress them in His deep displeasure: 'Yet I have set My King On My holy hill of Zion.' " (Ps. 2:4-6) The psalmist speaks of the *millennial Zion* where the King will initially be enthroned (Isa. 9:7; Mtt. 25:31; Luke 1:32-33).

God chose Zion as his eternal dwelling place (Ps. 132:13), the site of His *Temple*[5.2.73]. See *The Temple Mount*[4.16.3]. God promised, in the strongest terms, that He would never forget the *earthly* Zion:

> But Zion said, "The LORD has forsaken me, and my Lord has forgotten me." "Can a woman forget her nursing child, and not have compassion on the son of her womb? Surely they may forget, yet I will not forget you. See, I have inscribed you on the palms *of My hands*; your walls *are* continually before Me." (Isa. 49:14-16)

> The sun shall be turned into darkness, and the moon into blood, before the coming of the great and awesome day of the LORD. And it shall come to pass *that* whoever calls on the name of the LORD shall be saved. For in Mount Zion and in Jerusalem there shall be deliverance, as the LORD has said, among the remnant whom the LORD calls. (Joel 2:31-32)

Micah describes a coming time of global peace: "They shall beat their swords into plowshares, and their spears into pruning hooks; nation shall not lift up sword against nation, neither shall they learn war anymore" (Mic. 4:3). He then describes the gathering of the outcasts of Israel and the establishment of His millennial reign in Zion. "So the LORD will reign over them in Mount Zion. From now on, even forever" (Mic. 4:8). It is from Zion that the Deliverer will come when He turns ungodliness from Jacob (Rom. 11:25). In many of the redemptive passages concerning Zion, Jerusalem is in view. Jerusalem is referred to as the *daughter of Zion* (Mtt. 21:5; John 12:15).

Isaiah also speaks of the millennial Zion:

> Many people shall come and say, "Come, and let us go up to the mountain of the LORD, to the house of the God of Jacob; He will teach us His ways, and we shall walk in His paths." For out of Zion shall go forth the law, and the word of the LORD from Jerusalem. **He shall judge between the nations, and rebuke many people**; they shall beat their swords into plowshares, and their spears into pruning hooks; nation shall not lift up sword against nation, neither shall they learn war anymore. (Isa. 2:3-4) [emphasis added]

We know these passage speak of an *earthly* scene because they speak of a need for righteous judgment and people being rebuked. Neither of these activities will take place in the eternal state where sin has been vanquished. It need hardly be said that there is no need for deliverance for the *heavenly* Zion because it has never been forsaken, forgotten, or come under attack like its earthly counterpart. Thus, God's promises to redeem and protect Zion relate to the *earth* and not *heaven*.[4]

Although the vast majority of passages concern the earthly Zion, there are some notable exceptions. The author of Hebrews mentions a heavenly scene wherein *Mount Zion* is equated with the city of the living God, the heavenly Jerusalem:

> But you have come to Mount Zion and to the city of the living God, the heavenly Jerusalem, to an innumerable company of angels, to the general assembly and church of the firstborn *who are* registered in heaven, to God the Judge of all, to the spirits of just men made perfect, to Jesus the Mediator of the new covenant, and to the blood of sprinkling that speaks better things than *that of* Abel. (Heb. 12:22-24)

This heavenly Mount Zion is probably in view in other passages which refer to a mountain which is in heaven and is associated with the rule of God (Eze. 28:13-15) and the heavenly Jerusalem and the eternal order (Rev. 21:10).

Since there is both an earthly and a heavenly Zion, which is in view here? The answer to this question carries with it considerable significance. If it is the earthly Zion, then the 144,000 have been protected by their seal throughout the horrors of the Tribulation. If it is the heavenly Zion, after having served out their intended ministry, the 144,000 were removed from the earth, probably through martyrdom.[5]

3.14.1.1 - A Heavenly Scene?

Evidence in favor of the heavenly Zion is as follows:[6]

1. If the 144,000 are the ones singing the new song (Rev. 14:3), they are said to be "before the four living creatures, and the elders" (Rev. 14:3). In every other mention of the living creatures and elders within the book of Revelation, they are in heaven (Rev. 5:6, 8, 11, 14; 7:11; 19:4).
2. It appears that the scene takes place "before the throne of God" (Rev. 14:3, 5). The natural conclusion is that this is the throne of the Father in heaven (Rev. 4:2-3; 5:1, 7; 19:4).[7]
3. The Lamb is *standing* , as it was previously seen in heaven in the midst of the throne (Rev. 5:6; 7:17), but in the Millennium the Lamb would more likely be seated on His throne, the

throne of David (Rev. 3:21).

4. The 144,000 are said to be redeemed *from the earth* (Rev. 4:3). They were redeemed *from among men* (Rev. 4:4). The implication is that they are no longer on the earth among men.

The problem with taking this as a heavenly scene (the heavenly Mount Zion) is how to explain the failure of the sealing of the 144,000 for protection (Rev. 7:1-3) which has now apparently resulted in their death? Perhaps this is not as large of a problem as it first appears.

A close study of Revelation 12 suggests that the faithful remnant which shall be protected throughout the Tribulation and find entry into the *Millennial Kingdom*[5.2.39] are those who flee to the wilderness—the woman who has a place prepared for her by God (Rev. 12:6). We saw that the 144,000 of Israel, who appear to have an evangelistic role, could not be a part of those kept in the wilderness. Because of their evangelistic mission, they will not be in Judea when the signal comes to flee to the mountains and subsequently the wilderness. Furthermore, if they did participate in the flight and subsequent hiding, how could they perform their evangelistic task among the Gentiles and Jews of the Diaspora?

Nowhere is it said that the seal which these receive is to protect them against death throughout the Tribulation and from all causes. Scripture only tells us they are to be protected from the direct effects of God's judgments poured upon the earth. This is why the four winds of the earth are held back until they are sealed (Rev. 7:1-3). Judgments upon *the earth, the sea, and the trees* may not proceed until they are protected. Moreover, they are said to be protected from the demonic locust judgment (Rev. 9:4). All of these dangers come directly from God and represent His wrath upon the *earth dwellers*[5.2.18]. They are to be protected from this "friendly fire" during their evangelistic mission. Does this necessarily mean that they are completely invincible for the entire duration of the Tribulation? If the example of the two powerful witnesses of God is any example, then perhaps not.[8]

> The sealing they received protects them only from the wrath of God, not from the wrath of the dragon and the beast (cf. Rev. 12:12). These are the same 144,000 as in Revelation 7, but they are also the same as the rest of the woman's seed in Revelation 12:17, the witnesses to whom the dragon has access because of their refusal to worship the beast (Rev. 13:15). . . . They are the vanguard who bear the brunt of the struggle against the beast and pay the price of their own lives.[9]

In the same way that the two witnesses are invincible *for the duration of their ministry* (Rev. 11:5), so too might these be. Like the two witnesses "when they finish their testimony" (Rev. 11:7), it may suit God's purpose that their ultimate witness to Him finds its expression in their bold martyrdom (Rev. 12:11).

On the other hand, the two witnesses are never said to be sealed for protection whereas these are. And why are these individuals singled out for special sealing if their ultimate fate is no different than the unsealed martyrs mentioned elsewhere (Rev. 6:9-11; 7:14; 11:7; 12:11; 15:2; 20:4)?

3.14.1.2 - A Scene Spanning both Heaven and Earth?

The scene before us can also be interpreted in a different way which splits the participants between both a heavenly and an earthly location. Such an interpretation understands the 144,000 to be upon the earth having survived the Tribulation due to God's special protection (Rev. 7:1-3). John is given a preview of the Lamb and the 144,000 on the earthly Mount Zion at the introduction of the *Millennial Kingdom*[5.2.39] to come. They are accompanied by thunderous praise from heaven.

This interpretation understands the *singers* to be the *harpists* in heaven, rather than the 144,000 on the earth. *They* who sing a new song before the throne, the four living creatures, and the elders (Rev. 14:3), refers to the nearest antecedent, the *harpists*, not the 144,000 who stand with the Lamb. (However, there is a significant textual variation at this verse which *see*[3.14.2].) "The text does not say that the 144,000 are in the same place as the singers, only that they hear the singers."[10] It is the heavenly chorus playing harps which sing the song in heaven commemorating God's special preservation of the 144,000 throughout the entire Tribulation and the accomplishment of their unique evangelistic task (see commentary on *Revelation 7:3*[3.7.3]). The heavenly harpists sing the new song and the 144,000 are the only ones who can *learn* the song from among those on earth.

> Some want to identify the singers as the redeemed ones themselves. The reasons for assigning this

> identity are the inability of anyone else to learn the song (Rev. 14:3) (Kiddle) and the analogy of Rev. 15:2 where the overcomers have harps (Beasley-Murray). This cannot be, however, because the song is sung in heaven and the 144,000 redeemed ones are on the earthly Mount Zion (Alford, Beckwith). The song is intelligible to the 144,000, but they are not the singers (Moffatt).[11]

The association of the song with the harpists has the advantage of coupling the pronoun (*they*) more closely to the antecedent (*harpists*). It also associates the singing with those who initiate the music and play the harps. It also explains who the 144,000 would *learn* the song from. "Who then are the harpers? They are the martyred company seen in connection with the fifth seal and they also include now their brethren which were slain during the great tribulation."[12] If John sees a preview of the 144,000 standing on Mount Zion at the *end* of the Tribulation, then their appearance follows upon the events of the Tribulation. Interestingly, a group of singing harpists in heaven is mentioned in the very next chapter, although they sing a different song (the song of Moses and of the Lamb). They are those who "have victory over the *Beast*[5.2.9], over his image, and over his mark, and over the number of his name" (Rev. 15:2). The harpists here, although singing a different song, are probably also from among the redeemed.[13]

The weaknesses of this view include:

1. The new song originates in the mouths of the harpists, who lack the firsthand experience of the redemption and preservation of the 144,000. In other passages, those who initiate songs are the ones who experienced redemption (Rev. 5:9-10; 15:2).
2. The statement mentioning the faultlessness of the 144,000 *before the throne of God* (Rev. 14:5) must be understood to describe their salvific position rather than their physical location in heaven. (However, this phrase does not even appear in the *NU*[5.2.49] or *MT*[5.2.45] texts, but only the *TR*[5.2.79] text. See commentary on *Revelation 14:5*[3.14.5].)
3. The need to make a distinction between *singing* the song and *learning* the song. If the 144,000 are said to be the only ones who can *learn* the song, how do we account for the harpists who initially learn in order to *sing*? A possible solution is that the 144,000 are the only ones *from among those on the earth* who can learn it because the song, originated by the harpists in heaven, commemorates their personal experience. It is uniquely their special privilege to sing it. See commentary on *Revelation 14:3*[3.14.3].
4. The emphasis placed on the uniqueness of the song and its association with redemption (Rev. 14:3) argues against its origin with any but the 144,000 themselves.
5. The majority of manuscripts (NU and MT texts) indicate that the voice or sound was *like* harpists playing on their harps. If this describes a *voice* (rather than the sound of a multitude), then *they* which sing in Rev. 14:3 cannot refer to the voice. See commentary on *Revelation 14:2*[3.14.2].

A variation of this view understands the harpists playing their harps from heaven and the 144,000 singing the new song in response from the earth. This view takes *they* (singers) of verse 3, *these* (virgins) of verse 4, and *their* (faultless ones) of verse 5 as all referring to the 144,000 of verse 1. The main weakness of this view is accounting for how the new song they sing can be said to be "before the throne, before the four living creatures, and the elders" (Rev. 14:3) when the singers are themselves on earth.

Mills suggests another variation: that the 144,000 are seen first on earth (Rev. 14:1), but then raptured to heaven to sing before the throne thereafter (Rev. 14:3).[14] While such an event is *possible*, there is little within the context of the passage itself to support such a notion.

The main advantage all of these variations have over a completely heavenly scene is that they interpret God's seal of the 144,000 to have provided for their full safety for the duration of the Tribulation so that they are not only spiritual firstfruits, but also among the first Jews which enter the Millennial Kingdom to form its initial population. If John is shown a prophetic scene with the 144,000 and the Lamb on the earthly Mount Zion in the Millennial Kingdom and the rest of the scene is the heavenly reaction above, then the sealed of Israel would have avoided death to enter the kingdom and now stand as evidence of God's promise to protect a faithful remnant:

> The first verse presents what appears to be a millennial scene, . . . with the 144,000 Jews standing on Mount Zion with the protective seal on their foreheads prominently displayed. This shows that Satan's attempt at total Jewish destruction will fail.[15]

> They are the "firstfruits" of the millennial reign. They connect the *dispensations*[5.2.15]—somewhat as Noah did, who passed through the judgment of the flood into a new order of things.[16]

In chapter fourteen the same group [the 144,000 from Revelation 7] is pictured at the termination of the tribulation, when the kingdom is established. The returning King is on Mount Zion, as was predicted of Him (Zec. 14:4. At His return the faithful witnesses gather to Him, having been redeemed (Rev. 14:4) and having faithfully witnessed in the midst of apostasy (Rev. 14:4-5).[17]

one hundred *and* forty-four thousand

These are the twelve thousand from each of the twelve tribes of Israel who received the "seal of the living God" (Rev. 7:2-8). Some suggest this group to be a different group of Jews than those who were sealed in chapter seven.[18] This is highly improbable: the same number are involved; they are said to be marked on their foreheads; and, with the exception of Dan, they include representatives of both Judah (the southern kingdom) and Israel (the northern kingdom).

his father's name

The MT and NU texts have, *the name of him [the Lamb] and the name of the Father of him.* Elsewhere, the TR text indicates that *both* the name of the Father and the Son will be written on the overcomer (Rev. 3:12). The name indicates their adoption into the family of God (John 1:12) as well as their identity with the Father (Rev. 22:4). Those who follow after unrighteousness deny their sonship by their perverse actions (Deu. 32:5-9). See commentary on *Revelation 3:12*[3.3.12].

written on their foreheads

Written is γεγραμμένον [*gegrammenon*], a perfect tense passive participle, *having been written upon* . The name was written on their foreheads in the past and now they stand so named. The time of the writing was undoubtedly when the 144,000 of Israel were sealed (Rev. 7:3). The name of God on their forehead is to be contrasted with those who received the mark of the Beast "on their right hand or on their foreheads" (Rev. 13:16). See commentary on *Revelation 7:3*[3.7.3].

3.14.2 - Revelation 14:2

a voice from heaven like the voice of many waters

A singular voice, not the seven thunders (Rev. 10:4), although elsewhere a (singular) voice describes a great multitude speaking in unison "as the sound of many waters" (Rev. 19:1). This voice could be that of such a multitude contributing to the scene of worship. Or it could be the same voice which called the two witnesses up to heaven after their resurrection (Rev. 11:12). Christ's voice which John heard was also as "the sound, φωνὴ [*phōnē*], 'voice' here] of many waters" (Rev. 1:15 cf. Eze. 1:24; 43:2). Here it is probably the voice of the Father since the Lamb is said to be on Mount Zion.

In some cases, the *voice from heaven* speaks down to earthly recipients (Rev. 11:12; 18:4) which would favor the view of the Lamb and the 144,000 being on the earthly Mount Zion. In other cases, the phrase merely indicates its originating authority as heard by John during the vision (Rev. 10:4; 14:13; 21:3).

like the voice of loud thunder

The sound John hears is *like* thunder, not actual thunder. Mighty angels have great voices which sound like that of a multitude (Dan. 10:6 cf. Rev. 19:6) or the roar of a lion (Rev. 10:3). A mighty voice, like that of the four living creatures (Rev. 6:1). The participation of the voice from heaven indicates the significance of the scene.

I heard the sound of harpists playing their harps

και φωνὴ ἤκουσα κιθαρῳδῶν [*kai phōnē ēkousa kitharōdōn*], *and [the] sound I heard of harpists.* The *MT*[5.2.45] and *NU*[5.2.49] texts read somewhat differently: καὶ ἡ φωνὴ ἣν ἤκουσα ὡς κιθαρῳδῶν [*kai hē phōnē hēn ēkousa hōs kitharōdōn*], *and the voice which I heard as harpists harping*. Does John hear a different sound from the preceding voice—the sound of *harpists* playing? Or is he merely describing further attributes of the voice—that the voice *sounded like* harpists playing? Adding to this complication is that φωνὴ [*phōnē*] can mean either "voice" or "sound." Often, such subtle textual differences are of little significance, but here there is great significance to the variations.

If John hears *harpists* playing their harps, then *they* which sing in the following verse could refer to the harpists (and not necessarily the 144,000 with the Lamb). On the other hand, if John is saying that the voice which he previously described sounds *like harpists*, then there may not actually be harpists. If the voice (singular) is in view rather than harpists (plural), then *they* (plural) which sing in the following verse probably refers to the 144,000. Another possibility is that the distinction between "voice" and "sound" in the English text (both translated from φωνὴ [*phōnē*] in the Greek) confuses the matter. Perhaps it is simply a *sound* which John hears. Thus, the MT and NU text could be translated:

> And I heard a sound from heaven, like the sound of many waters and like the sound of loud thunder, and the sound which I heard was like harpists playing on their harps.

This would possibly describe a heavenly multitude which includes both singers and harps. If so, then *they* who sing in the next verse could refer to this multitude. See commentary on *Revelation 14:1*[3.14.1].

harps

The four living creatures and twenty-four elders are said to have harps (Rev. 5:8). So do those who have victory over the *Beast*[5.2.9], his image, and his mark—who are evidently martyred prior to the bowl judgments (Rev. 15:2). Harps were often used in worship in the *OT*[5.2.51] (2S. 6:5; 1Chr. 25:1-7; Ps. 33:2; 43:4; 57:8-9; 98:5; 147:7; 149:3; 150:3-6). Here, the harps are probably played by a multitude in heaven.

3.14.3 - Revelation 14:3

They sang

ᾄδουσιν [*adousin*], present tense, *they are singing*. Isaiah indicated that the ransomed (*redeemed* , below) would return to Zion with singing (Isa. 35:10; 51:11). Those who have been redeemed from amidst great difficulty respond with songs of great praise. "For the LORD has redeemed Jacob, and ransomed him from the hand of one stronger than he. Therefore they shall come and sing in the height of Zion" (Jer. 31:11-12a). If the harpists are the singers in heaven, then they sing in commemoration of the unique experience of the 144,000 on earth. If the 144,000 are singing in heaven, the song they sing is probably motivated by their similar experience to those who had victory over the *Beast*[5.2.9] through martyrdom (Rev. 15:3). Or, if this is a millennial scene and they sing from the earth, they sing because they were protected for the entire duration of the Tribulation. God brought them "through the sea" as when Israel was pursued by Pharaoh:

> So the Lord saved Israel that day out of the hand of the Egyptians, and Israel saw the Egyptians dead on the seashore. Thus Israel saw the great work which the Lord had done in Egypt; so the people feared the Lord, and believed the Lord and His servant Moses. Then Moses and the children of Israel sang this song to the Lord, and spoke, saying: "I will sing to the Lord, for He has triumphed gloriously! The horse and its rider He has thrown into the sea!" (Ex. 14:30-15:1)

See commentary on *Revelation 14:1*[3.14.1].

a new song

The twenty-four elders, probably representatives from among the Church, "sang a new song" (Rev. 5:9). The subject of their song was redemption (Rev. 5:8-10). Here we see one of the purposes of trials and tribulations—to produce in us a *new song* of praise to God (Ps. 40:3; 98:1; 144:9). These new songs often express themes of redemption and salvation. "The song is that of victory after conflict with the dragon, beast, and false prophet: never sung before, for such a conflict had never been fought before; therefore *new*."[19]

as it were

This phrase is missing from the *MT*[5.2.45] text and about half of the manuscripts which contribute to the *NU*[5.2.49] text.

before the throne

Which throne is this? The nearest previous mention of a throne related to God is His throne in heaven to which the child was caught up (Rev. 12:5 cf. Rev. 1:4; 3:21; 4:2-10; 5:1, 6-7, 11-13; 6:16; 7:9-17; 8:3). Every other mention of a throne in conjunction with the living creatures and elders is the Father's throne in heaven (Rev. 5:6, 11; 7:11; 14:3; 19:4).

before the four living creatures

These are the four ζῳ´ων [*zōōn*] , "living ones," who attend the throne in heaven (Rev. 4:6, 8-9; 5:6, 8, 11, 14; 6:1, 6; 7:11; 8:9; 14:3; 15:7; 19:4). See commentary on *Revelation 4:6*[3.4.6].

and the elders

The twenty-four elders who sit on thrones before the Father's throne. See commentary on *Revelation 4:4*[3.4.4].

and no one could learn that song

Why could no one else learn the song?[20] We suggest that the song is highly personal to the experiences of these 144,000 Jewish evangelists from the time of the Tribulation. In the same way that the twenty-four elders could sing the song of redemption: "For you were slain, and have redeemed **us** to God by Your blood out of every tribe and tongue and people and nation, and have made us priests to our God; and we shall reign on the earth," [emphasis added] only these men could sing about the keeping power of God that these had experienced. "Only those who had gone through that Tribulation could understand the song which celebrated it."[21]

Those who have been forgiven much or have endured intense danger and persecution are best able to appreciate the gifts of God which many others take for granted. Without such experiences, we tend more toward Simon the Pharisee than the woman who washed Jesus' feet with her tears (Luke 7:36-48). Are you going through immense hardships? Remember that God is sovereign and every tear you shed will surely contribute toward His glory and your subsequent ministry to others (Rom. 8:28).

who were redeemed

οἱ ἀγορασμένοι [*hoi agorasmenoi*], perfect passive participle, *the ones having been purchased.* Prior to Jeremiah's presentation of the New Covenant to Israel (Jer. 31:31), he relates a time when God promises to save the remnant of Israel and gather them to Mount Zion. He refers to His gathered flock as the redeemed of Jacob, those who were ransomed (Jer. 31:6-13). Their return will be accompanied by rejoicing and singing. This is not to be spiritualized as applying to the general family of faith, it is *Jacob* who is the object of these promises. Isaiah also indicates the power of redemption as fuel for praise: "And the ransomed of the LORD shall return, And come to Zion with singing, With everlasting joy on their heads. They shall obtain joy and gladness, And sorrow and sighing shall flee away" (Isa. 35:10 cf. Isa. 51:11).

3.14.4 - Revelation 14:4

not defiled with women

Defiled is Ἐμολύνθησαν [*Emolynthēsan*]: "Causing something to be dirty soil, smear, stain; metaphorically, as keeping the life spotless."[22] The same word describes those in the church at Sardis who "had not defiled their garments" (Rev. 3:4). Their faithful service of the Lamb was exemplary and motivated by their consuming obedience to His will, because they "follow the Lamb wherever He goes." This does not indicate that they were sinless, for they are among those needing redemption. This verse does not negate the divine institution and blessing upon married sexual relations for "marriage is honorable among all, and the bed undefiled; but fornicators and adulterers God will judge" (Heb. 13:4). Perhaps these minister at a time when the institution of marriage has all but fallen by the wayside (not inconceivable if present trends continue) and relations with women are almost exclusively outside of the bounds of marriage in their time? Theirs is a time characterized by fornication (Rev. 9:21), perhaps pagan rites of old are flourishing once again, but on a global basis:

> We have more than once, in the Epistles to the Assemblies, and on Revelation 9:20, 21, said that Fornication will be part of the great religious system of *Anti-Christ*[5.2.3] in the coming time of trouble and temptation; as it formed an obligatory part of the great pagan systems of idolatry. Idolatry was not a

> mere sin into which people gradually sunk; but it was a Satanic device into which people rose in order to gratify the lusts of the flesh under the cloak of religion.[23]
>
> The worship of Antichrist during the Tribulation will be unspeakably vile and perverse. As it did in the fertility cults of ancient times, sexual sin will apparently run rampant. Even in the current grossly immoral day, we can hardly imagine what the deviant sexual perversion of the Tribulation will be like. With all divine restraint removed (2Th. 2:6-7) and the unbelieving world judgmentally abandoned by God (cf. Rom. 1:24, 26, 28), sin will be released like a flood, inundating the world.[24]
>
> But in the fearful days of abandonment "as in the days of Noah"—when lust and violence will again fill the whole earth (as we see beginning *now!*) how wonderful to behold this company of 144,000 who have chosen to be entirely separated unto the Lamb and unto His Father, and who *are* thus, despite the days![25]

In their complete dedication to the service of the Lamb, they voluntarily chose to forgo relations with women in order to focus completely on their unique God-given task during the Tribulation.

they are virgins

These are *physical* virgins, for why else would it be said of this particular group of saints that they are virgins? *All the saints* are virgins in the spiritual sense of being set aside and dedicated to God. "I have betrothed you to one husband, that I may present *you as* a chaste virgin to Christ" (2Cor. 11:2).

Jesus explained, "there are eunuchs who were born thus from *their* mother's womb, and there are eunuchs who were made eunuchs by men, and there are eunuchs who have made themselves eunuchs for the kingdom of heaven's sake. He who is able to accept *it*, let him accept *it*" (Mtt. 19:12) "Not only is there virgin purity of life, but there is also virgin love—undivided heart affection for the Lamb."[26] These are eunuchs for the kingdom of heaven's sake. By both choice and gifting, they were enabled to give their full focus to ministry at the time of the end.

> Do not deprive one another except with consent for a time, that you may give yourselves to fasting and prayer; and come together again so that Satan does not tempt you because of your lack of self-control. But I say this as a concession, not as a commandment. For I wish that all men were even as I myself. But each one has his own gift from God, one in this manner and another in that. . . . But as God has distributed to each one, as the Lord has called each one, so let him walk. And so I ordain in all the churches. . . . But I want you to be without care. He who is unmarried cares for the things of the Lord—how he may please the Lord. (1Cor. 7:5-7, 17, 32)

who follow the Lamb wherever He goes

This speaks of their complete obedience to do the will of the Lamb. In the same way that the Lamb followed the Father (John 4:34), so these followed the Lamb. Those who fully follow God are blessed. Joshua and Caleb were allowed into the Promised Land because they followed God fully (Num. 14:24). A scribe claimed he would follow Jesus "wherever You go," but there is always a cost to such discipleship (Mtt. 8:19-22; Luke 9:57-62). Those who would know and serve the Master must first of all be *followers*, "My sheep hear My voice, and I know them, and they follow Me" (John 10:27). "If anyone serves Me, let him follow Me; and where I am there My servant will be also" (John 12:26).

These are among the rest of the woman's offspring who kept the commands of God. See commentary on *Revelation 12:17*[3.12.17]. If this scene is in heaven (see commentary on *Revelation 14:1*[3.14.1]), then their obedience had ultimately cost them their lives. Unlike Peter, they had not denied their Lord, but had followed the Lamb even through the portal of death and into eternal life:

> Simon Peter said to Him, "Lord, where are You going?" Jesus answered him, "Where I am going you cannot follow Me now, but you shall follow Me afterward." Peter said to Him, "Lord, why can I not follow You now? I will lay down my life for Your sake." Jesus answered him, "Will you lay down your life for My sake? Most assuredly, I say to you, the rooster shall not crow till you have denied Me three times." (John 13:36-38)

These were redeemed

ἠγοράσθησαν [*ēgorasthēsan*]: "Literally *buy, purchase, do business in the marketplace*"[27] (1Cor. 6:20; Eph. 1:14). The purchase price was the Lamb's blood (Acts 20:28; Rev. 1:5; 5:9; 12:11). See commentary on *Revelation 1:5*[3.1.5].

firstfruits

Ἀπαρχὴ [*Aparchē*]: "In Mosaic ceremonial law, a *technical term*[5.2.72] for the first portion of grain and fruit harvests and flocks offered to God . . . figuratively, of persons as the first of a set or category first: as the first converts in an area (Rom. 16.5)."[28] The firstfruits was the first portion of a harvest which was dedicated to God. It demonstrated the priority which was given to God because the first of that which had been long awaited was bypassed by the harvester and given to God (Lev. 23:10-14). By honoring God with one's firstfruits, the resulting blessing would provide a greater yield. The nation of Israel is said to be the firstfruits of God's increase which would eventually include multitudes of redeemed Gentiles (Jer. 2:3). James indicated that the early church was "a kind of firstfruits of His creatures" (Jas. 1:18). In the time since, the harvest has spread to multitudes around the world. Here, after the Church Age and the fullness of the Gentiles has come in (Rom. 11:25), these represent the firstfruits of the spiritual awakening of Israel in preparation for the *Millennial Kingdom*[5.2.39] to follow (Eze. 37).[29]

> For I do not desire, brethren, that you should be ignorant of this mystery, lest you should be wise in your own opinion, that blindness in part has happened to Israel until the fullness of the Gentiles has come in. And so all Israel will be saved, as it is written: "The Deliverer will come out of Zion, and He will turn away ungodliness from Jacob." (Rom. 11:25-26)

They may also be considered firstfruits from the perspective of their unique preservation through the Tribulation enabling them to contribute to the initial Jewish population which enters the Millennial Kingdom in their natural bodies and subsequently populates the kingdom (Isa. 65:20, 23).

> These sealed Jews [Rev. 7:4-8] are those who come to faith in Jesus as Messiah during the Tribulation period. They are further described as "first fruits unto God and to the Lamb" (Rev. 14:4), indicating that they compose the first stage of a final harvest of Jewish souls to be gathered later at the Lord's coming in glory. . . . These comprise the "remnant" of Jews "who keep the commandments of God, and have the testimony of Jesus Christ" (Rev. 12:17b).[30]

See commentary on *Revelation 7:4*[3.7.4], *Revelation 11:13*[3.11.13], and *Revelation 20:4*[3.20.4].

3.14.5 - Revelation 14:5

in their mouth

Scripture implicates the mouth as the organ which speaks forth the heart: "Brood of vipers! How can you, being evil, speak good things? For out of the abundance of the heart the mouth speaks" (Mtt. 12:34); "These people draw near to Me with their mouth, and honor Me with *their* lips, but their heart is far from Me" (Mtt. 15:8); "But those things which proceed out of the mouth come from the heart, and they defile a man" (Mtt. 15:18); "For with the heart one believes unto righteousness, and with the mouth confession is made unto salvation" (Rom. 10:10). The tendency of the tongue toward evil, and the immense difficulty with which it is harnessed is a frequent theme of Scripture.[31]

These are standing upon Mount Zion, God's holy hill:

> LORD, who may abide in Your *tabernacle*[5.2.69]? **Who may dwell in Your holy hill?** He who walks uprightly, and works righteousness, and speaks the truth in his heart; **He *who* does not backbite with his tongue**, nor does evil to his neighbor, nor does he take up a reproach against his friend. (Ps. 15:1-3) [emphasis added]

May their obedient and dedicated state before the Lamb be ever before us as motivation in our walk during the present age!

was found no deceit

Their mouths are to be contrasted with the blasphemous mouth of the *Beast*[5.2.9]. See commentary on *Revelation 13:5*[3.13.5]. Unlike the masses upon the earth at the time of their ministry, they do not mouth the lie (2Th. 2:11). Their mouths are like that of wisdom and of the Lamb:

> Listen, for I will speak of excellent things, and from the opening of my lips *will come* right things; for my mouth will speak truth; wickedness *is* an abomination to my lips. All the words of my mouth *are* with righteousness; nothing crooked or perverse *is* in them. (Pr. 8:6-8)

> And they made His grave with the wicked-But with the rich at His death, because He had done no

> violence, nor *was any* deceit in His mouth. (Isa. 53:9)

They are firstfruits in at least two ways: they are the first among many redeemed Jews during the Tribulation and they are the first among a purified Israel which will result from the time of *Jacob's Trouble*[2.13.4]:

> I will leave in your midst a meek and humble people, and they shall trust in the name of the LORD. The remnant of Israel shall do no unrighteousness and speak no lies, nor shall a deceitful tongue be found in their mouth; for they shall feed *their* flocks and lie down, and no one shall make *them* afraid. (Zep. 3:12-13)

They represent the early stages of the glorious promise made to Israel as part of her New Covenant:

> But this *is* the covenant that I will make with the house of Israel after those days, says the LORD: I will put My law in their minds, and write it on their hearts; and I will be their God, and they shall be My people. No more shall every man teach his neighbor, and every man his brother, saying, 'Know the LORD,' for they all shall know Me, from the least of them to the greatest of them, says the LORD. For I will forgive their iniquity, and their sin I will remember no more. (Jer. 31:33-34)

without fault

Ἄμωμοι [*Amōmoi*], used "of the absence of defects in sacrificial animals,"[32] spotless. Applied to these, it denotes being *blameless*.[33] "In the *Septuagint*[5.2.65], *amomos* is used as an ethical term and consistently refers to the holy behavior of the faithful (Ps. 119:1; Pr. 11:5) and, on occasion, is even applied as a title of honor to God himself (Ps. 18:30). . . . Christ was *amomos* because there was no spot or blemish in him. Thus he could ask: 'Which of you convicts Me of sin?' (John 8:46)."[34] As exemplary as their conduct has been during their ministry, this speaks of something far beyond what they themselves were able to exhibit.

before the throne of God

This phrase does not appear in the *NU*[5.2.49] or *MT*[5.2.45] texts, but only in the *TR*[5.2.79] text. It may have been added in an attempt to equate the 144,000 with those who sing before the throne, the living creatures, and the elders (Rev. 14:3). However, the singers may be the harpists. See commentary on *Revelation 14:1*[3.14.1].

The phrase "without fault before the throne of God" can be seen in terms of a heavenly scale of perfection. On one end is *fault*. On the other end is *God*. How can these two be found together? Only because the central mechanism of the scale is the *cross of Christ*, the "tree of life!" Having been redeemed and washed by His blood (Rev. 1:5), they stand clothed in the perfection of the Son before the Father. All their sins are cast behind them (Isa. 38:17) and they are without spot or wrinkle (Eph. 5:27). They are holy and blameless in His sight (Col. 1:22). They are "faultless before the presence of God" (Jude 1:24).

3.14.6 - Revelation 14:6

another angel

The most recent individual angel we encountered was the seventh angel who sounded his trumpet in Revelation 11:15. Another angel (*eagle* , *MT*[5.2.45] and *NU*[5.2.49] texts) flew with a similar message of warning for the *earth dwellers*[5.2.18] concerning the woes attending the sounding of the final three trumpets (Rev. 8:13).

in the midst of heaven

Μεσουρανήματι [*Mesouranēmati*]: "The highest point of the sun's circuit in the sky zenith, midair, directly overhead."[35]

having the everlasting gospel

The gospel is founded upon the New Covenant, which is an eternal covenant (Heb. 13:20) resulting in eternal life (Isa. 51:6; Tit. 1:1-3).

to preach

Εὐαγγέλιον [*Euangelion*]: "To announce good news."[36] The angel *gospelled the gospel* to those below on the earth. Not only was his message one of good news, but the very fact of his delivery of the message was a manifestation of that good news. For this angel on his lonely mission above the ravaged earth below stands as a beacon to the grace and mercy of God. He has not left these on the earth during the final week of His wrath without recourse. In the midst of terrible devastation and turmoil, He has not left those who have not yet heard subject to the well-intentioned, but often ineffective, witness of men. He provides a supernatural messenger who will finally fulfill the gospel mandate to all the earth (see below). "There is no record that it is believed or heeded. It may not be. Noah was a 'preacher of righteousness,' in view of the coming flood; but no one believed him except his own family."[37]

to those who dwell on the earth

The gospel is preached to the same individuals who are undergoing the time of testing (Rev. 3:10). A key purpose of the time of testing is to turn those who will be turned to salvation and to manifest those who are hardened and will continue to reject it. See *Earth Dwellers*[3.3.10.1].

to every nation, tribe, tongue, and people

Those over whom the *Beast*[5.2.9] was granted authority (Rev. 13:7) receive the gospel message from a supernatural source. Although it is the Church's mandate to preach the gospel to every creature (Mark 16:15; Luke 24:47; Acts 1:8) and to make disciples of all nations (Mtt. 28:19), it will not be her who ultimately fulfills the words of Jesus concerning the gospel reaching the entire world prior to the end:[38]

> Then many false prophets will rise up and deceive many. And because lawlessness will abound, the love of many will grow cold. But he who endures to the end shall be saved. And this **gospel of the kingdom** will be preached in all the world as a witness to all the nations, and then the end will come. (Mtt. 24:11-14 cf. Mark 13:10) [emphasis added]

The gospel message of the angel, founded upon the redeeming power of Christ's work on the cross, will likely include a significant emphasis upon the coming kingdom about to be ushered in on earth. In this, it will have much in common with that which was preached by John the Baptist and the disciples before they realized the destiny of Jesus upon the cross (Mtt. 3:1-2; 4:17, 23; 9:35; 10:7):[39]

> The "gospel of the kingdom" as announced by John (Mtt. 3:3), by the disciples who were specially commissioned (Mtt. 10:7), by the seventy (Luke 10:9), and by the Lord (Mtt. 4:17) proclaimed the good news that the promised kingdom was "at hand." The Lord indicates this same good news will be announced again. . . . Although the news at the first advent was restricted to Israel, prior to the second advent it will be announced not only to Israel but to the whole world. This preaching . . . marks the beginning of the final step in the realization of the theocratic kingdom program.[40]

See *The Arrival of God's Kingdom*[2.4.3].

> While the majority of the Church's teachers are loudly proclaiming that "the day of the Lord" will not come till the world's conversion comes, the Spirit and truth of God are declaring that day shall not come until the apostasy comes (2Th. 2:3). While the majority of the Church's teachers are maintaining that the world is not yet good enough for Christ, the Spirit is declaring in the Word that the world is not yet bad enough.[41]

See *Trouble Ahead*[2.13.1].

3.14.7 - Revelation 14:7

Fear God and give glory to Him

It seems unlikely that the words that John heard the angel say constitute the entire gospel message delivered to the *earth dwellers*[5.2.18]. Rather, it summarizes what their response should be. The specifics of the gospel message itself are not recorded. The warning of the angel occurs before the institution of the mark of the *Beast*[5.2.9]. Those who hear the angel and respond in faith are those who are found in the opening verses of the next chapter doing this very thing!

> They sing the song of Moses, the servant of God, and the song of the Lamb, saying: "Great and marvelous *are* Your works, Lord God Almighty! Just and true *are* Your ways, O King of the saints! **Who shall not fear You, O Lord, and glorify Your name?** For *You* alone *are* holy. For all nations shall come and worship before You, for Your judgments have been manifested." (Rev. 15:3-4) [emphasis added]

These who *hear and fear* have victory over the beast, his image, his mark, and the number of his name.

the hour of His judgment has come

Has come is ἦλθεν [*ēlthen*], prophetic aorist. The time of His judgment is certain and *imminent*[5.2.30], as if it is already underway. Now is the time of decision.

> The nations were angry, and Your wrath has come, and the time of the dead, that they should be judged, and that you should reward Your servants the prophets and the saints, and those who fear Your name, small and great, and should destroy those who destroy the earth. (Rev. 11:18)

worship Him who made heaven and earth

The Creator-creature distinction is the basis for all worship (Ne. 9:6; Acts 14:14). Only the Creator is worthy of worship. Worship of all else is idolatry. See commentary on *Revelation 4:11*[3.4.11].

The angel declares an important truth which great portions of the Church now compromise. Although readily admitting God as Creator, their Creator God is not that of the Scriptures, but a god of their own creation. They endorse the belief that both the universe and the earth are billions of years old and that God used, and continues to use, blind processes (accidental mutation and natural selection) to bring about His creative work.[42] Instead of upholding the clear Scriptural teaching of a six-day creation (Ex. 20:11), they accommodate flawed science and relegate the need for a Creator God into a smaller and smaller sphere, even embracing unscriptural ideas such as the existence of soulless *pre-Humans* before Adam.[43] These naively contribute to the ultimate state of godlessness of the earth dwellers at the end.

The blindness of the earth dwellers to the Creator in the book of Revelation can already be seen in our own times. Great effort and expenditure is underway to find life on Mars and to search the far reaches of space for signs of intelligence. All the while, here on earth, advances such as those in microbiology, bioengineering, and genetics shout "INTELLIGENCE!" Lacking a belief in a Creator, the creature naturally seeks to elevate something else in His place. Such is the pattern of idolatry which will manifest itself in the last times as worship to the *image of the Beast*[5.2.29] when he is brought to life (Rev. 13:14-15).

3.14.8 - Revelation 14:8

Babylon

Here is the first mention of Babylon found in this book. Some suggest that "Babylon" should not be understood in a literal sense, but as denoting a spiritual location describing the centers of commercial success and sin attending each age of history (Rev. 17:5). Some see "Babylon" as a code word for the city of *Rome*. Some believe "Babylon" means *Jerusalem*. Others are unsure what it means, or that its identification is important. It is our view that "Babylon" describes the literal city of history on the banks of the Euphrates River, originating with the kingdom of Babel established by Nimrod (Gen. 10:8-10). The city has had great influence throughout history, both in political and religious realms, and is to be rebuilt in the time of the end and to ultimately suffer God's wrath. See *The Identity of Babylon*[4.1.3]. See *#5 - Five Fallen Kings*[4.3.2.5].

is fallen, is fallen

Ἔπεσεν ἔπεσεν [*Epesen epesen*] , prophetic aorist verbs. The judgment of Babylon has not yet occurred, but it is so certain that it is stated as a past event (Rev. 16:19; 18:2-3). When her destruction comes, it will be sudden (Jer. 51:8), "in one hour" (Rev. 18:10), "in one hour she is made desolate" (Rev. 18:18), "her plagues will come in one day" (Rev. 18:8). Isaiah made the same declaration when he foresaw Babylon's ultimate destruction at God's threshing floor at the end of the age (Isa. 21:9-10). "The full thrust of which awaits the coming 'time of Jacob's trouble' (Jer. 30:5-7), the Great Tribulation, when Babylon, . . . will be destroyed by the Lion of the tribe of Judah at His second advent."[44] This is a preview and declaration of the final destruction of Babylon to follow (Rev. 18:2). See *The Destruction of Babylon*[4.1.2].

that great city

Babylon of the time of the end will be a great city, also called the *Harlot*[5.2.25]. "And the woman which you saw is **that great city** which reigns over the kings of the earth" [emphasis added] (Rev. 17:18 cf.

Rev. 18:10, 18, 16, 18-19, 21). See *The Great Harlot*[4.1.4]. The phrase "great city" emphasizes the arrogance of humanism in its pride of accomplishment apart from God. Nebuchadnezzar's declaration —followed by his judgment of seven years living as a beast—is a typological preview of this final week.

> The king spoke, saying, "Is not this **great Babylon**, that I have built for a royal dwelling by my mighty power and for the honor of my majesty?" While the word *was still* in the king's mouth, a voice fell from heaven: "King Nebuchadnezzar, to you it is spoken: the kingdom has departed from you! And they shall drive you from men, and your dwelling *shall be* with the beasts of the field. They shall make you eat grass like oxen; and seven times shall pass over you, until you know that the Most High rules in the kingdom of men, and gives it to whomever He chooses." That very hour the word was fulfilled concerning Nebuchadnezzar; he was driven from men and ate grass like oxen; his body was wet with the dew of heaven till his hair had grown like eagles' *feathers* and his nails like birds' *claws*. (Dan. 4:30-33) [emphasis added]

At the height of his arrogant independence, Nebuchadnezzar was made like unto a beast. So too, at the time of the end, the *Beast*[5.2.9], the final representative of the rule of man apart from God, rises to the apex of arrogance and blasphemy (see commentary on *Revelation 13:5*[3.13.5]). When he makes a 7-year covenant with Israel (Dan. 9:27), God's response is to usher in the Tribulation bringing seven years of intense judgment upon the realm of those who follow the Beast.

Jerusalem is also called a "great city" (Rev. 11:8; 16:19)[45] as is the New Jerusalem (Rev. 21:10).

she has made all nations drink of the wine of the wrath of her fornication

There is a close relationship between the nations and the intoxicating drink which Babylon offers: "I will show you the judgment of the great harlot, who sits on many waters, with whom the kings of the earth committed fornication, and the inhabitants of the earth were made drunk with the wine of her fornication" (Rev. 17:1b-2); "He has judged the great harlot who corrupted the earth with her fornication" (Rev. 19:2); "For all the nations have drunk of the wine of the wrath of her fornication, the kings of the earth have committed fornication with her, and the merchants of the earth have become rich through the abundance of her luxury" (Rev. 18:3). It is called "the wine of the wrath of her fornication." Although it primarily intoxicates the nations to participate in her *fornication* (Rev. 17:4), it is also brings them under God's *wrath* for their participation. See commentary on *Revelation 16:19*[3.16.19].

Although fornication emphasizes her spiritual idolatry, it also includes commercial aspects as is recorded for the city of Tyre: "And it shall be, at the end of seventy years, that the Lord will deal with Tyre. She will return to her hire, and commit fornication with all the kingdoms of the world on the face of the earth" (Isa. 23:17). See *Her Harlotry*[4.1.4.1].

In the same way that God gives up the godless who refuse to acknowledge Him as Creator (Rom. 1:18-24), so too in His sovereign permission, He uses Babylon to promote the drunkenness of the nations which already rage against Him (Ps. 2:1): "Babylon *was* a golden cup in the LORD'S hand, that made all the earth drunk. The nations drank her wine; therefore the nations are deranged" (Jer. 51:7). Because Babylon has made all nations drink her wine, God will make *her* drink *His* wine (see commentary on *Revelation 14:10*[3.14.10]).

> The mass hysteria, or drunkenness which permitted mobs to give themselves to such men as Hitler, Stalin and Mussolini, will head up in that mass-drunkenness which will bow to the image of the *Antichrist*[5.2.3] and accept a brand upon the forehead or hand as a sign of subservience to him. To all such, God will give another wine to drink.[46]

3.14.9 - Revelation 14:9

then a third angel followed

The first angel brought the *carrot* (Rev. 14:6), now the third brings the *stick*! Those who would not respond to God's gracious offer of salvation are now warned of the eternal significance of worshiping the *Beast*[5.2.9] and taking his mark. Unfortunately, many at the time of the end will follow in the well-worn pattern of those before them who continued to ignore God's gracious warning:

> However I have sent to you all My servants the prophets, rising early and sending *them*, saying, "Oh, do not do this abominable thing that I hate!" But they did not listen or incline their ear to turn from their wickedness, to burn no incense to other gods. So My fury and My anger were poured out and kindled in the cities of Judah and in the streets of Jerusalem; and they are wasted *and* desolate, as it is this day. (Jer. 44:4-6)

If anyone worships the beast

See commentary on *Revelation 13:4*[3.13.4].

and his image

See commentary on *Revelation 13:14*[3.13.14] and *Revelation 13:15*[3.13.15].

and receives *his* mark on his forehead or on his hand

See commentary on *Revelation 13:16*[3.13.16].

3.14.10 - Revelation 14:10

he himself shall also drink of the wine of the wrath of God

He himself, emphasis is placed upon the individual who worships the beast. He will be held individually responsible for his actions which will result in receiving God's wrath and eternal damnation (see below). "The devotees of the *Beast*[5.2.9] are here warned and threatened with punishments of so terrible a character that the very mention of them is enough to make one's flesh creep."[47] The reception of God's judgment is often described as *drinking* from His cup (Ps. 75:8; Isa. 51:17, 22-23; Jer. 25:15-17, 28; Hab. 2:16; Rev. 16:19).

> But God *is* the Judge: He puts down one, and exalts another. For in the hand of the LORD *there is* a cup, and the wine is red; it is fully mixed, and He pours it out; surely its dregs shall the wicked of the earth drain *and* drink down. (Ps. 75:7-8)

Throughout history God has warned kings that unless they "kiss the Son," they would perish "when His wrath is kindled but a little" (Ps. 2:12). The ultimate fulfillment of this warning will be during the *Campaign of Armageddon*[4.5].

Having drunk from the cup, the recipient is the object of God's wrath (Job 21:20) and staggers with drunkenness, becoming mad so as to participate in the ultimate folly of his own destruction (Jer. 25:16, 27; Zec. 12:2-4). "You have made us drink the wine of confusion" (Ps. 60:3).

> "In their excitement I will prepare their feasts; I will make them drunk, that they may rejoice, and sleep a perpetual sleep and not awake," says the LORD. "I will bring them down like lambs to the slaughter, like rams with male goats." (Jer. 51:39-40)

> "And I will make drunk her princes and wise men, her governors, her deputies, and her mighty men. And they shall sleep a perpetual sleep and not awake," says the King, Whose name *is* the LORD of hosts. (Jer. 51:57)

This passage explains why, in the *sequence of seals, trumpets, and bowls*[2.14.2], it is the *bowls* which are last. Each of the final seven bowls comprises a portion of the final *cup* of God's wrath. In "the seven last plagues . . . the wrath of God is complete" (Rev. 15:1). They are "the bowls of the wrath of God" which are poured out on the earth (Rev. 16:1). The wrath is manifest in Christ's treading of "the winepress of the fierceness and wrath of Almighty God" (Rev. 19:15 cf. Isa. 63:1-6). See commentary on *Revelation 11:18*[3.11.18].

wrath . . . indignation

God's wrath is frequently mentioned in association with the judgments poured out during the Tribulation (Rev. 6:16; 11:18). Here, it denotes the wrath which is specifically associated with the worship of the Beast, which probably occurs after the abomination of desolation at the midpoint of the Tribulation. See *Events of the 70th Week of Daniel*[2.13.5.4].

Wrath is θυμοῦ [*thymou*], *indignation* is ὀργῆς [*orgēs*]:

> *Thymos* refers to turbulent commotion, the boiling agitation of the feelings . . . that will either subside and disappear or else settle down into *orge*, which is more of an abiding and settled habit of mind ("an enduring anger") that is focused on revenge. . . . In his discussion of the two words, Origin arrived at the

> same conclusion: "*Thymos* differs from *orge* in that *thymos* is anger [*orge*] rising in vapor and burning up, while *orge* is a yearning for revenge." Jerome said: "*Thymos* is incipient anger and displeasure fermenting in the mind; *orge* however, when *thymos* has subsided, is that which longs for revenge and desires to injure the one thought to have caused harm."[48]

poured out full strength

Κεκερασμένου ἀκράτου [*Kekerasmenou akratou*], *having been poured unmixed [undiluted]*, to "cause to be fully experienced."[49] This is a frightful phrase, for it indicates those who worship the Beast will undergo the *full force* of God's wrath. The contents of the cup are not diluted, but of full intensity! "whereas wine was so commonly mixed with water that to *mix* wine is used in Greek for to *pour out* wine; this wine of God's wrath is undiluted; there is no drop of water to cool its heat. Naught of grace or hope is blended with it."[50] They will experience divine wrath without restraint: eternal torment by the Power of powers, the author of a myriad of supernovas.

He shall be tormented with fire and brimstone

Those who worship the Beast will be tormented with *fire and brimstone* indicating their ultimate destination. They will be "cast into the lake of fire and brimstone where the beast and the false prophet *are*. And they will be tormented day and night forever and ever" (Rev. 20:10). Those who worship the Beast and take his mark are *irredeemable*. Even though they have not yet died, their fate in the Lake of Fire is sealed. See *Beast Worshipers are Unique*[4.4.3.4]. They will "have their part in the lake which burns with fire and brimstone, which is the second death" (Rev. 21:8). As we saw in the previous chapter, those who worship the Beast "have not been written in the *Book of Life*[5.2.10]" (see commentary on *Revelation 13:8*[3.13.8]), thus they are destined for the Lake of Fire. "Anyone not found written in the Book of Life was cast into the lake of fire" (Rev. 20:15).

Those who refuse to worship the Beast during this time of intense persecution and pressure will do so only because they have given their worship to Jesus Christ. The cost of doing so will often be their physical life. The benefit will be their eternal life and participation in the first resurrection. "Blessed and holy is he who has part in the first resurrection. Over such, the second death has no power" (Rev. 20:6a). See commentary on *Revelation 3:11*[3.3.11].

The fire and brimstone with which they are tormented is no less real than that which rains down upon Sodom and Gomorrah (Gen. 19:24-25) and Gog and his troops (Eze. 38:22) and which those taken in such judgments *continue to suffer forever* (Jude 1:7).

in the presence of the holy angels and in the presence of the Lamb

Isaiah speaks of a time when all flesh shall come to worship before the LORD, but also go forth and look upon the corpses of the men who transgressed against God. Somehow, these who are "cast into outer darkness" (Mtt. 8:12; 22:13; 25:30) are visible to the redeemed throughout eternity (Isa. 66:24).[51] The damned will also see the blessed who enter the kingdom, whereas they themselves are thrust out (Luke 13:28). Perhaps awareness of the alternative which the damned missed will contribute to their torment, similar to the way in which the rich man could see Lazarus in Abraham's bosom (Luke 16:23). Although the holy angels and the Lamb will be present to see the torment of the damned, the damned will not benefit from an awareness of the presence of God (2Th. 1:8-9) for this is the ultimate blessing reserved for the redeemed. "The *tabernacle*[5.2.69] of God *is* with men, and He will dwell with them, and they shall be His people" (Rev. 21:3). See *The Abiding Presence of God*[4.16.2], *New Jerusalem*[4.16.5.11].

3.14.11 - Revelation 14:11

the smoke of their torment ascends forever and ever

This phrase speaks of eternal judgment, like that which will ultimately befall the land of Edom and the city of Babylon (Isa. 34:10; Rev. 19:3). The "goats," representing those among the *Beast*[5.2.9] worshipers who remain alive upon the earth at the return of Jesus to take up the throne of David (Mtt. 25:31), will be sent "into everlasting fire prepared for the devil and his angels" (Mtt. 24:41b cf. Rev. 20:10). The fire is *everlasting* (Isa. 66:24; Dan. 12:2; Mtt. 3:12; Mtt. 25:41; Mark 9:44-46; 2Th. 1:9; 2Pe. 2:17; Jude 1:13), but does not annihilate those who suffer its torment, for the Beast and the *False*

Prophet[5.2.20] are the first to experience its effects and have endured under it for one thousand years when they are joined by others (Rev. 19:20 cf. Rev. 20:10, 15). The answer to the question of how the damned could be due eternal torment might be found, in part, by understanding their hardened condition—which is without repentance:

> In the next world the wicked, with all restraint removed, will go headlong into sin, blaspheming and cursing God, growing worse and worse as they sink deeper and deeper into the bottomless pit. Endless punishment is the penalty for ENDLESS sinning.[52]
>
> I wish to present a paragraph or two from one of my teachers, Dr. R. A. Torrey. I sat in class as a boy of eighteen and heard Dr. Torrey lecture on the future destiny of unbelievers. . . . He said, "In conclusion, two things are certain. First, the more closely men walk with God and the more devoted they become to His service, the more likely they are to believe this doctrine. Many men tell us they love their fellow men too much to believe this doctrine; but the men who show their love in more practical ways than sentimental protestations about it, the men who show their love for their fellow men as Jesus Christ showed His, by laying down their lives for them, *they* believe it, even as Jesus Christ Himself believed it.
>
> Second, men who accept a loose doctrine regarding the ultimate penalty of Sin (Restorationism or Universalism or Annihilationism) lose their power for God. They may be very clever at argument and zealous in proselytizing, but they are poor at soul-saving. They are seldom found beseeching men to be reconciled to God. They are more likely to be found trying to upset the faith of those already won by the efforts of others, then winning men who have no faith at all. If you really believe the doctrine of endless, conscious torment of the impenitent, and the doctrine really gets hold of you, you will work as you never worked before for the salvation of the lost. If you in any wise abate this doctrine, it will abate your zeal."[53]

have no rest day and night, who worship the beast

Neither do the four living creatures in the presence of God rest day or night, but they are blessed to render ceaseless worship to God (Rev. 4:8). Those who gave their worship to the Beast have no rest. Instead of offering glorious worship to God, they suffer intense torment without relief. Their torment is eternal (Mtt. 25:41; Mark 9:43-44; Jude 1:7; Rev. 20:10). The beast worshipers may have rest during the brief time of the end, but will have no rest thereafter. The saints will experience extreme duress during the brief time of the end, but thereafter will "rest from their labors" (Rev. 14:13).

who worship the beast

See commentary on *Revelation 13:4*[3.13.4].

and his image

See commentary on *Revelation 13:14*[3.13.14] and *Revelation 13:15*[3.13.15].

and whoever receives the mark of his name

See commentary on *Revelation 13:16*[3.13.16].

3.14.12 - Revelation 14:12

Here is the patience of the saints

The patience of the saints is found in their acceptance of God's sovereign control over their lives (Rev. 13:10) and in the knowledge that God will avenge their blood at the hands of those who rejected Him (as here). As terrible as it might be, the awful experience of the saints at the hands of the *Beast*[5.2.9] (see *#20 - Saints*[4.3.2.20]) cannot compare with the doom which meets the Beast worshipers. See commentary on *Revelation 13:10*[3.13.10].

who keep the commandments of God and the faith of Jesus

Their faith is evident by their works—keeping God's commandments (Luke 6:46; Jas. 2:18). During this time, the woman who flees to the wilderness has offspring which "keep the commandments of God and have the testimony of Jesus Christ" (Rev. 12:17). Here, the phrase denotes those who are not just of Israel (her offspring), but also Gentile believers: all the saints of the end.

3.14.13 - Revelation 14:13

I heard a voice from heaven saying to me

This is probably the same voice which told John to "seal up the things which the seven thunders uttered" (Rev. 10:4), and called the two witnesses up to heaven (Rev. 11:12). The voice is undoubtedly that of God, either the Father or the Lamb, for it says, "Come out of her [Babylon] **my people**, lest you share in her sins, and lest you receive of her plagues" [emphasis added] (Rev. 18:4). There is great comfort in the statement which follows because it comes from the highest authority.

Write

It was Jesus who first told John to "write in a book" (Rev. 11:1 cf. Rev. 1:19; 2:1, 8, 12, 18; 3:1, 7, 14). Thus, it may be the Lamb which is speaking here.

blessed *are* the dead who die in the Lord

Who die is ἀποθνήσκοντες [*apothnēskontes*], *those presently dying*. Although there are many blessings for believers mentioned in this book (Rev. 1:3; 16:15; 19:9; 22:7, 14), these receive a special blessing in recognition of the severe conditions they find themselves in. This is a unique time of incomparable Christian persecution coming upon the earth, "Those who 'die in the Lord *henceforth*,' do so as martyrs."[54] The victory of the saints will not be in influencing the social institutions of the globe toward service of God—as lofty a goal as that might be. It will be found in their cleaving to the Lamb through thick and thin, in living and dying. No more so than at the end of present history when the world issues one last blasphemous attempt to throw off the Father and His Christ. This recognition by God underscores the horrors of the reign of the *Beast*[5.2.9] which includes unprecedented slaughter of Christians by the Beast (Rev. 13:7), his image (Rev. 13:15), and the *Harlot*[5.2.25] (Rev. 17:6). "Hence the special Benediction here pronounced upon all such as die rather than yield to the temptations and threats of the Beast and the *False Prophet*[5.2.20]. 'Worship, or be slain' is their cry. 'Be slain, and be blessed' is God's encouraging reply to them."[55] Those who die during this time receive special mention at the commencement of the *Millennial Kingdom*[5.2.39], having undergone martyrdom (Rev. 20:4). "Precious in the sight of the LORD *is* the death of His saints" (Ps. 116:15). See *#20 - Saints*[4.3.2.20].

"Yes," says the Spirit

The third Person of the Trinity joins in bestowing this special blessing upon the saints, most of whom will give their ultimate testimony in their martyrdom (Rev. 12:11; 15:2). Participation of the Holy Spirit in this blessing is of great significance, for it indicates His intimate involvement in the lives of the saints during the trials of the end. For it is only by the Spirit that those who are martyred are able to hold their testimony to the end (Rev. 12:11; 20:4).

that they may rest

Immediately upon death, all those of the faith obtain *rest* (Isa. 57:1; Dan. 12:13; Luke 23:43). This book stands in complete agreement with the teaching of Paul: "We are confident, yes, well pleased rather to be absent from the body and to be present with the Lord" (2Cor. 5:8); "For I am hard-pressed between the two, having a desire to depart and be with Christ, *which is* far better" (Php. 1:23). The martyrs attending the opening of the fifth seal are found under the altar in heaven (Rev. 6:9). The ones coming out of the Great Tribulation are immediately before the throne of God (Rev. 7:14). Those who overcome the Beast and his image (by death) are seen straightway in heaven (Rev. 15:1-3).

Scripture denies the Roman Catholic doctrine of purgatory:

> The righteous who die "in the Lord" do not suffer torment or punishment after death, as in purgatory. There is no such place as purgatory known to Scripture, and even the *Apocrypha*[5.2.5] contains firm testimony against such a view in a remarkable statement at Wisdom 3:1, "But the souls of the righteous are in the hand of God, and there shall no torment touch them."[56]

Those who are washed in the blood of the Lamb are *completely and permanently washed!* To infer that anyone, having trusted in Christ, must subsequently continue to pay for sin is completely unscriptural. It is doubly blasphemous:

1. It denies the sufficiency of Christ's one-time sacrifice for sin—thereby demeaning His perfect

work.

2. It infers that men could contribute something of merit on their own behalf *beyond that which Christ already obtained.*

The doctrine of purgatory is both a denial of Christ's *perfect* work and a vain attempt to add man's *imperfect* work. At its heart, it is motivated by greed and the desire to control the Biblically ignorant:

> The collection of [Roman Catholic] relics in 1509 included 5,005 fragments, the viewing of which reduced one's time in purgatory by 1,443 years. By 1518 it is estimated that there were 17,443 pieces on display in twelve aisles. Included among them were such remarkable relics as a veil sprinkled with the blood of Christ, a twig of Moses' burning bush, and a piece of bread from the Last Supper. By 1520 the collection had grown—despite Luther's opposition—to 19,013 holy pieces. Those who viewed the relics on All Saint's Day and made the required contribution would receive from the pope an indulgence that would reduce time spent in purgatory—either by themselves or others—by up to 1,902,202 years and 270 days.[57]

their works follow them

God is intimately familiar with their works (Rev. 2:2).

> I have fought the good fight, I have finished the race, I have kept the faith. Finally, there is laid up for me the crown of righteousness, which the Lord, the righteous Judge, will give to me on that Day, and not to me only but also to all who have loved His appearing. (2Ti. 4:7-8)

> For God *is* not unjust to forget your work and labor of love which you have shown toward His name, *in that* you have ministered to the saints, and do minister. (Heb. 6:10)

3.14.14 - Revelation 14:14

a while cloud

Clouds are often associated with God, and particularly the Son of Man (Mtt. 24:30; Luke 21:27; Rev. 1:7). See commentary on *Revelation 1:7*[3.1.7].

***One* like the Son of Man**

A clear indication that none other than Jesus is sitting on the cloud (Dan. 7:13; Mtt. 26:64). The reason that Son of Man oversees the harvest of wheat is that it is He who sowed the good seed (Mtt. 13:37).

having on His head a golden crown

Crown is στέφανον [*stephanon*]. See *Crowns*[4.6].

3.14.15 - Revelation 14:15

another angel came out of the temple

When angels come out of the temple on a mission, this is an indication of their divine mandate. The seven angels with the seven last plagues come out of the heavenly temple (Rev. 15:6). It is a voice from the temple which gives them final authority to "pour out the bowls of the wrath of God on the earth" (Rev. 16:1). The harvest of both the faithful and the ungodly are initiated by the Father, from within the temple.

for the time has come

The longsuffering and grace of God and His desire that all should have opportunity to repent now finally draws to a close for He knows that no more will come (2Pe. 3:9). His mercy withholds judgment, but his justice and righteousness make it unavoidable (Rev. 16:7). "But of that day and hour no one knows, not even the angels in heaven, nor the Son, but only the Father" (Mark 13:32). This is the end of the age, the long period when both good and evil were allowed to grow side-by-side. Now there will be a separation in preparation for the *Millennial Kingdom*[5.2.39] to follow:

> "Again, the kingdom of heaven is like a dragnet that was cast into the sea and gathered some of every kind, which, when it was full, they drew to shore; and they sat down and gathered the good into vessels, but threw the bad away. So it will be at the end of the age. The angels will come forth, separate the wicked from among the just, and cast them into the furnace of fire. There will be wailing and gnashing of teeth." (Mtt. 13:47-50)

All who remain alive on the face of the planet must now identify with one or the other of the two criminals crucified with Christ. All the world stands guilty. Those in the first harvest, like the repentant thief on the cross (Luke 23:42), turn in desperation to Christ for cleansing of their sins. They are the wheat. Those in the second harvest (the vintage of wrath) are like the thief who continues to revile Christ (Luke 23:39). They are the tares which are gathered for destruction.

for the harvest of the earth is ripe

The harvest is used throughout the Scriptures to symbolize the final gathering and separation of that which is desirable and productive (wheat) from that which is useless and for the fire (tares, chaff). The judgment attending the harvest is often represented by the threshing floor where the grain is separated from the outer husk (2S. 24:16; 1Chr. 21:15; Jer. 51:33; Dan. 2:35; Mic. 4:12).[58]

> For thus says the LORD of hosts, the God of Israel: "The daughter of Babylon *is* like a threshing floor *When it is* time to thresh her; yet a little while and the time of her harvest will come." (Jer. 51:33)

The long age so central to Jesus' teaching concerning the "kingdom of heaven" (Mtt. 13:24, 31, 33, 44-45, 47, 52) has now drawn to a close. (See *The Arrival of God's Kingdom*[2.4.3].) It is now the time of the harvest. "But when the grain ripens, immediately he puts in the sickle, because the harvest has come" (Mark 4:26).

At the harvest at the end of the age, there are both wheat and tares. The harvest includes a reaping of both and their separation. The wheat is gathered and preserved, the tares are gathered and destroyed.

> But when the grain had sprouted and produced a crop, then the tares also appeared. So the servants of the owner came and said to him, 'Sir, did you not sow good seed in your field? How then does it have tares?' He said to them, 'An enemy has done this.' The servants said to him, 'Do you want us then to go and gather them up?' But he said, 'No, lest while you gather up the tares you also uproot the wheat with them. Let both grow together until the harvest, and at the time of harvest I will say to the reapers, "First gather together the tares and bind them in bundles to burn them, but gather the wheat into my barn." ' (Mtt. 13:26-30)

It seems best to understand the two harvests depicted here as two aspects of the final harvest at the end of the age: a harvest of redemption and a harvest of wrath.[59] Those who view both as harvests of judgment have difficulty explaining why there should be two such harvests of wrath and what, if anything, can be said to differ between them? When the two harvests are compared, we see that Jesus is specifically associated with the first harvest—for it was He who sowed the good grain. Unlike the second harvest, there is no hint of wrath associated with the first harvest: no angel from the altar, no power over fire, no grapes, no trampling, no blood. The only possible negative aspect concerning the first harvest is that it is said to be *ripe*, ἐξηράνθη [*exēranthē*] from ζηραίνω [*zērainō*], which means *to dry up or wither* and is used to describe plants without good roots (Mark 4:6).[60] However, since the first harvest involves not grapes, but by implication wheat, this could just be a description of what naturally occurs when wheat reaches its maturity. All things considered, it seems best to understand these as two *different* harvests, one to gather faithful wheat and the other to destroy wild grapes. We are in agreement with Alford:

> What is the distinction between the two ingatherings? And why do we read of the casting into the wine-press of God's wrath in the second case, and of no corresponding feature in the other? Again, why is the agency so different—the Son of man on the white cloud with a golden crown in the one case, the mere angel in the other? Besides, the two ingatherings seem quite distinct. The former is over before the other begins. On the whole then, though I would not pronounce decidedly, I must incline to think that the harvest is the ingathering of the saints, God's harvest, reaped from the earth: described here thus generally, before the vintage of wrath which follows.[61]

3.14.16 - Revelation 14:16

He who sat on the cloud

The Son of Man is the one who reaps the first harvest of the saved. Although He is intimately involved with the first harvest, Scripture reveals that angels carry out the details of both harvests.

the earth was reaped

The reaping which takes place is worldwide. "And He will send His angels with a great sound of a trumpet, and they will gather together His elect from the four winds, from one end of heaven to the other" (Mtt. 24:31). One view connects this event with the resurrection of the saved dead prior to the *Millennial Kingdom*[5.2.39] (cf. Rev. 20:4).

> This, then, is our Lord's return at the end of the tribulation to harvest the bodies of the saints who die during the tribulation (Rev. 14:13) so as to reunite them with their souls, which, up to this point, will have been under the altar before God (Rev. 6:9). This reaping is the gathering of the harvest into Christ's barn (Mtt. 13:30). . . . The living redeemed will still be on earth, but the bodies of all deceased saints will have been resurrected and taken to Heaven. This addresses the state of all the saved during the tribulation.[62]

The saints which remain alive at the end of the Tribulation participate in the Sheep and Goat Judgment and enter the Millennial Kingdom in their natural bodies (Mtt. 25:31-34).

3.14.17 - Revelation 14:17

another angel came out of the temple in heaven

The authority to issue the command to reap the vintage of wrath is equally dependent upon the authority of God. See commentary on *Revelation 14:15*[3.14.15]. Jesus taught that the angels would be involved in the final harvest:

> The enemy who sowed them [the tares] is the devil, the harvest is the end of the age, and the reapers are the angels. Therefore as the tares are gathered and burned in the fire, so it will be at the end of this age. The Son of Man will send out His angels, and they will gather out of His kingdom all things that offend, and those who practice lawlessness, and will cast them into the furnace of fire. There will be wailing and gnashing of teeth. Then the righteous will shine forth as the sun in the kingdom of their Father. He who has ears to hear, let him hear! (Mtt. 13:39-43)

> The Son of Man will send out His angels, and they will gather out of His kingdom all things that offend, and those who practice lawlessness and will cast them into the furnace of fire. There will be wailing and gnashing of teeth. . . . So it will be at the end of the age. The angels will come forth, separate the wicked from among the just. (Mtt. 13:41-42, 49).

This second angel initiates the gathering of the tares, the removal of the ungodly who are "taken":

> "Even so will it be in the day when the Son of Man is revealed. In that day, he who is on the housetop, and his goods *are* in the house, let him not come down to take them away. And likewise the one who is in the field, let him not turn back. Remember Lot's wife. Whoever seeks to save his life will lose it, and whoever loses his life will preserve it. I tell you, in that night there will be two *men* in one bed: the one will be taken and the other will be left. Two *women* will be grinding together: the one will be taken and the other left. Two *men* will be in the field: the one will be taken and the other left." And they answered and said to Him, "Where, Lord?" So He said to them, "Wherever the body is, there the eagles will be gathered together." (Luke 17:30-37 cf. Mtt. 24:28)

As in the days of Noah, those whom are *taken* are taken in judgment (Mtt. 24:38-39; Luke 21:26-27). The "eagles will be gathered together" to feast on the carrion of the dead (Job 39:30; Rev. 19:17-18).[63]

3.14.18 - Revelation 14:18

another angel came out from the altar

The mention of the altar connects the upcoming vintage of wrath with the cry of the souls under the altar at the opening of the fifth seal. "And they cried with a loud voice, saying, 'How long, O Lord, holy and true, until You judge and avenge our blood on those who dwell on the earth?' " (Rev. 6:10). God had told them that they should rest until the remaining number of their fellow servants would be killed as they were. That time has now come.

who had power over fire

This may be the same angel who offered the prayers of the saints with incense "upon the golden altar which was before the throne" (Rev. 8:3). There, after offering the prayers, he filled his censer with fire from the altar and threw it to the earth prefiguring the series of trumpet judgments (Rev. 8:4-6). Similarly, it was "a voice from the four horns of the golden altar which is before God" which resulted in the release of the four angels bound at the Euphrates bringing the plague of demonic horsemen. This final vintage of wrath is also motivated by mountains of prayer by the saints of all times and ages for righteous judgment and vindication by God.

This is the baptism of fire spoken of by John the Baptist. In his warning to the Pharisees and Sadducees who were coming to his baptism, he indicated that the One following after him would initiate two baptisms. Every person living would receive one or the other.

> I indeed baptize you with water unto repentance, but He who is coming after me is mightier than I, whose sandals I am not worthy to carry. He will baptize you with the Holy Spirit and fire. His winnowing fan is in His hand, and He will thoroughly clean out His threshing floor, and gather His wheat into the barn; **but He will burn up the chaff with unquenchable fire.** (Mtt. 3:11-12) [emphasis added]

> John answered, saying to all, "I indeed baptize you with water; but One mightier than I is coming, whose sandal strap I am not worthy to loose. He will baptize you with the Holy Spirit and fire. His winnowing fan *is* in His hand, and He will thoroughly clean out His threshing floor, and gather the wheat into His barn; **but the chaff He will burn with unquenchable fire**." (Luke 3:16-17) [emphasis added]

> The term *and with fire* is better translated "or with fire." The immediate context certainly indicates that to be baptized with fire is the result of judgment (notice the reference to purging and burning in the next verse). Other than the visible tongues (billows) of fire which appeared over the disciples' heads at Pentecost, references to fire burning up unprofitable chaff refer to judgment rather than cleansing. The threshing fan (Mtt. 3:12) refers to a wooden shovel used for tossing grain into the wind in order to blow away the lighter chaff, leaving the good grain to settle in a pile. The chaff would then be swept up and burned, the unquenchable fire refers to the eternal punishment of hell or the lake of fire.[64]

gather the clusters of the vine of the earth

Joel foresaw the vintage of wrath associated with the *Day of the Lord*[5.2.14]:

> Let the nations be wakened, and come up to the Valley of Jehoshaphat; for there I will sit to judge all the surrounding nations. Put in the sickle, for the harvest is ripe. Come, go down; for the winepress is full, the vats overflow-For their wickedness *is* great. Multitudes, multitudes in the valley of decision! For the day of the LORD *is* near in the valley of decision. (Joel 3:12-14)

The reason that these vines will be trodden is that they are wild grapes. Like His chosen nation Israel, those on the earth had not born the fruit God intended.

> For their vine *is* of the vine of Sodom and of the fields of Gomorrah; their grapes *are* grapes of gall, their clusters *are* bitter. Their wine *is* the poison of serpents, and the cruel venom of cobras. (Deu. 32:32-33)

> Now let me sing to my Well-beloved a song of my Beloved regarding His vineyard: My Well-beloved has a vineyard on a very fruitful hill. He dug it up and cleared out its stones, and planted it with the choicest vine. He built a tower in its midst, and also made a winepress in it; so He expected *it* to bring forth *good* grapes, but it brought forth wild grapes. And now, O inhabitants of Jerusalem and men of Judah, judge, please, between Me and My vineyard. What more could have been done to My vineyard that I have not done in it? Why then, when I expected *it* to bring forth *good* grapes, did it bring forth wild grapes? **And now, please let Me tell you what I will do to My vineyard: I will take away its hedge, and it shall be burned; *And* break down its wall, and it shall be trampled down.** (Isa. 5:1-5) [emphasis added]

for her grapes are fully ripe

God allows evil to have its full fruit for several reasons. First, He provides ample opportunity for the godless to repent and seek forgiveness and restoration. Secondly, He allows the depth of sin to have its full development in those who have forever turned their back on redemption. "But in the fourth generation they shall return here, for the iniquity of the Amorites *is* not yet complete" (Gen. 15:16). Although His patience and mercy are abundant, He must eventually judge in order to vindicate His character: "The righteous shall rejoice when he sees the vengeance; He shall wash his feet in the blood of the wicked, so that men will say, 'Surely *there is* a reward for the righteous; surely He is God who judges in the earth' " (Ps. 58:10-11).

3.14.19 - Revelation 14:19

threw it *into* the great winepress of the wrath of God

This is not a fruitful winepress, for it is the winepress *of the wrath of God* . This is the time of the treading of the grapes of wrath, the final conflagration when God wipes out all His enemies at the second advent of Christ (Isa. 34:2-8; 63:1-6; Joel 3:12-14; Zep. 3:8; Rev. 19:15). See *Grapes of Wrath*[4.5.5].

3.14.20 - Revelation 14:20

outside the city

The city is Jerusalem. Like unclean and accursed things, these will be disposed of outside the city.

> For the bodies of those animals, whose blood is brought into the sanctuary by the high priest for sin, are burned outside the camp. Therefore Jesus also, that He might sanctify the people with His own blood, suffered outside the gate. Therefore let us go forth to Him, outside the camp, bearing His reproach. (Heb. 13:11-13)

> The valley of Jehoshaphat was outside Jerusalem and it is there that the fullest vengeance of God shall be poured out, "the press is full" (Joel 3:13).[65]

> The judgment of the nations in Joel 3:12-14 (which supplies the dual figures of harvest and vintage) takes place in the valley of Jehoshaphat, which traditions links with the Kidron valley lying between Jerusalem and the Mount of Olives. Zechariah 14:1-4 places the final battle on the outskirts of Jerusalem.[66]

See *Campaign of Armageddon*[4.5].

and blood came out

The bloodshed associated with the judgment which falls at the *Campaign of Armageddon*[4.5] at the close of the Tribulation period is unprecedented:

> The sword of the LORD is filled with blood, it is made overflowing with fatness, with the blood of lambs and goats, with the fat of the kidneys of rams. For the LORD has a sacrifice in Bozrah, and a great slaughter in the land of Edom. The wild oxen shall come down with them, and the young bulls with the mighty bulls; their land shall be soaked with blood, and their dust saturated with fatness. For *it is* the day of the LORD'S vengeance, the year of recompense for the cause of Zion. (Isa. 34:6-8)

It results in the staining of Jesus garments (Isa. 63:1-6; Rev. 19:13). See *Blood Stained Garments*[4.5.5.1].

up to the horses bridles

Possibly a reference to the armies in heaven who follow after Christ on white horses (Rev. 19:14). More likely, a reference to the horses of Christ's enemies.

one thousand six hundred furlongs

Furlong is σταδίων [*stadiōn*], a distance of one-eighth of a mile (185 meters)[67]. The total distance is approximately 200 miles.[68]

> The blood stretches for 1,600 furlongs, which is approximately two hundred miles. The two hundred miles may refer to the entire area from the Valley of Armageddon to Bozrah, which is about two hundred miles. Another possible explanation is that it refers to the round trip distance between Jerusalem and Bozrah. The fighting will begin in Jerusalem and move to Bozrah (100 miles), and with the Second Coming, will return back from Bozrah to the Valley of Jehoshaphat (another 100 miles). But the best explanation is based on Jeremiah 49:20-22 . . . In the context (see Jer. 49:13-14), this passage is dealing with the Campaign of Armageddon. The massive blood-letting that begins at Bozrah begins moving south down the Arabah until it empties in the Red Sea at the present-day cities of Eilat and Akaba. The distance from there to Jerusalem is about two hundred miles.[69]

> Armageddon is in the north of Palestine [Rev. 16:14-16], the valley of Jehoshaphat is in the south. Bozrah is named by Isaiah as the place where the Lord treads the winepress [Isa. 63:1-6]. And the distance between the farthest points of this "front" is 1600 furlongs.[70]

> What is signified is a vast destruction of human life over a circumscribed area. Certainly what is stated of the vast slaughter is beyond anything ever known.[71]

Although it is possible that this description is *hyperbole*[5.2.27], one must ask why then does Scripture mention this precise distance? Besides implicating the areas that might be involved (above), it would seem to indicate the magnitude of the final slaughter of all the ungodly. Attempts to understand the exact magnitude of the judgment are nearly impossible, but can provide some insight into the immensity of the slaughter:

> Let us consider the biblical portrayal of the size of this disaster: this river of blood is 184 miles long, and its depth is the height of a horse's bit. Now, if a horse's bit is four feet high, we can calculate the volume required to fill a blood stream of varying widths, and as we know that the typical quantity of blood in a person is six quarts, we can then calculate how many people it would take to supply the blood. The blood from one billion human beings would make a stream not even twenty yards wide over this length of 184 miles (a trough 4' deep with radiused sides would average 53 feet in width to hold the blood from one billion humans). If these figures are taken literally—and surely, when we recognize the literality of fulfilled prophecy in Daniel, they must be—then it is clear that God portrays the slaying of all unregenerate mankind. Notably, as the width is not given, we cannot determine the population of the earth at this time.[72]

See *Campaign of Armageddon*[4.5].

> Child of Adam, hear, and be admonished now while salvation is so freely offered. Be not deceived, for God is not mocked. Those impieties of thine, those guilty sports and gaieties, will yet have to be confronted before the judgment seat. Those gatherings in the gaming-hells and drink-shops of Satan, those sneers and witty jests at sacred things, those fiery lusts burning on the altars of carnal pleasure, are all written down in the account-books of eternity to be brought forth in the great day. . . . Think, O man, O woman, how would you fare were He this night to strike! If not *in the city*, in reconciliation with the King, outside is only death and damnation, and nothing can make it different.[73]

Notes

1 J. A. Seiss, *The Apocalypse: Lectures on the Book of Revelation* (Grand Rapids, MI: Zondervan Publishing House, 1966), 349.

2 "The word 'Zion' is first used of the stronghold or fortress of the ancient city Jebus. Though the Jebusites considered their city impregnable, David was able to conquer it. He lived in the fortress and named the city 'the city of David.' In time the word 'Zion' took on a broader meaning. It came to mean the entire city of Jerusalem, not just the fortress in it. The word was even used at times of a group such as 'the daughters of Zion' (Isa. 3:16-17), that is, female inhabitants in the city. Later the word came to mean the entire Jewish nation."—Mal Couch, *"Israelology in the Book of Revelation,"* in Mal Couch, ed., *A Bible Handbook to Revelation* (Grand Rapids, MI: Kregel Publications, 2001), 180.

3 Merrill F. Unger, *Unger's Commentary on the Old Testament* (Chattanooga, TN: AMG Publishers, 2002), s.v. "Zion."

4 By the same logic, we know that passages such as Isaiah 62 record promises which will be fulfilled in the earthly Jerusalem rather than the New Jerusalem. For what need has the heavenly city ever had for watchmen on its walls (Isa. 62:6)?

5 Although it is possible they could have been taken up directly to heaven, the text is completely silent as to this possibility.

6 "The Vision is in heaven; for the singers stand before the Throne, and they are with the Lamb. He is not yet descended to the Earth. This decides the point that it is the heavenly Zion which is here referred to. The *Temple*[5.2.73] on Earth was close to Mount Zion; so the Temple in heaven is correspondingly near to the heavenly Zion."—E. W. Bullinger, *Commentary On Revelation* (Grand Rapids, MI: Kregel Publications, 1984, 1935), Rev. 14:1. "Some writers take it as the earthly site of a millennial reign, but the entire scene is one of praise before the throne in heaven."—Robert H. Mounce, *The Book of Revelation* (Grand Rapids, MI: William B. Eerdmans Publishing Co., 1977), Rev. 14:1.

7 The phrase "before the throne of God" in Rev. 14:5 does not appear in the *NU*[5.2.49] or *MT*[5.2.45] texts, but appears only in the *TR*[5.2.79] text.

8 Thomas holds to an unusual interpretation: he takes the 144,000 to be on *earth*, but also has them *slain.* The entire problem with having them in heaven is because their seal would not have protected them. Most who take them to be on the earth do so partly out of deference to the effectiveness of their sealing—they survive the Tribulation.

9 Robert L. Thomas, *Revelation 8-22* (Chicago, IL: Moody Press, 1995), Rev. 14:1.

[10] Thomas, *Revelation 8-22*, Rev. 14:1.

[11] Thomas, *Revelation 8-22*, Rev. 14:3.

[12] Arno C. Gaebelein, *The Revelation* (Neptune, NJ: Loizeaux Brothers, 1961), 86.

[13] "We gather that the harp-singers of chaps. xiv. and xv. are the same company."—Walter Scott, *Exposition of The Revelation* (London, England: Pickering & Inglis, n.d.), Rev. 15:2.

[14] "We first find the 144,000 on earth (Mount Zion) and then in Heaven (before the throne). Now, this is remarkable, for it suggests that the Lamb will gather them together in Jerusalem in order to transport them to Heaven. It suggests, too, that these 144,000 will be raptured from Jerusalem, for there is no mention of them dying."—Monty S. Mills, *Revelations: An Exegetical Study of the Revelation to John* (Dallas, TX: 3E Ministries, 1987), Rev. 14:1.

[15] Arnold G. Fruchtenbaum, *The Footsteps of Messiah*, rev ed. (Tustin, CA: Ariel Ministries, 2003), 269.

[16] William R. Newell, *Revelation: Chapter by Chapter* (Grand Rapids, MI: Kregel Publications, 1994,c1935), 210.

[17] J. Dwight Pentecost, *Things to Come: A Study in Biblical Eschatology* (Grand Rapids, MI: Zondervan Publishing House, 1958), 300.

[18] "The two distinct companies—of Israel and the Gentiles—were beheld by the Seer in separate visions (Rev. 7). The elect company from the twelve tribes (Rev. 7:4-8), is not only distinct from their Gentile associates (Rev. 7:9-17), but is equally distinct from the 144,000 from amongst Judah who emerge out of the horrors of the coming hour of trial standing on Mount Zion. There are two Jewish companies of equal number. The hundred and forty-four thousand of *Israel*) (Rev. 7) and the hundred and forty-four thousand of *Judah* (Rev. 14)."—Scott, *Exposition of The Revelation*, 158.

[19] A. R. Fausset, *"The Revelation of St. John the Divine,"* in Robert Jamieson, A. R. Fausset, and David Brown, *A Commentary, Critical and Explanatory, on the Old and New Testaments* (Oak Harbor, WA: Logos Research Systems, Inc., 1997, 1877), Rev. 14:3.

[20] "During the time of the First and Second Temples, a number of the Levites played on two types of harps, singing arcane melodies that no one else was permitted to learn. This knowledge was passed from father to son, until the destruction of the Second *Temple*[5.2.73]."—Randall Price, *The Coming Last Days Temple* (Eugene, OR: Harvest House Publishers, 1999), 390.

[21] Bullinger, *Commentary On Revelation*, Rev. 14:3.

[22] Timothy Friberg, Barbara Friberg, and Neva F. Miller, *Analytical Lexicon of the Greek New Testament* (Grand Rapids, MI: Baker Books, 2000), 266.

[23] Bullinger, *Commentary On Revelation*, Rev. 14:4.

[24] John MacArthur, *Revelation 12-22 : The MacArthur New Testament Commentary* (Chicago, IL: Moody Press, 2000), Rev. 14:4.

[25] Newell, *Revelation: Chapter by Chapter*, 216.

[26] Scott, *Exposition of The Revelation*, Rev. 14:4.

[27] Friberg, *Analytical Lexicon of the Greek New Testament*, 33.

[28] Friberg, *Analytical Lexicon of the Greek New Testament*, 61.

[29] Some disagree: "Adams explains: 'The 144,000 cannot be interpreted as Jews who will some day escape persecution in a yet future age. In no intelligible sense could such a group of Jews be considered "firstfruits." Historically, the firstfruits of the Christian church were among the Jews—in fact among the very Jews who are here mentioned: those in Jerusalem, who escaped the destruction in 70 A.D. How artificial to twist "firstfruits" into the very *last* fruits of the Christian era!' "—Steve Gregg, *Revelation Four Views: A Parallel Commentary* (Nashville, TN: Thomas Nelson, 1997), 316. The problem with Adams' view is it completely ignores the distinction which Scripture makes between the Church and Israel. Those Jewish believers who frequent the pages of the *NT*[5.2.48] are members of the Church, not the restored revived Israel. This is Paul's point throughout three full chapters of Romans (Romans 9, 10, and 11). Furthermore, if these are uniquely preserved throughout the Tribulation, they form an initial Jewish population of the Millennial Kingdom. They serve as "firstfruits" of that *physical Jewish population* in a unique way.

[30] William Varner, *Jacob's Dozen: A Prophetic Look at the Tribes of Israel* (Bellmawr, NJ: Friends of Israel

Gospel Ministry, 1987), 103.

31 Concerning the need to tame the tongue: Ps. 5:9; 17:3; 19:14; 39:1; 120:1-7; 141:3; Pr. 10:19, 31-32; 15:2, 4; 15:28; 18:21; 21:23; Isa. 6:5, 7; 59:3; Mtt. 12:34-35; 15:18; Jas. 1:26; 3:6-3:8.

32 Frederick William Danker, and Walter Bauer, *A Greek-English Lexicon of the New Testament and Other Early Christian Literature* (Chicago, IL: University of Chicago Press, 2000), 47.

33 Danker, *A Greek-English Lexicon of the New Testament and Other Early Christian Literature*, 47.

34 Richard Chenevix Trench, *Commentary on the Epistles to the Seven Churches in Asia* (Eugene, OR: Wipf and Stock Publishers, 1861), 402.

35 Friberg, *Analytical Lexicon of the Greek New Testament*, 259.

36 Danker, *A Greek-English Lexicon of the New Testament and Other Early Christian Literature*, 317.

37 Newell, *Revelation: Chapter by Chapter*, 220.

38 Why? Because she will be absent from the earth at the time of the end, having been taken in the *Rapture*[4.14].

39 "This is the good news that God purposes to set up on the earth, in fulfilment of the Davidic Covenant (2S. 7:16, and refs.), a kingdom, political, spiritual, Israelitish, universal, over which God's Son, David's heir, shall be King, and which shall be, for one thousand years, the manifestation of the righteousness of God in human affairs. . . . Two preachings of this Gospel are mentioned, one past, beginning with the ministry of John the Baptist, continued by our Lord and His disciples, and ending with the Jewish rejection of the King. The other is yet future (Mtt. 24:14), during the great tribulation, and immediately preceding the coming of the King in glory."—C. I. Scofield, *The Scofield Study Bible* (New York, NY: Oxford University Press, 2002, 1909), Rev. 14:6.

40 Pentecost, *Things to Come: A Study in Biblical Eschatology*, 472.

41 Bullinger, *Commentary On Revelation*, 110.

42 Ignoring the fact that accidents of mutation result in a net *loss* of information whereas evolution requires a *gain* in information.

43 "To revert to the problem of the Pithecanthropus, the Swanscombe man, the Neanderthal and all the rest (possibly even the Cro-magnon man, who is apparently to be classed as *Homo sapiens*, but whose remains seem to date back at least to 20,000 B.C.) it seems best to regard these races as all prior to Adam's time, and not involved in the Adamic covenant. We must leave the question open, in view of the cultural remains, whether these pre-Adamic creatures had souls (or, to use the trichotomic terminology, spirits)."—Archer, G. Jr., *A Survey of Old Testament Introduction*, rev. ed., (Chicago, IL: Moody Press, 1985), pp. 204-205 cited in *Creation Magazine*, 24(4), September-November 2002, p. 45. [*www.AnswersInGenesis.org*] "My acceptance of Adam and Eve as historical is not incompatible with my belief that several forms of pre-Adamic 'hominid' seem to have existed for thousands of years previously. . . . It is conceivable that God created Adam out of one of them. . . . I think you may even call some of them Homo sapiens. . ." John Stott, *Understanding the Bible*, rev. ed., (Sydney: Scripture Union Publishing, 1984), p. 49 cited in *Creation Magazine*, 24(4), September-November 2002, p. 43. [*www.AnswersInGenesis.org*]

44 Unger, *Unger's Commentary on the Old Testament*, Jer. 21:10.

45 Interpreters are divided as to whether Rev. 16:19 describes two categories of cities (Babylon and the cities of the nations) or three (Jerusalem, the cities of the Gentile nations, and Babylon).

46 Donald Grey Barnhouse, *Revelation* (Grand Rapids, MI: Zondervan Publishing House, 1971), Rev. 14:9.

47 Scott, *Exposition of The Revelation*, Rev. 14:9.

48 Trench, *Commentary on the Epistles to the Seven Churches in Asia*, 146.

49 Friberg, *Analytical Lexicon of the Greek New Testament*, 228.

50 Fausset, "*The Revelation of St. John the Divine*," Rev. 14:8.

51 God is omnipresent, even in hell: "Where can I go from Your Spirit? Or where can I flee from Your presence? If I ascend into heaven, You *are* there; If I make my bed in hell, behold, You *are there*. *If* I take the wings of the morning, *and* dwell in the uttermost parts of the sea, even there Your hand shall lead me, and Your right hand shall hold me. If I say, 'Surely the darkness shall fall on me,' even the night shall be light about me; indeed, the darkness shall not hide from You, but the night shines as the day; the darkness and the light *are* both alike *to You*" (Ps. 139:7-12). Yet something more is in view here, for the *holy angels*, who lack

omnipresence, are also said to have access to the damned.

52 Loraine Boettner, *The Reformed Doctrine of Predestination* (Phillipsburg, NJ: Presbyterian and Reformed Publishing Company, 1932), 79.

53 Barnhouse, *Revelation*, Rev. 14:11.

54 Scott, *Exposition of The Revelation*, Rev. 14:13.

55 Bullinger, *Commentary On Revelation*, Rev. 14:13.

56 Jerome Smith, *The New Treasury of Scripture Knowledge* (Nashville, TN: Thomas Nelson Publishers, 1992), Rev. 14:13.

57 William R. Estep, *Renaissance and Reformation* (Grand Rapids, MI: Eerdman's Publishing Company, 1986), 117.

58 The Church can take great comfort in the fact that Ruth, the Gentile bride of Boaz (a type of the kinsman-redeemer Christ), was at his feet during the time of threshing (Ru. 3:2-7).

59 Seiss disagrees: "That this is the [a harvest of redemption] seems to me very improbable, if not entirely out of the question. According to the record up to this point, the great harvest of the good seed has already been reaped. The Living Ones, the Elders, the innumerable multitude, the Manchild, and the 144,000 all of whom are the good seed, are in heaven before this reaping comes."—Seiss, *The Apocalypse: Lectures on the Book of Revelation*, 358. Seiss would have us believe that not a single believer remains upon the earth at the time of this harvest! How could that be? For the second harvest is most certainly the second advent of Christ, including the *Campaign of Armageddon*[4.5] which occurs at the end of the Tribulation. There are still saints alive on the earth at the time of Christ's second advent because they are those who enter the Millennial Kingdom and form its initial population (Mtt. 25:31-34).

60 Danker, *A Greek-English Lexicon of the New Testament and Other Early Christian Literature*, 548.

61 John F. Walvoord, *The Revelation of Jesus Christ* (Chicago, IL: Moody Press, 1966), Rev. 14:14.

62 Mills, *Revelations: An Exegetical Study of the Revelation to John*, Rev. 14:16.

63 Concerning birds feasting on carrion in judgment: Deu. 28:26; Job 39:30; Eze. 32:4; 39:4, 17-20; Jer. 7:33; 12:9; 15:3; 16:4; 19:7; Mtt. 24:28; Luke 17:37; Rev. 19:17-18.

64 Jerry Falwell, Edward D. Hindson, and Michael Woodrow Kroll, eds., *KJV Bible Commentary* (Nashville, TN: Thomas Nelson, 1997, c1994), Mtt. 3:11.

65 Scott, *Exposition of The Revelation*, Rev. 14:19.

66 Mounce, *The Book of Revelation*, Rev. 14:19.

67 Trent C. Butler, Chad Brand, Charles Draper, and Archie England, eds., *Broadman and Holman Illustrated Bible Dictionary* (Nashville, TN: Broadman and Holman Publishers, 2003), 1666.

68 Several witnesses read 1606 stadia, a few read 1200 stadia. [Bruce M. Metzger, *A Textual Commentary on the Greek New Testament* (Stuttgart, Germany: Deutsche Bibelgesellschaft, 1994), Rev. 14:20].

69 Fruchtenbaum, *The Footsteps of Messiah*, 360.

70 Barnhouse, *Revelation*, Rev. 14:20.

71 Scott, *Exposition of The Revelation*, Rev. 14:20.

72 Mills, *Revelations: An Exegetical Study of the Revelation to John*, Rev. 14:20.

73 Seiss, *The Apocalypse: Lectures on the Book of Revelation*, 365.

ISBN 0-9788864-1-0
90000>
9 780978 886417

CPSIA information can be obtained
at www.ICGtesting.com
Printed in the USA
BVHW011053170719
553683BV00012B/477/P